TWENTY-THREE
PLAYS

An Introductory Anthology

TWENTY-THREE PLAYS

Edited by

Otto Reinert
UNIVERSITY OF WASHINGTON, SEATTLE

Peter Arnott
TUFTS UNIVERSITY

Little, Brown and Company
BOSTON · LB · TORONTO

Library of Congress Catalog Card No. 78-50417

First Printing

*Published simultaneously in Canada
by Little, Brown & Company (Canada) Limited*

Printed in the United States of America

Preface

Any selection of plays for a book like this is arbitrary — up to a point. Ours seeks to represent the main ages, cultures, dramatic modes, and theater styles of Western drama from the Greeks till today. Not all the plays are "great," but some of them are, and we think all are worth knowing. Our selection has been guided by readers' responses to a series of earlier anthologies.

In order to accommodate different classroom needs, the book appears in two editions. The longer, *Twenty-Three Plays*, is intended for courses exclusively on drama; the shorter, *Thirteen Plays*, for courses that deal with other literary genres as well, courses on the history of the theater, and courses in which a core text is supplemented with the teacher's choice of plays in individual volumes.

Eleven of the plays in the longer edition and six in the shorter were included in Otto Reinert's *Classic Through Modern Drama*. We have kept some of the critical commentaries for those plays and revised and replaced others. As before, the commentaries follow the individual plays, but we have added Forewords that relate each play to its contemporary theater. The Introduction has been revised and expanded and includes a new section on "Illusion and Convention" and a new "Anatomy of a Scene." The biographical notes and the bibliographies in the Appendix (including listings of recordings and screen versions) have been updated. An Index of Dramatic Terms appears on the inside back cover.

In everything we say about drama here we make two basic assumptions: first, that it is *literature*, and, second, that its literary uniqueness is its po-

tential for becoming a *performance*. In our play analyses we have tried to
be specific and inclusive without being intrusive and dogmatic — to suggest
and not to pre-empt. Like drama itself, our book is, and in more than one
sense, an effort of collaboration. The rest is up to our readers.

ACKNOWLEDGMENTS

We would like to acknowledge the helpful suggestions and comments of
instructors who have used the earlier anthologies, including David Berndt,
Robert Bender, Joseph M. Blimm, William R. Brown, Thomas Chase,
Thomas A. Copeland, Lynn Elliott, William Fordyce, H. Ramsey Fowler,
Elissa S. Guralnick, William H. Henry, Jr., Haskell Hinnant, Camille S.
Jordan, A. J. Kershner, Jr., Timothy Materer, Catharine W. McCue, Dan-
iel McDonald, Thomas J. O'Brien, Mark Polnoroff, Frank E. Ross, Helen
Saliba, David A. Samuelson, Roger H. Schutz, George D. Slawson, John
Stark, Charles Stagg, Douglas O. Street, Miceal F. Vaughan, Frederick M.
Warner, and Raymond J. Wilson III. Special thanks go to the people at
Little, Brown who were particularly supportive and encouraging, including
Dale Anderson, Charles H. Christensen, Elizabeth Philipps, Barbara Son-
nenschein, and Margaret N. Zusky.

Otto Reinert
Peter Arnott

Contents

CONTENTS

CONTENTS

Appendix   1209

Index of Dramatic Terms

inside back cover

Introduction

A Definition of Drama

Drama is the least purely literary of the literary genres. As written words, it is literature; as words spoken in a spectacle, it is theater. Separate the two, and we no longer have drama. The literary part moves toward a closet play, a script not actable and not meant to be. The theater part moves toward pantomime or dance or opera or the mechanics of mere showmanship. As words in the theater, drama is an ambiguous art, a hybrid — at the same time speech and spectacle, poetry and show business, church and circus.

A novel or a poem is read (or listened to in recital). A play can be either read or performed, but performance affects its status as literature. Dialogue can be performed as written, actors speaking the lines set down for the characters they impersonate, but stage directions do not survive the transfer from script to stage. And the more "literary" they are, the more they lose in the transfer. Their referents in performance — speech manner, movement, costume, makeup, lighting, set — are creations of the theater. The only way an audience can register the "trepidation" in Linda Loman's voice as she calls out her husband's name at the beginning of *Death of a Salesman* and the "casual irritation" in his is through the timbre and inflection in the voices of the two performers. Only the actor's face can express Biff's "hopeless glance" at his brother near the end of the play. And the transparent walls of the Loman house are more believable as part of a symbolic but actual stage set than as something visualized in the imagination.

These distinctions can be misleading if they are taken to be absolute. Films generally subordinate words to photography, and yet film scripts have been published to be read. At what point of verbal artistry do they cease being scenario and production notes and become drama? Conversely, isn't some drama covered by the old definition of theater as "three boards and a passion"? Isn't there more to a dramatic character than the words he speaks? Is *Act Without Words*, Beckett's mime, not drama just because its words are acted out and not spoken? Couldn't it rather be said to be drama *because* its words are visible?

The ambiguity of drama keeps alive the old debate between literary people and people of the theater, each claiming that drama belongs to *them*. Arbitrating between them is a little like deciding whether the United States is a republic or a democracy. Does the drama make the theater or the theater the drama? On the one hand: Without the playwright's art of words, there would be no need for the arts of the theater. People talking is the basic dramatic action, and wordless activity — swordplay, love-making, silence — derives its significance from the talk it interrupts. On the other hand: The words were written to be performed. They don't fulfill their destiny till they have become subject to the opportunities, temptations, and limitations of the physical playhouse. And performance is a collaborative effort, the joint product of many arts. The images the dramatist works with make up, in Ronald Peacock's words, "a composite form, using different 'arts' to one end." What the dramatist writes is a performable script, and if the script fails on stage for other reasons than mere ineptness of staging, it probably fails as dramatic literature, too.

DRAMA AND THEATER

Anthropologists trace the origin of theater and drama to wordless action: ritual dances and mimes performed by masked player-priests in fertility rites, ceremonies for the dead, and calls to the gods for good fortune in war and hunting. Children reenact those ancient beginnings when they "play at" being someone or something other than themselves. Aristotle (384–322 B.C.), the first theorist of drama, thought of art as the human response to a deep need to imitate experience and of drama as the most directly imitative (mimetic) of all the arts. He considered speech only one of its three media, more important than music and spectacle but no more basic. The word "drama" comes from a Greek verb, *dran*, meaning "to do" or "act" or "perform." "Theater" comes from the Greek *theatron*, "a place for viewing." There is nothing in either etymology about an art of words. Put them together, and we get a definition of drama as "doings in a place for viewing," or, more elegantly, "observed action."

Whether used about plays or about real-life events, the adjective "dramatic" refers to a quality of action rather than of language: an urgent, exciting course of events moving through striking changes toward crisis and resolution. The climax of a TV crime show, Everyman's search for something that will save his soul, the last days of Watergate — are all dramatic. A dramatic situation is one in which further action lies coiled like a tensed spring. It is Oedipus sending away for the old shepherd, Hamlet setting the mousetrap for the king, Helmer in A *Doll's House* reading Krogstad's letter, the family in *The Cherry Orchard* waiting for news about the auction. Drama, says Suzanne Langer, is "a complex of impending acts," a dynamic pattern in the process of being completed.

To the arguments from anthropology and dictionary can be added the argument from experience. One of the couplets in the prologue Samuel Johnson wrote for the opening of David Garrick's new theater in London in 1747 is as true now as it was then:

> The Drama's Laws the Drama's Patrons give,
> For we that live to please must please to live.

The fate of plays is decided in the theater and not in the study; successful playwrights get rich in the box office and not in the bookstore. Even the good reader of drama — *particularly* the good reader — knows how much he misses when he misses the performance, and he knows also that what he gains — time for thoughtful response — does not make up for it. However vivid and subtle his imagination, it can never match the theater's immediacy of spectacle and living voices. The stage is a place where fantasy becomes fact and fact fantasy, an imaginary place with real people in it, with life happening here and now. Take the drama out of the theater, and you take away our chance to enjoy good acting, good directing, good design, and the special communion good theater establishes among strangers sharing the same excitement. The drama is not complete till the personnel of the theater finishes what the playwright began. Words are the raw material for drama, but the drama itself is actors moving and speaking on a stage before an audience.

This is one view of drama. Giving the other won't settle the issue between the literary and the theatrical factions, but it may throw further light on drama's double nature.

There are concepts that common sense and practical experience cannot define adequately, and the origin of something does not necessarily determine its evolved nature. Even the definition of drama as an "art of words in the theater" implies that it is an art of words before it is anything else.

Not because performance presupposes something to be performed. So it does, but the theater's obvious retort to that is that the primitive ritual, the prescribed procedure, was preverbal, a choreographic rather than a literary "script." It is more to the point that for all practical purposes the history of drama begins with the earliest extant texts of Greek tragedies from the fifth century B.C. The ambiguity of word and action in those plays is apparent in what Aristotle writes about them; he is more concerned with their thought and expression than with their stagecraft. In his *Rhetoric* he aligns acting and music as arts that must both be appreciated by the ear. And surely the ancient Greek spectator thought of himself as "hearing" as well as "seeing" the play. It is true that different cultures have made different balances. A cultivated Elizabethan spectator would have needed much convincing that a play could be considered literature. His French counterpart a century later would have needed no convincing at all. If Aristotle hinted to his century that the theater was largely for the ear, Gordon Craig, the British stage designer, and Elmer Rice, the American playwright, have told ours that it is largely for the eye. But the common view in most ages of western theater has been that spoken or chanted words are intrinsic to drama and that the history of drama, therefore, is part of the literary history of our culture. And for the last three hundred years or so, the word "drama" in common English usage has meant something like "a literary composition in dialogue form, actable before an audience."

"Actable," not "enacted." On that distinction rests the argument that the literary component in drama takes precedence over the theatrical component. We can have theater without drama; pantomime, ballet, and burlesque are all forms of theater that may be dramatic but are not drama. Spectator sports may be considered in the same category. And we can have drama without performance, as we do in a book like this. Stagecraft is the midwife of drama, not its mother. The play is no more the enactment than the symphony is the concert.

Like symphonies, most plays have been written to be performed, but the potential performance is complete in the playwright's words, just as the melody, harmony, rhythm, tempo, and orchestration "are" in the composer's written score. The only difference is that for most of us it is easier to "see" and "hear" the play in our imagination as we read the script than it is to "hear" the music in our imagination as we read the score. Both symphonies and plays are forever-possible-but-never-to-be-realized performances, "ideal" performances in the philosophical sense, inherent in the score or script and independent of the artists who perform them. They all invite performance, and many deserve it, but any performance, however faithful or inspired, is inevitably different from — both more and less than — the work itself. Scores and scripts may be altered by the performing artists, but that does not prove they were not autonomous works of art to begin with. Some people will argue anything, but to say that *Hamlet* is not a play till it is acted seems as unreasonable as to say that it is not literature till it is read. The imagination can do anything the stage can do. It does things differently; some things it does better. In adaptability and resourcefulness the theater in the mind rivals any real theater.

Such comparisons don't matter when we attend a good performance of a good play. Then we no longer feel the tension between the art of words and the arts of the theater — between the intellectual and the sensory elements in drama — as conflict or division, but as complementarity. And when that happens, the whole controversy over what drama "really" is comes to seem rather silly.

DRAMA AND LITERATURE

Plays and movies based on prose fiction prove that performability is not unique to drama. But, at least in theory, the art of poet and novelist goes beyond dialogue and description of stageables. The lyric poet explores his own inner world of feeling and sensation, a subjective world different in kind from the externalized, objective world of drama. The novelist or the epic poet can suspend action indefinitely, do without dialogue and events and physical setting altogether ("epics of the mind"), and discourse on any kind and any number of subjects in slow or quick sequence. He can judge and analyze his characters in authorial comment, enter at will into their hearts and minds, and just as easily exit back into straight narrative. And if he never uses any of these freedoms, he is in effect a playwright, whether he calls his work a play or not.

For if the novelist has the option of being an all-knowing, all-managing god of the world he creates, the dramatist must be content to be a god shut out from his. His play shows and tells itself; his characters speak for themselves. If they are not credible, self-motivating human fictions, what is before us is hardly a play at all but a lecture or a polemic or a confession or an act of exhibitionism. The dramatist's voice and vision are multiple. Drama is his medium because it is open options, changing tensions, dialectics in motion. As dramatist, he is incapable of single-mindedness. He is skeptical of "Truth" but loves the process by which truths are born. He'll rather observe than interpret. Obsessed with morality, he will not moralize. He is Keats's man of "negative capability," "capable of being in uncertainties, Mysteries, doubts, without any irritable reaching after fact & reason." In another letter, Keats says of the "poetical Character" that it "has no self — it is every thing and nothing. . . . It has as much delight in conceiving an Iago as an Imogen. What shocks the virtuous philosopher delights the chameleon Poet." Keats's "Poet" has the soul and the instincts of a *dramatist*. Drama is the dramatist's act of self-transcendence. His art is a public art, unlike the private arts of the lyric poet and the fiction writer. His sense of life is too large and disinterested for mere self-expression to be enough for it, and when we understand his play it is because we make the right inferences.

For he couldn't intrude himself into his play even if he wanted to. It offers itself, directly, as "life," not as somebody's presentation of life. Its integrity is absolute. To paraphrase S. W. Dawson: Whatever the *significance* of the drama, it has no *reference* to anything outside of itself; everything in it is relevant, and nothing relevant is not in it.

A chorus or some other framing character — even when acted by the playwright himself — who interprets the action for us is still a part of the audible spectacle of on-going life on stage — is *in* the play, not *outside* it. Because of the special nature of the functions a chorus can serve (whether a single character or a group), its status as a dramatic device has often been conspicuously misinterpreted. It can save time. It can cover a great deal of expository material in a single direct address to the audience, allowing the author to get more quickly to what the play is about. It can offer pithy summaries that reduce the risk that we miss important points. It can draw morals and relate the immediate action to a wider frame of reference. (In different ways, both the Chorus in *Oedipus the King* and the Singer in *The Caucasian Chalk Circle* do this.) But it is still part of the play. It can serve as a bridge between the play's world and the world of the audience, but it belongs to the play, not to the world it connects the play with. It is a dramatic device. Critics have referred to the chorus as "the ideal spectator." This makes sense if it means simply that the chorus is a character or a group of characters in the play who are interested in and perhaps affected by the action but not participating in that action. The statement does *not* make sense — in fact, confuses the whole issue — if it means that the chorus is an objective authority standing outside of the play and telling us what the play is about. Even the most cursory reading of the script of any play using a chorus shows that the chorus is not *that*. Consider, for example, the way the members of the Chorus in *Oedipus the King* flounder in the dark, through most of the play, about matters on which we are far better informed than they. Or the way they hail the news of Oedipus' discovery on Mount Cithairon with almost hysterical glee — glee which will shortly turn out to be disastrously ill-founded.

But our recognition of the chorus as part of the play doesn't prevent us from making the relevant distinctions between it and the other characters. In Brecht's *Caucasian Chalk Circle*, for example, we understand that the Singer, obviously a "chorus" figure, belongs on a different plane of reality from that of Grusha and Azdak, whose stories he tells in the play's "inner" action. There is every reason we should accept his version of their stories, but that doesn't mean that he "is" Brecht. He is both a character in the "outer" action (about the two kolkhozes) and a technical device Brecht uses to get his ethico-political fable told in a certain way. Similarly, the Messenger and the Doctor who expound the Christian doctrine in *Everyman* are more than just prologue and epilogue figures. Like Everyman himself, they are in the play, parts of the playwright's artifact. But because they comment on, rather than interact with, the title character, they give us a perspective on the action different from that of characters like Fellowship and Kindred and Good Deeds — a larger, wiser, more detached perspective. This division of the characters into two groups roughly corresponding to the "inner" and the "outer" groups in Brecht's play makes *Everyman* a more complex play *in form* than plays that in other respects are more complex than it. In *Everyman*, the Messenger and the Doctor are at the same

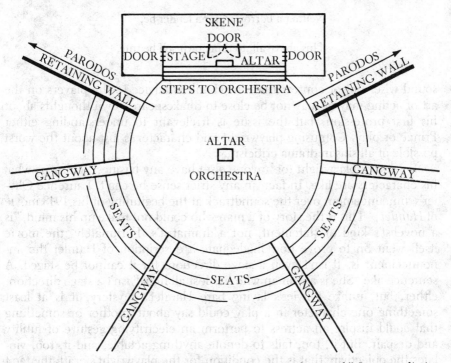

The open-air Greek theater was virtually "theater in the round." Its most distinctive feature was the orchestra *(literally, "dancing-place"), a circular, stone-paved floor on which the chorus went through its complex evolutions. A* parodos *("entry-way") right and left allowed for processional entrances and exits. The audience — 15,000 or more — sat on steeply tiered seats built into the surrounding hillside. On the rim of the orchestra stood the* skene *(literally, "hut" or "tent") which provided dressing-room space for the actors, doors for their entrances, and a simple, formal, architectural background for them to play against. There was no scenery in the modern sense of the word. A low platform gave the actors prominence and set them apart from the chorus.*

time a kind of chorus and a kind of "presenter" figures, and the action they present moves from Heaven to Earth. In contrast, every character in *Hamlet* belongs to the same court world at Elsinore. None of them stands outside the action and comments on it.

But if even presenter or commentator figures like the Messenger and the Doctor and Brecht's Singer are part of the dramatic fiction rather than stand-ins for the dramatist, there is obviously no sense in trying to look for the dramatist in disguise in any of his characters of the more common kind. Sophocles is no more Oedipus than he is Teiresias or Jocasta or the Chorus. Nora Helmer's confusion and distress are not Ibsen's. Neither Marat nor Sade speaks for Peter Weiss — or both do. In *Hamlet*, Polonius's words of advice to his departing son,

Neither a borrower nor a lender be,

. . .

This above all, to thine own self be true,

. . .

sound wiser out of context than in. Hamlet's advice to the players on the art of acting may or may not be close to Shakespeare's own thoughts about his first profession, but the issue is irrelevant to understanding either Prince or play. Confusing playwright and character is just about the worst possible of all sins in drama criticism.

Nor does a playwright (or anyone else) have any business telling us what his characters are like. In fact, in any strict sense he can't. Laurence Olivier's announcement over the soundtrack at the beginning of his 1948 movie of *Hamlet*, "This is the story of a man who could not make up his mind," is a novelist's kind of statement, not a dramatist's. Fortunately, the movie itself went on to prove how inadequate a description of Hamlet the announcement is. It isn't even a stage direction, for it cannot be staged. A sentence like "She is a woman who has lost all hope" isn't a stage direction, either, but, unlike Olivier's laying bare Hamlet's mystery, it is at least something one character in a play could say about another or something that could inspire an actress to perform an electrifying gesture of futility and despair. But it, too, fails to denote anything actable, and it, too, violates the objectivity that is the condition for the playwright's craft: the tacit agreement between him and us that for the duration of the make-believe he doesn't exist at all. That agreement makes it impossible for a critic to talk about the tone of a play, for tone, in literary criticism, refers to the quality of an author's language that reflects his attitude to his subject matter.

Not all plays observe objectivity so strictly. Modern playwrights, particularly, like to write stage directions that presume to the novelist's all-knowingness. The ending of Bernard Shaw's *Candida* is a flagrant example. When the heroine has sent her would-be lover, a young poet, "into the night" and turns to her husband, Shaw tells us, "They embrace. But they do not know the secret in the poet's heart." The first of these two sentences is stageable, a genuine stage direction. But no theatrical ingenuity can stage the second, except as words flashed on a screen, like the subtitles in old silent movies. The point is not that Shaw's plays occasionally include bits of novels, but that performability is the quality all plays have in common. The playgoer can only watch and listen; Shaw's comment on the final tableau in *Candida* does not exist for him till it is somehow translated into the language of the theater: sights and sounds. That a reader can make Shaw's words a part of his experience of the play only shows that reading a play may include nondramatic elements. The distinction is, if one likes, "academic," "purely theoretical." It certainly does not turn *Candida* into something else than a play. But to abandon this distinction is to abandon an effort to make a general distinction between drama and the other literary kinds. We *want* to be theoretical at this point: We are outlining a theory of drama.

On the other hand, plays that for technical reasons cannot be staged, or staged in their entirety, on any existing stage, or plays that if staged would overtax the patience, subtlety, or quickness of apprehension of an audience, aren't therefore *not* drama. Anyone putting on Milton's *Samson Agonistes* (ignoring the author's statement that he didn't intend it for the stage) risks disaster at the box office, but the work is still drama: a system of speaking parts developing a stageable action. Goethe's *Faust*, to take another example, has hardly ever been staged in its entirety, and the author, though a man of some practical stage experience, admitted that he was writing *against* the theater rather than *for* it. But *Faust* is still drama. Criteria for stageability are obviously relative. Consider, for example, how greatly film has extended the range of what can be shown an audience and how much of the difference between stage and screen resides in the simple fact that the camera moves around and the spectator does not. Even within the limits of the stage itself, technological advances create new possibilities. Byron's plays, regarded as ruinous in their own time because of their demands for a succession of fantastic and elaborate settings, have been successfully mounted in recent years by using back-projections to replace built sets. It is hardly a coincidence that the flowering of naturalistic drama during the last decades of the nineteenth century coincided with the replacement of gas by electricity as a means for lighting the stage and with the development of the revolving stage. Both greatly enhanced the theater's potential for a bright, versatile, and realistic stage picture.

A subtler but at least as important a kind of stageability is not a matter of finance, technical resources, and audience taste, but of language. All verbal language is speakable, but only a small part of it is dramatic in the sense of "fit to be spoken on a stage." The distinction has nothing to do with the difference between prose and verse. Shakespeare's verse is dramatic; Spenser's and Pope's and Wordsworth's is not. Ibsen's prose is dramatic; Henry James's and Proust's and Faulkner's is not.

There are many ways for language to be dramatic. Perhaps it is most potently so when it seems to be a *part of*, and not just *about*, the action — when we react to sentence rhythm and cadence, dialogue pace and length of speeches, as we do to events; when they are agents of the drama. Speech sound and speech pattern intensify emotion in the exchange between Oedipus and the old Herdsman.

HERDSMAN: No, master, in heaven's name, ask no more questions.
OEDIPUS: You are a dead man if I have to ask again.
HERDSMAN: It was a child of the house of Laius.
OEDIPUS: A slave? Or one of his own family?
HERDSMAN: I am near to saying what should not be said.

OEDIPUS: And I to hearing; but it must be heard.
HERDSMAN: They said it was Laius' son. But go inside
   And ask your wife; for she could tell you all.
OEDIPUS: You mean she gave it you?
HERDSMAN: She did, my lord.
OEDIPUS: But why?
HERDSMAN: For me to make away with it.
OEDIPUS: Her child!
HERDSMAN: She feared an evil prophecy.

The sound of human speech is not meaningful in itself, but given certain characters in certain situations it can add not just force but meaning to the words spoken. As the two voices here carry the speakers to revelation, the movement of the speech seems to echo the dread urgency of the sense. One voice is old, broken, and reluctant; the other is strong, short, and harsh, yet sounding less imperious than impelled.

The effect is different, because the characters and their circumstance are different, in the scene in *Hamlet* in which Horatio tells Hamlet of the appearance of the Ghost. But the way our ears, even in a reading, pick up the dramatic quality of speech accent and pace is similar:

HAMLET:
   My father, methinks I see my father.
HORATIO: Where, my lord?
HAMLET: In my mind's eye, Horatio.
HORATIO: I saw him once. 'A was a goodly king.
HAMLET: 'A was a man, take him for all in all,
   I shall not look upon his like again.
HORATIO: My lord, I think I saw him yesternight.
HAMLET: Saw? Who?
HORATIO: My lord, the King your father.   (I, ii, 182–91)

The same is true of some of the exchanges between Nora and Dr. Rank in the "silk stocking scene" in the middle of the second act of *A Doll's House*:

NORA *(after a brief pause)*: Why did you smile just then?
RANK: I didn't. It was you who laughed.
NORA: No, it was you who smiled, Dr. Rank!
RANK *(gets up)*: I see you're more of a mischief-maker than I thought.
NORA: I feel like mischief today.
RANK: So it seems.

         . . .

RANK *(leaning over her)*: Nora — do you really think he's the only one — ?
NORA *(with a slight start)*: Who — ?
RANK: — who'd gladly give his life for you.
NORA *(heavily)*: I see.

The richness, tension, and momentum of drama in such passages aren't all accounted for by situation and semantics.

The language of imagery and metaphor is more commonly associated with lyric and epic poetry than with drama, but a great poet can use it for subtle dramatic effects. When Hamlet, expostulating with his mother the queen in the bedroom scene in Act III, calls her adultery

> . . . an act
> That blurs the grace and blush of modesty,
> Calls virtue hypocrite, takes off the rose
> From the fair forehead of an innocent love,
> And sets a blister there, . . .   (III, iv, 41–45)

his words are more than "poetic" vituperation; they say that Gertrude's betrayal has sullied her son's love. The active verbs tell us what Gertrude has done; the passive nouns tell us to whom she has done it — to Ophelia, certainly, in Hamlet's imagination, but not *just* to Ophelia. It is not that no woman really is modest, pure, and fair, but that Hamlet no longer can think so. The images of corrupted girlhood express the cynicism that saps his will.

When, as in these examples, figurative language resonates in a larger dramatic context, we have poetic drama, whether in verse or prose. The painted harlot, the secret sickness, the overgrown garden, and the rotten realm in *Hamlet* are as crucial to the meaning of the whole play as the reason or reasons for Hamlet's delayed revenge. Or, rather, they take us as close to those reasons as any psychoanalytical theory can. And what Fortinbras says about the dead Hamlet in the last scene,

> Let four captains
> Bear Hamlet like a soldier to the stage,
> For he was likely, had he been put on,
> To have proved most royal; and for his passage
> The soldiers' music and the rite of war
> Speak loudly for him.   (V, ii, 372–76)

and the circumstances under which he says it insinuate an identity between the dead and the living prince that affects our sense of what is tragic about Hamlet's death as strongly as does Horatio's "Good night, sweet prince, / And flights of angels sing thee to thy rest." It is not a question of choosing one obituary speech over the other but of seeing how both together enrich our sense of Hamlet's character and of the fitness of his end. He dies in the arms of his scholar friend, and his epitaph is spoken by his soldier successor. There is a pattern, and it is exactly right.

Such interaction of words and scene, juxtaposition of images, allusiveness, and density of word texture help drama compensate for the brevity, simplicity, and explicitness it must observe in order to remain performable. If plays, for obvious reasons, cannot rival novels in length, in substance and subtlety of thought, or in intricacy of structure, they can probe souls as deeply, and for all their pace and compression their metaphorical universe can be as grand and compelling. As modern means of travel have expanded our capacity for seeing the world by shrinking its dimensions, so metaphor both creates and contracts imaginary space. Take from *Phaedra* the imagery of sun and monsters, from *A Doll's House* the black clothing that makes the wearer invisible, from *Major Barbara* the munition-maker Undershaft's claim that the Salvation Army motto, "Blood and Fire," might be his own, and from *Death of a Salesman* the scene in which Willy the salesman tries to become the planter of his small, dark garden, and what is left is in each case a lesser play. We can't always say exactly what has been lost, but we know it is poetry *of* as well as *in* the theater.

Like other good literature, good drama compels the surrender of our imaginations to the author's, but the language of drama is unique in being limited to the performable, including the instantly intelligible. The characteristics of drama are objectivity, brevity, pace, and continuousness. Poems and fiction can achieve the urgency of drama's human encounters, its impact of destinies in the making, only by being, precisely, dramatic.

DRAMA AND THE READER

Reading and seeing plays aren't really all that different. If they were, courses in drama wouldn't be taught anywhere but in the theater and publishing play anthologies would be worse than senseless.

But it is true that the newcomer to reading drama may feel lost at first as he tries to make sense out of conversations he knows nothing about — neither who the speakers are nor what they are talking about. And he may feel that seeing the stage directions and having the chance to ponder the dialogue at his leisure and to check back in the script for what he missed or may have forgotten don't really compensate him for the absence of the looks and the voices of actors, that help him keep the characters apart during the opening scenes of the play in performance. Nor is there an author to guide his reading, as there can be in novels. But as he reads on, he discovers that he understands the play by a process that is much the same whether he is a reader or a spectator-listener. What the characters say and do begins to make sense as he learns more about them, but he learns more about them only through what they say and do. Much of the peculiar enjoyment of drama is in that paradox. After a while, the characters become more than a list of names. They reveal their antecedents, their past and current relationships, their motives and purposes. They assume plot identity and "character." Their gestures become meaningful, their silences eloquent; what they might have said and done but didn't becomes a form of action. Absent characters exert pressure on the plot. The color of a scarf, a hat lying on a chair, the sound of an ax, groupings at a party, somebody's fiddling with a glass, a closed door, an unopened letter — all become charged with drama. Reading like that takes attention, imagination, and (above all) practice. One of the reader's rewards is that seeing and reading plays no longer seem like either-or propositions. He finds that each makes the other more enjoyable and that it is both fun and instructive to compare "book" and production. He matches his stage in the mind with the actual stage.

Because there is a performance waiting to get on stage inside every play, drama probably poses a greater challenge to the reader's imaginative participation than do the other literary genres. But understanding and enjoying *any* literary work call for all our faculties of response: intellectual, emotional, and sensory. We can't all respond equally well, but we can all make the effort to engage more than the top of our minds and the shallows of our souls. To do that with works from ages and cultures different from our own we need some background and may want more, but the lines between some and more and need and want may be hard to draw in given cases. Because of drama's potential for theater, the lines are often clearer when we read plays than when we read fiction or poems.

What kinds of background do we need? Obviously, it helps to know something about the size, shape, technical resources, and manner of staging of the theater for which the work was originally written. All plays (other than closet drama) have been written with a particular kind of performance in mind. We understand the play better if we get answers to such questions as, How was the stage space arranged? What scenic and mechanical apparatus could the author expect? How was the audience accommodated in relation to the stage? What was the distribution of seating room and standing room, the size of the audience, the theater acoustics? How· were the actors accustomed to speak their lines and conceive of their relationship to their roles, to the audience? These things are important because, although a library would classify them as "theater history" and keep them apart from "dramatic literature," they have always had a great influence, not so much on *what* the author writes but on *how* he writes it. For example, we can gain a clearer understanding of the dramatic values of the Chorus in *Oedipus the King* if we know the physical location of its performance in the Greek theater and its relationship to the actors of the individual parts. Reconstructing the setting for *Everyman* tells us not merely about the mechanics of the medieval stage but also something about the workings of the medieval mind. When we know that Molière, who ran his own troupe and almost certainly was the best comic actor in it, did not play the title role in his own *Tartuffe* but the apparently secondary role of Orgon, we learn something about the balance of interests in the play and about the way the playwright wanted us to look at it.

There are those who stress the inseparability of a play and its original playhouse home to such an extent that they insist that the only valid standard for judging a play is the performance the playwright had in mind when he wrote it. But we can't always know that, and the further back we go in history, the less we know. We know a great deal about how A *Doll's House* was originally staged: We have photographs and reviews of the early productions and inventories of costumes and props and production notes, including Ibsen's suggestions for staging. We know much less about how

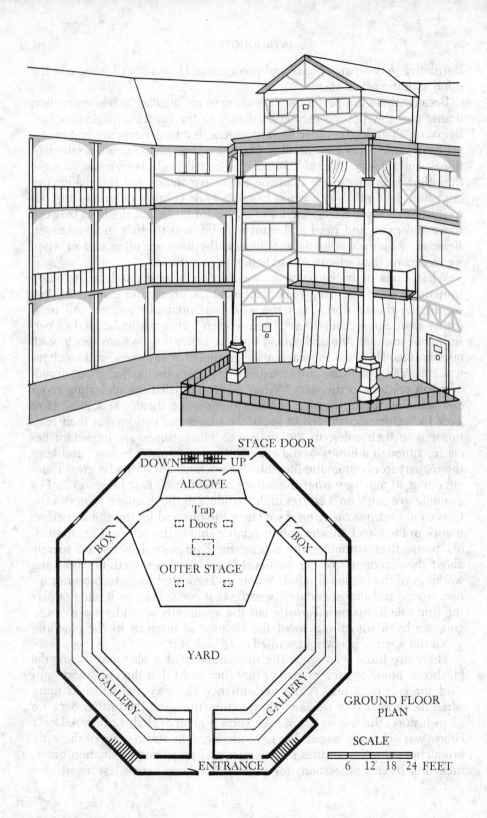

STAGE DOOR

DOWN   UP

ALCOVE

Trap
Doors

BOX   BOX

OUTER STAGE

GALLERY   GALLERY

YARD

GROUND FLOOR
PLAN

SCALE

ENTRANCE   6 12 18 24 FEET

Tartuffe was first performed. Rival scholars may offer reconstructions of the original stage for *Hamlet* so different, not merely in detail but in general principles, that it is hard to believe they are based on the same evidence. Even if exact reconstruction were possible, people have changed. A modern audience thrust into an Elizabethan playhouse would not react in the Elizabethan way. One reason (among many) is that such an audience's idea of the play would subtly but inevitably have been influenced by the many different productions of the play, in different theaters, each speaking to its own age, between Elizabethan times and ours. We have inherited not just a script but a tradition of the script in the theater. So not only is perfect archaeological reconstruction impossible, it is ultimately futile too. Nor is the playwright's authority absolute, even in cases in which we know how he thought his play should be produced. We can't always be sure he actually had his way, and we don't have to assume that his thoughts were or are better than anybody else's. Not all playwrights are talented or experienced in the crafts of the theater. They are not even necessarily the best critics of others' performance of their work. Intention is not accomplishment. All this means that even under the best of circumstances, modern attempts to duplicate older stages and stage productions must be a tentative thing, based on inferences and more or less educated guesses. That is all right, as long as we don't think that what we have is an authentic replica.

Certainly, we should bear in mind that knowledge of theater history — production details as well as general principles and the way both affect the playwright's modes of expression — makes a play easier to understand. The same is true of other aspects of the contemporary culture: social conditions, religious beliefs, moral and intellectual assumptions. The more we know about the culture reflected in what we read (or see and hear), the richer and truer our reading. It is true that we can never know everything and that it takes more than knowledge to "become" the playwright's contemporary, but we still have the obligation to try to learn as much as we can. Each culture, age, and reader, even the same reader at different times, reads a literary work differently, and the more we know about the

Although individual Elizabethan playhouses varied in shape and detail, they had several important features in common. The audience was accommodated in three tiers of galleries surrounding the playing-area, or, for the lowest admission price, as standees in the central, open courtyard. A deep-thrust stage carried the action into the center of the audience; this was partly canopied, to protect expensive costumes from the vagaries of the English weather. The tiring-house (i.e., attiring-house, or dressing-rooms) opened onto the stage and offered additional acting areas. Most theaters probably had an inner-below, a curtained alcove or shallow inner stage, in which scenic set-pieces could be changed during the action. An upper level provided for such scenes as the balcony in Romeo and Juliet, or castle walls in Shakespeare's history plays. The topmost floor of the tiring house held ropes and pulleys for "flying" entrances, and perhaps a separate musicians' gallery.

work the less likely we are to misread it. Scholarship helps preserve the identity of a literary work against the anarchy of interpretation that threatens it from reader ignorance and idiosyncrasy. A play's continued life as a unique work of art is at stake.

But such knowledge is not a precondition for the working of the dramatic imagination. Even when the images in our minds during our reading of a play can be translated into stage actualities, they are not ordinarily images of such actualities. Most of us don't imagine a stage castle, crypt, or kitchen, but the real thing — Hamlet, not some modern actor playing Hamlet. The exceptions are the theater workers — director, designer, actor, and others — who read with a particular production project in mind and the reader who has just come from a successful performance of the play. This is the reader who concerns us here. His imagination will be channeled by his memory of the hundreds of big and small details of staging and acting that together make up one of the theater's ways of "doing" the script. There is nothing wrong with that, either — in fact, there is a great deal that is right — as long as he realizes that the remembered performance both adds to and takes away from his reading experience: He loses in variety and inclusiveness what he gains in intensity. A good theater production is the joint creation of a team of professionals working together to a single artistic end. What they create is a *particular* meaning, however complex and comprehensive, lying latent in the script. It is not, and in the nature of things it cannot be, *all* of that script's meaning. Before we can have a believable, exciting stage Hamlet, somebody must choose among possible interpretations, approaches, and emphases — accepting, rejecting, adapting, combining. Otherwise, the character of the Prince of Denmark shatters into fragments and the play goes with it. Once again we are up against the disparity between the ideal and the actual, literature and theater. The script is inclusive, absolute, and permanent; the performance is selective, tentative, and temporary.

For all his disadvantages, then, the play reader has the advantage over the spectator that he retains the sovereignty of his imagination. He is not at the mercy of the theater company's vagaries of taste and interpretation. Of course, that only means that he is at the mercy of his own, and chances are that the play he puts on in the theater of his mind will be smaller and duller than the play he might see in the theater. Every reader runs that risk, and that challenge. But the point is that he does so because he is free to use his imagination. Its function has not been taken over by suppliers of theater — and taken over all the more completely and irresistibly the more imaginative and professionally expert they are. By themselves, words put the imagination to work. In the theater, they only feed it.

Obviously, a good play production can help us imagine what we found unimaginable before, or it can cool and contain an imagination that catches fire too easily. Our argument has not been that reading a play is always better than seeing-and-hearing it in the theater — "better" in the sense of more enjoyable and meaningful, and truer to the "pure" drama the playwright wrote — but only that a reading can be enjoyable, meaningful, and true. Anyone who considers reading a play a sorry making-do with second best and a playscript nothing more than a blueprint for an evening in the theater has abdicated his rights as a reader. Drama is not the only form of theater, and the theater is not the only home of drama.

ILLUSION AND CONVENTION

As there is a tension in drama itself between script and performance, so there is a tension between illusion and convention in our experience of it. Both tensions involve subtle but vital ambiguities.

Illusion is what we respond to when we take the stage happenings to be real. Convention is what we are aware of when we realize that those happenings have only been made to seem so. A convention is, literally, a "coming together," a meeting of minds — in this case, an agreement between the theater personnel and its customers that for the duration of the performance stage conditions are to be considered conditions in a real world. Conventions create illusion. They change people, things, and facts into something other than what they are. In this transformed reality Richard Burton is Hamlet, space in a downtown theater is a hall in the castle at Elsinore in long-ago Denmark, the ten-minute intermission spans weeks, and the light that floods the stage from lamps over our heads is the light of the sun. Conventions are the grammar of drama, the rules of the game, and sometimes it is more important to realize that there *are* rules than to know exactly *what* they are.

Conventions are more important in drama than in poetry and fiction because the sensory nature of an actual or imagined stage performance places the drama under a heavier obligation to create an illusion of reality. That can make it both easier and harder on the illusion-makers. The mere "thereness" of people and things on stage lends them credibility, but it can also happen that something acceptable to the imagination turns gross or silly or otherwise wrong on stage. More than one production of *Hamlet* has stumbled over the ghost of Hamlet's father.

Conventions change. Yesterday's conventions are today's absurdities and tomorrow's brilliant innovations. Some come about in response to technical necessity and disappear when there is no longer any need for them. Shakespeare had to use verbal imagery to get information about weather and season and place and time of day over to his audience (the opening lines of *Hamlet* are an example). A modern theater does it by means of scene design and electric lights. Other conventions reflect the assumptions and practices of a particular culture. The chorus in Greek tragedy probably owed its importance, first, to the evolution of drama from choral song and to certain uses of theater space associated with that tradition and, second, to the custom in the Athenian city-state of debating important issues in an assembly. The difference between Hamlet's blank verse speech and the Gravedigger's prose says something about the stratification of Elizabethan society. When foreigners in movies speak to each other in heavily accented English, it is because Hollywood knows that moviegoers want realism and don't know foreign languages.

Historically, most of Western drama falls into three divisions, each kind with its own set of conventions. In the *ceremonial* tradition (Greek, Renaissance, and neoclassical tragedy), aristocrats of noble or ignoble ambition and speaking a verse language charged with image and metaphor and allusion live and die in actions of greater significance, dignity, and intensity than ordinary actions. The plays ritualize human life. Their characters and their destinies take on archetypal dimensions: They enact universal patterns of experience. Oedipus, Hamlet, and Phaedra are examples. The *imitative* or *mimetic* tradition (forms of older comedy and the Ibsen-Chekhov-Shaw heritage in modern drama) reproduces the sensory surfaces of daily life and pretends that what happens on stage happens in reality; dialogue is overheard rather than listened to. (That is not all these plays do, but they do do that.) Other common terms for this kind of drama are *realism* and *naturalism*.* In the *expressionistic* tradition (allegorical and symbolic drama, some of Strindberg's and O'Neill's plays, and some aspects of contemporary absurdism), the stage represents the single subjective consciousness. Abstractionism and stylization, dream sequences, montage techniques, and fluidity and freedom of time and place are all conventions that insinuate an inner rather than an outer environment. The real world matters only insofar as it contributes items to the mind. The plays are mirrors to the soul.

When we say that a play creates "an illusion of life," we don't mean that we can't tell life and play apart. If we really couldn't, we wouldn't be able to make the statement in the first place and actors playing villains would risk assault from angry audiences. Small children and others who think they are actually present at the supposed scene of the action may seem to be proving the power of illusion and to be paying a kind of compliment to the arts of the theater. But they aren't really responding either to art or to reality; they are just confused.

What we *do* mean is that the people responsible for the stage representation are doing their jobs so well that we are willing to go along with the pretense. The conventions work; we accept the illusion. The psychology of illusion is complex and elusive. Does it involve what Coleridge called our

---

* "Realism" and "naturalism" both refer to art that seeks *verisimilitude* (literally, "semblance to truth"), or lifelikeness, to the world verifiable by sense experience. But sometimes "naturalism" refers not just to "formal realism" but also to a philosophy that regards human beings and their behavior as fully accountable for in terms of natural (as against supernatural) causes. The naturalist argues that the individual is a product of a certain combination of hereditary and environmental forces, over which he has virtually no control. This philosophical naturalism and materialism are closely related. Both are in opposition to idealism.

"willing suspension of disbelief," or does it depend on our disengaging ourselves from the issue of belief and nonbelief altogether? In any case, we
seem to be creatures who, given half a chance, are unable *not* to believe in
the make-believe. We do so because it is fun and because it allows us temporary relief from our own fretful selfhoods. And it isn't difficult, since
conventions are part of our daily life. If they weren't, we would hardly
accept them in the theater. It is by convention we take a photograph to be
a record of something seen, even though its rectangular frame is not the
frame in which our eyes transmit sights to our brain. By convention kids in
the comics don't grow up and grown-ups don't grow old. By convention
green light means "go" and red "stop." *Half* a chance, however, is all we
give ourselves when viewing plays. We attend them in a state of divided
consciousness. The plot fascinates us, we empathize with the characters,
we delight in our ability to pretend that both are real — while all along we
know perfectly well they are not, that the stage, to quote Dr. Johnson
again, "is only a stage, and the players only players." It is precisely the
knowing sophisticate in us that allows the child in us to surrender to the
magic of the fake reality on stage. The two of them together adopt an
attitude of naive and wide-eyed expectancy. Whenever a play performance
engages our imagination, there are other "players" in the theater than
those on stage.

There are conventions in every play. A play that tried to do without
them would depend for its effect on the audience's awareness of the conventions it was doing without. It would, in fact, submit itself to a convention more rigid and demanding than any it violated, for it would have to try
holding its audience without ever lapsing into the plausibility and coherence observed by conventional plays. If we didn't expect to see conventions at work, we wouldn't be in the theater at all. If all we wanted was a
good look at "real life" we'd go visiting our next-door neighbor. For the fun
of theater is not in being deluded but in admiring the art of those who
pretend to be trying to delude us. We'd rather have two men inside a
horse's hide than a real horse, not because the fake horse is more practical
(which it is) but because it is a device of art, and art is what we are in the
theater for. The real horse in an imaginary place mixes up artistic modes,
making each seem incongruous. The frank artifice goes better with the
other props, which also *are* not, but only *mark* or *signify*, the real thing.

Our illusion is never total, anyway; if it were, we'd miss the fun of appre-
ciating the skill of those who make it possible. All Hollywood's talent and
money can't convince us that the beautiful woman on screen is Cleopatra
and not Elizabeth Taylor or that King Kong is anything other than a contraption of plastic and wires and synthetic fur. When the hero is facing
certain death (from the Mafia, from an avalanche), a small voice inside us
keeps telling us he'll get away because the movie has still another hour to
run. We know that even a TV documentary has been edited. And the
biggest and most basic of all conventions in the realistic theater is the pre-

tense that the stage is not a stage, that the people on it are not actors and actresses, and that they say and do what they say and do because they know that no outsiders are watching and listening to them — manifest falsehoods all, as well we know.

In other words, illusion and convention are distinguishable in theory only; in any actual experience of drama they cannot be kept apart. It is a mistake, therefore, to think of plays as falling into place somewhere along a line that stretches from pure illusion at one end to pure convention at the other. There *is* a polarity, but illusion and convention are not the poles. "Realism" and "nonrealism" have gained wide currency, but they are, strictly speaking, a little misleading, since in a meaningful sense dreams and desires, memories and fears, are just as "real" as promissory notes and arms factories, cherry trees and refrigerators. The terms we used before, *mimesis*, or *imitation*, and *expression*, more accurately get at the distinction we are trying to make between the two main modes of drama. Mimetic drama pretends to be unaware of the form it imposes upon presumably raw sense experience. Expressive drama is concerned with the meaning and value such experience assumes in the consciousness. A *Doll's House* represents one kind, *Oedipus the King* and *Everyman* in different ways the other. But, again, the polarity is absolute only in theory. Few plays are consistently close to either extreme. There are, after all, recognizable sensory data both on the classical Greek state and on the pageant stage of the medieval liturgical drama: on both stages human beings speak and move. Conversely, Ibsen's theater shows the pressure of certain social forces on individuals and their relationships, and it expresses, at least by implication, an interpretation and evaluation of what it shows. It is more than a mere inventory of domestic items in a nineteenth-century middle-class home.

The fact that most of our popular drama on TV, in the movies, and on the stage continues the realistic tradition of the late nineteenth century probably accounts for the lingering prejudice against convention as "artificial" and "conformist" and against nonrealistic plays as "odd," "obscure," and "hard to get involved with." There are people who admit the conventional nature of all drama who yet feel that the only acceptable conventions are those that serve verisimilitude — that look least like artifice, that hide themselves behind familiar surfaces where everything seems probable and verifiable. But if such people object to the neoclassical convention of the three unities — the rule that the action of a play be confined to a single plot, a single place, and a single day — then, in all fairness, they should also object to the presentation on film and television of human beings as disembodied heads in closeups and to the three-walled rooms that have served as the setting for most of western drama after the Renaissance. There is every reason to think that playgoers of the past would have found a conventional modern theater just as "unnatural" as we presume to find their choruses and blank verse and soliloquies and asides. Why wouldn't they? For in our theater an audience that is not supposed to be there peeks through a proscenium arch into an artificially lighted box where paid professionals enact rehearsed goings-on as if they were real. Stage naturalism is never all that natural.

And it is the old way that has age and prestige on its side. Realism-naturalism is a late development in our theatrical culture; it is not much more than a hundred years old, and it is already waning. Ibsen and Shaw wanted to confront their contemporaries with certain social problems and to that end wrote plays that could pass for reasonable facsimiles of life in that society. These plays were not, of course, *really* documentaries, but all the circumstantial detail of their surface — furniture and dress and manners and small talk — made them look as if they were. For the most original and important dramatists of the present age significant reality is elsewhere: in myths and symbols and in ideologies and vast, collective, transcendent forces beyond our control and understanding. Their quest is not for immediate but for ultimate reality; they are interested in the physical and social facts only as a means of getting at the other reality beyond. Contemporary drama is reaching back to the ancient rituals in which drama is thought to have begun. Phaedra's environment is much less like ours than Nora Helmer's is, but for all that a modern woman may find it easier to relate to Phaedra than to Nora. If she does and if she asks herself why that should be so, she may decide that the details of dated realism in Ibsen's play have come between her and Nora and that behind the apparent differences in their circumstances there is kinship between Racine's and Ibsen's heroines. Speech and spectacle in *Oedipus the King* include none of the lifelike commonplaces of the Helmer home, for its place of action is not an ordinary living room where people talk about jobs and household expenses but a region of the soul where god and man meet.

This all means that plays that openly show their conventions can be as illusionistic as plays that hide theirs. Against all our experience and common sense, an opera, in which people sing at each other and the part of the heroine who is dying from consumption is sung by a vibrant soprano, commands our willing suspension of disbelief. In *Oedipus the King* the actors wear masks (or did in the original production), at intervals the action is interrupted by a body of performers who comment on it in a single voice, all the characters speak verse, and a man who has just blinded himself and who in real life would be suffering extremes of physical and mental anguish expresses himself in formal and stately words of moving eloquence. In a good production of the play, the idea that none of this is real because it doesn't copy a reality we are familiar with is irrelevant. The words, the spectacle, the action make up an illusion — precisely, an *illusion* — of a reality we believe in because it expresses an experience true to human nature. There is nothing really very strange in this. The imagination is a wonderfully adaptive faculty that finds it just as easy to believe in the "reality" of obvious conventions as not to be bothered by the conventions hiding in the apparent reality.

From the point of view of the practical theater, it can be harder to create a realistic than a nonrealistic illusion. A director who wants to stage *Oedipus the King* with the performers' faces showing, instead of being covered by masks, has to find an actress whose face will be equally convincing as Oedipus's wife's and as his mother's. There was no such problem in the original production. A male actor put on a mask which by convention signified "female" and which served as the face of *all* women, young and old. The example suggests that a director does wisely in not trying to impose an alien convention on a play — the sort of thing represented by a hippie *Everyman*, *Hamlet* in modern dress, and *A Doll's House* as an ancient male-female rite. By avoiding such changes, he not only respects the integrity of the play; he also makes it easier on himself and his cast.

For similar reasons, the conventions that govern plays of inner psychic experience may meet less resistance from a modern, literal-minded audience than the conventions of a traditional tragedy like *Oedipus the King*. In Sophocles' play, the images of human life, however heightened, intensified, and splendidly articulated, still keep some semblance to the real world our senses know. But *Everyman* is so obviously not an image of that kind of reality that we don't judge it by that reality's criteria. We may have seen death, but we have not seen Death, and few of us will claim to have seen God. How can we object, then, to seeing Death costumed as (say) a skeleton or to God with a gold helmet? As allegory, an extended metaphor for the larger truths behind the fleeting and fragile appearance of the real world, the play is perfectly credible. *Act Without Words*, too, is safe from being judged and found wanting by realistic standards, even though Beckett renders the irreducibles of life not in didactic dialogue and allegorical encounters but in homely symbols — a tree, some boxes, a length of rope, a carafe labeled "Water," — and basic actions — simple physical responses to physical stimuli. The sensory immediacy of all this is undeniable, but that, obviously, is not their whole significance. *The Ghost Sonata* is never quite without items from the ordinary, reliable world of the senses, but what Strindberg shows is not that world itself but the way it might appear in a troubled dream — now beautiful and benign, now misshapen and sinister. In *Death of a Salesman* scenes set in an objective present alternate with scenes set in the past that Willy Loman's breaking mind remembers (the happy scenes with Linda and the boys, the Boston hotel scene) or imagines (the scenes with Ben). Like Willy, we may find ourselves playing pinochle with a neighbor, but we are not likely to interrupt the game and start talking with a dead brother. Miller juxtaposes the mimetic and the expressive conventions within the same scene. Charley and the card game and the kitchen furniture belong to realism, the hallucinated Ben to expressionism. That is all right. Because the contrast is effectively making a point about Willy's psychology, it seems justified, not discordant. It doesn't break the play apart. Our tolerance is helped by the fact that both Charley and Ben, the "real" and the "unreal" character, appear on the same stage among the same props and that both are played by live actors. The theater is the great equalizer, making differences between conventions disappear in its rendering of all kinds of human experience in the same inclusive, physical idiom.

Like playwrights, actors, too, work within conventions. With certain plays at certain times an actor may conceive of his task as that of reproducing, as closely as possible, the surface appearances of actuality, representing a character "drawn from life" and assumed to have an off-stage past that explains his present and determines his future. In this acting convention the actor seeks to submerge his own real-life identity into that of his role — "to be" rather than "to act," as the slogan has it. This, in essence, is the theory of acting practiced and taught by the Russian director Constantin Stanislavsky (1863–1938), perhaps the single most important influence on twentieth-century acting.

But there have also been actors — Greek actors, certainly; Elizabethan, probably — who have thought of their craft as the communication of human actions and feelings by an agreed-upon set of gestures, movements, and speech manners; in short, conventions. Their stage is not a copy of the real world but a symbol, meaningful only to audiences who accept the conventions the stage flaunts. If Stanislavsky's theater is mimetic, this one is expressive.

In modern theater theory Bertolt Brecht's "epic" theater with its devices for *Verfremdung* (distancing, alienation) is sometimes thought of as the antithesis to Stanislavsky's realism. But Brecht capitalizes on convention not so much in order to avoid mimesis as to remind us that the illusion we surrender to is a *theater* illusion. A Brechtian actor plays up his double function: He is both an impersonator of a fictional character, *and* a professional mime who "demonstrates" (Brecht's word) how a character like that would behave in given situations. Brecht's theater is *theatricalist* in the way it openly acknowledges its function as a place for the production of dramatic artifacts. It makes a principle out of what is challenge and irony in the Father's speeches in Pirandello's *Six Characters in Search of an Author*. Pirandello's set is a stage during rehearsal. The rehearsal is interrupted by the arrival of a family of six, who call themselves characters in a play, and the drama is in the conflicting claims of the reality of "life" (the theater company) and the reality of "art" (the family). The stage, says the Father, is just a stage, the actors just actors, and their art a bad imitation of life. No actor can ever "be" him or any other character. Stage realism is a fraud.

From one viewpoint, Brecht's theater is less artificial than realistic

drama, for it owns up to what it actually is. From another, it only acknowledges the fact that all art, quite properly, is artificial — that is, "made by
art," the product of conscious craftsmanship which executes an idea or a
perception in pigment or clay or words on a stage. The two kinds of theater
differ in their ideological and artistic premises, in the kind of illusion they
try to create, and in the ways in which they go about creating it. But both
make use of conventions, ways of accommodating life to stage.

"Life" in drama, then, can be defined as generously as we and the people
of the theater agree it can be defined. That is what illusion and convention
are all about. Whoever during a performance is bothered by the obviously
painted landscape, or by the hero's apparent deafness to the villain's stage
whisper, or by the fewness of soldiers in battle scenes, or by too perfectly
timed exits and entrances, or by the casual use of time and space in *Everyman* and *Marat/Sade* — just isn't playing the game of make-believe. He
refuses to grant the play the right to define its own truth as an image of
human life — to be metaphor rather than mimicry. The play and the theater both will survive his refusal. The loss is his: the enjoyment of his imagination.

Perhaps Brecht's *Verfremdung* theory might help to convert him. To
make sure that his plays *confronted* audiences with reality rather than simply provided them with a pretext for *escaping* from it, Brecht employed a
number of devices to break the illusion of life. Among them are shifts back
and forth between drama and narrative, direct address to the audience,
and scenes and speeches that call attention to the performance as performance. The theory is that such devices will keep our attention fixed on the
left-wing propaganda of the play and prevent us from sloppily emoting in
empathy and suspense. As long as we realize that the play is only a play
and not real life, we remain, presumably, at a safe "esthetic distance" from
it. In *The Caucasian Chalk Circle* the interruptions of the dramatized episodes by the Singer's songs and recited summaries are meant to keep us
from mistaking the old fable "told" us for our enlightenment and entertainment for spontaneous happenings in the present.

It is hard to believe that Brecht was so naive as to think that only his
Verfremdung technique stood between his audience and a confusion of
play and life. True, he does sometimes sound as if he really thought that
the only reason people engage their emotions when they attend plays is
that they respond to the events on stage as if they were events in real life.
But this is polemics. What he is really doing in his plays is deliberately
exploiting for theatrical ends the illusion-convention duality of all drama.
He keeps us on a teeter-totter: Now we are engaged, now some *Verfremdung* device kicks us out of the illusion and we stand back to observe and
reflect. We cannot for long remain either enchanted or detached. And so
we are what Brecht wants us to be: alert, aware, critical. As long as we are
allowed our moments of delighted make-believe, we don't mind. And there
are worse ways of experiencing drama.

ACTION AND PLOT

The world of drama is not the scientist's world of matter and motion, or the philosopher's object for contemplation, or a marketplace or pleasure palace, or a place of pain and evil ripe for change, though there is a little of each of these in it. It is a place for speech in action (or, in Pirandello's phrase, "spoken action").

The place may be large and crowded, as in *Hamlet*, *The Caucasian Chalk Circle*, and *Marat/Sade* (*panoramic* plays), or it may be small, closed, and sparsely populated as in *Tartuffe*, *A Doll's House*, and *Riders to the Sea* (*focused* plays). The speech may be the heightened utterance of verse or colloquial prose, or a single play may employ both, as *Hamlet* does. Variety in kinds of discourse may serve characterization, point up the double level of action (as in *The Caucasian Chalk Circle*), or mark a range of abstract values (verse suggesting nobility, passion; prose meanness, reason).

Dramatic action is a comprehensive concept that includes but goes beyond physical activity. Aristotle's *Poetics* (c. 330 B.C.) defines poetry (i.e., imaginative literature in general) as "imitation of men in action." Drama differs from epic in its manner of imitation: epic *narrates* and *describes*, drama *shows* and *enacts*. In Aristotle's words: it "presents all [its] characters as living and moving before us."

Aristotle's "imitation" (Greek *mimesis*) has always been a controversial concept, but its context in the *Poetics* suggests that Aristotle had in mind something other than just a slice of life. Imitation is not the random reproduction of the sensory surface we would get if we posted a tape recorder and a movie camera on a busy street corner. We would be recording actuality; we would not be making art. Aristotle's imitation, rather, is an artist's deliberate selection and arrangement of images in a pattern that makes up a whole and coherent and humanly relevant course of events. The pattern is an action (Greek *praxis*) that represents Nature, and Nature, in this classical (and neoclassical) sense, is the sum of all the changeless laws under which we manifest our humanity, our "human nature." In our human view of things, "Nature" stands for the order, for the informing principle, of our existence, for the way things *are*. Art imitates this ultimate reality in order to help us orient ourselves in it.

This interpretation of "imitation" gains in plausibility if we assume, as many scholars have, that Aristotle wrote the *Poetics* in vindication of poetry against Plato's charges in the *Ion* and in Book X of *The Republic*. According to Plato, poetry is neither an art nor a skill but the product of the kind of madness people call inspiration. By exciting people's passions it threatens the order and stability of the state. Its fictions have inferior status as images of reality, because they are copies of the world of the senses, which itself is only an imperfect and impermanent copy of the eternal forms (or ideas) in the mind of God. Plato's poet, in other words, has no mind or will of his own, and what he utters in his frenzy is politically and psychologically subversive and philosophically trivial.

In contrast, Aristotle's detailed analyses of dramatic forms and techniques in the *Poetics* suggest, first, that he held the art of drama to be a craft with discoverable rules. Second, his theory of imitation assumes the significance of the *content* of drama. Third, his theory of *catharsis* (purgation) suggests that he attributed to at least tragic drama a psychotherapeutic function: By vicariously participating in the stage action, the spectator harmlessly expends potentially dangerous psychic energy in a release of tensions. Fourth, the effectiveness of catharsis depends on the spectator's emotional involvement in the action, and that, in turn, depends on a degree of moral and psychological plausibility in the main character (*protagonist*). We must be able to project ourselves, to some extent, into his situation and feelings. In other words, Aristotle seems to have regarded "poetry" (including drama) as a poet's deliberate artifact, philosophically relevant, and psychologically both salutary and realistic. As a theory of art, the *Poetics* recognizes what Plato's indictment did not: that a configuration of particular copies of sensory reality can have a meaning beyond that of asserting the existence of their originals. A whole can be greater than the sum of its parts. A curved wall can be built with square bricks.

A play is a patterning of language, event, character, and spectacle, each part a function of the other three. *Plot* (Aristotle's *mythos*) is the sequence of events by which the play reaches resolution. It is what makes a difference between a play and a mere collection of happenings. *Action* is what the plot amounts to. To define the action of a play is to distill its plot and state its meaning at the same time — to "essentialize" it. In *The Idea of a Theater* Francis Fergusson suggests that this is best done in an infinitive phrase, because infinitives suggest purpose and purpose makes for plot movement. The action in *Everyman* is "to give God an account of your life," in *Phaedra* "to acknowledge the power of Venus," in *The Man of Mode* "to control one's group for pleasure and power," in *A Doll's House* "to experience 'the wonderful,' " in *Riders to the Sea* "to learn to live with death at sea," in *Six Characters* "to live on stage," in *Marat/Sade* "to reenact the French Revolution."

Plots may be small or large, simple or complex, fast or slow, compact or diffuse. For all their obvious differences, *Oedipus the King*, *Everyman*, and *A Doll's House* all have plots that proceed by a single line of cause and effect. The phrase "the persecution and assassination of Jean-Paul Marat" suggests that there is the same kind of plot in Weiss's play, but the title action is only a skeletal plot, a structure to be constantly fractured by the formalities of the staged reenactment of the historical event, by the inmates' interruptions of the reenactment, and by the action-stopping songs and debates. As the madhouse stage reenacts the lunacy of history, the whole noisy spectacle turns the nominal plot into a chaos of conflicts. Aristotle defines plot as "the soul of tragedy," but plot in Aristotle's sense is clearly not the "soul" of Weiss's play.

Or plots may subordinate story-telling to the creation of a sense of active human presence. In *Tartuffe*, Molière takes his two main characters through their paces, by turns absurd, pathetic, and sinister. Plot here is the interaction of character and event in a succession of scenes exhibiting hypocrisy and gullibility in the round. A flow of social trivia carries the passive characters in Chekhov's *Cherry Orchard* to a decisive event. The discrepancy between their fixed psychology and moving time gives point and continuity to the sequence. Molière and Chekhov don't rely on the convenient convention that life runs in plots. They build drama by juxtaposing scenes of ironically different styles, tones, and content.

Sometimes a single dramatic action consists of two or more analogous, mutually reflective plots. In *Hamlet*, three young men, each with a father to avenge, undertake different kinds of revenge and react differently to the obstacles in their way. Their situations are similar enough to make their dissimilarities of character seem significant. In *Major Barbara*, Barbara, standing for "soul," and Cusins, standing for "mind," are converted to Undershaft's gospel of hard facts along plot lines that first run parallel, then diverge, and finally come together. In *The Cherry Orchard*, a variety of frustrations, isolations, and apathies cohere in a single image of waste and futility. Plot unity is clearly not the same thing in all plays.

Traditional anatomies of plays divide plots into four parts: (1) *exposition*, introducing the characters with their past and present situations; (2) *complication*, interweaving their fortunes in a "thickening" of the plot; (3) *reversal* (Greek *peripeteia*), the point at which the protagonist's fortune changes from good to bad (tragedy) or from bad to good (comedy); and (4) *denouement*, tying up loose ends, allowing the audience to calm down after the excitement. Alternative terms are *protasis* (premise or proposition), *epitasis* (intensification or "stretching"), and *catastrophe*. Simpler still is a division of the plot into a *rising* and a *falling* phase.

Other common terms in analyses of dramatic structure include *crisis*, the point in the complication at which the outcome of the plot is irreversibly determined; *recognition* (Greek *anagnorisis*), the protagonist's realization that his fortune has decisively turned and that he shares in the responsibility for the turn; and *climax*, the point in the play at which audience emotion is most intense. The climax usually coincides, as we would expect, either with the crisis or with the recognition. All three coincide in the last act of *A Doll's House*, when Helmer's reaction to the news of Nora's forgery opens her (and our) eyes to the nature of their marriage.

Good plots are complex, organic structures, in which the parts alternate, overlap, and merge. A particularly compact kind of plot structure is the *retrospective*, in which most of the dialogue amounts to a "looking back" on the past that has led to the present crisis. In retrospective plays, like

Oedipus the King, *A Doll's House*, and *Death of a Salesman*, exposition and complication virtually coincide; past circumstance affecting the present lives of the characters keeps coming to light almost till the end of the play: the two shepherds on Mount Cithairon, Nora's loan, the woman in the Boston hotel room. The revealed and reconsidered past are what such plays are about. In Sophocles' and Ibsen's plays, the retrospectiveness is limited to the dialogue, but whenever Willy Loman's memories are staged in expressionistic representations of what goes on in a mind that is losing its hold on reality, the spectacle, too, is retrospective.

Retrospective plays pick up their stories just before they "break"; their action is foreshortened. The dramatic situation is charged from the beginning; they are "plays of ripe condition" or "fifth-act plays." The second of these two terms recognizes that the whole action in a retrospective play is made up of plot matter which in chronologically structured plays normally is found in the last act. For example, in the nonretrospective *Hamlet* and *The Caucasian Chalk Circle*, *story* and *play* are very nearly the same, but the story of Nora and Helmer in *A Doll's House* has begun long before the play begins and is, as it were, over before the play is over. For what comes between Helmer's discovery of Nora's "crime" and Nora's final leaving is not further plot development but retrospective discussion. The drama is no longer in forward-moving events but in backward-looking debate.

This is to say that traditional plot analysis doesn't work equally well for all plays, not even for all older plays. For some of the most original modern plays it doesn't work at all. Nothing (or almost nothing) precedes the complication in *The Ghost Sonata* and *Dutchman*. Distinguishing between crisis and reversal in *The Caucasian Chalk Circle* is pointless. Nor can any traditional plot paradigm deal with Brecht's play-within-the-play structure, or with the variant of that structure in *Six Characters*, or with the diffuse plot of *The Cherry Orchard*, or with the scenography of repetition and paralysis in *Act Without Words*, or with the complicated time schemes and actor-audience relationships in *Marat/Sade*. Much of what is most powerful in modern drama is more like an image than a process — a static image of a condition from which there is no escape, rather than a sequence of events moving toward a conclusion. Happenings make a shape rather than a line, as if drama were approaching the mode of lyrics. The dynamic Aristotelian plot structure, with "beginning," "middle," and "end" in unilinear and coherent sequence toward a meaningful climax and conclusion, has been shattered in plays in which reality appears exploded — fragments in incidental arrangements, a chaos of feelings and events, random words and motion.

But that description, too, needs to be qualified. For to a contemporary, at least, the history of modern drama reads like a story of continuing revolt and counterrevolt, of constantly new experimentation, of a succession of avant-gardisms, each of which defies the very idea of any formal tradition. But recognizing the nature of modern drama isn't quite the same as admitting that traditional plot analysis, aside from having a certain historical interest, is quite useless in dealing with western drama of the last hundred years or so. Understanding the historical importance of traditional plot analysis is important to understanding the implications for our own drama of its current neglect or near-neglect. And its major terms correspond to the order of beginning, middle, and end, into which our own lives divide whenever we try to make sense of them. No doubt that is why the terms *are* major.

The *story* of *Oedipus the King* is the entire chronicle of the fulfillment of the oracle's prophecy from its first announcement to Laius and Jocasta till their son's final exit, self-blinded and self-banished. The *action* is the quest for Laius's killer, the human cause of the blight on Thebes. A definition of it by one of Fergusson's infinitive phrases points up the analogy between it and the action of *Hamlet:* "to purge the infected realm." The *plot* is the tight, causal chain of events that piece by piece unfolds the past. The *exposition* begins as the play opens, but with Teiresias's entry (line 289) it takes on the function of *complication* as well and leads in a single dramatic movement to the *reversal-recognition* when Oedipus talks with the Herdsman. For it is Teiresias's veiled allusion to an unspeakable secret in Oedipus's past (exposition) that sets the quest for Laius's killer in motion (complication), and Oedipus's fortune turns (reversal) the moment he learns the secret (recognition). The *crisis* comes when Oedipus, in the pride of his self-made fortune, refuses to heed Jocasta's warning against inquiring further into his origin. The *climax* of the play (or of any play) cannot be objectively determined, for the climax, unlike the crisis, the reversal, and the recognition, is not an intrinsic part of the play structure. Most people probably locate the climax in *Oedipus the King* either at the crisis or at the reversal-recognition. Earlier, we noted the same kind of convergence of crucial plot moments in the last act of *A Doll's House*. The *denouement* in Sophocles' play includes the Second Messenger's report on Jocasta's suicide and Oedipus's blinding himself, the exchange between Oedipus and the Chorus, Oedipus's final soliloquy, Creon's taking charge, Oedipus's banishment and last exit, and the concluding choric statement of the moral of the play.

A sound plot structure builds suspense, but it also survives it. It is the mark of superior plays that we want to see or read them more than once. There is so much *to* them that they reward, even if they don't require, repeated experience. And there is nothing odd about preferring seeing yet another *Hamlet* to seeing a brand new play. What we lose in thrill, we gain in understanding. Our minds are composed enough to attend to the whole pattern of developing events and not just to their final outcome, and we discover that our knowledge of the outcome heightens our awareness of the uncertainties that precede it. If our knowledge kills one kind of suspense, it creates another. With familiarity we are also in a better position to appreciate the playwright's *dramaturgy* — his skill in crafting his plot —

and *scenography* — his use of stage space, movement, color, line, and light as integral parts of his play. The football fan goes to the game not just to learn who wins and by what score but to watch the game being played and to judge and enjoy the skill of coach and players. Just so, the lover of drama seeks vicarious experience in artistic form and not just information. The ideal spectator, it could be argued, attends both kinds of game in a state of disinterested fascination.

Character and Conflict

When everything in a play seems appropriate to everything else, the play observes *dramatic decorum*. Manners fit period and place and social class. Speech is suitable to the age, sex, personality, and circumstance of the speaker as well as to the general level of language in the play: "high" (serious, eloquent) in tragedy, "middle" (colloquial) or "low" (vulgar, farcical) in comedy. Ideally, the collaboration and mutual appropriateness of the play constituents produce a single, consistent, and believable image of a piece of human reality. Such congruity of parts does not by itself make for a great play (or even, in the ways that really count, for a *whole* play), but it is difficult to think of a single great play that is without it.

If there is one relationship between basic play elements that ultimately determines what is and is not decorum in all the other relationships, it is that between character and plot. Character and plot are what the "men" and the "action" in Aristotle's definition of drama refer to. The definition, probably wisely, leaves unresolved the chicken-and-egg issue of which of the two comes first; in drama, as in the other arts, there must be just about as many different creative processes as there are creative artists. But it *does* suggest that plot reveals character, that we *are* what we *do*. There are moral philosophers who will object to that, but it is an indispensable premise for drama. No wonder Aristotle considered plot "the soul of the tragedy."

If one advantage of defining dramatic action in an infinitive phrase, as Fergusson suggests we do, is that it calls attention to *purpose* as the motor force of the play, another is the implied definition of "character" as something like "will in action" or "directed psychic energy." This definition is preferable to rival definitions, such as "plot ingredient" or "moral and mental constitution" or "a set of actions and speeches performed by an actor in order to elicit a certain affective response from an audience." For, unlike them, "will in action" recognizes the dynamics of the play as a movement of the soul — Fergusson's "changing life of the psyche." A play with that kind of plot movement observes decorum of the kind it can't do without and still be an action. Without it, the play is only figures moving and speaking on a stage where things happen. We sharpen our perceptions both of the action and of ourselves when we reverse the old equation of life with a play. For if, as Shakespeare's Jaques puts the equation in *As You Like It*,

"All the world's a stage, and all the men and women merely players," then, there on the stage before us, is our world with us in it.

The changes in "the life of the psyche" come about through the soul's interaction with other souls. In drama, such interaction is typically in the form of conflict; conflict is what plays are about. The conflict in *Oedipus the King* is most simply defined as one between man and god: The king's belief in the efficacy of reason and in the virtue of doing one's duty is smashed by a mysterious, immovable, supernatural force. Or we may think of the conflict as *dramatic irony*, a kind of complexity, or doubleness, in our view of the action, resulting from our awareness of a discrepancy between what a character *thinks* is the case and what *is* the case. Here we see that what Oedipus *thinks* his purpose, to purge Thebes, will accomplish — "By avenging him [the murdered Laius] I protect myself" — is at odds with what it *does* accomplish. To Oedipus himself, until the last piece of the puzzle falls into place, the conflict is between his wise and noble intent and the obstacles in its way.

In tragedy, the human will involved in the conflict is heroically uncompromising and therefore (it seems) doomed. In comedy, it is either successful (Undershaft's in *Major Barbara*) or frustrated (Tartuffe's) and, if frustrated, either reformable (Barbara's) or unreformable (Tartuffe's). Character against god, against nature (sea, mountain, hunger, tiger), against society, against another character, and against itself, describe the main kinds of conflict.

Conflict may be as simple as in a fairy tale or a western, or as complex as in *Hamlet*. It may be morally unequivocal (*Tartuffe*, *The Caucasian Chalk Circle*), ambiguous (*Oedipus the King*, *Phaedra*, *Major Barbara*), or neutral (*The Cherry Orchard*, *Riders to the Sea*, *Dutchman*). It may be elemental, political, philosophical, sexual, or metaphysical. In form it may be allegorical or realistic or fantastic. It may be of public significance (*Marat/Sade*) or private (*The Importance of Being Earnest*). Drama is unthinkable without conflict, for dramatic action is the movement of opposing forces toward a resolution of their opposition — in the hero's death or the villain's defeat, or in a configuration of circumstances in which the transcendent power that shapes our lives appears as order and meaning or as chaos, darkness, and silence.

Conflict creates suspense. Suspense is what we feel when we can't wait to find out what will happen, yet realize how much we enjoy the wait and how much our enjoyment depends on our certainty that we will find out in the end. Suspended between contrary feelings that reinforce one another, we count on the playwright to keep coming up with happenings that surprise us even as they seem to be the only possible consequences of what has happened before. Part of our fun is in exercising our privilege to be difficult customers: to be excited and exacting at the same time. The playwright's success in pleasing us depends on his skill in weaving character and event together in a tough, bright fabric of strong but intricate design.

Brecht's Azdak in *The Caucasian Chalk Circle* is a good example of a character whose plot function is to act plausibly and unexpectedly at the same time. Dirty, drunken, ignorant, cowardly, boot-licking, and bribe-taking, he doesn't seem like much of a judge. But then we realize that the chalk circle test is morally more relevant to the case than establishing biological motherhood and that all along Azdak has been acting on impulses of earthy common sense and good nature. Divorcing Grusha and the peasant she married of necessity is obviously divorcing the "right" and not the "wrong" couple; this way Grusha is free to marry Simon, and the old couple can go on enjoying "not liking" one another. Azdak's justice is the justice of man and not of law; perhaps that is why we approve of it. The subversive in us cheers when his incompetence and corruption turn wrong to right; like us, he prefers Grusha, with her courage and indignation, lovingness and good looks, to the disagreeable Natella Abashwili. Thanks to this selfish, ribald, superbly indestructible anarchist, generosity and natural feeling triumph over a cruel and greedy establishment. About the happy ending we say: "That works; it's not a trick. I didn't foresee it, but now that I see it I believe it."

The speakable word and the stageable spectacle are the media of drama, but its substance is a conflict we witness in a number of ways: partly as safe and superior beings enjoying dramatic irony at the expense of puppets who don't know what is happening to them; partly as observers feeling both suspense and sympathy, commiserating with those who suffer, rejoicing with the happy, relishing the downfall of the bad; and partly as fellow knaves and fools — there, but for the grace of God, *we* strut and fret.

ANATOMY OF A SCENE

The actor who played the butler Merriman in the original production of *The Importance of Being Earnest* recalled that on the opening night, "My first speech, 'Mr. Ernest Worthing has just driven over from the station. He has brought his luggage with him,' was received with the loudest and most sustained laugh that I have ever experienced, culminating in a round of applause; and as I came off Wilde said to me, 'I'm so glad you got that laugh. It shows they have followed the plot.'"

Wilde understood what some of his critics have not: in *Earnest* the plot is the play. Anyone who doesn't look forward to a feast of funny confusion the moment Merriman announces Algernon's arrival has been left behind by the play, however amused he may be by its effervescent dialogue. The plot is of the kind in which a crazy but impeccable logic of manners and sentiment moves events toward a resolution that unties all knots and leaves no loose ends. (The only exception is Algernon's unchanged Christian name, which leaves him unqualified to be Cecily's husband. If Wilde needs excuses for not doing the impossible, the facts are that Cecily no longer seems to mind, that Dr. Chasuble is ready for the christening in case she does, and that Algernon turns out to be, as he has claimed, Jack's younger brother.)

What makes one of the cleverest intrigues in all of English comedy all the more brilliant is the way Wilde has put it together from a hoard of old clichés: love at — or before — first sight, a formidable parent, a menial from the past solving the family mystery, a lost infant restored, impostors, overheard conversation, mistaken identity. Wilde turns this creaky contraption into something pert and brisk and joyful. Instead of the soggy pathos and dastardly schemes of Victorian melodrama, we have a bright, fast farce that deflates stuffiness. Even those who find nothing more than the "trivial comedy" of Wilde's subtitle in his play won't find anything thin or trite in his plot.

Fine plot carpentry of this sort is not the only or even the most important mode of drama. The interweaving strands of Shakespearean imagery, the agility of Shavian dialectics, the separate moments of poignant social realism in Chekhov — these are all material for dramatic texture rather than structure. Beckett's and Weiss's plays challenge the old axiom that drama can't do without plot and character. Tight, causal intrigue wouldn't fit either Weiss's multileveled spectacle of violent disjunction or Beckett's wordless fable about man's solitary, tantalizing existence, and neither of the two plays has or needs characters that can be "explained." Wilde's kind of plot ingenuity isn't even the main means to strong structure. The tragic movement in Racine's *Phaedra* is not generated by any mechanics of close-knit intrigue but by the gathering momentum of psychologically determined and fatefully timed confrontations and confessions.

But strong and complex plots are major vehicles for form and meaning in plays as different in other respects as *Oedipus the King*, *Hamlet*, *A Doll's House*, and *The Caucasian Chalk Circle*. The linked revelations that take the foundling king in Sophocles' play to the final, fearful question, "Who were my parents?", the cause-and-effect sequence of moves and countermoves in Hamlet's secret combat with his uncle-king, the exposed past that reveals the impassable rift between husband and wife in *A Doll's House*, and the long action in Brecht's play that leads up to the moment in Section III when the Ironshirts ask Grusha if little Michael is her son and both she and we know that if she answers yes she will lose Simon Shashava and if she answers no she will lose Michael — these are all plots where tensions build toward release. Because well-plotted intrigue is a literary instrument for precision, manipulating people and events so as to precisely fit one to the other, it lends itself better than other constituents of drama to an illustration of drama as technique. The phase in Wilde's plot that brings the two young couples together and temporarily settles the name business is an example.*

---

* The reader should turn to Merriman's speech in Act II, "A Miss Fairfax has just called to see Mr. Worthing" (p. 521), and read to Lady Bracknell's entry early in Act III (p. 529).

It is very much to the point that these scenes cannot be considered apart from the scenes that precede and follow. We miss the fun following Merriman's announcement to Cecily of Gwendolen's arrival unless we have certain plot facts clearly in mind.

Gwendolen's unexpected arrival at Jack's country house is the third such arrival in this act. Each leads only to such encounters as will postpone the moment when all confusion is untangled. Such postponement is what we want, of course; we haven't yet had our fill of fun. First, Algernon meets Cecily, confident that Jack, who could expose him, is still in town. Next, Jack meets Miss Prism and Dr. Chasuble, who at this stage of plot development are the only "safe" recipients of his news about his brother's death. And now Gwendolen meets Cecily alone; the presence of others would dissipate the dramatic force of their meeting.

No fewer than three "Ernest Worthings" are active in the plot at this point, and, what is equally remarkable, none of them is real. There is Algernon posing as Jack's wicked younger brother; there is that same brother dead in Paris "from a severe chill"; and there is Jack himself, engaged to Gwendolen under his town name since the day before. Both Cecily and Gwendolen are determined to marry an Ernest, but neither knows of the other's determination. As Gwendolen is engaged to Ernest-Jack, so Cecily has just become engaged to Ernest-Algernon. And as Gwendolen is ignorant that Cecily's "Ernest" is her own cousin Algernon, so Cecily is ignorant that Gwendolen's "Ernest" is her own "dear Uncle Jack." The wonder is not that we don't balk at accepting all of this but that no special lenience on our part is required. Everything accords perfectly with motive and circumstance.

No doubt our acceptance has been purchased partly with our anticipation of what will happen when two romantic, high-spirited, and extraordinarily articulate young women discover they are both engaged to be married to the same man. But our awareness of their unawareness is not all we enjoy.

There is not a soft spot in the entire structure. The quick switch from Gwendolen's and Cecily's instant, effusive friendship to their crisp, mutual disdain makes both funnier — just as Jack's entry in his "garb of woe" earlier in the act gains in comic effect by coming right after we have seen the brother he is in mourning for romancing with Cecily and being led into the house to be fed. In the purity of their extremes, Gwendolen's and Cecily's successive attitudes of intimacy and distance are just right. Nothing is fuzzy or hard to understand about their mutual ignorances, false assumptions, and mistaken inferences. It is a sign of Wilde's superb artistic control over his delicate material in this scene that he manages their nearly identical syntax and rhetoric, both in gushing friendship and in venomous politeness, without visible strain.

The physical action is just as carefully patterned, adding a kind of choreography to speech and sentiment. Early in the scene, while Cecily and Gwendolen are standing up, they are first strangers and then rivals; in the interval, while they are sitting down, they are friends. Later, instead of seatings and risings, we get the manual business of the tea table. All this action is indicated in stage directions so patently symmetrical as to call for stylized performance. There are no actual stage walks in the scene, but the two actresses would be true to the spirit of the script if they were to move and gesture in balletlike ways. What Wilde is doing is giving us the visual equivalent of the elaborate, formal artifice of manners in high society. The rehearsed look of the human spectacle is pretty much its point.

When Jack and Algernon enter, the ballet becomes more like a real dance. Jack "offers to kiss" Gwendolen; Gwendolen, "drawing back," asks him if he is engaged to marry Cecily; Jack tells her no; Gwendolen "offers her cheek"; Cecily tells her that Jack's name is Jack and not Ernest; Gwendolen "recedes." On Algernon's entry, he and Cecily go through the same sequence of questions and answers and physical movements, with Gwendolen now in Cecily's earlier role as catty informant. These symmetrical ceremonies of love's labors lost come to an end when Cecily and Gwendolen go into the house, together as "sisters" now that they have discovered that rather than being engaged to the same man, neither of them is engaged to any man at all. The brothers — they are, of course, actual brothers, but nobody knows that yet — are left bickering outside.

Act III opens with a third, indoor "movement" in the courtship dance. Once again, concerted emotions are shown in concerted physical action. Jack and Algernon face Gwendolen and Cecily. Standing and speaking together, the women tell the men that their "Christian names are still an insuperable barrier." Together, the men promise to have themselves rechristened. Together, the women are overcome with admiration and tenderness. The couples move together in embrace, only to "separate in alarm" a moment later when Merriman's announcement of Lady Bracknell's entrance marks the end of one phase in the plot and the beginning of another.

That Wilde's play is not a faithful picture of upper-class behavior in late Victorian England needs saying only in order to emphasize the importance of its artificiality. By long-standing convention, farce may freely make use of single-minded motivation, unvarying mannerisms, timed coincidences, and outrageous misunderstandings. That these things are obvious contrivances is, in the case of *Earnest*, an asset rather than a liability. They remove life on stage from the sober urgencies of our life outside the theater and take us to a realm of elegance and precious silliness, where we are free to enjoy untroubled laughter. Our laughter is all the happier because we know that we have understood something bright and beautiful. We are secretly pleased with ourselves for being clever enough to appreciate Wilde's clever and elegant wit. His play is a lighthearted game, played under exceedingly difficult rules, that never once insults our intelligence, offends our sensibilities, or disappoints our expectations.

There is still another dimension to our enjoyment. Because Wilde's art serves as a screen between us and the frivolities on stage, we can take his characters seriously in a way we couldn't if they were supposed to be "real people." Like other literary characters, Wilde's are only constituent moving parts in a shaped pattern of action. More than most plays, *The Importance of Being Earnest* forces that recognition on us. And because that is *all* they are, what they say and do can *mean* more than the random words and events in our own lives, lived among the uncontrollable recalcitrance of the real. Only if we see characters in this way, both as people and as artifacts mimicking people, can we experience their world as one made by art. If we don't, we risk turning literature into a daydream substituting for life. But if we do, we may begin to understand what Wilde meant when he said that his "trivial comedy" was "for serious people."

TRAGEDY AND COMEDY

Defining tragedies as plays that end unhappily and comedies as plays that end happily isn't as simpleminded a distinction as it sounds. There are, of course, perspectives in which the two come together in a view of human life as simultaneously terrible and joyous, but the mixed view does not cancel the original distinction. Some people argue that the insignificance of the individual in the modern world precludes tragedy and the enormity of our public events comedy. We are, they say, capable only of tragicomedy, of doubt but not of faith, of angst but not of awe; we neither laugh nor cry but only sneer and snivel. But if this were altogether so, we would scarcely respond as we do to the great tragedies and comedies of the past.

We are not the first to feel the ambivalence of the human condition. The primitive rites celebrating and propitiating the powers controlling the natural cycles of sun and rain, spring and fall, life and death, gave birth, presumably, to both comedy and tragedy. In the Dionysian theater of ancient Athens, suffering and ribaldry were part of the same performance, dramatizing the oneness of spirit and flesh in a civic-religious ceremony simultaneously mystical and obscene. Tragic man's freedom comes through his perception of himself in the hands of the gods. Homer and Dante and Cervantes and Dr. Johnson knew as well as Brecht and Beckett today that the comedy and the tragedy of life cannot be kept apart. Shakespeare and Molière wrote tragicomedy long before Ibsen and Chekhov. In their refusal to deal with one of its ingredients apart from the other, they were accepting, not rejecting, the old distinction. It is one that men and women have always reached for when they have wanted to make shaped images — something to take hold of and look at — out of their sense of their own lives. Body and soul, suffering and joy, the sublime and the ridiculous, still name what we see when we look at our strange and various lot. We live among antitheses, and our environment gets to us.

So tragedy and comedy do more than classify plays. They stand for ways, more complementary than contrasting, of looking at life. Tragic man is a paradox. Exercising freedom of will, he is the plaything of fate. Fallible and mortal, his spirit rises above error and misfortune. Acting on his virtue, he incurs guilt. Divided within by conflicting impulses and imperatives, he pits his naked strength against whatever enrages and inhibits him. His "tragic flaw" (what Aristotle called *hamartia*) is built into his nature. Incapable of compromise, he demands that an imperfect world conform to his notions of right and good but is defeated because wrong and evil are the world's warp and woof. It is both his folly and his greatness that he wants to impose absolutes on a contingent and relativistic existence. The final paradox about him is that he says about his condition: "I don't believe in the invincibility of evil, but I do believe in the inevitability of my own defeat."

Why both his belief and his disbelief should prove true to his experience is the question all tragedy asks and no tragedy answers. Plays that do answer, vindicating the order of things, are moving away from tragedy and toward religious drama. *Hamlet* is a more tragic play than *Everyman*, and a "Christian tragedy" is a contradiction in terms. Tragic man presses his human potential beyond its limits in an assertion of himself in the face of the unanswering unknown. If he does so unknowingly, he may be a fool; if deliberately, a villain; but as long as there is something great and noble about his quest, he may still be tragic.

The hero's high social rank in traditional tragedy is not a sign of the playwright's aristocratic bias but a symbol of the hero's superior human quality. In addition, it carries the suggestion that his destiny involves others than himself. How do we know? Because he is a king. Tragic man matters. When Aristotle distinguished between tragedy as imitating men as "better" than they are in real life and comedy as "worse," he didn't have in mind qualities of birth or intellect or rank or even morals, but of soul. The tragic hero suffers *because* he is "better." There is about him a quality of too much — too much ambition or imagination or sensitivity or passion or idealism or courage or capacity for suffering. The mystery at the center of the tragic universe is the nature of the justice that decrees that such abundance of soul must inevitably destroy itself. That is why a plot of mere disaster or mishap is not tragic. Such a plot may be moving or painful and its victim pathetic, but it is not tragic unless we can feel that there is some kind of fitness, ironic or not, between the protagonist's character and his fate. We require a connection. The tragic action must follow some kind of cosmic or existential logic.

The mystery is the subject of the kind of tragedy that questions the rules of the game. Why is there evil in the world? Why do the innocent suffer? Why is our highest virtue ever the instrument of our greatest pain? What obedience do we owe powers that are malign, arbitrary, indifferent? This is what we might call *existential* or *Promethean* tragedy (from the demigod

Prometheus in ancient myth, whose championship of man angered Zeus).
It recognizes man's helplessness but asserts his dignity by protesting against
it. There are elements of Promethean tragedy in the works of Sophocles,
Shakespeare, Racine, and other older writers of tragedy, but for clearer,
less ambiguous, examples we go, no doubt significantly, to modern plays:
Camus's *Caligula* and Sartre's *Flies*, Beckett's *Waiting for Godot* and *Act
Without Words*, Weiss's *Marat/Sade*, and Stoppard's *Rosencrantz and Guildenstern Are Dead*. These plays (and others like them) expose the apparent
absurdity of an existence that baffles and debases and scourges human
beings beyond what any possible guilt of transgression would warrant. Im-
plicitly or explicitly they refuse the option that we resign ourselves to the
discrepancy between intrinsic virtue and extrinsic evil. Promethean man
knows his resistance is futile, but that only stiffens his stance.

The other main kind of tragedy takes the option of resignation. It affirms
the meaning and justice of the cosmic order and finds compensation for
the final calamity in the classical (Aeschylean) formula of "Wisdom
through suffering." At the end comes the moment of recognition when the
hero and we understand and accept his destiny. Though the ways of gods
with men are severe and inscrutable, they witness to the operation of eternal laws, one of which is a law of compensation operating in human
affairs. Catastrophe enlightens, and we leave the play solemn but not depressed. This is tragedy of *catharsis*, purging our souls of fear, rebellious-
ness, and self-pity. We submit to things as they mysteriously and
immutably are. *Oedipus the King* and *Riders to the Sea* are examples.

And yet, we sense in Sophocles' play — not all the time, but sometimes
— the presence as well of something like the Promethean spirit of revolt
against the deity. We hear its voice in Oedipus's final anguish: crushed, yet
questioning; admitting guilt, yet feeling innocent. We hear it in the humble
bewilderment of the Chorus. It is evident most of all in the circumstances
of the story, that will not allow us to feel that the king so fearfully punished
ever knowingly did wrong or ever stopped trying to do right.

The ambiguous tragedy in *Oedipus the King* suggests that the distinction
between Promethean and cathartic tragedy is more useful in the abstract
— as a means to clarifying basic tragic concepts — than in critical practice. On the highest level of tragic drama it ceases to be meaningful. In
fact, it is arguable that the coming together of the two kinds in one, single, complex tragic effect is what *makes* a tragedy great. Hamlet's and
Phaedra's dilemmas, trapping them in paralyzing self-disgust, belong to the
Promethean dimension of the tragedy. Yet the ultimate thrust of either
play is not a Promethean indictment of the world order at the bar of human justice, and no one can seriously argue that Hamlet and Phaedra are
protagonists of modern absurdist metaphysical farce. Tragedies of such
comprehensiveness and complexity transcend the whole issue. If we want
to dissect them at all, we incline to borrow Friedrich Nietzsche's famous
dichotomy (in *The Birth of Tragedy*) between Apollo and Dionysus, each

god representing one side of the irreducible human antithesis: Apollo, reason, order, discipline; Dionysus, passion, instinct, ecstasy. Tragedy, says Nietzsche, is born when the orgiastic Dionysian energy is disciplined to clarity and harmony by the Apollonian voice.

Cultural pessimists like to point to the absence of great tragedy from modern drama. And if we accept Robert Heilman's distinction (in *Tragedy and Melodrama*) between tragedy as that which we do to ourselves and melodrama as that which is done to us, there is undoubtedly an element of melodrama in existential tragedy: paranoid man feeling sorry for himself and blaming someone or something other than himself for his troubles. There is a falling-off here from older tragedy. Our tragic protagonist is not a king or a prince but a common man, literally Arthur Miller's "lo-man." And he speaks — with none of Oedipus's or Hamlet's or Phaedra's eloquence — for those of us who feel more acted upon than acting and for whom complexity of vision has become simplicity, queries querulousness, and selfhood sentimentality. But not all contemporary protagonists of serious drama are whining victims without insight and dignity. In this collection, Beckett's and Weiss's are not.

The domain of tragedy is metaphysics: solitary and unaccommodated man confronting the riddling contradictions of his being. Comedy deals with the physical and the social: with man's triumphs and tribulations as gregarious animal. "The world," said Horace Walpole in the eighteenth century, "is a comedy to those who think and a tragedy to those who feel." He did not mean that tragedy is mindless and comedy without emotional appeal. He meant that the issues tragedy raises cannot be solved by rational analysis but relate to our awareness of living troubled and precarious lives of uncertain meaning and purpose. And he meant that comedy engages our critical faculties and sharpens our perceptions of the differences between what we are and what we try or pretend to be.

Comedy celebrates this life in all its variety and resiliency. It cherishes food, drink, and sex no less than virtue and sentiment, courage and kindness, wit and fancy. The eccentric who deviates from good nature and good sense and opposes his crotchets to the flow of life is a common figure in comedy. In some major comedies — Ben Jonson's and Molière's are obvious examples — he is the central character. His eccentricity, his "humor" — that is, bias of temperament and personality — is both the source and the substance of the comedy. Henri Bergson, the early twentieth-century French philosopher, had this kind of humor comedy in mind when he said that comic laughter follows our perception of "something mechanical encrusted upon the living." The comedy is in the incongruous spectacle of a human being reducing himself to an automaton. Orgon in *Tartuffe*, Sir Fopling Folly in *The Man of Mode*, and Stephen Undershaft in *Major Barbara* are examples.

The spirit of comedy tolerates everything except intolerance. Fanatics and killjoys are its enemies. It laughs vice and folly out of countenance but welcomes the reformed sinner and fool to its happy community of the virtuous and the wise. Our amusement is thoughtful. Comedy shows us human imperfection not so much in order to lash it as to remind us we all have a share in it. If the tragic virtue is integrity, the comic is charity. Comedy makes us laugh at ourselves when we are selfish or vicious or fatuous. Some great comedies do what is harder and sometimes more important: make us laugh at ourselves when we are at our best and know we are. Moral complacency is no safer from the irreverent comic spirit than moral iniquity is.

Where the laughter turns shrill and bitter, the comedy is about to become *satire*, for satire is inspired by righteous indignation rather than by good-natured amusement. It ridicules and chastises in order to reform. Satiric comedy tends toward tragicomedy, or "problem comedy," in its vision of a world in which human depravity seems to be the major agent of the action. Some of Shakespeare's and Jonson's comedies and Molière's *Tartuffe* are so "dark" that they are only doubtfully comedies at all. If satire marks one end of the comic spectrum, the festive, as in Shakespeare's romantic comedies, Etherege's *The Man of Mode*, and Wilde's *The Importance of Being Earnest*, marks the other. The happy endings of *festive comedies* signify the triumph of love and freedom, truth and harmony, in a society redeemed from hate and tyranny, deception and discord. Most comedies fall somewhere between the two poles. In *Tartuffe*, the satire on Orgon, the unjust, despotic father, yields to festive comedy when he acknowledges his errors and blesses Mariane's and Valère's romance. The world of war and revolution, brutality and injustice, through which Grusha makes her way with little Michael in *The Caucasian Chalk Circle*, is set right by Azdak's plain folk justice, which lets her keep the child she has saved and lets her marry the man she loves.

Of these two endings that of *Tartuffe* is the more typical. It is a version of the archetype about young love overcoming obstacles and being reconciled to a relenting authority figure. The lovers' faithful fortitude triumphs over lechery and greed. Blocking figures — a parent, a vindictive lover or mistress, an evil schemer — are either reconciled to the festive group (like Orgon) or cast out from it (like Tartuffe). A final ceremony — a wedding, a banquet, a dance — symbolizes the harmony and benevolence of the re-formed social group. A generation shift has taken place or is about to, and with it a shift in social power. The old, declined in vitality and set in their ways, yield — in the happiest comedies, gracefully — to the flexible and fun- and freedom-loving young. The redeemed society celebrates the happiness of the young couple, whose union promises the continuation of the life cycle. As sex and liking meet in love, so do love and social order meet in the institution of marriage, guaranteeing the viability of society.

Melodrama and *farce* are in some respects simpler versions of tragedy and comedy. Characters in melodrama are easily recognizable moral types: the chaste maid, the lustful count, the cruel capitalist, the honest apprentice, the pathetic parent, the exploited orphan. It is easy to manipulate characters of such facile emotional appeal in suspenseful and sensational plots. *Farce* is comedy that capitalizes on slapstick, double take, and contrived intrigue moving at breakneck speed. Characterization is shallow in farce, too, but the emphasis here is less on the moral absolutes of melodrama and more on the exhibition of people reduced to puppets, hilariously victimized not by villainous cunning so much as by preposterous whims of coincidence, the orneriness of the physical world, and their own and other people's plain silliness.

There is a place in the serious dramatic repertory for both melodrama and farce. Superior plays in both genres often have strong and ingenious plots and generate moral force. Tragedy and comedy sometimes include elements of both. The melodramatics of situation and sentiment in *A Doll's House* are devices for precipitating the Helmers' marital crisis. The wholesale dying at the end of *Hamlet* is not without an aspect of melodrama. In *Major Barbara*, several figures of farce serve Shaw's satire on the English upper class: Lady Britomart, the insensitive, self-pitying matriarch; Stephen, the bigot; Charles Lomax, the imbecile. *The Importance of Being Earnest* makes a clearer (and not just a funnier) social comment by being all farce, virtually untainted by social realism. Some of the Azdak scenes in *The Caucasian Chalk Circle* come close to being pure farce, both physically and verbally. The same might be said of some of the scenes in *Tartuffe*. Perhaps the most crucial point about *Marat/Sade* is that it renders an important historical event as grotesque farce. The world of drama is a large and profuse landscape rather than a tidy garden with different kinds of plays each in its own plot.

Still, both our reason and our imagination want to retain the basic division of drama into tragedy and comedy. It helps us discriminate not just among plays but among life experiences and our responses to them. Comedy moves in a circle: Life renews itself. Tragedy moves in a straight line: Nothing follows the defeat of the heroic will. At the end of *Tartuffe*, Cléante hopes for Tartuffe's reform, and Orgon looks forward to Mariane's and Valère's wedded bliss. But after Hamlet dies, "the rest is silence." In comedy, vice and folly are psychological rather than metaphysical realities, and the adaptive social structure survives the threat they have posed to the joy of life. In tragedy, the spirit, in acceptance or in rejection, undergoes what the Elizabethan poet and dramatist Fulke Greville called "the wearisome condition of humanity: . . . created sick, commanded to be sound." But both say that we endure.

Sophocles

OEDIPUS THE KING

Translated by Peter Arnott

FOREWORD

To an Athenian of the fifth century B.C. a theatrical performance was at the same time religious ritual, community service, and entertainment. The theater was a place for the worship of Dionysus, god of fertility and rebirth, and participation in the production of plays in the god's honor was a privilege and obligation reserved for free citizens.* In Greek society women were relegated to an inferior place. Men alone, therefore, made up the casts and choruses of the plays, and scholars have debated whether women were even allowed in the audience. The most important of the Dionysiac festivals was the Greater or City Dionysia, celebrated for five or six days every spring. Though the pattern of this festival changed over the years and came eventually to include comedy, tragedy provided its main substance. Three playwrights were chosen to compete for first prize with four plays each, three tragedies, sometimes but not always related in subject matter, and one satyr play, which burlesqued parts of the old myths dramatized in the tragedies.

The origins of Greek tragedy were undoubtedly more complex than we can now see. Tragedy seems to mean literally "goat song," perhaps a song

---

* The origin of Greek drama in the cult of Dionysus has been disputed by some scholars, but there is general agreement that the Dionysiac festival was the exclusive setting for theatrical performance.

for the prize of a goat, perhaps delivered by a chorus dressed as goats, or at least in goat skins. The performers of these early choruses, or *dithyrambs*, may have looked something like the chorus in the later satyr plays, who were costumed as satyrs, shaggy and obscene woodland creatures, half human and half animal. In the tetralogies of historical times the ribaldry of the satyr plays complemented the solemnity of the tragedies. We may think of them as the libidinal, orgiastic component in the celebration of the many ways in which the physical and psychic forces personified by anthropomorphic gods shaped human destiny.

Though the choruses of later tragedy changed markedly from these hypothetical beginnings, they continued, with their combination of song, dance, and recitative, to provide Greek drama with its most characteristic feature. Besides the chorus, however, other forms must have contributed to the development of Greek tragedy. Tradition records the existence of Thespis, a sixth-century figure who may have been the first individual to step out of the chorus and take a solo part. He may even have been the representative of a wholly distinct acting tradition, which merged with the chorus to make Greek tragedy as we know it.

Thus, the Dionysiac theater was a ceremony of word, song, and spectacle that united the entire community in a ritual expression of a range of religious experience — from springtime joy in nature's revived fecundity to pride and terror in man's capacity for good and evil, and awe before the vast mysteries behind his being. Most of the surviving Greek tragedies are not *about* Dionysus. Some of the later ones seem either to ignore the conventional deities, or to offer rationalist challenges to their existence. All the plays, however, testify to man's subservience to forces greater than himself, however we may choose to describe those forces. When characters arrive with relevant news just when the plot calls for it, when the sole survivor of the old fight at the crossroads turns out to be the same man who saved the infant Oedipus from exposure on Cithairon, when the shepherd is forced to recognize the messenger from Corinth who brings the news of King Polybus's death to Thebes as his fellow shepherd to whom he gave the baby, and when Jocasta prays to Apollo for delivery from defilement moments before the defiler is found and expelled from the city, a Greek spectator would not have felt these coincidences of timing and identity as outrageous implausibilities but as testimony to Apollo's direction of events and vindication of his oracle in Delphi and his priest Teiresias against Oedipus's and Jocasta's impious disbelief.

Aristotle credits Aeschylus, Sophocles' immediate predecessor, with the introduction of a second actor (*deuteragonist*) — a virtual prerequisite for the development of flexible dialogue and complex plot. (Plot, says Aristotle, some one hundred years after the great age of Greek tragedy, is "the soul of tragedy," and character is the second most important element.) Sophocles added a third actor, which Aeschylus also used in his last plays.

In early tragedy the lyrical element, sung by the chorus, must have predominated over acting in the modern sense, and even in Sophocles the part of the chorus as the community voice, a kind of audience representative on stage — concerned but ignorant, affected by what happens but not directly participating in it — remains of crucial importance. Aeschylus reduced the number of the chorus from fifty to twelve or fifteen. The chorus moved in slow and stately measures to the accompaniment of flutes, while chanting the odes, reflective lyrics dealing with the inscrutable ways of gods with men and usually having specific reference to the action immediately preceding. In dialogue passages the leader, *coryphaeus*, probably spoke for the whole chorus. The odes were divided into stanzas, called *strophes* and *antistrophes*, delivered, respectively, as the chorus moved first in one and then in the opposite direction. The odes alternated with *episodes*, in which the plot proper was carried forward. The first of the episodes was called the *prologos*, the last the *exodos*; there were typically five episodes in a tragedy. It is probably an anachronism to think of the odes as having also the function of separating the different episodes, like a curtain in a modern theater, though no doubt that is one of the ways in which they work for a modern audience or reader.

We have only limited knowledge of the physical properties of the Dionysiac theater in Athens during the age of Aeschylus, Sophocles, and Euripides, the third great tragic playwright. The audience — perhaps as many as 15,000 — sat on benches in rising concentric half circles on the southern slope of the Acropolis. The plays were performed before a long, low, wooden building (*skene*) that served both as dressing room and as conventional backdrop for the action — thus in *Oedipus the King* as the palace front. Before the *skene* was the main circular acting area, the *orchestra*, with an altar for Dionysus in the center. In the time of the great tragedians there may already have been a low raised stage separating the main action from the choral action; this feature grew more prominent in later stage architecture. Both actors and chorus wore masks, not for reasons of acoustics, as was once believed, but as conventional indicators of age, temperament, and sex — men, as we have noted, played women's parts. The masks must also have created an effect of depersonalized, universal myth. The performers were dressed in long, colored robes that made little pretense of being realistic costumes. Deprived of such visual assistance in identifying characters, the audience would be thrown back on the words — it will be apparent how often, in Greek tragedy, we are *told* things which in modern drama we would be *shown*, including the characters' names, for the Greek theater had no written programs. Actors, often including the playwright himself, normally played several roles in each performance. They had to be highly skilled semiprofessionals, for the performance of several plays in one day was physically strenuous, made great demands on the voice, and lasted most of the daylight hours.

DRAMATIS PERSONAE

PRIEST

OEDIPUS, King of Thebes

CREON, brother of Jocasta

CHORUS OF THEBAN ELDERS

TEIRESIAS, a blind prophet

JOCASTA, wife of Oedipus

FIRST MESSENGER

HERDSMAN

SECOND MESSENGER

ANTIGONE and ISMENE, daughters of OEDIPUS and JOCASTA
(nonspeaking parts)

CITIZENS OF THEBES, ATTENDANTS

Scene: Before the palace of Oedipus in Thebes.

A crowd of Theban citizens — priests, young men and children — kneel in supplication before the palace, wearing wreaths and carrying branches. Enter OEDIPUS *from the palace to address them.*

OEDIPUS: My children, in whom old Cadmus[1] is reborn,
Why have you come with wreathed boughs[2] in your hands
To sit before me as petitioners?
The town is full of smoke from altar-fires
And voices crying, and appeals to heaven.   5
I thought it, children, less than just to hear
Your cause at second-hand, but come in person —
I, Oedipus, a name that all men know.
Speak up, old man; for you are qualified
To be their spokesman. What is in your minds?   10
Are you afraid? In need? Be sure I am ready
To do all I can. I should truly be hard-hearted
To have no pity on such prayers as these.
PRIEST: Why, Oedipus, my country's lord and master,
You see us, of all ages, sitting here   15
Before your altars — some too young to fly
Far from the nest, and others bent with age,
Priests — I of Zeus[3] — and these, who represent
Our youth. The rest sit with their boughs
In the city squares, at both of Pallas'[4] shrines,   20

From *Sophocles: Oedipus the King and Antigone*, Peter D. Arnott, trans. and ed., Arlington Heights, Ill.: AHM Publishing Corp., 1960. Reprinted by permission of the publisher, AHM Publishing Corporation.

[1] legendary founder of Thebes. He killed the dragon guarding the site and sowed its teeth in the ground. From them sprang up armed men who fought each other. All were killed except five, who became the ancestors of the Thebans.

[2] branches entwined with wool, the customary symbol of supplication

[3] king of the gods

[4] Athena, goddess of wisdom

And where Ismenus'⁵ ashes tell the future.
The storm, as you can see, has hit our land
Too hard; she can no longer raise her head
Above the waves of this new sea of blood.
A blight is on the blossoms of the field,   25
A blight is on the pastured herds, on wives
In childbed; and the curse of heaven, plague,
Has struck, and runs like wildfire through the city,
Emptying Cadmus' house, while black Death reaps
The harvest of our tears and lamentations.   30
Not that we see you as a god, these boys
And I, who sit here at your feet for favors,
But as one pre-eminent in life's affairs
And in man's dealings with the powers above.
For it was you who came to Cadmus' town   35
And freed us from the monster who enslaved us
With her song,⁶ relying on your wits, and knowing
No more than we. Some god was at your side,
As men believe, when you delivered us.
So now, great Oedipus, giant among men,   40
We beg you, all of us who come in prayer,
Find us some remedy — a whisper heard
From heaven, or any human way you know.
In men proved by experience we see
A living promise, both in word and deed.   45
Greatest of men, give our city back its pride!
Look to your name! This country now remembers
Your former zeal, and hails you as her savior.
Never leave us with a memory of your reign
As one that raised and let us fall again,   50
But lift our city up, and keep it safe.
You came to make us happy years ago,
Good omens; show you are the same man still.
If you continue in your present power
Better a land with citizens than empty.   55
For city walls without their men are nothing,
Or empty ships, when once the crew has gone.
OEDIPUS: Poor children, I already know too well
The desires that bring you here. Yes, I have seen
Your sufferings; but suffer as you may,   60
There is not one of you who knows my pain.
Your griefs are private, every man here mourns
For himself, and for no other; but my heart grieves
At once for the state, and for myself, and you.
So do not think you rouse me from my sleep.   65

⁵ river near Thebes. Here the reference is   river, where divination by burnt offerings
to the prophetic shrine of Apollo by the   was practiced
                                      ⁶ the Sphinx and the riddle

Let me tell you, I have wept, yes, many tears,
And sent my mind exploring every path.
My anxious thought found but one hope of cure
On which I acted — sent Creon, Menoeceus' son,
My own wife's brother, to Apollo's shrine   70
At Delphi,[7] with commission to enquire
What I could say or do to save this town.
Now I am counting the days, and growing anxious
To know what he is doing. It is strange
He should delay so long beyond his time.   75
But when he comes, I shall be no true man
If I fail to take the course the god has shown us.
PRIEST: Well said, and timely! My friends are signaling
  This very moment that Creon is in sight.
OEDIPUS: O Lord Apollo, let him bring us news   80
  Glad as his face, to give our town good fortune.
PRIEST: I think he brings us comfort; otherwise
  He would not wear so thick a crown of laurel.[8]

(*Enter* CREON)

OEDIPUS: We shall soon know, he is close enough to hear us.
  Prince, brother of my house, Menoeceus' son,   85
  What is the news you bring us from the god?
CREON: Good news! Our sorrows, heavy as they are,
  With proper care may yet end happily.
OEDIPUS: What is the oracle? So far you have said nothing
  To raise my spirits or to dampen them.   90
CREON: If you wish to have it here and now, in public,
  I am ready to speak; if not, to go inside.
OEDIPUS: Speak before all. The sorrows of my people
  I count of greater weight than life itself.
CREON: Then, by your leave, I speak as I was told.   95
  Phoebus[9] commands us, in plain terms, to rid
  Our land of some pollution, nourished here,
  He says, and not to keep a thing past cure.
OEDIPUS: How shall we purge ourselves? What stain is this?
CREON: By banishing a man, or taking life   100
  For life, since murder brought this storm on us.
OEDIPUS: Who is the man whose fate the god reveals?
CREON: Our country once had Laius for its king,
  My lord, before you came to guide this city.
OEDIPUS: I have been told as much; I never saw him.   105
CREON: Laius was murdered. Phoebus tells us plainly
  To find his murderers and punish them.

---

[7] most famous and prosperous of Greek oracular shrines, believed to stand at the geographical center of the earth

[8] leaves from Apollo's sacred tree

[9] Apollo

OEDIPUS: Where on earth are they? An ancient crime,
    A scent grown cold; where shall we find it now?
CREON: Here, in this land, he said; seek it, and we   110
    Shall find; seek not, and it shall be hidden.
OEDIPUS: And where did Laius meet his bloody end?
    In the country? The palace? Traveling abroad?
CREON: He left us on a visit, as he said,
    To Delphi, and he never came back home.   115
OEDIPUS: Could no-one tell you? Had he no companion,
    No witness, who could give you facts to work on?
CREON: All were killed but one, who ran away in fright,
    And will swear to only one thing that he saw.
OEDIPUS: What was that? One thing might give the clue to more   120
    If we had some encouragement, some small beginning.
CREON: He said they met with bandits; it was not
    By one man's hands that Laius died, but many.
OEDIPUS: What bandit would have taken such a risk
    Unless he were bribed — by someone here, in Thebes?   125
CREON: It was suspected; but then our troubles came
    And there was no-one to avenge dead Laius.
OEDIPUS: It must have been great trouble, that could make you
    Leave the death of royalty unsolved!
CREON: The Sphinx, whose riddles made us turn our minds   130
    To things at home, and abandon mysteries.
OEDIPUS: Then I shall start afresh, and once again
    Find secrets out. Apollo and you too
    Have rightly taken up the dead man's cause.
    You will see me working with you, as is just,   135
    To avenge the land, and give the god his due.
    It is not on some far-distant friend's behalf
    But on my own, that I shall purge this stain.
    The man whose hand killed Laius might some time
    Feel a desire to do the same to me,   140
    And so by avenging him I protect myself.
    Waste no more time, my children, take away
    Your branches and your wreaths, and leave my steps.
    Have Cadmus' people summoned here and tell them
    I will see to everything. We shall be happy now,   145
    God helping us, or be forever damned.   (*Exeunt* OEDIPUS *and* CREON)
PRIEST: Let us arise, my sons. He promises
    The favors that we first came here to ask.
    May Phoebus who has sent this oracle
    Come to save Thebes, and cure us of the plague!   150
                (*Exeunt. Enter* CHORUS OF THEBAN ELDERS)
CHORUS: Sweet voice of Zeus, what word do you bring
    From golden Pytho[10] to glorious Thebes?

  [10] Delphi

I am heart-shaken, torn on the rack of fear.
Apollo, Healer, to whom men cry,
I tremble before you; what will it please you   155
To send us? Some new visitation?
Or something out of the past, come due
In fullness of time? Tell me, Voice undying,
The child of golden Hope.

Daughter of Zeus, to you first I cry,   160
Immortal Athena; and then her sister
Artemis,[11] guardian of our land, enthroned
In honor in our assemblies; Apollo,
Heavenly archer; now shine on us all three,
Champions strong against death; if ever   165
In time gone by you stood between Thebes
And threatened disaster, turning the fire
Of pestilence from us, come now!

For my sorrows have grown past counting.
The plague is on all our people, and wit   170
Can devise no armor. No more the good earth
Brings forth its crops; women groan in their barren labors,
And you may see, like flying birds,
Souls speeding, one by one,
To join the sunset god; their flight   175
Is faster than the racing flame.

Thebes dies a new death each moment; her children
Lie in the dust, death's agents, and no-one
Spares them a tear; their wives and gray-haired mothers
Flock screaming to the altars, and pray for their own lives.   180
Above the counterpoint of tears
There rings out clear the healing chant.
Show us, golden child of Zeus,
The smiling face of comfort!

Grim Death is marching on us, not now with clashing shields   185
But blasts of fiery breath, and the cry goes up around him.
Turn him away from us, drive him from our land!
Come, fair wind, and blow him away
To the vasty halls of the western ocean
Or the Thracian seas,[12] where sailors fear to go.   190
For if night has left any harm undone
Day treads on its heels to finish the work.
Zeus our Father, lord of the bright lightning,
Come with your thunder and destroy!

---

[11] goddess of childbirth and of wild things   garded as having his home in this wild re-
[12] off the north-east coast of Greece, noto-   gion.
riously treacherous. Ares, god of war, was re-

And we pray Apollo the archer to string his golden bow   195
And send invincible arrows to fight for us in the field,
And Artemis' blazing torches, that she carries
To light her way through the Lycian mountains.[13]
On the god with gold-bound hair I call,
Bacchus,[14] whose name we have made our own,   200
Who comes with a cry of maidens dancing.
Bright comforter, bring the joyous light
Of your torch, stand with us against our foe,
The rogue-god, whom his brothers shun!

(*Enter* OEDIPUS)

OEDIPUS: You pray; now for answer. If you are prepared   205
  To accept what I say, and be your own physician,
  Cure may be yours, and respite from your pain.
  I must speak as a stranger to your story, one
  Unacquainted with the facts; I could not press
  My enquiries far alone, without some clue.   210
  But now I am a Theban among Thebans
  And make this proclamation to the sons
  Of Cadmus: if anyone among you knows
  Who murdered Laius, son of Labdacus,
  I order him to make a full disclosure.   215
  If he should fear to implicate himself
  By confessing, why, nothing unpleasant will happen;
  He will leave the land unharmed, and that is all.
  If anybody knows another guilty —
  An alien perhaps — then let him not keep silent.   220
  He will earn a reward and my gratitude besides.
  But if you refuse to talk; if anyone
  Is frightened into shielding self or friend,
  Pay good attention to the consequences.
  As lord and master of this land of Thebes   225
  I declare this man, whoever he may be
  An outlaw; order you to break off speech
  With him, to excommunicate him from your prayers
  And sacrifices, to deny him holy water,
  To drive him from your doors, remembering   230
  That this is our pollution, which the god
  This day revealed to me in oracles.
  In this I show myself on heaven's side,
  One with the murdered man. My solemn curse
  Is on the killer, whether he is hiding   235
  In lonely guilt or has accomplices.
  May he reap the harm he sowed, and die unblest.
  And what is more, I pray that if this man

[13] in Asia Minor

[14] Dionysus, god of wine, traditionally

born in Thebes from the union of Zeus and a
mortal woman, Semele

Should live among my household with my knowledge,
The curse I swore just now should fall on me.   240
I lay the responsibility on you,
For my sake, and the gods', and for our country
Turned to a stricken, god-forsaken waste.
For even if heaven had not shown its hand
Fitness alone forbade such negligence   245
When one so noble, and your king, had died.
You should have held enquiries. Now since I
Have fallen heir to the power which once was his,
Sleep in his bed, and take his bride to wife,
And since, if he had not been disappointed   250
In his succession, we two would have had
A bond between us, children of one mother,
But as it was, his fortune struck him down,
For all these reasons, I shall fight for him
As I would for my own father, leave no stone   255
Unturned to find the man who shed his blood
In honor of the son of Labdacus,
Of Polydorus, Cadmus, and Agenor.
For those who disobey my words I pray
The gods to send no harvest to their fields,   260
Their wives no children, but to let them die
In present misery, or worse to come.
But as for you, the rest of Cadmus' children,
Who think as I do, may our ally, Right,
And all the gods be with you evermore.   265
CHORUS: You put me on my oath and I must speak.
I did not kill him, nor can I point to the man
Who did. It was for Phoebus, who sent the question,
To answer it, and find the murderer.
OEDIPUS: What you say is fair enough, but no man living   270
Can force the gods to speak when they do not want to.
CHORUS: By your leave, a second best occurs to me. . . .
OEDIPUS: Second or third best, do not keep it from us!
CHORUS: I know Teiresias has powers of vision
Second only to Phoebus. A man who asked of him,   275
My lord, might find his questions answered.
OEDIPUS: Another thing that I have not neglected.
On Creon's bidding I have sent men twice
To bring him; it is strange he is not yet come.
CHORUS: We have nothing else but vague and ancient rumors.   280
OEDIPUS: What are they? I must examine every story.
CHORUS: He is said to have been killed by men on the road.
OEDIPUS: Yes, so I hear; but no-one knows who did it.
CHORUS: If he has any fear in him, a curse
Such as you swore will bring him out of hiding.   285
OEDIPUS: Words will not scare a man when actions do not.
CHORUS: But here is one to convict him. They are bringing

The prophet here at last, the man of god,
The only one who has the truth born in him.

(*Enter* TEIRESIAS, *led by a boy*)

OEDIPUS: Teiresias, all things are known to you,   290
Open and secret, things of heaven and earth.
Blind though you are, you sense how terrible
A plague is on us; and in you, great prophet,
We find our only means of self-defence.
We sent — perhaps my messengers have told you —   295
To Phoebus; he replied, by one way only
Could Thebes secure deliverance from the plague,
By hunting down the murderers of Laius
And killing them or driving them abroad.
So grudge us nothing of your bird-cry lore[15]   300
Or any means of prophecy you know.
Come, save the city; save yourself and me,
And heal the foulness spread by Laius' blood.
We are in your hands. Man knows no finer task
Than helping friends with all his might and means.   305
TEIRESIAS: How terrible is wisdom when it turns
Against you! All of this I know, but let it
Slip from my mind, or I should not have come here.
OEDIPUS: What is it? Why have you come in so black a mood?
TEIRESIAS: Send me home. It will be easiest for each of us   310
To bear his own burden to the end, believe me.
OEDIPUS: A fine way to talk! You do your motherland
No kindness by withholding information.
TEIRESIAS: When I see you opening your mouth at the wrong moment
I take care to avoid a like mistake.   315
OEDIPUS: By heaven, if you know something, do not turn away!
You see us all on our knees imploring you.
TEIRESIAS: Yes, for you all know nothing. I shall never
Reveal my sorrows — not to call them yours.
OEDIPUS: What do you say? You know and will not talk?   320
Do you mean to turn traitor and betray the state?
TEIRESIAS: I wish to cause no pain — to either of us.
So why ask useless questions? My lips are sealed.
OEDIPUS: Why, you old reprobate, you could provoke
A stone to anger! Will you never speak?   325
Can nothing touch you? Is there no end to this?
TEIRESIAS: You blame my temper, but you fail to recognize
Your own working in you; no, you criticize me!
OEDIPUS: And who would not be angry when he hears you
Talking like this, and holding Thebes in contempt?   330
TEIRESIAS: These things will happen, if I speak or not.

---

[15] omens were commonly deduced from
the flight of birds

OEDIPUS: Then if they must, it is your duty to tell me.
TEIRESIAS: This discussion is at an end. Now, if you like,
   You may be as angry as your heart knows how.
OEDIPUS: Then in my anger I will spare you none   335
   Of my suspicions. This is what I think;
   You helped contrive the plot — no, did it all
   Except the actual killing. If you had
   Your eyesight I should say you did that too.
TEIRESIAS: Indeed? Then listen to what I say. Obey   340
   Your own pronouncement, and from this day on
   Speak not to me or any man here present.
   You are the curse, the defiler of this land.
OEDIPUS: You dare fling this at me? Have you no fear?
   Where can you hope for safety after this?   345
TEIRESIAS: I am safe enough. My strength is in my truth.
OEDIPUS: Who put you up to this? No skill of yours!
TEIRESIAS: You did — by forcing me to speak against my will.
OEDIPUS: What was it? Say it again, I must be sure.
TEIRESIAS: Did you not understand? Or are you tempting me? 350
OEDIPUS: I have not quite grasped it. Tell it me again.
TEIRESIAS: You hunt a murderer; it is yourself.
OEDIPUS: You will pay for uttering such slanders twice.
TEIRESIAS: Shall I say something else, to make you angrier still?
OEDIPUS: Say what you like, it is a waste of breath.   355
TEIRESIAS: You have been living in unimagined shame
   With your nearest, blind to your own degradation.
OEDIPUS: How long do you think such taunts will go unpunished?
TEIRESIAS: For ever, if there is any strength in truth.
OEDIPUS: In truth, but not in you. You have no strength,   360
   Failing in sight, in hearing, and in mind.
TEIRESIAS: And you are a fool to say such things to me,
   Things that the world will soon hurl back at you!
OEDIPUS: You live in the dark; you are incapable
   Of hurting me or any man with eyes.   365
TEIRESIAS: Your destiny is not to fall by me.
   That is Apollo's task, and he is capable.
OEDIPUS: Who is behind this? You? Or is it Creon?
TEIRESIAS: Your ruin comes not from Creon, but yourself.
OEDIPUS: Oh wealth! Oh monarchy! Talent which outruns 370
   Its rivals in the cutthroat game of life,
   How envy dogs your steps, and with what strength,
   When tempted by the power the city gave
   Into my hands, a gift, and never asked for,
   The man I trusted, Creon, my earliest friend,   375
   Yearns to depose me, plots behind my back,
   Makes accomplices of conjurers like this
   Who sells his tricks to the highest bidder, who looks
   Only for profits, and in his art is blind.
   Let us hear where you have proved yourself a seer! 380

Why did you not, when the Singing Bitch[16] was here,
Utter one word to set your people free?
For this was not a riddle to be solved
By the first-comer; it cried out for divination.
You were tried and found wanting; neither birds   385
Nor voices from heaven could help you. Then I came,
I, ignorant Oedipus, and put a stop to her
By using my wits, no lessons from the birds!
And it is I you try to depose, assuming
That you will have a place by Creon's throne.   390
You and your mastermind will repent your zeal
To purge this land. You are old, by the look of you;
If not, you would have learnt the price of boldness.
CHORUS: It seems to me that this man's words were spoken
In anger, Oedipus, and so were yours.   395
This is not what we need; we ask to know
How we can best obey the oracle.
TEIRESIAS: King though you are, the right of speech must be
The same for all. Here, I am my own master.
I live in Apollo's service, not in yours,   400
And have no need of Creon to endorse me.
Listen to me; you taunt me with my blindness,
But you have eyes, and do not see your sorrows,
Or where you live, or what is in your house.
Do you know whose son you are? You are abhorrent   405
To your kin on earth and under it, and do not know.
One day your mother's and your father's curse,
A two-tongued lash, will run you out of Thebes,
And you who see so well will then be blind.
What place will not give shelter to your cries?   410
What corner of Cithairon[17] will not ring with them,
When you have understood the marriage song which brought you
From prosperous voyage to uneasy harbor?
And a throng of sorrows that you cannot guess
Will drag you down and level you with those   415
You have begotten, and your proper self.
So go your way; heap mockery and insult
On Creon and my message; you will be crushed
More miserably than any man on earth.
OEDIPUS: Am I to listen to such things from him   420
Without protest? Out of my sight this instant! Leave my house!
Go back where you came from, and be damned!
TEIRESIAS: I would never have come here, if you had not called me.
OEDIPUS: If I had known you would rave like this, it would have been
A long time before I asked you to my house.   425

---

[16] the Sphinx   [17] mountain near Thebes where Oedipus
                                         was exposed

TEIRESIAS: I am what I am. I pass for a fool to you,
　　But as sane enough for the parents who begot you.
OEDIPUS: Who were they? Wait! What is my father's name?
TEIRESIAS: This day will give you parents and destroy you.
OEDIPUS: All the time you talk in riddles, mysteries.   430
TEIRESIAS: And who can decipher riddles better than you?
OEDIPUS: Yes, laugh at that! There you will find my greatness!
TEIRESIAS: And it is just this luck that has destroyed you.
OEDIPUS: I saved the city; nothing else can matter.
TEIRESIAS: Very well then, I shall go. Boy, take me home.   435
OEDIPUS: Yes, let him take you. Here you are in the way,
　　A hindrance; out of sight is out of mind.
TEIRESIAS: I will go when my errand is done. I do not fear
　　Your frown. There is no way that you can harm me.
　　Listen to me: the man you have sought so long,   440
　　Threatening, issuing your proclamations
　　About the death of Laius — he is here,
　　Passing for an alien, but soon to be revealed
　　A Theban born; and he will find no pleasure
　　In this turn of fortune. He who now has eyes   445
　　Will be blind, who now is rich, a beggar,
　　And wander abroad with a stick to find his way.
　　He will be revealed as father and as brother
　　Of the children in his home, as son and husband
　　Of the woman who bore him, his father's murderer   450
　　And successor to his bed. Now go away
　　And think about these things; and if you find I lie
　　Then you can say that I am no true prophet.

　　　　　　　　　　　　　　　(Exeunt TEIRESIAS and OEDIPUS)

CHORUS: Who is the man denounced
　　By the voice of god from the Delphian rock?
　　Who is the man with bloody hands   455
　　Guilty of horrors the tongue cannot name?
　　It is time for him to run
　　Faster of foot than the horses of the storm,
　　For the Son of Zeus is leaping upon him   460
　　With fire and lightning, and at his side
　　The Fates, remorseless avengers.

　　Fresh from Parnassus'[18] snows
　　The call blazes forth: the hunt is up!
　　Search every place for the unknown man!   465
　　He doubles among the wild woods for cover,
　　From hole to hole in the hills,
　　A rogue bull running a lost race, trying
　　To shake off the sentence ringing in his ears

---

[18] mountain near Delphi celebrated as the
home of Apollo and the Muses, and also as
the haunt of Dionysus

Pronounced by the shrine at earth's center, forever   470
Haunting him, goading him on.

The wise man with his birds and omens
Leaves me troubled and afraid,
Unable to believe or disbelieve.
What can I say? I fly from hope to fear.   475
Dark is the present, dark the days to come.
There is no quarrel that I know of
Now or in the past between
Labdacus' house and the son of Polybus,
Nothing that I could use as proof   480
Against Oedipus' reputation
In avenging Labdacus' line, and solving
The riddle of Laius' death.

To Zeus and Apollo all things are known,
They see the doings of mankind.   485
But who is to say that a human prophet
Knows any more of the future than I?
Though some men, I know, are wiser than others.
But I shall never join with his accusers
Until they have made good their charge.   490
We saw his wisdom tried and tested
When he fought the girl with wings.[19]
Thebes took him then to her heart, and I
Will never name him guilty.

(*Enter* CREON)

CREON: Citizens, I hear that Oedipus our king   495
  Lays monstrous charges against me, and am here
  In indignation. If in the present crisis
  He thinks I have injured him in any way
  By word or action calculated to harm him,
  I would rather die before my time is up   500
  Than bear this stigma. Such malicious slander
  Touches me on more than one tender spot.
  What hurts me most is this — to have my friends
  And you and my city brand me as a traitor.
CHORUS: This insult was probably spoken under stress,   505
  In anger, not with deliberate intent.
CREON: And what about the taunt that the seer was coerced
  Into lying by my design? Who started it?
CHORUS: It was said — I do not know how seriously.
CREON: Did he lay this charge against me steady-eyed?   510
  Did he sound as if he knew what he was saying?

[19] the Sphinx

CHORUS: I know nothing about it. I do not look at what
　　My masters do. Here he comes himself, from the palace.

(*Enter* OEDIPUS)

OEDIPUS: You! And what brings you here? Can you put on
　　So bold a face, to visit your victim's house,   515
　　Shown up for what you are, a murderer
　　Openly plotting to rob me of my crown?
　　In heaven's name, what did you take me for?
　　A fool? A coward? to entertain such schemes?
　　Do you think I would let you work behind my back   520
　　Unnoticed, or not take precautions once I knew?
　　Then is it not senseless, this attempt of yours
　　To bid for the throne alone and unsupported?
　　It takes men and money to make a revolution.
CREON: Wait! You have said your say; it is now your turn   525
　　To listen. Learn the facts and then pass judgment.
OEDIPUS: Smooth talker! But I have no inclination
　　To learn from you, my bitter enemy.
CREON: One thing let me say, before we go any further. . . .
OEDIPUS: One thing you must never say — that you are honest!   530
CREON: If you think there is any virtue in stubbornness
　　Devoid of reason, you have little sense.
OEDIPUS: If you think you can wrong one of your family
　　And get away unpunished, you are mad.
CREON: Justly said, I grant you. But give me some idea,   535
　　What injury do you say that I have done you?
OEDIPUS: Did you suggest it would be advisable
　　To bring the prophet here, or did you not?
CREON: I did; and I am still of the same opinion.
OEDIPUS: And how many years ago was it that Laius. . . .   540
CREON: That Laius what? I cannot follow you.
OEDIPUS: Was lost to his people by an act of violence.
CREON: That would take us a long way back into the past.
OEDIPUS: And was the prophet practicing in those days?
CREON: As skillfully as today, with equal honor.   545
OEDIPUS: And did he then make any mention of me?
CREON: Not at any time when I was there to hear him.
OEDIPUS: But did you not investigate the murder?
CREON: We were bound to, of course, but discovered nothing.
OEDIPUS: And why did this know-all not tell his story then? 550
CREON: I prefer not to talk about things I do not know.
OEDIPUS: You know one thing well enough that you could tell me.
CREON: What is it? If I know, I shall keep nothing back.
OEDIPUS: This: if you had not put your heads together
　　We should never have heard about my killing Laius.   555
CREON: If he says so, you know best. Now let me ask
　　And you must answer as I answered you.
OEDIPUS: Ask what you like. I am innocent of murder.

CREON: Come now; are not you married to my sister?
OEDIPUS: A question to which I can hardly answer no. 560
CREON: And you rule the country with her, equally?
OEDIPUS: I give her everything that she could wish for.
CREON: Do I, the third, not rank with both of you?
OEDIPUS: You do; which makes your treachery the worse.
CREON: Not if you reason with yourself as I do. 565
  First ask yourself this question: would any man
  Be king in constant fear, when he could live
  In peace and quiet, and have no less power?
  I want to be a king in everything
  But name — and I have no desire for that, 570
  Nor has any man who knows what is good for him.
  As it is, I am carefree. You give me all I want,
  But as king I should have many tiresome obligations.
  Then why should I find monarchy more desirable
  Than power and influence without the trouble? 575
  So far I have not been misguided enough
  To hanker after dishonorable gains.
  As it is, all wish me well and greet me kindly,
  And people with suits to you call first on me
  For there are all their chances of success. 580
  So why should I give up one life for the other?
  No man with any sense would stoop to treason.
  I have no love for such ideas, nor would I
  Associate with any man who did.
  Do you look for proof of this? Then go to Delphi 585
  And ask if I quoted the oracle correctly.
  And another thing; if you find that I have made
  A plot with the prophet, there will be two voices
  To sentence me to death — yours and my own.
  But do not convict me out of mere suspicion! 590
  It is hardly just to label good men bad
  Or bad men good, according to your whim.
  Mark my words: the man who drops an honest friend
  Cuts out his heart, the thing he loves the best.
  But you will learn this sure enough in time, 595
  For time alone can tell an honest man
  While one day is enough to show a villain.
CHORUS: Good advice, my lord, for one who keeps a watch
  For pitfalls. Hasty thoughts are dangerous.
OEDIPUS: When conspirators make haste to set plots moving 600
  I must make haste myself to counteract them.
  If I waited and did nothing it would mean
  Success for him and ruin for myself.
CREON: Then what do you want? My banishment from Thebes?
OEDIPUS: No, not your banishment. I want your death! 605
CREON: There speaks a man who will not listen to reason.
OEDIPUS: No, you must show the world what comes of envy!

CREON: I think you must be mad.

OEDIPUS: And I think sane.

CREON: Then hear me sensibly.

OEDIPUS: Hear you, a traitor?

CREON: Suppose you are wrong?

OEDIPUS: Kings must still be obeyed.   610

CREON: Kings, but not tyrants.

OEDIPUS: City, oh my city!

CREON: My city also. I have rights here too.

CHORUS: Stop this, my lords. I can see Jocasta coming
   From the palace just in time. Let her advise you,
   Put your quarrel aside and be friends again.   615

(*Enter* JOCASTA)

JOCASTA: Have you both gone out of your minds? What is the sense
   Of bandying insults? Are you not ashamed
   To start a private feud, when Thebes is ailing?
   Come inside. And Creon, you must go back home.
   Do not make a mortal grievance out of nothing.   620

CREON: Sister, your husband Oedipus thinks fit
   To make me suffer one way or the other —
   To drive me into banishment or kill me.

OEDIPUS: Exactly. I have caught him plotting mischief —
   A criminal attempt on the royal person.   625

CREON: May heaven's anger strike me dead this minute
   If I have done anything to deserve this charge!

JOCASTA: In the gods' name, Oedipus, believe what he says!
   If not from respect of the oath he has sworn,
   For the sake of your wife and everyone here!   630

CHORUS: Listen to reason, my lord;
   I beg you, be guided by us.

OEDIPUS: You ask for a favor; what is it?

CHORUS: He has been no fool in the past;
   He is strong in his oath; respect him.   635

OEDIPUS: Do you know what it is you ask?

CHORUS: I do.

OEDIPUS: Then explain yourselves; what do you mean?

CHORUS: Your friend has invoked a curse on his head.
   Do not brand him traitor on rumor alone.

OEDIPUS: You must know, by asking this   640
   You are asking my exile or death.

CHORUS: No, by the Sun, the first among gods!
   May I die the death that men fear most,
   Shunned, unclean in the sight of heaven,
   If I have such thoughts in my mind.   645
   But my heart is heavy at our country's dying
   If you add new troubles to her present load.

OEDIPUS: Let him go then; but I am signing my own death warrant
   Or condemning myself to exile and disgrace.

Your voice has moved me where his oath could not.   650
    As for him, wherever he may go, I hate him.
CREON: Now we have seen you — wild when you lose your temper,
    And yielding with bad grace. Such a nature as yours
    Is its own worst enemy, and so it should be.
OEDIPUS: Get out, and leave me in peace.
CREON: I am going.   655
    They know I am honest, though you will not see it.   (*Exit*)
CHORUS: Now quickly, my lady, take him inside.
JOCASTA: Not before I know what has happened.
CHORUS: There were words, a vague suspicion,
    False, but injustice stings.   660
JOCASTA: On both sides?
CHORUS: Yes.
JOCASTA: What was said?
CHORUS: Our country has troubles enough.
    Better let sleeping dogs lie.
OEDIPUS: You meant well enough, but see where it leads you,
    Checking me, blunting the edge of my anger.   665
CHORUS: I have said it before and say it again:
    Men would think that my wits had wandered,
    Would think me insane, to abandon you.
    Our beloved country was sinking fast
    Till you took the helm; and now you may prove   670
    Our guide and salvation again.
JOCASTA: Tell me as well, my lord, in heaven's name,
    What can have set such fury working in you?
OEDIPUS: I will tell you; you are more to me than they are.
    It is Creon, and the way he is plotting against me.   675
JOCASTA: Go on, and tell me how this quarrel started.
OEDIPUS: He says that I am Laius' murderer.
JOCASTA: Does he speak from knowledge or from hearsay only?
OEDIPUS: Neither; he sent a mischief-making prophet.
    He is taking care to keep his own mouth clean.   680
JOCASTA: You can relieve your mind of all such fears.
    Listen, and learn from me: no human being
    Is gifted with the art of prophecy.
    Once an oracle came to Laius — I will not say
    From Apollo himself, but from his ministers —   685
    To say a child would be born to him and me
    By whose hand it was fated he should die.
    And Laius, as rumor goes, was killed by bandits,
    From another land, at a place where three roads meet.
    And as for our son, before he was in this world   690
    Three days, Laius pinned his ankles together
    And had him abandoned on the trackless mountain.
    So in this case Apollo's purpose failed —
    That the child should kill his father, or that Laius
    Should be murdered by his son, the fear that haunted him.   695

So much for oracles which map our future!
Then take no notice of such things; whatever the god
Finds needful, he will show without assistance.
OEDIPUS: Oh wife, the confusion that is in my heart,
The fearful apprehension, since I heard you speak!   700
JOCASTA: What is it? What have I said to startle you?
OEDIPUS: I thought I heard you telling me that Laius
Was murdered at a place where three roads meet.
JOCASTA: Such was the story. People tell it still.
OEDIPUS: What country was it where the thing was done?   705
JOCASTA: In the land called Phocis, at the meeting-point
Of the roads from Delphi and from Daulia.
OEDIPUS: And how many years have gone by since it happened?
JOCASTA: It was just before you first appeared in Thebes
To rule us; that is when we heard of it.   710
OEDIPUS: Oh Zeus, what have you planned to do with me?
JOCASTA: Oedipus, what is it? Why has this upset you?
OEDIPUS: Do not ask me yet; but tell me about Laius.
What did he look like? How far gone in years?
JOCASTA: A tall man, with his hair just turning gray,   715
To look at, not so different from you.
OEDIPUS: Oh, what have I done? I think that I have laid
A dreadful curse on myself and never knew it!
JOCASTA: What are you saying? It frightens me to look at you.
OEDIPUS: I am terrified the prophet sees too well.   720
I shall know better if you tell me one thing more.
JOCASTA: You frighten me; but ask and I will tell you.
OEDIPUS: Did he ride with a handful of men, or with a band
Of armed retainers, as a chieftain should?
JOCASTA: There were five in all — a herald one of them,   725
And a single carriage in which Laius rode.
OEDIPUS: Oh, now I see it all. Jocasta, answer me,
Who was the man who told you what had happened?
JOCASTA: A servant — the only one who returned alive.
OEDIPUS: Is he with us? Is he in our household now?   730
JOCASTA: No, he is not. When he came back and found
You ruling here in Thebes and Laius dead
He wrung me by the hand and begged me send him
Into the country where we graze our sheep
As far as possible from the sight of Thebes.   735
I let him go away; slave though he was
He could have asked far more and had it granted.
OEDIPUS: I want him here, as fast as he can come.
JOCASTA: That can be seen to. What is in your mind?
OEDIPUS: I fear I have already said   740
More than I should; that is why I want to see him.
JOCASTA: He shall come then; but I too have a right
To know what lies heavy on your heart, my lord.
OEDIPUS: I shall keep nothing from you, now my apprehension

Has gone so far. Who else should I confide in   745
Unless in you, when this crisis is upon me?
My father's name was Polybus of Corinth,
My mother a Dorian,[20] Merope. In that city
I lived as first in honor, till one day
There happened something — worth surprise perhaps,   750
But not such anger as it roused in me.
A man at dinner, too far gone in wine,
Jeered in his cups, I was my father's bastard.
It preyed on my mind; and I restrained myself
That day as best I could, but in the morning   755
Went questioning my parents. They were angry
At such a taunt, and the man who let it fly,
So on their part I was satisfied; but still
The slander rankled as it spread and grew.
And so I went, without my parents' knowledge,   760
On a journey to Delphi. Phoebus sent me away
No wiser than I came, but something else
He showed me, sad and strange and terrible:
That I was doomed to mate with my own mother,
Bring an abhorrent brood into the world;   765
That I should kill the father who begat me.
When I heard, I fled from Corinth, ever since
Marking its whereabouts only by the stars,
To find some place where I should never see
This evil oracle's calamities fulfilled,   770
And in my travels reached that very place
Where, as you tell me, Laius met his death.
Wife, I shall tell the truth: I was on my way
And had nearly come to the joining of the roads
When there met me, from the opposite direction,   775
A herald, and a man in a horse-drawn carriage
Exactly as you described. The fellow in front
And the old man tried to push me out of the way.
I lost my temper, hit out at the one
Who jostled me, the driver; when the old man saw it,   780
He watched me, from the carriage, coming past
And brought his double goad down on my head —
But took it back with interest! One swift blow
From the good staff in my hand, and over he went
Clean out of the chariot, sprawling on his back,   785
And I killed every man in sight. If this stranger
Should turn out to have anything to do with Laius,
Who is more wretched than this man before you,
And who could be more hateful to the gods,
A man no citizen, no stranger even,   790

[20] one of the oldest Greek tribes; Oedipus
says this with some pride

May take into his house or speak with him
But drive him from their doors; and this, this curse
Was laid on me by no-one but myself.
And now my hands, by which he met his death,
Defile his bed. Am I not evil? Am I not   795
Foul through and through, when I must go to exile
And in that exile never see my people,
Or set foot in my homeland — for if I do
I must marry my mother, murder Polybus,
The father who gave me life and livelihood.   800
Then if you saw in Oedipus the prey
Of some tormenting power, would you be wrong?
Never, oh never, pure and awful gods,
Let me see that day; no, let me rather vanish
Out of the sight of men, before I see   805
This dreadful visitation come upon me.
CHORUS: This is fearful, my lord; but do not give up hope
    Until you have questioned the man who saw it done.
OEDIPUS: Yes, that is all the hope I have left me now,
    To wait the coming of this man, our shepherd.   810
JOCASTA: And when he comes, what would you have from him?
OEDIPUS: I will tell you. If I find his story tallies
    With yours, then it will mean that I am safe.
JOCASTA: And what is so important in my story?
OEDIPUS: You said that Laius, as he told the tale,   815
    Was killed by robbers. If he stands by this,
    That there were more than one, I did not kill him;
    You could not make one man a company.
    But if he names one solitary traveler
    There is no more doubt; the deed swings back to me.   820
JOCASTA: You can be sure that this is what he said.
    He cannot go back on it, all the city heard him.
    I was not the only one. But even supposing
    We find he tells a different tale today,
    My lord, he can never show that Laius' death   825
    Ran true to prophecy. Phoebus expressly said
    That he was doomed to die at my child's hands;
    But that unhappy babe went to his death
    Before he did; then how could he have killed him?
    So when it comes to oracles, after this   830
    I shall keep both eyes fixed firmly on the front.
OEDIPUS: You speak good sense. But all the same, send someone
    To bring the peasant here; do as I say.
JOCASTA: I will send at once. Come now, let us go home.
    Would I ever fail to do anything you wanted?   (Exeunt) 835
CHORUS: I pray that this may crown my every day,
    In all my words and deeds to walk
    Pure-hearted, in proper fear;
    For thus we are commanded from on high

By laws created in the shining heavens,   840
Who know no other father but Olympus,[21]
In their birth owing nothing to mortals
Nor sleeping though forgotten; great the god
Within them, and he grows not old.

Out of insolence is born the tyrant,   845
Insolence grown fat in vain
On things immoderate, unfit.
For a man who has mounted to the highest places
Must fall to meet his destiny below
Where there can be no help, no footing.   850
But honest ambition let us keep,
For thus the state is served; O Lord Apollo
Guide and strengthen me all my days.

But I pray that the man whose hands and tongue
Are arrogant, careless of retribution,   855
Who blasphemes in the holy places,
May fall upon evil days, the reward
Of the sin of self-conceit.
If he goes the wrong way to gain his ends,
And follows unholy courses, laying   860
Profaning hands on things he should not touch,
Could any man boast his life was safe
From the arrows of angry heaven?
But when such things as these are held in honor
Why should I sing the praises of the gods?   865

No longer shall I visit with my prayers
The inviolate shrine at the center of the world,[22]
Or Abae's[23] temple, or Olympia,[24]
If the prophecy should fail to come to pass
As spoken, for all the world to see.   870
O Zeus, if you are rightly called
The Almighty, the ruler of mankind,
Look to these things; and let them not escape
Your power eternal; for the oracles
Once told of Laius are forgotten, slighted;   875
Apollo is divested of his glory
And man turns his face away from heaven.[25]

(*Enter* JOCASTA)

JOCASTA: Elders of Thebes, I have a mind to pay
   A visit to the holy shrines, with gifts

---

[21] mountain home of the gods
[22] Delphi
[23] near Thebes, site of temple and oracle of Apollo
[24] home of the temple of Zeus and the famous Olympic Games
[25] a fair description of the growing agnosticism of Sophocles' own time

Of incense and wreathed branches in my hands.   880
For Oedipus has let his mind succumb
To all manner of fears, and will not judge the present
By what has gone before, like a sensible man,
But is the prey of every fearful rumor.
There is nothing more that I can say to help him,   885
And so I bring offerings to you, Apollo —
The nearest to us — and request this favor:
Show us how we can find a clean way out,
For now we are afraid to see him frightened,
Like sailors who see panic in their steersman.   890

(*Enter* MESSENGER)

MESSENGER: Could you tell me, my friends, where a man might find
  The palace of King Oedipus — better still,
  Where the king himself is, if you happen to know?
CHORUS: This is his house, and the king is indoors.
  This lady is the mother of his children.   895
MESSENGER: May heaven bless Oedipus' honored queen
  Her whole life long with every happiness!
JOCASTA: Stranger, I wish you the same; so fair a greeting
  Deserves no less. But tell us why you come.
  What have you to ask of us, or tell us?   900
MESSENGER: Good news for your house, my lady, and your husband!
JOCASTA: What news is this? Who sent you here to us?
MESSENGER: I come from Corinth; what I have to tell
  Will please you, no doubt; but there is sadness too.
JOCASTA: Pleasure and pain at once? What is this message?   905
MESSENGER: The people living in the Isthmian land[26]
  Will have him for their king; so goes the story.
JOCASTA: Why? Is old Polybus no longer king?
MESSENGER: No, death has claimed him. He is in his grave.
JOCASTA: What are you saying? Oedipus' father dead?   910
MESSENGER: If I am lying, may I die myself!
JOCASTA: Maid, run away and tell this to your master
  As fast as you can. Oh gods, where are
  Your oracles now? This is the man that Oedipus
  Has shunned for years, for fear of killing him,   915
  And now he is dead, and Oedipus never touched him!

(*Enter* OEDIPUS)

OEDIPUS: Jocasta, dearest wife, why have you sent
  For me, and called me from the palace?
JOCASTA: Listen to this man here, and learn from his words
  To what these holy oracles have come!   920
OEDIPUS: This man? Who is he? What has he to say?

---

[26] Corinth, situated on the narrow neck of
land which joins the two parts of Greece

JOCASTA: From Corinth; his message is that Polybus,
    Your father, lives no longer — he is dead!
OEDIPUS: What? Stranger, let me have it from your mouth.
MESSENGER: If this is where I must begin my message,   925
    I assure you, Polybus is dead and gone.
OEDIPUS: Did it happen by foul play? Or was he sick?
MESSENGER: When a man is old his life hangs by a thread.
OEDIPUS: Poor Polybus. He died of illness, then?
MESSENGER: That and old age. He had lived a long life.   930
OEDIPUS: Oh, wife, why should we ever spare a glance
    For the shrine of Delphi, or the birds that scream
    Above our heads? On their showing, I was doomed
    To be my father's murderer; but he
    Is dead and buried, and here am I, who never   935
    Laid hand on sword. Unless perhaps he died
    Through pining for me; thus I could have killed him.
    But as they stand, the oracles have gone
    To join him underground, and they are worthless!
JOCASTA: Did I not tell you so a long while since?   940
OEDIPUS: You did, but I was led astray through fear.
JOCASTA: Then do not take them any more to heart.
OEDIPUS: But my mother's bed . . . how should I not fear that?
JOCASTA: What has a man to fear, when life is ruled
    By chance, and the future is unknowable?   945
    The best way is to take life as it comes.
    So have no fear of marriage with your mother.
    Many men before this time have dreamt that they
    Have shared their mother's bed. The man to whom
    These things are nothing lives the easiest life.   950
OEDIPUS: It would be well enough to talk in such a way
    If my mother were not living. As she is,
    Though your words make sense, I have good cause to fear.
JOCASTA: But your father's death is a ray of light in darkness.
OEDIPUS: A bright one; but I fear the living woman.   955
MESSENGER: Who is this woman that you are afraid of?
OEDIPUS: Merope, old man, the wife of Polybus.
MESSENGER: And what is there in her to make you afraid?
OEDIPUS: A terrifying oracle from heaven.
MESSENGER: May it be told? Or are you sworn to silence?   960
OEDIPUS: Why should it not? Apollo told me once
    That I was doomed to marry with my mother
    And shed my father's blood with these my hands.
    And that is why I put my home in Corinth
    Behind me — for the best, but all the same   965
    There is nothing so sweet as the sight of parents' faces.
MESSENGER: Was it for fear of this you left our city?
OEDIPUS: It was; and to avoid my father's murder.
MESSENGER: Then had I better not remove your fear,
    My lord, since I am here with friendly purpose?   970

OEDIPUS: If so you would deserve reward, and have it.
MESSENGER: Indeed, this was my principal reason for coming,
   To do myself some good when you came home.
OEDIPUS: I shall never come. I must not see my parents.
MESSENGER: My son, I see you are making a mistake —   975
OEDIPUS: What do you mean, old man? In god's name tell me.
MESSENGER: — if you shrink from going home because of this.
OEDIPUS: I am terrified of proving Phoebus true.
MESSENGER: Of the guilt and shame that will come to you
   through your parents?
OEDIPUS: You have it, old man; that fear is always with me.   980
MESSENGER: Then let me tell you that these fears are groundless!
OEDIPUS: How can they be, if I were born their son?
MESSENGER: Because there is none of Polybus' blood in you.
OEDIPUS: Are you telling me that he was not my father?
MESSENGER: No more than I — one thing we had in common.   985
OEDIPUS: What could he have in common with a nobody?
MESSENGER: Why, I am not your father, and neither was he.
OEDIPUS: But then . . . he called me son . . . what made him do it?
MESSENGER: He took you as a present from my hands.
OEDIPUS: He had such love . . . for an adopted son?   990
MESSENGER: He had no sons of his own; this moved his heart.
OEDIPUS: You gave me to him — had you bought me?
   Found me?
MESSENGER: I found you, in the wild woods of Cithairon.
OEDIPUS: What led your wanderings to such a place?
MESSENGER: I was in charge of sheep there, on the mountain.   995
OEDIPUS: A shepherd, going from place to place for hire?
MESSENGER: But your preserver at that time, my son.
OEDIPUS: Why? What was matter with me when you found me?
MESSENGER: Your ankles are best witnesses of that.
OEDIPUS: Oh, why do you have to talk of that old trouble?   1000
MESSENGER: They were pinned together, and I cut you loose.
OEDIPUS: A shameful mark I carried from my cradle.
MESSENGER: And from this chance you took the name you bear.
OEDIPUS: Who did this to me? My father or my mother?
MESSENGER: The man who gave you me knows; I do not.   1005
OEDIPUS: You took me from someone else? You did not find me?
MESSENGER: No, another shepherd passed you on to me.
OEDIPUS: Who was this man? Can you identify him?
MESSENGER: We knew him, I think, as one of Laius' people.
OEDIPUS: You mean the king who used to rule this country?   1010
MESSENGER: The very same. This man was Laius' herdsman.
OEDIPUS: And is he still alive for me to see him?
MESSENGER: You in this country would best know of that.
OEDIPUS: My people, is there anyone here present
   Who knows the herdsman he is talking of,   1015
   Who has seen him in the country or the town?
  Come, tell me; it is time to solve this riddle.
CHORUS: I think he means no other than the man

You already want to see. Jocasta here
Would be best qualified to tell you that. ·   1020
OEDIPUS: My lady, do you know the man we mean —
The man we just sent for; is he speaking of him?
JOCASTA: Why ask who he means? Do not bother with it.
This story is not worth thinking of; it is nothing.
OEDIPUS: No, that can never be. I have the clues   1025
Here in my hand. I must find out my birth.
JOCASTA: No, by the gods! If you care for your own safety
Ask no more questions. I have suffered enough.
OEDIPUS: Take courage. If my mother was a slave, and hers,
And hers before her, you are still pure-born.   1030
JOCASTA: Listen, please listen to me! Do not do this!
OEDIPUS: No-one could stop me finding out the truth.
JOCASTA: It is for your sake; I advise you for the best.
OEDIPUS: If this is your best, I have no patience with it.
JOCASTA: I pray you may never find out who you are.'   1035
OEDIPUS: Go, somebody, and fetch the herdsman here.
Leave her to glory in her wealthy birth!
JOCASTA: Accursed! Accursed! I have no other name
To call you; you will never hear me again.   (Exit)
CHORUS: What can have made her leave you, Oedipus,   1040
In this burst of frantic grief? I have a fear
That from her silence there will break a storm.
OEDIPUS: Let break what will! As for my parentage,
Humble though it may be, I want to know it.
She is a woman, with a woman's pride,   1045
And is ashamed, no doubt, of my low birth. ·
But I proclaim myself the child of Luck,
My benefactress; this is no dishonor.
Yes, Luck is my mother, and the months, my cousins,
Saw me first humble and then saw me great.   1050
With such a parentage I could not be false
To myself again, or let this secret rest.
CHORUS: If I am any judge of the future,
If my mind does not play me false,
Cithairon, tomorrow at the full moon's rising,   1055
By Olympus, you will need no second telling
That Oedipus boasts of your kinship, hailing you
As nurse and mother.
And we shall be there with dances in your honor
Because you have found favor in our king's sight.   1060
Apollo, hear us when we pray,
And bless our good intentions!

Which of the nymphs, the long-lived ones,
Lay with the mountain-wanderer Pan[27]
To bring you to birth? Or was it Loxias?[28]   1065

[27] primitive nature deity, half man, half   [28] Apollo
goat

He is a god who loves the upland pastures.
Or was it Cyllene's lord,[29] or the god
Of the Bacchanals,[30] dwelling
High in the hilltops, who received you,
A new-born treasure, from the arms of a nymph   1070
Of Helicon,[31] the favorite
Companions of his pleasure?

(*Enter attendants with* HERDSMAN)

OEDIPUS: Elders, if I, who never saw the man,
  May make a guess, I think I see the herdsman
  We have sought so long; he is well advanced in years —   1075
  This answers the description — and besides
  I recognize the men escorting him
  As servants of my own. But you may well
  Have the advantage of me, if you have seen him before;
CHORUS: I know him, no mistake. He worked for Laius,   1080
  As honest a shepherd as you could hope to find.
OEDIPUS: First let me hear from you, my Corinthian friend.
  Is this your man?
MESSENGER: The one you see before you.
OEDIPUS: Come here, old man, and look me in the face.
  Answer my questions. You once worked for Laius?   1085
HERDSMAN: I did; and I was palace-bred, not bought.
OEDIPUS: In what employment? How did you spend your time?
HERDSMAN: For the best part of my life I watched the flocks.
OEDIPUS: What part of the country did you mostly work in?
HERDSMAN: Sometimes Cithairon, sometimes round about.   1090
OEDIPUS: Have you seen this man in those parts, to your knowledge?
HERDSMAN: Who? Doing what? What man are you talking about?
OEDIPUS: This man in front of you. Have you ever met him?
HERDSMAN: Not to remember off-hand. I cannot say.
MESSENGER: Small wonder, master. But let me refresh   1095
  His failing memory. I have no doubt
  That he recalls the time we spent together
  In the country round Cithairon. He had two flocks,
  And I, his mate, had one. Three years we did this,
  For six months at a time, from spring to fall.   1100
  Then, for the winter, I used to drive my flocks
  Home to my fold, he his to that of Laius.
  Did it happen as I say, or did it not?
HERDSMAN: Yes, true; but it was many years ago.
MESSENGER: Now tell me: do you remember giving me   1105
  A boy for me to bring up as my own?
HERDSMAN: What now? What has put that question in your head?

---

[29] Hermes, the messenger god, born on   [31] mountain sacred to Apollo and the
Mount Cyllene   Muses
[30] frenzied women who worshipped Dionysus

MESSENGER: That child, my friend, is the man you see before you.

HERDSMAN: Curse you! Do not say another word!

OEDIPUS: Old man, do not reprove him. Your words stand   1110
   In greater need of admonition than his.

HERDSMAN: And where do I offend, most noble master?

OEDIPUS: In not telling of the boy he asks about.

HERDSMAN: This meddler does not know what he is saying.

OEDIPUS: If you will not speak to oblige me I must make you.   1115

HERDSMAN: No, no, for god's sake; you would not hurt an old man?

OEDIPUS: Quickly, somebody, tie his arms behind him.

HERDSMAN: Unhappy man, what more do you want to know?

OEDIPUS: This child he talks of; did you give it him?

HERDSMAN: I did; and I wish that day had been my last.   1120

OEDIPUS: It will come to that, unless you tell the truth.

HERDSMAN: I shall do myself more harm by telling you.

OEDIPUS: It seems he is determined to waste our time.

HERDSMAN: No, no! I told you once, I gave it him.

OEDIPUS: Where did you get it? Your home or another's?   1125

HERDSMAN: It was not mine. Somebody gave it me.

OEDIPUS: Who? Which one of my people? Where does he live?

HERDSMAN: No, master, in heaven's name, ask no more questions.

OEDIPUS: You are a dead man if I have to ask again.

HERDSMAN: It was a child of the house of Laius.   1130

OEDIPUS: A slave? Or one of his own family?

HERDSMAN: I am near to saying what should not be said.

OEDIPUS: And I to hearing; but it must be heard.

HERDSMAN: They said it was Laius' son. But go inside
   And ask your wife; for she could tell you all.   1135

OEDIPUS: You mean she gave it you?

HERDSMAN: She did, my lord.

OEDIPUS: But why?

HERDSMAN: For me to make away with it.

OEDIPUS: Her child!

HERDSMAN: She feared an evil prophecy.

OEDIPUS: What was it?

HERDSMAN: That the son should kill his father.

OEDIPUS: Then why did you give him up to this old man?   1140

HERDSMAN: For pity, master, thinking he would take
   The child home, out of Thebes; but he preserved him
   For a fate worse than any other. If you are truly
   The man he says, then know you were born accursed.   *(Exit)*

OEDIPUS: Oh, oh, then everything has come out true.   1145
   Light, I shall not look on you again.
   I have been born where I should not be born,
   I have married where I should not marry,
   I have killed whom I should not kill; now all is clear.   *(Exit)*

CHORUS: You that are born into this world,   1150
   I count you in your lives as nothing worth.
   What man has ever won for himself
   More of happiness than this,

To seem, and having seemed, to pass?
For Oedipus, when I look at you   1155
And the fate which fell upon you, can I
Call any human being happy?

Zeus knows, his arrow went straight to its mark
And all of life's blessings became his prize.
He killed the girl with the crooked claws,   1160
The riddle-monger, and stood up among us
A tower of strength to drive death from our land,
For which we called you our king, paid you honors
The greatest we knew; in the proud land
Of Thebes you were lord and master.   1165

Now who has a sadder tale to tell?
A life turned upside down,
The door flung wide to misfortune,
The hounds of fate let loose.
Oh Oedipus, famous Oedipus,   1170
The same ample shelter sufficed
For father and son, a bed for the mating.
How could the furrows your father sowed
Have endured you so long in silence?

Time sees all, and has found you out   1175
Despite yourself, passing sentence
On the marriage that is no marriage,
Where begetter is one with begotten.
Laius' child, oh Laius' child,
Better if I had not seen you,   1180
For when all is said, he that gave me new life
Has taken all my joy in living.

(*Enter* SECOND MESSENGER)

MESSENGER: Ancestral and most honorable lords,
    Such things you will see and hear of; such a weight
    Of grief is yours, if like true sons of Thebes   1185
    You still care for the house of Labdacus.
    I think there is no river wide enough
    To wash this palace clean, so many are
    The horrors it hides, or soon will bring to light,
    Done willfully, from choice; no sufferings   1190
    Hurt more than those we bring upon ourselves.
CHORUS: Those that we know already claim their weight
    Of tears. What more have you to add to these?
MESSENGER: A tale which can be very briefly told
    And heard: our royal lady Jocasta is dead.   1195
CHORUS: Oh miserable queen; what was the cause?

MESSENGER: By her own hand. The worst of what has happened
    You shall be spared, you were not there to see it.
    But you shall hear as much as I recall
    About the sufferings of the wretched queen.   1200
    Past caring what she did, she rushed inside
    The hall, and made straight for her marriage bed,
    Head in hands, and fingers tearing at her hair.
    Once in the room she slammed the doors behind her
    And called on Laius rotting in his grave,   1205
    Remembering a once begotten child
    By whom the father should die, and leave the mother
    To bear his son's cursed children; she bewailed
    The bed where she had borne a double brood,
    Husband by husband, children by her child,   1210
    And then she died — I cannot tell you how,
    For Oedipus burst on us with a cry
    And we had no chance to watch her agonies.
    We had eyes for none but him, as he ran from one
    To another, demanding a sword, and where   1215
    He might find his wife — his mother, not his wife,
    The womb that gave him and his children birth.
    In his frenzy he was guided by some power
    More than human — not by any of us who stood there.
    With a dreadful cry, as though a hand had pointed,   1220
    He sprang at the double doors, forced back the bolts
    Till the sockets gave, and ran into the room.
    And there inside we saw the woman hanging,
    Her body swinging in a twist of rope.
    When he saw, a shuddering cry welled up inside him;   1225
    He cut the noose that held her; when she lay
    Cold on the ground, we saw a ghastly sight.
    He tore away the golden brooches from
    Her dress, that she had used as ornaments,
    And lifted them, and plunged them in his eyes   1230
    With words like these: "You shall not see again
    Such horrors as I did, saw done to me,
    But stare in darkness on forbidden faces,
    Meet those I longed to find, and pass them by."
    And to this tune he raised his hands and struck   1235
    His eyes again and again; with every blow
    Blood spurted down his cheeks. It did not fall
    In slow and sluggish drops, but all at once
    Black blood came pouring like a shower of hail.
    This storm has broken on two people's heads,   1240
    Not one alone; both man and wife have suffered.
    Till now, the happiness they inherited
    Was happiness indeed; and now, today,
    Tears, ruin, death, disgrace, as many ills
    As there are names for them; not one is lacking.   1245

CHORUS: How is he now? Is he in peace from pain?
MESSENGER: He shouts for the doors to be opened, for every man
   In Thebes to see his father's murderer,
   His mother's — heaven forbid I speak that word.
   He means to cast himself from Thebes, to stay   1250
   In this house no more, a self-inflicted curse.
   But his strength is gone; he needs someone to guide
   His steps, the pain is more than he can bear.
   And this too he will show you. See, the doors
   Are opening, and soon you will see a sight   1255
   To move your tears, though you recoil from it.

(Enter OEDIPUS, blind)

CHORUS: Oh sufferings dreadful to see,
   Most dreadful of all that ever
   Greeted my eyes. Wretched king,
   What insanity possessed you?   1260
   What demon, in one colossal spring
   Pounced on your ill-fated life?
   Unhappy king,
   I cannot even look you in the face,
   Though there are still many questions to be asked,   1265
   Many things left unsaid, much remaining to be seen,
   You fill me with such shuddering.
OEDIPUS: Oh, oh, the pain, the pain!
   Where do my poor legs take me?
   Where do the wild winds scatter my words?   1270
   Oh, my fate, where have you leapt with me?
CHORUS: To a dreadful place that must not be named,
   To a place unfit for the eyes of man.
OEDIPUS: Oh, this fog,
   This horrible darkness all around me,   1275
   Unspeakable visitation
   Blown by an evil wind; I am powerless.
   Oh, when I remember my sorrows
   I feel again the points in my eyes.
CHORUS: No wonder; in such sorrows you must have   1280
   Evils redoubled to endure and mourn.
OEDIPUS: Oh, my friend,
   You are my faithful servant still,
   Blind Oedipus' patient nurse.
   I know you are here, I can feel your presence.   1285
   Although I am in the darkness
   I can recognize your voice.
CHORUS: Oh man of wrath, how could you bring yourself
   To blind your eyes? What demon drove you on?
OEDIPUS: It was Apollo, my friends, Apollo   1290
   Who contrived my ruin, who worked my fall.
   But no-one blinded my eyes

But myself, in my own grief.
What use are eyes to me, who could never
See anything pleasant again? 1295
CHORUS: Yes, it was as you say.
OEDIPUS: What is there left for me to see,
  To love? Who still has a kindly word,
  My friends, for me?
  Take me away from this land, my friends, 1300
  Take me with all the speed you may,
  For Oedipus is no more,
  Contaminated, cursed,
  Unclean in heaven's sight.
CHORUS: Knowledge and pain; they hurt you equally. 1305
  I wish your path and mine had never crossed.
OEDIPUS: Cursed be the man who struck the cruel chains
  From my feet as I lay abandoned,
  And saved me from death, gave me back
  To the world of the living — why? 1310
  If I had died then, I should never
  Have grieved myself or my loved ones so.
CHORUS: I too would have had it so.
OEDIPUS: I would not have shed my father's blood
  Or heard men call me my mother's husband. 1315
  And now I am
  God-shunned, the son of a mother defiled,
  Have taken my turn in my mother's bed.
  If there is any sorrow
  Greater than all others 1320
  It belongs to Oedipus.
CHORUS: I cannot praise your judgment. You would be
  Far better dead than living still and blind.
OEDIPUS: Do not tell me I am wrong. What I have done
  Is best as it is. Give me no more advice. 1325
  If I had sight, I know not with what eyes
  I would have looked upon my father, when
  I walked among the dead, or my sad mother,
  For sins so great cannot be paid by hanging.
  Or do you think the sight of children born 1330
  As mine were born could give me any joy?
  No, never to these eyes of mine again,
  Nor the proud wall of our city, nor the holy
  Statues of our gods; these I, ten times accursed,
  I, who was noblest of the sons of Thebes, 1335
  Have set behind me by my own command
  That all cast out the sinner, the man revealed
  By heaven as unclean, as Laius' son.
  And tainted thus for all the world to see
  How could I look my people in the face? 1340
  I could not. If I could have stopped my ears,

My fount of hearing, I would not have rested
Till I had made a prison of this body
Barred against sight and sound. How happy the mind
That can so live, beyond the reach of suffering.   1345
Cithairon, why did you shelter me? Why did you not
Kill me there, where you found me, so that I might never
Show to mankind the seret of my birth?
Oh Polybus, Corinth, the ancestral home
Men called my father's; oh, how fair of face   1350
Was I, your child, and how corrupt beneath!
For now I am found evil, evil born.
Those three roads, and the hidden clump of trees,
The wood, the narrow place where three paths met,
Who drank from my own hands the father's blood,   1355
And so, my own blood; do you still remember
The things you saw me do? Then I came here
To do other things besides. Oh marriage, marriage,
You gave me birth, and after I was born
Bore children to your child, and brought to light   1360
Sons, fathers, brothers in a web of incest,
Than which men know nothing more abominable.
But what is sin to do is sin to speak of.
For heaven's love, hide me in some wilderness,
Or strike me dead, or throw me in the sea,   1365
Where you will never set eyes on me again.
Come, do not shrink from touching my poor body.
Please; do not be afraid. My sufferings
Are all my own, no-one will be infected.
CHORUS: No. Here is Creon, in time to listen to you,   1370
    Ready to act or advise. Now you are gone
    He is the only one we have to turn to.
OEDIPUS: Oh, what words can I find to say to him?
    What proof of my good faith? I have been found
    An arrant traitor to him in the past.   1375

(*Enter* CREON *with* ATTENDANTS)

CREON: Oedipus, I have not come to jeer at you
    Or throw your past misconduct in your face.

(*To the* CHORUS)

As for you, if you have no sense of decency
To a fellow man, at least have some respect
For holy sunlight, giver of warmth and life.   1380
Do not leave this pollution uncovered, an offence
To earth, to light, to the pure rain from heaven.
Take him indoors as quickly as you can.
Propriety forbids he should be made
A public spectacle. These things are for his family.   1385
OEDIPUS: Listen: since you have removed my apprehension

And behave so nobly to a man so low,
Grant me this favor — for your good, not for mine.
CREON: What is it you are so anxious to have me do?
OEDIPUS: Lose no more time; drive me away from Thebes 1390
To some place where nobody will know my name.
CREON: Believe me, I would have done so; but first I wanted
To find out from the god what I should do.
OEDIPUS: The will of god is clear enough already.
Kill the parricide, the sinner; and that am I. 1395
CREON: So he said. But all the same, now things have gone
So far, it is better that we seek clear guidance.
OEDIPUS: You will go to the god? For a poor wretch like myself?
CREON: I will. Perhaps you will believe him this time.
OEDIPUS: I do. And I will urge your duties on you. 1400
The woman inside — bury her as you would wish
To be buried yourself. It is right, she is your sister.
But as for me, never sentence my father's city
To have me within its walls, as long as I live,
But leave me to the hills, to my Cithairon 1405
As men now call it — destined for my grave
By my father and mother when they were alive.
They tried to kill me; let me die the way they wanted.
But I am sure of one thing; no disease,
Nothing can kill me now. I would not have been saved 1410
From death, unless it were for some strange destiny.
But let my destiny go where it will.
As for my children — Creon, do not trouble yourself
About my sons. They are men, they can never lack
A livelihood, wherever they may be. 1415
But my two girls, my poor unhappy daughters,
Who never knew what it was to eat a meal
Away from their father's side, but had their share
Of every little thing I had myself. . . .
Please look after them. And I beg this favor now, 1420
Let me lay my hands on them and weep with them.
Please, my lord,
Please, noble heart. If I could touch them now
I should think they were with me, as if I could see them.

(*Enter* ANTIGONE *and* ISMENE)

What is that? 1425
Oh you gods; is it my darlings that I hear
Sobbing? Has Creon taken pity on me
And sent my darlings, sent my children to me?
Am I right?
CREON: Yes, I had them brought to you; I knew 1430
They would delight you as they always have done.
OEDIPUS: Bless you for your trouble. May you find
A kinder fate than what has come to me.

Where are you now, my children? Over here:
Come to these hands of mine, your brother's hands,   1435
Whose offices have made your father's eyes
That were once so bright, to see as they see now.
For the truth is out; your father, stupid, blind,
Begot you in the womb where he was born.
Sight have I none, but tears I have for you   1440
When I think of how you will be forced to live
At men's hands in the bitter days to come.
What gathering of the folk will you attend,
What festival that will not send you home
In tears, instead of making holiday?   1445
And when the time has come for you to marry,
Show me the man, my children, bold enough
To take upon his own head such disgrace,
The stain that you and your brothers will inherit.
What sorrow is not ours? Your father killed   1450
His father, sowed his seed in her
Where he was sown as seed, and did beget you
In the selfsame place where he was once begotten.
That is how men will talk. Then who will marry you?
No-one, my children. Marriage is not for you.   1455
You must be barren till your lives are done.
Son of Menoeceus, you are the only father
These girls have left, for we, their parents,
Are both of us gone. So do not let them wander
Beggared and husbandless. They are your kin.   1460
And do not level them with my misfortunes
But pity them. You see how young they are.
You are the only friend they have in the world.
Touch me, kind heart, in token of your promise.
Children, if you were old enough to understand,   1465
There is much I could say to help you. As it is,
Pray after me — to live with moderation
And better fortune than your father did.

CREON: Your time is up. Dry your tears and go indoors.
OEDIPUS: It is hard, but I must obey.
CREON: There must be moderation in all things.   1470
OEDIPUS: I shall go on one condition.
CREON: Tell me what it is.
OEDIPUS: Send me away from Thebes to live.
CREON: That is for the gods to say.
OEDIPUS: They will be glad to see me gone.
CREON: Then your wish will soon be granted.
OEDIPUS: You agree then?
CREON: When I do not know, I do not speak.
OEDIPUS: Take me away, it is time.
CREON: Come along. Leave your children here.   1475
OEDIPUS: Never part us!

CREON: Do not ask to have everything your way.
   Your time for giving orders is over.   (*Exeunt*)
CHORUS: People of this city, look, this man is Oedipus,
   Who guessed the famous riddle, who rose to greatness,
   Envy of all in the city who saw his good fortune.   1480
   And now what a fearful storm of disaster has struck him.
   That is why we wait until we see the final day,
   Not calling anybody happy who is mortal
   Until he has passed the last milestone without calamity.

AFTERWORD

Oedipus the King was written about 430 B.C., when Sophocles was in his sixties. Though it deals with an earlier episode in the story of the House of Laius, it followed *Antigone* in composition, and the two plays are not parts of the same tetralogy. Sophocles did not win the prize for the tetralogy to which *Oedipus the King* belongs. In his *Poetics*, the most important classical treatment of the theory of tragedy, Aristotle discusses *Oedipus the King* as a model tragedy: a unified dramatization of formal complexity of a story of a certain magnitude concerning a good but not perfect man who comes to grief because of some error (*hamartia*) and which effects the purgation (*katharsis*) of the emotions of pity and fear in the audience. The exact meaning of catharsis has been much debated, but the medical denotation of Aristotle's term suggests that he had in mind some kind of soul therapy: witnessing the tragic action unfold to catastrophe in a scene of recognition (*anagnorisis*), the spectator harmlessly expends his subrational passions in vicarious suffering. Because moral enlightenment is the intended effect of this feeling of there-but-for-the-grace-of-God-go-I and because it depends on a degree of audience identification, the protagonist can be neither vicious nor perfect. Suffering vice commands no sympathy, and suffering perfection would seem merely preposterous.

When a playwright dramatizes a traditional story well known to his audience he must forego major plot invention and alteration and all attempts to surprise his audience in the more obvious ways. He is tied to the received facts. But in compensation he can dispense with the laborious exposition that clutters many an original play of more modern times. With the tragic myth given he can proceed at once to essentials: the dramatization not of a story but of its meaning. The old myth of man's vain effort to circumvent the divine will is in Sophocles's treatment a tautly suspenseful revelation of the unredeemability of the past, of the fateful continuity in a human life. There is the pathos of innocent ignorance and impotence in the scene where the two shepherds meet again, the Corinthian effusively reminiscing about the distant days when they tended their flocks together on Cithairon, the Theban scared and reluctant at the approach of the disastrous revelation he sees coming. The retrospective structure orders the narrative into a metaphor for the way the past doesn't just *produce* but *is* the present. The hours on stage comprise all of Oedipus's life. It is difficult to think of another play in which unity of time as a formal property of the drama contributes more to the meaning. Every step Oedipus takes to solve the old murder mystery, every new confrontation with those he summons to appear with pieces of the past, every one of their chance disclosures, brings him closer both to the solution he seeks and to the self-discovery he does not foresee. When the last piece falls into place the detective has become the criminal, his success his doom, his happy ignorance tragic knowledge, and the evil without the evil within.

Such a summary description of the plot points up its heavily ironic nature. Dramatic irony operates whenever the audience is aware of some circumstance in plot or character that gives a speech a meaning beyond or at odds with that which the speaker consciously intends, or charges a situation with a significance unsuspected by the character caught in it. The more hostile the covert significance is to the unwitting ironist and the farther he is from realizing it, the more poignant the irony. In Oedipus's words to the citizen suppliants in the beginning, "There is not one of you who knows my pain," we hear not just the king's concern for his stricken people and his self-involvement in their fate, we also perceive the dreadful accuracy of his description of himself. Our perception depends on our knowledge of the outcome, but the alert reader can anticipate the outcome in the persistent pattern of ironies — Oedipus cursing Laius's murderer, promising to take revenge for the dead king "As I would for my own father," and berating Teiresias for his arrogance, mocking his blindness, and accusing him of complicity in the murder. Far from being an inept, premature giveaway of the plot, Sophocles' method engages our interest in the dramatic form as an image of the frailty of man's defenses, the folly of his feelings of security and power — *hubris* is the Greek word — and the strange inevitability of his fate. Our suspense concerning the manner in which the ironies will complete themselves in the unraveling of the directed past is of a subtler kind than that produced by ignorance of outcome. If we miss the grim geometry in all this, the plot will seem only like a set of brutal facts manipulated for shock effect — not so much an irrelevant as an inadequate response.

Irony is a rhetorical device for holding different or opposite truths in suspension, for focusing on the discrepancy between what seems to be and what is. It is therefore properly the sustaining mode of a tragedy of self-ignorance. At the beginning of the play Oedipus has a clear and single purpose: to find Laius's murderer. When he later begins to pursue his own parentage the obvious irony is that this wise and self-assured man doesn't realize that his purpose has changed. The deeper irony is that it hasn't *really* changed, since the answer to the question of whose son he is is also the answer to the question of who killed Laius. Pride motivates both quests. He undertakes the first because he pities his people and wants to protect himself against Laius's fate but above all because he is King Oedipus of the "name that all men know," the conqueror of the Sphinx with a reputation as Thebes's savior to maintain, and sure of his own ability to discover the truth. That the Priest in the opening scene finds it proper to remind him that he is not one of the immortal gods says something perhaps about the respect he commands and expects to command. For the same reason he is later willing to risk learning that he is low-born; his achievements, he feels, will cancel any possible ignominy of birth. He is proud of being a self-made man, superior to what he takes to be Jocasta's aristocratic prejudice.

> As for my parentage,
> Humble though it may be, I want to know it.

His two quests turn out to have been one when he learns that he is the child not of "luck" but of the man he has slain and of the woman he has married. He was the one man clever enough to identify "man" from the clues in the Sphinx's riddle,* yet he has never known his own identity. The recognition scene imparts the old tragic wisdom that knowledge is suffering, an early, dark, and bitter variant of the Socratic "know thyself." One could define an abiding tension in western consciousness by these two views: faith in knowledge as a way to virtue and the good life, and the conviction that ultimate self-knowledge is painful. The Socratic ethic assumes progress through moral endeavor. Tragedy questions man's ability to perfect himself and his institutions through learning and self-discipline, and it demands a high price for enlightenment. The wage of noble striving is death. The tragic temper is devastating to a philosophy of amelioration and is hard to reconcile with a belief in a just and benevolent providence, but it is not unsupportable by the facts of history. Socrates was, as he recognized himself, a non-tragic figure. Coming to him — or to Plato's accounts of him — from Greek tragedy one is struck by a sense of the Socratic fallacy, a quality of innocence in his concept of man's nature.

Does Oedipus suffer justly? In committing parricide and incest he has violated the most sacred of the taboos governing family life. Freud used his name for the most primary of interpersonal conflicts, the child's sexual jealousy of the parent of his own sex, and equated his crime with each man's original sin. But since Oedipus is clearly innocent of evil intent, can the god be called just who exacts such suffering for crimes thus committed? How can he be held responsible for a destiny decreed for him before his birth and for the god's manipulation of events in such a way that the means by which he and his parents try to avert his destiny become the very means by which it is fulfilled? Why should Oedipus have to pay for his

---

* "Who moves on four in the morning, on two at noon, and on three in the evening?"

parents' impiety in ignoring Apollo's warning and in seeking to frustrate the god's will by abandoning their child? Does retribution in *Oedipus the King* strike the right victim?

It does if we make a distinction between divine *foreknowledge* and divine *preordination*. The god in his wisdom, knowing the kind of man Oedipus was, could know what his destiny was. But the god did not *determine* or *order* that destiny. Related to this view is that which sees Oedipus as the maker of his own misfortune and the whole play as a critique of rationalism. Sophocles' control of his subject matter is shown in the intricate chain of causality by which he moves his plot, but the plot concerns a king who thought he could control his destiny but discovered he was wrong. It is not the acts themselves that cause Oedipus's suffering, for he has lived happily for years after killing his father and marrying his mother; it is the finding out. He may have been doomed to do what he did but not to discover what he had done. He thinks he can outwit the god. Anger subverts his reason in his encounters with Laius, Teiresias, and Creon. He fails to see the possible connection between the drunken Corinthian's taunt that he is the son of an unknown father and the words of the Delphic oracle. His purpose is diverted when his pride is involved. He refuses to heed Teiresias's and Jocasta's warnings to leave the past alone. Intellectual pride and a hasty temper constitute his tragic flaw. Sophocles's tragedy, like so many of Shakespeare's, implies that character is fate. That Oedipus means well is true, but good intentions have never guaranteed protection against evil consequences.

That, however, is precisely the problem of divine justice in the play. If Oedipus regards the unsolved murder of Laius as a challenge to his ingenuity and determination, he also undertakes the investigation because he is not callous enough to ignore his people's plea for help. He suffers not *in spite* of but *because* of his exercise of kingly responsibility. True, if he had not been king he would not have had the responsibility, and he became king because he was headstrong. But that is not the whole truth. When all his vulnerabilities of mind and temper have been listed there remains a sense in which he is the victim both of circumstances over which he had no control and of his own virtues.

But Oedipus blinds himself in an agony of shame and guilty horror. Beyond his bewildered, "Oh, my fate, where have you leapt with me?" it doesn't occur to anyone to question the justice of his fate. He accepts the fact that he is a pollution of which Thebes must cleanse herself. The god's punishment of the city that has innocently harbored the violator of natural law is a blight of infertility on crops, beasts, and humans. And at the end Oedipus's personal tragedy restores the city to health; once again he saves Thebes, just as he set out to do. We are aware in all of this of the workings of a supernatural order that is ruthless but neither arbitrary nor malign. That Oedipus is an abomination in the eyes of god and men alike is a matter neither of morality nor of justice, but it is a fact that must be heeded. The universe is not obliged to fit man's sense of fair play. The will of the gods is inscrutable, but it must be obeyed. "Neither destiny nor Oedipus is acquitted or condemned" is how one critic puts the affirmation in *Oedipus the King* of an order that passes human understanding. The metaphysical implications of the title of Jean Cocteau's modern play version of the story about Oedipus, *The Infernal Machine*, would have made small sense to the Greeks.

When enlightenment crashes in on Oedipus, he obliterates his sight of the world he thought he controlled. Like Shakespeare's Gloucester (in *King Lear*) he learns that "he stumbled when he saw." And like Teiresias, Apollo's priest-prophet, whose experience of both male and female existence gives him an understanding that transcends that of ordinary men, and whose blindness is a symbol of inner vision, so Oedipus, too, at the end of his life is a figure whom great suffering has sanctified. In *Oedipus at Colonus* the aged king is still in exile and still irascible and imperious. But his destiny has taken him beyond tragedy, and his death is a holy mystery. Our questions of divine justice are not answered, but they are silenced. After Jocasta learns the truth and realizes that she can't keep it from her still ignorant son-husband, she goes to her suicide without further words. And the messenger from Corinth, the cheerful bringer of good news who finds himself turning into an instrument of catastrophe, can only listen in silent, mounting horror as Oedipus examines the old shepherd. At the end we think of him as slinking away, shaken and ignored.

Human guilt and innocence are ambiguous and inextricable; before the absolute, pride and power and virtue are equally helpless. The voice that stays with us is that of the Chorus, lost, awed, grieving for humanity, recognizing its "blindness":

> You that are born into this world.
> I count you in your lives as nothing worth.
> What man has ever won for himself
> More of happiness than this,
> To seem, and having seemed, to pass?

Anonymous

EVERYMAN

FOREWORD

Everyman is the most famous of all English morality plays, a type of allegorical drama that flourished in western Europe during the late Middle Ages. Morality plays derived from an older liturgical drama and contributed in turn to the development of Elizabethan drama. *Everyman* may have been based on a contemporary Dutch play, dated about 1500. The earliest extant texts of the English play were printed in the early sixteenth century. The play has had successful stagings in our time, including a famous adaptation by the German playwright Hugo von Hofmannsthal.

Medieval drama was independent of the drama of antiquity but had, like it, a religious origin. After the collapse of classical civilization, theatrical activity was largely limited to performances by strolling bands of actors and minstrels — *mimes* — heirs to the decadent traditions of the late Roman theater. The Catholic Church was against such vulgar vagabond spectacles and looked upon the remaining Roman theaters as temples of sin, but it was the Church itself that revived serious drama. As ancient drama began in ritual spectacle and song, so medieval drama began as a development of the potential drama in the celebration of the Mass and in antiphonal singing. From as early as the tenth century there is a record of clerical impersonation of characters from the Bible and the acting out of brief Biblical scenes in chanted speech before the congregation. Such dramatizations of Biblical stories, with words and melodies added, are called *tropes*. The first recorded trope is known, from its opening words, as the "Quem Quaeritis" ("Whom Seek Ye?"), an enactment of the meeting of the three Marys and the Angel at Christ's empty tomb on Easter morning. Tropes later developed into short plays, known today, whether in Latin or (later) the vernacular, as *liturgical* plays. (Scholars used to distinguish between *mystery plays*, based on Scripture, including the life of Christ, and *miracle plays*, based on saints' lives. But the terminology was never consistent and is today generally considered more confusing than helpful.) With the change in language from Latin to the vernacular the plays could serve to make Christian lore imaginatively real for illiterate audiences who knew no Latin. After the Pope instituted the Feast of Corpus Christi in 1264, plays became part of the annual celebration of the Feast in early summer. As the liturgical plays grew more elaborate, performance moved out of the church and the church precincts to the marketplace, and departures from the Biblical script became common, including the introduction of comic characters often represented with earthy realism. After 1210 the English clergy were no longer allowed to participate in profane theatricals, and the staging of the liturgical plays was wholly taken over by the town guilds. Members of a guild performed one of the plays in a larger cycle. The sacred story assigned a guild to stage was often one that was felt to be appropriate to the guild's particular craft, as when the fishmongers and bakers enacted the story of Christ feeding the multitude in the wilderness and the carpenters enacted the Crucifixion. The cycle plays were usually staged on platforms on wheels ("pageants"), appearing in sequence before stationary audiences along a route through the town. The surviving liturgical plays were parts of the cycles given in the towns of Coventry, Wakefield, Chester, and York in the Midlands and northern England. *The Second Shepherd's Play*, from the Wakefield (or Towneley) cycle, is probably the cycle play most familiar to modern readers. The cycle plays were at their height from about 1300 to 1450.

Despite the strong religious content in a play like *Everyman*, the morality represents a later stage in the gradual secularization of the old liturgical plays; and its successor in the development of English drama, the sixteenth-century *interlude*, carries secularization still further in its change from religious to more purely intellectual subject matter. Rather than episodes from the Bible or from saints' lives the moralities are dramatic allegorizations of universal moral and religious concepts — usually some version of the struggle between good and evil for man's soul on its perilous journey through life to salvation or perdition. The characters are personified abstracts with names like Youth, Mankind, Everyman, Good and Bad Angel, World, Vanity, Vice, and Death.

Although *Everyman* is now one of the most familiar medieval plays in performance, there is no surviving record of its original staging. Our knowledge of similar plays suggests that it may have been done on a long, shallow stage against a row of scenic units ("mansions") representing the

abodes of the principal characters — perhaps a tavern for Fellowship, a
private house for Kindred and Cousin, a church for Confession, and so
forth. Clearly there must be a grave-trap into which Everyman descends at
his death; this could also serve for Death's entrance and the place where
Good Deeds is first discovered, "cold in the ground." All these places
would be on view at the same time, and Everyman, passing from one to
another, would draw attention to whichever was needed for the immediate
action. An elevated platform doubtless held God, dressed in ecclesiastical
vestments, and his angels, who would call Everyman up to them after his
resurrection. Costumes must have relied heavily on familiar medieval symbolism, particularly Death, with drum and bloodstained shroud; other
characters have easily recognizable counterparts in the art of the time.

CHARACTERS

GOD

MESSENGER	KINDRED	KNOWLEDGE	DISCRETION
DEATH	COUSIN	CONFESSION	FIVE WITS
EVERYMAN	GOODS	BEAUTY	ANGEL
FELLOWSHIP	GOOD DEEDS	STRENGTH	DOCTOR

*Here Beginneth a Treatise how the High Father of Heaven Sendeth Death to
Summon Every Creature to Come and Give Account of their Lives in this
World, and is in Manner of a Moral Play.*

MESSENGER: I pray you all give your audience,
  And hear this matter with reverence,
  By figure[1] a moral play:
  The *Summoning of Everyman* called it is,
  That of our lives and ending shows   5
  How transitory we be all day.
  This matter is wondrous precious,
  But the intent of it is more gracious,
  And sweet to bear away.
  The story saith: Man, in the beginning   10
  Look well, and take good heed to the ending,
  Be you never so gay!
  Ye think sin in the beginning full sweet,
  Which in the end causeth the soul to weep,
  When the body lieth in clay.   15

From *Everyman and the Medieval Miracle
Plays*, edited by A. C. Cawley. An Everyman's Library Edition. Published in the
United States by E. P. Dutton and reprinted
with their permission.
  [1] form

Here shall you see how Fellowship and Jollity,
Both Strength, Pleasure, and Beauty,
Will fade from thee as flower in May;
For ye shall hear how our Heaven King
Calleth Everyman to a general reckoning: 20
Give audience, and hear what he doth say.   (*Exit.*)

(GOD *speaketh:*)

GOD: I perceive, here in my majesty,
How that all creatures be to me unkind,
Living without dread in worldly prosperity:
Of ghostly[2] sight the people be so blind,   25
Drowned in sin, they know me not for their God;
In worldly riches is all their mind,
They fear not my righteousness, the sharp rod.
My law that I showed, when I for them died,
They forget clean,[3] and shedding of my blood red;   30
I hanged between two, it cannot be denied;
To get them life I suffered[4] to be dead;
I healed their feet, with thorns hurt was my head.
I could do no more than I did, truly;
And now I see the people do clean forsake me: 35
They use the seven deadly sins damnable,
As pride, covetise, wrath, and lechery
Now in the world be made commendable;
And thus they leave of angels the heavenly company.
Every man liveth so after his own pleasure,   40
And yet of their life they be nothing[5] sure:
I see the more that I them forbear
The worse they be from year to year.
All that liveth appaireth[6] fast;
Therefore I will, in all the haste,   45
Have a reckoning of every man's person;
For, and[7] I leave the people thus alone
In their life and wicked tempests,
Verily they will become much worse than beasts;
For now one would by envy another up eat;   50
Charity they do all clean forget.
I hoped well that every man
In my glory should make his mansion,
And thereto I had them all elect;
But now I see, like traitors deject,   55
They thank me not for the pleasure that I to them meant,
Nor yet for their being I them have lent.
I proffered the people great multitude of mercy,
And few there be that asketh it heartily.

---

[2] spiritual   [5] not at all
[3] completely, altogether   [6] becomes worse
[4] allowed myself   [7] if

They be so cumbered with wordly riches 60
That needs on them I must do justice,
On every man living without fear.
Where art thou, Death, thou mighty messenger?

(*Enter* DEATH.)

DEATH: Almighty God, I am here at your will,
Your commandment to fulfil. 65
GOD: Go thou to Everyman,
And show him, in my name,
A pilgrimage he must on him take,
Which he in no wise[8] may escape;
And that he bring with him a sure reckoning 70
Without delay or any tarrying. (GOD *withdraws*.)
DEATH: Lord, I will in the world go run overall,[9]
And cruelly outsearch both great and small;
Every man will I beset that liveth beastly
Out of God's laws, and dreadeth not folly. 75
He that loveth riches I will strike with my dart,
His sight to blind, and from heaven to depart[10] —
Except that alms be his good friend —
In hell for to dwell, world without end.
Lo, yonder I see Everyman walking. 80
Full little he thinketh on my coming;
His mind is on fleshly lusts and his treasure,
And great pain it shall cause him to endure
Before the Lord, Heaven King.

(*Enter* EVERYMAN.)

Everyman, stand still! Whither art thou going 85
Thus gaily? Hast thou thy Maker forget?
EVERYMAN: Why askest thou?
Wouldest thou wit?[11]
DEATH: Yea, sir; I will show you:
In great haste I am sent to thee 90
From God out of his majesty.
EVERYMAN: What, sent to me?
DEATH: Yea, certainly.
Though thou have forget him here,
He thinketh on thee in the heavenly sphere,
As, ere we depart, thou shalt know. 95
EVERYMAN: What desireth God of me?
DEATH: That shall I show thee:
A reckoning he will needs have
Without any longer respite. 100

---

[8] manner   [10] separate
[9] everywhere   [11] know

EVERYMAN: To give a reckoning longer leisure I crave;
  This blind[12] matter troubleth my wit.
DEATH: On thee thou must take a long journey;
  Therefore thy book of count[13] with thee thou bring,
  For turn again thou cannot by no way.   105
  And look thou be sure of thy reckoning,
  For before God thou shalt answer, and show
  Thy many bad deeds, and good but a few;
  How thou hast spent thy life, and in what wise,
  Before the chief Lord of paradise.   110
  Have ado[14] that we were in that way,[15]
  For, wit thou well, thou shalt make none[16] attorney.
EVERYMAN: Full unready I am such reckoning to give.
  I know thee not. What messenger art thou?
DEATH: I am Death, that no man dreadeth,[17]   115
  For every man I rest,[18] and no man spareth;
  For it is God's commandment
  That all to me shall be obedient.
EVERYMAN: O Death, thou comest when I had thee least in mind!
  In thy power it lieth me to save;   120
  Yet of my good will I give thee, if thou will be kind:
  Yea, a thousand pound shalt thou have,
  And defer this matter till another day.
DEATH: Everyman, it may not be, by no way.
  I set not by[19] gold, silver, nor riches,   125
  Ne by pope, emperor, king, duke, ne princes;
  For, and I would receive gifts great,
  All the world I might get;
  But my custom is clean contrary.
  I give thee no respite. Come hence, and not tarry.   130
EVERYMAN: Alas, shall I have no longer respite?
  I may say Death giveth no warning!
  To think on thee, it maketh my heart sick,
  For all unready is my book of reckoning.
  But twelve year and I might have abiding,   135
  My counting-book I would make so clear
  That my reckoning I should not need to fear.
  Wherefore, Death, I pray thee, for God's mercy,
  Spare me till I be provided of remedy.
DEATH: Thee availeth not to cry, weep, and pray;   140
  But haste thee lightly[20] that thou were gone that journey,
  And prove thy friends if thou can;
  For, wit thou well, the tide abideth no man,

---

[12] obscure
[13] account
[14] see to it
[15] on that journey
[16] have no

[17] dreads no man
[18] arrest
[19] do not care for
[20] quickly

And in the world each living creature
For Adam's sin must die of nature.[21]   145

EVERYMAN: Death, if I should this pilgrimage take,
And my reckoning surely make,
Show me, for[22] saint charity,
Should I not come again shortly?

DEATH: No, Everyman; and thou be once there,   150
Thou mayst never more come here,
Trust me verily.

EVERYMAN: O gracious God in the high seat celestial,
Have mercy on me in this most need!
Shall I have no company from this vale terrestrial   155
Of mine acquaintance, that way me to lead?

DEATH: Yea, if any be so hardy
That would go with thee and bear thee company.
Hie[23] thee that thou were gone to God's magnificence,
Thy reckoning to give before his presence.   160
What, weenest[24] thou thy life is given thee,
And thy worldly goods also?

EVERYMAN: I had wend[25] so, verily.

DEATH: Nay, nay; it was but lent thee;
For as soon as thou art go,   165
Another a while shall have it, and then go therefro,[26]
Even as thou hast done.
Everyman, thou art mad! Thou hast thy wits five,
And here on earth will not amend thy life;
For suddenly I do come.   170

EVERYMAN: O wretched caitiff, whither shall I flee,
That I might scape this endless sorrow?
Now, gentle Death, spare me till to-morrow,
That I may amend me
With good advisement.[27]   175

DEATH: Nay, thereto I will not consent,
Nor no man will I respite;
But to the heart suddenly I shall smite
Without any advisement.
And now out of thy sight I will me hie;   180
See thou make thee ready shortly,
For thou mayst say this is the day
That no man living may scape away.   (*Exit* DEATH.)

EVERYMAN: Alas, I may well weep with sighs deep!
Now have I no manner of company   185
To help me in my journey, and me to keep;
And also my writing is full unready.

---

[21] as a natural thing
[22] in the name of
[23] hurry
[24] think

[25] thought
[26] from it
[27] reflection

How shall I do now for to excuse me?
I would to God I had never be get![28]
To my soul a full great profit it had be;   190
For now I fear pains huge and great.
The time passeth. Lord, help, that all wrought!
For though I mourn it availeth nought.
The day passeth, and is almost ago;[29]
I wot not well what for to do.   195
To whom were I best my complaint to make?
What and I to Fellowship thereof spake,
And showed him of this sudden chance?
For in him is all mine affiance;[30]
We have in the world so many a day   200
Be good friends in sport and play.
I see him yonder, certainly.
I trust that he will bear me company;
Therefore to him will I speak to ease my sorrow.
Well met, good Fellowship, and good morrow!   205

(FELLOWSHIP *speaketh:*)

FELLOWSHIP: Everyman, good morrow, by this day!
  Sir, why lookest thou so piteously?
  If any thing be amiss, I pray thee me say,
  That I may help to remedy.
EVERYMAN: Yea, good Fellowship, yea;   210
  I am in great jeopardy.
FELLOWSHIP: My true friend, show to me your mind;
  I will not forsake thee to my life's end,
  In the way of good company.
EVERYMAN: That was well spoken, and lovingly.   215
FELLOWSHIP: Sir, I must needs know your heaviness;[31]
  I have pity to see you in any distress.
  If any have you wronged, ye shall revenged be,
  Though I on the ground be slain for thee —
  Though that I know before that I should die.   220
EVERYMAN: Verily, Fellowship, gramercy.
FELLOWSHIP: Tush! by thy thanks I set not a straw.
  Show me your grief, and say no more.
EVERYMAN: If I my heart should to you break,[32]
  And then you to turn your mind from me,   225
  And would not me comfort when ye hear me speak,
  Then should I ten times sorrier be.
FELLOWSHIP: Sir, I say as I will do indeed.
EVERYMAN: Then be you a good friend at need:
  I have found you true herebefore.   230

---

[28] been born   [31] sorrow
[29] gone   [32] open
[30] trust

FELLOWSHIP: And so ye shall evermore;
 For, in faith, and thou go to hell,
 I will not forsake thee by the way.
EVERYMAN: Ye speak like a good friend; I believe you well.
 I shall deserve it, and I may.   235
FELLOWSHIP: I speak of no deserving, by this day!
 For he that will say, and nothing do,
 Is not worthy with good company to go;
 Therefore show me the grief of your mind,
 As to your friend most loving and kind.   240
EVERYMAN: I shall show you how it is:
 Commanded I am to go a journey,
 A long way, hard and dangerous,
 And give a strait count, without delay,
 Before the high Judge, Adonai.[33]   245
 Wherefore, I pray you, bear me company,
 As ye have promised, in this journey.
FELLOWSHIP: That is matter indeed. Promise is duty;
 But, and I should take such a voyage on me,
 I know it well, it should be to my pain;   250
 Also it maketh me afeard, certain.
 But let us take counsel here as well as we can,
 For your words would fear[34] a strong man.
EVERYMAN: Why, ye said if I had need
 Ye would me never forsake, quick[35] ne dead, 255
 Though it were to hell, truly.
FELLOWSHIP: So I said, certainly,
 But such pleasures be set aside, the sooth to say;
 And also, if we took such a journey,
 When should we come again?   260
EVERYMAN: Nay, never again, till the day of doom.
FELLOWSHIP: In faith, then will not I come there!
 Who hath you these tidings brought?
EVERYMAN: Indeed, Death was with me here.
FELLOWSHIP: Now, by God that all hath bought, 265
 If Death were the messenger,
 For no man that is living to-day
 I will not go that loath journey —
 Not for the father that begat me!
EVERYMAN: Ye promised otherwise, pardie.[36]   270
FELLOWSHIP: I wot well I said so, truly;
 And yet if thou wilt eat, and drink, and make good cheer,
 Or haunt to women the lusty company,[37]
 I would not forsake you while the day is clear,[38]
 Trust me verily.   275

[33] Hebrew name for God
[34] frighten
[35] alive
[36] by God

[37] frequent the pleasant company of women
[38] until daybreak

EVERYMAN: Yea, thereto ye would be ready!
　　To go to mirth, solace, and play,
　　Your mind will sooner apply,
　　Than to bear me company in my long journey.
FELLOWSHIP: Now, in good faith, I will not that way.　　　　　　　　　　280
　　But and thou will murder, or any man kill,
　　In that I will help thee with a good will.
EVERYMAN: O, that is a simple advice indeed.
　　Gentle fellow, help me in my necessity!
　　We have loved long, and now I need;　　　　　　　　　　　　　　　285
　　And now, gentle Fellowship, remember me.
FELLOWSHIP: Whether ye have loved me or no,
　　By Saint John, I will not with thee go.
EVERYMAN: Yet, I pray thee, take the labour, and do so much for me
　　To bring me forward,[39] for saint charity,　　　　　　　　　　　290
　　And comfort me till I come without the town.
FELLOWSHIP: Nay, and thou would give me a new gown,
　　I will not a foot with thee go;
　　But, and thou had tarried, I would not have left thee so.
　　And as now God speed thee in thy journey,　　　　　　　　　　295
　　For from thee I will depart as fast as I may.
EVERYMAN: Whither away, Fellowship? Will thou forsake me?
FELLOWSHIP: Yea, by my fay![40] To God I betake[41] thee.
EVERYMAN: Farewell, good Fellowship; for thee my heart is sore.
　　Adieu for ever! I shall see thee no more.　　　　　　　　　　　300
FELLOWSHIP: In faith, Everyman, farewell now at the ending;
　　For you I will remember that parting is mourning.　　(Exit FELLOWSHIP.)
EVERYMAN: Alack! shall we thus depart indeed —
　　Ah Lady, help! — without any more comfort?
　　Lo, Fellowship forsaketh me in my most need.　　　　　　　　　305
　　For help in this world whither shall I resort?
　　Fellowship herebefore with me would merry make,
　　And now little sorrow for me doth he take.
　　It is said, "In prosperity men friends may find,
　　Which in adversity be full unkind."　　　　　　　　　　　　　310
　　Now whither for succour shall I flee,
　　Sith that[42] Fellowship hath forsaken me?
　　To my kinsmen I will, truly,
　　Praying them to help me in my necessity;
　　I believe that they will do so,　　　　　　　　　　　　　　　315
　　For kind[43] will creep where it may not go.
　　I will go say, for yonder I see them.
　　Where be ye now, my friends and kinsmen?

(Enter KINDRED and COUSIN.)

KINDRED: Here be we now at your commandment.

[39] escort me　　　　　　　　　　[42] since
[40] faith　　　　　　　　　　　　　[43] kinship, family
[41] commend

Cousin, I pray you show us your intent   320
  In any wise, and do not spare.⁴⁴
COUSIN: Yea, Everyman, and to us declare
  If ye be disposed to go anywhither;
  For, wit you well, we will live and die together.
KINDRED: In wealth and woe we will with you hold,   325
  For over his kin a man may be bold.⁴⁵
EVERYMAN: Gramercy, my friends and kinsmen kind.
  Now shall I show you the grief of my mind:
  I was commanded by a messenger,
  That is a high king's chief officer;   330
  He bade me go a pilgrimage, to my pain,
  And I know well I shall never come again;
  Also I must give a reckoning strait,
  For I have a great enemy⁴⁶ that hath me in wait,
  Which intendeth me for to hinder.   335
KINDRED: What account is that which ye must render?
  That would I know.
EVERYMAN: Of all my works I must show
  How I have lived and my days spent;
  Also of ill deeds that I have used⁴⁷   340
  In my time, sith life was me lent;
  And of all virtues that I have refused.
  Therefore, I pray you, go thither with me
  To help to make mine account, for saint charity.
COUSIN: What, to go thither? Is that the matter?   345
  Nay, Everyman, I had liefer⁴⁸ fast⁴⁹ bread and water
  All this five year and more.
EVERYMAN: Alas, that ever I was bore!⁵⁰
  For now shall I never be merry,
  If that you forsake me.   350
KINDRED: Ah, sir, what ye be a merry man!
  Take good heart to you, and make no moan.
  But one thing I warn you, by Saint Anne —
  As for me, ye shall go alone.
EVERYMAN: My Cousin, will you not with me go?   355
COUSIN: No, by our Lady! I have the cramp in my toe.
  Trust not to me, for, so God me speed,
  I will deceive you in your most need.
KINDRED: It availeth not us to tice.⁵¹
  Ye shall have my maid with all my heart;   360
  She loveth to go to feasts, there to be nice,⁵²
  And to dance, and abroad to start:⁵³

---

⁴⁴ hold back
⁴⁵ a man may freely command the services
of his family
⁴⁶ i.e., the Devil
⁴⁷ practiced
⁴⁸ rather
⁴⁹ have nothing but
⁵⁰ born
⁵¹ entice
⁵² wanton
⁵³ rush

I will give her leave to help you in that journey,
If that you and she may agree.
EVERYMAN: Now show me the very effect of your mind: 365
Will you go with me, or abide behind?
KINDRED: Abide behind? Yea, that will I, and I may!
Therefore farewell till another day. (*Exit* KINDRED.)
EVERYMAN: How should I be merry or glad?
For fair promises men to me make, 370
But when I have most need they me forsake.
I am deceived; that maketh me sad.
COUSIN: Cousin Everyman, farewell now,
For verily I will not go with you.
Also of mine own an unready reckoning 375
I have to account; therefore I make tarrying.
Now God keep thee, for now I go. (*Exit* COUSIN.)
EVERYMAN: Ah, Jesus, is all come hereto?
Lo, fair words maketh fools fain,[54]
They promise, and nothing will do, certain. 380
My kinsmen promised me faithfully
For to abide with me steadfastly,
And now fast away do they flee:
Even so Fellowship promised me.
What friend were best me of to provide?[55] 385
I lose my time here longer to abide.
Yet in my mind a thing there is:
All my life I have loved riches;
If that my Good[56] now help me might,
He would make my heart full light. 390
I will speak to him in this distress —
Where art thou, my Goods and riches?

(GOODS *speaks from a corner:*)

GOODS: Who calleth me? Everyman? What! hast thou haste?
I lie here in corners, trussed and piled so high,
And in chests I am locked so fast, 395
Also sacked in bags. Thou mayst see with thine eye
I cannot stir; in packs low I lie.
What would ye have? Lightly me say.
EVERYMAN: Come hither, Good, in all the haste thou may,
For of counsel I must desire thee. 400
GOODS: Sir, and ye in the world have sorrow or adversity,
That can I help you to remedy shortly.
EVERYMAN: It is another disease that grieveth me;
In this world it is not, I tell thee so.
I am sent for, another way to go, 405
To give a strait count general
Before the highest Jupiter of all;

[54] glad   [56] goods, possessions
[55] to provide me with

And all my life I have had joy and pleasure in thee,
Therefore, I pray thee, go with me;
For, peradventure, thou mayst before God Almighty   410
My reckoning help to clean and purify;
For it is said ever among[57]
That money maketh all right that is wrong.
GOODS: Nay, Everyman, I sing another song.
I follow no man in such voyages;   415
For, and I went with thee,
Thou shouldst fare much the worse for me;
For because on me thou did set thy mind,
Thy reckoning I have made blotted and blind,
That thine account thou cannot make truly;   420
And that hast thou for the love of me.
EVERYMAN: That would grieve me full sore,
When I should come to that fearful answer.
Up, let us go thither together.
GOODS: Nay, not so! I am too brittle, I may not endure;   425
I will follow no man one foot, be ye sure.
EVERYMAN: Alas, I have thee loved, and had great pleasure
All my life-days on good and treasure.
GOODS: That is to thy damnation, without leasing,
For my love is contrary to the love everlasting;   430
But if thou had me loved moderately during,
As to the poor to give part of me,
Then shouldst thou not in this dolour be,
Nor in this great sorrow and care.
EVERYMAN: Lo, now was I deceived ere I was ware,   435
And all I may wite[58] misspending of time.
GOODS: What, weenest thou that I am thine?
EVERYMAN: I had wend so.
GOODS: Nay, Everyman, I say no.
As for a while I was lent thee;   440
A season thou hast had me in prosperity.
My condition is man's soul to kill;
If I save one, a thousand I do spill.
Weenest thou that I will follow thee?
Nay, not from this world, verily.   445
EVERYMAN: I had wend otherwise.
GOODS: Therefore to thy soul Good is a thief;
For when thou art dead, this is my guise[59] —
Another to deceive in this same wise
As I have done thee, and all to his soul's reprief.[60]   450
EVERYMAN: O false Good, cursed may thou be,
Thou traitor to God, that hast deceived me
And caught me in thy snare!

---

[57] at times
[58] blame on

[59] practice
[60] shame

GOODS: Marry, thou brought thyself in care,
   Whereof I am glad;   455
   I must needs laugh, I cannot be sad.
EVERYMAN: Ah, Good, thou hast had long my heartly love;
   I gave thee that which should be the Lord's above.
   But wilt thou not go with me indeed?
   I pray thee truth to say.   460
GOODS: No, so God me speed!
   Therefore farewell, and have good day.   (*Exit* GOODS.)
EVERYMAN: O, to whom shall I make my moan
   For to go with me in that heavy journey?
   First Fellowship said he would with me gone;   465
   His words were very pleasant and gay,
   But afterward he left me alone.
   Then spake I to my kinsmen, all in despair,
   And also they gave me words fair;
   They lacked no fair speaking,   470
   But all forsook me in the ending.
   Then went I to my Goods, that I loved best,
   In hope to have comfort, but there had I least;
   For my Goods sharply did me tell
   That he bringeth many into hell.   475
   Then of myself I was ashamed,
   And so I am worthy to be blamed;
   Thus may I well myself hate.
   Of whom shall I now counsel take?
   I think that I shall never speed.   480
   Till that I go to my Good Deed.
   But, alas, she is so weak
   That she can neither go nor speak;
   Yet will I venture on her now.
   My Good Deeds, where be you?   485

(GOOD DEEDS *speaks from the ground:*)

GOOD DEEDS: Here I lie, cold in the ground;
   Thy sins hath me sore bound,
   That I cannot stir.
EVERYMAN: O Good Deeds, I stand in fear!
   I must you pray of counsel,   490
   For help now should come right well.
GOOD DEEDS: Everyman, I have understanding
   That ye be summoned account to make
   Before Messias, of Jerusalem King;
   And you do by me,[61] that journey with you will I take.   495
EVERYMAN: Therefore I come to you, my moan to make;
   I pray you that ye will go with me.
GOOD DEEDS: I would full fain, but I cannot stand, verily.

[61] as I advise

EVERYMAN: Why, is there anything on you fall?
GOOD DEEDS: Yea, sir, I may thank you of[62] all;   500
    If ye had perfectly cheered me,
    Your book of count full ready had be.
    Look, the books of your works and deeds eke![63]
    Behold how they lie under the feet,
    To your soul's heaviness.   505
EVERYMAN: Our Lord Jesus help me!
    For one letter here I cannot see.
GOOD DEEDS: There is a blind reckoning in time of distress.
EVERYMAN: Good Deeds, I pray you help me in this need,
    Or else I am for ever damned indeed;   510
    Therefore help me to make reckoning
    Before the Redeemer of all thing,
    That King is, and was, and ever shall.
GOOD DEEDS: Everyman, I am sorry of your fall,
    And fain would I help you, and I were able.   515
EVERYMAN: Good Deeds, your counsel I pray you give me.
GOOD DEEDS: That shall I do verily;
    Though that on my feet I may not go,
    I have a sister that shall with you also,
    Called Knowledge, which shall with you abide,   520
    To help you to make that dreadful reckoning.

    (*Enter* KNOWLEDGE.)

KNOWLEDGE: Everyman, I will go with thee, and be thy guide,
    In thy most need to go by thy side.
EVERYMAN: In good condition I am now in every thing,
    And am wholly content with this good thing,   525
    Thanked be God my creator.
GOOD DEEDS: And when she hath brought you there
    Where thou shalt heel thee of thy smart,[64]
    Then go you with your reckoning and your Good Deeds together,
    For to make you joyful at heart   530
    Before the blessed Trinity.
EVERYMAN: My Good Deeds, gramercy!
    I am well content, certainly,
    With your words sweet.
KNOWLEDGE: Now go we together lovingly   535
    To Confession, that cleansing river.
EVERYMAN: For joy I weep; I would we were there!
    But, I pray you, give me cognition
    Where dwelleth that holy man, Confession.
KNOWLEDGE: In the house of salvation: 540
    We shall find him in that place,
    That shall us comfort, by God's grace.

---

[62] for
[63] also
[64] pain

(KNOWLEDGE *takes* EVERYMAN *to* CONFESSION.)

Lo, this is Confession. Kneel down and ask mercy,
For he is in good conceit[65] with God Almighty.
EVERYMAN: O glorious fountain, that all uncleanness doth clarify,   545
Wash from me the spots of vice unclean,
That on me no sin may be seen.
I come with Knowledge for my redemption,
Redempt with heart and full contrition;
For I am commanded a pilgrimage to take,   550
And great accounts before God to make.
Now I pray you, Shrift,[66] mother of salvation,
Help my Good Deeds for my piteous exclamation.
CONFESSION: I know your sorrow well, Everyman.
Because with Knowledge ye come to me,   555
I will you comfort as well as I can,
And a precious jewel I will give thee,
Called penance, voider of adversity;
Therewith shall your body chastised be,
With abstinence and perseverance in God's service.   560
Here shall you receive that scourge of me,
Which is penance strong that ye must endure,
To remember thy Saviour was scourged for thee
With sharp scourges, and suffered it patiently;
So must thou, ere thou scape that painful pilgrimage.   565
Knowledge, keep him in this voyage,
And by that time Good Deeds will be with thee.
But in any wise be siker[67] of mercy,
For your time draweth fast; and ye will saved be,
Ask God mercy, and he will grant truly.   570
When with the scourge of penance man doth him[68] bind,
The oil of forgiveness then shall he find.
EVERYMAN: Thanked be God for his gracious work!
For now I will my penance begin;
This hath rejoiced and lighted my heart,   575
Though the knots be painful and hard within.
KNOWLEDGE: Everyman, look your penance that ye fulfil,
What pain that ever it to you be;
And Knowledge shall give you counsel at will
How your account ye shall make clearly.   580
EVERYMAN: O eternal God, O heavenly figure,
O way of righteousness, O goodly vision,
Which descended down in a virgin pure
Because he would every man redeem,
Which Adam forfeited by his disobedience: 585
O blessed Godhead, elect and high divine,

---

[65] esteem   [67] sure
[66] confession   [68] himself

Forgive my grievous offence;
Here I cry thee mercy in this presence.
O ghostly treasure, O ransomer and redeemer,
Of all the world hope and conductor,[69]   590
Mirror of joy, and founder of mercy,
Which enlumineth heaven and earth thereby,[70]
Hear my clamorous complaint, though it late be;
Receive my prayers, of thy benignity;
Though I be a sinner most abominable,   595
Yet let my name be written in Moses' table.
O Mary, pray to the Maker of all thing,
Me for to help at my ending;
And save me from the power of my enemy,
For Death assaileth me strongly.   600
And, Lady, that I may by mean of thy prayer
Of your Son's glory to be[71] partner,
By the means of his passion, I it crave;
I beseech you help my soul to save.
Knowledge, give me the scourge of penance;   605
My flesh therewith shall give acquittance:[72]
I will now begin, if God give me grace.
KNOWLEDGE: Everyman, God give you time and space!
  Thus I bequeath you in the hands of our Saviour;
  Now may you make your reckoning sure.   610
EVERYMAN: In the name of the Holy Trinity,
  My body sore punished shall be:
  Take this, body, for the sin of the flesh!

(*Scourges himself.*)

Also thou delightest to go gay and fresh,
And in the way of damnation thou did me bring,   615
Therefore suffer now strokes and punishing.
Now of penance I will wade the water clear,
To save me from purgatory, that sharp fire.

(GOOD DEEDS *rises from the ground.*)

GOOD DEEDS: I thank God, now I can walk and go,
  And am delivered of my sickness and woe.   620
  Therefore with Everyman I will go, and not spare;
  His good works I will help him to declare.
KNOWLEDGE: Now, Everyman, be merry and glad!
  Your Good Deeds cometh now; ye may not be sad.
  Now is your Good Deeds whole and sound,   625
  Going upright upon the ground.
EVERYMAN: My heart is light, and shall be evermore;
  Now will I smite faster than I did before.

[69] guide   [71] be
[70] besides   [72] atonement

GOOD DEEDS: Everyman, pilgrim, my special friend,
  Blessed be thou without end;   630
  For thee is preparate the eternal glory.
  Ye have me made whole and sound,
  Therefore I will bide by thee in every stound.[73]
EVERYMAN: Welcome, my Good Deeds; now I hear thy voice,
  I weep for very sweetness of love.   635
KNOWLEDGE: Be no more sad, but ever rejoice;
  God seeth thy living in his throne above.
  Put on this garment to thy behoof,[74]
  Which is wet with your tears,
  Or else before God you may it miss,   640
  When ye to your journey's end come shall.
EVERYMAN: Gentle Knowledge, what do ye it call?
KNOWLEDGE: It is a garment of sorrow:
  From pain it will you borrow;[75]
  Contrition it is,   645
  That getteth forgiveness;
  It pleaseth God passing well.
GOOD DEEDS: Everyman, will you wear it for your heal?
EVERYMAN: Now blessed be Jesu, Mary's Son,
  For now have I on true contrition.   650
  And let us go now without tarrying;
  Good Deeds, have we clear our reckoning?
GOOD DEEDS: Yea, indeed, I have it here.
EVERYMAN: Then I trust we need not fear;
  Now, friends, let us not part in twain.   655
KNOWLEDGE: Nay, Everyman, that will we not, certain.
GOOD DEEDS: Yet must thou lead with thee
  Three persons of great might.
EVERYMAN: Who should they be?
GOOD DEEDS: Discretion and Strength they hight,[76]   660
  And thy Beauty may not abide behind.
KNOWLEDGE: Also ye must call to mind
  Your Five Wits as for your counsellors.
GOOD DEEDS: You must have them ready at all hours.
EVERYMAN: How shall I get them hither?   665
KNOWLEDGE: You must call them all together,
  And they will hear you incontinent.[77]
EVERYMAN: My friends, come hither and be present,
  Discretion, Strength, my Five Wits,[78] and Beauty.

(*Enter* BEAUTY, STRENGTH, DISCRETION *and* FIVE WITS.)

BEAUTY: Here at your will we be all ready.   670
  What will ye that we should do?

---

[73] always (or: in every attack)   [76] are called
[74] advantage   [77] immediately
[75] take   [78] senses

GOOD DEEDS: That ye would with Everyman go,
   And help him in his pilgrimage.
   Advise you, will ye with him or not in that voyage?
STRENGTH: We will bring him all thither,   675
   To his help and comfort, ye may believe me.
DISCRETION: So will we go with him all together.
EVERYMAN: Almighty God, lofed[79] may thou be!
   I give thee laud that I have hither brought
   Strength, Discretion, Beauty, and Five Wits. Lack I nought.   680
   And my Good Deeds, with Knowledge clear,
   All be in my company at my will here;
   I desire no more to[80] my business.
STRENGTH: And I, Strength, will by you stand in distress,
   Though thou would in battle fight on the ground.   685
FIVE WITS: And though it were through the world round,
   We will not depart for sweet ne sour.
BEAUTY: No more will I unto death's hour,
   Whatsoever thereof befall.
DISCRETION: Everyman, advise you first of all;   690
   Go with a good advisement and deliberation.
   We all give you virtuous monition
   That all shall be well.
EVERYMAN: My friends, harken what I will tell:
   I pray God reward you in his heavenly sphere.   695
   Now harken, all that be here,
   For I will make my testament
   Here before you all present:
   In alms half my good I will give with my hands twain
   In the way of charity, with good intent,   700
   And the other half still shall remain
   In queth,[81] to be returned there[82] it ought to be.
   This I do in despite of the fiend of hell,
   To go quit out of his peril
   Ever after and this day.   705
KNOWLEDGE: Everyman, harken what I say:
   Go to priesthood, I you advise,
   And receive of him in any wise
   The holy sacrament and ointment together.
   Then shortly see ye turn again hither;   710
   We will all abide you here.
FIVE WITS: Yea, Everyman, hie you that ye ready were.
   There is no emperor, king, duke, ne baron,
   That of God hath commission
   As hath the least priest in the world being;   715
   For of the blessed sacraments pure and benign
   He beareth the keys, and thereof hath the cure[83]

[79] praised   [82] where
[80] for   [83] charge
[81] bequest

For man's redemption — it is ever sure —
Which God for our soul's medicine
Gave us out of his heart with great pine.   720
Here in this transitory life, for thee and me,
The blessed sacraments seven there be:
Baptism, confirmation, with priesthood good,
And the sacrament of God's precious flesh and blood,
Marriage, the holy extreme unction, and penance;   725
These seven be good to have in remembrance,
Gracious sacraments of high divinity.
EVERYMAN: Fain would I receive that holy body,
And meekly to my ghostly father I will go.
FIVE WITS: Everyman, that is the best that ye can do.   730
God will you to salvation bring,
For priesthood exceedeth all other thing:
To us Holy Scripture they do teach,
And converteth man from sin heaven to reach;
God hath to them more power given   735
Than to any angel that is in heaven.
With five words[84] he may consecrate,
God's body in flesh and blood to make,
And handleth his Maker between his hands.
The priest bindeth and unbindeth all bands,   740
Both in earth and in heaven.
Thou ministers[85] all the sacraments seven;
Though we kissed thy feet, thou were worthy;
Thou art surgeon that cureth sin deadly:
No remedy we find under God   745
But all only[86] priesthood.
Everyman, God gave priests that dignity,
And setteth them in his stead among us to be;
Thus be they above angels in degree.

(EVERYMAN *goes to the priest to receive the last sacraments*.)

KNOWLEDGE: If priests be good, it is so,[87] surely.   750
But when Jesus hanged on the cross with great smart,
There he gave out of his blessed heart
The same sacrament in great torment:
He sold them not to us, that Lord omnipotent.
Therefore Saint Peter the apostle doth say   755
That Jesu's curse hath all they
Which God their Saviour do buy or sell,
Or they for any money do take or tell.[88]
Sinful priests giveth the sinners example bad;
Their children sitteth by other men's fires, I have heard;   760

---

[84] i.e., *Hoc est enim corpus meum* (Lat.   [86] except
"For this is my body"; from the sacrament of   [87] i.e., "above angels in degree"
the Eucharist)   [88] count
  [85] administer

And some haunteth women's company
With unclean life, as lusts of lechery:
These be with sin made blind.
FIVE WITS: I trust to God no such may we find;   765
   Therefore let us priesthood honour,
   And follow their doctrine for our souls' succour.
   We be their sheep, and they shepherds be
   By whom we all be kept in surety.
   Peace, for yonder I see Everyman come,
   Which hath made true satisfaction.   770
GOOD DEEDS: Methink it is he indeed.

(*Re-enter* EVERYMAN.)

EVERYMAN: Now Jesu be your alder speed![89]
   I have received the sacrament for my redemption,
   And then mine extreme unction:
   Blessed be all they that counselled me to take it!   775
   And now, friends, let us go without longer respite;
   I thank God that ye have tarried so long.
   Now set each of you on this rood[90] your hand,
   And shortly follow me:
   I go before there I would be; God be our guide!   780
STRENGTH: Everyman, we will not from you go
   Till ye have done this voyage long.
DISCRETION: I, Discretion, will bide by you also.
KNOWLEDGE: And though this pilgrimage be never so strong,[91]
   I will never part you fro.   785
STRENGTH: Everyman, I will be as sure by thee
   As ever I did by Judas Maccabee.[92]

(EVERYMAN *comes to his grave*.)

EVERYMAN: Alas, I am so faint I may not stand;
   My limbs under me doth fold.
   Friends, let us not turn again to this land,   790
   Not for all the world's gold;
   For into this cave must I creep
   And turn to earth, and there to sleep.
BEAUTY: What, into this grave? Alas!
EVERYMAN: Yea, there shall ye consume, more and less.[93]   795
BEAUTY: And what, should I smother here?
EVERYMAN: Yea, by my faith, and never more appear.
   In this world live no more we shall,
   But in heaven before the highest Lord of all.

[89] help to all of you
[90] cross
[91] hard, difficult
[92] Jewish religious and national leader against Syria in the 2nd century B.C. He told his men that "the success of war is not in the multitude: but strength cometh from heaven" (Apocrypha, I Maccabees 3:19)
[93] high and low

BEAUTY: I cross out all this; adieu, by Saint John!   800
   I take my cap in my lap, and am gone.
EVERYMAN: What, Beauty, whither will ye?
BEAUTY: Peace, I am deaf; I look not behind me,
   Not and thou wouldest give me all the gold in thy chest.   (*Exit* BEAUTY.)
EVERYMAN: Alas, whereto may I trust?   805
   Beauty goeth fast away from me;
   She promised with me to live and die.
STRENGTH: Everyman, I will thee also forsake and deny;
   Thy game liketh me not at all.
EVERYMAN: Why, then, ye will forsake me all?   810
   Sweet Strength, tarry a little space.
STRENGTH: Nay, sir, by the rood of grace!
   I will hie me from thee fast,
   Though thou weep till thy heart to-brast.[94]
EVERYMAN: Ye would ever bide by me, ye said.   815
STRENGTH: Yea, I have you far enough conveyed.
   Ye be old enough, I understand,
   Your pilgrimage to take on hand;
   I repent me that I hither came.
EVERYMAN: Strength, you to displease I am to blame;   820
   Yet promise is debt, this ye well wot.
STRENGTH: In faith, I care not.
   Thou art but a fool to complain;
   You spend your speech and waste your brain.
   Go thrust thee into the ground!   (*Exit* STRENGTH.)   825
EVERYMAN: I had wend surer I should you have found.
   He that trusteth in his Strength
   She him deceiveth at the length.
   Both Strength and Beauty forsaketh me;
   Yet they promised me fair and lovingly.   830
DISCRETION: Everyman, I will after Strength be gone;
   As for me, I will leave you alone.
EVERYMAN: Why, Discretion, will ye forsake me?
DISCRETION: Yea, in faith, I will go from thee,
   For when Strength goeth before   835
   I follow after evermore.
EVERYMAN: Yet, I pray thee, for the love of the Trinity,
   Look in my grave once piteously.
DISCRETION: Nay, so nigh will I not come;
   Farewell, every one!   (*Exit* DISCRETION.)   840
EVERYMAN: O, all thing faileth, save God alone —
   Beauty, Strength, and Discretion;
   For when Death bloweth his blast,
   They all run from me full fast.
FIVE WITS: Everyman, my leave now of thee I take;   845
   I will follow the other, for here I thee forsake.

---

[94] broke to pieces

EVERYMAN: Alas, then may I wail and weep,
  For I took you for my best friend.
FIVE WITS: I will no longer thee keep;
  Now farewell, and there an end. (*Exit* FIVE WITS.) 850
EVERYMAN: O Jesu, help! All hath forsaken me.
GOOD DEEDS: Nay, Everyman; I will bide with thee.
  I will not forsake thee indeed;
  Thou shalt find me a good friend at need.
EVERYMAN: Gramercy, Good Deeds! Now may I true friends see. 855
  They have forsaken me, every one;
  I loved them better than my Good Deeds alone.
  Knowledge, will ye forsake me also?
KNOWLEDGE: Yea, Everyman, when ye to Death shall go;
  But not yet, for no manner of danger. 860
EVERYMAN: Gramercy, Knowledge, with all my heart.
KNOWLEDGE: Nay, yet I will not from hence depart
  Till I see where ye shall become.
EVERYMAN: Methink, alas, that I must be gone
  To make my reckoning and my debts pay, 865
  For I see my time is nigh spent away.
  Take example, all ye that this do hear or see,
  How they that I loved best do forsake me,
  Except my Good Deeds that bideth truly.
GOOD DEEDS: All earthly things is but vanity: 870
  Beauty, Strength, and Discretion do man forsake,
  Foolish friends, and kinsmen, that fair spake —
  All fleeth save Good Deeds, and that am I.
EVERYMAN: Have mercy on me, God most mighty;
  And stand by me, thou mother and maid, holy Mary. 875
GOOD DEEDS: Fear not; I will speak for thee.
EVERYMAN: Here I cry God mercy.
GOOD DEEDS: Short[95] our end, and minish our pain;
  Let us go and never come again.
EVERYMAN: Into thy hands, Lord, my soul I commend; 880
  Receive it, Lord, that it be not lost.
  As thou me boughtest, so me defend,
  And save me from the fiend's boast,
  That I may appear with that blessed host
  That shall be saved at the day of doom. 885
  In manus tuas, of mights most
  For ever, *commendo spiritum meum*.[96] (*He sinks into his grave.*)
KNOWLEDGE: Now hath he suffered that we all shall endure;
  The Good Deeds shall make all sure.
  Now hath he made ending; 890
  Methinketh that I hear angels sing,
  And make great joy and melody
  Where Everyman's soul received shall be.

[95] shorten   [96] into thy hands I commend my spirit
(Luke 23:46)

ANGEL: Come, excellent elect spouse, to Jesu!
   Hereabove thou shalt go   895
   Because of thy singular virtue.
   Now the soul is taken the body fro,
   Thy reckoning is crystal-clear.
   Now shalt thou into the heavenly sphere,
   Unto the which all ye shall come   900
   That liveth well before the day of doom.

   (*Enter* DOCTOR.)

DOCTOR: This moral men may have in mind.
   Ye hearers, take it of worth,[97] old and young,
   And forsake Pride, for he deceiveth you in the end;
   And remember Beauty, Five Wits, Strength, and Discretion,   905
   They all at the last do every man forsake,
   Save[98] his Good Deeds there doth he take.
   But beware, for and they be small
   Before God, he hath no help at all;
   None excuse may be there for every man.   910
   Alas, how shall he do then?
   For after death amends may no man make,
   For then mercy and pity doth him forsake.
   If his reckoning be not clear when he doth come,
   God will say: '*Ite, maledicti, in ignem eternum.*'[99]   915
   And he that hath his account whole and sound,
   High in heaven he shall be crowned;
   Unto which place God bring us all thither,
   That we may live body and soul together.
   Thereto help the Trinity!   920
   Amen, say ye, for saint charity.

Thus Endeth this Moral Play of EVERYMAN.

AFTERWORD

A superficial reading of *Everyman* may leave an impression of nothing more than a quaintly pious but long-winded and simple-minded statement of venerable Christian platitudes, dotted with undigested bits of Church polemic against the selling of holy office. The sacerdotal bias may be felt to be intrusive and the insistent didacticism stifling to any genuinely dramatic treatment of character and event.

Clearly, it is the sequence of encounters between Everyman and the

---

[97] value it
[98] unless

[99] depart, ye cursed, into everlasting fire (Matthew 25:41)

personified forces that the medieval mind thought of as governing a Christian life that constitutes the action of the play. Just as clearly, it is an action contrived as an *exemplum* for the good of the spectator's soul rather than from any interest in plot or psychology for their own sakes. But it is also the stark simplicity of the dramatic movement and the single-mindedness of the didactic thrust that account for the play's naive but massive strength. In the words of the Messenger-Prologue, its "matter" is "wondrous precious": Everyman's eternal life is at stake. Dramatic tension is established the moment he is given the command to set his spiritual house in order, and for all the length of some of the individual episodes that follow, the pace and the tension thereafter never slacken. The fact that he is, after all, given respite to repent is not so much inconsistent with the initial premise of imminent doom as it is a way of making the spiritual drama possible at all. Faced with the alternatives of Heaven and Hell, Everyman, it could be argued, can claim small moral merit for his deathbed repentance, but to stress that point is to miss the deeper significance of the allegory and to ignore its didactic purpose. Death's challenge becomes a means to salvation, a further token of God's mercy to sinful man. The spectacle of Everyman's response is meant to summon us to eschatological fear, not to moral judgment. Moreover, we hardly think of the action as proceeding in worldly time. *Everyman* is a specimen of dramatic expressionism in the sense that its scene is the human soul and its time the timeless moment when the guilty conscience confronts death.

With sure sense of dramatic economy the playwright gives us only a few glimpses of Everyman's earlier, self-indulgent life as Fellowship's companion in reveling and violence. What he dramatizes is the impingement of God's will on the world. The lesson of the play is that life is only a loan, for which the borrower is accountable. The repeated encounters with worldly associates (extrinsic, in the form of friends, kin, and material possessions; intrinsic, in the form of properties of mind and body), who all fail the ultimate test of loyalty, have an incremental effect. The distinct point of reversal comes midway through the action as Everyman, with the help of Knowledge, Confession, and Penance (the last a potential rather than an actual personification), raises his Good Deeds from the ground. It is followed by a further complication — dramatically if not theologically unexpected — when his spiritual advisers leave him on the brink of his grave. Everyman is to face God's judgment alone, accompanied only — a distinct Catholic touch — by his Good Deeds. To say why Everyman is able to bear the second desertion better than the first is to define the nature of his growing spiritual strength. His foolish complacency and sensualism collapse in despair, and rehabilitation comes through the mustering of his inner resources.

The form of the play reflects its spiritual movement. The action begins with God in His Heaven and ends with Everyman sinking into his grave, but the downward movement is reversed when the Angel, in the next-to-the-last speech in the play, receives the redeemed and rising soul into "the heavenly sphere." And both descending and ascending action are analogous to Everyman's psychological movement from worldly folly through despair to the faith manifest in the Latin phrases he intones as he submits to death. The symmetrical form takes in even the two "presenter" figures, who speak directly to the theater audience: the Messenger (Prologue), immediately preceding God, and the Doctor (Epilogue), immediately following the Angel. The total structure is a V-shape reflecting the drama of man's fall and redemption in the symbolical "world" of the medieval mansion stage: Theater (Messenger) — Heaven (God) — Earth (Everyman) — Heaven (Angel) — Theater (Doctor).

The characters come alive in little touches of psychological realism. There is the contrast between Everyman's reluctance to tell Fellowship about his predicament and his friend's effusive and ironically unsolicited professions of loyalty. There are Death's solemn colloquialisms, the nice distinctions in tone and attitude between Cousin and Kindred, the almost human pathos in God's "I could do no more than I did, truly." Among them, the personified abstractions cover a range of wryly perceived human realities. And if it is true that the verse hobbles, it is also true that its very roughness contributes to the mood of homespun earnestness and to the anxious concern with the one thing that matters in a Christian life. Musical lilt would have worked against the purpose of the play. Nor is the prosody quite so haphazard as it may seem at first: the shorter, three-stressed line and the masculine endings have a way of turning up in passages of special momentousness.

Everyman himself is both an individual and all mankind, both the single and the collective object of God's care. His character encompasses the two sides of man's nature. He is blindly selfish, fallen, appetitive man, the thoughtless hedonist who answers Death's question if he had really thought that his worldly possessions were his to keep, "I had wend so, verily." But he is also man potentially resurrect, God's blessed pensioner:

> I hoped well that every man
> In my glory should make his mansion
> And thereto I had them all elect.

The irregularity in grammar — "every man" is the antecedent for "them" — brings together the simultaneous singular and plural significance of the title pronoun that is the play's key figure of speech, the vehicle for its terrifying relevance. The personification is more than a stale allegorical convention. The longer one considers the play, the more one becomes conscious of how much compressed tension, psychological insight, theological sophistication, and formal beauty the naive surface conceals. Goods says:

> I lie here in corners, trussed and piled so high.
> And in chests I am locked so fast,
> Also sacked in bags.

The lines don't just visualize wealth for us, they also insinuate the truth that material possessions are spiritually inert and therefore literally incapable of accompanying Everyman on his final journey. A small, vivid fact has unobtrusively become a large symbol. There is nothing simple-minded about such artistry.

The brevity of life, the vanity of the world, the treacherous falling-off of the gifts it offers, the sense of living under sentence of death, the desire to warn us all — these are traditional motifs in Christian forensics. But even nonbelievers can understand the critic who said that after *Everyman* all other plays somehow seem to deal with inessentials.

William Shakespeare

THE TRAGEDY OF HAMLET, PRINCE OF DENMARK

FOREWORD

In addition to providing his colleagues with plays to act in, Shakespeare was an actor himself in the theatrical company of which he was a shareholding member. Before 1603 the company was known as the Chamberlain's Men, and after the succession of King James I as the King's Men. If it ever occurred to Shakespeare to label his profession, chances are that he would have thought of himself as a man of the theater rather than as an author. What little evidence there is of his acting career suggests that he took secondary parts. According to tradition, he was the original Ghost in *Hamlet* vis à vis Richard Burbage's Prince.

In 1598–99 the Chamberlain's Men removed the lumber from an older theater building north of the Thames to a site on the Bankside (part of modern Southwark) south of the river and used it to build the Globe Theater, which remained its exclusive home for the next ten years. In 1609 the company began to give performances in the Blackfriars Theater within the city precincts during the winter season. In 1613 the Globe was burned down during a performance of Shakespeare's *Henry VIII*. The second Globe was built the following year. It survived until 1644, when it was pulled down during the regime of the theater-hating Puritans.

We don't know the exact shape and size of the first Globe, in which *Hamlet* was presumably first performed. Exactly what the original Globe playhouse looked like has been an issue of scholarly controversy in this century. The description that follows covers features which modern research fairly confidently has established as typical of the London playhouses in late Elizabethan and Jacobean times. There is no reason to believe that they were all essentially identical in structure.

The only Elizabethan theater for which a building contract has been preserved is the Fortune, built in 1600. But because it was explicitly modeled on the Globe, the contractors, unfortunately for us, did not specify other details of construction than those in which the Fortune was to differ from the Globe. From the fact that the Fortune contract calls for a square structure, we may infer that the Globe was not square. We know there were other round or polygonal theaters in Elizabethan London. An engraved panorama of London in the early 1610's designates a round building as the Globe, but the accuracy of the view is in doubt.

The Globe probably had three-tiered galleries with seats for those who could afford them; the poorer of the audience ("the groundlings") watched the performance standing in the "pit," the unroofed courtyard which the galleries surrounded on all sides. On one side, the third story of the building housed the musicians and the trumpeter who announced the beginning of the play. The second story was an upper stage, or "balcony." On the ground floor was a "tiring-house," or dressing room, for the actors. Either two or three doors connected the tiring-house with the "apron," a platform stage that was the main acting area and that extended perhaps the entire length of the tiring-house and projected half way into the open yard. (The Fortune stage was forty-three feet wide and about twenty-seven feet deep.) The platform was raised five to six feet above the ground to make room for entries and exits of ghosts and demons through a trapdoor in the stage floor. During a performance the space below the apron was covered by curtains. Part of the apron was covered by a roof set on posts, "the heavens." A particularly uncertain point in the reconstruction of the Elizabethan playhouse is whether an inner stage or recess back of the apron was used for action set in such places as bedrooms, studies, and caves, or whether such scenes were acted in semi-permanent booths or pavilions on the apron itself, with curtain walls that could be pulled to open the interior to the view of the audience. Such structures would represent a development of the "mansions" on the pageant stage of the medieval liturgical plays and the later moralities, which were still being performed in Stratford during Shakespeare's youth.

Costumes were often sumptuous, and there was some use of props. One contemporary list of props includes a rock, "three tombs," a "Hell mouth," a cage, a bay tree, a "wooden canopy," an altar, a bed, and two "moss banks." But there was no illusionistic scene painting, and considering the facts that performances took place in daylight, that adolescent boys played women's parts, and that technical devices for creating realistic effects were limited, the whole production must have been stylized, creating a symbolic rather than a lifelike "world." The largest Elizabethan playhouses could seat about 2,000 spectators or perhaps more. For all that, they were intimate theaters, in which actor and audience were both physically and psychologically closer than in a modern, picture-frame structure, where an audience seated in darkness faces an artificially lighted peekbox stage. And the absence of elaborate sets and technical machinery and of act and scene divisions made for a fluid, uncluttered, and fast-paced dramatic form.

DRAMATIS PERSONAE

CLAUDIUS, King of Denmark

HAMLET, son to the late, and nephew to the present, King

POLONIUS, Lord Chamberlain

HORATIO, friend to Hamlet

LAERTES, son to Polonius

VOLTEMAND
CORNELIUS
ROSENCRANTZ
GUILDENSTERN } courtiers
OSRIC
A GENTLEMAN
A PRIEST

MARCELLUS } officers
BARNARDO

FRANCISCO, a soldier

REYNALDO, servant to Polonius

PLAYERS

TWO CLOWNS, gravediggers

FORTINBRAS, Prince of Norway

A NORWEGIAN CAPTAIN

ENGLISH AMBASSADORS

GERTRUDE, Queen of Denmark, mother to Hamlet

OPHELIA, daughter to Polonius

GHOST OF HAMLET'S FATHER

LORDS, LADIES, OFFICERS, SOLDIERS, SAILORS, MESSENGERS, ATTENDANTS

Scene: Elsinore

ACT I

SCENE 1. [A GUARD PLATFORM OF THE CASTLE.]

Enter BARNARDO *and* FRANCISCO, *two sentinels.*

BARNARDO: Who's there?

FRANCISCO: Nay, answer me. Stand and unfold[1]* yourself.

BARNARDO: Long live the King![2]

FRANCISCO: Barnardo?

BARNARDO: He.

FRANCISCO: You come most carefully upon your hour.

BARNARDO: 'Tis now struck twelve. Get thee to bed, Francisco.

FRANCISCO: For this relief much thanks. 'Tis bitter cold,
    And I am sick at heart.

* [These are Professor Edward Hubler's notes for the Signet edition of *Hamlet.* — Editor's note.]

[1] disclose

[2] (perhaps a password, perhaps a greeting)

BARNARDO: Have you had quiet guard?
FRANCISCO: Not a mouse stirring.   10
BARNARDO: Well, good night.
   If you do meet Horatio and Marcellus,
   The rivals[3] of my watch, bid them make haste.

(*Enter* HORATIO *and* MARCELLUS.)

FRANCISCO: I think I hear them. Stand, ho! Who is there?
HORATIO: Friends to this ground.
MARCELLUS: And liegemen to the Dane.[4]   15
FRANCISCO: Give you[5] good night.
MARCELLUS: O, farewell, honest soldier.
   Who hath relieved you?
FRANCISCO: Barnardo hath my place.
   Give you good night.   (*Exit* FRANCISCO.)
MARCELLUS: Holla, Barnardo!
BARNARDO: Say ——
   What, is Horatio there?
HORATIO: A piece of him.
BARNARDO: Welcome, Horatio. Welcome, good Marcellus.   20
MARCELLUS: What, has this thing appeared again tonight?
BARNARDO: I have seen nothing.
MARCELLUS: Horatio says 'tis but our fantasy,
   And will not let belief take hold of him
   Touching this dreaded sight twice seen of us;   25
   Therefore I have entreated him along
   With us to watch the minutes of this night,
   That, if again this apparition come,
   He may approve[6] our eyes and speak to it.
HORATIO: Tush, tush, 'twill not appear.
BARNARDO: Sit down awhile,   30
   And let us once again assail your ears,
   That are so fortified against our story,
   What we have two nights seen.
HORATIO: Well, sit we down,
   And let us hear Barnardo speak of this.
BARNARDO: Last night of all,   35
   When yond same star that's westward from the pole[7]
   Had made his course t' illume that part of heaven
   Where now it burns, Marcellus and myself.
   The bell then beating one ——

(*Enter* GHOST.)

MARCELLUS: Peace, break thee off. Look where it comes again.   40
BARNARDO: In the same figure like the king that's dead.
MARCELLUS: Thou art a scholar; speak to it, Horatio.

---

[3] partners   [6] confirm
[4] loyal subjects to the King of Denmark   [7] polestar
[5] God give you

BARNARDO: Looks 'a not like the king? Mark it, Horatio.

HORATIO: Most like: it harrows me with fear and wonder.

BARNARDO: It would be spoke to.

MARCELLUS: Speak to it, Horatio.   45

HORATIO: What art thou that usurp'st this time of night,
Together with that fair and warlike form
In which the majesty of buried Denmark[8]
Did sometimes march? By heaven I charge thee, speak.

MARCELLUS: It is offended.

BARNARDO: See, it stalks away.   50

HORATIO: Stay! Speak, speak. I charge thee, speak.   (*Exit* GHOST.)

MARCELLUS: 'Tis gone and will not answer.

BARNARDO: How now, Horatio? You tremble and look pale.
Is not this something more than fantasy?
What think you on't?   55

HORATIO: Before my God, I might not this believe
Without the sensible and true avouch[9]
Of mine own eyes.

MARCELLUS: Is it not like the King?

HORATIO: As thou art to thyself.
Such was the very armor he had on   60
When he the ambitious Norway[10] combated:
So frowned he once, when, in an angry parle,[11]
He smote the sledded Polacks[12] on the ice.
'Tis strange.

MARCELLUS: Thus twice before, and jump[13] at this dead hour,   65
With martial stalk hath he gone by our watch.

HORATIO: In what particular thought to work I know not;
But, in the gross and scope[14] of my opinion,
This bodes some strange eruption to our state.

MARCELLUS: Good now, sit down, and tell me he that knows,   70
Why this same strict and most observant watch
So nightly toils the subject[15] of the land,
And why such daily cast of brazen cannon
And foreign mart[16] for implements of war,
Why such impress[17] of shipwrights, whose sore task   75
Does not divide the Sunday from the week,
What might be toward[18] that this sweaty haste
Doth make the night joint-laborer with the day?
Who is't that can inform me?

HORATIO: That can I.   80
At least the whisper goes so: our last king,
Whose image even but now appeared to us,
Was, as you know, by Fortinbras of Norway,

---

[8] the buried King of Denmark
[9] sensory and true proof
[10] King of Norway
[11] parley
[12] Poles in sledges
[13] just

[14] general drift
[15] makes the subjects toil
[16] trading
[17] forced service
[18] in preparation

Thereto pricked on by a most emulate pride,
Dared to the combat; in which our valiant Hamlet
(For so this side of our known world esteemed him)   85
Did slay this Fortinbras, who, by a sealed compact
Well ratified by law and heraldry,[19]
Did forfeit, with his life, all those his lands
Which he stood seized[20] of, to the conqueror;
Against the which a moiety competent[21]   90
Was gagèd[22] by our King, which had returned
To the inheritance of Fortinbras,
Had be been vanquisher, as, by the same comart[23]
And carriage of the article designed,[24]
His fell to Hamlet. Now, sir, young Fortinbras,   95
Of unimprovèd[25] mettle hot and full,
Hath in the skirts[26] of Norway here and there
Sharked up[27] a list of lawless resolutes,[28]
For food and diet, to some enterprise
That hath a stomach in't;[29] which is no other,   100
As it doth well appear unto our state,
But to recover of us by strong hand
And terms compulsatory, those foresaid lands
So by his father lost; and this, I take it,
Is the main motive of our preparations,   105
The source of this our watch, and the chief head[30]
Of this posthaste and romage[31] in the land.
BARNARDO: I think it be no other but e'en so;
Well may it sort[32] that this portentous figure
Comes armèd through our watch so like the King   110
That was and is the question of these wars.
HORATIO: A note it is to trouble the mind's eye:
In the most high and palmy state of Rome,
A little ere the mightiest Julius fell,
The graves stood tenantless, and the sheeted dead   115
Did squeak and gibber in the Roman streets;[33]
As stars with trains of fire and dews of blood,
Disasters[34] in the sun; and the moist star,[35]
Upon whose influence Neptune's empire stands,
Was sick almost to doomsday with eclipse.   120
And even the like precurse[36] of feared events,

---

[19] heraldic law (governing the combat)
[20] possessed
[21] equal portion
[22] engaged, pledged
[23] agreement
[24] import of the agreement drawn up
[25] untried
[26] borders
[27] collected indiscriminately (as a shark gulps its prey)
[28] desperadoes
[29] i.e., requires courage
[30] fountainhead, origin
[31] bustle
[32] befit
[33] (the break in the sense which follows this line suggests that a line has dropped out)
[34] threatening signs
[35] moon
[36] precursor, foreshadowing

As harbingers[37] preceding still[38] the fates
And prologue to the omen[39] coming on,
Have heaven and earth together demonstrated
Unto our climatures[40] and countrymen.   125

(*Enter* GHOST.)

But soft, behold, lo where it comes again!
I'll cross it,[41] though it blast me. — Stay, illusion.

(*It spreads his*[42] *arms.*)

If thou hast any sound or use of voice,
Speak to me.
If there be any good thing to be done   130
That may to thee do ease and grace to me,
Speak to me.
If thou art privy to thy country's fate,
Which happily[43] foreknowing may avoid,
O, speak!   135
Or if thou hast uphoarded in thy life
Extorted[44] treasure in the womb of earth,
For which, they say, you spirits oft walk in death,

(*The cock crows.*)

Speak of it. Stay and speak. Stop it, Marcellus.
MARCELLUS: Shall I strike at it with my partisan?[45]   140
HORATIO: Do, if it will not stand.
BARNARDO: 'Tis here.
HORATIO: 'Tis here.
MARCELLUS: 'Tis gone.   (*Exit* GHOST.)
We do it wrong, being so majestical,
To offer it the show of violence,
For it is as the air, invulnerable,   145
And our vain blows malicious mockery.
BARNARDO: It was about to speak when the cock crew.
HORATIO: And then it started, like a guilty thing
Upon a fearful summons. I have heard,
The cock, that is the trumpet to the morn,   150
Doth with his lofty and shrill-sounding throat
Awake the god of day, and at his warning,
Whether in sea or fire, in earth or air,
Th' extravagant and erring[46] spirit hies

---

[37] forerunners
[38] always
[39] calamity
[40] regions
[41] (1) cross its path, confront it, (2) make the sign of the cross in front of it
[42] i.e., its, the ghost's (though possibly what is meant is that Horatio spreads his own arms, making a cross of himself)
[43] haply, perhaps
[44] ill-won
[45] pike (a long-handled weapon)
[46] out of bounds and wandering

To his confine; and of the truth herein   155
This present object made probation.[47]
MARCELLUS: It faded on the crowing of the cock.
  Some say that ever 'gainst[48] that season comes
  Wherein our Savior's birth is celebrated,
  This bird of dawning singeth all night long,   160
  And then, they say, no spirit dare stir abroad,
  The nights are wholesome, then no planets strike,[49]
  No fairy takes,[50] nor witch hath power to charm:
  So hallowed and so gracious is that time.
HORATIO: So have I heard and do in part believe it.   165
  But look, the morn in russet mantle clad
  Walks o'er the dew of yon high eastward hill.
  Break we our watch up, and by my advice
  Let us impart what we have seen tonight
  Unto young Hamlet, for upon my life   170
  This spirit, dumb to us, will speak to him.
  Do you consent we shall acquaint him with it,
  As needful in our loves, fitting our duty?
MARCELLUS: Let's do't, I pray, and I this morning know
  Where we shall find him most convenient.   (*Exeunt.*)   175

SCENE 2. [THE CASTLE.]

Flourish.[1] *Enter* CLAUDIUS, *King of Denmark*, GERTRUDE *the Queen*, COUN-
CILORS, POLONIUS *and his son* LAERTES, HAMLET, *cum aliis*[2] [*including* VOL-
TEMAND *and* CORNELIUS].

KING: Though yet of Hamlet our dear brother's death
  The memory be green, and that it us befitted
  To bear our hearts in grief, and our whole kingdom
  To be contracted in one brow of woe,
  Yet so far hath discretion fought with nature   5
  That we with wisest sorrow think on him
  Together with remembrance of ourselves.
  Therefore our sometime sister,[3] now our Queen,
  Th' imperial jointress[4] to this warlike state,
  Have we, as 'twere, with a defeated joy,   10
  With an auspicious[5] and a dropping eye,
  With mirth in funeral, and with dirge in marriage,
  In equal scale weighing delight and dole,
  Taken to wife. Nor have we herein barred
  Your better wisdoms, which have freely gone   15

---

[47] proof
[48] just before
[49] exert an evil influence
[50] bewitches
[1] fanfare of trumpets

[2] with others (Latin)
[3] my (the royal "we") former sister-in-law
[4] joint tenant, partner
[5] joyful

With this affair along. For all, our thanks.
Now follows that you know young Fortinbras,
Holding a weak supposal of our worth,
Or thinking by our late dear brother's death
Our state to be disjoint and out of frame,⁶ 20
Colleaguèd with this dream of his advantage,⁷
He hath not failed to pester us with message,
Importing the surrender of those lands
Lost by his father, with all bands of law,
To our most valiant brother. So much for him. 25
Now for ourself and for this time of meeting.
Thus much the business is: we have here writ
To Norway, uncle of young Fortinbras —
Who, impotent and bedrid, scarcely hears
Of this his nephew's purpose — to suppress 30
His further gait⁸ herein, in that the levies,
The lists, and full proportions⁹ are all made
Out of his subject,¹⁰ and we here dispatch
You, good Cornelius, and you, Voltemand,
For bearers of this greeting to old Norway, 35
Giving to you no further personal power
To business with the King, more than the scope
Of these delated articles¹¹ allow.
Farewell, and let your haste commend your duty.
CORNELIUS, VOLTEMAND: In that, and all things, will we show our duty. 40
KING: We doubt it nothing. Heartily farewell.

(*Exit* VOLTEMAND *and* CORNELIUS.)

And now, Laertes, what's the news with you?
You told us of some suit. What is't, Laertes?
You cannot speak of reason to the Dane
And lose your voice.¹² What wouldst thou beg, Laertes, 45
That shall not be my offer, not thy asking?
The head is not more native¹³ to the heart,
The hand more instrumental to the mouth,
Than is the throne of Denmark to thy father.
What wouldst thou have, Laertes?
LAERTES: My dread lord, 50
Your leave and favor to return to France,
From whence, though willingly I came to Denmark
To show my duty in your coronation,
Yet now I must confess, that duty done,
My thoughts and wishes bend again toward France 55
And bow them to your gracious leave and pardon.

⁶ order
⁷ superiority
⁸ proceeding
⁹ supplies for war
¹⁰ i.e., out of old Norway's subjects and
realm

¹¹ detailed documents
¹² waste your breath
¹³ related

KING: Have you your father's leave? What says Polonius?
POLONIUS: He hath, my lord, wrung from me my slow leave
  By laborsome petition, and at last
  Upon his will I sealed my hard consent.[14]
  I do beseech you give him leave to go.   60
KING: Take thy fair hour, Laertes. Time be thine,
  And thy best graces spend it at thy will.
  But now, my cousin[15] Hamlet, and my son ——
HAMLET [*aside*]: A little more than kin, and less than kind![16]   65
KING: How is it that the clouds still hang on you?
HAMLET: Not so, my lord. I am too much in the sun.[17]
QUEEN: Good Hamlet, cast thy nighted color off,
  And let thine eye look like a friend on Denmark.
  Do not forever with thy vailèd lids[18]   70
  Seek for thy noble father in the dust.
  Thou know'st 'tis common; all that lives must die,
  Passing through nature to eternity.
HAMLET: Ay, madam, it is common.[19]
QUEEN: If it be,
  Why seems it so particular with thee?   75
HAMLET: Seems, madam? Nay, it is. I know not "seems."
  'Tis not alone my inky cloak, good mother,
  Nor customary suits of solemn black,
  Nor windy suspiration[20] of forced breath,
  No, nor the fruitful river in the eye,   80
  Nor the dejected havior of the visage,
  Together with all forms, moods, shapes of grief,
  That can denote me truly. These indeed seem,
  For they are actions that a man might play,
  But I have that within which passes show;   85
  These but the trappings and the suits of woe.
KING: 'Tis sweet and commendable in your nature, Hamlet,
  To give these mourning duties to your father,
  But you must know your father lost a father,
  That father lost, lost his, and the survivor bound   90
  In filial obligation for some term
  To do obsequious[21] sorrow. But to persever
  In obstinate condolement[22] is a course
  Of impious stubbornness. 'Tis unmanly grief.
  It shows a will most incorrect to heaven,   95
  A heart unfortified, a mind impatient,

---

[14] to his desire I gave my reluctant consent
[15] kinsman
[16] (pun on the meanings "kindly" and "natural"; though doubly related — *more than kin* — Hamlet asserts that he neither resembles Claudius in nature nor feels kindly toward him)

[17] sunshine of royal favor (with a pun on "son")
[18] lowered
[19] (1) universal, (2) vulgar
[20] heavy sighing
[21] suitable to obsequies (funerals)
[22] mourning

An understanding simple and unschooled.
For what we know must be and is as common
As any the most vulgar²³ thing to sense,
Why should we in our peevish opposition   100
Take it to heart? Fie, 'tis a fault to heaven,
A fault against the dead, a fault to nature,
To reason most absurd, whose common theme
Is death of fathers, and who still hath cried,
From the first corse²⁴ till he that died today,   105
"This must be so." We pray you throw to earth
This unprevailing²⁵ woe, and think of us
As of a father, for let the world take note
You are the most immediate to our throne,
And with no less nobility of love   110
Than that which dearest father bears his son
Do I impart toward you. For your intent
In going back to school in Wittenberg,
It is most retrograde²⁶ to our desire,
And we beseech you, bend you²⁷ to remain   115
Here in the cheer and comfort of our eye,
Our chiefest courtier, cousin, and our son.
QUEEN: Let not thy mother lose her prayers, Hamlet.
   I pray thee stay with us, go not to Wittenberg.
HAMLET: I shall in all my best obey you, madam.   120
KING: Why, 'tis a loving and a fair reply.
   Be as ourself in Denmark. Madam, come.
   This gentle and unforced accord of Hamlet
   Sits smiling to my heart, in grace whereof
   No jocund health that Denmark drinks today,   125
   But the great cannon to the clouds shall tell,
   And the King's rouse²⁸ the heaven shall bruit²⁹ again,
   Respeaking earthly thunder. Come away. (*Flourish. Exeunt all but* HAMLET.)
HAMLET: O that this too too sullied³⁰ flesh would melt,
   Thaw, and resolve itself into a dew,   130
   Or that the Everlasting had not fixed
   His canon³¹ 'gainst self-slaughter. O God, God,
   How weary, stale, flat, and unprofitable
   Seem to me all the uses of this world!
   Fie on't, ah, fie, 'tis an unweeded garden   135
   That grows to seed. Things rank and gross in nature
   Possess it merely.³² That it should come to this:
   But two months dead, nay, not so much, not two,

²³ common
²⁴ corpse
²⁵ unavailing
²⁶ contrary
²⁷ incline
²⁸ deep drink
²⁹ announce noisily

³⁰ (Q2 [Second Quarto] has *sallied*, here modernized to *sullied*, which makes sense and is therefore given; but the Folio reading, *solid*, which fits better with *melt*, is quite possibly correct)
³¹ law
³² entirely

So excellent a king, that was to this
Hyperion[33] to a satyr, so loving to my mother   140
That he might not beteem[34] the winds of heaven
Visit her face too roughly. Heaven and earth,
Must I remember? Why, she would hang on him
As if increase of appetite had grown
By what it fed on; and yet within a month —   145
Let me not think on't; frailty, thy name is woman —
A little month, or ere those shoes were old
With which she followed my poor father's body
Like Niobe,[35] all tears, why she, even she —
O God, a beast that wants discourse of reason[36]   150
Would have mourned longer — married with my uncle,
My father's brother, but no more like my father
Than I to Hercules. Within a month,
Ere yet the salt of most unrighteous tears
Had left the flushing[37] in her gallèd eyes,   155
She married. O, most wicked speed, to post[38]
With such dexterity to incestuous[39] sheets!
It is not, nor it cannot come to good.
But break my heart, for I must hold my tongue.

(*Enter* HORATIO, MARCELLUS, *and* BARNARDO.)

HORATIO: Hail to your lordship!
HAMLET: I am glad to see you well.   160
  Horatio — or I do forget myself.
HORATIO: The same, my lord, and your poor servant ever.
HAMLET: Sir, my good friend, I'll change[40] that name with you.
  And what make you from Wittenberg, Horatio?
  Marcellus.   165
MARCELLUS: My good lord!
HAMLET: I am very glad to see you. [*To* BARNARDO.] Good even, sir.
  But what, in faith, make you from Wittenberg?
HORATIO: A truant disposition, good my lord.
HAMLET: I would not hear your enemy say so,   170
  Nor shall you do my ear that violence
  To make it truster[41] of your own report
  Against yourself. I know you are no truant.
  But what is your affair in Elsinore?
  We'll teach you to drink deep ere you depart.   175
HORATIO: My lord, I came to see your father's funeral.
HAMLET: I prithee do not mock me, fellow student.
  I think it was to see my mother's wedding.

[33] the sun god, a model of beauty
[34] allow
[35] a mother who wept profusely at the death of her children
[36] lacks reasoning power
[37] stopped reddening
[38] hasten
[39] (canon law considered marriage with a deceased brother's widow to be incestuous)
[40] exchange
[41] believer

HORATIO: Indeed, my lord, it followed hard upon.
HAMLET: Thrift, thrift, Horatio. The funeral baked meats   180
    Did coldly furnish forth the marriage tables.
    Would I had met my dearest[42] foe in heaven
    Or ever I had seen that day, Horatio!
    My father, methinks I see my father.
HORATIO: Where, my lord?
HAMLET: In my mind's eye, Horatio.   185
HORATIO: I saw him once. 'A[43] was a goodly king.
HAMLET: 'A was a man, take him for all in all,
    I shall not look upon his like again.
HORATIO: My lord, I think I saw him yesternight.
HAMLET: Saw? Who?   190
HORATIO: My lord, the King your father.
HAMLET: The King my father?
HORATIO: Season your admiration[44] for a while
    With an attent ear till I may deliver
    Upon the witness of these gentlemen
    This marvel to you.
HAMLET: For God's love let me hear!   195
HORATIO: Two nights together had these gentlemen,
    Marcellus and Barnardo, on their watch
    In the dead waste and middle of the night
    Been thus encountered. A figure like your father,
    Armèd at point exactly, cap-a-pe,[45]   200
    Appears before them, and with solemn march
    Goes slow and stately by them. Thrice he walked
    By their oppressed and fear-surprisèd eyes,
    Within his truncheon's length,[46] whilst they, distilled[47]
    Almost to jelly with the act[48] of fear,   205
    Stand dumb and speak not to him. This to me
    In dreadful[49] secrecy impart they did,
    And I with them the third night kept the watch,
    Where, as they had delivered, both in time,
    Form of the thing, each word made true and good,   210
    The apparition comes. I knew your father.
    These hands are not more like.
HAMLET: But where was this?
MARCELLUS: My lord, upon the platform where we watched.
HAMLET: Did you not speak to it?
HORATIO: My lord, I did;
    But answer made it none. Yet once methought   215
    If lifted up it[50] head and did address

---

[42] most intensely felt
[43] he
[44] control your wonder
[45] head to foot
[46] space of a short staff

[47] reduced
[48] action
[49] terrified
[50] its

Itself to motion like as it would speak:
But even then the morning cock crew loud,
And at the sound it shrunk in haste away
And vanished from our sight.
HAMLET: 'Tis very strange.   220
HORATIO: As I do live, my honored lord, 'tis true,
  And we did think it writ down in our duty
  To let you know of it.
HAMLET: Indeed, indeed, sirs, but this troubles me.
  Hold you the watch tonight?
ALL: We do, my lord.   225
HAMLET: Armed, say you?
ALL: Armed, my lord.
HAMLET: From top to toe?
ALL: My lord, from head to foot.
HAMLET: Then saw you not his face.
HORATIO: O, yes, my lord. He wore his beaver[51] up.   230
HAMLET: What, looked he frowningly?
HORATIO: A countenance more in sorrow than in anger.
HAMLET: Pale or red?
HORATIO: Nay, very pale.
HAMLET: And fixed his eyes upon you?
HORATIO: Most constantly.
HAMLET: I would I had been there.   235
HORATIO: It would have much amazed you.
HAMLET: Very like, very like. Stayed it long?
HORATIO: While one with moderate haste might tell[52] a hundred.
BOTH: Longer, longer.
HORATIO: Not when I saw't.
HAMLET: His beard was grizzled,[53] no?   240
HORATIO: It was as I have seen it in his life,
  A sable silvered.[54]
HAMLET: I will watch tonight.
  Perchance 'twill walk again.
HORATIO: I warr'nt it will.
HAMLET: If it assume my noble father's person,
  I'll speak to it though hell itself should gape   245
  And bid me hold my peace. I pray you all,
  If you have hitherto concealed this sight,
  Let it be tenable[55] in your silence still,
  And whatsomever else shall hap tonight,
  Give it an understanding but no tongue;   250
  I will requite your loves. So fare you well.
  Upon the platform 'twixt eleven and twelve
  I'll visit you.

---

[51] visor, face guard   [54] black mingled with white
[52] count   [55] held
[53] gray

ALL: Our duty to your honor.

HAMLET: Your loves, as mine to you. Farewell.   (*Exeunt [all but* HAMLET].)

My father's spirit — in arms? All is not well.   255

I doubt[56] some foul play. Would the night were come!

Till then sit still, my soul. Foul deeds will rise,

Though all the earth o'erwhelm them, to men's eyes.   (*Exit.*)

SCENE 3. [A ROOM.]

Enter LAERTES *and* OPHELIA, *his sister.*

LAERTES: My necessaries are embarked. Farewell.

And, sister, as the winds give benefit

And convoy[1] is assistant, do not sleep,

But let me hear from you.

OPHELIA: Do you doubt that?

LAERTES: For Hamlet, and the trifling of his favor,   5

Hold it a fashion and a toy[2] in blood,

A violet in the youth of primy[3] nature,

Forward,[4] not permanent, sweet, not lasting,

The perfume and suppliance[5] of a minute,

No more.   10

OPHELIA: No more but so?

LAERTES: Think it no more.

For nature crescent[6] does not grow alone

In thews[7] and bulk, but as this temple[8] waxes,

The inward service of the mind and soul

Grows wide withal. Perhaps he loves you now,   15

And now no soil nor cautel[9] both besmirch

The virtue of his will; but you must fear,

His greatness weighed,[10] his will is not his own.

For he himself is subject to his birth.

He may not, as unvalued[11] persons do,   20

Carve for himself; for on his choice depends

The safety and health of this whole state;

And therefore must his choice be circumscribed

Unto the voice and yielding of that body

Whereof he is the head. Then if he says he loves you,   25

It fits your wisdom so far to believe it

As he in his particular act and place

May give his saying deed, which is no further

Than the main voice of Denmark goes withal.

[56] suspect
[1] conveyance
[2] idle fancy
[3] springlike
[4] premature
[5] diversion
[6] growing
[7] muscles and sinews
[8] i.e., the body
[9] deceit
[10] high rank considered
[11] of low rank

Then weigh what loss your honor may sustain   30
If with too credent[12] ear you list his songs,
Or lose your heart, or your chaste treasure open
To his unmastered importunity.
Fear it, Ophelia, fear it, my dear sister,
And keep you in the rear of your affection,   35
Out of the shot and danger of desire.
The chariest maid is prodigal enough
If she unmask her beauty to the moon.
Virtue itself scapes not calumnious strokes.
The canker[13] galls the infants of the spring   40
Too oft before their buttons[14] be disclosed,
And in the morn and liquid dew of youth
Contagious blastments are most imminent.
Be wary then; best safety lies in fear;
Youth to itself rebels, though none else near.   45
OPHELIA: I shall the effect of this good lesson keep
As watchman to my heart, but, good my brother,
Do not, as some ungracious[15] pastors do,
Show me the steep and thorny way to heaven,
Whiles, like a puffed and reckless libertine,   50
Himself the primrose path of dalliance treads
And recks not his own rede.[16]

(*Enter* POLONIUS.)

LAERTES: O, fear me not.
I stay too long. But here my father comes.
A double blessing is a double grace;
Occasion smiles upon a second leave.   55
POLONIUS: Yet here, Laertes? Aboard, aboard, for shame!
The wind sits in the shoulder of your sail,
And you are stayed for. There — my blessing with thee,
And these few precepts in thy memory
Look thou character.[17] Give thy thoughts no tongue,   60
Nor any unproportioned[18] thought his act.
Be thou familiar, but by no means vulgar.
Those friends thou hast, and their adoption tried,
Grapple them unto thy soul with hoops of steel,
But do not dull thy palm with entertainment   65
Of each new-hatched, unfledged courage.[19] Beware
Of entrance to a quarrel; but being in,
Bear't that th' opposèd may beware of thee.
Give every man thine ear, but few thy voice;
Take each man's censure,[20] but reserve thy judgment.   70

---

[12] credulous
[13] cankerworm
[14] buds
[15] lacking grace
[16] does not heed his own advice

[17] inscribe
[18] unbalanced
[19] gallant youth
[20] opinion

Costly thy habit as thy purse can buy,
But not expressed in fancy; rich, not gaudy,
For the apparel oft proclaims the man,
And they in France of the best rank and station
Are of a most select and generous, chief in that.[21]   75
Neither a borrower nor a lender be,
For loan oft loses both itself and friend,
And borrowing dulleth edge of husbandry.[22]
This above all, to thine own self be true,
And it must follow, as the night the day,   80
Thou canst not then be false to any man.
Farewell. My blessing season this[23] in thee!
LAERTES: Most humbly do I take my leave, my lord.
POLONIUS: The time invites you. Go, your servants tend.[24]
LAERTES: Farewell, Ophelia, and remember well   85
What I have said to you.
OPHELIA: 'Tis in my memory locked,
And you yourself shall keep the key of it.
LAERTES: Farewell.   (*Exit* LAERTES.)
POLONIUS: What is't, Ophelia, he hath said to you?
OPHELIA: So please you, something touching the Lord Hamlet.   90
POLONIUS: Marry,[25] well bethought.
'Tis told me he hath very oft of late
Given private time to you, and you yourself
Have of your audience been most free and bounteous.
If it be so — as so 'tis put on me,   95
And that in way of caution — I must tell you
You do not understand yourself so clearly
As it behooves my daughter and your honor.
What is between you? Give me up the truth.
OPHELIA: He hath, my lord, of late made many tenders[26]   100
Of his affection to me.
POLONIUS: Affection pooh! You speak like a green girl,
Unsifted[27] in such perilous circumstance.
Do you believe his tenders, as you call them?
OPHELIA: I do not know, my lord, what I should think.   105
POLONIUS: Marry, I will teach you. Think yourself a baby
That you have ta'en these tenders for true pay
Which are not sterling. Tender yourself more dearly,
Or (not to crack the wind of the poor phrase)
Tend'ring it thus you'll tender me a fool.[28]   110

[21] show their fine taste and their gentle-manly instincts more in that than in any other point of manners (Kittredge)
[22] thrift
[23] make fruitful this (advice)
[24] attend
[25] (a light oath, from "By the Virgin Mary")

[26] offers (in line 103 it has the same meaning, but in line 106 Polonius speaks of *tenders* in the sense of counters or chips; in line 109 *Tend'ring* means "holding," and *tender* means "give," "present")
[27] untried
[28] (1) present me with a fool, (2) present me with a baby

OPHELIA: My lord, he hath importuned me with love
  In honorable fashion.
POLONIUS: Ay, fashion you may call it. Go to, go to.
OPHELIA: And hath given countenance to his speech, my lord,
  With almost all the holy vows of heaven.   115
POLONIUS: Ay, springes to catch woodcocks.[29] I do know,
  When the blood burns, how prodigal the soul
  Lends the tongue vows. These blazes, daughter,
  Giving more light than heat, extinct in both,
  Even in their promise, as it is a-making,   120
  You must not take for fire. From this time
  Be something scanter of your maiden presence.
  Set your entreatments[30] at a higher rate
  Than a command to parley. For Lord Hamlet,
  Believe so much in him that he is young,   125
  And with a larger tether may he walk
  Than may be given you. In few, Ophelia,
  Do not believe his vows, for they are brokers,[31]
  Not of that dye[32] which their investments[33] show,
  But mere implorators[34] of unholy suits,   130
  Breathing like sanctified and pious bonds,[35]
  The better to beguile. This is for all:
  I would not, in plain terms, from this time forth
  Have you so slander[36] any moment leisure
  As to give words or talk with the Lord Hamlet.   135
  Look to't, I charge you. Come your ways.
OPHELIA: I shall obey, my lord.   (*Exeunt.*)

SCENE 4. [A GUARD PLATFORM.]

Enter HAMLET, HORATIO, *and* MARCELLUS.

HAMLET: The air bites shrewdly;[1] it is very cold.
HORATIO: It is a nipping and an eager[2] air.
HAMLET: What hour now?
HORATIO: I think it lacks of twelve.
MARCELLUS: No, it is struck.
HORATIO: Indeed? I heard it not. It then draws near the season   5
  Wherein the spirit held his wont to walk.

  (*A flourish of trumpets, and two pieces go off.*)

  What does this mean, my lord?
HAMLET: The King doth wake[3] tonight and takes his rouse,[4]

---

[29] snares to catch stupid birds
[30] interviews
[31] procurers
[32] i.e., kind
[33] garments
[34] solicitors

[35] pledges
[36] disgrace
[1] bitterly
[2] sharp
[3] hold a revel by night
[4] carouses

Keeps wassail, and the swagg'ring upspring[5] reels,
And as he drains his draughts of Rhenish[6] down   10
The kettledrum and trumpet thus bray out
The triumph of his pledge.[7]

HORATIO: Is it a custom?

HAMLET: Ay, marry, is't,
But to my mind, though I am native here
And to the manner born, it is a custom   15
More honored in the breach than the observance.
This heavy-headed revel east and west
Makes us traduced and taxed of[8] other nations.
They clepe[9] us drunkards and with swinish phrase
Soil our addition,[10] and indeed it takes   20
From our achievements, though performed at height,
The pith and marrow of our attribute.[11]
So oft it chances in particular men
That for some vicious mole[12] of nature in them,
As in their birth, wherein they are not guilty,   25
(Since nature cannot choose his origin)
By the o'ergrowth of some complexion,[13]
Oft breaking down the pales[14] and forts of reason,
Or by some habit that too much o'erleavens[15]
The form of plausive[16] manners, that (these men,   30
Carrying, I say, the stamp of one defect,
Being nature's livery, or fortune's star[17])
Their virtues else, be they are pure as grace,
As infinite as man may undergo,
Shall in the general censure[18] take corruption   35
From that particular fault. The dram of evil
Doth all the noble substance of a doubt,
To his own scandal.[19]

(*Enter* GHOST.)

HORATIO: Look, my lord, it comes.

HAMLET: Angels and ministers of grace defend us!
Be thou a spirit of health[20] or goblin damned,   40
Bring with thee airs from heaven or blasts from hell,
Be thy intents wicked or charitable,
Thou com'st in such a questionable[21] shape

---

[5] a dance
[6] Rhine wine
[7] the achievement (of drinking a wine cup in one draught) of his toast
[8] blamed by
[9] call
[10] reputation (literally, "title of honor")
[11] reputation
[12] blemish
[13] natural disposition
[14] enclosures

[15] mixes with, corrupts
[16] pleasing
[17] nature's equipment (i.e., "innate"), or a person's destiny determined by the stars
[18] popular judgment
[19] (though the drift is clear, there is no agreement as to the exact meaning of these lines)
[20] good spirit
[21] (1) capable of discourse, (2) dubious

That I will speak to thee. I'll call thee Hamlet,
King, father, royal Dane. O, answer me!   45
Let me not burst in ignorance, but tell
Why thy canonized[22] bones, hearsèd in death,
Have burst their cerements,[23] why the sepulcher
Wherein we saw thee quietly interred
Hath oped his ponderous and marble jaws   50
To cast thee up again. What may this mean
That thou, dead corse, again in complete steel,
Revisits thus the glimpses of the moon,
Making night hideous, and we fools of nature
So horridly to shake our disposition[24]   55
With thoughts beyond the reaches of our souls?
Say, why is this? Wherefore? What should we do?

(GHOST *beckons* HAMLET.)

HORATIO: It beckons you to go away with it,
    As if it some impartment[25] did desire
    To you alone.
MARCELLUS: Look with what courteous action   60
    It waves you to a more removèd ground.
    But do not go with it.
HORATIO: No, by no means.
HAMLET: It will not speak. Then I will follow it.
HORATIO: Do not, my lord.
HAMLET: Why, what should be the fear?
    I do not set my life at a pin's fee,   65
    And for my soul, what can it do to that,
    Being a thing immortal as itself?
    It waves me forth again. I'll follow it.
HORATIO: What if it tempt you toward the flood, my lord,
    Or to the dreadful summit of the cliff   70
    That beetles[26] o'er his base into the sea,
    And there assume some other horrible form,
    Which might deprive your sovereignty of reason[27]
    And draw you into madness? Think of it.
    The very place puts toys[28] of desperation,   75
    Without more motive, into every brain
    That looks so many fathoms to the sea
    And hears it roar beneath.
HAMLET: It waves me still.
    Go on; I'll follow thee.
MARCELLUS: You shall not go, my lord.
HAMLET: Hold off your hands.   80

---

[22] buried according to the canon or ordinance of the church
[23] waxed linen shroud
[24] disturb us

[25] communication
[26] juts out
[27] destroy the sovereignty of your reason
[28] whims, fancies

HORATIO: Be ruled. You shall not go.
HAMLET: My fate cries out
   And makes each petty artere[29] in this body
   As hardy as the Nemean lion's nerve.[30]
   Still am I called! Unhand me, gentlemen.
   By heaven, I'll make a ghost of him that lets[31] me!   85
   I say, away! Go on. I'll follow thee.   (*Exit* GHOST, *and* HAMLET.)
HORATIO: He waxes desperate with imagination.
MARCELLUS: Let's follow. 'Tis not fit thus to obey him.
HORATIO: Have after! To what issue will this come?
MARCELLUS: Something is rotten in the state of Denmark.   90
HORATIO: Heaven will direct it.
MARCELLUS: Nay, let's follow him.   (*Exeunt.*)

SCENE 5. [THE BATTLEMENTS.]

Enter GHOST *and* HAMLET.

HAMLET: Whither wilt thou lead me? Speak; I'll go no further.
GHOST: Mark me.
HAMLET: I will.
GHOST: My hour is almost come,
   When I to sulf'rous and tormenting flames
   Must render up myself.
HAMLET: Alas, poor ghost.
GHOST: Pity me not, but lend thy serious hearing   5
   To what I shall unfold.
HAMLET: Speak. I am bound to hear.
GHOST: So art thou to revenge, when thou shalt hear.
HAMLET: What?
GHOST: I am thy father's spirit,
   Doomed for a certain term to walk the night,   10
   And for the day confined to fast in fires,
   Till the foul crimes[1] done in my days of nature
   Are burnt and purged away. But that I am forbid
   To tell the secrets of my prison house,
   I could a tale unfold whose lightest word   15
   Would harrow up thy soul, freeze thy young blood,
   Make thy two eyes like stars start from their spheres,[2]
   Thy knotted and combinèd locks to part,
   And each particular hair to stand an end
   Like quills upon the fearful porpentine.[3]   20
   But this eternal blazon[4] must not be

---

[29] artery
[30] sinews of the mythical lion slain by Hercules
[31] hinders
[1] sins

[2] (in Ptolemaic astronomy, each planet was fixed in a hollow transparent shell concentric with the earth)
[3] timid porcupine
[4] revelation of eternity

To ears of flesh and blood. List, list, O, list!
If thou didst ever thy dear father love ——
HAMLET: O God!
GHOST: Revenge his foul and most unnatural murder.   25
HAMLET: Murder?
GHOST: Murder most foul, as in the best it is,
  But this most foul, strange, and unnatural.
HAMLET: Haste me to know't, that I, with wings as swift
  As meditation[5] or the thoughts of love,   30
  May sweep to my revenge.
GHOST: I find thee apt,
  And duller shouldst thou be than the fat weed
  That roots itself in ease on Lethe wharf,[6]
  Wouldst thou not stir in this. Now, Hamlet, hear.
  'Tis given out that, sleeping in my orchard,   35
  A serpent stung me. So the whole ear of Denmark
  Is by a forgèd process[7] of my death
  Rankly abused. But know, thou noble youth,
  The serpent that did sting thy father's life
  Now wears his crown.
HAMLET: O my prophetic soul!   40
  My uncle?
GHOST: Ay, that incestuous, that adulterate[8] beast,
  With witchcraft of his wits, with traitorous gifts —
  O wicked wit and gifts, that have the power
  So to seduce! — won to his shameful lust   45
  The will of my most seeming-virtuous queen.
  O Hamlet, what a falling-off was there,
  From me, whose love was of that dignity
  That it went hand in hand even with the vow
  I made to her in marriage, and to decline   50
  Upon a wretch whose natural gifts were poor
  To those of mine.
  But virtue, as it never will be moved,
  Though lewdness[9] court it in a shape of heaven,
  So lust, though to a radiant angel linked,   55
  Will sate itself in a celestial bed
  And prey on garbage.
  But soft, methinks I scent the morning air;
  Brief let me be. Sleeping within my orchard,
  My custom always of the afternoon,   60
  Upon my secure[10] hour thy uncle stole
  With juice of cursed hebona[11] in a vial,
  And in the porches of my ears did pour

---

[5] thought
[6] bank of the river of forgetfulness in Hades
[7] false account

[8] adulterous
[9] lust
[10] unsuspecting
[11] a poisonous plant

The leperous distillment, whose effect
Holds such an enmity with blood of man   65
That swift as quicksilver it courses through
The natural gates and alleys of the body,
And with a sudden vigor it doth posset[12]
And curd, like eager[13] droppings into milk,
The thin and wholesome blood. So did it mine,   70
And a most instant tetter[14] barked about
Most lazarlike[15] with vile and loathsome crust
All my smooth body.
Thus was I, sleeping, by a brother's hand
Of life, of crown, of queen at once dispatched,   75
Cut off even in the blossoms of my sin,
Unhouseled, disappointed, unaneled,[16]
No reck'ning made, but sent to my account
With all my imperfections on my head.
O, horrible! O, horrible! Most horrible!   80
If thou hast nature in thee, bear it not.
Let not the royal bed of Denmark be
A couch for luxury[17] and damnèd incest.
But howsomever thou pursues this act,
Taint not thy mind, nor let thy soul contrive   85
Against thy mother aught. Leave her to heaven
And to those thorns that in her bosom lodge
To prick and sting her. Fare thee well at once.
The glowworm shows the matin[18] to be near
And 'gins to pale his uneffectual fire.   90
Adieu, adieu, adieu. Remember me.   (Exit.)
HAMLET: O all you host of heaven! O earth! What else?
And shall I couple hell? O fie! Hold, hold, my heart,
And you, my sinews, grow not instant old,
But bear me stiffly up. Remember thee?   95
Ay, thou poor ghost, whiles memory holds a seat
In this distracted globe.[19] Remember thee?
Yea, from the table[20] of my memory
I'll wipe away all trivial fond[21] records,
All saws[22] of books, all forms, all pressures[23] past   100
That youth and observation copied there,
And thy commandment all alone shall live
Within the book and volume of my brain,
Unmixed with baser matter. Yes, by heaven!
O most pernicious woman!   105

[12] curdle
[13] acid
[14] scab
[15] leperlike
[16] without the sacrament of communion,
unabsolved, without extreme unction
[17] lust

[18] morning
[19] i.e., his head
[20] tablet, notebook
[21] foolish
[22] maxims
[23] impressions

O villain, villain, smiling, damnèd villain!
My tables — meet it is I set it down
That one may smile, and smile, and be a villain.
At least I am sure it may be so in Denmark. [*Writes.*]
So, uncle, there you are. Now to my word: 110
It is "Adieu, adieu, remember me."
I have sworn't.

HORATIO AND MARCELLUS (*within*): My lord, my lord!

(*Enter* HORATIO *and* MARCELLUS.)

MARCELLUS: Lord Hamlet!
HORATIO: Heavens secure him!
HAMLET: So be it!
MARCELLUS: Illo, ho, ho,[24] my lord!   115
HAMLET: Hillo, ho, ho, boy! Come, bird, come.
MARCELLUS: How is't, my noble lord?
HORATIO: What news, my lord?
HAMLET: O, wonderful!
HORATIO: Good my lord, tell it.
HAMLET: No, you will reveal it.
HORATIO: Not I, my lord, by heaven.
MARCELLUS: Nor I, my lord.   120
HAMLET: How say you then? Would heart of man once think it?
  But you'll be secret?
BOTH: Ay, by heaven, my lord.
HAMLET: There's never a villain dwelling in all Denmark
  But he's an arrant knave.
HORATIO: There needs no ghost, my lord, come from the grave   125
  To tell us this.
HAMLET: Why, right, you are in the right;
  And so, without more circumstance[25] at all,
  I hold it fit that we shake hands and part:
  You, as your business and desire shall point you,
  For every man hath business and desire
  Such as it is, and for my own poor part,   130
  Look you, I'll go pray.
HORATIO: These are but wild and whirling words, my lord.
HAMLET: I am sorry they offend you, heartily;
  Yes, faith, heartily.
HORATIO: There's no offense, my lord.   135
HAMLET: Yes, by Saint Patrick, but there is, Horatio,
  And much offense too. Touching this vision here,
  It is an honest ghost,[26] that let me tell you.
  For your desire to know what is between us,
  O'ermaster't as you may. And now, good friends,   140
  As you are friends, scholars, and soldiers,
  Give me one poor request.

---

[24] (falconer's call to his hawk)   [26] i.e., not a demon in his father's shape
[25] details

HORATIO: What is't, my lord? We will.

HAMLET: Never make known what you have seen tonight.

BOTH: My lord, we will not.

HAMLET: Nay, but swear't.

HORATIO: In faith,   145

My lord, not I.

MARCELLUS: Nor I, my lord — in faith.

HAMLET: Upon my sword.

MARCELLUS: We have sworn, my lord, already.

HAMLET: Indeed, upon my sword, indeed.

   (GHOST *cries under the stage.*)

GHOST: Swear.

HAMLET: Ha, ha, boy, say'st thou so? Art thou there, truepenny?[27]   150

Come on. You hear this fellow in the cellarage.

Consent to swear.

HORATIO: Propose the oath, my lord.

HAMLET: Never to speak of this that you have seen.

Swear by my sword.

GHOST [*beneath*]: Swear.   155

HAMLET: *Hic et ubique?*[28] Then we'll shift our ground;

Come hither, gentlemen,

And lay your hands again upon my sword.

Swear by my sword

Never to speak of this that you have heard.   160

GHOST [*beneath*]: Swear by his sword.

HAMLET: Well said, old mole! Canst work i' th' earth so fast?

A worthy pioner![29] Once more remove, good friends.

HORATIO: O day and night, but this is wondrous strange!

HAMLET: And therefore as a stranger give it welcome.   165

There are more things in heaven and earth, Horatio,

Than are dreamt of in your philosophy.

But come:

Here as before, never, so help you mercy,

How strange or odd some'er I bear myself   170

(As I perchance hereafter shall think meet

To put an antic disposition[30] on),

That you, at such times seeing me, never shall

With arms encumb'red[31] thus, or this headshake,

Or by pronouncing of some doubtful phrase,   175

As "Well, well, we know," or "We could, and if we would,"

Or "If we list to speak," or "There be, an if they might,"

Or such ambiguous giving out, to note

That you know aught of me — this do swear,

So grace and mercy at your most need help you.   180

GHOST [*beneath*]: Swear.

---

[27] honest fellow   [30] fantastic behavior
[28] here and everywhere (Latin)   [31] folded
[29] digger of mines

[They swear.]

HAMLET: Rest, rest, perturbèd spirit. So, gentlemen
  With all my love I do commend me[32] to you,
  And what so poor a man as Hamlet is
  May do t' express his love and friending to you,   185
  God willing, shall not lack. Let us go in together,
  And still your fingers on your lips, I pray.
  The time is out of joint. O cursèd spite,
  That ever I was born to set it right!
  Nay, come, let's go together.   *(Exeunt.)*   190

ACT II

SCENE 1. [A ROOM.]

Enter old POLONIUS, *with his man* REYNALDO.

POLONIUS: Give him this money and these notes, Reynaldo.
REYNALDO: I will, my lord.
POLONIUS: You shall do marvell's[1] wisely, good Reynaldo,
  Before you visit him, to make inquire
  Of his behavior.
REYNALDO: My lord, I did intend it.   5
POLONIUS: Marry, well said, very well said. Look you sir,
  Inquire me first what Danskers[2] are in Paris,
  And how, and who, what means, and where they keep,[3]
  What company, at what expense; and finding
  By this encompassment[4] and drift of question   10
  That they do know my son, come you more nearer
  Than your particular demands[5] will touch it.
  Take you as 'twere some distant knowledge of him,
  As thus, "I know his father and his friends,
  And in part him." Do you mark this, Reynaldo?   15
REYNALDO: Ay, very well, my lord.
POLONIUS: "And in part him, but," you may say, "not well,
  But if't be he I mean, he's very wild,
  Addicted so and so." And there put on him
  What forgeries[6] you please; marry, none so rank   20
  As may dishonor him — take heed of that —
  But, sir, such wanton, wild, and usual slips
  As are companions noted and most known
  To youth and liberty.

---

[32] entrust myself   [4] circling
[1] marvelous(ly)   [5] questions
[2] Danes   [6] inventions
[3] dwell

REYNALDO: As gaming, my lord.

POLONIUS: Ay, or drinking, fencing, swearing, quarreling,   25
     Drabbing.[7] You may go so far.

REYNALDO: My lord, that would dishonor him.

POLONIUS: Faith, no, as you may season it in the charge.
     You must not put another scandal on him,
     That he is open to incontinency.[8]   30
     That's not my meaning. But breathe his faults so quaintly[9]
     That they may seem the taints of liberty,
     The flash and outbreak of a fiery mind,
     A savageness in unreclaimèd blood,
     Of general assault.[10]

REYNALDO: But, my good lord ——   35

POLONIUS: Wherefore should you do this?

REYNALDO: Ay, my lord,
     I would know that.

POLONIUS: Marry, sir, here's my drift,
     And I believe it is a fetch of warrant.[11]
     You laying these slight sullies on my son
     As 'twere a thing a little soiled i' th' working,   40
     Mark you,
     Your party in converse, him you would sound,
     Having ever seen in the prenominate crimes[12]
     The youth you breathe of guilty, be assured
     He closes with you in this consequence:[13]   45
     "Good sir," or so, or "friend," or "gentleman" —
     According to the phrase or the addition[14]
     Of man and country —

REYNALDO: Very good, my lord.

POLONIUS: And then, sir, does 'a[15] this — 'a does —
     What was I about to say? By the mass, I was about to say something!   50
     Where did I leave?

REYNALDO: At "closes in the consequence," at "friend or so," and "gentleman."

POLONIUS: At "closes in the consequence" — Ay, marry!
     He closes thus: "I know the gentleman;
     I saw him yesterday, or t'other day,
     Or then, or then, with such or such, and, as you say,   55
     There was 'a gaming, there o'ertook in's rouse,
     There falling out at tennis"; or perchance,
     "I saw him enter such a house of sale,"
     Videlicet,[16] a brothel, or so forth.   60
     See you now —

---

[7] wenching
[8] habitual licentiousness
[9] ingeniously, delicately
[10] common to all men
[11] justifiable device
[12] if he has ever seen in the aforementioned crimes

[13] he falls in with you in this conclusion
[14] title
[15] he
[16] namely

Your bait of falsehood take this carp of truth,
And thus do we of wisdom and of reach,[17]
With windlasses[18] and with assays of bias,[19]
By indirections find directions out.   65
So, by my former lecture and advice,
Shall you my son. You have me, have you not?
REYNALDO: My lord, I have.
POLONIUS: God bye ye, fare ye well.
REYNALDO: Good my lord.
POLONIUS: Observe his inclination in yourself.[20]   70
REYNALDO: I shall, my lord.
POLONIUS: And let him ply his music.
REYNALDO: Well, my lord.
POLONIUS: Farewell.   (*Exit* REYNALDO.)

(*Enter* OPHELIA.)

                              How now, Ophelia, what's the matter?
OPHELIA: O my lord, my lord, I have been so affrighted!
POLONIUS: With what, i' th' name of God?   75
OPHELIA: My lord, as I was sewing in my closet,[21]
    Lord Hamlet, with his doublet all unbraced,[22]
    No hat upon his head, his stockings fouled,
    Ungartered, and down-gyvèd[23] to his ankle,
    Pale as his shirt, his knees knocking each other,   80
    And with a look so piteous in purport,[24]
    As if he had been loosèd out of hell
    To speak of horrors — he comes before me.
POLONIUS: Mad for thy love?
OPHELIA: My lord, I do not know,
    But truly I do fear it.
POLONIUS: What said he?   85
OPHELIA: He took me by the wrist and held me hard;
    Then goes he to the length of all his arm,
    And with his other hand thus o'er his brow
    He falls to such perusal of my face
    As 'a would draw it. Long stayed he so.   90
    At last, a little shaking of mine arm,
    And thrice his head thus waving up and down,
    He raised a sigh so piteous and profound
    As it did seem to shatter all his bulk
    And end his being. That done, he lets me go,   95
    And, with his head over his shoulder turned,
    He seemed to find his way without his eyes,

[17] far-reaching awareness(?)
[18] circuitous courses
[19] indirect attempts (metaphor from bowling; *bias* = curved course)
[20] for yourself

[21] private room
[22] jacket entirely unlaced
[23] hanging down like fetters
[24] expression

For out o' doors he went without their helps,
And to the last bended their light on me.
POLONIUS: Come, go with me. I will go seek the King.   100
This is the very ecstasy[25] of love,
Whose violent property fordoes[26] itself
And leads the will to desperate undertakings
As oft as any passions under heaven
That does afflict our natures. I am sorry.   105
What, have you given him any hard words of late?
OPHELIA: No, my good lord; but as you did command,
I did repel his letters and denied
His access to me.
POLONIUS: That hath made him mad.
I am sorry that with better heed and judgment   110
I had not quoted[27] him. I feared he did but trifle
And meant to wrack thee; but beshrew my jealousy.[28]
By heaven, it is as proper[29] to our age
To cast beyond ourselves[30] in our opinions
As it is common for the younger sort   115
To lack discretion. Come, go we to the King.
This must be known, which, being kept close, might move
More grief to hide than hate to utter love.[31]
Come.   (*Exeunt.*)

SCENE 2. [THE CASTLE.]

Flourish. Enter KING *and* QUEEN, ROSENCRANTZ, *and* GUILDENSTERN [*with others*].

KING: Welcome, dear Rosencrantz and Guildenstern.
Moreover that[1] we much did long to see you,
The need we have to use you did provoke
Our hasty sending. Something have you heard
Of Hamlet's transformation: so call it,   5
Sith[2] nor th' exterior nor the inward man
Resembles that it was. What it should be,
More than his father's death, that thus hath put him
So much from th' understanding of himself,
I cannot dream of. I entreat you both   10
That, being of so[3] young days brought up with him,
And sith so neighbored to his youth and havior,[4]

[25] madness
[26] quality destroys
[27] noted
[28] curse on my suspicions
[29] natural
[30] to be overcalculating
[31] (the general meaning is that while tell-

ing the King of Hamlet's love may anger the King, more grief would come from keeping it secret)
[1] beside the fact that
[2] since
[3] from such
[4] behavior in his youth

That you vouchsafe your rest[5] here in our court
Some little time, so by your companies
To draw him on to pleasures, and to gather   15
So much as from occasion you may glean,
Whether aught to us unknown afflicts him thus,
That opened[6] lies within our remedy.
QUEEN: Good gentlemen, he hath much talked of you,
And sure I am, two men there is not living   20
To whom he more adheres. If it will please you
To show us so much gentry[7] and good will
As to expend your time with us awhile
For the supply and profit of our hope,
Your visitation shall receive such thanks   25
As fits a king's remembrance.
ROSENCRANTZ: Both your Majesties
Might, by the sovereign power you have of us,
Put your dread pleasures more into command
Than to entreaty.
GUILDENSTERN: But we both obey,
And here give up ourselves in the full bent[8]   30
To lay our service freely at your feet,
To be commanded.
KING: Thanks, Rosencrantz and gentle Guildenstern.
QUEEN: Thanks, Guildenstern and gentle Rosencrantz.
And I beseech you instantly to visit   35
My too much changèd son. Go, some of you,
And bring these gentlemen where Hamlet is.
GUILDENSTERN: Heavens make our presence and our practices
Pleasant and helpful to him!
QUEEN: Ay, amen!
     (*Exeunt* ROSENCRANTZ *and* GUILDENSTERN [*with some* ATTENDANTS].)

     (*Enter* POLONIUS.)

POLONIUS: Th' ambassadors from Norway, my good lord,   40
Are joyfully returned.
KING: Thou still[9] hast been the father of good news.
POLONIUS: Have I, my lord? Assure you, my good liege,
I hold my duty, as I hold my soul,
Both to my God and to my gracious king;   45
And I do think, or else this brain of mine
Hunts not the trail of policy so sure[10]
As it hath used to do, that I have found
The very cause of Hamlet's lunacy.

---

[5] consent to remain
[6] revealed
[7] courtesy
[8] entirely (the figure is of a bow bent to its capacity)

[9] always
[10] does not follow clues of political doings with such sureness

KING: O, speak of that! That do I long to hear.   50
POLONIUS: Give first admittance to th' ambassadors.
   My news shall be the fruit to that great feast.
KING: Thyself do grace to them and bring them in.   [*Exit* POLONIUS.]
   He tells me, my dear Gertrude, he hath found
   The head and source of all your son's distemper.   55
QUEEN: I doubt[11] it is no other but the main,[12]
   His father's death and our o'erhasty marriage.
KING: Well, we shall sift him.

   (*Enter* POLONIUS, VOLTEMAND, *and* CORNELIUS.)

                     Welcome, my good friends.
   Say, Voltemand, what from our brother Norway?
VOLTEMAND: Most fair return of greetings and desires.   60
   Upon our first,[13] he sent out to suppress
   His nephew's levies, which to him appeared
   To be a preparation 'gainst the Polack;
   But better looked into, he truly found
   It was against your Highness, whereat grieved,   65
   That so his sickness, age, and impotence
   Was falsely borne in hand,[14] sends out arrests
   On Fortinbras; which he, in brief, obeys,
   Receives rebuke from Norway, and in fine,[15]
   Makes vow before his uncle never more   70
   To give th' assay[16] of arms against your Majesty.
   Whereon old Norway, overcome with joy,
   Gives him threescore thousand crowns in annual fee
   And his commission to employ those soldiers,
   So levied as before, against the Polack,   75
   With an entreaty, herein further shown,   [*Gives a paper.*]
   That it might please you to give quiet pass
   Through your dominions for this enterprise,
   On such regards of safety and allowance[17]
   As therein are set down.
KING: It likes us well;   80
   And at our more considered time[18] we'll read,
   Answer, and think upon this business.
   Meantime, we thank you for your well-took labor.
   Go to your rest; at night we'll feast together.
   Most welcome home!   (*Exeunt* AMBASSADORS.)
POLONIUS: This business is well ended.   85
   My liege and madam, to expostulate[19]
   What majesty should be, what duty is,

---

[11] suspect
[12] principal point
[13] first audience
[14] deceived
[15] finally

[16] trial
[17] i.e., conditions
[18] time proper for considering
[19] discuss

Why day is day, night night, and time is time,
Were nothing but to waste night, day, and time.
Therefore, since brevity is the soul of wit,[20]   90
And tediousness the limbs and outward flourishes,
I will be brief. Your noble son is mad.
Mad call I it, for, to define true madness,
What is't but to be nothing else but mad?
But let that go.
QUEEN: More matter, with less art.   95
POLONIUS: Madam, I swear I use no art at all.
That he's mad, 'tis true: 'tis true 'tis pity,
And pity 'tis 'tis true — a foolish figure.[21]
But farewell it, for I will use no art.
Mad let us grant him then; and now remains   100
That we find out the cause of this effect,
Or rather say, the cause of this defect,
For this effect defective comes by cause.
Thus it remains, and the remainder thus.
Perpend.[22]   105
I have a daughter: have, while she is mine,
Who in her duty and obedience, mark,
Hath given me this. Now gather, and surmise.

([*Reads*] *the letter*.)

"To the celestial, and my soul's idol, the most beautified
Ophelia" —

That's an ill phrase, a vile phrase; "beautified" is a vile phrase. But you shall   110
hear. Thus:

"In her excellent white bosom, these, &c."

QUEEN: Came this from Hamlet to her?
POLONIUS: Good madam, stay awhile. I will be faithful.

           "Doubt thou the stars are fire,   115
              Doubt that the sun doth move;
           Doubt[23] truth to be a liar,
              But never doubt I love.

O dear Ophelia, I am ill at these numbers.[24] I have not art to reckon my
groans; but that I love thee best, O most best, believe it. Adieu.   120
                        Thine evermore, most dear lady,
              whilst this machine[25] is to him, HAMLET."

This in obedience hath my daughter shown me,
And more above[26] hath his solicitings,

---

[20] wisdom, understanding   [24] unskilled in verses
[21] figure of rhetoric   [25] complex device (here, his body)
[22] consider carefully   [26] in addition
[23] suspect

As they fell out by time, by means, and place,   125
All given to mine ear.

KING: But how hath she
Received his love?

POLONIUS: What do you think of me?

KING: As of a man faithful and honorable.

POLONIUS: I would fain prove so. But what might you think,
When I had seen this hot love on the wing   130
(As I perceived it, I must tell you that,
Before my daughter told me), what might you,
Or my dear Majesty your Queen here, think,
If I had played the desk or table book,[27]
Or given my heart a winking,[28] mute and dumb,   135
Or looked upon this love with idle sight?
What might you think? No, I went round to work
And my young mistress thus I did bespeak:
"Lord Hamlet is a prince, out of thy star.[29]
This must not be." And then I prescripts gave her,   140
That she should lock herself from his resort,
Admit no messengers, receive no tokens.
Which done, she took the fruits of my advice,
And he, repellèd, a short tale to make,
Fell into a sadness, then into a fast,   145
Thence to a watch,[30] thence into a weakness,
Thence to a lightness,[31] and, by this declension,
Into the madness wherein now he raves,
And all we mourn for.

KING: Do you think 'tis this?

QUEEN: It may be, very like.   150

POLONIUS: Hath there been such a time, I would fain know that,
That I have positively said " 'Tis so,"
When it proved otherwise?

KING: Not that I know.

POLONIUS [pointing to his head and shoulder]: Take this from this, if this be
    otherwise.
If circumstances lead me, I will find   155
Where truth is hid, though it were hid indeed
Within the center.[32]

KING: How may we try it further?

POLONIUS: You know sometimes he walks four hours together
Here in the lobby.

QUEEN: So he does indeed.

POLONIUS: At such a time I'll loose my daughter to him.   160
Be you and I behind an arras[33] then.

---

[27] i.e., been a passive recipient of secrets
[28] closing of the eyes
[29] sphere
[30] wakefulness

[31] mental derangement
[32] center of the earth
[33] tapestry hanging in front of a wall

Mark the encounter. If he love her not,
And be not from his reason fall'n thereon,
Let me be no assistant for a state
But keep a farm and carters.

KING: We will try it.   165

(*Enter* HAMLET *reading on a book*.)

QUEEN: But look where sadly the poor wretch comes reading.
POLONIUS: Away, I do beseech you both, away.   (*Exit* KING *and* QUEEN.)
 I'll board him presently.[34] O, give me leave.
 How does my good Lord Hamlet?
HAMLET: Well, God-a-mercy.   170
POLONIUS: Do you know me, my lord?
HAMLET: Excellent well. You are a fishmonger.[35]
POLONIUS: Not I, my lord.
HAMLET: Then I would you were so honest a man.
POLONIUS: Honest, my lord?   175
HAMLET: Ay, sir. To be honest, as this world goes, is to be one man picked out
 of ten thousand.
POLONIUS: That's very true, my lord.
HAMLET: For if the sun breed maggots in a dead dog, being a good kissing
 carrion[36] —— Have you a daughter?   180
POLONIUS: I have, my lord.
HAMLET: Let her not walk i' th' sun. Conception[37] is a blessing, but as your
 daughter may conceive, friend, look to't.
POLONIUS [*aside*]: How say you by that? Still harping on my daughter. Yet he
 knew me not at first. 'A said I was a fishmonger. 'A is far gone, far gone. And   185
 truly in my youth I suffered much extremity for love, very near this. I'll
 speak to him again. — What do you read, my lord?
HAMLET: Words, words, words.
POLONIUS: What is the matter, my lord?
HAMLET: Between who?   190
POLONIUS: I mean the matter[38] that you read, my lord.
HAMLET: Slanders, sir; for the satirical rogue says here that old men have gray
 beards, that their faces are wrinkled, their eyes purging thick amber and
 plumtree gum, and that they have a plentiful lack of wit, together with most
 weak hams. All which, sir, though I most powerfully and potently believe,   195
 yet I hold it not honesty[39] to have it thus set down; for you yourself, sir,
 should be old as I am if, like a crab, you could go backward.
POLONIUS [*aside*]: Though this be madness, yet there is method in't. Will you
 walk out of the air, my lord?
HAMLET: Into my grave.   200

---

[34] accost him at once
[35] dealer in fish (slang for a procurer)
[36] (perhaps the meaning is "a good piece of flesh to kiss," but many editors emend *good* to *god*, taking the word to refer to the sun)
[37] (1) understanding, (2) becoming pregnant

[38] (Polonius means "subject matter," but Hamlet pretends to take the word in the sense of "quarrel")
[39] decency

POLONIUS: Indeed, that's out of the air. [*Aside.*] How pregnant[40] sometimes his replies are! A happiness[41] that often madness hits on, which reason and sanity could not so prosperously be delivered of. I will leave him and suddenly contrive the means of meeting between him and my daughter. — My lord, I will take my leave of you.   205

HAMLET: You cannot take from me anything that I will more willingly part withal — except my life, except my life, except my life.

(*Enter* GUILDENSTERN *and* ROSENCRANTZ.)

POLONIUS: Fare you well, my lord.

HAMLET: These tedious old fools!

POLONIUS: You go to seek the Lord Hamlet? There he is.   210

ROSENCRANTZ [*to* POLONIUS]: God save you, sir!   [*Exit* POLONIUS.]

GUILDENSTERN: My honored lord!

ROSENCRANTZ: My most dear lord!

HAMLET: My excellent good friends! How dost thou, Guildenstern? Ah, Rosencrantz! Good lads, how do you both?   215

ROSENCRANTZ: As the indifferent[42] children of the earth.

GUILDENSTERN: Happy in that we are not overhappy.
On Fortune's cap we are not the very button.

HAMLET: Nor the soles of her shoe?

ROSENCRANTZ: Neither, my lord.   220

HAMLET: Then you live about her waist, or in the middle of her favors?

GUILDENSTERN: Faith, her privates[43] we.

HAMLET: In the secret parts of Fortune? O, most true! She is a strumpet. What news?

ROSENCRANTZ: None, my lord, but that the world's grown honest.   225

HAMLET: Then is doomsday near. But your news is not true. Let me question more in particular. What have you, my good friends, deserved at the hands of Fortune that she sends you to prison hither?

GUILDENSTERN: Prison, my lord?

HAMLET: Denmark's a prison.   230

ROSENCRANTZ: Then is the world one.

HAMLET: A goodly one, in which there are many confines, wards,[44] and dungeons, Denmark being one o' th' worst.

ROSENCRANTZ: We think not so, my lord.

HAMLET: Why, then 'tis none to you, for there is nothing either good or bad but 235
thinking makes it so. To me it is a prison.

ROSENCRANTZ: Why then your ambition makes it one. 'Tis too narrow for your mind.

HAMLET: O God, I could be bounded in a nutshell and count myself a king of infinite space, were it not that I have bad dreams.   240

GUILDENSTERN: Which dreams indeed are ambition, for the very substance of the ambitious is merely the shadow of a dream.

HAMLET: A dream itself is but a shadow.

---

[40] meaningful
[41] apt turn of phrase
[42] ordinary

[43] ordinary men (with a pun on "private parts")
[44] cells

ROSENCRANTZ: Truly, and I hold ambition of so airy and light a quality that it is but a shadow's shadow. 245

HAMLET: Then are our beggars bodies, and our monarchs and outstretched heroes the beggars' shadows.[45] Shall we to th' court? For, by my fay,[46] I cannot reason.

BOTH: We'll wait upon you.

HAMLET: No such matter. I will not sort you with the rest of my servants, for, to 250 speak to you like an honest man, I am most dreadfully attended. But in the beaten way of friendship, what make you at Elsinore?

ROSENCRANTZ: To visit you, my lord; no other occasion.

HAMLET: Beggar that I am, I am even poor in thanks, but I thank you; and sure, dear friends, my thanks are too dear a halfpenny.[47] Were you not sent for? Is 255 it your own inclining? Is it a free visitation? Come, come, deal justly with me. Come, come; nay, speak.

GUILDENSTERN: What should we say, my lord?

HAMLET: Why anything — but to th' purpose. You were sent for, and there is a kind of confession in your looks, which your modesties have not craft 260 enough to color. I know the good King and Queen have sent for you.

ROSENCRANTZ: To what end, my lord?

HAMLET: That you must teach me. But let me conjure you by the rights of our fellowship, by the consonancy of our youth, by the obligation of our ever-preserved love, and by what more dear a better proposer can charge you 265 withal, be even and direct with me, whether you were sent for or no.

ROSENCRANTZ [aside to GUILDENSTERN]: What say you?

HAMLET [aside]: Nay then, I have an eye of you. — If you love me, hold not off.

GUILDENSTERN: My lord, we were sent for. 270

HAMLET: I will tell you why; so shall my anticipation prevent your discovery,[48] and your secrecy to the King and Queen molt no feather. I have of late, but wherefore I know not, lost all my mirth, forgone all custom of exercises; and indeed, it goes so heavily with my disposition that this goodly frame, the earth, seems to me a sterile promontory; this most excellent canopy, the air, 275 look you, this brave o'erhanging firmament, this majestical roof fretted[49] with golden fire: why, it appeareth nothing to me but a foul and pestilent congregation of vapors. What a piece of work is a man, how noble in reason, how infinite in faculties, in form and moving how express[50] and admirable, in action how like an angel, in apprehension how like a god: the beauty of 280 the world, the paragon of animals; and yet to me, what is this quintessence of dust? Man delights not me; nor woman neither, though by your smiling you seem to say so.

ROSENCRANTZ: My lord, there was no such stuff in my thoughts.

HAMLET: Why did ye laugh then, when I said "Man delights not me"? 285

ROSENCRANTZ: To think, my lord, if you delight not in man, what lenten[51]

---

[45] i.e., by your logic, beggars (lacking ambition) are substantial, and great men are elongated shadows
[46] faith
[47] i.e., not worth a halfpenny

[48] forestall your disclosure
[49] adorned
[50] exact
[51] meager

entertainment the players shall receive from you. We coted[52] them on the
way, and hither are they coming to offer you service.

HAMLET: He that plays the king shall be welcome; his Majesty shall have tribute
of me; the adventurous knight shall use his foil and target;[53] the lover shall   290
not sigh gratis; the humorous man[54] shall end his part in peace; the clown
shall make those laugh whose lungs are tickle o' th' sere;[55] and the lady shall
say her mind freely, or[56] the blank verse shall halt[57] for't. What players are
they?

ROSENCRANTZ: Even those you were wont to take such delight in, the tragedi-   295
ans of the city.

HAMLET: How chances it they travel? Their residence, both in reputation and
profit, was better both ways.

ROSENCRANTZ: I think their inhibition[58] comes by the means of the late innovation.[59]   300

HAMLET: Do they hold the same estimation they did when I was in the city? Are
they so followed?

ROSENCRANTZ: No indeed, are they not.

HAMLET: How comes it? Do they grow rusty?

ROSENCRANTZ: Nay, their endeavor keeps in the wonted pace, but there is, sir,   305
an eyrie[60] of children, little eyases, that cry out on the top of question[61] and
are most tyrannically[62] clapped for't. These are now the fashion, and so
berattle the common stages[63] (so they call them) that many wearing rapiers
are afraid of goosequills[64] and dare scarce come thither.

HAMLET: What, are they children? Who maintains 'em? How are they   310
escoted?[65] Will they pursue the quality[66] no longer than they can sing? Will
they not say afterwards, if they should grow themselves to common players
(as it is most like, if their means are no better), their writers do them wrong
to make them exclaim against their own succession?[67]

ROSENCRANTZ: Faith, there has been much to-do on both sides, and the nation   315
holds it no sin to tarre[68] them to controversy. There was, for a while, no
money bid for argument[69] unless the poet and the player went to cuffs in the
question.

HAMLET: Is't possible?

GUILDENSTERN: O, there has been much throwing about of brains.   320

HAMLET: Do the boys carry it away?

---

[52] overtook
[53] shield
[54] i.e., eccentric man (among stock characters in dramas were men dominated by a
"humor" or odd trait)
[55] on hair trigger (sere = part of the gun-
lock)
[56] else
[57] limp
[58] hindrance
[59] (probably an allusion to the companies
of child actors that had become popular and
were offering serious competition to the
adult actors)

[60] nest
[61] unfledged hawks that cry shrilly above
others in matters of debate
[62] violently
[63] cry down the public theaters (with the
adult acting companies)
[64] pens (of satirists who ridicule the public
theaters and their audiences)
[65] financially supported
[66] profession of acting
[67] future
[68] incite
[69] plot of a play

ROSENCRANTZ: Ay, that they do, my lord — Hercules and his load[70] too.

HAMLET: It is not very strange, for my uncle is King of Denmark, and those
that would make mouths at him while my father lived give twenty, forty,
fifty, a hundred ducats apiece for his picture in little. 'Sblood,[71] there is   325
something in this more than natural, if philosophy could find it out.

(A flourish.)

GUILDENSTERN: There are the players.

HAMLET: Gentlemen, you are welcome to Elsinore. Your hands, come then.
Th' appurtenance of welcome is fashion and ceremony. Let me comply[72]
with you in this garb,[73] lest my extent[74] to the players (which I tell you must   330
show fairly outwards) should more appear like entertainment than yours.
You are welcome. But my uncle-father and aunt-mother are deceived.

GUILDENSTERN: In what, my dear lord?

HAMLET: I am but mad north-northwest:[75] when the wind is southerly I know a
hawk from a handsaw.[76]   335

(Enter POLONIUS.)

POLONIUS: Well be with you, gentlemen.

HAMLET: Hark you, Guildenstern, and you too; at each ear a hearer. That great
baby you see there is not yet out of his swaddling clouts.

ROSENCRANTZ: Happily[77] he is the second time come to them, for they say an
old man is twice a child.   340

HAMLET: I will prophesy he comes to tell me of the players. Mark it. — You say
right, sir; a Monday morning, 'twas then indeed.

POLONIUS: My lord, I have news to tell you.

HAMLET: My lord, I have news to tell you. When Roscius[78] was an actor in
Rome ——   345

POLONIUS: The actors are come hither, my lord.

HAMLET: Buzz, buzz.[79]

POLONIUS: Upon my honor ——

HAMLET: Then came each actor on his ass ——

POLONIUS: The best actors in the world, either for tragedy, comedy, history,   350
pastoral, pastoral-comical, historical-pastoral, tragical-historical, tragical-
comical-historical-pastoral; scene individable,[80] or poem unlimited.[81] Seneca[82] cannot be too heavy, nor Plautus[83] too light. For the law of writ and
the liberty,[84] these are the only men.

[70] i.e., the whole world (with a reference to the Globe Theater, which had a sign that represented Hercules bearing the globe)
[71] by God's blood
[72] be courteous
[73] outward show
[74] behavior
[75] i.e., on one point of the compass only
[76] (hawk can refer not only to a bird but to a kind of pickax; handsaw — a carpenter's tool — may involve a similar pun on "hernshaw," a heron)
[77] perhaps

[78] a famous Roman comic actor
[79] (an interjection, perhaps indicating that the news is old)
[80] plays observing the unities of time, place, and action
[81] plays not restricted by the tenets of criticism
[82] Roman tragic dramatist
[83] Roman comic dramatist
[84] (perhaps "for sticking to the text and for improvising"; perhaps "for classical plays and for modern loosely written plays")

HAMLET: O Jephthah, judge of Israel,[85] what a treasure hadst thou!   355
POLONIUS: What a treasure had he, my lord?
HAMLET: Why,

> "One fair daughter, and no more,
>   The which he lovèd passing well."

POLONIUS [aside]: Still on my daughter.   360
HAMLET: Am I not i' th' right, old Jephthah?
POLONIUS: If you call me Jephthah, my lord, I have a daughter that I love
    passing well.
HAMLET: Nay, that follows not.
POLONIUS: What follows then, my lord?   365
HAMLET: Why,

> "As by lot, God wot,"

and then, you know,

> "It came to pass, as most like it was."

The first row of the pious chanson[86] will show you more, for look where   370
my abridgment[87] comes.

(*Enter the* PLAYERS.)

You are welcome, masters, welcome, all. I am glad to see thee well. Welcome, good friends. O, old friend, why, thy face is valanced[88] since I saw
thee last. Com'st thou to beard me in Denmark? What, my young lady[89] and
mistress? By'r Lady, your ladyship is nearer to heaven than when I saw you   375
last by the altitude of a chopine.[90] Pray God your voice, like a piece of
uncurrent gold, be not cracked within the ring.[91] — Masters, you are all
welcome. We'll e'en to't like French falconers, fly at anything we see. We'll
have a speech straight. Come, give us a taste of your quality. Come, a passionate speech.   380
PLAYER: What speech, my good lord?
HAMLET: I heard thee speak me a speech once, but it was never acted, or if it
was, not above once, for the play, I remember, pleased not the million; 'twas
caviare to the general,[92] but it was (as I received it, and others, whose judgments in such matters cried in the top of[93] mine) an excellent play, well   385
digested in the scenes, set down with as much modesty as cunning.[94] I remember one said there were no sallets[95] in the lines to make the matter
savory; nor no matter in the phrase that might indict the author of affectation, but called it an honest method, as wholesome as sweet, and by very
much more handsome than fine.[96] One speech in't I chiefly loved. 'Twas   390

---

[85] the title of a ballad on the Hebrew judge
who sacrificed his daughter (see Judges 11)
    [86] stanza of the scriptural song
    [87] (1) i.e., entertainers, who abridge the
time, (2) interrupters
    [88] fringed (with a beard)
    [89] i.e., boy for female roles
    [90] thick-soled shoe
    [91] (a coin was unfit for legal tender if a
crack extended from the edge through the

ring enclosing the monarch's head. Hamlet,
punning on *ring*, refers to the change of
voice that the boy actor will undergo)
    [92] i.e., too choice for the multitude
    [93] overtopping
    [94] restraint as art
    [95] salads, spicy jests
    [96] well-proportioned rather than orna-
mented

Aeneas' tale to Dido, and thereabout of it especially when he speaks of
Priam's slaughter. If it live in your memory, begin at this line — let me see,
let me see:

> "The rugged Pyrrhus, like th' Hyrcanian beast[97] ——"

'Tis not so; it begins with Pyrrhus: 395

> "The rugged Pyrrhus, he whose sable[98] arms,
> Black as his purpose, did the night resemble
> When he lay couchèd in th' ominous horse,[99]
> Hath now this dread and black complexion smeared
> With heraldry more dismal.[100] Head to foot   400
> Now is he total gules, horridly tricked[101]
> With blood of fathers, mothers, daughters, sons,
> Baked and impasted[102] with the parching streets,
> That lend a tyrannous and a damnèd light
> To their lord's murder. Roasted in wrath and fire,   405
> And thus o'ersizèd[103] with coagulate gore,
> With eyes like carbuncles, the hellish Pyrrhus
> Old grandsire Priam seeks."

So, proceed you.

POLONIUS: Fore God, my lord, well spoken, with good accent and good discretion.   410

PLAYER:

> "Anon he finds him,
> Striking too short at Greeks. His antique sword,
> Rebellious to his arm, lies where it falls
> Repugnant to command.[104] Unequal matched,
> Pyrrhus at Priam drives, in rage strikes wide,   415
> But with the whiff and wind of his fell sword
> Th' unnervèd father falls. Then senseless Ilium,[105]
> Seeming to feel this blow, with flaming top
> Stoops to his base,[106] and with a hideous crash
> Takes prisoner Pyrrhus' ear. For lo, his sword,   420
> Which was declining on the milky head
> Of reverend Priam, seemed i' th' air to stick.
> So as a painted tyrant[107] Pyrrhus stood,
> And like a neutral to his will and matter[108]
> Did nothing.   425
> But as we often see, against[109] some storm,
> A silence in the heavens, the rack[110] stand still,
> The bold winds speechless, and the orb below

---

[97] i.e., tiger (Hyrcania was in Asia)
[98] black
[99] i.e., wooden horse at the siege of Troy
[100] ill-omened
[101] all red, horridly adorned
[102] encrusted
[103] smeared over

[104] disobedient
[105] insensate Troy
[106] collapses (*his* = its)
[107] tyrant in a picture
[108] task
[109] just before
[110] clouds

As hush as death, anon the dreadful thunder
Doth rend the region, so after Pyrrhus' pause,   430
A rousèd vengeance sets him new awork,
And never did the Cyclops' hammers fall
On Mars's armor, forged for proof eterne,[111]
With less remorse than Pyrrhus' bleeding sword
Now falls on Priam.   435
Out, out, thou strumpet Fortune! All you gods,
In general synod[112] take away her power,
Break all the spokes and fellies[113] from her wheel,
And bowl the round nave[114] down the hill of heaven,
As low as to the fiends."   440

POLONIUS: This is too long.
HAMLET: It shall to the barber's, with your beard. — Prithee say on. He's for a
jig or a tale of bawdry, or he sleeps. Say on; come to Hecuba.
PLAYER:

"But who (ah woe!) had seen the mobled[115] queen — "

HAMLET: "The mobled queen"?   445
POLONIUS: That's good. "Mobled queen" is good.
PLAYER:

"Run barefoot up and down, threat'ning the flames
With bisson rheum,[116] a clout[117] upon that head
Where late the diadem stood, and for a robe,
About her lank and all o'erteemèd[118] loins,   450
A blanket in the alarm of fear caught up —
Who this had seen, with tongue in venom steeped
'Gainst Fortune's state would treason have pronounced.
But if the gods themselves did see her then,
When she saw Pyrrhus make malicious sport   455
In mincing with his sword her husband's limbs,
The instant burst of clamor that she made
(Unless things mortal move them not at all)
Would have made milch[119] the burning eyes of heaven
And passion in the gods."   460

POLONIUS: Look, whe'r[120] he has not turned his color, and has tears in's eyes.
Prithee no more.
HAMLET: 'Tis well. I'll have thee speak out the rest of this soon. Good my lord,
will you see the players well bestowed?[121] Do you hear? Let them be well
used, for they are the abstract and brief chronicles of the time. After your   465
death you were better have a bad epitaph than their ill report while you live.

[111] eternal endurance
[112] council
[113] rims
[114] hub
[115] muffled
[116] blinding tears

[117] rag
[118] exhausted with childbearing
[119] moist (literally, "milk-giving")
[120] whether
[121] housed

POLONIUS: My lord, I will use them according to their desert.

HAMLET: God's bodkin,[122] man, much better! Use every man after his desert,
and who shall scape whipping? Use them after your own honor and dignity.
The less they deserve, the more merit is in your bounty. Take them in.   470

POLONIUS: Come, sirs.

HAMLET: Follow him, friends. We'll hear a play tomorrow. [*Aside to* PLAYER.]
Dost thou hear me, old friend! Can you play *The Murder of Gonzago?*

PLAYER: Ay, my lord.

HAMLET: We'll ha't tomorrow night. You could for a need study a speech of   475
some dozen or sixteen lines which I would set down and insert in't, could
you not?

PLAYER: Ay, my lord.

HAMLET: Very well. Follow that lord, and look you mock him not. My good
friends, I'll leave you till night. You are welcome to Elsinore.   480

                              (*Exeunt* POLONIUS *and* PLAYERS.)

ROSENCRANTZ: Good my lord.   (*Exeunt* [ROSENCRANTZ *and* GUILDENSTERN].)

HAMLET: Ay, so, God bye to you. — Now I am alone.
O, what a rogue and peasant slave am I!
Is it not monstrous that this player here,
But in a fiction, in a dream of passion,[123]   485
Could force his soul so to his own conceit[124]
That from her working all his visage wanned,
Tears in his eyes, distraction in his aspect,
A broken voice, and his whole function[125] suiting
With forms[126] to his conceit? And all for nothing!   490
For Hecuba!
What's Hecuba to him, or he to Hecuba,
That he should weep for her! What would he do
Had he the motive and the cue for passion
That I have? He would drown the stage with tears   495
And cleave the general ear with horrid speech,
Make mad the guilty and appall the free,[127]
Confound the ignorant, and amaze indeed
The very faculties of eyes and ears.
Yet I,   500
A dull and muddy-mettled[128] rascal, peak
Like John-a-dreams,[129] unpregnant of[130] my cause,
And can say nothing. No, not for a king,
Upon whose property and most dear life
A damned defeat was made. Am I a coward?   505
Who calls me villain? Breaks my pate across?
Plucks off my beard and blows it in my face?
Tweaks me by the nose? Gives me the lie i' th' throat
As deep as to the lungs? Who does me this?

---

[122] by God's little body
[123] imaginary emotion
[124] imagination
[125] action
[126] bodily expressions

[127] terrify (make pale?) the guiltless
[128] weak-spirited
[129] mope like a dreamer
[130] unquickened by

Ha, 'swounds,[131] I should take it, for it cannot be   510
But I am pigeon-livered[132] and lack gall
To make oppression bitter, or ere this
I should ha' fatted all the region kites[133]
With this slave's offal. Bloody, bawdy villain!
Remorseless, treacherous, lecherous, kindless[134] villain!   515
O, vengeance!
Why, what an ass am I! This is most brave,[135]
That I, the son of a dear father murdered,
Prompted to my revenge by heaven and hell,
Must, like a whore, unpack my heart with words   520
And fall a-cursing like a very drab,[136]
A stallion![137] Fie upon't, foh! About,[138] my brains.
Hum ——
I have heard that guilty creatures sitting at a play
Have by the very cunning of the scene   525
Been struck so to the soul that presently[139]
They have proclaimed their malefactions.
For murder, though it have no tongue, will speak
With most miraculous organ. I'll have these players
Play something like the murder of my father   530
Before mine uncle. I'll observe his looks,
I'll tent[140] him to the quick. If 'a do blench,[141]
I know my course. The spirit that I have seen
May be a devil, and the devil hath power
T' assume a pleasing shape, yea, and perhaps   535
Out of my weakness and my melancholy,
As he is very potent with such spirits,
Abuses me to damn me. I'll have grounds
More relative[142] than this. The play's the thing
Wherein I'll catch the conscience of the king.   (*Exit.*) 540

ACT III

SCENE 1. [THE CASTLE.]

Enter KING, QUEEN, POLONIUS, OPHELIA; ROSENCRANTZ, GUILDENSTERN, LORDS.

KING: And can you by no drift of conference[1]
    Get from him why he puts on this confusion,

---

[131] by God's wounds
[132] gentle as a dove
[133] kites (scavenger birds) of the sky
[134] unnatural
[135] fine
[136] prostitute
[137] male prostitute (perhaps one should adopt the Folio reading, *scullion* = kitchen wench)
[138] to work
[139] immediately
[140] probe
[141] flinch
[142] (probably "pertinent," but possibly "able to be related plausibly")
[1] management of conversation

Grating so harshly all his days of quiet
With turbulent and dangerous lunacy?
ROSENCRANTZ: He does confess he feels himself distracted,   5
But from what cause 'a will by no means speak.
GUILDENSTERN: Nor do we find him forward to be sounded,[2]
But with a crafty madness keeps aloof
When we would bring him on to some confession
Of his true state.
QUEEN: Did he receive you well?   10
ROSENCRANTZ: Most like a gentleman.
GUILDENSTERN: But with much forcing of his disposition.[3]
ROSENCRANTZ: Niggard of question,[4] but of our demands
Most free in his reply.
QUEEN: Did you assay[5] him
To any pastime?   15
ROSENCRANTZ: Madam, it so fell out that certain players
We o'erraught[6] on the way; of these we told him,
And there did seem in him a kind of joy
To hear of it. They are here about the court,
And, as I think, they have already order   20
This night to play before him.
POLONIUS: 'Tis most true,
And he beseeched me to entreat your Majesties
To hear and see the matter.
KING: With all my heart, and it doth much content me
To hear him so inclined.   25
Good gentlemen, give him a further edge
And drive his purpose into these delights.
ROSENCRANTZ: We shall, my lord.
                        (*Exeunt* ROSENCRANTZ *and* GUILDENSTERN.)
KING: Sweet Gertrude, leave us too,
For we have closely[7] sent for Hamlet hither,
That he, as 'twere by accident, may here   30
Affront[8] Ophelia.
Her father and myself (lawful espials[9])
Will so bestow ourselves that, seeing unseen,
We may of their encounter frankly judge
And gather by him, as he is behaved,   35
If't be th' affliction of his love or no
That thus he suffers for.
QUEEN: I shall obey you.
And for your part, Ophelia, I do wish
That your good beauties be the happy cause

---

[2] willing to be questioned   [6] overtook
[3] effort   [7] secretly
[4] uninclined to talk   [8] meet face to face
[5] tempt   [9] spies

Of Hamlet's wildness. So shall I hope your virtues   40
Will bring him to his wonted way again,
To both your honors.
OPHELIA: Madam, I wish it may.   [*Exit* QUEEN.]
POLONIUS: Ophelia, walk you here. — Gracious, so please you,
We will bestow ourselves. [*To* OPHELIA.] Read on this book,
That show of such an exercise may color[10]   45
Your loneliness. We are oft to blame in this,
'Tis too much proved, that with devotion's visage
And pious action we do sugar o'er
The devil himself.
KING [*aside*]:   O, 'tis too true.
How smart a lash that speech doth give my conscience!   50
The harlot's cheek, beautied with plast'ring art,
Is not more ugly to the thing that helps it
Than is my deed to my most painted word.
O heavy burden!
POLONIUS: I hear him coming. Let's withdraw, my lord.   55
                                    [*Exeunt* KING *and* POLONIUS.]

(*Enter* HAMLET.)

HAMLET: To be, or not to be: that is the question:
Whether 'tis nobler in the mind to suffer
The slings and arrows of outrageous fortune,
Or to take arms against a sea of troubles,
And by opposing end them. To die, to sleep —   60
No more — and by a sleep to say we end
The heartache, and the thousand natural shocks
That flesh is heir to! 'Tis a consummation
Devoutly to be wished. To die, to sleep —
To sleep — perchance to dream: ay, there's the rub,[11]   65
For in that sleep of death what dreams may come
When we have shuffled off this mortal coil,[12]
Must give us pause. There's the respect[13]
That makes calamity of so long life:[14]
For who would bear the whips and scorns of time,   70
Th' oppressor's wrong, the proud man's contumely,
The pangs of despised love, the law's delay,
The insolence of office, and the spurns
That patient merit of th' unworthy takes,
When he himself might his quietus[15] make   75

[10] act of devotion may give a plausible hue to (the book is one of devotion)
[11] impediment (obstruction to a bowler's ball)
[12] (1) turmoil, (2) a ring of rope (here the flesh encircling the soul)
[13] consideration
[14] (1) makes calamity so long-lived, (2) makes living so long a calamity
[15] full discharge (a legal term)

With a bare bodkin?[16] Who would fardels[17] bear,
To grunt and sweat under a weary life,
But that the dread of something after death,
The undiscovered country, from whose bourn[18]
No traveler returns, puzzles the will,   80
And makes us rather bear those ills we have,
Than fly to others that we know not of?
Thus conscience[19] does make cowards of us all,
And thus the native hue of resolution
Is sicklied o'er with the pale cast[20] of thought,   85
And enterprises of great pitch[21] and moment,
With this regard[22] their currents turn awry,
And lose the name of action. — Soft you now,
The fair Ophelia! — Nymph, in thy orisons[23]
Be all my sins remembered.
OPHELIA: Good my lord,   90
  How does your honor for this many a day?
HAMLET: I humbly thank you; well, well, well.
OPHELIA: My lord, I have remembrances of yours
  That I have longèd long to redeliver.
  I pray you now, receive them.
HAMLET: No, not I,   95
  I never gave you aught.
OPHELIA: My honored lord, you know right well you did,
  And with them words of so sweet breath composed
  As made these things more rich. Their perfume lost,
  Take these again, for to the noble mind   100
  Rich gifts wax poor when givers prove unkind.
  There, my lord.
HAMLET: Ha, ha! Are you honest?[24]
OPHELIA: My lord?
HAMLET: Are you fair?   105
OPHELIA: What means your lordship?
HAMLET: That if you be honest and fair, your honesty should admit no dis-
  course to your beauty.[25]
OPHELIA: Could beauty, my lord, have better commerce than with honesty?
HAMLET: Ay, truly; for the power of beauty will sooner transform honesty from   110
  what it is to a bawd[26] than the force of honesty can translate beauty into his
  likeness. This was sometime a paradox, but now the time gives it proof. I did
  love you once.
OPHELIA: Indeed, my lord, you made me believe so.

---

[16] dagger
[17] burdens
[18] region
[19] self-consciousness, introspection
[20] color
[21] height (a term from falconry)
[22] consideration

[23] prayers
[24] (1) are you modest, (2) are you chaste, (3) have you integrity
[25] your modesty should permit no approach to your beauty
[26] procurer

HAMLET: You should not have believed me, for virtue cannot so inoculate[27] our   115
    old stock but we shall relish of it.[28] I loved you not.

OPHELIA: I was the more deceived.

HAMLET: Get thee to a nunnery. Why wouldst thou be a breeder of sinners? I
    am myself indifferent honest,[29] but yet I could accuse me of such things that
    it were better my mother had not borne me: I am very proud, revengeful,   120
    ambitious, with more offenses at my beck[30] than I have thoughts to put them
    in, imagination to give them shape, or time to act them in. What should
    such fellows as I do crawling between earth and heaven? We are arrant
    knaves all; believe none of us. Go thy ways to a nunnery. Where's your
    father?   125

OPHELIA: At home, my lord.

HAMLET: Let the doors be shut upon him, that he may play the fool nowhere
    but in's own house. Farewell.

OPHELIA: O help him, you sweet heavens!

HAMLET: If thou dost marry, I'll give thee this plague for thy dowry: be thou as   130
    chaste as ice, as pure as snow, thou shalt not escape calumny. Get thee to a
    nunnery. Go, farewell. Or if thou wilt needs marry, marry a fool, for wise
    men know well enough what monsters[31] you make of them. To a nunnery,
    go, and quickly too. Farewell.

OPHELIA: Heavenly powers, restore him!   135

HAMLET: I have heard of your paintings too, well enough. God hath given you
    one face, and you make yourselves another. You jig and amble, and you lisp;
    you nickname God's creatures and make your wantonness your ignorance.[32]
    Go to, I'll no more on't; it hath made me mad. I say we will have no moe[33]
    marriage. Those that are married already — all but one — shall live. The   140
    rest shall keep as they are. To a nunnery, go.   (*Exit.*)

OPHELIA: O what a noble mind is here o'erthrown!
    The courtier's, soldier's, scholar's, eye, tongue, sword,
    Th' expectancy and rose[34] of the fair state,
    The glass of fashion, and the mold of form,[35]   145
    Th' observed of all observers, quite, quite down!
    And I, of ladies most deject and wretched,
    That sucked the honey of his musicked vows,
    Now see that noble and most sovereign reason
    Like sweet bells jangled, out of time and harsh,   150
    That unmatched form and feature of blown[36] youth
    Blasted with ecstasy.[37] O, woe is me
    T' have seen what I have seen, see what I see!

(*Enter* KING *and* POLONIUS.)

---

[27] graft
[28] smack of it (our old sinful nature)
[29] moderately virtuous
[30] call
[31] horned beasts, cuckolds
[32] excuse your wanton speech by pretending ignorance

[33] more
[34] i.e., fair hope
[35] the mirror of fashion, and the pattern of excellent behavior
[36] blooming
[37] madness

KING: Love? His affections[38] do not that way tend,
  Nor what he spake, though it lacked form a little,   155
  Was not like madness. There's something in his soul
  O'er which his melancholy sits on brood,
  And I do doubt[39] the hatch and the disclose
  Will be some danger; which for to prevent,
  I have in quick determination   160
  Thus set it down: he shall with speed to England
  For the demand of our neglected tribute.
  Haply the seas, and countries different,
  With variable objects, shall expel
  This something-settled[40] matter in his heart,   165
  Whereon his brains still beating puts him thus
  From fashion of himself. What think you on't?
POLONIUS: It shall do well. But yet do I believe
  The origin and commencement of his grief
  Sprung from neglected love. How now, Ophelia?   170
  You need not tell us what Lord Hamlet said;
  We heard it all. My lord, do as you please,
  But if you hold it fit, after the play,
  Let his queen mother all alone entreat him
  To show his grief. Let her be round[41] with him,   175
  And I'll be placed, so please you, in the ear
  Of all their conference. If she find him not,[42]
  To England send him, or confine him where
  Your wisdom best shall think.
KING: It shall be so.
  Madness in great ones must not unwatched go.   (Exeunt.)   180

SCENE 2. [THE CASTLE.]

Enter HAMLET *and three of the* PLAYERS.

HAMLET: Speak the speech, I pray you, as I pronounced it to you, trippingly on
  the tongue. But if you mouth it, as many of our players do, I had as lief the
  town crier spoke my lines. Nor do not saw the air too much with your hand,
  thus, but use all gently, for in the very torrent, tempest, and (as I may say)
  whirlwind of your passion, you must acquire and beget a temperance that   5
  may give it smoothness. O, it offends me to the soul to hear a robustious
  periwig-pated[1] fellow tear a passion to tatters, to very rags, to split the ears of
  the groundlings,[2] who for the most part are capable of[3] nothing but inexplic-

---

[38] inclinations
[39] fear
[40] somewhat settled
[41] blunt
[42] does not find him out

[1] boisterous wig-headed
[2] those who stood in the pit of the theater
(the poorest and presumably most ignorant
of the audience)
[3] are able to understand

able dumb shows[4] and noise. I would have such a fellow whipped for
o'erdoing Termagant. It out-herods Herod.[5] Pray you avoid it.   10

PLAYER: I warrant your honor.

HAMLET: Be not too tame neither, but let your own discretion be your tutor.
Suit the action to the word, the word to the action, with this special observance, that you o'erstep not the modesty of nature. For anything so o'erdone
is from[6] the purpose of playing, whose end, both at the first and now, was   15
and is, to hold, as 'twere, the mirror up to nature; to show virtue her own
feature, scorn her own image, and the very age and body of the time his
form and pressure.[7] Now, this overdone, or come tardy off, though it makes
the unskillful laugh, cannot but make the judicious grieve, the censure of the
which one must in your allowance o'erweigh a whole theater of others. O,   20
there be players that I have seen play, and heard others praise, and that
highly (not to speak it profanely), that neither having th' accent of Christians, nor the gait of Christian, pagan, nor man, have so strutted and bellowed that I have thought some of Nature's journeymen[8] had made men,
and not made them well, they imitated humanity so abominably.   25

PLAYER: I hope we have reformed that indifferently[9] with us, sir.

HAMLET: O, reform it altogether! And let those that play your clowns speak no
more than is set down for them, for there be of them that will themselves
laugh, to set on some quantity of barren spectators to laugh too, though in
the meantime some necessary question of the play be then to be considered.   30
That's villainous and shows a most pitiful ambition in the fool that uses it.
Go make you ready.   (*Exeunt* PLAYERS.)

(*Enter* POLONIUS, GUILDENSTERN, *and* ROSENCRANTZ.)

How now, my lord? Will the King hear this piece of work?

POLONIUS: And the Queen too, and that presently.

HAMLET: Bid the players make haste.   (*Exit* POLONIUS.)   35
Will you two help to hasten them?

ROSENCRANTZ: Ay, my lord.   (*Exeunt they two.*)

HAMLET: What, ho, Horatio!

(*Enter* HORATIO.)

HORATIO: Here, sweet lord, at your service.

HAMLET: Horatio, thou art e'en as just a man   40
As e'er my conversation coped withal.[10]

HORATIO: O, my dear lord ——

HAMLET: Nay, do not think I flatter.
For what advancement[11] may I hope from thee,
That no revenue hast but thy good spirits
To feed and clothe thee? Why should the poor be flattered?   45

---

  [4] (it had been the fashion for actors to
preface plays or parts of plays with silent
mime)

  [5] (boisterous characters in the old mystery
plays)

  [6] contrary to

  [7] image, impress

  [8] workers not yet masters of their craft

  [9] tolerably

  [10] met with

  [11] promotion

No, let the candied[12] tongue lick absurd pomp,
And crook the pregnant[13] hinges of the knee
Where thrift[14] may follow fawning. Dost thou hear?
Since my dear soul was mistress of her choice
And could of men distinguish her election,   50
S' hath sealed thee[15] for herself, for thou hast been
As one, in suff'ring all, that suffers nothing,
A man that Fortune's buffets and rewards
Hast ta'en with equal thanks; and blest are those
Whose blood[16] and judgment are so well commeddled[17]   55
That they are not a pipe for Fortune's finger
To sound what stop she please. Give me that man
That is not passion's slave, and I will wear him
In my heart's core, ay, in my heart of heart,
As I do thee. Something too much of this —   60
There is a play tonight before the king.
One scene of it comes near the circumstance
Which I have told thee, of my father's death.
I prithee, when thou seest that act afoot,
Even with the very comment[18] of thy soul   65
Observe my uncle. If his occulted[19] guilt
Do not itself unkennel in one speech,
It is a damnèd ghost that we have seen,
And my imaginations are as foul
As Vulcan's stithy.[20] Give him heedful note,   70
For I mine eyes will rivet to his face,
And after we will both our judgments join
In censure of his seeming.[21]
HORATIO: Well, my lord.
If 'a steal aught the whilst this play is playing,
And scape detecting, I will pay the theft.   75

(*Enter Trumpets and Kettledrums*, KING, QUEEN, POLONIUS, OPHELIA, RO-
SENCRANTZ, GUILDENSTERN, *and other* LORDS *attendant with his* GUARD
carrying torches. Danish March. Sound a Flourish.)

HAMLET: They are coming to the play: I must be idle;[22]
    Get you a place.
KING: How fares our cousin Hamlet?
HAMLET: Excellent, i' faith, of the chameleon's dish;[23] I eat the air, promise-
    crammed; you cannot feed capons so.   80
KING: I have nothing with this answer, Hamlet; these words are not mine.
HAMLET: No, nor mine now. [*To* POLONIUS.] My lord, you played once i' th'
    university, you say?

---

[12] sugared, flattering
[13] (1) pliant, (2) full of promise of good
fortune
[14] profit
[15] she (the soul) has set a mark on you
[16] passion
[17] blended

[18] deepest wisdom
[19] hidden
[20] forge, smithy
[21] judgment on his looks
[22] play the fool
[23] air (on which chameleons were thought
to live)

POLONIUS: That did I, my lord, and was accounted a good actor.

HAMLET: What did you enact?   85

POLONIUS: I did enact Julius Caesar. I was killed i' th' Capitol; Brutus killed me.

HAMLET: It was a brute part of him to kill so capital a calf there. Be the players ready?

ROSENCRANTZ: Ay, my lord. They stay upon your patience.

QUEEN: Come hither, my dear Hamlet, sit by me.   . 90

HAMLET: No, good mother. Here's metal more attractive.[24]

POLONIUS [*to the* KING]: O ho! Do you mark that?

HAMLET: Lady, shall I lie in your lap?

[*He lies at* OPHELIA'*s feet.*]

OPHELIA: No, my lord.

HAMLET: I mean, my head upon your lap?   95

OPHELIA: Ay, my lord.

HAMLET: Do you think I meant country matters?[25]

OPHELIA: I think nothing, my lord.

HAMLET: That's a fair thought to lie between maids' legs.

OPHELIA: What is, my lord?   100

HAMLET: Nothing.

OPHELIA: You are merry, my lord.

HAMLET: Who, I?

OPHELIA: Ay, my lord.

HAMLET: O God, your only jig-maker![26] What should a man do but be merry?   105
For look you how cheerfully my mother looks, and my father died within's two hours.

OPHELIA: Nay, 'tis twice two months, my lord.

HAMLET: So long? Nay then, let the devil wear black, for I'll have a suit of sables.[27] O heavens! Die two months ago, and not forgotten yet? Then   110
there's hope a great man's memory may outlive his life half a year. But, by'r Lady, 'a must build churches then, or else shall 'a suffer not thinking on, with the hobbyhorse,[28] whose epitaph is "For O, for O, the hobbyhorse is forgot!"

(*The trumpets sound. Dumb show follows:*
Enter a KING *and a* QUEEN *very lovingly, the* QUEEN *embracing him, and he her. She kneels; and makes show of protestation unto him. He takes her up, and declines his head upon her neck. He lies him down upon a bank of flow-ers. She, seeing him asleep, leaves him. Anon come in another man: takes off his crown, kisses it, pours poison in the sleeper's ears, and leaves him. The* QUEEN *returns, finds the* KING *dead, makes passionate action. The* POISONER, *with some three or four, come in again, seem to condole with her. The dead body is carried away. The* POISONER *woos the* QUEEN *with gifts; she seems harsh awhile, but in the end accepts love. Exeunt.*)

[24] magnetic
[25] rustic doings (with a pun on the vulgar word for the pudendum)
[26] composer of songs and dances (often a fool, who performed them)
[27] (pun on "black" and "luxurious furs")
[28] mock horse worn by a performer in the morris dance

OPHELIA: What means this, my lord?   115
HAMLET: Marry, this is miching mallecho;[29] it means mischief.
OPHELIA: Belike this show imports the argument[30] of the play.

(*Enter* PROLOGUE.)

HAMLET: We shall know by this fellow. The players cannot keep counsel; they'll
   tell all.
OPHELIA: Will 'a tell us what this show meant?   120
HAMLET: Ay, or any show that you will show him. Be not you ashamed to show,
   he'll not shame to tell you what it means.
OPHELIA: You are naught,[31] you are naught; I'll mark the play.
PROLOGUE: For us, and for our tragedy,
   Here stooping to your clemency,   125
   We beg your hearing patiently.   [*Exit.*]
HAMLET: Is this a prologue, or the posy of a ring?[32]
OPHELIA: 'Tis brief, my lord.
HAMLET: As woman's love.

(*Enter* [*two Players as*] KING *and* QUEEN.)

PLAYER KING: Full thirty times hath Phoebus' cart[33] gone round   130
   Neptune's salt wash[34] and Tellus'[35] orbèd ground,
   And thirty dozen moons with borrowed sheen
   About the world have times twelve thirties been,
   Since love our hearts, and Hymen did our hands,
   Unite commutual in most sacred bands.   135
PLAYER QUEEN: So many journeys may the sun and moon
   Make us again count o'er ere love be done!
   But woe is me, you are so sick of late,
   So far from cheer and from your former state,
   That I distrust[36] you. Yet, though I distrust,   140
   Discomfort you, my lord, it nothing must.
   For women fear too much, even as they love,
   And women's fear and love hold quantity,
   In neither aught, or in extremity.[37]
   Now what my love is, proof[38] hath made you know,   145
   And as my love is sized, my fear is so.
   Where love is great, the littlest doubts are fear,
   Where little fears grow great, great love grows there.
PLAYER KING: Faith, I must leave thee, love, and shortly too;
   My operant[39] powers their functions leave to do: 150
   And thou shalt live in this fair world behind,

[29] sneaking mischief
[30] plot
[31] wicked, improper
[32] motto inscribed in a ring
[33] the sun's chariot
[34] the sea
[35] Roman goddess of the earth
[36] am anxious about

[37] (perhaps the idea is that women's anxiety is great or little in proportion to their love. The previous line, unrhymed, may be a false start that Shakespeare neglected to delete)
[38] experience
[39] active

Honored, beloved, and haply one as kind
For husband shalt thou ——
PLAYER QUEEN: O, confound the rest!
Such love must needs be treason in my breast.
In second husband let me be accurst!   155
None wed the second but who killed the first.
HAMLET [*aside*]: That's wormwood.[40]
PLAYER QUEEN: The instances[41] that second marriage move[42]
Are base respects of thrift,[43] but none of love.
A second time I kill my husband dead   160
When second husband kisses me in bed.
PLAYER KING: I do believe you think what now you speak,
But what we do determine oft we break.
Purpose is but the slave to memory,
Of violent birth, but poor validity,[44]   165
Which now like fruit unripe sticks on the tree,
But fall unshaken when they mellow be.
Most necessary 'tis that we forget
To pay ourselves what to ourselves is debt.
What to ourselves in passion we propose,   170
The passion ending, doth the purpose lose.
The violence of either grief or joy
Their own enactures[45] with themselves destroy:
Where joy most revels, grief doth most lament;
Grief joys, joy grieves, on slender accident.   175
This world is not for aye, nor 'tis not strange
That even our loves should with our fortunes change,
For 'tis a question left us yet to prove,
Whether love lead fortune, or else fortune love.
The great man down, you mark his favorite flies;   180
The poor advanced makes friends of enemies;
And hitherto doth love on fortune tend,
For who not needs shall never lack a friend;
And who in want a hollow friend doth try,
Directly seasons him[46] his enemy.   185
But, orderly to end where I begun,
Our wills and fates do so contrary run
That our devices still are overthrown;
Our thoughts are ours, their ends none of our own.
So think thou wilt no second husband wed,   190
But die thy thoughts when thy first lord is dead.
PLAYER QUEEN: Nor earth to me give food, nor heaven light,
Sport and repose lock from me day and night,
To desperation turn my trust and hope,

---

[40] a bitter herb   [44] strength
[41] motives   [45] acts
[42] induce   [46] ripens him into
[43] considerations of profit

An anchor's[47] cheer in prison be my scope,   195
Each opposite that blanks[48] the face of joy
Meet what I would have well, and it destroy:
Both here and hence pursue me lasting strife,
If, once a widow, ever I be wife!
HAMLET: If she should break it now!   200
PLAYER KING: 'Tis deeply sworn. Sweet, leave me here awhile;
My spirits grow dull, and fain I would beguile
The tedious day with sleep.
PLAYER QUEEN: Sleep rock thy brain,

([He] sleeps.)

And never come mischance between us twain!   (Exit.)
HAMLET: Madam, how like you this play?   205
QUEEN: The lady doth protest too much, methinks.
HAMLET: O, but she'll keep her word.
KING: Have you heard the argument?[49] Is there no offense in't?
HAMLET: No, no, they do but jest, poison in jest; no offense i' th' world.
KING: What do you call the play?   210
HAMLET: The Mousetrap. Marry, how? Tropically.[50] This play is the image of a
murder done in Vienna: Gonzago is the Duke's name; his wife, Baptista. You
shall see anon. 'Tis a knavish piece of work, but what of that? Your Majesty,
and we that have free[51] souls, it touches us not. Let the galled jade winch;[52]
our withers are unwrung.   215

(Enter LUCIANUS.)

This is one Lucianus, nephew to the King.
OPHELIA: You are as good as a chorus, my lord.
HAMLET: I could interpret[53] between you and your love, if I could see the pup-
pets dallying.
OPHELIA: You are keen,[54] my lord, you are keen.   220
HAMLET: It would cost you a groaning to take off mine edge.
OPHELIA: Still better, and worse.
HAMLET: So you mistake[55] your husbands. — Begin, murderer. Leave thy
damnable faces and begin. Come, the croaking raven doth bellow for re-
venge.
LUCIANUS: Thoughts black, hands apt, drugs fit, and time agreeing,   225
Confederate season,[56] else no creature seeing,
Thou mixture rank, of midnight weeds collected,
With Hecate's ban[57] thrice blasted, thrice infected,

---

[47] anchorite's, hermit's
[48] adverse thing that blanches
[49] plot
[50] figuratively (with a pun on "trap")
[51] innocent
[52] chafed horse wince

[53] (like a showman explaining the action of puppets)
[54] (1) sharp, (2) sexually aroused
[55] err in taking
[56] the opportunity allied with me
[57] the curse of the goddess of sorcery

Thy natural magic and dire property[58]
On wholesome life usurps immediately.   230

(*Pours the poison in his ears.*)

HAMLET: 'A poisons him i' th' garden for his estate. His name's Gonzago. The
story is extant, and written in very choice Italian. You shall see anon how
the murderer gets the love of Gonzago's wife.
OPHELIA: The King rises.
HAMLET: What, frighted with false fire?[59]   235
QUEEN: How fares my lord?
POLONIUS: Give o'er the play.
KING: Give me some light. Away!
POLONIUS: Lights, lights, lights!   (*Exeunt all but* HAMLET *and* HORATIO.)
HAMLET:

     Why, let the strucken deer go weep,   240
        The hart ungallèd play:
     For some must watch, while some must sleep;
        Thus runs the world away.

Would not this, sir, and a forest of feathers[60] — if the rest of my fortunes
turn Turk[61] with me — with two Provincial roses[62] on my razed[63] shoes, get   245
me a fellowship in a cry[64] of players?
HORATIO: Half a share.
HAMLET: A whole one, I.

     For thou dost know, O Damon dear,   250
        This realm dismantled was
     Of Jove himself; and now reigns here
        A very, very — pajock.[65]

HORATIO: You might have rhymed.[66]
HAMLET: O good Horatio, I'll take the ghost's word for a thousand pound. Didst   255
perceive?
HORATIO: Very well, my lord.
HAMLET: Upon the talk of poisoning?
HORATIO: I did very well note him.
HAMLET: Ah ha! Come, some music! Come, the recorders![67]   260
For if the King like not the comedy,
Why then, belike he likes it not, perdy.[68]
Come, some music!

(*Enter* ROSENCRANTZ *and* GUILDENSTERN.)

GUILDENSTERN: Good my lord, vouchsafe me a word with you.

---

[58] nature
[59] blank discharge of firearms
[60] (plumes were sometimes part of a costume)
[61] i.e., go bad, treat me badly
[62] rosettes like the roses of Provence (?)
[63] ornamented with slashes
[64] pack, company
[65] peacock
[66] i.e., rhymed "was" with "ass"
[67] flutelike instruments
[68] by God (Fr. *par dieu*)

HAMLET: Sir, a whole history.   265

GUILDENSTERN: The King, sir ——

HAMLET: Ay, sir, what of him?

GUILDENSTERN: Is in his retirement marvelous distemp'red.

HAMLET: With drink, sir?

GUILDENSTERN: No, my lord, with choler.[69]   270

HAMLET: Your wisdom should show itself more richer to signify this to the doctor, for for me to put him to his purgation would perhaps plunge him into more choler.

GUILDENSTERN: Good my lord, put your discourse into some frame,[70] and start not so wildly from my affair.   275

HAMLET: I am tame, sir; pronounce.

GUILDENSTERN: The Queen, your mother, in most great affliction of spirit hath sent me to you.

HAMLET: You are welcome.

GUILDENSTERN: Nay, good my lord, this courtesy is not of the right breed. If it shall please you to make me a wholesome answer, I will do your mother's commandment: if not, your pardon and my return shall be the end of my business.   280

HAMLET: Sir, I cannot.

ROSENCRANTZ: What, my lord?   285

HAMLET: Make you a wholesome[71] answer; my wit's diseased. But, sir, such answer as I can make, you shall command, or rather, as you say, my mother. Therefore no more, but to the matter. My mother, you say ——

ROSENCRANTZ: Then thus she says: your behavior hath struck her into amazement and admiration.[72]   290

HAMLET: O wonderful son, that can so stonish a mother! But is there no sequel at the heels of this mother's admiration? Impart.

ROSENCRANTZ: She desires to speak with you in her closet ere you go to bed.

HAMLET: We shall obey, were she ten times our mother. Have you any further trade with us?   295

ROSENCRANTZ: My lord, you once did love me.

HAMLET: And do still, by these pickers and stealers.[73]

ROSENCRANTZ: Good my lord, what is your cause of distemper? You do surely bar the door upon your own liberty, if you deny your griefs to your friend.

HAMLET: Sir, I lack advancement.[74]   300

ROSENCRANTZ: How can that be, when you have the voice of the King himself for your succession in Denmark?

(*Enter the* PLAYERS *with recorders.*)

HAMLET: Ay, sir, but "while the grass grows" — the proverb[75] is something musty. O, the recorders. Let me see one. To withdraw[76] with you — why do you go about to recover the wind[77] of me as if you would drive me into a toil?[78]   305

---

[69] anger (but Hamlet pretends to take the word in its sense of "biliousness")
[70] order, control
[71] sane
[72] wonder
[73] i.e., hands (with reference to the prayer: "Keep my hands from picking and stealing")
[74] promotion
[75] ("While the grass groweth, the horse starveth")
[76] speak in private
[77] get on the windward side (as in hunting)
[78] snare

GUILDENSTERN: O my lord, if my duty be too bold, my love is too unmannerly.[79]

HAMLET: I do not well understand that. Will you play upon this pipe?

GUILDENSTERN: My lord, I cannot.

HAMLET: I pray you.

GUILDENSTERN: Believe me, I cannot.   310

HAMLET: I pray you.

GUILDENSTERN: Believe me, I cannot.

HAMLET: I do beseech you.

GUILDENSTERN: I know no touch of it, my lord.

HAMLET: It is as easy as lying. Govern these ventages[80] with your fingers and 315
thumb, give it breath with your mouth, and it will discourse most eloquent
music. Look you, these are the stops.

GUILDENSTERN: But these cannot I command to any utt'rance of harmony; I
have not the skill.

HAMLET: Why, look you now, how unworthy a thing you make of me! You   320
would play upon me; you would seem to know my stops; you would pluck out
the heart of my mystery; you would sound me from my lowest note to the
top of my compass;[81] and there is much music, excellent voice, in this little
organ,[82] yet cannot you make it speak. 'Sblood, do you think I am easier to
be played on than a pipe? Call me what instrument you will, though you can 325
fret[83] me, you cannot play upon me.

(*Enter* POLONIUS.)

God bless you, sir!

POLONIUS: My lord, the Queen would speak with you, and presently.

HAMLET: Do you see yonder cloud that's almost in shape of a camel?

POLONIUS: By th' mass and 'tis, like a camel indeed.   330

HAMLET: Methinks it is like a weasel.

POLONIUS: It is backed like a weasel.

HAMLET: Or like a whale.

POLONIUS: Very like a whale.

HAMLET: Then I will come to my mother by and by. [*Aside.*] They fool me to 335
the top of my bent.[84] — I will come by and by.[85]

POLONIUS: I will say so.   (*Exit.*)

HAMLET: "By and by" is easily said. Leave me, friends. [*Exeunt all but* HAMLET.]
'Tis now the very witching time of night,
When churchyards yawn, and hell itself breathes out   340
Contagion to this world. Now could I drink hot blood
And do such bitter business as the day
Would quake to look on. Soft, now to my mother.
O heart, lose not thy nature; let not ever
The soul of Nero[86] enter this firm bosom.   345

[79] i.e., if these questions seem rude, it is because my love for you leads me beyond good manners
[80] vents, stops on a recorder
[81] range of voice
[82] i.e., the recorder
[83] (with a pun alluding to the frets, or ridges, that guide the fingering on some instruments)
[84] they compel me to play the fool to the limit of my capacity
[85] very soon
[86] Roman emperor who had his mother murdered

Let me be cruel, not unnatural;
I will speak daggers to her, but use none.
My tongue and soul in this be hypocrites:
How in my words somever she be shent,[87]
To give them seals[88] never, my soul, consent!   (*Exit.*)   350

SCENE 3. [THE CASTLE.]

Enter KING, ROSENCRANTZ, *and* GUILDENSTERN.

KING: I like him not, nor stands it safe with us
To let his madness range. Therefore prepare you.
I your commission will forthwith dispatch,
And he to England shall along with you.
The terms[1] of our estate may not endure   5
Hazard so near's[2] as doth hourly grow
Out of his brows.
GUILDENSTERN: We will ourselves provide.
Most holy and religious fear it is
To keep those many many bodies safe
That live and feed upon your Majesty.   10
ROSENCRANTZ: The single and peculiar[3] life is bound
With all the strength and armor of the mind
To keep itself from noyance,[4] but much more
That spirit upon whose weal depends and rests
The lives of many. The cess of majesty[5]   15
Dies not alone, but like a gulf[6] doth draw
What's near it with it; or it is a massy wheel
Fixed on the summit of the highest mount,
To whose huge spokes ten thousand lesser things
Are mortised and adjoined, which when it falls,   20
Each small annexment, petty consequence,
Attends[7] the boist'rous ruin. Never alone
Did the King sigh, but with a general groan.
KING: Arm[8] you, I pray you, to this speedy voyage,
For we will fetters put about this fear,   25
Which now goes too free-footed.
ROSENCRANTZ: We will haste us.   (*Exeunt* GENTLEMEN.)

(*Enter* POLONIUS.)

POLONIUS: My lord, he's going to his mother's closet.
Behind the arras I'll convey myself

87 rebuked
88 confirm them with deeds
1 conditions
2 near us
3 individual, private

4 injury
5 cessation (death) of a king
6 whirlpool
7 waits on, participates in
8 prepare

To hear the process.[9] I'll warrant she'll tax him home,[10]
And, as you said, and wisely was it said,   30
'Tis meet that some more audience than a mother,
Since nature makes them partial, should o'erhear
The speech of vantage.[11] Fare you well, my liege.
I'll call upon you ere you go to bed
And tell you what I know.

KING: Thanks, dear my lord.   (*Exit* [POLONIUS].)   35
O, my offense is rank, it smells to heaven;
It hath the primal eldest curse[12] upon't,
A brother's murder. Pray can I not,
Though inclination be as sharp as will.
My stronger guilt defeats my strong intent,   40
And like a man to double business bound
I stand in pause where I shall first begin,
And both neglect. What if this cursèd hand
Were thicker than itself with brother's blood,
Is there not rain enough in the sweet heavens   45
To wash it white as snow? Whereto serves mercy
But to confront[13] the visage of offense?
And what's in prayer but this twofold force,
To be forestallèd ere we come to fall,
Or pardoned being down? Then I'll look up.   50
My fault is past. But, O, what form of prayer
Can serve my turn? "Forgive me my foul murder"?
That cannot be, since I am still possessed
Of those effects[14] for which I did the murder,
My crown, mine own ambition, and my queen.   55
May one be pardoned and retain th' offense?
In the corrupted currents of this world
Offense's gilded hand may shove by justice,
And oft 'tis seen the wicked prize itself
Buys out the law. But 'tis not so above.   60
There is no shuffling;[15] there the action lies
In his true nature, and we ourselves compelled,
Even to the teeth and forehead of our faults,
To give in evidence. What then? What rests?[16]
Try what repentance can. What can it not?   65
Yet what can it when one cannot repent?
O wretched state! O bosom black as death!
O limèd[17] soul, that struggling to be free
Art more engaged![18] Help, angels! Make assay.[19]

---

[9] proceedings
[10] censure him sharply
[11] from an advantageous place
[12] (curse of Cain, who killed Abel)
[13] oppose
[14] things gained

[15] trickery
[16] remains
[17] caught (as with birdlime, a sticky substance spread on boughs to snare birds)
[18] ensnared
[19] an attempt

Bow, stubborn knees, and, heart with strings of steel, 70
Be soft as sinews of the newborn babe.
All may be well. [*He kneels.*]

(*Enter* HAMLET.)

HAMLET: Now might I do it pat, now 'a is a-praying,
And now I'll do't. And so 'a goes to heaven,
And so am I revenged. That would be scanned.[20] 75
A villain kills my father, and for that
I, his sole son, do this same villain send
To heaven.
Why, this is hire and salary, not revenge.
'A took my father grossly, full of bread,[21] 80
With all his crimes broad blown,[22] as flush[23] as May;
And how his audit[24] stands, who knows save heaven?
But in our circumstance and course of thought,
'Tis heavy with him; and am I then revenged,
To take him in the purging of his soul, 85
When he is fit and seasoned for his passage?
No.
Up, sword, and know thou a more horrid hent.[25]
When he is drunk asleep, or in his rage,
Or in th' incestuous pleasure of his bed, 90
At game a-swearing, or about some act
That has no relish[26] of salvation in't —
Then trip him, that his heels may kick at heaven,
And that his soul may be as damned and black
As hell, whereto it goes. My mother stays. 95
This physic[27] but prolongs thy sickly days. (*Exit.*)
KING [*rises*]: My words fly up, my thoughts remain below.
Words without thoughts never to heaven go. (*Exit.*)

SCENE 4. [THE QUEEN'S CLOSET.]

Enter [QUEEN] GERTRUDE *and* POLONIUS.

POLONIUS: 'A will come straight. Look you lay home[1] to him.
Tell him his pranks have been too broad[2] to bear with,
And that your Grace hath screened and stood between
Much heat and him. I'll silence me even here.
Pray you be round with him. 5
HAMLET (*within*): Mother, Mother, Mother!

---

[20] ought to be looked into
[21] i.e., worldly gratification
[22] sins in full bloom
[23] vigorous
[24] account
[25] grasp (here, occasion for seizing)

[26] flavor
[27] (Claudius's purgation by prayer, as Hamlet thinks in line 85)
[1] thrust (rebuke) him sharply
[2] unrestrained

QUEEN: I'll warrant you; fear me not. Withdraw; I hear him coming.

[POLONIUS *hides behind the arras*.]

(*Enter* HAMLET.)

HAMLET: Now, Mother, what's the matter?

QUEEN: Hamlet, thou hast thy father much offended.

HAMLET: Mother, you have my father much offended.   10

QUEEN: Come, come, you answer with an idle[3] tongue.

HAMLET: Go, go, you question with a wicked tongue.

QUEEN: Why, how now, Hamlet?

HAMLET: What's the matter now?

QUEEN: Have you forgot me?

HAMLET: No, by the rood,[4] not so!   15

    You are the Queen, your husband's brother's wife,

    And, would it were not so, you are my mother.

QUEEN: Nay, then I'll set those to you that can speak.

HAMLET: Come, come, and sit you down. You shall not budge.

    You go not till I set you up a glass[5]

    Where you may see the inmost part of you!   20

QUEEN: What wilt thou do? Thou wilt not murder me?

    Help, ho!

POLONIUS [*behind*]: What, ho! Help!

HAMLET [*draws*]: How now? A rat? Dead for a ducat, dead!

([*Makes a pass through the arras and*] *kills* POLONIUS.)

POLONIUS [*behind*]: O, I am slain!

QUEEN: O me, what hast thou done?   25

HAMLET: Nay, I know not. Is it the King?

QUEEN: O, what a rash and bloody deed is this!

HAMLET: A bloody deed — almost as bad, good Mother,

    As kill a king, and marry with his brother.

QUEEN: As kill a king?

HAMLET: Ay, lady, it was my word.   30

[*Lifts up the arras and sees* POLONIUS.]

    Thou wretched, rash, intruding fool, farewell!

    I took thee for thy better. Take thy fortune.

    Thou find'st to be too busy is some danger. —

    Leave wringing of your hands. Peace, sit you down

    And let me wring your heart, for so I shall   35

    If it be made of penetrable stuff,

    If damnèd custom have not brazed[6] it so

    That it be proof[7] and bulwark against sense.[8]

QUEEN: What have I done that thou dar'st wag thy tongue

    In noise so rude against me?

HAMLET: Such an act   40

---

[3] foolish

[4] cross

[5] mirror

[6] hardened like brass

[7] armor

[8] feeling

That blurs the grace and blush of modesty,
Calls virtue hypocrite, takes off the rose
From the fair forehead of an innocent love,
And sets a blister[9] there, makes marriage vows
As false as dicers' oaths. O, such a deed   45
As from the body of contraction[10] plucks
The very soul, and sweet religion makes
A rhapsody[11] of words! Heaven's face does glow
O'er this solidity and compound mass
With heated visage, as against the doom   50
Is thoughtsick at the act.[12]
QUEEN: Ay me, what act,
That roars so loud and thunders in the index?[13]
HAMLET: Look here upon this picture, and on this,
The counterfeit presentment[14] of two brothers.
See what a grace was seated on this brow: 55
Hyperion's curls, the front[15] of Jove himself,
An eye like Mars, to threaten and command,
A station[16] like the herald Mercury
New lighted on a heaven-kissing hill —
A combination and a form indeed   60
Where every god did seem to set his seal
To give the world assurance of a man.
This was your husband. Look you now what follows.
Here is your husband, like a mildewed ear
Blasting his wholesome brother. Have you eyes?   65
Could you on this fair mountain leave to feed,
And batten[17] on this moor? Ha! Have you eyes?
You cannot call it love, for at your age
The heyday[18] in the blood is tame, it's humble,
And waits upon the judgment, and what judgment   70
Would step from this to this? Sense[19] sure you have,
Else could you not have motion, but sure that sense
Is apoplexed,[20] for madness would not err,
Nor sense to ecstasy[21] was ne'er so thralled
But it reserved some quantity of choice   75
To serve in such a difference. What devil was't
That thus hath cozened you at hoodman-blind?[22]
Eyes without feeling, feeling without sight,

[9] brands (as a harlot)
[10] marriage contract
[11] senseless string
[12] i.e., the face of heaven blushes over this
earth (compounded of four elements), the
face hot, as if Judgment Day were near, and
it is thoughtsick at the act
[13] prologue
[14] represented image

[15] forehead
[16] bearing
[17] feed gluttonously
[18] excitement
[19] feeling
[20] paralyzed
[21] madness
[22] cheated you at blindman's buff

Ears without hands or eyes, smelling sans[23] all,
Or but a sickly part of one true sense   80
Could not so mope.[24]
O shame, where is thy blush? Rebellious hell,
If thou canst mutine in a matron's bones,
To flaming youth let virtue be as wax
And melt in her own fire. Proclaim no shame   85
When the compulsive ardor[25] gives the charge,
Since frost itself as actively doth burn,
And reason panders will.[26]

QUEEN: O Hamlet, speak no more.
Thou turn'st mine eyes into my very soul,
And there I see such black and grainèd[27] spots   90
As will not leave their tinct.[28]

HAMLET: Nay, but to live
In the rank sweat of an enseamed[29] bed,
Stewed in corruption, honeying and making love
Over the nasty sty —

QUEEN: O, speak to me no more.
These words like daggers enter in my ears.   95
No more, sweet Hamlet.

HAMLET: A murderer and a villain,
A slave that is not twentieth part the tithe[30]
Of your precedent lord, a vice[31] of kings,
A cutpurse of the empire and the rule,
That from a shelf the precious diadem stole   100
And put it in his pocket —

QUEEN: No more.

(*Enter* GHOST.)

HAMLET: A king of shreds and patches —
Save me and hover o'er me with your wings,
You heavenly guards! What would your gracious figure?

QUEEN: Alas, he's mad.   105

HAMLET: Do you not come your tardy son to chide,
That, lapsed in time and passion, lets go by
Th' important acting of your dread command?
O, say!

GHOST: Do not forget. This visitation   110
Is but to whet thy almost blunted purpose.
But look, amazement on thy mother sits.
O, step between her and her fighting soul!

[23] without
[24] be stupid
[25] compelling passion
[26] reason acts as a procurer for desire
[27] dyed in grain (fast dyed)
[28] color

[29] (perhaps "soaked in grease," i.e., sweaty;
perhaps "much wrinkled")
[30] tenth part
[31] (like the Vice, a fool and mischief-
maker in the old morality plays)

Conceit[32] in weakest bodies strongest works.
Speak to her, Hamlet.

HAMLET: How is it with you, lady?   115

QUEEN: Alas, how is't with you,
That you do bend your eye on vacancy,
And with th' incorporal[33] air do hold discourse?
Forth at your eyes your spirits wildly peep,
And as the sleeping soldiers in th' alarm   120
Your bedded hair[34] like life in excrements[35]
Start up and stand an end.[36] O gentle son,
Upon the heat and flame of thy distemper
Sprinkle cool patience. Whereon do you look?

HAMLET: On him, on him! Look you, how pale he glares!   125
His form and cause conjoined, preaching to stones,
Would make them capable.[37] — Do not look upon me,
Lest with this piteous action you convert
My stern effects.[38] Then what I have to do
Will want true color; tears perchance for blood.   130

QUEEN: To whom do you speak this?

HAMLET: Do you see nothing there?

QUEEN: Nothing at all; yet all that is I see.

HAMLET: Nor did you nothing hear?

QUEEN: No, nothing but ourselves.

HAMLET: Why, look you there! Look how it steals away!
My father, in his habit[39] as he lived!   135
Look where he goes even now out at the portal!   (*Exit* GHOST.)

QUEEN: This is the very coinage of your brain.
This bodiless creation ecstasy
Is very cunning in.

HAMLET: Ecstasy?
My pulse as yours doth temperately keep time   140
And makes as healthful music. It is not madness
That I have uttered. Bring me to the test,
And I the matter will reword, which madness
Would gambol[40] from. Mother, for love of grace,
Lay not that flattering unction[41] to your soul,   145
That not your trespass but my madness speaks.
It will but skin and film the ulcerous place
Whiles rank corruption, mining[42] all within,
Infects unseen. Confess yourself to heaven,
Repent what's past, avoid what is to come,   150

---

[32] imagination
[33] bodiless
[34] hairs laid flat
[35] outgrowths (here, the hair)
[36] on end
[37] receptive
[38] divert my stern deeds

[39] garment (Q1, although a "bad" quarto, is probably correct in saying that at line 102 the ghost enters "in his nightgown," i.e., dressing gown)
[40] start away
[41] ointment
[42] undermining

And do not spread the compost[43] on the weeds
To make them ranker. Forgive me this my virtue.
For in the fatness of these pursy[44] times
Virtue itself of vice must pardon beg,
Yea, curb[45] and woo for leave to do him good.　　　　155
QUEEN: O Hamlet, thou hast cleft my heart in twain.
HAMLET: O, throw away the worser part of it,
And live the purer with the other half.
Good night — but go not to my uncle's bed.
Assume a virtue, if you have it not.　　　　　　　　160
That monster custom, who all sense doth eat,
Of habits devil, is angel yet in this,
That to the use[46] of actions fair and good
He likewise gives a frock or livery[47]
That aptly is put on. Refrain tonight,　　　　　　　165
And that shall lend a kind of easiness
To the next abstinence; the next more easy;
For use almost can change the stamp of nature,
And either[48] the devil, or throw him out
With wondrous potency. Once more, good night,　　170
And when you are desirous to be blest,
I'll blessing beg of you. — For this same lord,
I do repent; but heaven hath pleased it so,
To punish me with this, and this with me,
That I must be their[49] scourge and minister.　　　175
I will bestow[50] him and will answer well
The death I gave him. So again, good night.
I must be cruel only to be kind.
Thus bad begins, and worse remains behind.
One word more, good lady.
QUEEN:　　　　　　　　What shall I do?　　　　180
HAMLET: Not this, by no means, that I bid you do:
Let the bloat King tempt you again to bed,
Pinch wanton on your cheek, call you his mouse,
And let him, for a pair of reechy[51] kisses,
Or paddling in your neck with his damned fingers,　185
Make you to ravel[52] all this matter out,
That I essentially am not in madness,
But mad in craft. 'Twere good you let him know,
For who that's but a queen, fair, sober, wise,
Would from a paddock,[53] from a bat, a gib,[54]　　190

---

[43] fertilizing substance
[44] bloated
[45] bow low
[46] practice
[47] characteristic garment (punning on "habits" in line 163)
[48] (probably a word is missing after either; among suggestions are "master," "curb," and "house"; but possibly either is a verb meaning "make easier")
[49] i.e., the heavens'
[50] stow, lodge
[51] foul (literally "smoky")
[52] unravel, reveal
[53] toad
[54] tomcat

Such dear concernings hide? Who would do so?
No, in despite of sense and secrecy,
Unpeg the basket on the house's top,
Let the birds fly, and like the famous ape,
To try conclusions,[55] in the basket creep   195
And break your own neck down.
QUEEN: Be thou assured, if words be made of breath,
And breath of life, I have no life to breathe
What thou hast said to me.
HAMLET: I must to England; you know that?
QUEEN: Alack,   200
I had forgot. 'Tis so concluded on.
HAMLET: There's letters sealed, and my two schoolfellows,
Whom I will trust as I will adders fanged,
They bear the mandate;[56] they must sweep my way
And marshal me to knavery. Let it work;   205
For 'tis the sport to have the enginer
Hoist with his own petar,[57] and 't shall go hard
But I will delve one yard below their mines
And blow them at the moon. O, 'tis most sweet
When in one line two crafts[58] directly meet.   210
This man shall set me packing:
I'll lug the guts into the neighbor room.
Mother, good night. Indeed, this counselor
Is now most still, most secret, and most grave,
Who was in life a foolish prating knave.   215
Come, sir, to draw toward an end with you.
Good night, Mother.
                    ([Exit the QUEEN. Then] exit HAMLET, tugging in POLONIUS.)

ACT IV

SCENE 1. [THE CASTLE.]

Enter KING *and* QUEEN, *with* ROSENCRANTZ *and* GUILDENSTERN.

KING: There's matter in these sighs. These profound heaves
You must translate; 'tis fit we understand them.
Where is your son?
QUEEN: Bestow this place on us a little while.
                    [*Exeunt* ROSENCRANTZ *and* GUILDENSTERN.]
Ah, mine own lord, what have I seen tonight!   5
KING: What, Gertrude? How does Hamlet?

---

[55] to make experiments   [58] (1) boats, (2) acts of guile, crafty
[56] command   schemes
[57] bomb

QUEEN: Mad as the sea and wind when both contend
    Which is the mightier. In his lawless fit,
    Behind the arras hearing something stir,
    Whips out his rapier, cries, "A rat, a rat!"   10
    And in this brainish apprehension[1] kills
    The unseen good old man.
KING: O heavy deed!
    It had been so with us, had we been there.
    His liberty is full of threats to all,
    To you yourself, to us, to every one.   15
    Alas, how shall this bloody deed be answered?
    It will be laid to us, whose providence[2]
    Should have kept short, restrained, and out of haunt[3]
    This mad young man. But so much was our love
    We would not understand what was most fit,   20
    But, like the owner of a foul disease,
    To keep it from divulging, let it feed
    Even on the pith of life. Where is he gone?
QUEEN: To draw apart the body he hath killed;
    O'er whom his very madness, like some ore   25
    Among a mineral[4] of metals base,
    Shows itself pure. 'A weeps for what is done.
KING: O Gertrude, come away!
    The sun no sooner shall the mountains touch
    But we will ship him hence, and this vile deed   30
    We must with all our majesty and skill
    Both countenance and excuse. Ho, Guildenstern!

(*Enter* ROSENCRANTZ *and* GUILDENSTERN.)

    Friends both, go join you with some further aid:
    Hamlet in madness hath Polonius slain,
    And from his mother's closet hath he dragged him.   35
    Go seek him out; speak fair, and bring the body
    Into the chapel. I pray you haste in this.
              [*Exeunt* ROSENCRANTZ *and* GUILDENSTERN.]
    Come, Gertrude, we'll call up our wisest friends
    And let them know both what we mean to do
    And what's untimely done . . .[5]   40
    Whose whisper o'er the world's diameter,
    As level as the cannon to his blank[6]
    Transports his poisoned shot, may miss our name
    And hit the woundless[7] air. O, come away!
    My soul is full of discord and dismay.   (*Exeunt.*) 45

---

[1] mad imagination
[2] foresight
[3] away from association with others
[4] vein of gold in a mine
[5] (evidently something has dropped out of the text. Capell's conjecture, "so, haply slander," is usually printed)
[6] white center of a target
[7] invulnerable

Scene 2. [The Castle.]

Enter HAMLET.

HAMLET: Safely stowed.
GENTLEMEN (*within*): Hamlet! Lord Hamlet!
HAMLET: But soft, what noise? Who calls on Hamlet?
  O, here they come.

(*Enter* ROSENCRANTZ *and* GUILDENSTERN.)

ROSENCRANTZ: What have you done, my lord, with the dead body?   5
HAMLET: Compounded it with dust, whereto 'tis kin.
ROSENCRANTZ: Tell us where 'tis, that we may take it thence
  And bear it to the chapel.
HAMLET: Do not believe it.
ROSENCRANTZ: Believe what?   10
HAMLET: That I can keep your counsel and not mine own. Besides, to be de-
  manded of[1] a sponge, what replication[2] should be made by the son of a king?
ROSENCRANTZ: Take you me for a sponge, my lord?
HAMLET: Ay, sir, that soaks up the King's countenance,[3] his rewards, his au-
  thorities. But such officers do the King best service in the end. He keeps   15
  them, like an ape, in the corner of his jaw, first mouthed, to be last swal-
  lowed. When he needs what you have gleaned, it is but squeezing you and,
  sponge, you shall be dry again.
ROSENCRANTZ: I understand you not, my lord.
HAMLET: I am glad of it: a knavish speech sleeps in a foolish ear.   20
ROSENCRANTZ: My lord, you must tell us where the body is and go with us to
  the King.
HAMLET: The body is with the King, but the King is not with the body. The
  King is a thing ——
GUILDENSTERN: A thing, my lord?   25
HAMLET: Of nothing. Bring me to him. Hide fox, and all after.[4]   (*Exeunt.*)

Scene 3. [The Castle.]

Enter KING, *and two or three.*

KING: I have sent to seek him and to find the body:
  How dangerous it is that this man goes loose!
  Yet must not we put the strong law on him:
  He's loved of the distracted[1] multitude,
  Who like not in their judgment, but their eyes,   5
  And where 'tis so, th' offender's scourge is weighed,
  But never the offense. To bear[2] all smooth and even,

[1] questioned by
[2] reply
[3] favor
[4] (a cry in a game such as hide-and-seek; Hamlet runs from the stage)

[1] bewildered, senseless
[2] carry out

This sudden sending him away must seem
Deliberate pause.³ Diseases desperate grown
By desperate appliance are relieved,   10
Or not at all.

(*Enter* ROSENCRANTZ, [GUILDENSTERN,] *and all the rest.*)

             How now? What hath befall'n?
ROSENCRANTZ: Where the dead body is bestowed, my lord,
  We cannot get from him.
KING: But where is he?
ROSENCRANTZ: Without, my lord; guarded, to know your pleasure.
KING: Bring him before us.
ROSENCRANTZ: Ho! Bring in the lord.   15

(*They enter.*)

KING: Now, Hamlet, where's Polonius?
HAMLET: At supper.
KING: At supper? Where?
HAMLET: Not where he eats, but where 'a is eaten. A certain convocation of
  politic⁴ worms are e'en at him. Your worm is your only emperor for diet. We   20
  fat all creatures else to fat us, and we fat ourselves for maggots. Your fat king
  and your lean beggar is but variable service⁵ — two dishes, but to one table.
  That's the end.
KING: Alas, alas!
HAMLET: A man may fish with the worm that hath eat of a king, and eat of the   25
  fish that hath fed of that worm.
KING: What dost thou mean by this?
HAMLET: Nothing but to show you how a king may go a progress⁶ through the
  guts of a beggar.
KING: Where is Polonius?   30
HAMLET: In heaven. Send thither to see. If your messenger find him not there,
  seek him i' th' other place yourself. But if indeed you find him not within this
  month, you shall nose him as you go up the stairs into the lobby.
KING [*to* ATTENDANTS]: Go seek him there.
HAMLET: 'A will stay till you come.   [*Exeunt* ATTENDANTS.]   35
KING: Hamlet, this deed, for thine especial safety,
  Which we do tender⁷ as we dearly grieve
  For that which thou hast done, must send thee hence
  With fiery quickness. Therefore prepare thyself.
  The bark is ready and the wind at help,   40
  Th' associates tend,⁸ and everything is bent
  For England.
HAMLET: For England?
KING: Ay, Hamlet.

---

³ planning
⁴ statesmanlike, shrewd
⁵ different courses

⁶ royal journey
⁷ hold dear
⁸ wait

HAMLET: Good.

KING: So is it, if thou knew'st our purposes.

HAMLET: I see a cherub[9] that sees them. But come, for England! Farewell, dear
Mother.   45

KING: Thy loving father, Hamlet.

HAMLET: My mother — father and mother is man and wife, man and wife is
one flesh, and so, my mother. Come, for England!   (*Exit.*)

KING: Follow him at foot;[10] tempt him with speed aboard.
Delay it not; I'll have him hence tonight.   50
Away! For everything is sealed and done
That else leans[11] on th' affair. Pray you make haste.

[*Exeunt all but the* KING.]

And, England, if my love thou hold'st at aught —
As my great power thereof may give thee sense,
Since yet thy cicatrice[12] looks raw and red   55
After the Danish sword, and thy free awe[13]
Pays homage to us — thou mayst not coldly set
Our sovereign process,[14] which imports at full
By letters congruing to that effect
The present[15] death of Hamlet. Do it, England,   60
For like the hectic[16] in my blood he rages,
And thou must cure me. Till I know 'tis done,
Howe'er my haps,[17] my joys were ne'er begun.   (*Exit.*)

SCENE 4. [A PLAIN IN DENMARK.]

Enter FORTINBRAS *with his* ARMY *over the stage.*

FORTINBRAS: Go, Captain, from me greet the Danish king.
Tell him that by his license Fortinbras
Craves the conveyance of[1] a promised march
Over his kingdom. You know the rendezvous.
If that his Majesty would aught with us,
We shall express our duty in his eye;[2]   5
And let him know so.

CAPTAIN: I will do't, my lord.

FORTINBRAS: Go softly[3] on.   [*Exeunt all but the* CAPTAIN.]

(*Enter* HAMLET, ROSENCRANTZ, &c.)

HAMLET: Good sir, whose powers[4] are these?

CAPTAIN: They are of Norway, sir.   10

HAMLET: How purposed, sir, I pray you?

[9] angel of knowledge	[16] fever
[10] closely	[17] chances, fortunes
[11] depends	[1] escort for
[12] scar	[2] before his eyes (i.e., in his presence)
[13] uncompelled submission	[3] slowly
[14] regard slightly our royal command	[4] forces
[15] instant	

CAPTAIN: Against some part of Poland.

HAMLET: Who commands them, sir?

CAPTAIN: The nephew to old Norway, Fortinbras.

HAMLET: Goes it against the main[5] of Poland, sir,　　　　　　　15
　　Or for some frontier?

CAPTAIN: Truly to speak, and with no addition,[6]
　　We go to gain a little patch of ground
　　That hath in it no profit but the name.
　　To pay five ducats, five, I would not farm it,　　　　　　　20
　　Nor will it yield to Norway or the Pole
　　A ranker[7] rate, should it be sold in fee.[8]

HAMLET: Why, then the Polack never will defend it.

CAPTAIN: Yes, it is already garrisoned.

HAMLET: Two thousand souls and twenty thousand ducats　　　25
　　Will not debate[9] the question of this straw.
　　This is th' imposthume[10] of much wealth and peace,
　　That inward breaks, and shows no cause without
　　Why the man dies. I humbly thank you, sir.　　　　　　*[Exit.]*

CAPTAIN: God bye you, sir.

ROSENCRANTZ:　　　　　　　Will't please you go, my lord?　　30

HAMLET: I'll be with you straight. Go a little before.　*[Exeunt all but* HAMLET.*]*
　　How all occasions do inform against me
　　And spur my dull revenge! What is a man,
　　If his chief good and market[11] of his time
　　Be but to sleep and feed? A beast, no more.　　　　　　　35
　　Sure he that made us with such large discourse,[12]
　　Looking before and after, gave us not
　　That capability and godlike reason
　　To fust[13] in us unused. Now, whether it be
　　Bestial oblivion,[14] or some craven scruple　　　　　　　40
　　Of thinking too precisely on th' event[15] —
　　A thought which, quartered, hath but one part wisdom
　　And ever three parts coward — I do not know
　　Why yet I live to say, "This thing's to do,"
　　Sith I have cause, and will, and strength, and means　　　45
　　To do't. Examples gross[16] as earth exhort me.
　　Witness this army of such mass and charge,[17]
　　Led by a delicate and tender prince,
　　Whose spirit, with divine ambition puffed,
　　Makes mouths at the invisible event,[18]　　　　　　　　50
　　Exposing what is mortal and unsure

---

[5] main part
[6] plainly
[7] higher
[8] outright
[9] settle
[10] abscess, ulcer
[11] profit
[12] understanding

[13] grow moldy
[14] forgetfulness
[15] outcome
[16] large, obvious
[17] expense
[18] makes scornful faces at (is contemptuous of) the unseen outcome

To all that fortune, death, and danger dare,
Even for an eggshell. Rightly to be great
Is not[19] to stir without great argument,[20]
But greatly[21] to find quarrel in a straw   55
When honor's at the stake. How stand I then,
That have a father killed, a mother stained,
Excitements[22] of my reason and my blood,
And let all sleep, while to my shame I see
The imminent death of twenty thousand men   60
That for a fantasy and trick of fame[23]
Go to their graves like beds, fight for a plot
Whereon the numbers cannot try the cause,
Which is not tomb enough and continent[24]
To hide the slain? O, from this time forth,   65
My thoughts be bloody, or be nothing worth!   (*Exit.*)

SCENE 5. [THE CASTLE.]

Enter HORATIO, [QUEEN] GERTRUDE, *and a* GENTLEMAN.

QUEEN: I will not speak with her.
GENTLEMAN: She is importunate, indeed distract.
   Her mood will needs be pitied.
QUEEN: What would she have?
GENTLEMAN: She speaks much of her father, says she hears
   There's tricks i' th' world, and hems, and beats her heart,   5
   Spurns enviously at straws,[1] speaks things in doubt[2]
   That carry but half sense. Her speech is nothing,
   Yet the unshapèd use of it doth move
   The hearers to collection;[3] they yawn[4] at it,
   And botch the words up fit to their own thoughts,   10
   Which, as her winks and nods and gestures yield them,
   Indeed would make one think there might be thought,
   Though nothing sure, yet much unhappily.
HORATIO: 'Twere good she were spoken with, for she may strew
   Dangerous conjectures in ill-breeding minds.   15
QUEEN: Let her come in.   [*Exit* GENTLEMAN.]
   [*Aside.*] To my sick soul (as sin's true nature is)
   Each toy seems prologue to some great amiss;[5]
   So full of artless jealousy[6] is guilt
   It spills[7] itself in fearing to be spilt.   20

---

[19] (the sense seems to require "not not")
[20] reason
[21] i.e., nobly
[22] incentives
[23] illusion and trifle of reputation
[24] receptacle, container
[1] objects spitefully to insignificant matters
[2] uncertainly

[3] i.e., yet the formless manner of it moves her listeners to gather up some sort of meaning
[4] gape (?)
[5] misfortune
[6] crude suspicion
[7] destroys

(*Enter* OPHELIA [*distracted*].)

OPHELIA: Where is the beauteous majesty of Denmark?
QUEEN: How now, Ophelia?
OPHELIA: (*She sings.*)

> How should I your truelove know
> From another one?
> By his cockle hat[8] and staff   25
> And his sandal shoon.[9]

QUEEN: Alas, sweet lady, what imports this song?
OPHELIA: Say you? Nay, pray you mark.

> He is dead and gone, lady,   (*Song.*)
> He is dead and gone;   30
> At his head a grass-green turf,
> At his heels a stone.

O, ho!
QUEEN: Nay, but Ophelia ——
OPHELIA: Pray you mark. [*Sings.*]   35

> White his shroud as the mountain snow ——

(*Enter* KING.)

QUEEN: Alas, look here, my lord.
OPHELIA:

> Larded[10] all with sweet flowers   (*Song.*)
> Which bewept to the grave did not go
> With truelove showers.   40

KING: How do you, pretty lady?
OPHELIA: Well, God dild[11] you! They say the owl was a baker's daughter.[12]
    Lord, we know what we are, but know not what we may be. God be at your
    table!
KING: Conceit[13] upon her father.   45
OPHELIA: Pray let's have no words of this, but when they ask you what it means,
    say you this:

> Tomorrow is Saint Valentine's day.[14]   (*Song.*)
> All in the morning betime,
> And I a maid at your window,   50
> To be your Valentine.

---

[8] (a cockleshell on the hat was the sign of a pilgrim who had journeyed to shrines overseas. The association of lovers and pilgrims was a common one)
[9] shoes
[10] decorated
[11] yield, i.e., reward

[12] (an allusion to a tale of a baker's daughter who begrudged bread to Christ and was turned into an owl)
[13] brooding
[14] Feb. 14 (the notion was that a bachelor would become the truelove of the first girl he saw on this day)

> Then up he rose and donned his clothes
> And dupped[15] the chamber door,
> Let in the maid, that out a maid
> Never departed more.   55

KING: Pretty Ophelia.

OPHELIA: Indeed, la, without an oath, I'll make an end on't:

[*Sings.*]   By Gis[16] and by Saint Charity,
>   Alack, and fie for shame!
>   Young men will do't if they come to't,   60
>   By Cock,[17] they are to blame.
>   Quoth she, "Before you tumbled me,
>   You promised me to wed."

He answers:

>   "So would I 'a' done, by yonder sun,   65
>   An thou hadst not come to my bed."

KING: How long hath she been thus?

OPHELIA: I hope all will be well. We must be patient, but I cannot choose but
weep to think they would lay him i' th' cold ground. My brother shall know
of it; and so I thank you for your good counsel. Come, my coach! Good   70
night, ladies, good night. Sweet ladies, good night, good night.   (*Exit.*)

KING: Follow her close; give her good watch, I pray you.   [*Exit* HORATIO.]
> O, this is the poison of deep grief; it springs
> All from her father's death — and now behold!
> O Gertrude, Gertrude,   75
> When sorrows come, they come not single spies,
> But in battalions: first, her father slain;
> Next, your son gone, and he most violent author
> Of his own just remove; the people muddied,[18]
> Thick and unwholesome in their thoughts and whispers   80
> For good Polonius' death, and we have done but greenly[19]
> In huggermugger[20] to inter him; poor Ophelia
> Divided from herself and her fair judgment,
> Without the which we are pictures or mere beasts:
> Last, and as much containing as all these,   85
> Her brother is in secret come from France,
> Feeds on his wonder,[21] keeps himself in clouds,
> And wants not buzzers[22] to infect his ear
> With pestilent speeches of his father's death,
> Wherein necessity, of matter beggared,[23]   90
> Will nothing stick[24] our person to arraign
> In ear and ear. O my dear Gertrude, this,

[15] opened (did up)
[16] (contraction of "Jesus")
[17] (1) God, (2) phallus
[18] muddled
[19] foolishly
[20] secret haste
[21] suspicion
[22] does not lack talebearers
[23] unprovided with facts
[24] will not hesitate

Like to a murd'ring piece,[25] in many places
Gives me superfluous death.   (*A noise within.*)

(*Enter a* MESSENGER.)

QUEEN: Alack, what noise is this?
KING: Attend, where are my Switzers?[26] Let them guard the door.   95
   What is the matter?
MESSENGER: Save yourself, my lord.
   The ocean, overpeering of his list,[27]
   Eats not the flats with more impiteous haste
   Than young Laertes, in a riotous head,[28]
   O'erbears your officers. The rabble call him lord,   100
   And, as the world were now but to begin,
   Antiquity forgot, custom not known,
   The ratifiers and props of every word,
   They cry, "Choose we! Laertes shall be king!"
   Caps, hands, and tongues applaud it to the clouds,   105
   "Laertes shall be king! Laertes king!" (*A noise within.*)
QUEEN: How cheerfully on the false trail they cry!
   O, this is counter,[29] you false Danish dogs!

(*Enter* LAERTES *with others.*)

KING: The doors are broke.
LAERTES: Where is this king? — Sirs, stand you all without.   110
ALL: No, let's come in.
LAERTES: I pray you give me leave.
ALL: We will, we will
LAERTES: I thank you. Keep the door.   [*Exeunt his* FOLLOWERS.]
                   O thou vile King,
   Give me my father.
QUEEN: Calmly, good Laertes.
LAERTES: That drop of blood that's calm proclaims me bastard,   115
   Cries cuckold[30] to my father, brands the harlot
   Even here between the chaste unsmirchèd brow
   Of my true mother.
KING: What is the cause, Laertes,
   That thy rebellion looks so giantlike?
   Let him go, Gertrude. Do not fear[31] our person.   120
   There's such divinity doth hedge a king
   That treason can but peep to[32] what it would,
   Acts little of his will. Tell me, Laertes,
   Why thou art thus incensed. Let him go, Gertrude.
   Speak, man.   125

[25] (a cannon that shot a kind of shrapnel)
[26] Swiss guards
[27] shore
[28] with a rebellious force
[29] (a hound runs counter when he follows
the scent backward from the prey)

[30] man whose wife is unfaithful
[31] fear for
[32] i.e., look at from a distance

LAERTES: Where is my father?
KING: Dead.
QUEEN: But not by him.
KING: Let him demand his fill.
LAERTES: How came he dead? I'll not be juggled with.
　To hell allegiance, vows to the blackest devil,
　Conscience and grace to the profoundest pit!
　I dare damnation. To this point I stand,   130
　That both the worlds I give to negligence,[33]
　Let come what comes, only I'll be revenged
　Most throughly for my father.
KING: Who shall stay you?
LAERTES: My will, not all the world's.   135
　And for my means, I'll husband them[34] so well
　They shall go far with little.
KING: Good Laertes,
　If you desire to know the certainty
　Of your dear father, is't writ in your revenge
　That swoopstake[35] you will draw both friend and foe,   140
　Winner and loser?
LAERTES: None but his enemies.
KING: Will you know them then?
LAERTES: To his good friends thus wide I'll ope my arms
　And like the kind life-rend'ring pelican[36]
　Repast[37] them with my blood.
KING: Why, now you speak   145
　Like a good child and a true gentleman.
　That I am guiltless of your father's death,
　And am most sensibly[38] in grief for it,
　It shall as level to your judgment 'pear
　As day does to your eye.   150

(A noise within: "Let her come in.")

LAERTES: How now? What noise is that?

(Enter OPHELIA.)

O heat, dry up my brains; tears seven times salt
Burn out the sense and virtue[39] of mine eye!
By heaven, thy madness shall be paid with weight
Till our scale turn the beam.[40] O rose of May,   155
Dear maid, kind sister, sweet Ophelia!
O heavens, is't possible a young maid's wits

[33] i.e., I care not what may happen (to me) in this world or the next   [37] feed
[34] use them economically   [38] acutely
[35] in a clean sweep   [39] power
[36] (thought to feed its young with its own blood)   [40] weigh down the bar (of the balance)

Should be as mortal as an old man's life?
Nature is fine[41] in love, and where 'tis fine,
It sends some precious instance[42] of itself   160
After the thing it loves.

OPHELIA:

> They bore him barefaced on the bier   (*Song.*)
> Hey non nony, nony, hey nony
> And in his grave rained many a tear ——

Fare you well, my dove!   165

LAERTES: Hadst thou thy wits, and didst persuade revenge,
It could not move thus.

OPHELIA: You must sing "A-down a-down, and you call him a-down-a." O, how the
wheel[43] becomes it! It is the false steward, that stole his master's daughter.

LAERTES: This nothing's more than matter.[44]   170

OPHELIA: There's rosemary, that's for remembrance. Pray you, love, remember. And there is pansies, that's for thoughts.

LAERTES: A document[45] in madness, thoughts and remembrance fitted.

OPHELIA: There's fennel[46] for you, and columbines. There's rue for you, and
here's some for me. We may call it herb of grace o' Sundays. O, you must   175
wear your rue with a difference. There's a daisy. I would give you some
violets, but they withered all when my father died. They say 'a made a good
end. [*Sings.*]

> For bonny sweet Robin is all my joy.

LAERTES: Thought and affliction, passion, hell itself,   180
She turns to favor[47] and to prettiness.

OPHELIA:

> And will 'a not come again?   (*Song.*)
> And will 'a not come again?
>   No, no, he is dead,
>   Go to thy deathbed,   185
> He never will come again.
>
> His beard was as white as snow,
> All flaxen was his poll[48]
>   He is gone, he is gone,
>   And we cast away moan.   190
> God 'a' mercy on his soul!

---

[41] refined, delicate
[42] sample
[43] (of uncertain meaning, but probably a turn or dance of Ophelia's, rather than Fortune's wheel)
[44] this nonsense has more meaning than matters of consequence
[45] lesson
[46] (the distribution of flowers in the ensuing lines has symbolic meaning, but the meaning is disputed. Perhaps *fennel*, flattery; *columbines*, cuckoldry; *rue*, sorrow for Ophelia and repentance for the Queen; *daisy*, dissembling; *violets*, faithfulness. For other interpretations, see J. W. Lever in *Review of English Studies*, New Series 3 [1952], pp. 123–29)
[47] charm, beauty
[48] white as flax was his head

And of all Christian souls, I pray God. God bye you.   [*Exit.*]

LAERTES: Do you see this, O God?

KING: Laertes, I must commune with your grief,

  Or you deny me right. Go but apart,   195

  Make choice of whom your wisest friends you will,

  And they shall hear and judge 'twixt you and me.

  If by direct or by collateral[49] hand

  They find us touched,[50] we will our kingdom give,

  Our crown, our life, and all that we call ours,   200

  To you in satisfaction; but if not,

  Be you content to lend your patience to us,

  And we shall jointly labor with your soul

  To give it due content.

LAERTES: Let this be so.

  His means of death, his obscure funeral —   205

  No trophy, sword, nor hatchment[51] o'er his bones,

  No noble rite nor formal ostentation[52] —

  Cry to be heard, as 'twere from heaven to earth,

  That I must call't in question.

KING: So you shall;

  And where th' offense is, let the great ax fall.   210

  I pray you go with me.   (*Exeunt.*)

SCENE 6. [THE CASTLE.]

(*Enter* HORATIO *and others.*)

HORATIO: What are they that would speak with me?

GENTLEMAN: Seafaring men, sir. They say they have letters for you.

HORATIO: Let them come in.   [*Exit* ATTENDANT.]

  I do not know from what part of the world

  I should be greeted, if not from Lord Hamlet.   5

(*Enter* SAILORS.)

SAILOR: God bless you, sir.

HORATIO: Let Him bless thee too.

SAILOR: 'A shall, sir, an't please Him. There's a letter for you, sir — it came from th' ambassador that was bound for England — if your name be Horatio, as I am let to know it is.   10

HORATIO [*reads the letter*]:

  "Horatio, when thou shalt have overlooked[1] this, give these fellows some means to the King. They have letters for him. Ere we were two days old at sea, a pirate of very warlike appointment[2] gave us chase. Finding ourselves too slow of sail, we put on a compelled valor, and in the grapple I boarded

---

[49] indirect
[50] implicated
[51] tablet bearing the coat of arms of the dead

[52] ceremony
[1] surveyed
[2] equipment

them. On the instant they got clear of our ship; so I alone became their   15
prisoner. They have dealt with me like thieves of mercy, but they knew what
they did: I am to do a good turn for them. Let the king have the letters I
have sent, and repair thou to me with as much speed as thou wouldest fly
death. I have words to speak in thine ear will make thee dumb; yet are they
much too light for the bore³ of the matter. These good fellows will bring   20
thee where I am. Rosencrantz and Guildenstern hold their course for England. Of them I have much to tell thee. Farewell.

         He that thou knowest thine, HAMLET."

Come, I will give you way for these your letters,
And do't the speedier that you may direct me   25
To him from whom you brought them.   *(Exeunt.)*

SCENE 7. [THE CASTLE.]

Enter KING *and* LAERTES.

KING: Now must your conscience my acquittance seal,
 And you must put me in your heart for friend,
 Sith you have heard, and with a knowing ear,
 That he which hath your noble father slain
 Pursued my life.
LAERTES: It well appears. But tell me   5
 Why you proceeded not against these feats
 So criminal and so capital¹ in nature,
 As by your safety, greatness, wisdom, all things else,
 You mainly² were stirred up.
KING: O, for two special reasons,
 Which may to you perhaps seem much unsinewed,³   10
 But yet to me they're strong. The Queen his mother
 Lives almost by his looks, and for myself —
 My virtue or my plague, be it either which —
 She is so conjunctive⁴ to my life and soul,
 That, as the star moves not but in his sphere,   15
 I could not but by her. The other motive
 Why to a public count⁵ I might not go
 Is the great love the general gender⁶ bear him,
 Who, dipping all his faults in their affection,
 Would, like the spring that turneth wood to stone,⁷   20
 Convert his gyves⁸ to graces; so that my arrows,
 Too slightly timbered⁹ for so loud a wind,

³ caliber (here, "importance")
¹ deserving death
² powerfully
³ weak
⁴ closely united
⁵ reckoning

⁶ common people
⁷ (a spring in Shakespeare's county was so charged with lime that it would petrify wood placed in it)
⁸ fetters
⁹ shafted

Would have reverted to my bow again,
And not where I had aimed them.
LAERTES: And so have I a noble father lost,   25
A sister driven into desp'rate terms,[10]
Whose worth, if praises may go back again,[11]
Stood challenger on mount of all the age
For her perfections. But my revenge will come.
KING: Break not your sleeps for that. You must not think   30
That we are made of stuff so flat and dull
That we can let our beard be shook with danger,
And think it pastime. You shortly shall hear more.
I loved your father, and we love ourself,
And that, I hope, will teach you to imagine ——   35

(*Enter a* MESSENGER *with letters.*)

How now? What news?
MESSENGER: Letters, my lord, from Hamlet:
These to your Majesty; this to the Queen.
KING: From Hamlet? Who brought them?
MESSENGER: Sailors, my lord, they say; I saw them not.
They were given me by Claudio; he received them   40
Of him that brought them.
KING: Laertes, you shall hear them. —
Leave us.   (*Exit* MESSENGER.)

[*Reads*.] "High and mighty, you shall know I am set naked[12] on your kingdom. Tomorrow shall I beg leave to see your kingly eyes; when I shall (first
asking your pardon thereunto) recount the occasion of my sudden and more   45
strange return.

                                            HAMLET."

What should this mean? Are all the rest come back?
Or is it some abuse,[13] and no such thing?
LAERTES: Know you the hand?
KING: 'Tis Hamlet's character.[14] "Naked"!   50
And in a postscript here, he says "alone."
Can you devise[15] me?
LAERTES: I am lost in it, my lord. But let him come.
It warms the very sickness in my heart
That I shall live and tell him to his teeth,   55
"Thus did'st thou."
KING: If it be so, Laertes
(As how should it be so? How otherwise?),
Will you be ruled by me?
LAERTES: Ay, my lord,
So you will not o'errule me to a peace.

---

[10] conditions   [13] deception
[11] revert to what is past   [14] handwriting
[12] destitute   [15] advise

KING: To thine own peace. If he be now returned,   60
　　As checking at[16] his voyage, and that he means
　　No more to undertake it, I will work him
　　To an exploit now ripe in my device,
　　Under the which he shall not choose but fall;
　　And for his death no wind of blame shall breathe,   65
　　But even his mother shall uncharge the practice[17]
　　And call it accident.
LAERTES:　　　　　　　My lord, I will be ruled;
　　The rather if you could devise it so
　　That I might be the organ.
KING:　　　　　　　　　It falls right.
　　You have been talked of since your travel much,   70
　　And that in Hamlet's hearing, for a quality
　　Wherein they say you shine. Your sum of parts
　　Did not together pluck such envy from him
　　As did that one, and that, in my regard,
　　Of the unworthiest siege.[18]
LAERTES:　　　　　　　What part is that, my lord?   75
KING: A very riband in the cap of youth,
　　Yet needful too, for youth no less becomes
　　The light and careless livery that it wears
　　Than settled age his sables and his weeds,[19]
　　Importing health and graveness. Two months since   80
　　Here was a gentleman of Normandy.
　　I have seen myself, and served against, the French,
　　And they can[20] well on horseback, but this gallant
　　Had witchcraft in't. He grew unto his seat,
　　And to such wondrous doing brought his horse   85
　　As had he been incorpsed and deminatured
　　With the brave beast. So far he topped my thought
　　That I, in forgery[21] of shapes and tricks,
　　Come short of what he did.
LAERTES:　　　　　　　A Norman was't?
KING: A Norman.   90
LAERTES: Upon my life, Lamord.
KING:　　　　　　　　　The very same.
LAERTES: I know him well. He is the brooch[22] indeed
　　And gem of all the nation.
KING: He made confession[23] of you,
　　And gave you such a masterly report,   95
　　For art and exercise in your defense,
　　And for your rapier most especial,
　　That he cried out 'twould be a sight indeed

---

[16] turning away from (a term in falconry)　　[20] do
[17] not charge the device with treachery　　[21] invention
[18] rank　　[22] ornament
[19] i.e., sober attire　　[23] report

If one could match you. The scrimers[24] of their nation
He swore had neither motion, guard, nor eye,   100
If you opposed them. Sir, this report of his
Did Hamlet so envenom with his envy
That he could nothing do but wish and beg
Your sudden coming o'er to play with you.
Now, out of this ——
LAERTES: What out of this, my lord?   105
KING: Laertes, was your father dear to you?
   Or are you like the painting of a sorrow,
   A face without a heart?
LAERTES: .   Why ask you this?
KING: Not that I think you did not love your father,
   But that I know love is begun by time,   110
   And that I see, in passages of proof,[25]
   Time qualifies[26] the spark and fire of it.
   There lives within the very flame of love
   A kind of wick or snuff[27] that will abate it,
   And nothing is at a like goodness still,[28]   115
   For goodness, growing to a plurisy,[29]
   Dies in his own too-much. That we would do
   We should do when we would, for this "would" changes,
   And hath abatements and delays as many
   As there are tongues, are hands, are accidents,   120
   And then this "should" is like a spendthrift sigh,[30]
   That hurts by easing. But to the quick[31] of th' ulcer —
   Hamlet comes back; what would you undertake
   To show yourself in deed your father's son
   More than in words?
LAERTES: To cut his throat i' th' church!   125
KING: No place indeed should murder sanctuarize;[32]
   Revenge should have no bounds. But, good Laertes,
   Will you do this? Keep close within your chamber.
   Hamlet returned shall know you are come home.
   We'll put on those[33] shall praise your excellence   130
   And set a double varnish on the fame
   The Frenchman gave you, bring you in fine[34] together
   And wager on your heads. He, being remiss,
   Most generous, and free from all contriving,
   Will not peruse the foils, so that with ease,   135
   Or with a little shuffling, you may choose

---

[24] fencers
[25] proved cases
[26] diminishes
[27] residue of burnt wick (which dims the light)
[28] always
[29] fullness, excess

[30] (sighing provides ease, but because it was thought to thin the blood and so shorten life it was spendthrift)
[31] sensitive flesh
[32] protect
[33] we'll incite persons who
[34] finally

A sword unbated,[35] and, in a pass of practice,[36]
Requite him for your father.

LAERTES: I will do't,
And for that purpose I'll anoint my sword.
I bought an unction of a mountebank,[37]   140
So mortal that, but dip a knife in it,
Where it draws blood, no cataplasm[38] so rare,
Collected from all simples[39] that have virtue[40]
Under the moon, can save the thing from death
That is but scratched withal. I'll touch my point   145
With this contagion, that, if I gall him slightly,
It may be death.

KING: Let's further think of this,
Weigh what convenience both of time and means
May fit us to our shape.[41] If this should fail,
And that our drift look through[42] our bad performance,   150
'Twere better not assayed. Therefore this project
Should have a back or second, that might hold
If this did blast in proof.[43] Soft, let me see.
We'll make a solemn wager on your cunnings —
I ha't!   155
When in your motion you are hot and dry —
As make your bouts more violent to that end —
And that he calls for drink, I'll have prepared him
A chalice for the nonce,[44] whereon but sipping,
If he by chance escape your venomed stuck,[45]   160
Our purpose may hold there. — But stay, what noise?

(*Enter* QUEEN.)

QUEEN: One woe doth tread upon another's heel.
So fast they follow. Your sister's drowned, Laertes.

LAERTES: Drowned! O, where?

QUEEN: There is a willow grows askant[46] the brook,   165
That shows his hoar[47] leaves in the glassy stream:
Therewith[48] fantastic garlands did she make
Of crowflowers, nettles, daisies, and long purples,
That liberal[49] shepherds give a grosser name,
But our cold maids do dead men's fingers call them.   170
There on the pendent boughs her crownet[50] weeds
Clamb'ring to hang, an envious sliver[51] broke,

---

[35] not blunted
[36] treacherous thrust
[37] quack
[38] poultice
[39] medicinal herbs
[40] (to heal)
[41] role
[42] purpose show through
[43] burst (fail) in performance
[44] occasion
[45] thrust
[46] aslant
[47] silver-gray
[48] i.e., with willow twigs
[49] free-spoken, coarse-mouthed
[50] coronet
[51] malicious branch

When down her weedy trophies and herself
Fell in the weeping brook. Her clothes spread wide,
And mermaidlike awhile they bore her up,   175
Which time she chanted snatches of old lauds,[52]
As one incapable[53] of her own distress,
Or like a creature native and indued[54]
Unto that element. But long it could not be
Till that her garments, heavy with their drink,   180
Pulled the poor wretch from her melodious lay
To muddy death.
LAERTES: Alas, then she is drowned?
QUEEN: Drowned, drowned.
LAERTES: Too much of water hast thou, poor Ophelia,
And therefore I forbid my tears; but yet   185
It is our trick;[55] nature her custom holds,
Let shame say what it will: when these are gone,
The woman[56] will be out. Adieu, my lord.
I have a speech o' fire, that fain would blaze,
But that this folly drowns it.   (*Exit*.)
KING: Let's follow, Gertrude.   190
How much I had to do to calm his rage!
Now fear I this will give it start again;
Therefore let's follow.   (*Exeunt*.)

ACT V

SCENE 1. [A CHURCHYARD.]

Enter two CLOWNS.[1]

CLOWN: Is she to be buried in Christian burial when she willfully seeks her own
  salvation?
OTHER: I tell thee she is. Therefore make her grave straight.[2] The crowner[3]
  hath sate on her, and finds it Christian burial.
CLOWN: How can that be, unless she drowned herself in her own defense?   5
OTHER: Why, 'tis found so.
CLOWN: It must be *se offendendo*;[4] it cannot be else. For here lies the point: if I
  drown myself wittingly, it argues an act, and an act hath three branches —
  it is to act, to do, to perform. Argal,[5] she drowned herself wittingly.
OTHER: Nay, but hear you, Goodman Delver.   10
CLOWN: Give me leave. Here lies the water — good. Here stands the man —

---

[52] hymns
[53] unaware
[54] in harmony with
[55] trait, way
[56] i.e., womanly part of me
[1] rustics

[2] straightway
[3] coroner
[4] (blunder for *se defendendo*, a legal term
  meaning "in self-defense")
[5] (blunder for Latin *ergo*, "therefore")

good. If the man go to this water and drown himself, it is, will he nill he,[6] he
goes; mark you that. But if the water come to him and drown him, he
drowns not himself. Argal, he that is not guilty of his own death, shortens
not his own life.   15

OTHER: But is this law?

CLOWN: Ay marry, is't — crowner's quest[7] law.

OTHER: Will you ha' the truth on't? If this had not been a gentlewoman, she
should have been buried out o' Christian burial.

CLOWN: Why, there thou say'st. And the more pity that great folk should have   20
count'nance[8] in this world to drown or hang themselves more than their
even-Christen.[9] Come, my spade. There is no ancient gentlemen but
gard'ners, ditchers, and gravemakers. They hold up[10] Adam's profession.

OTHER: Was he a gentleman?

CLOWN: 'A was the first that ever bore arms.[11]   25

OTHER: Why, he had none.

CLOWN: What, art a heathen? How dost thou understand the Scripture?
The Scripture says Adam digged. Could he dig without arms? I'll put another question to thee. If thou answerest me not to the purpose, confess
thyself ——

OTHER: Go to.   30

CLOWN: What is he that builds stronger than either the mason, the shipwright,
or the carpenter?

OTHER: The gallowsmaker, for that frame outlives a thousand tenants.

CLOWN: I like thy wit well, in good faith. The gallows does well. But how does it
well? It does well to those that do ill. Now thou dost ill to say the gallows is   35
built stronger than the church. Argal, the gallows may do well to thee. To't
again, come.

OTHER: Who builds stronger than a mason, a shipwright, or a carpenter?

CLOWN: Ay, tell me that, and unyoke.[12]

OTHER: Marry, now I can tell.   40

CLOWN: To't.

OTHER: Mass,[13] I cannot tell.

(*Enter* HAMLET *and* HORATIO *afar off.*)

CLOWN: Cudgel thy brains no more about it, for your dull ass will not mend his
pace with beating. And when you are asked this question next, say "a grave-
maker." The houses he makes lasts till doomsday. Go, get thee in, and fetch   45
me a stoup[14] of liquor.   [*Exit other* CLOWN.]

      In youth when I did love, did love,   (*Song.*)
        Methought it was very sweet
      To contract — O — the time for — a — my behove,[15]
        O, methought there — a — was nothing — a — meet.   50

---

[6] will he or will he not (whether he will or
will not)
  [7] inquest
  [8] privilege
  [9] fellow Christian
  [10] keep up

[11] had a coat of arms (the sign of a gentleman)
  [12] i.e., stop work for the day
  [13] by the mass
  [14] tankard
  [15] advantage

HAMLET: Has this fellow no feeling of his business? 'A sings in grave-making.
HORATIO: Custom hath made it in him a property of easiness.[16]
HAMLET: 'Tis e'en so. The hand of little employment hath the daintier sense.[17]
CLOWN:

> But age with his stealing steps   (*Song*.)
>   Hath clawed me in his clutch,
> And hath shipped me into the land,   55
>   As if I had never been such.

[*Throws up a skull*.]

HAMLET: That skull had a tongue in it, and could sing once. How the knave
jowls[18] it to the ground, as if 'twere Cain's jawbone, that did the first murder!
This might be the pate of a politician, which this ass now o'erreaches,[19] one   60
that would circumvent God, might it not?
HORATIO: It might, my lord.
HAMLET: Or of a courtier, which could say "Good morrow, sweet lord! How
dost thou, sweet lord?" This might be my Lord Such-a-one, that praised my
Lord Such-a-one's horse when 'a went to beg it, might it not?   65
HORATIO: Ay, my lord.
HAMLET: Why, e'en so, and now my Lady Worm's, chapless,[20] and knocked
about the mazzard[21] with a sexton's spade. Here's fine revolution, an we had
the trick to see't. Did these bones cost no more the breeding but to play at
loggets[22] with them? Mine ache to think on't.   70
CLOWN:

> A pickax and a spade, a spade,   (*Song*.)
>   For and a shrouding sheet;
> O, a pit of clay for to be made
>   For such a guest is meet.

[*Throws up another skull*.]

HAMLET: There's another. Why may not that be the skull of a lawyer? Where be   75
his quiddities[23] now, his quillities,[24] his cases, his tenures,[25] and his tricks?
Why does he suffer this mad knave now to knock him about the sconce[26]
with a dirty shovel, and will not tell him of his action of battery? Hum! This
fellow might be in's time a great buyer of land, with his statutes, his recogni-
zances, his fines,[27] his double vouchers, his recoveries. Is this the fine[28] of   80
his fines, and the recovery of his recoveries, to have his fine pate full of fine

[16] easy for him
[17] is more sensitive (because it is not cal-
loused)
[18] hurls
[19] (1) reaches over, (2) has the advantage
over
[20] lacking the lower jaw
[21] head
[22] (a game in which small pieces of wood
were thrown at an object)

[23] subtle   arguments   (Lat. *quidditas*,
"whatness")
[24] fine distinctions
[25] legal means of holding land
[26] head
[27] his documents giving a creditor control
of a debtor's land, his bonds of surety, his
documents changing an entailed estate into
fee simple (unrestricted ownership)
[28] end

dirt? Will his vouchers vouch him no more of his purchases, and double ones too, than the length and breadth of a pair of indentures?[29] The very convey-ances[30] of his lands will scarcely lie in this box, and must th' inheritor him-self have no more, ha?

HORATIO: Not a jot more, my lord.   85

HAMLET: Is not parchment made of sheepskins?

HORATIO: Ay, my lord, and of calveskins too.

HAMLET: They are sheep and calves which seek out assurance[31] in that. I will speak to this fellow. Whose grave's this, sirrah?

CLOWN: Mine, sir. [*Sings.*]   90

> O, a pit of clay for to be made
> For such a guest is meet.

HAMLET: I think it be thine indeed, for thou liest in't.

CLOWN: You lie out on't, sir, and therefore 'tis not yours. For my part, I do not lie in't, yet it is mine.   95

HAMLET: Thou dost lie in't, to be in't and say it is thine. 'Tis for the dead, not for the quick;[32] therefore thou liest.

CLOWN: 'Tis a quick lie, sir; 'twill away again from me to you.

HAMLET: What man dost thou dig it for?

CLOWN: For no man, sir.   100

HAMLET: What woman then?

CLOWN: For none neither.

HAMLET: Who is to be buried in't?

CLOWN: One that was a woman, sir; but, rest her soul, she's dead.

HAMLET: How absolute[33] the knave is! We must speak by the card,[34] or equivo-   105
cation[35] will undo us. By the Lord, Horatio, this three years I have took note of it, the age is grown so picked[36] that the toe of the peasant comes so near the heel of the courtier he galls his kibe.[37] How long hast thou been a grave-maker?

CLOWN: Of all the days i' th' year, I came to't that day that our last king Hamlet   110
overcame Fortinbras.

HAMLET: How long is that since?

CLOWN: Cannot you tell that? Every fool can tell that. It was that very day that young Hamlet was born — he that is mad, and sent into England.

HAMLET: Ay, marry, why was he sent into England?   115

CLOWN: Why, because 'a was mad. 'A shall recover his wits there; or, if 'a do not, 'tis no great matter there.

HAMLET: Why?

CLOWN: 'Twill not be seen in him there. There the men are as mad as he.

HAMLET: How came he mad?   120

CLOWN: Very strangely, they say.

HAMLET: How strangely?

---

[29] contracts
[30] legal documents for the transference of land
[31] safety
[32] living

[33] positive, decided
[34] by the compass card, i.e., exactly
[35] ambiguity
[36] refined
[37] sore on the back of the heel

CLOWN: Faith, e'en with losing his wits.

HAMLET: Upon what ground?

CLOWN: Why, here in Denmark. I have been sexton here, man and boy, thirty   125
years.

HAMLET: How long will a man lie i' th' earth ere he rot?

CLOWN: Faith, if 'a be not rotten before 'a die (as we have many pocky corses[38]
nowadays that will scarce hold the laying in), 'a will last you some eight year
or nine year. A tanner will last you nine year.   130

HAMLET: Why he, more than another?

CLOWN: Why, sir, his hide is so tanned with his trade that 'a will keep out water
a great while, and your water is a sore decayer of your whoreson dead body.
Here's a skull now hath lien you i' th' earth three and twenty years.

HAMLET: Whose was it?   135

CLOWN: A whoreson mad fellow's it was. Whose do you think it was?

HAMLET: Nay, I know not.

CLOWN: A pestilence on him for a mad rogue! 'A poured a flagon of Rhenish on
my head once. This same skull, sir, was, sir, Yorick's skull, the King's jester.

HAMLET: This?   140

CLOWN: E'en that.

HAMLET: Let me see. [Takes the skull.] Alas, poor Yorick! I knew him, Horatio,
a fellow of infinite jest, of most excellent fancy. He hath borne me on his
back a thousand times. And now how abhorred in my imagination it is! My
gorge rises at it. Here hung those lips that I have kissed I know not how oft. 145
Where be your gibes now? Your gambols, your songs, your flashes of merriment that were wont to set the table on a roar? Not one now to mock your
own grinning? Quite chapfall'n?[39] Now get you to my lady's chamber, and
tell her, let her paint an inch thick, to this favor[40] she must come. Make her
laugh at that. Prithee, Horatio, tell me one thing.   150

HORATIO: What's that, my lord?

HAMLET: Dost thou think Alexander looked o' this fashion i' th' earth?

HORATIO: E'en so.

HAMLET: And smelt so? Pah! [Puts down the skull.]

HORATIO: E'en so, my lord.   155

HAMLET: To what base uses we may return, Horatio! Why may not imagination
trace the noble dust of Alexander till 'a find it stopping a bunghole?

HORATIO: 'Twere to consider too curiously,[41] to consider so.

HAMLET: No, faith, not a jot, but to follow him thither with modesty enough,[42]
and likelihood to lead it; as thus: Alexander died, Alexander was buried,   160
Alexander returneth to dust; the dust is earth; of earth we make loam; and
why of that loam whereto he was converted might they not stop a beer
barrel?

Imperious Caesar, dead and turned to clay,
Might stop a hole to keep the wind away.   165
O, that that earth which kept the world in awe

[38] bodies of persons who had been infected   [40] facial appearance
with the pox (syphilis)   [41] minutely
[39] (1) down in the mouth, (2) jawless   [42] without exaggeration

Should patch a wall t' expel the winter's flaw![43]
But soft, but soft awhile! Here comes the King.

(*Enter* KING, QUEEN, LAERTES, *and a coffin, with* LORDS *attendant* [*and a*
DOCTOR OF DIVINITY].)

The Queen, the courtiers. Who is this they follow?
And with such maimèd[44] rites? This doth betoken   170
The corse they follow did with desp'rate hand
Fordo it[45] own life. 'Twas of some estate.[46]
Couch[47] we awhile, and mark.   [*Retires with* HORATIO.]
LAERTES: What ceremony else?
HAMLET: That is Laertes,
A very noble youth. Mark.   175
LAERTES: What ceremony else?
DOCTOR: Her obsequies have been as far enlarged
As we have warranty. Her death was doubtful,[48]
And, but that great command o'ersways the order,
She should in ground unsanctified been lodged   180
Till the last trumpet. For charitable prayers,
Shards,[49] flints, and pebbles should be thrown on her.
Yet here she is allowed her virgin crants,[50]
Her maiden strewments,[51] and the bringing home
Of bell and burial.   185
LAERTES: Must there no more be done?
DOCTOR: No more be done.
We should profane the service of the dead
To sing a requiem and such rest to her
As to peace-parted souls.
LAERTES: Lay her i' th' earth,
And from her fair and unpolluted flesh   190
May violets spring! I tell thee, churlish priest,
A minist'ring angel shall my sister be
When thou liest howling!
HAMLET: What, the fair Ophelia?
QUEEN: Sweets to the sweet! Farewell. [*Scatters flowers.*]
I hoped thou shouldst have been my Hamlet's wife.   195
I thought thy bride bed to have decked, sweet maid,
And not have strewed thy grave.
LAERTES: O, treble woe
Fall ten times treble on that cursèd head
Whose wicked deed thy most ingenious sense[52]
Deprived thee of! Hold off the earth awhile,   200
Till I have caught her once more in mine arms.

[43] gust   [48] suspicious
[44] incomplete   [49] broken pieces of pottery
[45] destroy its   [50] garlands
[46] high rank   [51] i.e., of flowers
[47] hide   [52] finely endowed mind

(Leaps in the grave.)

Now pile your dust upon the quick and dead
Till of this flat a mountain you have made
T'o'ertop old Pelion[53] or the skyish head
Of blue Olympus.   205
HAMLET *(coming forward)*:
                    What is he whose grief
Bears such an emphasis, whose phrase of sorrow
Conjures the wand'ring stars,[54] and makes them stand
Like wonder-wounded hearers? This is I,
Hamlet the Dane.   210
LAERTES: The devil take thy soul!

[Grapples with him.][55]

HAMLET: Thou pray'st not well.
I prithee take thy fingers from my throat,
For, though I am not splenitive[56] and rash,
Yet have I in me something dangerous,
Which let thy wisdom fear. Hold off thy hand.   215
KING: Pluck them asunder.
QUEEN: Hamlet, Hamlet!
ALL: Gentlemen!
HORATIO: Good my lord, be quiet.

[Attendants part them.]

HAMLET: Why, I will fight with him upon this theme
Until my eyelids will no longer wag.
QUEEN: O my son, what theme?   220
HAMLET: I loved Ophelia. Forty thousand brothers
Could not with all their quantity of love
Make up my sum. What wilt thou do for her?
KING: O, he is mad, Laertes.
QUEEN: For love of God forbear him.   225
HAMLET: 'Swounds, show me what thou't do.
Woo't weep? Woo't fight? Woo't fast? Woo't tear thyself?
Woo't drink up eisel?[57] Eat a crocodile?
I'll do't. Dost thou come here to whine?
To outface me with leaping in her grave?   230
Be buried quick with her, and so will I.
And if thou prate of mountains, let them throw
Millions of acres on us, till our ground,

---

[53] (according to classical legend, giants in their fight with the gods sought to reach heaven by piling Mount Pelion and Mount Ossa on Mount Olympus)
[54] planets
[55] (Q1, a bad quarto, presumably reporting a version that toured, has a previous direction saying "Hamlet leaps in after Laertes." Possibly he does so, somewhat hysterically.

But such a direction — absent from the two good texts, Q2 and F — makes Hamlet the aggressor, somewhat contradicting his next speech. Perhaps Laertes leaps out of the grave to attack Hamlet)
[56] fiery (the spleen was thought to be the seat of anger)
[57] vinegar

Singeing his pate against the burning zone,[58]
Make Ossa like a wart! Nay, an thou'lt mouth,   235
I'll rant as well as thou.
QUEEN: This is mere madness;
And thus a while the fit will work on him.
Anon, as patient as the female dove
When that her golden couplets are disclosed,[59]
His silence will sit drooping.
HAMLET: Hear you, sir.   240
What is the reason that you use me thus?
I loved you ever. But it is no matter.
Let Hercules himself do what he may,
The cat will mew, and dog will have his day.
KING: I pray thee, good Horatio, wait upon him.   (*Exit* HAMLET *and* HORATIO.)   245
[*To* LAERTES.] Strengthen your patience in our last night's speech.
We'll put the matter to the present push.[60]
Good Gertrude, set some watch over your son.
This grave shall have a living[61] monument.
An hour of quiet shortly shall we see;   250
Till then in patience our proceeding be.   (*Exeunt.*)

Scene 2. [The Castle.]

Enter HAMLET *and* HORATIO.

HAMLET: So much for this, sir; now shall you see the other.
    You do remember all the circumstance?
HORATIO: Remember it, my lord!
HAMLET: Sir, in my heart there was a kind of fighting
    That would not let me sleep. Methought I lay   5
    Worse than the mutines in the bilboes.[1] Rashly
    (And praised be rashness for it) let us know,
    Our indiscretion sometime serves us well
    When our deep plots do pall,[2] and that should learn us
    There's a divinity that shapes our ends,   10
    Rough-hew them how we will.
HORATIO: That is most certain.
HAMLET: Up from my cabin,
    My sea gown scarfed about me, in the dark
    Groped I to find out them, had my desire,
    Fingered[3] their packet, and in fine[4] withdrew   15
    To mine own room again, making so bold,
    My fears forgetting manners, to unseal

[58] sun's orbit
[59] (the dove lays two eggs, and the newly hatched [*disclosed*] young are covered with golden down)
[60] immediate test
[61] lasting (with perhaps also a reference to the plot against Hamlet's life)

[1] mutineers in fetters
[2] fail
[3] stole
[4] finally

Their grand commission; where I found, Horatio —
Ah, royal knavery! — an exact command,
Larded[5] with many several sorts of reasons,   20
Importing Denmark's health, and England's too,
With, ho, such bugs and goblins in my life,[6]
That on the supervise,[7] no leisure bated,[8]
No, not to stay the grinding of the ax,
My head should be struck off.   25

HORATIO: Is't possible?

HAMLET: Here's the commission; read it at more leisure.
But wilt thou hear now how I did proceed?

HORATIO: I beseech you.

HAMLET: Being thus benetted round with villains,
Or[9] I could make a prologue to my brains,   30
They had begun the play. I sat me down,
Devised a new commission, wrote it fair.
I once did hold it, as our statists[10] do,
A baseness to write fair,[11] and labored much
How to forget that learning, but, sir, now   35
It did me yeoman's service. Wilt thou know
Th' effect[12] of what I wrote?

HORATIO: Ay, good my lord.

HAMLET: An earnest conjuration from the King,
As England was his faithful tributary,
As love between them like the palm might flourish,   40
As peace should still her wheaten garland wear
And stand a comma[13] 'tween their amities,
And many suchlike as's of great charge,[14]
That on the view and knowing of these contents,
Without debatement further, more or less,   45
He should those bearers put to sudden death,
Not shriving[15] time allowed.

HORATIO: How was this sealed?

HAMLET: Why, even in that was heaven ordinant.[16]
I had my father's signet in my purse,
Which was the model[17] of that Danish seal,   50
Folded the writ up in the form of th' other,
Subscribed it, gave't th' impression, placed it safely,
The changeling never known. Now, the next day
Was our sea fight, and what to this was sequent
Thou knowest already.   55

---

[5] enriched
[6] such bugbears and imagined terrors if I were allowed to live
[7] reading
[8] delay allowed
[9] ere
[10] statesmen
[11] clearly
[12] purport
[13] link
[14] (1) serious exhortation, (2) heavy burden (punning on as's and "asses")
[15] absolution
[16] ruling
[17] counterpart

HORATIO: So Guildenstern and Rosencrantz go to't.

HAMLET: Why, man, they did make love to this employment.
They are not near my conscience; their defeat
Does by their own insinuation[18] grow.
'Tis dangerous when the baser nature comes 60
Between the pass[19] and fell[20] incensèd points
Of mighty opposites.

HORATIO: Why, what a king is this!

HAMLET: Does it not, think thee, stand me now upon[21] —
He that hath killed my king, and whored my mother,
Popped in between th' election[22] and my hopes, 65
Thrown out his angle[23] for my proper life,[24]
And with such coz'nage[25] — is't not perfect conscience
To quit[26] him with this arm? And is't not to be damned
To let this canker of our nature come
In further evil? 70

HORATIO: It must be shortly known to him from England
What is the issue of the business there.

HAMLET: It will be short; the interim's mine,
And a man's life's no more than to say "one."
But I am very sorry, good Horatio, 75
That to Laertes I forgot myself,
For by the image of my cause I see
The portraiture of his. I'll court his favors.
But sure the bravery[27] of his grief did put me
Into a tow'ring passion. 80

HORATIO: Peace, who comes here?

(*Enter young* OSRIC, *a courtier*.)

OSRIC: Your lordship is right welcome back to Denmark.

HAMLET: I humbly thank you, sir. [*Aside to* HORATIO.]
Dost know this waterfly?

HORATIO [*aside to* HAMLET]: No, my good lord.

HAMLET [*aside to* HORATIO]: Thy state is the more gracious, for 'tis a vice to 85
know him. He hath much land, and fertile. Let a beast be lord of beasts, and
his crib shall stand at the king's mess.[28] 'Tis a chough,[29] but, as I say, spacious[30] in the possession of dirt.

OSRIC: Sweet lord, if your lordship were at leisure, I should impart a thing to
you from his Majesty. 90

HAMLET: I will receive it, sir, with all diligence of spirit. Put your bonnet to his
right use. 'Tis for the head.

OSRIC: I thank your lordship, it is very hot.

---

[18] meddling
[19] thrust
[20] cruel
[21] become incumbent upon me
[22] (the Danish monarchy was elective)
[23] fishing line
[24] my own life

[25] trickery
[26] pay back
[27] bravado
[28] table
[29] jackdaw (here, chatterer)
[30] well off

HAMLET: No, believe me, 'tis very cold; the wind is northerly.

OSRIC: It is indifferent cold, my lord, indeed.   95

HAMLET: But yet methinks it is very sultry and hot for my complexion.[31]

OSRIC: Exceedingly, my lord; it is very sultry, as 'twere — I cannot tell how. But, my lord, his Majesty bade me signify to you that 'a has laid a great wager on your head. Sir, this is the matter ——

HAMLET: I beseech you remember.   100

[HAMLET *moves him to put on his hat*.]

OSRIC: Nay, good my lord; for my ease, in good faith. Sir, here is newly come to court Laertes — believe me, an absolute gentleman, full of most excellent differences,[32] of very soft society and great showing. Indeed, to speak feelingly[33] of him, he is the card[34] or calendar of gentry; for you shall find in him the continent[35] of what part a gentleman would see.   105

HAMLET: Sir, his definement[36] suffers no perdition[37] in you, though I know, to divide him inventorially would dozy[38] th' arithmetic of memory, and yet but yaw neither in respect of his quick sail.[39] But, in the verity of extolment, I take him to be a soul of great article,[40] and his infusion[41] of such dearth and rareness as, to make true diction[42] of him, his semblable[43] is his mirror, and   110 who else would trace him, his umbrage,[44] nothing more.

OSRIC: Your lordship speaks most infallibly of him.

HAMLET: The concernancy,[45] sir? Why do we wrap the gentleman in our more rawer breath?

OSRIC: Sir?   115

HORATIO: Is't not possible to understand in another tongue? You will to't,[46] sir, really.

HAMLET: What imports the nomination of this gentleman?

OSRIC: Of Laertes?

HORATIO [*aside to* HAMLET]: His purse is empty already. All's golden words are   120 spent.

HAMLET: Of him, sir.

OSRIC: I know you are not ignorant ——

HAMLET: I would you did, sir; yet, in faith, if you did, it would not much approve[47] me. Well, sir?   125

OSRIC: You are not ignorant of what excellence Laertes is ——

HAMLET: I dare not confess that, lest I should compare with him in excellence; but to know a man well were to know himself.

OSRIC: I mean, sir, for his weapon; but in the imputation[48] laid on him by them, in his meed[49] he's unfellowed.   130

---

[31] temperament
[32] distinguishing characteristics
[33] justly
[34] chart
[35] summary
[36] description
[37] loss
[38] dizzy
[39] i.e., and yet only stagger despite all (*yaw neither*) in trying to overtake his virtues
[40] (literally, "item," but here perhaps "traits" or "importance")

[41] essential quality
[42] description
[43] likeness
[44] shadow
[45] meaning
[46] will get there
[47] commend
[48] reputation
[49] merit

HAMLET: What's his weapon?

OSRIC: Rapier and dagger.

HAMLET: That's two of his weapons — but well.

OSRIC: The King, sir, hath wagered with him six Barbary horses, against the which he has impawned,[50] as I take it, six French rapiers and poniards, with their assigns,[51] as girdle, hangers,[52] and so. Three of the carriages,[53] in faith, are very dear to fancy, very responsive[54] to the hilts, most delicate carriages, and of very liberal conceit.[55]

HAMLET: What call you the carriages?

HORATIO [*aside to* HAMLET]: I knew you must be edified by the margent[56] ere you had done.

OSRIC: The carriages, sir, are the hangers.

HAMLET: The phrase would be more germane to the matter if we could carry a cannon by our sides. I would it might be hangers till then. But on! Six Barbary horses against six French swords, their assigns, and three liberal-conceited carriages — that's the French bet against the Danish. Why is this all impawned, as you call it?

OSRIC: The King, sir, hath laid, sir, that in a dozen passes between yourself and him he shall not exceed you three hits; he hath laid on twelve for nine, and it would come to immediate trial if your lordship would vouchsafe the answer.

HAMLET: How if I answer no?

OSRIC: I mean, my lord, the opposition of your person in trial.

HAMLET: Sir, I will walk here in the hall. If it please his Majesty, it is the breathing time of day with me.[57] Let the foils be brought, the gentleman willing, and the King hold his purpose, I will win for him an I can; if not, I will gain nothing but my shame and the odd hits.

OSRIC: Shall I deliver you e'en so?

HAMLET: To this effect, sir, after what flourish your nature will.

OSRIC: I commend my duty to your lordship.

HAMLET: Yours, yours.   [*Exit* OSRIC.]

He does well to commend it himself; there are no tongues else for's turn.

HORATIO: This lapwing[58] runs away with the shell on his head.

HAMLET: 'A did comply, sir, with his dug[59] before 'a sucked it. Thus has he, and many more of the same breed that I know the drossy age dotes on, only got the tune of the time and, out of an habit of encounter,[60] a kind of yeasty[61] collection, which carries them through and through the most fanned and winnowed opinions; and do but blow them to their trial, the bubbles are out.[62]

---

[50] wagered
[51] accompaniments
[52] straps hanging the sword to the belt
[53] (an affected word for hangers)
[54] corresponding
[55] elaborate design
[56] i.e., marginal (explanatory) comment
[57] time when I take exercise
[58] (the new-hatched lapwing was thought to run around with half its shell on its head)

[59] he was ceremoniously polite to his mother's breast
[60] out of his own superficial way of meeting and conversing with people
[61] frothy
[62] i.e., they are blown away (the reference is to the "yeasty collection")

(*Enter a* LORD.)

LORD: My lord, his Majesty commended him to you by young Osric, who   170
    brings back to him that you attend him in the hall. He sends to know if your
    pleasure hold to play with Laertes, or that you will take longer time.

HAMLET: I am constant to my purposes; they follow the King's pleasure. If his
    fitness speaks, mine is ready; now or whensoever, provided I be so able as
    now.   175

LORD: The King and Queen and all are coming down.

HAMLET: In happy time.

LORD: The Queen desires you to use some gentle entertainment[63] to Laertes
    before you fall to play.

HAMLET: She well instructs me.   [*Exit* LORD.]   180

HORATIO: You will lose this wager, my lord.

HAMLET: I do not think so. Since he went into France I have been in continual
    practice. I shall win at the odds. But thou wouldst not think how ill all's here
    about my heart. But it is no matter.

HORATIO: Nay, good my lord ——   185

HAMLET: It is but foolery, but it is such a kind of gaingiving[64] as would perhaps
    trouble a woman.

HORATIO: If your mind dislike anything, obey it. I will forestall their repair
    hither and say you are not fit.

HAMLET: Not a whit, we defy augury. There is special providence in the fall of a 190
    sparrow.[65] If it be now, 'tis not to come; if it be not to come, it will be now; if
    it be not now, yet it will come. The readiness is all. Since no man of aught
    he leaves knows, what is't to leave betimes?[66] Let be.

(*A table prepared.* [*Enter*] *Trumpets, Drums, and* OFFICERS *with cushions;*
KING, QUEEN, [OSRIC,] *and all the State,* [*with*] *foils, daggers,* [*and stoups of
wine borne in*]; *and* LAERTES.)

KING: Come, Hamlet, come, and take this hand from me.

[*The* KING *puts* LAERTES' *hand into* HAMLET'S.]

HAMLET: Give me your pardon, sir. I have done you wrong,   195
    But pardon't, as you are a gentleman.
    This presence[67] knows, and you must needs have heard,
    How I am punished with a sore distraction
    What I have done.
    That might your nature, honor, and exception[68]   200
    Roughly awake, I here proclaim was madness.
    Was't Hamlet wronged Laertes? Never Hamlet.
    If Hamlet from himself be ta'en away,

---

[63] to be courteous
[64] misgiving
[65] (cf. Matthew 10:29: "Are not two sparrows sold for a farthing? and one of them
shall not fall on the ground without your
Father")

[66] early
[67] royal assembly
[68] disapproval

And when he's not himself does wrong Laertes,
Then Hamlet does it not, Hamlet denies it.   205
Who does it then? His madness. If't be so,
Hamlet is of the faction[69] that is wronged;
His madness is poor Hamlet's enemy.
Sir, in this audience,
Let my disclaiming from a purposed evil   210
Free me so far in your most generous thoughts
That I have shot my arrow o'er the house
And hurt my brother.

LAERTES: I am satisfied in nature,
Whose motive in this case should stir me most
To my revenge. But in my terms of honor   215
I stand aloof, and will no reconcilement
Till by some elder masters of known honor
I have a voice and precedent[70] of peace
To keep my name ungored. But till that time
I do receive your offered love like love,   220
And will not wrong it.

HAMLET: I embrace it freely,
And will this brother's wager frankly play.
Give us the foils. Come on.

LAERTES: Come, one for me.

HAMLET: I'll be your foil,[71] Laertes. In mine ignorance
Your skill shall, like a star i' th' darkest night,   225
Stick fiery off[72] indeed.

LAERTES: You mock me, sir.

HAMLET: No, by this hand.

KING: Give them the foils, young Osric. Cousin Hamlet,
You know the wager?

HAMLET: Very well, my lord.
Your grace has laid the odds o' th' weaker side.   230

KING: I do not fear it, I have seen you both;
But since he is bettered,[73] we have therefore odds.

LAERTES: This is too heavy; let me see another.

HAMLET: This likes me well. These foils have all a length?

(*Prepare to play.*)

OSRIC: Ay, my good lord.   235

KING: Set me the stoups of wine upon that table.
If Hamlet give the first or second hit,
Or quit[74] in answer of the third exchange,
Let all the battlements their ordnance fire.

---

[69] party, side
[70] authoritative opinion justified by precedent
[71] (1) blunt sword, (2) background (of metallic leaf) for a jewel

[72] stand out brilliantly
[73] has improved (in France)
[74] repay, hit back

The King shall drink to Hamlet's better breath,   240
And in the cup an union[75] shall he throw
Richer than that which four successive kings
In Denmark's crown have worn. Give me the cups,
And let the kettle[76] to the trumpet speak,
The trumpet to the cannoneer without,   245
The cannons to the heavens, the heaven to earth,
"Now the King drinks to Hamlet." Come, begin.

(*Trumpets the while.*)

And you, the judges, bear a wary eye.
HAMLET: Come on, sir.
LAERTES: Come, my lord.

(*They play.*)

HAMLET: One.
LAERTES: No.
HAMLET: Judgment?
OSRIC: A hit, a very palpable hit.

(*Drum, trumpets, and shot. Flourish; a piece goes off.*)

LAERTES: Well, again.   250
KING: Stay, give me drink. Hamlet, this pearl is thine.
Here's to thy health. Give him the cup.
HAMLET: I'll play this bout first; set it by awhile.
Come.

[*They play.*]

                Another hit. What say you?
LAERTES: A touch, a touch; I do confess't.   255
KING: Our son shall win.
QUEEN: He's fat,[77] and scant of breath.
Here, Hamlet, take my napkin, rub thy brows.
The Queen carouses to thy fortune, Hamlet.
HAMLET: Good madam!
KING: Gertrude, do not drink.
QUEEN: I will, my lord; I pray you pardon me. [*Drinks.*]   260
KING [*aside*]: It is the poisoned cup; it is too late.
HAMLET: I dare not drink yet, madam — by and by.
QUEEN: Come, let me wipe thy face.
LAERTES: My lord, I'll hit him now.
KING: I do not think't.
LAERTES [*aside*]: And yet it is almost against my conscience.   265
HAMLET: Come for the third, Laertes. You do but dally.
I pray you pass with your best violence;
I am sure you make a wanton[78] of me.
LAERTES: Say you so? Come on.

---

[75] pearl
[76] kettledrum

[77] (1) sweaty, (2) out of training
[78] spoiled child

([*They*] *play*.)

OSRIC: Nothing neither way.   270
LAERTES: Have at you now!

(*In scuffling they change rapiers*, [*and both are wounded*].)

KING: Part them. They are incensed.
HAMLET: Nay, come — again!

[*The* QUEEN *falls*.]

OSRIC: Look to the Queen there, ho!
HORATIO: They bleed on both sides. How is it, my lord?
OSRIC: How is't, Laertes?
LAERTES: Why, as a woodcock to mine own springe,[79] Osric.   275
   I am justly killed with mine own treachery.
HAMLET: How does the Queen?
KING: She sounds[80] to see them bleed.
QUEEN: No, no, the drink, the drink! O my dear Hamlet!
   The drink, the drink! I am poisoned.   [*Dies*.]
HAMLET: O villainy! Ho! Let the door be locked.   280
   Treachery! Seek it out.

[LAERTES *falls*.]

LAERTES: It is here, Hamlet. Hamlet, thou art slain;
   No med'cine in the world can do thee good.
   In thee there is not half an hour's life.
   The treacherous instrument is in thy hand,   285
   Unbated and envenomed. The foul practice[81]
   Hath turned itself on me. Lo, here I lie,
   Never to rise again. Thy mother's poisoned.
   I can no more. The King, the King's to blame.
HAMLET: The point envenomed too?   290
   Then, venom, to thy work. (*Hurts the* KING.)
ALL: Treason! Treason!
KING: O, yet defend me, friends, I am but hurt.
HAMLET: Here, thou incestuous, murd'rous, damnèd Dane,
   Drink off this potion. Is thy union here?   295
   Follow my mother.   (KING *dies*.)
LAERTES: He is justly served.
   It is a poison tempered[82] by himself.
   Exchange forgiveness with me, noble Hamlet.
   Mine and my father's death come not upon thee,
   Nor thine on me!   (*Dies*.)   300
HAMLET: Heaven make thee free of it! I follow thee.
   I am dead, Horatio. Wretched Queen, adieu!
   You that look pale and tremble at this chance,
   That are but mutes[83] or audience to this act,

---

[79] snare   [82] mixed
[80] swoons   [83] performers who have no words to speak
[81] deception

Had I but time (as this fell sergeant,[84] Death,   305
Is strict in his arrest) O, I could tell you —
But let it be. Horatio, I am dead;
Thou livest; report me and my cause aright
To the unsatisfied.[85]
HORATIO: Never believe it.
I am more an antique Roman[86] than a Dane.   310
Here's yet some liquor left.
HAMLET: As th' art a man,
Give me the cup. Let go. By heaven, I'll ha't!
O God, Horatio, what a wounded name,
Things standing thus unknown, shall live behind me!
If thou didst ever hold me in thy heart,   315
Absent thee from felicity[87] awhile,
And in this harsh world draw thy breath in pain,
To tell my story.   (A *march afar off*. [*Exit* OSRIC.])
              What warlike noise is this?

(*Enter* OSRIC.)

OSRIC: Young Fortinbras, with conquest come from Poland,
To th' ambassadors of England gives   320
This warlike volley.
HAMLET: O, I die, Horatio!
The potent poison quite o'ercrows[88] my spirit.
I cannot live to hear the news from England,
But I do prophesy th' election lights
On Fortinbras. He has my dying voice.   325
So tell him, with th' occurrents,[89] more and less,
Which have solicited[90] — the rest is silence.   (*Dies*.)
HORATIO: Now cracks a noble heart. Good night, sweet Prince,
And flights of angels sing thee to thy rest.

[*March within*.]

Why does the drum come hither?   330

(*Enter* FORTINBRAS, *with the* AMBASSADORS *with Drum, Colors, and* ATTEN-
DANTS.)

FORTINBRAS: Where is this sight?
HORATIO: What is it you would see?
If aught of woe or wonder, cease your search.
FORTINBRAS: This quarry[91] cries on havoc.[92] O proud Death,
What feast is toward[93] in thine eternal cell
That thou so many princes at a shot   335

---

[84] dread sheriff's officers
[85] uninformed
[86] (with reference to the old Roman fashion of suicide)
[87] i.e., the felicity of death
[88] overpowers (as a triumphant cock crows over its weak opponent)

[89] occurrences
[90] incited
[91] heap of slain bodies
[92] proclaims general slaughter
[93] in preparation

So bloodily hast struck?
AMBASSADOR: The sight is dismal;
And our affairs from England come too late.
The ears are senseless that should give us hearing
To tell him his commandment is fulfilled,
That Rosencrantz and Guildenstern are dead.   340
Where should we have our thanks?
HORATIO: Not from his[94] mouth,
Had it th' ability of life to thank you.
He never gave commandment for their death.
But since, so jump[95] upon this bloody question,
You from the Polack wars, and you from England,   345
Are here arrived, give order that these bodies
High on a stage[96] be placèd to the view,
And let me speak to th' yet unknowing world
How these things came about. So shall you hear
Of carnal, bloody, and unnatural acts,   350
Of accidental judgments, casual[97] slaughters,
Of deaths put on by cunning and forced cause,
And, in this upshot, purposes mistook
Fall'n on th' inventors' heads. All this can I
Truly deliver.
FORTINBRAS: Let us haste to hear it,   355
And call the noblest to the audience.
For me, with sorrow I embrace my fortune.
I have some rights of memory[98] in this kingdom,
Which now to claim my vantage doth invite me.
HORATIO: Of that I shall have also cause to speak,   360
And from his mouth whose voice will draw on[99] more.
But let this same be presently performed,
Even while men's minds are wild, lest more mischance
On[100] plots and errors happen.
FORTINBRAS: Let four captains
Bear Hamlet like a soldier to the stage,   365
For he was likely, had he been put on,[101]
To have proved most royal; and for his passage[102]
The soldiers' music and the rite of war
Speak loudly for him.
Take up the bodies. Such a sight as this   370
Becomes the field,[103] but here shows much amiss.
Go, bid the soldiers shoot.

(*Exeunt marching; after the which a peal of ordnance are shot off.*)

FINIS

[94] (Claudius's)   [99] vote will influence
[95] precisely   [100] on top of
[96] platform   [101] advanced (to the throne)
[97] not humanly planned, chance   [102] death
[98] remembered claims   [103] battlefield

AFTERWORD

When we think of great drama, *Hamlet* is the play likely to come to mind first. In our culture it is *the* play. That a tragedy holds this special place is not strange, for tragedy is a dialogue with the absolute, in which man wrests wisdom and dignity from the inscrutables that defeat him. Tragedy, said Milton, "hath been ever held the gravest, moralest, and most profitable of all other poems." Nor is it surprising that the tragedy is one of Shakespeare's, for no other voice speaks so closely to so many of our deepest concerns as his. What may not be so obvious is why *Hamlet* has been singled out for distinction among all Shakespeare's tragedies. *Othello* has more strength and poignancy of plot; *Antony and Cleopatra* more lyrical intensity and larger imagery of word and action; *King Lear* rawer suffering, greater moral passion, and more titanic utterance. What is the reason for *Hamlet*'s unique prestige?

The answer, to judge from two hundred years of criticism, is Hamlet himself, the brightest, wittiest, and most attractive of all Shakespeare's tragic heroes, and the hardest to understand. It is not that his motives are unfathomable or that his thought lies too deep for words, for though what he does may surprise us, his actions are always unmistakably his, and his soliloquies express recognizable emotions and rather commonplace thoughts of the satire-against-the-world variety. His language is vivid, precise, and imaginative, sometimes racy and violent, but not dense, and his metaphors are striking but not obscure. The mystery of Hamlet is a *gestalt* of the whole situation of a young man of exquisite sensibility and intelligence called upon to redeem a world from which he feels alienated. Between his intent and his act lies the riddle.

Hamlet is the only intellectual among Shakespeare's tragic protagonists. More than the others, he lives in a world his mind has made. Life at Elsinore, with its various activities — statecraft, preparations for war, court ceremonials, and the comings and goings of embassies, old friends, and traveling players — is "weary, stale, flat, and unprofitable"; Denmark is an "unweeded garden"; and after the Ghost reveals Claudius's crime, Denmark is also a "prison" ruled by a "vice of kings," the "serpent" in old Hamlet's orchard of innocence, a Cain, whose willing consort is Hamlet's own mother. The corrupted garden-prison holds his mind: "O God, I could be bounded in a nutshell and count myself a king of infinite space, were it not that I have bad dreams." His disgust extends to existence itself. The world's "goodly frame" under a "most excellent canopy, . . . this brave, o'erhanging firmament," has become a "sterile promontory" under "a foul and pestilential congregation of vapors." In the most famous of his soliloquies, human life is a catalogue of moral and physical ills. Man is a victim of the cruel paradox of his being. "Infinite in faculties," he is yet nothing but "this quintessence of dust," "crawling between earth and heaven." Because Hamlet's sentience is finer than what it perceives, he is sick with thought, and his madness is more than a ruse. In his affronted and divided imagination, he is a riddle no more to others than to himself. "You would pluck out the heart of my mystery," he cries to Guildenstern and will not and cannot unlock his secret.

The record of *Hamlet* criticism is much more, of course, than the futile record of Guildenstern's folly. Still, if more has been written about *Hamlet* than about any other play, it is because the mystery remains. There is a residue of unexpounded and unexpoundable meaning at the end of even the most searching analysis of any great tragedy. It is part, we feel, of what makes the play great. If this quality of elusive enigma behind the accessible coherence of character and event seems stronger in *Hamlet* than in other plays, the reason is that Hamlet's own singular radiance leaves us more aware of tragic human waste and gives greater urgency to the questions we address to ultimate justice. Shakespeare's other tragic heroes are all, in different ways and to different extents, complicit in the evil that causes their suffering, but Hamlet's debilitation of will and befoulment of imagination are the consequence of his mother's and his uncle's corrupted appetites. His world has failed his trust, but he accepts responsibility for its redemption and dies effecting it.

The reason so high a price is exacted has often been said to be a flaw in Hamlet himself. A different man, like Laertes or Fortinbras, would have swept to his revenge. By "thinking too precisely on th' event" Hamlet fails to act. When he traces "the noble dust of Alexander" to the bung in a beer barrel, he is still, we may feel, a victim of that terrible reflective clairvoyance that for three long acts has disabled him for the task he is supposed to perform. What good is any human action in the face of the inevitable charnel house realities that the Gravedigger's shovel unearths? Horatio's reply to Hamlet's vision of futility, " 'Twere to consider too curiously to consider so," deepens our sense of Hamlet's tragic isolation. Even the one man whom he wears in his "heart of hearts" refuses to follow him in his pursuit of the ultimate questions. His isolation becomes neither less absolute nor less tragic when we say that common sense sides with Horatio: Some queries are better left alone; things are as they are in their inexplicable oddity.

But there is a curious quality about Hamlet's mood in the graveyard scene. He no longer rages against himself for failing to take action against the king. Instead of disgust with the world and himself, there is a kind of stoical acceptance, a resignation to Providence, a realization that "the readiness is all." His absence at sea has changed him. He now confronts the visible evidence that man is the quintessence of dust in a spirit of almost playful fatalism. He has passed through suffering and — like all tragic heroes in the moment of recognition — left mere common sense behind. His mind in Act V is no less penetrating and lucid than before, and it has gained a new composure.

A successfully resolute Hamlet would of course have been the hero of a melodrama, and it is tragedy we want. And what, perhaps, finally defines our sense of what is tragic in the story of Hamlet is not pity that the "vicious mole" of too scrupulous thinking in the nature of the sweet and noble prince caused him fatally to delay his revenge, but rather terror that our existence is such that the highest and finest thought has such consequences. This is to say that the philosophical thrust of the play involves something like an anti-theodicy: Rather than justifying the ways of the universe to rebellious man, *Hamlet* is the tragedy of an imagination required to impose value on a dark existence, to resurrect a fallen world. Hamlet's telling Rosencrantz and Guildenstern that "there is nothing either good or bad but thinking makes it so" does not mean that a desperate solipsism is his tragic flaw. Rather, it means that the flaw is in a condition that compels the mind to such desperate freedom.

There are tragedies from the past from which we feel we can infer certain philosophical verities shared alike by playwright and audience. With all their differences, such tragedies share an implicit belief in a hierarchy of created things, sustained by stable laws that human nature, in its difficult duality of mind and body, must come to terms with or else suffer. Such shared assumptions presumably made for a community not just of belief but of feeling and imagination that could relate life on stage meaningfully to the entire life of society beyond the stage. In *Hamlet*, too, we are aware of such assumptions, but in *Hamlet* we also feel that they are being tested in a way that is not quite the way in which they are being tested in such plays as Aeschylus's *Oresteia*, Sophocles' Theban plays, Shakespeare's own *King Lear*, and Racine's and Ibsen's dramatizations of the destructive conflict between reason and passion in the human soul. Those other tragedies build tragic worlds that are if anything more severe than that of *Hamlet*, and they are no less unflinching or inclusive in their vision of the human predicament. The difference is Hamlet's position of guiltlessness among evil. In no other tragedy do we get a stronger sense of the mysterious fact that man may suffer not despite but because of his virtue. And so we say that still another reason for the unique hold *Hamlet* has on us is that it is the most modern of older tragedies. We take to the element of metaphysical protest in it. We see Hamlet's dilemma as our own: to be or not to be in a world of intolerable seeming. And we like to think of ourselves as victims of that same sickness of the time that paralyzes his enterprise and nearly unbalances his superb mind.

But here a doubt arises. If we claim kinship with Hamlet as existential man deadlocked in absurdity, how did earlier ages see him? Does what we find in the play tell us why it has always seemed more challenging and absorbing than other plays — why it has become, in T.S. Eliot's words, "the Mona Lisa of literature"?

Perhaps it does, because the fashionable terminology in which we try to express our sense of life as grotesque and violent futility may obscure what our experience has in common with that of earlier times. Reviewing the main issues in *Hamlet* criticism, we discover continuity, not always of opinion, but of concern, where we too readily may have been assuming discontinuity. Past responses to the play are proof that our age has no monopoly on psychological perplexity and metaphysical anxiety.

The main problem for the critic of *Hamlet* has always been how to account for Hamlet's delayed revenge, however differently critics may have phrased the problem. For Dr. Johnson in the eighteenth century, the delay was a flaw that made Hamlet himself "rather an instrument than an agent" and which rendered his feigned madness dramatically pointless. The Romantics, in a characteristic shift in critical interest, were the first to locate the problem in psychology rather than in dramaturgy, and there it remained until well into the twentieth century. For Goethe, Hamlet was a sensitive soul unfit for the great task of revenge: "There is an oak-tree planted in a precious vase, . . . the roots expand, the vase is shattered." For other Romantic critics, the play was a "tragedy of thought" (Schlegel) and Hamlet himself "the prince of speculative philosophers" (Hazlitt), nearly neurotic in his excessive meditativeness, and defeating his purpose by "continually resolving to do, yet doing nothing but resolve" (Coleridge). A. C. Bradley read *Hamlet* as a tragedy of blighted idealism. It is the play, he says, that "most brings home to us at once the sense of the soul's infinity, and the sense of doom which not only circumscribes that infinity but appears to be its offspring." Ernest Jones, Freud's collaborator and biographer, saw in Hamlet the victim of an Oedipus complex, who has transferred his ambivalent feelings about his real father to the usurper of his father's place. Because the King has achieved what Hamlet subconsciously desires, the taboo on incest and parricide keeps Hamlet from accomplishing his conscious intent. Laurence Olivier's interpretation of Hamlet in his film version of the play was influenced by this Freudian view.

Psychological criticism of *Hamlet* has achieved a number of valuable insights, nowhere more than in Bradley's study, which marks the culmination of this kind of criticism. But it leads both to narrowness and to overinterpretation because of the fallacy of its tacit assumption that a character in literature is a real person rather than a verbal construct. Unlike people in real life Hamlet will have "life" for as long as Shakespeare's play is being read and staged, but by the same token his life is confined to the words Shakespeare wrote. That is why Bradley's query, "Where was Hamlet at the time of his father's death?" is both unanswerable and irrelevant. Hamlet's whereabouts at the time is not among the facts Shakespeare chose to make part of the imaginary world of *Hamlet*. Had he had real-life existence, it would be logical to say of Hamlet that he either was or was not at (say) Wittenberg when his father died. The conditions of physical life leave no other alternatives, and the alternatives are mutually exclusive. But because he is a creation of Shakespeare's imagination, the proposition does not apply. It isn't just that the text will not admit a definite answer; it will not admit the question. As a fiction Hamlet is not to be supposed to occupy

or to have occupied a particular piece of space at a particular time unless
words in the play tell us he does or did — the way we learn that Hamlet
and Horatio at one time were fellow students at Wittenberg and the way we
learn that at one time during the action Hamlet is on board a ship headed
for England.

There is an attraction in bestowing the full concreteness of real existence
on literary characters who capture our imagination. We pay tribute to the
author's ability to create an illusion of life when we do so. But by taking the
literary work as a record of reality we are denying it its own particular
mode of existence and are violating its integrity as an image — not a copy
— of reality. In reaction against Bradley's extrapolated Hamlet, modern
critics have seen that "the Prince of Denmark without *Hamlet*" represents
a hardly less disabling approach to the play than its proverbial reverse. The
Hamlet character is a function of life at the court of Elsinore, just as that
life is largely defined for us by Hamlet's attitude toward it and behavior in
it. When the sentinel in the opening scene is "sick at heart," when Polonius sends Reynaldo to Paris to spy on Laertes, when the Queen in adding
her thanks to her husband's innocently reduces Rosencrantz and Guildenstern to the interchangeable nonentities they are by inverting the order of
their names, when it is said that the dead Polonius will stink up the castle
unless his body is found, and when the King speaks of Hamlet as the raging
"hectic in my blood," the verbal images establish the moral climate of the
Danish court no less relevantly than Hamlet's own direct comments on it.
The error of the psychological critics was not their recognition of the central importance of the title character but their tendency to abstract him
from his dramatic context in trying to account for his psychology and de-
riving from that psychology lessons on how to live.

Twentieth-century criticism of Shakespeare is, as a body, much too rich
and versatile to be adequately described in a few sentences, but a few examples of post-Bradleyan approaches may suggest its range. Historical criticism has given new perspectives on old problems. The delayed revenge was
a conventional feature in Elizabethan revenge tragedy, and Shakespeare's
contemporaries are less likely to have regarded Hamlet's procrastination as
a psychological puzzle than as a plot device without which Shakespeare
would have had no play. Shakespeare may also have sought to add topical
relevance to his exploitation of a popular dramatic convention by so altering his source as to make the action reflect political hesitancy in high
places — a powerful topic during the last years of Queen Elizabeth's reign,
when the rebellious Earl of Essex threatened the stability of the state.
T. S. Eliot refused to grant *Hamlet* a place among Shakespeare's masterpieces on the neoclassical grounds that great literature is depersonalized
emotion and a son's disgust with his mother's sexual sin is an emotion that
has not found, and perhaps could not find, adequate expression in the plot
that came to Shakespeare's hand. For some reason, Shakespeare was unable to turn the old story into a stageable equivalent for Hamlet's feeling;

he failed to find — Eliot's phrase has entered the critical vocabulary — an "objective correlative" for it, and the enigmatic quality of the play is a sign of artistic failure rather than of success. Eliot's sense of disparity between act and feeling in *Hamlet* has not been shared by those critics who, without constituting a single school of criticism, have added to our understanding of the play by treating it as a complex, multi-level formal structure, in which verbal and scenic imagery, rhetoric, plot patterns, and Renaissance concepts about man, the state, and the universe collaborate in an extended metaphor of human life as a system of rival ethical norms in conflict.

One of the distinctive strengths of current Shakespearean criticism — or so, at least, it appears to a contemporary — is its recognition of the value of critical pluralism. Textual criticism and history of ideas, political and social history, and scholarly findings on the Elizabethan playhouse and on its literary and theatrical conventions are requisite tools for a responsible, close study of the way in which the particular verbal textures cumulatively build the inclusive meaning of the plays. Before he can argue that Hamlet is a conventional revenger figure, or the scapegoat prince of archetypal myth who must die in order to redeem his diseased land, or a soul divided against itself and made indecisive by a conflict between Christian conscience and the imperative of a more primitive ethos for private revenge, the critic must be sure he is working with a sound text of a play that was written for a certain kind of theater.

Hamlet was entered in the Stationers' Register on July 26, 1602. The Register was a list of the titles members of the company, or guild, of booksellers intended to publish. Its main purpose was to protect the publisher-bookseller's copyright, but it also facilitated the government's control over printed matter. *Hamlet* does not appear in the list of Shakespeare's plays included in *Palladis Tamia*, a kind of miscellany or commonplace book on literary and other topics, which Francis Meres, a schoolmaster divine, wrote in 1598. Since Meres lists just about every play that we know or have good reasons for believing that Shakespeare had written by 1598 (the only exceptions are the three *Henry VI* plays and *The Taming of the Shrew*, which may be the play that Meres calls "Love labours wonne"), a reasonable inference is that Shakespeare wrote *Hamlet* after Meres compiled his list. There have been arguments for a more accurate date for the composition of the play within the 1598–1602 period, but in the absence of conclusive evidence it must suffice here to say that scholars consider 1601–02 a likely date.

The play first appeared in print in 1603 in a corrupt and almost certainly unauthorized (pirated) text, the First (or "bad") Quarto, which is only a little more than half the length of the Second Quarto, which appeared in two imprints in 1604 and 1605, respectively. ("Quarto" and "folio" are printer's terms referring to the format of the printed sheets.) The Second Quarto was probably based on Shakespeare's own unrevised manuscript. It includes some 200 lines not in the Folio edition published in 1623. The Folio was a collection of all but one of Shakespeare's plays, which was prepared by two of Shakespeare's colleagues in the King's Men, John Hemminge and Henry Condell. On the other hand, the Folio includes eighty-five lines not in the Second Quarto. Presumably, both sets of cuts were authentic — that is, representing Shakespeare's own editing of his play. Shakespeare did not regard his plays as books to be printed but as scripts to be performed, and the discrepancies between the Second Quarto and the Folio texts are accounted for if we consider both texts acting versions used at different times during provincial tours. There are no divisions into acts and scenes in either of the two quartos, and in the Folio such divisions are restricted to the beginning of the first two acts. Modern editions of *Hamlet* are based on both the Second Quarto and the Folio.

As with all his plays (except, possibly, the first, *Love's Labor Lost*), Shakespeare found his plot in older sources. His most immediate source was an earlier *Hamlet* play, written, probably by Thomas Kyd, some time before 1590. There are references to this play in several contemporary sources, but no one today believes the references to be to Shakespeare's play. The ultimate source for this *Ur-Hamlet* (or "original" *Hamlet*) is a legendary Scandinavian story first given literary form about 1200 in a *Danish History* written in Latin by the Danish historian Saxo Grammaticus. Saxo's history was first printed in 1514. In 1576 the Frenchman Belleforest wrote an adaptation of it for his *Histoires Tragiques*, from which, or possibly through an English intermediary, it came to the author of *Ur-Hamlet*. The Ghost, we know, was an important figure in *Ur-Hamlet*. Except for it and the play-within-the-play, all the major features of Shakespeare's plot are in both Saxo and Belleforest, but there are also differences. In the early narrative versions Hamlet is a teen-ager, the murder of his father by his uncle is public knowledge, Hamlet feigns madness to save his life, the King suspects the sham and tries to expose it by using a light-virtued girl as a lure, and in the end Hamlet, with aid from England, succeeds in killing his uncle by burning down the royal hall where the King sits drinking with his men.

A seventeenth-century German play, *Der Bestrafte Brudermord (Fratricide Punished)*, apparently derives from *Ur-Hamlet* and thus allows us to make at least general inferences about its content. But since *Ur-Hamlet* is not extant, we don't know the exact extent of Shakespeare's indebtedness to it. Very likely it was quite strong. By all indications, *Ur-Hamlet* was a typical revenge drama in the tradition of Seneca's tragedies, which had been translated into English in 1580 and almost immediately had become a vogue. One reason for attributing *Ur-Hamlet* to Thomas Kyd is his *Spanish Tragedy* (probably 1586–87), in which the ghost of a murdered son appears to his father for revenge and the father feigns madness in order to get at his enemies. With its revenge plot, midnight scenes, ghostly apparitions, brooding violence, real and dissembled madness, treachery, poison, eavesdropping, and a stage full of corpses at the end, Shakespeare's *Hamlet* obviously belongs to the same genre. Shakespeare's achievement was the transformation of his sensationalist source into what Maynard Mack calls "a paradigm of the life of man."

The plot of *Hamlet* is not a model of compact unilinearity; if it had been, it could not have served as vehicle for a view of life as a mesh of interlocking destinies in a fallen and disordered world of disguised purpose and capricious fate. The plot's shape is huge, its harmony of proportion is not self-evident, and its pace is irregular. But it does have shaped coherence.

Gradually, other lives are drawn into and destroyed by the clash of the "mighty opposites" of criminal and avenger: the Queen, the Polonius family, Rosencrantz and Guildenstern. The conflict spreads to involve the political relations between Denmark and England. In the background, and intermittently entering the on-stage action, Fortinbras gathers and moves his Norwegian forces. Because his effective military bustle contrasts with Hamlet's fretful inaction, it is as if Hamlet's ordeal is being given symbolic sanction as a form of heroic warfare when Fortinbras at the end orders a soldier's funeral for the dead Prince. The analogy-with-difference between Hamlet, Fortinbras, and Laertes, all young men with a father to avenge, has both a cohesive and a thematic function, with Fortinbras occupying an intermediary position between Hamlet's scrupulous reflectiveness and Laertes's fickle and febrile rashness. But the main coherence of action in the play is in Hamlet's inner movement through three phases, divided by distinct breaks in the surface continuity of plot: a lapse in time between Acts I and II, and the hero's absence both from the stage and from Denmark between IV, 5 and V, 1. In the first phase, Hamlet's world-weary melancholia finds its object and its potential relief when the Ghost reveals the King's crime (Act I). In the second, his purpose dissipates itself in procrastination interrupted by futile bursts of violence (against Ophelia, Polonius, and the Queen) and self-reproach (Acts II–IV). In the third, his new calm of mind after his return from sea leads to his acceptance of Laertes's challenge and the consequent accomplishment of his avenger's mission in catastrophe (Act V). Alternating between active and passive suffering, the reluctant righter of the disjointed world undergoes a purgatory of the spirit, until the "cursed spite" that directs his fate is laid to rest in his tragic triumph.

If stages in Hamlet's progress of soul define the tragic action, imagery defines the kind of world in which the action takes place. The master image of the play is that of deceptive appearance — guilt masking itself as innocence, disease as health, corruption as wholesomeness. The king who rules this world sees himself as a painted harlot. It is a world in which human motives must be forever scanned, where the worth of any action is in doubt, and where justice itself becomes suspect and arbitrary. Disaster and death follow in the path of the noble avenger; he harrows the Danish court like some mortal disease. On the melodrama of the old story Shakespeare's consistent image patterns have grafted a philosophical problem play.

When the Queen in Act I tries to dispel her son's depression by reminding him that a father's death is a natural occurrence that should not "seem particular" to him, Hamlet replies that he knows not "seems." The reply is ironic, for he knows little else. He is surrounded by false or uncertain appearance. The Ghost who looks like his father may be a demon from Hell come to lure his soul to perdition. His mother, once the seeming paragon of chaste fidelity, is actually frail flesh incarnate, her lust blistering even "the fair forehead of an innocent love." Ophelia paints her face and lets herself be used as a decoy. A joyful reunion with old friends turns into an encounter with enemy spies. When Hamlet finds the King at prayer, the moment of retribution seems at hand. Then reflection intervenes: Killing the villain at his prayer would be to send his soul straight to Heaven and would seem like a poor kind of revenge. But here is seeming within seeming. The appearance of prayer is false; this *was* the moment for striking. Hamlet visits his mother, who seems to be alone but isn't. He lunges at the King behind the arras, but it isn't the King. He is to be sent to England to recover his wits, but actually to be killed. After his return, Laertes and he are to seal their reconciliation in a friendly exercise of arms, but the illusion of deadly combat is reality, and the refreshing drink is poison.

Such is the nature of Hamlet's world that he who knows not "seems" himself partakes in the general deceptiveness. He begins his revenge by dissembling madness. Deadly hatred motivates his "antic disposition," not love, as Polonius thinks. He uses a troupe of professional make-believers to expose the King's pretended innocence. What looks like an evening's pleasant entertainment for the court is actually the King's confrontation with his own crime; that is the mirror the players' art holds up to the King's corrupted nature. After the mousetrap scene, the King realizes that Hamlet is a guileful and dangerous enemy and not the madcap fooler with a secret that he had seemed to be. Hamlet sends his unsuspecting companions to their execution in England. He equivocates with Laertes when he tells him it was his madness and not his true self that killed Polonius. Where, finally, is the dividing line between lunacy and sanity, guilt and innocence, illusion and reality, right and wrong? Is Hamlet simply play-acting when he rages against Ophelia, or is he relieving his mind of pained outrage at the deceptiveness that taints even his love?

The mere seemingness of all things is one main motif. Another is the image of "rank corruption," which, "mining all within, / Infects unseen" until it finally breaks out. It first appears in Horatio's early speech that the coming of the Ghost "bodes some strange eruption to our state," words that prophetically describe the entire course of events that follow. It is implicit in Marcellus's words after the second appearance of the Ghost, "Something is rotten in the state of Denmark," and in the Ghost's description of the way his brother poisoned him. It turns up in other passages as well.

The deception motif and the image of concealed corruption slowly ripening meet in King Claudius, the smiling villain who is the secret ulcer that infects the entire body politic. In Renaissance concepts of monarchy, the king embodies his nation. In Rosencrantz's words:

> The cess of majesty
> Dies not alone, but like a gulf doth draw
> What's near it with it. . . .
>   Never alone
> Did the King sigh, but with a general groan.

The spreading infection that follows the evil act of murdering a king disintegrates the murderer-usurper's realm on all its levels. The state is first threatened with invasion, then with Laertes's rebellion, and is, in the end, in fact invaded. Natural family relationships turn unnatural following the initial violence done to brother by brother: Wife is set against husband, mother (and "father") against son, and lovers are separated. On the level of individual life Ophelia's madness is a dissolution of the natural order in the self — chaos subverting the harmonious microcosm of man.

On the surface, all seems fair in Claudius's Denmark. He has succeeded to the throne and married his brother's wife with the approval of the whole Council. (Whether the union is to be considered incestuous or not is one of the play's many uncertainties.) He rules with wisdom, authority, and proper pomp. His first political act is a piece of successful diplomacy. But corruption "inward breaks": Ruling without the grace of God, he is unable to pray; guilt-ridden, he is forever draining goblets of wine; self-loathing, he prefers to execute his designs through others.

The graveyard scene at the beginning of Act V visualizes the exhumation of the hidden corruption in anticipation of the climax at the end. Its macabre comedy — jokes among skulls — has human life itself as theme. The emperor's might, the lawyer's tricks, the jester's songs and gibes, the lady's beauty — all end in bones, mold, and stench. What the Gravedigger discloses symbolizes the reality of Claudius's rotten realm, and Clown and Prince, the two supreme realists in the play, share the same task. The deception that masks Denmark's sickness with fair appearance is the same deception that masks the growing corruption within all life. Hamlet completes his task only when he is already dying and leaves his purged heritage politically powerless, as if the restoration of innocence were not a viable condition. His death is an escape from an existence in which he has been both an exile and a prisoner.

Molière

TARTUFFE

Translated by Richard Wilbur

FOREWORD

Tartuffe represents the neoclassical drama of seventeenth-century France. From Italian stagecraft of the Renaissance, the French theater during the reign of Louis XIV developed most of the features of the conventional modern theater: a deep box stage framed by a proscenium arch, with the audience seated in front; a curtain; wings for movable sets; artificial light; elaborate painted scenery and backstage mechanical devices for special effects; actresses in female roles. It also took over some of the dramatic conventions of the Italian theater, particularly the three unities and — in comedy — the characters of the *commedia dell'arte*, semi-farces in which characters and plot were established stereotypes but the dialogue was improvised during performance. In *Tartuffe*, we recognize Orgon, the foolish and tyrannical father, Valère and Mariane, the nice if somewhat bland young lovers, and Dorine, the pert and clever maid, as descendants from their stock Italian prototypes.

Tartuffe had a complicated birth. An early version of its present first three acts made up the whole play when it was first given at Versailles in 1664. King Louis himself was amused, but the religious bigots at court took offense and prevailed upon him to ban the play. "The King," says a contemporary, "could not in his delicate carefulness for the things that concern religion suffer vice to be made so like virtue, that one might be taken for the other." The play was, however, given private readings and even performances during the next few years, probably in a five-act version. For a public performance of the play (in five acts) in 1667 Molière had changed his title to *The Impostor*, to leave no one in doubt that he was attacking only false piety, and dressed Tartuffe as a fop rather than in priest-like black, but again he drew the ire of the religious authorities. Only in 1669 did the King permit the play, with its original title restored and in its present form, to be freely performed. It immediately became Molière's biggest box-office hit, and has continued to be one of the most frequently revived works from the French repertory. Perhaps for the wrong reasons, it has always been popular during periods of discontent with the establishment. Napoleon watched it with qualified approval shortly after the French Revolution. It was a great favorite in a Russia which had just shaken off its czars. In our time, it has had a new spate of revivals for audiences who have become dissatisfied with contemporary manifestations of hypocrisy.

CHARACTERS

MME PERNELLE, Orgon's mother
ORGON, Elmire's husband
ELMIRE, Orgon's wife
DAMIS, Orgon's son, Elmire's stepson
MARIANE, Orgon's daughter, Elmire's
    stepdaughter, in love with Valère
VALÈRE, in love with Mariane

CLÉANTE, Orgon's brother-in-law
TARTUFFE, a hypocrite
DORINE, Mariane's lady's-maid
M. LOYAL, a bailiff
A POLICE OFFICER
FLIPOTE, Mme Pernelle's maid

The scene throughout: ORGON's *house in Paris*

ACT I

SCENE 1

MADAME PERNELLE and FLIPOTE, her maid
ELMIRE   DORINE   CLÉANTE
MARIANE   DAMIS

MADAME PERNELLE: Come, come, Flipote; it's time I left this place.
ELMIRE: I can't keep up, you walk at such a pace.
MADAME PERNELLE: Don't trouble, child; no need to show me out.
    It's not your manners I'm concerned about
ELMIRE: We merely pay you the respect we owe.   5
    But, Mother, why this hurry? Must you go?
MADAME PERNELLE: I must. This house appalls me. No one in it
    Will pay attention for a single minute.
    Children, I take my leave much vexed in spirit.
    I offer good advice, but you won't hear it.   10
    You all break in and chatter on and on.
    It's like a madhouse with the keeper gone.
DORINE: If . . .
MADAME PERNELLE: Girl, you talk too much, and I'm afraid
    You're far too saucy for a lady's-maid.
    You push in everywhere and have your say.   15
DAMIS: But . . .
MADAME PERNELLE: You, boy, grow more foolish every day.
    To think my grandson should be such a dunce!
    I've said a hundred times, if I've said it once,
    That if you keep the course on which you've started,
    You'll leave your worthy father broken-hearted.   20
MARIANE: I think . . .
MADAME PERNELLE: And you, his sister, seem so pure,
    So shy, so innocent, and so demure.
    But you know what they say about still waters.
    I pity parents with secretive daughters.
ELMIRE: Now, Mother . . .
MADAME PERNELLE: And as for you, child, let me add   25
    That your behavior is extremely bad,
    And a poor example for these children, too.
    Their dear, dead mother did far better than you.
    You're much too free with money, and I'm distressed
    To see you so elaborately dressed.   30
    When it's one's husband that one aims to please,
    One has no need of costly fripperies.
CLÉANTE: Oh, Madame, really . . .
MADAME PERNELLE: You are her brother, Sir,
    And I respect and love you; yet if I were
    My son, this lady's good and pious spouse,   35
    I wouldn't make you welcome in my house.

You're full of worldly counsels which, I fear,
Aren't suitable for decent folk to hear.
I've spoken bluntly, Sir; but it behooves us
Not to mince words when righteous fervor moves us.   40
DAMIS: Your man Tartuffe is full of holy speeches . . .
MADAME PERNELLE: And practises precisely what he preaches.
He's a fine man, and should be listened to.
I will not hear him mocked by fools like you.
DAMIS: Good God! Do you expect me to submit   45
To the tyranny of that carping hypocrite?
Must we forgo all joys and satisfactions
Because that bigot censures all our actions?
DORINE: To hear him talk — and he talks all the time —
There's nothing one can do that's not a crime.   50
He rails at everything, your dear Tartuffe.
MADAME PERNELLE: Whatever he reproves deserves reproof.
He's out to save your souls, and all of you
Must love him, as my son would have you do.
DAMIS: Ah no, Grandmother, I could never take   55
To such a rascal, even for my father's sake.
That's how I feel, and I shall not dissemble.
His every action makes me seethe and tremble
With helpless anger, and I have no doubt
That he and I will shortly have it out.   60
DORINE: Surely it is a shame and a disgrace
To see this man usurp the master's place —
To see this beggar who, when first he came,
Had not a shoe or shoestring to his name
So far forget himself that he behaves   65
As if the house were his, and we his slaves.
MADAME PERNELLE: Well, mark my words, your souls would fare far better
If you obeyed his precepts to the letter.
DORINE: You see him as a saint. I'm far less awed;
In fact, I see right through him. He's a fraud.   70
MADAME PERNELLE: Nonsense!
DORINE: His man Laurent's the same, or worse;
I'd not trust either with a penny purse.
MADAME PERNELLE: I can't say what his servant's morals may be;
His own great goodness I can guarantee.
You all regard him with distaste and fear   75
Because he tells you what you're loath to hear,
Condemns your sins, points out your moral flaws,
And humbly strives to further Heaven's cause.
DORINE: If sin is all that bothers him, why is it
He's so upset when folk drop in to visit?   80
Is Heaven so outraged by a social call
That he must prophesy against us all?
I'll tell you what I think: if you ask me,
He's jealous of my mistress' company.

MADAME PERNELLE: Rubbish! (*To* ELMIRE.) He's not alone, child, in
     complaining   85
   Of all your promiscuous entertaining.
   Why, the whole neighborhood's upset, I know,
   By all these carriages that come and go,
   With crowds of guests parading in and out
   And noisy servants loitering about.   90
   In all of this, I'm sure there's nothing vicious;
   But why give people cause to be suspicious?
CLÉANTE: They need no cause; they'll talk in any case.
   Madam, this world would be a joyless place
   If, fearing what malicious tongues might say,   95
   We locked our doors and turned our friends away.
   And even if one did so dreary a thing,
   D'you think those tongues would cease their chattering?
   One can't fight slander; it's a losing battle;
   Let us instead ignore their tittle-tattle.   100
   Let's strive to live by conscience' clear decrees,
   And let the gossips gossip as they please.
DORINE: If there is talk against us, I know the source:
   It's Daphne and her little husband, of course.
   Those who have greatest cause for guilt and shame   105
   Are quickest to besmirch a neighbor's name.
   When there's a chance for libel, they never miss it;
   When something can be made to seem illicit
   They're off at once to spread the joyous news,
   Adding to fact what fantasies they choose.   110
   By talking up their neighbor's indiscretions
   They seek to camouflage their own transgressions,
   Hoping that others' innocent affairs
   Will lend a hue of innocence to theirs,
   Or that their own black guilt will come to seem   115
   Part of a general shady color-scheme.
MADAME PERNELLE: All that is quite irrelevant. I doubt
   That anyone's more virtuous and devout
   Than dear Orante; and I'm informed that she
   Condemns your mode of life most vehemently.   120
DORINE: Oh, yes, she's strict, devout, and has no taint
   Of worldliness; in short, she seems a saint.
   But it was time which taught her that disguise;
   She's thus because she can't be otherwise.
   So long as her attractions could enthrall,
   She flounced and flirted and enjoyed it all,
   But now that they're no longer what they were
   She quits a world which fast is quitting her,
   And wears a veil of virtue to conceal
   Her bankrupt beauty and her lost appeal.   130
   That's what becomes of old coquettes today:
   Distressed when all their lovers fall away,

They see no recourse but to play the prude,
And so confer a style on solitude.
Thereafter, they're severe with everyone,   135
Condemning all our actions, pardoning none,
And claiming to be pure, austere, and zealous
When, if the truth were known, they're merely jealous,
And cannot bear to see another know
The pleasures time has forced them to forgo.   140
MADAME PERNELLE (*initially to* ELMIRE): That sort of talk is what you like to
     hear;
Therefore you'd have us all keep still, my dear,
While Madam rattles on the livelong day.
Nevertheless, I mean to have my say.
I tell you that you're blest to have Tartuffe   145
Dwelling, as my son's guest, beneath this roof;
That Heaven has sent him to forestall its wrath
By leading you, once more, to the true path;
That all he reprehends is reprehensible,
And that you'd better heed him, and be sensible.   150
These visits, balls, and parties in which you revel
Are nothing but inventions of the Devil.
One never hears a word that's edifying:
Nothing but chaff and foolishness and lying,
As well as vicious gossip in which one's neighbor   155
Is cut to bits with epee, foil, and saber.
People of sense are driven half-insane
At such affairs, where noise and folly reign
And reputations perish thick and fast.
As a wise preacher said on Sunday last,   160
Parties are Towers of Babylon, because
The guests all babble on with never a pause;
And then he told a story which, I think . . .
(*To* CLÉANTE.) I heard that laugh, Sir, and I saw that wink!
Go find your silly friends and laugh some more!   165
Enough; I'm going; don't show me to the door.
I leave this household much dismayed and vexed;
I cannot say when I shall see you next.
(*Slapping* FLIPOTE.) Wake up, don't stand there gaping into space!
I'll slap some sense into that stupid face.   170
Move, move, you slut.

Scene 2

CLÉANTE
DORINE

CLÉANTE: I think I'll stay behind;
I want no further pieces of her mind.
How that old lady . . .

DORINE: Oh, what wouldn't she say
   If she could hear you speak of her that way!
   She'd thank you for the *lady*, but I'm sure   5
   She'd find the *old* a little premature.
CLÉANTE: My, what a scene she made, and what a din!
   And how this man Tartuffe has taken her in!
DORINE: Yes, but her son is even worse deceived;
   His folly must be seen to be believed.   10
   In the late troubles, he played an able part
   And served his king with wise and loyal heart,
   But he's quite lost his senses since he fell
   Beneath Tartuffe's infatuating spell.
   He calls him brother, and loves him as his life,   15
   Preferring him to mother, child, or wife.
   In him and him alone will he confide;
   He's made him his confessor and his guide;
   He pets and pampers him with love more tender
   Than any pretty mistress could engender,   20
   Gives him the place of honor when they dine,
   Delights to see him gorging like a swine,
   Stuffs him with dainties till his guts distend,
   And when he belches, cries "God bless you, friend!"
   In short, he's mad; he worships him; he dotes;   25
   His deeds he marvels at, his words he quotes,
   Thinking each act a miracle, each word
   Oracular as those that Moses heard.
   Tartuffe, much pleased to find so easy a victim,
   Has in a hundred ways beguiled and tricked him,   30
   Milked him of money, and with his permission
   Established here a sort of Inquisition.
   Even Laurent, his lackey, dares to give
   Us arrogant advice on how to live;
   He sermonizes us in thundering tones   35
   And confiscates our ribbons and colognes.
   Last week he tore a kerchief into pieces
   Because he found it pressed in a *Life of Jesus:*
   He said it was a sin to juxtapose
   Unholy vanities and holy prose.   40

Scene 3

ELMIRE   DAMIS   DORINE
MARIANE   CLÉANTE

ELMIRE (*to* CLÉANTE): You did well not to follow; she stood in the door
   And said *verbatim* all she'd said before.
   I saw my husband coming. I think I'd best
   Go upstairs now, and take a little rest.

CLÉANTE: I'll wait and greet him here; then I must go.   5
    I've really only time to say hello.
DAMIS: Sound him about my sister's wedding, please.
    I think Tartuffe's against it, and that he's
    Been urging Father to withdraw his blessing.
    As you well know, I'd find that most distressing.   10
    Unless my sister and Valère can marry,
    My hopes to wed *his* sister will miscarry,
    And I'm determined . . .
DORINE: He's coming.

SCENE 4

ORGON
CLÉANTE
DORINE

ORGON: Ah, Brother, good-day.
CLÉANTE: Well, welcome back. I'm sorry I can't stay.
    How was the country? Blooming, I trust, and green?
ORGON: Excuse me, Brother; just one moment.
    (*To* DORINE.)   Dorine . . .
    (*To* CLÉANTE.) To put my mind at rest, I always learn   5
    The household news the moment I return.
    (*To* DORINE.) Has all been well, these two days I've been gone?
    How are the family? What's been going on?
DORINE: Your wife, two days ago, had a bad fever,
    And a fierce headache which refused to leave her.   10
ORGON: Ah. And Tartuffe?
DORINE: Tartuffe? Why, he's round and red,
    Bursting with health, and excellently fed.
ORGON: Poor fellow!
DORINE: That night, the mistress was unable
    To take a single bite at the dinner-table.
    Her headache-pains, she said, were simply hellish.   15
ORGON: Ah. And Tartuffe?
DORINE: He ate his meal with relish,
    And zealously devoured in her presence
    A leg of mutton and a brace of pheasants.
ORGON: Poor fellow!
DORINE: Well, the pains continued strong,
    And so she tossed and tossed the whole night long,   20
    Now icy-cold, now burning like a flame.
    We sat beside her bed till morning came.
ORGON: Ah. And Tartuffe?
DORINE: Why, having eaten, he rose
    And sought his room, already in a doze,
    Got into his warm bed, and snored away   25
    In perfect peace until the break of day.

ORGON: Poor fellow!
DORINE: After much ado, we talked her
   Into dispatching someone for the doctor.
   He bled her, and the fever quickly fell.
ORGON: Ah. And Tartuffe?
DORINE: He bore it very well.   30
   To keep his cheerfulness at any cost,
   And make up for the blood *Madame* had lost,
   He drank, at lunch, four beakers full of port.
ORGON: Poor fellow!
DORINE: Both are doing well, in short.
   I'll go and tell *Madame* that you've expressed   35
   Keen sympathy and anxious interest.

SCENE 5

ORGON
CLÉANTE

CLÉANTE: That girl was laughing in your face, and though
   I've no wish to offend you, even so
   I'm bound to say that she had some excuse.
   How can you possibly be such a goose?
   Are you so dazed by this man's hocus-pocus   5
   That all the world, save him, is out of focus?
   You've given him clothing, shelter, food, and care;
   Why must you also . . .
ORGON: Brother, stop right there.
   You do not know the man of whom you speak.
CLÉANTE: I grant you that. But my judgment's not so weak   10
   That I can't tell, by his effect on others . . .
ORGON: Ah, when you meet him, you two will be like brothers!
   There's been no loftier soul since time began.
   He is a man who . . . a man who . . . an excellent man.
   To keep his precepts is to be reborn,   15
   And view this dunghill of a world with scorn.
   Yes, thanks to him I'm a changed man indeed.
   Under his tutelage my soul's been freed
   From earthly loves, and every human tie:
   My mother, children, brother, and wife could die,   20
   And I'd not feel a single moment's pain.
CLÉANTE: That's a fine sentiment, Brother; most humane.
ORGON: Oh, had you seen Tartuffe as I first knew him,
   Your heart, like mine, would have surrendered to him.
   He used to come into our church each day   25
   And humbly kneel nearby, and start to pray.
   He'd draw the eyes of everybody there
   By the deep fervor of his heartfelt prayer;
   He'd sigh and weep, and sometimes with a sound

Of rapture he would bend and kiss the ground;   30
And when I rose to go, he'd run before
To offer me holy-water at the door.
His serving-man, no less devout than he,
Informed me of his master's poverty;
I gave him gifts, but in his humbleness   35
He'd beg me every time to give him less.
"Oh, that's too much," he'd cry, "too much by twice!
I don't deserve it. The half, Sir, would suffice."
And when I wouldn't take it back, he'd share
Half of it with the poor, right then and there.   40
At length, Heaven prompted me to take him in
To dwell with us, and free our souls from sin.
He guides our lives, and to protect my honor
Stays by my wife, and keeps an eye upon her;
He tells me whom she sees, and all she does,   45
And seems more jealous than I ever was!
And how austere he is! Why, he can detect
A mortal sin where you would least suspect;
In smallest trifles, he's extremely strict.
Last week, his conscience was severely pricked   50
Because, while praying, he had caught a flea
And killed it, so he felt, too wrathfully.
CLÉANTE: Good God, man! Have you lost your common sense —
Or is this all some joke at my expense?
How can you stand there and in all sobriety . . .   55
ORGON: Brother, your language savors of impiety.
Too much free-thinking's made your faith unsteady,
And as I've warned you many times already,
'Twill get you into trouble before you're through.
CLÉANTE: So I've been told before by dupes like you: 60
Being blind, you'd have all others blind as well;
The clear-eyed man you call an infidel,
And he who sees through humbug and pretense
Is charged, by you, with want of reverence.
Spare me your warnings, Brother; I have no fear   65
Of speaking out, for you and Heaven to hear,
Against affected zeal and pious knavery.
There's true and false in piety, as in bravery,
And just as those whose courage shines the most
In battle, are the least inclined to boast,   70
So those whose hearts are truly pure and lowly
Don't make a flashy show of being holy.
There's a vast difference, so it seems to me,
Between true piety and hypocrisy:
How do you fail to see it, may I ask?   75
Is not a face quite different from a mask?
Cannot sincerity and cunning art,
Reality and semblance, be told apart?

Are scarecrows just like men, and do you hold
That a false coin is just as good as gold?   80
Ah, Brother, man's a strangely fashioned creature
Who seldom is content to follow Nature,
But recklessly pursues his inclination
Beyond the narrow bounds of moderation,
And often, by transgressing Reason's laws,   85
Perverts a lofty aim or noble cause.
A passing observation, but it applies.
ORGON: I see, dear Brother, that you're profoundly wise;
    You harbor all the insight of the age.
    You are our one clear mind, our only sage,   90
    The era's oracle, its Cato too,
    And all mankind are fools compared to you.
CLÉANTE: Brother, I don't pretend to be a sage,
    Nor have I all the wisdom of the age.
    There's just one insight I would dare to claim: 95
    I know that true and false are not the same;
    And just as there is nothing I more revere
    Than a soul whose faith is steadfast and sincere,
    Nothing that I more cherish and admire
    Than honest zeal and true religious fire,   100
    So there is nothing that I find more base
    Than specious piety's dishonest face —
    Than these bold mountebanks, these histrios
    Whose impious mummeries and hollow shows
    Exploit our love of Heaven, and make a jest   105
    Of all that men think holiest and best;
    These calculating souls who offer prayers
    Not to their Maker, but as public wares,
    And seek to buy respect and reputation
    With lifted eyes and sighs of exaltation;   110
    These charlatans, I say, whose pilgrim souls
    Proceed, by way of Heaven, toward earthly goals,
    Who weep and pray and swindle and extort,
    Who preach the monkish life, but haunt the court,
    Who make their zeal the partner of their vice —   115
    Such men are vengeful, sly, and cold as ice,
    And when there is an enemy to defame
    They cloak their spite in fair religion's name,
    Their private spleen and malice being made
    To seem a high and virtuous crusade,   120
    Until, to mankind's reverent applause,
    They crucify their foe in Heaven's cause.
    Such knaves are all too common; yet, for the wise,
    True piety isn't hard to recognize,
    And, happily, these present times provide us   125
    With bright examples to instruct and guide us.
    Consider Ariston and Périandre;

Look at Oronte, Alcidamas, Clitandre;
Their virtue is acknowledged; who could doubt it?
But you won't hear them beat the drum about it.   130
They're never ostentatious, never vain,
And their religion's moderate and humane;
It's not their way to criticize and chide:
They think censoriousness a mark of pride,
And therefore, letting others preach and rave,   135
They show, by deeds, how Christians should behave.
They think no evil of their fellow man,
But judge of him as kindly as they can.
They don't intrigue and wangle and conspire;
To lead a good life is their one desire;   140
The sinner wakes no rancorous hate in them;
It is the sin alone which they condemn;
Nor do they try to show a fiercer zeal
For Heaven's cause than Heaven itself could feel.
These men I honor, these men I advocate   145
As models for us all to emulate.
Your man is not their sort at all, I fear:
And, while your praise of him is quite sincere,
I think that you've been dreadfully deluded.
ORGON: Now then, dear Brother, is your speech concluded?   150
CLÉANTE: Why, yes.
ORGON: Your servant, Sir. (*He turns to go.*)
CLÉANTE: No, Brother; wait.
  There's one more matter. You agreed of late
  That young Valère might have your daughter's hand.
ORGON: I did.
CLÉANTE: And set the date, I understand.
ORGON: Quite so.
CLÉANTE: You've now postponed it; is that true?   155
ORGON: No doubt.
CLÉANTE: The match no longer pleases you?
ORGON: Who knows?
CLÉANTE: D'you mean to go back on your word?
ORGON: I won't say that.
CLÉANTE: Has anything occurred
  Which might entitle you to break your pledge?
ORGON: Perhaps.
CLÉANTE: Why must you hem, and haw, and hedge?   160
  The boy asked me to sound you in this affair . . .
ORGON: It's been a pleasure.
CLÉANTE: But what shall I tell Valère?
ORGON: Whatever you like.
CLÉANTE: But what have you decided?
  What are your plans?
ORGON: I plan, Sir, to be guided
  By Heaven's will.

CLÉANTE: Come, Brother, don't talk rot.   165
   You've given Valère your word; will you keep it, or not?
ORGON: Good day.
CLÉANTE: This looks like poor Valère's undoing;
   I'll go and warn him that there's trouble brewing.

ACT II

SCENE 1

ORGON

MARIANE

ORGON: Mariane.
MARIANE: Yes, Father?
ORGON: A word with you; come here.
MARIANE: What are you looking for?
ORGON (*peering into a small closet*):   Eavesdroppers, dear.
   I'm making sure we shan't be overheard.
   Someone in there could catch our every word.
   Ah, good, we're safe. Now, Mariane, my child,   5
   You're a sweet girl who's tractable and mild,
   Whom I hold dear, and think most highly of.
MARIANE: I'm deeply grateful, Father, for your love.
ORGON: That's well said, Daughter; and you can repay me
   If, in all things, you'll cheerfully obey me.   10
MARIANE: To please you, Sir, is what delights me best.
ORGON: Good, good. Now, what d'you think of Tartuffe, our guest?
MARIANE: I, Sir?
ORGON: Yes. Weigh your answer; think it through.
MARIANE: Oh, dear. I'll say whatever you wish me to.
ORGON: That's wisely said, my Daughter. Say of him, then,   15
   That he's the very worthiest of men,
   And that you're fond of him, and would rejoice
   In being his wife, if that should be my choice.
   Well?
MARIANE: What?
ORGON: What's that?
MARIANE: I . . .
ORGON: Well?
MARIANE: Forgive me, pray.
ORGON: Did you not hear me?
MARIANE: Of *whom*, Sir, must I say   20
   That I am fond of him, and would rejoice
   In being his wife, if that should be your choice?
ORGON: Why, of Tartuffe.
MARIANE: But, Father, that's false, you know.
   Why would you have me say what isn't so?

ORGON: Because I am resolved it shall be true. 25
  That it's my wish should be enough for you.
MARIANE: You can't mean, Father . . .
ORGON: Yes, Tartuffe shall be
  Allied by marriage to this family,
  And he's to be your husband, is that clear?
  It's a father's privilege . . . 30

SCENE 2

DORINE
ORGON
MARIANE

ORGON (*to* DORINE):   What are you doing in here?
  Is curiosity so fierce a passion
  With you, that you must eavesdrop in this fashion?
DORINE: There's lately been a rumor going about —
  Based on some hunch or chance remark, no doubt — 5
  That you mean Mariane to wed Tartuffe.
  I've laughed it off, of course, as just a spoof.
ORGON: You find it so incredible?
DORINE: Yes, I do.
  I won't accept that story, even from you.
ORGON: Well, you'll believe it when the thing is done. 10
DORINE: Yes, yes, of course. Go on and have your fun.
ORGON: I've never been more serious in my life.
DORINE: Ha!
ORGON: Daughter, I mean it; you're to be his wife.
DORINE: No, don't believe your father; it's all a hoax.
ORGON: See here, young woman . . .
DORINE: Come, Sir, no more jokes; 15
  You can't fool us.
ORGON: How dare you talk that way?
DORINE: All right, then: we believe you, sad to say.
  But how a man like you, who looks so wise
  And wears a moustache of such splendid size,
  Can be so foolish as to . . .
ORGON: Silence, please! 20
  My girl, you take too many liberties.
  I'm master here, as you must not forget.
DORINE: Do let's discuss this calmly; don't be upset.
  You can't be serious, Sir, about this plan.
  What should that bigot want with Mariane? 25
  Praying and fasting ought to keep him busy.
  And then, in terms of wealth and rank, what is he?
  Why should a man of property like you
  Pick out a beggar son-in-law?
ORGON: That will do.

Speak of his poverty with reverence.   30
His is a pure and saintly indigence
Which far transcends all worldly pride and pelf.
He lost his fortune, as he says himself,
Because he cared for Heaven alone, and so
Was careless of his interests here below.   35
I mean to get him out of his present straits
And help him to recover his estates —
Which, in his part of the world, have no small fame.
Poor though he is, he's a gentleman just the same.
DORINE: Yes, so he tells us; and, Sir, it seems to me   40
Such pride goes very ill with piety.
A man whose spirit spurns this dungy earth
Ought not to brag of lands and noble birth;
Such worldly arrogance will hardly square
With meek devotion and the life of prayer.   45
. . . But this approach, I see, has drawn a blank;
Let's speak, then, of his person, not his rank.
Doesn't it seem to you a trifle grim
To give a girl like her to a man like him?
When two are so ill-suited, can't you see   50
What the sad consequence is bound to be?
A young girl's virtue is imperilled, Sir,
When such a marriage is imposed on her;
For if one's bridegroom isn't to one's taste,
It's hardly an inducement to be chaste,   55
And many a man with horns upon his brow
Has made his wife the thing that she is now.
It's hard to be a faithful wife, in short,
To certain husbands of a certain sort,
And he who gives his daughter to a man she hates   60
Must answer for her sins at Heaven's gates.
Think, Sir, before you play so risky a role.
ORGON: This servant-girl presumes to save my soul!
DORINE: You would do well to ponder what I've said.
ORGON: Daughter, we'll disregard this dunderhead.   65
Just trust your father's judgment. Oh, I'm aware
That I once promised you to young Valère;
But now I hear he gambles, which greatly shocks me;
What's more, I've doubts about his orthodoxy.
His visits to church, I note, are very few.   70
DORINE: Would you have him go at the same hours as you,
And kneel nearby, to be sure of being seen?
ORGON: I can dispense with such remarks, Dorine.
(To MARIANE.) Tartuffe, however, is sure of Heaven's blessing,
And that's the only treasure worth possessing.   75
This match will bring you joys beyond all measure;
Your cup will overflow with every pleasure;
You two will interchange your faithful loves

Like two sweet cherubs, or two turtle-doves.
No harsh word shall be heard, no frown be seen,   80
And he shall make you happy as a queen.
DORINE: And she'll make him a cuckold, just wait and see.
ORGON: What language!
DORINE: Oh, he's a man of destiny;
He's *made* for horns, and what the stars demand
Your daughter's virtue surely can't withstand.   85
ORGON: Don't interrupt me further. Why can't you learn
That certain things are none of your concern?
DORINE: It's for your own sake that I interfere.

(*She repeatedly interrupts* ORGON *just as he is turning to speak to his
daughter:*)

ORGON: Most kind of you. Now, hold your tongue, d'you hear?
DORINE: If I didn't love you . . .
ORGON: Spare me your affection.   90
DORINE: I love you, Sir, in spite of your objection.
ORGON: Blast!
DORINE: I can't bear, Sir, for your honor's sake,
To let you make this ludicrous mistake.
ORGON: You mean to go on talking?
DORINE: If I didn't protest
This sinful marriage, my conscience couldn't rest.   95
ORGON: If you don't hold your tongue, you little shrew . . .
DORINE: What, lost your temper? A pious man like you?
ORGON: Yes! Yes! You talk and talk. I'm maddened by it.
Once and for all, I tell you to be quiet.
DORINE: Well, I'll be quiet. But I'll be thinking hard.   100
ORGON: Think all you like, but you had better guard
That saucy tongue of yours, or I'll . . .
(*Turning back to* MARIANE.)   Now, child,
I've weighed this matter fully.
DORINE (*aside*):   It drives me wild
That I can't speak.

(ORGON *turns his head, and she is silent.*)

ORGON: Tartuffe is no young dandy,
But, still, his person . . .
DORINE (*aside*):   Is as sweet as candy.   105
ORGON: Is such that, even if you shouldn't care
For his other merits . . .

(*He turns and stands facing* DORINE, *arms crossed.*)

DORINE (*aside*):   They'll make a lovely pair.
If I were she, no man would marry me
Against my inclination, and go scot-free.
He'd learn, before the wedding-day was over,   110
How readily a wife can find a lover.

ORGON (*to* DORINE): It seems you treat my orders as a joke.
DORINE: Why, what's the matter? 'Twas not to you I spoke.
ORGON: What *were* you doing?
DORINE: Talking to myself, that's all.
ORGON: Ah! (*Aside*.) One more bit of impudence and gall,   115
    And I shall give her a good slap in the face.

(*He puts himself in position to slap her;* DORINE, *whenever he glances at her,
stands immobile and silent:*)

    Daughter, you shall accept, and with good grace,
    The husband I've selected . . . Your wedding-day . . .
    (*To* DORINE.) Why don't you talk to yourself?
DORINE: I've nothing to say.
ORGON: Come, just one word.
DORINE: No thank you, Sir. I pass.   120
ORGON: Come, speak; I'm waiting.
DORINE: I'd not be such an ass.
ORGON (*turning to* MARIANE): In short, dear Daughter, I mean to be obeyed,
    And you must bow to the sound choice I've made.
DORINE (*moving away*): I'd not wed such a monster, even in jest.

(ORGON *attempts to slap her, but misses*.)

ORGON: Daughter, that maid of yours is a thorough pest;   125
    She makes me sinfully annoyed and nettled.
    I can't speak further; my nerves are too unsettled.
    She's so upset me by her insolent talk,
    I'll calm myself by going for a walk.

SCENE 3

DORINE

MARIANE

DORINE (*returning*): Well, have you lost your tongue, girl? Must I play
    Your part, and say the lines you ought to say?
    Faced with a fate so hideous and absurd,
    Can you not utter one dissenting word?
MARIANE: What good would it do? A father's power is great.   5
DORINE: Resist him now, or it will be too late.
MARIANE: But . . .
DORINE: Tell him one cannot love at a father's whim;
    That you shall marry for yourself, not him;
    That since it's you who are to be the bride,
    It's you, not he, who must be satisfied;   10
    And that if his Tartuffe is so sublime,
    He's free to marry him at any time.
MARIANE: I've bowed so long to Father's strict control,
    I couldn't oppose him now, to save my soul.

DORINE: Come, come, Mariane. Do listen to reason, won't you?   15
    Valère has asked your hand. Do you love him, or don't you?
MARIANE: Oh, how unjust of you! What can you mean
    By asking such a question, dear Dorine?
    You know the depth of my affection for him;
    I've told you a hundred times how I adore him.   20
DORINE: I don't believe in everything I hear;
    Who knows if your professions were sincere?
MARIANE: They were, Dorine, and you do me wrong to doubt it;
    Heaven knows that I've been all too frank about it.
DORINE: You love him, then?
MARIANE: Oh, more than I can express.   25
DORINE: And he, I take it, cares for you no less?
MARIANE: I think so.
DORINE: And you both, with equal fire,
    Burn to be married?
MARIANE: That is our one desire.
DORINE: What of Tartuffe, then? What of your father's plan?
MARIANE: I'll kill myself, if I'm forced to wed that man.   30
DORINE: I hadn't thought of that recourse. How splendid!
    Just die, and all your troubles will be ended!
    A fine solution. Oh, it maddens me
    To hear you talk in that self-pitying key.
MARIANE: Dorine, how harsh you are! It's most unfair.   35
    You have no sympathy for my despair.
DORINE: I've none at all for people who talk drivel
    And, faced with difficulties, whine and snivel.
MARIANE: No doubt I'm timid, but it would be wrong . . .
DORINE: True love requires a heart that's firm and strong.   40
MARIANE: I'm strong in my affection for Valère,
    But coping with my father is his affair.
DORINE: But if your father's brain has grown so cracked
    Over his dear Tartuffe that he can retract
    His blessing, though your wedding-day was named,   45
    It's surely not Valère who's to be blamed.
MARIANE: If I defied my father, as you suggest,
    Would it not seem unmaidenly, at best?
    Shall I defend my love at the expense
    Of brazenness and disobedience?
    Shall I parade my heart's desires, and flaunt . . .   50
DORINE: No, I ask nothing of you. Clearly you want
    To be Madame Tartuffe, and I feel bound
    Not to oppose a wish so very sound.
    What right have I to criticize the match?
    Indeed, my dear, the man's a brilliant catch.   55
    Monsieur Tartuffe! Now, there's a man of weight!
    Yes, yes, Monsieur Tartuffe, I'm bound to state,
    Is quite a person; that's not to be denied;

'Twill be no little thing to be his bride.   60
The world already rings with his renown;
He's a great noble — in his native town;
His ears are red, he has a pink complexion,
And all in all, he'll suit you to perfection.
MARIANE: Dear God!
DORINE: Oh, how triumphant you will feel   65
   At having caught a husband so ideal!
MARIANE: Oh, do stop teasing, and use your cleverness
   To get me out of this appalling mess.
   Advise me, and I'll do whatever you say.
DORINE: Ah no, a dutiful daughter must obey   70
   Her father, even if he weds her to an ape.
   You've a bright future; why struggle to escape?
   Tartuffe will take you back where his family lives,
   To a small town aswarm with relatives —
   Uncles and cousins whom you'll be charmed to meet.   75
   You'll be received at once by the elite,
   Calling upon the bailiff's wife, no less —
   Even, perhaps, upon the mayoress,
   Who'll sit you down in the *best* kitchen chair.
   Then, once a year, you'll dance at the village fair   80
   To the drone of bagpipes — two of them, in fact —
   And see a puppet-show, or an animal act.
   Your husband . . .
MARIANE: Oh, you turn my blood to ice!
   Stop torturing me, and give me your advice.
DORINE (*threatening to go*): Your servant, Madam.
MARIANE: Dorine, I beg of you . . .   85
DORINE: No, you deserve it; this marriage must go through.
MARIANE: Dorine!
DORINE: No.
MARIANE: Not Tartuffe! You know I think him . . .
DORINE: Tartuffe's your cup of tea, and you shall drink him.
MARIANE: I've always told you everything, and relied . . .
DORINE: No. You deserve to be tartuffified.   90
MARIANE: Well, since you mock me and refuse to care,
   I'll henceforth seek my solace in despair:
   Despair shall be my counsellor and friend,
   And help me bring my sorrows to an end.

   (*She starts to leave.*)

DORINE: There now, come back; my anger has subsided.   95
   You do deserve some pity, I've decided.
MARIANE: Dorine, if Father makes me undergo
   This dreadful martyrdom, I'll die, I know.
DORINE: Don't fret; it won't be difficult to discover
   Some plan of action . . . But here's Valère, your lover.   100

SCENE 4

VALÈRE
MARIANE
DORINE

VALÈRE: Madame, I've just received some wondrous news
    Regarding which I'd like to hear your views.
MARIANE: What news?
VALÈRE: You're marrying Tartuffe.
MARIANE: I find
    That Father does have such a match in mind.
VALÈRE: Your father, Madam . . .
MARIANE: . . . has just this minute said   5
    That it's Tartuffe he wishes me to wed.
VALÈRE: Can he be serious?
MARIANE: Oh, indeed he can;
    He's clearly set his heart upon the plan.
VALÈRE: And what position do you propose to take, Madam?
MARIANE: Why — I don't know.
VALÈRE: For heaven's sake —   10
    You don't know?
MARIANE: No.
VALÈRE: Well, well!
MARIANE: Advise me, do.
VALÈRE: Marry the man. That's my advice to you.
MARIANE: That's your advice?
VALÈRE: Yes.
MARIANE: Truly?
VALÈRE: Oh, absolutely.
    You couldn't choose more wisely, more astutely.
MARIANE: Thanks for this counsel; I'll follow it, of course.   15
VALÈRE: Do, do; I'm sure 'twill cost you no remorse.
MARIANE: To give it didn't cause your heart to break.
VALÈRE: I gave it, Madam, only for your sake.
MARIANE: And it's for your sake that I take it, Sir.
DORINE (*withdrawing to the rear of the stage*): Let's see which fool will prove the
    stubborner.
VALÈRE: So! I am nothing to you, and it was flat   20
    Deception when you . . .
MARIANE: Please, enough of that.
    You've told me plainly that I should agree
    To wed the man my father's chosen for me,
    And since you've designed to counsel me so wisely,
    I promise, Sir, to do as you advise me.   25
VALÈRE: Ah, no, 'twas not by me that you were swayed.
    No, your decision was already made;
    Though now, to save appearances, you protest
    That you're betraying me at my behest.   30

MARIANE: Just as you say.
VALÈRE:　　　　　　　　Quite so. And I now see
　That you were never truly in love with me.
MARIANE: Alas, you're free to think so if you choose.
VALÈRE: I choose to think so, and here's a bit of news:
　You've spurned my hand, but I know where to turn　35
　For kinder treatment, as you shall quickly learn.
MARIANE: I'm sure you do. Your noble qualities
　Inspire affection . . .
VALÈRE:　　　　　　　　Forget my qualities, please.
　They don't inspire you overmuch, I find.
　But there's another lady I have in mind　40
　Whose sweet and generous nature will not scorn
　To compensate me for the loss I've borne.
MARIANE: I'm no great loss, and I'm sure that you'll transfer
　Your heart quite painlessly from me to her.
VALÈRE: I'll do my best to take it in my stride.　45
　The pain I feel at being cast aside
　Time and forgetfulness may put an end to.
　Or if I can't forget, I shall pretend to.
　No self-respecting person is expected
　To go on loving once he's been rejected.　50
MARIANE: Now, that's a fine, high-minded sentiment.
VALÈRE: One to which any sane man would assent.
　Would you prefer it if I pined away
　In hopeless passion till my dying day?
　Am I to yield you to a rival's arms　55
　And not console myself with other charms?
MARIANE: Go then: console yourself; don't hesitate.
　I wish you to; indeed, I cannot wait.
VALÈRE: You wish me to?
MARIANE:　　　　　　　　Yes.
VALÈRE:　　　　　　　　　　That's the final straw.
　Madam, farewell. Your wish shall be my law.　60

(*He starts to leave, and then returns: this repeatedly:*)

MARIANE: Splendid.
VALÈRE (*coming back again*):
　　　　　　　　This breach, remember, is of your making;
　It's you who've driven me to the step I'm taking.
MARIANE: Of course.
VALÈRE (*coming back again*):
　　　　　　　　Remember, too, that I am merely
　Following your example.
MARIANE:　　　　　　　　I see that clearly.
VALÈRE: Enough. I'll go and do your bidding, then.　65
MARIANE: Good.
VALÈRE (*coming back again*):
　　　　　　　　You shall never see my face again.

MARIANE: Excellent.
VALÈRE (*walking to the door, then turning about*):
                                      Yes?
MARIANE: What?
VALÈRE: What's that? What did you say?
MARIANE: Nothing. You're dreaming.
VALÈRE: Ah. Well, I'm on my way.
    Farewell, *Madame*.

(*He moves slowly away*.)

MARIANE: Farewell.
DORINE (*to* MARIANE):   If you ask me,
    Both of you are as mad as mad can be.
    Do stop this nonsense, now. I've only let you   70
    Squabble so long to see where it would get you.
    Whoa there, Monsieur Valère!

(*She goes and seizes* VALÈRE *by the arm; he makes a great show of resistance*.)

VALÈRE: What's this, Dorine?
DORINE: Come here.
VALÈRE: No, no, my heart's too full of spleen.
    Don't hold me back; her wish must be obeyed.   75
DORINE: Stop!
VALÈRE: It's too late now; my decision's made.
DORINE: Oh, pooh!
MARIANE (*aside*):   He hates the sight of me, that's plain.
    I'll go, and so deliver him from pain.
DORINE (*leaving* VALÈRE, *running after* MARIANE):
    And now *you* run away! Come back.
MARIANE: No, no.
    Nothing you say will keep me here. Let go!   80
VALÈRE (*aside*): She cannot bear my presence, I perceive.
    To spare her further torment, I shall leave.
DORINE (*leaving* MARIANE, *running after* VALÈRE): Again! You'll not escape, Sir;
        don't you try it.
    Come here, you two. Stop fussing, and be quiet.

(*She takes* VALÈRE *by the hand, then* MARIANE, *and draws them together*.)

VALÈRE (*to* DORINE): What do you want of me?
MARIANE (*to* DORINE):   What is the point of this?   85
DORINE: We're going to have a little armistice.
    (*To* VALÈRE.) Now weren't you silly to get so overheated?
VALÈRE: Didn't you see how badly I was treated?
DORINE (*to* MARIANE): Aren't you a simpleton, to have lost your head?
MARIANE: Didn't you hear the hateful things he said?   90
DORINE (*to* VALÈRE): You're both great fools. Her sole desire, Valère,
    Is to be yours in marriage. To that I'll swear.

(*To* MARIANE.) He loves you only, and he wants no wife
But you, Mariane. On that I'll stake my life.
MARIANE (*to* VALÈRE): Then why you advised me so, I cannot see.   95
VALÈRE (*to* MARIANE): On such a question, why ask advice of *me?*
DORINE: Oh, you're impossible. Give me your hands, you two.
    (*To* VALÈRE.)   Yours first.
VALÈRE (*giving* DORINE *his hand*): But why?
DORINE (*to* MARIANE):   And now a hand from you.
MARIANE (*also giving* DORINE *her hand*):
    What are you doing?
DORINE: There: a perfect fit.
    You suit each other better than you'll admit.   100

(VALÈRE *and* MARIANE *hold hands for some time without looking at each other.*)

VALÈRE (*turning toward* MARIANE): Ah, come, don't be so haughty.
    Give a man
    A look of kindness, won't you, Mariane?

(MARIANE *turns toward* VALÈRE *and smiles.*)

DORINE : I tell you, lovers are completely mad!
VALÈRE (*to* MARIANE): Now come, confess that you were very bad
    To hurt my feelings as you did just now.   105
    I have a just complaint, you must allow.
MARIANE: *You* must allow that you were most unpleasant . . .
DORINE: Let's table that discussion for the present;
    Your father has a plan which must be stopped.
MARIANE: Advise us, then; what means must we adopt?   110
DORINE: We'll use all manner of means, and all at once.
    (*To* MARIANE.) Your father's addled; he's acting like a dunce.
    Therefore you'd better humor the old fossil.
    Pretend to yield to him, be sweet and docile,
    And then postpone, as often as necessary,   115
    The day on which you have agreed to marry.
    You'll thus gain time, and time will turn the trick.
    Sometimes, for instance, you'll be taken sick,
    And that will seem good reason for delay;
    Or some bad omen will make you change the day —   120
    You'll dream of muddy water, or you'll pass
    A dead man's hearse, or break a looking-glass.
    If all else fails, no man can marry you
    Unless you take his ring and say "I do."
    But now, let's separate. If they should find   125
    Us talking here, our plot might be divined.
    (*To* VALÈRE.) Go to your friends, and tell them what's occurred,
    And have them urge her father to keep his word.
    Meanwhile, we'll stir her brother into action,
    And get Elmire, as well, to join our faction.   130
    Good-bye.

VALÈRE (*to* MARIANE):
> Though each of us will do his best,
> It's your true heart on which my hopes shall rest.

MARIANE (*to* VALÈRE): Regardless of what Father may decide,
> None but Valère shall claim me as his bride.

VALÈRE: Oh, how those words content me! Come what will . . .   135

DORINE: Oh, lovers, lovers! Their tongues are never still.
> Be off, now.

VALÈRE (*turning to go, then turning back*):
> One last word . . .

DORINE: No time to chat:
> *You* leave by this door; and *you* leave by that.

(DORINE *pushes them, by the shoulders, toward opposing doors.*)

ACT III

SCENE 1

DAMIS

DORINE

DAMIS: May lightning strike me even as I speak,
> May all men call me cowardly and weak,
> If any fear or scruple holds me back
> From settling things, at once, with that great quack!

DORINE: Now, don't give way to violent emotion.   5
> Your father's merely talked about this notion,
> And words and deeds are far from being one.
> Much that is talked about is left undone.

DAMIS: No, I must stop that scoundrel's machinations;
> I'll go and tell him off; I'm out of patience.   10

DORINE: Do calm down and be practical. I had rather
> My mistress dealt with him — and with your father.
> She has some influence with Tartuffe, I've noted.
> He hangs upon her words, seems most devoted,
> And may, indeed, be smitten by her charm.   15
> Pray Heaven it's true! 'Twould do our cause no harm.
> She sent for him, just now, to sound him out
> On this affair you're so incensed about;
> She'll find out where he stands, and tell him, too,
> What dreadful strife and trouble will ensue   20
> If he lends countenance to your father's plan.
> I couldn't get in to see him, but his man
> Says that he's almost finished with his prayers.
> Go, now. I'll catch him when he comes downstairs.

DAMIS: I want to hear this conference, and I will.   25

DORINE: No, they must be alone.
DAMIS: Oh, I'll keep still.
DORINE: Not you. I know your temper. You'd start a brawl,
  And shout and stamp your foot and spoil it all.
  Go on.
DAMIS: I won't; I have a perfect right . . .
DORINE: Lord, you're a nuisance! He's coming; get out of sight.   30

(DAMIS *conceals himself in a closet at the rear of the stage*.)

SCENE 2

TARTUFFE
DORINE

TARTUFFE (*observing* DORINE, *and calling to his manservant offstage*):
  Hang up my hair-shirt, put my scourge in place,
  And pray, Laurent, for Heaven's perpetual grace.
  I'm going to the prison now, to share
  My last few coins with the poor wretches there.
DORINE (*aside*): Dear God, what affectation! What a fake!   5
TARTUFFE: You wished to see me?
DORINE: Yes . . .
TARTUFFE (*taking a handkerchief from his pocket*):
                                    For mercy's sake,
  Please take this handkerchief, before you speak.
DORINE: What?
TARTUFFE: Cover that bosom, girl. The flesh is weak,
  And unclean thoughts are difficult to control.
  Such sights as that can undermine the soul.   10
DORINE: Your soul, it seems, has very poor defenses,
  And flesh makes quite an impact on your senses.
  It's strange that you're so easily excited;
  My own desires are not so soon ignited,
  And if I saw you naked as a beast,   15
  Not all your hide would tempt me in the least.
TARTUFFE: Girl, speak more modestly; unless you do,
  I shall be forced to take my leave of you.
DORINE: Oh, no, it's I who must be on my way;
  I've just one little message to convey.   20
  Madame is coming down, and begs you, Sir,
  To wait and have a word or two with her.
TARTUFFE: Gladly.
DORINE (*aside*):   *That* had a softening effect!
  I think my guess about him was correct.
TARTUFFE: Will she be long?
DORINE: No: that's her step I hear.   25
  Ah, here she is, and I shall disappear.

SCENE 3

ELMIRE

TARTUFFE

TARTUFFE: May Heaven, whose infinite goodness we adore,
 Preserve your body and soul forevermore,
 And bless your days, and answer thus the plea
 Of one who is its humblest votary.
ELMIRE: I thank you for that pious wish. But please,   5
 Do take a chair and let's be more at ease.

(*They sit down.*)

TARTUFFE: I trust that you are once more well and strong?
ELMIRE: Oh, yes: the fever didn't last for long.
TARTUFFE: My prayers are too unworthy, I am sure,
 To have gained from Heaven this most gracious cure;   10
 But lately, Madam, my every supplication
 Has had for object your recuperation.
ELMIRE: You shouldn't have troubled so. I don't deserve it.
TARTUFFE: Your health is priceless, Madam, and to preserve it
 I'd gladly give my own, in all sincerity.   15
ELMIRE: Sir, you outdo us all in Christian charity.
 You've been most kind. I count myself your debtor.
TARTUFFE: 'Twas nothing, Madam. I long to serve you better.
ELMIRE: There's a private matter I'm anxious to discuss.
 I'm glad there's no one here to hinder us.   20
TARTUFFE: I too am glad; it floods my heart with bliss
 To find myself alone with you like this.
 For just this chance I've prayed with all my power —
 But prayed in vain, until this happy hour.
ELMIRE: This won't take long, Sir, and I hope you'll be   25
 Entirely frank and unconstrained with me.
TARTUFFE: Indeed, there's nothing I had rather do
 Than bare my inmost heart and soul to you.
 First, let me say that what remarks I've made
 About the constant visits you are paid   30
 Were prompted not by any mean emotion,
 But rather by a pure and deep devotion,
 A fervent zeal . . .
ELMIRE: No need for explanation.
 Your sole concern, I'm sure, was my salvation.
TARTUFFE (*taking* ELMIRE's *hand and pressing her fingertips*): Quite so;
 and such great fervor do I feel . . .   35
ELMIRE: Ooh! Please! You're pinching!
TARTUFFE: 'Twas from excess of zeal.
 I never meant to cause you pain, I swear.
 I'd rather . . .

(*He places his hand on* ELMIRE's *knee.*)

ELMIRE: What can your hand be doing there?
TARTUFFE: Feeling your gown; what soft, fine-woven stuff!
ELMIRE: Please, I'm extremely ticklish. That's enough.   40

(*She draws her chair away;* TARTUFFE *pulls his after her.*)

TARTUFFE (*fondling the lace collar of her gown*): My, my, what lovely
     lacework on your dress!
The workmanship's miraculous, no less.
I've not seen anything to equal it.
ELMIRE: Yes, quite. But let's talk business for a bit.
They say my husband means to break his word   45
And give his daughter to you, Sir. Had you heard?
TARTUFFE: He did once mention it. But I confess
I dream of quite a different happiness.
It's elsewhere, Madam, that my eyes discern
The promise of that bliss for which I yearn.   50
ELMIRE: I see: you care for nothing here below.
TARTUFFE: Ah, well — my heart's not made of stone, you know.
ELMIRE: All your desires mount heavenward, I'm sure,
In scorn of all that's earthly and impure.
TARTUFFE: A love of heavenly beauty does not preclude   55
A proper love for earthly pulchritude;
Our senses are quite rightly captivated
By perfect works our Maker has created.
Some glory clings to all that Heaven has made;
In you, all Heaven's marvels are displayed.   60
On that fair face, such beauties have been lavished,
The eyes are dazzled and the heart is ravished;
How could I look on you, O flawless creature,
And not adore the Author of all Nature,
Feeling a love both passionate and pure   65
For you, his triumph of self-portraiture?
At first, I trembled lest that love should be
A subtle snare that Hell had laid for me;
I vowed to flee the sight of you, eschewing
A rapture that might prove my soul's undoing;   70
But soon, fair being, I became aware
That my deep passion could be made to square
With rectitude, and with my bounden duty.
I thereupon surrendered to your beauty.
It is, I know, presumptuous on my part   75
To bring you this poor offering of my heart,
And it is not my merit, Heaven knows,
But your compassion on which my hopes repose.
You are my peace, my solace, my salvation;
On you depends my bliss — or desolation;   80
I bide your judgment and, as you think best,
I shall be either miserable or blest.
ELMIRE: Your declaration is most gallant, Sir,

But don't you think it's out of character?
You'd have done better to restrain your passion
And think before you spoke in such a fashion.   85
It ill becomes a pious man like you . . .
TARTUFFE: I may be pious, but I'm human too:
With your celestial charms before his eyes,
A man has not the power to be wise.   90
I know such words sound strangely, coming from me,
But I'm no angel, nor was meant to be,
And if you blame my passion, you must needs
Reproach as well the charms on which it feeds.
Your loveliness I had no sooner seen   95
Than you became my soul's unrivalled queen;
Before your seraph glance, divinely sweet,
My heart's defenses crumbled in defeat,
And nothing fasting, prayer, or tears might do
Could stay my spirit from adoring you.   100
My eyes, my sighs have told you in the past
What now my lips make bold to say at last,
And if, in your great goodness, you will deign
To look upon your slave, and ease his pain, —
If, in compassion for my soul's distress,   105
You'll stoop to comfort my unworthiness,
I'll raise to you, in thanks for that sweet manna,
An endless hymn, an infinite hosanna.
With me, of course, there need be no anxiety,
No fear of scandal or of notoriety.   110
These young court gallants, whom all the ladies fancy,
Are vain in speech, in action rash and chancy;
When they succeed in love, the world soon knows it;
No favor's granted them but they disclose it
And by the looseness of their tongues profane   115
The very altar where their hearts have lain.
Men of my sort, however, love discreetly,
And one may trust our reticence completely.
My keen concern for my good name insures
The absolute security of yours;   120
In short, I offer you, my dear Elmire,
Love without scandal, pleasure without fear.
ELMIRE: I've heard your well-turned speeches to the end,
And what you urge I clearly apprehend.
Aren't you afraid that I may take a notion   125
To tell my husband of your warm devotion,
And that, supposing he were duly told,
His feelings toward you might grow rather cold?
TARTUFFE: I know, dear lady, that your exceeding charity
Will lead your heart to pardon my temerity;   130
That you'll excuse my violent affection
As human weakness, human imperfection;

    And that — O fairest! — you will bear in mind
    That I'm but flesh and blood, and am not blind.
ELMIRE: Some women might do otherwise, perhaps,   135
    But I shall be discreet about your lapse;
    I'll tell my husband nothing of what's occurred
    If, in return, you'll give your solemn word
    To advocate as forcefully as you can
    The marriage of Valère and Mariane,   140
    Renouncing all desire to dispossess
    Another of his rightful happiness,
    And . . .

SCENE 4

DAMIS

ELMIRE

TARTUFFE

DAMIS (*emerging from the closet where he has been hiding*):
          No! We'll not hush up this vile affair;
    I heard it all inside that closet there,
    Where Heaven, in order to confound the pride
    Of this great rascal, prompted me to hide.
    Ah, now I have my long-awaited chance   5
    To punish his deceit and arrogance,
    And give my father clear and shocking proof
    Of the black character of his dear Tartuffe.
ELMIRE: Ah no, Damis; I'll be content if he
    Will study to deserve my leniency.   10
    I've promised silence — don't make me break my word;
    To make a scandal would be too absurd.
    Good wives laugh off such trifles, and forget them;
    Why should they tell their husbands, and upset them?
DAMIS: You have your reasons for taking such a course,   15
    And I have reasons, too, of equal force.
    To spare him now would be insanely wrong.
    I've swallowed my just wrath for far too long
    And watched this insolent bigot bringing strife
    And bitterness into our family life.   20
    Too long he's meddled in my father's affairs,
    Thwarting my marriage-hopes, and poor Valère's.
    It's high time that my father was undeceived,
    And now I've proof that can't be disbelieved —
    Proof that was furnished me by Heaven above.   25
    It's too good not to take advantage of.
    This is my chance, and I deserve to lose it
    If, for one moment, I hesitate to use it.
ELMIRE: Damis . . .
DAMIS: No, I must do what I think right.

Madam, my heart is bursting with delight,   30
And, say whatever you will, I'll not consent
To lose the sweet revenge on which I'm bent.
I'll settle matters without more ado;
And here, most opportunely, is my cue.

Scene 5

ORGON   TARTUFFE
DAMIS   ELMIRE

DAMIS: Father, I'm glad you've joined us. Let us advise you
   Of some fresh news which doubtless will surprise you.
   You've just now been repaid with interest
   For all your loving-kindness to our guest.
   He's proved his warm and grateful feelings toward you;   5
   It's with a pair of horns he would reward you.
   Yes, I surprised him with your wife, and heard
   His whole adulterous offer, every word.
   She, with her all too gentle disposition,
   Would not have told you of his proposition;   10
   But I shall not make terms with brazen lechery,
   And feel that not to tell you would be treachery.
ELMIRE: And I hold that one's husband's peace of mind
   Should not be spoilt by tattle of this kind.
   One's honor doesn't require it: to be proficient   15
   In keeping men at bay is quite sufficient.
   These are my sentiments, and I wish, Damis,
   That you had heeded me and held your peace.

Scene 6

ORGON
DAMIS
TARTUFFE

ORGON: Can it be true, this dreadful thing I hear?
TARTUFFE: Yes, Brother, I'm a wicked man, I fear:
   A wretched sinner, all depraved and twisted,
   The greatest villain that has ever existed.
   My life's one heap of crimes, which grows each minute;   5
   There's naught but foulness and corruption in it;
   And I perceive that Heaven, outraged by me,
   Has chosen this occasion to mortify me.
   Charge me with any deed you wish to name;
   I'll not defend myself, but take the blame.   10
   Believe what you are told, and drive Tartuffe
   Like some base criminal from beneath your roof;

Yes, drive me hence, and with a parting curse:
I shan't protest, for I deserve far worse.
ORGON (*to* DAMIS): Ah, you deceitful boy, how dare you try   15
  To stain his purity with so foul a lie?
DAMIS: What! Are you taken in by such a bluff?
  Did you not hear . . . ?
ORGON: Enough, you rogue, enough!
TARTUFFE: Ah, Brother, let him speak: you're being unjust.
  Believe his story; the boy deserves your trust.   20
  Why, after all, should you have faith in me?
  How can you know what I might do, or be?
  Is it on my good actions that you base
  Your favor? Do you trust my pious face?
  Ah, no, don't be deceived by hollow shows;   25
  I'm far, alas, from being what men suppose;
  Though the world takes me for a man of worth,
  I'm truly the most worthless man on earth.
  (*To* DAMIS.) Yes, my dear son, speak out now: call me the chief
  Of sinners, a wretch, a murderer, a thief;   30
  Load me with all the names men most abhor;
  I'll not complain; I've earned them all, and more;
  I'll kneel here while you pour them on my head
  As a just punishment for the life I've led.
ORGON (*to* TARTUFFE): This is too much, dear Brother.
  (*To* DAMIS.)   Have you no heart?   35
DAMIS: Are you so hoodwinked by this rascal's art . . . ?
ORGON: Be still, you monster.
  (*To* TARTUFFE.)   Brother, I pray you, rise.
  (*To* DAMIS.) Villain!
DAMIS: But . . .
ORGON: Silence!
DAMIS: Can't you realize . . . ?
ORGON: Just one word more, and I'll tear you limb from limb.
TARTUFFE: In God's name, Brother, don't be harsh with him.   40
  I'd rather far be tortured at the stake
  Than see him bear one scratch for my poor sake.
ORGON (*to* DAMIS): Ingrate!
TARTUFFE: If I must beg you, on bended knee,
  To pardon him . . .
ORGON (*falling to his knees, addressing* TARTUFFE):
                        Such goodness cannot be!
  (*To* DAMIS.) Now, *there's* true charity!
DAMIS: What, you . . . ?
ORGON: Villain, be still!   45
  I know your motives; I know you wish him ill:
  Yes, all of you — wife, children, servants, all —
  Conspire against him and desire his fall,
  Employing every shameful trick you can
  To alienate me from this saintly man.   50

Ah, but the more you seek to drive him away,
The more I'll do to keep him. Without delay,
I'll spite this household and confound its pride
By giving him my daughter as his bride.
DAMIS: You're going to force her to accept his hand?   55
ORGON: Yes, and this very night, d'you understand?
I shall defy you all, and make it clear
That I'm the one who gives the orders here.
Come, wretch, kneel down and clasp his blessed feet,
And ask his pardon for your black deceit.   60
DAMIS: I ask that swindler's pardon? Why, I'd rather . . .
ORGON: So! You insult him, and defy your father!
A stick! A stick! (*To* TARTUFFE.) No, no — release me, do.
(*To* DAMIS.) Out of my house this minute! Be off with you,
And never dare set foot in it again.   65
DAMIS: Well, I shall go, but . . .
ORGON: Well, go quickly, then.
I disinherit you; an empty purse
Is all you'll get from me — except my curse!

SCENE 7

ORGON
TARTUFFE

ORGON: How he blasphemed your goodness! What a son!
TARTUFFE : Forgive him, Lord, as I've already done.
(*To* ORGON.) You can't know how it hurts when someone tries
To blacken me in my dear Brother's eyes.
ORGON: Ahh!
TARTUFFE: The mere thought of such ingratitude   5
Plunges my soul into so dark a mood . . .
Such horror grips my heart . . . I gasp for breath,
And cannot speak, and feel myself near death.
ORGON: (*He runs, in tears, to the door through which he has just driven
his son.*) You blackguard! Why did I spare you? Why did I not
Break you in little pieces on the spot?   10
Compose yourself, and don't be hurt, dear friend.
TARTUFFE: These scenes, these dreadful quarrels, have got to end.
I've much upset your household, and I perceive
That the best thing will be for me to leave.
ORGON: What are you saying!
TARTUFFE: They're all against me here;   15
They'd have you think me false and insincere.
ORGON: Ah, what of that? Have I ceased believing in you?
TARTUFFE: Their adverse talk will certainly continue,
And charges which you now repudiate
You may find credible at a later date.   20
ORGON: No, Brother, never.

TARTUFFE: Brother, a wife can sway
   Her husband's mind in many a subtle way.
ORGON: No, no.
TARTUFFE: To leave at once is the solution;
   Thus only can I end their persecution.
ORGON: No, no, I'll not allow it; you shall remain.   25
TARTUFFE: Ah, well; 'twill mean much martyrdom and pain,
   But if you wish it . . .
ORGON: Ah!
TARTUFFE: Enough; so be it.
   But one thing must be settled, as I see it.
   For your dear honor, and for our friendship's sake,
   There's one precaution I feel bound to take.   30
   I shall avoid your wife, and keep away . . .
ORGON: No, you shall not, whatever they may say.
   It pleases me to vex them, and for spite
   I'd have them see you with her day and night.
   What's more, I'm going to drive them to despair   35
   By making you my only son and heir;
   This very day, I'll give to you alone
   Clear deed and title to everything I own.
   A dear, good friend and son-in-law-to-be
   Is more than wife, or child, or kin to me.   40
   Will you accept my offer, dearest son?
TARTUFFE: In all things, let the will of Heaven be done.
ORGON: Poor fellow! Come, we'll go draw up the deed.
   Then let them burst with disappointed greed!

ACT IV

Scene 1

CLÉANTE
TARTUFFE

CLÉANTE: Yes, all the town's discussing it, and truly,
   Their comments do not flatter you unduly.
   I'm glad we've met, Sir, and I'll give my view
   Of this sad matter in a word or two.
   As for who's guilty, that I shan't discuss;   5
   Let's say it was Damis who caused the fuss;
   Assuming, then, that you have been ill-used
   By young Damis, and groundlessly accused,
   Ought not a Christian to forgive, and ought
   He not to stifle every vengeful thought?   10
   Should you stand by and watch a father make
   His only son an exile for your sake?
   Again I tell you frankly, be advised:

The whole town, high and low, is scandalized;
This quarrel must be mended, and my advice is   15
Not to push matters to a further crisis.
No, sacrifice your wrath to God above,
And help Damis regain his father's love.

TARTUFFE: Alas, for my part I should take great joy
In doing so. I've nothing against the boy.   20
I pardon all, I harbor no resentment;
To serve him would afford me much contentment.
But Heaven's interest will not have it so:
If he comes back, then I shall have to go.
After his conduct — so extreme, so vicious —   25
Our further intercourse would look suspicious.
God knows what people would think! Why, they'd describe
My goodness to him as a sort of bribe;
They'd say that out of guilt I made pretense
Of loving-kindness and benevolence —   30
That, fearing my accuser's tongue, I strove
To buy his silence with a show of love.

CLÉANTE: Your reasoning is badly warped and stretched,
And these excuses, Sir, are most far-fetched.
Why put yourself in charge of Heaven's cause?   35
Does Heaven need our help to enforce its laws?
Leave vengeance to the Lord, Sir; while we live,
Our duty's not to punish, but forgive;
And what the Lord commands, we should obey
Without regard to what the world may say.   40
What! Shall the fear of being misunderstood
Prevent our doing what is right and good?
No, no; let's simply do what Heaven ordains,
And let no other thoughts perplex our brains.

TARTUFFE: Again, Sir, let me say that I've forgiven   45
Damis, and thus obeyed the laws of Heaven;
But I am not commanded by the Bible
To live with one who smears my name with libel.

CLÉANTE: Were you commanded, Sir, to indulge the whim
Of poor Orgon, and to encourage him   50
In suddenly transferring to your name
A large estate to which you have no claim?

TARTUFFE: 'Twould never occur to those who know me best
To think I acted from self-interest.
The treasures of this world I quite despise;   55
Their specious glitter does not charm my eyes;
And if I have resigned myself to taking
The gift which my dear Brother insists on making,
I do so only, as he well understands,
Lest so much wealth fall into wicked hands,   60
Lest those to whom it might descend in time
Turn it to purposes of sin and crime,

And not, as I shall do, make use of it
For Heaven's glory and mankind's benefit.
CLÉANTE: Forget these trumped-up fears. Your argument   65
Is one the rightful heir might well resent;
It *is* a moral burden to inherit
Such wealth, but give Damis a chance to bear it.
And would it not be worse to be accused
Of swindling, than to see that wealth misused?   70
I'm shocked that you allowed Orgon to broach
This matter, and that you feel no self-reproach;
Does true religion teach that lawful heirs
May freely be deprived of what is theirs?
And if the Lord has told you in your heart   75
That you and young Damis must dwell apart,
Would it not be the decent thing to beat
A generous and honorable retreat,
Rather than let the son of the house be sent,
For your convenience, into banishment?   80
Sir, if you wish to prove the honesty
Of your intentions . . .
TARTUFFE: Sir, it is half-past three.
I've certain pious duties to attend to,
And hope my prompt departure won't offend you.
CLÉANTE (*alone*): Damn.

SCENE 2

ELMIRE   CLÉANTE
MARIANE   DORINE

DORINE: Stay, Sir, and help Mariane, for Heaven's sake!
She's suffering so, I fear her heart will break.
Her father's plan to marry her off tonight
Has put the poor child in a desperate plight.
I hear him coming. Let's stand together, now,   5
And see if we can't change his mind, somehow,
About this match we all deplore and fear.

SCENE 3

ORGON   MARIANE   DORINE
ELMIRE   CLÉANTE

ORGON: Hah! Glad to find you all assembled here.
(*To* MARIANE.) This contract, child, contains your happiness,
And what it says I think your heart can guess.
MARIANE (*falling to her knees*): Sir, by that Heaven which sees me here
distressed,
And by whatever else can move your breast,   5

Do not employ a father's power, I pray you,
To crush my heart and force it to obey you,
Nor by your harsh commands oppress me so
That I'll begrudge the duty which I owe —
And do not so embitter and enslave me   10
That I shall hate the very life you gave me.
If my sweet hopes must perish, if you refuse
To give me to the one I've dared to choose,
Spare me at least — I beg you, I implore —
The pain of wedding one whom I abhor;   15
And do not, by a heartless use of force,
Drive me to contemplate some desperate course.

ORGON (*feeling himself touched by her*): Be firm, my soul. No human
   weakness, now.

MARIANE: I don't resent your love for him. Allow
   Your heart free rein, Sir; give him your property,   20
   And if that's not enough, take mine from me;
   He's welcome to my money; take it, do,
   But don't, I pray, include my person too.
   Spare me, I beg you; and let me end the tale
   Of my sad days behind a convent veil.   25

ORGON: A convent! Hah! When crossed in their amours,
   All lovesick girls have the same thought as yours.
   Get up! The more you loathe the man, and dread him,
   The more ennobling it will be to wed him.
   Marry Tartuffe, and mortify your flesh!   30
   Enough; don't start that whimpering afresh.

DORINE: But why . . . ?

ORGON: Be still, there. Speak when you're spoken to.
   Not one more bit of impudence out of you.

CLÉANTE: If I may offer a word of counsel here . . .

ORGON: Brother, in counseling you have no peer;   35
   All your advice is forceful, sound, and clever;
   I don't propose to follow it, however.

ELMIRE (*to* ORGON): I am amazed, and don't know what to say;
   Your blindness simply takes my breath away.
   You are indeed bewitched, to take no warning   40
   From our account of what occurred this morning.

ORGON: Madam, I know a few plain facts, and one
   Is that you're partial to my rascal son;
   Hence, when he sought to make Tartuffe the victim
   Of a base lie, you dared not contradict him.   45
   Ah, but you underplayed your part, my pet;
   You should have looked more angry, more upset.

ELMIRE: When men make overtures, must we reply
   With righteous anger and a battle-cry?
   Must we turn back their amorous advances   50
   With sharp reproaches and with fiery glances?
   Myself, I find such offers merely amusing,

And make no scenes and fusses in refusing;
My taste is for good-natured rectitude,
And I dislike the savage sort of prude　　　　　　　　　　　　55
Who guards her virtue with her teeth and claws,
And tears men's eyes out for the slightest cause:
The Lord preserve me from such honor as that,
Which bites and scratches like an alley-cat!
I've found that a polite and cool rebuff　　　　　　　　　　　60
Discourages a lover quite enough.

ORGON: I know the facts, and I shall not be shaken.

ELMIRE: I marvel at your power to be mistaken.
Would it, I wonder, carry weight with you
If I could *show* you that our tale was true?　　　　　　　　65

ORGON: Show me?

ELMIRE:　　　　　　Yes.

ORGON:　　　　　　　　Rot.

ELMIRE:　　　　　　　　　　　Come, what if I found a way
To make you see the facts as plain as day?

ORGON: Nonsense.

ELMIRE:　　　　　　Do answer me; don't be absurd.
I'm not now asking you to trust our word.
Suppose that from some hiding-place in here　　　　　　　70
You learned the whole sad truth by eye and ear —
What would you say of your good friend, after that?

ORGON : Why, I'd say . . . nothing, by Jehoshaphat!
It can't be true.

ELMIRE:　　　　　You've been too long deceived,
And I'm quite tired of being disbelieved.　　　　　　　　75
Come now: let's put my statements to the test,
And you shall see the truth made manifest.

ORGON: I'll take that challenge. Now do your uttermost.
We'll see how you make good your empty boast.

ELMIRE (*to* DORINE): Send him to me.

DORINE:　　　　　　　　　　He's crafty; it may be hard　　80
To catch the cunning scoundrel off his guard.

ELMIRE: No, amorous men are gullible. Their conceit
So blinds them that they're never hard to cheat.
Have him come down (*To* CLÉANTE & MARIANE.) Please leave us, for a bit.

SCENE 4

ELMIRE
ORGON

ELMIRE: Pull up this table, and get under it.

ORGON: What?

ELMIRE:　　　　It's essential that you be well-hidden.

ORGON: Why there?

ELMIRE: Oh, Heavens! Just do as you are bidden.
  I have my plans; we'll soon see how they fare.
  Under the table, now; and once you're there,
  Take care that you are neither seen nor heard.   5
ORGON: Well, I'll indulge you, since I gave my word
  To see you through this infantile charade.
ELMIRE: Once it is over, you'll be glad we played.
  (*To her husband, who is now under the table*.) I'm going to act quite
    strangely, now, and you   10
  Must not be shocked at anything I do.
  Whatever I may say, you must excuse
  As part of that deceit I'm forced to use.
  I shall employ sweet speeches in the task
  Of making that impostor drop his mask;   15
  I'll give encouragement to his bold desires,
  And furnish fuel to his amorous fires.
  Since it's for your sake, and for his destruction,
  That I shall seem to yield to his seduction,
  I'll gladly stop whenever you decide   20
  That all your doubts are fully satisfied.
  I'll count on you, as soon as you have seen
  What sort of man he is, to intervene,
  And not expose me to his odious lust
  One moment longer than you feel you must.   25
  Remember: you're to save me from my plight
  Whenever . . . He's coming! Hush! Keep out of sight!

Scene 5

TARTUFFE

ELMIRE

ORGON

TARTUFFE: You wish to have a word with me, I'm told.
ELMIRE: Yes. I've a little secret to unfold.
  Before I speak, however, it would be wise
  To close that door, and look about for spies.

(TARTUFFE *goes to the door, closes it, and returns*.)

  The very last thing that must happen now   5
  Is a repetition of this morning's row.
  I've never been so badly caught off guard.
  Oh, how I feared for you! You saw how hard
  I tried to make that troublesome Damis
  Control his dreadful temper, and hold his peace.   10
  In my confusion, I didn't have the sense
  Simply to contradict his evidence;
  But as it happened, that was for the best,

And all has worked out in our interest.
This storm has only bettered your position; 15
My husband doesn't have the least suspicion,
And now, in mockery of those who do,
He bids me be continually with you.
And that is why, quite fearless of reproof,
I now can be alone with my Tartuffe, 20
And why my heart — perhaps too quick to yield —
Feels free to let its passion be revealed.
TARTUFFE: Madam, your words confuse me. Not long ago,
  You spoke in quite a different style, you know.
ELMIRE: Ah, Sir, if that refusal made you smart, 25
  It's little that you know of woman's heart,
  Or what that heart is trying to convey
  When it resists in such a feeble way!
  Always, at first, our modesty prevents
  The frank avowal of tender sentiments; 30
  However high the passion which inflames us,
  Still, to confess its power somehow shames us.
  Thus we reluct, at first, yet in a tone
  Which tells you that our heart is overthrown,
  That what our lips deny, our pulse confesses, 35
  And that, in time, all noes will turn to yesses.
  I fear my words are all too frank and free,
  And a poor proof of woman's modesty;
  But since I'm started, tell me, if you will —
  Would I have tried to make Damis be still, 40
  Would I have listened, calm and unoffended,
  Until your lengthy offer of love was ended,
  And been so very mild in my reaction,
  Had your sweet words not given me satisfaction?
  And when I tried to force you to undo 45
  The marriage-plans my husband has in view,
  What did my urgent pleading signify
  If not that I admired you, and that I
  Deplored the thought that someone else might own
  Part of a heart I wished for mine alone? 50
TARTUFFE: Madam, no happiness is so complete
  As when, from lips we love, come words so sweet;
  Their nectar floods my every sense, and drains
  In honeyed rivulets through all my veins.
  To please you is my joy, my only goal; 55
  Your love is the restorer of my soul;
  And yet I must beg leave, now, to confess
  Some lingering doubts as to my happiness.
  Might this not be a trick? Might not the catch
  Be that you wish me to break off the match 60
  With Mariane, and so have feigned to love me?
  I shan't quite trust your fond opinion of me

Until the feelings you've expressed so sweetly
Are demonstrated somewhat more concretely,
And you have shown, by certain kind concessions,   65
That I may put my faith in your professions.
ELMIRE (*She coughs, to warn her husband.*) Why be in such a hurry?
    Must my heart
Exhaust its bounty at the very start?
To make that sweet admission cost me dear,
But you'll not be content, it would appear,   70
Unless my store of favors is disbursed
To the last farthing, and at the very first.
TARTUFFE: The less we merit, the less we dare to hope,
And with our doubts, mere words can never cope.
We trust no promised bliss till we receive it;   75
Not till a joy is ours can we believe it.
I, who so little merit your esteem,
Can't credit this fulfillment of my dream,
And shan't believe it, Madam, until I savor
Some palpable assurance of your favor.   80
ELMIRE: My, how tyrannical your love can be,
And how it flusters and perplexes me!
How furiously you take one's heart in hand,
And make your every wish a fierce command!
Come, must you hound and harry me to death?   85
Will you not give me time to catch my breath?
Can it be right to press me with such force,
Give me no quarter, show me no remorse,
And take advantage, by your stern insistence,
Of the fond feelings which weaken my resistance?   90
TARTUFFE: Well, if you look with favor upon my love,
Why, then, begrudge me some clear proof thereof?
ELMIRE: But how can I consent without offense
To Heaven, toward which you feel such reverence?
TARTUFFE: If Heaven is all that holds you back, don't worry.   95
I can remove that hindrance in a hurry.
Nothing of that sort need obstruct our path.
ELMIRE: Must one not be afraid of Heaven's wrath?
TARTUFFE: Madam, forget such fears, and be my pupil,
And I shall teach you how to conquer scruple.   100
Some joys, it's true, are wrong in Heaven's eyes;
Yet Heaven is not averse to compromise;
There is a science, lately formulated,
Whereby one's conscience may be liberated,
And any wrongful act you care to mention   105
May be redeemed by purity of intention.
I'll teach you, Madam, the secrets of that science;
Meanwhile, just place on me your full reliance.
Assuage my keen desires, and feel no dread:
The sin, if any, shall be on my head.   110

(ELMIRE *coughs, this time more loudly*.)

You've a bad cough.

ELMIRE: Yes, yes. It's bad indeed.

TARTUFFE (*producing a little paper bag*): A bit of licorice may be what you
    need.

ELMIRE: No, I've a stubborn cold, it seems. I'm sure it
    Will take much more than licorice to cure it.

TARTUFFE: How aggravating.

ELMIRE: Oh, more than I can say.   115

TARTUFFE: If you're still troubled, think of things this way:
    No one shall know our joys, save us alone,
    And there's no evil till the act is known;
    It's scandal, Madam, which makes it an offense,
    And it's no sin to sin in confidence.   120

ELMIRE (*having coughed once more*): Well, clearly I must do as you require,
    And yield to your importunate desire.
    It is apparent, now, that nothing less
    Will satisfy you, and so I acquiesce.
    To go so far is much against my will;   125
    I'm vexed that it should come to this; but still,
    Since you are so determined on it, since you
    Will not allow mere language to convince you,
    And since you ask for concrete evidence, I
    See nothing for it, now, but to comply.   130
    If this is sinful, if I'm wrong to do it,
    So much the worse for him who drove me to it.
    The fault can surely not be charged to me.

TARTUFFE: Madam, the fault is mine, if fault there be,
    And . . .

ELMIRE: Open the door a little, and peek out;   135
    I wouldn't want my husband poking about.

TARTUFFE: Why worry about the man? Each day he grows
    More gullible; one can lead him by the nose.
    To find us here would fill him with delight,
    And if he saw the worst, he'd doubt his sight.   140

ELMIRE: Nevertheless, do step out for a minute
    Into the hall, and see that no one's in it.

SCENE 6

ORGON

ELMIRE

ORGON (*coming out from under the table*): That man's a perfect monster, I
    must admit!
    I'm simply stunned. I can't get over it.

ELMIRE: What, coming out so soon? How premature!
    Get back in hiding, and wait until you're sure.

Stay till the end, and be convinced completely;   5
We mustn't stop till things are proved concretely.
ORGON: Hell never harbored anything so vicious!
ELMIRE: Tut, don't be hasty. Try to be judicious.
Wait, and be certain that there's no mistake.
No jumping to conclusions, for Heaven's sake!   10

(*She places* ORGON *behind her, as* TARTUFFE *re-enters.*)

SCENE 7

TARTUFFE
ELMIRE
ORGON

TARTUFFE (*not seeing* ORGON): Madam, all things have worked out to
    perfection;
I've given the neighboring rooms a full inspection;
No one's about; and now I may at last . . .
ORGON (*intercepting him*): Hold on, my passionate fellow, not so fast!
I should advise a little more restraint.   5
Well, so you thought you'd fool me, my dear saint!
How soon you wearied of the saintly life —
Wedding my daughter, and coveting my wife!
I've long suspected you, and had a feeling
That soon I'd catch you at your double-dealing.   10
Just now, you've given me evidence galore;
It's quite enough; I have no wish for more.
ELMIRE (*To* TARTUFFE): I'm sorry to have treated you so slyly,
But circumstances forced me to be wily.
TARTUFFE: Brother, you can't think . . .
ORGON: No more talk from you;   15
Just leave this household, without more ado.
TARTUFFE: What I intended . . .
ORGON: That seems fairly clear.
Spare me your falsehoods and get out of here.
TARTUFFE: No, I'm the master, and you're the one to go!
This house belongs to me, I'll have you know,   20
And I shall show you that you can't hurt *me*
By this contemptible conspiracy,
That those who cross me know not what they do,
And that I've means to expose and punish you,
Avenge offended Heaven, and make you grieve   25
That ever you dared order me to leave.

SCENE 8

ELMIRE
ORGON

ELMIRE: What was the point of all that angry chatter?
ORGON: Dear God, I'm worried. This is no laughing matter.
ELMIRE: How so?
ORGON: I fear I understood his drift.
  I'm much disturbed about that deed of gift.
ELMIRE: You gave him . . . ?
ORGON: Yes, it's all been drawn and signed.   5
  But one thing more is weighing on my mind.
ELMIRE: What's that?
ORGON: I'll tell you; but first let's see if there's
  A certain strong-box in his room upstairs.

ACT V

SCENE 1

ORGON
CLÉANTE

CLÉANTE: Where are you going so fast?
ORGON: God knows!
CLÉANTE: Then wait;
  Let's have a conference, and deliberate
  On how this situation's to be met.
ORGON: That strong-box has me utterly upset;
  This is the worst of many, many shocks.   5
CLÉANTE: Is there some fearful mystery in that box?
ORGON: My poor friend Argas brought that box to me
  With his own hands, in utmost secrecy;
  'Twas on the very morning of his flight.
  It's full of papers which, if they came to light,   10
  Would ruin him — or such is my impression.
CLÉANTE: Then why did you let it out of your possession?
ORGON: Those papers vexed my conscience, and it seemed best
  To ask the counsel of my pious guest.
  The cunning scoundrel got me to agree   15
  To leave the strong-box in his custody,
  So that, in case of an investigation,
  I could employ a slight equivocation
  And swear I didn't have it, and thereby,
  At no expense to conscience, tell a lie.   20
CLÉANTE: It looks to me as if you're out on a limb.
  Trusting him with that box, and offering him
  That deed of gift, were actions of a kind

Which scarcely indicate a prudent mind.
With two such weapons, he has the upper hand,   25
And since you're vulnerable, as matters stand,
You erred once more in bringing him to bay.
You should have acted in some subtler way.
ORGON: Just think of it: behind that fervent face,
A heart so wicked, and a soul so base!   30
I took him in, a hungry beggar, and then . . .
Enough, by God! I'm through with pious men:
Henceforth I'll hate the whole false brotherhood,
And persecute them worse than Satan could.
CLÉANTE: Ah, there you go — extravagant as ever!   35
Why can you not be rational? You never
Manage to take the middle course, it seems,
But jump, instead, between absurd extremes.
You've recognized your recent grave mistake
In falling victim to a pious fake;   40
Now, to correct that error, must you embrace
An even greater error in its place,
And judge our worthy neighbors as a whole
By what you've learned of one corrupted soul?
Come, just because one rascal made you swallow   45
A show of zeal which turned out to be hollow,
Shall you conclude that all men are deceivers,
And that, today, there are no true believers?
Let atheists make that foolish inference;
Learn to distinguish virtue from pretense,   50
Be cautious in bestowing admiration,
And cultivate a sober moderation.
Don't humor fraud, but also don't asperse
True piety; the latter fault is worse,
And it is best to err, if err one must,   55
As you have done, upon the side of trust.

Scene 2

DAMIS
ORGON
CLÉANTE

DAMIS: Father, I hear that scoundrel's uttered threats
Against you; that he pridefully forgets
How, in his need, he was befriended by you,
And means to use your gifts to crucify you.
ORGON: It's true, my boy. I'm too distressed for tears.   5
DAMIS: Leave it to me, Sir; let me trim his ears.
Faced with such insolence, we must not waver.
I shall rejoice in doing you the favor
Of cutting short his life, and your distress.

CLÉANTE: What a display of young hotheadedness!   10
  Do learn to moderate your fits of rage.
  In this just kingdom, this enlightened age,
  One does not settle things by violence.

SCENE 3

MADAME PERNELLE	DORINE	ORGON
MARIANE	DAMIS	CLÉANTE
ELMIRE		

MADAME PERNELLE: I hear strange tales of very strange events.
ORGON: Yes, strange events which these two eyes beheld.
  The man's ingratitude is unparalleled.
  I save a wretched pauper from starvation,
  House him, and treat him like a blood relation,   5
  Shower him every day with my largesse,
  Give him my daughter, and all that I possess;
  And meanwhile the unconscionable knave
  Tries to induce my wife to misbehave;
  And not content with such extreme rascality,   10
  Now threatens me with my own liberality,
  And aims, by taking base advantage of
  The gifts I gave him out of Christian love,
  To drive me from my house, a ruined man,
  And make me end a pauper, as he began.   15
DORINE: Poor fellow!
MADAME PERNELLE: No, my son, I'll never bring
  Myself to think him guilty of such a thing.
ORGON: How's that?
MADAME PERNELLE: The righteous always were maligned.
ORGON: Speak clearly, Mother. Say what's on your mind.
MADAME PERNELLE: I mean that I can smell a rat, my dear.   20
  You know how everybody hates him, here.
ORGON: That has no bearing on the case at all.
MADAME PERNELLE: I told you a hundred times, when you were small,
  That virtue in this world is hated ever;
  Malicious men may die, but malice never.   25
ORGON: No doubt that's true, but how does it apply?
MADAME PERNELLE: They've turned you against him by a clever lie.
ORGON: I've told you, I was there and saw it done.
MADAME PERNELLE: Ah, slanderers will stop at nothing, Son.
ORGON: Mother, I'll lose my temper . . . For the last time,   30
  I tell you I was witness to the crime.
MADAME PERNELLE: The tongues of spite are busy night and noon,
  And to their venom no man is immune.
ORGON: You're talking nonsense. Can't you realize
  I saw it; saw it; saw it with my eyes?   35
  Saw, do you understand me? Must I shout it
  Into your ears before you'll cease to doubt it?

MADAME PERNELLE: Appearances can deceive, my son. Dear me,
   We cannot always judge by what we see.
ORGON: Drat! Drat!
MADAME PERNELLE: One often interprets things awry;   40
   Good can seem evil to a suspicious eye.
ORGON: Was I to see his pawing at Elmire
   As an act of charity?
MADAME PERNELLE: Till his guilt is clear,
   A man deserves the benefit of the doubt.
   You should have waited, to see how things turned out.   45
ORGON: Great God in Heaven, what more proof did I need?
   Was I to sit there, watching, until he'd . . .
   You drive me to the brink of impropriety.
MADAME PERNELLE: No, no, a man of such surpassing piety
   Could not do such a thing. You cannot shake me.   50
   I don't believe it, and you shall not make me.
ORGON: You vex me so that, if you weren't my mother,
   I'd say to you . . . some dreadful thing or other.
DORINE: It's your turn now, Sir, not to be listened to;
   You'd not trust us, and now she won't trust you.   55
CLÉANTE: My friends, we're wasting time which should be spent
   In facing up to our predicament.
   I fear that scoundrel's threats weren't made in sport.
DAMIS: Do you think he'd have the nerve to go to court?
ELMIRE: I'm sure he won't: they'd find it all too crude   60
   A case of swindling and ingratitude.
CLÉANTE: Don't be too sure. He won't be at a loss
   To give his claims a high and righteous gloss;
   And clever rogues with far less valid cause
   Have trapped their victims in a web of laws.   65
   I say again that to antagonize
   A man so strongly armed was most unwise.
ORGON: I know it; but the man's appalling cheek
   Outraged me so, I couldn't control my pique.
CLÉANTE: I wish to Heaven that we could devise   70
   Some truce between you, or some compromise.
ELMIRE: If I had known what cards he held, I'd not
   Have roused his anger by my little plot.
ORGON (to DORINE, as M. LOYAL enters): What is that fellow looking for?
      Who is he?
   Go talk to him — and tell him that I'm busy.   75

SCENE 4

MONSIEUR LOYAL	DAMIS	ELMIRE
MADAME PERNELLE	MARIANE	CLÉANTE
ORGON	DORINE	

MONSIEUR LOYAL: Good day, dear sister. Kindly let me see
   Your master.

DORINE: He's involved with company,
  And cannot be disturbed just now, I fear.
MONSIEUR LOYAL: I hate to intrude; but what has brought me here
  Will not disturb your master, in any event.   5
  Indeed, my news will make him most content.
DORINE: Your name?
MONSIEUR LOYAL: Just say that I bring greetings from
  Monsieur Tartuffe, on whose behalf I've come.
DORINE (*to* ORGON): Sir, he's a very gracious man, and bears
  A message from Tartuffe, which, he declares,   10
  Will make you most content.
CLÉANTE: Upon my word,
  I think this man had best be seen, and heard.
ORGON: Perhaps he has some settlement to suggest.
  How shall I treat him? What manner would be best?
CLÉANTE: Control your anger, and if he should mention   15
  Some fair adjustment, give him your full attention.
MONSIEUR LOYAL: Good health to you, good Sir. May Heaven confound
  Your enemies, and may your joys abound.
ORGON (*aside, to* CLÉANTE): A gentle salutation: it confirms
  My guess that he is here to offer terms.   20
MONSIEUR LOYAL: I've always held your family most dear;
  I served your father, Sir, for many a year.
ORGON: Sir, I must ask your pardon; to my shame,
  I cannot now recall your face or name.
MONSIEUR LOYAL: Loyal's my name; I come from Normandy,   25
  And I'm a bailiff, in all modesty.
  For forty years, praise God, it's been my boast
  To serve with honor in that vital post,
  And I am here, Sir, if you will permit
  The liberty, to serve you with this writ . . .   30
ORGON: To — *what?*
MONSIEUR LOYAL: Now, please, Sir, let us have no friction:
  It's nothing but an order of eviction.
  You are to move your goods and family out
  And make way for new occupants, without
  Deferment or delay, and give the keys . . .   35
ORGON: I? Leave this house?
MONSIEUR LOYAL: Why yes, Sir, if you please.
  This house, Sir, from the cellar to the roof,
  Belongs now to the good Monsieur Tartuffe,
  And he is lord and master of your estate
  By virtue of a deed of present date,   40
  Drawn in due form, with clearest legal phrasing . . .
DAMIS: Your insolence is utterly amazing!
MONSIEUR LOYAL: Young man, my business here is not with you,
  But with your wise and temperate father, who,
  Like every worthy citizen, stands in awe   45
  Of justice, and would never obstruct the law.
ORGON: But . . .

MONSIEUR LOYAL: Not for a million, Sir, would you rebel
  Against authority; I know that well.
  You'll not make trouble, Sir, or interfere
  With the execution of my duties here.   50
DAMIS: Someone may execute a smart tattoo
  On that black jacket of yours, before you're through.
MONSIEUR LOYAL: Sir, bid your son be silent. I'd much regret
  Having to mention such a nasty threat
  Of violence, in writing my report.   55
DORINE (*aside*): This man Loyal's a most disloyal sort!
MONSIEUR LOYAL: I love all men of upright character,
  And when I agreed to serve these papers, Sir,
  It was your feelings that I had in mind.
  I couldn't bear to see the case assigned   60
  To someone else, who migh esteem you less
  And so subject you to unpleasantness.
ORGON: What's more unpleasant than telling a man to leave
  His house and home?
MONSIEUR LOYAL: You'd like a short reprieve?
  If you desire it, Sir, I shall not press you,   65
  But wait until tomorrow to dispossess you.
  Splendid. I'll come and spend the night here, then,
  Most quietly, with half a score of men.
  For form's sake, you might bring me, just before
  You go to bed, the keys to the front door.   70
  My men, I promise, will be on their best
  Behavior, and will not disturb your rest.
  But bright and early, Sir, you must be quick
  And move out all your furniture, every stick:
  The men I've chosen are both young and strong,   75
  And with their help it shouldn't take you long.
  In short, I'll make things pleasant and convenient,
  And since I'm being so extremely lenient,
  Please show me, Sir, a like consideration,
  And give me your entire cooperation.   80
ORGON (*aside*): I may be all but bankrupt, but I vow
  I'd give a hundred louis, here and now,
  Just for the pleasure of landing one good clout
  Right on the end of that complacent snout.
CLÉANTE: Careful; don't make things worse.
DAMIS: My bootsole itches   85
  To give that beggar a good kick in the breeches.
DORINE: Monsieur Loyal, I'd love to hear the whack
  Of a stout stick across your fine broad back.
MONSIEUR LOYAL: Take care: a woman too may go to jail if
  She uses threatening language to a bailiff.   90
CLÉANTE: Enough, enough, Sir. This must not go on.
  Give me that paper, please, and then begone.

MONSIEUR LOYAL: Well, *au revoir*. God give you all good cheer!
ORGON: May God confound you, and him who sent you here!

SCENE 5

ORGON	ELMIRE	DORINE
CLÉANTE	MADAME PERNELLE	DAMIS
MARIANE		

ORGON: Now, Mother, was I right or not? This writ
  Should change your notion of Tartuffe a bit.
  Do you perceive his villainy at last?
MADAME PERNELLE: I'm thunderstruck. I'm utterly aghast.
DORINE: Oh, come, be fair. You mustn't take offense   5
  At this new proof of his benevolence.
  He's acting out of selfless love, I know.
  Material things enslave the soul, and so
  He kindly has arranged your liberation
  From all that might endanger your salvation.   10
ORGON: Will you not ever hold your tongue, you dunce?
CLÉANTE: Come, you must take some action, and at once.
ELMIRE: Go tell the world of the low trick he's tried.
  The deed of gift is surely nullified
  By such behavior, and public rage will not   15
  Permit the wretch to carry out his plot.

SCENE 6

VALÈRE	ELMIRE	DAMIS
ORGON	MARIANE	DORINE
CLÉANTE	MADAME PERNELLE	

VALÈRE: Sir, though I hate to bring you more bad news,
  Such is the danger that I cannot choose.
  A friend who is extremely close to me
  And knows my interest in your family
  Has, for my sake, presumed to violate   5
  The secrecy that's due to things of state,
  And sends me word that you are in a plight
  From which your one salvation lies in flight.
  That scoundrel who's imposed upon you so
  Denounced you to the King an hour ago   10
  And, as supporting evidence, displayed
  The strong-box of a certain renegade
  Whose secret papers, so he testified,
  You had disloyally agreed to hide.
  I don't know just what charges may be pressed,   15

But there's a warrant out for your arrest;
Tartuffe has been instructed, furthermore,
To guide the arresting officer to your door.
CLÉANTE: He's clearly done this to facilitate
His seizure of your house and your estate.   20
ORGON: That man, I must say, is a vicious beast!
VALÈRE: Quick, Sir; you mustn't tarry in the least.
My carriage is outside, to take you hence;
This thousand louis should cover all expense.
Let's lose no time, or you shall be undone;   25
The sole defense, in this case, is to run.
I shall go with you all the way, and place you
In a safe refuge to which they'll never trace you.
ORGON: Alas, dear boy, I wish that I could show you
My gratitude for everything I owe you.   30
But now is not the time; I pray the Lord
That I may live to give you your reward.
Farewell, my dears; be careful . . .
CLÉANTE: Brother, hurry.
We shall take care of things; you needn't worry.

SCENE 7

THE OFFICER	ELMIRE	DORINE
TARTUFFE	MARIANE	CLÉANTE
VALÈRE	MADAME PERNELLE	DAMIS
ORGON		

TARTUFFE: Gently, Sir, gently; stay right where you are.
No need for haste; your lodging isn't far.
You're off to prison, by order of the Prince.
ORGON: This is the crowning blow, you wretch; and since
It means my total ruin and defeat,   5
Your villainy is now at last complete.
TARTUFFE: You needn't try to provoke me; it's no use.
Those who serve Heaven must expect abuse.
CLÉANTE: You are indeed most patient, sweet, and blameless.
DORINE: How he exploits the name of Heaven! It's shameless.   10
TARTUFFE: Your taunts and mockeries are all for naught;
To do my duty is my only thought.
MARIANE: Your love of duty is most meritorious,
And what you've done is little short of glorious.
TARTUFFE: All deeds are glorious, Madam, which obey   15
The sovereign prince who sent me here today.
ORGON: I rescued you when you were destitute;
Have you forgotten that, you thankless brute?
TARTUFFE: No, no, I well remember everything;
But my first duty is to serve my King.   20

That obligation is so paramount
That other claims, beside it, do not count;
And for it I would sacrifice my wife,
My family, my friend, or my own life.
ELMIRE: Hypocrite!
DORINE: All that we most revere, he uses   25
To cloak his plots and camouflage his ruses.
CLÉANTE: If it is true that you are animated
By pure and loyal zeal, as you have stated,
Why was this zeal not roused until you'd sought
To make Orgon a cuckold, and been caught?   30
Why weren't you moved to give your evidence
Until your outraged host had driven you hence?
I shan't say that the gift of all his treasure
Ought to have damped your zeal in any measure;
But if he is a traitor, as you declare,   35
How could you condescend to be his heir?
TARTUFFE (*to the* OFFICER): Sir, spare me all this clamor; it's growing shrill.
Please carry out your orders, if you will.
OFFICER: Yes, I've delayed too long, Sir. Thank you kindly.
You're just the proper person to remind me.   40
Come, you are off to join the other boarders
In the King's prison, according to his orders.
TARTUFFE: Who? I, Sir?
OFFICER: Yes.
TARTUFFE: To prison? This can't be true!
OFFICER: I owe an explanation, but not to you.
(*To* ORGON.) Sir, all is well; rest easy, and be grateful.   45
We serve a Prince to whom all sham is hateful,
A Prince who sees into our inmost hearts,
And can't be fooled by any trickster's arts.
His royal soul, though generous and human,
Views all things with discernment and acumen;   50
His sovereign reason is not lightly swayed,
And all his judgments are discreetly weighed.
He honors righteous men of every kind,
And yet his zeal for virtue is not blind,
Nor does his love of piety numb his wits   55
And make him tolerant of hypocrites.
'Twas hardly likely that this man could cozen
A King who's foiled such liars by the dozen.
With one keen glance, the King perceived the whole
Perverseness and corruption of his soul,   60
And thus high Heaven's justice was displayed:
Betraying you, the rogue stood self-betrayed.
The King soon recognized Tartuffe as one
Notorious by another name, who'd done
So many vicious crimes that one could fill   65
Ten volumes with them, and be writing still.

But to be brief: our sovereign was appalled
By this man's treachery toward you, which he called
The last, worst villainy of a vile career,
And bade me follow the impostor here   70
To see how gross his impudence could be,
And force him to restore your property.
Your private papers, by the King's command,
I hereby seize and give into your hand.
The King, by royal order, invalidates   75
The deed which gave this rascal your estates,
And pardons, furthermore, your grave offense
In harboring an exile's documents.
By these decrees, our Prince rewards you for
Your loyal deeds in the late civil war,   80
And shows how heartfelt is his satisfaction
In recompensing any worthy action,
How much he prizes merit, and how he makes
More of men's virtues than of their mistakes.
DORINE: Heaven be praised!
MADAME PERNELLE: I breathe again, at last.   85
ELMIRE: We're safe.
MARIANE: I can't believe the danger's past.
ORGON (to TARTUFFE): Well, traitor, now you see . . .
CLÉANTE: Ah, Brother, please,
Let's not descend to such indignities.
Leave the poor wretch to his unhappy fate,
And don't say anything to aggravate   90
His present woes; but rather hope that he
Will soon embrace an honest piety,
And mend his ways, and by a true repentance
Move our just King to moderate his sentence.
Meanwhile, go kneel before your sovereign's throne   95
And thank him for the mercies he has shown.
ORGON: Well said: let's go at once and, gladly kneeling,
Express the gratitude which all are feeling.
Then, when that first great duty has been done,
We'll turn with pleasure to a second one,   100
And give Valère, whose love has proven so true,
The wedded happiness which is his due.

AFTERWORD

For us, living in a more liberal — or indifferent — age than that of Louis
XIV, the implications of Tartuffe's hypocrisy are likely to be less controversial than they were for some of Molière's contemporaries, though they are
hardly less meaningful. Tartuffe threatens a family with ruin, almost dis-

rupts the basic social unit, breaks natural bonds. He is himself a solitary outsider, familyless, friendless, loveless, without any social context. But the fact that he is not related to anybody or anything before Orgon picks him up is not, somehow, a cause for pity. Rather, it makes him a sinister, anti-social figure, lone evil against the vital group.

Behind the deliberate artifice of the whole play, behind the farcical intrigue, the stylization of character, and the fluent and funny couplet verse, is a dark moral fable for which the comic conventions of the neoclassical theater shockingly serve as an almost perfect vehicle. Tartuffe's mask of devoutness conceals a monster of greed, lechery, and ingratitude; but the human grotesque is an actual menace: the caricature has the power to destroy. The bourgeois society reflected in the play is a fallen world, in which evil deception is both plausible and resourceful because its main victim fails to temper religious zeal with worldly wisdom. Piety becomes monomania.

This is only one of the play's many ironies. Shared fear almost separates the lovers when their romance is threatened. Honesty provokes self-righteous wrath in Orgon. Orgon's folly forces the faithful Elmire to play the role of adulterous coquette — and forces Orgon to listen to her performance. M. Loyal is a model of politeness while he dispossesses Orgon of his house; the public bailiff is "loyal" only to hypocritical villainy. Where plain speaking has been forbidden, sarcasm — the rhetoric for devious meaning — becomes the voice of wise virtue, like Dorine's. The most richly ironic scene in the whole play is Scene 6 in Act III, but the richness is largely a matter of implications that carry us beyond the realm of high comedy to which the scene ostensibly belongs. When Damis denounces Tartuffe to his father as Elmire's would-be seducer, Tartuffe readily admits his sinfulness in such sweeping terms of self-abasement that Orgon becomes only further convinced of his Christian humility and turns Damis out of the house. The villain uses truth as a means to deception. This is the sort of thing that places *Tartuffe*, like *The Misanthrope*, though for different reasons, among Molière's problem comedies: In *Tartuffe*, a villain pretends to be a good man; in *The Misanthrope*, a good man appears to be a fool. Our laughter may well be uncomfortable. Somehow it implicates us in the vice and folly on stage.

Formally, what is most striking about the play is the delay of Tartuffe's appearance for more than two acts. The delay represents a daring piece of dramaturgy, for though the gain in audience suspense is obvious, there is also the risk of anticlimax when the title character *does* appear. But his first speech, "Hang up my hair-shirt, put my scourge in place, / And pray, Laurent, for Heaven's perpetual grace," brilliantly justifies the device. False unction is on display forever in this penitent ascetic with a valet.

The little scene reveals a major characteristic of Molière's comic art. What his characters are they are with an intensity and thoroughness and sharpness of outline that establish their identity once and for all. We are dealing in blacks and whites. There are no complexities or ambiguities or

subtle depths. Virtue and wisdom exist less for their own sake than as antitheses to vice and folly, and if the gulls appear as stereotypes that is no
more than their own doing. They are diminishers of their own humanity.
The opening dialogue between old Madame Pernelle and the various members of the household, in which they all take turns trying to interrupt the
old lady's harangue but only succeed in drawing her fire, represents a patterning of speech that is obviously unnatural but which nevertheless justifies itself not only as a certain rhythm of dialogue but also as a method by
which human attitudes are clearly defined and contrasted. Molière is not
interested in photographic realism or in doing justice to the infinite complexities of the human soul, in discovering the good that surely must reside
somewhere even in a bigot. He is interested in providing us with a memorable spectacle of hypocrisy, gullibility, and obstinacy in action. The long,
stilted speeches, the alternating passages of fast, cut-and-thrust dialogue,
the exaggerations and oversimplifications and contrivances of situation and
character, these are all deliberate formalizations of the dramatist's art, devices that both heighten the comedy — or farce, if one likes — and extend
the anatomy of basic human attitudes. Take a famous scene that presents
some characteristic difficulties in the way of enjoying Molière — Scene 4
in Act I. Orgon has just returned from a trip to the country and asks the
maid Dorine how everyone has been during his absence. Dorine tells him
his wife has had an attack of fever, to which he replies, "Ah! And
Tartuffe?" Dorine says he is comfortable and in excellent health, and Orgon exclaims, "Poor fellow!" This sequence of four speeches is repeated
three times. Again a pattern is established, and we gather an impression of
Orgon's perversion of values.

But is the scene funny? Does it reflect actual human behavior, even allowing the playwright the privilege of exaggeration for heightened effect?
What does it *mean* to say "Poor fellow" about someone you have just been
told is perfectly well and content? Why is the speech repeated?

The exchange is, obviously, a shortcut to characterization as well as a
piece of verbal slapstick. But if it were only that, we would not be dealing
with great comedy. We are, though, and the reason is that we can feel the
unnaturalness and idiocy of Orgon's replies to be functional to Molière's
theme. Orgon's affection for Tartuffe, to the point of ignoring and even
injuring his own family, *is* a form of lunacy. His response to the news of
his wife's illness is no more insane than his later decision to give his daughter in marriage to a man who is hateful to her or to disinherit his son in
favor of that man and to entrust him with a friend's secrets. While Dorine's
speeches in the scene are full and flavorful, vivid with concrete detail, Orgon's are limited to five words, two set phrases, the expression of a small
and frozen attitude. He listens and yet does not listen. What Dorine tells
him about Tartuffe does not reach him as meaning; it only triggers a piece
of pious cant; he answers automatically, totally inadequate to the human
situation. He speaks like a man hypnotized, or under a spell. There is po-

etic justice (as Dorine points out) in the scene in which Madame Pernelle obstinately refuses to believe that Tartuffe could have designs on Elmire, even after her son has been convinced by the evidence of his own eyes. If, after the spell has been broken, Orgon is frustrated by his equally stubborn mother into contemplating the absurdity of his own previous behavior, this is precisely Molière's point. Orgon has only himself to blame for his troubles and for his flatness of character. In a sense, the play is about inflexibility of spirit as much as it is about hypocrisy.

Against Orgon's obstinate stupidity and unnaturalness of feeling and against the increasingly sinister presence of Tartuffe (consider the function and effect of M. Loyal in this connection), the play asserts the primary value of sane moderation in human relationships. Three characters represent these values: Cléante, the voice of wisdom and restraint, whose most significant speech is the one in which he objects to Orgon's vow never again to trust a pious man; Dorine, who constantly deflates stuffiness and pretension and who saves Valère and Mariane from their own foolish pride; and Elmire, who refuses to become hysterical over Tartuffe's advances and succeeds in opening Orgon's eyes by using herself as bait to lure Tartuffe into giving himself away. These three combine goodness with intelligence and strength. In contrast, there are the good characters who suffer because of some excess of feeling: Damis's rash anger, like his father's later, ends in his discomfiture and the temporary strengthening of Tartuffe's hand; and Mariane has to be rescued from her own despair. Valère's character is ambivalent in this respect. He and Mariane are too stubbornly proud to manage their own romance, but at the very end of the play he passes from folly to a kind of heroism and becomes Tartuffe's contrast (*foil*, in the technical term): Tartuffe repays Orgon's kindness with ingratitude; Valère repays Orgon's injustice with kindness.

If Cléante is Molière's spokesman (*raisonneur*), it becomes significant that he and his allies are rendered helpless against the efficacy of evil at the end. The best they can hope for is some way of coming to terms with Tartuffe. To recover what Orgon's error has cost them appears impossible. For a moment in Act V, the play seems about to turn into a kind of tragedy — the family to be destroyed by the evil intruder. At this point Molière does something that courses in writing drama warn against; he introduces a *deus ex machina*, a person (or fact) who has not entered the action before and who steps in to resolve a deadlocked situation. In this case, the god from the wings is King Louis XIV, represented by the officer who arrests Tartuffe. Nothing earlier in the play has led us to expect this development. Is it, therefore, more than fulsome flattery of Molière's royal patron as the earthly representative of divine providence and an awkward way out of a plot that threatened to master the supposed writer of comedy? It is certainly not playing the game according to the rules of detective fiction.

Again one must keep in mind Molière's artistic end — not plausibility but communication of wisdom in effective drama. The fact that outside help is needed, that the all-powerful hand of the king must interfere to keep evil from succeeding against innocence, becomes a plot metaphor for the simple truth that discovery of one's error and sincere remorse for it do not necessarily rectify its consequences. We are moving here on the very edge of comedy, where the forces of stupidity and evil somehow seem more substantial than those of reason and goodness. The comedy turns serious. Innocent, gullible, well-meaning man is unable to cope with evil alone. He needs kingly help.

Jean Racine

PHAEDRA

Translated by Peter Arnott

FOREWORD

In France, as in England, a professional, secular theater emerged from the community performances of sacred drama in the Middle Ages, but took rather longer to do so. By the time of Racine's first play, in 1663, the commercial theater was firmly established in Paris, under royal patronage and appealing to a cultivated clientele, but still on a more limited basis than in London. For most of the period there were only three permanent companies. Racine began by writing for Molière, then switched allegiances to an older and more conventional theater, the Hôtel de Bourgogne, with which he remained for the rest of his professional career. The Hôtel de Bourgogne had established a style for the performance of tragedy. Stage movement was reduced to a minimum. Actors confined themselves to a few stylized gestures — we notice, in *Phaedra*, how little physical action is suggested by the text — and, like their Greek predecessors, relied largely on the power of the voice. Lines, written in carefully constructed rhyming couplets, were delivered in a kind of singsong recitative. If we could revive these performances today, we should doubtless feel we were listening to dramatic oratorio rather than drama proper. Circumscribed by tiny stages and, in obedience to the fashionable doctrine of the three unities, by unchanging sets, French classical tragedy worked in terms of an artificial, constricted world, populated largely by kings and queens speaking a kind of language never heard in real life. *Phaedra*, which exemplifies all these qualities, was written in 1677. It was Racine's last play for the professional theater, and though accepted somewhat hesitantly by its original audience, has since been hailed as his greatest work and the tragic masterpiece of its time.

CHARACTERS

THESEUS, King of Athens
PHAEDRA, his wife
HIPPOLYTUS, son of Theseus by a former wife
ARICIA, princess of the Athenian royal line

THERAMENES, tutor of Hippolytus
OENONE, nurse and confidante of Phaedra
ISMENE, confidante of Aricia
PANOPE, lady-in-waiting to Phaedra
GUARDS

The scene is in Troezen, an Athenian dependency in the Peloponnesus

ACT I

SCENE 1

HIPPOLYTUS
THERAMENES

HIPPOLYTUS:
My resolution's made, Theramenes,
Old friend; I must be moving on.
Say my adieux to the delights of Troezen.[1]
Such are the apprehensions that beset me
I blush to contemplate my idle days.   5
Six long months separated from my father,
My love would know his fate, but finds no answer,
Not even the land where he is lying hidden.
THERAMENES:
What land is left for you to search, my lord?
Already, at the proper dictates of your fears   10
I've combed each inch of Corinth's neighbor sea,
Sought Theseus from the dwellers on the shores
Where Acheron tunnels dark down to the underworld.

Racine's *Phaedra*, translated by Peter Arnott. Copyright © 1978 by Peter Arnott.
Caution: This play in its printed form is designed for the reading public only. All dramatic rights to it are fully protected by copyright, and no public or private performance — professional or amateur — may be given without the written permission of the author.

[1] The city of Troezen was an Athenian dependency in the southern half of Greece, and the birthplace of Theseus

Traveled to Elis, and through Taenarus[2]
Far to the waters that saw Icarus fall.   15
With what new hope, under what happy skies
Do you think to find the path his feet have trod?
Why, who's to say? Perhaps your royal father
Wishes his absence to remain a mystery,
And while with you we tremble for his life   20
Our carefree hero, hiding some new love
Is waiting till the woman he's seduced . . .

HIPPOLYTUS:
No more, Theramenes. Speak no ill of Theseus.
He shed his follies and his youth together.
Whatever's keeping him, is nothing shameful.   25
Phaedra has cured him of inconstancy;
She's feared no rival for a long time now.
Well then: in seeking him I'll do my duty
And leave this place that I have come to dread.

THERAMENES:
My lord! Since when have you had cause to fear   30
This peaceful place your boyhood loved so well
And where I've seen you rather spend your days
Than in Athens, and the noisy pomp of court?

HIPPOLYTUS:
Those happy days are gone. Things wear new faces
Since first the gods delivered to these shores   35
The daughter of Minos and Pasiphaë.

THERAMENES:
I know. You have clear cause to be aggrieved.
Phaedra provokes you, and offends your sight,
Your father's jealous wife, who scarcely saw you
Before she proved her power and had you banished.   40
But the hate she had for you in days gone by
Has either vanished or been laid to sleep.
Besides, what dangers can a dying woman,
And one who wants to die, enforce on you?
Phaedra is sick, and will not tell us why.   45
Can she be plotting any harm against you?

HIPPOLYTUS:
No, she's no enemy for me to fear.
Another woman routs Hippolytus;
Her name — I'll tell you — is Aricia,
The last survivor of a nest of traitors.   50

THERAMENES:
My lord, are you against her too?
Has Pallas' beautiful daughter ever
Been tainted with her brothers' treachery?
She's lovely and innocent; why should you hate her?

[2] The river Acheron and Cape Taenarus were traditional entrances to the Underworld

HIPPOLYTUS:

   If I hated her, I should not run away.   55

THERAMENES:

   My lord, by your leave, I can suggest a reason.
   Has something happened to the proud Hippolytus,
   Relentless enemy of the laws of love
   The yoke that Theseus wore so many times?
   Has Venus, so long slighted by your pride,   60
   Reduced you to the common rank of men
   To justify your father at the last?
   My lord, are you in love?

HIPPOLYTUS:

                  You dare say that!
   My friend who knew me since I first drew breath?
   Can you ask me to betray so shamefully   65
   Such proud, uncompromising principles?
   The Amazon my mother gave me suck
   This pride at which you wonder with her milk,
   And reaching riper years I saw myself
   To be the man I was, and found it good.   70
   Bound to me by unseeking loyalty
   You used to tell me stories of my father;
   You know how my heart hung on every word
   And warmed to tales of his heroic deeds
   When you depicted that brave warrior   75
   Consoling mankind for the death of Hercules:
   Slaughter of monsters, punishment of rovers,
   Procrustes and Cercyon, Scyron, Sinnis,[3]
   Epidaurus littered with its giant's bones,
   Crete reeking with the blood of Minotaur;   80
   But when you told less admirable tales,
   The easy vows pledged in a hundred places,
   Helen of Sparta ravished from her parents,
   Periboea weeping upon Salamis,
   So many others, even their names forgotten,   85
   Too trusting spirits cheated by his passion,
   Ariadne weeping in the wilderness,
   Then Phaedra, taken under better omens,
   You know how sadly I listened to this story
   And urged you often to pass over it,   90
   Happy, if I could only wipe from mind
   This sordid chapter of so fair a tale.
   Now shall I see these fetters fall on me?
   Does Heaven wish to humble me so low?
   Such weakling sighs would sound the worse from me.   95
   Theseus has high-heaped honors to condone him;

---

[3] Most of this list of monsters and marauders had been killed by Theseus when he first traveled from Troezen to Athens to inherit his kingdom

But I have slain no monsters to this day
As he has done, to give my weakness license.
But even if my proud heart could be softened
Should I choose Aricia for my conqueror?   100
Rather my errant thoughts should have remembered
The eternal barrier that stands between us.
My father holds her dangerous, and imposes
Stern laws to stop her brothers' line in her.
He fears the tainted branch will bear green shoots   105
And seeks to bury their name with their sister.
She's bound his ward till the day the grave receives her.
No torch will ever light her wedding day.
Should I wed her cause, and flout my father's anger,
Set myself up as a bold example,   110
Launch my youth on the shifting shoals of love . . .

THERAMENES:
My lord, once your appointed hour is come
The last thing Heaven cares about is reason.
Your father tried to close your eyes; instead
He opened them! His animosity   115
Fanned into life the flame of independence,
And lent enchantment to his enemy.
But come, why fear an honorable love
And shrink to venture what has sweets to give?
Will you always keep your chastity for guide?   120
Why fear to tread the path of Hercules?
Many a manly heart's gone down to Venus!
Where would you be yourself, you renegade,
If Antiope had stood firm against her laws
And never burned with maiden love for Theseus?   125
Why talk as if you still depised such things?
All's changed, admit it; these last few days
We've hardly seen you as we used to do
Racing your chariot at the waterside
Or in the mastery of Neptune's art,[4]   130
Breaking an untamed courser to the bit.
The forests ring less often to our cries;
Your eyes are heavy with an inner fire;
There's no more doubt of it, you're hot in love,
Heartsick almost to death, and still pretending.   135
Has fair Aricia found the way to please you?

HIPPOLYTUS:
I go, Theramenes. My quest is calling me.

THERAMENES:
Won't you see Phaedra before you leave,
My Lord?

---

[4] Not swimming, but horsemanship; Neptune was originally also god of horses

HIPPOLYTUS:

>   I intend to. You may so inform her.
> Let's see her, since my duty so obliges.   140
> But here's Oenone: what's upset her now?

Scene 2

HIPPOLYTUS
THERAMENES
OENONE

OENONE:

>   My lord, can any sorrow match with mine?
> The queen is nearly at life's end; I watch
> Beside her night and day in vain; she's dying
> Of some unspoken sickness in my arms.
> Her mind is prey to long delirium.   5
> Torn by her fitful temper from her bed
> She cries for daylight, bidding me to keep
> All people from her melancholy path.
> She's here.

HIPPOLYTUS:

>   So be it. I shall leave her here alone,
> And not inflict on her a face she hates.   10

Scene 3

PHAEDRA
OENONE

PHAEDRA:

>   No further, Oenone; let us stay here;
> I cannot stand, my strength is going;
> The daylight blinds my eyes, my knees
> Are trembling, giving beneath me.

OENONE:

>   Almighty gods, let these tears be enough!   5

PHAEDRA:

>   How heavy these veils, these baubles hang on me.
> What interfering fingers tied these knots
> And worked this weight of hair upon my brow?
> They plague me, hurt me; all things meet to hurt me.

OENONE:

>   Now see how one wish wars against the other!   10
> You've nothing but your own caprice to blame.
> You made us dress you, cursed our laggard hands.
> It was you recalled your former strength and wanted
> To see the light and to be seen again.

And now you see it. Do you want to hide 15
And hate the light you came out here to find?

PHAEDRA:

Proud shining father of a fated line,
My mother dared to boast herself your child.
Perhaps you blush to see me in my sorrow.
Sun, I have come to pay my last respects. 20

OENONE:

Will you never lose that cruel longing?
Must I always see you bidding life farewell
And looking forward to your funeral?

PHAEDRA:

Oh gods, what would I give to sit
Beneath the shadow of a spreading tree 25
And feed my eyes upon the chariot
Trailing brave dust-clouds, flying on its course!

OENONE:

My lady!

PHAEDRA:

I'm mad; where am I, what have I said?
My wits have wandered after my desires.
They're gone; the gods have stolen them away. 30
See how I blush, Oenone; I'm ashamed
To make this exhibition of my grief.

OENONE:

Blush for your silence, if you blush at all.
It only aggravates your misery.
You spurn our help, you're deaf to all we say; 35
Would you be friendless when you end your days?
What madness checks them midway in their course?
What spell, what poison has polluted them?
Darkness has hidden heaven three times over
Since sleep last won admittance to your eyes; 40
Three times new day dispelled the shades of night
Since your wasting body last took nourishment.
What deadly purpose is possessing you?
By what right do you seek to kill yourself?
You offend against the gods who gave you life, 45
Betray the husband of your marriage-bond,
And worst of all, betray your wretched children,
Abandoning them to a tyrant's yoke.
Remember, the day that robs them of their mother
Will be a glad day for the foreign woman's son, 50
That haughty enemy of you and yours,
The son the Amazon carried in her womb,
Hippolytus . . .

PHAEDRA:

Oh, gods!

OENONE:

Ah, that has stung you!

PHAEDRA:

You fool, what name have you let pass your lips?

OENONE:

Oh, yes, you've every reason to be angry. 55
I like to see you shudder at his name.
Live on; let love join duty to revive you.
Live; never let a Scythian woman's son
Impose his despotism on your sons, and rule
The purest blood of Greece, the blood of gods. 60
No time to lose; there's death in every moment.
Make haste, restore the vigor you have lost;
Your days are wasting, but the torch of life
Is not yet spent, and still can be rekindled.

PHAEDRA:

I've kept my guilt alive too long already. 65

OENONE:

What, is there something preying on your mind?
What have you done to give you such remorse?
Your hands were never stained with innocent blood!

PHAEDRA:

My hands are still clean, the gods be praised!
Would to Heaven my heart were so. 70

OENONE:

But what could you conceive so horrible
That even now the thought of it appalls you?

PHAEDRA:

I've told you enough. Spare me the rest.
I'll die before I confess such horrors.

OENONE:

Then die. Stay true to your inhuman silence. 75
But find somebody else to close your eyes.
Your light is almost spent; but I shall be
Before you on the steep way to the dead land.
There are a thousand open ways to death;
The shortest shall be mine by right of sorrow. 80
Oh, you are hard. Have I ever broken a promise?
Remember how I held you in my arms
When you were born; I left my home, my children,
Abandoned everything to follow you.
Is this how you reward your faithful servant? 85

PHAEDRA:

What do you hope to gain by forcing me?
You'd run from me screaming if I spoke.

OENONE:

What could you say more horrible
Than watching you die before my eyes?

PHAEDRA:

If you knew my crime, the burden I must bear, 90
I should die just the same, and die more guilty.

OENONE:
My lady, I pray you by the tears I've shed
For you, and by the knees to which I cling;
Deliver me from this uncertainty.

PHAEDRA:
Your wish, not mine. Get up.

OENONE:
                                    I'm listening.   95

PHAEDRA:
Heaven, what shall I tell her? Where shall I start?

OENONE:
You do me an injustice. What's to fear?

PHAEDRA:
Hatred of Venus, and her fatal anger!
Mother, what dark ways you walked for love!

OENONE:
Let us forget them, and in time to come   100
Inter this memory in lasting silence.

PHAEDRA:
My sister Ariadne, racked by love,
Abandoned on the shore and left to die!

OENONE:
What are you doing? What torments your mind
To make you cry against your family?   105

PHAEDRA:
Venus has spoken. Last of my sad line
And the unhappiest, I too shall die.

OENONE:
Are you in love?

PHAEDRA:
                        In love? I am possessed.

OENONE:
With whom?

PHAEDRA:
                        Now you will hear the crowning horror.
I love — I tremble at the very name —   110
I love —

OENONE:
                Love whom?

PHAEDRA:
                                You know the Amazon's son,
The prince I persecuted for so long . . .

OENONE:
Hippolytus! Great gods!

PHAEDRA:
                                It was you who spoke his name.

OENONE:
Just Heaven! The blood has frozen in my veins:
All's lost; there is a curse upon your house;   115

A curse was on the ship that came for you,
A curse upon its landfall: what possessed them
Ever to court the perils of your shore?

PHAEDRA:

My trouble had a longer way to go.
I had scarcely sealed my marriage bond with Theseus,   120
Secure in seeming happiness and peace,
When Athens showed me my antagonist.
I saw him, blushed and turned pale at his sight;
A fear arose in my distracted mind;
My eyes no longer saw, I could not speak.   125
I felt my body turn to ice and fire,
Knew Venus and her all-devouring flame,
The torments destined for her chosen victims.
I thought to turn them off by tireless prayer,
Built her a temple, made it beautiful,   130
And hourly stood among the sacrifices
To hunt my reason in their gutted bodies.
Poor remedies for passion past all healing!
In vain my hands burnt incense at her altars;
My lips invoked the goddess, but my heart   135
Hippolytus. I saw him everywhere;
His image knelt beside me at the altar.
I offered all to this forbidden god.
I hid from him; and then the final blow,
I scanned his father's face to see the son.   140
At last I dared revolt against myself,
And spurred my heart to attack him. To secure
The exile of the enemy I worshipped
I played the cruel stepmother, and urged
His banishment. My clamorous insistence   145
Tore him at last from the paternal bosom.
I breathed again, Oenone; with him gone
My days more easy walked in innocence.
Compliant to my lord, I hid my hurt
And bore the fruits of this damned union.   150
But all in vain! The ways of Fate are hard.
I came to Troezen at my husband's side
And saw my banished enemy again.
My wound was living, and began to bleed.
No more is it a subtle, secret passion   155
But Venus incarnate, battened on her prey.
I loathe my crime as it is fit I should;
I hold my life in hate, abhor this love,
And wished to keep my fair name still by dying
And hide this dark love from the eyes of day.   160
I yielded to your tears and your entreaties.
You know it all now, and I am not sorry,
If it will spare me your unjust reproaches,

Allow me to await my death in peace
And stop your useless efforts to rekindle   165
This spark of life which soon will be extinguished.

SCENE 4

PHAEDRA
OENONE
PANOPE

PANOPE:
I would have wished to keep sad news from you,
My lady, but it must be told.
Death has taken your conquering husband.
You are the last to hear it.
OENONE:
                         Panope,
What are you saying?
PANOPE:
                    The Queen is wasting time   5
To offer prayers for Theseus' safe return.
Hippolytus, his son, has just discovered
His death from vessels newly come to port.
PHAEDRA:
Heaven!
PANOPE:
          Athens is at odds to choose a lord.
One party is voting for your son, the prince.   10
Others, forgetful of the constitution,
Make bold to clamor for the foreign woman's son.
There's even talk that a presumptuous faction
Is planning to offer Aricia the throne.
I thought that I should warn you of this crisis.   15
Hippolytus is leaving on the instant.
If he once shows himself in this new storm
He'll have the fickle people at his back.
OENONE:
Panope, the Queen has heard enough.
She will not be neglectful of your warning.   20
My lady, I'd done begging you to live,
And was resigned to follow you to the grave.
I'd no more arguments to change your mind.
But this new loss makes new necessities.
Your fortune's changed, and wears a different face: 25
The king is dead, and you must take his place.
You have an obligation to your son,
A slave without you; if you live, a king.
Whose arm will steady him in this sad time?
Whose ready hand will wipe away his tears?   30

His innocence will cry out to the gods
And call the wrath of ancestors upon you.
Live! you've no cause now to accuse yourself.
Your love's a lawful love like any other.
Theseus has severed by his death the ties   35
That made your love a foul and guilty thing.
Hippolytus holds little terror now;
You'll not be guilty if you look at him.
Perhaps it is because he thinks you hate him
He goes to give a leader to the rebels.   40
Redeem his error and restore his spirit.
Troezen is his, as king of this fair land,
But the splendid ramparts that Minerva built
He knows must be your son's by right of law.
You have an honest cause, a common fight.   45
Join forces, fight Aricia together!

PHAEDRA:

I'll let myself be led by your advice.
Live, then, if I can be brought back to life,
And if a mother's love at this sad time
Can lend new vigor to my failing heart.   50

ACT II

SCENE 1

ARICIA
ISMENE

ARICIA:

Hippolytus has asked to see me here?
Hippolytus wants *me*? To say goodbye?
Are you telling the truth, Ismene? Are you sure?

ISMENE:

This is the first effect of Theseus' death
My lady; now you can expect the hearts   5
He sundered from you to come flying home
From every side. At last Aricia
Is mistress of her destiny, and soon
Will see Greece bowed in homage at her feet.

ARICIA:

Ismene, this is no empty rumor?   10
My slavery is over? He is dead?

ISMENE:

No lie, my lady. Your gods are kind at last.
Theseus has gone to join your brothers' ghosts.

ARICIA:

How did it happen?

ISMENE:
           They are spreading stories
About his death, things no one could believe —   15
How he was drowned while chasing some new light
Of love, a faithless husband to the last.
They even say — the rumor's everywhere —
He went down with Peirithous to Hades
To see the gloomy waters of Cocytus,[1]   20
A live man walking in the shadow world,
But could not leave that melancholy place
Or cross again the bourn of no return.

ARICIA:
I cannot think a man could penetrate
The abyss of the dead before his time.   25
What spell could lure him to those fearful shores?

ISMENE:
He's dead. You are the only one to doubt it.
Athens laments his passing, Troezen knows
And already hails Hippolytus as king.
In the palace Phaedra trembles for her son   30
And asks advice of her bewildered friends.

ARICIA:
And do you think Hippolytus will be
More human than his father, loose my shackles,
And feel for my distress?

ISMENE:
            I know he will.

ARICIA:
Do you know Hippolytus? He has no heart.   35
A foolish hope, to look for help from him.
He has no time for women. Why should I
Be singled out as worthy of his favors?
You see how long he has avoided us
And left no place unvisited but ours.   40

ISMENE:
I know everything they say about his coldness.
But I've watched this proud Hippolytus in your presence.
His reputation for indifference
Only increased my curiosity.
His presence gave the lie to his report.   45
The moment you looked at him he was uneasy.
He vainly tried to tear his eyes away
But still stood gazing, and his looks spoke love.
The name of lover may affront his manhood,
But lover's in his eyes, if not his tongue.   50

ARICIA:
How hungrily my heart hangs on your words,

[1] Another of the rivers of the Underworld

Ismene, though there's little substance in them.
You know me; could you think it possible
That the sad plaything of a callous fate
Who fed on bitter fruit and drank of tears   55
Should ever know the foolish cares of love?
The last descendant of an earth-born king
I was the sole survivor of the war,
Saw taken in the flower of their youth
Six brothers, high hope of a noble house.   60
The sword reaped harvest, and the sodden earth
Swallowed the sad draught of my brothers' blood.
And since their death, you know the stern decree
Forbidding any man in Greece to love me.
They feared one day the sister's reckless flames   65
Might breathe new life into her brothers' ashes.
But you also know with what disdainful eye
I looked upon my conqueror's suspicions;
For all my life I have been shy of love,
And often rendered thanks for his injustice   70
That so happily enforced my own misgivings.
That was a time before I saw his son.
Not that I loved him for his looks alone,
Enamored of his eyes, his storied grace,
Gifts with which nature chose to honor him   75
But he himself mistrusted and seemed blind to.
I love and prize more precious things in him,
His father's virtues, not his weaknesses.
I love, I will confess, that selfless pride
That never bowed beneath the yoke of love.   80
Phaedra has little cause to preen herself
On winning Theseus' sighs, but I am made
Of prouder stuff, and scorn the easy triumph ·
Of conquering a love so lightly given
Or entering so vulnerable a heart.   85
No; but to make a stubborn spirit bend,
Acquaint an unfeeling heart with pains of love,
Bind him with chains that steal away his soul
And see him struggle in the welcome yoke,
This is my ambition and my challenge.   90
Disarming Hercules would be cheap game
Beside the conquest of Hippolytus,
For things too quickly and too often won
Yield slender glory in the victor's eyes.
But, oh, Ismene, what a fool am I;   95
I shall have only too much opposition,
And you may hear me, humbled by defeat,
Lament this pride I so admire today.
Could Hippolytus love me? By what happy chance
Could I have swayed him. . . .   100

ISMENE:
   He can answer that himself.
   He's coming.

SCENE 2

HIPPOLYTUS
ARICIA
ISMENE

HIPPOLYTUS:
   Madam, I felt I could not leave without
   A word to you of what your future holds
   In store. My father's dead; my fears spoke true
   And hit the reason for his too long absence.
   Nothing but death could dim his shining deeds   5
   And hide him so long from the universe.
   At last the gods yield to the third grim Fate
   Hercules' friend, companion and successor.
   Even your hatred must allow him virtues
   And will not grudge the titles he has won.   10
   I have one consolation in my mourning,
   That I can liberate you from your bondage
   And revoke the law whose strictness I deplored.
   Now you can give yourself, and give your heart.
   By right of my dominion here in Troezen.   15
   The legacy of my forefather Pittheus
   Which recognized me instantly as king,
   I leave you as free — no, freer than myself.
ARICIA:
   Hold back your bounty; so much overwhelms me.
   To honor my poor state so generously,   20
   My lord, would place me further than you think
   Beneath the laws from which you would exempt me.
HIPPOLYTUS:
   Athens is caught between a choice of kings.
   There's talk of you, or me, or Phaedra's son.
ARICIA:
   Of me, my lord?
HIPPOLYTUS:
                  I do not fool myself.   25
   There's an exclusive law that would debar me;
   Greece throws my foreign mother in my face!
   But if my brother were my only rival,
   My lady, I have rights undeniable
   Over him, that I'd preserve in spite of law.   30
   But there's a curb more constitutional
   On my temerity. I yield to you
   Or rather, I restore to you a place,

A scepter handed to your ancestors
By the legendary mortal born of Earth.
From them it passed to Aegeus[1] by adoption.   35
Athens, protected and enlarged by Theseus,
Was glad to own so generous a king,
And let your luckless brothers fall from mind.
Her walls are yours now for the entering.
This long feud's taken toll enough of tears;   40
Her soil's too rich already with your blood
Where it was shed upon the reeking field.
Now Troezen's at my call; the isle of Crete
Will offer Phaedra's son a rich retreat.   45
Attica's yours; I go, your minister,
To knit the torn affections of our people.

ARICIA:

Your words have left me lost and wondering;
I'm half afraid this is some cheating dream.
Am I awake? Is this your true intent?   50
What god was in you, lord, to think of it?
How right is all the world to sing your praises,
And yet how far the tale falls short of truth!
You're willing to renounce your rights for me?
Could I ask more than that you do not hate me   55
And that you should have made your heart a stranger
To enmity so long. . . .

HIPPOLYTUS:

                   Hate you, my lady?
However vividly men paint my pride
Do you think I was begotten on some monster?
What heart so savage and what hate so strong   60
Could not be softened by a sight of you?
What proof have I against such sweet deception. . . .

ARICIA:

My lord?

HIPPOLYTUS:

                   I've gone too far.
Passion has proved stronger than my reason.
But madam, now that I have broken silence   65
I must go on as I started, and reveal
A secret that I can no longer keep.
There stands before you an unhappy prince
Whom headstrong pride has modeled in her image.
I, who disdained to walk the ways of love   70
And mocked her prisoners these many years
Who wept to see the wreck of foolish men
And thought that I could stand safe on the shore
For ever, and watch others fight the storm;

[1] Theseus's father

Now I am captive to the common law.   75
How sadly do I see myself translated!
For near six months, irresolute, ashamed,
The shafts of love embedded in my heart,
I struggled vainly against you, against myself,
Fled from your presence, sought you in your absence;   80
Your face was with me in the clustered trees,
By day, and in the shadows of the night
I saw again the charms I would avoid.
Hippolytus the rebel is your slave.
And what has come of all this care and pain?   85
I seek myself, but can no longer find.
My bow, my spear, my chariot call in vain.
My cries re-echo lonely through the forest;
My steeds grow lazy and forget my voice.
Perhaps the telling of so wild a love   90
Will make you blush to hear what you have worked.
This is a clumsy way to give a heart,
And a strange captive for so fair a bond.
But the gift should be more precious in your eyes.
Imagine that I speak a foreign tongue;   95
Do not reject these halting protestations
That but for you would never have been spoken.

SCENE 3

HIPPOLYTUS	THERAMENES
ARICIA	ISMENE

THERAMENES:
   My lord, I am precursor of the Queen.
   She wants you.
HIPPOLYTUS:
               Me!
THERAMENES:
                 I cannot read her mind.
   Her people have been asking for you. Phaedra
   Would have a word with you before you go.
HIPPOLYTUS:
   Phaedra! What can I say to her? And what can she   5
   Expect . . .
ARICIA:
            My lord, you cannot refuse to listen.
   Although you know her for your enemy
   You owe her tears at least the form of pity.
HIPPOLYTUS:
   Yet you are going. And I leave, still unknowing
   Whether I have offended my adored one   10
   Or if the heart I leave here in your hands . . .

ARICIA:

Go, Prince, pursue your generous intent.
Make Athens tributary to my power.
All that you would give me, I accept;
But you have given me a gift more precious   15
Than all the might and majesty of empire.

SCENE 4

HIPPOLYTUS
THERAMENES

HIPPOLYTUS:

Is everything ready? But here's the Queen.
Go see that all's prepared for our departure.
Run, give the signal, and hurry back
To rescue me from this unwelcome meeting.

SCENE 5

PHAEDRA
HIPPOLYTUS
OENONE

PHAEDRA:

He's there. My blood runs backwards in my veins.
When I see him I forget what I must say.

OENONE:

Remember your son. You are his only hope.

PHAEDRA:

They tell me you depart upon the instant,
My lord. I came to join my tears with yours   5
And teach you something of a mother's fears.
My son is fatherless; and some day soon
He'll have to look upon his mother's death.
So young, he has a thousand enemies.
You are the only shield he has against them.   10
But in my mind there lurks a guilty fear
I may have stopped your ears against his cries.
I dread to think your just resentment may
Pursue in him your hatred for his mother.

HIPPOLYTUS:

Madam, I could never harbor thoughts so base.   15

PHAEDRA:

You hate me, but I'll not complain of that,
My lord; you've seen me bent on your destruction;
You could not read the writing in my heart.
I went out of my way to have you hate me;
Could not suffer the same roof to shelter us;   20

At home, abroad, I declared myself against you;
I wished you seas away, and in my presence
Forbade the very mention of your name.
But if the punishment must match the crime,
If you can only hate where you are hated,   25
Never was woman more deserving pity
And less deserving of your enmity.

HIPPOLYTUS:

A mother jealous of her children's rights
I know will rarely make allowances
For a stepson, madam. Second marriages   30
Breed strange suspicions. Any other woman
Would have felt the same resentment, and perhaps
Have made me more acquainted with ill-usage.

PHAEDRA:

My lord, I make bold to declare it now:
Heaven exempts me from this common law!   35
It is another care that troubles me.

HIPPOLYTUS:

Madam, the time for mourning is not yet.
Your husband still may look upon the sun.
Heaven may grace our prayers, and send him home.
Neptune is watching over him; my father   40
Will never pray his guardian in vain.

PHAEDRA:

Nobody sees the dead land twice, my lord.
If Theseus' eyes have seen those somber shores
You waste your prayers. No god can bring him back,
For Acheron is greedy of his prey.   45
But he's not dead; he breathes again in you.
I think I see my husband standing here;
I see him, speak to him; my heart — I'm wandering,
My lord; my passion speaks in spite of me.

HIPPOLYTUS:

Such are the powerful effects of love.   50
Though dead, he's ever present to your eyes.
Your heart is burning still with love of him.

PHAEDRA:

Yes, prince, I waste, I burn for Theseus' love.
I love him — not the Theseus Hades saw,
The fickle lover of a thousand conquests   55
Who sought to sully Pluto's marriage bed,
But faithful, proud — perhaps a little shy,
Youthful and handsome, winning every heart,
Made in the likeness of the gods, or yours.
He had your bearing, had your eyes, your speech;   60
His face wore this same tint of modesty
When he crossed the waters to our land of Crete,
A fit man for the love of Minos' daughters!

What were you doing then? When he assembled
The flower of Greece, where was Hippolytus?   65
Why were you still so young you could not sail
Upon the ship that carried him ashore?
By your hand then the Minotaur had died
Despite the windings of his vast retreat;
To save you from perplexity my sister   70
In your hands would have placed the fatal thread.[1]
But no: in this I should have been before her,
Love would have given me first inspiration.
I should have been your help, Prince, I your guide
To learn the windings of the labyrinth;   75
What cares I would have lavished on your head!
And sought more surety for love than thread!
Companion in the danger you must seek
I should have gone before you on your way,
And Phaedra would have plumbed the labyrinth   80
With you, and we'd emerge or die together!

HIPPOLYTUS:

Gods! What are you saying? Can you forget
That Theseus is my father, and your husband?

PHAEDRA:

What makes you think I have forgotten it?
Would I be so prodigal of my good name?   85

HIPPOLYTUS:

Forgive me, madam. I confess with shame
I set a wrong construction on your words.
I am confused, and cannot bear your eyes.
I go.

PHAEDRA:

    Oh, cruel! You understand too well.
I've said enough to keep you safe from error.
Well then; know Phaedra and her passion whole.   90
I love. But never think I love myself
For loving you, or think it innocent,
Nor yet that love's insanity has drawn
More poison from my spiritless submission.   95
I am the prey of the avenging gods.
You could never hate me as I loathe myself.
Gods be my witness, gods who in my heart
Kindled the fire that has destroyed my race;
The gods who win cruel glory for themselves   100
From mortal frailty, and love to tempt us.
Look in your mind. Recall what's passed between us.
I did not run from you. I drove you out.
I wished to seem a monster in your sight
And rouse your hate, the better to resist you.   105

---

[1] Ariadne had given Theseus a spool of thread to help him find his way back out of the labyrinth

And what has come of all my fruitless pain?
You hate me more, and I love you no less.
Your sufferings only lent you new enchantment.
I've pined, I've burnt, in love's hot fires, in tears;
You only need to look at me to know   110
If you could bring yourself to look at me.
Well? do you imagine I confessed these things,
These shameful things, because I wanted to?
Afraid for my son, lest I should be found wanting,
I came here to entreat you not to hate him.   115
Poor purpose for a heart obsessed with love!
I could only talk to you about yourself.
Take vengeance, punish this abhorrent passion.
Be worthy of the hero who begot you,
Remove this loathsome monster from the world!   120
The wife of Theseus loves Hippolytus!
Have faith, the monster never can escape you.
Here is my heart. Here's where your hand must strike.
I feel it thrusting forward to your arm,
In eagerness to expiate its crime.   125
Strike. But if you think it unworthy of your blows,
If your hatred grudges me so sweet a punishment,
Or if my base blood will pollute your hands,
Lend me your sword, if you will not your arm;
Give it me!

OENONE:
       What are you doing? Oh, just gods!   130
There's someone coming. Have no witnesses.
Come in, away, or your good name is lost.

SCENE 6

HIPPOLYTUS
THERAMENES

THERAMENES:
   Is that Phaedra running, being dragged away?
   What's this, my lord? I see you are distressed.
   Where is your sword? What leaves you pale and speechless?
HIPPOLYTUS:
   Theramenes, let's run. That such a thing could be!
   I'm sick to look upon myself.   5
   Phaedra — oh, no, great gods! this is a thing
   To be interred forever in oblivion.
THERAMENES:
   The sail's spread ready, if you're set to go,
   But, my lord, Athens has declared herself.
   The chiefs have sounded every tribe's opinion.   10
   Your brother carries it. The day is Phaedra's.

HIPPOLYTUS:
  Phaedra!
THERAMENES:
       A herald charged with Athens' will
Is coming to give the state into her hands.
Her son is king, my lord.
HIPPOLYTUS:
              Gods, are you blind?
Is this the way that you reward her virtue?   15
THERAMENES:
But there's a whisper that the king's alive.
Theseus has been seen, they say, in Epirus.
But my lord, I looked there: I know full well . . .
HIPPOLYTUS:
No matter. Keep ears open and miss nothing.
Let's test this rumor, run it to its source.   20
If there's no cause for me to change my plans
We'll take our leave, and at whatever cost
Place the scepter in more worthy hands.

ACT III

Scene 1

PHAEDRA
OENONE

PHAEDRA:
  Tell them to find themselves another queen!
Leave me alone! You want the world to see me?
Is this your way to woo me from my grief?
No, better hide me; I've said all too much.
My passion burst its boundaries; I said   5
Things better left unspoken. Oh, the way
He listened to me; and how deviously
He strove to turn a deaf ear to my speech,
Praying for nothing but a quick release.
And how his blushes multiplied my shame!   10
What made you turn me from my deadly purpose?
Oh, when his sword was poised above my breast,
Did he turn pale, and snatch the sword away?
No: my hand need only touch it once
To make it an abomination in his eyes.   15
He would have been defiled by touching it.
OENONE:
  Madam, this melancholy prepossession
Only fans the flames of your obsession.
Be your father's daughter. It were better

To seek distraction in more noble duties.   20
Spite this fool who runs from his good fortune.
Be queen, and govern the affairs of state.

PHAEDRA:
Should I be queen? Should I control the state,
Who am not able to control myself?
Whose feeble intellect has abdicated?   25
Who's strangled in the halter of her shame
Almost to dying?

OENONE:
              Run away.

PHAEDRA:
                  I cannot.

OENONE:
You banished him, but cannot run away?

PHAEDRA:
Too late for that. He knows my desperate passion.
The barriers of modesty are down.   30
I spread my shame before my captor's eyes.
Hope crept into my heart in spite of me.
It was you who summoned back my failing strength,
Caught my soul already winging from my lips,
And found the way to cheat me back to life   35
By hinting that I could enjoy his love.

OENONE:
Guilty or innocent, is there anything
That I would not have done to save your life?
But if you know a slight, could you forget
How he stood cruel and supercilious   40
To watch you all but grovel at his feet,
Insufferable in his outlandish pride?
If Phaedra could have seen him with my eyes!

PHAEDRA:
Oenone, that's a vice he can outgrow;
He's forest-bred, and has a native wildness.   45
A hard school reared him, and he's learned hard ways.
His ears are strangers to the sound of love.
Perhaps surprise prevented him from speaking;
Perhaps my protestations were too passionate.

OENONE:
Remember that his mother was a savage!   50

PHAEDRA:
Yes, Scythian; but she knew how to love.

OENONE:
He has a rooted hatred for our sex.

PHAEDRA:
Then I shall have no cause to fear a rival.
Oenone, your advice is out of season.
Serve my infatuation, not my reason.   55

His heart is proof against love's embassies,
So let's seek out a spot more sensitive.
The thought of monarchy had power to move him;
Athens attracted him, he could not hide it;
His ships' prows were already pointing there 　60
And sails spread to the pleasure of the breeze.
Help me; go and seek out this young pretender,
Oenone, flash the crown before his eyes.
The sacred diadem is his to wear;
I only ask the honor of crowning him. 　65
Give him the power I am incapable
Of keeping for myself; he'll teach my son
How monarchs must comport themselves; perhaps
He will agree to take his father's place.
I yield both son and mother to his hands, 　70
Try every way to move him. Arguments
From you will be more welcome than from me.
Press him with sad tales of a dying Phaedra
And feel no shame to play the suppliant.
I'll answer all; I have no hope but you. 　75
Go, for my future hangs on your return.

Scene 2

PHAEDRA

PHAEDRA:
Remorseless witness of my degradation,
Venus, have I sunk low enough to please you?
Your cruelty can go no further now.
Your triumph's perfect and your conquest won.
Cruel deity, if you desire new glory 　5
Attack a less complaisant enemy.
Hippolytus rejects you, braves your wrath
And never bowed his knee before your shrine.
Venus, revenge; our causes now are one.
Make him know love.
　　　　　　　　What, back again so soon, 　10
Oenone? He detests me, will not hear you.

Scene 3

PHAEDRA
OENONE

OENONE:
You must suppress these hopeless thoughts of love,
My lady, and recall your former virtue.
The King we all thought dead is here to see.

Theseus is living! Theseus is in Troezen!
The folk come flocking for a sight of him.   5
I was going on your orders to Hippolytus
When a thousand shouting voices bruised the skies . . .

PHAEDRA:

Stop there, Oenone. My husband is alive,
And I have spoken love, dishonored him.
He is alive. That is all I need to know.   10

OENONE:

What?

PHAEDRA:

      I told you so; but no, you would not have it.
Your tears prevailed upon my penitence.
I could have died this morning and been pitied,
But listened to you, and now must die dishonored.

OENONE:

Die?

PHAEDRA:

      Oh, just gods, what have I done today?   15
My husband will confront me with his son;
I'll see the witness of my lawless love
And he'll see me, how I accost his father,
Heart heavy with the sighs he would not hear,
And eyes wet with the tears that he rejected.   20
He has an interest in Theseus' honor;
Do you think he'll keep the secret of my love
Suffer treason to his father and his king?
Will he repress his loathing? If he did
It will still come out. I know what I have done,   25
Oenone; I'm not one of these brazen women
Who find serenity amid their crimes
And keep their countenance without a blush.
I know my passion, have it constantly
Before my mind. These walls, these vaulted roofs   30
Already seem as if they would give tongue,
As my accusers, and are only waiting
Until my husband comes to undeceive him.
Die, then. Come death, and all this horror's done.
To end my life. Is this so sad a thing?   35
Death holds no terrors for the unhappy ones.
I only fear the name I leave behind me,
A bitter legacy for my poor children.
The blood of Jupiter must swell their hearts;
But though they pride themselves on noble blood   40
It's no light load to have a guilty mother.
I fear that accusations all too true
Will one day taunt them with their mother's crimes
And they'll have such a bitter load to bear
That neither one will dare to lift his eyes.   45

OENONE:

No doubt of that. I feel for both of them.
Never was fear more justified than yours.
But why expose your sons to such a slight?
Why do you mean to be your own accuser?
For that will do it. They'll say Phaedra's guilt   50
Was such she could not face her husband's wrath.
Your death will gratify Hippolytus
And lend his story substance. Face to face
With him, I should be easily confounded.
I'd see him gloating in his victory   55
Telling your shame in every eager ear.
No! let a thunderbolt destroy me first!
Be honest with me. Do you love him still?
How do you look on his presumption now?

PHAEDRA:

I see a monster, an abomination.   60

OENONE:

Then why allow him an unblemished victory?
You fear him. Be before him with the charge
He comes to level against you today.
Who'll call you liar? Everything's against him;
His sword, by lucky chance left in your hands;   65
His father, long by you forewarned against him;
The banishment you brought on him already.

PHAEDRA:

How can I hurt him? He is innocent.

OENONE:

I'll do it all; I only ask your silence.
I am unhappy too, I have a conscience;   70
I'd rather face a thousand deaths than this.
But if it's this cruel remedy or lose you
Your life's a prize that pays the price for all.
I'll speak; and angered by the tale I tell
Theseus will send his son to banishment.   75
A vengeful father is a father still;
His anger will be easily appeased.
But even if the innocent must bleed
What's that beside the threat to your good name?
Honor's a jewel too dear for compromise.   80
Whatever he proposes, you obey,
My lady, and to save your threatened name
Bury the rest, yes, bury virtue too.
They're coming; I see Theseus.

PHAEDRA:

                              I, Hippolytus.
My judgment's written in his callous eyes.   85
Do as you wish. I yield myself to you.
In this distress, I can do no more for myself.

SCENE 4

THESEUS   THERAMENES
PHAEDRA   OENONE
HIPPOLYTUS

THESEUS:
  Now fortune's smiling fair on me again,
  My lady, and in your arms —
PHAEDRA:
               Do not go on, my lord.
  Restrain your raptures, lest they be defiled.
  I am unworthy of your sweet caresses.
  You have been wronged; while you have been away   5
  Malicious fortune has not spared your wife.
  I am unfit to please you or come near you.
  My only thought is that you should not see me.

SCENE 5

THESEUS
HIPPOLYTUS

THESEUS:
  What way is this to welcome home your father,
  My son?
HIPPOLYTUS:
          Only Phaedra can resolve this riddle.
  But if my prayers have any power to move you
  Allow me, lord to look on her no more,
  But suffer me to take my fears away   5
  And live in any other land but hers.
THESEUS:
  You want to leave me?
HIPPOLYTUS:
          I did not seek her out.
  You were the one who brought her to these shores,
  And thought it good, my lord, when you departed,
  To trust Aricia and the Queen to Troezen.   10
  I was commanded to take care of them.
  I have fulfilled my charge; so what's to keep me?
  I've pitted my young manhood long enough
  Against poor game, for want of any better.
  Time now to leave my leisure years behind   15
  And blood my spear in more resplendent conquests.
  Even before you had attained my years
  More than one tyrant, more than one wild beast
  Had felt the heavy summons of your arm.

You were already the oppressor's scourge,
Protector of the peoples of two seas.   20
Men traveled free, and plied their trade in peace.
Hercules heard the fame of your achievements
And rested easy, leaving you his load.
But I, the unknown son of famous father   25
Still have far to go to emulate my mother!
So let me try my manhood; give it space.
If there's one monster that has slipped your hands
Let me lay his skin before your feet in triumph
Or else die honorably, and leave to men   30
This memory as my memorial,
To cry to all the world I was your son!

THESEUS:

What do I see? What evil's in this place
To make my family shrink before my face?
Gods, why did you free me from imprisonment   35
If fear and coldness wait to welcome me?
I had one friend; but he, with lust's effrontery
Looked covetously on Epirus' queen.
Reluctantly I helped his amorous intent,
But angry destiny had blinded us.   40
The king caught me unready, weaponless.
I wept sad tears to watch Peirithous
Flung by this savage to the cruel beasts
Who fed on his unhappy victims' blood.
Me he kept captive in his caves, so dark   45
And deep, they border on the realm of death.
Six months, and then the gods took note of me.
I found a way to cheat my jailor's eyes
And cleansed the world of this offense to nature.
His body served as browsing for his beasts.   50
And when I turned in glad anticipation
To all the gods had given me most precious;
When — how shall I say it — I came heart-whole
To enter on possession of my dreams,
I've nothing but constraint to welcome me.   55
They run from me, draw back from my embraces.
And you have lent me something of your fear;
I would as soon be prisoner again.
Come, speak. Here's Phaedra crying I've been wronged.
Who was the traitor? Why was I not revenged?   60
Has Greece, that used my arm so many times,
Given asylum to the criminal?
You have no answer. Has my son — my son —
Come to an understanding with my enemies?
Come in. This burden of suspicion is too great.   65
We'll find the crime and criminal together.
Phaedra can tell the cause of her distress.

Scene 6

HIPPOLYTUS
THERAMENES

HIPPOLYTUS:

What did she mean? Her words have petrified me.
Is Phaedra still the servant of her passions?
Will she accuse me and destroy herself?
Gods! What will the King say? With what deadly poison
Has love contaminated all our house?   5
And what of me, who love his enemy?
He left one son, and he has found another.
My mind is full of dark presentiments.
Let's go and see if by some happy art
I can awake my father's tenderness   10
And tell him of a love he would suppress
But one that all his power can never conquer.

ACT IV

Scene 1

THESEUS
OENONE

THESEUS:

What are you saying? This traitor, this hothead
Plotted this outrage on his father's honor?
Oh destiny, how hard you dog my steps!
I am uncertain where to go or stay.
Oh father-love! Oh, foul ingratitude!   5
To dare do this, to sink his thoughts so low!
To gain the goal of his black passion, he
Would have cast all scruples off and ravished her.
I knew the sword, the servant of his lust,
The sword I hung on him for prouder purposes.   10
Had every bond of blood no power to hold him?
And Phaedra did not want to have him punished!
Phaedra kept silence, and protected him!

OENONE:

It was his father Phaedra was protecting!
Ashamed of having drawn upon herself   15
Such passionate intent and lustful eyes.
Phaedra was dying; death couched in her hand
To quench the pure light in her living eyes.
I saw her arm go up and ran to save her.
I alone had art to keep her for your love.   20
Sad for her grief and your anxiety
I've played unwilling spokesman to her tears.

THESEUS:

Traitor! He could not keep his countenance.
He quaked with fear as he accosted me.
His frigid welcome froze my father's heart.
But this guilty passion that's devouring him: 25
Had he already made it known in Athens?

OENONE:

My lord, remember how my lady cried.
Her hate was born out of this guilty love.

THESEUS:

And then it broke out hot again in Troezen.   30

OENONE:

My lord, I've told you all the story now.
It's hard to leave my lady in her grief.
Permit me go take my place beside her.

Scene 2

THESEUS
HIPPOLYTUS

THESEUS:

He's here. Great gods! to see that noble bearing
What eye would not have been deceived as mine?
So: must the holy mark of virtue now
Be blazoned on a base adulterer's brow,
And is there no sure sign by which a man   5
Might look into men's hearts and know a traitor?

HIPPOLYTUS:

What is the reason for this melancholy,
My lord, that can so cloud your stately brow?
Can you not trust your secret to my care?

THESEUS:

Traitor, you dare to look me in the face?   10
You prodigy of nature, on whose head
The skies long since should have unleashed their fury;
Of all marauders that I purged from earth
The only one that's left alive to plague me!
After the fever of your horrid lust   15
Carried you panting to your father's bed
You dare to flaunt your hated face before me
And haunt the place still heavy with your crime?
You should be searching under foreign skies
For lands that have not echoed Theseus' name.   20
Fly, traitor; do not tempt my hatred here
Or brave the wrath I struggle to restrain.
My name is black enough for all eternity
For having fathered such a profligate
Without your death to shame my memory   25
And dim the luster of my noble deeds.

Fly; if you do not want a sudden death
To add you to the tally of my vengeance.
Take care this star above us never sees you
Set your incautious foot within this place.   30
Away, I tell you, never come again;
Rid my realm of the pollution of your presence.
And you, great Neptune; if ever in time past
I purged the human refuse from your shores,
Remember, to reward my glad success   35
You pledged yourself to gratify my prayers.
Through the long bitterness of prison days
I never called on your immortal power,
Hoarding the aid which you had promised me;
I kept your prayers for time of urgency.   40
That time has come. Avenge a father's sorrow,
This traitor I surrender to your wrath.
Stifle his lustful cravings in his blood
And by your fury I shall know you kind.

HIPPOLYTUS:

She dares to charge me with adultery?   45
Here's too much horror, it has left me dumb.
So many sudden unexpected blows
Have robbed me of my tongue and stopped my voice.

THESEUS:

Traitor, you hoped that Phaedra would be weak
And keep the secret of your filthy lust.   50
Then when you ran, you should not have left your sword
Behind, a hostile witness in her hands,
Or better, should have crowned your villainy
By severing her speech and life at once.

HIPPOLYTUS:

My lawful anger at so black a lie   55
Might well call truth to be my advocate.
But I must keep a secret that concerns you.
For your sake I am dumb, so do not press me,
My lord, or bring fresh torments on yourself.
Review my life, remember what I am.   60
Small crimes are harbingers of greater crimes.
And he who violates the laws of men
Will end by flouting the commands of Heaven.
There are degrees in crime as well as virtue.
Virtue and innocence were never turned   65
In one brief moment to licentiousness;
One day's too short to see an honest man
Turn coward, murderer, incestuous.
My mother was a lady chaste and noble
And I have not disgraced her honest name.   70
Pittheus, who passed throughout the world for wise,
Adopted me, and deigned to be my tutor.
I've no wish to paint myself in glowing colors,

But if I have inherited any virtue,
My lord, I think I have made manifest   75
My hatred of this crime they impute to me.
It is for this Greece knows Hippolytus.
I've pushed the austere rigor of my days
So far it borders upon boorishness.
Men find my humor too uncompromising;   80
The day is not more pure than is my heart.
They'd laugh to see Hippolytus in love . . .

THESEUS:

Coward, this very arrogance condemns you.
Now I can see what lies behind your coldness.
Phaedra alone charmed your lascivious eyes.   85
Your heart, indifferent to any other,
Looked scornfully upon an honest love.

HIPPOLYTUS:

No, father. This heart — from you I cannot hide it —
Has not despised an honorable love.
Here at your feet I own my true offense.   90
My heart is pledged to serve Aricia.
Pallas' daughter has prevailed upon your son.
I worship her; defying your commands
I'll never love another if not her.

THESEUS:

You love her? No, this is some clumsy trick.   95
You accuse yourself to make me think you honest.

HIPPOLYTUS:

Six months, my lord, I've loved her from a distance,
And came with misgivings to confess to you.
What? Can I say nothing to convince you?
What oath, then, must I swear to satisfy you?   100
By earth, by heaven, by the breathing world . . .

THESEUS:

All criminals fall back on perjury.
Stop, stop, spare me these busy protestations,
If this is all that your hypocrisy
Can plead in your defense.   105

HIPPOLYTUS:

You call me hypocrite and treacherous.
Phaedra knows better in her heart of hearts.

THESEUS:

Such arrogance I cannot stomach.

HIPPOLYTUS:

How long will be my exile, then, and where?

THESEUS:

You could put the pillars of Hercules between us;   110
And still be too close for my peace of mind.

HIPPOLYTUS:

But if you yield me to the calumny
Of such a charge, where shall I look for friends?

THESEUS:

    Go find friends to damn you with their praises,

    Who applaud adultery and honor incest,   115

    Traitors and renegades outside the law,

    Fit company for criminals like you.

HIPPOLYTUS:

    You still talk of incest and adultery?

    Then I'll be still. But Phaedra had a mother,

    Phaedra is sprung from stock, you know too well,   120

    More full of these obscenities than mine!

THESEUS:

    What, is there nothing sacred to your rage?

    For the last time, remove yourself from my sight.

    Traitor, GET OUT; or else your father's anger

    Will have you flung out like a common felon.   125

Scene 3

THESEUS

THESEUS:

    Unhappy boy, you go to certain death.

    Beside the waters where the very gods

    Walk trembling, Neptune pledged his word to me

    And he will keep it. In your shadow treads

    An ever-present and avenging god.   5

    I loved you once; in spite of your offense

    My heart already weeps for what must be.

    But you have left no way but to condemn you.

    Did ever father suffer greater wrong?

    Just gods, who look upon my load of sorrow,   10

    How could I have begotten such a son?

Scene 4

THESEUS
PHAEDRA

PHAEDRA:

    My lord, I come with cause to be afraid.

    I heard you shouting even where I stood

    And feared that threat had given birth to deed.

    If there's still time, have mercy on your son.

    Spare your own blood, I make so bold to pray you,   5

    And never let me hear him cry aloud

    Or sentence me to sorrow all my days

    For having raised his father's hands against him.

THESEUS:

    No, madam, my hand's still clean of my own blood,

And yet the criminal has not gone free.   10
A god shall be his executioner.
This Neptune owes me. You shall be avenged.
PHAEDRA:
This Neptune owes you! Have your angry prayers . . .
THESEUS:
So apprehensive that they go unanswered?
Make one with me and let us pray together.   15
Read over the black roster of his crimes
And fan the sullen furnace of my wrath.
There's more he's done that you yet know not of;
He tells me that your mouth's a nest of lies,
Insists Aricia is mistress of his heart,   20
That he loves her!
PHAEDRA:
                    What!
THESEUS:
                        He told me to my face.
But I'm not one to be put off so lightly.
Let's pray that Neptune's punishment be swift.
I shall go back to kneel before his shrine
And press him to fulfill his godly word.   25

Scene 5

PHAEDRA

PHAEDRA:
He's gone. But what's this tolling in my ears?
What dormant fire is waking in my heart?
What thunderbolt, oh gods, what word of death?
I flew with every fiber of my being
Intent to save his son; I tore myself   5
Out of Oenone's startled arms, and yielded
To the remorse that was tormenting me.
How far would I have gone towards confessing?
Perhaps, if he had not cut off my words,
Truth would have stumbled timid from my lips.   10
Oh, he can love; but he cannot love me!
Aricia has his heart! Aricia!
Gods! When he cased his cold ingratitude
In eye so scornful and in brow so stern
I thought his heart was ever shut to love   15
And barred to every woman as to me.
But another woman bent his stubborn spirit!
Another woman taught his cold eyes smile!
Perhaps his heart is anybody's prize,
Accessible to everyone but me!   20
And I would take it on me to defend him!

SCENE 6

PHAEDRA
OENONE

PHAEDRA:
Oenone, do you know what I've discovered?

OENONE:
No, but I fear the worse, to tell the truth.
I blenched to think what took you from me so
And feared your passion might destroy you.

PHAEDRA:
Who would believe it, Oenone? I have a rival.   5

OENONE:
What?

PHAEDRA:
      No doubt of it. Hippolytus is in love.
This imperturbable antagonist
From whom I could not wring one gentle word,
Who was indifferent to all my prayers,
This tiger that I trembled to approach   10
Has yielded, owned a conqueror, surrendered.
Aricia found the watchword to his heart.

OENONE:
Aricia!

PHAEDRA:
      Here is yet untasted sorrow.
New agonies to fill my future days.
All I endured, my terror and my passion,   15
Love's fever and the anguish of remorse,
The intolerable slight of cold refusal,
Was but a premonition of this hell.
In love! What witchcraft did they use to blind me?
How did they keep their tryst, what time, what place?   20
You knew. Why did you let me fool myself?
Could you not tell me of their assignations?
Did nobody see them whispering together,
Courting each other's company, and going
Deep in the forest where no man could spy?   25
But no, their love was open to the world.
Their sighs were innocent, the heavens smiled,
They felt no shame to walk the ways of love,
Nor came there any cloud to mar their days.
While I was cast out of the breathing world   30
To cower in dark corners from the sun,
Without appeal to any god but Death,
I waited only for my time to die.
My food was bitterness, my water tears;
But even in my anguish prying eyes   35
Would never leave me sorrow at my leisure.
I tasted furtively that bitter pleasure

And put a calm face on my heavy heart.
How many times I would have wept, but dared not!

OENONE:

Their love is hopeless. How can they enjoy it?   40
They'll have to part.

PHAEDRA:

                   But ever be in love.
As I speak — the thought's a dagger in my heart —
They mock the fury of a woman scorned,
And though separation stares them in the face
Whisper a thousand words of never parting.   45
Their happiness is my humiliation,
Oenone. Feel for my frustrated love.
Aricia must be destroyed, my husband's wrath
Be roused again against this nest of traitors.
And let him not rest easy with half measures;   50
The sister's crime is greater than her brothers'.
I'll take my jealousy to him and beg —
What am I doing? Have I lost my mind?
I, jealous? I ask Theseus to avenge me?
My husband lives, and still I'm hot in love.   55
In love with whom? Where would I give my heart?
At every word my hair stands on my head.
Now I have reached the pinnacle of crime;
My breath blows incest and deceitfulness.
There's murder in my hands, they cry for vengeance,   60
To cool their fever in the blood of innocents.
What right have I to live, to look upon
This pure, bright sun, the founder of my race?
I claim the king and father of the gods
For my progenitor; throughout the universe,   65
Throughout wide heaven are my ancestors.
Where can I hide? in the dark underworld?
No, there's my father, in his ruthless hands
The urn of judgment given him by Fate,
Minos,[1] before whose court pale men must come.   70
How his ghost will cry out in astonishment
To see his daughter present in his sight,
Compelled to tell the tally of her crimes,
So new, so strange, unheard of even in Hell.
What will you say, my father, when you see me?   75
I can imagine how the dreadful urn
Will tumble from your hands; I can imagine
How you will cast about for some new punishment,
To be your own child's executioner.
Forgive! A cruel god has crushed your house.   80
Behold his vengeance in your daughter's frenzy.

---

[1] Phaedra's father, the great Cretan lawgiver, was made one of the judges in the Underworld after his death

I'm driven by the shame of my offense
That never tasted any of its joys.
Hounded by sorrows till my dying breath
I make a living penance of my days.   85

OENONE:
My lady, there is nothing here to fear.
Look with new eyes. This is no mortal sin.
You fell in love. We cannot fight our fate.
You were bewitched and not accountable.
Is this so strange and wonderful a thing?   90
Are you the only woman in the world
Whom love has won? To err is only human.
You are mortal, so accept your mortal lot.
The very gods, the gods of high Olympus
Who thunder terror into sinners' ears   95
Have known the stirrings of illicit love.

PHAEDRA:
What words are these? What are you hinting now?
You mean to feed me poison to the end,
My evil genius? Look what you have made me.
You called me back to the daylight that I fled;   100
Your voice was louder than the voice of duty.
I fled Hippolytus, you made me see him.
What have you done? How could you be so bold
To bear false witness, bring his life in danger?
For this may be his death; a father's curse   105
Flung out in anger may have been fulfilled.
I'll hear no more from you. I hate you. Go.
Leave me to bear my burden by myself.
May heaven pay you in your own bad coin
And may your punishment be an example   110
To all who pander to the weaknesses of princes
By fawning artifice, and smooth their path to crime,
Vile flatterers, the most pernicious gift
That angry Heaven could have made to kings.

OENONE:
Oh, gods, I did all, left my all for her.   115
Is this my recompense? I have deserved it.

ACT V

SCENE 1

HIPPOLYTUS
ARICIA
ISMENE

ARICIA:
Your life's in danger; how can you be silent
And leave your father in his error? He loves you.

You are cruel, if you can count my tears as nothing
And consent so calmly to our separation.
Go, leave Aricia to her misery,   5
But if you go, yet take precaution for your life.
Defend your honor from these calumnies
And force your father to revoke the curse.
It's not too late. What whim is this, to leave
A clear field to the woman who accused you?   10
Tell Theseus the truth.

HIPPOLYTUS:
                        What more can I tell him?
Parade his cuckoldry before the world,
Or watch my father turning red with shame
Because I could not bring myself to lie?
No one but you has fathomed this fearful secret,   15
The gods and you my only confidants.
Here's proof of love, I could not keep from you
Things I could scarcely whisper to myself.
Forget my tale, if such a thing can be,
My lady, never open those chaste lips   20
To tell so horrible a circumstance.
The gods are just. Let's trust ourselves to them.
For their sakes they must show me innocent.
Sooner or later Phaedra must be punished
With the ignominy she has deserved.   25
This is the only thing I ask of you.
In all things else I give my anger rein.
Break the chains of slavery that bind you,
Follow me boldly, share my punishment.
Leave this funereal polluted place   30
Where virtue sucks contagion from the air.
Turn my disgrace to your advantage, run;
In the confusion they've no eyes for you.
I can secure for you the means of flight.
There are no sentries set on you but mine   35
And allies strong to help us; Sparta calls
And Argos welcomes us with open arms.
Let's carry our complaint to common friends.
Phaedra must never link our shattered fortunes
To drive us both from the ancestral throne,   40
And promise to her son my head and yours.
The chance is fair, if we are shrewd to grasp it.
Why so mistrustful? Can you hesitate?
Your interests alone have made me bold;
When I am all on fire, must you be cold?   45
Do you fear to follow in an exile's path?

ARICIA:
My lord, how sweet such banishment would be!

If I could link my destiny to yours
I'd live enraptured and forget the world.
But that sweet bond has not yet made us one.   50
Could I with honor run away with you?
There's no law stern enough to censure me
For slipping from the clutches of your father.
I owe him nothing, he's no kin to me.
Flight is a virtue, when you fly from tyrants,   55
But my lord, you love me; and my reputation. . . .

HIPPOLYTUS:

No, no, I do not hold your name so cheap.
I come to you with nobler purposes.
Fly from your enemies; come with me as my wife.
Heaven has made us outcasts in misfortune;   60
We'll ask no man's permission to be wed.
It does not take a feast to make a wedding.
At Troezen's gates, among the monuments
Where ancient princes of my line lie buried
There stands a temple that the liar shuns,   65
A place where no man dares foreswear himself,
For perjury meets sudden punishment.
There's no curb stronger on a lying tongue,
For there it goes in fear of instant death.
There, if you trust me, we will go to pledge   70
The solemn testimony of our love.
The god men worship there shall be our witness.
We'll pray together that he be our father.
I'll call upon the highest of the gods,
Virgin Diana, Juno, Queen of Heaven,   75
And all divinities, to see our love
And guarantee that I will keep my oath.

ARICIA:

Here comes the king. Go, Prince, and lose no time.
I'll stay a while to cover my departure.
Leave me a guide, someone that I can trust   80
To prop my fears and lead my steps towards you.

SCENE 2

THESEUS
ARICIA
ISMENE

THESEUS:

Lighten my darkness, gods, and grant my eyes
Some glimmer of the truth!

ARICIA:

Have a care for everything, Ismene, and be ready.

Scene 3

THESEUS
ARICIA

THESEUS:

My lady, you look pale, and lost for words.
What was Hippolytus doing here?

ARICIA:

Saying goodbye to me forever.

THESEUS:

So it was your eyes tamed his rebel heart,
Your happy arts that taught him first to love.   5

ARICIA:

My lord, I cannot gloss the truth for you.
Your prejudices never passed to him.
He did not treat me like a criminal.

THESEUS:

Oh yes. He swore he'd love you till his death.
But put no faith in that. His fickle heart   10
Has sworn the same to other women too.

ARICIA:

It has, my lord?

THESEUS:

               You should have kept him constant.
Have you no shame, to share his love with her?

ARICIA:

Have you no shame, to let malicious tongues
Work damage on his fair young days? Are you   15
So unacquainted with his heart? Are you
So poor a judge of guilt and innocence?
Are yours the only eyes that must be blind
To virtue that has dazzled other men?
You must not throw him to his slanderers!   20
Give yourself pause, take back your fatal prayer.
Take care, my lord, take care; unsmiling Heaven
May hate you well enough to bring your curse
To pass; for often in its anger it will take
The victims that we offer; Heaven's gifts   25
Are often punishments to fit our crimes.

THESEUS:

No use. There can be no excuse for him.
Love's blinded you to his depravity.
But I have witnesses that I can trust.
I've seen tears flow, tears that could not be liars.   30

ARICIA:

Have a care, my lord. Your all-conquering hand
Delivered men from monsters without number.
But all are not destroyed; you have left one
Alive. . . . Your son, my lord, forbids me to go on.

I have been well schooled in his deference   35
And should embarrass him if I continued.
I copy his discretion, and withdraw,
Before I am compelled to break my silence.

SCENE 4

THESEUS

THESEUS:

What did she mean? What secret lay behind
Her words, so often started, never finished?
Is this some empty pretext to confuse me?
Are they conspirators to torture me?
But though I steel myself to punish them   5
There is a voice speaks low within my heart.
I pity them, and yet I must disguise it;
I pity them, and yet I know not why!
Let's go make new inquiry of Oenone;
For I would have more light upon this crime.   10
Guards, bring Oenone to me privately.

SCENE 5

THESEUS
PANOPE

PANOPE:

I have no notion what the Queen intends,
My lord, but I am frightened by her frenzy.
Despair has thrown his shadow over her
And death is written white upon her face.
Oenone, driven from her in disgrace   5
Has thrown herself into the sea and drowned.
The reason for her madness no one knows;
The waves have stolen her from our sight forever.

THESEUS:

What tale is this?

PANOPE:

                    The Queen was not appeased;
The pain grew wild and fitful in her heart.   10
Sometimes as balm to her unspoken sorrow
She embraced her sons, and bathed them in her tears
And then as suddenly forgot her love
And pushed them off as if she hated them.
She wandered aimless and irresolute;   15
Her eyes were wild and never recognized us.
Three times she tried to write, then changed her mind
And three times tore the letter she had started.
See her, my lord, we beg; she needs your help.

THESEUS:

Oenone dead, and Phaedra near to dying?   20
Bring back my son, let him defend himself;
Let him but speak to me and I will listen!
Neptune, be tardy with your deadly gifts,
For I'd be happy they were not fulfilled.
Perhaps I trusted in false witnesses   25
And lifted my cruel hands to you too soon.
Oh, then my curse would have a bitter answer.

SCENE 6

THESEUS
THERAMENES

THESEUS:

Is it you, Theramenes? Where is my son?
I made you tutor of his tender years.
But why these tears? Why do I see you weep?
How is my son?

THERAMENES:

              Your care has come too late.
To help. You waste your love. Hippolytus   5
Is dead.

THESEUS:

       Oh gods.

THERAMENES:

I saw him die; the dearest of creation,
And I make bold to tell you, lord, least guilty.

THESEUS:

My son is dead? What, were the gods so greedy
That even as I stretched my arms to him   10
They could not bide their time, but he must die?
How was he taken? How did Heaven strike him down?

THERAMENES:

We had that minute passed the gates of Troezen.
He rode his chariot; his dejected men
Borrowed his silence, and surrounded him.   15
Moodily he followed the Mycenae road
And let the reins hang on the horses' backs.
His noble steeds, who formerly were seen
High-stepping to his call and mettlesome,
Now paced with drooping head and down-cast eye   20
As sympathetic to his melancholy.
Then from the waters' depths a fearful cry
Came shattering the stillness of the air,
And from the bowels of the earth a voice
Gave tongue in kind, and bellowed a reply.   25
The blood was frozen in our hearts; the hair
Rose on our horses' backs, they sniffed the air;

And then the surface of the water heaved
And bubbled, and a liquid mountain rose.
The wave came in, broke, and before our eyes　　　　　　30
Threw up a raging monster in the surf,
His huge head barbed and menacing with horns,
A plate of yellow scales upon his body,
A man-devouring bull, a fiery dragon.
The heavens shuddered at the savage beast,　　　　　　35
Earth trembled, and the very air was rank.
The sea that carried him crept back in fear.
All fled, threw courage to the winds as vain
And sought asylum in the shrine nearby.
Only Hippolytus, his father's son,　　　　　　40
Reined in his horses, took his hunting spear,
Thrust at the beast, and with unerring aim
Gave him a gaping wound upon the flank.
The monster, writhing in his pain and fury,
Rolled bellowing before the horses' feet,　　　　　　45
Thrusting his flaming mouth into their faces,
Which covered them with fire and blood and smoke.
They were panic-stricken, and for once struck deaf
Ran heedless of their master's hand and voice,
He spent his strength to hold them but in vain.　　　　　　50
Their mouths frothed blood until the bit was red.
Some saw among the melee, so they say,
A god who struck goads in their sweaty flanks.
Fear carried them pell mell across the rocks.
The axle shrieked and snapped; Hippolytus　　　　　　55
Saw his chariot go down in splinters,
And he fell with it, tangled in the reins.
Forgive my emotion. Till my dying day
That cruel sight will fill my eyes with tears.
I saw your son, my lord, I saw your son,　　　　　　60
Dragged by horses that had eaten from his hand.
He tried to call them, but his voice alarmed them.
They bolted; his body was one bleeding wound.
At last they slackened their precipitous flight
And stopped, not far from those time-honored tombs　　　　　　65
Where lie the dusty relics of dead kings.
Heart in mouth I ran, his escort after me.
His blood lay spotted on the road to guide us;
The rocks were red with it, the ugly thorns
Were hung with scarlet drops and matted hair.　　　　　　70
I came and called him. He stretched out his hand;
His eye half opened and then closed again.
"Heaven," he said, "has taken my blameless life.
Comfort Aricia when I am gone.
Friend, if the scales fall from my father's eyes　　　　　　75
And he mourns the sad death of his slandered son,
To appease my death and my unhappy ghost

Tell him to treat his prisoner with kindness.
And give her back . . ." On this the prince fell dead;
My arms held nothing but a broken heap of bones,   80
Sad trophy of the anger of the gods.
Even a father's eyes would not have known him.

THESEUS:

My son; dear promise that I have destroyed,
Merciless gods, who took me at my word,
To what remorse have I condemned my days.   85

THERAMENES:

Then came Aricia in fear and dread,
My lord, a fugitive before your wrath
To take her husband in the sight of Heaven.
She drew near, saw the red and reeking earth,
She saw — oh, sad sight for a lover's eyes —   90
Hippolytus stretched out so white, so broken.
For a moment she could not believe the disaster
Or recognize the brave youth she had loved.
She saw Hippolytus but sought him still.
But at last she knew too well that it was he   95
And turned a mute accusing glance to Heaven,
Cold, moaning to herself and near to death
She fainted at the feet of her dear love.
Ismene was by; Ismene, bathed in tears
Called her to life — no, to her grief again.   100
And I; I came here, out of love with life,
To tell you of a hero's dying wish,
My lord, and to discharge the bitter duty
He trusted to me with his dying breath.
But I can see his enemy approaching.   105

Scene 7

THESEUS	PANOPE
PHAEDRA	GUARDS
THERAMENES	

THESEUS:

Well, you have won. My son has lost his life.
Oh, I have room to fear; presentiments
That he is guiltless fill my heart with dread.
But he is dead, my lady; take your victim;
Be joyful in his slaughter, whether he   5
Deserved to die, or whether he did not.
I'll think him guilty since you tell me so.
His death has given me cause enough to weep
Without uncovering to truth's harsh eyes
Things which could never restore him to my tears   10
And well might make my burden heavier.

Let me go far from you and from this land
Where I'll not see my son's torn bloody ghost.
Confounded, with this memory to haunt me,
I'd gladly hide me from the universe.   15
My fame but makes my punishment the greater;
Were I unknown, I'd hide myself the better.
I hate the gifts the gods have showered upon me
And go to mourn their murderous bequests,
Nor will I ask them anything again;   20
Their fatal gifts could never recompense
The sum of what they took from me this day.

PHAEDRA:
No, Theseus. Now the time has come to break
This conspiracy of silence, and restore
Your son his innocence. He did no crime.   25

THESEUS:
God help me, I condemned him on your word.
Murderess! Do you think you will be forgiven . . .

PHAEDRA:
Time's precious, Theseus; listen to me now.
Your son was chaste and dutiful. It was I
That cast on him my lewd incestuous eyes.   30
Heaven lit the flame within my breast
And that accursed Oenone did the rest.
She feared that once Hippolytus had learned
My passion, he'd reveal this fearful love.
She took advantage of my weak compliance   35
And ran to you with lying accusations.
She paid her due, and running from my wrath
Found in the waves too easy punishment.
The sword by now would have cut off my life
But I let virtue falsely be suspected.   40
I wished to bare my penitence to you
Then take the slow way to the underworld.
I drank, set coursing through my burning veins
A poison Medea brought with her to Athens.
Its venom has already reached my heart.   45
Now everything is misted to my sight,
The heavens, and the husband I have wronged,
And death that steals the luster from my eyes
Makes clean again the light that they polluted.

PANOPE:
She's dead, my lord.

THESEUS:
                 And of so black a cause   50
The memory can never die with her.
So let me go, shown up for what I am,
To wash his bleeding body in my tears,
To make atonement for my fearful curse

And do my humble best to honor him.   55
The better to appease his angry ghost,
All enmity of families forgotten,
Henceforth Aricia shall be my daughter.

AFTERWORD

We have called *Hamlet*, deservedly, *the* play. On the same terms a
Frenchman would be likely to name *Phaedra the* French play. Though it
has never equaled *Hamlet*'s multitude of revivals or attracted the same universal interest, it has, for centuries, served as the French theater's touch-
stone, model, or talking-point, compelling the attention even of those who
profess to despise it. It is the greatest surviving example of a particular
concept of tragedy: what tragedy should be about, and how it should be
presented.

People used to assume that nobody could like *both* Shakespeare and Racine; their plays were too different. Shakespeare's were the product of a
robust native tradition of popular theater; Racine's of classical learning,
private pieties, and the elaborate ceremonial that governed both art and
conduct at the sophisticated court of an absolute king. Speech in Shakespeare is free and flowing blank verse; Racine's alexandrine (six-footed)
couplets are stately and sonorous but too regular to create an illusion of
spontaneity. Shakespeare is flexible, abundant, and immediate; Racine
rigid, sparse, and abstract. Shakespeare is "the poet of nature"; Racine is
the poet of rules and restraint. These contrasts are quite unfair to Racine,
but there is just enough truth in them to account for their prevalence —
certainly among people in the English-speaking world, for whom "the
Bard" abides splendidly alone on the highest peak of dramatic art.

Even the most superficial comparison of *Hamlet* and *Phaedra* shows the
plays moving in different worlds. That of *Hamlet* is vast. We stay at or near
the court of Denmark throughout, but we always have a sense of a larger
world outside, impinging on the one we observe. In *Phaedra* our attention
is focused on a very limited set of actions taking place in a carefully controlled environment. *Hamlet*'s range of physical action is much the larger.
A ghost is seen. Actors perform a play. A girl goes mad and drowns. An
army marches from Norway. An old man is stabbed to death. A duel is
fought. In *Phaedra* the characters stand around and talk. *Hamlet* has many
characters, drawn from the whole spectrum of society, with language and
behavior appropriate to their origins. *Phaedra* has few, and they are all
royalty and high-ranking aristocrats; no place for a Gravedigger here. And
they all express themselves in the same high, courtly style.

From a certain standpoint, these things may look like limitations in
Phaedra, and we may wonder why French playwrights denied themselves

so many aspects of Shakespeare's wider world, so many obvious tools of the dramatist's trade. But the French saw these limitations as desirable, or, rather, not as limitations at all, but as a process of selection, a trimming away of inessentials, in order to concentrate on the crux of the tragedy. To them, Shakespeare's plots jumped and sprawled, raced and lagged; Racine's were exquisitely tight and balanced structures, of even pace and compelling cogency. Where Elizabethan playwrights took their inspiration from the dispersive world view of the medieval pageant plays, the French turned their backs on their own medieval heritage and reverted, happily and consciously, to an earlier dramatic form. They believed they were recreating the essence of the classical dramas of ancient Greece and Rome.

In turning to classical models, seventeenth-century French playwrights were responsive to the thrust of their time. It was an age of tidying, of ordering. In politics, France was transformed from a factional state, teetering on the brink of civil war, into the most absolute monarchy the post-classical world has known. Everyone, from the great nobles down, was put firmly in his allotted place, and Louis XIV, at the apex of the social pyramid, saw himself as a new Augustus. In town planning, Paris began to change from a medieval jumble into something like the city we know today. New palaces, mansions, public squares, and arcades sprang up, embodying in their architectural principles the same sense of order. In the arts, now seen as an instrument of national prestige, the lumber of the Middle Ages was discarded, and new shapes began to appear. These were based on classical models, because in them the desired virtues of form, order, clarity, and symmetry were most apparent.

Thus French playwrights turned eagerly to classical plays, or at least to classical themes. Some things they dropped, notably the Greek chorus, no longer viable in a theater of different architecture and with a more commercial orientation. But they retained the Greek concept of a tragic action limited in physical scope and confined to a minimal number of characters. The concept was reinforced by French and Italian commentators on Aristotle, who hammered out of the *Poetics* the famous "three unities." These were rules for dramatic construction far more limiting than any the Greek playwrights obeyed or would have welcomed. By the rule of *unity of action*, a play should have one principal plot, without irrelevancies or subplots. By the rule of *unity of place*, the action should be confined to one location, preferably to a single room. By the rule of *unity of time*, dramatic time should come as close as possible to real time; in any case, the time of the action should not exceed one single day. *Phaedra* observes these rules, though it is perhaps arguable that the Hippolytus-Aricia plot is subsidiary to the main plot about Phaedra and Hippolytus.

But if Racine achieved concentration and unity at the cost of Shakespearean spaciousness, the smaller compass of his play is not impoverishment, and its singleness of effect is not simplicity. The central situation — Phaedra's illicit love — doesn't change till the end, but there is movement in the play nevertheless, though it is spatial rather than temporal. Racine takes us around his subject, making us see it from different angles and at different distances. And the tragic world he creates in *Phaedra* is as passional, ambiguous, and mysterious as any in Shakespeare. "All the characters ever do is reason," say people who lack a taste for Racinian drama. That is not true, but even if it were, it wouldn't matter as much as the objectors think, for what the characters reason *about* is their passion.

Like other neoclassical artists, Racine sought to express the universals in human life — to "follow Nature." That meant, not slavishly to copy the incidental appearance of things, but to reveal the changeless reality beneath by making the sensory surface transparent. What people have in common seemed more important than what separates them. Consensus ranked above idiosyncrasy, tradition above innovation. Social order and stability distinguished civilization from savagery. Political division is one of the evils in *Phaedra*, and Hippolytus's death is tragic partly because his marriage to Aricia would have brought a happy ending to an old dynastic feud. It was in keeping with this bias for the ordered and for the general that neoclassical dramatists so cheerfully observed the unity of place. The idea was not that everything happened in the *same* place, but that the stage, left unlocalized, could be *any* place. "Realism," in the modern, post-Ibsenite sense, was not one of the artistic ideals of the age. Precisely because real life is particular, transient, and chaotic, it was the business of art to deal with the general, the permanent, and the ordered. To the extent that verisimilitude really *is* "like life," a neoclassicist would have found it *un*-natural — a merely mechanical record of passing trifles.

We are not surprised, then, to find that *Phaedra*, as a play reflecting neoclassical values in politics, morals, social relationships, and art, has a conscious and carefully structured form. Modern readers often find it frigid and artificial — though perhaps more so in reading than in performance. But if French critics for so long considered Shakespeare merely a gifted barbarian and his plays shapeless and sprawling, it was because Racine in his plays organized life as strictly, and with as rigid a symmetry, as contemporary landscape gardeners organized trees, flowers, and water in the grounds of Versailles. Nature had been ordered into Art.

Racine, who read Greek well, took the story of Phaedra from a famous original, Euripides' *Hippolytus*. In it he found a play built on symmetry and with the precision of deliberative speech, offering first one side of the case, then the other, and attempting to strike a balance between them. The human action is framed by long monologues by the two goddesses Aphrodite (Latin Venus) and Artemis (Latin Diana), one the goddess of Love, the other of Chastity and the hunt. In her Prologue Aphrodite declares her intention to punish Hippolytus, the hunter, for his indifference to love (there is no Aricia in Euripides). In her Epilogue Artemis vows to get even with her rival goddess for the death of the Prince by killing one of Aphrodite's favorites. Phaedra, the woman who loves too much, is bal-

anced against Hippolytus, the young man who loves too little. Racine has
eliminated Euripides' goddesses as on-stage characters, but in the rest of
his play he extends Euripides' symmetry. Characters are neatly paired off:
Each principal has a *confidant*. Hippolytus is matched with Theramenes,
Phaedra with Oenone, Aricia with Ismene. Only Theseus, the King, stands
alone. He is the pivot around whom the others revolve. His entrance, significantly, marks the mathematical center of the play.

Just as character matches character, so plot matches plot. Phaedra has
an illicit passion for Hippolytus; Hippolytus has a guilty love for Aricia.
Scene balances scene; character responds to character. Hippolytus reveals
to Theramenes his love for Aricia; Phaedra reveals to Oenone her love for
Hippolytus. Next, Hippolytus declares his love to Aricia and Phaedra hers
to Hippolytus. It is all very much like the remorseless geometrical convolu-
tions of the grand ballet, which was the favorite courtly art of the time.
Symmetrical imagery spans the whole play. Phaedra makes her first entrance calling to the sun. She dies with a farewell to the light.

What is universal in her story has something to do with her extraordinary character and circumstance. Were she more "average," her story
would seem smaller: the sad case of a nice woman freaked out on sex. As it
is, her story is one of those that touch our lives before we know them.
They are part of the heritage we grow into, and when we *do* get to know
them, they seem not so much to have anticipated our own experience as
having always been part of it. It is almost as if without them we would not
have available to us certain modes of feeling and perceiving, certain qualities of consciousness. They discover ourselves to ourselves, ordering what
was shapeless in us, expressing what was dumb. Phaedra, torn between
obligation and inclination, has become one of the archetypes of our culture, a basic model for a certain kind of metaphysical fate and a certain
kind of moral crisis. She is the virtuous, high-minded mortal fallen into the
terrible hands of the goddess of love.

In his Preface to the play, Racine says that he changed Euripides' play in
order to ennoble Phaedra's character and make it more complex. In Euripides the mortals are little more than pawns in the hands of the goddesses;
in Racine the action is wholly human. We learn of Venus's fearful power
only through Phaedra's assertion of it. Venus, in consequence, turns into
something like sexual passion incarnate, the personification of an irresistible force in human life. Or a cynic might say she is just a convenient
pretext for Phaedra to disclaim responsibility for her criminal lust. At any
rate, Racine's Phaedra is much less unequivocally than Euripides' the victim of "remorseless Venus," "the prey of the avenging gods."

Morals are therefore more ambiguous in Racine's play than in
Euripides'. Racine in the Preface describes his heroine as "neither entirely
guilty, nor entirely innocent." She loathes her passion for Hippolytus, but
she yields to it. She blames Venus for it, but she is unable not to feel guilty
about it. She fatefully abandons virtuous silence when she declares her

love; yet she has some justification in the appearance of things. Theseus is presumed dead (a motif not in Euripides), and there would be political advantage in a marriage between his widow and his son. But silence, too, can be both morally reprehensible and fateful. Jealousy of Aricia keeps Phaedra from telling Theseus that Oenone's accusation of his son is false. Hippolytus has more estimable reasons for his unwillingness to tell his father about his love for Aricia and about Phaedra's attempt at seduction — in one case, a sense of filial duty; in the other, a sense of honor and pity. Still, his silence has consequences as catastrophic as Phaedra's. It is as if whether in speech or in silence human will and human virtue were powerless to stop the infernal machine Venus has set in motion.

Divine justice, however, is not really an issue in the play. The closest it comes to being so is in Phaedra's feeling that her suffering is an inherited curse. Her past is tainted with family guilt. She comes of a "fated line," whose ancestor was Phoebus Apollo, the sun god, from whose bright face she seeks to hide her "dark love." The darkness in her comes from her parents. Her father was Minos, in life the semidivine King of Crete, and in death the judge of the dead souls in Hades, the underworld. Her mother was Pasiphaë, who changed herself into a cow to satisfy her passion for a bull. The unnatural mating resulted in the birth of the Minotaur, half human and half bull.* As the Minotaur in its twin nature is a physical monster, so is Phaedra a kind of moral monster in her dividedness: half guilt and half innocence, half reason and half passion, half jealousy and half remorse. But it also makes for the tragic irony of her destiny.

Her husband Theseus is similarly ambivalent — both a heroic killer of monsters and a faithless seducer and adulterer. It is fitting that monster imagery pervades this play about an unfaithful wife, a vengeful father, and a disobedient son. Like the Minotaur, whose half sister Phaedra is, the monster from the sea that causes Hippolytus's death is half bull. At one time or another, most of the major characters in the play refer to themselves and others as "monsters," and Aricia darkly hints to Theseus that one monster still remains for him to overcome: Phaedra's adulterous, incestuous passion. It is ironic that this society dedicated to honor, virtue, and reason seems to be dominated by "monsters" — by the unnatural, the submoral, the subrational. The old myth contributes to the play's quality of tragedy of fate.

Yet it isn't altogether that. We suggested above that by keeping the god-

---

* When the throne of Crete was in dispute, Neptune, god of the Ocean, signified his support of Minos by sending him a bull to sacrifice. When Minos couldn't bring himself to kill the handsome animal, Neptune, to punish him, made Pasiphaë lust for it. Minos confined the Minotaur in the labyrinth Daedalus built for him. He defeated Athens in war and agreed to make peace only on condition that Athens every nine years send seven young men to Crete as food for the monster. Theseus, Prince of Athens, slew the Minotaur and found his way out of the labyrinth by means of a ball of thread given him by Ariadne, Minos' daughter. On his return voyage to Athens he deserted Ariadne (whether innocently or not is not clear). He married Hippolyta (or Antiope), Queen of the Amazons. Hippolytus was their son. After Hippolyta's death, Theseus married Phaedra, Ariadne's sister.

dess of love off stage Racine set the door ajar for a psychological explanation of his heroine's character. In this view, Oenone comes to seem like a projection of the practical, less scrupulous side of her mistress. To some extent the same is true of Theramenes in relation to Hippolytus. On the one hand, these *confidant* figures, loyal servant-advisers of the principals, are conventional devices: pretexts for the principals to talk about themselves and sounding boards for their opinions. In this capacity they serve one of the functions of the vanished Greek chorus. On the other hand, they are stage embodiments of the conflict of soul in the principals. There is a sense in which Phaedra's exchanges with Oenone are inner dialogues and Oenone's suicide represents the death of the scheming sensualist in Phaedra and the liberation of the noble and self-transcending woman she was before she became Venus's captive. Venus and Oenone direct her destiny and frustrate her moral will. Venus gives divine sanction to her desire, and that desire finds a resourceful ally in Oenone's shrewd and practical intelligence. It is as if human life were being shaped both by an external, supernatural force and by an internal, psychological one. The two come together in Theramenes' description of Hippolytus's death. The runaway horses symbolize the power of Phaedra's reinless lust to destroy the innocent.

There is still another point to be made about the *confidants* — one that has to do with the characteristically neoclassical features of the play. Euripides has nobles *and* commoners in his play. His Prince Hippolytus engages in a meaningful dialogue with an old huntsman. Phaedra's Nurse, in the Greek original, is a prototype for Juliet's Nurse in *Romeo and Juliet*, an earthy old busybody, a woman of the people. Racine promotes her, as Oenone, to the rank of courtly lady-in-waiting. Like his other characters, she is drawn from the upper aristocracy. The change doesn't just reflect modish snobbishness or the feeling that only the rich and powerful were worth writing tragedies about. Undoubtedly, there was something of that; the King, after all, subsidized the theaters, and the plays were designed to appeal to an aristocratic clientele. But there was also a question of focus. The underlying idea was that kings and queens, being in positions of enormous power and responsibility, revealed in heightened form the agony of the decisions we all have to make. At different points in the play both Theramenes and Oenone give advice to their superiors based on what ordinary men and women would do. "You love Aricia? Why not. It's only human." "So you've fallen in love with a man you shouldn't. It happens to everybody." But it is precisely because Phaedra and Hippolytus are *not* ordinary people that they can't take the ordinary way out. And when Theseus, as King, makes a mistake in judgment, the consequences are catastrophic. By virtue of their great station, these characters make us see great issues more clearly, their high social rank having its counterpart in their highly refined moral sensibility and discrimination. They are human nature writ large.

One of the clichés of criticism is that Racine is untranslatable. In the widest sense, any author is: No language can reproduce all the shades and nuances of another. But Racine is more difficult than most, because of the verse form he uses. French playwrights and critics at the time shared the conviction that tragedy required a special language, a heightened, dignified, supremely articulate voice. Again, decorum required it. Prose and colloquialisms would demean the nobility of the tragic characters and the tragic genre — another reason the French found Shakespeare, with his coarse clowns in tragedy, unsatisfactory.

The rhyme in Racine's alexandrines divides long speeches into pairs of lines, coruscating with epigrammatic brilliance but much harder to build crescendos with than Shakespeare's blank verse. Even in translation a comparison of one of Phaedra's tirades with one of Hamlet's soliloquies will reveal the difference in thought patterns imposed by the two verse forms. Within each of Racine's couplets, with very rare exceptions, the first line contains a complete thought, matched by another complete thought in the second. The rhyme points the balance. Unrhymed verse, like blank verse, finds it difficult to reproduce this. Rhyme is more difficult in English, anyway, which may be why we have come to associate it with the lighter dramatic forms (as in Gilbert's *Trial by Jury*, pages 415–430. Most English translators of Racine either avoid the rhyme altogether, or they use it selectively. What is important is the balance, and the translator must do everything he can to preserve it.

These formal characteristics of Racine's dramatic language are annoyances only if we allow them to be. They are not to be mistaken for superficial mechanics or incidental ornaments. They are the outward expressions of the inner substance of the play. Why did the French playwrights deliberately choose to write scenes of high passion in so apparently constricted a verse form? Because the force of an explosion is greater when it is confined. Just as they made the action more intense by limiting it in variety and scope and in time and space, so they intensified their language by constraining it within a strict form of stresses and rhymes. When passionate feelings are thus constrained, something exciting happens. The feelings seem to try to burst their bonds, to escape from the discipline imposed by the verse. In addition, the couplet form invites antithetical expression, and a play like *Phaedra* is, as we have seen, a drama of antitheses: passion-reason, love-duty, king-subject, man-woman, father-son, principal-*confidant*. Because of all this, the tension in the play between the rational form and the eruptive irrationality of the substance is perfectly true to the principle of dramatic decorum.

Which takes us back to the heart of the play: Passion subverting Reason, the libidinal psyche bursting social and moral law. Phaedra and Hippolytus share the same fault: They both love where they shouldn't — Phaedra her husband's son, Hippolytus his father's enemy. The painful situation catches the tragic dilemma of Racine's age. Reason and order were its sovereign social values — patterns to govern our lives by, flouted at our peril.

Ideally, they were vested in authority figures. In *Phaedra* that means Theseus, as King, as husband, and as father. Love is the passion most likely to
make us stray from our path of duty and responsibility. No wonder that in
the rigidly hierarchical society of Louis XIV's France, in which everybody,
from meanest peasant to exalted Sun King, had his prescribed duties to
perform within the social scheme, the conflict between love and duty became the standard tragic plot.

In *Phaedra*, the sense of obligation is deficient on either side, with disastrous results. Both Phaedra and Hippolytus know what they *should* be
doing. Hippolytus is miserably conscious that his love for Aricia, defensible
though it may seem to us, amounts to a defection from duty to an authority
that is at the same time royal and paternal. Phaedra, even at the height of
her dementia, is aware of how far she falls short of the ideals of queenship.
Theseus himself, this glittering, magnetic figure, trailing clouds of glory, is
shown us (in Hippolytus's speech to Theramenes in Act I) as a man who in
the past was led astray by passion. In the present situation he makes the
grievous mistake of letting his anger with his son overcome his reason.

We today may find all this silly rather than tragic, for we are far more
skeptical of moral imperatives than Racine's age was — particularly in the
outward form they assume here. Yet *Phaedra* still commands attention because the authoritarian code of ethics on which Phaedra and Hippolytus
are wrecked is more than a reflection of the official mores of the contemporary upper classes. It is also more than a reflection of Racine's inability,
despite his conscious repudiation, to free himself completely from the belief in divine predestination that the austere Jansenist sect had indoctri-
nated him with in his childhood. If that were all it was, the play would no
doubt be historically and biographically "interesting," but it would hardly
move us because of its relevance to our own deepest concerns. If it does
move us, it is because the code, *as* a piece of the historical past, is also a
plot device for the expression of a timeless human dilemma. We use other
terms than the philosophers and theologians of Racine's age for describing
our sense of our own psychic dividedness. For divine power over human
life our secular age has substituted notions about heredity and environmental conditioning. Those are *our* psychological determinants. But even they
are relevant to a discussion of the extent to which Phaedra is responsible
for her fatal passion. One critic has suggested — not altogether flippantly
— that Phaedra's fault is not her love for Hippolytus — that she cannot
help — but her talking about it. That would make her a victim, not of
Venus, not of an ancestral curse, not of tainted heredity, but of her own
social error. We don't have to decide that the critic is either right or wrong.
Among other things, what makes Racine's version of the old story so great
is that it is large enough to accommodate more than a single interpretation. In that it resembles the human reality it seeks to imitate.

That is why in our single-minded pursuit of such critical arguments we
risk losing sight of the transcendent humanity of the characters. None of

our convenient pigeon-holes will ultimately hold them. Even within the spare and apparently contrived framework of the play, they remain insistently, stubbornly human — making their own statements about themselves, doing what they do because they are what they are. Hippolytus is a proud but basically insecure young man, half resentful of his father's glorious image, staggered to find that he, like everyone else, can fall in love. Phaedra, victim or destroyer, caught in a region of anguish somewhere between her ancestor Apollo, god of light, and her father Minos, prince of darkness, succumbs to an all-too-human jealousy. What finally pushes her over the edge is not the fact that Hippolytus rejects her love but the fact that she learns he can love somebody else.

Finally, we should see the play — which is, after all, about people in authority and the difficulties and the consequences of their decision-making — also as in some sense a political allegory, a lesson for its own time and perhaps for ours. In an age of autocratic monarchy, it was vital that the King made the right decisions. Theseus made the wrong one. It was vital that the right person had the King's ear. Both Theseus and Phaedra listen to the wrong people. There must have been several in the audience who smarted when Phaedra cast off Oenone with bitter remarks about pernicious flatterers. It has even been suggested that this was Racine's last commercial play because he was warned off by those he had offended at court; they may have felt he was getting too close to the mark. Perhaps we should interpret Theseus's curse, too, in terms of the age. The question is sometimes asked how a professedly rationalist playwright, writing for a rationalist age, could use as the mainspring of his plot the super-human powers bestowed on Theseus by his patron deity. On the most elementary level, Racine *had* to use the curse; it was an essential part of the play he used as model. But on another level the curse can be seen as a metaphor for the total, crushing power that can be wielded by people in absolute authority. In that light Racine's allegory remains valid even today. Voltaire was to argue, in the next century, that tragedy should have some redeeming power — that some good should come out of the suffering. In *Phaedra* we see this in Theseus. Phaedra and Hippolytus are destroyed, but the King must live on with the consciousness of his error. In the last lines of the play, we see this chastening effect already at work. In Theseus's final acceptance of Aricia, daughter of an enemy house, there is hope for the state's redemption and for his.

Sir George Etherege

THE MAN OF MODE; OR, SIR FOPLING FLUTTER

A Comedy

FOREWORD

In 1660, eleven years after King Charles I had been executed by the Puritan Parliament, his son returned from exile in France and, as most of the nation cheered, assumed the throne of his father. The whole period from 1660 until about 1700 takes its name from this restoration of the House of Stuart, but actually the Restoration restored very little else. In literary history, particularly, 1660 is one of those dates that definitely divide one age from another. For the ordinary Englishman in 1660 the painful memories of the Civil War and of Cromwell's military dictatorship were overlaid with relief that the Puritans' repression of delight in things of this world had come to an end. He now took his models for behavior and his tastes in art from the Stuart court, which had learned its sophisticated and easygoing ways in the country where most of the Cavaliers had waited out the fall of the Commonwealth. In the prevailing tone of Restoration literature such few voices of Puritanism as remained — Milton's, Bunyan's — sound strangely alien.

But the Puritan interlude was not easily dismissed, as witnessed by the stridency with which the new literary fashions presumed that it could be. In 1660, pre–Civil War times were still less than a generation past, but already the image of the Elizabethans was receding into semi-nostalgic memory as that of "the Giant Race before the Flood." As if in quest of a continuum that had been broken, Restoration authors like John Dryden were given to comparing their own accomplishment with those of the au-

thors of what they referred to as "the last age." A cliché of such comparisons was the Restoration writers' pride in their greater refinement of language and in their more scrupulous observation of the decorum of the
classical genres. But together with their public air of condescension toward
Spenser's quaintly archaic allegory, Shakespeare's "wildness," and Donne's
harshness and obscurity went an awareness that their predecessors had
been graced with a robust vitality departed from their own lesser age. This
ambivalence of self-assessment is one of the recurrent themes of Restoration literary criticism. The times themselves fostered it.

Charles II was a man of charm and intelligence, and he was personally
popular, but it did not take many years of the restored monarchy to make it
clear that his reign was no golden age. In retrospect, a series of public
catastrophes in the middle years of his first decade as king seemed like ill
omens borne out by future events: the Plague in 1665, the Great Fire of
London in 1666, the burning of English ships by a Dutch flotilla in the
Thames estuary in 1667. Charles was a good-natured, unprincipled, and
pragmatic libertine who considered it his main task as king to hang on to
the throne he had regained. His finances were in such a mess that he had
to sacrifice British and Protestant interests as the price for getting funds
from Louis XIV of France, and only his manipulation of men and money
preserved the legitimate succession to the throne and kept religious and
political factionalism — these were the years of the rise of political parties
— from breaking out in a renewal of civil war. His brother, who succeeded
him in 1685, was a less adroit politician as well as a rigid Roman Catholic
and lost his throne in the Revolution of 1688. But long before, the glorious
promise of the Restoration had turned into a shabby and violent reality. It
was an age in which public events and the private actions of public men
easily could breed cynical disillusionment in the sensible and the sensitive,
and very often they did. Some of the best Restoration plays are evidence.

The history of the Restoration theater is mainly the story of the shifting
fortunes of the two theatrical companies that, by royal patents issued
shortly after the Restoration in 1660, held a monopoly on public productions of plays and operas throughout the period. In 1682 the King's Company, weakened by internal dissension and the loss of its theater by fire,
was forced to merge with the Duke's Company; actually, the merger
amounted to the absorption of the weaker company by the stronger. The
United Company remained the only licensed company acting in London
till 1695, when a dissident group of actors led by Thomas Betterton, the
leading actor of his generation, broke out and reestablished theatrical competition. The scarcity and smallness of Restoration theaters compared with
those of Elizabethan London are the most striking evidence we have that
the new age drew a much more narrow audience than the old.

Unlike the Elizabethan playhouse, such as Shakespeare's Globe, the
Restoration playhouse was an enclosed structure where performance took
place by artificial light. The largest of them, the Theatre Royal in Drury

Lane, could hold perhaps close to 1,000 spectators. The Duke's house in Dorset Garden was only a little smaller but much more elaborate. A modified version of the apron, the main acting area projecting into the audience, was a feature taken over from the Elizabethan playhouse. There was no upper stage. The deep, raked inner stage was separated from the apron by a proscenium arch with a curtain which was drawn when the performance began and which remained open until it ended. Costumes were elaborate, and the stage design attempted at least a degree of realistic illusion in the use of props and painted "flats" or "shutters." The latter were wings that moved in grooves before the fixed, painted backdrop. The use of "machines" for special, spectacular effects was frequent and popular. Boxes ran around the theater room on three sides, the most expensive seats being those in the side boxes opening directly on the apron. The Restoration equivalents of the Elizabethan groundlings sat on benches on the floor in front of the stage. Below the apron was a pit for the orchestra, which played before the curtain opened and between acts.

An immensely popular innovation was the introduction of actresses, which occurred within a year or two of the reopening of the theaters. It is said that this was done on Charles II's personal initiative. Several Restoration actors and actresses gained reputations for brilliant acting, but their social standing remained low and even perilous; they were held answerable for roles that the royal Master of Revels considered seditious or otherwise offensive, and actresses were considered fair game for the rakes. Because of the short run of even successful new plays, the companies had to operate on a repertory system, which put considerable strain on the actors. A play that ran for twelve consecutive nights was considered a hit. The playwright's sole income from his play came from the box office take on the third night. A performance was usually a pretty rowdy affair: orange-women vended their wares, footmen boisterously held seats for their masters, people came and went and moved about — the fops to be seen, the rakes to pick up girls, friends to talk, all of them intentionally or not disturbing the actors on stage and those spectators who had come to see and hear the play. Criticism of play and performance was immediate and uninhibited and sometimes took physical form. There were occasional brawls. Playwrights and actors had to strive for strong effects in order to hold the attention of the spectators, many of whom were there not just for theatrical amusement. In general, the physical features of the Restoration playhouse were those of the baroque theater of contemporary France, with certain native features retained from the pre-Commonwealth theater. In physical structure and in manner of staging it may be said that the London Restoration theater represented something like a midpoint between the Elizabethan and the conventional modern playhouse.

PROLOGUE

BY SIR CARR SCROOPE,[1]
BARONET

Like dancers on the ropes poor poets fare,
Most perish young, the rest in danger are;
This (one would think) should make our authors wary,
But, gamester-like, the giddy fools miscarry.
A lucky hand or two so tempts 'em on,
They cannot leave off play till they're undone.
With modest fears a Muse does first begin,
Like a young wench newly entice'd to sin;
But tickl'd once with praise, by her good will,
The wanton fool would never more lie still.
'Tis an old mistress you'll meet here to-night,
Whose charms you once have look'd on with delight.
But now of late such dirty drabs[2] have known ye,
A Muse o'th' better sort's ashamed to own ye.
Nature well drawn, and wit, must now give place
To gaudy nonsense and to dull grimace;
Nor is it strange that you should like so much
That kind of wit, for most of yours is such.
But I'm afraid that while to France we go, ⎫
To bring you home fine dresses, dance, and show, ⎬
The stage, like you, will but more foppish[3] grow. ⎭
Of foreign wares, why should we fetch the scum.
When we can be so richly serv'd at home?
For heav'n be thank'd, 'tis not so wise an age
But your own follies may supply the stage.
Tho' often plough'd, there's no great fear the soil
Should barren grow by the too frequent toil;
While at your doors are to be daily found
Such loads of dunghill to manure the ground.
'Tis by your follies that we players thrive,
As the physicians by diseases live;
And as each year some new distemper reigns,
Whose friendly poison helps to increase their gains,
So, among you, there starts up every day
Some new, unheard-of fool for us to play.
Then, for your own sakes be not too severe,
Nor what you all admire at home, damn here;
Since each is fond of his own ugly face,
Why should you, when we hold it, break the glass?

From *Restoration Plays*, edited by Brice Harris, 1953, Random House, Inc., publishers.

[1] (1649–80) courtier and minor poet

[2] whores

[3] silly and affected (particularly in dress and speech)

THE ACTORS' NAMES

GENTLEMEN:	GENTLEWOMEN:	WAITING WOMEN:
MR. DORIMANT	LADY TOWNLEY	PERT and
MR. MEDLEY	EMILIA	BUSY
OLD HARRY BELLAIR	MRS. LOVEIT	TOM, a Shoemaker
YOUNG HARRY BELLAIR	BELLINDA	NAN, an Orange-Woman
SIR FOPLING FLUTTER	LADY WOODVILL, and	THREE SLOVENLY BUL-
	HARRIET, her daughter	LIES
		TWO CHAIRMEN
		MR. SMIRK, a Parson
		HANDY, a Valet-de-chambre
		PAGES, FOOTMEN, &c.

ACT I

*Scene: A dressing-room; a table covered with a toilet,
clothes laid ready.*

Enter DORIMANT *in his gown and slippers, with a note in his hand, made up;*[1] *repeating verses.*

DORIMANT:

> Now for some ages had the pride of Spain
> Made the sun shine on half the world in vain.[2]

(Then looking on the note.)

"For Mrs. Loveit." What a dull, insipid thing is a billet-doux written in cold blood, after the heat of the business is over! It is a tax upon good nature which I have here been labouring to pay, and have done it, but with as much regret as ever fanatic[3] paid the Royal Aid or church duties. 'Twill have the same fate, I know, that all my notes to her have had of late: 'twill not be thought kind enough. 'Faith, women are i'the right when they jealously examine our letters, for in them we always first discover our decay of passion. — Hey! who waits?[4]

(Enter HANDY.*)*

HANDY: Sir —— .
DORIMANT: Call a footman.
HANDY: None of 'em are come yet.
DORIMANT: Dogs! Will they ever lie snoring abed till noon?

---

[1] completed and ready to be sent

[2] (from a poem by the Cavalier poet Edmund Waller [1606–87]. Dorimant quotes Waller's "smooth" couplets throughout the play. These notes will identify the author of a quotation only when he is *not* Waller)

[3] Puritan (the Puritans were opposed to both the monarchy and the Church of England)

[4] is in attendance

HANDY: 'Tis all one, Sir; if they're up, you indulge 'em so they're ever poaching after
   whores all the morning.

DORIMANT: Take notice henceforward who's wanting in his duty; the next clap he
   gets, he shall rot for an example. What vermin are those chattering without?

HANDY: Foggy[5] Nan, the orange-woman, and Swearing Tom, the shoemaker.

DORIMANT: Go, call in that overgrown jade with the flasket[6] of guts before her; fruit
   is refreshing in a morning.   (*Exit* HANDY.)

          It is not that I love you less
          Than when before your feet I lay ——

(*Enter* ORANGE-WOMAN *and* HANDY.)

—— How now, double tripe,[7] what news do you bring?

ORANGE-WOMAN: News! Here's the best fruit has come to town t'year; gad, I was up
   before four o'clock this morning and bought all the choice i'the market.

DORIMANT: The nasty refuse of your shop.

ORANGE-WOMAN: You need not make mouths at it; I assure you, 'tis all culled ware.

DORIMANT: The citizens[8] buy better on a holiday in their walk to Tottenham.[9]

ORANGE-WOMAN: Good or bad, 'tis all one; I never knew you commend anything.
   Lord! would the ladies had heard you talk of 'em as I have done! (*Sets down the
   fruit.*) Here, bid your man give me an angel.[10]

DORIMANT: Give the bawd[11] her fruit again.

ORANGE-WOMAN: Well, on my conscience, there never was the like of you! God's my
   life, I had almost forgot to tell you there is a young gentlewoman lately come to
   town with her mother, that is so taken with you.

DORIMANT: Is she handsome?

ORANGE-WOMAN: Nay, gad, there are few finer women, I tell you but so, and a
   hugeous fortune, they say. Here, eat this peach. It comes from the stone; 'tis
   better than any Newington[12] y'have tasted.

DORIMANT (*taking the peach*): This fine woman, I'll lay my life, is some awkward,
   ill-fashioned country toad who, not having above four dozen of black hairs on
   her head, has adorned her baldness with a large, white fruz,[13] that she may look
   sparkishly in the forefront of the King's box at an old play.

ORANGE-WOMAN: Gad, you'd change your note quickly if you did but see her.

DORIMANT: How came she to know me?

ORANGE-WOMAN: She saw you yesterday at the Change;[14] she told me you came and
   fooled with the woman at the next shop.

DORIMANT: I remember there was a mask[15] observed me, indeed. Fooled, did she
   say?

ORANGE-WOMAN: Ay; I vow she told me twenty things you said, too, and acted with
   head and with her body so like you ——

[5] flabby
[6] basket
[7] (1) paunch, (2) trash
[8] tradespeople
[9] lower middle-class suburb north of London
[10] gold coin worth about ten shillings
[11] (young orange-women were often prostitutes, and old ones often procured girls for their male customers)
[12] town in Kent, famous for its orchards
[13] wig of short, curled hair
[14] the New Exchange, a fashionable shopping area near the Strand
[15] i.e., a masked woman (cf. "vizard," note 25, this act)

(*Enter* MEDLEY.)

MEDLEY: Dorimant, my life, my joy, my darling sin! how dost thou?

ORANGE-WOMAN: Lord, what a filthy trick these men have got of kissing one another! (*She spits*.)

MEDLEY: Why do you suffer this cartload of scandal to come near you and make your neighbors think you so improvident to need a bawd?

ORANGE-WOMAN: Good, now! we shall have it you did but want[16] him to help you! Come, pay me for my fruit.

MEDLEY: Make us thankful for it, huswife, bawds are as much out of fashion as gentlemen-ushers; none but old formal ladies use the one, and none but foppish old stagers[17] employ the other. Go! You are an insignificant brandy bottle.

DORIMANT: Nay, there you wrong her; three quarts of Canary is her business.

ORANGE-WOMAN: What you please, gentlemen.

DORIMANT: To him! give him as good as he brings.

ORANGE-WOMAN: Hang him, there is not such another heathen in the town again, except it be the shoemaker without.

MEDLEY: I shall see you hold up your hand at the bar next sessions for murder, huswife; that shoemaker can take his oath you are in fee with the doctors to sell green fruit to the gentry that the crudities may breed diseases.

ORANGE-WOMAN: Pray, give me my money.

DORIMANT: Not a penny! When you bring the gentlewoman hither you spoke of, you shall be paid.

ORANGE-WOMAN: The gentlewoman! the gentlewoman may be as honest[18] as your sisters for aught as I know. Pray, pay me, Mr. Dorimant, and do not abuse me so; I have an honester way[19] of living — you know it.

MEDLEY: Was there ever such a resty[20] bawd?

DORIMANT: Some jade's tricks she has, but she makes amends when she's in good humour. —— Come, tell me the lady's name and Handy shall pay you.

ORANGE-WOMAN: I must not; she forbid me.

DORIMANT: That's a sure sign she would have you.

MEDLEY: Where does she live?

ORANGE-WOMAN: They lodge at my house.

MEDLEY: Nay, then she's in a hopeful way.

ORANGE-WOMAN: Good Mr. Medley, say your pleasure of me, but take heed how you affront my house! God's my life! — "in a hopeful way"!

DORIMANT: Prithee, peace! What kind of woman's the mother?

ORANGE-WOMAN: A goodly grave gentlewoman. Lord, how she talks against the wild young men o' the town! As for your part, she thinks you an arrant devil; should she see you, on my conscience she would look if you had not a cloven foot.

DORIMANT: Does she know me?

ORANGE-WOMAN: Only by hearsay; a thousand horrid stories have been told her of you, and she believes 'em all.

MEDLEY: By the character this should be the famous Lady Woodvill and her daughter Harriet.

ORANGE-WOMAN: The devil's in him for guessing, I think.

---

[16] need
[17] veterans, old hands
[18] chaste

[19] i.e., than being a bawd
[20] lazy, sluggish

DORIMANT: Do you know 'em?

MEDLEY: Both very well; the mother's a great admirer of the forms and civility of the last age.

DORIMANT: An antiquated beauty may be allowed to be out of humour at the freedoms of the present. This is a good account of the mother; pray, what is the daughter?

MEDLEY: Why, first, she's an heiress — vastly rich.

DORIMANT: And handsome?

MEDLEY: What alteration a twelvemonth may have bred in her I know not, but a year ago she was the beautifullest creature I ever saw: a fine, easy, clean shape; light brown hair in abundance; her features regular; her complexion clear and lively; large, wanton eyes; but above all, a mouth that has made me kiss it a thousand times in imagination; teeth white and even, and pretty, pouting lips, with a little moisture ever hanging on them, that look like the Provins rose fresh on the bush, ere the morning sun has quite drawn up the dew.

DORIMANT: Rapture! mere[21] rapture!

ORANGE-WOMAN: Nay, gad, he tells you true; she's a delicate creature.

DORIMANT: Has she wit?

MEDLEY: More than is usual in her sex, and as much malice. Then, she's as wild as you would wish her, and has a demureness in her looks that makes it so surprising.

DORIMANT: Flesh and blood cannot hear this and not long to know her.

MEDLEY: I wonder what makes her mother bring her up to town; an old doting keeper cannot be more jealous of his mistress.

ORANGE-WOMAN: She made me laugh yesterday; there was a judge came to visit 'em, and the old man, she told me, did so stare upon her, and when he saluted[22] her smacked so heartily. Who would think it of 'em?

MEDLEY: God-a-mercy, judge!

DORIMANT: Do 'em right; the gentlemen of the long robe have not been wanting by their good examples to countenance the crying sin o' the nation.

MEDLEY: Come, on with your trappings; 'tis later than you imagine.

DORIMANT: Call in the shoemaker, Handy.

ORANGE-WOMAN: Good Mr. Dorimant, pay me. Gad, I had rather give you my fruit than stay to be abused by that foul-mouthed rogue; what you gentlemen say, it matters not much, but such a dirty fellow does one more disgrace.

DORIMANT: Give her ten shillings, and be sure you tell the young gentlewoman I must be acquainted with her.

ORANGE-WOMAN: Now do you long to be tempting this pretty creature. Well, heavens mend you!

MEDLEY: Farewell, bog![23]   (*Exit* ORANGE-WOMAN *and* HANDY.)

Dorimant, when did you see your *pisaller*,[24] as you call her, Mrs. Loveit?

DORIMANT: Not these two days.

MEDLEY: And how stand affairs between you?

DORIMANT: There has been great patching of late, much ado; we make a shift to hang together.

MEDLEY: I wonder how her mighty spirit bears it.

---

[21] sheer
[22] kissed
[23] soggy person

[24] (Fr. "to go worst") a substitute for someone better

DORIMANT: Ill enough, on all conscience; I never knew so violent a creature.

MEDLEY: She's the most passionate in her love and the most extravagant in her jealousy of any woman I ever heard of. What note is that?

DORIMANT: An excuse I am going to send her for the neglect I am guilty of.

MEDLEY: Prithee, read it.

DORIMANT: No; but if you will take the pains, you may.

MEDLEY (*reads*):

> I never was a lover of business, but now I have a just reason to hate it, since it has kept me these two days from seeing you. I intend to wait upon you in the afternoon, and in the pleasure of your conversation forget all I have suffered during this tedious absence.

This business of yours, Dorimant, has been with a vizard[25] at the playhouse; I have had an eye on you. If some malicious body should betray you, this kind note would hardly make your peace with her.

DORIMANT: I desire no better.

MEDLEY: Why, would her knowledge of it oblige you?

DORIMANT: Most infinitely; next to the coming to a good understanding with a new mistress, I love a quarrel with an old one. But the devil's in't, there has been such a calm in my affairs of late, I have not had the pleasure of making a woman so much as break her fan, to be sullen, or forswear herself, these three days.

MEDLEY: A very great misfortune. Let me see; I love mischief well enough to forward this business myself. I'll about it presently, and though I know the truth of what y'ave done will set her a-raving, I'll heighten it a little with invention, leave her in a fit o' the mother,[26] and be here again before y'are ready.

DORIMANT: Pray, stay; you may spare yourself the labour. The business is undertaken already by one who will manage it with as much address, and I think with a little more malice, than you can.

MEDLEY: Who i'the devil's name can this be!

DORIMANT: Why, the vizard — that very vizard you saw me with.

MEDLEY: Does she love mischief so well as to betray herself to spite another?

DORIMANT: Not so neither, Medley. I will make you comprehend the mystery: this mask, for a farther confirmation of what I have been these two days swearing to her, made me yesterday at the playhouse make her a promise before her face utterly to break off with Loveit, and, because she tenders[27] my reputation and would not have me do a barbarous thing, has contrived a way to give me a handsome occasion.

MEDLEY: Very good.

DORIMANT: She intends about an hour before me, this afternoon, to make Loveit a visit, and, having the privilege, by reason of a professed friendship between 'em, to talk of her concerns ——

MEDLEY: Is she a friend?

DORIMANT: Oh, an intimate friend!

MEDLEY: Better and better; pray, proceed.

DORIMANT: She means insensibly[28] to insinuate[29] a discourse of me and artificially[30]

---

[25] a masked woman, usually a prostitute
[26] hysteria
[27] is solicitous about
[28] slyly
[29] introduce in a devious way
[30] artfully

raise her jealousy to such a height that, transported with the first motions of her passion, she shall fly upon me with all the fury imaginable as soon as ever I enter; the quarrel being thus happily begun, I am to play my part, confess and justify all my roguery, swear her impertinence and ill-humour makes her intolerable, tax her with the next fop that comes into my head, and in a huff march away, slight her, and leave her to be taken by whosoever thinks it worth his time to lie down before her.

MEDLEY: This vizard is a spark and has a genius that makes her worthy of yourself, Dorimant.

(*Enter* HANDY, SHOEMAKER, *and* FOOTMAN.)

DORIMANT: You rogue there who sneak like a dog that has flung down a dish, if you do not mend your waiting, I'll uncase[31] you and turn you loose to the wheel of fortune. Handy, seal this and let him run with it presently.   (*Exit* FOOTMAN.)

MEDLEY: Since y'are resolved on a quarrel, why do you send her this kind note?

DORIMANT: To keep her at home in order to the business — (*To the* SHOEMAKER.) How now, you drunken sot?

SHOEMAKER: 'Zbud,[32] you have no reason to talk; I have not had a bottle of sack[33] of yours in my belly this fortnight.

MEDLEY: The orange-woman says your neighbours take notice what a heathen you are, and design to inform the bishop and have you burned for an atheist.

SHOEMAKER: Damn her, dunghill, if her husband does not remove her, she stinks so, the parish intend to indict him for a nuisance.

MEDLEY: I advise you like a friend; reform your life. You have brought the envy of the world upon you by living above yourself. Whoring and swearing are vices too genteel for a shoemaker.

SHOEMAKER: 'Zbud, I think you men of quality will grow as unreasonable as the women. You would ingross[34] the sins of the nation; poor folks can no sooner be wicked but th'are railed at by their betters.

DORIMANT: Sirrah,[35] I'll have you stand i'the pillory for this libel!

SHOEMAKER: Some of you deserve it, I'm sure; there are so many of 'em, that our journeymen nowadays, instead of harmless ballads, sing nothing but your damned lampoons.

DORIMANT: Our lampoons, you rogue!

SHOEMAKER: Nay, good Master, why should not you write your own commentaries as well as Cæsar?

MEDLEY: The rascal's read, I perceive.

SHOEMAKER: You know the old proverb — ale and history.[36]

DORIMANT: Draw on my shoes, Sirrah.

SHOEMAKER: Here's a shoe —— !

DORIMANT: Sits with more wrinkles than there are in an angry bully's forehead!

SHOEMAKER: 'Zbud, as smooth as your mistress's skin does upon her! So; strike your foot in home. 'Zbud, if e'er a monsieur of 'em all[37] make more fashionable ware, I'll be content to have my ears whipped off with my own paring knife.

---

[31] strip (of his livery; i.e., dismiss from service)

[32] by God's blood

[33] dry white wine

[34] monopolize

[35] a term of address used to one's inferiors

[36] ("Truth is in ale as in history")

[37] any Frenchman

MEDLEY: And served up in a ragout instead of coxcombs to a company of French shoemakers for a collation.

SHOEMAKER: Hold, hold! Damn 'em, caterpillars![38] let 'em feed upon cabbage. Come Master, your health this morning next my heart now!

DORIMANT: Go, get you home and govern your family better! Do not let your wife follow you to the ale-house, beat your whore, and lead you home in triumph.

SHOEMAKER: 'Zbud, there's never a man i'the town lives more like a gentleman with his wife than I do. I never mind her motions,[39] she never inquires into mine; we speak to one another civilly, hate one another heartily, and because 'tis vulgar to lie and soak[40] together, we have each of us our several[41] settle-bed.[42]

DORIMANT: Give him half a crown.

MEDLEY: Not without[43] he will promise to be bloody drunk.

SHOEMAKER: "Tope"[44] 's the word i'the eye of the world, for my master's honor, Robin!

DORIMANT: Do not debauch my servants, Sirrah.

SHOEMAKER: I only tip him the wink;[45] he knows an ale-house from a hovel.

(*Exit* SHOEMAKER.)

DORIMANT: My clothes, quickly.

MEDLEY: Where shall we dine today?

(*Enter* YOUNG BELLAIR.)

DORIMANT: Where you will; here comes a good third man.

YOUNG BELLAIR: Your servant, gentlemen.

MEDLEY: Gentle Sir, how will you answer this visit to your honourable mistress? 'Tis not her interest you should keep company with men of sense who will be talking reason.

YOUNG BELLAIR: I do not fear[46] her pardon; do you but grant me yours for my neglect of late.

MEDLEY: Though y'ave made us miserable by the want of your good company, to show you I am free from all resentment, may the beautiful cause of our misfortune give you all the joys happy lovers have shared ever since the world began.

YOUNG BELLAIR: You wish me in heaven, but you believe me on my journey to hell.

MEDLEY: You have a good strong faith, and that may contribute much towards your salvation. I confess I am but of an untoward[47] constitution, apt to have doubts and scruples, and in love they are no less distracting than in religion. Were I so near marriage, I should cry out by fits as I ride in my coach, "Cuckold, cuckold!" with no less fury than the mad fanatic does "glory!" in Bethlem.[48]

YOUNG BELLAIR: Because religion makes some run mad must I live an atheist?

MEDLEY: Is it not great indiscretion for a man of credit, who may have money enough on his word, to go and deal with Jews, who for little sums make men enter into bonds and give judgments?

---

[38] ravagers, extortioners
[39] doings
[40] drink
[41] separate
[42] daybed
[43] unless
[44] (1) to drink heavily, (2) to pledge (the Shoemaker is either improving upon Medley's vulgar language or accepting his condition that he spend the money on drink; or he intends both meanings)
[45] give him a hint
[46] worry about
[47] disinclined (to believe in the religion of marriage)
[48] Bethlehem Hospital for the insane (often "Bedlam")

YOUNG BELLAIR: Preach no more on this text. I am determined, and there is no hope of my conversion.

DORIMANT (*to* HANDY, *who is fiddling about him*): Leave your unnecessary fiddling; a wasp that's buzzing about a man's nose at dinner is not more troublesome than thou art.

HANDY: You love to have your clothes hang just, Sir.

DORIMANT: I love to be well dressed, Sir, and think it no scandal to my understanding.

HANDY: Will you use the essence[49] or orange flower water?

DORIMANT: I will smell as I do to-day, no offence to the ladies' noses.

HANDY: Your pleasure, Sir.   (*Exit* HANDY.)

DORIMANT: That a man's excellency should lie in neatly tying of a ribband or a cravat![50] How careful's nature in furnishing the world with necessary coxcombs![51]

YOUNG BELLAIR: That's a mighty pretty suit of yours, Dorimant.

DORIMANT: I am glad't has your approbation.

YOUNG BELLAIR: No man in town has a better fancy in his clothes than you have.

DORIMANT: You will make me have an opinion of my genius.

MEDLEY: There is a great critic, I hear, in these matters, lately arrived piping hot from Paris.

YOUNG BELLAIR: Sir Fopling Flutter, you mean.

MEDLEY: The same.

YOUNG BELLAIR: He thinks himself the pattern of modern gallantry.

DORIMANT: He is indeed the pattern of modern foppery.

MEDLEY: He was yesterday at the play, with a pair of gloves up to his elbows, and a periwig[52] more exactly curled than a lady's head newly dressed for a ball.

YOUNG BELLAIR: What a pretty lisp he has!

DORIMANT: Ho! that he affects in imitation of the people of quality of France.

MEDLEY: His head stands, for the most part, on one side, and his looks are more languishing than a lady's when she lolls at stretch in her coach or leans her head carelessly against the side of a box i'the playhouse.

DORIMANT: He is a person indeed of great acquired follies.

MEDLEY: He is like many others, beholding to his education for making him so eminent a coxcomb; many a fool had been lost to the world had their indulgent parents wisely bestowed neither learning nor good breeding on 'em.

YOUNG BELLAIR: He has been, as the sparkish[53] word is, "brisk[54] upon the ladies" already. He was yesterday at my Aunt Townley's and gave Mrs. Loveit a catalogue of his good qualities under the character of a complete gentleman, who, according to Sir Fopling, ought to dress well, dance well, fence well, have a genius for love letters, and agreeable voice for a chamber, be very amorous, something[55] discreet, but not over-constant.

MEDLEY: Pretty ingredients to make an accomplished person!

DORIMANT: I am glad he pitched upon Loveit.

YOUNG BELLAIR: How so?

DORIMANT: I wanted a fop to lay to her charge, and this is as pat as may be.

---

[49] perfume
[50] silk scarf worn around the neck
[51] conceited fools, fops
[52] wig
[53] fashionable (with derogatory overtones: foppish)
[54] lively, forward
[55] somewhat

YOUNG BELLAIR: I am confident she loves no man but you.

DORIMANT: The good fortune were enough to make me vain, but that I am in my nature modest.

YOUNG BELLAIR: Hark you, Dorimant. —— With your leave, Mr. Medley; 'tis only a secret concerning a fair lady.

MEDLEY: Your good breeding, Sir, gives you too much trouble; you might have whispered without all this ceremony.

YOUNG BELLAIR (*to* DORIMANT): How stand your affairs with Bellinda of late?

DORIMANT: She's a little jilting baggage.

YOUNG BELLAIR: Nay, I believe her false enough, but she's ne'er the worse for your purpose; she was with you yesterday in a disguise at the play.

DORIMANT: There we fell out and resolved never to speak to one another more.

YOUNG BELLAIR: The occasion?

DORIMANT: Want of courage to meet me at the place appointed. These young women apprehend[56] loving as much as the young men do fighting, at first; but, once entered, like them too, they all turn bullies straight.

(*Enter* HANDY.)

HANDY (*to* YOUNG BELLAIR): Sir, your man without[57] desires to speak with you.

YOUNG BELLAIR: Gentlemen, I'll return immediately.   (*Exit* YOUNG BELLAIR.)

MEDLEY: A very pretty fellow this.

DORIMANT: He's handsome, well-bred, and by much the most tolerable of all the young men that do not abound in wit.

MEDLEY: Ever well dressed, always complaisant,[58] and seldom impertinent. You and he are grown very intimate, I see.

DORIMANT: It is our mutual interest to be so: it makes the women think the better of his understanding, and judge more favourably of my reputation; it makes him pass upon some for a man of very good sense, and I upon others for a very civil person.

MEDLEY: What was that whisper?

DORIMANT: A thing which he would fain have known, but I did not think it fit to tell him; it might have frighted him from his honourable intentions of marrying.

MEDLEY: Emilia, give her her due, has the best reputation of any young woman about the town who has beauty enough to provoke detraction; her carriage[59] is unaffected, her discourse modest, not at all censorious nor pretending, like the counterfeits of the age.

DORIMANT: She's a discreet maid, and I believe nothing can corrupt her but a husband.

MEDLEY: A husband?

DORIMANT: Yes, a husband: I have known many women make a difficulty of losing a maidenhead, who have afterwards made none of making a cuckold.

MEDLEY: This prudent consideration, I am apt to think, has made you confirm poor Bellair in the desperate resolution he has taken.

DORIMANT: Indeed, the little hope I found there was of her, in the state she was in, has made me by my advice contribute something towards the changing of her condition.

---

[56] are apprehensive about

[57] outside

[58] pleasant, obliging

[59] conduct, deportment

(*Enter* YOUNG BELLAIR.)

Dear Bellair, by heavens, I thought we had lost thee; men in love are never to be reckoned on when we would form a company.

YOUNG BELLAIR: Dorimant, I am undone. My man has brought the most surprising news i'the world.

DORIMANT: Some strange misfortune is befallen your love.

YOUNG BELLAIR: My father came to town last night and lodges i'the very house where Emilia lies.

MEDLEY: Does he know it is with her you are in love?

YOUNG BELLAIR: He knows I love, but knows not whom, without some officious sot has betrayed me.

DORIMANT: Your Aunt Townley is your confidante and favours the business.

YOUNG BELLAIR: I do not apprehend any ill office from her. I have received a letter in which I am commanded by my father to meet him at my aunt's this afternoon. He tells me farther he has made a match for me and bids me resolve to be obedient to his will or expect to be disinherited.

MEDLEY: Now's your time, Bellair; never had lover such an opportunity of giving a generous proof of his passion.

YOUNG BELLAIR: As how, I pray?

MEDLEY: Why, hang[60] an estate, marry Emilia out of hand, and provoke your father to do what he threatens; 'tis but despising a coach, humbling yourself to a pair of goloshes,[61] being out of countenance when you meet your friends, pointed at and pitied wherever you go by all the amorous fops that know you, and your fame will be immortal.

YOUNG BELLAIR: I could find in my heart to resolve not to marry at all.

DORIMANT: Fie, fie! That would spoil a good jest and disappoint the well-natured town of an occasion of laughing at you.

YOUNG BELLAIR: The storm I have so long expected hangs o'er my head and begins to pour down upon me; I am on the rack and can have no rest till I'm satisfied in what I fear. Where do you dine?

DORIMANT: At Long's or Locket's.[62]

MEDLEY: At Long's let it be.

YOUNG BELLAIR: I'll run and see Emilia and inform myself how matters stand. If my misfortunes are not so great as to make me unfit for company, I'll be with you.　　　　　　　　　　　　　　　　　　　　(*Exit* YOUNG BELLAIR.)

(*Enter a* FOOTMAN *with a letter.*)

FOOTMAN (*to* DORIMANT): Here's a letter, Sir.

DORIMANT: The superscription's right: "For Mr. Dorimant."

MEDLEY: Let's see; the very scrawl and spelling of a true-bred whore.

DORIMANT: I know the hand; the style is admirable, I assure you.

MEDLEY: Prithee, read it.

DORIMANT (*reads*):

I told you you dud not love me, if you dud, you would have seen me again ere

---

[60] never mind, "damn!"　　　　　　　　　　　[62] fashionable London taverns
[61] wooden shoes

now. I have no money and am very mallicolly; pray send me a guynie to see the operies.

> Your servant to command,
> MOLLY.

MEDLEY: Pray, let the whore have a favourable answer, that she may spark it in a box and do honour to her profession.

DORIMANT: She shall, and perk up[63] i'the face of quality. Is the coach at door?

HANDY: You did not bid me send for it.

DORIMANT: Eternal blockhead! (HANDY *offers to go out*.) Hey, sot ——

HANDY: Did you call me, Sir?

DORIMANT: I hope you have no just exception to the name, Sir?

HANDY: I have sense, Sir.

DORIMANT: Not so much as a fly in winter. —— How did you come, Medley?

MEDLEY: In a chair.

FOOTMAN: You may have a hackney coach if you please, Sir.

DORIMANT: I may ride the elephant if I please, Sir. Call another chair and let my coach follow to Long's.

> Be calm, ye great parents, etc.

> (*Exeunt, singing.*)

ACT II

SCENE 1

Enter my LADY TOWNLEY *and* EMILIA.

LADY TOWNLEY: I was afraid, Emilia, all had been discovered.

EMILIA: I tremble with the apprehension still.

LADY TOWNLEY: That my brother should take lodgings i'the very house where you lie!

EMILIA: 'Twas lucky we had timely notice to warn the people to be secret. He seems to be a mighty good-humoured old man.

LADY TOWNLEY: He ever had a notable smirking way with him.

EMILIA: He calls me rogue, tells me he can't abide me, and does so bepat me.

LADY TOWNLEY: On my word, you are much in his favour then.

EMILIA: He has been very inquisitive, I am told, about my family, my reputation, and my fortune.

LADY TOWNLEY: I am confident he does not i'the least suspect you are the woman his son's in love with.

EMILIA: What should make him, then, inform himself so particularly of me?

LADY TOWNLEY: He was always of a very loving temper himself; it may be he has a doting fit upon him — who knows?

EMILIA: It cannot be.

[63] show off

(*Enter* YOUNG BELLAIR.)

LADY TOWNLEY: Here comes my nephew. —— Where did you leave your father?

YOUNG BELLAIR: Writing a note within. Emilia, this early visit looks as if some kind jealousy would not let you rest at home.

EMILIA: The knowledge I have of my rival gives me a little cause to fear your constancy.

YOUNG BELLAIR: My constancy! I vow ——

EMILIA: Do not vow. Our love is frail as is our life and full as little in our power; and are you sure you shall outlive this day?

YOUNG BELLAIR: I am not; but when we are in perfect health, 'twere an idle thing to fright ourselves with the thoughts of sudden death.

LADY TOWNLEY: Pray, what has passed between you and your father i'the garden?

YOUNG BELLAIR: He's firm in his resolution, tells me I must marry Mrs. Harriet, or swears he'll marry himself and disinherit me. When I saw I could not prevail with him to be more indulgent, I dissembled an obedience to his will, which has composed his passion and will give us time, and, I hope, opportunity, to deceive him.

(*Enter* OLD BELLAIR *with a note in his hand.*)

LADY TOWNLEY: Peace, here he comes!

OLD BELLAIR: Harry, take this and let your man carry it for me to Mr. Fourbe's[1] chamber, my lawyer i'the Temple.[2]   (*Exit* YOUNG BELLAIR.)
(*To* EMILIA.) Neighbour, a dod![3] I am glad to see thee here. Make much of her, Sister; she's one of the best of your acquaintance. I like her countenance and her behaviour well; she has a modesty that is not common i'this age, a dod, she has!

LADY TOWNLEY: I know her value, Brother, and esteem her accordingly.

OLD BELLAIR: Advise her to wear a little more mirth in her face; a dod, she's too serious.

LADY TOWNLEY: The fault is very excusable in a young woman.

OLD BELLAIR: Nay, a dod, I like her ne'er the worse. A melancholy beauty has her charms. I love a pretty sadness in a face, which varies now and then, like changeable colours, into a smile.

LADY TOWNLEY: Methinks you speak very feelingly, Brother.

OLD BELLAIR: I am but five and fifty, Sister, you know, an age not altogether unsensible. — (*To* EMILIA.) Cheer up, sweetheart! I have a secret to tell thee may chance to make thee merry. We three will make collation together anon; i'the meantime, mum,[4] I can't abide you! go, I can't abide you!

(*Enter* YOUNG BELLAIR.)

Harry, come! you must along with me to my Lady Woodvill's. I am going to slip the boy at a mistress.

YOUNG BELLAIR: At a wife, Sir, you would say.

OLD BELLAIR: You need not look so glum, Sir; a wife is no curse when she brings the blessing of a good estate with her; but an idle town flirt, with a painted face, a

---

[1] i.e., Mr. Cheat (Fr.)
[2] the lawyers' quarter in London
[3] Ah, God! (cf. "egad!")
[4] not a word!

rotten reputation, and a crazy fortune, a dod! is the devil and all, and such a one I hear you are in league with.

YOUNG BELLAIR: I cannot help detraction, Sir.

OLD BELLAIR: Out! A pise[5] o' their breeches, there are keeping[6] fools enough for such flaunting baggages, and they are e'en too good for 'em. — (*To* EMILIA.) Remember 'night. Go, y'are a rogue, y'are a rogue! Fare you well, fare you well! —— Come, come, come along, Sir!   (*Exeunt* OLD *and* YOUNG BELLAIR.)

LADY TOWNLEY: On my word, the old man comes on apace; I'll lay my life he's smitten.

EMILIA: This is nothing but the pleasantness of his humour.

LADY TOWNLEY: I know him better than you. Let it work; it may prove lucky.

(*Enter a* PAGE.)

PAGE: Madam, Mr. Medley has sent to know whether a visit will not be troublesome this afternoon.

LADY TOWNLEY: Send him word his visits never are so.   (*Exit* PAGE.)

EMILIA: He's a very pleasant man.

LADY TOWNLEY: He's a very necessary man among us women; he's not scandalous i'the least, perpetually contriving to bring good company together, and always ready to stop up a gap at ombre;[7] then, he knows all the little news o'the town.

EMILIA: I love to hear him talk o'the intrigues; let 'em be never so dull in themselves, he'll make 'em pleasant i'the relation.

LADY TOWNLEY: But he improves things so much one can take no measure of the truth from him. Mr. Dorimant swears a flea or a maggot is not made more monstrous by a magnifying glass than a story is by his telling it.

(*Enter* MEDLEY.)

EMILIA: Hold, here he comes.

LADY TOWNLEY: Mr. Medley.

MEDLEY: Your servant, Madam.

LADY TOWNLEY: You have made yourself a stranger of late.

EMILIA: I believe you took a surfeit of ombre last time you were here.

MEDLEY: Indeed, I had my bellyful of that termagant, Lady Dealer. There never was so unsatiable a carder;[8] an old gleeker[9] never loved to sit to't like her. I have played with her now at least a dozen times till she's worn out all her fine complexion and her tour[10] would keep in curl no longer.

LADY TOWNLEY: Blame her not, poor woman; she loves nothing so well as a black ace.[11]

MEDLEY: The pleasure I have seen her in when she has had hope in drawing for a matadore!

---

[5] pox (?)
[6] i.e., mistress-keeping
[7] a card game with forty cards played by 3 persons (cf. Alexander Pope's *Rape of the Lock*, Canto III)
[8] card-player
[9] one of the players in a three-handed card game
[10] crescent-shaped front of false hair
[11] (the black aces were two of the three highest trumps, or matadors, in ombre)

EMILIA: 'Tis as pretty sport to her as persuading masks off is to you, to make discoveries.

LADY TOWNLEY: Pray, where's your friend Mr. Dorimant?

MEDLEY: Soliciting his affairs; he's a man of great employment, has more mistresses now depending than the most eminent lawyer in England has causes.

EMILIA: Here has been Mrs. Loveit so uneasy and out of humour these two days.

LADY TOWNLEY: How strangely love and jealousy rage in that poor woman!

MEDLEY: She could not have picked out a devil upon earth so proper to torment her; he's made her break a dozen or two of fans already, tear half a score points[12] in pieces, and destroy hoods and knots[13] without number.

LADY TOWNLEY: We heard of a pleasant serenade he gave her t'other night.

MEDLEY: A Danish serenade with kettle-drums and trumpets.

EMILIA: Oh, barbarous!

MEDLEY: What! You are of the number of the ladies whose ears are grown so delicate since our operas you can be charmed with nothing but *flûtes douces*[14] and French hautboys?[15]

EMILIA: Leave your raillery, and tell us, is there any new wit come forth, songs or novels?

MEDLEY: A very pretty piece of gallantry, by an eminent author, called *The Diversions of Bruxelles*, very necessary to be read by all old ladies who are desirous to improve themselves at questions and commands,[16] blindman's bluff, and the like fashionable recreations.

EMILIA: Oh, ridiculous!

MEDLEY: Then there is *The Art of Affectation*, written by a late beauty of quality, teaching you how to draw up your breasts, stretch up your neck, to thrust out your breech, to play with your head, to toss up your nose, to bite your lips, to turn up your eyes, to speak in a silly, soft tone of a voice, and use all the foolish French words that will infallibly make your person and conversation charming; with a short apology at the latter end in the behalf of young ladies who notoriously wash[17] and paint though they have naturally good complexions.

EMILIA: What a deal of stuff you tell us!

MEDLEY: Such as the town affords, Madam. The Russians, hearing the great respect we have for foreign dancing, have lately sent over some of their best balladines,[18] who are now practising a famous ballet which will be suddenly danced at the Bear Garden.

LADY TOWNLEY: Pray, forbear your idle stories, and give us an account of the state of love as it now stands.

MEDLEY: Truly, there has been some revolutions in those affairs, great chopping and changing[19] among the old, and some new lovers whom malice, indiscretion, and misfortune have luckily brought into play.

LADY TOWNLEY: What think you of walking into the next room and sitting down before you engage in this business?

MEDLEY: I wait upon you, and I hope (though women are commonly unreasonable)

---

[12] pieces of lace
[13] bows of ribbon
[14] (Fr.) soft flutes
[15] oboes
[16] a parlor game

[17] use cosmetic washes
[18] ballet dancers
[19] (1) buying and selling, (2) changing frequently

by the plenty of scandal I shall discover, to give you very good content,
ladies.   (*Exeunt*)

SCENE 2

Enter MRS. LOVEIT *and* PERT. MRS. LOVEIT *putting up*[1] *a letter, then pulling
out her pocket-glass and looking in it.*

MRS. LOVEIT: Pert.

PERT: Madam?

MRS. LOVEIT: I hate myself, I look so ill today.

PERT: Hate the wicked cause on't, that base man Mr. Dorimant, who makes you
torment and vex yourself continually.

MRS. LOVEIT: He is to blame, indeed.

PERT: To blame to be two days without sending, writing, or coming near you, contrary to his oath and covenant! 'Twas to much purpose to make him swear! I'll lay
my life there's not an article but he has broken — talked to the vizards i'the pit,
waited upon the ladies from the boxes to their coaches, gone behind the scenes,
and fawned upon those little insignificant creatures, the players. 'Tis impossible
for a man of his inconstant temper to forbear, I'm sure.

MRS. LOVEIT: I know he is a devil, but he has something of the angel yet undefaced
in him, which makes him so charming and agreeable that I must love him, be he
never so wicked.

PERT: I little thought, Madam, to see your spirit tamed to this degree, who banished
poor Mr. Lackwit but for taking up another lady's fan in your presence.

MRS. LOVEIT: My knowing of such odious fools contributes to the making of me love
Dorimant the better.

PERT: Your knowing of Mr. Dorimant, in my mind, should rather make you hate all
mankind.

MRS. LOVEIT: So it does, besides himself.

PERT: Pray, what excuse does he make in his letter?

MRS. LOVEIT: He has had business.

PERT: Business in general terms would not have been a current[2] excuse for another.
A modish man is always very busy when he is in pursuit of a new mistress.

MRS. LOVEIT: Some fop has bribed you to rail at him. He had business; I will believe
it, and will forgive him.

PERT: You may forgive him anything, but I shall never forgive him his turning me
into ridicule, as I hear he does.

MRS. LOVEIT: I perceive you are of the number of those fools his wit has made his
enemies.

PERT: I am of the number of those he's pleased to rally, Madam, and if we may
believe Mr. Wagfan and Mr. Caperwell, he sometimes makes merry with yourself
too, among his laughing companions.

MRS. LOVEIT: Blockheads are as malicious to witty men as ugly women are to the
handsome; 'tis their interest, and they make it their business to defame 'em.

PERT: I wish Mr. Dorimant would not make it his business to defame you.

---

[1] putting away   [2] valid

MRS. LOVEIT: Should he, I had rather be made infamous by him than owe my reputation to the dull discretion of those fops you talk of.

(*Enter* BELLINDA.)

Bellinda! (*Running to her.*)
BELLINDA: My dear!
MRS. LOVEIT: You have been unkind of late.
BELLINDA: Do not say unkind — say unhappy.
MRS. LOVEIT: I could chide you. Where have you been these two days?
BELLINDA: Pity me rather, my dear, where I have been — so tired with two or three country gentlewomen, whose conversation has been more unsufferable than a country fiddle.
MRS. LOVEIT: Are they relations?
BELLINDA: No, Welsh acquaintance I made when I was last year at St. Winifred's. They have asked me a thousand questions of the modes and intrigues of the town, and I have told 'em almost as many things for news that hardly were so when their gowns were in fashion.
MRS. LOVEIT: Provoking creatures! How could you endure 'em?
BELLINDA (*aside*): Now to carry on my plot. Nothing but love could make me capable of so much falsehood. 'Tis time to begin, lest Dorimant should come before her jealousy has stung her. — (*Laughs, and then speaks on.*) I was yesterday at a play with 'em, where I was fain to show 'em the living as the man at Westminster does the dead: "That is Mrs. Such-a-one, admired for her beauty; that is Mr. Such-a-one, cried up for a wit; That is sparkish Mr. Such-a-one, who keeps reverend Mrs. Such-a-one; and there sits fine Mrs. Such-a-one who was lately cast off by my Lord Such-a-one."
MRS. LOVEIT: Did you see Dorimant there?
BELLINDA: I did, and imagine you were there with him and have no mind to own it.
MRS. LOVEIT: What should make you think so?
BELLINDA: A lady masked in a pretty *déshabillé*,[3] whom Dorimant entertained with more respect than the gallants do a common vizard.
MRS. LOVEIT (*aside*): Dorimant at the play entertaining a mask! Oh, heavens!
BELLINDA (*aside*): Good!
MRS. LOVEIT: Did he stay all the while?
BELLINDA: Till the play was done, and then led her out, which confirms me it was you.
MRS. LOVEIT: Traitor!
PERT: Now you may believe he had business, and you may forgive him too.
MRS. LOVEIT: Ingrateful, perjured man!
BELLINDA: You seem so much concerned, my dear, I fear I have told you unawares what I had better have concealed for your quiet.
MRS. LOVEIT: What manner of shape had she?
BELLINDA: Tall and slender. Her motions were very genteel; certainly she must be some person of condition.
MRS. LOVEIT: Shame and confusion be ever in her face when she shows it!

---

[3] (Fr.) loose, low-cut, sometimes "see-through" dress

BELLINDA: I should blame your discretion for loving that wild man, my dear, but they say he has a way so bewitching that few can defend their hearts who know him.

MRS. LOVEIT: I will tear him from mine or die i'the attempt.

BELLINDA: Be more moderate.

MRS. LOVEIT: Would I had daggers, darts, or poisoned arrows in my breast, so I could but remove the thoughts of him from thence!

BELLINDA: Fie, fie! your transports are too violent, my dear; this may be but an accidental gallantry, and 'tis likely ended at her coach.

PERT: Should it proceed farther, let your comfort be, the conduct Mr. Dorimant affects will quickly make you know your rival, ten to one let you see her ruined, her reputation exposed to the town — a happiness none will envy her but yourself, Madam.

MRS. LOVEIT: Whoe'er she be, all the harm I wish her is, may she love him as well as I do and may he give her as much cause to hate him.

PERT: Never doubt the latter end of your curse, Madam.

MRS. LOVEIT: May all the passions that are raised by neglected love — jealousy, indignation, spite, and thirst of revenge — eternally rage in her soul, as they do now in mine. (*Walks up and down with a distracted air.*)

(*Enter a* PAGE.)

PAGE: Madam, Mr. Dorimant ——

MRS. LOVEIT: I will not see him.

PAGE: I told him you were within, Madam.

MRS. LOVEIT: Say you lied — say I'm busy — shut the door — say anything!

PAGE: He's here, Madam.

(*Enter* DORIMANT.)

DORIMANT:

> They taste of death who do at heaven arrive;
> But we this paradise approach alive.

(*To* MISTRESS LOVEIT.) What, dancing *The Galloping Nag* without a fiddle? (*Offers to catch her by the hand; she flings away and walks on, he pursuing her.*) I fear this restlessness of the body, Madam, proceeds from an unquietness of the mind. What unlucky accident puts you out of humour? A point ill washed, knots spoiled i'the making up, hair shaded awry, or some other little mistake in setting you in order?

PERT: A trifle, in my opinion, Sir, more inconsiderable than any you mention.

DORIMANT: O Mrs. Pert! I never knew you sullen enough to be silent; come, let me know the business.

PERT: The business, Sir, is the business that has taken you up these two days. How have I seen you laugh at men of business, and now to become a man of business yourself!

DORIMANT: We are not masters of our own affections; our inclinations daily alter: now we love pleasure, and anon we shall dote on business. Human frailty will have it so, and who can help it?

MRS. LOVEIT: Faithless, inhuman, barbarous man ——

DORIMANT (*aside*): Good! Now the alarm strikes.

MRS. LOVEIT: Without sense of love, of honour, or of gratitude, tell me, for I will know, what devil masked she was you were with at the play yesterday?

DORIMANT: Faith, I resolved as much as you, but the devil was obstinate and would not tell me.

MRS. LOVEIT: False in this as in your vows to me! — you do know.

DORIMANT: The truth is, I did all I could to know.

MRS. LOVEIT: And dare you own it to my face? Hell and furies! (*Tears her fan in pieces.*)

DORIMANT: Spare your fan, Madam; you are growing hot and will want it to cool you.

MRS. LOVEIT: Horror and distraction seize you! Sorrow and remorse gnaw your soul, and punish all your perjuries to me! (*Weeps.*)

DORIMANT (*turning to* BELLINDA):

> So thunder breaks the cloud in twain
> And makes a passage for the rain.[4]

(*To* BELLINDA.) Bellinda, you are the devil that have raised this storm; you were at the play yesterday and have been making discoveries to your dear.

BELLINDA: Y'are the most mistaken man i'the world.

DORIMANT: It must be so, and here I vow revenge — resolve to pursue and persecute you more impertinently than ever any loving fop did his mistress, hunt you i'the Park, trace you i'the Mail,[5] dog you in every visit you make, haunt you at the plays and i'the drawing-room, hang my nose in your neck and talk to you whether you will or no, and ever look upon you with such dying[6] eyes till your friends grow jealous of me, send you out of town, and the world suspect your reputation. — (*In a lower voice.*) At my Lady Townley's when we go from hence. (*He looks kindly on* BELLINDA.)

BELLINDA: I'll meet you there.

DORIMANT: Enough.

MRS. LOVEIT (*pushing* DORIMANT *away*): Stand off! You sha' not stare upon her so.

DORIMANT: Good; there's one made jealous already.

MRS. LOVEIT: Is this the constancy you vowed?

DORIMANT: Constancy at my years! 'Tis not a virtue in season; you might as well expect the fruit the autumn ripens i'the spring.

MRS. LOVEIT: Monstrous principle!

DORIMANT: Youth has a long journey to go, Madam; should I have set up my rest at the first inn I lodged at, I should never have arrived at the happiness I now enjoy.

MRS. LOVEIT: Dissembler, damned dissembler!

DORIMANT: I am so, I confess; good nature and good manners corrupt me. I am honest in my inclinations, and would not, wer't not to avoid offence, make a lady a little in years believe I think her young, willfully mistake art for nature, and seem as fond of a thing I am weary of as when I doted on't in earnest.

MRS. LOVEIT: False man!

---

[4] (from a poem by Matthew Roydon, a minor Elizabethan poet)

[5] the Mall, a walk bordering St. James's Park

[6] swooning

DORIMANT: True woman!

MRS. LOVEIT: Now you begin to show yourself.

DORIMANT: Love gilds us over and makes us show fine things to one another for a time, but soon the gold wears off and then again the native brass appears.

MRS. LOVEIT: Think on your oaths, your vows and protestations, perjured man!

DORIMANT: I made 'em when I was in love.

MRS. LOVEIT: And therefore ought they not to bind? Oh, impious!

DORIMANT: What we swear at such a time may be a certain proof of a present passion, but, to say truth, in love there is no security to be given for the future.

MRS. LOVEIT: Horrid and ingrateful, begone, and never see me more!

DORIMANT: I am not one of those troublesome coxcombs who, because they were once well received, take the privilege to plague a woman with their love ever after. I shall obey you, Madam, though I do myself some violence.

(*He offers to go and* MRS. LOVEIT *pulls him back.*)

MRS. LOVEIT: Come back! You sha' not go! Could you have the ill-nature to offer it?

DORIMANT: When love grows diseased, the best thing we can do is to put it to a violent death. I cannot endure the torture of a lingering and consumptive passion.

MRS. LOVEIT: Can you think mine sickly?

DORIMANT: Oh, 'tis desperately ill. What worse symptoms are there than your being always uneasy when I visit you, your picking quarrels with me on slight occasions, and in my absence kindly listening to the impertinences of every fashionable fool that talks to you?

MRS. LOVEIT: What fashionable fool can you lay to my charge?

DORIMANT: Why, the very cock-fool of all those fools — Sir Fopling Flutter.

MRS. LOVEIT: I never saw him in my life but once.

DORIMANT: The worse woman you, at first sight to put on all your charms, to entertain him with that softness in your voice, and all that wanton kindness in your eyes you so notoriously affect when you design a conquest.

MRS. LOVEIT: So damned a lie did never malice yet invent. Who told you this?

DORIMANT: No matter. That ever I should love a woman that can dote on a senseless caper, a tawdry French ribband, and a formal cravat!

MRS. LOVEIT: You make me mad.

DORIMANT: A guilty conscience may do much. Go on, be the game-mistress o' the town, and enter[7] all our young fops as fast as they come from travel.

MRS. LOVEIT: Base and scurrilous!

DORIMANT: A fine mortifying reputation 'twill be for a woman of your pride, wit, and quality!

MRS. LOVEIT: This jealousy's a mere pretence, a cursed trick of your own devising. I know you.

DORIMANT: Believe it and all the ill of me you can: I would not have a woman have the least good thought of me that can think well of Fopling. Farewell! Fall to, and much good may do[8] you with your coxcomb.

MRS. LOVEIT: Stay, oh stay! and I will tell you all.

DORIMANT: I have been told too much already.   (*Exit* DORIMANT.)

MRS. LOVEIT: Call him again!

---

[7] initiate   [8] may it do

PERT: E'en[9] let him go — a fair riddance.

MRS. LOVEIT: Run, I say! call him again! I will have him called!

PERT: The devil should carry him away first were it my concern.　　　　(Exit PERT.)

BELLINDA: He's frighted me from the very thoughts of loving men. For heaven's sake, my dear, do not discover what I told you! I dread his tongue as much as you ought to have done his friendship.

(Enter PERT.)

PERT: He's gone, Madam.

MRS. LOVEIT: Lightning blast him!

PERT: When I told him you desired him to come back, he smiled, made a mouth at me, flung into his coach, and said ——

MRS. LOVEIT: What did he say?

PERT: "Drive away!" and then repeated verses.

MRS. LOVEIT: Would I had made a contract to be a witch when first I entertained this greater devil, monster, barbarian! I could tear myself in pieces. Revenge — nothing but revenge can ease me. Plague, war, famine, fire — all that can bring universal ruin and misery on mankind — with joy I'd perish to have you in my power but this moment.　　　　(Exit MRS. LOVEIT.)

PERT: Follow, Madam; leave her not in this outrageous passion!

(PERT gathers up the things.)

BELLINDA (aside): He's given me the proof which I desired of his love,

> But 'tis a proof of his ill-nature too.
> I wish I had not seen him use her so.
> I sigh to think that Dorimant may be
> One day as faithless and unkind to me.　　　　(Exeunt.)

ACT III

SCENE 1

Scene: LADY WOODVILL's lodgings.

Enter HARRIET and BUSY, her woman.

BUSY: Dear Madam, let me set that curl in order.

HARRIET: Let me alone; I will shake 'em all out of order.

BUSY: Will you never leave this wildness?

HARRIET: Torment me not.

BUSY: Look! There's a knot falling off.

HARRIET: Let it drop.

BUSY: But one pin, dear Madam.

HARRIET: How do I daily suffer under thy officious fingers!

[9] just

BUSY: Ah, the difference that is between you and my Lady Dapper! how uneasy she is if the least thing be amiss about her!

HARRIET: She is indeed most exact; nothing is ever wanting to make her ugliness remarkable.

BUSY: Jeering people say so.

HARRIET: Her powdering, painting, and her patching[1] never fail in public to draw the tongues and eyes of all the men upon her.

BUSY: She is, indeed, a little too pretending.

HARRIET: That women should set up for beauty as much in spite of nature as some men have done for wit!

BUSY: I hope without offence one may endeavour to make one's self agreeable.

HARRIET: Not when 'tis impossible. Women then ought to be no more fond of dressing than fools should be of talking; hoods and modesty, masks and silence, things that shadow and conceal — they should think of nothing else.

BUSY: Jesu! Madam, what will your mother think is become of you? For heaven's sake go in again!

HARRIET: I won't.

BUSY: This is the extravagantest thing that ever you did in your life, to leave her and a gentleman who is to be your husband.

HARRIET: My husband! Hast thou so little wit to think I spoke what I meant when I overjoyed her in the country with a low curtsey and "What you please, Madam; I shall ever be obedient"?

BUSY: Nay, I know not, you have so many fetches.[2]

HARRIET: And this was one, to get her up to London! Nothing else, I assure thee.

BUSY: Well, the man, in my mind, is a fine man.

HARRIET: The man indeed wears his clothes fashionably and has a pretty, negligent way with him, very courtly and much affected; he bows, and talks, and smiles so agreeably, as he thinks.

BUSY: I never saw anything so genteel.

HARRIET: Varnished over with good breeding, many a blockhead makes a tolerable show.

BUSY: I wonder you do not like him.

HARRIET: I think I might be brought to endure him, and that is all a reasonable woman should expect in a husband; but there is duty i'the case, and like the haughty Merab,[3] I

Find much aversion in my stubborn mind,

Which

Is bred by being promis'd and design'd.[4]

BUSY: I wish you do not design your own ruin. I partly guess your inclinations, Madam — that Mr. Dorimant ——

HARRIET: Leave your prating and sing some foolish song or other.

BUSY: I will — the song you love so well ever since you saw Mr. Dorimant.

---

[1] sticking small pieces of black silk on the face as beauty spots

[2] dodges, tricks

[3] Saul's daughter, promised to David but married to someone else (I Sam. 18:17–19)

[4] (from *The Davideis*, an unfinished epic poem by Abraham Cowley [1618–67])

Song

When first Amintas charm'd my heart,
My heedless sheep began to stray;
The wolves soon stole the greatest part,
And all will now be made a prey.

Ah, let not love your thoughts possess,
'Tis fatal to a shepherdess;
The dang'rous passion you must shun,
Or else like me be quite undone.

HARRIET: Shall I be paid down by a covetous parent for a purchase? I need no land; no, I'll lay myself out[5] all in love. It is decreed —

(*Enter* YOUNG BELLAIR.)

YOUNG BELLAIR: What generous resolution are you making, Madam?

HARRIET: Only to be disobedient, Sir.

YOUNG BELLAIR: Let me join hands with you in that.

HARRIET: With all my heart; I never thought I should have given you mine so willingly. Here I, Harriet ——

YOUNG BELLAIR: And I, Harry ——

HARRIET: Do solemnly protest ——

YOUNG BELLAIR: And vow ——

HARRIET: That I with you ——

YOUNG BELLAIR: And I with you ——

BOTH: Will never marry.

HARRIET: A match!

YOUNG BELLAIR: And no match! How do you like this indifference now?

HARRIET: You expect I should take it ill, I see.

YOUNG BELLAIR: 'Tis not unnatural for you women to be a little angry: you miss a conquest, though you would slight the poor man were he in your power.

HARRIET: There are some, it may be, have an eye like Bart'lomew[6] — big enough for the whole fair; but I am not of the number, and you may keep your gingerbread. 'Twill be more acceptable to the lady whose dear image it wears, Sir.

YOUNG BELLAIR: I must confess, Madam, you came a day after the fair.[7]

HARRIET: You own then you are in love?

YOUNG BELLAIR: I do.

HARRIET: The confidence is generous, and in return I could almost find in my heart to let you know my inclinations.

YOUNG BELLAIR: Are you in love?

HARRIET: Yes, with this dear town, to that degree I can scarce endure the country in landscapes and in hangings.

YOUNG BELLAIR: What a dreadful thing 'twould be to be hurried back to Hampshire!

HARRIET: Ah, name it not!

YOUNG BELLAIR: As for us, I find we shall agree well enough. Would we could do something to deceive the grave people!

---

[5] spend myself

[6] Bartholomew Cokes, a glutton and curiosity-seeker in Ben Jonson's comedy *Bartholomew Fair* (1614) (the title of the play refers to the fair held annually about the time of St. Bartholomew's Day, August 24, in Smithfield, north of London)

[7] (proverbial)

HARRIET: Could we delay their quick proceeding, 'twere well. A reprieve is a good step towards the getting of a pardon.

YOUNG BELLAIR: If we give over the game, we are undone. What think you of playing it on booty?[8]

HARRIET: What do you mean?

YOUNG BELLAIR: Pretend to be in love with one another; 'twill make some dilatory excuses we may feign pass the better.

HARRIET: Let us do't, if it be but for the dear pleasure of dissembling.

YOUNG BELLAIR: Can you play your part?

HARRIET: I know not what it is to love, but I have made pretty remarks[9] by being now and then where lovers meet. Where did you leave their gravities?[10]

YOUNG BELLAIR: I'th' next room. Your mother was censuring our modern gallant.

(*Enter* OLD BELLAIR *and* LADY WOODVILL.)

HARRIET: Peace! here they come. I will lean against this wall and look bashfully down upon my fan, while you, like an amorous spark, modishly entertain me.

LADY WOODVILL: Never go about to excuse 'em; come, come, it was not so when I was a young woman.

OLD BELLAIR: A dod, they're something disrespectful ——

LADY WOODVILL: Quality was then considered, and not rallied by every fleering[11] fellow.

OLD BELLAIR: Youth will have its jest, a dod, it will.

LADY WOODVILL: 'Tis good breeding now to be civil to none but players and Exchange women; they are treated by 'em as much above their condition as others are below theirs.

OLD BELLAIR: Out! a pise on 'em! talk no more. The rogues ha' got an ill habit of preferring beauty no matter where they find it.

LADY WOODVILL: See your son and my daughter; they have improved their acquaintance since they were within.

OLD BELLAIR: A dod, methinks they have! Let's keep back and observe.

YOUNG BELLAIR: Now for a look and gestures that may persuade 'em I am saying all the passionate things imaginable.

HARRIET: Your head a little more on one side. Ease yourself on your left leg and play with your right hand.

YOUNG BELLAIR: Thus, is it not?

HARRIET: Now set your right leg firm on the ground, adjust your belt, then look about you.

YOUNG BELLAIR: A little exercising will make me perfect.

HARRIET: Smile, and turn to me again very sparkish.

YOUNG BELLAIR: Will you take your turn and be instructed?

HARRIET: With all my heart!

YOUNG BELLAIR: At one motion play your fan, roll your eyes, and then settle a kind look upon me.

HARRIET: So!

YOUNG BELLAIR: Now spread your fan, look down upon it, and tell the sticks with a finger.

HARRIET: Very modish!

---

[8] two players conspiring to cheat a third
[9] observations
[10] i.e., their parents
[11] jeering, snickering

YOUNG BELLAIR: Clap your hand up to your bosom, hold down your gown. Shrug a little, draw up your breasts, and let 'em fall again gently, with a sigh or two, etc.

HARRIET: By the good instructions you give, I suspect you for one of those malicious observers who watch people's eyes, and from innocent looks make scandalous conclusions.

YOUNG BELLAIR: I know some, indeed, who out of mere love to mischief are as vigilant as jealousy itself, and will give you an account of every glance that passes at a play and i'th' Circle.[12]

HARRIET: 'Twill not be amiss now to seem a little pleasant.

YOUNG BELLAIR: Clap your fan, then, in both your hands, snatch it to your mouth, smile, and with a lively motion fling your body a little forwards. So! Now spread it, fall back on the sudden, cover your face with it and break out into a loud laughter — take up, look grave, and fall a-fanning of yourself. — Admirably well acted!

HARRIET: I think I am pretty apt at these matters.

OLD BELLAIR: A dod, I like this well!

LADY WOODVILL: This promises something.

OLD BELLAIR: Come! there is love i'th' case, a dod there is, or will be. What say you, young lady?

HARRIET: All in good time, Sir; you expect we should fall to and love as game-cocks fight, as soon as we are set together. A dod, y'are unreasonable!

OLD BELLAIR: A dod, Sirrah, I like thy wit well.

(*Enter a* SERVANT.)

SERVANT: The coach is at the door, Madam.

OLD BELLAIR: Go, get you and take the air together.

LADY WOODVILL: Will not you go with us?

OLD BELLAIR: Out! a pise! A dod, I ha' business and cannot. We shall meet at night at my sister Townley's.

YOUNG BELLAIR (*aside*): He's going to Emilia. I overheard him talk of a collation. (*Exeunt.*)

SCENE 2

Enter LADY TOWNLEY, EMILIA, *and* MR. MEDLEY.

LADY TOWNLEY: I pity the young lovers we last talked of, though to say truth their conduct has been so indiscreet they deserve to be unfortunate.

MEDLEY: Y'have had an exact account, from the great lady i'th' box down to the little orange wench.

EMILIA: Y'are a living libel, a breathing lampoon. I wonder you are not torn in pieces.

MEDLEY: What think you of setting up an office of intelligence for these matters? The project may get money.

[12] (1) a circular path in Hyde Park, (2) a small social set, coterie

LADY TOWNLEY: You would have great dealings with country ladies.

MEDLEY: More than Muddiman[1] has with their husbands.

(*Enter* BELLINDA.)

LADY TOWNLEY: Bellinda, what has become of you? We have not seen you here of late with your friend Mrs. Loveit.

BELLINDA: Dear creature, I left her but now so sadly afflicted!

LADY TOWNLEY: With her old distemper, jealousy!

MEDLEY: Dorimant has played her some new prank.

BELLINDA: Well, that Dorimant is certainly the worst man breathing.

EMILIA: I once thought so.

BELLINDA: And do you not think so still?

EMILIA: No, indeed!

BELLINDA: Oh, Jesu!

EMILIA: The town does him a great deal of injury, and I will never believe what it says of a man I do not know, again, for his sake.

BELLINDA: You make me wonder.

LADY TOWNLEY: He's a very well-bred man.

BELLINDA: But strangely ill-natured.

EMILIA: Then he's a very witty man.

BELLINDA: But a man of no principles.

MEDLEY: Your man of principles is a very fine thing, indeed.

BELLINDA: To be preferred to men of parts by women who have regard to their reputation and quiet. Well, were I minded to play the fool, he should be the last man I'd think of.

MEDLEY: He has been the first in many ladies' favours, though you are so severe, Madam.

LADY TOWNLEY: What he may be for a lover, I know not; but he's a very pleasant acquaintance, I am sure.

BELLINDA: Had you seen him use Mrs. Loveit as I have done, you would never endure him more.

EMILIA: What, he has quarreled with her again!

BELLINDA: Upon the slightest occasion; he's jealous of Sir Fopling.

LADY TOWNLEY: She never saw him in her life but yesterday, and that was here.

EMILIA: On my conscience, he's the only man in town that's her aversion! How horribly out of humour she was all the while he talked to her!

BELLINDA: And somebody has wickedly told him ――

EMILIA: Here he comes.

(*Enter* DORIMANT.)

MEDLEY: Dorimant! you are luckily come to justify yourself: here's a lady ――

BELLINDA: Has a word or two to say to you from a disconsolate person.

DORIMANT: You tender your reputation too much, I know, Madam, to whisper with me before this good company.

BELLINDA: To serve Mrs. Loveit I'll make a bold venture.

DORIMANT: Here's Medley, the very spirit of scandal.

---

[1] (1629–92) editor of a popular scandal sheet and newsletter

BELLINDA: No matter!

EMILIA: 'Tis something you are unwilling to hear, Mr. Dorimant.

LADY TOWNLEY: Tell him, Bellinda, whether he will or no.

BELLINDA (aloud): Mrs. Loveit ——

DORIMANT: Softly! these are laughers; you do not know 'em.

BELLINDA (to DORIMANT apart): In a word, y'ave made me hate you, which I thought you never could have done.

DORIMANT: In obeying your commands.

BELLINDA: 'Twas a cruel part you played. How could you act it?

DORIMANT: Nothing is cruel to a man who could kill himself to please you. Remember five o'clock to-morrow morning!

BELLINDA: I tremble when you name it.

DORIMANT: Be sure you come!

BELLINDA: I sha'not.

DORIMANT: Swear you will!

BELLINDA: I dare not.

DORIMANT: Swear, I say!

BELLINDA: By my life — by all the happiness I hope for ——

DORIMANT: You will.

BELLINDA: I will!

DORIMANT: Kind!

BELLINDA: I am glad I've sworn. I vow I think I should ha' failed you else!

DORIMANT: Surprisingly kind! In what temper did you leave Loveit?

BELLINDA: Her raving was prettily[2] over, and she began to be in a brave[3] way of defying you and all your works. Where have you been since you went from thence?

DORIMANT: I looked in at the play.

BELLINDA: I have promised, and must return to her again.

DORIMANT: Persuade her to walk in the Mail this evening.

BELLINDA: She hates the place and will not come.

DORIMANT: Do all you can to prevail with her.

BELLINDA: For what purpose?

DORIMANT: Sir Fopling will be here anon; I'll prepare him to set upon her there before me.

BELLINDA: You persecute her too much, but I'll do all you'll ha' me.

DORIMANT (aloud): Tell her plainly 'tis grown so dull a business I can drudge on no longer.

EMILIA: There are afflictions in love, Mr. Dorimant.

DORIMANT: You women make em, who are commonly as unreasonable in that as you are at play — without the advantage be on your side, a man can never quietly give over when he's weary.

MEDLEY: If you would play[4] without being obliged to complaisance, Dorimant, you should play in public places.

---

[2] fairly well

[3] fine

[4] (both Medley here and Dorimant in his reply use "play" as a double entendre, meaning both gambling and sex. Medley means that if Dorimant wants to feel free to quit the game when he feels like it he should not involve either his partner or himself too deeply)

DORIMANT: Ordinaries[5] were a very good thing for that, but gentlemen do not of late frequent 'em. The deep play is now in private houses.

(BELLINDA *offering to steal away*.)

LADY TOWNLEY: Bellinda, are you leaving us so soon?

BELLINDA: I am to go to the Park with Mrs. Loveit, Madam.   (*Exit* BELLINDA.)

LADY TOWNLEY: This confidence will go nigh to spoil this young creature.

MEDLEY: 'Twill do her good, Madam. Young men who are brought up under practising lawyers prove the abler counsel when they come to be called to the bar themselves.

DORIMANT: The town has been very favourable to you this afternoon, my Lady Townley; you use to have an *embarras*[6] of chairs and coaches at your door, an uproar of footmen in your hall, and a noise of fools above here.

LADY TOWNLEY: Indeed, my house is the general rendezvous, and next to the playhouse is the common refuge of all the young idle people.

EMILIA: Company is a very good thing, Madam, but I wonder you do not love it a little more chosen.

LADY TOWNLEY: 'Tis good to have an universal taste; we should love wit, but for variety be able to divert ourselves with the extravagancies of those who want[7] it.

MEDLEY: Fools will make you laugh.

EMILIA: For once or twice, but the repetition of their folly after a visit or two grows tedious and unsufferable.

LADY TOWNLEY: You are a little too delicate, Emilia.

(*Enter a* PAGE.)

PAGE: Sir Fopling Flutter, Madam, desires to know if you are to be seen.

LADY TOWNLEY: Here's the freshest fool in town, and one who has not cloyed you yet. —— Page!

PAGE: Madam!

LADY TOWNLEY: Desire him to walk up.   (*Exit* PAGE.)

DORIMANT: Do not you fall on him, Medley, and snub him. Soothe him up in his extravagance; he will show the better.

MEDLEY: You know I have a natural indulgence for fools and need not this caution, Sir.

(*Enter* SIR FOPLING FLUTTER *with his* PAGE *after him*.)

SIR FOPLING: Page, wait without.   (*Exit* PAGE.)

(*To* LADY TOWNLEY.) Madam, I kiss your hands. I see yesterday was nothing of chance; the *belles assemblées*[8] form themselves here every day. (*To* EMILIA.) Lady, your servant. —— Dorimant, let me embrace thee! Without lying, I have not met with any of my acquaintance who retain so much of Paris as thou dost — the very air thou hadst when the marquise mistook thee i'th' Tuileries and cried, "Hey, Chevalier!" and then begged thy pardon.

---

[5] taverns
[6] (Fr.) bothersome excess
[7] lack
[8] (Fr.) elegant gatherings

DORIMANT: I would fain wear in fashion as long as I can, Sir; 'tis a thing to be valued in men as well as baubles.[9]

SIR FOPLING: Thou art a man of wit and understand the town. Prithee, let thee and I be intimate; there is no living without making some good man the confidant of our pleasures.

DORIMANT: 'Tis true! but there is no man so improper for such a business as I am.

SIR FOPLING: Prithee, why hast thou so modest an opinion of thyself?

DORIMANT: Why, first, I could never keep a secret in my life; and then, there is no charm so infallibly makes me fall in love with a woman as my knowing a friend loves her. I deal honestly with you.

SIR FOPLING: Thy humour's very gallant, or let me perish! I knew a French count so like thee!

LADY TOWNLEY: Wit, I perceive, has more power over you than beauty, Sir Fopling, else you would not have let this lady stand so long neglected.

SIR FOPLING (*to* EMILIA): A thousand pardons, Madam; some civility's due of course upon the meeting a long absent friend. The *éclat*[10] of so much beauty, I confess, ought to have charmed me sooner.

EMILIA: The *brillant*[11] of so much good language, Sir, has much more power than the little beauty I can boast.

SIR FOPLING: I never saw anything prettier than this high work on your *point d'Espagne*.[12]

EMILIA: 'Tis not so rich as *point de Venise*.[13]

SIR FOPLING: Not altogether, but looks cooler and is more proper for the season. —— Dorimant, is not that Medley?

DORIMANT: The same, Sir.

SIR FOPLING: Forgive me, Sir; in this *embarras* of civilities I could not come to have you in my arms sooner. You understand an equipage[14] the best of any man in town, I hear.

MEDLEY: By my own you would not guess it.

SIR FOPLING: There are critics who do not write, Sir.

MEDLEY: Our peevish poets will scarce allow it.

SIR FOPLING: Damn 'em, they'll allow no man wit who does not play the fool like themselves and show it! Have you taken notice of the gallesh[15] I brought over?

MEDLEY: Oh, yes! 't has quite another air than th' English makes.

SIR FOPLING: 'Tis as easily known from an English tumbril[16] as an Inns of Court man[17] is from one of us.

DORIMANT: Truly; there is a *bel air*[18] in galleshes as well as men.

MEDLEY: But there are few so delicate to observe it.

SIR FOPLING: The world is generally very *grossier*[19] here, indeed.

LADY TOWNLEY: He's very fine.

EMILIA: Extreme proper.

---

[9] trinkets
[10] (Fr.) splendor
[11] (Fr.) sparkle
[12] (Fr.) Spanish lace
[13] (Fr.) Venetian lace
[14] (1) carriage (with or without horses and attendant servants), (2) retinue
[15] calèche, light carriage with a folding hood, buggy
[16] dung-cart
[17] i.e., lawyer
[18] (Fr.) graceful style
[19] (Fr.) coarse

SIR FOPLING: A slight suit I made to appear in at my first arrival — not worthy your consideration, ladies.

DORIMANT: The pantaloon[20] is very well mounted.

SIR FOPLING: The tassels are new and pretty.

MEDLEY: I never saw a coat better cut.

SIR FOPLING: It makes me show long-waisted, and, I think, slender.

DORIMANT: That's the shape our ladies dote on.

MEDLEY: Your breech, though, is a handful too high, in my eye, Sir Fopling.

SIR FOPLING: Peace, Medley! I have wished it lower a thousand times, but a pox on't! 'twill not be.

LADY TOWNLEY: His gloves are well fringed, large and graceful.

SIR FOPLING: I was always eminent for being *bien ganté*.[21]

EMILIA: He wears nothing but what are originals of the most famous hands in Paris.

SIR FOPLING: You are in the right, Madam.

LADY TOWNLEY: The suit!

SIR FOPLING: Barroy.[22]

EMILIA: The garniture![23]

SIR FOPLING: Le Gras.

MEDLEY: The shoes!

SIR FOPLING: Piccar.

DORIMANT: The periwig!

SIR FOPLING: Chedreux.

LADY TOWNLEY: } The gloves!
EMILIA:

SIR FOPLING: Orangerie[24] — you know the smell, ladies. —— Dorimant, I could find in my heart for an amusement to have a gallantry with some of our English ladies.

DORIMANT: 'Tis a thing no less necessary to confirm the reputation of your wit than a duel will be to satisfy the town of your courage.

SIR FOPLING: Here was a woman yesterday ——

DORIMANT: Mistress Loveit.

SIR FOPLING: You have named her.

DORIMANT: You cannot pitch on a better for your purpose.

SIR FOPLING: Prithee, what is she?

DORIMANT: A person of quality, and one who has a rest of reputation enough to make the conquest considerable; besides, I hear she likes you too.

SIR FOPLING: Methoughts she seemed, though, very reserved and uneasy all the time I entertained her.

DORIMANT: Grimace and affectation! You will see her i'th' Mail to-night.

SIR FOPLING: Prithee, let thee and I take the air together.

DORIMANT: I am engaged to Medley, but I'll meet you at St. James's and give you some information upon the which you may regulate your proceedings.

SIR FOPLING: All the world will be in the Park to-night. Ladies, 'twere pity to keep so

---

[20] trousers
[21] (Fr.) well-gloved
[22] (Barroy, Le Gras, Piccar, and Chedreux were the proprietors of fashionable shops in Paris)
[23] ornament
[24] (Fr.) "Orange House" (perhaps the name of a perfume shop)

much beauty longer within doors and rob the Ring[25] of all those charms that should adorn it. —— Hey, Page!

(*Enter* PAGE.)

See that all my people be ready.   (PAGE *goes out again*.)
— Dorimant, *au revoir*.   (*Exit*.)

MEDLEY: A fine mettled coxcomb.

DORIMANT: Brisk and insipid.

MEDLEY: Pert and dull.

EMILIA: However you despise him, gentlemen, I'll lay my life he passes for a wit with many.

DORIMANT: That may very well be; Nature has her cheats, stums[26] a brain, and puts sophisticate[27] dulness often on the tasteless multitude for true wit and good humour. Medley, come!

MEDLEY: I must go a little way; I will meet you i'the Mail.

DORIMANT: I'll walk through the garden thither. — (*To the women*.) We shall meet anon and bow.

LADY TOWNLEY: Not to-night. We are engaged about a business the knowledge of which may make you laugh hereafter.

MEDLEY: Your servant, ladies.

DORIMANT: *Au revoir*, as Sir Fopling says.   (*Exeunt* MEDLEY *and* DORIMANT.)

LADY TOWNLEY: The old man will be here immediately.

EMILIA: Let's expect[28] him i'th' garden.

LADY TOWNLEY: Go! you are a rogue.

EMILIA: I can't abide you.   (*Exeunt*.)

SCENE 3

Scene: The Mail.

Enter HARRIET *and* YOUNG BELLAIR, *she pulling him*.

HARRIET: Come along.

YOUNG BELLAIR: And leave your mother!

HARRIET: Busy will be sent with a hue and cry after us, but that's no matter.

YOUNG BELLAIR: 'Twill look strangely in me.

HARRIET: She'll believe it a freak of mine and never blame your manners.

YOUNG BELLAIR: What reverend acquaintance is that she has met?

HARRIET: A fellow-beauty of the last king's time,[1] though by the ruins you would hardly guess it.   (*Exeunt*.)

(*Enter* DORIMANT *and crosses the stage*.
Enter YOUNG BELLAIR *and* HARRIET.)

YOUNG BELLAIR: By this time your mother is in a fine taking.

---

[25] (cf. note 12, Scene 1 in this act)
[26] re-ferments (as with wine that has grown vapid)
[27] adulterated, artificial
[28] wait for
[1] i.e., the reign of Charles I (1625–49)

HARRIET: If your friend Mr. Dorimant were but here now, that she might find me talking with him!

YOUNG BELLAIR: She does not know him, but dreads him, I hear, of all mankind.

HARRIET: She concludes if he does but speak to a woman, she's undone — is on her knees every day to pray heaven defend me from him.

YOUNG BELLAIR: You do not apprehend him so much as she does?

HARRIET: I never saw anything in him that was frightful.

YOUNG BELLAIR: On the contrary, have you not observed something extreme delightful in his wit and person?

HARRIET: He's agreeable and pleasant, I must own, but he does so much affect being so, he displeases me.

YOUNG BELLAIR: Lord, Madam! all he does and says is so easy and so natural.

HARRIET: Some men's verses seem so to the unskillful, but labour i'the one and affectation in the other to the judicious plainly appear.

YOUNG BELLAIR: I never heard him accused of affectation before.

(*Enter* DORIMANT *and stares upon her.*)

HARRIET: It passes on the easy town, who are favourably pleased in him to call it humour.   (*Exeunt* YOUNG BELLAIR *and* HARRIET.)

DORIMANT: 'Tis she! it must be she — that lovely hair, that easy shape, those wanton eyes, and all those melting charms about her mouth which Medley spoke of! I'll follow the lottery and put in for a prize with my friend Bellair.

(*Exeunt* DORIMANT *repeating:*)

In love the victors from the vanquish'd fly;
They fly that wound, and they pursue that die.

(*Enter* YOUNG BELLAIR *and* HARRIET *and after them* DORIMANT *standing at a distance.*)

YOUNG BELLAIR: Most people prefer High Park[2] to this place.

HARRIET: It has the better reputation, I confess; but I abominate the dull diversions there — the formal bows, the affected smiles, the silly bywords and amorous tweers[3] in passing. Here one meets with a little conversation now and then.

YOUNG BELLAIR: These conversations have been fatal to some of your sex, Madam.

HARRIET: It may be so; because some who want temper[4] have been undone by gaming, must others who have it wholly deny themselves the pleasure of play?

DORIMANT (*coming up gently and bowing to her*): Trust me, it were unreasonable, Madam.

HARRIET: (*She starts and looks grave.*) Lord, who's this?

YOUNG BELLAIR: Dorimant!

DORIMANT: Is this the woman your father would have you marry?

YOUNG BELLAIR: It is.

DORIMANT: Her name?

YOUNG BELLAIR: Harriet.

DORIMANT: I am not mistaken; she's handsome.

[2] Hyde Park   [4] lack self-control
[3] leers

YOUNG BELLAIR: Talk to her; her wit is better than her face. We were wishing for you but now.

DORIMANT (*to* HARRIET): Overcast with seriousness o'the sudden! A thousand smiles were shining in that face but now; I never saw so quick a change of weather.

HARRIET (*aside*): I feel as great a change within, but he shall never know it.

DORIMANT: You were talking of play, Madam. Pray, what may be your stint?[5]

HARRIET: A little harmless discourse in public walks, or at most an appointment in a box, barefaced,[6] at the playhouse: you are for masks and private meetings, where women engage for all they are worth, I hear.

DORIMANT: I have been used to deep play, but I can make one at small game when I like my gamester well.

HARRIET: And be so unconcerned you'll ha' no pleasure in't.

DORIMANT: Where there is a considerable sum to be won, the hope of drawing people in makes every trifle considerable.

HARRIET: The sordidness of men's natures, I know, makes 'em willing to flatter and comply with the rich, though they are sure never to be the better for 'em.

DORIMANT: 'Tis in their power to do us good, and we despair not but at some time or other they may be willing.

HARRIET: To men who have fared in this town like you, 'twould be a great mortification to live on hope. Could you keep a Lent for a mistress?

DORIMANT: In expectation of a happy Easter and, though time be very precious, think forty days well lost to gain your favour.

HARRIET: Mr. Bellair, let us walk; 'tis time to leave him. Men grow dull when they begin to be particular.

DORIMANT: Y'are mistaken; flattery will not ensue, though I know y'are greedy of the praises of the whole Mail.

HARRIET: You do me wrong.

DORIMANT: I do not. As I followed you, I observed how you were pleased when the fops cried, "She's handsome, very handsome! by God she is!" and whispered aloud your name; the thousand several forms[7] you put your face into; then, to make yourself more agreeable, how wantonly you played with your head, flung back your locks, and looked smilingly over your shoulder at 'em!

HARRIET: I do not go begging the men's, as you do the ladies', good liking, with a sly softness in your looks and a gentle slowness in your bows as you pass by 'em — as thus, Sir. (*Acts him.*) Is not this like you?

(*Enter* LADY WOODVILL *and* BUSY.)

YOUNG BELLAIR: Your mother, Madam. (*Pulls* HARRIET; *she composes herself.*)

LADY WOODVILL: Ah, my dear child Harriet!

BUSY: Now is she so pleased with finding her again she cannot chide her.

LADY WOODVILL: Come away!

DORIMANT: 'Tis now but high Mail,[8] Madam, the most entertaining time of all the evening.

HARRIET: I would fain see that Dorimant, Mother, you so cry out of for a monster; he's in the Mail, I hear.

LADY WOODVILL: Come away then! The plague is here and you should dread the infection.

[5] limit
[6] i.e., without a mask
[7] expressions
[8] the most popular hour in the Mall

YOUNG BELLAIR: You may be misinformed of the gentleman.

LADY WOODVILL: Oh, no! I hope you do not know him. He is the prince of all the devils in the town — delights in nothing but in rapes and riots!

DORIMANT: If you did but hear him speak, Madam!

LADY WOODVILL: Oh, he has a tongue, they say, would tempt the angels to a second fall.

(*Enter* SIR FOPLING *with his equipage, six* FOOTMEN *and a* PAGE.)

SIR FOPLING: Hey! Champagne, Norman, La Rose, La Fleur, La Tour, La Verdure!
—— Dorimant ——

LADY WOODVILL: Here, here he is among this rout! He names him! Come away, Harriet; come away!   (*Exeunt* LADY WOODVILL, HARRIET,
                                                                                        BUSY, *and* YOUNG BELLAIR.)

DORIMANT: This fool's coming has spoiled all. She's gone, but she has left a pleasing image of herself behind that wanders in my soul — it must not settle there.

SIR FOPLING: What reverie is this? Speak, man!

DORIMANT:

> Snatcht from myself, how far behind
> Already I behold the shore!

(*Enter* MEDLEY.)

MEDLEY: Dorimant, a discovery! I met with Bellair.

DORIMANT: You can tell me no news, Sir; I know all.

MEDLEY: How do you like the daughter?

DORIMANT: You never came so near truth in your life as you did in her description.

MEDLEY: What think you of the mother?

DORIMANT: Whatever I think of her, she thinks very well of me, I find.

MEDLEY: Did she know you?

DORIMANT: She did not; whether she does now or no, I know not. Here was a pleasant scene towards,[9] when in came Sir Fopling, mustering up his equipage, and at the latter end named me and frighted her away.

MEDLEY: Loveit and Bellinda are not far off; I saw 'em alight at St. James's.

DORIMANT: Sir Fopling! Hark you, a word or two. (*Whispers.*) Look you do not want assurance.[10]

SIR FOPLING: I never do on these occasions.

DORIMANT: Walk on; we must not be seen together. Make your advantage of what I have told you. The next turn you will meet the lady.

SIR FOPLING: Hey! Follow me all!   (*Exeunt* SIR FOPLING *and his equipage.*)

DORIMANT: Medley, you shall see good sport anon between Loveit and this Fopling.

MEDLEY: I thought there was something toward, by that whisper.

DORIMANT: You know a worthy principle of hers?

MEDLEY: Not to be so much as civil to a man who speaks to her in the presence of him she professes to love.

DORIMANT: I have encouraged Fopling to talk to her to-night.

MEDLEY: Now you are here, she will go nigh to beat him.

DORIMANT: In the humour she's in, her love will make her do some very extravagant thing doubtless.

---

[9] in progress   [10] an air of confidence

MEDLEY: What was Bellinda's business with you at my Lady Townley's?

DORIMANT: To get me to meet Loveit here in order to an *éclaircissement*.[11] I made some difficulty of it and have prepared this encounter to make good my jealousy.

MEDLEY: Here they come.

(*Enter* MRS. LOVEIT, BELLINDA, *and* PERT.)

DORIMANT: I'll meet her and provoke her with a deal of dumb civility in passing by, then turn short and be behind her when Sir Fopling sets upon her ——

> See how unregarded now
> That piece of beauty passes.[12]

(*Exeunt* DORIMANT and MEDLEY.)

BELLINDA: How wonderful respectfully he bowed!

PERT: He's always over-mannerly when he has done a mischief.

BELLINDA: Methoughts, indeed, at the same time he had a strange, despising countenance.

PERT: The unlucky[13] look he thinks becomes him.

BELLINDA: I was afraid you would have spoke to him, my dear.

MRS. LOVEIT: I would have died first; he shall no more find me the loving fool he has done.

BELLINDA: You love him still?

MRS. LOVEIT: No!

PERT: I wish you did not.

MRS. LOVEIT: I do not, and I will have you think so. — What made you hale me to this odious place, Bellinda?

BELLINDA: I hate to be hulched up[14] in a coach; walking is much better.

MRS. LOVEIT: Would we could meet Sir Fopling now!

BELLINDA: Lord, would you not avoid him?

MRS. LOVEIT: I would make him all the advances that may be.

BELLINDA: That would confirm Dorimant's suspicion, my dear.

MRS. LOVEIT: He is not jealous; but I will make him so, and be revenged a way he little thinks on.

BELLINDA (*aside*): If she should make him jealous, that may make him fond of her again. I must dissuade her from it. —— Lord, my dear, this will certainly make him hate you.

MRS. LOVEIT: 'Twill make him uneasy, though he does not care for me. I know the effects of jealousy on men of his proud temper.

BELLINDA: 'Tis a fantastic remedy; its operations are dangerous and uncertain.

MRS. LOVEIT: 'Tis the strongest cordial we can give to dying love: it often brings it back when there's no sign of life remaining. But I design not so much the reviving of his, as my revenge.

(*Enter* SIR FOPLING *and his equipage*.)

---

[11] (Fr.) clarification
[12] (opening lines of Sonnet I by Sir John Suckling [1609–42], like Waller a Cavalier poet)
[13] mischievous
[14] hunched up

SIR FOPLING: Hey! Bid the coachman send home four of his horses and bring the coach to Whitehall; I'll walk over the Park. —— Madam, the honour of kissing your fair hands is a happiness I missed this afternoon at my Lady Townley's.

MRS. LOVEIT: You were very obliging, Sir Fopling, the last time I saw you there.

SIR FOPLING: The preference was due to your wit and beauty. —— Madam, your servant; there never was so sweet an evening.

BELLINDA: 'T has drawn all the rabble of the town hither.

SIR FOPLING: 'Tis pity there's not an order made that none but the *beau monde*[15] should walk here.

MRS. LOVEIT: 'Twould add much to the beauty of the place. See what a sort of nasty fellows are coming!

(*Enter four ill-fashioned* FELLOWS, *singing:*)

'Tis not for kisses alone,[16] etc.

MRS. LOVEIT: Fo! Their periwigs are scented with tobacco so strong ——

SIR FOPLING: It overcomes our pulvillio.[17] Methinks I smell the coffee-house they come from.

1 MAN: Dorimant's convenient,[18] Madam Loveit.

2 MAN: I like the oily buttock[19] with her.

3 MAN: What spruce prig[20] is that?

1 MAN: A caravan[21] lately come from Paris.

2 MAN: Peace! they smoke.[22]   (*All of them coughing; exeunt singing:*)

There's something else to be done,[23] etc.

(*Enter* DORIMANT *and* MEDLEY.)

DORIMANT: They're engaged.

MEDLEY: She entertains him as if she liked him!

DORIMANT: Let us go forward — seem earnest in discourse and show ourselves; then you shall see how she'll use him.

BELLINDA: Yonder's Dorimant, my dear.

MRS. LOVEIT (*aside*): I see him. He comes insulting, but I will disappoint him in his expectation. (*To* SIR FOPLING.) I like this pretty, nice humour of yours, Sir Fopling. —— With what a loathing eye he looked upon those fellows!

SIR FOPLING: I sat near one of 'em at a play to-day and was almost poisoned with a pair of cordovan[24] gloves he wears.

MRS. LOVEIT: Oh, filthy cordovan! How I hate the smell! (*Laughs in a loud, affected way.*)

SIR FOPLING: Did you observe, Madam, how their cravats hung loose an inch from their neck and what a frightful air it gave 'em?

MRS. LOVEIT: Oh, I took particular notice of one that is always spruced up with a deal of dirty sky-coloured ribband.

BELLINDA: That's one of the walking flageolets[25] who haunt the Mail o'nights.

[15] (Fr.) the fashionable world, society
[16] (the first line of an anonymous bawdy song)
[17] scented powder
[18] i.e., mistress
[19] "lush lay"
[20] fop
[21] traveling company
[22] observe, take notice of (us)
[23] (another line from the same song)
[24] horse leather from Cordova, Spain
[25] small wind instrument

MRS. LOVEIT: Oh, I remember him; h'has a hollow tooth enough to spoil the sweetness of an evening.

SIR FOPLING: I have seen the tallest walk the streets with a dainty pair of boxes[26] neatly buckled on.

MRS. LOVEIT: And a little foot-boy at his heels, pocket-high, with a flat cap, a dirty face ——

SIR FOPLING: And a snotty nose.

MRS. LOVEIT: Oh, odious! — There's many of my own sex with that Holborn equipage trig to Gray's Inn Walks and now and then travel hither on a Sunday.

MEDLEY: She takes no notice of you.

DORIMANT: Damn her! I am jealous of a counterplot.

MRS. LOVEIT: Your liveries are the finest, Sir Fopling — oh, that page! that page is the prettily'st dressed — they are all Frenchmen.

SIR FOPLING: There's one damned English blockhead among 'em; you may know him by his mien.

MRS. LOVEIT: Oh, that's he — that's he! What do you call him?

SIR FOPLING: Hey — I know not what to call him ——

MRS. LOVEIT: What's your name?

FOOTMAN: John Trott, Madam.

SIR FOPLING: Oh, unsufferable! Trott, Trott, Trott! There's nothing so barbarous as the names of our English servants. —— What countryman are you, Sirrah?

FOOTMAN: Hampshire, Sir.

SIR FOPLING: Then Hampshire be your name. Hey, Hampshire!

MRS. LOVEIT: Oh, that sound — that sound becomes the mouth of a man of quality!

MEDLEY: Dorimant, you look a little bashful on the matter.

DORIMANT: She dissembles better than I thought she could have done.

MEDLEY: You have tempted her with too luscious a bait. She bites at the coxcomb.

DORIMANT: She cannot fall from loving me to that.

MEDLEY: You begin to be jealous in earnest.

DORIMANT: Of one I do not love ——

MEDLEY: You did love her.

DORIMANT: The fit has long been over.

MEDLEY: But I have known men fall into dangerous relapses when they have found a woman inclining to another.

DORIMANT (*to himself*): He guesses the secret of my heart. I am concerned, but dare not show it, lest Bellinda should mistrust all I have done to gain her.

BELLINDA (*aside*): I have watched his look and find no alteration there. Did he love her, some signs of jealousy would have appeared.

DORIMANT: I hope this happy evening, Madam, has reconciled you to the scandalous Mail. We shall have you now hankering[27] here again ——

MRS. LOVEIT: Sir Fopling, will you walk?

SIR FOPLING: I am all obedience, Madam.

MRS. LOVEIT: Come along then, and let's agree to be malicious on all the ill-fashioned things we meet.

SIR FOPLING: We'll make a critique on the whole Mail, Madam

MRS. LOVEIT: Bellinda, you shall engage[28] ——

BELLINDA: To the reserve of[29] our friends, my dear.

---

[26] wooden shoes
[27] hanging about expectantly and longingly
[28] i.e., be one of us, participate
[29] excluding

MRS. LOVEIT: No! no exceptions!

SIR FOPLING: We'll sacrifice all to our diversion.

MRS. LOVEIT: All — all.

SIR FOPLING: All.

BELLINDA: All? Then let it be.   (*Exeunt* SIR FOPLING, MRS. LOVEIT,
                                    BELLINDA, *and* PERT, *laughing*.)

MEDLEY: Would you had brought some more of your friends, Dorimant, to have been witnesses of Sir Fopling's disgrace and your triumph.

DORIMANT: 'Twere unreasonable to desire you not to laugh at me; but pray do not expose me to the town this day or two.

MEDLEY: By that time you hope to have regained your credit.

DORIMANT: I know she hates Fopling and only makes use of him in hope to work me on again; had it not been for some powerful considerations which will be removed to-morrow morning, I had made her pluck off this mask and show the passion that lies panting under.

(*Enter a* FOOTMAN.)

MEDLEY: Here comes a man from Bellair with news of your last adventure.

DORIMANT: I am glad he sent him; I long to know the consequence of our parting.

FOOTMAN: Sir, my master desires you to come to my Lady Townley's presently and bring Mr. Medley with you. My Lady Woodvill and her daughter are there.

MEDLEY: Then all's well, Dorimant.

FOOTMAN: They have sent for the fiddles and mean to dance. He bid me tell you, Sir, the old lady does not know you, and would have you own yourself to be Mr. Courtage. They are all prepared to receive you by that name.

DORIMANT: That foppish admirer of quality, who flatters the very meat at honourable tables and never offers love to a woman below a lady-grandmother.

MEDLEY: You know the character you are to act, I see.

DORIMANT: This is Harriet's contrivance — wild, witty, lovesome, beautiful, and young! —— Come along, Medley.

MEDLEY: This new woman would well supply the loss of Loveit.

DORIMANT: That business must not end so; before to-morrow sun is set I will revenge and clear it.

> And you and Loveit, to her cost, shall find,
> I fathom all the depths of womankind.   (*Exeunt*.)

ACT IV

SCENE 1

The Scene opens with the Fiddles playing a Country Dance.

Enter DORIMANT *and* LADY WOODVILL, YOUNG BELLAIR *and* MRS. HARRIET, OLD BELLAIR *and* EMILIA, MR. MEDLEY *and* LADY TOWNLEY, *as having just ended the Dance.*

OLD BELLAIR: So, so, so! — a smart bout, a very smart bout, a dod!

LADY TOWNLEY: How do you like Emilia's dancing, Brother?

OLD BELLAIR: Not at all — not at all!

LADY TOWNLEY: You speak not what you think, I am sure.

OLD BELLAIR: No matter for that; go, bid her dance no more. It don't become her — it don't become her. Tell her I say so. (*Aside.*) A dod, I love her!

DORIMANT (*to* LADY WOODVILL): All people mingle nowadays, Madam. And in public places women of quality have the least respect showed 'em.

LADY WOODVILL: I protest you say the truth, Mr. Courtage.

DORIMANT: Forms and ceremonies, the only things that uphold quality and greatness, are now shamefully laid aside and neglected.

LADY WOODVILL: Well, this is not the women's age, let 'em think what they will. Lewdness is the business now; love was the business in my time.

DORIMANT: The women, indeed, are little beholding to the young men of this age; they're generally only dull admirers of themselves, and make their court to nothing but their periwigs and their cravats, and would be more concerned for the disordering of 'em, though on a good occasion, than a young maid would be for the tumbling of her head or handkercher.[1]

LADY WOODVILL: I protest you hit 'em.

DORIMANT: They are very assiduous to show themselves at court, well dressed, to the women of quality, but their business is with the stale mistresses of the town, who are prepared to receive their lazy addresses by industrious old lovers who have cast 'em off and made 'em easy.

HARRIET: He fits my mother's humour so well, a little more and she'll dance a kissing dance with him anon.

MEDLEY: Dutifully observed, Madam.

DORIMANT: They pretend to be great critics in beauty. By their talk you would think they liked no face, and yet can dote on an ill one if it belong to a laundress or a tailor's daughter. They cry, "A woman's past her prime at twenty, decayed at four-and-twenty, old and unsufferable at thirty."

LADY WOODVILL: Unsufferable at thirty! That they are in the wrong, Mr. Courtage, at five-and-thirty, there are living proofs enough to convince 'em.

DORIMANT: Ay, Madam. There's Mrs. Setlooks, Mrs. Droplip, and my Lady Lowd; show me among all our opening buds a face that promises so much beauty as the remains of theirs.

LADY WOODVILL: The depraved appetite of this vicious age tastes nothing but green fruit, and loathes it when 'tis kindly[2] ripened.

DORIMANT: Else so many deserving women, Madam, would not be so untimely neglected.

LADY WOODVILL: I protest, Mr. Courtage, a dozen such good men as you would be enough to atone for that wicked Dorimant and all the under debauchees of the town.

(HARRIET, EMILIA, YOUNG BELLAIR, MEDLEY, LADY TOWNLEY *break out into a laughter.*)

—— What's the matter there?

MEDLEY: A pleasant mistake, Madam, that a lady has made, occasions a little laughter.

OLD BELLAIR: Come, come, you keep 'em idle! They are impatient till the fiddles play again.

---

[1] a small scarf worn around the neck   [2] naturally, seasonably

DORIMANT: You are not weary, Madam?

LADY WOODVILL: One dance more; I cannot refuse you, Mr. Courtage.

(*They dance. After the dance*, OLD BELLAIR, *singing and dancing up to* EMILIA.)

EMILIA: You are very active, Sir.

OLD BELLAIR: A dod, Sirrah! when I was a young fellow I could ha' capered up to my woman's gorget.[3]

DORIMANT: You are willing to rest yourself, Madam ——

LADY TOWNLEY: We'll walk into my chamber and sit down.

MEDLEY: Leave us Mr. Courtage; he's a dancer, and the young ladies are not weary yet.

LADY WOODVILL: We'll send him out again.

HARRIET: If you do not quickly, I know where to send for Mr. Dorimant.

LADY WOODVILL: This girl's head, Mr. Courtage, is ever running on that wild fellow.

DORIMANT: 'Tis well you have got her a good husband, Madam; that will settle it.   (*Exeunt* LADY TOWNLEY, LADY WOODVILL, *and* DORIMANT.)

OLD BELLAIR (*to* EMILIA): A dod, sweetheart, be advised and do not throw thyself away on a young, idle fellow.

EMILIA: I have no such intention, Sir.

OLD BELLAIR: Have a little patience! Thou shalt have the man I spake of. A dod, he loves thee and will make a good husband — but no words!

EMILIA: But, Sir ——

OLD BELLAIR: No answer — out a pise! peace! and think on't.

(*Enter* DORIMANT.)

DORIMANT: Your company is desired within, Sir.

OLD BELLAIR: I go, I go! Good Mr. Courtage, fare you well! — (*To* EMILIA.) Go, I'll see you no more!

EMILIA: What have I done, Sir?

OLD BELLAIR: You are ugly, you are ugly! — Is she not, Mr. Courtage?

EMILIA: Better words or I shan't abide you.

OLD BELLAIR: Out a pise; a dod, what does she say? Hit her a pat for me there.   (*Exit* OLD BELLAIR.)

MEDLEY: You have charms for the whole family.

DORIMANT: You'll spoil all with some unseasonable jest, Medley.

MEDLEY: You see I confine my tongue and am content to be a bare spectator, much contrary to my nature.

EMILIA: Methinks, Mr. Dorimant, my Lady Woodvill is a little fond of you.

DORIMANT: Would her daughter were!

MEDLEY: It may be you may find her so. Try her — you have an opportunity.

DORIMANT: And I will not lose it. —— Bellair, here's a lady has something to say to you.

YOUNG BELLAIR: I wait upon her. —— Mr. Medley, we have both business with you.

DORIMANT: Get you together then. (*To* HARRIET.) That demure curtsey is not amiss in jest, but do not think in earnest it becomes you.

---

[3] a woman's ornamental collar or neckpiece

HARRIET: Affectation is catching, I find; from your grave bow I got it.

DORIMANT: Where had you all that scorn and coldness in your look?

HARRIET: From nature, Sir; pardon my want of art. I have not learnt those soft-nesses and languishings which now in faces are so much in fashion.

DORIMANT: You need 'em not; you have a sweetness of your own, if you would but calm your frowns and let it settle.

HARRIET: My eyes are wild and wandering like my passions, and cannot yet be tied to rules of charming.

DORIMANT: Women, indeed, have commonly a method of managing those messen-gers of love. Now they will look as if they would kill, and anon they will look as if they were dying. They point and rebate[4] their glances, the better to invite us.

HARRIET: I like this variety well enough, but hate the set face that always looks as it would say, "Come love me!" — a woman who at plays makes the *doux yeux*[5] to a whole audience and at home cannot forbear 'em to her monkey.

DORIMANT: Put on a gentle smile and let me see how well it will become you.

HARRIET: I am sorry my face does not please you as it is, but I shall not be complai-sant and change it.

DORIMANT: Though you are obstinate, I know 'tis capable of improvement, and shall do you justice, Madam, if I chance to be at Court when the critics of the Circle pass their judgment; for thither you must come.

HARRIET: And expect to be taken in pieces, have all my features examined, every motion censured, and on the whole be condemned to be but pretty, or a beauty of the lowest rate. What think you?

DORIMANT: The women — nay, the very lovers who belong to the drawing-room — will maliciously allow you more than that: they always grant what is apparent, that they may the better be believed when they name concealed faults they can-not easily be disproved in.

HARRIET: Beauty runs as great a risk exposed at Court as wit does on the stage, where the ugly and the foolish all are free to censure.

DORIMANT (*aside*): I love her and dare not let her know it; I fear sh'as an ascendant o'er me and may revenge the wrongs I have done her sex. (*To her.*) Think of making a party,[6] Madam; love will engage.

HARRIET: You make me start! I did not think to have heard of love from you.

DORIMANT: I never knew what 'twas to have a settled ague[7] yet, but now and then have had irregular fits.

HARRIET: Take heed! sickness after long health is commonly more violent and dan-gerous.

DORIMANT (*aside*): I have took the infection from her, and feel the disease now spreading in me. (*To her.*) Is the name of love so frightful that you dare not stand it?

HARRIET: 'Twill do little execution out of your mouth on me, I am sure.

DORIMANT: It has been fatal ——

HARRIET: To some easy women, but we are not all born to one destiny. I was in-formed you use to laugh at love and not make it.

DORIMANT: The time has been, but now I must speak ——

---

[4] blunt
[5] (Fr.) soft eyes

[6] joining the social circle
[7] fever

HARRIET: If it be on that idle subject, I will put on my serious look, turn my head carelessly from you, drop my lip, let my eyelids fall and hang half o'er my eyes — thus — while you buzz a speech of an hour long in my ear, and I answer never a word. Why do you not begin?

DORIMANT: That the company may take notice how passionately I make advances of love, and how disdainfully you receive 'em!

HARRIET: When your love's grown strong enough to make you bear being laughed at, I'll give you leave to trouble me with it. Till when pray forbear, Sir.

(*Enter* SIR FOPLING *and others in masks*.)

DORIMANT: What's here — masquerades?

HARRIET: I thought that foppery had been left off, and people might have been in private with a fiddle.

DORIMANT: 'Tis endeavoured to be kept on foot still by some who find themselves the more acceptable the less they are known.

YOUNG BELLAIR: This must be Sir Fopling.

MEDLEY: That extraordinary habit shows it.

YOUNG BELLAIR: What are the rest?

MEDLEY: A company of French rascals whom he picked up in Paris and has brought over to be his dancing equipage on these occasions. Make him own himself; a fool is very troublesome when he presumes he is incognito.

SIR FOPLING (*to* HARRIET): Do you know me?

HARRIET: Ten to one but I guess at you?

SIR FOPLING: Are you women as fond of a vizard as we men are?

HARRIET: I am very fond of a vizard that covers a face I do not like, Sir.

YOUNG BELLAIR: Here are no masks, you see, Sir, but those which came with you. This was intended a private meeting; but because you look like a gentleman, if you will discover yourself and we know you to be such, you shall be welcome.

SIR FOPLING (*pulling off his mask*): Dear Bellair!

MEDLEY: Sir Fopling! How came you hither?

SIR FOPLING: Faith, as I was coming late from Whitehall, after the King's *couchée*,[8] one of my people told me he had heard fiddles at my Lady Townley's, and ——

DORIMANT: You need not say any more, Sir.

SIR FOPLING: Dorimant, let me kiss thee.

DORIMANT: Hark you, Sir Fopling —— (*Whispers.*)

SIR FOPLING: Enough, enough, Courtage. —— A pretty kind of young woman that, Medley. I observed her in the Mail — more *éveillée*[9] than our English women commonly are. Prithee, what is she?

MEDLEY: The most noted coquette in town. Beware of her.

SIR FOPLING: Let her be what she will, I know how to take my measures. In Paris the mode is to flatter the *prude*, laugh at the *faux-prude*,[10] make serious love to the *demi-prude*,[11] and only rally with the *coquette*.[12] Medley, what think you?

MEDLEY: That for all this smattering of the mathematics, you may be out in your judgment at tennis.

---

[8] (Fr.) evening reception
[9] (Fr.) lively
[10] (Fr.) sham-prude

[11] (Fr.) half-prude
[12] (Fr.) flirt

SIR FOPLING: What a *coq-à-l'âne*[13] is this? I talk of women and thou answer'st tennis.

MEDLEY: Mistakes will be for want of apprehension.

SIR FOPLING: I am very glad of the acquaintance I have with this family.

MEDLEY: My lady truly is a good woman.

SIR FOPLING: Ah, Dorimant — Courtage, I would say — would thou hadst spent the last winter in Paris with me! When thou wert there, La Corneus and Sallyes were the only habitudes[14] we had: a comedian would have been a *bonne fortune*.[15] No stranger ever passed his time so well as I did some months before I came over. I was well received in a dozen families where all the women of quality used to visit; I have intrigues to tell thee more pleasant than ever thou read'st in a novel.

HARRIET: Write 'em, Sir, and oblige us women. Our language wants such little stories.

SIR FOPLING: Writing, Madam, 's a mechanic part of wit. A gentleman should never go beyond a song or a *billet*.

HARRIET: Bussy was a gentleman.

SIR FOPLING: Who, d'Ambois?[16]

MEDLEY: Was there ever such a brisk blockhead?

HARRIET: Not d'Ambois, Sir, but Rabutin[17] — he who writ the loves of France.

SIR FOPLING: That may be, Madam; many gentlemen do things that are below 'em. Damn your authors, Courtage; women are the prettiest things we can fool away our time with.

HARRIET: I hope ye have wearied yourself to-night at Court, Sir, and will not think of fooling with anybody here.

SIR FOPLING: I cannot complain of my fortune there, Madam. —— Dorimant ——

DORIMANT: Again!

SIR FOPLING: Courtage — a pox on't! — I have something to tell thee. When I had made my court within, I came out and flung myself upon the mat under the state[18] i'th' outward room, i'th' midst of half a dozen beauties who were withdrawn to jeer among themselves, as they called it.

DORIMANT: Did you know 'em?

SIR FOPLING: Not one of 'em, by heavens! — not I. But they were all your friends.

DORIMANT: How are you sure of that?

SIR FOPLING: Why, we laughed at all the town — spared nobody but yourself. They found me a man for their purpose.

DORIMANT: I know you are malicious, to your power.[19]

SIR FOPLING: And faith, I had occasion to show it, for I never saw more gaping fools at a ball or on a birthday.

DORIMANT: You learned who the women were?

SIR FOPLING: No matter; they frequent the drawing-room.[20]

DORIMANT: And entertain themselves pleasantly at the expense of all the fops who come there.

SIR FOPLING: That's their business. Faith, I sifted 'em,[21] and find they have a sort of wit among them. —— Ah, filthy! (*Pinches a tallow candle.*)

---

[13] (Fr. "from rooster to donkey") string of nonsense

[14] familiar relations

[15] (Fr.) piece of good luck

[16] Bussy d'Ambois, the title hero of a play by George Chapman (1607)

[17] Roger de Rabutin (1618–93), Comte de Bussy, wrote the *Histoire Amoreuse des Gaules*

[18] canopy

[19] as malicious as you know how to be

[20] i.e., court assembly

[21] tried them out

DORIMANT: Look, he has been pinching the tallow candle.

SIR FOPLING: How can you breathe in a room where there's grease frying? —— Dorimant, thou art intimate with my lady; advise her, for her own sake and the good company that comes hither, to burn wax lights.

HARRIET: What are these masquerades who stand so obsequiously at a distance?

SIR FOPLING: A set of balladines whom I picked out of the best in France and brought over with a *flûte-douce* or two — my servants. They shall entertain you.

HARRIET: I had rather see you dance yourself, Sir Fopling.

SIR FOPLING: And I had rather do it — all the company knows it — but, Madam ——

MEDLEY: Come, come, no excuses, Sir Fopling!

SIR FOPLING: By heavens, Medley ——

MEDLEY: Like a woman I find you must be struggled with before one brings you to what you desire.

HARRIET (*aside*): Can he dance?

EMILIA: And fence and sing too, if you'll believe him.

DORIMANT: He has no more excellence in his heels than in his head. He went to Paris a plain, bashful English blockhead, and is returned a fine undertaking[22] French fop.

MEDLEY: I cannot prevail.

SIR FOPLING: Do not think it want of complaisance, Madam.

HARRIET: You are too well bred to want that, Sir Fopling. I believe it want of power.

SIR FOPLING: By heavens, and so it is! I have sat up so damned late and drunk so cursed hard since I came to this lewd town, that I am fit for nothing but low dancing now — a *courante*, a *bourrée*, or a *menuet*.[23] But St. André tells me, if I will but be regular, in one month I shall rise again. Pox on this debauchery! (*Endeavours at a caper.*)

EMILIA: I have heard your dancing much commended.

SIR FOPLING: It had the good fortune to please in Paris. I was judged to rise within an inch as high as the Basque in an entry I danced there.

HARRIET: I am mightily taken with this fool; let us sit. —— Here's a seat, Sir Fopling.

SIR FOPLING: At your feet, Madam; I can be nowhere so much at ease. —— By your leave, gown.

HARRIET: }
EMILIA: } Ah, you'll spoil it!

SIR FOPLING: No matter; my clothes are my creatures. I make 'em to make my court to you ladies. —— Hey! *Qu'on commence!*[24] (*Dance.*) —— To an English dancer, English motions. I was forced to entertain[25] this fellow, one of my set miscarrying.[26] —— Oh, horrid! Leave your damned manner of dancing and put on the French air: have you not a pattern before you? —— Pretty well! imitation in time may bring him to something.

(*After the dance, enter* OLD BELLAIR, LADY WOODVILL, *and* LADY TOWNLEY.)

OLD BELLAIR: Hey, a dod, what have we here — a mumming?[27]

---

[22] enterprising
[23] (all "low" dances because they are slow and stately)
[24] (Fr.) begin!
[25] employ
[26] having an accident
[27] costumed play-acting

LADY WOODVILL: Where's my daughter? Harriet!

DORIMANT: Here, here, Madam! I know not but under these disguises there may be dangerous sparks; I gave the young lady warning.

LADY WOODVILL: Lord! I am so obliged to you, Mr. Courtage.

HARRIET: Lord, how you admire this man!

LADY WOODVILL: What have you to except against him?

HARRIET: He's a fop.

LADY WOODVILL: He's not a Dorimant, a wild extravagant fellow of the times.

HARRIET: He's a man made up of forms and commonplaces sucked out of the remaining lees of the last age.

LADY WOODVILL: He's so good a man that, were you not engaged ——

LADY TOWNLEY: You'll have but little night to sleep in.

LADY WOODVILL: Lord, 'tis perfect day.[28]

DORIMANT (aside): The hour is almost come I appointed Bellinda, and I am not so foppishly in love here to forget. I am flesh and blood yet.

LADY TOWNLEY: I am very sensible,[29] Madam.

LADY WOODVILL: Lord, Madam!

HARRIET: Look! in what a struggle is my poor mother yonder!

YOUNG BELLAIR: She has much ado to bring out the compliment.

DORIMANT: She strains hard for it.

HARRIET: See, see! her head tottering, her eyes staring, and her under lip trembling ——

DORIMANT: Now — now she's in the very convulsions of her civility. (Aside.) 'Sdeath, I shall lose Bellinda! I must fright her hence; she'll be an hour in this fit of good manners else. (To LADY WOODVILL.) Do you not know Sir Fopling, Madam?

LADY WOODVILL: I have seen that face — oh, heaven! 'tis the same we met in the Mail. How came he here?

DORIMANT: A fiddle, in this town, is a kind of fop-call; no sooner it strikes up but the house is besieged with an army of masquerades straight.

LADY WOODVILL: Lord! I tremble, Mr. Courtage. For certain, Dorimant is in the company.

DORIMANT: I cannot confidently say he is not. You had best be gone. I will wait upon you; your daughter is in the hands of Mr. Bellair.

LADY WOODVILL: I'll see her before me. —— Harriet, come away.

YOUNG BELLAIR: Lights! Lights!

LADY TOWNLEY: Light, down there!

OLD BELLAIR: A dod, it needs not ——

DORIMANT: Call my Lady Woodvill's coach to the door quickly.

> (Exeunt YOUNG BELLAIR, HARRIET, LADY TOWNLEY, DORIMANT, and LADY WOODVILL.)

OLD BELLAIR: Stay, Mr. Medley: let the young fellows do that duty; we will drink a glass of wine together. 'Tis good after dancing. What mumming spark is that?

MEDLEY: He is not to be comprehended in few words.

SIR FOPLING: Hey, La Tour!

MEDLEY: Whither away, Sir Fopling?

---

[28] broad daylight

[29] i.e., of the honor you have done me by being my guest

SIR FOPLING: I have business with Courtage.

MEDLEY: He'll but put the ladies into their coach and come up again.

OLD BELLAIR: In the meantime I'll call for a bottle. (*Exit* OLD BELLAIR.)

(*Enter* YOUNG BELLAIR.)

MEDLEY: Where's Dorimant?

YOUNG BELLAIR: Stolen home. He has had business waiting for him there all this night, I believe, by an impatience I observed in him.

MEDLEY: Very likely; 'tis but dissembling drunkenness, railing at his friends, and the kind soul will embrace the blessing and forget the tedious expectation.

SIR FOPLING: I must speak with him before I sleep.

YOUNG BELLAIR: Emilia and I are resolved on that business.

MEDLEY: Peace! here's your father.

(*Enter* OLD BELLAIR *and* BUTLER *with a bottle of wine.*)

OLD BELLAIR: The women are all gone to bed. —— Fill, boy! —— Mr. Medley, begin a health.

MEDLEY (*whispers*): To Emilia!

OLD BELLAIR: Out a pise! she's a rogue, and I'll not pledge you.

MEDLEY: I know you will.

OLD BELLAIR: A dod, drink it, then!

SIR FOPLING: Let us have the new bacchic.

OLD BELLAIR: A dod, that is a hard word. What does it mean, Sir?

MEDLEY: A catch or drinking-song.

OLD BELLAIR: Let us have it then.

SIR FOPLING: Fill the glasses round and draw up in a body. —— Hey, music!

(*They sing.*)

> The pleasures of love and the joys of good wine
> To perfect our happiness wisely we join.
> We to beauty all day
> Give the sovereign sway
> And her favourite nymphs devoutly obey.
> At the plays we are constantly making our court,
> And when they are ended we follow the sport
> To the Mall and the Park,
> Where we love till 'tis dark;
> Then sparkling champagne
> Puts an end to their reign;
> It quickly recovers
> Poor languishing lovers;
> Makes us frolic and gay, and drowns all our sorrow.
> But alas! we relapse again on the morrow.
> > Let every man stand
> > With his glass in his hand,
> And briskly discharge at the word of command:
> > Here's a health to all those
> > Whom to-night we depose!

Wine and beauty by turns great souls should inspire;
Present all together! and now, boys, give fire!

OLD BELLAIR: A dod, a pretty business and very merry!

SIR FOPLING: Hark you, Medley, let you and I take the fiddles and go waken Dorimant.

MEDLEY: We shall do him a courtesy, if it be as I guess. For after the fatigue of this night he'll quickly have his belly full and be glad of an occasion to cry, "Take away, Handy!"

YOUNG BELLAIR: I'll go with you, and there we'll consult about affairs, Medley.

OLD BELLAIR (*looks on his watch*): A dod, 'tis six o'clock!

SIR FOPLING: Let's away, then.

OLD BELLAIR: Mr. Medley, my sister tells me you are an honest man — and a dod, I love you. Few words and hearty — that's the way with old Harry, old Harry.

SIR FOPLING: Light your flambeaux.[30] Hey!

OLD BELLAIR: What does the man mean?

MEDLEY: 'Tis day, Sir Fopling.

SIR FOPLING: No matter; our serenade will look the greater.

(*Exeunt omnes.*)

SCENE 2

Scene: DORIMANT'*s lodging. A table, a candle, a
toilet, etc.* HANDY, *tying up linen.*

Enter DORIMANT *in his gown, and* BELLINDA.

DORIMANT: Why will you be gone so soon?

BELLINDA: Why did you stay out so late?

DORIMANT: Call a chair, Handy. —— What makes you tremble so?

BELLINDA: I have a thousand fears about me. Have I not been seen, think you?

DORIMANT: By nobody but myself and trusty Handy.

BELLINDA: Where are all your people?

DORIMANT: I have dispersed 'em on sleeveless[1] errands. What does that sigh mean?

BELLINDA: Can you be so unkind to ask me? Well — (*sighs*) — were it to do again ——

DORIMANT: We should do it, should we not?

BELLINDA: I think we should — the wickeder man you to make me love so well. Will you be discreet now?

DORIMANT: I will.

BELLINDA: You cannot.

DORIMANT: Never doubt it.

BELLINDA: I will not expect it.

DORIMANT: You do me wrong.

BELLINDA: You have no more power to keep the secret than I had not to trust you with it.

[30] torches

[1] useless (Dorimant has made sure that all his servants are out of the way)

DORIMANT: By all the joys I have had and those you keep in store ——

BELLINDA: You'll do for my sake what you never did before.

DORIMANT: By that truth thou hast spoken, a wife shall sooner betray herself to her husband.

BELLINDA: Yet I had rather you should be false in this than in another thing you promised me.

DORIMANT: What's that?

BELLINDA: That you would never see Loveit more but in public places — in the Park, at Court and plays.

DORIMANT: 'Tis not likely a man should be fond of seeing a damned old play when there is a new one acted.

BELLINDA: I dare not trust your promise.

DORIMANT: You may ——

BELLINDA: This does not satisfy me. You shall swear you never will see her more.

DORIMANT: I will, a thousand oaths. By all ——

BELLINDA: Hold! You shall not, now I think on't better.

DORIMANT: I will swear!

BELLINDA: I shall grow jealous of the oath and think I owe your truth to that, not to your love.

DORIMANT: Then, by my love; no other oath I'll swear.

(*Enter* HANDY.)

HANDY: Here's a chair.

BELLINDA: Let me go.

DORIMANT: I cannot.

BELLINDA: Too willingly, I fear.

DORIMANT: Too unkindly feared. When will you promise me again?

BELLINDA: Not this fortnight.

DORIMANT: You will be better than your word.

BELLINDA: I think I shall. Will it not make you love me less? (*Starting.*) Hark! what fiddles are these? (*Fiddles without.*)

DORIMANT: Look out, Handy.   (*Exit* HANDY *and returns.*)

HANDY: Mr. Medley, Mr. Bellair, and Sir Fopling; they are coming up.

DORIMANT: How got they in?

HANDY: The door was open for the chair.

BELLINDA: Lord, let me fly!

DORIMANT: Here, here, down the back stairs! I'll see you into your chair.

BELLINDA: No, no! Stay and receive 'em. And be sure you keep your word and never see Loveit more. Let it be a proof of your kindness.

DORIMANT: It shall. —— Handy, direct her. (*Kissing her hand.*) Everlasting love go along with thee.   (*Exeunt* BELLINDA *and* HANDY.)

(Enter YOUNG BELLAIR, MEDLEY, and SIR FOPLING.)

YOUNG BELLAIR: Not abed yet?

MEDLEY: You have had an irregular fit, Dorimant.

DORIMANT: I have.

YOUNG BELLAIR: And is it off already?

DORIMANT: Nature has done her part, gentlemen; when she falls kindly to work, great cures are effected in little time, you know.

SIR FOPLING: We thought there was a wench in the case, by the chair that waited. Prithee, make us a *confidence*.[2]

DORIMANT: Excuse me.

SIR FOPLING: *Le sage*[3] Dorimant! Was she pretty?

DORIMANT: So pretty she may come to keep her coach and pay parish duties[4] if the good humour of the age continue.

MEDLEY: And be of the number of the ladies kept by public-spirited men for the good of the whole town.

SIR FOPLING (*dancing by himself*): Well said, Medley.

YOUNG BELLAIR: See Sir Fopling dancing!

DORIMANT: You are practising and have a mind to recover, I see.

SIR FOPLING: Prithee, Dorimant, why hast not thou a glass hung up here? A room is the dullest thing without one.

YOUNG BELLAIR: Here is company to entertain you.

SIR FOPLING: But I mean in case of being alone. In a glass a man may entertain himself ——

DORIMANT: The shadow of himself, indeed.

SIR FOPLING: Correct the errors of his motions and his dress.

MEDLEY: I find, Sir Fopling, in your solitude you remember the saying of the wise man, and study yourself.

SIR FOPLING: 'Tis the best diversion in our retirements. Dorimant, thou art a pretty fellow and wear'st thy clothes well, but I never saw thee have a handsome cravat. Were they made up like mine, they'd give another air to thy face. Prithee, let me send my man to dress thee but one day; by heavens, an Englishman cannot tie a ribbon.

DORIMANT: They are something clumsy fisted ——

SIR FOPLING: I have brought over the prettiest fellow that ever spread a toilet. He served some time under Merille, the greatest *genie* in the world for a *valet-de-chambre*.

DORIMANT: What! he who formerly belonged to the Duke of Candale?

SIR FOPLING: The same, and got him his immortal reputation.

DORIMANT: Y'have a very fine brandenburgh[5] on, Sir Fopling.

SIR FOPLING: It serves to wrap me up after the fatigue of a ball.

MEDLEY: I see you often in it, with your periwig tied up.

SIR FOPLING: We should not always be in a set dress; 'tis more *en cavalier*[6] to appear now and then in a *déshabillé*.

MEDLEY: Pray, how goes your business with Loveit?

SIR FOPLING: You might have answered yourself in the Mail last night. Dorimant, did you not see the advances she made me? I have been endeavouring at a song.

DORIMANT: Already!

SIR FOPLING: 'Tis my *coup d'essai*[7] in English: I would fain have thy opinion of it.

DORIMANT: Let's see it.

SIR FOPLING: Hey, page, give me my song. —— Bellair, here; thou hast a pretty voice — sing it.

YOUNG BELLAIR: Sing it yourself, Sir Fopling.

[2] take us into your confidence
[3] (Fr.) prudent, discreet
[4] i.e., become rich and respectable
[5] morning gown
[6] (Fr.) stylish, fitting for a man-about-town
[7] (Fr.) first effort

SIR FOPLING: Excuse me.

YOUNG BELLAIR: You learnt to sing in Paris.

SIR FOPLING: I did — of Lambert, the greatest master in the world. But I have his own fault, a weak voice, and care not to sing out of a *ruelle*.[8]

DORIMANT (*aside*): A *ruelle* is a pretty cage for a singing fop, indeed.

YOUNG BELLAIR (*reads the song*):

> How charming Phillis is, how fair!
>   Ah, that she were as willing
> To ease my wounded heart of care,
>   And make her eyes less killing.
> I sigh, I sigh, I languish now,
>   And love will not let me rest;
> I drive about the Park and bow,
>   Still as[9] I meet my dearest.

SIR FOPLING: Sing it! sing it, man; it goes to a pretty new tune which I am confident was made by Baptiste.[10]

MEDLEY: Sing it yourself, Sir Fopling; he does not know the tune.

SIR FOPLING: I'll venture.

(SIR FOPLING *sings*.)

DORIMANT: Ay, marry! now 'tis something. I shall not flatter you, Sir Fopling; there is not much thought in't, but 'tis passionate and well turned.

MEDLEY: After the French way.

SIR FOPLING: That I aimed at. Does it not give you a lively image of the thing? Slap! down goes the glass, and thus we are at it.

DORIMANT: It does, indeed, I perceive, Sir Fopling. You'll be the very head of the sparks who are lucky in compositions of this nature.

(*Enter* SIR FOPLING'S FOOTMAN.)

SIR FOPLING: La Tour, is the bath ready?

FOOTMAN: Yes, Sir.

SIR FOPLING: *Adieu donc, mes chers*.[11]   (*Exit* SIR FOPLING.)

MEDLEY: When have you your revenge on Loveit, Dorimant?

DORIMANT: I will but change my linen and about it.

MEDLEY: The powerful considerations which hindered have been removed then?

DORIMANT: Most luckily this morning. You must along with me; my reputation lies at stake there.

MEDLEY: I am engaged to Bellair.

DORIMANT: What's your business?

MEDLEY: Ma-tri-mony, an't[12] like you.

DORIMANT: It does not, Sir.

YOUNG BELLAIR: It may in time, Dorimant: what think you of Mrs. Harriet?

DORIMANT: What does she think of me?

YOUNG BELLAIR: I am confident she loves you.

---

[8] (Fr.) lady's select circle
[9] whenever
[10] Jean Baptiste Lully (1633–87), composer and master of music at Louis XIV's court
[11] (Fr.) goodbye then, dear fellows
[12] if it

DORIMANT: How does it appear?

YOUNG BELLAIR: Why, she's never well but when she's talking of you — but then, she finds all the faults in you she can. She laughs at all who commend you — but then, she speaks ill of all who do not.

DORIMANT: Women of her temper betray themselves by their over-cunning. I had once a growing love with a lady who would always quarrel with me when I came to see her, and yet was never quiet if I stayed a day from her.

YOUNG BELLAIR: My father is in love with Emilia.

DORIMANT: That is a good warrant for your proceedings. Go on and prosper; I must to Loveit. Medley, I am sorry you cannot be a witness.

MEDLEY: Make her meet Sir Fopling again in the same place and use him ill before me.

DORIMANT: That may be brought about, I think. I'll be at your aunt's anon and give you joy, Mr. Bellair.

YOUNG BELLAIR: You had not best think of Mrs. Harriet too much; without church security there's no taking up there.

DORIMANT: I may fall into the snare too. But ——

> The wise will find a difference in our fate;
> You wed a woman, I a good estate.   (*Exeunt.*)

SCENE 3

Enter the chair with BELLINDA; *the men set it down and open it.* BELLINDA *starting.*

BELLINDA (*surprised*): Lord, where am I? — in the Mail! Whither have you brought me?

1 CHAIRMAN: You gave us no directions, Madam.

BELLINDA (*aside*): The fright I was in made me forget it.

1 CHAIRMAN: We use to carry a lady from the Squire's hither.

BELLINDA (*aside*): This is Loveit: I am undone if she sees me. — Quickly, carry me away!

1 CHAIRMAN: Whither, an't like your honour?

BELLINDA: Ask no questions ——

(*Enter* MRS. LOVEIT'S FOOTMAN.)

FOOTMAN: Have you seen my lady, Madam?

BELLINDA: I am just come to wait upon her.

FOOTMAN: She will be glad to see you, Madam. She sent me to you this morning to desire your company, and I was told you went out by five o'clock.

BELLINDA (*aside*): More and more unlucky!

FOOTMAN: Will you walk in, Madam?

BELLINDA: I'll discharge my chair and follow. Tell your mistress I am here.

              (*Exit* FOOTMAN.)

(*Gives the* CHAIRMAN *money.*) Take this, and if ever you should be examined, be sure you say you took me up in the Strand over against the Exchange, as you will answer it[1] to Mr. Dorimant.

---

[1] be held accountable for it

CHAIRMAN: We will, an't like your honour.   (*Exeunt* CHAIRMEN.)
BELLINDA: Now to come off, I must on ——

> In confidence and lies some hope is left;
> 'Twere hard to be found out in the first theft.   (*Exit*.)

ACT V

Scene 1

Enter MRS. LOVEIT *and* PERT, *her woman*.

PERT: Well! in my eyes Sir Fopling is no such despicable person.
MRS. LOVEIT: You are an excellent judge!
PERT: He's as handsome a man as Mr. Dorimant, and as great a gallant.
MRS. LOVEIT: Intolerable! Is't not enough I submit to his impertinences, but must I be plagued with yours too?
PERT: Indeed, Madam ——
MRS. LOVEIT: 'Tis false, mercenary malice ——

(*Enter her* FOOTMAN.)

FOOTMAN: Mrs. Bellinda, Madam.
MRS. LOVEIT: What of her?
FOOTMAN: She's below.
MRS. LOVEIT: How came she?
FOOTMAN: In a chair; Ambling Harry brought her.
MRS. LOVEIT: He bring her! His chair stands near Dorimant's door and always brings me from thence. —— Run and ask him where he took her up.

(*Exit* FOOTMAN.)

Go! there is no truth in friendship neither. Women, as well as men, all are false —— or all are so to me, at least.
PERT: You are jealous of her too?
MRS. LOVEIT: You had best tell her I am. 'Twill become the liberty you take of late. This fellow's bringing of her, her going out by five o'clock — I know not what to think.

(*Enter* BELLINDA.)

Bellinda, you are grown an early riser, I hear.
BELLINDA: Do you not wonder, my dear, what made me abroad so soon?
MRS. LOVEIT: You do not use to be so.
BELLINDA: The country gentlewomen I told you of (Lord, they have the oddest diversions!) would never let me rest till I promised to go with them to the markets this morning to eat fruit and buy nosegays.
MRS. LOVEIT: Are they so fond of a filthy nosegay?
BELLINDA: They complain of the stinks of the town, and are never well but when they have their noses in one.
MRS. LOVEIT: There are essences and sweet waters.

BELLINDA: Oh, they cry out upon perfumes, they are unwholesome; one of 'em was falling into a fit with the smell of these *nerolii*.[1]

MRS. LOVEIT: Methinks in complaisance you should have had a nosegay too.

BELLINDA: Do you think, my dear, I could be so loathsome to trick myself up with carnations and stock-gillyflowers? I begged their pardon and told them I never wore anything but orange flowers and tuberose. That which made me willing to go was a strange desire I had to eat some fresh nectarines.

MRS. LOVEIT: And had you any?

BELLINDA: The best I ever tasted.

MRS. LOVEIT: Whence came you now?

BELLINDA: From their lodgings, where I crowded out of a coach and took a chair to come and see you, my dear.

MRS. LOVEIT: Whither did you send for that chair?

BELLINDA: 'Twas going by empty.

MRS. LOVEIT: Where do these country gentlewomen lodge, I pray?

BELLINDA: In the Strand over against the Exchange.

PERT: That place is never without a nest of 'em. They are always, as one goes by, fleering in balconies or staring out of windows.

(*Enter* FOOTMAN.)

MRS. LOVEIT (*to the* FOOTMAN): Come hither! (*Whispers.*)

BELLINDA (*aside*): This fellow by her order has been questioning the chairmen. I threatened 'em with the name of Dorimant; if they should have told truth, I am lost forever.

MRS. LOVEIT: In the Strand, said you?

FOOTMAN: Yes, Madam; over against the Exchange.   (*Exit* FOOTMAN.)

MRS. LOVEIT (*aside*): She's innocent, and I am much to blame.

BELLINDA (*aside*): I am so frighted, my countenance will betray me.

MRS. LOVEIT: Bellinda, what makes you look so pale?

BELLINDA: Want of my usual rest and jolting up and down so long in an odious hackney.

(FOOTMAN *returns.*)

FOOTMAN: Madam, Mr. Dorimant.

MRS. LOVEIT: What makes him here?

BELLINDA (*aside*): Then I am betrayed, indeed. He's broke his word, and I love a man that does not care for me!

MRS. LOVEIT: Lord, you faint, Bellinda!

BELLINDA: I think I shall — such an oppression here on the sudden.

PERT: She has eaten too much fruit, I warrant you.

MRS. LOVEIT: Not unlikely.

PERT: 'Tis that lies heavy on her stomach.

MRS. LOVEIT: Have her into my chamber, give her some surfeit water,[2] and let her lie down a little.

PERT: Come, Madam! I was a strange devourer of fruit when I was young — so ravenous ——   (*Exeunt* BELLINDA, *and* PERT, *leading her off.*)

---

[1] essence of orange flowers   [2] remedy for indigestion

MRS. LOVEIT: Oh, that my love would be but calm awhile, that I might receive this man with all the scorn and indignation he deserves!

(*Enter* DORIMANT.)

DORIMANT: Now for a touch of Sir Fopling to begin with. Hey, page, give positive order that none of my people stir. Let the *canaille*[3] wait as they should do. Since noise and nonsense have such powerful charms,

> I, that I may successful prove,
> Transform myself to what you love.

MRS. LOVEIT: If that would do, you need not change from what you are: you can be vain and loud enough.

DORIMANT: But not with so good a grace as Sir Fopling. Hey, Hampshire! Oh, that sound, that sound becomes the mouth of a man of quality![4]

MRS. LOVEIT: Is there a thing so hateful as a senseless mimic?

DORIMANT: He's a great grievance indeed to all who, like yourself, Madam, love to play the fool in quiet.

MRS. LOVEIT: A ridiculous animal, who has more of the ape than the ape has of the man in him!

DORIMANT: I have as mean an opinion of a sheer mimic as yourself; yet were he all ape, I should prefer him to the gay, the giddy, brisk, insipid noisy fool you dote on.

MRS. LOVEIT: Those noisy fools, however you despise 'em, have good qualities which weigh more (or ought at least) with us women than all the pernicious wit you have to boast of.

DORIMANT: That I may hereafter have a just value for their merit, pray do me the favour to name 'em.

MRS. LOVEIT: You'll despise 'em as the dull effects of ignorance and vanity; yet I care not if I mention some. First, they really admire us, while you at best but flatter us well.

DORIMANT: Take heed! Fools can dissemble too.

MRS. LOVEIT: They may, but not so artificially as you. There is no fear they should deceive us. Then, they are assiduous, Sir; they are ever offering us their service, and always waiting on our will.

DORIMANT: You owe that to their excessive idleness. They know not how to entertain themselves at home, and find so little welcome abroad they are fain to fly to you who countenance 'em, as a refuge against the solitude they would be otherwise condemned to.

MRS. LOVEIT: Their conversation, too, diverts us better.

DORIMANT: Playing with your fan, smelling to your gloves, commending your hair, and taking notice how 'tis cut and shaded after the new way ——

MRS. LOVEIT: Were it sillier than you can make it, you must allow 'tis pleasanter to laugh at others than to be laughed at ourselves, though never so wittily. Then, though they want skill to flatter us, they flatter themselves so well they save us the labour. We need not take that care and pains to satisfy 'em of our love, which we so often lose on you.

---

[3] (Fr.) rabble   [4] (cf. III, 3, p. 374)

DORIMANT: They commonly, indeed, believe too well of themselves, and always better of you than you deserve.

MRS. LOVEIT: You are in the right. They have an implicit faith in us which keeps 'em from prying narrowly into our secrets and saves us the vexatious trouble of clearing doubts which your subtle and causeless jealousies every moment raise.

DORIMANT: There is an inbred falsehood in women which inclines 'em still to them whom they may most easily deceive.

MRS. LOVEIT: The man who loves above his quality does not suffer more from the insolent impertinence of his mistress than the woman who loves above her understanding does from the arrogant presumptions of her friend.

DORIMANT: You mistake the use of fools; they are designed for properties,[5] and not for friends. You have an indifferent[6] stock of reputation left yet. Lose it all like a frank gamester on the square; 'twill then be time enough to turn rook[7] and cheat it up again on a good, substantial bubble.[8]

MRS. LOVEIT: The old and the ill-favoured are only fit for properties, indeed, but young and handsome fools have met with kinder fortunes.

DORIMANT: They have, to the shame of your sex be it spoken! 'Twas this, the thought of this, made me by a timely jealousy endeavour to prevent the good fortune you are providing for Sir Fopling. But against a woman's frailty all our care is vain.

MRS. LOVEIT: Had I not with a dear experience bought the knowledge of your falsehood, you might have fooled me yet. This is not the first jealousy you have feigned, to make a quarrel with me and get a week to throw away on some such unknown, inconsiderable slut as you have been lately lurking with at plays.

DORIMANT: Women, when they would break off with a man, never want th' address to turn the fault on him.

MRS. LOVEIT: You take a pride of late in using of me ill, that the town may know the power you have over me, which now (as unreasonably as yourself) expects that I (do me all the injuries you can) must love you still.

DORIMANT: I am so far from expecting that you should, I begin to think you never did love me.

MRS. LOVEIT: Would the memory of it were so wholly worn out in me, that I did doubt it too! What made you come to disturb my growing quiet?

DORIMANT: To give you joy of your growing infamy.

MRS. LOVEIT: Insupportable! Insulting devil! — this from you, the only author of my shame! This from another had been but justice, but from you 'tis a hellish and inhumane outrage. What have I done?

DORIMANT: A thing that puts you below my scorn, and makes my anger as ridiculous as you have made my love.

MRS. LOVEIT: I walked last night with Sir Fopling.

DORIMANT: You did, Madam, and you talked and laughed aloud, "Ha, ha, ha!" — Oh, that laugh! that laugh! that laugh becomes the confidence of a woman of quality.

MRS. LOVEIT: You who have more pleasure in the ruin of a woman's reputation than in the endearments of her love, reproach me not with yourself — and I defy you to name the man can lay a blemish on my fame.

[5] "things" to be used
[6] moderate

[7] sharper
[8] dupe

DORIMANT: To be seen publicly so transported with the vain follies of that notorious fop, to me is an infamy below the sin of prostitution with another man.

MRS. LOVEIT: Rail on! I am satisfied in the justice of what I did; you had provoked me to't.

DORIMANT: What I did was the effect of a passion whose extravagancies you have been willing to forgive.

MRS. LOVEIT: And what I did was the effect of a passion you may forgive if you think fit.

DORIMANT: Are you so indifferent grown?

MRS. LOVEIT: I am.

DORIMANT: Nay, then 'tis time to part. I'll send you back your letters you have so often asked for. I have two or three of 'em about me.

MRS. LOVEIT: Give 'em me.

DORIMANT: You snatch as if you thought I would not. There! and may the perjuries in 'em be mine if e'er I see you more! (*Offers to go; she catches him.*)

MRS. LOVEIT: Stay!

DORIMANT: I will not.

MRS. LOVEIT: You shall.

DORIMANT: What have you to say?

MRS. LOVEIT: I cannot speak it yet.

DORIMANT: Something more in commendation of the fool. —— Death, I want patience; let me go!

MRS. LOVEIT: I cannot. (*Aside.*) I can sooner part with the limbs that hold him. —— I hate that nauseous fool; you know I do.

DORIMANT: Was it the scandal you were fond of then?

MRS. LOVEIT: Y'had raised my anger equal to my love — a thing you ne'er could do before, and in revenge I did — I know not what I did. Would you would not think on't any more!

DORIMANT: Should I be willing to forget it, I shall be daily minded of it; 'twill be a commonplace for all the town to laugh at me, and Medley, when he is rhetorically drunk, will ever be declaiming on it in my ears.

MRS. LOVEIT: 'Twill be believed a jealous spite. Come, forget it.

DORIMANT: Let me consult my reputation; you are too careless of it. (*Pauses.*) You shall meet Sir Fopling in the Mail again to-night.

MRS. LOVEIT: What mean you?

DORIMANT: I have thought on it, and you must. 'Tis necessary to justify my love to the world. You can handle a coxcomb as he deserves when you are not out of humour, Madam.

MRS. LOVEIT: Public satisfaction for the wrong I have done you! This is some new device to make me more ridiculous.

DORIMANT: Hear me!

MRS. LOVEIT: I will not.

DORIMANT: You will be persuaded.

MRS. LOVEIT: Never!

DORIMANT: Are you so obstinate?

MRS. LOVEIT: Are you so base?

DORIMANT: You will not satisfy my love?

MRS. LOVEIT: I would die to satisfy that; but I will not, to save you from a thousand racks, do a shameless thing to please your vanity.

DORIMANT: Farewell, false woman!

MRS. LOVEIT: Do! go!

DORIMANT: You will call me back again.

MRS. LOVEIT: Exquisite fiend, I knew you came but to torment me!

(*Enter* BELLINDA *and* PERT.)

DORIMANT (*surprised*): Bellinda here!

BELLINDA (*aside*): He starts and looks pale! The sight of me has touched his guilty soul.

PERT: 'Twas but a qualm, as I said — a little indigestion; the surfeit water did it, Madam, mixed with a little mirabilis.[9]

DORIMANT (*aside*): I am confounded, and cannot guess how she came hither!

MRS. LOVEIT: 'Tis your fortune, Bellinda, ever to be here when I am abused by this prodigy of ill-nature.

BELLINDA: I am amazed to find him here. How has he the face to come near you?

DORIMANT (*aside*): Here is fine work towards! I never was at such a loss before.

BELLINDA: One who makes a public profession of breach of faith and ingratitude — I loathe the sight of him.

DORIMANT (*aside*): There is no remedy: I must submit to their tongues now, and some other time bring myself off as well as I can.

BELLINDA: Other men are wicked, but then, they have some sense of shame. He is never well but when he triumphs — nay, glories to a woman's face in his villainies.

MRS. LOVEIT: You are in the right, Bellinda, but methinks your kindness for me makes you concern yourself too much with him.

BELLINDA: It does indeed, my dear. His barbarous carriage to you yesterday made me hope you ne'er would see him more, and the very next day to find him here again, provokes me strangely. But because I know you love him, I have done.

DORIMANT: You have reproached me handsomely, and I deserve it for coming hither; but ——

PERT: You must expect it, Sir. All women will hate you for my lady's sake.

DORIMANT (*aside to* BELLINDA): Nay, if she begins too, 'tis time to fly; I shall be scolded to death else. — I am to blame in some circumstances, I confess; but as to the main, I am not so guilty as you imagine. I shall seek a more convenient time to clear myself.

MRS. LOVEIT: Do it now. What impediments are here?

DORIMANT: I want time, and you want temper.

MRS. LOVEIT: These are weak pretences.

DORIMANT: You were never more mistaken in your life; and so farewell.

(DORIMANT *flings off.*)

MRS. LOVEIT: Call a footman, Pert, quickly; I will have him dogged.

PERT: I wish you would not, for my quiet and your own.

MRS. LOVEIT: I'll find out the infamous cause of all our quarrels, pluck her mask off, and expose her barefaced to the world!   (*Exit* PERT.)

BELLINDA (*aside*): Let me but escape this time, I'll never venture more.

MRS. LOVEIT: Bellinda, you shall go with me.

---

[9] *aqua mirabilis* (Lat. "wonder water"), another remedy for indigestion

BELLINDA: I have such a heaviness hangs on me with what I did this morning, I would fain go home and sleep, my dear.

MRS. LOVEIT: Death and eternal darkness! I shall never sleep again. Raging fevers seize the world and make mankind as restless all as I am!   (*Exit* MRS. LOVEIT.)

BELLINDA: I knew him false and helped to make him so. Was not her ruin enough to fright me from the danger? It should have been, but love can take no warning.   (*Exit* BELLINDA.)

SCENE 2

Scene: LADY TOWNLEY's *house.*

Enter MEDLEY, YOUNG BELLAIR, LADY TOWNLEY, EMILIA, *and* CHAPLAIN.

MEDLEY: Bear up, Bellair, and do not let us see that repentance in thine we daily do in married faces.

LADY TOWNLEY: This wedding will strangely surprise my brother when he knows it.

MEDLEY: Your nephew ought to conceal it for a time, Madam; since marriage has lost its good name, prudent men seldom expose their own reputations till 'tis convenient to justify their wives.

OLD BELLAIR (*without*): Where are you all there? Out, a dod! will nobody hear?

LADY TOWNLEY: My brother! Quickly, Mr. Smirk, into this closet! you must not be seen yet.   (SMIRK *goes into the closet.*[1])

(*Enter* OLD BELLAIR *and* LADY TOWNLEY's PAGE.)

OLD BELLAIR: Desire Mr. Fourbe to walk into the lower parlour; I will be with him presently. (*To* YOUNG BELLAIR.) Where have you been, Sir, you could not wait on me to-day?

YOUNG BELLAIR: About a business.

OLD BELLAIR: Are you so good at business? A dod, I have a business, too, you shall dispatch out of hand, Sir. —— Send for a parson, Sister; my Lady Woodvill and her daughter are coming.

LADY TOWNLEY: What need you huddle up[2] things thus?

OLD BELLAIR: Out a pise! youth is apt to play the fool, and 'tis not good it should be in their power.

LADY TOWNLEY: You need not fear your son.

OLD BELLAIR: He's been idling this morning, and a dod, I do not like him. (*To* EMILIA.) How dost thou do, sweetheart?

EMILIA: You are very severe, Sir — married in such haste.

OLD BELLAIR: Go to, thou'rt a rogue, and I will talk with thee anon. Here's my Lady Woodvill come.

(*Enter* LADY WOODVILL, HARRIET, *and* BUSY.)

Welcome, Madam; Mr. Fourbe's below with the writings.

LADY WOODVILL: Let us down and make an end then.

OLD BELLAIR: Sister, show the way. (*To* YOUNG BELLAIR, *who is talking to* HARRIET.)

---

[1] small, private room   [2] hurry

Harry, your business lies not there yet. —— Excuse him till we have done, lady, and then, a dod, he shall be for thee. Mr. Medley, we must trouble you to be a witness.

MEDLEY: I luckily came for that purpose, Sir.

> (*Exeunt* OLD BELLAIR, MEDLEY, YOUNG BELLAIR,
> LADY TOWNLEY, *and* LADY WOODVILL.)

BUSY: What will you do, Madam?

HARRIET: Be carried back and mewed³ up in the country again — run away here — anything rather than be married to a man I do not care for! Dear Emilia, do thou advise me.

EMILIA: Mr. Bellair is engaged, you know.

HARRIET: I do, but know not what the fear of losing an estate may fright him to.

EMILIA: In the desperate condition you are in, you should consult with some judicious man. What think you of Mr. Dorimant?

HARRIET: I do not think of him at all.

BUSY (*aside*): She thinks of nothing else, I am sure.

EMILIA: How fond your mother was of Mr. Courtage!

HARRIET: Because I contrived the mistake to make a little mirth, you believe I like the man.

EMILIA: Mr. Bellair believes you love him.

HARRIET: Men are seldom in the right when they guess at a woman's mind. Would she whom he loves loved him no better!

BUSY (*aside*): That's e'en well enough, on all conscience.

EMILIA: Mr. Dorimant has a great deal of wit.

HARRIET: And takes a great deal of pains to show it.

EMILIA: He's extremely well fashioned.

HARRIET: Affectedly grave, or ridiculously wild and apish.

BUSY: You defend him still against your mother!

HARRIET: I would not were he justly rallied, but I cannot hear anyone undeservedly railed at.

EMILIA: Has your woman learnt the song you were so taken with?

HARRIET: I was fond of a new thing; 'tis dull at second hearing.

EMILIA: Mr. Dorimant made it.

BUSY: She knows it, Madam, and has made me sing it at least a dozen times this morning.

HARRIET: Thy tongue is as impertinent as thy fingers.

EMILIA: You have provoked her.

BUSY: 'Tis but singing the song and I shall appease her.

EMILIA: Prithee, do.

HARRIET: She has a voice will grate your ears worse than a cat-call, and dresses so ill she's scarce fit to trick up a yeoman's daughter on a holiday.

(BUSY *sings*.)

Song
BY SIR C. S.
As Amoret with Phillis sat,
    One evening on the plain,

---

³ cooped

> And saw the charming Strephon wait
>   To tell the nymph his pain;
>
> The threat'ning danger to remove,
>   She whisper'd in her ear,
> "Ah, Phillis, if you would not love,
>   This shepherd do not hear!
>
> "None ever had so strange an art,
>   His passion to convey
> Into a list'ning virgin's heart,
>   And steal her soul away.
>
> "Fly, fly betimes,[4] for fear you give
>   Occasion for your fate."
> "In vain," she said; "in vain I strive!
>   Alas, 'tis now too late."

(*Enter* DORIMANT.)

DORIMANT:

>   Music so softens and disarms the mind ——

HARRIET:

>   That not one arrow does resistance find.

DORIMANT: Let us make use of the lucky minute, then.

HARRIET (*aside, turning from* DORIMANT): My love springs with my blood into my face; I dare not look upon him yet.

DORIMANT: What have we here? the picture of celebrated beauty giving audience in public to a declared lover?

HARRIET: Play the dying fop and make the piece complete, Sir.

DORIMANT: What think you if the hint were well improved — the whole mystery of making love pleasantly designed and wrought in a suit of hangings?[5]

HARRIET: 'Twere needless to execute fools in effigy who suffer daily in their own persons.

DORIMANT (*to* EMILIA, *aside*): Mrs. Bride, for such I know this happy day has made you ——

EMILIA (*aside*): Defer the formal joy you are to give me, and mind your business with her. (*Aloud.*) Here are dreadful preparations, Mr. Dorimant — writings, sealing, and a parson sent for.

DORIMANT: To marry this lady ——

BUSY: Condemned she is, and what will become of her I know not, without you generously engage in a rescue.

DORIMANT: In this sad condition, Madam, I can do no less than offer you my service.

HARRIET: The obligation is not great; you are the common sanctuary for all young women who run from their relations.

DORIMANT: I have always my arms open to receive the distressed. But I will open my

---

[4] in time   [5] set of draperies or tapestries

heart and receive you, where none yet did ever enter. You have filled it with a secret, might I but let you know it ——

HARRIET: Do not speak it if you would have me believe it; your tongue is so famed for falsehood, 'twill do the truth an injury. (*Turns away her head.*)

DORIMANT: Turn not away, then, but look on me and guess it.

HARRIET: Did you not tell me there was no credit to be given to faces? that women nowadays have their passions as much at will as they have their complexions, and put on joy and sadness, scorn and kindness, with the same ease they do their paint and patches? Are they the only counterfeits?

DORIMANT: You wrong your own while you suspect my eyes. By all the hope I have in you, the inimitable colour in your cheeks is not more free from art than are the sighs I offer.

HARRIET: In men who have been long hardened in sin we have reason to mistrust the first signs of repentance.

DORIMANT: The prospect of such a heaven will make me persevere and give you marks that are infallible.

HARRIET: What are those?

DORIMANT: I will renounce all the joys I have in friendship and in wine, sacrifice to you all the interest I have in other women ——

HARRIET: Hold! Though I wish you devout, I would not have you turn fanatic. Could you neglect these a while and make a journey into the country?

DORIMANT: To be with you, I could live there and never send one thought to London.

HARRIET: Whate'er you say, I know all beyond High Park's a desert to you, and that no gallantry can draw you farther.

DORIMANT: That has been the utmost limit of my love; but now my passion knows no bounds, and there's no measure to be taken of what I'll do for you from anything I ever did before.

HARRIET: When I hear you talk thus in Hampshire I shall begin to think there may be some truth enlarged upon.

DORIMANT: Is this all? Will you not promise me ——

HARRIET: I hate to promise; what we do then is expected from us and wants much of the welcome it finds when it surprises.

DORIMANT: May I not hope?

HARRIET: That depends on you and not on me, and 'tis to no purpose to forbid it. (*Turns to* BUSY.)

BUSY: Faith, Madam, now I perceive the gentleman loves you too, e'en let him know your mind, and torment yourselves no longer.

HARRIET: Dost think I have no sense of modesty?

BUSY: Think, if you lose this you may never have another opportunity.

HARRIET: May he hate me (a curse that frights me when I speak it), if ever I do a thing against the rules of decency and honour.

DORIMANT (*to* EMILIA): I am beholding to you for your good intentions, Madam.

EMILIA: I thought the concealing of our marriage from her might have done you better service.

DORIMANT: Try her again.

EMILIA: What have you resolved, Madam? The time draws near.

HARRIET: To be obstinate and protest against this marriage.

(*Enter* LADY TOWNLEY *in haste.*)

LADY TOWNLEY (*to* EMILIA): Quickly, quickly! let Mr. Smirk out of the closet.

(SMIRK *comes out of the closet*.)

HARRIET: A parson! Had you laid him in here?

DORIMANT: I knew nothing of him.

HARRIET: Should it appear you did, your opinion of my easiness may cost you dear.

(*Enter* OLD BELLAIR, YOUNG BELLAIR, MEDLEY, *and* LADY WOODVILL.)

OLD BELLAIR: Out a pise! the canonical hour[6] is almost past. Sister, is the man of God come?

LADY TOWNLEY: He waits your leisure.

OLD BELLAIR: By your favour, Sir. —— A dod, a pretty spruce[7] fellow. What may we call him?

LADY TOWNLEY: Mr. Smirk — my Lady Biggot's chaplain.

OLD BELLAIR: A wise woman! a dod, she is. The man will serve for the flesh as well as the spirit. Please you, Sir, to commission a young couple to go to bed together a God's name? —— Harry!

YOUNG BELLAIR: Here, Sir.

OLD BELLAIR: Out a pise! Without your mistress in your hand!

SMIRK: Is this the gentleman?

OLD BELLAIR: Yes, Sir.

SMIRK: Are you not mistaken, Sir?

OLD BELLAIR: A dod, I think not, Sir.

SMIRK: Sure, you are, Sir!

OLD BELLAIR: You look as if you would forbid the banns, Mr. Smirk. I hope you have no pretension to the lady.

SMIRK: Wish him joy, Sir; I have done him the good office to-day already.

OLD BELLAIR: Out a pise! What do I hear?

LADY TOWNLEY: Never storm, Brother; the truth is out.

OLD BELLAIR: How say you, Sir? Is this your wedding day?

YOUNG BELLAIR: It is, Sir.

OLD BELLAIR: And a dod, it shall be mine too. (*To* EMILIA.) Give me thy hand, sweetheart. What dost thou mean? Give my thy hand, I say.

(EMILIA *kneels and* YOUNG BELLAIR.)

LADY TOWNLEY: Come, come! give her your blessing; this is the woman your son loved and is married to.

OLD BELLAIR: Ha! cheated! cozened! and by your contrivance, Sister!

LADY TOWNLEY: What would you do with her? She's a rogue and you can't abide her.

MEDLEY: Shall I hit her a pat for you, Sir?

OLD BELLAIR: A dod, you are all rogues, and I never will forgive you.

LADY TOWNLEY: Whither? Whither away?

MEDLEY: Let him go and cool awhile.

LADY WOODVILL (*to* DORIMANT): Here's a business broke out now, Mr. Courtage; I am made a fine fool of.

[6] (the hours from 8 A.M. to 3 P.M. were the legal marriage hours in English parish churches)

[7] neat, dapper

DORIMANT: You see the old gentleman knew nothing of it.

LADY WOODVILL: I find he did not. I shall have some trick put upon me if I stay in this wicked town any longer. —— Harriet, dear child, where art thou? I'll into the country straight.

OLD BELLAIR: A dod, Madam, you shall hear me first.

(*Enter* MRS. LOVEIT *and* BELLINDA.)

MRS. LOVEIT: Hither my man dogged him.

BELLINDA: Yonder he stands, my dear.

MRS. LOVEIT: I see him (*Aside*.) and with him the face that has undone me. Oh, that I were but where I might throw out the anguish of my heart! Here it must rage within and break it.

LADY TOWNLEY: Mrs. Loveit! Are you afraid to come forward?

MRS. LOVEIT: I was amazed to see so much company here in a morning. The occasion sure is extraordinary.

DORIMANT (*aside*): Loveit and Bellinda! The devil owes me a shame to-day and I think never will have done paying it.

MRS. LOVEIT: Married! dear Emilia! How am I transported with the news!

HARRIET (*to* DORIMANT): I little thought Emilia was the woman Mr. Bellair was in love with. I'll chide her for not trusting me with the secret.

DORIMANT: How do you like Mrs. Loveit?

HARRIET: She's a famed mistress of yours, I hear.

DORIMANT: She has been, on occasion.

OLD BELLAIR (*to* LADY WOODVILL): A dod, Madam, I cannot help it.

LADY WOODVILL: You need make no more apologies, Sir.

EMILIA (*to* MRS. LOVEIT): The old gentleman's excusing himself to my Lady Woodvill.

MRS. LOVEIT: Ha, ha, ha! I never heard of anything so pleasant!

HARRIET (*to* DORIMANT): She's extremely overjoyed at something.

DORIMANT: At nothing. She is one of those hoyting[8] ladies who gaily fling themselves about and force a laugh when their aching hearts are full of discontent and malice.

MRS. LOVEIT: O heaven! I was never so near killing myself with laughing. —— Mr. Dorimant, are you a brideman?

LADY WOODVILL: Mr. Dorimant! — Is this Mr. Dorimant, Madam?

MRS. LOVEIT: If you doubt it, your daughter can resolve you, I suppose.

LADY WOODVILL: I am cheated too — basely cheated!

OLD BELLAIR: Out a pise! what's here? More knavery yet?

LADY WOODVILL: Harriet, on my blessing come away, I charge you!

HARRIET: Dear Mother, do but stay and hear me.

LADY WOODVILL: I am betrayed and thou art undone, I fear.

HARRIET: Do not fear it; I have not, nor never will, do anything against my duty — believe me, dear Mother, do!

DORIMANT (*to* MRS. LOVEIT): I had trusted you with this secret but that I knew the violence of your nature would ruin my fortune, as now unluckily it has. I thank you, Madam.

MRS. LOVEIT: She's an heiress, I know, and very rich.

---

[8] loud and restless   [9] material advantage

DORIMANT: To satisfy you, I must give up my interest[9] wholly to my love. Had you been a reasonable woman, I might have secured 'em both and been happy.

MRS. LOVEIT: You might have trusted me with anything of this kind — you know you might. Why did you go under a wrong name?

DORIMANT: The story is too long to tell you now. Be satisfied, this is the business; this is the mask has kept me from you.

BELLINDA (*aside*): He's tender of my honour though he's cruel to my love.

MRS. LOVEIT: Was it no idle mistress, then?

DORIMANT: Believe me, a wife to repair the ruins of my estate, that needs it.

MRS. LOVEIT: The knowledge of this makes my grief hang lighter on my soul, but I shall never more be happy.

DORIMANT: Bellinda!

BELLINDA: Do not think of clearing yourself with me; it is impossible. Do all men break their words thus?

DORIMANT: Th'extravagant words they speak in love. 'Tis as unreasonable to expect we should perform all we promise then, as do all we threaten when we are angry. When I see you next ——

BELLINDA: Take no notice of me, and I shall not hate you.

DORIMANT: How came you to Mrs. Loveit?

BELLINDA: By a mistake the chairmen made for want of my giving them directions.

DORIMANT: 'Twas a pleasant one. We must meet again.

BELLINDA: Never.

DORIMANT: Never!

BELLINDA: When we do, may I be as infamous as you are false.

LADY TOWNLEY: Men of Mr. Dorimant's character always suffer in the general opinion of the world.

MEDLEY: You can make no judgment of a witty man from common fame, considering the prevailing faction, Madam.

OLD BELLAIR: A dod, he's in the right.

MEDLEY: Besides, 'tis a common error among women to believe too well of them they know, and too ill of them they don't.

OLD BELLAIR: A dod, he observes well.

LADY TOWNLEY: Believe me, Madam, you will find Mr. Dorimant as civil a gentleman as you thought Mr. Courtage.

HARRIET: If you would but know him better ——

LADY WOODVILL: You have a mind to know him better! Come away! You shall never see him more.

HARRIET: Dear Mother, stay!

LADY WOODVILL: I wo'not[10] be consenting to your ruin.

HARRIET: Were my fortune in your power ——

LADY WOODVILL: Your person is.

HARRIET: Could I be disobedient, I might take it out of yours and put it into his.

LADY WOODVILL: 'Tis that you would be at; you would marry this Dorimant.

HARRIET: I cannot deny it; I would, and never will marry any other man.

LADY WOODVILL: Is this the duty that you promised?

HARRIET: But I will never marry him against your will.

[10] will not

LADY WOODVILL (*aside*): She knows the way to melt my heart. — (*To* HARRIET.) Upon yourself light your undoing!

MEDLEY (*to* OLD BELLAIR): Come, Sir, you have not the heart any longer to refuse your blessing.

OLD BELLAIR: A dod, I ha' not. —— Rise, and God bless you both! Make much of her, Harry; she deserves thy kindness. (*To* EMILIA.) A dod, Sirrah, I did not think it had been in thee.

(*Enter* SIR FOPLING *and's* PAGE.)

SIR FOPLING: 'Tis a damned windy day. —— Hey, page, is my periwig right?

PAGE: A little out of order, Sir.

SIR FOPLING: Pox o' this apartment! It wants an antechamber to adjust oneself in. (*To* MRS. LOVEIT.) Madam, I came from your house, and your servants directed me hither.

MRS. LOVEIT: I will give order hereafter they shall direct you better.

SIR FOPLING: The great satisfaction I had in the Mail last night has given me much disquiet since.

MRS. LOVEIT: 'Tis likely to give me more than I desire.

SIR FOPLING (*aside*): What the devil makes her so reserved? —— Am I guilty of an indiscretion, Madam?

MRS. LOVEIT: You will be of a great one if you continue your mistake, Sir.

SIR FOPLING: Something puts you out of humour.

MRS. LOVEIT: The most foolish, inconsiderable thing that ever did.

SIR FOPLING: Is it in my power?

MRS. LOVEIT: To hang or drown it. Do one of 'em and trouble me no more.

SIR FOPLING: So *fière*?[11] *Serviteur*,[12] Madam! —— Medley, where's Dorimant?

MEDLEY: Methinks the lady has not made you those advances to-day she did last night, Sir Fopling.

SIR FOPLING: Prithee, do not talk of her!

MEDLEY: She would be a *bonne fortune*.

SIR FOPLING: Not to me at present.

MEDLEY: How so?

SIR FOPLING: An intrigue now would be but a temptation to me to throw away that vigour on one which I mean shall shortly make my court to the whole sex in a ballet.

MEDLEY: Wisely considered, Sir Fopling.

SIR FOPLING: No one woman is worth the loss of a cut in a caper.

MEDLEY: Not when 'tis so universally designed.

LADY WOODVILL: Mr. Dorimant, everyone has spoke so much in your behalf that I can no longer doubt but I was in the wrong.

MRS. LOVEIT: There's nothing but falsehood and impertinence in this world; all men are villains or fools. Take example from my misfortunes. Bellinda, if thou wouldst be happy, give thyself wholly up to goodness.

HARRIET (*to* MRS. LOVEIT): Mr. Dorimant has been your God Almighty long enough; 'tis time to think of another.

MRS. LOVEIT: Jeered by her! I will lock myself up in my house and never see the world again.

[11] (Fr.) haughty   [12] (Fr.) servant

HARRIET: A nunnery is the more fashionable place for such a retreat, and has been the fatal consequence of many a *belle passion*.[13]

MRS. LOVEIT (*aside*): Hold, heart, till I get home! Should I answer, 'twould make her triumph greater. (*Is going out.*)

DORIMANT: Your hand, Sir Fopling ——

SIR FOPLING: Shall I wait upon you, Madam?

MRS. LOVEIT: Legion of fools, as many devils take thee! (*Exit* MRS. LOVEIT.)

MEDLEY: Dorimant, I pronounce thy reputation clear; and henceforward when I would know anything of woman, I will consult no other oracle.

SIR FOPLING: Stark mad, by all that's handsome! —— Dorimant, thou hast engaged me in a pretty business.

DORIMANT: I have not leisure now to talk about it.

OLD BELLAIR: Out a pise! What does this man of mode do here again?

LADY TOWNLEY: He'll be an excellent entertainment within, Brother, and is luckily come to raise the mirth of the company.

LADY WOODVILL: Madam, I take my leave of you.

LADY TOWNLEY: What do you mean, Madam?

LADY WOODVILL: To go this afternoon part of my way to Hartly.

OLD BELLAIR: A dod, you shall stay and dine first! Come, we will all be good friends, and you shall give Mr. Dorimant leave to wait upon you and your daughter in the country.

LADY WOODVILL: If his occasions bring him that way, I have now so good an opinion of him, he shall be welcome.

HARRIET: To a great rambling, lone house that looks as it were not inhabited, the family's so small. There you'll find my mother, an old lame aunt, and myself, Sir, perched up on chairs at a distance in a large parlour, sitting moping like three or four melancholy birds in a spacious volary.[14] Does not this stagger your resolution?

DORIMANT: Not at all, Madam. The first time I saw you you left me with the pangs of love upon me, and this day my soul has quite given up her liberty.

HARRIET: This is more dismal than the country! Emilia, pity me, who am going to that sad place. Methinks I hear the hateful noise of rooks already — kaw, kaw, kaw! There's music in the worst cry[15] in London — My dill and cowcumbers to pickle!

OLD BELLAIR: Sister, knowing of this matter, I hope you have provided us some good cheer.

LADY TOWNLEY: I have, Brother, and the fiddles too.

OLD BELLAIR: Let 'em strike up, then; the young lady shall have a dance before she departs.

(*Dance.*)

(*After the dance.*) —— So! now we'll in and make this an arrant[16] wedding-day. (*To the pit.*)

> And if these honest gentlemen rejoice,
> A dod, the boy has made a happy choice.

(*Exeunt omnes.*)

---

[13] (Fr.) strong passion
[14] large birdcage

[15] i.e., of the street-vendors
[16] downright, regular

EPILOGUE

BY MR. DRYDEN

Most modern wits such monstrous fools have shown,[1]
They seem'd not of heav'n's making, but their own.
Those nauseous harlequins[2] in farce may pass,
But there goes more to a substantial ass.
Something of man must be expos'd to view
That, gallants, they may more resemble you.
Sir Fopling is a fool so nicely writ,
The ladies would mistake him for a wit;
And when he sings, talks loud, and cocks,[3] would cry,
"I vow, methinks he's pretty company!
So brisk, so gay, so travell'd, so refin'd,
As[4] he took pains to graff[5] upon his kind."
True fops help nature's work and go to school,
To file[6] and finish God A'mighty's fool.
Yet none Sir Fopling him, or him, can call;
He's knight o'th' shire,[7] and represents ye all.
From each he meets, he culls whate'er he can;
Legion's his name, a people in a man.
His bulky folly gathers as it goes
And, rolling o'er you, like a snowball grows.
His various modes from various fathers follow;
One taught the toss, and one the new French wallow.[8]
His sword-knot,[9] this; his cravat, this design'd;
And this, the yard-long snake[10] he twirls behind.
From one the sacred periwig he gain'd,
Which wind ne'er blew, nor touch of hat profan'd.
Another's diving bow he did adore,
Which with a shog[11] casts all the hair before[12]
Till he with full decorum brings it back,
And rises with a water spaniel shake.
As for his songs (the ladies' dear delight),
Those sure he took from most of you who write.
Yet every man is safe from what he feared,
For no one fool is hunted from the herd.

---

[1] shown themselves
[2] stock comic characters in Italian commedia dell'arte, part lovers and part clowns, wearing multicolored dress
[3] struts
[4] as if
[5] graft
[6] polish
[7] parliamentary representative
[8] rolling gait
[9] ribbon or tassel tied to the hilt of a sword
[10] i.e., the pigtail of his wig
[11] shake
[12] forward, in front

AFTERWORD

Restoration comedy denotes a large and varied body of plays, but what users of the term most commonly have in mind are the prose plays of witty dialogue and sexual intrigue among Londoners of high fashion, written by George Etherege, William Wycherley, and William Congreve. Less pure (the adjective refers to genre, not to morals) contributions to this kind of comedy were made by Dryden and other, lesser, playwrights. Thomas Shadwell tried to adapt the older comedy of humors by Ben Jonson to the new taste for stage naughtiness in sprawling plays of naive social gusto. A little later John Vanbrugh and George Farquhar, modifying their models, wrote comedies whose provincial settings, spacious structures, and incipient sentimentalizations of marriage place them only on the fringes of the comedy of sex as it is more narrowly defined by plays like *The Man of Mode* and Wycherley's *The Country Wife*. Even in Congreve's last plays, including *The Way of the World*, which is sometimes considered the epitome of Restoration comedy of sex but really is not, the earlier treatment of sex as a gay and cruel game for social control is beginning to give way to more conventionally decent attitudes.

Dryden's praise of Shakespeare's "large and comprehensive" soul in the *Essay of Dramatic Poesy* (1668) is a recognition of that inclusiveness of a disinterested imagination that makes one world of the whole of Shakespearean drama. The same gathering vision is not evident in the drama of Dryden's own age, which may be why so many critics have been reluctant to call it "great." Dryden himself was an extraordinarily versatile playwright, who wrote superior plays in almost every genre he attempted. Too much of a pragmatist and skeptic to lock his creative impulse in a single form, his versatility was that of a gifted professional who had to please his fickle audiences or starve, and who was lucky enough to take delight in the forced exercise of his craft in a variety of dramatic and theatrical styles, rather than that of a genius so large of soul that nothing less than a universe of human situations, values, and voices was commensurate with his sense of life. In Dryden's drama in particular and in Restoration drama in general our impression of variety comes from sets of separate, smaller grasps of experience, fragmented and ambiguously felt, products of an anxious and sometimes meretricious search for expressive form. It is no accident that interest in Restoration drama has reached a new height in our own time.

A main reason for this impression of uncertain and scattering dramatic energies is the fact that Restoration drama seems (in the words of a modern critic) "positively schizophrenic" in its pursuit of two kinds of plays that seem completely at odds with one another. The same audiences that flocked to see rakes and their gamesome ladies elegantly seduce one another and exchange witty repartee in fashionable London parks and drawing rooms among cuckolds, fops, amorous harridans, country boors, tyrannical parents, and mercenary clergymen, apparently took equal pleasure in plays in rhymed couplets declaimed by royal characters of absolute virtue or villainy in exotic lands who were engaged in a bewildering turbulent succession of martial and romantic intrigue. What the spectator was supposed to get from these plays was the equivalent in drama of Homer's and Virgil's epics, "imitations of the highest patterns of human life" and with "love and valor" therefore as their proper subjects. That is why they are called *heroic* plays and why their verse is *heroic* couplets. What the spectator actually did get was frenetic melodrama, in which the skillful interweaving of military and erotic plots, the splendid costumes and the shifting spectacle, and the passional couplet eloquence achieved a kind of preposterous but spellbinding integrity. The very exclusiveness of their consistent extravagance of sentiment and event turns the best of these plays into superb theatricals of color, movement, and fine words. But this is not the highest kind of dramatic merit, and, paradoxically, the cynical frivolities of the comedies of bad sexual manners somehow seem more serious and more relevant to deeper concerns in human life than the larger-than-life feelings and the resounding platitudes of the heroic plays. The immediate problem, however, is to account for the coexistence of both types of drama in Restoration London. Rather remarkably, both attained their clearest form and their greatest popular success in the mid-1670s.

Perhaps the best explanation is the simplest one. The sex comedies and the heroic plays appealed respectively to the two sides of the Restoration playgoer's divided feelings about his society, as if illustrating Aristotle's point that human reality lies between its polarized extremes in the two genres of drama, tragedy showing men as "better" than they are in real life and comedy as "worse." The comedies enjoyed the patronage of licentious aristocrats so secure in their station and so casual about propriety that they did not mind having their outrageous manners mimicked on the public stage. The commoners in the audience were still on the rebound from years of Puritan censorship; for a long time after 1660 going to the theater was a way of repudiating the Commonwealth, which (not altogether successfully) had closed the theaters and banned all shows in 1642. Now, with a mixture, perhaps, of envy and titillated glee, they enjoyed the spectacle of the loose living of their social betters. The satiric implications of the scene with the Shoemaker in Act I of *The Man of Mode* can hardly have been lost on the social levellers and the thoughtful cynics in the audience: When man is reduced to a bundle of physical appetites fine gentlemen must protect their status by monopolizing sin, lest class distinctions disappear in a democracy of vice.

But the libertine image, in the comedies, of man as a scheming sensualist gratifying his passions in a social world whose glitter only covers the brutalities of the primeval Hobbesian jungle was balanced in the heroic plays by the spectacle of heroes and heroines of surpassing bravery, fidelity, and chaste love, embodiments of pure Platonic essences of virtue. In their triumphs, moral or factual or both at the same time, the playgoer could feel his soul purified and ennobled by vicariously sharing in a life more just and heroic than that presided over by a lazy and corrupt king who indiscriminately paraded blue-blooded duchesses and an ex–orange-woman and actress like Nell Gwyn as his royal mistresses. Both kinds of plays presented a limited view of life; they were successful precisely to the extent that their particular ethos could be felt to be simple and severely "closed" and exclusive. And, again, to the extent that it really was so the drama missed true excellence.

In this view, the sex comedies and the heroic plays appear much less as opposites inexplicably flourishing together than as complementary reductives for audiences of divided and troubled moral and social, political and religious, allegiances. And this view allows us to discover similarities behind the obvious differences. For example, the furious bombast of the frustrated villains, male and female, in the heroic play sounds very much like the outbursts of the jealous cockolds and the abandoned mistresses in the sex comedies. And the rake-hero's intrigues for sexual conquest and mastery of his social group in the comedies bespeak the same fierce desire for conquest of both empire and beauteous queen that motivates the heroic hero. Dryden's ten-act *Conquest of Granada* (1670–71) is perhaps the most perfect example of heroic drama, and its hero Almanzor has more than a little — not everything, but something — in common with Etherege's Dorimant. Almanzor's grand rhetoric of simile and antithesis shares with Dorimant's flip cadences of perfectly polished prose the function of expressing the hero's uncompromising pride and single-minded drive of selfhood. The concepts underlying both characters owe a debt to Hobbes's view of natural man as a creature of aggressive egoism moved by the impulses of his body. Thus, on closer inspection, the apparent schizophrenia of Restoration drama reveals significant signs of a complex and unified sensibility. In the small number of dramatic masterpieces from the age this unity-in-complexity is achieved within the conventions of a single dramatic form.

Etherege's *Man of Mode* opened at the Duke's theater in Dorset Garden on April 11, 1676. Thomas Betterton played Dorimant in a manner which, it was widely believed, Etherege and he intended as a representation of John Wilmot, Earl of Rochester, courtier, poet, and the most notorious of Charles II's playboy friends.

The play offers an admirable test case for the critical status of Restoration sex comedy in general. If it, commonly regarded as one of the two or three finest specimens of its kind, fails to survive critical scrutiny, the whole case for the sex comedies as something more than salacious frivolity collapses.

One of the axioms of neoclassical criticism was that the function of literature is to teach morality delightfully, "to please and instruct," as the Horatian dictum had it — not necessarily by direct didacticism but at least by implicit example. In 1698, in a long pamphlet entitled A *Short View of the Immorality and Profaneness of the English Stage*, Jeremy Collier, a blunt-spoken clergyman of strong moral convictions and no critical subtlety, attacked a number of Restoration playwrights and plays for their corrupting influence on good Christians. He charged them with indecency and profanity of language and for slandering the clergy and the nobility, but what really fired his indignation was their violation of poetic justice, a moralistic concept of criticism that obliged the playwright to improve upon the sadly arbitrary state of things in a fallen world by rigorously rewarding virtue and punishing vice. But in a play like *The Man of Mode* not only is whoring held up as the model behavior of a complete gentleman, it is also shown to be the way to social and sexual success. After getting rid of one mistress and acquiring another the hero is rewarded with the love and quite possibly the hand of a bright and beautiful heiress. What wholesome lesson can an audience bring away from watching such unblushing exploits? As it happens, Etherege escaped Collier's censure, presumably because he was dead by the time Collier wrote and the clergyman was generous enough to attack only living authors. But had Etherege been around to defend himself (Congreve was and was chastised for plays no bawdier than Etherege's), *The Man of Mode* would almost certainly have been one of Collier's exhibits of stage immorality. It is hard to say whether Collier was cause or effect in the change in popular taste in comedy that followed the Collier controversy — whether, that is, he initiated the change or at least hastened its accomplishment or just seized the opportunity for fame by speaking up on behalf of a new trend that would have been just as successful had he never written. Probably he did a bit of both. At any rate, the fact is that after about 1700 comedy turned benevolent and sentimental, reforming its rakes in firm endorsements of pre-marital chastity and marital fidelity.

Collier's polemical method was to cite passages out of context as examples of behavior and language that every right-thinking, God-fearing person would abominate in real life. In equating art with life Collier absurdly overstated his case, but the issues he raised are real and those which subsequent generations of critics, particularly in the nineteenth century, have focused on. A pleasant but ultimately self-defeating argument in defense of the comedies is that of Charles Lamb in one of the *Essays of Elia* (1822). There is, says Lamb, really no moral issue involved at all, since the world of the comedies is a "Utopia of gallantry, where pleasure is duty, and the manners perfect freedom, . . . altogether a speculative scene of things, which has no reference whatever to the world that is." But in claiming the immunity of the amoral for the comedies, this kind of argument makes them trivial or even meaningless; one cannot take seriously — in fact, it is difficult to conceive of — plays that have "no reference whatever" to the world of real men and women. Far more destructively than Collier's angry bluster, Lamb's smiling acceptance of them as delightful romps in a fairyland of fornication reduces them to escape literature, to the self-indulgent irresponsibilities of pornography. Thomas Macaulay would have none of Lamb's argument. The trouble with the morality of a play like *The Country Wife*, he says in a review in 1841, is that it reflects a world "which is a great deal too real." And a playwright of genius "makes an ill use of his powers" when he glamorizes sexual profligacy "by uniting it with beauty, grace, dignity, spirit, a high social position, popularity, literature, wit, taste, knowledge of the world, brilliant success in every undertaking." This is almost straight Collier; the playwright is still being faulted for ignoring poetic justice.

Modern critics have generally felt that judging a work of literature in terms of its presumed effects on its audience inevitably leads to arguments over the intrinsic merits and the pragmatic value of whatever ideology the work is supposed to propound and that this is a futile exercise as far as understanding *literature* is concerned. They prefer to deal with the values implicit in the structures of the work itself. As a result, opposition to Restoration sex comedy today does not take the form of Collier's and the Victorians' disapproval of its looseness of manners but develops the implications of Lamb's dangerous apology and turns them against the plays. The comedies of wit and intrigue, says L. C. Knights in an influential essay ("Restoration Comedy: The Reality and the Myth," 1946), have "no significant relation to the best thought of the time." Their dialogue isn't really *about* anything; there is only a general air of cynicism "without the tough strength of disillusion." Their language, compared with that of Elizabethan comedy, which also could be both witty and racy (racier, in fact; there are few dirty words in the Restoration comedies), betrays their intellectual thinness in the monotony of the mechanical see-saw pattern of balanced antithesis.* "The criticism that defenders of Restoration comedy need to answer," Knights concludes, "is not that the comedies are 'immoral,' but that they are trivial, gross and dull."

Some linked, general observations bearing upon the argument over the what and why of content in the comedies are called for at this point. First, the critic who feels that at least a few of them are serious and superior drama is not obliged to argue that they have no pornographic appeal at all — that is, that they never or nowhere stimulate the sexual imagination as an end in itself. Second, he does not have to believe that the playwrights were innocent of any intent to provide stage pornography or, if he decides that they were not, to deny that they had any thought of exploiting it for

---

* The kind of antithetical style that Knights has in mind is much more prominent in Congreve's style than in Etherege's, but there are at least two illustrations of it in *The Man of Mode*. In Act III, Dorimant tells Sir Fopling Flutter that an affair with a lady is "a thing no less necessary to confirm the reputation of your wit than a duel will be to satisfy the town of your courage." And in Act V, Mrs. Loveit tells Dorimant that "the man who loves above his quality does not suffer more from the insolent impertinence of his mistress than the woman who loves above her understanding does from the arrogant presumptions of her friend."

money or popularity. He can make these concessions and still feel that the plays have something of more importance to say. Third, such concessions do not force him to argue that the only redeeming value of the plays is the way they document the manners of their debauched age, or expose the depravity of their upper-class audiences under cover of amusing them with smut, or both at the same time. Though it is difficult today to determine how accurately the comedies reflected actual behavior in the fast, young set among the idle rich in Charles II's London, there is evidence that they probably were as truthful to the social facts of their time as successful comedies of manners in any age generally are. And there certainly is satire in *The Man of Mode*, not just in such obvious figures of fun as Sir Fopling and Old Bellair but also in the insinuated image of the life of selfish hedonism as a fretful, futile round of alternating anxiety and ennui. But pornography and social history and realistic satire do not exhaust the play's meaning, and there are other possible responses to the notion that Dorimant is the play's model of a perfect gentleman than either moral outrage or cynical scorn.

Elizabethan comedy had sought to romanticize the sexual urge and Jacobean tragic melodrama to criminalize it as lust. Restoration sex comedy, developing the conventions in such earlier city comedies as those of James Shirley, a late Jacobean playwright, sought not so much to reconcile romance and lust as to use the tensions between them to delineate the behavior of people forced to accommodate their desires to the rules of society. In *The Man of Mode*, the main plot about Dorimant and the subplot about Emilia and Young Bellair are partly analogous, because both use dissembling as plot motif, and partly in counterpoint, because one is libidinal and the other romantic in motivation. The play roughly observes the unity of time not because the playwright is mechanically obeying a rule of neoclassical play-making or because Dorimant's erotic escapades are so many and complicated that crowding them all together within the space of some twenty-four hours amounts to a triumph of ingenious plotting, but because Etherege wants to sharpen our sense of the energy behind Dorimant's egoistical enterprise. Everything in the play goes to turning an essentially simple story of the tentative taming of a rake into a comprehensive and ambivalent image of man as social animal. A scheme of values is being wryly anatomized in which man's highest achievement is the gratification of his ego and his senses in a manner acceptable to his elegant and sophisticated but jealously censorious peers. Human relationships are largely determined by the requirement that people conceal their selfishly appetitive "nature" by the "art" of good manners. As in any age in which the nature-art dichotomy is felt to be a central problem of social ethics, English neoclassical comedy tends to be comedy of manners: plays in which mastery of or submission to, conformity with or deviation from, a group code distinguishes between social success and failure, between an "in" group of gentlemen of true wit and young ladies wise and attractive enough to win the game of love and the "outs" of foppish would-be-wits and cast-off mistresses. Because the delicate game is *social*, the emphasis in such comedies is on dialogue and behavior — on gossip, argument, repartee, epigram, innuendo, dress, deportment, and food — rather than on fullness of characterization and elaborate intrigue.

Sex is a major concern in these plays because success in sex depends both on the expression of the appetitive self and on graceful social control. That is why sex in a play like *The Man of Mode* stands for more than itself. Its many metaphorical disguises include business, gambling, play-acting, religion, warfare, and the eating of fruit. The range and frequency of the sexual innuendo in the dialogue suggest, two centuries before Freud, the libidinal nature of man's psychic force in all its manifestations. The most serious challenge to Dorimant's glamorous position in his circle is how he can manage to end his affair with Loveit in such a way that Medley, the suave and detached arbiter in matters of "reputation" in the play, will acquit him of the imputation that Loveit dropped him rather than he her. And when Loveit breaks her fan in a fit of jealousy, she disarms herself of an object that is both a cooling device and an instrument for subtle coquetry, woman's weapon in the duel of flirtation. Her act symbolizes a fatal loss of rational control of her passions.

Such episodes have philosophical implications. The play assumes one of the psychological commonplaces of classical and Christian humanism. Man is a creature of both reason and passion, suspended somewhere between the stations of angels and beasts in the great scheme of things, "created half to rise, and half to fall," as Alexander Pope was to put it in the *Essay on Man*, the most concise poetic compendium of neoclassical concepts of human nature. Man's passions move his soul; it is his moral obligation to use his reason to guide the movement. As a social being, he wins the good life when he achieves a maximum of personal freedom within the limits set by necessary social restraint.

Dorimant is charming, witty, educated, intelligent, graceful, and romantic, but he is also arrogant, heartless, ambitious, lecherous, mercenary, and inconstant — a "devil" with "something of the angel yet undefaced in him." It is this duality in human nature that *The Man of Mode* is all about. In the game of sex, the two sides of human nature interpenetrate: wit, a faculty of reason, the angelic element, is a major sexual attraction; sexual conquest, an act of passion, the animal element, is part of the conqueror's mastery of his social group. Because his business is pleasure, pleasure becomes his business — that is, an occupation of serious social and economic consequences, in which, inevitably, there are losses as well as gains. Marriage links sex and money. Though wealth, or at least a sufficiency, is taken for granted — no one has to work for a living in Restoration comedy — an estate is an important consideration in choosing a wife for both Dorimant and Young Bellair. The conventionally ambivalent treatment of marriage in the sex comedies is involved in this business-pleasure dichotomy/equation. The fashionable attitude is that marriage breeds boredom, cuckolds, and neglected wives. Stylish couples politely hate and ignore one another. And yet, marriage is a goal sought after by most of the heroes and heroines, and most of them end up romantically married. Those who don't, like Horner in Wycherley's *Country Wife*, seem, for that reason, only qualified social successes. Marriage both is and is not romantic bliss, both is and is not a matter of pecuniary interest.

One reason why marriage is a calculated risk is man's desire for sexual variety. His inconstancy of affection is a function of his awareness of mortality; by variety he can sustain an illusion of richness of life within his limited span. There is irony affecting both the Emilia–Young Bellair marriage and the possible match between Harriet and Dorimant in the fact that the play leaves open the question of whether Dorimant's love will survive the trial of a stay among the rooks in Hampshire with old Lady Woodvill and "an old lame aunt" or whether he will return to his customary haunts, the boudoirs in London, and attempt a discreet affair with Emilia, who now, as a married woman, may, by the theory Dorimant expounds to Medley in Act I, be available for seduction. This would not be out of either his or her character. On the very verge of his provisional engagement to Harriet, Dorimant tells Bellinda they "must meet again," and early in the play Emilia tells her lover, "Do not vow. Our love is frail as is our life and full as little in our power." The losers in the game of sex are those who presume on the permanence of passion. "Constancy at my years!" Dorimant protests to Loveit. " 'Tis not a virtue in season; . . . Youth has a long journey to go, Madam." The fools in the play are, in one way or another, "humor" characters, whose fixity of emotion limits their social agility and testifies to their paucity of soul and sense. Lady Woodvill and Old Bellair are harmless and gullible blocking characters near the end of their journey, one a superannuate, the other a silly pretender to a young girl's love. More pathetic are the two characters who are too shallow and rigid for the code they affect: Sir Fopling, who is nothing but a fop, and Loveit, trapped in her jealous passion. The only concession the play makes to those whom age or character disqualifies for the perils and pleasures of the love game is Lady Townley, Young Bellair's worldly-wise aunt, a spectator-adviser figure who opens her house to the frolics of youth. Bellinda, sensuous, sentimental, and resourceful, worried about her reputation and troubled by her falseness to Loveit, in love with Dorimant but unable to keep him, belongs neither with the wits nor with the fools. The most complex of Dorimant's three conquests, she elicits sympathy and interest of a kind that the brittle decorum of the play can barely contain.

When Dorimant at the end of Act III turns from a rhapsody on Harriet's charms to plans for revenge on Loveit, and when at Lady Townley's party in Act IV he breaks off his courtship of Harriet to keep his early morning assignation with Bellinda, it seems almost pointless to be shocked by his fickleness and insincerity. He is sincerely living his libertine philosophy: "I am flesh and blood yet." A little earlier a group of maskers has arrived at Lady Townley's and has been asked to remove their masks because the occasion is not a masquerade. But it is: Dorimant is there as "Mr. Court-age," assiduous in his attentions to Lady Woodvill but about to pretend "business." Libertinism requires dissembling: Loveit acts infatuation with Sir Fopling in the park; Bellinda pretends friendship with Loveit; Emilia conceals her marriage; Harriet "acts" Dorimant when they first meet; less innocently, she is the author of Dorimant's deception of her mother; and she and Young Bellair, another of the less equivocally "nice" young people in the play, deliberately fool their parents in a charade of wooing.

To maintain his reputation as masterful seducer Dorimant must turn his public self as a sober and courteous "Mr. Courtage" into a vindictive and promiscuous Machiavel; his chosen role leaves him no other choice. The "foppery" he despises includes, by his own definition, being deeply in love, and it may be that he is so committed to the brilliant part he has cast himself in that he has lost the freedom to love strongly enough to "bear," as Harriet puts it to him in Act IV, "being laughed at." If he has, he may yet fail her test. Her comment is the most probing comment in the whole play on the code it dramatizes. That both Dorimant and Sir Fopling could qualify for the part of title hero says something about the constrictive qual-ity of the former's performance. When the "four ill-fashioned fellows" in Act III vulgarly comment on Sir Fopling's appearance before exiting as suddenly as they entered, we catch a glimpse of what a man of mode looks like in the perspective of a broader social scene. There is a difference in style and intelligence of performance, certainly, but in a deeper sense is Dorimant's dissembling really so very different from Sir Fopling's foolish pretense to sexual irresistibility and fine manners? Dorimant's success as exemplary gentleman depends on his walking a narrow line between fop-pery and the crude sensualism of his social inferiors, like the whore who writes to him in Act I, asking for money for the "operies" to cure her "mallicolly." Between Sir Fopling and the Shoemaker, Dorimant has not much room to move. Sir Fopling is a caricature of a fine gentleman, and yet in the eyes of the world that Dorimant both commands and obeys he is his plausible rival for Loveit's affections. "She cannot fall from loving me to that" is his own incredulous but worried comment on her performance with Sir Fopling in the Mall. The Shoemaker is the brute inside every fine gentleman, aping the ways of his betters in practicing the vices natural to all men, provoking his genteel customer to a rudeness of manner rather below his own.

The ambivalence of Dorimant's personality and situation is at the center of the social exhibit that Etherege's play asks us to contemplate — neither to censure nor to admire but to contemplate. To say that it simply discloses — intentionally or not — the grossness, the triviality, the cruelty, and the hypocrisy of Dorimant and his set is to miss the ironic poise of its view of social man. If Dorimant is as "wicked" as he is "charming," he is also as "charming" as he is "wicked"; the two epithets demand equal rights. No tidy hierarchy of moral absolutes that we may want to erect will fit a plot in which a virtuous young woman falls in love at first sight with an accomplished rake, is brought to his knowledge by a woman who is probably a bawd, causes him to remove from the fashionable "town" to the unfashionable "country" because he wants to marry her, and may tame him by her "wildness." Harriet's and Dorimant's romance is as tentative and inconclusive as the balance between his sexual anarchy and her sexual order — between the self's instinctive predatoriness and its disciplined sociality. *The Man of Mode* is a play that uses the artifices of manners in a small and exclusive social class to pose the problem of how the jungle of society can become a genuine civilization, and it does so without suggesting that this can ever be anything other than a fragile and uncertain achievement. Such a play has a "significant relation to the best thought" of an age that habitually thought in antitheses and whose uneasy civic peace was the result of compromises. Its relevance to our own age could be similarly argued.

Sir William S. Gilbert

TRIAL BY JURY

FOREWORD

The second half of the nineteenth century saw a vogue for comic opera, or operetta, in Europe, a fashion America was eagerly to follow. The most distinguished practitioners of this highly popular form were, in France, Jacques Offenbach, and in England the unlikely but productive partnership of W. S. Gilbert and Sir Arthur Sullivan. Gilbert had been trained as a lawyer before turning to the theater — how often the two professions are allied! — and had also written a quantity of light humorous verse. Sullivan, while still young, had already established a reputation as a serious composer. Throughout his life he preferred to regard himself in this light; he composed hymns, incidental music to Shakespeare, and a serious opera, *Ivanhoe*, which had a limited success in its time, and deserves to be considered as one of the few English contributions to this art form. Gilbert and Sullivan were brought together for *Thespis*, a musical burlesque of Greek themes, which now survives only as a libretto. This first venture failed, but the two men collaborated again on *Trial by Jury* in 1875. This was an enormous success, and led to a long series of joint works, managed by the astute entrepreneur Richard D'Oyly Carte, who in 1881 built the Savoy Theatre to house the operettas. The theater still stands, and the works are still known as the Savoy Operas. Among other claims to distinction, the Savoy was the first London theater to use electric light — something which at first terrified audiences, but soon came to be accepted as a valuable and flexible extension of the stage designer's craft.

This was also the period when the director, a figure we now take for granted, was beginning to emerge. Gilbert, as well as writing the libretti, took full responsibility for staging the works. He was a tyrannical director, controlling every movement of the principals and chorus and insisting on something still revolutionary at that time — that individual performances should be subordinated to the ensemble effect. Painstaking in attending to detail and remorseless in weeding out everything he considered spurious or irrelevant, he represented a new spirit that was also beginning to make itself felt in the serious theater. His productions can still be studied in the prompt books of the D'Oyly Carte Opera Company, which reproduce Gilbert's original staging virtually unchanged.

DRAMATIS PERSONAE

THE LEARNED JUDGE	USHER
THE PLAINTIFF	FOREMAN OF THE JURY
THE DEFENDANT	ASSOCIATE
COUNSEL FOR THE PLAINTIFF	FIRST BRIDESMAID

SCENE — A *Court of Justice*
BARRISTERS, ATTORNEYS, JURYMEN *and* PUBLIC *discovered.*

CHORUS:
    Hark, the hour of ten is sounding;
    Hearts with anxious fears are bounding,
    Hall of Justice crowds surrounding,
        Breathing hope and fear —
    For to-day in this arena,   5
    Summoned by a stern subpœna,
    Edwin, sued by Angelina,
        Shortly will appear.

    (*Enter* USHER.)

SOLO — USHER:
    Now, Jurymen, hear my advice —
    All kinds of vulgar prejudice   10
        I pray you set aside:
    With stern judicial frame of mind,
    From bias free of every kind,
        This trial must be tried.
CHORUS:
    From bias free of every kind,   15
    This trial must be tried.

    (*During Chorus,* USHER *sings fortissimo,* "Silence in Court!")

USHER:

Oh listen to the plaintiff's case:
Observe the features of her face —
        The broken-hearted bride.
Condole with her distress of mind.   20
From bias free of every kind,
        This trial must be tried!

CHORUS:

From bias free, &c.

USHER:

And when amid the plaintiff's shrieks,
The ruffianly defendant speaks —   25
        Upon the other side;
What *he* may say you needn't mind —
From bias free of every kind,
        This trial must be tried!

CHORUS:

From bias free, &c.   30

(*Enter* DEFENDANT.)

RECITATIVE — DEFENDANT:

Is this the Court of the Exchequer?

ALL:

It is!

DEFENDANT (*aside*):

Be firm, be firm my pecker,
Your evil star's in the ascendant!

ALL:

Who are you?   35

DEFENDANT:

I'm the Defendant!

CHORUS OF JURYMEN (*shaking their fists*):

Monster, dread our damages.
        We're the jury,
        Dread our fury!

DEFENDANT:

Hear me, hear me, if you please,   40
        These are very strange proceedings —
For permit me to remark
        On the merits of my pleadings,
You're at present in the dark.

[JURYMEN] (DEFENDANT *beckons to* JURYMEN — *they leave the box and gather
        round him as they sing the following*): —
That's a very true remark —   45
        On the merits of his pleadings
        We're entirely in the dark!
        Ha! ha! — ho! ho!

SONG — DEFENDANT:

When first my old, old love I knew,

My bosom welled with joy; 50
My riches at her feet I threw —
   I was a love-sick boy!
No terms seemed too extravagant
   Upon her to employ —
I used to mope, and sigh, and pant, 55
   Just like a love-sick boy!
      Tink-a-Tank — Tink-a-Tank.
But joy incessant palls the sense;
   And love, unchanged will cloy,
And she became a bore intense 60
   Unto her love-sick boy!
With fitful glimmer burnt my flame,
   And I grew cold and coy,
At last, one morning, I became
   Another's love-sick boy. 65
      Tink-a-Tank — Tink-a-Tank.
CHORUS OF JURYMEN (*advancing stealthily*):
Oh, I was like that when a lad!
   A shocking young scamp of a rover,
I behaved like a regular cad;
   But that sort of thing is all over. 70
I am now a respectable chap
   And shine with a virtue resplendent
And, therefore, I haven't a rap
   Of sympathy with the defendant!
      He shall treat us with awe, 75
      If there isn't a flaw,
Singing so merrily — Trial-la-law!
Trial-la-law — Trial-la-law!
Singing so merrily — Trial-la-law!

(*They enter the jury-box.*)

RECIT. — USHER (*on Bench*):
Silence in Court, and all attention lend. 80
Behold your Judge! In due submission bend!

(*Enter* JUDGE *on Bench.*)

CHORUS:
All hail great Judge!
   To your bright rays,
We never grudge
   Ecstatic praise.
      All hail! 85
May each decree
   As statute rank,
And never be
   Reversed in Banc.
      All hail! 90

RECIT. — JUDGE:
 For these kind words accept my thanks, I pray,
 A Breach of Promise we've to try to-day.
 But firstly, if the time you'll not begrudge,
 I'll tell you how I came to be a Judge.   95
ALL:
 He'll tell us how he came to be a Judge!
JUDGE:
 Let me speak!
ALL:
 Let him speak, &c.
SONG — JUDGE:
 When I, good friends, was called to the bar,
  I'd an appetite fresh and hearty,   100
 But I was, as many young barristers are,
  An impecunious party.
 I'd a swallow-tail coat of a beautiful blue —
  A brief which I bought of a booby —
 A couple of shirts and a collar or two,   105
  And a ring that looked like a ruby!
CHORUS:
 A couple of shirts, &c.
JUDGE:
 In Westminster Hall I danced a dance,
  Like a semi-despondent fury:
 For I thought I never should hit on a chance   110
  Of addressing a British Jury —
 But I soon got tired of third class journeys,
  And dinners of bread and water;
 So I fell in love with a rich attorney's
  Elderly, ugly daughter.   115
CHORUS:
 So he fell in love, &c.
JUDGE:
 The rich attorney, he jumped with joy,
  And replied to my fond professions:
 "You shall reap the reward of your pluck, my boy,
  At the Bailey and Middlesex Sessions.   120
 You'll soon get used to her looks," said he,
  "And a very nice girl you'll find her!
 She may very well pass for forty-three
  In the dusk, with a light behind her!"
CHORUS:
 She may very well, &c.   125
JUDGE:
 The rich attorney was good as his word;
  The briefs came trooping gaily,
 And every day my voice was heard
  At the Sessions or Ancient Bailey.

All thieves who could my fees afford   130
    Relied on my orations,
And many a burglar I've restored
    To his friends and his relations.
CHORUS:
And many a burglar, &c.
JUDGE:
At length I became as rich as the Gurneys —   135
    An incubus then I thought her,
So I threw over that rich attorney's
    Elderly, ugly daughter.
The rich attorney my character high
    Tried vainly to disparage —   140
And now, if you please, I'm ready to try
    This Breach of Promise of Marriage!
CHORUS:
And now, if you please, &c.
JUDGE:
For now I'm a Judge!
ALL:
And a good Judge too!   145
JUDGE:
Yes, now I'm a Judge!
ALL:
And a good Judge too!
JUDGE:
Though all my law be fudge,
Yet I'll never, never budge,
But I'll live and die a Judge!   150
ALL:
And a good Judge too!
JUDGE (*pianissimo*):
It was managed by a job —
ALL:
And a good job too!
JUDGE:
It was managed by a job!
ALL:
And a good job too!   155
JUDGE:
It is patent to the mob,
That my being made a nob,
Was effected by a job.
ALL:
And a good job too!

(*Enter* COUNSEL FOR PLAINTIFF. *He takes his place in front row of Counsel's seats.*)

RECIT. — COUNSEL:
>Swear thou the Jury!   160

USHER:
>Kneel, Jurymen, oh, kneel!

(*All the* JURY *kneel in the Jury-box, and so are hidden from audience.*)

USHER:
>Oh, will you swear by yonder skies,
>Whatever question may arise,
>'Twixt rich and poor — 'twixt low and high,
>That you will well and truly try.   165

JURY (*raising their hands, which alone are visible*):
>To all of this we make reply,
>By the dull slate of yonder sky:
>That we will well and truly try.

(*All rise with the last note.*)

RECIT. — COUNSEL:
>Where is the Plaintiff?
>Let her now be brought.   170

RECIT. — USHER:
>Oh Angelina! Come thou into Court!
>>Angelina! Angelina!

(*Enter the* BRIDESMAIDS)

CHORUS OF BRIDESMAIDS:
>Comes the broken flower —
>>Comes the cheated maid —
>Though the tempest lower,   175
>>Rain and cloud will fade!
>Take, oh maid, these posies:
>>Though thy beauty rare
>Shame the blushing roses —
>>They are passing fair!   180
>>>Wear the flowers till they fade;
>Happy be thy life, oh maid!

(*The* JUDGE, *having taken a great fancy to* 1ST BRIDESMAID, *sends her a note by* USHER, *which she reads, kisses rapturously, and places in her bosom.*)

(*Enter* PLAINTIFF.)

SOLO — PLAINTIFF:
>O'er the season vernal,
>>Time may cast a shade;
>Sunshine, if eternal,   185
>>Makes the roses fade;
>Time may do his duty;
>>Let the thief alone —
>Winter hath a beauty,

That is all his own.   190
    Fairest days are sun and shade:
    I am no unhappy maid!

(The JUDGE, *having by this time transferred his admiration to* PLAINTIFF,
directs the USHER *to take the note from* 1ST BRIDESMAID *and hand it to* PLAIN-
TIFF, *who reads it, kisses it rapturously, and places it in her bosom.*)

CHORUS OF BRIDESMAIDS:
    Wear the flowers, &c.
JUDGE:
    Oh never, never, never, since I joined the human race,
    Saw I so exquisitely fair a face.   195
THE JURY (*shaking their forefingers at him*):
    Ah, sly dog! Ah, sly dog!
JUDGE (*to* JURY):
    How say you? Is she not designed for capture?
FOREMAN (*after consulting with the* JURY):
    We've but one word, my lord, and that is — Rapture!
PLAINTIFF (*curtseying*):
    Your kindness, gentlemen, quite overpowers!
THE JURY:
    We love you fondly, and would make you ours!   200
THE BRIDESMAIDS (*shaking their forefingers at* JURY):
    Ah, sly dogs! Ah, sly dogs!
THE JURY (*shaking their fists at* DEFENDANT):
    Monster! Monster! Dread our fury!
    There's the Judge and we're the Jury!
      Come, substantial damages!
      Substantial damages!   205
        Damages! dam ——
USHER:
    Silence in Court!
RECIT. — COUNSEL FOR PLAINTIFF:
    May it please you, my lud!
      Gentlemen of the jury!
(*Aria.*)
    With a sense of deep emotion,   210
      I approach this painful case;
    For I never had a notion
      That a man could be so base,
    Or deceive a girl confiding,
    Vows, *etcetera*, deriding.   215
ALL:
    He deceived a girl confiding,
    Vows, *etcetera*, deriding.
COUNSEL:
    See my interesting client.
      Victim of a heartless wile!
    See the traitor all defiant   220
      Wear a supercilious smile!

Sweetly smiled my client on him,
Coyly woo'd and gently won him.

ALL:

Sweetly smiled, &c.

COUNSEL:

Swiftly fled each honeyed hour   225
 Spent with this unmanly male!
Camberwell became a bower,
 Peckham an Arcadian Vale,
Breathing concentrated otto! —
An existence *à la* Watteau.   230

ALL:

Bless us, concentrated otto! &c.

COUNSEL:

Picture, then, my client naming,
 And insisting on the day;
Picture him excuses framing —
 Going from her far away;   235
Doubly criminal to do so,
For the maid had bought her *trousseau!*

ALL:

Doubly criminal, &c.

(PLAINTIFF *falls sobbing on* COUNSEL'*s breast.*)

COUNSEL (*to* PLAINTIFF):

Cheer up, my pretty — oh cheer up!

JURY:

Cheer up, cheer up, we love you!   240

(COUNSEL *leads* PLAINTIFF *fondly into Witness-box, he takes a tender leave of
her, and resumes his place in Court.*) (PLAINTIFF *reels as if about to faint.*)

JUDGE:

That she is reeling
 Is plain to me!

FOREMAN:

If faint you're feeling
 Recline on me!

(*She falls sobbing on to the* FOREMAN'*s breast.*)

PLAINTIFF (*feebly*):

I shall recover   245
 If left alone.

ALL (*shaking their fists at* DEFENDANT):

Oh, perjured lover,
Atone! atone!

FOREMAN:

Just like a father
 I wish to be.   250

(*Kissing her.*)

JUDGE (*approaching her*):
  Or, if you'd rather
    Recline on me!

(*She jumps on to Bench, sits down by the* JUDGE, *and falls sobbing on his breast.*)

COUNSEL:
  Oh! fetch some water
  From far Cologne!
ALL:
  For this sad slaughter   255
  Atone! atone!
JURY (*shaking fists at* DEFENDANT):
  Monster, monster, dread our fury,
  There's the Judge, and we're the Jury!
SONG — DEFENDANT:
  Oh, gentlemen, listen, I pray,
    Though I own that my heart has been ranging,   260
  Of nature the laws I obey,
    For nature is constantly changing.
  The moon in her phases is found,
    The time and the wind and the weather,
  The months in succession come round,   265
    And you don't find two Mondays together.
      Ah! Consider the moral, I pray,
        Nor bring a young fellow to sorrow,
      Who loves this young lady to-day,
        And loves that young lady to-morrow.   270
BRIDESMAIDS (*rushing forward, and kneeling to* JURY):
      Consider the moral, &c.
DEFENDANT:
  You cannot eat breakfast all day,
    Nor is it the act of a sinner,
  When breakfast is taken away,
    To turn his attention to dinner;   275
  And it's not in the range of belief,
    To look upon him as a glutton,
  Who, when he is tired of beef,
    Determines to tackle the mutton.
      Ah! But this I am willing to say,   280
        If it will appease her sorrow,
      I'll marry this lady to-day,
        And I'll marry the other to-morrow!
BRIDESMAIDS:
      But this he is willing to say, &c.
RECIT. — JUDGE:
  That seems a reasonable proposition
  To which, I think, your client may agree.   285
COUNSEL:
  But, I submit, m'lud, with all submission,

To marry two at once is Burglaree!
(*Referring to law book.*)
In the reign of James the Second,
It was generally reckoned   290
   As a rather serious crime
To marry two wives at a time.

(*Hands book up to* JUDGE, *who reads it.*)

ALL:
  Oh, man of learning!

(*Quartette.*)

JUDGE:
  A nice dilemma we have here,
  That calls for all our wit: 295
COUNSEL:
  And at this stage, it don't appear
  That we can settle it.
DEFENDANT:
  If I to wed the girl am loth
  A breach 'twill surely be ——
PLAINTIFF:
  And if he goes and marries both,   300
  It counts as Burglaree!
ALL:
  A nice dilemma, &c.

(DUET — *plaintiff and* DEFENDANT)

PLAINTIFF (*embracing him rapturously*):
  I love him — I love him — with fervour unceasing.
    I worship and madly adore;
    My blind adoration is ever increasing,   305
    My loss I shall ever deplore.
  Oh, see what a blessing, what love and caressing
    I've lost, and remember it, pray,
  When you I'm addressing, are busy assessing
    The damages Edwin must pay!   310
DEFENDANT (*repelling her furiously*):
  I smoke like a furnace — I'm always in liquor —
    A ruffian — a bully — a sot;
  I'm sure I should thrash her, perhaps I should kick her,
    I am such a very bad lot!
  I'm not prepossessing, as you may be guessing,   315
    She couldn't endure me a day;
  Recall my professing, when you are assessing
    The damages Edwin must pay!

(*She clings to him passionately; after a struggle, he throws her off into arms of*
COUNSEL.)

JURY:
> We would be fairly acting,
> But this is most distracting!
> If, when in liquor, he would kick her,   .
>> That is an abatement.

PUBLIC:
> She loves him, and madly adores, &c.

RECIT. — JUDGE:
> The question, gentlemen — is one of liquor;
>> You ask for guidance — this is my reply:
> He says, when tipsy, he would thrash and kick her,
>> Let's make him tipsy, gentlemen, and try!

COUNSEL:
> With all respect
> I do object!

PLAINTIFF:
> I do object!

DEFENDANT:
> I don't object!

ALL:
> With all respect
> We do object!

JUDGE (*tossing his books and papers about*):
> All the legal furies seize you!
> No proposal seems to please you,
> I can't sit up here all day,
> I must shortly get away.
> Barristers, and you, attorneys,
> Set out on your homeward journeys;
> Gentle, simple-minded usher,
> Get you, if you like, to Rus*sher!*
> Put your briefs upon the shelf,
> I will marry her myself!

(*He comes down from Bench to floor of Court. He embraces* ANGELINA.)

(FINALE)

PLAINTIFF:
> Oh, joy unbounded,
> With wealth surrounded,
> The knell is sounded
>> Of grief and woe.

COUNSEL:
> With love devoted
> On you he's doted.
> To castle moated
>> Away they go.

DEFENDANT:
> I wonder whether

They'll live together
In marriage tether
  In manner true! 355
USHER:
  It seems to me, sir,
  Of such as she, sir,
  A judge is he, sir,
      And a good judge too
CHORUS:
  Oh, joy unbounded, &c. 360
JUDGE:
  Yes, I am a Judge.
ALL:
  And a good Judge too!
JUDGE:
  Yes, I am a Judge.
ALL:
  And a good Judge too!
JUDGE:
  Though homeward as you trudge, 365
  You declare my law is fudge.
  Yet of beauty I'm a judge.
ALL:
  And a good Judge too!
JUDGE:
  Though defendant is a snob.
ALL:
  And a great snob too! 370
JUDGE:
  Though defendant is a snob.
  I'll reward him from my fob.
ALL:
  So we've settled with the job,
  And a good job too!

CURTAIN.

AFTERWORD

Trial by Jury, an innovatory and seminal work, deserves consideration in this volume on two counts: first as musical theater, second as satirical comedy. At the theater's earliest beginnings, drama and music could not be considered as things apart. Greek tragedies were "musicals" in the sense that the chorus sang and danced and the actors, too, broke into song at moments of high emotion. We cannot even begin to reconstruct the original nature of these performances, as the music has been lost and only the words remain. Thereafter the two forms of expression began to diverge.

Drama came to consist purely of the spoken word, and opera, as we know it, did not originate till certain Italian composers of the Renaissance tried to reproduce the effect they thought Greek tragedy must originally have created. But drama was not too set in its spoken patterns and opera went its separate way as a somewhat precious and artificial by-product of theater appealing to a select and largely aristocratic audience.

There were more popular forms, such as the ballad opera in England and the *vaudeville* in France — the latter, with a shift of meaning, adding a new word to the American vocabulary — which combined music and drama in various proportions. These, however, rarely attracted the attention of serious artists or won a lasting place in any repertory. One of the major achievements of Gilbert and Sullivan was that they raised musical theater to a high level of both popular and critical esteem by using plots based on sharp observations of contemporary life and music containing some of the most memorable tunes ever written. We noted Gilbert's function as director, and his attention to the concept of the total work as something larger than the sum of its individual performances. But the same attitude was present in the works from their inception. Earlier opera had been conceived largely in terms of set pieces for the principals, with the chorus filling in the gaps. *Trial by Jury* integrated soloists and chorus in a way that had scarcely been attempted before. The chorus now played a major part in the action, presenting a musico-dramatic work in which all elements were combined into a harmonious whole.

The scores of the Gilbert and Sullivan operettas followed a well-established English pattern in parodying the serious music of the time. They are full of echoes and parodies of Handel, of patriotic songs, of drawing-room ballads, and of fashionable Italian composers. Gilbert's libretti, following the same mode, deserve inclusion in the literature of satirical comedy. They are indeed faithful to an ancient, and perhaps fundamental, purpose of comedy in ridiculing things that in ordinary life are held sacred, thus acting as a safety valve for emotions that might otherwise find a more dangerous outlet. The earliest comedies we possess, those of the Greek Aristophanes, are of such a kind. No respecters of persons, they poured scorn on some of the most powerful individuals and the most prestigious institutions in the Athenian city-state, showing prominent politicians as buffoons and heaping even the gods with ridicule. Some critics argue that Gilbert was influenced by his own classical education in applying the Aristophanic spirit of censure to British institutions.

On the surface, *Trial by Jury* hardly seems a work of considerable extent or purpose. It is very short — less than thirty minutes, with a brisk conductor. It reads like a light-hearted piece of foolery, perhaps somewhat coy by our standards, and relying a little too heavily on the pun, a form of humor adored by the Victorians but deprecated by us. On closer examination, however, the work appears as a scathing indictment of the English legal system, informed by Gilbert's own apprenticeship. The issue is an action for breach of promise, once a popular type of case, now largely vanished from the courts. A young man is sued for having first promised to marry a girl and then reneged. It appears in the course of the action, however, that the defendant is the most honest man present. The jury is composed of middle-class hypocrites who understand the temptation all too well, but now have to pretend to be above it. The learned judge, by his own admission, has based his career on the same offense. Vacuous court functionaries are prepared to browbeat the jury into submission. (Read the Usher's song, totally prejudiced against the defendant, but always with the refrain, "From bias free of every kind, This trial must be tried.") Learned counsel is full of erudite and elegant argument that has nothing to do with the case. The plaintiff bride makes the most flagrant appeals to the court's emotions, and the case is eventually decided on the basis of self-interest. And this operetta was only the beginning. Gilbert's later work went on to satirize every pillar of the British establishment — army, navy, civil service, parliamentary democracy, university education, and even a royal reception.

Thus an apparently slight work induces serious reflections on the conditions under which satire can flourish. That Gilbert gave some offense to officialdom may be surmised from the fact that he was awarded a knighthood reluctantly, and very late in life; Sullivan had received his honor much earlier. The fact remains that the operettas enjoyed an immense popular success on *every* level of society, and that, in a period when censorship of the London theater was at its strongest, no attempt was made to keep these works from the stage, or alter their content in any substantial way. Ironically, the most serious protest that Gilbert ever received was from a foreign power. *The Mikado*, his most popular work, was resented by the Japanese government on the grounds that it ridiculed their royal family. In reality, *The Mikado* was an easily recognizable parody of British institutions, barely concealed beneath its Japanese coloring.

It can be argued that such satiric attacks are only possible when society feels itself so impregnable from outside assault that it can tolerate any attacks from within. This is certainly true of Aristophanes' society; his most trenchant plays were written when the Athenian hegemony was at its most powerful and seemed destined to last forever. When Athens eventually became involved in a disastrous war, Aristophanes' writing conspicuously changed direction, and the critical content of his plays diminished to virtually nothing. By the same token, Gilbert wrote when the British Empire was at the peak of its power. There were no major wars between the Crimean War in the 1850s and the Boer War in the 1890s, the country was prosperous, and Queen Victoria seemed to be immortal. Why not, then, make friendly fun of institutions that were apparently unshakeable? Gilbert, in any case, made his satire more palatable by creating a kind of fantasy world in which (as in *Alice's Adventures in Wonderland*, with whose author Gilbert once nearly collaborated) familiar personages and institutions were seen in a fairyland setting that removed the attacks from immediate reality. Even *Trial by Jury*, in which the setting and mechanics of courtroom procedure are drawn from life, ended in the original production with the descent of cupids wearing legal wigs.

Gilbert was protected by another well-established principle of play writing: When the dramatist wishes to make social comment, comedy is safer than serious drama. Though its attack may be barbed, comedy affects to speak in jest. The point is perfectly made by a story about Bernard Shaw. At the opening night of one of his more penetrating plays, he was greeted by a delighted lady from the audience with "Mr. Shaw, you are a very funny man!" "Madam," replied Shaw, "the funniest thing is that I am completely serious." Laughter is often the sugar coating that makes the pill acceptable. We need only compare the plaudits lavished on Gilbert with the odium heaped upon his near contemporary, Ibsen. Both, in their different ways, were exposing a society riddled with complacency and speaking in platitudes. But Ibsen wrote tragedy in prose, and Gilbert wrote musical comedy; and if comedy is safe, music is safer still. The point has been made by many critics that musical theater makes it possible to say things that could be said only with great difficulty in any other medium, perhaps because they are too delicate, perhaps because they are too offensive. But the musical form, because it is removed from everyday experience, acts as a filter between the author and his audience. Every author who wishes to reform his public is faced with a dilemma. If he is too subtle, he will not make his point, if he is too blatant, his audience will be offended and refuse to listen to him. Music provides an acceptable solution. It is noticeable that whenever the theater has been subjected to extreme censorship, it has tended to retreat behind music, and that some of the more sensitive issues in the modern theater have been dealt with in musical drama.

The Realistic Theater
and Its Aftermath

At this point it is appropriate to say something about changing modes of stage presentation, for with Ibsen the theater of past ages comes to an end and that of our own age begins. In the earlier plays we have considered, from *Oedipus the King* through *Phaedra*, we have seen a wide range of theatrical styles. Each culture has evolved its own mode of staging based on the social patterns and artistic preconceptions of the time. These modes could in no true sense be called "realistic." Actors conceived their roles in terms of formal postures and gestures. They spoke lines written for the most part in a heightened poetic language, only rarely in ordinary prose, and for tragedy at least they used a special, incantatory voice. Costumes were formal robes. Stage settings, if they were used at all, were formal backgrounds for the action rather than pictorial representations of the supposed locale.

In Ibsen's theater we see an obvious difference. In *A Doll's House*, an important part of the author's purpose is that the settings, costumes, and general milieu must be as realistic as possible. We must believe that we are seeing a slice of someone else's everyday life. The decor becomes a part of the action. Actors no longer play *against* a setting but *in* it. They are viewed as part of their surroundings, and these surroundings are spelled out for us in literal detail. We hear about the furniture, the ornaments, the mailbox. The play's most important moment is provided not by the actors but by the set — the sound of a door slamming offstage. Compare this with *Oedipus the King* or *Phaedra*, in which the setting is of minimal importance. True, one could stage *Phaedra* against a reproduction of Louis XIV's

Versailles, and it would be not at all inappropriate. But one could stage it just as well against a plain curtain. To set *A Doll's House* in a scenic void is to invite miscomprehension or disaster. From the latter part of the nineteenth century realism became not merely *a* style but *the* style.

This was no overnight revolution, but the product of more than a century of restlessness and dissatisfaction. By the 1760s the theater had grown lazy. Conventional gestures and speech-patterns that had once had an organic relationship with the culture that evolved them tended to remain in currency long after their useful life had passed. They became fossilized into a kind of artificial stage behavior that no longer responded to the needs and expectations of the audience. (One may see the same kind of thing today in opera: Too often, a twentieth-century audience is forced to watch what is essentially a nineteenth-century production.) Actors learned performances, like lines, by rote, being content merely to reproduce the stances, gestures and inflections that their predecessors had used before them. The stage became further and further removed from real life. Dickens, in his play-reporting, shows how these shoddy, second-hand attitudes had permeated the theater of his own day. For a view of the theater at its lowest ebb, the reader may profitably turn to the account of the *Hamlet* production in *Great Expectations*.

At the same time, eighteenth-century critics were beginning to object to a similar carelessness in stage settings. They found it inappropriate that items from the old stock sets were used in careless proximity, whatever the nature of the piece; that an architectural frieze should frame what purported to be a woodland glade. These discrepancies became more blatant as the contents of the plays themselves changed. The Romantic period brought, in drama as in lyric poetry, an insistence on the workings and forces of nature. If man was to be shown as a product of his natural environment, then this environment had to be shown, and shown forcefully, on the stage. Thus designers began to move outside the painted walls of the old conventional interiors to display rivers, forests, mountain peaks and open skies, evolving new methods of construction and lighting to do so. In time, interior designs began to acquire a corresponding realism. In the nineteenth century the naturalistic movement argued, no less forcibly, that man must be seen as a product of his *urban* environment. Émile Zola, in his novel *Thérèse Raquin*, spends chapters not in telling the story but in establishing the sordid Paris slum in which his characters live and which enforces a pattern of behavior upon them; living where they do, they cannot help being what they are. Once again, the theater followed suit. Stage settings acquired real furniture, rubbed and worn with use. Stage costumes could now be worn in the street and pass for real. This attitude even extended to works not apparently conceived in the realistic mode. We see how, even in Gilbert's direction of a comic operetta like *Trial by Jury*, there is a new insistence on getting all the physical details right. Designers of *Hamlet* now started to worry about the period in which the play was supposed to be set, and to ask how people lived in the historical Danish court.

Actors also changed their ways. As late as the 1840s a Shakespearean actor might still have been using gestures and inflections that had been in vogue two hundred years before. This now became impossible. An actor of the new school was asked to work from the life, to explore his character as though he were a real person and to establish a personal identification with him. Acting was now perceived as an ensemble art, rather than a collection of individual performances. Actors were asked to relate to each other, as well as to the audience, and to function as a homogeneous and mutually responsive group. Consequently we see in the modern theater the emergence of the director, with the responsibility of assembling every aspect of the production into a cohesive whole.

The realistic mode has predominated into our time and has been given additional emphasis by the *total* realism now accessible to film and television. But the arts are never static for long, and already, by the end of the nineteenth century, a reaction against realism had started to appear. This happened most obviously in painting. Various schools challenged the supremacy of realism by asserting that their function was to show the essence of the subject, not its surface appearance. Thus Cézanne reduced nature to elementary geometrical shapes, and the impressionists worked in patterns of light and shade; the expressionists turned to harsh color and angular drawing, and the surrealists arranged natural objects in bizarre juxtapositions. Just so, in the theater, some writers felt that the limitations of realism were too severe, and sought various ways of escape. The advent of the cinema both encouraged realism in the performing arts and gave ammunition to its opponents. It could now be argued that realism should be left to the film, which did it to perfection. Thus the twentieth-century theater has turned increasingly to purely theatrical devices — to open stages, with mere indications of scenery; to ritual; to masks and choruses; to actor-audience participation. The plays that follow, therefore, cover a wide spectrum of approaches. Some, like A *Doll's House* and *Major Barbara*, uphold realism. Others, like *The Ghost Sonata*, just as clearly oppose it. And others still, though they may *seem* to be realistic plays (*Virginia Woolf*, *The Dumb Waiter*) are using the techniques of realism to do quite other things.

Henrik Ibsen

A DOLL'S HOUSE

Translated by Otto Reinert

FOREWORD

In a century when the theater had remained largely aloof from public issues, Ibsen brought it back with a jolt to social awareness. The favored form of his time was the "well-made play" — Oscar Wilde's *The Importance of Being Earnest* is an illustrious example — the kind of play in which craftsmanship took precedence over content. Ibsen put back the content. As a Norwegian, he lived in a country only recently independent, and still susceptible to models from abroad. He learned much from the French writers and their formulae — many of their virtues and some of their vices. His originality lay in the subjects that he chose to write about, some of which had previously been considered unmentionable. Victorien Sardou, one of Ibsen's models, could entertain Paris audiences with *Let's Get a Divorce*, but this was a frivolous romp that no one was expected to take seriously. *A Doll's House* treats the breakup of a marriage in a very different light. Its notoriety spread far beyond Norway, and the play still retains some of its original shock value in countries where women's emancipation is still a current issue. A key factor in the development of the modern theater has been the rapidity of modern communications. By Ibsen's time the appearance of a new and provocative work could almost simultaneously shock audiences in New York and London, in Paris and Berlin. In England Ibsen's works were championed by the critic William Archer and translated by him, unfortunately into a rather heavy style, which blinded generations to the lightness and wit that Ibsen can display at need. These plays influenced the young Bernard Shaw, who in his treatise *The Quintessence of Ibsenism* and in his own plays insisted on the theater's responsibility to fulfil its social obligations.

THE CHARACTERS

TORVALD HELMER, a lawyer
NORA, his wife
DR. RANK
MRS. LINDE
KROGSTAD

THE HELMERS' THREE SMALL CHILDREN
The children's NURSE, Anne-Marie
A HOUSEMAID
A PORTER

The Scene: The Helmers' living room

ACT I

A pleasant living room, tastefully but not expensively furnished. A door on the rear wall, right, leads to the front hall; another door, left, to HELMER's *study. Between the two doors a piano. A third door in the middle of the left wall; further front a window. Near the window a round table and a small couch. Toward the rear of the right wall a fourth door; further front a tile stove with a rocking chair and a couple of armchairs in front of it. Between the stove and the door a small table. Copperplate etchings on the walls. A whatnot with porcelain figurines and other small objects. A small bookcase with de luxe editions. A rug on the floor; fire in the stove. Winter day.*

The doorbell rings, then the sound of the front door opening. NORA, *dressed for outdoors, enters, humming cheerfully. She carries several packages, which she puts down on the table, right. She leaves the door to the front hall open; there a* PORTER *is seen holding a Christmas tree and a basket. He gives them to the* MAID, *who has let them in.*

NORA: Be sure to hide the Christmas tree, Helene. The children mustn't see it till after we've trimmed it tonight. (*Opens her purse; to the* PORTER.) How much?
PORTER: Fifty øre.
NORA: Here's a crown. No, keep the change. (*The* PORTER *thanks her, leaves.* NORA *closes the door. She keeps laughing quietly to herself as she takes off her coat, etc. She takes a bag of macaroons from her pocket and eats a couple. She walks cautiously over to the door to the study and listens.*) Yes, he's home. (*Resumes her humming, walks over to the table, right.*)
HELMER (*in his study*): Is that my little lark twittering out there?
NORA (*opening some of the packages*): That's right.
HELMER: My squirrel bustling about?

NORA: Yes.

HELMER: When did squirrel come home?

NORA: Just now. (*Puts the bag of macaroons back in her pocket, wipes her mouth.*) Come out here, Torvald. I want to show you what I've bought.

HELMER: I'm busy right now! (*After a little while he opens the door and looks in, pen in hand.*) Bought, eh? All that? So little wastrel has been throwing money around again?

NORA: Oh, but Torvald, this Christmas we can be a little extravagant, can't we? It's the first Christmas we haven't had to watch every penny.

HELMER: I don't know about that. We certainly don't have money to throw away.

NORA: Yes, Torvald, we do. A little, anyway. Just a tiny little bit? Now that you're going to get that big salary and all and make lots and lots of money.

HELMER: Starting at New Year's, yes. But payday isn't till the end of the quarter.

NORA: That doesn't matter. We can always borrow.

HELMER: Nora! (*Goes over to her and playfully pulls her ear.*) There you go being irresponsible again. Suppose I borrowed a thousand crowns today and you spent it all for Christmas and on New Year's Eve a tile from the roof laid me out cold?

NORA (*putting her hand over his mouth*): I won't have you say such horrid things.

HELMER: But suppose it happened. Then what?

NORA: If it did, I wouldn't care whether we owed money or not.

HELMER: But what about the people I had borrowed from?

NORA: Who cares about them! They are strangers!

HELMER: Nora, Nora, you *are* a woman. No, really! You know how I feel about that. No debts! A home in debt isn't a free home, and if it isn't free it isn't beautiful. We've managed nicely so far, you and I, and that's the way we'll go on. It won't be for much longer.

NORA (*walks over toward the stove*): All right, Torvald. Whatever you say.

HELMER (*follows her*): Come, come, my little songbird mustn't droop her wings. What's this? Can't have a pouty squirrel in the house, you know. (*Takes out his wallet.*) Nora, what do you think I have here?

NORA (*turns around quickly*): Money!

HELMER: Here. (*Gives her some bills.*) Don't you think I know Christmas is expensive?

NORA (*counting*): Ten — twenty — thirty — forty. Thank you, thank you, Torvald. This helps a lot.

HELMER: I certainly hope so.

NORA: It does, it does! But I want to show you what I got. It was cheap, too. Look. New clothes for Ivar. And a sword. And a horse and a trumpet for Bob. And a doll and a little bed for Emmy. It isn't any good, but it wouldn't last, anyway. And here's some dress material and scarves for the maids. I feel bad about old Anne-Marie, though. She really should be getting much more.

HELMER: And what's in here?

NORA (*cries*): Not till tonight!

HELMER: I see. But now what does my little spendthrift have in mind for herself?

NORA: Oh, nothing. I really don't care.

HELMER: Of course you do. Tell me what you'd like. Within reason.

NORA: Oh, I don't know. Really, I don't. The only thing —

HELMER: Well?

NORA (*fiddling with his buttons, without looking at him*): If you really want to give me something, you might — you could —

HELMER: All right, let's have it.

NORA (*quickly*): Some money, Torvald. Just as much as you think you can spare. Then I'll buy myself something one of these days.

HELMER: No, really, Nora —

NORA: Oh yes, please, Torvald. Please? I'll wrap the money in pretty gold paper and hang it on the tree. Won't that be nice?

HELMER: What's the name for little birds that are always spending money?

NORA: Wastrels, I know. But please let's do it my way, Torvald. Then I'll have time to decide what I need most. Now that's sensible, isn't it?

HELMER (*smiling*): Oh, very sensible. That is, if you really bought yourself something you could use. But it all disappears in the household expenses or you buy things you don't need. And then you come back to me for more.

NORA: Oh, but Torvald —

HELMER: That's the truth, dear little Nora, and you know it. (*Puts his arm around her.*) My wastrel is a little sweetheart, but she *does* go through an awful lot of money awfully fast. You've no idea how expensive it is for a man to keep a wastrel.

NORA: That's not fair, Torvald. I really save all I can.

HELMER (*laughs*): Oh, I believe that. All you can. Meaning, exactly nothing!

NORA (*hums, smiles mysteriously*): You don't know all the things we songbirds and squirrels need money for, Torvald.

HELMER: You know, you're funny. Just like your father. You're always looking for ways to get money, but as soon as you do, it runs through your fingers and you can never say what you spent it for. Well, I guess I'll just have to take you the way you are. It's in your blood. Yes, that sort of thing is hereditary, Nora.

NORA: In that case, I wish I had inherited many of Daddy's qualities.

HELMER: And I don't want you any different from just what you are — my own sweet little songbird. Hey! — I think I just noticed something. Aren't you looking — what's the word? — a little — sly — ?

NORA: I am?

HELMER: You definitely are. Look at me.

NORA (*looks at him*): Well?

HELMER (*wagging a finger*): Little sweet-tooth hasn't by any chance been on a rampage today, has she?

NORA: Of course not. Whatever makes you think that?

HELMER: A little detour by the pastryshop maybe?

NORA: No, I assure you, Torvald —

HELMER: Nibbled a little jam?

NORA: Certainly not!

HELMER: Munched a macaroon or two?

NORA: No, really, Torvald, honestly —

HELMER: All right. Of course I was only joking.

NORA (*walks toward the table, right*): You know I wouldn't do anything to displease you.

HELMER: I know. And I have your promise. (*Over to her.*) All right, keep your little Christmas secrets to yourself, Nora darling. They'll all come out tonight, I suppose, when we light the tree.

NORA: Did you remember to invite Rank?

HELMER: No, but there's no need to. He knows he'll have dinner with us. Anyway,

I'll see him later this morning. I'll ask him then. I did order some good wine. Oh Nora, you've no idea how much I'm looking forward to tonight!

NORA: Me too! And the children, Torvald! They'll have such a good time!

HELMER: You know, it *is* nice to have a good, safe job and a comfortable income. Feels good just thinking about it. Don't you agree?

NORA: Oh, it's wonderful!

HELMER: Remember last Christmas? For three whole weeks you shut yourself up every evening till long after midnight, making ornaments for the Christmas tree and I don't know what else. Some big surprise for all of us, anyway. I'll be damned if I've ever been so bored in my whole life!

NORA: I wasn't bored at all.

HELMER (*smiling*): But you've got to admit you didn't have much to show for it in the end.

NORA: Oh, don't tease me again about that! Could I help it that the cat got in and tore up everything?

HELMER: Of course you couldn't, my poor little Nora. You just wanted to please the rest of us, and that's the important thing. But I *am* glad the hard times are behind us. Aren't you?

NORA: Oh yes. I think it's just wonderful.

HELMER: This year I won't be bored and lonely. And you won't have to strain your dear eyes and your delicate little hands —

NORA (*claps her hands*): No I won't, will I, Torvald? Oh, how wonderful, how lovely, to hear you say that! (*Puts her arm under his.*) Let me tell you how I think we should arrange things, Torvald. Soon as Christmas is over — (*The doorbell rings.*) Someone's at the door. (*Straightens things up a bit.*) A caller, I suppose. Bother!

HELMER: Remember, I'm not home.

THE MAID (*in the door to the front hall*): Ma'am, there's a lady here —

NORA: All right. Ask her to come in.

THE MAID (*to* HELMER): And the Doctor just arrived.

HELMER: Is he in the study?

THE MAID: Yes, sir.

(HELMER *exits into his study.* THE MAID *shows* MRS. LINDE *in and closes the door behind her as she leaves.* MRS. LINDE *is in travel dress.*)

MRS. LINDE (*timid and a little hesitant*): Good morning, Nora.

NORA (*uncertainly*): Good morning.

MRS. LINDE: I don't believe you know who I am.

NORA: No — I'm not sure — Though I know I should — Of course! Kristine! It's you!

MRS. LINDE: Yes, it's me.

NORA: And I didn't even recognize you! I had no idea! (*In a lower voice.*) You've changed, Kristine.

MRS. LINDE: I'm sure I have. It's been nine or ten long years.

NORA: Has it really been that long? Yes, you're right. I've been so happy these last eight years. And now you're here. Such a long trip in the middle of winter. How brave!

MRS. LINDE: I got in on the steamer this morning.

NORA: To have some fun over the holidays, of course. That's lovely. For we *are* going to have fun. But take off your coat! You aren't cold, are you? (*Helps her.*) There, now! Let's sit down here by the fire and just relax and talk. No, you sit there. I want the rocking chair. (*Takes her hands.*) And now you've got your old face back. It was just for a minute, right at first — Though you are a little more pale, Kristine. And maybe a little thinner.

MRS. LINDE: And much, much older, Nora.

NORA: Maybe a little older. Just a teeny-weeny bit, not much. (*Interrupts herself, serious.*) Oh, but how thoughtless of me, chatting away like this! Sweet, good Kristine, can you forgive me?

MRS. LINDE: Forgive you what, Nora?

NORA (*in a low voice*): You poor dear, you lost your husband, didn't you?

MRS. LINDE: Three years ago, yes.

NORA: I know. I saw it in the paper. Oh please believe me, Kristine. I really meant to write you, but I never got around to it. Something was always coming up.

MRS. LINDE: Of course, Nora. I understand.

NORA: No, that wasn't very nice of me. You poor thing, all you must have been through. And he didn't leave you much, either, did he?

MRS. LINDE: No.

NORA: And no children?

MRS. LINDE: No.

NORA: Nothing at all, in other words?

MRS. LINDE: Not so much as a sense of loss — a grief to live on —

NORA (*incredulous*): But Kristine, how can that *be*?

MRS. LINDE (*with a sad smile, strokes* NORA's *hair*): That's the way it sometimes is, Nora.

NORA: All alone. How awful for you. I have three darling children. You can't see them right now, though; they're out with their nurse. But now you must tell me everything —

MRS. LINDE: No, no; I'd rather listen to you.

NORA: No, you begin. Today I won't be selfish. Today I'll think only of you. Except there's one thing I've just got to tell you first. Something marvelous that's happened to us just these last few days. You haven't heard, have you?

MRS. LINDE: No; tell me.

NORA: Just think. My husband's been made manager of the Mutual Bank.

MRS. LINDE: Your husband — ! Oh, I'm so glad!

NORA: Yes, isn't that great? You see, private law practice is so uncertain, especially when you won't have anything to do with cases that aren't — you know — quite nice. And of course Torvald won't do that, and I quite agree with him. Oh, you've no idea how delighted we are! He takes over at New Year's, and he'll be getting a big salary and all sorts of extras. From now on we'll be able to live in quite a different way — exactly as we like. Oh, Kristine! I feel so carefree and happy! It's lovely to have lots and lots of money and not have to worry about a thing! Don't you agree?

MRS. LINDE: It would be nice to have enough, at any rate.

NORA: No, I don't mean just enough. I mean lots and lots!

MRS. LINDE (*smiles*): Nora, Nora, when are you going to be sensible? In school you spent a great deal of money.

NORA (*quietly laughing*): Yes, and Torvald says I still do. (*Raises her finger at* MRS. LINDE.) But "Nora, Nora" isn't so crazy as you all think. Believe me, we've had nothing to be extravagant with. We've both had to work.

MRS. LINDE: You too?

NORA: Yes. Oh, It's been little things mostly — sewing, crocheting, embroidery — that sort of thing. (*Casually.*) And other things too. You know, of course, that Torvald left government service when we got married? There was no chance of promotion in his department, and of course he had to make more money than he had been making. So for the first few years he worked altogether too hard. He took jobs on the side and worked day and night. It turned out to be too much for him. He became seriously ill. The doctors told him he needed to go south.

MRS. LINDE: That's right; you spent a year in Italy, didn't you?

NORA: Yes, we did. But you won't believe how hard it was to get away. Ivar had just been born. But of course we had to go. Oh, it was a wonderful trip. And it saved Torvald's life. But it took a lot of money, Kristine.

MRS. LINDE: I'm sure it did.

NORA: Twelve hundred dollars of the old money.[1] Four thousand eight hundred crowns. That's a lot.

MRS. LINDE: Yes. So it's lucky you have it when something like that happens.

NORA: Well, actually we got the money from Daddy.

MRS. LINDE: I see. That was about the time your father died, I believe.

NORA: Yes, just about then. And I couldn't even go and take care of him. I was expecting little Ivar any day. And I had poor Torvald to look after, desperately sick and all. My dear, good Daddy! I never saw him again, Kristine. That's the saddest thing that's happened to me since I got married.

MRS. LINDE: I know you were very fond of him. But then you went to Italy?

NORA: Yes, for now we had the money, and the doctors urged us to go. So we left about a month later.

MRS. LINDE: And when you came back your husband was well again?

NORA: Healthy as a horse!

MRS. LINDE: But — the doctor?

NORA: What do you mean?

MRS. LINDE: I thought the maid said it was the doctor, that gentleman who came the same time I did.

NORA: Oh, that's Doctor Rank. He doesn't come as a doctor. He's our closest friend. He looks in at least once every day. No, Torvald hasn't been sick once since then. And the children are strong and healthy, too, and so am I. (*Jumps up and claps her hands.*) Oh god, Kristine! Isn't it wonderful to be alive and happy! Isn't it just lovely! — But now I'm being mean again, talking only about myself and my things. (*Sits down on a footstool close to* MRS. LINDE *and puts her arms on her lap.*) Please, don't be angry with me! Tell me, is it really true that you didn't care for your husband? Then why did you marry him?

MRS. LINDE: Mother was still alive, but she was bedridden and helpless. And I had my two younger brothers to look after. I didn't think I had the right to turn him down.

NORA: No, I suppose. So he had money then?

MRS. LINDE: He was quite well off, I think. But it was an uncertain business, Nora. When he died, the whole thing collapsed and there was nothing left.

NORA: And then — ?

---

[1] In 1875 Norway joined the international monetary union based on the gold standard. The monetary unit changed from the old silver specie dollar ("*Daler*") to the crown ("*Krone*"), redeemable in gold. As Nora's remark implies, there were four crowns to a dollar.

MRS. LINDE: Well, I had to manage as best I could. With a little store and a little school and anything else I could think of. The last three years have been one long work day for me, Nora, without any rest. But now it's over. My poor mother doesn't need me any more. She passed away. And the boys are on their own too. They've both got jobs and support themselves.

NORA: What a relief for you —

MRS. LINDE: No, not relief. Just a great emptiness. Nobody to live for any more. (*Gets up, restlessly.*) That's why I couldn't stand it any longer in that little hole. It's got to be easier to find something to keep me busy and occupy my thoughts here in town. With a little luck I should be able to find a good, steady job — something in an office —

NORA: Oh but Kristine, that's exhausting work, and you look worn out already. It would be much better if you went to a resort.

MRS. LINDE (*walks over to the window*): I don't have a Daddy who can give me the money, Nora.

NORA (*getting up*): Oh, don't be angry with me.

MRS. LINDE (*over to her*): Dear Nora, don't *you* be angry with *me*. That's the worst thing about my kind of situation: you become so bitter. You've nobody to work for, and yet you have to look out for yourself, somehow. You got to keep on living, and so you become selfish. Do you know — when you told me about your husband's new position I was delighted not so much for your sake as for my own.

NORA: Why was that? Oh, I see. You think maybe Torvald can give you a job?

MRS. LINDE: That's what I had in mind.

NORA: And he will too, Kristine. Just leave it to me. I'll be ever so subtle about it. I'll think of something nice to tell him, something he'll like. I so much want to help you.

MRS. LINDE: That's very good of you, Nora — making an effort like that for me. Especially since you've known so little trouble and hardship in your own life.

NORA: I — have known so little — ?

MRS. LINDE (*smiling*): Oh well, some sewing or whatever it was. You're still a child, Nora.

NORA (*with a toss of her head, walks away*): You shouldn't sound so superior.

MRS. LINDE: I shouldn't?

NORA: You're just like all the others. None of you think I'm good for anything really serious.

MRS. LINDE: Well, now —

NORA: That I've never been through anything difficult.

MRS. LINDE: But Nora! You just told me all your troubles!

NORA: That's nothing! (*Lowers her voice.*) I haven't told you about *it*.

MRS. LINDE: It? What's that? What do you mean?

NORA: You patronize me, Kristine, and that's not fair. You're proud that you worked so long and so hard for your mother.

MRS. LINDE: I don't think I patronize anyone. But it *is* true that I'm both proud and happy that I could make mother's last years comparatively easy.

NORA: And you're proud of all you did for your brothers.

MRS. LINDE: I think I have the right to be.

NORA: And so do I. But now I want to tell you something, Kristine. I have something to be proud and happy about too.

MRS. LINDE: I don't doubt that for a moment. But what exactly do you mean?

NORA: Not so loud! Torvald mustn't hear — not for anything in the world. Nobody must know about this, Kristine. Nobody but you.

MRS. LINDE: But what is it?

NORA: Come here. (*Pulls her down on the couch beside her.*) You see, I *do* have something to be proud and happy about. I've saved Torvald's life.

MRS. LINDE: Saved — ? How do you mean — "saved"?

NORA: I told you about our trip to Italy. Torvald would have died if he hadn't gone.

MRS. LINDE: I understand that. And so your father gave you the money you needed.

NORA (*smiles*): Yes, that's what Torvald and all the others think. But —

MRS. LINDE: But what?

NORA: Daddy didn't give us a penny. *I* raised that money.

MRS. LINDE: *You* did? That whole big amount?

NORA: Twelve hundred dollars. Four thousand eight hundred crowns. *Now* what do you say?

MRS. LINDE: But Nora, how could you? Did you win the state lottery?

NORA (*contemptuously*): State lottery! (*Snorts.*) What would be so great about that?

MRS. LINDE: Where did it come from then?

NORA (*humming and smiling, enjoying her secret*): Hmmm. Tra-la-la-la-la!

MRS. LINDE: You certainly couldn't have borrowed it.

NORA: Oh? And why not?

MRS. LINDE: A wife can't borrow money without her husband's consent.

NORA (*with a toss of her head*): Oh, I don't know — take a wife with a little bit of a head for business — a wife who knows how to manage things —

MRS. LINDE: But Nora, I don't understand at all —

NORA: You don't have to. I didn't say I borrowed the money, did I? I could have gotten it some other way. (*Leans back.*) An admirer may have given it to me. When you're as tolerably goodlooking as I am —

MRS. LINDE: Oh, you're crazy.

NORA: I think you're dying from curiosity, Kristine.

MRS. LINDE: I'm beginning to think you've done something very foolish, Nora.

NORA (*sits up*): Is it foolish to save your husband's life?

MRS. LINDE: I say it's foolish to act behind his back.

NORA: But don't you see: he couldn't be told! You're missing the whole point, Kristine. We couldn't even let him know how seriously ill he was. The doctors came to *me* and told me his life was in danger, that nothing could save him but a stay in the south. Don't you think I tried to work on him? I told him how lovely it would be if I could go abroad like other young wives. I cried and I begged. I said he'd better remember what condition I was in, that he had to be nice to me and do what I wanted. I even hinted he could borrow the money. But that almost made him angry with me. He told me I was being irresponsible and that it was his duty as my husband not to give in to my whims and moods — I think that's what he called it. All right, I said to myself, you've got to be saved somehow, and so I found a way —

MRS. LINDE: And your husband never learned from your father that the money didn't come from him?

NORA: Never. Daddy died that same week. I thought of telling him all about it and ask him not to say anything. But since he was so sick — It turned out I didn't have to —

MRS. LINDE: And you've never told your husband?

NORA: Of course not! Good heavens, how could I? He, with his strict principles! Besides, you know how men are. Torvald would find it embarrassing and humiliating to learn that he owed me anything. It would upset our whole relationship. Our happy, beautiful home would no longer be what it is.

MRS. LINDE: Aren't you ever going to tell him?

NORA (*reflectively, half smiling*): Yes — one day, maybe. Many, many years from now, when I'm no longer young and pretty. Don't laugh! I mean when Torvald no longer feels about me the way he does now, when he no longer thinks it's fun when I dance for him and put on costumes and recite for him. Then it will be good to have something in reserve — (*Interrupts herself.*) Oh, I'm just being silly! That day will never come. — Well, now, Kristine, what do you say about my great secret? Don't you think I'm good for something too? — By the way, you wouldn't believe all the worry I've had because of it. It's been very hard to meet my obligations on schedule. You see, in business there's something called quarterly interest and something called installments on the principal, and those things are terribly hard to come up with. I've had to save a little here and a little there, whenever I could. I couldn't use much of the housekeeping money, for Torvald has to eat well. And I couldn't use what I got for clothes for the children. They have to look nice, and I didn't think it would be right to spend less than I got — the sweet little things!

MRS. LINDE: Poor Nora! So you had to take it from your own allowance?

NORA: Yes, of course. After all, it was my affair. Every time Torvald gave me money for a new dress or what have you, I never used more than half of it. I always bought the cheapest, simplest things for myself. Thank god, everything looks good on me, so Torvald never noticed. But it was hard many times, Kristine, for it's fun to have pretty clothes. Don't you think?

MRS. LINDE: Certainly.

NORA: Anyway, I had other ways of making money too. Last winter I was lucky enough to get some copying work. So I locked the door and sat up writing every night till quite late. God! I often got so tired — ! But it was great fun, too, working and making money. It was almost like being a man.

MRS. LINDE: But how much have you been able to pay off this way?

NORA: I couldn't tell you exactly. You see, it's very difficult to keep track of that kind of business. All I know is I have been paying off as much as I've been able to scrape together. Many times I just didn't know what to do. (*Smiles.*) Then I used to imagine a rich old gentleman had fallen in love with me —

MRS. LINDE: What! What old gentleman?

NORA: Phooey! And now he was dead and they were reading his will, and there it said in big letters, "All my money is to be paid in cash immediately to the charming Mrs. Nora Helmer."

MRS. LINDE: But dearest Nora — who *was* this old gentleman?

NORA: For heaven's sake, Kristine, don't you see! There *was* no old gentleman. He was just somebody I made up when I couldn't think of any way to raise the money. But never mind him. The old bore can be anyone he likes to for all I care. I have no use for him or his last will, for now I don't have a single worry in the world. (*Jumps up.*) Dear god, what a lovely thought that is! To be able to play and have fun with the children, to have everything nice and pretty in the house, just the way Torvald likes it! Not a care! And soon spring will be here, and the air will be blue and high. Maybe we can travel again. Maybe I'll see the ocean again! Oh, yes, yes! — it's wonderful to be alive and happy!

(*The doorbell rings.*)

MRS. LINDE (*getting up*): There's the doorbell. Maybe I better be going.

NORA: No, please stay. I'm sure it's just someone for Torvald —

THE MAID (*in the hall door*): Excuse me, ma'am. There's a gentleman here who'd like to see Mr. Helmer.

NORA: You mean the Bank Manager.

THE MAID: Sorry, ma'am; the Bank Manager. But I didn't know — since the Doctor is with him —

NORA: Who is the gentleman?

KROGSTAD (*appearing in the door*): It's just me, Mrs. Helmer.

(MRS. LINDE *starts, looks, turns away toward the window.*)

NORA (*takes a step toward him, tense, in a low voice*): You? What do you want? What do you want with my husband?

KROGSTAD: Bank business — in a way. I have a small job in the Mutual, and I understand your husband is going to be our new boss —

NORA: So it's just — ?

KROGSTAD: Just routine business, ma'am. Nothing else.

NORA: All right. In that case, why don't you go through the door to the office. (*Dismisses him casually as she closes the door. Walks over to the stove and tends the fire.*)

MRS. LINDE: Nora — who was that man?

NORA: His name's Krogstad. He's a lawyer.

MRS. LINDE: So it *was* him.

NORA: Do you know him?

MRS. LINDE: I used to — many years ago. For a while he worked as a clerk in our part of the country.

NORA: Right. He did.

MRS. LINDE: He has changed a great deal.

NORA: I believe he had a very unhappy marriage.

MRS. LINDE: And now he's a widower, isn't he?

NORA: With many children. There now; it's burning nicely again. (*Closes the stove and moves the rocking chair a little to the side.*)

MRS. LINDE: They say he's into all sorts of business.

NORA: Really? Maybe so. I wouldn't know. But let's not talk about business. It's such a bore.

RANK (*appears in the door to* HELMER'S *study*): No, I don't want to be in the way. I'd rather talk to your wife a bit. (*Closes the door and notices* MRS. LINDE.) Oh, I beg your pardon. I believe I'm in the way here too.

NORA: No, not at all. (*Introduces them.*) Doctor Rank. Mrs. Linde.

RANK: Aha. A name often heard in this house. I believe I passed you on the stairs coming up.

MRS. LINDE: Yes. I'm afraid I climb stairs very slowly. They aren't good for me.

RANK: I see. A slight case of inner decay, perhaps?

MRS. LINDE: Overwork, rather.

RANK: Oh, is that all? And now you've come to town to relax at all the parties?

MRS. LINDE: I have come to look for a job.

RANK: A proven cure for overwork, I take it?

MRS. LINDE: One has to live, Doctor.

RANK: Yes, that seems to be the general opinion.

NORA: Come on, Doctor Rank — you want to live just as much as the rest of us.

RANK: Of course I do. Miserable as I am, I prefer to go on being tortured as long as possible. All my patients feel the same way. And that's true of the moral invalids too. Helmer is talking with a specimen right this minute.

MRS. LINDE (*in a low voice*): Ah!

NORA: What do you mean?

RANK: Oh, this lawyer, Krogstad. You don't know him. The roots of his character are decayed. But even he began by saying something about having *to live* — as if it were a matter of the highest importance.

NORA: Oh? What did he want with Torvald?

RANK: I don't really know. All I heard was something about the Bank.

NORA: I didn't know that Krog — that this Krogstad had anything to do with the Mutual Bank.

RANK: Yes, he seems to have some kind of job there. (*To* MRS. LINDE.) I don't know if you are familiar in your part of the country with the kind of person who is always running around trying to sniff out cases of moral decrepitude and as soon as he finds one puts the individual under observation in some excellent position or other. All the healthy ones are left out in the cold.

MRS. LINDE: I should think it's the sick who need looking after the most.

RANK (*shrugs his shoulders*): There we are. That's the attitude that turns society into a hospital.

(NORA, *absorbed in her own thoughts suddenly starts giggling and clapping her hands.*)

RANK: What's so funny about that? Do you even know what society is?

NORA: What do I care about your stupid society! I laughed at something entirely different — something terribly amusing. Tell me, Doctor Rank — all the employees in the Mutual Bank, from now on they'll all be dependent on Torvald, right?

RANK: Is that what you find so enormously amusing?

NORA (*smiles and hums*): That's my business, that's my business! (*Walks around.*) Yes, I do think it's fun that we — that Torvald is going to have so much influence on so many people's lives. (*Brings out the bag of macaroons.*) Have a macaroon, Doctor Rank.

RANK: Well, well — macaroons. I thought they were banned around here.

NORA: Yes, but these were some that Kristine gave me.

MRS. LINDE: What! I?

NORA: That's all right. Don't look so scared. You couldn't know that Torvald won't let me have macaroons. He's afraid they'll ruin my teeth. But who cares! Just once in a while — ! Right, Doctor Rank? Have one! (*Puts a macaroon into his mouth.*) You too, Kristine. And one for me. A very small one. Or at most two. (*Walks around again.*) Yes, I really feel very, very happy. Now there's just one thing I'm dying to do.

RANK: Oh? And what's that?

NORA: Something I want to say so Torvald could hear.

RANK: And why can't you?

NORA: I don't dare to, for it's not nice.

MRS. LINDE: Not nice?

RANK: In that case, I guess you'd better not. But surely to the two of us — ? What is it you'd like to say to Helmer?

NORA: I want to say, "goddammit!"

RANK: Are you out of your mind!

MRS. LINDE: For heaven's sake, Nora!

RANK: Say it. Here he comes.

NORA (*hiding the macaroons*): Shhh!

(HELMER *enters from his study, carrying his hat and overcoat.*)

NORA (*going to him*): Well, dear, did you get rid of him?

HELMER: Yes, he just left.

NORA: Torvald, I want you to meet Kristine. She's just come to town.

HELMER: Kristine — ? I'm sorry; I don't think —

NORA: Mrs. Linde, Torvald dear. Mrs. Kristine Linde.

HELMER: Ah, yes. A childhood friend of my wife's, I suppose.

MRS. LINDE: Yes, we've known each other for a long time.

NORA: Just think; she has come all this way just to see you.

HELMER: I'm not sure I understand —

MRS. LINDE: Well, not really —

NORA: You see, Kristine is an absolutely fantastic secretary, and she would so much like to work for a competent executive and learn more than she knows already —

HELMER: Very sensible, I'm sure, Mrs. Linde.

NORA: So when she heard about your appointment — there was a wire — she came here as fast as she could. How about it, Torvald? Couldn't you do something for Kristine? For my sake? Please?

HELMER: Quite possibly. I take it you're a widow, Mrs. Linde?

MRS. LINDE: Yes.

HELMER: And you've had office experience?

MRS. LINDE: Some — yes.

HELMER: In that case I think it's quite likely that I'll be able to find you a position.

NORA (*claps her hands*): I knew it! I knew it!

HELMER: You've arrived at a most opportune time, Mrs. Linde.

MRS. LINDE: Oh, how can I ever thank you —

HELMER: Not at all, not at all. (*Puts his coat on.*) But today you'll have to excuse me —

RANK: Wait a minute; I'll come with you. (*Gets his fur coat from the front hall, warms it by the stove.*)

NORA: Don't be long, Torvald.

HELMER: An hour or so, no more.

NORA: Are you leaving, too, Kristine?

MRS. LINDE (*putting on her things*): Yes, I better go and find a place to stay.

HELMER: Good. Then we'll be going the same way.

NORA (*helping her*): I'm sorry this place is so small, but I don't think we very well could —

MRS. LINDE: Of course! Don't be silly, Nora. Goodbye, and thank you for everything.

NORA: Goodbye. We'll see you soon. You'll be back this evening, of course. And you too, Doctor Rank; right? If you feel well enough? Of course you will. Just wrap yourself up.

(*General small talk as all exit into the hall. Children's voices are heard on the stairs.*)

NORA: There they are! There they are! (*She runs and opens the door.* THE NURSE ANNE-MARIE *enters with the children.*) Come in! Come in! (*Bends over and kisses them.*) Oh, you sweet, sweet darlings! Look at them, Kristine! Aren't they beautiful?

RANK: No standing around in the draft!

HELMER: Come along, Mrs. Linde. This place isn't fit for anyone but mothers right now.

(DOCTOR RANK, HELMER, *and* MRS. LINDE *go down the stairs.* THE NURSE *enters the living room with the* CHILDREN. NORA *follows, closing the door behind her.*)

NORA: My, how nice you all look! Such red cheeks! Like apples and roses. (*The children all talk at the same time.*) You've had so much fun? I *bet* you have. Oh, isn't that nice! You pulled both Emmy and Bob on your sleigh? Both at the same time? That's very good, Ivar. Oh, let me hold her for a minute, Anne-Marie. My sweet little doll baby! (*Takes the smallest of the children from* THE NURSE *and dances with her.*)Yes, yes, of course; Mama'll dance with you too, Bob. What? You threw snowballs? Oh, I wish I'd been there! No, no; *I* want to take their clothes off, Anne-Marie. Please let me; I think it's so much fun. You go on in. You look frozen. There's hot coffee on the stove.

(THE NURSE *exits into the room to the left.* NORA *takes the children's wraps off and throws them all around. They all keep telling her things at the same time.*)

NORA: Oh, really? A big dog ran after you? But it didn't bite you? Of course not. Dogs don't bite sweet little doll babies. Don't peek at the packages, Ivar! What's in them? Wouldn't you like to know! No, no; that's something terrible! Play? You want to play? What do you want to play? Okay, let's play hide-and-seek. Bob hides first. You want *me* to? All right. I'll go first.

(*Laughing and shouting,* NORA *and the children play in the living room and in the adjacent room, right. Finally,* NORA *hides herself under the table; the children rush in, look for her, can't find her. They hear her low giggle, run to the table, lift the rug that covers it, see her. General hilarity. She crawls out, pretends to scare them. New delight. In the meantime there has been a knock on the door between the living room and the front hall, but nobody has noticed. Now the door is opened halfway;* KROGSTAD *appears. He waits a little. The play goes on.*)

KROGSTAD: Pardon me, Mrs. Helmer —

NORA (*with a muted cry turns around, jumps up*): Ah! What do you want?

KROGSTAD: I'm sorry. The front door was open. Somebody must have forgotten to close it —

NORA (*standing up*): My husband isn't here, Mr. Krogstad.

KROGSTAD: I know.

NORA: So what do you want?

KROGSTAD: I'd like a word with you.

NORA: With — ! (*To the children.*) Go in to Anne-Marie. What? No, the strange man won't do anything bad to mama. When he's gone we'll play some more. (*She takes the children into the room to the left and closes the door.*)

NORA (*tense, troubled*): You want to speak with me?

KROGSTAD: Yes I do.

NORA: Today — ? It isn't the first of the month yet.

KROGSTAD: No, it's Christmas Eve. It's up to you what kind of holiday you'll have.

NORA: What do you want? I can't possibly —

KROGSTAD: Let's not talk about that just yet. There's something else. You do have a few minutes, don't you?

NORA: Yes. Yes, of course. That is, —

KROGSTAD: Good. I was sitting in Olsen's restaurant when I saw your husband go by.

NORA: Yes — ?

KROGSTAD: — with a lady.

NORA: What of it?

KROGSTAD: May I be so free as to ask: wasn't that lady Mrs. Linde?

NORA: Yes.

KROGSTAD: Just arrived in town?

NORA: Yes, today.

KROGSTAD: She's a good friend of yours, I understand?

NORA: Yes, she is. But I fail to see —

KROGSTAD: I used to know her myself.

NORA: I know that.

KROGSTAD: So you know that. I thought as much. In that case, let me ask you a simple question. Is Mrs. Linde going to be employed in the bank?

NORA: What makes you think you have the right to cross examine me like this, Mr. Krogstad — you, one of my husband's employees? But since you ask, I'll tell you. Yes, Mrs. Linde is going to be working in the bank. And it was I who recommended her, Mr. Krogstad. Now you know.

KROGSTAD: So I was right.

NORA (*walks up and down*): After all, one does have a little influence, you know. Just because you're a woman, it doesn't mean that — Really, Mr. Krogstad, people in a subordinate position should be careful not to offend someone who — oh well —

KROGSTAD: — has influence?

NORA: Exactly.

KROGSTAD (*changing his tone*): Mrs. Helmer, I must ask you to be good enough to use your influence on my behalf.

NORA: Oh? What do you mean?

KROGSTAD: I want you to make sure that I am going to keep my subordinate position in the bank.

NORA: I don't understand. Who is going to take your position away from you?

KROGSTAD: There's no point in playing ignorant with me, Mrs. Helmer. I can very well appreciate that your friend would find it unpleasant to run into me. So now I know who I can thank for my dismissal.

NORA: But I assure you —

KROGSTAD: Never mind. I just want to say you still have time. I advise you to use your influence to prevent it.

NORA: But Mr. Krogstad, I don't have any influence — none at all.

KROGSTAD: No? I thought you just said —

NORA: Of course I didn't mean it that way. I! Whatever makes you think that I have any influence of that kind on my husband?

KROGSTAD: I went to law school with your husband. I have no reason to think that the Bank Manager is less susceptible than other husbands.

NORA: If you're going to insult my husband, I'll have to ask you to leave.

KROGSTAD: You're brave, Mrs. Helmer.

NORA: I'm not afraid of you any more. After New Year's I'll be out of this thing with you.

KROGSTAD (more controlled): Listen, Mrs. Helmer. If necessary, I'll fight as for my life to keep my little job in the bank.

NORA: So it seems.

KROGSTAD: It isn't just the money; that's really the smallest part of it. There is something else — Well, I guess I might as well tell you. It's like this. I'm sure you know, like everybody else, that some years ago I committed — an impropriety.

NORA: I believe I've heard it mentioned.

KROGSTAD: The case never came to trial, but from that moment all doors were closed to me. So I took up the kind of business you know about. I had to do something, and I think I can say about myself that I have not been among the worst. But now I want to get out of all that. My sons are growing up. For their sake I must get back as much of my good name as I can. This job in the bank was like the first rung on the ladder. And now your husband wants to kick me down and leave me back in the mud again.

NORA: But I swear to you, Mr. Krogstad; it's not at all in my power to help you.

KROGSTAD: That's because you don't want to. But I have the means to force you.

NORA: You don't mean you're going to tell my husband I owe you money?

KROGSTAD: And if I did?

NORA: That would be a mean thing to do. (Almost crying.) That secret, which is my joy and my pride — for him to learn about it in such a coarse and ugly way — to learn it from you — ! It would be terribly unpleasant for me.

KROGSTAD: Just unpleasant?

NORA (heatedly): But go ahead! Do it! It will be worse for you than for me. When my husband realizes what a bad person you are, you're certainly going to lose your job.

KROGSTAD: I asked you if it was just domestic unpleasantness you were afraid of?

NORA: When my husband finds out, of course he'll pay off the loan, and then we won't have anything more to do with you.

KROGSTAD (stepping closer): Listen, Mrs. Helmer — either you have a very bad memory, or you don't know much about business. I think I had better straighten you out on a few things.

NORA: What do you mean?

KROGSTAD: When your husband was ill, you came to me to borrow twelve hundred dollars.

NORA: I knew nobody else.

KROGSTAD: I promised to get you the money —

NORA: And you did.

KROGSTAD: — I promised to get you the money on certain conditions. At the time you were so anxious about your husband's health and so set on getting him away that I doubt very much that you paid much attention to the details of our transaction. That's why I remind you of them now. Anyway, I promised to get you the money if you would sign an I.O.U., which I drafted.

NORA: And which I signed.

KROGSTAD: Good. But below your signature I added a few lines, making your father security for the loan. Your father was supposed to put his signature to those lines.

NORA: Supposed to — ? He did.

KROGSTAD: I had left the date blank. That is, your father was to date his own signature. You recall that, don't you, Mrs. Helmer?

NORA: I guess so —

KROGSTAD: I gave the note to you. You were to mail it to your father. Am I correct?

NORA: Yes.

KROGSTAD: And of course you did so right away, for no more than five or six days later you brought the paper back to me, signed by your father. Then I paid you the money.

NORA: Well? And haven't I been keeping up with the payments?

KROGSTAD: Fairly well, yes. But to get back to what we were talking about — those were difficult days for you, weren't they, Mrs. Helmer?

NORA: Yes, they were.

KROGSTAD: Your father was quite ill, I believe.

NORA: He was dying.

KROGSTAD: And died shortly afterwards?

NORA: That's right.

KROGSTAD: Tell me, Mrs. Helmer; do you happen to remember the date of your father's death? I mean the exact day of the month?

NORA: Daddy died on September 29.

KROGSTAD: Quite correct. I have ascertained that fact. That's why there is something peculiar about this (*takes out a piece of paper*), which I can't account for.

NORA: Peculiar? How? I don't understand —

KROGSTAD: It seems very peculiar, Mrs. Helmer, that your father signed this promissory note three days after his death.

NORA: How so? I don't see what —

KROGSTAD: Your father died on September 29. Now look. He has dated his signature October 2. Isn't that odd?

(NORA *remains silent*)

KROGSTAD: Can you explain it?

(NORA *still silent*)

KROGSTAD: I also find it striking that the date and the month and the year are not in your father's handwriting but in a hand I think I recognize. Well, that might be explained. Your father may have forgotten to date his signature and somebody else may have done it here, guessing at the date before he had learned of your father's death. That's all right. It's only the signature itself that matters. And that is genuine, isn't it, Mrs. Helmer? Your father *did* put his name to this note?

NORA (*after a brief silence tosses her head back and looks defiantly at him*): No, he didn't. I wrote Daddy's name.

KROGSTAD: Mrs. Helmer — do you realize what a dangerous admission you just made?

NORA: Why? You'll get your money soon.

KROGSTAD: Let me ask you something. Why didn't you mail this note to your father?

NORA: Because it was impossible. Daddy was sick — you know that. If I had asked him for his signature I would have had to tell him what the money was for. But I couldn't tell him, as sick as he was, that my husband's life was in danger. That was impossible. Surely you can see that.

KROGSTAD: Then it would have been better for you if you had given up your trip abroad.

NORA: No, that was impossible! That trip was to save my husband's life. I couldn't give it up.

KROGSTAD: But didn't you realize that what you did amounted to fraud against me?

NORA: I couldn't let that make any difference. I didn't care about you at all. I hated the way you made all those difficulties for me, even though you knew the danger my husband was in. I thought you were cold and unfeeling.

KROGSTAD: Mrs. Helmer, obviously you have no clear idea of what you have done. Let me tell you that what I did that time was no more and no worse. And it ruined my name and reputation.

NORA: You! Are you trying to tell me that you did something brave once in order to save your wife's life?

KROGSTAD: The law doesn't ask about motives.

NORA: Then it's a bad law.

KROGSTAD: Bad or not — if I produce this note in court you'll be judged according to the law.

NORA: I refuse to believe you. A daughter shouldn't have the right to spare her dying old father worry and anxiety? A wife shouldn't have the right to save her husband's life? I don't know the laws very well, but I'm sure that somewhere they make allowance for cases like that. And you, a lawyer, don't know that? I think you must be a bad lawyer, Mr. Krogstad.

KROGSTAD: That may be. But business — the kind of business you and I have with one another — don't you think I know something about that? Very well. Do what you like. But let me tell you this: if I'm going to be kicked out again, you'll keep me company. (*He bows and exits through the front hall.*)

NORA (*pauses thoughtfully; then, with a defiant toss of her head*): Oh, nonsense! Trying to scare me like that! I'm not all that silly. (*Starts picking up the children's clothes; soon stops.*) But — ? No! That's impossible! I did it for love!

THE CHILDREN (*in the door to the left*): Mama, the strange man just left. We saw him.

NORA: Yes, yes; I know. But don't tell anybody about the strange man. Do you hear? Not even Daddy.

THE CHILDREN: We won't. But now you'll play with us again, won't you, mama?

NORA: No, not right now.

THE CHILDREN: Oh, but mama — you promised.

NORA: I know, but I can't just now. Go to your own room. I've so much to do. Be nice now, my little darlings. Do as I say. (*She nudges them gently into the other room and closes the door. She sits down on the couch, picks up a piece of embroidery, makes a few stitches, then stops.*) No! (*Throws the embroidery down, goes to the hall door and calls out:*) Helene! Bring the Christmas tree in here, please! (*Goes to the table, left, opens the drawer, halts.*) No — that's impossible!

THE MAID (*with the Christmas tree*): Where do you want it, ma'am?

NORA: There. The middle of the floor.

THE MAID: You want anything else?

NORA: No, thanks. I have everything I need. (THE MAID *goes out.* NORA *starts trimming the tree.*) I want candles — and flowers — That awful man! Oh, nonsense!

There's nothing wrong. This will be a lovely tree. I'll do everything you want me to, Torvald. I'll sing for you — dance for you —

(HELMER, *a bundle of papers under his arm, enters from outside.*)

NORA: Ah — you're back already?

HELMER: Yes. Has anybody been here?

NORA: Here? No.

HELMER: That's funny. I saw Krogstad leaving just now.

NORA: Oh? Oh yes, that's right. Krogstad was here for just a moment.

HELMER: I can tell from your face that he came to ask you to put in a word for him.

NORA: Yes.

HELMER: And it was supposed to be your own idea, wasn't it? You were not to tell me he'd been here. He asked you that too, didn't he?

NORA: Yes, Torvald, but —

HELMER: Nora, Nora, how could you! Talking to a man like that and making him promises! And lying to me about it afterwards — !

NORA: Lying — ?

HELMER: Didn't you say nobody had been here? (*Shakes his finger at her.*) My little songbird must never do that again. Songbirds are supposed to have clean beaks to chirp with — no false notes. (*Puts his arm around her waist.*) Isn't that so? Of course it is. (*Lets her go.*) And that's enough about that. (*Sits down in front of the fireplace.*) Ah, it's nice and warm in here. (*Begins to leaf through his papers.*)

NORA (*busy with the tree. After a brief pause*): Torvald.

HELMER: Yes.

NORA: I'm looking forward so much to the Stenborgs' costume party day after tomorrow.

HELMER: And I can't wait to find out what you're going to surprise me with.

NORA: Oh, that silly idea!

HELMER: Oh?

NORA: I can't think of anything. It all seems so foolish and pointless.

HELMER: Ah, my little Nora admits that?

NORA (*behind his chair, her arms on the back of the chair*): Are you very busy, Torvald?

HELMER: Well —

NORA: What are all those papers?

HELMER: Bank business.

NORA: Already?

HELMER: I've asked the board to give me the authority to make certain changes in organization and personnel. That's what I'll be doing over the holidays. I want it all settled before New Year's.

NORA: So that's why this poor Krogstad —

HELMER: Hm.

NORA (*leisurely playing with the hair on his neck*): If you weren't so busy, Torvald, I'd ask you for a great, big favor.

HELMER: Let's hear it, anyway.

NORA: I don't know anyone with better taste than you, and I want so much to look nice at the party. Couldn't you sort of take charge of me, Torvald, and decide what I'll wear — help me with my costume?

HELMER: Aha! Little Lady Obstinate is looking for someone to rescue her?

NORA: Yes, Torvald. I won't get anywhere without your help.

HELMER: All right. I'll think about it. We'll come up with something.

NORA: Oh, you *are* nice! (*Goes back to the Christmas tree. A pause.*) Those red flowers look so pretty. — Tell me, was it really all that bad what this Krogstad fellow did?

HELMER: He forged signatures. Do you have any idea what that means?

NORA: Couldn't it have been because he felt he had to?

HELMER: Yes, or like so many others he may simply have been thoughtless. I'm not so heartless as to condemn a man absolutely because of a single imprudent act.

NORA: Of course not, Torvald!

HELMER: People like him can redeem themselves morally by openly confessing their crime and taking their punishment.

NORA: Punishment — ?

HELMER: But that was not the way Krogstad chose. He got out of it with tricks and evasions. That's what has corrupted him.

NORA: So you think that if — ?

HELMER: Can't you imagine how a guilty person like that has to lie and fake and dissemble wherever he goes — putting on a mask before everybody he's close to, even his own wife and children? It's this thing with the children that's the worst part of it, Nora.

NORA: Why is that?

HELMER: Because when a man lives inside such a circle of stinking lies he brings infection into his own home and contaminates his whole family. With every breath of air his children inhale the germs of something ugly.

NORA (*moving closer behind him*): Are you so sure of that?

HELMER: Of course I am. I have seen enough examples of that in my work. Nearly all young criminals have had mothers who lied.

NORA: Why mothers — particularly?

HELMER: Most often mothers. But of course fathers tend to have the same influence. Every lawyer knows that. And yet, for years this Krogstad has been poisoning his own children in an atmosphere of lies and deceit. That's why I call him a lost soul morally. (*Reaches out for her hands.*) And that's why my sweet little Nora must promise me never to take his side again. Let's shake on that. — What? What's this? Give me your hand! There! Now that's settled. I assure you, I would find it impossible to work in the same room with that man. I feel literally sick when I'm around people like that.

NORA (*withdraws her hand and goes to the other side of the Christmas tree*): It's so hot in here. And I have so much to do.

HELMER (*gets up and collects his papers*): Yes, and I really should try to get some of this reading done before dinner. I must think about your costume too. And maybe just possibly I'll have something to wrap in gilt paper and hang on the Christmas tree. (*Puts his hand on her head.*) Oh my adorable little songbird! (*Enters his study and closes the door.*)

NORA (*after a pause, in a low voice*): It's all a lot of nonsense. It's not that way at all. It's impossible. It has to be impossible.

THE NURSE (*in the door, left*): The little ones are asking ever so nicely if they can't come in and be with their mama.

NORA: No, no, no! Don't let them in here! You stay with them, Anne-Marie.

THE NURSE: If you say so, ma'am. (*Closes the door.*)

NORA (*pale with terror*): Corrupt my little children — ! Poison my home — ? (*Brief pause; she lifts her head.*) That's not true. Never. Never in a million years.

ACT II

The same room. The Christmas tree is in the corner by the piano, stripped, shabby-looking, with burnt-down candles. NORA's *outdoor clothes are on the couch.* NORA *is alone. She walks around restlessly. She stops by the couch and picks up her coat.*

NORA (*drops the coat again*): There's somebody now! (*Goes to the door, listens.*) No. Nobody. Of course not — not on Christmas. And not tomorrow either.[1] — But perhaps — (*Opens the door and looks.*) No, nothing in the mailbox. All empty. (*Comes forward.*) How silly I am! Of course he isn't serious. Nothing like that could happen. After all, I have three small children.

(THE NURSE *enters from the room, left, carrying a big carton.*)

THE NURSE: Well, at last I found it — the box with your costume.
NORA: Thanks. Just put it on the table.
THE NURSE (*does so*): But it's all a big mess, I'm afraid.
NORA: Oh, I wish I could tear the whole thing to little pieces!
NURSE: Heavens! It's not as bad as all that. It can be fixed all right. All it takes is a little patience.
NORA: I'll go over and get Mrs. Linde to help me.
NURSE: Going out again? In this awful weather? You'll catch a cold.
NORA: That might not be such a bad thing. How are the children?
NURSE: The poor little dears are playing with their presents, but —
NORA: Do they keep asking for me?
NURSE: Well, you know, they're used to being with their mama.
NORA: I know. But Anne-Marie, from now on I can't be with them as much as before.
NURSE: Oh well. Little children get used to everything.
NORA: You think so? Do you think they'll forget their mama if I were gone alto-gether?
NURSE: Goodness me — gone altogether?
NORA: Listen, Anne-Marie; something I've often wondered about. How could you bring yourself to leave your child with strangers?
NURSE: But I had to, if I were to nurse you.
NORA: Yes, but how could you *want* to?
NURSE: When I could get such a nice place? When something like that happens to a poor young girl, she'd better be grateful for whatever she gets. For *he* didn't do a thing for me — the louse!
NORA: But your daughter has forgotten all about you, hasn't she?
NURSE: Oh no! Not at all! She wrote to me both when she was confirmed and when she got married.

---

[1] In Norway both December 25 and 26 are legal holidays.

NORA (*putting her arms around her neck*): You dear old thing — you were a good
mother to me when I was little.

NURSE: Poor little Nora had no one else, you know.

NORA: And if my little ones didn't, I know you'd — oh, I'm being silly! (*Opens the
carton*.) Go in to them, please. I really should —. Tomorrow you'll see how
pretty I'll be.

NURSE: I know. There won't be anybody at that party half as pretty as you, ma'am.
(*Goes out, left*.)

NORA (*begins to take clothes out of the carton. In a moment she throws it all down*.)
If only I dared to go out. If only I knew nobody would come — that nothing
would happen while I was gone. — How silly! Nobody'll come. Just don't think
about it. Brush the muff. Beautiful gloves. Beautiful gloves. Forget it. Forget it.
One, two, three, four, five, six — (*Cries out*.) There they are! (*Moves toward the
door, stops irresolutely*.)

(MRS. LINDE *enters from the hall. She has already taken off her coat*.)

NORA: Oh, it's you, Kristine. There's no one else out there, is there? I'm so glad
you're here.

MRS. LINDE: They told me you'd asked for me.

NORA: I just happened to walk by. I need your help with something — badly. Let's
sit here on the couch. Look. Torvald and I are going to a costume party tomorrow night — at Consul Stenborg's upstairs — and Torvald wants me to go as a
Neapolitan fisher girl and dance the Tarantella. I learned it when we were on
Capri, don't you know.

MRS. LINDE: Well, well! So you'll be putting on a whole show?

NORA: Yes. Torvald thinks I should. Look, here's the costume. Torvald had it
made for me while we were there. But it's all so torn and everything. I just don't
know —

MRS. LINDE: Oh that can be fixed. It's not that much. The trimmings have come
loose in a few places. Do you have needle and thread? Ah, here we are. All set.

NORA: I really appreciate it, Kristine.

MRS. LINDE (*sewing*): So you'll be in disguise tomorrow night, eh? You know — I
may come by for just a moment, just to look at you. — Oh dear, I haven't even
thanked you for the nice evening last night.

NORA (*gets up, moves around*): Oh I don't know. I don't think last night was as nice
as it usually is. — You should have come to town a little earlier, Kristine. — Yes,
Torvald knows how to make it nice and pretty around here.

MRS. LINDE: You too, I should think. After all, you're your father's daughter. By the
way, is Dr. Rank always as depressed as he was last night?

NORA: No, last night was unusual. He's a very sick man, you know — very sick.
Poor Rank, his spine is rotting away or something. Tuberculosis, I think. You
see, his father was a nasty old man with mistresses and all that sort of thing.
Rank has been sickly ever since he was a little boy.

MRS. LINDE (*dropping her sewing to her lap*): But dearest Nora, where have you
learned about things like that?

NORA (*still walking about*): Oh, you know — with three children you sometimes get
to talk with — other wives. Some of them know quite a bit about medicine. So
you pick up a few things.

MRS. LINDE (*resumes her sewing. After a brief pause*): Does Dr. Rank come here every day?

NORA: Every single day. He's Torvald's oldest and best friend, after all. And my friend too, for that matter. He's part of the family, almost.

MRS. LINDE: But tell me, is he quite sincere? I mean, isn't he the kind of man who likes to say nice things to people?

NORA: No, not at all. Rather the opposite, in fact. What makes you say that?

MRS. LINDE: When you introduced us yesterday, he told me he'd often heard my name mentioned in this house. But later on it was quite obvious that your husband really had no idea who I was. So how could Dr. Rank — ?

NORA: You're right, Kristine, but I can explain that. You see, Torvald loves me so very much that he wants me all to himself. That's what he says. When we were first married he got jealous, almost, when I as much as mentioned anybody from back home that I was fond of. So of course I soon stopped doing that. But with Dr. Rank I often talk about home. You see, he likes to listen to me.

MRS. LINDE: Look here, Nora. In many ways you're still a child. After all, I'm quite a bit older than you and have had more experience. I want to give you a piece of advice. I think you should get out of this thing with Dr. Rank.

NORA: Get out of what thing?

MRS. LINDE: Several things in fact, if you want my opinion. Yesterday you said something about a rich admirer who was going to give you money —

NORA: One who doesn't exist, unfortunately. What of it?

MRS. LINDE: Does Dr. Rank have money?

NORA: Yes he does.

MRS. LINDE: And no dependents?

NORA: No. But — ?

MRS. LINDE: And he comes here every day?

NORA: Yes, I told you that already.

MRS. LINDE: But how can that sensitive man be so tactless?

NORA: I haven't the slightest idea what you're talking about.

MRS. LINDE: Don't play games with me, Nora. Don't you think I know who you borrowed the twelve hundred dollars from?

NORA: Are you out of your mind! The very idea — ! A friend of both of us who sees us every day — ! What a dreadfully uncomfortable position that would be!

MRS. LINDE: So it really isn't Dr. Rank?

NORA: Most certainly not! I would never have dreamed of asking him — not for a moment. Anyway, he didn't have any money then. He inherited it afterwards.

MRS. LINDE: Well, I still think that may have been lucky for you, Nora dear.

NORA: The idea! It would never have occurred to me to ask Dr. Rank — . Though I'm sure that if I *did* ask him —

MRS. LINDE: But of course you won't.

NORA: Of course not. I can't imagine that would ever be necessary. But I am quite sure that if I told Dr. Rank —

MRS. LINDE: Behind your husband's back?

NORA: I must get out of — this other thing. That's also behind his back. I *must* get out of it.

MRS. LINDE: That's what I told you yesterday. But —

NORA (*walking up and down*): A man manages these things so much better than a woman —

MRS. LINDE: One's husband, yes.

NORA: Silly, silly! (*Stops.*) When you've paid off all you owe, you get your I.O.U. back; right?

MRS. LINDE: Yes, of course.

NORA: And you can tear it into a hundred thousand little pieces and burn it — that dirty, filthy paper!

MRS. LINDE (*looks hard at her, puts down her sewing, rises slowly*): Nora — you're hiding something from me.

NORA: Can you tell?

MRS. LINDE: Something's happened to you, Nora, since yesterday morning. What is it?

NORA (*going to her*): Kristine! (*Listens.*) Shhh. Torvald just came back. Listen. Why don't you go in to the children for a while. Torvald can't stand having sewing around. Get Anne-Marie to help you.

MRS. LINDE (*gathers some of the sewing things together*): All right, but I'm not leaving here till you and I have talked.

(*She goes out left, just as* HELMER *enters from the front hall.*)

NORA (*towards him*): I have been waiting and waiting for you, Torvald.

HELMER: Was that the dressmaker?

NORA: No, it was Kristine. She's helping me with my costume. Oh Torvald, just wait till you see how nice I'll look!

HELMER: I told you. Pretty good idea I had, wasn't it?

NORA: Lovely! Marvellous! And wasn't it nice of me to go along with it?

HELMER (*his hand under her chin*): Nice? To do what your husband tells you? All right, you little rascal; I know you didn't mean it that way. But don't let me interrupt you. I suppose you want to try it on.

NORA: And you'll be working?

HELMER: Yes. (*Shows her a pile of papers.*) Look. I've been down to the bank. (*Is about to enter his study.*)

NORA: Torvald.

HELMER (*halts*): Yes?

NORA: What if your little squirrel asked you ever so nicely —

HELMER: For what?

NORA: Would you do it?

HELMER: Depends on what it is.

NORA: Squirrel would run around and do all sorts of fun tricks if you'd be nice and agreeable.

HELMER: All right. What is it?

NORA: Lark would chirp and twitter in all the rooms, up and down —

HELMER: So what? Lark does that anyway.

NORA: I'll be your elfmaid and dance for you in the moonlight, Torvald.

HELMER: Nora, don't tell me it's the same thing you mentioned this morning?

NORA (*closer to him*): Yes, Torvald. I beg you!

HELMER: You really have the nerve to bring that up again?

NORA: Yes. You've just got to do as I say. You *must* let Krogstad keep his job.

HELMER: My dear Nora. It's his job I intend to give to Mrs. Linde.

NORA: I know. And that's ever so nice of you. But can't you just fire somebody else?

HELMER: This is incredible! You just don't give up, do you? Because *you* make some foolish promise, *I* am supposed to — !

NORA: That's not the reason, Torvald. It's for your own sake. That man writes for the worst newspapers. You've said so yourself. There's no telling what he may do to you. I'm scared to death of him.

HELMER: Ah, I understand. You're afraid because of what happened before.

NORA: What do you mean?

HELMER: You're thinking of your father, of course.

NORA: Yes. Yes, you're right. Remember the awful things they wrote about Daddy in the newspapers? I really think they might have forced him to resign if the ministry hadn't sent you to look into the charges and if you hadn't been so helpful and understanding.

HELMER: My dear little Nora, there is a world of difference between your father and me. Your father's official conduct was not above reproach. Mine is, and I intend it to stay that way as long as I hold my position.

NORA: Oh, but you don't know what vicious people like him may think of. Oh, Torvald! Now all of us could be so happy together here in our own home, peaceful and carefree. Such a good life, Torvald, for you and me and the children! That's why I implore you —

HELMER: And it's exactly because you plead for him that you make it impossible for me to keep him. It's already common knowledge in the bank that I intend to let Krogstad go. If it gets out that the new manager has changed his mind because of his wife —

NORA: Yes? What then?

HELMER: No, of course, that wouldn't matter at all as long as little Mrs. Pighead here got her way! Do you want me to make myself look ridiculous before my whole staff — make people think I can be pushed around by just anybody — by outsiders? Believe me, I'd soon find out what the consequences would be! Besides, there's another thing that makes it absolutely impossible for Krogstad to stay on in the bank now that I'm in charge.

NORA: What's that?

HELMER: I suppose in a pinch I could overlook his moral shortcomings —

NORA: Yes, you could; couldn't you, Torvald?

HELMER: And I understand he's quite a good worker, too. But we've known each other for a long time. It's one of those imprudent relationships you get into when you're young that embarrass you for the rest of your life. I guess I might as well be frank with you: he and I are on a first name basis. And that tactless fellow never hides the fact even when other people are around. Rather, he seems to think it entitles him to be familiar with me. Every chance he gets he comes out with his damn "Torvald, Torvald." I'm telling you, I find it most awkward. He would make my position in the bank intolerable.

NORA: You don't really mean any of this, Torvald.

HELMER: Oh? I don't? And why not?

NORA: No, for it's all so petty.

HELMER: What! Petty? You think I'm being petty!

NORA: No, I *don't* think you are petty, Torvald dear. That's exactly why I —

HELMER: Never mind. You think my reasons are petty, so it follows that I must be petty too. Petty! Indeed! By god, I'll put an end to this right now! (*Opens the door to the front hall and calls out.*) Helene!

NORA: What are you doing?

HELMER (*searching among his papers*): Making a decision. (THE MAID *enters*.) Here. Take this letter. Go out with it right away. Find somebody to deliver it. But quick. The address is on the envelope. Wait. Here's money.

THE MAID: Very good, sir. (*She takes the letter and goes out.*)

HELMER (*collecting his papers*): There now, little Mrs. Obstinate!

NORA (*breathless*): Torvald — what was that letter?

HELMER: Krogstad's dismissal.

NORA: Call it back, Torvald! There's still time! Oh Torvald, please — call it back! For my sake, for your own sake, for the sake of the children! Listen to me, Torvald! Do it! You don't know what you're doing to all of us!

HELMER: Too late.

NORA: Yes. Too late.

HELMER: Dear Nora, I forgive you this fear you're in, although it really is an insult to me. Yes, it is! It's an insult to think that I am scared of a shabby scrivener's revenge. But I forgive you, for it's such a beautiful proof how much you love me. (*Takes her in his arms.*) And that's the way it should be, my sweet darling. Whatever happens, you'll see that when things get really rough I have both strength and courage. You'll find out that I am man enough to shoulder the whole burden.

NORA (*terrified*): What do you mean by that?

HELMER: All of it, I tell you —

NORA (*composed*): You'll never have to do that.

HELMER: Good. Then we'll share the burden, Nora — like husband and wife, the way it ought to be. (*Caresses her.*) Now are you satisfied? There, there, there. Not that look in your eyes — like a frightened little dove. It's all your own foolish imagination. — Why don't you practise the Tarantella — and your tambourine, too. I'll be in the inner office. When I close both doors I won't hear a thing. You may make as much noise as you like. (*Turning in the doorway.*) And when Rank comes, why don't you tell him where to find me. (*He nods to her, enters his study carrying his papers, and closes the door.*)

NORA (*transfixed by terror, whispers*): He would do it. He'll do it. He'll do it in spite of the whole world. — No, this mustn't happen. Anything rather than that! There must be a way — ! (*The doorbell rings.*) Doctor Rank! Anything rather than that! Anything — anything at all!

(*She passes her hand over her face, pulls herself together, and opens the door to the hall.* DR. RANK *is out there, hanging up his coat. Darkness begins to fall during the following scene.*)

NORA: Hello there, Dr. Rank. I recognized your ringing. Don't go in to Torvald yet. I think he's busy.

RANK: And you?

NORA (*as he enters and she closes the door behind him*): You know I always have time for you.

RANK: Thanks. I'll make use of that as long as I can.

NORA: What do you mean by that? "As long as you can"?

RANK: Does that frighten you?

NORA: Well, it's a funny expression. As if something was going to happen.

RANK: Something is going to happen that I've long been expecting. But I admit I hadn't thought it would come quite so soon.

NORA (*seizes his arm*): What is it you've found out? Dr. Rank — tell me!

RANK (*sits down by the stove*): I'm going downhill fast. There's nothing to be done about that.

NORA (*with audible relief*): So it's *you* —

RANK: Who else? No point in lying to myself. I'm in worse shape than any of my other patients, Mrs. Helmer. These last few days I've been making up my inner status. Bankrupt. Chances are that within a month I'll be rotting up in the cemetery.

NORA: Shame on you! Talking that horrid way!

RANK: The thing itself is horrid — damn horrid. The worst of it, though, is all that other horror that comes first. There is only one more test I need to make. After that I'll have a pretty good idea when I'll start coming apart. There is something I want to say to you. Helmer's refined nature can't stand anything hideous. I don't want him in my sick room.

NORA: Oh but Dr. Rank —

RANK: I don't want him there. Under no circumstance. I'll close my door to him. As soon as I have full certainty that the worst is about to begin I'll give you my card with a black cross on it. Then you'll know the last, horrible destruction has started.

NORA: Today you're really quite impossible. And I had hoped you'd be in a particularly good mood.

RANK: With death on my hands? Paying for someone else's sins? Is there justice in that? And yet there isn't a single family that isn't ruled by that same law of ruthless retribution, in one way or another.

NORA (*puts her hands over her ears*): Poppycock! Be fun! Be fun!

RANK: Well, yes. You may just as well laugh at the whole thing. My poor, innocent spine is suffering for my father's frolics when he was a young lieutenant.

NORA (*over by the table, left*): Right. He was addicted to asparagus and goose liver paté, wasn't he?

RANK: And truffles.

NORA: Of course. Truffles. And oysters too, I think.

RANK: And oysters. Obviously.

NORA: And all the port and champagne that go with it. It's really too bad that goodies like that ruin your backbone.

RANK: Particularly an unfortunate backbone that never enjoyed any of it.

NORA: Ah yes, that's the saddest part of it all.

RANK (*looks searchingly at her*): Hm —

NORA (*after a brief pause*): Why did you smile just then?

RANK: I didn't. It was you who laughed.

NORA: No, it was you who smiled, Dr. Rank!

RANK (*gets up*): I see you're more of a mischief-maker than I thought.

NORA: I feel like mischief today.

RANK: So it seems.

NORA (*with both her hands on his shoulders*): Dear, dear Dr. Rank, don't you go and die and leave Torvald and me.

RANK: Oh, you won't miss me for very long. Those who go away are soon forgotten.

NORA (*with an anxious look*): Do you believe that?

RANK: You'll make new friends, and then —

NORA: Who'll make new friends?

RANK: Both you and Helmer, once I'm gone. You yourself seem to have made a good start already. What was this Mrs. Linde doing here last night?

NORA: Aha — Don't tell me you're jealous of poor Kristine?

RANK: Yes I am. She'll be my successor in this house. As soon as I have made my excuses, that woman is likely to —

NORA: Shh — not so loud. She's in there.

RANK: Today too? There you are!

NORA: She's mending my costume. My god, you really *are* unreasonable. (*Sits down on the couch.*) Now be nice, Dr. Rank. Tomorrow you'll see how beautifully I'll dance, and then you are to pretend I'm dancing just for you — and for Torvald too, of course. (*Takes several items out of the carton.*) Sit down, Dr. Rank; I want to show you something.

RANK (*sitting down*): What?

NORA: Look.

RANK: Silk stockings.

NORA: Flesh-colored. Aren't they lovely? Now it's getting dark in here, but tomorrow — No, no. You only get to see the foot. Oh well, you might as well see all of it.

RANK: Hm.

NORA: Why do you look so critical? Don't you think they'll fit?

RANK: That's something I can't possibly have a reasoned opinion about.

NORA (*looks at him for a moment*): Shame on you. (*Slaps his ear lightly with the stocking.*) That's what you get. (*Puts the things back in the carton.*)

RANK: And what other treasures are you going to show me?

NORA: Nothing at all, because you're naughty. (*She hums a little and rummages in the carton.*)

RANK (*after a brief silence*): When I sit here like this, talking confidently with you, I can't imagine — I can't possibly imagine what would have become of me if I hadn't had you and Helmer.

NORA (*smiles*): Well, yes — I do believe you like being with us.

RANK (*in a lower voice, lost in thought*): And then to have to go away from it all —

NORA: Nonsense. You're not going anywhere.

RANK (*as before*): — and not leave behind as much as a poor little token of gratitude, hardly a brief memory of someone missed, nothing but a vacant place that anyone can fill.

NORA: And what if I were to ask you — ? No —

RANK: Ask me what?

NORA: For a great proof of your friendship —

RANK: Yes, yes — ?

NORA: No, I mean — for an enormous favor —

RANK: Would you really for once make me as happy as all that?

NORA: But you don't even know what it is.

RANK: Well, then; tell me.

NORA: Oh, but I can't, Dr. Rank. It's altogether too much to ask — It's advice and help and a favor —

RANK: So much the better. I can't even begin to guess what it is you have in mind. So for heaven's sake tell me! Don't you trust me?

NORA: Yes, I trust you more than anybody I know. You are my best and most faithful friend. I know that. So I will tell you. All right, Dr. Rank. There is something you can help me prevent. You know how much Torvald loves me — beyond all words. Never for a moment would he hesitate to give his life for me.

RANK (*leaning over her*): Nora — do you really think he's the only one — ?

NORA (*with a slight start*): Who — ?

RANK: — who'd gladly give his life for you.

NORA (*heavily*): I see.

RANK: I have sworn an oath to myself to tell you before I go. I'll never find a better occasion. — All right, Nora; now you know. And now you also know that you can confide in me, more than in anyone else.

NORA (*gets up. In a calm, steady voice*): Let me get by.

RANK (*makes room for her but remains seated*): Nora —

NORA (*in the door to the front hall*): Helene, bring the lamp in here, please. (*Walks over to the stove.*) Oh, dear Dr. Rank. That really wasn't very nice of you.

RANK (*gets up*): That I have loved you as much as anybody — was that not nice?

NORA: No, not that. But that you told me. There was no need for that.

RANK: What do you mean? Have you known — ?

(THE MAID *enters with the lamp, puts it on the table, and goes out.*)

RANK: Nora — Mrs. Helmer — I'm asking you: did you know?

NORA: Oh, how can I tell what I knew and didn't know! I really can't say — But that you could be so awkward, Dr. Rank! Just when everything was so comfortable.

RANK: Well, anyway, now you know that I'm at your service with my life and soul. And now you must speak.

NORA (*looks at him*): After what just happened?

RANK: I beg you — let me know what it is.

NORA: There is nothing I can tell you now.

RANK: Yes, yes. You mustn't punish me this way. Please let me do for you whatever anyone *can* do.

NORA: Now there is nothing you can do. Besides, I don't think I really need any help, anyway. It's probably just my imagination. Of course that's all it is. I'm sure of it! (*Sits down in the rocking chair, looks at him, smiles.*) Well, well, well, Dr. Rank! What a fine gentleman you turned out to be! Aren't you ashamed of yourself, now that we have light?

RANK: No, not really. But perhaps I ought to leave — and not come back?

NORA: Don't be silly; of course not! You'll come here exactly as you have been doing. You know perfectly well that Torvald can't do without you.

RANK: Yes, but what about you?

NORA: Oh, I always think it's perfectly delightful when you come.

RANK: That's the very thing that misled me. You are a riddle to me. It has often seemed to me that you'd just as soon be with me as with Helmer.

NORA: Well, you see, there are people you love, and then there are other people you'd almost rather be with.

RANK: Yes, there is something in that.

NORA: When I lived home with Daddy, of course I loved him most. But I always thought it was so much fun to sneak off down to the maids' room, for they never gave me good advice and they always talked about such fun things.

RANK: Aha! So it's *their* place I have taken.

NORA (*jumps up and goes over to him*): Oh dear, kind Dr. Rank, you know very well I didn't mean it that way. Can't you see that with Torvald it is the way it used to be with Daddy?

(THE MAID *enters from the front hall.*)

THE MAID: Ma'am! (*Whispers to her and gives her a caller's card.*)

NORA (*glances at the card*): Ah! (*Puts it in her pocket.*)

RANK: Anything wrong?

NORA: No, no; not at all. It's nothing — just my new costume —

RANK: But your costume is lying right there!

NORA: Oh yes, that one. But this is another one. I ordered it. Torvald mustn't know —

RANK: Aha. So that's the great secret.

NORA: That's it. Why don't you go in to him, please. He's in the inner office. And keep him there for a while —

RANK: Don't worry. He won't get away. (*Enters* HELMER's *study.*)

NORA (*to* THE MAID): You say he's waiting in the kitchen?

THE MAID: Yes. He came up the back stairs.

NORA: But didn't you tell him there was somebody with me?

THE MAID: Yes, but he wouldn't listen.

NORA: He won't leave?

THE MAID: No, not till he's had a word with you, ma'am.

NORA: All right. But try not to make any noise. And, Helene — don't tell anyone he's here. It's supposed to be a surprise for my husband.

THE MAID: I understand, ma'am — (*She leaves.*)

NORA: The terrible is happening. It's happening, after all. No, no, no. It can't happen. It won't happen. (*She bolts the study door.*)

(THE MAID *opens the front hall door for* KROGSTAD *and closes the door behind him. He wears a fur coat for traveling, boots, and a fur hat.*)

NORA (*toward him*): Keep your voice down. My husband's home.

KROGSTAD: That's all right.

NORA: What do you want?

KROGSTAD: To find out something.

NORA: Then hurry. What?

KROGSTAD: I expect you know I've been fired.

NORA: I couldn't prevent it, Mr. Krogstad. I fought for you as long and as hard as I could, but it didn't do any good.

KROGSTAD: Your husband doesn't love you any more than that? He knows what I can do to you, and yet he runs the risk —

NORA: Surely you didn't think I'd tell him?

KROGSTAD: No, I really didn't. It wouldn't be like Torvald Helmer to show that kind of guts —

NORA: Mr. Krogstad, I insist that you show respect for my husband.

KROGSTAD: By all means. All due respect. But since you're so anxious to keep this a secret, may I assume that you are a little better informed than yesterday about exactly what you have done?

NORA: Better than *you* could ever teach me.

KROGSTAD: Of course. Such a bad lawyer as I am —

NORA: What do you want of me?

KROGSTAD: I just wanted to see how you were, Mrs. Helmer. I've been thinking about you all day. You see, even a bill collector, a pen pusher, a — anyway, someone like me — even he has a little of what they call a heart.

NORA: Then show it. Think of my little children.

KROGSTAD: Have you and your husband thought of mine? Never mind. All I want to tell you is that you don't need to take this business too seriously. I have no intention of bringing charges right away.

NORA: Oh no, you wouldn't; would you? I knew you wouldn't.

KROGSTAD: The whole thing can be settled quite amicably. Nobody else needs to know anything. It will be between the three of us.

NORA: My husband must never find out about this.

KROGSTAD: How are you going to prevent it? Maybe you can pay me the balance on the loan?

NORA: No, not right now.

KROGSTAD: Or do you have some way of raising the money in the next few days?

NORA: None I intend to make use of.

KROGSTAD: It wouldn't do you any good, anyway. Even if you had the cash in your hand right this minute, I wouldn't give you your note back. It wouldn't make any difference *how* much money you offered me.

NORA: Then you'll have to tell me what you plan to use the note *for*.

KROGSTAD: Just keep it; that's all. Have it on hand, so to speak. I won't say a word to anybody else. So if you've been thinking about doing something desperate —

NORA: I have.

KROGSTAD: — like leaving house and home —

NORA: I have!

KROGSTAD: — or even something worse —

NORA: How did you know?

KROGSTAD: — then: don't.

NORA: How did you know I was thinking of *that*?

KROGSTAD: Most of us do, right at first. I did, too, but when it came down to it I didn't have the courage —

NORA (*tonelessly*): Nor do I.

KROGSTAD (*relieved*): See what I mean? I thought so. You don't either.

NORA: I don't. I don't.

KROGSTAD: Besides, it would be very silly of you. Once that first domestic blow-up is behind you —. Here in my pocket is a letter for your husband.

NORA: Telling him everything?

KROGSTAD: As delicately as possible.

NORA (*quickly*): He mustn't get that letter. Tear it up. I'll get you the money somehow.

KROGSTAD: Excuse me, Mrs. Helmer. I thought I just told you —

NORA: I'm not talking about the money I owe you. Just let me know how much money you want from my husband, and I'll get it for you.

KROGSTAD: I want no money from your husband.

NORA: Then, what *do* you want?

KROGSTAD: I'll tell you, Mrs. Helmer. I want to rehabilitate myself; I want to get up in the world; and your husband is going to help me. For a year and a half I haven't done anything disreputable. All that time I have been struggling with the most miserable circumstances. I was content to work my way up step by step. Now I've been kicked out, and I'm no longer satisfied just getting my old job back. I want more than that; I want to get to the top. I'm quite serious. I want the bank to take me back but in a higher position. I want your husband to create a new job for me —

NORA: He'll never do that!

KROGSTAD: He will. I know him. He won't dare not to. And once I'm back inside and he and I are working together, you'll see! Within a year I'll be the manager's right hand. It will be Nils Krogstad and not Torvald Helmer who'll be running the Mutual Bank!

NORA: You'll never see that happen!

KROGSTAD: Are you thinking of — ?

NORA: Now I *do* have the courage.

KROGSTAD: You can't scare me. A fine, spoiled lady like you —

NORA: You'll see, you'll see!

KROGSTAD: Under the ice, perhaps? Down in that cold, black water? Then spring comes, and you float up again — hideous, ugly, unrecognizable, hair all gone —

NORA: You don't frighten me.

KROGSTAD: Nor you me. One doesn't do that sort of thing, Mrs. Helmer. Besides, what good would it do? He'd still be in my power.

NORA: Afterwards? When I'm no longer — ?

KROGSTAD: Aren't you forgetting that your reputation would be in my hands?

(NORA *stares at him, speechless.*)

KROGSTAD: All right; now I've told you what to expect. So don't do anything foolish. When Helmer gets my letter I expect to hear from him. And don't you forget that it's your husband himself who forces me to use such means again. That I'll never forgive him. Goodbye, Mrs. Helmer. (*Goes out through the hall.*)

NORA (*at the door, opens it a little, listens*): He's going. And no letter. Of course not! That would be impossible! (*Opens the door more.*) What's he doing? He's still there. Doesn't go down. Having second thoughts — ? Will he — ?

(*The sound of a letter dropping into the mailbox. Then* KROGSTAD's *steps are heard going down the stairs, gradually dying away.*)

NORA (*with a muted cry runs forward to the table by the couch. Brief pause*): In the mailbox. (*Tiptoes back to the door to the front hall.*) There it is. Torvald, Torvald — now we're lost!

MRS. LINDE (*enters from the left, carrying* NORA's *Capri costume*): There now. I think it's all fixed. Why don't we try it on you —

NORA (*in a low, hoarse voice*): Kristine, come here.

MRS. LINDE: What's wrong with you? You look quite beside yourself.

NORA: Come over here. Do you see that letter? There, look — through the glass in the mailbox.

MRS. LINDE: Yes, yes; I see it.

NORA: That letter is from Krogstad.

MRS. LINDE: Nora — it was Krogstad who lent you the money!

NORA: Yes, and now Torvald will find out about it.

MRS. LINDE: Oh believe me, Nora. That's the best thing for both of you.

NORA: There's more to it than you know. I forged a signature —

MRS. LINDE: Oh my god — !

NORA: I just want to tell you this, Kristine, that you must be my witness.

MRS. LINDE: Witness? How? Witness to what?

NORA: If I lose my mind — and that could very well happen —

MRS. LINDE: Nora!

NORA: — or if something were to happen to me — something that made it impossible for me to be here —

MRS. LINDE: Nora, Nora! You're not yourself!

NORA: — and if someone were to take all the blame, assume the whole responsibility — Do you understand — ?

MRS. LINDE: Yes, yes; but how can you think — !

NORA: — then you are to witness that that's not so, Kristine. I am not beside myself. I am perfectly rational, and what I'm telling you is that nobody else has known about this. I've done it all by myself, the whole thing. Just remember that.

MRS. LINDE: I will. But I don't understand any of it.

NORA: Oh, how could you! For it's the wonderful that's about to happen.

MRS. LINDE: The wonderful?

NORA: Yes, the wonderful. But it's so terrible, Kristine. It mustn't happen for anything in the whole world!

MRS. LINDE: I'm going over to talk to Krogstad right now.

NORA: No, don't. Don't go to him. He'll do something bad to you.

MRS. LINDE: There was a time when he would have done anything for me.

NORA: He!

MRS. LINDE: Where does he live?

NORA: Oh, I don't know — Yes, wait a minute (*reaches into her pocket.*) — here's his card. — But the letter; the letter — !

HELMER (*in his study, knocks on the door*): Nora!

NORA (*cries out in fear*): Oh, what is it? What do you want?

HELMER: That's all right. Nothing to be so scared about. We're not coming in. For one thing, we can't. You've bolted the door, you know. Are you trying on your costume?

NORA: Yes — yes, I am. I'm going to be so pretty, Torvald.

MRS. LINDE (*looking at the card*): He lives just around the corner.

NORA: I know, but it's no use. Nothing can save us now. The letter is in the mailbox.

MRS. LINDE: And your husband has the key?

NORA: Yes. He always keeps it with him.

MRS. LINDE: Krogstad must ask for his letter back, unread. He's got to think up some pretext or other —

NORA: But this is just the time of day when Torvald —

MRS. LINDE: Delay him. Go in to him. I'll be back as soon as I can. (*She hurries out through the hall door.*)

NORA (*walks over to* HELMER's *door, opens it, and peeks in*): Torvald!

HELMER (*still offstage*): Well, well! So now one's allowed in one's own living room again. Come on, Rank. Now we'll see — (*In the doorway.*) But what's this?

NORA: What, Torvald dear?

HELMER: Rank prepared me for a splendid metamorphosis.

RANK (*in the doorway*): That's how I understood it. Evidently I was mistaken.

NORA: Nobody gets to admire me in my costume before tomorrow.

HELMER: But, dearest Nora — you look all done in. Have you been practising too hard?

NORA: No, I haven't practised at all.

HELMER: But you'll have to, you know.

NORA: I know it, Torvald. I simply must. But I can't do a thing unless you help me. I have forgotten everything.

HELMER: Oh it will all come back. We'll work on it.

NORA: Oh yes, please, Torvald. You just have to help me. Promise? I am so nervous. That big party —. You mustn't do anything else tonight. Not a bit of business. Don't even touch a pen. Will you promise, Torvald?

HELMER: I promise. Tonight I'll be entirely at your service — you helpless little thing. — Just a moment, though. First I want to — (*Goes to the door to the front hall.*)

NORA: What are you doing out there?

HELMER: Just looking to see if there's any mail.

NORA: No, no! Don't, Torvald!

HELMER: Why not?

NORA: Torvald, I beg you. There is no mail.

HELMER: Let me just look, anyway. (*Is about to go out.*)

(NORA *by the piano, plays the first bars of the Tarantella dance.*)

HELMER (*halts at the door*): Aha!

NORA: I won't be able to dance tomorrow if I don't get to practise with you.

HELMER (*goes to her*): Are you really all that scared, Nora dear?

NORA: Yes, so terribly scared. Let's try it right now. There's still time before we eat. Oh please, sit down and play for me, Torvald. Teach me, coach me, the way you always do.

HELMER: Of course I will, my darling, if that's what you want. (*Sits down at the piano.*)

NORA (*takes the tambourine out of the carton, as well as a long, many-colored shawl. She quickly drapes the shawl around herself. She leaps into the middle of the floor and cries*): Play for me! I want to dance!

(HELMER *plays and* NORA *dances.* DOCTOR RANK *stands by the piano behind* HELMER *and watches.*)

HELMER (*playing*): Slow down, slow down!

NORA: Can't!

HELMER: Not so violent, Nora!

NORA: It has to be this way.

HELMER (*stops playing*): No, no. This won't do at all.

NORA (*laughing, swinging her tambourine*): What did I tell you?

RANK: Why don't you let me play.

HELMER (*getting up*): Good idea. Then I can direct her better.

(RANK *sits down at the piano and starts playing.* NORA *dances more and more wildly.* HELMER *stands by the stove, repeatedly correcting her. She doesn't seem to hear. Her hair comes loose and falls down over her shoulders. She doesn't notice but keeps on dancing.* MRS. LINDE *enters.*)

MRS. LINDE (*stops by the door, dumbfounded*): Ah — !

NORA (*dancing*): We're having such fun, Kristine!

HELMER: My dearest Nora, you're dancing as if it were a matter of life and death!

NORA: It is! It is!

HELMER: Rank, stop. This is sheer madness. Stop, I say!

(RANK *stops playing;* NORA *suddenly stops dancing.*)

HELMER (*goes over to her*): If I hadn't seen it I wouldn't have believed it. You've forgotten every single thing I ever taught you.

NORA (*tosses away the tambourine*): See? I told you.

HELMER: Well! You certainly need coaching.

NORA: Didn't I tell you I did? Now you've seen for yourself. I'll need your help till the very minute we're leaving for the party. Will you promise, Torvald?

HELMER: You can count on it.

NORA: You're not to think of anything except me — not tonight and not tomorrow. You're not to read any letters — not to look in the mailbox —

HELMER: Ah, I see. You're still afraid of that man.

NORA: Yes — yes, that too.

HELMER: Nora, I can tell from looking at you. There's a letter from him out there.

NORA: I don't know. I think so. But you're not to read it now. I don't want anything ugly to come between us before it's all over.

RANK (*to* HELMER *in a low voice*): Better not argue with her.

HELMER (*throws his arm around her*): The child shall have her way. But tomorrow night, when you've done your dance —

NORA: Then you'll be free.

THE MAID (*in the door, right*): Dinner can be served any time, ma'am.

NORA: We want champagne, Helene.

THE MAID: Very good, ma'am. (*Goes out.*)

HELMER: Aha! Having a party, eh?

NORA: Champagne from now till sunrise! (*Calls out.*) And some macaroons, Helene. Lots! — just this once.

HELMER (*taking her hands*): There, there — I don't like this wild — frenzy — Be my own sweet little lark again, the way you always are.

NORA: Oh, I will. But you go on in. You too, Dr. Rank. Kristine, please help me put up my hair.

RANK (*in a low voice to* HELMER *as they go out*): You don't think she is — you know — expecting — ?

HELMER: Oh no. Nothing like that. It's just this childish fear I was telling you about. (*They go out, right.*)

NORA: Well?

MRS. LINDE: Left town.

NORA: I saw it in your face.

MRS. LINDE: He'll be back tomorrow night. I left him a note.

NORA: You shouldn't have. I don't want you to try to stop anything. You see, it's a kind of ecstasy, too, this waiting for the wonderful.

MRS. LINDE: But what is it you're waiting *for*?

NORA: You wouldn't understand. Why don't you go in to the others. I'll be there in a minute.

(MRS. LINDE *enters the dining room, right.*)

NORA (*stands still for a little while, as if collecting herself. She looks at her watch*): Five o'clock. Seven hours till midnight. Twenty-four more hours till next midnight. Then the Tarantella is over. Twenty-four plus seven — thirty-one more hours to live.

HELMER (*in the door, right*): What's happening to my little lark?

NORA (*to him, with open arms*): Here's your lark!

ACT III

The same room. The table by the couch and the chairs around it have been moved to the middle of the floor. A lighted lamp is on the table. The door to the front hall is open. Dance music is heard from upstairs. MRS. LINDE *is seated by the table, idly leafing through the pages of a book. She tries to read but seems unable to concentrate. Once or twice she turns her head in the direction of the door, anxiously listening.*

MRS. LINDE (*Looks at her watch*): Not yet. It's almost too late. If only he hasn't — (*Listens again.*) Ah! There he is. (*She goes to the hall and opens the front door carefully. Quiet footsteps on the stairs. She whispers.*) Come in. There's nobody here.

KROGSTAD (*in the door*): I found your note when I got home. What's this all about?

MRS. LINDE: I've got to talk to you.

KROGSTAD: Oh? And it has to be here?

MRS. LINDE: It couldn't be at my place. My room doesn't have a separate entrance. Come in. We're quite alone. The maid is asleep and the Helmers are at a party upstairs.

KROGSTAD (*entering*): Really? The Helmers are dancing tonight, are they?

MRS. LINDE: And why not?

KROGSTAD: You're right. Why not, indeed.

MRS. LINDE: All right, Krogstad. Let's talk, you and I.

KROGSTAD: I didn't know we had anything to talk about.

MRS. LINDE: We have much to talk about.

KROGSTAD: I didn't think so.

MRS. LINDE: No, because you've never really understood me.

KROGSTAD: What was there to understand? What happened was perfectly commonplace. A heartless woman jilts a man when she gets a more attractive offer.

MRS. LINDE: Do you think I'm all that heartless? And do you think it was easy for me to break with you?

KROGSTAD: No?

MRS. LINDE: You really thought it was?

KROGSTAD: If it wasn't, why did you write the way you did that time?

MRS. LINDE: What else could I do? If I had to make a break, I also had the duty to destroy whatever feelings you had for me.

KROGSTAD (*clenching his hands*): So that's the way it was. And you did — *that* — just for money!

MRS. LINDE: Don't forget I had a helpless mother and two small brothers. We couldn't wait for you, Krogstad. You know yourself how uncertain your prospects were then.

KROGSTAD: All right. But you still didn't have the right to throw me over for somebody else.

MRS. LINDE: I don't know. I have asked myself that question many times. Did I have
that right?

KROGSTAD (*in a lower voice*): When I lost you I lost my footing. Look at me now. A
shipwrecked man on a raft.

MRS. LINDE: Rescue may be near.

KROGSTAD: It *was* near. Then you came.

MRS. LINDE: I didn't know that, Krogstad. Only today did I find out it's your job I'm
taking over in the bank.

KROGSTAD: I believe you when you say so. But now that you *do* know, aren't you
going to step aside?

MRS. LINDE: No, for it wouldn't do you any good.

KROGSTAD: Whether it would or not — I would do it.

MRS. LINDE: I have learned common sense. Life and hard necessity have taught me
that.

KROGSTAD: And life has taught me not to believe in pretty speeches.

MRS. LINDE: Then life has taught you a very sensible thing. But you do believe in
actions, don't you?

KROGSTAD: How do you mean?

MRS. LINDE: You referred to yourself just now as a shipwrecked man.

KROGSTAD: It seems to me I had every reason to do so.

MRS. LINDE: And I am a shipwrecked woman. No one to grieve for, no one to care
for.

KROGSTAD: You made your choice.

MRS. LINDE: I had no other choice that time.

KROGSTAD: Let's say you didn't. What then?

MRS. LINDE: Krogstad, how would it be if we two shipwrecked people got together?

KROGSTAD: What's this!

MRS. LINDE: Two on one wreck are better off than each on his own.

KROGSTAD: Kristine!

MRS. LINDE: Why do you think I came to town?

KROGSTAD: Surely not because of me?

MRS. LINDE: If I'm going to live at all I must work. All my life, for as long as I can
remember, I have worked. That's been my one and only pleasure. But now that
I'm all alone in the world I feel only this terrible emptiness and desolation. There
is no joy in working just for yourself. Krogstad — give me someone and something to work for.

KROGSTAD: I don't believe in this. I think you're just another hysterical female being
noble and sacrificing yourself.

MRS. LINDE: Did you ever know me to be hysterical?

KROGSTAD: You really could do this? Listen — do you know about my past? All
of it?

MRS. LINDE: Yes.

KROGSTAD: Do you also know what people think of me around here?

MRS. LINDE: A little while ago you sounded as if you thought that together with me
you might have become a different person.

KROGSTAD: I'm sure of it.

MRS. LINDE: Couldn't that still be?

KROGSTAD: Kristine — do you know what you are doing? Yes, I see you do. And you really think you have the courage — ?

MRS. LINDE: I need someone to be a mother to, and your children need a mother. You and I need one another. Nils, I believe in you — in the real you. Together with you I dare to do anything.

KROGSTAD (*seizes her hands*): Thanks, thanks, Kristine — now I know I'll raise myself in the eyes of others. — Ah, but I forget — !

MRS. LINDE (*listening*): Shh! — There's the Tarantella. You must go; hurry!

KROGSTAD: Why? What is it?

MRS. LINDE: Do you hear what they're playing up there? When that dance is over they'll be down.

KROGSTAD: All right. I'm leaving. The whole thing is pointless, anyway. Of course you don't know what I'm doing to the Helmers.

MRS. LINDE: Yes, Krogstad; I do know.

KROGSTAD: Still, you're brave enough — ?

MRS. LINDE: I very well understand to what extremes despair can drive a man like you.

KROGSTAD: If only it could be undone!

MRS. LINDE: It could, for your letter is still out there in the mailbox.

KROGSTAD: Are you sure?

MRS. LINDE: Quite sure. But —

KROGSTAD (*looks searchingly at her*): Maybe I'm beginning to understand. You want to save your friend at any cost. Be honest with me. That's it, isn't it?

MRS. LINDE: Krogstad, you may sell yourself once for somebody else's sake, but you don't do it twice.

KROGSTAD: I'll ask for my letter back.

MRS. LINDE: No, no.

KROGSTAD: Yes, of course. I'll wait here till Helmer comes down. Then I'll ask him for my letter. I'll tell him it's just about my dismissal — that he shouldn't read it.

MRS. LINDE: No, Krogstad. You are not to do that.

KROGSTAD: But tell me — wasn't that the real reason you wanted to meet me here?

MRS. LINDE: At first it was, because I was so frightened. But that was yesterday. Since then I have seen the most incredible things going on in this house. Helmer must learn the whole truth. This miserable secret must come out in the open; those two must come to a full understanding. They simply can't continue with all this concealment and evasion.

KROGSTAD: All right; if you want to take that chance. But there is one thing I *can* do, and I'll do it right now.

MRS. LINDE (*listening*): But hurry! Go! The dance is over. We aren't safe another minute.

KROGSTAD: I'll be waiting for you downstairs.

MRS. LINDE: Yes, do. You must see me home.

KROGSTAD: I've never been so happy in my whole life. (*He leaves through the front door. The door between the living room and the front hall remains open.*)

MRS. LINDE (*straightens up the room a little and gets her things ready*): What a change! Oh yes! — what a change! People to work for — to live for — a home to bring happiness to. I can't wait to get to work — ! If only they'd come soon — (*Listens.*) Ah, there they are. Get my coat on — (*Puts on her coat and hat.*)

(HELMER's and NORA's voices are heard outside. A key is turned in the lock, and HELMER almost forces NORA into the hall. She is dressed in her Italian costume, with a big, black shawl over her shoulders. He is in evening dress under an open, black cape.)

NORA (in the door, still resisting): No, no, no! I don't want to! I want to go back upstairs. I don't want to leave so early.

HELMER: But dearest Nora —

NORA: Oh please, Torvald — please! I'm asking you as nicely as I can — just another hour!

HELMER: Not another minute, sweet. You know we agreed. There now. Get inside. You'll catch a cold out here. (She still resists, but he guides her gently into the room.)

MRS. LINDE: Good evening.

NORA: Kristine!

HELMER: Ah, Mrs. Linde. Still here?

MRS. LINDE: I know. I really should apologize, but I so much wanted to see Nora in her costume.

NORA: You've been waiting up for me?

MRS. LINDE: Yes, unfortunately I didn't get here in time. You were already upstairs, but I just didn't feel like leaving till I had seen you.

HELMER (removing NORA's shawl): Yes, do take a good look at her, Mrs. Linde. I think I may say she's worth looking at. Isn't she lovely?

MRS. LINDE: She certainly is —

HELMER: Isn't she a miracle of loveliness, though? That was the general opinion at the party, too. But dreadfully obstinate — that she is, the sweet little thing. What can we do about that? Will you believe it — I practically had to use force to get her away.

NORA: Oh Torvald, you're going to be sorry you didn't give me even half an hour more.

HELMER: See what I mean, Mrs. Linde? She dances the Tarantella — she is a tremendous success — quite deservedly so, though perhaps her performance was a little too natural — I mean, more than could be reconciled with the rules of art. But all right! The point is: she's a success, a tremendous success. So should I let her stay after that? Weaken the effect? Of course not. So I take my lovely little Capri girl — I might say, my capricious little Capri girl — under my arm — a quick turn around the room — a graceful bow in all directions, and — as they say in the novels — the beautiful apparition is gone. A finale should always be done for effect, Mrs. Linde, but there doesn't seem to be any way of getting that into Nora's head. Poooh — ! It's hot in here. (Throws his cape down on a chair and opens the door to his study.) Why, it's dark! Oh yes — of course. Excuse me — (Goes inside and lights a couple of candles.)

NORA (in a hurried, breathless whisper): Well?

MRS. LINDE (in a low voice): I have talked to him.

NORA: And — ?

MRS. LINDE: Nora — you've got to tell your husband everything.

NORA (no expression in her voice): I knew it.

MRS. LINDE: You have nothing to fear from Krogstad. But you must speak.

NORA: I'll say nothing.

MRS. LINDE: Then the letter will.

NORA: Thank you, Kristine. Now I know what I have to do. Shh!

HELMER (*returning*): Well, Mrs. Linde, have you looked your fill?

MRS. LINDE: Yes. And now I'll say goodnight.

HELMER: So soon? Is that your knitting?

MRS. LINDE (*takes it*): Yes, thank you. I almost forgot.

HELMER: So you knit, do you?

MRS. LINDE: Oh yes.

HELMER: You know — you ought to take up embroidery instead.

MRS. LINDE: Oh? Why?

HELMER: Because it's so much more beautiful. Look. You hold the embroidery so — in your left hand. Then with your right you move the needle — like this — in an easy, elongated arc — you see?

MRS. LINDE: Maybe you're right —

HELMER: Knitting, on the other hand, can never be anything but ugly. Look here: arms pressed close to the sides — the needles going up and down — there's something Chinese about it somehow —. That really was an excellent champagne they served us tonight.

MRS. LINDE: Well; goodnight, Nora. And don't be obstinate any more.

HELMER: Well said, Mrs. Linde!

MRS. LINDE: Goodnight, sir.

HELMER (*sees her to the front door*): Goodnight, goodnight. I hope you'll get home all right? I'd be very glad to — but of course you don't have far to walk, do you? Goodnight, goodnight. (*She leaves. He closes the door behind her and returns to the living room.*) There! At last we got rid of her. She really is an incredible bore, that woman.

NORA: Aren't you very tired, Torvald?

HELMER: No, not in the least.

NORA: Not sleepy either?

HELMER: Not at all. Quite the opposite. I feel enormously — animated. How about you? Yes, you do look tired and sleepy.

NORA: Yes, I am very tired. Soon I'll be asleep.

HELMER: What did I tell you? I was right, wasn't I? Good thing I didn't let you stay any longer.

NORA: Everything you do is right.

HELMER (*kissing her forehead*): Now my little lark is talking like a human being. But did you notice what splendid spirits Rank was in tonight?

NORA: Was he? I didn't notice. I didn't get to talk with him.

HELMER: Nor did I — hardly. But I haven't seen him in such a good mood for a long time. (*Looks at her, comes closer to her.*) Ah! It does feel good to be back in our own home again, to be quite alone with you — Oh, how lovely you are! — my exciting young woman!

NORA: Don't look at me like that, Torvald!

HELMER: Am I not to look at my most precious possession? All that loveliness that is mine, nobody's but mine, all of it mine!

NORA (*walks to the other side of the table*): I won't have you talk to me like that tonight.

HELMER (*follows her*): The Tarantella is still in your blood. I can tell. That only makes you all the more alluring. Listen! The guests are beginning to leave. (*Softly.*) Nora — darling — soon the whole house will be quiet.

NORA: I hope so.

HELMER: Yes, don't you, my darling? Do you know — when I'm at a party with you, like tonight — do you know why I hardly ever talk to you, why I keep away from you, only look at you once in a while — a few stolen glances — do you know why I do that? It's because I pretend that you are my secret love, my young, secret bride-to-be, and nobody has the slightest suspicion that there is anything between us.

NORA: Yes, I know. All your thoughts are with me.

HELMER: Then when we're leaving and I lay your shawl around your delicate young shoulders — around that wonderful curve of your neck — then I imagine you're my young bride, that we're coming away from the wedding, that I am taking you to my home for the first time — that I am alone with you for the first time — quite alone with you, you young, trembling beauty! I have desired you all evening — all my longing has only been for you. When you were dancing the Tarantella, chasing, inviting — my blood was on fire; I couldn't stand it any longer — that's why I brought you down so early —

NORA: Leave me now, Torvald. Please! I don't want all this.

HELMER: What do you mean? You're only playing your little teasing bird game with me; aren't you, Nora? Don't want to? I'm your husband, aren't I?

(*There is a knock on the front door.*)

NORA (*with a start*): Did you hear that — ?

HELMER (*on his way to the hall*): Who is it?

RANK (*outside*): It's me. May I come in for a moment?

HELMER (*in a low voice, annoyed*): Oh, what does he want now? (*Aloud.*) Just a minute. (*Opens the door.*) Well! How good of you not to pass by our door.

RANK: I thought I heard your voice, so I felt like saying hello. (*Looks around.*) Ah yes — this dear, familiar room. What a cozy, comfortable place you have here, you two.

HELMER: Looked to me as if you were quite comfortable upstairs too.

RANK: I certainly was. And why not? Why not enjoy all you can in this world? As much as you can and for as long as you can, anyway. Excellent wine.

HELMER: The champagne, particularly.

RANK: You noticed that too? Incredible how much I managed to put away.

NORA: Torvald drank a lot of champagne tonight, too.

RANK: Did he?

NORA: Yes, he did, and then he's always so much fun afterwards.

RANK: Well, why not have some fun in the evening after a well spent day?

HELMER: Well spent? I'm afraid I can't claim that.

RANK (*slapping him lightly on the shoulder*): But you see, I can!

NORA: Dr. Rank, I believe you have been conducting a scientific test today.

RANK: Exactly.

HELMER: What do you know — little Nora talking about scientific experiments!

NORA: May I congratulate you on the result?

RANK: You may indeed.

NORA: It was a good one?

RANK: The best possible for both doctor and patient—certainty.

NORA (*a quick query*): Certainty?

RANK: Absolute certainty. So why shouldn't I have myself an enjoyable evening afterwards?

NORA: I quite agree with you, Dr. Rank. You should.

HELMER: And so do I. If only you don't pay for it tomorrow.

RANK: Oh well — you get nothing for nothing in this world.

NORA: Dr. Rank — you are fond of costume parties, aren't you?

RANK: Yes, particularly when there is a reasonable number of amusing disguises.

NORA: Listen — what are the two of us going to be the next time?

HELMER: You frivolous little thing! Already thinking about the next party!

RANK: You and I? That's easy. You'll be Fortune's Child.

HELMER: Yes, but what is a fitting costume for that?

RANK: Let your wife appear just the way she always is.

HELMER: Beautiful. Very good indeed. But how about yourself? Don't you know what you'll go as?

RANK: Yes, my friend. I know precisely what I'll be.

HELMER: Yes?

RANK: At the next masquerade I'll be invisible.

HELMER: That's a funny idea.

RANK: There's a certain black hat — you've heard about the hat that makes you invisible, haven't you? You put that on, and nobody can see you.

HELMER (*suppressing a smile*): I guess that's right.

RANK: But I'm forgetting what I came for. Helmer, give me a cigar — one of your dark Havanas.

HELMER: With the greatest pleasure. (*Offers him his case.*)

RANK (*takes one and cuts off the tip*): Thanks.

NORA (*striking a match*): Let me give you a light.

RANK: Thanks. (*She holds the match; he lights his cigar.*) And now goodbye!

HELMER: Goodbye, goodbye, my friend.

NORA: Sleep well, Dr. Rank.

RANK: I thank you.

NORA: Wish me the same.

RANK: You? Well, if you really want me to —. Sleep well. And thanks for the light.
(*He nods to both of them and goes out.*)

HELMER (*in a low voice*): He had had quite a bit to drink.

NORA (*absently*): Maybe so.

(HELMER *takes out his keys and goes out into the hall.*)

NORA: Torvald — what are you doing out there?

HELMER: Emptying the mailbox. It is quite full. There wouldn't be room for the newspapers in the morning —

NORA: Are you going to work tonight?

HELMER: You know very well I won't. — Say! What's this? Somebody's been at the lock.

NORA: The lock — ?

HELMER: Sure. Why, I wonder. I hate to think that any of the maids —. Here's a broken hairpin. It's one of yours, Nora.

NORA (*quickly*): Then it must be one of the children.

HELMER: You better make damn sure they stop that. Hm, hm. — There! I got it open, finally. (*Gathers up the mail, calls out to the kitchen:*) Helene? — Oh Helene — turn out the light here in the hall, will you? (*He comes back into the living room and closes the door.)* Look how it's been piling up. *(Shows her the bundle of letters. Starts leafing through it.)* What's this?

NORA *(by the window)*: The letter! Oh no, no, Torvald!

HELMER: Two calling cards — from Rank.

NORA: From Dr. Rank?

HELMER *(looking at them)*: "Doctor of Medicine Rank!" They were on top. He must have put them there when he left just now.

NORA: Anything written on them?

HELMER: A black cross above the name. What a macabre idea. Like announcing his own death.

NORA: That's what it is.

HELMER: Hm? You know about this? Has he said anything to you?

NORA: That card means he's saying goodbye to us. He'll lock himself up to die.

HELMER: My poor friend. I knew of course he wouldn't be with me very long. But so soon —. And this hiding himself away like a wounded animal —

NORA: When it has to be, it's better it happens without words. Don't you think so, Torvald?

HELMER *(walking up and down)*: He'd grown so close to us. I find it hard to think of him as gone. With his suffering and loneliness he was like a clouded background for our happy sunshine. Well, it may be better this way. For him, at any rate. *(Stops.)* And perhaps for us, too, Nora. For now we have nobody but each other. *(Embraces her.)* Oh you — my beloved wife! I feel I just can't hold you close enough. Do you know, Nora — many times I have wished some great danger threatened you, so I could risk my life and blood and everything — everything, for your sake.

NORA *(frees herself and says in a strong and firm voice)*: I think you should go and read your letters now, Torvald.

HELMER: No, no — not tonight. I want to be with you, my darling.

NORA: With the thought of your dying friend — ?

HELMER: You are right. This has shaken both of us. Something not beautiful has come between us. Thoughts of death and dissolution. We must try to get over it — out of it. Till then — we'll each go to our own room.

NORA *(her arms around his neck)*: Torvald — goodnight! Goodnight!

HELMER *(kisses her forehead)*: Goodnight, my little songbird. Sleep well, Nora. Now I'll read my letters. *(He goes into his room, carrying the mail. Closes the door.)*

NORA *(her eyes desperate, her hands groping, finds* HELMER's *black cloak and throws it around her; she whispers, quickly, brokenly, hoarsely)*: Never see him again. Never. Never. Never. *(Puts her shawl over her head.)* And never see the children again, either. Never; never. — The black, icy water — fathomless — this — ! If only it was all over. — Now he has it. Now he's reading it. No, no; not yet. Torvald — goodbye — you — the children —

(She is about to hurry through the hall, when HELMER *flings open the door to his room and stands there with an open letter in his hand.)*

HELMER: Nora!

NORA *(cries out)*: Ah — !

HELMER: What is it? You know what's in this letter?

NORA: Yes, I do! Let me go! Let me out!

HELMER *(holds her back)*: Where do you think you're going?

NORA (*trying to tear herself loose from him*): I won't let you save me, Torvald!

HELMER (*tumbles back*): True! Is it true what he writes? Oh my god! No, no — this can't possibly be true.

NORA: It is true. I have loved you more than anything else in the whole world.

HELMER: Oh, don't give me any silly excuses.

NORA (*taking a step towards him*): Torvald — !

HELMER: You wretch! What have you done!

NORA: Let me go. You are not to sacrifice yourself for me. You are not to take the blame.

HELMER: No more playacting. (*Locks the door to the front hall.*) You'll stay here and answer me. Do you understand what you have done? Answer me! Do you understand?

NORA (*gazes steadily at him with an increasingly frozen expression*): Yes. Now I'm beginning to understand.

HELMER (*walking up and down*): What a dreadful awakening. All these years — all these eight years — she, my pride and my joy — a hypocrite, a liar — oh worse! worse! — a criminal! Oh, the bottomless ugliness in all this! Damn! Damn! Damn!

(NORA *silent, keeps gazing at him.*)

HELMER (*stops in front of her*): I ought to have guessed that something like this would happen. I should have expected it. All your father's loose principles — Silence! You have inherited every one of your father's loose principles. No religion, no morals, no sense of duty —. Now I am being punished for my leniency with him. I did it for your sake, and this is how you pay me back.

NORA: Yes. This is how.

HELMER: You have ruined all my happiness. My whole future — you've thrown it away. Oh, it's terrible to think about. I am at the mercy of an unscrupulous man. He can do with me whatever he likes, demand anything of me, command me and dispose of me just as he pleases — I dare not say a word! To go down so miserably, to be destroyed — all because of an irresponsible woman!

NORA: When I am gone from the world, you'll be free.

HELMER: No noble gestures, please. Your father was always full of such phrases too. What good would it do me if you were gone from the world, as you put it? Not the slightest bit of good at all. He could still make the whole thing public, and if he did I wouldn't be surprised if people thought I'd been your accomplice. They might even think it was my idea — that it was I who urged you to do it! And for all this I have you to thank — you, whom I've borne on my hands through all the years of our marriage. Now do you understand what you've done to me?

NORA (*with cold calm*): Yes.

HELMER: I just can't get it into my head that this is happening; it's all so incredible. But we have to come to terms with it somehow. Take your shawl off. Take it off, I say! I have to satisfy him one way or another. The whole affair must be kept quiet at whatever cost. — And as far as you and I are concerned, nothing must seem to have changed. I'm talking about appearances, of course. You'll go on living here; that goes without saying. But I won't let you bring up the children; I dare not trust you with them. — Oh! Having to say this to one I have loved so much, and whom I still — ! But all that has to be past. It's not a question of happiness any more but of hanging on to what can be salvaged — pieces, appearances — (*The doorbell rings.* HELMER *jumps.*) What's that? So late. Is the worst — ? Has he — ! Hide, Nora! Say you're sick.

(NORA *doesn't move.* HELMER *opens the door to the hall.*)

THE MAID (*half dressed, out in the hall*): A letter for your wife, sir.

HELMER: Give it to me. (*Takes the letter and closes the door.*) Yes, it's from him. But I won't let you have it. I'll read it myself.

NORA: Yes — you read it.

HELMER (*by the lamp*): I hardly dare. Perhaps we're lost, both you and I. No; I've got to know. (*Tears the letter open, glances through it, looks at an enclosure, a cry of joy.*) Nora!

(NORA *looks at him with a question in her eyes.*)

HELMER: Nora! — No, I must read it again. — Yes, yes; it is so! I'm saved! Nora, I'm saved!

NORA: And I?

HELMER: You too, of course; we're both saved, both you and I. Look! He's returning your note. He writes that he's sorry, he regrets, a happy turn in his life — oh, it doesn't matter what he writes. We're saved, Nora! Nobody can do anything to you now. Oh Nora, Nora —. No, I want to get rid of this disgusting thing first. Let me see — (*Looks at the signature.*) No, I don't want to see it. I don't want it to be more than a bad dream, the whole thing. (*Tears up the note and both letters, throws the pieces in the stove, and watches them burn.*) There! Now it's gone. — He wrote that ever since Christmas Eve —. Good god, Nora, these must have been three terrible days for you.

NORA: I have fought a hard fight these last three days.

HELMER: And been in agony and seen no other way out than —. No, we won't think of all that ugliness. We'll just rejoice and tell ourselves it's over, it's all over! Oh, listen to me, Nora. You don't seem to understand. It's over. What *is* it? Why do you look like that — that frozen expression on your face? Oh my poor little Nora, don't you think I know what it is? You can't make yourself believe that I have forgiven you. But I have, Nora; I swear to you, I have forgiven you for everything. Of course I know that what you did was for love of me.

NORA: That is true.

HELMER: You have loved me the way a wife ought to love her husband. You just didn't have the wisdom to judge the means. But do you think I love you any less because you don't know how to act on your own? Of course not. Just lean on me. I'll advise you; I'll guide you. I wouldn't be a man if I didn't find you twice as attractive because of your womanly helplessness. You mustn't pay any attention to the hard words I said to you right at first. It was just that first shock when I thought everything was collapsing all around me. I have forgiven you, Nora. I swear to you — I really have forgiven you.

NORA: I thank you for your forgiveness. (*She goes out through the door, right.*)

HELMER: No, stay — (*Looks into the room she entered.*) What are you doing in there?

NORA (*within*): Getting out of my costume.

HELMER (*by the open door*): Good, good. Try to calm down and compose yourself, my poor little frightened songbird. Rest safely; I have broad wings to cover you with. (*Walks around near the door.*) What a nice and cozy home we have, Nora.

Here's shelter for you. Here I'll keep you safe like a hunted dove I have rescued from the hawk's talons. Believe me: I'll know how to quiet your beating heart. It will happen by and by, Nora; you'll see. Why, tomorrow you'll look at all this in quite a different light. And soon everything will be just the way it was before. I won't need to keep reassuring you that I have forgiven you; you'll feel it yourself. Did you really think I could have abandoned you, or even reproached you? Oh, you don't know a real man's heart, Nora. There is something unspeakably sweet and satisfactory for a man to know deep in himself that he has forgiven his wife — forgiven her in all the fullness of his honest heart. You see, that way she becomes his very own all over again — in a double sense, you might say. He has, so to speak, given her a second birth; it is as if she had become his wife and his child, both. From now on that's what you'll be to me, you lost and helpless creature. Don't worry about a thing, Nora. Only be frank with me, and I'll be your will and your conscience. — What's this? You're not in bed? You've changed your dress — !

NORA (*in an everyday dress*): Yes, Torvald. I have changed my dress.

HELMER: But why — now — this late — ?

NORA: I'm not going to sleep tonight.

HELMER: But my dear Nora —

NORA (*looks at her watch*): It isn't all that late. Sit down here with me, Torvald. You and I have much to talk about. (*Sits down at the table.*)

HELMER: Nora — what is this all about? That rigid face —

NORA: Sit down. This will take a while. I have much to say to you.

HELMER (*sits down, facing her across the table*): You worry me, Nora. I don't understand you.

NORA: No, that's just it. You don't understand me. And I have never understood you — not till tonight. No, don't interrupt me. Just listen to what I have to say. — This is a settling of accounts, Torvald.

HELMER: What do you mean by that?

NORA (*after a brief silence*): Doesn't one thing strike you, now that we are sitting together like this?

HELMER: What would that be?

NORA: We have been married for eight years. Doesn't it occur to you that this is the first time that you and I, husband and wife, are having a serious talk?

HELMER: Well — serious —. What do you mean by that?

NORA: For eight whole years — longer, in fact — ever since we first met, we have never talked seriously to each other about a single serious thing.

HELMER: You mean I should forever have been telling you about worries you couldn't have helped me with anyway?

NORA: I am not talking about worries. I'm saying we have never tried seriously to get to the bottom of anything together.

HELMER: But dearest Nora, I hardly think that would have been something *you* —

NORA: That's the whole point. You have never understood me. Great wrong has been done to me, Torvald. First by Daddy and then by you.

HELMER: What! by us two? We who have loved you more than anyone else?

NORA (*shakes her head*): You never loved me — neither Daddy nor you. You only thought it was fun to be in love with me.

HELMER: But, Nora — what an expression to use!

NORA: That's the way it has been, Torvald. When I was home with Daddy, he told me all his opinions, and so they became my opinions too. If I disagreed with him I kept it to myself, for he wouldn't have liked that. He called me his little doll baby, and he played with me the way I played with my dolls. Then I came to your house —

HELMER: What a way to talk about our marriage!

NORA (*imperturbably*): I mean that I passed from Daddy's hands into yours. You arranged everything according to your taste, and so I came to share it — or I pretended to; I'm not sure which. I think it was a little of both, now one and now the other. When I look back on it now, it seems to me I've been living here like a pauper — just a hand-to-mouth kind of existence. I have earned my keep by doing tricks for you, Torvald. But that's the way you wanted it. You have great sins against me to answer for, Daddy and you. It's your fault that nothing has become of me.

HELMER: Nora, you're being both unreasonable and ungrateful. Haven't you been happy here?

NORA: No, never. I thought I was, but I wasn't.

HELMER: Not — not happy!

NORA: No; just having fun. And you have always been very good to me. But our home has never been more than a playroom. I have been your doll wife here, just the way I used to be Daddy's doll child. And the children have been my dolls. I thought it was fun when you played with me, just as they thought it was fun when I played with them. That's been our marriage, Torvald.

HELMER: There is something in what you are saying — exaggerated and hysterical though it is. But from now on things will be different. Playtime is over; it's time for growing up.

NORA: Whose growing up — mine or the children's?

HELMER: Both yours and the children's, Nora darling.

NORA: Oh Torvald, you're not the man to bring me up to be the right kind of wife for you.

HELMER: How can you say that?

NORA: And I — ? What qualifications do I have for bringing up the children?

HELMER: Nora!

NORA: You said so yourself a minute ago — that you didn't dare to trust me with them.

HELMER: In the first flush of anger, yes. Surely, you're not going to count that.

NORA: But you were quite right. I am *not* qualified. Something else has to come first. Somehow I have to grow up myself. And you are not the man to help me do that. That's a job I have to do by myself. And that's why I'm leaving you.

HELMER (*jumps up*): What did you say!

NORA: I have to be by myself if I am to find out about myself and about all those other things too. So I can't stay here any longer.

HELMER: Nora, Nora!

NORA: I'm leaving now. I'm sure Kristine will put me up for tonight.

HELMER: You're out of your mind! I won't let you! I forbid you!

NORA: You can't forbid me anything any more; it won't do any good. I'm taking my own things with me. I won't accept anything from you, either now or later.

HELMER: But this is madness!

NORA: Tomorrow I'm going home — I mean back to my old home town. It will be easier for me to find some kind of job there.

HELMER: Oh, you blinded, inexperienced creature — !

NORA: I must see to it that I get experience, Torvald.

HELMER: Leaving your home, your husband, your children! Not a thought of what people will say!

NORA: I can't worry about that. All I know is that I have to leave.

HELMER: Oh, this is shocking! Betraying your most sacred duties like this!

NORA: And what do you consider my most sacred duties?

HELMER: Do I need to tell you that? They are your duties to your husband and your children.

NORA: I have other duties equally sacred.

HELMER: You do not. What duties would they be?

NORA: My duties to myself.

HELMER: You are a wife and a mother before you are anything else.

NORA: I don't believe that any more. I believe I am first of all a human being, just as much as you — or at any rate that I must try to become one. Oh, I know very well that most people agree with you, Torvald, and that it says something like that in all the books. But what people say and what the books say is no longer enough for me. I have to think about these things myself and see if I can't find the answers.

HELMER: You mean to tell me you don't know what your proper place in your own home is? Don't you have a reliable guide in such matters? Don't you have religion?

NORA: Oh but Torvald — I don't really know what religion is.

HELMER: What's this?

NORA: All I know is what the Reverend Hansen told me when he prepared me for confirmation. He said that religion was *this* and it was *that*. When I get by myself, away from here, I'll have to look into that, too. I have to decide if what the Reverend Hansen said was right, or anyway if it is right for *me*.

HELMER: Oh, this is unheard of in a young woman! If religion can't guide you, let me appeal to your conscience. For surely you have moral feelings? Or — answer me — maybe you don't?

NORA: Well, you see, Torvald, I don't really know what to say. I just don't know. I am confused about these things. All I know is that my ideas are quite different from yours. I have just found out that the laws are different from what I thought they were, but in no way can I get it into my head that those laws are right. A woman shouldn't have the right to spare her dying old father or save her husband's life! I just can't believe that.

HELMER: You speak like a child. You don't understand the society you live in.

NORA: No, I don't. But I want to find out about it. I have to make up my mind who is right, society or I.

HELMER: You are sick, Nora; you have a fever. I really don't think you are in your right mind.

NORA: I have never felt so clearheaded and sure of myself as I do tonight.

HELMER: And clearheaded and sure of yourself you're leaving your husband and your children?

NORA: Yes.

HELMER: Then there is only one possible explanation.

NORA: What?

HELMER: You don't love me any more.

NORA: No; that's just it.

HELMER: Nora! How can you say that!

NORA: I am sorry, Torvald, for you have always been so good to me. But I can't help it. I don't love you any more.

HELMER (*with forced composure*): And this too is a clear and sure conviction?

NORA: Completely clear and sure. That's why I don't want to stay here any more.

HELMER: And are you ready to explain to me how I came to forfeit your love?

NORA: Certainly, I am. It was tonight, when the wonderful didn't happen. That was when I realized you were not the man I thought you were.

HELMER: You have to explain. I don't understand.

NORA: I have waited patiently for eight years, for I wasn't such a fool that I thought the wonderful is something that happens any old day. Then this — thing — came crashing in on me, and then there wasn't a doubt in my mind that now — now comes the wonderful. When Krogstad's letter was in that mailbox, never for a moment did it even occur to me that you would submit to his conditions. I was so absolutely certain that you would say to him: make the whole thing public — tell everybody. And when that had happened —

HELMER: Yes, then what? When I had surrendered my wife to shame and disgrace — !

NORA: When that had happened, I was absolutely certain that you would stand up and take the blame and say, "I am the guilty one."

HELMER: Nora!

NORA: You mean I never would have accepted such a sacrifice from you? Of course not. But what would my protests have counted against yours? *That* was the wonderful I was hoping for in terror. And to prevent that I was going to kill myself.

HELMER: I'd gladly work nights and days for you, Nora — endure sorrow and want for your sake. But nobody sacrifices his *honor* for his love.

NORA: A hundred thousand women have done so.

HELMER: Oh, you think and talk like a silly child.

NORA: All right. But you don't think and talk like the man I can live with. When you had gotten over your fright — not because of what threatened *me* but because of the risk to *you* — and the whole danger was past, then you acted as if nothing at all had happened. Once again I was your little songbird, your doll, just as before, only now you had to handle her even more carefully, because she was so frail and weak. (*Rises.*) Torvald — that moment I realized that I had been living here for eight years with a stranger and had borne him three children — Oh, I can't stand thinking about it! I feel like tearing myself to pieces!

HELMER (*heavily*): I see it, I see it. An abyss has opened up between us. — Oh but Nora — surely it can be filled?

NORA: The way I am now I am no wife for you.

HELMER: I have it in me to change.

NORA: Perhaps — if your doll is taken from you.

HELMER: To part — to part from you! No, no, Nora! I can't grasp that thought!

NORA (*goes out, right*): All the more reason why it has to be. (*She returns with her street clothes and a small bag, which she sets down on the chair by the table.*)

HELMER: Nora, Nora! Not now! Wait till tomorrow.

NORA (*putting on her coat*): I can't spend the night in a stranger's rooms.

HELMER: But couldn't we live here together like brother and sister — ?

NORA (*tying on her hat*): You know very well that wouldn't last long —. (*Wraps her shawl around her.*) Goodbye, Torvald. I don't want to see the children. I know I leave them in better hands than mine. The way I am now I can't be anything to them.

HELMER: But some day, Nora — some day — ?

NORA: How can I tell? I have no idea what's going to become of me.

HELMER: But you're still my wife, both as you are now and as you will be.

NORA: Listen, Torvald — when a wife leaves her husband's house, the way I am doing now, I have heard he has no further legal responsibilities for her. At any rate, I now release you from all responsibility. You are not to feel yourself obliged to me for anything, and I have no obligations to you. There has to be full freedom on both sides. Here is your ring back. Now give me mine.

HELMER: Even this?

NORA: Even this.

HELMER: Here it is.

NORA: There. So now it's over. I'm putting the keys here. The maids know everything about the house — better than I. Tomorrow, after I'm gone, Kristine will come over and pack my things from home. I want them sent after me.

HELMER: Over! It's all over! Nora, will you never think of me?

NORA: I'm sure I'll often think of you and the children and this house.

HELMER: May I write to you, Nora?

NORA: No — never. I won't have that.

HELMER: But send you things — ? You must let me —

NORA: Nothing, nothing —

HELMER: — help you, when you need help —

NORA: I told you, no; I won't have it. I'll accept nothing from strangers.

HELMER: Nora — can I never again be more to you than a stranger?

NORA (*picks up her bag*): Oh Torvald — then the most wonderful of all would have to happen —

HELMER: Tell me what that would be — !

NORA: For that to happen, both you and I would have to change so that — Oh Torvald, I no longer believe in the wonderful.

HELMER: But I *will* believe. Tell me! Change, so that — ?

NORA: So that our living together would become a true marriage. Goodbye. (*She goes out through the hall.*)

HELMER (*sinks down on a chair near the door and covers his face with his hands*): Nora! Nora! (*Looks around him and gets up.*) All empty. She's gone. (*With sudden hope.*) The most wonderful — ? !

(*From downstairs comes the sound of a heavy door slamming shut.*)

AFTERWORD

Some things in A *Doll's House* have dated, but the issue Nora and Helmer debate in the last scene is not one of them.

NORA: I have other duties equally sacred.

HELMER: You do not. What duties would they be?

NORA: My duties to myself.
HELMER: You are a wife and a mother before you are anything else.
NORA: I don't believe that any more. I believe I am first of all a human being, just as
   much as you — or at any rate that I must try to become one.

There is still bite in that. But if a century-old play about a social problem seems relevant to our current situation, it must be because we have made less progress than we thought or because the problem is of a kind that affirmative action and consciousness-raising won't solve. The first is the Women's Lib explanation. The second turns the play into a tragedy about selfhood violated by social forms and self-violated by its own social needs. It sees Nora's being a woman as incidental — a reflection of a situation that happened (or still happens) to be a fact of life in our society rather than an essential premise for a drama about a type of human deprivation that only women suffer. Both explanations are valid and important.

I like to think that both together account for our willingness to put up with the old-fashioned technical crudities in the play. The most obvious are the contrivances of the blackmailing plot (fateful letter, reformed villain), the heavy-handed symbols (bedraggled Christmas tree, frenzied dancing, doffed masquerade costume), the too obviously planted speeches that later bloom into dramatic irony (Helmer being fatuously masculine), and the small talk portentously charged with deeper meaning (Nora's "Soon I'll be asleep," Rank's "Thanks for the light.") Unfriendly critics regard this sort of thing as heavy-handed use of the mechanical tricks of the French "well-made" drama of the middle years of the nineteenth century. During his youth in Norway, Ibsen had helped stage a number of these plays by Scribe, Augier, Dumas *fils*, and others in theaters in Bergen and Oslo. Other ironies are less transparent. The family crisis comes at Christmas, of all times. Krogstad first enters just as Nora has savored her freedom from worry. The "shipwrecked" older couple get together in a true marriage just as the "happy" younger couple discover the falseness of theirs and separate. Krogstad calls the kind of high-minded self-sacrifice Nora expects from Helmer "female hysteria," and Mrs. Linde doesn't disagree.

But what critics mainly have found fault with in the play are Nora's sudden change from squirrel and lark to calm and wise debater, and the lack of any real dramatic function for Dr. Rank. Both objections can be answered. Those who find Nora's change unbelievable miss the first-act clues to her suppressed frustration (the hidden macaroons) and resentment (the impulse to profanity). They fail, that is, to see how alien the role she is playing is to her deeper nature. That the *play* at the same time changes from busy melodrama to quiet discussion may seem like a more dubious asset, turning the debate scene between husband and wife into something more like an epilogue that analyzes what has gone before than an integral part of the action. Yet the fact that the change *is* drastic underscores the nature and the importance of the change in Nora.

It is true that Dr. Rank ultimately affects neither the blackmailing plot nor the fate of the Helmers' marriage, that his quasi-Darwinian notion of the survival of the morally fittest (in Act I) is only vaguely relevant to the story of the Helmers, and that we don't need his love for Nora to convince us that there is more to her than Helmer's little wastrel and wanton. On the other hand, if Nora might not have seemed less nice without her scenes with Rank, she would have seemed less complex. Also, lonely and dying, Rank is a contrast to his friends' marriage (as Helmer notices) — a contrast that turns ironic at the end when we see that it has been more apparent than real. Finally, his physical and Nora's moral corruption are analogous illustrations of the ruthless laws of heredity; both are children of corrupt fathers. And tainted heredity is one of the major themes in the play; the air of fatality and sad decay that attends the scenes with Rank isn't just gratuitous sentimentality. But all such considerations aside, it is surely impossible *not* to feel that A *Doll's House* would be a smaller play without Dr. Rank. Something about him doesn't come under the purview of mere interpretation and formal analysis.

And whatever the faults of Ibsen's craftsmanship, few of them seriously interfere with the drama about Nora. The action of that drama is the transformation of a doll and a pet into a potential woman. At the end Nora sets out in quest of herself in a world of which she knows little more than that it is a place where the evil "impossible" does happen and "the wonderful" she has waited for in terror and ecstasy does not. This is tragic irony and not feminist propaganda.

It has been the misfortune of A *Doll's House* that it made drama history on its first appearance for reasons that ever since have obscured its tragic quality and fixed its status as that of a play with a message. It was not the first nineteenth-century play to deal with a topical issue in realistic form. It wasn't even the first such play Ibsen wrote. Two years earlier, in 1877, he had exposed small-town bigotry and hypocritical business ethics in *Pillars of Society*. But it was the first play to make a powerful whole out of the three indispensable ingredients of the social problem play: truthfulness to the realities of contemporary middle-class life, a controversial "meaning," and a tight and exciting plot — realism, relevance, and suspense. It was the first of the three plays, all written around 1880, in which Ibsen moved western drama out of the doldrums of bedroom farce, gothic melodrama, and blank verse pseudotragedy where it had languished for some 150 years. Together with *Ghosts* and *An Enemy of the People* it established the social problem play as the dominant form of drama for the next third of a century. By the time illness put an end to Ibsen's career in 1900, drama had caught up with the contemporary novel in artistry, significance, and prestige. More than any other single playwright of his time he had restored drama to its traditional function: an imitation of human life in serious action.

But the controversy set off by the publication of A *Doll's House* late in 1879 concerned practical reform rather than Aristotelian poetics. Theater directors immediately sensed the box office potential in Ibsen's new play; within weeks of its publication in book form it was being acted on a number of European stages. Everywhere people took sides for or against Nora. There doesn't seem to have been much exaggeration in a famous contemporary description of the effect of the play: "The door Nora Helmer slammed shut on her marriage sent shock waves through thousands of homes." Lawyers debated whether any court of justice would actually convict her of forgery. Anxious hostesses asked their dinner guests not to discuss her. Announcing that *she* would never abandon *her* children, a famous German actress refused to appear as Nora unless Ibsen provided a new ending.*

A social problem play presents a particular instance of a general condition. Its dialogue includes discussion of the rightness or wrongness of the forms and rules of social relationships, and the outcome of its action is "proof" that, given certain characters caught in certain circumstances, the prevailing social conventions have distressing consequences. If Ibsen's earliest working note for A *Doll's House* is typical, it would seem that a social problem play originates in the playwright's perception of a general, abstract social truth rather than in an image, an action, or a character. The set of notes is headed, "Notes for the contemporary tragedy," and the first note reads:

There are two kinds of moral law, two kinds of conscience: one male, the other, entirely different, female. They don't understand one another, but in the world of practical affairs a woman is judged by man's law, as if she were not a woman but a man.

Because social problem plays are plays about consequences, they commonly have a retrospective structure. A *Doll's House* is an example — so much so that it became a model. The classical prototype for a retrospective play is Sophocles' *Oedipus the King*. Ibsen's "Messenger from Corinth" is Mrs. Linde, whose innocent arrival precipitates the catastrophe. Because they compress a long story to its brief climax — the charged past exploding in the complacent present — retrospective plays usually have a small cast, a small time span, and a single setting. But concentration tends to strain plausibility; in both Sophocles and Ibsen we are aware of the playwright's manipulation of the comings and goings of his characters to meet the demands of his plot. This is obviously more of a handicap to Ibsen's realism than to Sophocles' myth. Ibsen was more successful in concealing the arti-

---

* He did. But he referred to it as a "barbaric outrage" and agreed to write it only because existing copyright laws gave him no control over his scripts outside of Scandinavia. Under the circumstance he preferred violating the play himself to having somebody else do it.

In the new German ending, Helmer forces Nora to take a last look at their sleeping children. When they wake up in the morning, he tells her, they will be motherless — "the way you were." At this, Nora drops her bag, sinks to her knees, and cries, "Oh, I'm committing a great sin against myself, but I can't leave them!" "Joyfully but softly," Helmer calls out, "Nora!" and the curtain falls.

fices of retrospectiveness in *Ghosts*, his next play. In it there are no irrelevant servants, no subplot, and no major character that has only a tenuous connection with the main plot. Inevitably, exposition takes up a large part of a retrospective play, for the rediscovery and reassessment of the past are precisely what such a play is about. Also inevitably, because one of the conventions of dramatic realism is lifelike speech, exposition in a realistic retrospective play is fragmented and discontinuous and often comes in the form of hints and innuendo.*

The philosophical premise for retrospective drama is the operation of laws of causality in human affairs. Its corollary is moral responsibility. Ibsen's major characters suffer because of what they and others did and did not do in the past. Nora suffers the consequences not just of her forgery but of her whole conditioning from girlhood on by a society run by men and also of the failure of that society to recognize that the moral law it has conditioned her to obey is different from its own male law. Yet that is the law society judges her by.

The backward-looking-ness of Ibsen's plays is therefore more than a device for a compact and suspenseful — a "well-made" — plot — just as the plot is not an end in itself but a means to catching and holding audience attention. The retrospective structure is an image-in-action of the moral nature of human reality. This is as true of *A Doll's House* and *Ghosts* as of Ibsen's later plays, in which social problems are less prominent or absent altogether. The common critical view that the sequence of Ibsen's last twelve plays reveals a change in the nature of the action from "social" to "psychological" and from external to internal oversimplifies a complex development. In an obvious sense all four of his problem plays dramatize the clash between an entrenched conservatism, unresponsive to changes in social and scientific thought, and a militant liberalism, nurtured by those changes and asserting the right of the individual freely to seek and live his own selfhood. But in *A Doll's House* and *Ghosts*, at least, the bitterest battles between tradition and rebellion are fought in the soul of the woman protagonist. They are "psychological" plays as much as they are "social," and to the extent they *are* social they offer diagnosis of existing conditions rather than programs for future reform. They are polemical only in the limited sense that they seek to offend the bigoted, upset the complacent, and make the unthinking think. In this they were being faithful to the rationale for the social problem play, as the Danish critic Georg Brandes had formulated it in one of a series of lectures on modern literature that he

---

* A good example is the story of Helmer's courtship of Nora. From a hint of Nora's in Act II and from Helmer's own admission in Act III — though neither one of them is aware of the implications of what he or she is saying — we learn that Helmer's love for Nora kept him from bringing charges against her father for what appears to have been misappropriation of public funds. This in spite of the fact that he was acting as the government's investigator of an official under suspicion. That Helmer, who regards himself as a paragon of professional integrity, once put love above duty is both a piece of rather complex irony and another instance of the unconscious hypocrisy of the male establishment.

gave in Copenhagen during the winter of 1871–72. Ibsen rarely admitted to being influenced by anyone, but after reading Brandes's published lectures he wrote to him to say how profoundly they had excited and stimulated him. Modern drama, Brandes had said, "has the obligation to submit problems to debate."

He did not add, "and to solve them," and Ibsen's plays prove that he had understood exactly what Brandes had and had not said. But Ibsen's readers and audiences have generally ignored the "open" endings of A Doll's House and Ghosts (we don't know what Nora and Mrs. Alving are going to do next or what is to become of them) and assumed that the plays answer the questions they ask.* Everybody "knows" that A Doll's House is a thesis play, a play with a message. There has even been general agreement on what the message is: a disenchanted, discontented wife should get out. The only disagreement has been over whether the message is a Good or a Bad Thing. For liberals, the play vindicates an individual's right to rebel against an oppressive social convention. For conservatives, it subverts the most sacred of social institutions, or — in updated terms — it challenges the ideal of family togetherness.

Ibsen expressed his frustration with this kind of persistent misunderstanding of his plays in a little speech at a dinner that the Norwegian Association for Women's Rights gave in his honor in 1898. Replying to their praise of him as a champion of their cause and particularly as the creator of Nora, he said:

> I have been more of a poet and less of a social philosopher than most people have been inclined to think. I am grateful for your toast, but I can't claim the honor of ever having worked consciously for women's rights. I'm not even sure I know what women's rights are. To me it has seemed a matter of human rights.

The speech must have disconcerted his hostesses. It is still useful reading. The last sentence quoted could be dismissed as a piece of the platitudinous sublime if it hadn't come from the author of A Doll's House. As it is, we think of Nora's right to face the bleak prospects that open on her last exit.

Given the public's (and sometimes the critics') insistence on reducing A Doll's House to polemics, it is not surprising that as women acquired property rights and the right to vote and were allowed outside the kitchen and the nursery and given a share in at least some of men's professional and sexual privileges, the play came to be regarded as just about the mustiest of Ibsen's major plays. And with the obsolescence of its polemics went the

---

* After A Doll's House, Ibsen said many years later, "I just had to write Ghosts." The situations in the two plays are complementary, and the plays have the same general theme and share at least one major plot motif. Mrs. Alving leaves her husband, whom she has never loved, but is persuaded to return. He turns into a debauchee. Years after his death, she seeks to redeem the ugly and shameful past through love of her son. But he has inherited syphilis from his father and suffers a physical collapse that demolishes his mind. In the final tableau his mother must choose between killing him (as he had asked her to do before the last attack) or taking care of him.

obsolescence of its art. To the new generation of playwrights Ibsen seemed like the writer of dreary semi-documentaries from a philistine age that had banished beauty and starved the imagination in its preference for "useful" literature. They felt muted and shackled on his kind of stage, where everything was supposed to sound like and look like what went on in the spectator's own hideously overfurnished rooms. By the time of World War I the very success of what used to be known as "Ibsenism," as art and ideology, had bred a reaction that was ready to consign Ibsen's own plays to literary history and to leave to "the father of modern drama" the sole parental function of being an authority figure to rebel against.

Today, once again, we know that the dignity, freedom, and self-respect that Helmer and his society denied Nora are still being denied countless women. Equality of the sexes is still more pious fiction than fact, and we wonder how the generations between Ibsen's and our own ever came to think otherwise. Sexual prejudices and fears and stereotypes may take subtler forms than they used to, but we know they are just as real. We even know what the really tough questions to ask of Ibsen's play are. Is Nora young and pretty and charming because Ibsen was a sexist at heart, who from well-meaning male insensitivity blurred the hard issues of Nora's case with sex appeal and trite romantic sentiment? Is there covert sexism in his notion about the "two moral laws, two kinds of conscience"? Doesn't the distinction he makes rest on a belief in a kind of separate-but-equal principle that allots to women the intuitive reasons of the heart and to men practical common sense in dealing with the real world? Isn't there a sense in which the German version of the ending, simply by being more believable, is a stronger indictment of male society than the ending we have? And did Ibsen feel something like that himself when in *Ghosts* he made the tragedy of the wife who stays so much grimmer than the tragedy in *A Doll's House* of the wife who leaves? Isn't it ironic that Nora could be said to give up more than she gains? For must we believe her when she says she has never been happy in her cozy marriage? And if she is self-deceived on this point, doesn't that add force to Ibsen's critique of social attitudes, including women's? Or do such questions only prove that those attitudes are still with us? The reasons modern feminists have helped revive interest in the play are more varied and sophisticated than those that prompted the Norwegian Women's Righters to toast Ibsen in 1898, and their skeptical questioning is more in Ibsen's spirit.

One of those reasons is political. Money is the play's overriding plot issue. Around the motif of Nora's loan cluster subordinate motifs that all have to do with money. They include Helmer's big new salary, Nora's father's casual money dealings, Nora's daydream (with its hint of prostitution) of a wealthy old admirer who will leave her all his money, Dr. Rank's inherited wealth (with a hint, given his other heritage, of a connection between money and moral and physical corruption), Krogstad's "miserable circumstances" that have reduced him to a shady money-lender and blackmailer, the economic necessities that have blighted Mrs. Linde's emotional life, and the nurse Anne-Marie's having to give up her child for material security. When the play ends Nora is beginning to experience both Mrs. Linde's and Anne-Marie's deprivations.

Nora's real crime is her venture into business, man's domain, forbidden women unless they enter as menials, like Mrs. Linde. In retribution, "bank business" in the shape of Krogstad enters and wrecks "the home" she should have stayed in.* Helmer's "dreadful awakening" in Act III is his discovery that Nora's "little Christmas secrets," which he had patronized so indulgently in Act I, include forgery — that his precious little sex object has committed a crime. When in the last scene he identifies his honor with his profession, Nora in crushing irony claims love as the motive for her dishonor. By the invidious poetic justice that operates in Helmer's banker's world of business rules and regulations, Mrs. Linde, who once gave up love for money, is at the end rewarded with love, husband, and children, while Nora loses both family and love because she once used money to save both. Sexism and capitalism are intimate allies in maintaining a socioeconomic order defined by the three institutions of bank, hospital, and nursery. The play's five major characters move or do not move within that triangle. Helmer is the servant of money who first dismisses Krogstad because he makes him sick and then replaces him with Mrs. Linde, who used to take care of her sick mother and in the future will restore Krogstad (who, according to Dr. Rank, belongs in a hospital) to moral health. Dr. Rank, the healer, is himself sick. Nora in her doll's house is a mother confined to the nursery. Ibsen's imagery defines bourgeois society as money-ridden, prostituting, and repressive, a society in which daughters take care of parents, mothers become like children, and men grow callous and sick. No wonder politically radical feminists like the play.

The finished play is less the story of a woman's tangle with men's legal system than Ibsen's early note suggested it was going to be. Its sphere of action is domestic and not judicial. Still, the legal issue is there, and Ibsen uses it to put society in a double bind. The issue is whether society should enact laws that would acknowledge the validity of woman's conscience and condone economic crimes committed from "womanly" motives. If Nora is right, the play puts society under obligation to pass such laws. If she is wrong, the play faults society for its failure to educate its women for informed and mature responsibilities. Either way, Nora wins and society loses.

But this is theory and thesis rather than drama. In the drama it is Nora who is the loser. Like others of Ibsen's tragic heroines she finds her world going to pieces when she comes to a larger understanding of herself and her situation. In her case the recognition comes through a particular disil-

---

* It may be worth noting that a literal translation of the Norwegian title of the play is "A Doll's *Home*" (*Et dukkehjem*).

lusionment: her discovery that the act that was her secret pride and joy is a disgraceful crime in the eyes of the man for whose sake she did it. This action is closer to the heart of the play than the demonstration that society's criminal code is humanly inadequate. Not to see this is once again to let the thesis play absorb the problem play and to let social polemics and satire crowd out the tragedy.

Obviously, the tragedy in *A Doll's House* is not the traditional kind in which a nobly indomitable spirit triumphs over adverse circumstance. Rather, it is of the muted, ambiguous, almost banal kind that Ibsen's heading for his working notes suggested it was when it referred to it as a "contemporary" tragedy. That is why those critics — Hermann Weigand, in *The Modern Ibsen*, is one of them — err who find Nora the wrong kind of heroine for realizing Ibsen's intentions. Their argument is that she is too selfish and silly through too much of the play (seven-eighths, to be exact) to serve as a victim who can enlist our sympathy and as a spokesperson who can enlist our agreement. They point to her behavior during the first minute or two of stage action. We see her being secretive ("Hide the Christmas tree"), careless with money when she has every reason not to be ("No; keep the change"), and slyly deceptive and duplicitous (the macaroon business). Later we see her being a thoughtlessly cruel little egoist with poor Mrs. Linde and a calculating coquette with both her husband and Dr. Rank. Her naiveté in business matters strains belief, and her notion of "the wonderful" is a silly schoolgirl's romantic nonsense. In her final scene with Helmer she cannot or will not give him credit for at least beginning to understand and to feel contrition. In fact, say some of these critics, Helmer is too nice for the part of villain. He is a professional success, a good and responsible provider, a playful and apparently ardent lover. He has intelligence, wit, taste, imagination, and a kind of easygoing, virile charm. Even Nora admits he has always "been good" to her. His affection for her is certainly infuriating in its condescension, but it is genuine affection nevertheless.

But Ibsen didn't intend for Nora to seem admirable in her role as doll-wife, nor for Helmer to seem like an ogre of a Victorian husband. Ibsen's case against male society is stronger and not weaker because of the good qualities he has allowed Helmer. By appearing to make a fair case he makes a convincing one: "even the best of husbands . . . !" And he avoids a character stereotype of liberal melodrama. It is even more important to realize that the qualities that the critics think disqualify Nora for the part of heroine in a polemical play are crucial to Ibsen's polemical point. They are symptoms of the damage sexists like her father and her husband and the Reverend Hansen have done to her personality. With the exception of Dr. Rank, the men in her life have conditioned her to conceal her natural impulses and honest opinions and bred into her habits of self-degradation. It is not at all strange that she enjoys Rank's company "almost as much as" Helmer's. We can't hold against her her dependent position in a conventional marriage, but we can be pained and saddened by her frivolous acceptance of her role — a less than human role, as Helmer's cute little animal names for her imply (perhaps a little too insistently). The system is vicious not so much because it allows men to "own" women as because it forces women to disown themselves. How thoroughly she has been brainwashed is evident in the scene where she gets indignant with Krogstad for suggesting that Helmer may take her opinions seriously.* Apparently perplexed, a recent reviewer, bothered by Nora's obvious defects of character and mind, asks, "How can we be sure that the Nora who leaves isn't still the same little selfish, play-acting, romantic fool that she was at the beginning?" The answer is that we can't.

What is more pathetic is that neither can she. She is not at the end a strong and confident champion of the Movement, a triumphant specimen of heroic and emancipated (or, in Bernard Shaw's ironic phrase, "unwomanly") womanhood. Her leaving home is a sad and lonely act of uncertain outcome and questionable morality, not an obvious "right" in either sense of the word. She leaves like the child Helmer says (and she admits) she is. Still hurting and confused from the loss of her faith in "the wonderful" and willful and intolerant and already hardened in her new and desperate commitment to herself, she ignores Helmer's obvious anguish and his fumbling but sincere promise of a new start and leaves her children to be brought up by a man she has convinced herself is a prig and a tyrant and a stifler of female souls (one of the children is a girl) and by a kindly but coarse old nurse, who has been so thoroughly squashed by the system that she can't even see herself as its innocent victim. Nora doesn't even have the strength and fury that come from certainty of being right. She is sure she must leave, but only because she has become unsure of everything else. All she knows is that if she was a pet and a plaything when she was a wife, she can no longer be a wife if she wants to become a woman. She leaves not in pride but in self-disgust. She looks back upon her marriage as a prostituting masquerade and as a "hand-to-mouth kind of existence. I have earned my keep by doing tricks for you, Torvald. . . . I realized that I had been living here for eight years with a stranger and had borne him three children — Oh, I can't stand thinking about it! I feel like tearing myself to pieces!" She hates herself for allowing herself to be sexually exploited. The self-destructive image echoes her repressed rage at Helmer's using her during her squirrel days. Then, too, her imagination was haunted by a desire to tear

---

* A much more complex instance is her silk stocking scene with Dr. Rank. Is she prostituting herself when she uses sexual titillation to get money, or is she heroically playing a demeaning role in order to rescue her family and herself from ruin? Is she being kind to Rank by remaining silent at the end, respecting his love for her too much to force him to put a price tag on it? Or is she being cruel from some mistaken notion of wifely honor that obliges her to be annoyed with him and to deny him the only pleasure it is still in her power to give him? If we can overlook its awkward and improbable conclusion, the scene is richly ambiguous — more so, perhaps, than any other scene in the play — and presents a nice critical problem.

things to pieces and to shatter the smugness of Helmer's benevolent sultanism by yelling "goddammit!" in his face.

If A Doll's House achieves something more subtle than a posing of Nora's absolute right against Helmer's absolute wrong, it becomes more and not less relevant to the feminist movement than when it is read as a strident tract. For then we see Nora as the product of social conventions and value systems that still stunt women's personal development, impoverish and trivialize their lives ("fun" is not happiness), and degrade them in their own eyes. Her tragedy is the tragedy of wasted human potential, and the ending does not reassure us that her future will redeem the waste. She is quite sincere when she feels that "nothing" has become of her, and we cannot prove her wrong. And when Ibsen lets his curtain come down not on the wife who leaves but on the desolate husband who stays behind, he is suggesting that men, no less than women, are victims of the system. That it is Helmer who now needs to believe in "the wonderful" is the ultimate irony in A Doll's House. For "the wonderful" happens when a man and a woman live together under one law, and nothing in the play suggests the likelihood of that coming to pass.*

---

* The Norwegian "det vidunderlige," which my translation here renders as "the wonderful," presents a crucial but frustrating challenge to the translator. It implies both something surpassingly desirable and something miraculous. "The wonderful" does not strongly enough suggest the unattainability of the ideal in the real world. But its most common alternative in English translations of Ibsen's play, "the miracle" or "the miraculous," loses most of the emotional charge of the original.

Oscar Wilde

THE IMPORTANCE OF BEING EARNEST

FOREWORD

When the joint careers of Gilbert and Sullivan were at their peak, that of
Oscar Wilde was in the ascendant. Like several great wits of the British
theater, Wilde was Irish born. Educated at Trinity College, Dublin, and
Oxford, he burst on the fashionable London world as poet, playwright,
socialite, and the most colorful spokesman of the aesthetic movement,
which dominated the closing decades of the century. Gilbert satirized this
movement in *Patience*, and Wilde's lecture tour in the United States whet-
ted the public interest for the American production of that work. *The Importance of Being Earnest*, Wilde's most brilliant comedy, opened in 1895.
While it was still playing to packed houses, Wilde became involved in a
series of court actions that were to destroy his career. Found guilty of ho-
mosexuality in a sensational trial, he was sentenced to prison. *The Importance of Being Earnest* continued to play, but with the author's name removed from the posters. The fashionable society that had once idolized
him now rejected him — the case touched a sensitive nerve, coming in the
wake of another, similar trial in which prominent members of the aristocracy had been involved — and after his release, Wilde spent his remaining
years in exile. He finally died miserably in Paris.

THE PERSONS OF THE PLAY

JOHN WORTHING, J.P.   LADY BRACKNELL
ALGERNON MONCRIEFF   HON. GWENDOLEN FAIRFAX
REV. CANON CHASUBLE, D.D.   CECILY CARDEW
MERRIMAN, Butler   MISS PRISM, Governess
LANE, Manservant

THE SCENES OF THE PLAY

ACT I
ALGERNON MONCRIEFF's *Flat in Half-Moon Street*, W.

ACT II
The Garden at the Manor House, Woolton

ACT III
Drawing-room at the Manor House, Woolton

TIME
The Present

ACT I

Scene — Morning-room in Algernon's flat in Half-Moon Street. The room is luxuriously and artistically furnished. The sound of a piano is heard in the adjoining room.

LANE is arranging afternoon tea on the table, and after the music has ceased, ALGERNON enters.

ALGERNON: Did you hear what I was playing, Lane?

LANE: I didn't think it polite to listen, sir.

ALGERNON: I'm sorry for that, for your sake. I don't play accurately — any one can play accurately — but I play with wonderful expression. As far as the piano is concerned, sentiment is my forte. I keep science for Life.

LANE: Yes, sir.

ALGERNON: And, speaking of the science of Life, have you got the cucumber sandwiches cut for Lady Bracknell?

LANE: Yes, sir. *(Hands them on a salver.)*

ALGERNON *(inspects them, takes two, and sits down on the sofa)*: Oh! . . . by the way, Lane, I see from your book that on Thursday night, when Lord Shoreman and Mr. Worthing were dining with me, eight bottles of champagne are entered as having been consumed.

LANE: Yes, sir; eight bottles and a pint.

ALGERNON: Why is it that at a bachelor's establishment the servants invariably drink the champagne? I ask merely for information.

LANE: I attribute it to the superior quality of the wine, sir. I have often observed that in married households the champagne is rarely of a first-rate brand.

ALGERNON: Good heavens! Is marriage so demoralizing as that?

LANE: I believe it *is* a very pleasant state, sir. I have had very little experience of it myself up to the present. I have only been married once. That was in consequence of a misunderstanding between myself and a young person.

ALGERNON (*languidly*): I don't know that I am much interested in your family life, Lane.

LANE: No, sir; it is not a very interesting subject. I never think of it myself.

ALGERNON: Very natural, I am sure. That will do, Lane, thank you.

LANE: Thank you, sir.

(LANE *goes out.*)

ALGERNON: Lane's views on marriage seem somewhat lax. Really, if the lower orders don't set us a good example, what on earth is the use of them? They seem, as a class, to have absolutely no sense of moral responsibility.

(*Enter* LANE.)

LANE: Mr. Ernest Worthing.

(*Enter* JACK. LANE *goes out.*)

ALGERNON: How are you, my dear Ernest? What brings you up to town?

JACK: Oh, pleasure, pleasure! What else should bring one anywhere? Eating as usual, I see, Algy!

ALGERNON (*stiffly*): I believe it is customary in good society to take some slight refreshment at five o'clock. Where have you been since last Thursday?

JACK (*sitting down on the sofa*): In the country.

ALGERNON: What on earth do you do there?

JACK (*pulling off his gloves*): When one is in town one amuses oneself. When one is in the country one amuses other people. It is excessively boring.

ALGERNON: And who are the people you amuse?

JACK (*airily*): Oh, neighbours, neighbours.

ALGERNON: Got nice neighbours in your part of Shropshire?

JACK: Perfectly horrid! Never speak to one of them.

ALGERNON: How immensely you must amuse them! (*Goes over and takes sandwich.*) By the way, Shropshire is your county, is it not?

JACK: Eh? Shropshire? Yes, of course. Hallo! Why all these cups? Why cucumber sandwiches? Why such reckless extravagance in one so young? Who is coming to tea?

ALGERNON: Oh! merely Aunt Augusta and Gwendolen.

JACK: How perfectly delightful!

ALGERNON: Yes, that is all very well; but I am afraid Aunt Augusta won't quite approve of your being here.

JACK: May I ask why?

ALGERNON: My dear fellow, the way you flirt with Gwendolen is perfectly disgraceful. It is almost as bad as the way Gwendolen flirts with you.

JACK: I am in love with Gwendolen. I have come up to town expressly to propose to her.

ALGERNON: I thought you had come up for pleasure? . . . I call that business.

JACK: How utterly unromantic you are!

ALGERNON: I really don't see anything romantic in proposing. It is very romantic to be in love. But there is nothing romantic about a definite proposal. Why, one may be accepted. One usually is, I believe. Then the excitement is all over. The very essence of romance is uncertainty. If ever I get married, I'll certainly try to forget the fact.

JACK: I have no doubt about that, dear Algy. The Divorce Court was specially invented for people whose memories are so curiously constituted.

ALGERNON: Oh! there is no use speculating on that subject. Divorces are made in Heaven — (JACK *puts out his hand to take a sandwich.* ALGERNON *at once interferes.*) Please don't touch the cucumber sandwiches. They are ordered specially for Aunt Augusta. (*Takes one and eats it.*)

JACK: Well, you have been eating them all the time.

ALGERNON: That is quite a different matter. She is my aunt. (*Takes plate from below.*) Have some bread and butter. The bread and butter is for Gwendolen. Gwendolen is devoted to bread and butter.

JACK (*advancing to table and helping himself*): And very good bread and butter it is too.

ALGERNON: Well, my dear fellow, you need not eat as if you were going to eat it all. You behave as if you were married to her already. You are not married to her already, and I don't think you ever will be.

JACK: Why on earth do you say that?

ALGERNON: Well, in the first place, girls never marry the men they flirt with. Girls don't think it right.

JACK: Oh, that is nonsense!

ALGERNON: It isn't. It is a great truth. It accounts for the extraordinary number of bachelors that one sees all over the place. In the second place, I don't give my consent.

JACK: Your consent!

ALGERNON: My dear fellow. Gwendolen is my first cousin. And before I allow you to marry her, you will have to clear up the whole question of Cecily. (*Rings bell.*)

JACK: Cecily! What on earth do you mean? What do you mean, Algy, by Cecily! I don't know any one of the name of Cecily.

(*Enter* LANE.)

ALGERNON: Bring me that cigarette case Mr. Worthing left in the smoking-room the last time he dined here.

LANE: Yes, sir.

(LANE *goes out.*)

JACK: Do you mean to say you have had my cigarette case all this time? I wish to goodness you had let me know. I have been writing frantic letters to Scotland Yard about it. I was very nearly offering a large reward.

ALGERNON: Well, I wish you would offer one. I happen to be more than usually hard up.

JACK: There is no good offering a large reward now that the thing is found.

(*Enter* LANE *with the cigarette case on a salver.* ALGERNON *takes it at once.* LANE *goes out.*)

ALGERNON: I think that is rather mean of you, Ernest, I must say. (*Opens case and examines it.*) However, it makes no matter, for, now that I look at the inscription inside, I find that the thing isn't yours after all.

JACK: Of course it's mine. (*Moving to him.*) You have seen me with it a hundred times, and you have no right whatsoever to read what is written inside. It is a very ungentlemanly thing to read a private cigarette case.

ALGERNON: Oh! it is absurd to have a hard and fast rule about what one should read and what one shouldn't. More than half of modern culture depends on what one shouldn't read.

JACK: I am quite aware of the fact, and I don't propose to discuss modern culture. It isn't the sort of thing one should talk of in private. I simply want my cigarette case back.

ALGERNON: Yes; but this isn't your cigarette case. This cigarette case is a present from someone of the name of Cecily, and you said you didn't know anyone of that name.

JACK: Well, if you want to know, Cecily happens to be my aunt.

ALGERNON: Your aunt!

JACK: Yes. Charming old lady she is, too. Lives at Tunbridge Wells. Just give it back to me, Algy.

ALGERNON (*retreating to back of sofa*): But why does she call herself little Cecily if she is your aunt and lives at Tunbridge Wells? (*Reading.*) "From little Cecily with her fondest love."

JACK (*moving to sofa and kneeling upon it*): My dear fellow, what on earth is there in that? Some aunts are tall, some aunts are not tall. That is a matter that surely an aunt may be allowed to decide for herself. You seem to think that every aunt should be exactly like your aunt! That is absurd. For Heaven's sake give me back my cigarette case. (*Follows* ALGERNON *round the room.*)

ALGERNON: Yes. But why does your aunt call you her uncle? "From little Cecily, with her fondest love to her dear Uncle Jack." There is no objection, I admit, to an aunt being a small aunt, but why an aunt, no matter what her size may be, should call her own nephew her uncle, I can't quite make out. Besides, your name isn't Jack at all; it is Ernest.

JACK: It isn't Ernest; it's Jack.

ALGERNON: You have always told me it was Ernest. I have introduced you to every one as Ernest. You answer to the name of Ernest. You look as if your name was Ernest. You are the most earnest-looking person I ever saw in my life. It is perfectly absurd your saying that your name isn't Ernest. It's on your cards. Here is one of them. (*Taking it from case.*) "Mr. Ernest Worthing, B.4, The Albany." I'll keep this as a proof that your name is Ernest if ever you attempt to deny it to me, or to Gwendolen, or to any else. (*Puts the card in his pocket.*)

JACK: Well, my name is Ernest in town and Jack in the country, and the cigarette case was given to me in the country.

ALGERNON: Yes, but that does not account for the fact that your small Aunt Cecily, who lives at Tunbridge Wells, calls you her dear uncle. Come, old boy, you had much better have the thing out at once.

JACK: My dear Algy, you talk exactly as if you were a dentist. It is very vulgar to talk like a dentist when one isn't a dentist. It produces a false impression.

ALGERNON: Well, that is exactly what dentists always do. Now, go on! Tell me the whole thing. I may mention that I have always suspected you of being a confirmed and secret Bunburyist; and I am quite sure of it now.

JACK: Bunburyist? What on earth do you mean by a Bunburyist?

ALGERNON: I'll reveal to you the meaning of that incomparable expression as soon as you are kind enough to inform me why you are Ernest in town and Jack in the country.

JACK: Well, produce my cigarette case first.

ALGERNON: Here it is. (*Hands cigarette case.*) Now produce your explanation, and pray make it improbable. (*Sits on sofa.*)

JACK: My dear fellow, there is nothing improbable about my explanation at all. In fact it's perfectly ordinary. Old Mr. Thomas Cardew, who adopted me when I was a little boy, made me in his will guardian to his granddaughter, Miss Cecily Cardew. Cecily, who addresses me as her uncle from motives of respect that you could not possibly appreciate, lives at my place in the country under the charge of her admirable governess, Miss Prism.

ALGERNON: Where is that place in the country, by the way?

JACK: That is nothing to you, dear boy. You are not going to be invited. . . . I may tell you candidly that the place is not in Shropshire.

ALGERNON: I suspected that, my dear fellow! I have Bunburyed all over Shropshire on two separate occasions. Now, go on. Why are you Ernest in town and Jack in the country?

JACK: My dear Algy, I don't know whether you will be able to understand my real motives. You are hardly serious enough. When one is placed in the position of guardian, one has to adopt a very high moral tone on all subjects. It's one's duty to do so. And as a high moral tone can hardly be said to conduce very much to either one's health or one's happiness, in order to get up to town I have always pretended to have a younger brother of the name of Ernest, who lives in the Albany, and gets into the most dreadful scrapes. That, my dear Algy, is the whole truth pure and simple.

ALGERNON: The truth is rarely pure and never simple. Modern life would be very tedious if it were either, and modern literature a complete impossibility!

JACK: That wouldn't be at all a bad thing.

ALGERNON: Literary criticism is not your forte, my dear fellow. Don't try it. You should leave that to people who haven't been at a University. They do it so well in the daily papers. What you really are is a Bunburyist. I was quite right in saying you were a Bunburyist. You are one of the most advanced Bunburyists I know.

JACK: What on earth do you mean?

ALGERNON: You have invented a very useful younger brother called Ernest, in order that you may be able to come up to town as often as you like. I have invented an invaluable permanent invalid called Bunbury, in order that I may be able to go down into the country whenever I choose. Bunbury is perfectly invaluable. If it wasn't for Bunbury's extraordinary bad health, for instance, I wouldn't be able to dine with you at Willis's to-night, for I have been really engaged to Aunt Augusta for more than a week.

JACK: I haven't asked you to dine with me anywhere to-night.

ALGERNON: I know. You are absurdly careless about sending out invitations. It is very foolish of you. Nothing annoys people so much as not receiving invitations.

JACK: You had much better dine with your Aunt Augusta.

ALGERNON: I haven't the smallest intention of doing anything of the kind. To begin with, I dined there on Monday, and once a week is quite enough to dine with one's own relations. In the second place, whenever I do dine there I am always treated as a member of the family, and sent down with either no woman at all, or two. In the third place, I know perfectly well whom she will place me next to, tonight. She will place me next Mary Farquhar, who always flirts with her own husband across the dinner-table. That is not very pleasant. Indeed, it is not even decent . . . and that sort of thing is enormously on the increase. The amount of women in London who flirt with their own husbands is perfectly scandalous. It looks so bad. It is simply washing one's clean linen in public. Besides, now that I know you to be a confirmed Bunburyist I naturally want to talk to you about Bunburying. I want to tell you the rules.

JACK: I'm not a Bunburyist at all. If Gwendolen accepts me, I am going to kill my brother, indeed I think I'll kill him in any case. Cecily is a little too much interested in him. It is rather a bore. So I am going to get rid of Ernest. And I strongly advise you to do the same with Mr. . . . with your invalid friend who has the absurd name.

ALGERNON: Nothing will induce me to part with Bunbury, and if you ever get married, which seems to me extremely problematic, you will be very glad to know Bunbury. A man who marries without knowing Bunbury has a very tedious time of it.

JACK: That is nonsense. If I marry a charming girl like Gwendolen, and she is the only girl I ever saw in my life that I would marry, I certainly won't want to know Bunbury.

ALGERNON: Then your wife will. You don't seem to realize, that in married life three is company and two is none.

JACK (*sententiously*): That, my dear young friend, is the theory that the corrupt French Drama has been propounding for the last fifty years.

ALGERNON: Yes, and that the happy English home has proved in half the time.

JACK: For heaven's sake, don't try to be cynical. It's perfectly easy to be cynical.

ALGERNON: My dear fellow, it isn't easy to be anything nowadays. There's such a lot of beastly competition about. (*The sound of an electric bell is heard.*) Ah! that must be Aunt Augusta. Only relatives, or creditors, ever ring in that Wagnerian manner. Now, if I get her out of the way for ten minutes, so that you can have an opportunity for proposing to Gwendolen, may I dine with you to-night at Willis's?

JACK: I suppose so, if you want to.

ALGERNON: Yes, but you must be serious about it. I hate people who are not serious about meals. It is so shallow of them.

(*Enter* LANE.)

LANE: Lady Bracknell and Miss Fairfax.

(ALGERNON *goes forward to meet them. Enter* LADY BRACKNELL *and* GWENDOLEN.)

LADY BRACKNELL: Good afternoon, dear Algernon, I hope you are behaving very well.

ALGERNON: I'm feeling very well, Aunt Augusta.

LADY BRACKNELL: That's not quite the same thing. In fact the two things rarely go together. (*Sees* JACK *and bows to him with icy coldness.*)

ALGERNON (*to* GWENDOLEN): Dear me, you are smart!

GWENDOLEN: I am always smart! Am I not, Mr. Worthing?

JACK: You're quite perfect, Miss Fairfax.

GWENDOLEN: Oh! I hope I am not that. It would leave no room for developments, and I intend to develop in many directions. (GWENDOLEN *and* JACK *sit down together in the corner.*)

LADY BRACKNELL: I'm sorry if we are a little late, Algernon, but I was obliged to call on dear Lady Harbury. I hadn't been there since her poor husband's death. I never saw a woman so altered; she looks quite twenty years younger. And now I'll have a cup of tea, and one of those nice cucumber sandwiches you promised me.

ALGERNON: Certainly, Aunt Augusta. (*Goes over to tea-table.*)

LADY BRACKNELL: Won't you come and sit here, Gwendolen?

GWENDOLEN: Thanks, mamma, I'm quite comfortable where I am.

ALGERNON (*picking up empty plate in horror*): Good heavens! Lane! Why are there no cucumber sandwiches? I ordered them specially.

LANE (*gravely*): There were no cucumbers in the market this morning, sir. I went down twice.

ALGERNON: No cucumbers!

LANE: No, sir. Not even for ready money.

ALGERNON: That will do, Lane, thank you.

LANE: Thank you, sir.

(*Goes out.*)

ALGERNON: I am greatly distressed, Aunt Augusta, about there being no cucumbers, not even for ready money.

LADY BRACKNELL: It really makes no matter, Algernon. I had some crumpets with Lady Harbury, who seems to me to be living entirely for pleasure now.

ALGERNON: I hear her hair has turned quite gold from grief.

LADY BRACKNELL: It certainly has changed its colour. From what cause I, of course, cannot say. (ALGERNON *crosses and hands tea.*) Thank you. I've quite a treat for you to-night, Algernon. I am going to send you down with Mary Farquhar. She is such a nice woman, and so attentive to her husband. It's delightful to watch them.

ALGERNON: I am afraid, Aunt Augusta, I shall have to give up the pleasure of dining with you to-night after all.

LADY BRACKNELL (*frowning*): I hope not, Algernon. It would put my table completely out. Your uncle would have to dine upstairs. Fortunately he is accustomed to that.

ALGERNON: It is a great bore, and, I need hardly say, a terrible disappointment to me, but the fact is I have just had a telegram to say that my poor friend Bunbury is very ill again. (*Exchanges glances with* JACK.) They seem to think I should be with him.

LADY BRACKNELL: It is very strange. This Mr. Bunbury seems to suffer from curiously bad health.

ALGERNON: Yes; poor Bunbury is a dreadful invalid.

LADY BRACKNELL: Well, I must say, Algernon, that I think it is high time that Mr. Bunbury made up his mind whether he was going to live or to die. This shilly-shallying with the question is absurd. Nor do I in any way approve of the modern sympathy with invalids. I consider it morbid. Illness of any kind is hardly a thing to be encouraged in others. Health is the primary duty of life. I am always telling that to your poor uncle, but he never seems to take much notice . . . as far as any improvement in his ailments goes. I should be much obliged if you would ask Mr. Bunbury, from me, to be kind enough not to have a relapse on Saturday, for

I rely on you to arrange my music for me. It is my last reception, and one wants something that will encourage conversation, particularly at the end of the season when every one has practically said whatever they had to say, which, in most cases, was probably not much.

ALGERNON: I'll speak to Bunbury, Aunt Augusta, if he is still conscious, and I think I can promise you he'll be all right by Saturday. Of course the music is a great difficulty. You see, if one plays good music, people don't listen, and if one plays bad music people don't talk. But I'll run over the programme I've drawn out, if you will kindly come into the next room for a moment.

LADY BRACKNELL: Thank you, Algernon. It is very thoughtful of you. (*Rising, and following* ALGERNON.) I'm sure the programme will be delightful, after a few expurgations. French songs I cannot possibly allow. People always seem to think that they are improper, and either look shocked, which is vulgar, or laugh, which is worse. But German sounds a thoroughly respectable language, and, indeed I believe is so. Gwendolen, you will accompany me.

GWENDOLEN: Certainly, mamma.

(LADY BRACKNELL *and* ALGERNON *go into the music-room,* GWENDOLEN *remains behind.*)

JACK: Charming day it has been, Miss Fairfax.

GWENDOLEN: Pray don't talk to me about the weather, Mr. Worthing. Whenever people talk to me about the weather, I always feel quite certain that they mean something else. And that makes me so nervous.

JACK: I do mean something else.

GWENDOLEN: I thought so. In fact, I am never wrong.

JACK: And I would like to be allowed to take advantage of Lady Bracknell's temporary absence. . . .

GWENDOLEN: I would certainly advise you to do so. Mamma has a way of coming back suddenly into a room that I have often had to speak to her about.

JACK (*nervously*): Miss Fairfax, ever since I met you I have admired you more than any girl . . . I have ever met since . . . I met you.

GWENDOLEN: Yes, I am quite well aware of the fact. And I often wish that in public, at any rate, you had been more demonstrative. For me you have always had an irresistible fascination. Even before I met you I was far from indifferent to you. (JACK *looks at her in amazement.*) We live, as I hope you know, Mr. Worthing, in an age of ideals. The fact is constantly mentioned in the more expensive monthly magazines, and has reached the provincial pulpits, I am told; and my ideal has always been to love some one of the name of Ernest. There is something in that name that inspires absolute confidence. The moment Algernon first mentioned to me that he had a friend called Ernest, I knew I was destined to love you.

JACK: You really love me, Gwendolen?

GWENDOLEN: Passionately!

JACK: Darling? You don't know how happy you've made me.

GWENDOLEN: My own Ernest!

JACK: But you don't really mean to say that you couldn't love me if my name wasn't Ernest?

GWENDOLEN: But your name is Ernest.

JACK: Yes, I know it is. But supposing it was something else? Do you mean to say you couldn't love me then?

GWENDOLEN (*glibly*): Ah! that is clearly a metaphysical speculation, and like most metaphysical speculations has very little reference at all to the actual facts of real life, as we know them.

JACK: Personally, darling, to speak quite candidly, I don't much care about the name of Ernest. . . . I don't think the name suits me at all.

GWENDOLEN: It suits you perfectly. It is a divine name. It has a music of its own. It produces vibrations.

JACK: Well, really, Gwendolen, I must say that I think there are lots of other much nicer names. I think Jack, for instance, a charming name.

GWENDOLEN: Jack? . . . No, there is very little music in the name Jack, if any at all, indeed. It does not thrill. It produces absolutely no vibrations. . . . I have known several Jacks, and they all, without exception, were more than usually plain. Besides, Jack is a notorious domesticity for John! And I pity any woman who is married to a man called John. She would probably never be allowed to know the entrancing pleasure of a single moment's solitude. The only really safe name is Ernest.

JACK: Gwendolen, I must get christened at once — I mean we must get married at once. There is no time to be lost.

GWENDOLEN: Married, Mr. Worthing?

JACK (*astounded*): Well . . . surely. You know that I love you, and you led me to believe, Miss Fairfax, that you were not absolutely indifferent to me.

GWENDOLEN: I adore you. But you haven't proposed to me yet. Nothing has been said at all about marriage. The subject has not even been touched on.

JACK: Well . . . may I propose to you now?

GWENDOLEN: I think it would be an admirable opportunity. And to spare you any possible disappointment, Mr. Worthing, I think it only fair to tell you quite frankly beforehand that I am fully determined to accept you.

JACK: Gwendolen!

GWENDOLEN: Yes, Mr. Worthing, what have you got to say to me?

JACK: You know what I have got to say to you.

GWENDOLEN: Yes, but you don't say it.

JACK: Gwendolen, will you marry me? (*Goes on his knees.*)

GWENDOLEN: Of course I will, darling. How long you have been about it! I am afraid you have had very little experience in how to propose.

JACK: My own one, I have never loved any one in the world but you.

GWENDOLEN: Yes, but men often propose for practice. I know my brother Gerald does. All my girl-friends tell me so. What wonderfully blue eyes you have, Ernest! They are quite, quite blue. I hope you will always look at me just like that, especially when there are other people present.

(*Enter* LADY BRACKNELL.)

LADY BRACKNELL: Mr. Worthing! Rise, sir, from this semi-recumbent posture. It is most indecorous.

GWENDOLEN: Mamma! (*He tries to rise; she restrains him.*) I must beg you to retire. This is no place for you. Besides, Mr. Worthing has not quite finished yet.

LADY BRACKNELL: Finished what, may I ask?

GWENDOLEN: I am engaged to Mr. Worthing, mamma. (*They rise together.*)

LADY BRACKNELL: Pardon me, you are not engaged to any one. When you do become engaged to some one, I, or your father, should his health permit him, will inform you of the fact. An engagement should come on a young girl as a surprise, pleasant or unpleasant, as the case may be. It is hardly a matter that she could be allowed to arrange for herself. . . . And now I have a few questions to put to you, Mr. Worthing. While I am making these inquiries, you, Gwendolen, will wait for me below in the carriage.

GWENDOLEN (*reproachfully*): Mamma!

LADY BRACKNELL: In the carriage, Gwendolen! (GWENDOLEN *goes to the door. She and* JACK *blow kisses to each other behind* LADY BRACKNELL's *back*. LADY BRACK-NELL *looks vaguely about as if she could not understand what the noise was. Finally turns round.*) Gwendolen, the carriage!

GWENDOLEN: Yes, mamma.

(*Goes out, looking back at* JACK.)

LADY BRACKNELL (*sitting down*): You can take a seat, Mr. Worthing.

(*Looks in her pocket for note-book and pencil.*)

JACK: Thank you, Lady Bracknell, I prefer standing.

LADY BRACKNELL (*pencil and note-book in hand*): I feel bound to tell you that you are not down on my list of eligible young men, although I have the same list as the dear Duchess of Bolton has. We work together, in fact. However, I am quite ready to enter your name, should your answers be what a really affectionate mother requires. Do you smoke?

JACK: Well, yes, I must admit I smoke.

LADY BRACKNELL: I am glad to hear it. A man should always have an occupation of some kind. There are far too many idle men in London as it is. How old are you?

JACK: Twenty-nine.

LADY BRACKNELL: A very good age to be married at. I have always been of opinion that a man who desires to get married should know either everything or nothing. Which do you know?

JACK (*after some hesitation*): I know nothing, Lady Bracknell.

LADY BRACKNELL: I am pleased to hear it. I do not approve of anything that tampers with natural ignorance. Ignorance is like a delicate exotic fruit; touch it and the bloom is gone. The whole theory of modern education is radically unsound. Fortunately in England, at any rate, education produces no effect whatsoever. If it did, it would prove a serious danger to the upper classes, and probably lead to acts of violence in Grosvenor Square. What is your income?

JACK: Between seven and eight thousand a year.

LADY BRACKNELL (*makes a note in her book*): In land, or in investments?

JACK: In investments, chiefly.

LADY BRACKNELL: That is satisfactory. What between the duties expected of one during one's lifetime, and the duties exacted from one after one's death, land has ceased to be either a profit or a pleasure. It gives one position, and prevents one from keeping it up. That's all that can be said about land.

JACK: I have a country house with some land, of course, attached to it, about fifteen hundred acres, I believe; but I don't depend on that for my real income. In fact, as far as I can make out, the poachers are the only people who make anything out of it.

LADY BRACKNELL: A country house! How many bedrooms? Well, that point can be cleared up afterwards. You have a town house, I hope? A girl with a simple, unspoiled nature, like Gwendolen, could hardly be expected to reside in the country.

JACK: Well, I own a house in Belgrave Square, but it is let by the year to Lady Bloxham. Of course, I can get it back whenever I like, at six months' notice.

LADY BRACKNELL: Lady Bloxham? I don't know her.

JACK: Oh, she goes about very little. She is a lady considerably advanced in years.

LADY BRACKNELL: Ah, nowadays that is no guarantee of respectability of character. What number in Belgrave Square?

JACK: 149.

LADY BRACKNELL (*shaking her head*): The unfashionable side. I thought there was something. However, that could easily be altered.

JACK: Do you mean the fashion, or the side?

LADY BRACKNELL (*sternly*): Both, if necessary, I presume. What are your politics?

JACK: Well, I am afraid I really have none. I am a Liberal Unionist.

LADY BRACKNELL: Oh, they count as Tories. They dine with us. Or come in the evening, at any rate. Now to minor matters. Are your parents living?

JACK: I have lost both my parents.

LADY BRACKNELL: To lose one parent, Mr. Worthing, may be regarded as a misfortune; to lose both looks like carelessness. Who was your father? He was evidently a man of some wealth. Was he born in what the Radical papers call the purple of commerce, or did he rise from the ranks of the aristocracy?

JACK: I am afraid I really don't know. The fact is, Lady Bracknell, I said I had lost my parents. It would be nearer the truth to say that my parents seem to have lost me. . . . I don't actually know who I am by birth. I was . . . well, I was found.

LADY BRACKNELL: Found!

JACK: The late Mr. Thomas Cardew, an old gentleman of a very charitable and kindly disposition, found me, and gave me the name of Worthing, because he happened to have a first-class ticket for Worthing in his pocket at the time. Worthing is a place in Sussex. It is a seaside resort.

LADY BRACKNELL: Where did the charitable gentleman who had a first-class ticket for this seaside resort find you?

JACK (*gravely*): In a hand-bag.

LADY BRACKNELL: A hand-bag?

JACK (*very seriously*): Yes, Lady Bracknell. I was in a hand-bag — a somewhat large, black leather hand-bag, with handles to it — an ordinary hand-bag in fact.

LADY BRACKNELL: In what locality did this Mr. James, or Thomas, Cardew come across this ordinary hand-bag?

JACK: In the cloak-room at Victoria Station. It was given to him in mistake for his own.

LADY BRACKNELL: The cloak-room at Victoria Station?

JACK: Yes. The Brighton line.

LADY BRACKNELL: The line is immaterial. Mr. Worthing, I confess I feel somewhat bewildered by what you have just told me. To be born, or at any rate bred, in a hand-bag, whether it had handles or not, seems to me to display a contempt for the ordinary decencies of family life that reminds one of the worst excesses of the French Revolution. And I presume you know what that unfortunate movement led to? As for the particular locality in which the hand-bag was found, a cloak-room at a railway station might serve to conceal a social indiscretion — has probably, indeed, been used for that purpose before now — but it could hardly be regarded as an assured basis for a recognized position in good society.

JACK: May I ask you then what you would advise me to do? I need hardly say I would do anything in the world to ensure Gwendolen's happiness.

LADY BRACKNELL: I would strongly advise you, Mr. Worthing, to try and acquire some relations as soon as possible, and to make a definite effort to produce at any rate one parent, of either sex, before the season is quite over.

JACK: Well, I don't see how I could possibly manage to do that. I can produce the hand-bag at any moment. It is in my dressing-room at home. I really think that should satisfy you, Lady Bracknell.

LADY BRACKNELL: Me, sir! What has it to do with me? You can hardly imagine that I and Lord Bracknell would dream of allowing our only daughter — a girl brought up with the utmost care — to marry into a cloak-room, and form an alliance with a parcel. Good morning, Mr. Worthing!

(LADY BRACKNELL *sweeps out in majestic indignation.*)

JACK: Good morning! (ALGERNON, *from the other room, strikes up the Wedding March.* JACK *looks perfectly furious, and goes to the door.*) For goodness' sake don't play that ghastly tune, Algy! How idiotic you are!

(*The music stops and* ALGERNON *enters cheerily.*)

ALGERNON: Didn't it go off all right, old boy? You don't mean to say Gwendolen refused you? I know it is a way she has. She is always refusing people. I think it is most ill-natured of her.

JACK: Oh, Gwendolen is as right as a trivet. As far as she is concerned, we are engaged. Her mother is perfectly unbearable. Never met such a Gorgon. . . . I don't really know what a Gorgon is like, but I am quite sure that Lady Bracknell is one. In any case, she is a monster, without being a myth, which is rather unfair. . . . I beg your pardon Algy, I suppose I shouldn't talk about your own aunt in that way before you.

ALGERNON: My dear boy, I love hearing my relations abused. It is the only thing that makes me put up with them at all. Relations are simply a tedious pack of people, who haven't got the remotest knowledge of how to live, nor the smallest instinct about when to die.

JACK: Oh, that is nonsense!

ALGERNON: It isn't!

JACK: Well, I won't argue about the matter. You always want to argue about things.

ALGERNON: That is exactly what things were originally made for.

JACK: Upon my word, if I thought that, I'd shoot myself. . . . (A *pause.*) You don't think there is any chance of Gwendolen becoming like her mother in about a hundred and fifty years, do you, Algy?

ALGERNON: All women become like their mothers. That is their tragedy. No man does. That's his.

JACK: Is that clever?

ALGERNON: It is perfectly phrased! and quite as true as any observation in civilized life should be.

JACK: I am sick to death of cleverness. Everybody is clever nowadays. You can't go anywhere without meeting clever people. The thing has become an absolute public nuisance. I wish to goodness we had a few fools left.

ALGERNON: We have.

JACK: I should extremely like to meet them. What do they talk about?

ALGERNON: The fools? Oh! about the clever people, of course.

JACK: What fools.

ALGERNON: By the way, did you tell Gwendolen the truth about your being Ernest in town, and Jack in the country?

JACK (*in a very patronizing manner*): My dear fellow, the truth isn't quite the sort of thing one tells to a nice, sweet, refined girl. What extraordinary ideas you have about the way to behave to a woman!

ALGERNON: The only way to behave to a woman is to make love to her, if she is pretty, and to someone else, if she is plain.

JACK: Oh, that is nonsense.

ALGERNON: What about your brother? What about the profligate Ernest?

JACK: Oh, before the end of the week I shall have got rid of him. I'll say he died in Paris of apoplexy. Lots of people die of apoplexy, quite suddenly, don't they?

ALGERNON: Yes, but it's hereditary, my dear fellow. It's a sort of thing that runs in families. You had much better say a severe chill.

JACK: You are sure a severe chill isn't hereditary, or anything of that kind?

ALGERNON: Of course it isn't!

JACK: Very well, then. My poor brother Ernest is carried off suddenly, in Paris, by a severe chill. That gets rid of him.

ALGERNON: But I thought you said that . . . Miss Cardew was a little too much interested in your poor brother Ernest? Won't she feel his loss a good deal?

JACK: Oh, that is all right. Cecily is not a silly romantic girl, I am glad to say. She has got a capital appetite, goes long walks, and pays no attention at all to her lessons.

ALGERNON: I would rather like to see Cecily.

JACK: I will take very good care you never do. She is excessively pretty, and she is only just eighteen.

ALGERNON: Have you told Gwendolen yet that you have an excessively pretty ward who is only just eighteen?

JACK: Oh! one doesn't blurt these things out to people. Cecily and Gwendolen are perfectly certain to be extremely great friends. I'll bet you anything you like that half an hour after they have met, they will be calling each other sister.

ALGERNON: Women only do that when they have called each other a lot of other things first. Now, my dear boy, if we want to get a good table at Willis's, we really must go and dress. Do you know it is nearly seven?

JACK (*irritably*): Oh! it always is nearly seven.

ALGERNON: I'm hungry.

JACK: I never knew you when you weren't. . . .

ALGERNON: What shall we do after dinner? Go to a theatre?

JACK: Oh no! I loathe listening.

ALGERNON: Well, let us go to the Club?

JACK: Oh, no! I hate talking.

ALGERNON: Well, we might trot round to the Empire at ten?

JACK: Oh, no! I can't bear looking at things. It is so silly.

ALGERNON: Well, what shall we do?

JACK: Nothing!

ALGERNON: It is awfully hard work doing nothing. However, I don't mind hard work where there is no definite object of any kind.

(*Enter* LANE.)

LANE: Miss Fairfax.

(*Enter* GWENDOLEN. LANE *goes out*.)

ALGERNON: Gwendolen, upon my word!

GWENDOLEN: Algy, kindly turn your back. I have something very particular to say to Mr. Worthing.

ALGERNON: Really, Gwendolen, I don't think I can allow this at all.

GWENDOLEN: Algy, you always adopt a strictly immoral attitude towards life. You are not quite old enough to do that. (ALGERNON *retires to the fire-place*.)

JACK: My own darling!

GWENDOLEN: Ernest, we may never be married. From the expression on mamma's face I fear we never shall. Few parents nowadays pay any regard to what their children say to them. The old-fashioned respect for the young is fast dying out. Whatever influence I ever had over mamma, I lost at the age of three. But although she may prevent us from becoming man and wife, and I may marry someone else, and marry often, nothing that she can possibly do can alter my eternal devotion to you.

JACK: Dear Gwendolen!

GWENDOLEN: The story of your romantic origin, as related to me by mamma, with unpleasing comments, has naturally stirred the deeper fibres of my nature. Your Christian name has an irresistible fascination. The simplicity of your character makes you exquisitely incomprehensible to me. Your town address at the Albany I have. What is your address in the country?

JACK: The Manor House, Woolton, Herfordshire.

(ALGERNON, *who has been carefully listening, smiles to himself, and writes the address on his shirt-cuff. Then picks up the Railway Guide*.)

GWENDOLEN: There is a good postal service, I suppose? It may be necessary to do something desperate. That of course will require serious consideration. I will communicate with you daily.

JACK: My own one!

GWENDOLEN: How long do you remain in town?

JACK: Till Monday.

GWENDOLEN: Good! Algy, you may turn round now.

ALGERNON: Thanks, I've turned round already.

GWENDOLEN: You may also ring the bell.

JACK: You will let me see you to your carriage, my own darling?

GWENDOLEN: Certainly.

JACK (*to* LANE, *who now enters*): I will see Miss Fairfax out.

LANE: Yes, sir.

(JACK *and* GWENDOLEN *go off*.)

(LANE *presents several letters on a salver to* ALGERNON. *It is to be surmised that they are bills, as* ALGERNON, *after looking at the envelopes, tears them up*.)

ALGERNON: A glass of sherry, Lane.

LANE: Yes, sir.

ALGERNON: To-morrow, Lane, I'm going Bunburying.

LANE: Yes, sir.

ALGERNON: I shall probably not be back till Monday. You can put up my dress clothes, my smoking jacket, and all the Bunbury suits . . .

LANE: Yes, sir. (*Handing sherry.*)

ALGERNON: I hope to-morrow will be a fine day, Lane.

LANE: It never is, sir.

ALGERNON: Lane, you're a perfect pessimist.

LANE: I do my best to give satisfaction, sir.

(*Enter* JACK. LANE *goes off.*)

JACK: There's a sensible, intellectual girl! the only girl I ever cared for in my life. (ALGERNON *is laughing immoderately.*) What on earth are you so amused at?

ALGERNON: Oh, I'm a little anxious about poor Bunbury, that is all.

JACK: If you don't take care, your friend Bunbury will get you into a serious scrape some day.

ALGERNON: I love scrapes. They are the only things that are never serious.

JACK: Oh, that's nonsense, Algy. You never talk anything but nonsense.

ALGERNON: Nobody ever does.

(JACK *looks indignantly at him, and leaves the room.* ALGERNON *lights a cigarette, reads his shirt-cuff, and smiles.*)

ACT DROP

ACT II

Scene — *Garden at the Manor House. A flight of grey stone steps leads up to the house. The garden, an old-fashioned one, full of roses. Time of year, July. Basket chairs, and a table covered with books, are set under a large yew-tree.*
   MISS PRISM *discovered seated at the table.* CECILY *is at the back, watering flowers.*

MISS PRISM (*calling*): Cecily, Cecily! Surely such a utilitarian occupation as the watering of flowers is rather Moulton's duty than yours? Especially at a moment when intellectual pleasures await you. Your German grammar is on the table. Pray open it at page fifteen. We will repeat yesterday's lesson.

CECILY (*coming over very slowly*): But I don't like German. It isn't at all a becoming language. I know perfectly well that I look quite plain after my German lesson.

MISS PRISM: Child, you know how anxious your guardian is that you should improve yourself in every way. He laid particular stress on your German, as he was leaving for town yesterday. Indeed, he always lays stress on your German when he is leaving for town.

CECILY: Dear Uncle Jack is so very serious! Sometimes he is so serious that I think he cannot be quite well.

MISS PRISM (*drawing herself up*): Your guardian enjoys the best of health, and his gravity of demeanour is especially to be commended in one so comparatively young as he is. I know no one who has a higher sense of duty and responsibility.

CECILY: I suppose that is why he often looks a little bored when we three are together.

MISS PRISM: Cecily! I am surprised at you. Mr. Worthing has many troubles in his life. Idle merriment and triviality would be out of place in his conversation. You must remember his constant anxiety about that unfortunate young man his brother.

CECILY: I wish Uncle Jack would allow that unfortunate young man, his brother, to come down here sometimes. We might have a good influence over him, Miss Prism. I am sure you certainly would. You know German, and geology, and things of that kind influence a man very much. (CECILY *begins to write in her diary.*)

MISS PRISM (*shaking her head*): I do not think that even I could produce any effect on a character that according to his own brother's admission is irretrievably weak and vacillating. Indeed I am not sure that I would desire to reclaim him. I am not in favour of this modern mania for turning bad people into good people at a moment's notice. As a man sows so let him reap. You must put away your diary, Cecily. I really don't see why you should keep a diary at all.

CECILY: I keep a diary in order to enter the wonderful secrets of my life. If I didn't write them down, I should probably forget all about them.

MISS PRISM: Memory, my dear Cecily, is the diary that we all carry about with us.

CECILY: Yes, but it usually chronicles the things that have never happened, and couldn't possibly have happened. I believe that Memory is responsible for nearly all the three-volume novels that Mudie sends us.

MISS PRISM: Do not speak slightingly of the three-volume novel, Cecily. I wrote one myself in earlier days.

CECILY: Did you really, Miss Prism? How wonderfully clever you are! I hope it did not end happily? I don't like novels that end happily. They depress me so much.

MISS PRISM: The good ended happily, and the bad unhappily. That is what Fiction means.

CECILY: I suppose so. But it seems very unfair. And was your novel ever published?

MISS PRISM: Alas! no. The manuscript unfortunately was abandoned. (CECILY *starts.*) I used the word in the sense of lost or mislaid. To your work, child, these speculations are profitless.

CECILY (*smiling*): But I see dear Dr. Chasuble coming up through the garden.

MISS PRISM (*rising and advancing*): Dr. Chasuble! This is indeed a pleasure.

(*Enter* CANON CHASUBLE.)

CHASUBLE: And how are we this morning? Miss Prism, you are, I trust, well?

CECILY: Miss Prism has just been complaining of a slight headache. I think it would do her so much good to have a short stroll with you in the Park, Dr. Chasuble.

MISS PRISM: Cecily, I have not mentioned anything about a headache.

CECILY: No, dear Miss Prism, I know that, but I felt instinctively that you had a headache. Indeed I was thinking about that, and not about my German lesson, when the Rector came in.

CHASUBLE: I hope, Cecily, you are not inattentive.

CECILY: Oh, I am afraid I am.

CHASUBLE: That is strange. Were I fortunate enough to be Miss Prism's pupil, I would hang upon her lips. (MISS PRISM *glares.*) I spoke metaphorically. — My metaphor was drawn from bees. Ahem! Mr. Worthing, I suppose, has not returned from town yet?

MISS PRISM: We do not expect him till Monday afternoon.

CHASUBLE: Ah yes, he usually likes to spend his Sunday in London. He is not one of those whose sole aim is enjoyment, as, by all accounts, that unfortunate young man his brother seems to be. But I must not disturb Egeria and her pupil any longer.

MISS PRISM: Egeria? My name is Laetitia, Doctor.

CHASUBLE (*bowing*): A classical allusion merely, drawn from the Pagan authors. I shall see you both no doubt at Evensong?

MISS PRISM: I think, dear Doctor, I will have a stroll with you. I find I have a headache after all, and a walk might do it good.

CHASUBLE: With pleasure, Miss Prism, with pleasure. We might go as far as the schools and back.

MISS PRISM: That would be delightful. Cecily, you will read your Political Economy in my absence. The chapter on the Fall of the Rupee you may omit. It is somewhat too sensational. Even these metallic problems have their melodramatic side.

(*Goes down the garden with* DR. CHASUBLE.)

CECILY (*picks up books and throws them back on table*): Horrid Political Economy! Horrid Geography! Horrid, horrid German!

(*Enter* MERRIMAN *with a card on a salver.*)

MERRIMAN: Mr. Ernest Worthing has just driven over from the station. He has brought his luggage with him.

CECILY (*takes the card and reads it*): "Mr. Ernest Worthing, B.4, The Albany, W." Uncle Jack's brother! Did you tell him Mr. Worthing was in town?

MERRIMAN: Yes, Miss. He seemed very much disappointed. I mentioned that you and Miss Prism were in the garden. He said he was anxious to speak to you privately for a moment.

CECILY: Ask Mr. Ernest Worthing to come here. I suppose you had better talk to the housekeeper about a room for him.

MERRIMAN: Yes, Miss.

(MERRIMAN *goes off.*)

CECILY: I have never met any really wicked person before. I feel rather frightened. I am so afraid he will look just like every one else.

(*Enter* ALGERNON, *very gay and debonair.*)

He does!

ALGERNON (*raising his hat*): You are my little cousin Cecily, I'm sure.

CECILY: You are under some strange mistake. I am not little. In fact, I believe I am more than usually tall for my age. (ALGERNON *is rather taken aback.*) But I am your cousin Cecily. You, I see from your card, are Uncle Jack's brother, my cousin Ernest, my wicked cousin Ernest.

ALGERNON: Oh! I am not really wicked at all, cousin Cecily. You mustn't think that I am wicked.

CECILY: If you are not, then you have certainly been deceiving us all in a very inexcusable manner. I hope you have not been leading a double life, pretending to be wicked and being really good all the time. That would be hypocrisy.

ALGERNON (*looks at her in amazement*): Oh! Of course I have been rather reckless.

CECILY: I am glad to hear it.

ALGERNON: In fact, now you mention the subject, I have been very bad in my own small way.

CECILY: I don't think you should be so proud of that, though I am sure it must have been very pleasant.

ALGERNON: It is much pleasanter being here with you.

CECILY: I can't understand how you are here at all. Uncle Jack won't be back till Monday afternoon.

ALGERNON: That is a great disappointment. I am obliged to go up by the first train on Monday morning. I have a business appointment that I am anxious . . . to miss!

CECILY: Couldn't you miss it anywhere but in London?

ALGERNON: No: the appointment is in London.

CECILY: Well, I know, of course, how important it is not to keep a business engagement, if one wants to retain any sense of the beauty of life, but still I think you had better wait till Uncle Jack arrives. I know he wants to speak to you about your emigrating.

ALGERNON: About my what?

CECILY: Your emigrating. He has gone up to buy your outfit.

ALGERNON: I certainly wouldn't let Jack buy my outfit. He has no taste in neckties at all.

CECILY: I don't think you will require neckties. Uncle Jack is sending you to Australia.

ALGERNON: Australia! I'd sooner die.

CECILY: Well, he said at dinner on Wednesday night, that you would have to choose between this world, the next world, and Australia.

ALGERNON: Oh, well! The accounts I have received of Australia and the next world are not particularly encouraging. This world is good enough for me, cousin Cecily.

CECILY: Yes, but are you good enough for it?

ALGERNON: I'm afraid I'm not that. That is why I want you to reform me. You might make that your mission, if you don't mind, Cousin Cecily.

CECILY: I'm afraid I've no time, this afternoon.

ALGERNON: Well, would you mind my reforming myself this afternoon?

CECILY: It is rather Quixotic of you. But I think you should try.

ALGERNON: I will. I feel better already.

CECILY: You are looking a little worse.

ALGERNON: That is because I am hungry.

CECILY: How thoughtless of me. I should have remembered that when one is going to lead an entirely new life, one requires regular and wholesome meals. Won't you come in?

ALGERNON: Thank you. Might I have a buttonhole first? I have never any appetite unless I have a buttonhole first.

CECILY: A Maréchal Niel? (*Picks up scissors.*)

ALGERNON: No, I'd sooner have a pink rose.

CECILY: Why? (*Cuts a flower.*)

ALGERNON: Because you are like a pink rose, Cousin Cecily.

CECILY: I don't think it can be right for you to talk to me like that. Miss Prism never says such things to me.

ALGERNON: Then Miss Prism is a short-sighted old lady. (CECILY *puts the rose in his buttonhole.*) You are the prettiest girl I ever saw.

CECILY: Miss Prism says that all good looks are a snare.

ALGERNON: They are a snare that every sensible man would like to be caught in.

CECILY: Oh, I don't think I would care to catch a sensible man. I shouldn't know what to talk to him about.

(*They pass into the house.* MISS PRISM *and* DR. CHASUBLE *return.*)

MISS PRISM: You are too much alone, dear Dr. Chasuble. You should get married. A misanthrope I can understand — a womanthrope, never!

CHASUBLE (*with a scholar's shudder*): Believe me, I do not deserve so neologistic a phrase. The precept as well as the practice of the Primitive Church was distinctly against matrimony.

MISS PRISM (*sententiously*): That is obviously the reason why the Primitive Church has not lasted up to the present day. And you do not seem to realize, dear Doctor, that by persistently remaining single, a man converts himself into a permanent public temptation. Men should be more careful; this very celibacy leads weaker vessels astray.

CHASUBLE: But is a man not equally attractive when married?

MISS PRISM: No married man is ever attractive except to his wife.

CHASUBLE: And often, I've been told, not even to her.

MISS PRISM: That depends on the intellectual sympathies of the woman. Maturity can always be depended on. Ripeness can be trusted. Young women are green. (DR. CHASUBLE *starts.*) I spoke horticulturally. My metaphor was drawn from fruits. But where is Cecily?

CHASUBLE: Perhaps she followed us to the schools.

(*Enter* JACK *slowly from the back of the garden. He is dressed in the deepest mourning, with crepe hatband and black gloves.*)

MISS PRISM: Mr. Worthing!

CHASUBLE: Mr. Worthing?

MISS PRISM: This is indeed a surprise. We did not look for you till Monday afternoon.

JACK (*shakes* MISS PRISM's *hand in a tragic manner*): I have returned sooner than I expected. Dr. Chasuble, I hope you are well?

CHASUBLE: Dear Mr. Worthing, I trust this garb of woe does not betoken some terrible calamity?

JACK: My brother.

MISS PRISM: More shameful debts and extravagance?

CHASUBLE: Still leading his life of pleasure?

JACK (*shaking his head*): Dead!

CHASUBLE: Your brother Ernest dead?

JACK: Quite dead.

MISS PRISM: What a lesson for him! I trust he will profit by it.

CHASUBLE: Mr. Worthing, I offer you my sincere condolence. You have at least the consolation of knowing that you were always the most generous and forgiving of brothers.

JACK: Poor Ernest! He had many faults, but it is a sad, sad blow.

CHASUBLE: Very sad indeed. Were you with him at the end?

JACK: No. He died abroad; in Paris, in fact. I had a telegram last night from the manager of the Grand Hotel.

CHASUBLE: Was the cause of death mentioned?

JACK: A severe chill, it seems.

MISS PRISM: As a man sows, so shall he reap.

CHASUBLE (*raising his hand*): Charity, dear Miss Prism, charity! None of us are perfect. I myself am peculiarly susceptible to draughts. Will the interment take place here?

JACK: No. He seems to have expressed a desire to be buried in Paris.

CHASUBLE: In Paris! (*Shakes his head.*) I fear that hardly points to any very serious state of mind at the last. You would no doubt wish me to make some slight allusion to this tragic domestic affliction next Sunday. (JACK *presses his hand convulsively*.) My sermon on the meaning of the manna in the wilderness can be adapted to almost any occasion, joyful, or, as in the present case, distressing. (*All sigh.*) I have preached it at harvest celebrations, christenings, confirmations, on days of humiliation and festal days. The last time I delivered it was in the Cathedral, as a charity sermon on behalf of the Society for the Prevention of Discontent among the Upper Orders. The Bishop, who was present, was much struck by some of the analogies I drew.

JACK: Ah! that reminds me, you mentioned christenings I think, Dr. Chasuble? I suppose you know how to christen all right? (DR. CHASUBLE *looks astounded.*) I mean, of course, you are continually christening, aren't you?

MISS PRISM: It is, I regret to say, one of the Rector's most constant duties in this parish. I have often spoken to the poorer classes on the subject. But they don't seem to know what thrift is.

CHASUBLE: But is there any particular infant in whom you are interested, Mr. Worthing? Your brother was, I believe, unmarried, was he not?

JACK: Oh yes.

MISS PRISM (*bitterly*): People who live entirely for pleasure usually are.

JACK: But it is not for any child, dear Doctor. I am very fond of children. No! the fact is, I would like to be christened myself, this afternoon, if you have nothing better to do.

CHASUBLE: But surely, Mr. Worthing, you have been christened already?

JACK: I don't remember anything about it.

CHASUBLE: But have you any grave doubts on the subject?

JACK: I certainly intend to have. Of course I don't know if the thing would bother you in any way, or if you think I am a little too old now.

CHASUBLE: Not at all. The sprinkling, and, indeed, the immersion of adults is a perfectly canonical practice.

JACK: Immersion!

CHASUBLE: You need have no apprehensions. Sprinkling is all that is necessary, or indeed I think advisable. Our weather is so changeable. At what hour would you wish the ceremony performed?

JACK: Oh, I might trot round about five if that would suit you.

CHASUBLE: Perfectly, perfectly! In fact I have two similar ceremonies to perform at that time. A case of twins that occurred recently in one of the outlying cottages on your own estate. Poor Jenkins the carter, a most hard-working man.

JACK: Oh! I don't see much fun in being christened along with other babies. It would be childish. Would half-past five do?

CHASUBLE: Admirably! Admirably! (*Takes out watch.*) And now, dear Mr. Worthing, I will not intrude any longer into a house of sorrow. I would merely beg you not to be too much bowed down by grief. What seem to us bitter trials are often blessings in disguise.

MISS PRISM: This seems to me a blessing of an extremely obvious kind.

(*Enter* CECILY *from the house.*)

CECILY: Uncle Jack! Oh, I am pleased to see you back. But what horrid clothes you have got on. Do go and change them.

MISS PRISM: Cecily!

CHASUBLE: My child! my child. (CECILY *goes towards* JACK; *he kisses her brow in a melancholy manner.*)

CECILY: What is the matter, Uncle Jack? Do look happy! You look as if you had a toothache, and I have got such a surprise for you. Who do you think is in the dining-room? Your brother!

JACK: Who?

CECILY: Your brother Ernest. He arrived about half an hour ago.

JACK: What nonsense! I haven't got a brother.

CECILY: Oh, don't say that. However badly he may have behaved to you in the past he is still your brother. You couldn't be so heartless as to disown him. I'll tell him to come out. And you will shake hands with him, won't you, Uncle Jack? (*Runs back into the house.*)

CHASUBLE: These are very joyful tidings.

MISS PRISM: After we had all been resigned to his loss, his sudden return seems to me peculiarly distressing.

JACK: My brother is in the dining-room? I don't know what it all means. I think it is perfectly absurd.

(*Enter* ALGERNON *and* CECILY *hand in hand. They come slowly up to* JACK.)

JACK: Good heavens! (*Motions* ALGERNON *away.*)

ALGERNON: Brother John, I have come down from town to tell you that I am very sorry for all the trouble I have given you, and I intend to lead a better life in the future. (JACK *glares at him and does not take his hand.*)

CECILY: Uncle Jack, you are not going to refuse your own brother's hand?

JACK: Nothing will induce me to take his hand. I think his coming down here disgraceful. He knows perfectly well why.

CECILY: Uncle Jack, do be nice. There is some good in everyone. Ernest has just been telling me about his poor invalid friend Mr. Bunbury whom he goes to visit so often. And surely there must be much good in one who is kind to an invalid, and leaves the pleasures of London to sit by a bed of pain.

JACK: Oh! he has been talking about Bunbury, has he?

CECILY: Yes, he has told me all about poor Mr. Bunbury, and his terrible state of health.

JACK: Bunbury! Well, I won't have him talk to you about Bunbury or about anything else. It is enough to drive one perfectly frantic.

ALGERNON: Of course I admit that the faults were all on my side. But I must say that I think that Brother John's coldness to me is peculiarly painful. I expected a more enthusiastic welcome, especially considering it is the first time I have come here.

CECILY: Uncle Jack, if you don't shake hands with Ernest I will never forgive you.

JACK: Never forgive me?

CECILY: Never, never, never!

JACK: Well, this is the last time I shall ever do it. (*Shakes hands with* ALGERNON *and glares.*)

CHASUBLE: It's pleasant, is it not, to see so perfect a reconciliation? I think we might leave the two brothers together.

MISS PRISM: Cecily, you will come with us.

CECILY: Certainly, Miss Prism. My little task of reconciliation is over.

CHASUBLE: You have done a beautiful action to-day, dear child.

MISS PRISM: We must not be premature in our judgements.

CECILY: I feel very happy.

(*They all go off except* JACK *and* ALGERNON.)

JACK: You young scoundrel, Algy, you must get out of this place as soon as possible. I don't allow any Bunburying here.

(*Enter* MERRIMAN.)

MERRIMAN: I have put Mr. Ernest's things in the room next to yours, sir. I suppose that is all right?

JACK: What?

MERRIMAN: Mr. Ernest's luggage, sir. I have unpacked it and put it in the room next to your own.

JACK: His luggage?

MERRIMAN: Yes, sir. Three portmanteaus, a dressing-case, two hatboxes, and a large luncheon-basket.

ALGERNON: I am afraid I can't stay more than a week this time.

JACK: Merriman, order the dog-cart at once. Mr. Ernest has been suddenly called back to town.

MERRIMAN: Yes, sir. (*Goes back into the house.*)

ALGERNON: What a fearful liar you are, Jack. I have not been called back to town at all.

JACK: Yes, you have.

ALGERNON: I haven't heard any one call me.

JACK: Your duty as a gentleman calls you back.

ALGERNON: My duty as a gentleman has never interfered with my pleasures in the smallest degree.

JACK: I can quite understand that.

ALGERNON: Well, Cecily is a darling.

JACK: You are not to talk of Miss Cardew like that. I don't like it.

ALGERNON: Well, I don't like your clothes. You look perfectly ridiculous in them. Why on earth don't you go up and change? It is perfectly childish to be in deep mourning for a man who is actually staying for a whole week with you in your house as a guest. I call it grotesque.

JACK: You are certainly not staying with me for a whole week as a guest or anything else. You have got to leave . . . by the four-five train.

ALGERNON: I certainly won't leave you so long as you are in mourning. It would be most unfriendly. If I were in mourning you would stay with me, I suppose. I should think it very unkind if you didn't.

JACK: Well, will you go if I change my clothes?

ALGERNON: Yes, if you are not too long. I never saw anybody take so long to dress, and with such little result.

JACK: Well, at any rate, that is better than being always over-dressed as you are.

ALGERNON: If I am occasionally a little over-dressed, I make up for it by being always immensely over-educated.

JACK: Your vanity is ridiculous, your conduct an outrage, and your presence in my garden utterly absurd. However, you have got to catch the four-five, and I hope you will have a pleasant journey back to town. This Bunburying, as you call it, has not been a great success for you.

(*Goes into the house.*)

ALGERNON: I think it has been a great success. I'm in love with Cecily, and that is everything. (*Enter* CECILY *at the back of the garden. She picks up the can and begins to water the flowers.*) But I must see her before I go, and make arrangements for another Bunbury. Ah, there she is.

CECILY: Oh, I merely came back to water the roses. I thought you were with Uncle Jack.

ALGERNON: He's gone to order the dog-cart for me.

CECILY: Oh, is he going to take you for a nice drive?

ALGERNON: He's going to send me away.

CECILY: Then have we got to part?

ALGERNON: I am afraid so. It's very painful parting.

CECILY: It is always painful to part from people whom one has known for a very brief space of time. The absence of old friends one can endure with equanimity. But even a momentary separation from any one to whom one has just been introduced is almost unbearable.

ALGERNON: Thank you.

(*Enter* MERRIMAN.)

MERRIMAN: The dog-cart is at the door, sir.

(ALGERNON *looks appealingly at* CECILY.)

CECILY: It can wait, Merriman . . . for . . . five minutes.

MERRIMAN: Yes, miss.   (*Exit* MERRIMAN.)

ALGERNON: I hope, Cecily, I shall not offend you if I state quite frankly and openly that you seem to me to be in every way the visible personification of absolute perfection.

CECILY: I think your frankness does you great credit, Ernest. If you will allow me, I will copy your remarks into my diary. (*Goes over to table and begins writing in diary.*)

ALGERNON: Do you really keep a diary? I'd give anything to look at it. May I?

CECILY: Oh no. (*Puts her hand over it.*) You see, it is simply a very young girl's record of her own thoughts and impressions, and consequently meant for publication. When it appears in volume form I hope you will order a copy. But pray, Ernest, don't stop. I delight in taking down from dictation. I have reached "absolute perfection." You can go on. I am quite ready for more.

ALGERNON (*somewhat taken aback*): Ahem! Ahem!

CECILY: Oh, don't cough, Ernest. When one is dictating one should speak fluently and not cough. Besides, I don't know how to spell a cough. (*Writes as* ALGERNON *speaks.*)

ALGERNON (*speaking very rapidly*): Cecily, ever since I first looked upon your wonderful and incomparable beauty, I have dared to love you wildly, passionately,
   devotedly, hopelessly.
CECILY: I don't think that you should tell me that you love me wildly, passionately,
   devotedly, hopelessly. Hopelessly doesn't seem to make much sense, does it?
ALGERNON: Cecily!

(*Enter* MERRIMAN.)

MERRIMAN: The dog-cart is waiting, sir.
ALGERNON: Tell it to come round next week, at the same hour.
MERRIMAN (*looks at* CECILY, *who makes no sign*): Yes, sir.

(MERRIMAN *retires*.)

CECILY: Uncle Jack would be very much annoyed if he knew you were staying on till
   next week, at the same hour.
ALGERNON: Oh, I don't care about Jack. I don't care for anybody in the whole world
   but you. I love you, Cecily. You will marry me, won't you?
CECILY: You silly boy! Of course. Why, we have been engaged for the last three
   months.
ALGERNON: For the last three months?
CECILY: Yes, it will be exactly three months on Thursday.
ALGERNON: But how did we become engaged?
CECILY: Well, ever since dear Uncle Jack first confessed to us that he had a younger
   brother who was very wicked and bad, you of course have formed the chief topic
   of conversation between myself and Miss Prism. And of course a man who is
   much talked about is always very attractive. One feels there must be something in
   him, after all. I daresay it was foolish of me, but I fell in love with you, Ernest.
ALGERNON: Darling! And when was the engagement actually settled?
CECILY: On the 14th of February last. Worn out by your entire ignorance of my
   existence, I determined to end the matter one way or the other, and after a long
   struggle with myself I accepted you under this dear old tree here. The next day I
   bought this little ring in your name, and this is the little bangle with the true
   lover's knot I promised you always to wear.
ALGERNON: Did I give you this? It's very pretty, isn't it?
CECILY: Yes, you've wonderfully good taste, Ernest. It's the excuse I've always given
   for your leading such a bad life. And this is the box in which I keep all your dear
   letters. (*Kneels at table, opens box, and produces letters tied up with blue ribbon*.)
ALGERNON: My letters! But, my own sweet Cecily, I have never written you any
   letters.
CECILY: You need hardly remind me of that, Ernest. I remember only too well that
   I was forced to write your letters for you. I wrote always three times a week, and
   sometimes oftener.
ALGERNON: Oh, do let me read them, Cecily?
CECILY: Oh, I couldn't possibly. They would make you far too conceited. (*Replaces
   box*.) The three you wrote me after I had broken off the engagement are so
   beautiful, and so badly spelled, that even now I can hardly read them without
   crying a little.
ALGERNON: But was our engagement ever broken off?

CECILY: Of course it was. On the 22nd of last March. You can see the entry if you like. (*Shows diary*.) "To-day I broke off my engagement with Ernest. I feel it is better to do so. The weather still continues charming."

ALGERNON: But why on earth did you break it off? What had I done? I had done nothing at all. Cecily, I am very much hurt indeed to hear you broke it off. Particularly when the weather was so charming.

CECILY: It would hardly have been a really serious engagement if it hadn't been broken off at least once. But I forgave you before the week was out.

ALGERNON (*crossing to her, and kneeling*): What a perfect angel you are, Cecily.

CECILY: You dear romantic boy. (*He kisses her, she puts her fingers through his hair.*) I hope your hair curls naturally, does it?

ALGERNON: Yes, darling, with a little help from others.

CECILY: I am so glad.

ALGERNON: You'll never break off our engagement again, Cecily?

CECILY: I don't think I could break it off now that I have actually met you. Besides, of course, there is the question of your name.

ALGERNON: Yes, of course. (*Nervously.*)

CECILY: You must not laugh at me, darling, but it had always been a girlish dream of mine to love some one whose name was Ernest. (ALGERNON *rises*, CECILY *also*.) There is something in that name that seems to inspire absolute confidence. I pity any poor married woman whose husband is not called Ernest.

ALGERNON: But, my dear child, do you mean to say you could not love me if I had some other name?

CECILY: But what name?

ALGERNON: Oh, any name you like — Algernon — for instance . . .

CECILY: But I don't like the name of Algernon.

ALGERNON: Well, my own dear, sweet, loving little darling, I really can't see why you should object to the name of Algernon. It is not at all a bad name. In fact, it is rather an aristocratic name. Half of the chaps who get into the Bankruptcy Court are called Algernon. But seriously, Cecily . . . (*moving to her*) if my name was Algy, couldn't you love me?

CECILY (*rising*): I might respect you, Ernest, I might admire your character, but I fear that I should not be able to give you my undivided attention.

ALGERNON: Ahem! Cecily! (*Picking up hat.*) Your Rector here is, I suppose, thoroughly experienced in the practice of all the rites and ceremonials of the Church?

CECILY: Oh, yes. Dr. Chasuble is a most learned man. He has never written a single book, so you can imagine how much he knows.

ALGERNON: I must see him at once on a most important christening — I mean on most important business.

CECILY: Oh!

ALGERNON: I shan't be away more than half an hour.

CECILY: Considering that we have been engaged since February the 14th, and that I only met you to-day for the first time, I think it is rather hard that you should leave me for so long a period as half an hour. Couldn't you make it twenty minutes?

ALGERNON: I'll be back in no time. (*Kisses her and rushes down the garden.*)

CECILY: What an impetuous boy he is! I like his hair so much I must enter his proposal in my diary.

(*Enter* MERRIMAN.)

MERRIMAN: A Miss Fairfax has just called to see Mr. Worthing. On very important business, Miss Fairfax states.

CECILY: Isn't Mr. Worthing in his library?

MERRIMAN: Mr. Worthing went over in the direction of the Rectory some time ago.

CECILY: Pray ask the lady to come out here; Mr. Worthing is sure to be back soon. And you can bring tea.

MERRIMAN: Yes, Miss.

(*Goes out.*)

CECILY: Miss Fairfax! I suppose one of the many good elderly women who are associated with Uncle Jack in some of his philanthropic work in London. I don't quite like women who are interested in philanthropic work. I think it is so forward of them.

(*Enter* MERRIMAN.)

MERRIMAN: Miss Fairfax.

(*Enter* GWENDOLEN. *Exit* MERRIMAN.)

CECILY (*advancing to meet her*): Pray let me introduce myself to you. My name is Cecily Cardew.

GWENDOLEN: Cecily Cardew? (*Moving to her and shaking hands.*) What a very sweet name! Something tells me that we are going to be great friends. I like you already more than I can say. My first impressions of people are never wrong.

CECILY: How nice of you to like me so much after we have known each other such a comparatively short time. Pray sit down.

GWENDOLEN (*still standing up*): I may call you Cecily, may I not?

CECILY: With pleasure!

GWENDOLEN: And you will always call me Gwendolen, won't you?

CECILY: If you wish.

GWENDOLEN: Then that is all quite settled, is it not?

CECILY: I hope so. (*A pause. They both sit down together.*)

GWENDOLEN: Perhaps this might be a favourable opportunity for my mentioning who I am. My father is Lord Bracknell. You have never heard of papa, I suppose?

CECILY: I don't think so.

GWENDOLEN: Outside the family circle, papa, I am glad to say, is entirely unknown. I think that is quite as it should be. The home seems to me to be the proper sphere for the man. And certainly once a man begins to neglect his domestic duties he becomes painfully effeminate, does he not? And I don't like that. It makes men so very attractive. Cecily, mamma, whose views on education are remarkably strict, has brought me up to be extremely shortsighted; it is part of her system; so do you mind my looking at you through my glasses?

CECILY: Oh! not at all, Gwendolen. I am very fond of being looked at.

GWENDOLEN (*after examining* CECILY *carefully through a lorgnette*): You are here on a short visit, I suppose.

CECILY: Oh no! I live here.

GWENDOLEN (*severely*): Really? Your mother, no doubt, or some female relative of advanced years, resides here also?

CECILY: Oh no! I have no mother, nor, in fact, any relations.

GWENDOLEN: Indeed?

CECILY: My dear guardian, with the assistance of Miss Prism, has the arduous task of looking after me.

GWENDOLEN: Your guardian?

CECILY: Yes, I am Mr. Worthing's ward.

GWENDOLEN: Oh! It is strange he never mentioned to me that he had a ward. How secretive of him! He grows more interesting hourly. I am not sure, however, that the news inspires me with feelings of unmixed delight. (*Rising and going to her.*) I am very fond of you, Cecily; I have liked you ever since I met you! But I am bound to state that now that I know that you are Mr. Worthing's ward, I cannot help expressing a wish you were — well, just a little older than you seem to be — and not quite so very alluring in appearance. In fact, if I may speak candidly ——

CECILY: Pray do! I think that whenever one has anything unpleasant to say, one should always be quite candid.

GWENDOLEN: Well, to speak with perfect candour, Cecily, I wish that you were fully forty-two, and more than usually plain for your age. Ernest has a strong upright nature. He is the very soul of truth and honor. Disloyalty would be as impossible to him as deception. But even men of the noblest possible moral character are extremely susceptible to the influence of the physical charms of others. Modern, no less than Ancient History, supplies us with many most painful examples of what I refer to. If it were not so, indeed, History would be quite unreadable.

CECILY: I beg your pardon, Gwendolen, did you say Ernest?

GWENDOLEN: Yes.

CECILY: Oh, but it is not Mr. Ernest Worthing who is my guardian. It is his brother — his elder brother.

GWENDOLEN (*sitting down again*): Ernest never mentioned to me that he had a brother.

CECILY: I am sorry to say they have not been on good terms for a long time.

GWENDOLEN: Ah! that accounts for it. And now that I think of it I have never heard any man mention his brother. The subject seems distasteful to most men. Cecily, you have lifted a load from my mind. I was growing almost anxious. It would have been terrible if any cloud had come across a friendship like ours, would it not? Of course you are quite, quite sure that it is not Mr. Ernest Worthing who is your guardian?

CECILY: Quite sure. (*A pause.*) In fact, I am going to be his.

GWENDOLEN (*inquiringly*): I beg your pardon?

CECILY (*rather shy and confidingly*): Dearest Gwendolen, there is no reason why I should make a secret of it to you. Our little country newspaper is sure to chronicle the fact next week. Mr. Ernest Worthing and I are engaged to be married.

GWENDOLEN (*quite politely, rising*): My darling Cecily, I think there must be some slight error. Mr. Ernest Worthing is engaged to me. The announcement will appear in the *Morning Post* on Saturday at the latest.

CECILY (*very politely, rising*): I am afraid you must be under some misconception. Ernest proposed to me exactly ten minutes ago. (*Shows diary.*)

GWENDOLEN (*examines diary through her lorgnette carefully*): It is very curious, for he asked me to be his wife yesterday afternoon at 5:30. If you would care to verify the incident, pray do so. (*Produces diary of her own.*) I never travel without my diary. One should always have something sensational to read in the train. I am so sorry, dear Cecily, if it is any disappointment to you, but I am afraid I have the prior claim.

CECILY: It would distress me more than I can tell you, dear Gwendolen, if it caused you any mental or physical anguish, but I feel bound to point out that since Ernest proposed to you he clearly has changed his mind.

GWENDOLEN (*meditatively*): If the poor fellow has been entrapped into any foolish promise I shall consider it my duty to rescue him at once, and with a firm hand.

CECILY (*thoughtfully and sadly*): Whatever unfortunate entanglement my dear boy may have got into, I will never reproach him with it after we are married.

GWENDOLEN: Do you allude to me, Miss Cardew, as an entanglement? You are presumptuous. On an occasion of this kind it becomes more than a moral duty to speak one's mind. It becomes a pleasure.

CECILY: Do you suggest, Miss Fairfax, that I entrapped Ernest into an engagement? How dare you? This is no time for wearing the shallow mask of manners. When I see a spade I call it a spade.

GWENDOLEN (*satirically*): I am glad to say that I have never seen a spade. It is obvious that our social spheres have been widely different.

(*Enter* MERRIMAN, *followed by the footman. He carries a salver, table cloth, and plate stand.* CECILY *is about to retort. The presence of the servants exercises a restraining influence, under which both girls chafe.*)

MERRIMAN: Shall I lay tea here as usual, Miss?

CECILY (*sternly, in a calm voice*): Yes, as usual.

(MERRIMAN *begins to clear table and lay cloth. A long pause.* CECILY *and* GWENDOLEN *glare at each other.*)

GWENDOLEN: Are there many interesting walks in the vicinity, Miss Cardew?

CECILY: Oh! yes! a great many. From the top of one of the hills quite close one can see five counties.

GWENDOLEN: Five counties! I don't think I should like that; I hate crowds.

CECILY (*sweetly*): I suppose that is why you live in town? (GWENDOLEN *bites her lip, and beats her foot nervously with her parasol.*)

GWENDOLEN (*looking round*): Quite a well-kept garden this is, Miss Cardew.

CECILY: So glad you like it, Miss Fairfax.

GWENDOLEN: I had no idea there were any flowers in the country.

CECILY: Oh, flowers are as common here, Miss Fairfax, as people are in London.

GWENDOLEN: Personally I cannot understand how anybody manages to exist in the country, if anybody who is anybody does. The country always bores me to death.

CECILY: Ah! This is what the newspapers call agricultural depression, is it not? I believe the aristocracy are suffering very much from it just at present. It is almost an epidemic amongst them, I have been told. May I offer you some tea, Miss Fairfax?

GWENDOLEN (*with elaborate politeness*): Thank you. (*Aside.*) Detestable girl! But I require tea!

CECILY (*sweetly*): Sugar?

GWENDOLEN (*superciliously*): No, thank you. Sugar is not fashionable any more. (CECILY *looks angrily at her, takes up the tongs and puts four lumps of sugar into the cup.*)

CECILY (*severely*): Cake or bread and butter?

GWENDOLEN (*in a bored manner*): Bread and butter, please. Cake is rarely seen at the best houses nowadays.

CECILY (*cuts a very large slice of cake and puts it on the tray*): Hand that to Miss Fairfax.

(MERRIMAN *does so, and goes out with footman.* GWENDOLEN *drinks the tea and makes a grimace. Puts down cup at once, reaches out her hand to the bread and butter, looks at it, and finds it is cake. Rises in indignation.*)

GWENDOLEN: You have filled my tea with lumps of sugar, and though I asked most distinctly for bread and butter, you have given me cake. I am known for the gentleness of my disposition, and the extraordinary sweetness of my nature, but I warn you, Miss Cardew, you may go too far.

CECILY (*rising*): To save my poor, innocent, trusting boy from the machinations of any other girl there are no lengths to which I would not go.

GWENDOLEN: From the moment I saw you I distrusted you. I felt that you were false and deceitful. I am never deceived in such matters. My first impressions of people are invariably right.

CECILY: It seems to me, Miss Fairfax, that I am trespassing on your valuable time. No doubt you have many other calls of a similar character to make in the neighbourhood.

(*Enter* JACK.)

GWENDOLEN (*catching sight of him*): Ernest! My own Ernest!

JACK: Gwendolen! Darling! (*Offers to kiss her.*)

GWENDOLEN (*drawing back*): A moment! May I ask if you are engaged to be married to this young lady? (*Points to* CECILY.)

JACK (*laughing*): To dear little Cecily! Of course not! What could have put such an idea into your pretty little head?

GWENDOLEN: Thank you. You may! (*Offers her cheek.*)

CECILY (*very sweetly*): I knew there must be some misunderstanding, Miss Fairfax. The gentleman whose arm is at present round your waist is my guardian, Mr. John·Worthing.

GWENDOLEN: I beg your pardon?

CECILY: This is Uncle Jack.

GWENDOLEN (*receding*): Jack! Oh!

(*Enter* ALGERNON.)

CECILY: Here is Ernest.

ALGERNON (*goes straight over to* CECILY *without noticing anyone else*): My own love! (*Offers to kiss her.*)

CECILY (*drawing back*): A moment, Ernest! May I ask you — are you engaged to be married to this young lady?

ALGERNON (*looking round*): To what young lady? Good heavens! Gwendolen!

CECILY: Yes: to good heavens, Gwendolen, I mean to Gwendolen.

ALGERNON (*laughing*): Of course not! What could have put such an idea into your pretty little head?

CECILY: Thank you. (*Presenting her cheek to be kissed.*) You may. (ALGERNON *kisses her.*)

GWENDOLEN: I felt there was some slight error, Miss Cardew. The gentleman who is now embracing you is my cousin, Mr. Algernon Moncrieff.

CECILY (*breaking away from Algernon*): Algernon Moncrieff! Oh!

(*The two girls move towards each other and put their arms round each other's waists as if for protection.*)

CECILY: Are you called Algernon?

ALGERNON: I cannot deny it.

CECILY: Oh!

GWENDOLEN: Is your name really John?

JACK (*standing rather proudly*): I could deny it if I liked. I could deny anything if I liked. But my name certainly is John. It has been John for years.

CECILY (*to* GWENDOLEN): A gross deception has been practised on both of us.

GWENDOLEN: My poor wounded Cecily!

CECILY: My sweet wronged Gwendolen!

GWENDOLEN (*slowly and seriously*): You will call me sister, will you not? (*They embrace.* JACK *and* ALGERNON *groan and walk up and down.*)

CECILY (*rather brightly*): There is just one question I would like to be allowed to ask my guardian.

GWENDOLEN: An admirable idea! Mr. Worthing, there is just one quesion I would like to be permitted to put to you. Where is your brother Ernest? We are both engaged to be married to your brother Ernest, so it is a matter of some importance to us to know where your brother Ernest is at present.

JACK (*slowly and hesitatingly*): Gwendolen — Cecily — it is very painful for me to be forced to speak the truth. It is the first time in my life that I have ever been reduced to such a painful position, and I am really quite inexperienced in doing anything of the kind. However, I will tell you quite frankly that I have no brother Ernest. I have no brother at all. I never had a brother in my life, and I certainly have not the smallest intention of ever having one in the future.

CECILY (*surprised*): No brother at all?

JACK (*cheerily*): None!

GWENDOLEN (*severely*): Had you never a brother of any kind?

JACK (*pleasantly*): Never. Not even of any kind.

GWENDOLEN: I am afraid it is quite clear, Cecily, that neither of us is engaged to be married to anyone.

CECILY: It is not a very pleasant position for a young girl suddenly to find herself in. Is it?

GWENDOLEN: Let us go into the house. They will hardly venture to come after us there.

CECILY: No, men are so cowardly, aren't they?

(*They retire into the house with scornful looks.*)

JACK: This ghastly state of things is what you call Bunburying, I suppose?

ALGERNON: Yes, and a perfectly wonderful Bunbury it is. The most wonderful Bunbury I have ever had in my life.

JACK: Well, you've no right whatsoever to Bunbury here.

ALGERNON: That is absurd. One has a right to Bunbury anywhere one chooses. Every serious Bunburyist knows that.

JACK: Serious Bunburyist? Good heavens!

ALGERNON: Well, one must be serious about something, if one wants to have any amusement in life. I happen to be serious about Bunburying. What on earth you are serious about I haven't got the remotest idea. About everything, I should fancy. You have such an absolutely trivial nature.

JACK: Well, the only small satisfaction I have in the whole of this wretched business is that your friend Bunbury is quite exploded. You won't be able to run down to the country quite so often as you used to do, dear Algy. And a very good thing too.

ALGERNON: Your brother is a little off colour, isn't he, dear Jack? You won't be able to disappear to London quite so frequently as your wicked custom was. And not a bad thing, either.

JACK: As for your conduct towards Miss Cardew, I must say that your taking in a sweet, simple, innocent girl like that is quite inexcusable. To say nothing of the fact that she is my ward.

ALGERNON: I can see no possible defence at all for your deceiving a brilliant, clever, thoroughly experienced young lady like Miss Fairfax. To say nothing of the fact that she is my cousin.

JACK: I wanted to be engaged to Gwendolen, that is all. I love her.

ALGERNON: Well, I simply wanted to be engaged to Cecily. I adore her.

JACK: There is certainly no chance of your marrying Miss Cardew.

ALGERNON: I don't think there is much likelihood, Jack, of you and Miss Fairfax being united.

JACK: Well, that is no business of yours.

ALGERNON: If it was my business, I wouldn't talk about it. (*Begins to eat muffins.*) It is very vulgar to talk about one's business. Only people like stockbrokers do that, and then merely at dinner parties.

JACK: How you can sit there, calmly eating muffins when we are in this horrible trouble, I can't make out. You seem to me to be perfectly heartless.

ALGERNON: Well, I can't eat muffins in an agitated manner. The butter would probably get on my cuffs. One should always eat muffins quite calmly. It is the only way to eat them.

JACK: I say it's perfectly heartless your eating muffins at all, under the circumstances.

ALGERNON: When I am in trouble, eating is the only thing that consoles me. Indeed, when I am in really great trouble, as any one who knows me intimately will tell you, I refuse everything except food and drink. At the present moment I am eating muffins because I am unhappy. Besides, I am particularly fond of muffins. (*Rising.*)

JACK (*rising*): Well, there is no reason why you should eat them all in that greedy way. (*Takes muffins from Algernon.*)

ALGERNON (*offering tea-cake*): I wish you would have tea-cake instead. I don't like tea-cake.

JACK: Good heavens! I suppose a man may eat his own muffins in his own garden.

ALGERNON: But you have just said it was perfectly heartless to eat muffins.

JACK: I said it was perfectly heartless of you, under the circumstances. That is a very different thing.

ALGERNON: That may be. But the muffins are the same. (*He seizes the muffin-dish from* JACK.)

JACK: Algy, I wish to goodness you would go.

ALGERNON: You can't possibly ask me to go without having some dinner. It's absurd. I never go without my dinner. No one ever does, except vegetarians and people like that. Besides I have just made arrangements with Dr. Chasuble to be christened at a quarter to six under the name of Ernest.

JACK: My dear fellow, the sooner you give up that nonsense the better. I made arrangements this morning with Dr. Chasuble to be christened myself at 5:30, and I naturally will take the name of Ernest. Gwendolen would wish it. We can't both be christened Ernest. It's absurd. Besides, I have a perfect right to be christened if I like. There is no evidence at all that I have ever been christened by anybody. I should think it extremely probable I never was, and so does Dr. Chasuble. It is entirely different in your case. You have been christened already.

ALGERNON: Yes, but I have not been christened for years.

JACK: Yes, but you have been christened. That is the important thing.

ALGERNON: Quite so. So I know my constitution can stand it. If you are not quite sure about your ever having been christened, I must say I think it rather dangerous your venturing on it now. It might make you very unwell. You can hardly have forgotten that someone very closely connected with you was very nearly carried off this week in Paris by a severe chill.

JACK: Yes, but you said yourself that a severe chill was not hereditary.

ALGERNON: It usen't to be, I know — but I daresay it is now. Science is always making wonderful improvements in things.

JACK (*picking up the muffin-dish*): Oh, that is nonsense; you are always talking nonsense.

ALGERNON: Jack, you are at the muffins again! I wish you wouldn't. There are only two left. (*Takes them.*) I told you I was particularly fond of muffins.

JACK: But I hate tea-cake.

ALGERNON: Why on earth then do you allow tea-cake to be served up for your guests? What ideas you have of hospitality!

JACK: Algernon! I have already told you to go. I don't want you here. Why don't you go!

ALGERNON: I haven't quite finished my tea yet! and there is still one muffin left. (JACK *groans, and sinks into a chair.* ALGERNON *continues eating.*)

ACT DROP

ACT III

Scene — Drawing-room at the Manor House.
  GWENDOLEN *and* CECILY *are at the window, looking out into the garden.*

GWENDOLEN: The fact that they did not follow us at once into the house, as any one else would have done, seems to me to show that they have some sense of shame left.

CECILY: They have been eating muffins. That looks like repentance.

GWENDOLEN (*after a pause*): They don't seem to notice us at all. Couldn't you cough?

CECILY: But I haven't got a cough.

GWENDOLEN: They're looking at us. What effrontery!

CECILY: They're approaching. That's very forward of them.

GWENDOLEN: Let us preserve a dignified silence.

CECILY: Certainly. It's the only thing to do now.

(*Enter* JACK *followed by* ALGERNON. *They whistle some dreadful popular air from a British Opera.*)

GWENDOLEN: This dignified silence seems to produce an unpleasant effect.

CECILY: A most distasteful one.

GWENDOLEN: But we will not be the first to speak.

CECILY: Certainly not.

GWENDOLEN: Mr. Worthing, I have something very particular to ask you. Much depends on your reply.

CECILY: Gwendolen, your common sense is invaluable. Mr. Moncrieff, kindly answer me the following question. Why did you pretend to be my guardian's brother?

ALGERNON: In order that I might have an opportunity of meeting you.

CECILY (*to* GWENDOLEN): That certainly seems a satisfactory explanation, does it not?

GWENDOLEN: Yes, dear, if you can believe him.

CECILY: I don't. But that does not affect the wonderful beauty of his answer.

GWENDOLEN: True. In matters of grave importance, style, not sincerity, is the vital thing. Mr. Worthing, what explanation can you offer to me for pretending to have a brother? Was it in order that you might have an opportunity of coming up to town to see me as often as possible?

JACK: Can you doubt it, Miss Fairfax?

GWENDOLEN: I have the gravest doubts upon the subject. But I intend to crush them. This is not the moment for German scepticism. (*Moving to* CECILY.) Their explanations appear to be quite satisfactory, especially Mr. Worthing's. That seems to me to have the stamp of truth upon it.

CECILY: I am more than content with what Mr. Moncrieff said. His voice alone inspires one with absolute credulity.

GWENDOLEN: Then you think we should forgive them?

CECILY: Yes. I mean no.

GWENDOLEN: True! I had forgotten. There are principles at stake that one cannot surrender. Which of us should tell them? The task is not a pleasant one.

CECILY: Could we not both speak at the same time?

GWENDOLEN: An excellent idea! I nearly always speak at the same time as other people. Will you take the time from me?

CECILY: Certainly. (GWENDOLEN *beats time with uplifted finger.*)

GWENDOLEN and CECILY (*speaking together*): Your Christian names are still an insuperable barrier. That is all!

JACK and ALGERNON (*speaking together*): Our Christian names! Is that all? But we are going to be christened this afternoon.

GWENDOLEN (*to* JACK): For my sake you are prepared to do this terrible thing?

JACK: I am.

CECILY (*to* ALGERNON): To please me you are ready to face this fearful ordeal?

ALGERNON: I am!

GWENDOLEN: How absurd to talk of the equality of the sexes! Where questions of self-sacrifice are concerned, men are infinitely beyond us.

JACK: We are. (*Clasps hands with* ALGERNON.)

CECILY: They have moments of physical courage of which we women know absolutely nothing.

GWENDOLEN (*to* JACK): Darling!

ALGERNON (*to* CECILY): Darling! (*They fall into each other's arms.*)

(*Enter* MERRIMAN. *When he enters he coughs loudly, seeing the situation.*)

MERRIMAN: Ahem! Ahem! Lady Bracknell.

JACK: Good heavens!

(*Enter* LADY BRACKNELL. *The couples separate in alarm. Exit* MERRIMAN.)

LADY BRACKNELL: Gwendolen! What does this mean?

GWENDOLEN: Merely that I am engaged to be married to Mr. Worthing, mamma.

LADY BRACKNELL: Come here. Sit down. Sit down immediately. Hesitation of any kind is a sign of mental decay in the young, of physical weakness in the old. (*Turns to* JACK.) Apprised, sir, of my daughter's sudden flight by her trusty maid, whose confidence I purchased by means of a small coin, I followed her at once by a luggage train. Her unhappy father is, I am glad to say, under the impression that she is attending a more than usually lengthy lecture by the University Extension Scheme on the Influence of a Permanent Income on Thought. I do not propose to undeceive him. Indeed I have never undeceived him on any question. I would consider it wrong. But of course, you will clearly understand that all communication between yourself and my daughter must cease immediately from this moment. On this point, as indeed on all points, I am firm.

JACK: I am engaged to be married to Gwendolen, Lady Bracknell!

LADY BRACKNELL: You are nothing of the kind, sir. And now as regards Algernon! . . . Algernon!

ALGERNON: Yes, Aunt Augusta.

LADY BRACKNELL: May I ask if it is in this house that your invalid friend Mr. Bunbury resides?

ALGERNON (*stammering*): Oh! No! Bunbury doesn't live here. Bunbury is somewhere else at present. In fact, Bunbury is dead.

LADY BRACKNELL: Dead! When did Mr. Bunbury die? His death must have been extremely sudden.

ALGERNON (*airily*): Oh! I killed Bunbury this afternoon. I mean poor Bunbury died this afternoon.

LADY BRACKNELL: What did he die of?

ALGERNON: Bunbury? Oh, he was quite exploded.

LADY BRACKNELL: Exploded! Was he the victim of a revolutionary outrage? I was not aware that Mr. Bunbury was interested in social legislation. If so, he is well punished for his morbidity.

ALGERNON: My dear Aunt Augusta, I mean he was found out! The doctors found out that Bunbury could not live, that is what I mean — so Bunbury died.

LADY BRACKNELL: He seems to have had great confidence in the opinion of his physicians. I am glad, however, that he made up his mind at the last to some definite course of action, and acted under proper medical advice. And now that we have finally got rid of this Mr. Bunbury, may I ask, Mr. Worthing, who is that young person whose hand my nephew Algernon is now holding in what seems to me a peculiarly unnecessary manner?

JACK: That lady is Miss Cecily Cardew, my ward. (LADY BRACKNELL *bows coldly to* CECILY.)

ALGERNON: I am engaged to be married to Cecily, Aunt Augusta.

LADY BRACKNELL: I beg your pardon?

CECILY: Mr. Moncrieff and I are engaged to be married, Lady Bracknell.

LADY BRACKNELL (*with a shiver, crossing to the sofa and sitting down*): I do not know whether there is anything peculiarly exciting in the air of this particular part of Herfordshire, but the number of engagements that go on seems to me considerably above the proper average that statistics have laid down for our guidance. I think some preliminary inquiry on my part would not be out of place. Mr. Worthing, is Miss Cardew at all connected with any of the larger railway stations in London? I merely desire information. Until yesterday I had no idea that there were any families or persons whose origin was a Terminus. (JACK *looks perfectly furious, but restrains himself.*)

JACK (*in a cold, clear voice*): Miss Cardew is the granddaughter of the late Mr. Thomas Cardew of 149 Belgrave Square, S.W.; Gervase Park, Dorking, Surrey; and the Sporran, Fifeshire, N.B.

LADY BRACKNELL: That sounds not unsatisfactory. Three addresses always inspire confidence, even in tradesmen. But what proof have I of their authenticity?

JACK: I have carefully preserved the Court Guides of the period. They are open to your inspection, Lady Bracknell.

LADY BRACKNELL (*grimly*): I have known strange errors in that publication.

JACK: Miss Cardew's family solicitors are Messrs. Markby, Markby, and Markby.

LADY BRACKNELL: Markby, Markby, and Markby? A firm of the very highest position in their profession. Indeed I am told that one of the Mr. Markbys is occasionally to be seen at dinner parties. So far I am satisfied.

JACK (*very irritably*): How extremely kind of you, Lady Bracknell! I have also in my possession, you will be pleased to hear, certificates of Miss Cardew's birth, baptism, whooping cough, registration, vaccination, confirmation, and the measles; both the German and the English variety.

LADY BRACKNELL: Ah! A life crowded with incident, I see; though perhaps somewhat too exciting for a young girl. I am not myself in favour of premature experiences. (*Rises, looks at her watch.*) Gwendolen! the time approaches for our departure. We have not a moment to lose. As a matter of form, Mr. Worthing, I had better ask you if Miss Cardew has any little fortune?

JACK: Oh! about a hundred and thirty thousand pounds in the Funds. That is all. Good-bye, Lady Bracknell. So pleased to have seen you.

LADY BRACKNELL (*sitting down again*): A moment, Mr. Worthing. A hundred and thirty thousand pounds! And in the Funds! Miss Cardew seems to me a most attractive young lady, now that I look at her. Few girls of the present day have any really solid qualities, any of the qualities that last, and improve with time. We live, I regret to say, in an age of surfaces. (*To* CECILY.) Come over here, dear. (CECILY *goes across.*) Pretty child! your dress is sadly simple, and your hair seems almost as Nature might have left it. But we can soon alter all that. A thoroughly experienced French maid produces a really marvellous result in a very brief space of time. I remember recommending one to young Lady Lancing, and after three months her own husband did not know her.

JACK (*aside*): And after six months nobody knew her.

LADY BRACKNELL (*glares at* JACK *for a few moments. Then bends, with a practised smile, to* CECILY): Kindly turn round, sweet child. (CECILY *turns completely round.*) No, the side view is what I want. (CECILY *presents her profile.*) Yes, quite as I expected. There are distinct social possibilities in your profile. The two weak points in our age are its want of principle and its want of profile. The chin a little higher, dear. Style largely depends on the way the chin is worn. They are worn very high, just at present. Algernon!

ALGERNON: Yes, Aunt Augusta!

LADY BRACKNELL: There are distinct social possibilities in Miss Cardew's profile.

ALGERNON: Cecily is the sweetest, dearest, prettiest girl in the whole world. And I don't care twopence about social possibilities.

LADY BRACKNELL: Never speak disrespectfully of Society, Algernon. Only people who can't get into it do that. (*To* CECILY.) Dear child, of course you know that Algernon has nothing but his debts to depend upon. But I do not approve of mercenary marriages. When I married Lord Bracknell I had no fortune of any kind. But I never dreamed for a moment of allowing that to stand in my way. Well, I suppose I must give my consent.

ALGERNON: Thank you, Aunt Augusta.

LADY BRACKNELL: Cecily, you may kiss me!

CECILY (*kisses her*): Thank you, Lady Bracknell.

LADY BRACKNELL: You may also address me as Aunt Augusta for the future.

CECILY: Thank you, Aunt Augusta.

LADY BRACKNELL: The marriage, I think, had better take place quite soon.

ALGERNON: Thank you, Aunt Augusta.

CECILY: Thank you, Aunt Augusta.

LADY BRACKNELL: To speak frankly, I am not in favour of long engagements. They give people the opportunity of finding out each other's character before marriage, which I think is never advisable.

JACK: I beg your pardon for interrupting you, Lady Bracknell, but this engagement is quite out of the question. I am Miss Cardew's guardian, and she cannot marry without my consent until she comes of age. That consent I absolutely decline to give.

LADY BRACKNELL: Upon what grounds, may I ask? Algernon is an extremely, I may almost say an ostentatiously, eligible young man. He has nothing, but he looks everything. What more can one desire?

JACK: It pains me very much to have to speak frankly to you, Lady Bracknell, about your nephew, but the fact is that I do not approve at all of his moral character. I suspect him of being untruthful. (ALGERNON *and* CECILY *look at him in indignant amazement*.)

LADY BRACKNELL: Untruthful! My nephew Algernon? Impossible! He is an Oxonian.

JACK: I fear there can be no possible doubt about the matter. This afternoon during my temporary absence in London on an important question of romance, he obtained admission to my house by means of the false pretence of being my brother. Under an assumed name he drank, I've just been informed by my butler, an entire pint bottle of my Perrier-Jouet, Brut, '89, a wine I was specially reserving for myself. Continuing his disgraceful deception, he succeeded in the course of the afternoon in alienating the affections of my only ward. He subsequently stayed to tea, and devoured every single muffin. And what makes his conduct all the more heartless is, that he was perfectly well aware from the first that I have no brother, that I never had a brother, and that I don't intend to have a brother, not even of any kind. I distinctly told him so myself yesterday afternoon.

LADY BRACKNELL: Ahem! Mr. Worthing, after careful consideration I have decided entirely to overlook my nephew's conduct to you.

JACK: That is very generous of you, Lady Bracknell. My own decision, however, is unalterable. I decline to give my consent.

LADY BRACKNELL (*to* CECILY): Come here, sweet child. (CECILY *goes over.*) How old are you, dear?

CECILY: Well, I am really only eighteen, but I always admit to twenty when I go to evening parties.

LADY BRACKNELL: You are perfectly right in making some slight alteration. Indeed, no woman should ever be quite accurate about her age. It looks so calculating. . . . (*In a meditative manner.*) Eighteen, but admitting to twenty at evening parties. Well, it will not be very long before you are of age and free from the restraints of tutelage. So I don't think your guardian's consent is, after all, a matter of any importance.

JACK: Pray excuse me, Lady Bracknell, for interrupting you again, but it is only fair to tell you that according to the terms of her grandfather's will Miss Cardew does not come legally of age till she is thirty-five.

LADY BRACKNELL: That does not seem to me to be a grave objection. Thirty-five is a very attractive age. London society is full of women of the very highest birth who have, of their own free choice, remained thirty-five for years. Lady Dumbleton is an instance in point. To my own knowledge she has been thirty-five ever since she arrived at the age of forty, which was many years ago now. I see no reason why our dear Cecily should not be even still more attractive at the age you mention than she is at present. There will be a large accumulation of property.

CECILY: Algy, could you wait for me till I was thirty-five?

ALGERNON: Of course I could, Cecily. You know I could.

CECILY: Yes, I felt instinctively, but I couldn't wait all that time. I hate waiting even five minutes for anybody. It always makes me rather cross. I am not punctual myself, I know, but I do like punctuality in others, and waiting, even to be married, is quite out of the question.

ALGERNON: Then what is to be done, Cecily?

CECILY: I don't know, Mr. Moncrieff.

LADY BRACKNELL: My dear Mr. Worthing, as Miss Cardew states positively that she cannot wait till she is thirty-five — a remark which I am bound to say seems to me to show a somewhat impatient nature — I would beg of you to reconsider your decision.

JACK: But my dear Lady Bracknell, the matter is entirely in your own hands. The moment you consent to my marriage with Gwendolen, I will most gladly allow your nephew to form an alliance with my ward.

LADY BRACKNELL (*rising and drawing herself up*): You must be quite aware that what you propose is out of the question.

JACK: Then a passionate celibacy is all that any of us can look forward to.

LADY BRACKNELL: That is not the destiny I propose for Gwendolen. Algernon, of course, can choose for himself. (*Pulls out her watch.*) Come, dear (GWENDOLEN *rises*), we have already missed five, if not six, trains. To miss any more might expose us to comment on the platform.

(*Enter* DR. CHASUBLE.)

CHASUBLE: Everything is quite ready for the christenings.

LADY BRACKNELL: The christenings, sir! Is not that somewhat premature?

CHASUBLE (*looking rather puzzled, and pointing to* JACK *and* ALGERNON): Both these gentlemen have expressed a desire for immediate baptism.

LADY BRACKNELL: At their age? The idea is grotesque and irreligious! Algernon, I forbid you to be baptized. I will not hear of such excesses. Lord Bracknell would be highly displeased if he learned that that was the way in which you wasted your time and money.

CHASUBLE: Am I to understand then that there are to be no christenings at all this afternoon?

JACK: I don't think that, as things are now, it would be of much practical value to either of us, Dr. Chasuble.

CHASUBLE: I am grieved to hear such sentiments from you, Mr. Worthing. They savour of the heretical views of the Anabaptists, views that I have completely refuted in four of my unpublished sermons. However, as your present mood seems to be one peculiarly secular, I will return to the church at once. Indeed, I have just been informed by the pew-opener that for the last hour and a half Miss Prism has been waiting for me in the vestry.

LADY BRACKNELL (*starting*): Miss Prism! Did I hear you mention a Miss Prism?

CHASUBLE: Yes, Lady Bracknell. I am on my way to join her.

LADY BRACKNELL: Pray allow me to detain you for a moment. This matter may prove to be one of vital importance to Lord Bracknell and myself. Is this Miss Prism a female of repellent aspect, remotely connected with education?

CHASUBLE (*somewhat indignantly*): She is the most cultivated of ladies, and the very picture of respectability.

LADY BRACKNELL: It is obviously the same person. May I ask what position she holds in your household?

CHASUBLE (*severely*): I am a celibate, madam.

JACK (*interposing*): Miss Prism, Lady Bracknell, has been for the last three years Miss Cardew's esteemed governess and valued companion.

LADY BRACKNELL: In spite of what I hear of her, I must see her at once. Let her be sent for.

CHASUBLE (*looking off*): She approaches; she is nigh.

(*Enter* MISS PRISM *hurriedly.*)

MISS PRISM: I was told you expected me in the vestry, dear Canon. I have been waiting for you there for an hour and three-quarters. (*Catches sight of* LADY BRACKNELL, *who has fixed her with a stony glare.* MISS PRISM *grows pale and quails. She looks anxiously round as if desirous to escape.*)

LADY BRACKNELL (*in a severe, judicial voice*): Prism! (MISS PRISM *bows her head in shame.*) Come here, Prism! (MISS PRISM *approaches in a humble manner.*) Prism! Where is that baby? (*General consternation. The Canon starts back in horror.* ALGERNON *and* JACK *pretend to be anxious to shield* CECILY *and* GWENDOLEN *from hearing the details of a terrible scandal.*) Twenty-eight years ago, Prism, you left Lord Bracknell's house, Number 104, Upper Grosvenor Square, in charge of a perambulator that contained a baby of the male sex. You never returned. A few weeks later, through the elaborate investigations of the Metropolitan police, the perambulator was discovered at midnight standing by itself in a remote corner of Bayswater. It contained the manuscript of a three-volume novel of more than usually revolting sentimentality. (MISS PRISM *starts in involuntary indignation.*) But the baby was not there. (*Every one looks at* MISS PRISM.) Prism! Where is that baby? (*A pause.*)

MISS PRISM: Lady Bracknell, I admit with shame that I do not know. I only wish I did. The plain facts of the case are these. On the morning of the day you mention, a day that is for ever branded on my memory, I prepared as usual to take the baby out in its perambulator. I had also with me a somewhat old, but capacious hand-bag in which I had intended to place the manuscript of a work of fiction that I had written during my few unoccupied hours. In a moment of mental abstraction, for which I can never forgive myself, I deposited the manuscript in the bassinette and placed the baby in the hand-bag.

JACK (*who has been listening attentively*): But where did you deposit the hand-bag?

MISS PRISM: Do not ask me, Mr. Worthing.

JACK: Miss Prism, this is a matter of no small importance to me. I insist on knowing where you deposited the hand-bag that contained that infant.

MISS PRISM: I left it in the cloak-room of one of the larger railway stations in London.

JACK: What railway station?

MISS PRISM (*quite crushed*): Victoria. The Brighton line. (*Sinks into a chair.*)

JACK: I must retire to my room for a moment. Gwendolen, wait here for me.

GWENDOLEN: If you are not too long, I will wait here for you all my life.

(*Exit* JACK *in great excitement.*)

CHASUBLE: What do you think this means, Lady Bracknell?

LADY BRACKNELL: I dare not even suspect, Dr. Chasuble. I need hardly tell you that in families of high position strange coincidences are not supposed to occur. They are hardly considered the thing.

(*Noises heard overhead as if some one was throwing trunks about. Every one looks up.*)

CECILY: Uncle Jack seems strangely agitated.

CHASUBLE: Your guardian has a very emotional nature.

LADY BRACKNELL: This noise is extremely unpleasant. It sounds as if he was having an argument. I dislike arguments of any kind. They are always vulgar, and often convincing.

CHASUBLE (*looking up*): It has stopped now. (*The noise is redoubled.*)

LADY BRACKNELL: I wish he would arrive at some conclusion.

GWENDOLEN: This suspense is terrible. I hope it will last.

(*Enter* JACK *with a hand-bag of black leather in his hand.*)

JACK (*rushing over to* MISS PRISM): Is this the hand-bag, Miss Prism? Examine it carefully before you speak. The happiness of more than one life depends on your answer.

MISS PRISM (*calmly*): It seems to be mine. Yes, here is the injury it received through the upsetting of a Gower Street omnibus in younger and happier days. Here is the stain on the lining caused by the explosion of a temperance beverage, an incident that occurred at Leamington. And here, on the lock, are my initials. I had forgotten that in an extravagant mood I had had them placed there. The bag is undoubtedly mine. I am delighted to have it so unexpectedly restored to me. It has been a great inconvenience being without it all these years.

JACK (*in a pathetic voice*): Miss Prism, more is restored to you than this hand-bag. I was the baby you placed in it.

MISS PRISM (*amazed*): You?

JACK (*embracing her*): Yes . . . mother!

MISS PRISM (*recoiling in indignant astonishment*): Mr. Worthing. I am unmarried!

JACK: Unmarried! I do not deny that is a serious blow. But after all, who has the right to cast a stone against one who has suffered? Cannot repentance wipe out an act of folly? Why should there be one law for men, and another for women? Mother, I forgive you. (*Tries to embrace her again.*)

MISS PRISM (*still more indignant*): Mr. Worthing, there is some error. (*Pointing to* LADY BRACKNELL.) There is the lady who can tell you who you really are.

JACK (*after a pause*): Lady Bracknell, I hate to seem inquisitive, but would you kindly inform me who I am?

LADY BRACKNELL: I am afraid that the news I have to give you will not altogether please you. You are the son of my poor sister, Mrs. Moncrieff, and consequently Algernon's elder brother.

JACK: Algy's elder brother! Then I have a brother after all. I knew I had a brother! I always said I had a brother! Cecily — how could you have ever doubted that I had a brother? (*Seizes hold of* ALGERNON.) Dr. Chasuble, my unfortunate brother. Miss Prism, my unfortunate brother. Gwendolen, my unfortunate brother. Algy, you young scoundrel, you will have to treat me with more respect in the future. You have never behaved to me like a brother in all your life.

ALGERNON: Well, not till to-day, old boy, I admit. I did my best, however, though I was out of practice.

(*Shakes hands.*)

GWENDOLEN (*to* JACK): My own! But what own are you? What is your Christian name, now that you have become some one else?

JACK: Good heavens! . . . I had quite forgotten that point. Your decision on the subject of my name is irrevocable, I suppose?

GWENDOLEN: I never change, except in my affections.

CECILY: What a noble nature you have, Gwendolen!

JACK: Then the question had better be cleared up at once. Aunt Augusta, a moment. At the time when Miss Prism left me in the hand-bag, had I been christened already?

LADY BRACKNELL: Every luxury that money could buy, including christening, had been lavished on you by your fond and doting parents.

JACK: Then I was christened! That is settled. Now, what name was I given? Let me know the worst.

LADY BRACKNELL: Being the eldest son you were naturally christened after your father.

JACK (*irritably*): Yes, but what was my father's Christian name?

LADY BRACKNELL (*meditatively*): I cannot at the present moment recall what the General's Christian name was. But I have no doubt he had one. He was eccentric, I admit. But only in later years. And that was the result of the Indian climate, and marriage, and indigestion, and other things of that kind.

JACK: Algy! Can't you recollect what our father's Christian name was?

ALGERNON: My dear boy, we were never even on speaking terms. He died before I was a year old.

JACK: His name would appear in the Army Lists of the period, I suppose, Aunt Augusta?

LADY BRACKNELL: The General was essentially a man of peace, except in his domestic life. But I have no doubt his name would appear in any military directory.

JACK: The Army Lists of the last forty years are here. These delightful records should have been my constant study. (*Rushes to bookcase and tears the books out.*) M. Generals . . . Mallam, Maxbohm, Magley — what ghastly names they have — Markby, Migsby, Mobbs, Moncrieff! Lieutenant 1840, Captain, Lieutenant-Colonel, Colonel, General 1869, Christian names, Ernest John. (*Puts book very quietly down and speaks quite calmly.*) I always told you, Gwendolen, my name was Ernest, didn't I? Well, it is Ernest after all. I mean it naturally is Ernest.

LADY BRACKNELL: Yes, I remember now that the General was called Ernest. I knew I had some particular reason for disliking the name.

GWENDOLEN: Ernest! My own Ernest! I felt from the first that you could have no other name!

JACK: Gwendolen, it is a terrible thing for a man to find out suddenly that all his life he has been speaking nothing but the truth. Can you forgive me?

GWENDOLEN: I can. For I feel that you are sure to change.

JACK: My own one!

CHASUBLE (*to* MISS PRISM): Laetitia! (*Embraces her.*)

MISS PRISM (*enthusiastically*): Frederick! At last!

ALGERNON: Cecily! (*Embraces her.*) At last!

JACK: Gwendolen! (*Embraces her.*) At last!

LADY BRACKNELL: My nephew, you seem to be displaying signs of triviality.

JACK: On the contrary, Aunt Augusta, I've now realized for the first time in my life the vital Importance of Being Earnest.

TABLEAU

CURTAIN

AFTERWORD

In considering Gilbert's *Trial by Jury*, we noted that its humor arises chiefly from taking an unfamiliar view of a familiar institution. The court of law, that traditional stronghold of equity and wisdom, is shown to be populated by fools and hypocrites; the judge is no less culpable than the defendant. One of Gilbert's favorite words to describe his own compositions, and one that many critics have applied to his work after him, was "topsey-turveydom" — turning things upside down. Dramatic theorists have argued that this word has a much wider application, as a fundamental of all comedy. We laugh when we are presented with a reversal of the norm, when the event runs contrary to expectation. The cinema has presented us with the most economical definition of this in the early work of Chaplin: The dignified man-about-town, wearing the top hat that is the ultimate symbol of social prestige, slips on a banana skin or falls into a swimming pool.

The Importance of Being Earnest clearly belongs to the same category. We see this most simply in the epigrams that are the staple of Wildean dialogue. Here, the author's usual trick is to take a quite ordinary statement and, at the last moment, substitute a totally unexpected word. It looks easy, until one tries to imitate it; very few writers have made a successful pastiche of Wilde. The same technique extends to other, larger aspects of the play. Wilde wrote for the same kind of audience that Gilbert knew: secure, complacent, basing its standards on certain established and apparently impregnable values, the most important of which was family tradition and pride of birth. Wilde accordingly has his hero trace his origin to that most mundane of objects, a handbag. In a period when women were, in theory, idolized but in practice usually treated as simpering idiots without minds or interests of their own, Wilde lets his women dominate the scene. Lady Bracknell is, of course, a dragon — it is interesting that, in an increasing number of modern revivals, the role has been played by a man — but Gwendolen is very much her mother's daughter. She virtually forces the proposal out of Jack in Act I, and it is her resolution that precipitates the crisis in Act II. Nor does Cecily lag far behind. Notice how the loquacious Algernon is struck speechless in her presence, and how, in spite of having been raised in rural seclusion, she is a worthy antagonist for the urban sophistication of Gwendolen. Individual scenes and incidents reveal the same kind of basic comic reversal. Mourning, which in Victorian times was a highly serious and ceremonial business, and even for us is no occasion for levity, becomes comic when Worthing appears in full regalia for the death of his mythical brother. Humor resides not in the subject matter, but in the point of view. At the end of the same act the tea party, that most demure of entertainments, becomes a battle royal, with sugar and cake as weapons.

To this extent, then, Gilbert and Wilde share certain comic convictions and techniques. But here the resemblance ends. In Trial by Jury we noted that Gilbert's humor was anarchic — an amiable anarchy, certainly, tempered by fantasy and music, but still fundamentally destructive. Although this aspect of Gilbert's writing was passed over by his contemporary audience, it is still a major component of his work and must be reckoned with. Wilde's play, though it may seem to be similarly anarchic in its subversion of traditional values, is in fact nothing of the kind. At the end, the pillars of Victorian respectability remain unshaken. The issue of Jack Worthing's birth, the fundamental question of the play, is solved with the utmost propriety: He is shown not merely to descend from respectable parents but to be related to Lady Bracknell, and what could be more respectable than that? The couples are neatly paired off. There are no repercussions, no questions left to ask.

The Importance of Being Earnest thus exists within its own self-contained world, which is in itself a mirror of the small self-contained world of upper

Victorian society; and though it seems to begin by questioning the values of that world, it ends by accepting them absolutely. There are no problems of the kind that beset more humble lives. Everyone is wealthy. No one has to struggle to earn a living, and the energies are left free to deal with romantic complications. Servants exist as convenient machinery on the periphery of the main action. It always seems to be summer afternoon. Politics are scarcely mentioned, save as the occasion for a mild joke whose point is that politics are pointless. The vast mass of the rest of society is presumed not to exist; the play stands outside of history, social or otherwise. It makes no kind of sense, for instance, to tell ourselves that Jack and Gwendolen's son will fight in the First World War. That belongs to a different world. Wilde's play leaves its audience amused, untouched and comfortable. How unlike the intellectual savagery of Molière, or the provocative, socially oriented contrariness of Shaw! Our century, which delights in exposing the hypocrisy of Victorian society and revealing the dark moral substratum of the time, may affect to take a more sinister view of Jack Worthing's double life. There are certainly tantalizing analogies with Victorian pornography: Bunbury, the *alter ego*, and the ward concealed in the country. We must remember, too, that Wilde himself led such a double life, frequenting the fashionable salons on one hand, the more sordid homosexual brothels on the other. But if any such considerations are implicit in the play — and this one must beg leave to doubt — they are not allowed to ruffle the serenity of its surface. Laughter is not disturbed by serious thought.

But is the play any the worse for that? If we do not treasure it for its sociological content, it has other pronounced virtues. Pure entertainment is one of the purposes of theater: not the only one, not the most important one, but certainly an honorable one. From time to time, audiences have gone to the playhouse simply to see themselves mirrored in a flattering way, to be reassured, to see the premises of the society which they accept, and to which they belong, shown in bright colors, with the virtues exaggerated and the failings only gently ridiculed. Conspicuous examples are a great deal of the comedy of Restoration England; most of the drama of nineteenth-century France, which provided an agreeable escape from the vexations of contemporary politics; and, in our century, the plays of Noel Coward, which, like Wilde's, exist in a moral and social vacuum. Wilde wrote to entertain the audience he knew, and with which, until his downfall, his own social life mingled. Nor was he the only one. It is no accident that, at his time, many leading figures of the stage prided themselves on being "gentlemanly actors," comporting themselves like minor members of the aristocracy and displaying appropriate manners and address both on stage and off. The Victorian lady would see the elegance of her gowns reproduced on the stage. The society host and hostess claimed wit and elegance in conversation; when they went to see Wilde's plays they would see people like themselves being very witty and elegant indeed. Wilde even panders to his audience so far as to introduce little in-jokes; they were intelligible only to the socially initiated, but we do not need to be cryptographers to understand the plays.

The substance of Wilde's plays is froth, social trivia touched by high art. When he tried to write seriously, he was often ludicrous. But the fact remains that, though Wilde's society has vanished, the plays survive. More than that, *The Importance of Being Earnest* has achieved that rare distinction of being a virtually guaranteed box office success. Why?

Surely the secret of its longevity lies in its construction. Though Wilde liked to pose as a dilettante, a natural genius, he was in fact (like most such people) a hard and careful worker, and one who never wasted good material — some of his favorite epigrams appear in play after play. Although *The Importance of Being Earnest* was written during illness and a period of some mental turmoil, it shows the same meticulous craftsmanship as the rest of his comedies. Originally conceived as a four-act play, the manuscript of which still survives, it was pared down to three before production. Wilde was careful to excise anything that, however witty in itself, was dramatically superfluous. The results are apparent in the final version. Not a word needs to be added, and the director cuts at his peril. This became obvious when the play was filmed. The adapters thought that, in deference to the new medium, a small amount of additional dialogue was necessary. But the interpolations stood out, not merely as inferior, but as redundant; Wilde had already said it all.

Critics assign *The Importance of Being Earnest* to the genre known as the *pièce bien faite*, the well-made play. This term is often used, rather unfairly, in a derogatory sense — *Oedipus the King*, for example, is a very well made play. In its precise critical significance, however, it implies a work constructed according to a well-tried and predictable formula: A situation is developed, complications ensue that build to a climax, and then, finally, all is resolved. In the hands of inferior dramatists the formula often appears obvious and contrived. Wilde's art is to conceal art. Each step in the plot development is carefully prepared for; each follows logically, given the nature of the characters, from what has preceded; and the resolution, though as artificial as anything that has ever appeared on the stage, carries the necessary conviction and surprise because Wilde has carefully planted it in the mouth of a character previously established as only a minor figure. Once again we see the comic effect of reversal; who would have expected the governess, prim, submissive, ultrarespectable, to have carried such a secret from her past, or to bring about the denouement so explosively?

Although the term "well-made play" is customarily associated with the escapist, art-for-amusement's-sake theater of the nineteenth century, its origins can be traced back far earlier — as far back as the fourth century B.C., when the comic playwrights, successors to the tragic playwrights of the great age, also wrote smart comedies drawn from the immediate social environment. Apart from the formulaic nature of the plot, there are certain other common characteristics of the genre that merit attention. One is the way in which character is subordinated to incident. In *The Importance of Being Earnest* characters are well and sharply defined, and interestingly differentiated. Jack/Ernest, for all his double life, is a somewhat ponderous character, taking his pleasures, like a true Englishman, heavily and seriously. Algernon, by contrast, is a butterfly, a glib and polished talker, never (until he meets Cecily) at a loss for words, who seems to take nothing seriously. The two girls, though equally matched in feminine wiles, consistently reveal the differences in their backgrounds. But these characters hardly influence or modify one another. Nobody *changes* as a result of the action; they are simply rearranged. Lady Bracknell, in spite of the shocks she has received, will obviously be just as formidable a mother-in-law as she was a mother. The motivating force is not character but incident, and usually incident that is the result of blind chance. We might compare the characters to balls on a pool table. Each has its distinctive color; one cannot be mistaken for another. Then some external, arbitrary force sets them in motion. They collide, bounce, reverberate, shoot off at angles, arrange themselves in various combinations; but they do not grow bigger or smaller, melt into one another or take a new shape. The dramatic interest lies in the various patterns that can be established using certain givens, and the impetus comes from outside, from the force of external circumstance, rather than from inside, the nature of the characters themselves.

Secondly, one may notice the reliance of the well-made play on physical objects to further the plot, again at the expense of character. In performance, the propmaster is one of the most important members of the company. Often, a whole scene revolves around some small material item, and a misplaced prop can spell disaster for the actor and the play. Perhaps this insistence reflects the reliance of a materialistic age on *things*, solid objects, which can be seen and handled in their three-dimensional reality. Certainly *The Importance of Being Earnest* relies on them. Note the cigarette case, with its revealing inscription, which forces Jack into an admission of the existence of his ward. Note how Algernon's intentions at the end of Act I are signaled by his thumbing through the railway timetable. And note, above all, how Jack's identity is ultimately established, not so much by Miss Prism's confession, as by the physical existence of the famous handbag. Compare this with another classic recognition scene, the revelation of the true identity of Oedipus in *Oedipus the King*. It is true that a physical token, the reference to Oedipus's pierced feet, triggers a recognition in Jocasta. But Oedipus's self-knowledge comes to him from things quite different: from his own conscience, from the growing awareness of his past, from the gradual breaking down of the barriers he has unconsciously built around his own identity. *Oedipus the King* can be played on a bare stage without props, costumes, or scenery and still make perfect dramatic sense. If we take away the props from Wilde's play, much of the action is reduced to incomprehensibility.

In summary, then, *The Importance of Being Earnest* is a perfect example of the kind of play we watch or read, not for its content, but for the skill of its execution. It is the measure of the dramatist's skill that he makes us believe in his people, and the ridiculous things that are happening to them, for as long as the action lasts. Perhaps Algernon Moncrieff delivers the most appropriate description of the work, in his remark to Jack Worthing: It is perfectly expressed, and as true as anything needs to be.

Anton Chekhov

THE CHERRY ORCHARD

Translated by Stark Young

FOREWORD

Chekhov's plays have come to be inseparably linked with a particular theater and its production style: the Moscow Art Theater, founded by Constantin Stanislavsky and Vladimir Nemerovich-Danchenko in 1898. In a way this association is unfair and unfortunate: Chekhov had many differences with Stanislavsky about how his plays should be presented, and the perpetuation of the Art Theater "style" has tended to restrict the possibility of other interpretations. Nevertheless, it was Stanislavsky who first brought Chekhov to serious public attention with his production of *The Sea-Gull*, the title of which also gave the theater its emblem, still embroidered on the front curtain. The Moscow Art Theater still flourishes, and in recent years has been seen far outside Russia; its Chekhov productions, despite the author's original doubts, are still accepted by many as definitive.

In an earlier section we referred to the emergence of the director in the modern theater. Stanislavsky was a leading figure in this movement. He insisted on total control, and considered no detail to be too trivial if it contributed to the finished production. Although he experimented in various directions, and encouraged such experimentation in others, he was fundamentally a realist, and brought to Chekhov's plays, as to others, a concern for a totally authentic environment in which the actors could identify themselves completely with the lives of the characters they portrayed. His production notes for Shakespeare's *Othello* show the care he lavished on reproducing the sounds and textures of Venice, including gondolas apparently floating down scenic canals. They also show how he asked the actors to start earlier than the beginning of the play and construct former "lives" for their characters that would explain and motivate their behavior in the drama itself. In the same way, his Chekhov productions showed the realistic theater at its best. He was once asked why he bothered to paint a portion of the setting that the audience could not see. "My actors can see it," he replied, "and it worries them." All the externals had to be right. The setting had to say something not merely about its time and place but about the people who lived there, just as a real room contains the reverberations of its inhabitants. For the actor, he insisted on meticulous study of the script until every nuance was explored. It might be months before the actor was allowed to lay his script aside. Actors were urged to employ "emotional recall," and find things in their own experience that could illuminate their character's behavior. This was acting from the inside out: a grasp of the character's psychology followed by its outward expression in logically conceived patterns of speech and action.

Stanislavsky's method, often canonized as "the Method," has been vastly influential, though often misunderstood or misinterpreted — people still argue over what Stanislavsky actually taught. It has become the foundation of much modern acting training, and in the United States, through Lee Strasberg and the Actors' Studio, has produced a number of distinguished actors.

CHARACTERS

RANEVSKAYA, LYUBOFF ANDREEVNA, a landowner
ANYA, her daughter, seventeen years old
VARYA, her adopted daughter, twenty-four years old
GAYEFF, LEONID ANDREEVICH, brother of Ranevskaya
LOPAHIN, YERMOLAY ALEXEEVICH, a merchant
TROFIMOFF, PYOTR SERGEEVICH, a student
SEMYONOFF-PISHTCHIK, BORIS BORISOVICH, a landowner

CHARLOTTA IVANOVNA, a governess
EPIHODOFF, SEMYON PANTELEEVICH, a clerk
DUNYASHA, a maid
FIERS, a valet, an old man of eighty-seven
YASHA, a young valet
A PASSERBY or STRANGER
THE STATIONMASTER
A POST-OFFICE CLERK
VISITORS, SERVANTS

Scene: The action takes place on the estate of L. A. Ranevskaya.

ACT I

A room that is still called the nursery. One of the doors leads into Anya's room. Dawn, the sun will soon be rising. It is May, the cherry trees are in blossom but in the orchard it is cold, with a morning frost. The windows in the room are closed. Enter Dunyasha with a candle and Lopahin with a book in his hand.

LOPAHIN: The train got in, thank God! What time is it?

DUNYASHA: It's nearly two. (*Blows out her candle.*) It's already daylight.

LOPAHIN: But how late was the train? Two hours at least. (*Yawning and stretching.*) I'm a fine one, I am, look what a fool thing I did! I drove here on purpose just to meet them at the station, and then all of a sudden I'd overslept myself! Fell asleep in my chair. How provoking! — You could have waked me up.

DUNYASHA: I thought you had gone. (*Listening.*) Listen, I think they are coming now.

LOPAHIN (*listening*): No — No, there's the luggage and one thing and another. (*A pause.*) Lyuboff Andreevna has been living abroad five years. I don't know what she is like now — She is a good woman. An easy-going, simple woman. I remember when I was a boy about fifteen, my father, who is at rest — in those days he ran a shop here in the village — hit me in the face with his fist, my nose was bleeding — We'd come to the yard together for something or other, and he was a little drunk. Lyuboff Andreevna, I can see her now, still so young, so slim, led me to the washbasin here in this very room, in the nursery. "Don't cry," she says, "little peasant, it will be well in time for your wedding" — (*A pause.*) Yes, little peasant — My father was a peasant truly, and here I am in a white waistcoat and yellow shoes. Like a pig rooting in a pastry shop — I've got this rich, lots of money, but if you really stop and think of it. I'm just a peasant — (*Turning the pages of a book.*) Here I was reading a book and didn't get a thing out of it. Reading and went to sleep. (*A pause.*)

DUNYASHA: And all night long the dogs were not asleep, they know their masters are coming.

LOPAHIN: What is it, Dunyasha, you're so —

DUNYASHA: My hands are shaking. I'm going to faint.

LOPAHIN: You're just so delicate, Dunyasha. And all dressed up like a lady, and your hair all done up! Mustn't do that. Must know your place.

(*Enter* EPIHODOFF, *with a bouquet: he wears a jacket and highly polished boots with a loud squeak. As he enters he drops the bouquet.*)

EPIHODOFF (*picking up the bouquet*): Look, the gardener sent these, he says to put them in the dining room. (*Giving the bouquet to* DUNYASHA.)

LOPAHIN: And bring me some kvass.

DUNYASHA: Yes, sir. (*Goes out.*)

EPIHODOFF: There is a morning frost now, three degrees of frost (*sighing*) and the cherries all in bloom. I cannot approve of our climate — I cannot. Our climate can never quite rise to the occasion. Listen, Yermolay Alexeevich, allow me to subtend, I bought myself, day before yesterday, some boots and they, I venture to assure you, squeak so that it is impossible. What could I grease them with?

LOPAHIN: Go on. You annoy me.

EPIHODOFF: Every day some misfortune happens to me. But I don't complain, I am used to it and I even smile.

(DUNYASHA *enters, serves* LOPAHIN *the kvass.*)

EPIHODOFF: I'm going. (*Stumbling over a chair and upsetting it.*) There (*as if triumphant*), there, you see, pardon the expression, a circumstance like that, among others — It is simply quite remarkable. (*Goes out.*)

DUNYASHA: And I must tell you, Yermolay Alexeevich, that Epihodoff has proposed to me.

LOPAHIN: Ah!

DUNYASHA: I don't know really what to — He is a quiet man but sometimes when he starts talking, you can't understand a thing he means. It's all very nice, and full of feeling, but just doesn't make any sense. I sort of like him. He loves me madly. He's a man that's unfortunate, every day there's something or other. They tease him around here, call him twenty-two misfortunes —

LOPAHIN (*cocking his ear*): Listen, I think they are coming —

DUNYASHA: They are coming! But what's the matter with me — I'm cold all over.

LOPAHIN: They're really coming. Let's go meet them. Will she recognize me? It's five years we haven't seen each other.

DUNYASHA (*excitedly*): I'm going to faint this very minute. Ah, I'm going to faint!

(*Two carriages can be heard driving up to the house.* LOPAHIN *and* DUNYASHA *hurry out. The stage is empty. In the adjoining rooms a noise begins.* FIERS *hurries across the stage, leaning on a stick; he has been to meet* LYUBOFF AN-DREEVNA, *and wears an old-fashioned livery and a high hat; he mutters something to himself, but you cannot understand a word of it. The noise offstage gets louder and louder. A voice: "Look! Let's go through here —"* LYUBOFF ANDREEVNA, ANYA *and* CHARLOTTA IVANOVNA, *with a little dog on a chain, all of them dressed for traveling,* VARYA, *in a coat and kerchief,* GAYEFF, SEMYON-OFF-PISHTCHIK, LOPAHIN, DUNYASHA, *with a bundle and an umbrella,* SERVANTS *with pieces of luggage — all pass through the room.*)

ANYA: Let's go through here. Mama, do you remember what room this is?

LYUBOFF ANDREEVNA (*happily, through her tears*): The nursery!

VARYA: How cold it is, my hands are stiff. (*To* LYUBOFF ANDREEVNA.) Your rooms, the white one and the violet, are just the same as ever, Mama.

LYUBOFF ANDREEVNA: The nursery, my dear beautiful room — I slept here when I was little — (*Crying.*) And now I am like a child — (*Kisses her brother and* VARYA, *then her brother again.*) And Varya is just the same as ever, looks like a nun. And I knew Dunyasha — (*Kisses* DUNYASHA.)

GAYEFF: The train was two hours late. How's that? How's that for good management?

CHARLOTTA (*to* PISHTCHIK): My dog he eats nuts too.

PISHTCHIK (*astonished*): Think of that!

(*Everybody goes out except* ANYA *and* DUNYASHA.)

DUNYASHA: We waited so long — (*Taking off* ANYA'S *coat and hat.*)

ANYA: I didn't sleep all four nights on the way. And now I feel so chilly.

DUNYASHA: It was Lent when you left, there was some snow then, there was frost, and now? My darling (*laughing and kissing her*), I waited so long for you, my joy, my life — I'm telling you now, I can't keep from it another minute.

ANYA (*wearily*): There we go again —

DUNYASHA: The clerk Epihodoff proposed to me after Holy Week.

ANYA: You're always talking about the same thing — (*Arranging her hair.*) I've lost all my hairpins — (*She is tired to the point of staggering.*)

DUNYASHA: I just don't know what to think. He loves me, loves me so!

ANYA (*looks in through her door, tenderly*): My room, my windows, it's just as if I had never been away. I'm home! Tomorrow morning I'll get up, I'll run into the orchard — Oh, if I only could go to sleep! I haven't slept all the way, I was tormented by anxiety.

DUNYASHA: Day before yesterday, Pyotr Sergeevich arrived.

ANYA (*joyfully*): Petya!

DUNYASHA: He's asleep in the bathhouse, he lives there. I am afraid, he says, of being in the way. (*Taking her watch from her pocket and looking at it.*) Somebody ought to wake him up. It's only that Varvara Mikhailovna told us not to. Don't you wake him up, she said.

VARYA (*enters with a bunch of keys at her belt*): Dunyasha, coffee, quick — Mama is asking for coffee.

DUNYASHA: This minute. (*Goes out.*)

VARYA: Well, thank goodness, you've come back. You are home again. (*Caressingly.*) My darling is back! My precious is back!

ANYA: I've had such a time.

VARYA: I can imagine!

ANYA: I left during Holy Week, it was cold then. Charlotta talked all the way and did her tricks. Why did you fasten Charlotta on to me — ?

VARYA: But you couldn't have traveled alone, darling; not at seventeen!

ANYA: We arrived in Paris, it was cold there and snowing. I speak terrible French. Mama lived on the fifth floor; I went to see her; there were some French people in her room, ladies, an old priest with his prayer book, and the place was full of tobacco smoke — very dreary. Suddenly I began to feel sorry for Mama, so sorry, I drew her to me, held her close and couldn't let her go. Then Mama kept hugging me, crying — yes —

VARYA (*tearfully*): Don't — oh, don't —

ANYA: Her villa near Menton she had already sold, she had nothing left, nothing. And I didn't have a kopeck left. It was all we could do to get here. And Mama doesn't understand! We sit down to dinner at a station and she orders, insists on the most expensive things and gives the waiters rouble tips. Charlotta does the same. Yasha too demands his share; it's simply dreadful. Mama has her butler, Yasha, we've brought him here —

VARYA: I saw the wretch.

ANYA: Well, how are things? Has the interest on the mortgage been paid?

VARYA: How could we?

ANYA: Oh, my God, my God — !

VARYA: In August the estate is to be sold —

ANYA: My God — !

LOPAHIN (*looking in through the door and mooing like a cow*): Moo-o-o — (*Goes away.*)

VARYA (*tearfully*): I'd land him one like that — (*Shaking her fist.*)

ANYA (*embracing* VARYA *gently*): Varya, has he proposed? (VARYA *shakes her head.*) But he loves you — Why don't you have it out with him, what are you waiting for?

VARYA: I don't think anything will come of it for us. He is very busy, he hasn't any
time for me — And doesn't notice me. God knows, it's painful for me to see him
— Everybody talks about our marriage, everybody congratulates us, and the truth
is, there's nothing to it — it's all like a dream — (*In a different tone.*) You have a
brooch looks like a bee.

ANYA (*sadly*): Mama bought it. (*Going toward her room, speaking gaily, like a child.*)
And in Paris I went up in a balloon!

VARYA: My darling is back! My precious is back! (DUNYASHA *has returned with the
coffee pot and is making coffee.* VARYA *is standing by the door.*) Darling, I'm busy
all day long with the house and I go around thinking things. If only you could be
married to a rich man, I'd be more at peace too, I would go all by myself to a
hermitage — then to Kiev — to Moscow, and I'd keep going like that from one
holy place to another — I would go on and on. Heavenly!

ANYA: The birds are singing in the orchard. What time is it now?

VARYA: It must be after two. It's time you were asleep, darling. (*Going into* ANYA's
room.) Heavenly!

YASHA (*enters with a lap robe and a traveling bag. Crossing the stage airily*): May I
go through here?

DUNYASHA: We'd hardly recognize you, Yasha; you've changed so abroad!

YASHA: Hm — And who are you?

DUNYASHA: When you left here, I was like that — (*Her hand so high from the floor.*)
I'm Dunyasha, Fyodor Kozoyedoff's daughter. You don't remember!

YASHA: Hm — You little peach! (*Looking around before he embraces her; she shrieks
and drops a saucer;* YASHA *hurries out.*)

VARYA (*at the door, in a vexed tone*): And what's going on here?

DUNYASHA (*tearfully*): I broke a saucer —

VARYA: That's good luck.

ANYA (*emerging from her room*): We ought to tell Mama beforehand. Petya is
here —

VARYA: I told them not to wake him up.

ANYA (*pensively*): Six years ago our father died, a month later our brother Grisha
was drowned in the river, such a pretty little boy, just seven. Mama couldn't bear
it, she went away, went away without ever looking back — (*Shuddering.*) How I
understand her, if she only knew I did. (*A pause.*) And Petya Trofimoff was
Grisha's tutor, he might remind —

FIERS (*enters in a jacket and white waistcoat. Going to the coffee urn, busy with it*):
The mistress will have her breakfast here — (*Putting on white gloves.*) Is the
coffee ready? (*To* DUNYASHA, *sternly.*) You! What about the cream?

DUNYASHA: Oh, my God — (*Hurrying out.*)

FIERS (*busy at the coffee urn*): Oh, you good-for-nothing — ! (*Muttering to himself.*)
Come back from Paris — And the master used to go to Paris by coach —
(*Laughing.*)

VARYA: Fiers, what are you — ?

FIERS: At your service. (*Joyfully.*) My mistress is back! It's what I've been waiting
for! Now I'm ready to die — (*Crying for joy.*)

(LYUBOFF ANDREEVNA, GAYEFF *and* SEMYONOFF-PISHTCHIK *enter;* SEMYONOFF-
PISHTCHIK *is in a sleeveless coat of fine cloth and wide trousers tucked into his
boots.* GAYEFF *enters; he makes gestures with his hands and body as if he were
playing billiards.*)

LYUBOFF ANDREEVNA: How is it? Let me remember — Yellow into the corner! Duplicate in the middle!

GAYEFF: I cut into the corner. Sister, you and I slept here in this very room once, and now I am fifty-one years old, strange as that may seem —

LOPAHIN: Yes, time passes.

GAYEFF: What?

LOPAHIN: Time, I say, passes.

GAYEFF: And it smells like patchouli here.

ANYA: I'm going to bed. Good night, Mama. (*Kissing her mother.*)

LYUBOFF ANDREEVNA: My sweet little child. (*Kissing her hands.*) You're glad you are home? I still can't get myself together.

ANYA: Good-by, Uncle.

GAYEFF (*kissing her face and hands*): God be with you. How like your mother you are! (*To his sister.*) Lyuba, at her age you were exactly like her.

(ANYA *shakes hands with* LOPAHIN *and* PISHTCHIK, *goes out and closes the door behind her.*)

LYUBOFF ANDREEVNA: She's very tired.

PISHTCHIK: It is a long trip, I imagine.

VARYA (*to* LOPAHIN *and* PISHTCHIK): Well, then, sirs? It's going on three o'clock, time for gentlemen to be going.

LYUBOFF ANDREEVNA (*laughing*): The same old Varya. (*Drawing her to her and kissing her.*) There, I'll drink my coffee, then we'll all go. (FIERS *puts a small cushion under her feet.*) Thank you, my dear. I am used to coffee. Drink it day and night. Thank you, my dear old soul. (*Kissing* FIERS.)

VARYA: I'll go see if all the things have come. (*Goes out.*)

LYUBOFF ANDREEVNA: Is it really me sitting here? (*Laughing.*) I'd like to jump around and wave my arms. (*Covering her face with her hands.*) But I may be dreaming! God knows I love my country, love it deeply, I couldn't look out of the car window, I just kept crying. (*Tearfully.*) However, I must drink my coffee. Thank you, Fiers, thank you, my dear old friend. I'm so glad you're still alive.

FIERS: Day before yesterday.

GAYEFF: He doesn't hear well.

LOPAHIN: And I must leave right now. It's nearly five o'clock in the morning, for Kharkov. What a nuisance! I wanted to look at you — talk — You are as beautiful as ever.

PISHTCHIK (*breathing heavily*): Even more beautiful — In your Paris clothes — It's a feast for the eyes —

LOPAHIN: Your brother, Leonid Andreevich here, says I'm a boor, a peasant money grubber, but that's all the same to me, absolutely. Let him say it. All I wish is you'd trust me as you used to, and your wonderful, touching eyes would look at me as they did. Merciful God! My father was a serf; belonged to your grandfather and your father; but you, your own self, you did so much for me once that I've forgotten all that and love you like my own kin — more than my kin.

LYUBOFF ANDREEVNA: I can't sit still — I can't. (*Jumping up and walking about in great excitement.*) I'll never live through this happiness — Laugh at me, I'm silly — My own little bookcase — ! (*Kissing the bookcase.*) My little table!

GAYEFF: And in your absence the nurse here died.

LYUBOFF ANDREEVNA (*sitting down and drinking coffee*): Yes, may she rest in Heaven! They wrote me.

GAYEFF: And Anastasy died. Cross-eyed Petrushka left me and lives in town now at the police officer's. (*Taking out of his pocket a box of hard candy and sucking a piece.*)

PISHTCHIK: My daughter, Dashenka — sends you her greetings —

LOPAHIN: I want to tell you something very pleasant, cheerful. (*Glancing at his watch.*) I'm going right away. There's no time for talking. Well, I'll make it two or three words. As you know, your cherry orchard is to be sold for your debts; the auction is set for August twenty-second, but don't you worry, my dear, you just sleep in peace, there's a way out of it. Here's my plan. Please listen to me. Your estate is only thirteen miles from town. They've run the railroad by it. Now if the cherry orchard and the land along the river were cut up into building lots and leased for summer cottages, you'd have at the very lowest twenty-five thousand roubles per year income.

GAYEFF: Excuse me, what rot!

LYUBOFF ANDREEVNA: I don't quite understand you, Yermolay Alexeevich.

LOPAHIN: At the very least you will get from the summer residents twenty-five roubles per year for a two-and-a-half acre lot, and if you post a notice right off, I'll bet you anything that by autumn you won't have a single patch of land free, everything will be taken. In a word, my congratulations, you are saved. The location is wonderful, the river's so deep. Except, of course, it all needs to be tidied up, cleared — For instance, let's say, tear all the old buildings down and this house, which is no good any more, and cut down the old cherry orchard —

LYUBOFF ANDREEVNA: Cut down? My dear, forgive me, you don't understand at all. If there's one thing in the whole province that's interesting — not to say remarkable — it's our cherry orchard.

LOPAHIN: The only remarkable thing about this cherry orchard is that it's very big. There's a crop of cherries once every two years and even that's hard to get rid of. Nobody buys them.

GAYEFF: This orchard is even mentioned in the encyclopedia.

LOPAHIN (*glancing at his watch*): If we don't cook up something and don't get somewhere, the cherry orchard and the entire estate will be sold at auction on the twenty-second of August. Do get it settled then! I swear there is no other way out. Not a one!

FIERS: There was a time, forty-fifty years ago when the cherries were dried, soaked, pickled, cooked into jam and it used to be —

GAYEFF: Keep quiet, Fiers.

FIERS: And it used to be that the dried cherries were shipped by the wagon-load to Moscow and to Kharkov. And the money there was! And the dried cherries were soft then, juicy, sweet, fragrant — They had a way of treating them then —

LYUBOFF ANDREEVNA: And where is that way now?

FIERS: They have forgotten it. Nobody remembers it.

PISHTCHIK (*to* LYUBOFF ANDREEVNA): What's happening in Paris? How is everything? Did you eat frogs?

LYUBOFF ANDREEVNA: I ate crocodiles.

PISHTCHIK: Think of it — !

LOPAHIN: Up to now in the country there have been only the gentry and the peasants, but now in summer the villa people too are coming in. All the towns, even the least big ones, are surrounded with cottages. In about twenty years very likely the summer resident will multiply enormously. He merely drinks tea on the porch now, but it might well happen that on this two-and-a-half acre lot of his, he'll go in for farming, and then your cherry orchard would be happy, rich, splendid —

GAYEFF (*getting hot*): What rot!

(*Enter* VARYA *and* YASHA.)

VARYA: Here, Mama. Two telegrams for you. (*Choosing a key and opening the old bookcase noisily.*) Here they are.

LYUBOFF ANDREEVNA: From Paris. (*Tearing up the telegrams without reading them.*) Paris, that's all over —

GAYEFF: Do you know how old this bookcase is, Lyuba? A week ago I pulled out the bottom drawer and looked, and there the figures were burned on it. The bookcase was made exactly a hundred years ago. How's that? Eh? You might celebrate its jubilee. It's an inanimate object, but all the same, be that as it may, it's a bookcase.

PISHTCHIK (*in astonishment*): A hundred years — ! Think of it — !

GAYEFF: Yes — quite something — (*Shaking the bookcase.*) Dear, honored bookcase! I salute your existence, which for more than a hundred years has been directed toward the clear ideals of goodness and justice; your silent appeal to fruitful endeavor has not flagged in all the course of a hundred years, sustaining (*tearfully*) through the generations of our family our courage and our faith in a better future and nurturing in us ideals of goodness and of a social consciousness.

(*A pause.*)

LOPAHIN: Yes.

LYUBOFF ANDREEVNA: You're the same as ever, Lenya.

GAYEFF (*slightly embarrassed*): Carom to the right into the corner pocket. I cut into the side pocket!

LOPAHIN (*glancing at his watch*): Well, it's time for me to go.

YASHA (*handing medicine to* LYUBOFF ANDREEVNA): Perhaps you'll take the pills now —

PISHTCHIK: You should never take medicaments, dear madam — They do neither harm nor good — Hand them here, dearest lady. (*He takes the pillbox, shakes the pills out into his palm, blows on them, puts them in his mouth and washes them down with kvass.*) There! Now!

LYUBOFF ANDREEVNA (*startled*): Why, you've lost your mind!

PISHTCHIK: I took all the pills.

LOPAHIN: Such a glutton!

(*Everyone laughs.*)

FIERS: The gentleman stayed with us during Holy Week, he ate half a bucket of pickles — (*Muttering.*)

LYUBOFF ANDREEVNA: What is he muttering about?

VARYA: He's been muttering like that for three years. We're used to it.

YASHA: In his dotage.

(CHARLOTTA IVANOVNA *in a white dress — she is very thin, her corset laced very tight — with a lorgnette at her belt, crosses the stage.*)

LOPAHIN: Excuse me, Charlotta Ivanovna, I haven't had a chance yet to welcome you. (*Trying to kiss her hand.*)

CHARLOTTA (*drawing her hand away*): If I let you kiss my hand, 'twould be my elbow next, then my shoulder —

LOPAHIN: No luck for me today. (*Everyone laughs.*) Charlotta Ivanovna, show us a trick!

CHARLOTTA: No. I want to go to bed. (*Exit.*)

LOPAHIN: In three weeks we shall see each other. (*Kissing* LYUBOFF ANDREEVNA's *hand.*) Till then, good-by. It's time. (*To* GAYEFF.) See you soon. (*Kissing* PISHTCHIK.) See you soon. (*Shaking* VARYA's *hand, then* FIERS' AND YASHA's.) I don't feel like going. (*To* LYUBOFF ANDREEVNA.) If you think it over and make up your mind about the summer cottages, let me know and I'll arrange a loan of something like fifty thousand roubles. Think it over seriously.

VARYA (*angrily*): Do go on, anyhow, will you!

LOPAHIN: I'm going, I'm going — (*Exit.*)

GAYEFF: Boor. However, pardon — Varya is going to marry him; it's Varya's little fiancé.

VARYA: Don't talk too much, Uncle.

LYUBOFF ANDREEVNA: Well, Varya, I should be very glad. He's a good man.

PISHTCHIK: A man, one must say truthfully — A most worthy — And my Dashenka — says also that — she says all sorts of things — (*Snoring but immediately waking up.*) Nevertheless, dearest lady, oblige me — With a loan of two hundred and forty roubles — Tomorrow the interest on my mortgage has got to be paid —

VARYA (*startled*): There's not any money, none at all.

LYUBOFF ANDREEVNA: Really, I haven't got anything.

PISHTCHIK: I'll find it, somehow. (*Laughing.*) I never give up hope. There, I think to myself, all is lost, I am ruined and lo and behold — a railroad is put through my land and — they paid me. And then, just watch, something else will turn up — if not today, then tomorrow — Dashenka will win two hundred thousand — She has a ticket.

LYUBOFF ANDREEVNA: We've finished the coffee, now we can go to bed.

FIERS (*brushing* GAYEFF's *clothes, reprovingly*): You put on the wrong trousers again. What am I going to do with you!

VARYA (*softly*): Anya is asleep. (*Opening the window softly.*) Already the sun's rising — it's not cold. Look, Mama! What beautiful trees! My Lord, what air! The starlings are singing!

GAYEFF (*opening another window*): The orchard is all white. You haven't forgotten, Lyuba? That long lane there runs straight — as a strap stretched out. It glistens on moonlight nights. Do you remember? You haven't forgotten it?

LYUBOFF ANDREEVNA (*looking out of the window on to the orchard*): Oh, my childhood, my innocence! I slept in this nursery and looked out on the orchard from here, every morning happiness awoke with me, it was just as it is now, then, nothing has changed. (*Laughing with joy.*) All, all white! Oh, my orchard! After a dark, rainy autumn and cold winter, you are young again and full of happiness. The heavenly angels have not deserted you — If I only could lift the weight from my breast, from my shoulders, if I could only forget my past!

GAYEFF: Yes, and the orchard will be sold for debt, strange as that may seem.

LYUBOFF ANDREEVNA: Look, our dear mother is walking through the orchard — In a white dress! (*Laughing happily.*) It's she.

GAYEFF: Where?

VARYA: God be with you, Mama!

LYUBOFF ANDREEVNA: There's not anybody, it only seemed so. To the right, as you turn to the summerhouse, a little white tree is leaning there, looks like a woman — (*Enter* TROFIMOFF, *in a student's uniform, well worn, and glasses.*) What a wonderful orchard! The white masses of blossoms, the sky all blue.

TROFIMOFF: Lyuboff Andreevna! (*She looks around at him.*) I will just greet you and go immediately. (*Kissing her hand warmly.*) I was told to wait until morning, but I hadn't the patience —

(LYUBOFF ANDREEVNA *looks at him puzzled.*)

VARYA (*tearfully*): This is Petya Trofimoff —

TROFIMOFF: Petya Trofimoff, the former tutor of your Grisha — Have I really changed so?

(LYUBOFF ANDREEVNA *embraces him; and crying quietly.*)

GAYEFF (*embarrassed*): There, there, Lyuba.

VARYA (*crying*): I told you, Petya, to wait till tomorrow.

LYUBOFF ANDREEVNA: My Grisha — My boy — Grisha — Son —

VARYA: What can we do, Mama? It's God's will.

TROFIMOFF (*in a low voice, tearfully*): There, there —

LYUBOFF ANDREEVNA (*weeping softly*): My boy was lost, drowned — Why? Why, my friend? (*More quietly.*) Anya is asleep there, and I am talking so loud — Making so much noise — But why, Petya? Why have you lost your looks? Why do you look so much older?

TROFIMOFF: A peasant woman on the train called me a mangy-looking gentleman.

LYUBOFF ANDREEVNA: You were a mere boy then, a charming young student, and now your hair's not very thick any more and you wear glasses. Are you really a student still? (*Going to the door.*)

TROFIMOFF: Very likely I'll be a perennial student.

LYUBOFF ANDREEVNA (*kissing her brother, then* VARYA): Well, go to bed — You've grown older too, Leonid.

PISHTCHIK (*following her*): So that's it, we are going to bed now. Oh, my gout! I'm staying here — I'd like, Lyuboff Andreevna, my soul, tomorrow morning — Two hundred and forty roubles —

GAYEFF: He's still at it.

PISHTCHIK: Two hundred and forty roubles — To pay interest on the mortgage.

LYUBOFF ANDREEVNA: I haven't any money, my dove.

PISHTCHIK: I'll pay it back, my dear — It's a trifling sum —

LYUBOFF ANDREEVNA: Oh, very well, Leonid will give — You give it to him, Leonid.

GAYEFF: Oh, certainly, I'll give it to him. Hold out your pockets.

LYUBOFF ANDREEVNA: What can we do, give it, he needs it — He'll pay it back.

(LYUBOFF ANDREEVNA, TROFIMOFF, PISHTCHIK *and* FIERS *go out.* GAYEFF, VARYA *and* YASHA *remain.*)

GAYEFF: My sister hasn't yet lost her habit of throwing money away. (*To* YASHA.) Get away, my good fellow, you smell like hens.

YASHA (*with a grin*): And you are just the same as you used to be, Leonid Andre-evich.

GAYEFF: What? (*To* VARYA.) What did he say?

VARYA (*to* YASHA): Your mother has come from the village, she's been sitting in the servants' hall ever since yesterday, she wants to see you —

YASHA: The devil take her!

VARYA: Ach, shameless creature!

YASHA: A lot I need her! She might have come tomorrow. (*Goes out.*)

VARYA: Mama is just the same as she was, she hasn't changed at all. If she could, she'd give everything she has.

GAYEFF: Yes — If many remedies are prescribed for an illness, you may know the illness is incurable. I keep thinking, I rack my brains, I have many remedies, a great many, and that means, really, I haven't any at all. It would be fine to inherit a fortune from somebody, it would be fine to marry off our Anya to a very rich man, it would be fine to go to Yaroslavl and try our luck with our old aunt, the Countess. Auntie is very, very rich.

VARYA (*crying*): If God would only help us!

GAYEFF: Don't bawl! Auntie is very rich but she doesn't like us. To begin with, Sister married a lawyer, not a nobleman — (ANYA *appears at the door.*) Married not a nobleman and behaved herself, you could say, not very virtuously. She is good, kind, nice, I love her very much, but no matter how much you allow for the extenuating circumstances, you must admit she's a depraved woman. You feel it in her slightest movement.

VARYA (*whispering*): Anya is standing in the door there.

GAYEFF: What? (*A pause.*) It's amazing, something got in my right eye. I am begin-ning to see poorly. And on Thursday, when I was in the District Court —

(ANYA *enters.*)

VARYA: But why aren't you asleep, Anya?

ANYA: I don't feel like sleeping. I can't.

GAYEFF: My little girl — (*Kissing* ANYA's *face and hands.*) My child — (*Tearfully.*) You are not my niece, you are my angel, you are everything to me. Believe me, believe —

ANYA: I believe you, Uncle. Everybody loves you, respects you — But dear Uncle, you must keep quiet, just keep quiet — What were you saying, just now, about my mother, about your own sister? What did you say that for?

GAYEFF: Yes, yes — (*Putting her hand up over his face.*) Really, it's terrible! My God! Oh, God, save me! And today I made a speech to the bookcase — So silly! And it was only when I finished it that I could see it was silly.

VARYA: It's true, Uncle, you ought to keep quiet. Just keep quiet. That's all.

ANYA: If you kept quiet, you'd have more peace.

GAYEFF: I'll keep quiet. (*Kissing* ANYA's *and* VARYA's *hands.*) I'll keep quiet. Only this, it's about business. On Thursday I was in the District Court; well, a few of us gathered around and a conversation began about this and that, about lots of things; apparently it will be possible to arrange a loan on a promissory note to pay the bank the interest due.

VARYA: If the Lord would only help us!

GAYEFF: Tuesday I shall go and talk it over again. (*To* VARYA) Don't bawl! (*To* ANYA.) Your mother will talk to Lopahin; of course, he won't refuse her . . . And as soon as you rest up, you will go to Yaroslavl to your great-aunt, the Countess. There, that's how we will move from three directions, and the business is in the bag. We'll pay the interest. I am convinced of that — (*Putting a hard candy in his mouth.*) On my honor I'll swear, by anything you like, that the estate shall not be sold! (*Excitedly.*) By my happiness, I swear! Here's my hand, call me a worthless, dishonorable man, if I allow it to come up for auction! With all my soul I swear it!

ANYA (*a quieter mood returns to her; she is happy*): How good you are, Uncle, how clever! (*Embracing her uncle.*) I feel easy now! I feel easy! I'm happy!

FIERS (FIERS *enters, reproachfully*): Leonid Andreevich, have you no fear of God? When are you going to bed?

GAYEFF: Right away, right away. You may go, Fiers. For this once I'll undress myself. Well, children, beddy bye — More details tomorrow, and now, go to bed. (*Kissing* ANYA *and* VARYA.) I am a man of the eighties — It is a period that's not admired, but I can say, nevertheless, that I've suffered no little for my convictions in the course of my life. It is not for nothing that the peasant loves me. One must know the peasant! One must know from what —

ANYA: Again, Uncle!

VARYA: You, Uncle dear, keep quiet.

FIERS (*angrily*): Leonid Andreevich!

GAYEFF: I'm coming, I'm coming — Go to bed. A double bank into the side pocket! A clean shot — (*Goes out,* FIERS *hobbling after him.*)

ANYA: I feel easy now. I don't feel like going to Yaroslavl; I don't like Great-aunt, but still I feel easy. Thanks to Uncle. (*Sits down.*)

VARYA: I must get to sleep. I'm going. And there was unpleasantness here during your absence. In the old servants' quarters, as you know, live only the old servants: Yephemushka, Polya, Yevstignay, well, and Karp. They began to let every sort of creature spend the night with them — I didn't say anything. But then I hear they've spread the rumor that I'd given orders to feed them nothing but beans. Out of stinginess, you see — And all that from Yevstignay — Very well, I think to myself. If that's the way it is, I think to myself, then you just wait. I call in Yevstignay — (*Yawning.*) He comes — How is it, I say, that you, Yevstignay — You're such a fool — (*Glancing at* ANYA.) Anitchka! — (*A pause.*) Asleep! (*Takes* ANYA *by her arm.*) Let's go to bed — Come on! — (*Leading her.*) My little darling fell asleep! Come on — (*They go. Far away beyond the orchard a shepherd is playing on a pipe.* TROFIMOFF *walks across the stage and, seeing* VARYA *and* ANYA, *stops.*) Shh — She is asleep — asleep — Let's go, dear.

ANYA (*softly, half dreaming*): I'm so tired — All the bells! — Uncle — dear — And Mama and Uncle — Varya.

VARYA: Come on, my dear, come on. (*They go into* ANYA's *room.*)

TROFIMOFF (*tenderly*): My little sun! My spring!

ACT II

A field. An old chapel, long abandoned, with crooked walls, near it a well, big stones that apparently were once tombstones, and an old bench. A road to the estate of GAYEFF *can be seen. On one side poplars rise, casting their shadows; the cherry orchard begins there. In the distance a row of telegraph poles; and far,*

*far away, faintly traced on the horizon, is a large town, visible only in the
clearest weather. The sun will soon be down.* CHARLOTTA, YASHA *and* DUNYASHA
are sitting on the bench; EPIHODOFF *is standing near and playing the guitar;
everyone sits lost in thought.* CHARLOTTA *wears an old peak cap* (fourrage); *she
has taken a rifle from off her shoulders and is adjusting the buckle on the strap.*

CHARLOTTA (*pensively*): I have no proper passport, I don't know how old I am — it
always seems to me I'm very young. When I was a little girl, my father and
mother traveled from fair to fair and gave performances, very good ones. And I
did *salto mortale* and different tricks. And when Papa and Mama died, a German
lady took me to live with her and began teaching me. Good. I grew up. And
became a governess. But where I came from and who I am I don't know — Who
my parents were, perhaps they weren't even married — I don't know. (*Taking a
cucumber out of her pocket and beginning to eat it.*) I don't know a thing. (*A
pause.*) I'd like so much to talk but there's not anybody. I haven't anybody.

EPIHODOFF (*playing the guitar and singing*): "What care I for the noisy world, what
care I for friends and foes." — How pleasant it is to play the mandolin!

DUNYASHA: That's a guitar, not a mandolin. (*Looking into a little mirror and powdering her face.*)

EPIHODOFF: For a madman who is in love this is a mandolin — (*Singing.*) "If only
my heart were warm with the fire of requited love."

(YASHA *sings with him.*)

CHARLOTTA: How dreadfully these people sing — Phooey! Like jackals.

DUNYASHA (*to* YASHA): All the same, what happiness to have been abroad.

YASHA: Yes, of course. I cannot disagree with you. (*Yawning and then lighting a
cigar.*)

EPIHODOFF: That's easily understood. Abroad everything long since attained its
complete development.

YASHA: That's obvious.

EPIHODOFF: I am a cultured man. I read all kinds of remarkable books, but the
trouble is I cannot discover my own inclinations, whether to live or to shoot
myself, but nevertheless, I always carry a revolver on me. Here it is — (*Showing
a revolver.*)

CHARLOTTA: That's done. Now I am going. (*Slinging the rifle over her shoulder.*)
You are a very clever man, Epihodoff, and a very terrible one; the women must
love you madly. Brrrr-r-r-r! (*Going.*) These clever people are all so silly, I haven't
anybody to talk with. I'm always alone, alone, I have nobody and — Who I am,
why I am, is unknown — (*Goes out without hurrying.*)

EPIHODOFF: Strictly speaking, not touching on other subjects, I must state about
myself, in passing, that fate treats me mercilessly, as a storm does a small ship. If,
let us suppose, I am mistaken, then why, to mention one instance, do I wake up
this morning, look and there on my chest is a spider of terrific size — There, like
that. (*Showing the size with both hands.*) And also I take some kvass to drink and
in it I find something in the highest degree indecent, such as a cockroach. (*A
pause.*) Have you read Buckle? (*A pause.*) I desire to trouble you, Avdotya Feodorovna, with a couple of words.

DUNYASHA: Speak.

EPIHODOFF: I have a desire to speak with you alone — (*Sighing.*)

DUNYASHA (*embarrassed*): Very well — But bring me my cape first — by the cupboard — It's rather damp here —

EPIHODOFF: Very well — I'll fetch it — Now I know what I should do with my revolver — (*Takes the guitar and goes out playing.*)

YASHA: Twenty-two misfortunes! Between us he's a stupid man, it must be said. (*Yawning.*)

DUNYASHA: God forbid he should shoot himself. (*A pause.*) I've grown so uneasy, I'm always fretting. I was only a girl when I was taken into the master's house, and now I've lost the habit of simple living — and here are my hands white, white as a lady's. I've become so delicate, fragile, ladylike, afraid of everything — Frightfully so. And, Yasha, if you deceive me, I don't know what will happen to my nerves.

YASHA (*kissing her*): You little cucumber! Of course every girl must behave properly. What I dislike above everything is for a girl to conduct herself badly.

DUNYASHA: I have come to love you passionately, you are educated, you can discuss anything. (*A pause.*)

YASHA (*yawning*): Yes, sir — To my mind it is like this: If a girl loves someone, it means she is immoral. (*A pause.*) It is pleasant to smoke a cigar in the clear air — (*Listening.*) They are coming here — It is the ladies and gentlemen —

(DUNYASHA *impulsively embraces him.*)

YASHA: Go to the house, as though you had been to bathe in the river, go by this path; otherwise, they might meet you and suspect me of making a rendezvous with you. That I cannot tolerate.

DUNYASHA (*with a little cough*): Your cigar has given me the headache. (*Goes out.*)

(YASHA *remains, sitting near the chapel.* LYUBOFF ANDREEVNA, GAYEFF *and* LOPAHIN *enter.*)

LOPAHIN: We must decide definitely, time doesn't wait. Why, the matter's quite simple. Are you willing to lease your land for summer cottages or are you not? Answer in one word, yes or no? Just one word!

LYUBOFF ANDREEVNA: Who is it smokes those disgusting cigars out here — ? (*Sitting down.*)

GAYEFF: The railroad running so near is a great convenience. (*Sitting down.*) We made a trip to town and lunched there — Yellow in the side pocket! Perhaps I should go in the house first and play one game —

LYUBOFF ANDREEVNA: You'll have time.

LOPAHIN: Just one word! (*Imploringly.*) Do give me your answer!

GAYEFF (*yawning*): What?

LYUBOFF ANDREEVNA (*looking in her purse*): Yesterday there was lots of money in it. Today there's very little. My poor Varya! For the sake of economy she feeds everybody milk soup, and in the kitchen the old people get nothing but beans, and here I spend money — senselessly — (*Dropping her purse and scattering gold coins.*) There they go scattering! (*She is vexed.*)

YASHA: Allow me, I'll pick them up in a second. (*Picking up the coins.*)

LYUBOFF ANDREEVNA: If you will, Yasha. And why did I go in town for lunch — ? Your restaurant with its music is trashy, the tablecloths smell of soap — Why drink so much, Lyonya? Why eat so much? Why talk so much? Today in the restaurant you were talking a lot again, and all of it beside the point. About the seventies, about the decadents. And to whom? Talking to waiters about the decadents!

LOPAHIN: Yes.

GAYEFF (*waving his hand*): I am incorrigible, that's evident — (*To* YASHA, *irritably*.) What is it? — You are forever swirling around in front of us!

YASHA (*laughing*): I cannot hear your voice without laughing.

GAYEFF (*to his sister*): Either I or he —

LYUBOFF ANDREEVNA: Go away. Go on —

YASHA (*giving* LYUBOFF ANDREEVNA *her purse*): I am going right away. (*Barely suppressing his laughter.*) This minute. (*Goes out.*)

LOPAHIN: The rich Deriganoff intends to buy your estate. They say he is coming personally to the auction.

LYUBOFF ANDREEVNA: And where did you hear that?

LOPAHIN: In town they are saying it.

GAYEFF: Our Yaroslavl aunt promised to send us something, but when and how much she will send, nobody knows —

LOPAHIN: How much will she send? A hundred thousand? Two hundred?

LYUBOFF ANDREEVNA: Well — maybe ten, fifteen thousand — we'd be thankful for that.

LOPAHIN: Excuse me, but such light-minded people as you are, such odd, unbusinesslike people, I never saw. You are told in plain Russian that your estate is being sold up and you just don't seem to take it in.

LYUBOFF ANDREEVNA: But what are we to do? Tell us what?

LOPAHIN: I tell you every day. Every day I tell you the same thing. Both the cherry orchard and the land have got to be leased for summer cottages, it has to be done right now, quick — The auction is right under your noses. Do you understand! Once you finally decide that there are to be summer cottages, you will get all the money you want, and then you'll be saved.

LYUBOFF ANDREEVNA: Summer cottages and summer residents — it is so trivial, excuse me.

GAYEFF: I absolutely agree with you.

LOPAHIN: I'll either burst out crying, or scream, or faint. I can't bear it! You are torturing me! (*To* GAYEFF.) You're a perfect old woman!

GAYEFF: What?

LOPAHIN: A perfect old woman! (*About to go.*)

LYUBOFF ANDREEVNA (*alarmed*): No, don't go, stay, my lamb, I beg you. Perhaps we will think of something!

LOPAHIN: What is there to think about?

LYUBOFF ANDREEVNA: Don't go, I beg you. With you here it is more cheerful anyhow — (*A pause.*) I keep waiting for something, as if the house were about to tumble down on our heads.

GAYEFF (*deep in thought*): Double into the corner pocket — Bank into the side pocket —

LYUBOFF ANDREEVNA: We have sinned so much —

LOPAHIN: What sins have you — ?

GAYEFF (*puts a hard candy into his mouth*): They say I've eaten my fortune up in hard candies — (*Laughing.*)

LYUBOFF ANDREEVNA: Oh, my sins — I've always thrown money around like mad, recklessly, and I married a man who accumulated nothing but debts. My hus band died from champagne — he drank fearfully — and to my misfortune I fell in love with another man. I lived with him, and just at that time — it was my first punishment — a blow over the head: right here in the river my boy was drowned and I went abroad — went away for good, never to return, never to see this river again — I shut my eyes, ran away, beside myself, and he after me — mercilessly, brutally. I bought a villa near Menton, because he fell ill there, and for three years I knew no rest day or night, the sick man exhausted me, my soul dried up. And last year when the villa was sold for debts, I went to Paris and there he robbed me of everything, threw me over, took up with another woman; I tried to poison myself — so stupid, so shameful — And suddenly I was seized with long-ing for Russia, for my own country, for my little girl — (*Wiping away her tears.*) Lord, Lord, have mercy, forgive me my sins! Don't punish me any more! (*Get-ting a telegram out of her pocket.*) I got this today from Paris, he asks forgiveness, begs me to return — (*Tears up the telegram.*) That sounds like music somewhere. (*Listening.*)

GAYEFF: It is our famous Jewish orchestra. You remember, four violins, a flute and a double bass.

LYUBOFF ANDREEVNA: Does it still exist? We ought to get hold of it sometime and give a party.

LOPAHIN (*listening*): Can't hear it — (*Singing softly.*) "And for money the Germans will frenchify a Russian." (*Laughing.*) What a play I saw yesterday at the theatre, very funny!

LYUBOFF ANDREEVNA: And most likely there was nothing funny about it. You shouldn't look at plays, but look oftener at yourselves. How gray all your lives are, what a lot of idle things you say!

LOPAHIN: That's true. It must be said frankly this life of ours is idiotic — (*A pause.*) My father was a peasant, an idiot, he understood nothing, he taught me nothing, he just beat me in his drunken fits and always with a stick. At bottom I am just as big a dolt and idiot as he was. I wasn't taught anything, my handwriting is vile, I write like a pig — I am ashamed for people to see it.

LYUBOFF ANDREEVNA: You ought to get married, my friend.

LOPAHIN: Yes — That's true.

LYUBOFF ANDREEVNA: To our Varya, perhaps. She is a good girl.

LOPAHIN: Yes.

LYUBOFF ANDREEVNA: She comes from simple people, and she works all day long, but the main thing is she loves you. And you, too, have liked her a long time.

LOPAHIN: Why not? I am not against it — She's a good girl. (*A pause.*)

GAYEFF: They are offering me a position in a bank. Six thousand a year — Have you heard that?

LYUBOFF ANDREEVNA: Not you! You stay where you are —

FIERS (*enters, bringing an overcoat. To* GAYEFF): Pray, Sir, put this on, it's damp.

GAYEFF (*putting on the overcoat*): You're a pest, old man.

FIERS: That's all right — This morning you went off without letting me know. (*Looking him over.*)

LYUBOFF ANDREEVNA: How old you've grown, Fiers!

FIERS: At your service.

LOPAHIN: She says you've grown very old!

FIERS: I've lived a long time. They were planning to marry me off before your papa was born. (*Laughing.*) And at the time the serfs were freed I was already the head footman. I didn't want to be freed then, I stayed with the masters — (A *pause*.) And I remember, everybody was happy, but what they were happy about they didn't know themselves.

LOPAHIN: In the old days it was fine. At least they flogged.

FIERS (*not hearing*): But, of course, the peasants stuck to the masters, the masters stuck to the peasants, and now everything is all smashed up, you can't tell about anything.

GAYEFF: Keep still, Fiers. Tomorrow I must go to town. They have promised to introduce me to a certain general who might make us a loan.

LOPAHIN: Nothing will come of it. And you can rest assured you won't pay the interest.

LYUBOFF ANDREEVNA: He's just raving on. There aren't any such generals.

(TROFIMOFF, ANYA *and* VARYA *enter*.)

GAYEFF: Here they come.

ANYA: There is Mama sitting there.

LYUBOFF ANDREEVNA (*tenderly*): Come, come — My darlings — (*Embracing* ANYA *and* VARYA) If you only knew how I love you both! Come sit by me — there — like that.

(*Everybody sits down.*)

LOPAHIN: Our perennial student is always strolling with the young ladies.

TROFIMOFF: It's none of your business.

LOPAHIN: He will soon be fifty and he's still a student.

TROFIMOFF: Stop your stupid jokes.

LOPAHIN: But why are you so peevish, you queer duck?

TROFIMOFF: Don't you pester me.

LOPAHIN (*laughing*): Permit me to ask you, what do you make of me?

TROFIMOFF: Yermolay Alexeevich, I make this of you: you are a rich man, you'll soon be a millionaire. Just as it is in the metabolism of nature, a wild beast is needed to eat up everything that comes his way; so you, too, are needed.

(*Everyone laughs.*)

VARYA: Petya, you'd better tell us about the planets.

LYUBOFF ANDREEVNA: No, let's go on with yesterday's conversation.

TROFIMOFF: What was it about?

GAYEFF: About the proud man.

TROFIMOFF: We talked a long time yesterday, but didn't get anywhere. In a proud man, in your sense of the word, there is something mystical. Maybe you are right, from your standpoint, but if we are to discuss it in simple terms, without whimsy, then what pride can there be, is there any sense in it, if man physiologically is poorly constructed, if in the great majority he is crude, unintelligent, profoundly miserable. One must stop admiring oneself. One must only work.

GAYEFF: All the same, you will die.

TROFIMOFF: Who knows? And what does it mean — you will die? Man may have a hundred senses, and when he dies only the five that are known to us may perish, and the remaining ninety-five go on living.

LYUBOFF ANDREEVNA: How clever you are, Petya!

LOPAHIN (*ironically*): Terribly!

TROFIMOFF: Humanity goes forward, perfecting its powers. Everything that's unattainable now will some day become familiar, understandable; it is only that one must work and must help with all one's might those who seek the truth. With us in Russia so far only a very few work. The great majority of the intelligentsia that I know are looking for nothing, doing nothing, and as yet have no capacity for work. They call themselves intelligentsia, are free and easy with the servants, treat the peasants like animals, educate themselves poorly, read nothing seriously, do absolutely nothing; about science they just talk and about art they understand very little. Every one of them is serious, all have stern faces; they all talk of nothing but important things, philosophize, and all the time everybody can see that the workmen eat abominably, sleep without any pillows, thirty or forty to a room, and everywhere there are bedbugs, stench, dampness, moral uncleanness — And apparently with us, all the fine talk is only to divert the attention of ourselves and of others. Show me where we have the day nurseries they are always talking so much about, where are the reading rooms? They only write of these in novels, for the truth is there are not any at all. There is only filth, vulgarity, orientalism — I am afraid of very serious faces and dislike them. I'm afraid of serious conversations. Rather than that let's just keep still.

LOPAHIN: You know I get up before five o'clock in the morning and work from morning till night. Well, I always have money, my own and other people's, on hand, and I see what the people around me are. One has only to start doing something to find out how few honest and decent people there are. At times when I can't go to sleep, I think: Lord, thou gavest us immense forests, unbounded fields and the widest horizons, and living in the midst of them we should indeed be giants —

LYUBOFF ANDREEVNA: You feel the need for giants — They are good only in fairy tales, anywhere else they only frighten us.

(*At the back of the stage* EPIHODOFF *passes by, playing the guitar.*)

LYUBOFF ANDREEVNA (*lost in thought*): Epihodoff is coming —
ANYA (*lost in thought*): Epihodoff is coming.
GAYEFF: The sun has set, ladies and gentlemen.
TROFIMOFF: Yes.
GAYEFF (*not loud and as if he were declaiming*): Oh, Nature, wonderful, you gleam with eternal radiance, beautiful and indifferent, you, whom we call Mother, combine in yourself both life and death, you give life and you take it away.
VARYA (*beseechingly*): Uncle!
ANYA: Uncle, you're doing it again!
TROFIMOFF: You'd better bank the yellow into the sidepocket.
GAYEFF: I'll be quiet, quiet.

(*All sit absorbed in their thoughts. There is only the silence.* FIERS *is heard muttering to himself softly. Suddenly a distant sound is heard, as if from the sky, like the sound of a snapped string, dying away, mournful.*)

LYUBOFF ANDREEVNA: What's that?
LOPAHIN: I don't know. Somewhere far off in a mine shaft a bucket fell. But somewhere very far off.
GAYEFF: And it may be some bird — like a heron.
TROFIMOFF: Or an owl —

LYUBOFF ANDREEVNA (*shivering*): It's unpleasant, somehow. (*A pause.*)

FIERS: Before the disaster it was like that. The owl hooted and the samovar hummed without stopping, both.

GAYEFF: Before what disaster?

FIERS: Before the emancipation. (*A pause.*)

LYUBOFF ANDREEVNA: You know, my friends, let's go. Twilight is falling. (*To* ANYA.) You have tears in your eyes — What is it, my dear little girl? (*Embracing her.*)

ANYA: It's just that, Mama. It's nothing.

TROFIMOFF: Somebody is coming.

(A STRANGER *appears in a shabby white cap, and an overcoat; he is a little drunk.*)

THE STRANGER: Allow me to ask you, can I go straight through here to the station?

GAYEFF: You can. Go by that road.

THE STRANGER: I am heartily grateful to you. (*Coughing.*) The weather is splendid — (*Declaiming.*) Brother of mine, suffering brother — Go out to the Volga, whose moans — (*To* VARYA.) Mademoiselle, grant a hungry Russian man some thirty kopecks —

(VARYA *is frightened and gives a shriek.*)

LOPAHIN (*angrily*): There's a limit to everything.

LYUBOFF ANDREEVNA (*flustered*): Take this — Here's this for you — (*Searching in her purse.*) No silver — It's all the same, here's a gold piece for you —

THE STRANGER: I am heartily grateful to you. (*Goes out. Laughter.*)

VARYA (*frightened*): I'm going — I'm going — Oh, Mama, you poor little Mama! There's nothing in the house for people to eat, and you gave him a gold piece.

LYUBOFF ANDREEVNA: What is to be done with me, so silly? I shall give you all I have in the house. Yermolay Alexeevich, you will lend me some this once more! —

LOPAHIN: Agreed.

LYUBOFF ANDREEVNA: Let's go, ladies and gentlemen, it's time. And here, Varya, we have definitely made a match for you, I congratulate you.

VARYA (*through her tears*): Mama, that's not something to joke about.

LOPAHIN: Achmelia, get thee to a nunnery.

GAYEFF: And my hands are trembling; it is a long time since I have played billiards.

LOPAHIN: Achmelia, oh nymph, in thine orisons be all my sins remember'd —

LYUBOFF ANDREEVNA: Let's go, my friends, it will soon be suppertime.

VARYA: He frightened me. My heart is thumping so!

LOPAHIN: I remind you, ladies and gentlemen: August twenty-second the cherry orchard will be auctioned off. Think about that! — Think! —

(*All go out except* TROFIMOFF *and* ANYA.)

ANYA (*laughing*): My thanks to the stranger, he frightened Varya, now we are alone.

TROFIMOFF: Varya is afraid we might begin to love each other and all day long she won't leave us to ourselves. With her narrow mind she cannot understand that we are above love. To sidestep the petty and illusory, which prevent our being free and happy, that is the aim and meaning of our life. Forward! We march on irresistibly toward the bright star that burns there in the distance. Forward! Do not fall behind, friends!

ANYA (*extending her arms upwards*): How well you talk! (*A pause.*) It's wonderful here today!

TROFIMOFF: Yes, the weather is marvelous.

ANYA: What have you done to me, Petya, why don't I love the cherry orchard any longer the way I used to? I loved it so tenderly, it seemed to me there was not a better place on earth than our orchard.

TROFIMOFF: All Russia is our orchard. The earth is immense and beautiful, and on it are many wonderful places. (*A pause.*) Just think, Anya: your grandfather, great-grandfather and all your ancestors were slave owners, in possession of living souls, and can you doubt that from every cherry in the orchard, from every leaf, from every trunk, human beings are looking at you, can it be that you don't hear their voices? To possess living souls, well, that depraved all of you who lived before and who are living now, so that your mother and you and your uncle no longer notice that you live by debt, at somebody else's expense, at the expense of those very people whom you wouldn't let past your front door — We are at least two hundred years behind the times, we have as yet absolutely nothing, we have no definite attitude toward the past, we only philosophize, complain of our sadness or drink vodka. Why, it is quite clear that to begin to live in the present we must first atone for our past, must be done with it; and we can atone for it only through suffering, only through uncommon, incessant labor. Understand that, Anya.

ANYA: The house we live in ceased to be ours long ago, and I'll go away, I give you my word.

TROFIMOFF: If you have the household keys, throw them in the well and go away. Be free as the wind.

ANYA (*transported*): How well you said that!

TROFIMOFF: Believe me, Anya, believe me! I am not thirty yet, I am young, I am still a student, but I have already borne so much! Every winter I am hungry, sick, anxious, poor as a beggar, and — where has destiny not chased me, where haven't I been! And yet, my soul has always, every minute, day and night, been full of inexplicable premonitions. I have a premonition of happiness, Anya, I see it already —

ANYA (*pensively*): The moon is rising.

(EPIHODOFF *is heard playing on the guitar, always the same sad song. The moon rises. Somewhere near the poplars* VARYA *is looking for* ANYA *and calling:* "Anya! Where are you?")

TROFIMOFF: Yes, the moon is rising. (*A pause.*) Here is happiness, here it comes, comes always nearer and nearer, I hear its footsteps now. And if we shall not see it, shall not come to know it, what does that matter? Others will see it!

VARYA (*off*): Anya! Where are you?

TROFIMOFF: Again, that Varya! (*Angrily.*) It's scandalous!

ANYA: Well, let's go to the river. It's lovely there.

TROFIMOFF: Let's go. (*They go out.*)

VARYA (*off*): Anya! Anya!

ACT III

The drawing room, separated by an arch from the ballroom. A chandelier is lighted. A Jewish orchestra is playing — the same that was mentioned in Act II. Evening. In the ballroom they are dancing grand rond. The voice of SE-MYONOFF-PISHTCHIK: *"Promenade à une paire!" They enter the drawing room: in the first couple are* PISHTCHIK *and* CHARLOTTA IVANOVNA; *in the second,* TROFI-MOFF *and* LYUBOFF ANDREEVNA; *in the third,* ANYA *with the* POST-OFFICE CLERK; *in the fourth,* VARYA *with the* STATIONMASTER, *et cetera —* VARYA *is crying softly and wipes away her tears while she is dancing.* DUNYASHA *is in the last couple through the drawing room.* PISHTCHIK *shouts: "Grand rond, balancez!" and "Les Cavaliers à genoux et remerciez vos dames!"*

FIERS in a frock coat goes by with seltzer water on a tray. PISHTCHIK *and* TROFIMOFF *come into the drawing room.*

PISHTCHIK: I am full-blooded, I have had two strokes already, and dancing is hard for me, but as they say, if you are in a pack of dogs, you may bark and bark, but you must still wag your tail. At that, I have the health of a horse. My dear father — he was a great joker — may he dwell in Heaven — used to talk as if our ancient line, the Semyonoff-Pishtchiks, were descended from the very horse that Caligula made a Senator — (*Sitting down.*) But here's my trouble: I haven't any money. A hungry dog believes in nothing but meat — (*Snoring but waking at once.*) And the same way with me — I can't talk about anything but money.

TROFIMOFF: Well, to tell you the truth, there is something of a horse about your figure.

PISHTCHIK: Well — a horse is a fine animal — You can sell a horse —

(*The sound of playing billiards comes from the next room.* VARYA *appears under the arch to the ballroom.*)

TROFIMOFF (*teasing*): Madam Lopahin! Madam Lopahin!

VARYA (*angrily*): A mangy-looking gentleman!

TROFIMOFF: Yes, I am a mangy-looking gentleman, and proud of it!

VARYA (*in bitter thought*): Here we have gone and hired musicians and what are we going to pay them with? (*Goes out.*)

TROFIMOFF (*to* PISHTCHIK): If the energy you have wasted in the course of your life trying to find money to pay the interest had gone into something else, you could very likely have turned the world upside down before you were done with it.

PISHTCHIK: Nietzsche — the philosopher — the greatest — the most celebrated — a man of tremendous mind — says in his works that one may make counterfeit money.

TROFIMOFF: And have you read Nietzsche?

PISHTCHIK: Well — Dashenka told me. And I'm in such a state now that I could make counterfeit money myself — Day after tomorrow three hundred and ten roubles must be paid — one hundred and thirty I've on hand — (*Feeling in his pockets, alarmed.*) The money is gone! I have lost the money! (*Tearfully.*) Where is the money? (*Joyfully.*) Here it is, inside the lining — I was in quite a sweat —

(LYUBOFF ANDREEVNA *and* CHARLOTTA IVANOVNA *come in.*)

LYUBOFF ANDREEVNA (*humming the lazginka, a Georgian dance*): Why does Leonid take so long? What's he doing in town? (*To* DUNYASHA.) Dunyasha, offer the musicians some tea —

TROFIMOFF: In all probability the auction did not take place.

LYUBOFF ANDREEVNA: And the musicians came at an unfortunate moment and we planned the ball at an unfortunate moment — Well, it doesn't matter. (*Sitting down and singing softly.*)

CHARLOTTA (*gives* PISHTCHIK *a deck of cards*): Here is a deck of cards for you, think of some one card.

PISHTCHIK: I have thought of one.

CHARLOTTA: Now, shuffle the deck. Very good. Hand it here; oh, my dear Monsieur Pishtchik. *Eins, zwei, drei!* Now look for it, it's in your coat pocket —

PISHTCHIK (*getting a card out of his coat pocket*): The Eight of Spades, that's absolutely right! (*Amazed.*) Fancy that!

CHARLOTTA (*holding a deck of cards in her palm; to* TROFIMOFF): Tell me quick now, which card is on top?

TROFIMOFF: What is it? Well — the Queen of Spades.

CHARLOTTA: Right! (*To* PISHTCHIK.) Well? Which card's on top?

PISHTCHIK: The Ace of Hearts.

CHARLOTTA: Right! (*Strikes the deck against her palm; the deck of cards disappears.*) And what beautiful weather we are having today!

(*A mysterious feminine voice answers her, as if from under the floor: "Oh, yes. The weather is splendid, madame." "You are so nice, you're my ideal —" The voice: "Madame, you too please me greatly."*)

THE STATIONMASTER (*applauding*): Madam Ventriloquist, bravo!

PISHTCHIK (*amazed*): Fancy that! Most charming Charlotta Ivanovna — I am simply in love with you.

CHARLOTTA: In love? (*Shrugging her shoulders.*) Is it possible that you can love? *Guter mensch aber schlechter musikant.*[1]

TROFIMOFF (*slapping* PISHTCHIK *on the shoulder*): You horse, you —

CHARLOTTA: I beg your attention, one more trick. (*Taking a lap robe from the chair.*) Here is a very fine lap robe — I want to sell it — (*Shaking it out.*) Wouldn't somebody like to buy it?

PISHTCHIK (*amazed*): Fancy that!

CHARLOTTA: *Eins, zwei, drei!*

(*She quickly raises the lowered robe, behind it stands* ANYA, *who curtseys, runs to her mother, embraces her and runs back into the ballroom amid the general delight.*)

LYUBOFF ANDREEVNA (*applauding*): Bravo, bravo —!

CHARLOTTA: Now again! *Eins, zwei, drei!*

(*Lifting the robe: behind it stands* VARYA, *she bows.*)

PISHTCHIK (*amazed*): Fancy that!

CHARLOTTA: That's all. (*Throwing the robe at* PISHTCHIK, *curtseying and running into the ballroom.*)

---

[1] "Good man but wretched performer."

PISHTCHIK (*hurrying after her*): You little rascal — What a girl! What a girl! (*Goes out.*)

LYUBOFF ANDREEVNA: And Leonid is not here yet. What he's doing in town so long, I don't understand! Everything is finished there, either the estate is sold by now, or the auction didn't take place. Why keep it from us so long?

VARYA (*trying to comfort her*): Uncle has bought it, I am sure of that.

TROFIMOFF (*mockingly*): Yes.

VARYA: Great-aunt sent him power of attorney to buy it in her name and transfer the debt. She did this for Anya. And I feel certain, God willing, that Uncle will buy it.

LYUBOFF ANDREEVNA: Our Yaroslavl great-aunt has sent fifteen thousand to buy the estate in her name — She doesn't trust us, but that wouldn't be enough to pay the interest even — (*Covering her face with her hands.*) Today my fate will be decided, my fate —

TROFIMOFF (*teasing* VARYA): Madam Lopahin!

VARYA (*angrily*): Perennial student! You have already been expelled from the University twice.

LYUBOFF ANDREEVNA: But why are you angry, Varya? He teases you about Lopahin, what of it? Marry Lopahin if you want to, he is a good man, interesting. If you don't want to, don't marry him; darling, nobody is making you do it.

VARYA: I look at this matter seriously, Mama, one must speak straight out. He's a good man, I like him.

LYUBOFF ANDREEVNA: Then marry him. What there is to wait for I don't understand!

VARYA: But I can't propose to him myself, Mama. It's two years now; everyone has been talking to me about him, everyone talks, and he either remains silent or jokes. I understand. He's getting rich, he's busy with his own affairs, and has no time for me. If there were money, ever so little, even a hundred roubles, I would drop everything, and go far away. I'd go to a nunnery.

TROFIMOFF: How saintly!

VARYA (*to* TROFIMOFF): A student should be intelligent! (*In a low voice, tearfully.*) How homely you have grown, Petya, how old you've got. (*To* LYUBOFF ANDREEVNA, *no longer crying.*) It is just that I can't live without working, Mama. I must be doing something every minute.

YASHA (YASHA *enters. Barely restraining his laughter*): Epihodoff has broken a billiard cue! — (*Goes out.*)

VARYA: But why is Epihodoff here? Who allowed him to play billiards? I don't understand these people — (*Goes out.*)

LYUBOFF ANDREEVNA: Don't tease her, Petya; you can see she has troubles enough without that.

TROFIMOFF: She is just too zealous. Sticking her nose into things that are none of her business. All summer she gave us no peace, neither me nor Anya; she was afraid a romance would spring up between us. What business is that of hers? And besides I haven't shown any signs of it. I am so remote from triviality. We are above love!

LYUBOFF ANDREEVNA: Well, then, I must be beneath love. (*Very anxiously.*) Why isn't Leonid here? Just to tell us whether the estate is sold or not? Calamity seems to me so incredible that I don't know what to think, I'm lost — I could scream this minute — I could do something insane. Save me, Petya. Say something, do say. . . .

TROFIMOFF: Whether the estate is sold today or is not sold — is it not the same? There is no turning back, the path is all grown over. Calm yourself, my dear, all that was over long ago. One mustn't deceive oneself, one must for once at least in one's life look truth straight in the eye.

LYUBOFF ANDREEVNA: What truth? You see where the truth is and where the un- truth is, but as for me, it's as if I had lost my sight, I see nothing. You boldly decide all important questions, but tell me, my dear boy, isn't that because you are young and haven't had time yet to suffer through any one of your problems? You look boldly ahead, and isn't that because you don't see and don't expect anything terrible, since life is still hidden from your young eyes? You are braver, more honest, more profound than we are, but stop and think, be magnanimous, have a little mercy on me, just a little. Why, I was born here. My father and mother lived here and my grandfather. I love this house, I can't imagine my life without the cherry orchard and if it is very necessary to sell it, then sell me along with the orchard — (*Embracing* TROFIMOFF *and kissing him on the forehead.*) Why, my son was drowned here — (*Crying.*) Have mercy on me, good, kind man.

TROFIMOFF: You know I sympathize with you from the bottom of my heart.

LYUBOFF ANDREEVNA: But that should be said differently, differently — (*Taking out her handkerchief; a telegram falls on the floor.*) My heart is heavy today, you can't imagine how heavy. It is too noisy for me here, my soul trembles at every sound, I tremble all over and yet I can't go off to myself, when I am alone the silence frightens me. Don't blame me, Petya — I love you as one of my own. I should gladly have given you Anya's hand, I assure you, only, my dear, you must study and finish your course. You do nothing. Fate simply flings you about from place to place, and that's so strange — Isn't that so? Yes? And you must do something about your beard, to make it grow somehow — (*Laughing.*) You look funny!

TROFIMOFF (*picking up the telegram*): I do not desire to be beautiful.

LYUBOFF ANDREEVNA: This telegram is from Paris. I get one every day. Yesterday and today too. That wild man has fallen ill again, something is wrong again with him — He asks forgiveness, begs me to come, and really I ought to make a trip to Paris and stay awhile near him. Your face looks stern, Petya, but what is there to do, my dear, what am I to do, he is ill, he is alone, unhappy and who will look after him there, who will keep him from doing the wrong thing, who will give him his medicine on time? And what is there to hide or keep still about? I love him, that's plain. I love him, love him — It's a stone about my neck, I'm sinking to the bottom with it, but I love that stone and live without it I cannot. (*Pressing* TROFIMOFF's *hand.*) Don't think harshly of me, Petya, don't say anything to me, don't —

TROFIMOFF (*tearfully*): Forgive my frankness, for God's sake! Why, he picked your bones.

LYUBOFF ANDREEVNA: No, no, no, you must not talk like that. (*Stopping her ears.*)

TROFIMOFF: But he is a scoundrel, only you, you are the only one that doesn't know it. He is a petty scoundrel, a nonentity —

LYUBOFF ANDREEVNA (*angry but controlling herself*): You are twenty-six years old or twenty-seven, but you are still a schoolboy in the second grade!

TROFIMOFF: Very well!

LYUBOFF ANDREEVNA: You should be a man — at your age you should understand people who love. And you yourself should love someone — you should fall in love! (*Angrily.*) Yes, yes! And there is no purity in you; you are simply smug, a ridiculous crank, a freak —

TROFIMOFF (*horrified*): What is she saying!

LYUBOFF ANDREEVNA: "I am above love!" You are not above love, Petya, you are, as our Fiers would say, just a good-for-nothing. Imagine, at your age, not having a mistress — !

TROFIMOFF (*horrified*): This is terrible! What is she saying! (*Goes quickly into the ballroom, clutching his head.*) This is horrible — I can't bear it, I am going — (*Goes out but immediately returns.*) All is over between us. (*Goes out into the hall.*)

LYUBOFF ANDREEVNA (*shouting after him*): Petya, wait! You funny creature, I was joking! Petya! (*In the hall you hear someone running up the stairs and suddenly falling back down with a crash. You hear* ANYA *and* VARYA *scream but immediately you hear laughter.*) What's that?

ANYA (ANYA *runs in. Laughing*): Petya fell down the stairs! (*Runs out.*)

LYUBOFF ANDREEVNA: What a funny boy that Petya is — ! (THE STATIONMASTER *stops in the center of the ballroom and begins to recite "The Sinner" by A. Tolstoi. They listen to him but he has recited only a few lines when the strains of a waltz are heard from the hall and the recitation is broken off. They all dance.* TROFI-MOFF, ANYA, VARYA *and* LYUBOFF ANDREEVNA *come in from the hall.*) But, Petya — but, dear soul — I beg your forgiveness — Let's go dance. (*She dances with* TROFIMOFF. ANYA *and* VARYA *dance.* FIERS *enters, leaving his stick by the side door.* YASHA *also comes into the drawing room and watches the dancers.*)

YASHA: What is it, Grandpa?

FIERS: I don't feel very well. In the old days there were generals, barons, admirals dancing at our parties, and now we send for the post-office clerk and the station-master, and even they are none too anxious to come. Somehow I've grown feeble. The old master, the grandfather, treated everybody with sealing-wax for all sicknesses. I take sealing-wax every day, have done so for twenty-odd years or more; it may be due to that that I'm alive.

YASHA: You are tiresome, Grandpa. (*Yawning.*) Why don't you go off and die?

FIERS: Aw, you — good-for-nothing! — (*Muttering.*)

(TROFIMOFF AND LYUBOFF ANDREEVNA *dance in the ballroom and then in the drawing room.*)

LYUBOFF ANDREEVNA: Merci. I'll sit down awhile — (*Sitting down.*) I'm tired.

ANYA (ANYA *enters. Agitated*): And just now in the kitchen some man was saying that the cherry orchard had been sold today.

LYUBOFF ANDREEVNA: Sold to whom?

ANYA: He didn't say who to. He's gone.

(*Dancing with* TROFIMOFF, *they pass into the ballroom.*)

YASHA: It was some old man babbling there. A stranger.

FIERS: And Leonid Andreevich is still not here, he has not arrived. The overcoat he has on is light, midseason — let's hope he won't catch cold. Ach, these young things!

LYUBOFF ANDREEVNA: I shall die this minute. Go, Yasha, find out who it was sold to.

YASHA: But he's been gone a long time, the old fellow. (*Laughing.*)

LYUBOFF ANDREEVNA (*with some annoyance*): Well, what are you laughing at? What are you so amused at?

YASHA: Epihodoff is just too funny. An empty-headed man. Twenty-two misfortunes!

LYUBOFF ANDREEVNA: Fiers, if the estate is sold, where will you go?

FIERS: Wherever you say, there I'll go.

LYUBOFF ANDREEVNA: Why do you look like that? Aren't you well? You know you ought to go to bed —

FIERS: Yes — (*With a sneer.*) I go to bed and without me who's going to serve, who'll take care of things? I'm the only one in the whole house.

YASHA (*to* LYUBOFF ANDREEVNA): Lyuboff Andreevna, let me ask a favor of you, do be so kind! If you ever go back to Paris, take me with you, please do! It's impossible for me to stay here. (*Looking around him, and speaking in a low voice.*) Why talk about it? You can see for yourself it's an uncivilized country, an immoral people and not only that, there's the boredom of it. The food they give us in that kitchen is abominable and there's that Fiers, too, walking about and muttering all kinds of words that are out of place. Take me with you, be so kind!

PISHTCHIK (*enters*): Allow me to ask you — for a little waltz, most beautiful lady — (LYUBOFF ANDREEVNA *goes with him.*) Charming lady, I must borrow a hundred and eighty roubles from you — will borrow — (*dancing*) a hundred and eighty roubles — (*They pass into the ballroom.*)

YASHA (*singing low*): "Wilt thou know the unrest in my soul!"

(*In the ballroom a figure in a gray top hat and checked trousers waves both hands and jumps about; there are shouts of "Bravo, Charlotta Ivanovna!"*)

DUNYASHA (*stopping to powder her face*): The young lady orders me to dance — there are a lot of gentlemen and very few ladies — but dancing makes my head swim and my heart thump. Fiers Nikolaevich, the post-office clerk said something to me just now that took my breath away.

(*The music plays more softly.*)

FIERS: What did he say to you?

DUNYASHA: You are like a flower, he says.

YASHA (*yawning*): What ignorance — ! (*Goes out.*)

DUNYASHA: Like a flower — I am such a sensitive girl, I love tender words awfully.

FIERS: You'll be getting your head turned.

(EPIHODOFF *enters.*)

EPIHODOFF: Avdotya Feodorovna, you don't want to see me — It's as if I were some sort of insect. (*Sighing.*) Ach, life!

DUNYASHA: What do you want?

EPIHODOFF: Undoubtedly you may be right. (*Sighing.*) But of course, if one considers it from a given point of view, then you, I will allow myself so to express it, forgive my frankness, absolutely led me into a state of mind. I know my fate, every day some misfortune happens to me, but I have long since become accustomed to that, and so I look on my misfortunes with a smile. You gave me your word and, although I —

DUNYASHA: I beg you, we'll talk later on, but leave me now in peace. I'm in a dream now. (*Playing with her fan.*)

EPIHODOFF: I have a something wrong happens every day — I will allow myself so to express it — I just smile, I even laugh.

VARYA (*enters from the ballroom*): You are not gone yet, Semyon? What a really disrespectful man you are! (*To* DUNYASHA.) Get out of here, Dunyasha. (*To* EPIHODOFF.) You either play billiards and break a cue or you walk about the drawing room like a guest.

EPIHODOFF: Allow me to tell you, you cannot make any demands on me.

VARYA: I'm not making any demands on you, I'm talking to you. All you know is to walk from place to place but not do any work. We keep a clerk, but what for, nobody knows.

EPIHODOFF (*offended*): Whether I work, whether I walk, whether I eat, or whether I play billiards are matters to be discussed only by people of understanding and my seniors.

VARYA: You dare to say that to me! (*Flying into a temper.*) You dare? So I don't understand anything? Get out of here! This minute!

EPIHODOFF (*alarmed*): I beg you to express yourself in a delicate manner.

VARYA (*beside herself*): This very minute, get out of here! Get out! (*He goes to the door; she follows him.*) Twenty-two misfortunes! Don't you dare breathe in here! Don't let me set eyes on you! (EPIHODOFF *has gone out, but his voice comes from outside the door:* "*I shall complain about you.*") Ah, you are coming back? (*Grabbing the stick that* FIERS *put by the door.*) Come on, come — come on, I'll show you — Ah, you are coming? You are coming? Take that then — !

(*She swings the stick, at the very moment when* LOPAHIN *is coming in.*)

LOPAHIN: Most humbly, I thank you.

VARYA (*angrily and ironically*): I beg your pardon!

LOPAHIN: It's nothing at all. I humbly thank you for the pleasant treat.

VARYA: It isn't worth your thanks. (*Moving away, then looking back and asking gently.*) I haven't hurt you?

LOPAHIN: No, it's nothing. There's a great bump coming, though.

(*Voices in the ballroom:* "*Lopahin has come back.*" "*Yermolay Alexeevich!*")

PISHTCHIK (*enters*): See what we see, hear what we hear — ! (*He and* LOPAHIN *kiss one another.*) You smell slightly of cognac, my dear, my good old chap. And we are amusing ourselves here too.

LYUBOFF ANDREEVNA (*enters*): Is that you, Yermolay Alexeevich? Why were you so long? Where is Leonid?

LOPAHIN: Leonid Andreevich got back when I did; he's coming.

LYUBOFF ANDREEVNA (*agitated*): Well, what? Was there an auction? Do speak!

LOPAHIN (*embarrassed, afraid of showing the joy he feels*): The auction was over by four o'clock — We were late for the train, had to wait till half-past nine. (*Sighing heavily.*) Ugh, my head's swimming a bit!

(GAYEFF *enters; with his right hand he carries his purchases, with his left he wipes away his tears.*)

LYUBOFF ANDREEVNA: Lyona, what? Lyona, eh? (*Impatiently, with tears in her eyes.*) Quick, for God's sake —

GAYEFF (*not answering her, merely waving his hand; to* FIERS, *crying*): Here, take it

— There are anchovies, some Kertch herrings — I haven't eaten anything all day — What I have suffered! (*The door into the billiard room is open; you hear the balls clicking and* YASHA's *voice: "Seven and eighteen!"* GAYEFF's *expression changes, he is no longer crying.*) I'm terribly tired. You help me change, Fiers. (*Goes to his room through the ballroom*, FIERS *behind him.*)

PISHTCHIK: What happened at the auction? Go on, tell us!

LYUBOFF ANDREEVNA: Is the cherry orchard sold?

LOPAHIN: It's sold.

LYUBOFF ANDREEVNA: Who bought it?

LOPAHIN: I bought it. (*A pause.* LYUBOFF ANDREEVNA *is overcome. She would have fallen had she not been standing near the chair and table.* VARYA *takes the keys from her belt, throws them on the floor in the middle of the drawing room and goes out.*) I bought it. Kindly wait a moment, ladies and gentlemen, everything is muddled up in my head, I can't speak — (*Laughing.*) We arrived at the auction, Deriganoff was already there. Leonid Andreevich had only fifteen thousand and Deriganoff right off bids thirty over and above indebtedness. I see how things are, I match him with forty thousand. He forty-five. I fifty-five. That is to say he raises it by fives, I by tens — So it ended. Over and above the indebtedness, I bid up to ninety thousand, it was knocked down to me. The cherry orchard is mine now. Mine! (*Guffawing.*) My God, Lord, the cherry orchard is mine! Tell me I'm drunk, out of my head, that I'm imagining all this — (*Stamps his feet.*) Don't laugh at me! If only my father and grandfather could rise from their graves and see this whole business, see how their Yermolay, beaten, half-illiterate Yermolay, who used to run around barefoot in winter, how that very Yermolay has bought an estate that nothing in the world can beat. I bought the estate where grandfather and father were slaves, where you wouldn't even let me in the kitchen. I am asleep, it's only some dream of mine, it only seems so to me — That's nothing but the fruit of your imagination, covered with the darkness of the unknown — (*Picking up the keys, with a gentle smile.*) She threw down the keys, wants to show she is not mistress any more — (*Jingling the keys.*) Well, it's all the same. (*The orchestra is heard tuning up.*) Hey, musicians, play, I want to hear you! Come on, everybody, and see how Yermolay Lopahin will swing the ax in the cherry orchard, how the trees will fall to the ground! We are going to build villas and our grandsons and great-grandsons will see a new life here — Music, play! (*The music is playing.* LYUBOFF ANDREEVNA *has sunk into a chair, crying bitterly.* LOPAHIN *reproachfully:*) Why, then, didn't you listen to me? My poor dear, it can't be undone now. (*With tears.*) Oh, if this could all be over soon, if somehow our awkward, unhappy life would be changed!

PISHTCHIK (*taking him by the arm, in a low voice*): She is crying. Come on in the ballroom, let her be by herself — Come on — (*Taking him by the arm and leading him into the ballroom.*)

LOPAHIN: What's the matter? Music, there, play up! (*Sarcastically.*) Everything is to be as I want it! Here comes the new squire, the owner of the cherry orchard. (*Quite accidentally, he bumps into the little table, and very nearly upsets the candelabra.*) I can pay for everything!

(*Goes out with* PISHTCHIK. *There is nobody left either in the ballroom or the drawing room but* LYUBOFF ANDREEVNA, *who sits all huddled up and crying bitterly. The music plays softly.* ANYA *and* TROFIMOFF *enter hurriedly.* ANYA *comes up to her mother and kneels in front of her.* TROFIMOFF *remains at the ballroom door.*)

ANYA: Mama — ! Mama, you are crying? My dear, kind, good Mama, my beautiful, I love you — I bless you. The cherry orchard is sold, it's not ours any more, that's true, true; but don't cry, Mama, you've your life still left you, you've your good, pure heart ahead of you — Come with me, come on, darling, away from here, come on — We will plant a new orchard, finer than this one, you'll see it, you'll understand; and joy, quiet, deep joy will sink into your heart, like the sun at evening, and you'll smile, Mama! Come, darling, come on!

ACT IV

The same setting as in Act I. There are neither curtains on the windows nor are there any pictures on the walls. Only a little furniture remains piled up in one corner as if for sale. A sense of emptiness is felt. Near the outer door, at the rear of the stage, is a pile of suitcases, traveling bags, and so on. The door on the left is open, and through it VARYA's *and* ANYA's *voices are heard.* LOPAHIN *is standing waiting.* YASHA *is holding a tray with glasses of champagne. In the hall* EPIHODOFF *is tying up a box, offstage at the rear there is a hum. It is the peasants who have come to say good-by.* GAYEFF's *voice: "Thanks, brothers, thank you."*

YASHA: The simple folk have come to say good-by. I am of the opinion, Yermolay Alexeevich, that the people are kind enough but don't understand anything.

(*The hum subsides.* LYUBOFF ANDREEVNA *enters through the hall with* GAYEFF; *she is not crying, but is pale, her face quivers, she is not able to speak.*)

GAYEFF: You gave them your purse, Lyuba. Mustn't do that! Mustn't do that!

LYUBOFF ANDREEVNA: I couldn't help it! I couldn't help it!

(*Both go out.*)

LOPAHIN (*calling through the door after them*): Please, I humbly beg you! A little glass at parting. I didn't think to bring some from town, and at the station I found just one bottle. Please! (*A pause.*) Well, then, ladies and gentlemen! You don't want it? (*Moving away from the door.*) If I'd known that, I wouldn't have bought it. Well, then I won't drink any either. (YASHA *carefully sets the tray down on a chair.*) At least, you have some, Yasha.

YASHA: To those who are departing! Pleasant days to those who stay behind! (*Drinking.*) This champagne is not the real stuff, I can assure you.

LOPAHIN: Eight roubles a bottle. (*A pause.*) It's devilish cold in here.

YASHA: They didn't heat up today; we are leaving anyway. (*Laughing.*)

LOPAHIN: What are you laughing about?

YASHA: For joy.

LOPAHIN: Outside it's October, but it's sunny and still, like summer. Good for building. (*Looking at his watch, then through the door.*) Ladies and gentlemen, bear in mind we have forty-six minutes in all till train time! Which means you have to go to the station in twenty minutes. Hurry up a little.

TROFIMOFF (*in an overcoat, entering from outside*): Seems to me it is time to go. The carriages are ready. The devil knows where my rubbers are. They've disappeared. (*In the door.*) Anya, my rubbers are not here! I can't find them.

LOPAHIN: And I have to go to Harkoff. I'm going on the same train with you. I'm going to live in Harkoff all winter. I've been dilly-dallying along with you, I'm tired of doing nothing. I can't be without work; look, I don't know what to do with my hands here, see, they are dangling somehow, as if they didn't belong to me.

TROFIMOFF: We are leaving right away, and you'll set about your useful labors again.

LOPAHIN: Here, drink a glass.

TROFIMOFF: I shan't.

LOPAHIN: It's to Moscow now?

TROFIMOFF: Yes. I'll see them off to town, and tomorrow to Moscow.

LOPAHIN: Yes — Maybe the professors are not giving their lectures. I imagine they are waiting till you arrive.

TROFIMOFF: That's none of your business.

LOPAHIN: How many years is it you've been studying at the University?

TROFIMOFF: Think of something newer. This is old and flat. (*Looking for his rubbers.*) You know, perhaps, we shall not see each other again; therefore, permit me to give you one piece of advice at parting! Don't wave your arms! Cure yourself of that habit — of arm waving. And also of building summer cottages, figuring that the summer residents will in time become individual landowners; figuring like that is arm waving too — Just the same, however, I like you. You have delicate soft fingers like an artist, you have a delicate soft heart —

LOPAHIN (*embracing him*): Good-by, my dear boy. Thanks for everything. If you need it, take some money from me for the trip.

TROFIMOFF: Why should I? There's no need for it.

LOPAHIN: But you haven't any!

TROFIMOFF: I have. Thank you. I got some for a translation. Here it is in my pocket. (*Anxiously.*) But my rubbers are gone.

VARYA (*from another room*): Take your nasty things! (*Throws a pair of rubbers on to the stage.*)

TROFIMOFF: But what are you angry about, Varya? Hm — Why, these are not my rubbers.

LOPAHIN: In the spring I planted twenty-seven hundred acres of poppies and now I've made forty thousand clear. And when my poppies were in bloom, what a picture it was! So look, as I say, I've made forty thousand, which means I'm offering you a loan because I can afford to. Why turn up your nose? I'm a peasant — I speak straight out.

TROFIMOFF: Your father was a peasant, mine — an apothecary — and from that absolutely nothing follows. (LOPAHIN *takes out his wallet.*) Leave it alone, leave it alone — If you gave me two hundred thousand even, I wouldn't take it. I am a free man. And everything that you all value so highly and dearly, both rich men and beggars, has not the slightest power over me, it's like a mere feather floating in the air. I can get along without you, I can pass you by, I am strong and proud. Humanity is moving toward the loftiest truth, toward the loftiest happiness that is possible on earth and I am in the front ranks.

LOPAHIN: Will you get there?

TROFIMOFF: I'll get there. (*A pause.*) I'll get there, or I'll show the others the way to get there.

(*In the distance is heard the sound of an ax on a tree.*)

LOPAHIN: Well, good-by, my dear boy. It's time to go. We turn up our noses at one another, but life keeps on passing. When I work a long time without stopping, my thoughts are clearer, and it seems as if I, too, know what I exist for, and, brother, how many people are there in Russia who exist, nobody knows for what? Well, all the same, it's not that that keeps things circulating. Leonid Andreevich, they say, has accepted a position — he'll be in a bank, six thousand a year — the only thing is he won't stay there, he's very lazy —

ANYA (*in the doorway*): Mama begs of you until she's gone, not to cut down the orchard.

TROFIMOFF: Honestly, haven't you enough tact to — (*Goes out through the hall.*)

LOPAHIN: Right away, right away — What people, really! (*Goes out after him.*)

ANYA: Has Fiers been sent to the hospital?

YASHA: I told them to this morning. They must have sent him.

ANYA (*to* EPIHODOFF, *who is passing through the room*): Semyon Panteleevich, please inquire whether or not they have taken Fiers to the hospital.

YASHA (*huffily*): This morning, I told Igor. Why ask ten times over!

EPIHODOFF: The venerable Fiers, according to my conclusive opinion, is not worth mending, he ought to join his forefathers. And I can only envy him. (*Putting a suitcase on a hatbox and crushing it.*) Well, there you are, of course. I knew it. (*Goes out.*)

YASHA (*mockingly*): Twenty-two misfortunes —

VARYA (*on the other side of the door*): Have they taken Fiers to the hospital?

ANYA: They have.

VARYA: Then why didn't they take the letter to the doctor?

ANYA: We must send it on after them — (*Goes out.*)

VARYA (*from the next room*): Where is Yasha? Tell him his mother has come, she wants to say good-by to him.

YASHA (*waving his hand*): They merely try my patience.

(DUNYASHA *has been busying herself with the luggage; now when* YASHA *is left alone, she goes up to him.*)

DUNYASHA: If you'd only look at me once, Yasha. You are going away — leaving me — (*Crying and throwing herself on his neck.*)

YASHA: Why are you crying? (*Drinking champagne.*) In six days I'll be in Paris again. Tomorrow we will board the express train and dash off out of sight; somehow, I can't believe it. *Vive la France!* It doesn't suit me here — I can't live here — Can't help that. I've seen enough ignorance — enough for me. (*Drinking champagne.*) Why do you cry? Behave yourself properly, then you won't be crying.

DUNYASHA (*powdering her face, looking into a small mirror*): Send me a letter from Paris. I loved you, Yasha, you know, loved you so! I am a tender creature, Yasha!

YASHA: They are coming here. (*Bustling about near the suitcases, humming low.*)

(LYUBOFF ANDREEVNA, GAYEFF, ANYA *and* CHARLOTTA IVANOVNA *enter.*)

GAYEFF: We should be going. There is very little time left. (*Looking at* YASHA.) Who is it smells like herring!

LYUBOFF ANDREEVNA: In about ten minutes let's be in the carriage — (*Glancing around the room.*) Good-by, dear house, old Grandfather. Winter will pass, spring will be here, but you won't be here any longer, they'll tear you down. How much these walls have seen! (*Kissing her daughter warmly.*) My treasure, you are beaming, your eyes are dancing like two diamonds. Are you happy? Very?

ANYA: Very! It's the beginning of a new life, Mama!

GAYEFF (*gaily*): Yes, indeed, everything is fine now. Before the sale of the cherry orchard, we all were troubled, distressed, and then when the question was settled definitely, irrevocably, we all calmed down and were even cheerful — I'm a bank official. I am a financier now — Yellow ball into the side pocket; anyway, Lyuba, you look better, no doubt about that.

LYUBOFF ANDREEVNA: Yes. My nerves are better, that's true. (*They hand her her hat and coat.*) I sleep well. Carry out my things, Yasha. It's time. (*To* ANYA.) My little girl, we shall see each other again soon — I am going to Paris, I shall live there on the money your Yaroslavl great-aunt sent for the purchase of the estate — long live Great-aunt! But that money won't last long.

ANYA: Mama, you'll come back soon, soon — Isn't that so? I'll prepare myself, pass the examination at high school, and then I'll work, I will help you. We'll read all sorts of books together. Mama, isn't that so? (*Kissing her mother's hands.*) We'll read in the autumn evenings, read lots of books, and a new, wonderful world will open up before us — (*Daydreaming.*) Mama, do come —

LYUBOFF ANDREEVNA: I'll come, my precious. (*Embracing her daughter.*)

(LOPAHIN *enters with* CHARLOTTA *who is softly humming a song.*)

GAYEFF: Lucky Charlotta: she's singing!

CHARLOTTA (*taking a bundle that looks like a baby wrapped up*): My baby, bye, bye — (*A baby's cry is heard: Ooah, ooah —!*) Hush, my darling, my dear little boy. (*Ooah, ooah —!*) I am so sorry for you! (*Throwing the bundle back.*) Will you please find me a position? I cannot go on like this.

LOPAHIN: We will find something, Charlotta Ivanovna, don't worry.

GAYEFF: Everybody is dropping us, Varya is going away. — All of a sudden we are not needed.

CHARLOTTA: I have no place in town to live. I must go away. (*Humming.*) It's all the same —

(PISHTCHIK *enters.*)

LOPAHIN: The freak of nature —!

PISHTCHIK (*out of breath*): Ugh, let me catch my breath — I'm exhausted — My honored friends — Give me some water —

GAYEFF: After money, I suppose? This humble servant will flee from sin! (*Goes out.*)

PISHTCHIK: It's a long time since I was here — Most beautiful lady — (*To* LOPAHIN.) You here —? Glad to see you — a man of the greatest intellect — Here — Take it — (*Giving* LOPAHIN *some money.*) Four hundred roubles — That leaves eight hundred and forty I still owe you —

LOPAHIN (*with astonishment, shrugging his shoulders*): I must be dreaming. But where did you get it?

PISHTCHIK: Wait — I'm hot — Most extraordinary event. Some Englishmen came and found on my land some kind of white clay — (*To* LYUBOFF ANDREEVNA.) And four hundred for you — Beautiful lady — Wonderful lady — (*Handing over the money.*) The rest later. (*Taking a drink of water.*) Just now a young man was saying on the train that some great philosopher recommends jumping off roofs

— "Jump!" he says, and "therein lies the whole problem." (*With astonishment.*) You don't say! Water!

LOPAHIN: And what Englishmen were they?

PISHTCHIK: I leased them the parcel of land with the clay for twenty-four years — And now, excuse me, I haven't time — I must run along — I'm going to Znoykoff's — To Kardamonoff's — I owe everybody — (*Drinking.*) I wish you well — I'll drop in on Thursday —

LYUBOFF ANDREEVNA: We are moving to town right away, and tomorrow I'm going abroad —

PISHTCHIK: What? (*Alarmed.*) Why to town? That's why I see furniture — Suitcases — Well, no matter — (*Tearfully.*) No matter — Men of the greatest minds — those Englishmen — No matter — Good luck! God will help you — No matter — Everything in this world comes to an end — (*Kissing* LYUBOFF ANDREEVNA's *hand.*) And should the report reach you that my end has come, think of that well-known horse and say: "There was once on earth a so and so — Semyonoff Pishtchik — The kingdom of Heaven be his." Most remarkable weather — yes — (*Going out greatly disconcerted, but immediately returning and speaking from the door.*) Dashenka sends her greetings! (*Goes out.*)

LYUBOFF ANDREEVNA: And now we can go. I am leaving with two worries. First, that Fiers is sick. (*Glancing at her watch.*) We still have five minutes —

ANYA: Mama, Fiers has already been sent to the hospital. Yasha sent him off this morning.

LYUBOFF ANDREEVNA: My second worry — is Varya. She is used to getting up early and working, and now without any work she is like a fish out of water. She has grown thin, pale and cries all the time, poor thing — (*A pause.*) You know this, Yermolay Alexeevich: I dreamed — of marrying her to you. And there was every sign of your getting married. (*Whispering to* ANYA, *who beckons to* CHARLOTTA; *both go out.*) She loves you, you are fond of her, and I don't know, don't know why it is you seem to avoid each other — I don't understand it!

LOPAHIN: I don't understand it either, I must confess. It's all strange somehow — If there's still time, I am ready right now even — Let's finish it up — and *basta*, but without you I feel I won't propose.

LYUBOFF ANDREEVNA: But that's excellent. Surely it takes only a minute. I'll call her at once.

LOPAHIN: And to fit the occasion there's the champagne. (*Looking at the glasses.*) Empty, somebody has already drunk them. (YASHA *coughs.*) That's what's called lapping it up —

LYUBOFF ANDREEVNA (*vivaciously*): Splendid! We'll go out — Yasha, *allez*! I'll call her — (*Through the door.*) Varya, drop everything and come here. Come on! (*Goes out with* YASHA.)

LOPAHIN (*looking at his watch*): Yes —

(*A pause. Behind the door you hear smothered laughter, whispering, finally* VARYA *enters.*)

VARYA (*looking at the luggage a long time*): That's strange, I just can't find it —

LOPAHIN: What are you looking for?

VARYA: I packed it myself and don't remember where. (*A pause.*)

LOPAHIN: Where do you expect to go now, Varvara Mikhailovna?

VARYA: I? To Regulin's. I agreed to go there to look after the house — As a sort of housekeeper.

LOPAHIN: That's in Yashnevo? It's nigh on to seventy miles. (*A pause.*) And here ends life in this house —

VARYA (*examining the luggage*): But where is it? Either I put it in the trunk, perhaps — Yes, life in this house is ended — it won't be any more —

LOPAHIN: And I am going to Harkoff now — By the next train. I've a lot to do. And I am leaving Epihodoff — on the ground here — I've hired him.

VARYA: Well!

LOPAHIN: Last year at this time it had already been snowing, if you remember, and now it's quiet, it's sunny. It's only that it's cold, about three degrees of frost.

VARYA: I haven't noticed. (*A pause.*) And besides our thermometer is broken — (*A pause. A voice from the yard through the door.*) Yermolay Alexeevich —

LOPAHIN (*as if he had been expecting this call for a long time*): This minute! (*Goes out quickly.*)

(VARYA, *sitting on the floor, putting her head on a bundle of clothes, sobs quietly. The door opens,* LYUBOFF ANDREEVNA *enters cautiously.*)

VARYA (*she is not crying any longer, and has wiped her eyes*): Yes, it's time, Mama. I can get to Regulin's today, if we are just not too late for the train — (*Through the door.*) Anya, put your things on! (ANYA, *then* GAYEFF *and* CHARLOTTA IVANOVNA *enter.* GAYEFF *has on a warm overcoat, with a hood. The servants gather, also the drivers.* EPIHODOFF *busies himself with the luggage.*) Now we can be on our way.

ANYA (*joyfully*): On our way!

GAYEFF: My friends, my dear, kind friends! Leaving this house forever, can I remain silent, can I restrain myself from expressing, as we say, farewell, those feelings that fill now my whole being —

ANYA (*beseechingly*): Uncle!

VARYA: Dear Uncle, don't!

GAYEFF (*dejectedly*): Bank the yellow into the side pocket — I am silent —

(TROFIMOFF *and then* LOPAHIN *enter.*)

TROFIMOFF: Well, ladies and gentlemen, it's time to go!

LOPAHIN: Epihodoff, my coat!

LYUBOFF ANDREEVNA: I'll sit here just a minute more. It's as if I had never seen before what the walls in this house are like, what kind of ceilings, and now I look at them greedily, with such tender love —

GAYEFF: I remember when I was six years old, on Trinity Day, I sat in this window and watched my father going to Church —

LYUBOFF ANDREEVNA: Are all the things taken out?

LOPAHIN: Everything, I think. (*Putting on his overcoat. To* EPIHODOFF.) Epihodoff, you see that everything is in order.

EPIHODOFF (*talking in a hoarse voice*): Don't worry, Yermolay Alexeevich!

LOPAHIN: Why is your voice like that?

EPIHODOFF: Just drank some water, swallowed something.

YASHA (*with contempt*): The ignorance —

LYUBOFF ANDREEVNA: We are going and there won't be a soul left here —

LOPAHIN: Till spring.

VARYA (*she pulls an umbrella out from a bundle, it looks as if she were going to hit someone;* LOPAHIN *pretends to be frightened*): What do you, what do you — I never thought of it.

TROFIMOFF: Ladies and gentlemen, let's get in the carriages — It's time! The train is coming any minute.

VARYA: Petya, here they are, your rubbers, by the suitcase. (*Tearfully.*) And how dirty yours are, how old — !

TROFIMOFF (*putting on the rubbers*): Let's go, ladies and gentlemen!

GAYEFF (*greatly embarrassed, afraid he will cry*): The train — The station — Cross into the side, combination off the white into the corner —

LYUBOFF ANDREEVNA: Let's go!

LOPAHIN: Everybody here? Nobody there? (*Locking the side door on the left.*) Things are stored here, it must be locked up, let's go!

ANYA: Good-by, house! Good-by, the old life!

TROFIMOFF: Long live the new life!

(*Goes out with* ANYA. VARYA *casts a glance around the room and, without hurrying, goes out.* YASHA *and* CHARLOTTA, *with her dog, go out.*)

LOPAHIN: And so, till spring. Out, ladies and gentlemen — Till we meet. (*Goes out.*)

(LYUBOFF ANDREEVNA *and* GAYEFF *are left alone. As if they had been waiting for this, they throw themselves on one another's necks sobbing, but smothering their sobs as if afraid of being heard.*)

GAYEFF (*in despair*): Oh, Sister, Sister —

LYUBOFF ANDREEVNA: Oh, my dear, my lovely, beautiful orchard! My life, my youth, my happiness, good-by!

ANYA (ANYA's *voice, gaily, appealingly*): Mama — !

TROFIMOFF (TROFIMOFF's *voice, gaily, excitedly*): Aaooch!

LYUBOFF ANDREEVNA: For the last time, just to look at the walls, at the window — My dear mother used to love to walk around in this room —

GAYEFF: Oh, Sister, Sister — !

ANYA (ANYA's *voice*): Mama — !

TROFIMOFF (TROFIMOFF's *voice, gaily, excitedly*): Aaooch!

LYUBOFF ANDREEVNA: We are coming! (*They go out.*)

(*The stage is empty. You hear the keys locking all the doors, then the carriages drive off. It grows quiet. In the silence you hear the dull thud of an ax on a tree, a lonely, mournful sound. Footsteps are heard. From the door on the right* FIERS *appears. He is dressed as usual, in a jacket and a white waistcoat, slippers on his feet. He is sick.*)

FIERS (*going to the door and trying the knob*): Locked. They've gone. (*Sitting down on the sofa.*) They forgot about me — No matter — I'll sit here awhile — And Leonid Andreevich, for sure, didn't put on his fur coat, he went off with his topcoat — (*Sighing anxiously.*) And I didn't see to it — The young saplings! (*He mutters something that cannot be understood.*) Life has gone by, as if I hadn't lived at all — (*Lying down.*) I'll lie down awhile — You haven't got any strength, nothing is left, nothing — Ach, you — good-for-nothing — (*He lies still.*)

(*There is a far-off sound as if out of the sky, the sound of a snapped string, dying away, sad. A stillness falls, and there is only the thud of an ax on a tree, far away in the orchard.*)

CURTAIN

AFTERWORD

The beginning of the second act of *The Cherry Orchard* is a particularly concise collocation of characteristics found in all of Chekhov's last four plays. Since the plays are so often misunderstood and since a main cause of misunderstanding is the failure to realize what Chekhov was doing and the assumption that he was trying to do something else, the passage may repay a closer look.

Its four characters are all employed in the Ranevskaya household, and all are minor: Charlotta, a governess of indeterminate youthfulness and cosmopolitan circus background; Epihodoff, a foolish clerk, whose dignity of speech and bearing continually collapses in pratfalls and jammed syntax; the maid Dunyasha, with whom Epihodoff is in love; and the brash young valet Yasha, Epihodoff's successful rival. They are together for no particular purpose. There is a touch of pathos in Charlotta's situation and perhaps in Epihodoff's, but none of the four is really an attractive character. They do not know each other very well and do not establish any close rapport. Their words bound off other words or drop, echoless, in a void of indifference and self-absorption. When Charlotta ends her opening monologue with a plea for human contact, Epihodoff breaks into song on the all-sufficiency of love. He is joined in singing by his rival Yasha. Dunyasha tells them they sound "like jackals." Alone with Yasha, Dunyasha tells him she loves him. Yasha replies that he considers a girl who is in love immoral. Talk is desultory, punctuated by pauses and yawns. The constant changes in topic are incoherent: foreign travel, suicide, a cockroach in a glass of beer, an early Victorian philosopher. The setting is desolate: sunset among forgotten tombstones near an abandoned chapel, the cherry orchard on one side and a large town looming on the horizon.

One hesitates calling such a passage a "scene," because "scene" suggests a distinct unit within a larger plot dynamic. But no plot is furthered by this casual group, no phase of action marked, no issue raised or concluded, no climax prepared. The impression of aimless and listless small talk remains even when the passage is seen in the context of the whole play. At its end Charlotta is as lost and lonely as she is here, and Epihodoff neither kills himself nor ever stops stumbling over or crushing things or tangling his sentences. Neither her rifle nor his revolver is ever mentioned again, let alone fired. The Epihodoff–Dunyasha–Yasha triangle ends in stalemate, like the other two tentative romances in the play, Lopahin's and Varya's, and Anya's and Trofimoff's. None of the four characters here influences the issue of whether or not the estate is to be sold or otherwise affects the destiny of the major characters.

To people used to the taut, significant action patterns of western drama from Sophocles through Shakespeare and Ibsen, Chekhov's status as major dramatist may seem puzzling. The tension between Mme Ranevskaya and her equally vague and ineffectual brother Gayeff on the one hand and the concerned and practical merchant Lopahin on the other on how to save the mortgaged estate provides *The Cherry Orchard* with more suspense and plot coherence than Chekhov's other important plays. Nevertheless, what coherence the play possesses is rather in the nature of frame than of substance. As in *The Sea-Gull*, *Uncle Vanya*, and *Three Sisters* most of the drama proceeds, like our sample passage, by incongruent juxtapositions of little banalities and irrelevancies, fatuities and incoherences — random fragments of life lifted on stage from a continuing flow of trivia to make an irregular, languid rhythm of inconsequence. Take the episode in Act I when Pishtchik swallows Mme Ranevskaya's (Lyuboff Andreevna's) pills.

PISHTCHIK: You should never take medicaments, dear madam — They do neither harm nor good — Hand them here, dearest lady. (*He takes the pillbox, shakes the pills out into his palm, blows on them, puts them in his mouth and washes them down with kvass.*) There! Now!
LYUBOFF ANDREEVNA (*startled*): Why, you've lost your mind!
PISHTCHIK: I took all the pills.
LOPAHIN: Such a glutton!

(*Everyone laughs.*)

And that is the end of the episode. The pills are not missed, we are never told what Mme Ranevskaya takes pills for, Pishtchik does not get sick, they do not alter his behavior in any way, nobody ever refers to them again. By the rules of sound play construction one should be shocked by such casualness and waste and demand to know the relevance of the incident. But its relevance is its non-relevance to anything beyond its own inanity. Of such isolated bits of humdrum life, as startling as they are pointless, is Chekhov's world made. No wonder he did not find Ibsen simple enough and refused him status as dramatist for not "knowing life." To judge by his own plays, what he objected to was the Norwegian's careful arrangement of the rich and immediate chaos of experience according to the demands of tightly plotted melodrama of thematic import, in which every event is a link in a causal chain and every speech reveals character or contributes to the theme. Economy of means to a significant end is the Ibsen hallmark. Chekhov is lavish with apparently useless character and incident. His plays are not unplanned, and their quality of improvised rambling is the result of scrupulous craftsmanship, but his realism is of the inclusive kind that not only can afford but needs items that have no other function than to make a moment of live drama. Near the close of Act II there is heard, "as if from the sky," a "mournful" sound, "like the sound of a snapped string." A few moments later, a drunken beggar appears. If only because of mere proximity, is there a connection between sound and man? What do they mean? How do they function in the drama? The questions are unanswerable, even — in the sense in which they usually are asked — impertinent. We can only say that without the sound and the beggar a dimension of reality would be gone from the scene. Instead of Ibsen's stripped and strictly functional casts Chekhov prodigally peoples the Ranevskaya estate with a chorus of semigrotesque retainers and hangers-on, for whom there is no more a definite function in the plot than there appears to be in the running of the household. The quartet in the opening of Act II are just four of them. He further diffuses the outline of his cast with unseen characters in a kind of ghostly attendance on those on stage: Mme Ranevskaya's dead little boy Grisha, her Paris lover, her and Gayeff's rich old aunt in Yaroslavl, Pishtchik's clever daughter Dashenka. Swayed by the dead and the absent, the characters we do see appear more real and less strong.

Thus, Chekhov builds drama by a kind of pointillism. If we look too close we see only specks of reality, but at a distance a pattern emerges. As sentiment is about to become pathos and tension approaches tragic intensity, a sudden incongruity deflates theme and mood — a moment of slapstick, a change in tempo, an unattuned image or speech, a new topic of conversation. In Act I, when Varya tells Anya of the family's precarious financial position — "In August the estate is to be sold" — Lopahin suddenly sticks his head through the door and moos like a cow. "I'd land him one like that," threatens Varya tearfully, shaking her fist. In Act III she does almost exactly that, by unlucky timing hitting him over the head with a broomstick just as he enters to tell the family that he has bought the estate. In Chekhov, typically, farce impinges on the peripety of the main drama. Lopahin's allusions to Hamlet and Ophelia represent the third coordinate in the system that defines his and Varya's abortive romance in terms partly farcical and partly poignant. Just as Lopahin, the serf's son, impatient with procrastination and a businessman of action, is no Prince Hamlet, so is the Ranevskaya estate that he seeks to set right both a more innocent and a pettier world than Denmark. And poor Varya is only a formidable and rather foolish nun. Tragic grandeur is further deflated by Lopahin's consistent failure to remember Ophelia's name.*

From such discord and ambivalence the play builds its larger patterns. Old Fiers considers the emancipation of the serfs in 1863 a disaster. In contrast, Trofimoff, the muddled revolutionary idealist, envisions a brighter Russian future built by liberty and dignified labor. Between past and future the present moves by ceaseless ebb and flow. In Act I, Mme Ranevskaya comes home; in Act IV she goes away. Arrival-departure frames the collection of discordant moments here as in Chekhov's other late plays. But departure is not conclusion. Though something passes, something also comes. The cherry trees fall by the blows of the axe that new enterprise wields. But how great is the loss? After all, the old recipe for drying cherries and keeping them "soft, . . . juicy, sweet, fragrant" is forgotten. But, then, is the main value of the orchard commercial? The

---

* He also misquotes Shakespeare's lines, a fact which the English translation here does not take notice of. See David Magarshack, *Chekhov the Dramatist* (New York, 1960), pp. 278–279.

beauty of the old order, but also its foolishness and gentle decadence, give way to Lopahin, the entrepreneur, the reluctant heir of the feudal past, including his own childhood and — though he does not know it — the old serf Fiers.

The pattern of change is framed by a still larger pattern. The play begins with Lopahin waking up and ends with Fiers falling asleep. What happens in the interval?

> We are such stuff
> As dreams are made on, and our little life
> Is rounded with a sleep.

That is, nothing — and everything. Is it just another odd fact that the first and the last act both take place in a room called "the Nursery" and that it is furnished in Act I and bare in Act IV? To Fiers at the end it is as if life has gone by and left him with a feeling of not having lived at all. Is *The Cherry Orchard* Chekhov's *Tempest* in a deeper sense than by being his last play? Lopahin has been taken to represent the new economic man, the proletarian become a rising merchant, a bourgeois forerunner of the Soviet revolution. Perhaps he is. There certainly is irony in his unawareness of his artistic inclinations and in his inability to escape his serf origin long enough to get himself a genteel wife, either Varya or her foster mother, Mme Ranevskaya herself, who is — as certain of his speeches hint — the woman he really loves. But to seize upon socio-economic symbolism or on Lopahin's psychology as the main theme is to lock Chekhov's kaleidoscope in one or the other of only two of its myriad constellations. Life may be "little" in Chekhov, as it is for most people, but the drama in which it is recorded is not impoverished. When people complain that "nothing happens" in Chekhov, one may be willing to see what they have in mind. But they are quite wrong.

What is true, however, is that Chekhov's manner of drama is one that makes heavy demands on the *reader*. Few great playwrights gain more from performance than he. His distinctive tonality is muted on the page. In the absence of exciting scenes and strong plot, interest has to depend on imaginative evocation of spectacle, movement, and voice, and this, for most of us, is a new and difficult challenge. If we fail to meet it, bewilderment and then boredom may follow. The strangeness and the number of the Russian names are further obstacles.

But even in performance there are people who find Chekhov too wanly elegiac, slow, and indefinite. Chekhov realized the danger himself and quarreled with the two directors of the Moscow Art Theater for not guarding sufficiently against it. One of them was Constantin Stanislavsky, whose naturalistic staging of *The Sea-Gull* in 1898 had established Chekhov's reputation as a dramatist and whose painstaking rehearsals, emphasis on ensemble acting, and insistence that the actor engage himself imaginatively and emotionally in his part (we call all this "Method" acting today) were to make him the single most important influence on modern acting. But to Chekhov he was the man who had "ruined" his *Cherry Orchard*. In an effort, perhaps, to avert the disaster he saw was coming he wrote to Stanislavsky's wife even before rehearsals began, in October, 1903: "I'm afraid my play has turned out to be not a drama but a comedy, and in places even a farce, and I fear Nemirovich-Danchenko [the literary director of the Theater] will never forgive me for that." What actually happened was, from Chekhov's point of view, even worse. So far from feeling any need for forgiving Chekhov for having written a comedy, it did not even occur to the two directors that he had not written a tragedy. Some weeks after the first performance of *The Cherry Orchard* in January, 1904, and about four months before his death, Chekhov wrote to his wife about the Stanislavsky production:

Take my *Cherry Orchard*. Is it my *Cherry Orchard*? With the exception of one or two parts nothing in it is mine. I am describing life, ordinary life, and not blank despondency. They either make me into a cry-baby or a bore. They invent something about me out of their own heads, anything they like, something I never thought of or dreamed about. This is beginning to make me angry.

There is in principle no reason why Stanislavsky and Nemirovich-Danchenko cannot have perceived the nature of *The Cherry Orchard* more clearly than Chekhov himself. But did they? Most producers have heeded the playwright's protests against a tragic *Cherry Orchard*, but few have staged it as a comedy or agreed with Chekhov that Lopahin's part is comical and the whole play "gay and frivolous." For most people, on either side of the footlights, Chekhov remains the twilight voice of old Russia, a bittersweet realist poet of mood and atmosphere, the sympathetic-ironic chronicler of the heartaches and frustrations and failures of decent but foolishly weak and confused people. What comedy there is in Chekhov is in a very minor key indeed, at most arch and acid, very rarely hearty. Trofimoff, for example, is an undoubted fool, and yet he is made the spokesman of genuine values: the blessings of work and love. Other visionary idealists in Chekhov are also presented as fatuous escapists into vague and wordy optimism.

From the vantage point of today we may wonder whether Chekhov, were he still alive, would have persisted in using "comedy" and "farce" as labels for *The Cherry Orchard*. To turn again to the opening of Act II, consider the following exchange:

CHARLOTTA: . . . Who my parents were, perhaps they weren't even married — I don't know. (*Taking a cucumber out of her pocket and beginning to eat it.*) I don't know a thing. (*A pause.*) I'd like so much to talk but there's not anybody. I haven't anybody.

EPIHODOFF (*playing the guitar and singing*): "What care I for the noisy world, what care I for friends and foes." — How pleasant it is to play the mandolin!

DUNYASHA: That's a guitar, not a mandolin. (*Looking into a little mirror and powdering her face.*)

EPIHODOFF: For a madman who is in love this is a mandolin — (*Singing.*) "If only my heart were warm with the fire of requited love."
(YASHA *sings with him.*)

This is quintessential Chekhov, but it might have come from a contemporary play of the absurd theater. Without a "proper passport" and with her sense of lostness and isolation in a meaningless existence — "Who I am, why I am, is unknown" — Charlotta becomes an almost Kafkaesque figure in a parable of modern man's existential agony. In her military cap, tinkering with a rifle, eating a cucumber, holding forth in unhappy monologue, she is a figure of pathetic farce as well. The incongruity is "absurd" in the modern, literary, sense. She and Epihodoff are equally lonely, but their monodies produce only discord. The scenic and verbal imagery of guitar and cigar, guns and pocket mirror, jackals, spider, cockroach, and a serving-maid's lily white, ladylike hands belongs in an odd, vaguely disturbing dream. "Absurd" also is people's failure to relate through language. Charlotta's sudden vaudeville tricks come to seem less like farcical interruptions than like symptoms of an isolation desperately battered by the inarticulate prisoner within. Epihodoff reads important books he cannot understand and which fail to convince him that life is worth living. For lack of human respondents Gayeff apostrophizes bookcases and Nature and hides his embarrassment in billiard jargon and candy. As means to overcome a breakdown in communication his antics resemble Charlotta's tricks. Since experience is wholly subjective, there can be no stable relationship between word and meaning:

DUNYASHA: That's a guitar, not a mandolin. . . .
EPIHODOFF: For a madman who is in love this is a mandolin — . . .

Even the lovers fail to communicate:

DUNYASHA: I have come to love you passionately, you are educated, you can discuss anything. (*A pause.*)
YASHA (*yawning*): Yes, sir — . . .

Certainly there is comedy here, even farce, but is that *all* there is?

The point is not that Chekhov anticipated the absurd theater some seventy years ago or that today's absurdists are indebted to him — not even, though this is true, that the absurd manner is not the invention of existential playwrights of the last two decades. The point of Chekhov's "absurdity" is the more general one that art always "is" and does not "mean" and that modern art has made a fetish and a program of what previous generations of artists tacitly took for granted.

Not that Chekhov, of course, is "meaningless" — literally — any more than are playwrights like Beckett and Pinter. Art cannot be "meaningless" — literally — and still remain art (which is why people who make nothing of the absurdists quite properly deny them status as dramatists). "Absurd" is a silly epithet for drama that takes reality too seriously to presume to subject it to interpretation or judgment or to arrangement by laws of narrative. The dictum that art be without meaning means that its meaning should be inviolately implicit and centripetal. The artist's image of reality does not derive its authority from a non-art original and does not justify itself by any intention of altering such an original, for however commendable an end. Chekhov was occasionally provoked into claiming for his plays a pragmatic value for lethargic, end-of-the-century Russian intelligentsia — object lessons in how *not* to manage the business of life — but their uncompromising objectivity suggests that the claim was only an effort to speak a language that dull producers could understand. With reference to this specific case: In the opening of Act II of *The Cherry Orchard* Chekhov is not telling us that life is trivial, futile, and solitary or asking us to do something about it. He is showing us some trivial, futile, and solitary moments in a scenic imitation of life. The distinction is all-important: ultimately that between an election poster and Rembrandt. "You ask me what life is?" he once wrote to his wife. "It is like asking what a carrot is. A carrot is a carrot; that's all we know." The artist records facts: people, places, things, words. But held in the artist's vision, they catch the comical or frightening but always vulnerable human pose — "the lust of the flesh and the soul's incurable loneliness" — between the quaint, incontrovertible events of birth and death. Our most vital drama, old and contemporary, claims to do no more and no less.

Bernard Shaw

MAJOR BARBARA

FOREWORD

For many writers after Ibsen the stage became a forum for the discussion
of social and political issues. Shaw became the most successful, and most
controversial, practitioner of this kind of drama in English. The British
stage of his time was still inhibited by a censorship that was not removed,
incredibly, until the late 1960s. Socially undesirable subjects were taboo.
Even *Oedipus the King* was suspect, because it dealt with murder and incest. Productions still lay under the heavy hand of Victorian realism. As a
professional iconoclast, Shaw thus found much to protest against. One of
his early plays, on the forbidden subject of prostitution, was banned. When
the Shakespeare Memorial Theatre at Stratford-on-Avon burned down, he
sent a telegram of congratulations, and affronted the public by his assertion that he was a better dramatist than Shakespeare. Throughout his long
career he delighted in taunting the political and artistic establishment.

At the same time, there was innovation and experimentation in the British theater, from which Shaw was able to profit. Harley Granville-Barker,
one of the most exciting directors of his time, staged some of Shaw's plays.
Gilbert Murray (who seems to have served as a model for Cusins in *Major
Barbara*) was for the first time offering English audiences intelligible and
playable translations of Greek tragedies. Shaw, though he affected
ignorance and dislike of the classics, was undoubtedly in sympathy with
them, for he himself wrote plays in which the plots (which Shaw referred
to contemptuously as "clockwork mice") were of less importance than

the arguments that the characters expressed. Shaw was a self-taught and successful public speaker, with a strong interest in economics. His characters became (sometimes a little incongruously) mouthpieces for the arguments he wanted to put across. He thought of his plays as dramatized debates.

Shaw was, however, astute enough to combine polemics with a sense of box-office. (He once told Sam Goldwyn, "You think only about art; I think only about money.") Most of his plays worked as argument *and* as neatly constructed entertainment, and had a considerable mass appeal. Two were turned into musical comedies. Several, including *Major Barbara*, were filmed. A Shaw Festival was created in England to perform a few of his plays every year. At the site of the festival Shaw planted a ceremonial tree, which died overnight — the fact was kept from him, but would have amused him. After his death, and the inevitable eclipse suffered by writers who have been successful in their lifetimes, his works have once more become established in the theater, not merely in star revivals but as the bread-and-butter of the average repertory company.

PREFACE TO MAJOR BARBARA
FIRST AID TO CRITICS

Before dealing with the deeper aspects of Major Barbara, let me, for the credit of English literature, make a protest against an unpatriotic habit into which many of my critics have fallen. Whenever my view strikes them as being at all outside the range of, say, an ordinary suburban churchwarden, they conclude that I am echoing Schopenhauer, Nietzsche, Ibsen, Strindberg, Tolstoy, or some other heresiarch in northern or eastern Europe.

I confess there is something flattering in this simple faith in my accomplishment as a linguist and my erudition as a philosopher. But I cannot countenance the assumption that life and literature are so poor in these islands that we must go abroad for all dramatic material that is not common and all ideas that are not superficial. I therefore venture to put my critics in possession of certain facts concerning my contact with modern ideas.

About half a century ago, an Irish novelist, Charles Lever, wrote a story entitled A Day's Ride: A Life's Romance. It was published by Charles Dickens in Household Words, and proved so strange to the public taste that Dickens pressed Lever to make short work of it. I read scraps of this novel when I was a child; and it made an enduring impression on me. The hero was a very romantic hero, trying to live bravely, chivalrously, and powerfully by dint of mere romance-fed imagination, without courage, without means, without knowledge, without skill, without anything real except his bodily appetites. Even in my childhood I found in this poor devil's unsuccessful encounters with the facts of life, a poignant quality that romantic fiction lacked. The book, in spite of its first failure, is not dead: I saw its title the other day in the catalogue of Tauchnitz.

Now why is it that when I also deal in the tragi-comic irony of the conflict between real life and the romantic imagination, critics never affiliate me to my countryman and immediate forerunner, Charles Lever, whilst they confidently derive me from a Norwegian author of whose language I do not know three words, and of whom I knew nothing until years after the Shavian *Anschauung* was already unequivocally declared in books full of what came, ten years later, to be perfunctorily labelled Ibsenism? I was not Ibsenist even at second hand; for Lever, though he may have read Henri Beyle, *alias* Stendhal, certainly never read Ibsen. Of the books that made Lever popular, such as Charles O'Malley and Harry Lorrequer, I know nothing but the names and some of the illustrations. But the story of the day's ride and life's romance of Potts (claiming alliance with Pozzo di Borgo) caught me and fascinated me as something strange and significant, though I already knew all about Alnaschar and Don Quixote and Simon Tappertit and many another romantic hero mocked by reality. From the plays of Aristophanes to the tales of Stevenson that mockery has been made familiar to all who are properly saturated with letters.

Where, then, was the novelty in Lever's tale? Partly, I think, in a new seriousness in dealing with Potts's disease. Formerly, the contrast between madness and sanity was deemed comic: Hogarth shews us how fashionable people went in parties to Bedlam to laugh at the lunatics. I myself have had a village idiot exhibited to me as something irresistibly funny. On the stage the madman was once a regular comic figure: that was how Hamlet got his opportunity before Shakespear touched him. The originality of Shakespear's version lay in his taking the lunatic sympathetically and seriously, and thereby making an advance towards the eastern consciousness of the fact that lunacy may be inspiration in disguise, since a man who has more brains than his fellows necessarily appears as mad to them as one who has less. But Shakespear did not do for Pistol and Parolles what he did for Hamlet. The particular sort of madman they represented, the romantic make-believer, lay outside the pale of sympathy in literature: he was pitilessly despised and ridiculed here as he was in the east under the name of Alnaschar, and was doomed to be, centuries later, under the name of Simon Tappertit. When Cervantes relented over Don Quixote, and Dickens relented over Pickwick, they did not become impartial: they simply changed sides, and became friends and apologists where they had formerly been mockers.

In Lever's story there is a real change of attitude. There is no relenting towards Potts: he never gains our affections like Don Quixote and Pickwick: he has not even the infatuate courage of Tappertit. But we dare not laugh at him, because, somehow, we recognize ourselves in Potts. We may, some of us, have enough nerve, enough muscle, enough luck, enough tact or skill or address or knowledge to carry things off better than he did; to impose on the people who saw through him; to fascinate Katinka (who cut Potts so ruthlessly at the end of the story); but for all that, we know that Potts plays an enormous part in ourselves and in the world, and that the social problem is not a problem of story-book heroes of the older pattern, but a problem of Pottses, and of how to make men of them. To fall back on my old phrase, we have the feeling — one that Alnaschar, Pistol, Parolles, and Tappertit never gave us — that Potts is a piece of really scientific natural history as distinguished from funny story telling. His author is not throwing a stone at a creature of another and inferior order, but making a confession, with the effect that the stone hits each of us full in the conscience and causes our self-esteem to smart very sorely. Hence the failure of Lever's book to please the readers of Household Words. That pain in the self-esteem nowadays causes critics to raise a cry of Ibsenism. I therefore assure them that the sensation first came to me from Lever and may have come to him from Beyle, or at least out of the Stendhalian atmosphere. I exclude the hypothesis of complete originality on Lever's part, because a man can no more be completely original in that sense than a tree can grow out of air.

Another mistake as to my literary ancestry is made whenever I violate the romantic convention that all women are angels when they are not devils; that they are better looking than men; that their part in courtship is entirely passive; and that the human female form is the most beautiful object in nature. Schopenhauer wrote a splenetic essay which, as it is neither polite nor profound, was probably intended to knock this nonsense violently on the head. A sentence denouncing the idolized form as ugly has been largely quoted. The English critics have read that sentence; and I must here affirm, with as much gentleness as the implication will bear, that it has yet to be proved that they have dipped any deeper. At all events, whenever an English playwright represents a young and marriageable woman as being anything but a romantic heroine, he is disposed of without further thought as an echo of Schopenhauer. My own case is a specially hard one, because, when I implore the critics who are obsessed with the Schopenhauerian formula to remember that playwrights, like sculptors, study their figures from life, and not from philosophic essays, they reply passionately that I am not a playwright and that my stage figures do not live. But even so, I may and do ask them why, if they must give the credit of my plays to a philosopher, they do not give it to an English philosopher? Long before I ever read a word by Schopenhauer, or even knew whether he was a philosopher or a chemist, the Socialist revival of the eighteen-eighties brought me into contact, both literary and personal, with Ernest Belfort Bax, an English Socialist and philosophic essayist, whose handling of modern feminism would provoke romantic protests from Schopenhauer himself, or even Strindberg. As a matter of fact I hardly noticed Schopenhauer's disparagements of women when they came under my notice later on, so thoroughly had Bax familiarized me with the homoist attitude, and forced me to recognize the extent to which public opinion, and consequently legislation and jurisprudence, is corrupted by feminist sentiment.

Belfort Bax's essays were not confined to the Feminist question. He was a ruthless critic of current morality. Other writers have gained sympathy for dramatic criminals by eliciting the alleged "soul of goodness in things evil"; but Bax would propound some quite undramatic and apparently shabby violation of our commercial law and morality, and not merely defend it with the most disconcerting ingenuity, but actually prove it to be a positive duty that nothing but the certainty of police persecution should prevent every right-minded man from at once doing on principle. The Socialists were naturally shocked, being for the most part morbidly moral people; but at all events they were saved later on from the delusion that nobody but Nietzsche had ever challenged our mercanto-Christian morality. I first heard the name of Nietzsche from a German mathematician, Miss Borchardt, who had read my Quintessence of Ibsenism, and told me that she saw what I had been reading: namely, Nietzsche's Jenseits von Gut und Böse. Which I protest I had never seen, and could not have read with any comfort, for want of the necessary German, if I had seen it.

Nietzsche, like Schopenhauer, is the victim in England of a single much quoted sentence containing the phrase "big blonde beast." On the strength of this alliteration it is assumed that Nietzsche gained his European reputation by a senseless glorification of selfish bullying as the rule of life, just as it is assumed, on the strength of the single word Superman (Übermensch) borrowed by me from Nietzsche, that I look for the salvation of society to the despotism of a single Napoleonic Superman, in spite of my careful demonstration of the folly of that outworn infatuation. But even the less recklessly superficial critics seem to believe that the modern objection to Christianity as a pernicious slave-morality was first put forward by Nietzsche. It was familiar to me before I ever heard of Nietzsche. The late Captain Wilson, author of several queer pamphlets, propagandist of a metaphysical system called Comprehensionism, and inventor of the term "Crosstianity" to distinguish the retrograde element in Christendom, was wont thirty years ago, in the discussions of the Dialectical Society, to protest earnestly against the beatitudes of the Sermon on the Mount as excuses for cowardice and servility, as destructive of our will, and consequently of our honor and manhood. Now it is true that Captain Wilson's moral criticism of Christianity was not a historical theory of it, like Nietzsche's; but this objection cannot be made to Stuart-Glennie, the successor of Buckle as a philosophic historian, who devoted his life to the elaboration and propagation of his theory that Christianity is part of an epoch (or rather an aberration, since it began as recently as 6000 B.C. and is already collapsing) produced by the necessity in which the numerically inferior white races found themselves to impose their domination on the colored races by priestcraft, making a virtue and a popular religion of drudgery and submissiveness in this world not only as a means of achieving saintliness of character but of securing a reward in heaven. Here was the slave-morality view formulated by a Scotch philosopher of my acquaintance long before we all began chattering about Nietzsche.

As Stuart-Glennie traced the evolution of society to the conflict of races, his theory made some sensation among Socialists — that is, among the only people who were seriously thinking about historical evolution at all — by its collision with the class-conflict theory of Karl Marx. Nietzsche, as I gather, regarded the slave-morality as having been invented and imposed on the world by slaves making a virtue of necessity and a religion of their servitude. Stuart-Glennie regarded the slave-morality as an invention of the superior white race to subjugate the minds of the inferior races whom they wished to exploit, and who would have destroyed them by force of numbers if their minds had not been subjugated. As this process is in operation still, and can be studied at first hand not only in our Church schools and in the struggle between our modern proprietary classes and the proletariat, but in the part played by Christian missionaries in reconciling the black races of Africa to their subjugation by European Capitalism, we can judge for ourselves whether the initiative came from above or below. My object here is not to argue the historical point, but simply to make our theatre critics ashamed of their habit of treating Britain as an intellectual void, and assuming that every philosophical idea, every historic theory, every criticism of our moral, religious and juridical institutions, must necessarily be either a foreign import, or else a fantastic sally (in rather questionable taste) totally unrelated to the existing body of thought. I urge them to remember that this body of thought is the slowest of growths and the rarest of blossomings, and that if there is such a thing on the philosophic plane as a matter of course, it is that no individual can make more than a minute contribution to it. In fact, their conception of clever persons parthenogenetically bringing forth complete original cosmogonies by dint of sheer "brilliancy" is part of that ignorant credulity which is the despair of the honest philosopher, and the opportunity of the religious impostor.

THE GOSPEL OF ST ANDREW UNDERSHAFT

It is this credulity that drives me to help my critics out with Major Barbara by telling them what to say about it. In the millionaire Undershaft I have represented a man who has become intellectually and spiritually as well as practically conscious of the irresistible natural truth which we all abhor and repudiate: to wit, that the greatest of our evils, and the worst of our crimes is poverty, and that our first duty, to which every other consideration should be sacrificed, is not to be poor. "Poor but honest," "the respectable poor," and such phrases are as intolerable and as immoral as "drunken but amiable," "fraudulent but a good after-dinner speaker," "splendidly criminal," or the like. Security, the chief pretence of civilization, cannot exist where the worst of dangers, the danger of poverty, hangs over everyone's head, and where the alleged protection of our persons from violence is only an accidental result of the existence of a police force whose real business is to force the poor man to see his children starve whilst idle people over-feed pet dogs with the money that might feed and clothe them.

It is exceedingly difficult to make people realize that an evil is an evil. For instance, we seize a man and deliberately do him a malicious injury: say, imprison him for years. One would not suppose that it needed any exceptional clearness of wit to recognize in this an act of diabolical cruelty. But in England such a recognition provokes a stare of surprise, followed by an explanation that the outrage is punishment or justice or something else that is all right, or perhaps by a heated attempt to argue that we should all be robbed and murdered in our beds if such stupid villainies as sentences of imprisonment were not committed daily. It is useless to argue that even if this were true, which it is not, the alternative to adding crimes of our own to the crimes from which we suffer is not helpless submission. Chickenpox is an evil; but if I were to declare that we must either submit to it or else repress it sternly by seizing everyone who suffers from it and punishing them by inoculation with smallpox, I should be laughed at; for though nobody could deny that the result would be to prevent chickenpox to some extent by making people avoid it much more carefully, and to effect a further apparent prevention by making them conceal it very anxiously, yet people would have sense enough to see that the deliberate propagation of smallpox was a creation of evil, and must therefore be ruled out in favor of purely humane and hygienic measures. Yet in the precisely parallel case of a man breaking into my house and stealing my wife's diamonds I am expected as a matter of course to steal ten years of his life, torturing him all the time. If he tries to defeat that monstrous retaliation by shooting me, my survivors hang him. The net result suggested by the police statistics is that we inflict atrocious injuries on the burglars we catch in order to make the rest take effectual precautions against detection; so that instead of saving our wives' diamonds from burglary we only greatly decrease our chances of ever getting them back, and increase our chances of being shot by the robber if we are unlucky enough to disturb him at his work.

But the thoughtless wickedness with which we scatter sentences of imprisonment, torture in the solitary cell and on the plank bed, and flogging, on moral invalids and energetic rebels, is as nothing compared to the silly levity with which we tolerate poverty as if it were either a wholesome tonic for lazy people or else a virtue to be embraced as St Francis embraced it. If a man is indolent, let him be poor. If he is drunken, let him be poor. If he is not a gentleman, let him be poor. If he is addicted to the fine arts or to pure science instead of to trade and finance, let him be poor. If he chooses to spend his urban eighteen shillings a week or his agricultural thirteen shillings a week on his beer and his family instead of saving it up for his old age, let him be poor. Let nothing be done for "the undeserving": let him be poor. Serve him right! Also — somewhat inconsistently — blessed are the poor!

Now what does this Let Him Be Poor mean? It means let him be weak. Let him be ignorant. Let him become a nucleus of disease. Let him be a standing exhibition and example of ugliness and dirt. Let him have rickety children. Let him be cheap and let him drag his fellows down to his own price by selling himself to do their work. Let his habitations turn our cities into poisonous congeries of slums. Let his daughters infect our young men with the diseases of the streets, and his sons revenge him by turning the nation's manhood into scrofula, cowardice, cruelty, hypocrisy, political imbecility, and all the other fruits of oppression and malnutrition. Let the undeserving become still less deserving; and let the deserving lay up for himself, not treasures in heaven, but horrors in hell upon earth. This being so, is it really wise to let him be poor? Would he not do ten times less harm as a prosperous burglar, incendiary, ravisher or murderer, to the utmost limits of humanity's comparatively negligible impulses in these directions? Suppose we were to abolish all penalties for such activities, and decide that poverty is the one thing we will not tolerate — that every adult with less than, say, £365 a year, shall be painlessly but inexorably killed, and every hungry half naked child forcibly fattened and clothed, would not that be an enormous improvement on our existing system, which has already destroyed so many civilizations, and is visibly destroying ours in the same way?

Is there any radicle of such legislation in our parliamentary system? Well, there are two measures just sprouting in the political soil, which may conceivably grow to something valuable. One is the institution of a Legal Minimum Wage. The other, Old Age Pensions. But there is a better plan than either of these. Some time ago I mentioned the subject of Universal Old Age Pensions to my fellow Socialist Cobden-Sanderson, famous as an artist-craftsman in book-binding and printing. "Why not Universal Pensions for Life?" said Cobden-Sanderson. In saying this, he solved the industrial problem at a stroke. At present we say callously to each citizen "If you want money, earn it" as if his having or not having it were a matter that concerned himself alone. We do not even secure for him the opportunity of earning it: on the contrary, we allow our industry to be organized in open dependence on the maintenance of "a reserve army of unemployed" for the sake of "elasticity." The sensible course would be Cobden-Sanderson's: that is, to give every man enough to live well on, so as to guarantee the community against the possibility of a case of the malignant disease of poverty, and then (necessarily) to see that he earned it.

Undershaft, the hero of Major Barbara, is simply a man who, having grasped the fact that poverty is a crime, knows that when society offered him the alternative of poverty or a lucrative trade in death and destruction, it offered him, not a choice between opulent villainy and humble virtue, but between energetic enterprise and cowardly infamy. His conduct stands the Kantian test, which Peter Shirley's does not. Peter Shirley is what we call the honest poor man. Undershaft is what we call the wicked rich one: Shirley is Lazarus, Undershaft Dives. Well, the misery of the world is due to the fact that the great mass of men act and believe as Peter Shirley acts and believes. If they acted and believed as Undershaft acts and believes, the immediate result would be a revolution of incalculable beneficence. To be wealthy, says Undershaft, is with me a point of honor for which I am prepared to kill at the risk of my own life. This preparedness is, as he says, the final test of sincerity. Like Froissart's medieval hero, who saw that "to rob and kill was a good life" he is not the dupe of that public sentiment against killing which is propagated and endowed by people who would otherwise be killed themselves, or of the mouth-honor paid to poverty and obedience by rich and insubordinate do-nothings who want to rob the poor without courage and command them without superiority. Froissart's knight, in placing the achievement of a good life before all the other duties — which indeed are not duties at all when they conflict with it, but plain wickednesses — behaved bravely, admirably, and, in the final analysis, public-spiritedly. Medieval society, on the other hand, behaved very badly indeed in organizing itself so stupidly that a good life could be achieved by robbing and pilling. If the knight's contemporaries had been all as resolute as he, robbing and pilling would have been the shortest way to the gallows, just as, if we were all as resolute and clearsighted as Undershaft, an attempt to live by means of what is called "an independent income" would be the shortest way to the lethal chamber. But as, thanks to our political imbecility and personal cowardice (fruits of poverty, both), the best imitation of a good life now procurable is life on an independent income, all sensible people aim at securing such an income, and are, of course, careful to legalize and moralize both it and all the actions and sentiments which lead to it and support it as an institution. What else can they do? They know, of course, that they are rich because others are poor. But they cannot help that: it is for the poor to repudiate poverty when they have had enough of it. The thing can be done easily enough: the demonstrations to the contrary made by the economists, jurists, moralists and sentimentalists hired by the rich to defend them, or even doing the work gratuitously out of sheer folly and abjectness, impose only on those who want to be imposed on.

The reason why the independent income-tax payers are not solid in defence of their position is that since we are not medieval rovers through a sparsely populated country, the poverty of those we rob prevents our having the good life for which we sacrifice them. Rich men or aristocrats with a developed sense of life — men like Ruskin and William Morris and Kropotkin — have enormous social appetites and very fastidious personal ones. They are not content with handsome houses: they want handsome cities. They are not content with bediamonded wives and blooming daughters: they complain because the charwoman is badly dressed, because the laundress smells of gin, because the sempstress is anemic, because every man they meet is not a friend and every woman not a romance. They turn up their noses at their neighbors' drains, and are made ill by the architecture of their neighbors' houses. Trade patterns made to suit vulgar people do not please them (and they can get nothing else): they cannot sleep nor sit at ease upon "slaughtered" cabinet makers' furniture. The very air is not good enough for them: there is too much factory smoke in it. They even demand abstract conditions: justice, honor, a noble moral atmosphere, a mystic nexus to replace the cash nexus. Finally they declare that though to rob and pill with your own hand on horseback and in steel coat may have been a good life, to rob and pill by the hands of the policeman, the bailiff, and the soldier, and to underpay them meanly for doing it, is not a good life, but rather fatal to all possibility of even a tolerable one. They call on the poor to revolt, and, finding the poor shocked at their ungentlemanliness, despairingly revile the proletariat for its "damned wantlessness" (verdammte Bedürfnislosigkeit).

So far, however, their attack on society has lacked simplicity. The poor do not share their tastes nor understand their art-criticisms. They do not want the simple life, nor the esthetic life; on the contrary, they want very much to wallow in all the costly vulgarities from which the elect souls among the rich turn away with loathing. It is by surfeit and not by abstinence that they will be cured of their hankering after unwholesome sweets. What they do dislike and despise and are ashamed of is poverty. To ask them to fight for the difference between the Christmas number of the Illustrated London News and the Kelmscott Chaucer is silly: they prefer the News. The difference between a stockbroker's cheap and dirty starched white shirt and collar and the comparatively costly and carefully dyed blue shirt of William Morris is a difference so disgraceful to Morris in their eyes that if they fought on the subject at all, they would fight in defence of the starch. "Cease to be slaves, in order that you may become cranks" is not a very inspiring call to arms; nor is it really improved by substituting saints for cranks. Both terms denote men of genius; and the common man does not want to live the life of a man of genius: he would much rather live the life of a pet collie if that were the only alternative. But he does want more money. Whatever else he may be vague about, he is clear about that. He may or may not prefer Major Barbara to the Drury Lane pantomime; but he always prefers five hundred pounds to five hundred shillings.

Now to deplore this preference as sordid, and teach children that it is sinful to desire money, is to strain towards the extreme possible limit of impudence in lying and corruption in hypocrisy. The universal regard for money is the one hopeful fact in our civilization, the one sound spot in our social conscience. Money is the most important thing in the world. It represents health, strength, honor, generosity and beauty as conspicuously and undeniably as the want of it represents illness, weakness, disgrace, meanness and ugliness. Not the least of its virtues is that it destroys base people as certainly as it fortifies and dignifies noble people. It is only when it is cheapened to worthlessness for some and made impossibly dear to others, that it becomes a curse. In short, it is a curse only in such foolish social conditions that life itself is a curse. For the two things are inseparable: money is the counter that enables life to be distributed socially: it is life as truly as sovereigns and bank notes are money. The first duty of every citizen is to insist on having money on reasonable terms; and this demand is not complied with by giving four men three shillings each for ten or twelve hours' drudgery and one man a thousand pounds for nothing. The crying need of the nation is not for better morals, cheaper bread, temperance, liberty, culture, redemption of fallen sisters and erring brothers, nor the grace, love and fellowship of the Trinity, but simply for enough money. And the evil to be attacked is not sin, suffering, greed, priest-craft, kingcraft, demagogy, monopoly, ignorance, drink, war, pestilence, nor any other of the scapegoats which reformers sacrifice, but simply poverty.

Once take your eyes from the ends of the earth and fix them on this truth just under your nose; and Andrew Undershaft's views will not perplex you in the least. Unless indeed his constant sense that he is only the instrument of a Will or Life Force which uses him for purposes wider than his own, may puzzle you. If so, that is because you are walking either in artificial Darwinian darkness, or in mere stupidity. All genuinely religious people have that consciousness. To them Undershaft the Mystic will be quite intelligible, and his perfect comprehension of his daughter the Salvationist and her lover the Euripidean republican natural and inevitable. That, however, is not new, even on the stage. What is new, as far as I know, is that article in Undershaft's religion which recognizes in Money the first need and in poverty the vilest sin of man and society.

This dramatic conception has not, of course, been attained *per saltum*. Nor has it been borrowed from Nietzsche or from any man born beyond the Channel. The late Samuel Butler, in his own department the greatest English writer of the latter half of the XIX century, steadily inculcated the necessity and morality of a conscientious Laodiceanism in religion and of an earnest and constant sense of the importance of money. It drives one almost to despair of English literature when one sees so extraordinary a study of English life as Butler's posthumous Way of All Flesh making so little impression that when, some years later, I produce plays in which Butler's extraordinarily fresh, free and future-piercing suggestions have an obvious share, I am met with nothing but vague cacklings about Ibsen and Nietzsche, and am only too thankful that they are not about Alfred de Musset and Georges Sand. Really, the English do not deserve to have great men. They allowed Butler to die practically unknown, whilst I, a comparatively insignificant Irish journalist, was leading them by the nose into an advertisement of me which has made my own life a burden. In Sicily there is a Via Samuele Butler. When an English tourist sees it, he either asks "Who the devil was Samuele Butler?" or wonders why the Sicilians should perpetuate the memory of the author of Hudibras.

Well, it cannot be denied that the English are only too anxious to recognize a man of genius if somebody will kindly point him out to them. Having pointed myself out in this manner with some success, I now point out Samuel Butler, and trust that in consequence I shall hear a little less in future of the novelty and foreign origin of the ideas which are now making their way into the English theatre through plays written by Socialists. There are living men whose originality and power are as obvious as Butler's and when they die that fact will be discovered. Meanwhile I recommend them to insist on their own merits as an important part of their own business.

THE SALVATION ARMY

When Major Barbara was produced in London, the second act was reported in an important northern newspaper as a withering attack on the Salvation Army, and the despairing ejaculation of Barbara deplored by a London daily as a tasteless blasphemy. And they were set right, not by the professed critics of the theatre, but by religious and philosophical publicists like Sir Oliver Lodge and Dr Stanton Coit, and strenuous Nonconformist journalists like William Stead, who not only understood the act as well as the Salvationists themselves, but also saw it in its relation to the religious life of the nation, a life which seems to lie not only outside the sympathy of many of our theatre critics, but actually outside their knowledge of society. Indeed nothing could be more ironically curious than the confrontation Major Barbara effected of the theatre enthusiasts with the religious enthusiasts. On the one hand was the playgoer, always seeking pleasure, paying exorbitantly for it, suffering unbearable discomforts for it, and hardly ever getting it. On the other hand was the Salvationist, repudiating gaiety and courting effort and sacrifice, yet always in the wildest spirits, laughing, joking, singing, rejoicing, drumming, and tambourining: his life flying by in a flash of excitement, and his death arriving as a climax of triumph. And, if you please, the playgoer despising the Salvationist as a joyless person, shut out from the heaven of the theatre, self-condemned to a life of hideous gloom; and the Salvationist mourning over the playgoer as over a prodigal with vine leaves in his hair, careering outrageously to hell amid the popping of champagne corks and the ribald laughter of sirens! Could misunderstanding be more complete, or sympathy worse misplaced?

Fortunately, the Salvationists are more accessible to the religious character of the drama than the playgoers to the gay energy and artistic fertility of religion. They can see, when it is pointed out to them, that a theatre, as a place where two or three are gathered together, takes from that divine presence an inalienable sanctity of which the grossest and profanest farce can no more deprive it than a hypocritical sermon by a snobbish bishop can desecrate Westminster Abbey. But in our professional playgoers this indispensable preliminary conception of sanctity seems wanting. They talk of actors as mimes and mummers, and, I fear, think of dramatic authors as liars and pandars, whose main business is the voluptuous soothing of the tired city speculator when what he calls the serious business of the day is over. Passion, the life of drama, means nothing to them but primitive sexual excitement: such phrases as "impassioned poetry" or "passionate love of truth" have fallen quite out of their vocabulary and been replaced by "passional crime" and the like. They assume, as far as I can gather, that people in whom passion has a larger scope are passionless and therefore uninteresting. Consequently they come to think of religious people as people who are not interesting and not amusing. And so, when Barbara cuts the regular Salvation Army jokes, and snatches a kiss from her lover across his drum, the devotees of the theatre think they ought to appear shocked, and conclude that the whole play is an elaborate mockery of the Army. And then either hypocritically rebuke me for mocking, or foolishly take part in the supposed mockery!

Even the handful of mentally competent critics got into difficulties over my demonstration of the economic deadlock in which the Salvation Army finds itself. Some of them thought that the Army would not have taken money from a distiller and a cannon founder: others thought it should not have taken it: all assumed more or less definitely that it reduced itself to absurdity or hypocrisy by taking it. On the first point the reply of the Army itself was prompt and conclusive. As one of its officers said, they would take money from the devil himself and be only too glad to get it out of his hands and into God's. They gratefully acknowledged that publicans not only give them money but allow them to collect it in the bar — sometimes even when there is a Salvation meeting outside preaching teetotalism. In fact, they questioned the verisimilitude of the play, not because Mrs. Baines took the money, but because Barbara refused it.

On the point that the Army ought not to take such money, its justification is obvious. It must take the money because it cannot exist without money, and there

is no other money to be had. Practically all the spare money in the country consists
of a mass of rent, interest, and profit, every penny of which is bound up with crime,
drink, prostitution, disease, and all the evil fruits of poverty, as inextricably as with
enterprise, wealth, commercial probity, and national prosperity. The notion that
you can earmark certain coins as tainted is an unpractical individualist superstition.
None the less the fact that all our money is tainted gives a very severe shock to
earnest young souls when some dramatic instance of the taint first makes them
conscious of it. When an enthusiastic young clergyman of the Established Church
first realizes that the Ecclesiastical Commissioners receive the rents of sporting
public houses, brothels, and sweating dens; or that the most generous contributor at
his last charity sermon was an employer trading in female labor cheapened by
prostitution as unscrupulously as a hotel keeper trades in waiters' labor cheapened
by tips, or commissionaires' labor cheapened by pensions; or that the only patron
who can afford to rebuild his church or his schools or give his boys' brigade a
gymnasium or a library is the son-in-law of a Chicago meat King, that young clergyman has, like Barbara, a very bad quarter hour. But he cannot help himself by
refusing to accept money from anybody except sweet old ladies with independent
incomes and gentle and lovely ways of life. He has only to follow up the income of
the sweet ladies to its industrial source, and there he will find Mrs Warren's profession and the poisonous canned meat and all the rest of it. His own stipend has the
same root. He must either share the world's guilt or go to another planet. He must
save the world's honor if he is to save his own. This is what all the Churches find
just as the Salvation Army and Barbara find it in the play. Her discovery that she is
her father's accomplice; that the Salvation Army is the accomplice of the distiller
and the dynamite maker; that they can no more escape one another than they can
escape the air they breathe; that there is no salvation for them through personal
righteousness, but only through the redemption of the whole nation from its vicious, lazy, competitive anarchy: this discovery has been made by everyone except
the Pharisees and (apparently) the professional playgoers, who still wear their Tom
Hood shirts and underpay their washerwomen without the slightest misgiving as to
the elevation of their private characters, the purity of their private atmospheres,
and their right to repudiate as foreign to themselves the coarse depravity of the
garret and the slum. Not that they mean any harm: they only desire to be, in their
little private way, what they call gentlemen. They do not understand Barbara's
lesson because they have not, like her, learnt it by taking their part in the larger life
of the nation.

BARBARA'S RETURN TO THE COLORS

Barbara's return to the colors may yet provide a subject for the dramatic historian
of the future. To go back to the Salvation Army with the knowledge that even the
Salvationists themselves are not saved yet; that poverty is not blessed, but a most
damnable sin; and that when General Booth chose Blood and Fire for the emblem
of Salvation instead of the Cross, he was perhaps better inspired than he knew:
such knowledge, for the daughter of Andrew Undershaft, will clearly lead to something hopefuller than distributing bread and treacle at the expense of Bodger.

It is a very significant thing, this instinctive choice of the military form of organization, this substitution of the drum for the organ, by the Salvation Army. Does it

not suggest that the Salvationists divine that they must actually fight the devil instead of merely praying at him? At present, it is true, they have not quite ascertained his correct address. When they do, they may give a very rude shock to that sense of security which he has gained from his experience of the fact that hard words, even when uttered by eloquent essayists and lecturers, or carried unanimously at enthusiastic public meetings on the motion of eminent reformers, break no bones. It has been said that the French Revolution was the work of Voltaire, Rousseau and the Encyclopedists. It seems to me to have been the work of men who had observed that virtuous indignation, caustic criticism, conclusive argument and instructive pamphleteering, even when done by the most earnest and witty literary geniuses, were as useless as praying, things going steadily from bad to worse whilst the Social Contract and the pamphlets of Voltaire were at the height of their vogue. Eventually, as we know, perfectly respectable citizens and earnest philanthropists connived at the September massacres because hard experience had convinced them that if they contented themselves with appeals to humanity and patriotism, the aristocracy, though it would read their appeals with the greatest enjoyment and appreciation, flattering and admiring the writers, would none the less continue to conspire with foreign monarchists to undo the revolution and restore the old system with every circumstance of savage vengeance and ruthless repression of popular liberties.

The nineteenth century saw the same lesson repeated in England. It had its Utilitarians, its Christian Socialists, its Fabians (still extant): it had Bentham, Mill, Dickens, Ruskin, Carlyle, Butler, Henry George, and Morris. And the end of all their efforts is the Chicago described by Mr Upton Sinclair, and the London in which the people who pay to be amused by my dramatic representation of Peter Shirley turned out to starve at forty because there are younger slaves to be had for his wages, do not take, and have not the slightest intention of taking, any effective step to organize society in such a way as to make that everyday infamy impossible. I, who have preached and pamphleteered like any Encyclopedist, have to confess that my methods are no use, and would be no use if I were Voltaire, Rousseau, Bentham, Marx, Mill, Dickens, Carlyle, Ruskin, Butler, and Morris all rolled into one, with Euripides, More, Montaigne, Molière, Beaumarchais, Swift, Goethe, Ibsen, Tolstoy, Jesus and the prophets all thrown in (as indeed in some sort I actually am, standing as I do on all their shoulders). The problem being to make heroes out of cowards, we paper apostles and artist-magicians have succeeded only in giving cowards all the sensations of heroes whilst they tolerate every abomination, accept every plunder, and submit to every oppression. Christianity, in making a merit of such submission, has marked only that depth in the abyss at which the very sense of shame is lost. The Christian has been like Dickens' doctor in the debtor's prison, who tells the newcomer of its ineffable peace and security: no duns; no tyrannical collectors of rates, taxes, and rent; no importunate hopes nor exacting duties; nothing but the rest and safety of having no farther to fall.

Yet in the poorest corner of this soul-destroying Christendom vitality suddenly begins to germinate again. Joyousness, a sacred gift long dethroned by the hellish laughter of derision and obscenity, rises like a flood miraculously out of the fetid dust and mud of the slums; rousing marches and impetuous dithyrambs rise to the heavens from people among whom the depressing noise called "sacred music" is a standing joke; a flag with Blood and Fire on it is unfurled, not in murderous rancor, but because fire is beautiful and blood a vital and splendid red; Fear, which we flatter by calling Self, vanishes; and transfigured men and women carry their gospel through a transfigured world, calling their leader General, themselves captains and brigadiers, and their whole body an Army: praying, but praying only for refreshment, for strength to fight, and for needful MONEY (a notable sign, that); preaching, but not preaching submission; daring ill-usage and abuse, but not putting up with more of it than is inevitable; and practising what the world will let them practise, including soap and water, color and music. There is danger in such activity; and where there is danger there is hope. Our present security is nothing, and can be nothing, but evil made irresistible.

WEAKNESSES OF THE SALVATION ARMY

For the present, however, it is not my business to flatter the Salvation Army. Rather must I point out to it that it has almost as many weaknesses as the Church of England itself. It is building up a business organization which will compel it eventually to see that its present staff of enthusiast-commanders shall be succeeded by a bureaucracy of men of business who will be no better than bishops, and perhaps a good deal more unscrupulous. That has always happened sooner or later to great orders founded by saints; and the order founded by St William Booth is not exempt from the same danger. It is even more dependent than the Church on rich people who would cut off supplies at once if it began to preach that indispensable revolt against poverty which must also be a revolt against riches. It is hampered by a heavy contingent of pious elders who are not really Salvationists at all, but Evangelicals of the old school. It still, as Commissioner Howard affirms, "sticks to Moses," which is flat nonsense at this time of day if the Commissioner means, as I am afraid he does, that the Book of Genesis contains a trustworthy scientific account of the origin of species, and that the god to whom Jephthah sacrificed his daughter is any less obviously a tribal idol than Dagon or Chemosh.

Further, there is still too much other-worldliness about the Army. Like Frederick's grenadier, the Salvationist wants to live for ever (the most monstrous way of crying for the moon); and though it is evident to anyone who has ever heard General Booth and his best officers that they would work as hard for human salvation as they do at present if they believed that death would be the end of them individually, they and their followers have a bad habit of talking as if the Salvationists were heroically enduring a very bad time on earth as an investment which will bring them in dividends later on in the form, not of a better life to come for the whole world, but of an eternity spent by themselves personally in a sort of bliss which would bore any active person to a second death. Surely the truth is that the Salvationists are unusually happy people. And is it not the very diagnostic of true salvation that it shall overcome the fear of death? Now the man who has come to believe that there is no such thing as death, the change so called being merely the transition to an exquisitely happy and utterly careless life, has not overcome the fear of death at all: on the contrary, it has overcome him so completely that he refuses to die on any terms whatever. I do not call a Salvationist really saved until he is ready to lie down cheerfully on the scrap heap, having paid scot and lot and something over, and let his eternal life pass on to renew its youth in the battalions of the future.

Then there is the nasty lying habit called confession, which the Army encourages because it lends itself to dramatic oratory, with plenty of thrilling incident. For my part, when I hear a convert relating the violences and oaths and blasphemies he was guilty of before he was saved, making out that he was a very terrible fellow then and is the most contrite and chastened of Christians now, I believe him no more than I believe the millionaire who says he came up to London or Chicago as a boy with only three halfpence in his pocket. Salvationists have said to me that Barbara in my play would never have been taken in by so transparent a humbug as Snobby Price; and certainly I do not think Snobby could have taken in any experienced Salvationist on a point on which the Salvationist did not wish to be taken in. But on the point of conversion all Salvationists wish to be taken in; for the more obvious the sinner the more obvious the miracle of his conversion. When you advertize a converted burglar or reclaimed drunkard as one of the attractions at an experience meeting, your burglar can hardly have been too burglarious or your drunkard too drunken. As long as such attractions are relied on, you will have your Snobbies claiming to have beaten their mothers when they were as a matter of prosaic fact habitually beaten by them, and your Rummies of the tamest respectability pretending to a past of reckless and dazzling vice. Even when confessions are sincerely autobiographic we should beware of assuming that the impulse to make them is pious or the interest of the hearers is wholesome. As well might we assume that the poor people who insist on shewing disgusting ulcers to district visitors are convinced hygienists, or that the curiosity which sometimes welcomes such exhibitions is a pleasant and creditable one. One is often tempted to suggest that those who pester our police superintendents with confessions of murder might very wisely be taken at their word and executed, except in the few cases in which a real murderer is seeking to be relieved of his guilt by confession and expiation. For though I am not, I hope, an unmerciful person, I do not think that the inexorability of the deed once done should be disguised by any ritual, whether in the confessional or on the scaffold.

And here my disagreement with the Salvation Army, and with all propagandists of the Cross (which I loathe as I loathe all gibbets) becomes deep indeed. Forgiveness, absolution, atonement, are figments: punishment is only a pretence of cancelling one crime by another; and you can no more have forgiveness without vindictiveness than you can have a cure without a disease. You will never get a high morality from people who conceive that their misdeeds are revocable and pardonable, or in a society where absolution and expiation are officially provided for us all. The demand may be very real; but the supply is spurious. Thus Bill Walker, in my play, having assaulted the Salvation Lass, presently finds himself overwhelmed with an intolerable conviction of sin under the skilled treatment of Barbara. Straightway he begins to try to unassault the lass and deruffianize his deed, first by getting punished for it in kind, and, when that relief is denied him, by fining himself a pound to compensate the girl. He is foiled both ways. He finds the Salvation Army as inexorable as fact itself. It will not punish him: it will not take his money. It will not tolerate a redeemed ruffian: it leaves him no means of salvation except ceasing to be a ruffian. In doing this, the Salvation Army instinctively grasps the central truth of Christianity and discards its central superstition: that central truth being the vanity of revenge and punishment, and that central superstition the salvation of the world by the gibbet.

For, be it noted, Bill has assaulted an old and starving woman also; and for this worse offence he feels no remorse whatever, because she makes it clear that her malice is as great as his own. "Let her have the law of me, as she said she would," says Bill: "what I done to her is no more on what you might call my conscience than sticking a pig." This shews a perfectly natural and wholesome state of mind on his part. The old woman, like the law she threatens him with, is perfectly ready to play the game of retaliation with him: to rob him if he steals, to flog him if he strikes, to murder him if he kills. By example and precept the law and public opinion teach him to impose his will on others by anger, violence, and cruelty, and to wipe off the moral score by punishment. That is sound Crosstianity. But this Crosstianity has got entangled with something which Barbara calls Christianity, and which unexpectedly causes her to refuse to play the hangman's game of Satan casting out Satan. She refuses to prosecute a drunken ruffian; she converses on equal terms with a blackguard to whom no lady should be seen speaking in the public street: in short, she imitates Christ. Bill's conscience reacts to this just as naturally as it does to the old woman's threats. He is placed in a position of unbearable moral inferiority, and strives by every means in his power to escape from it, whilst he is still quite ready to meet the abuse of the old woman by attempting to smash a mug on her face. And that is the triumphant justification of Barbara's Christianity as against our system of judicial punishment and the vindictive villainthrashings and "poetic justice" of the romantic stage.

For the credit of literature it must be pointed out that the situation is only partly novel. Victor Hugo long ago gave us the epic of the convict and the bishop's candlesticks, of the Crosstian policeman annihilated by his encounter with the Christian Valjean. But Bill Walker is not, like Valjean, romantically changed from a demon into an angel. There are millions of Bill Walkers in all classes of society today; and the point which I, as a professor of natural psychology, desire to demonstrate, is that Bill, without any change in his character or circumstances whatsoever, will react one way to one sort of treatment and another way to another.

In proof I might point to the sensational object lesson provided by our commercial millionaires today. They begin as brigands: merciless, unscrupulous, dealing out ruin and death and slavery to their competitors and employees, and facing desperately the worst that their competitors can do to them. The history of the English factories, the American Trusts, the exploitation of African gold, diamonds, ivory and rubber, outdoes in villainy the worst that has ever been imagined of the buccaneers of the Spanish Main. Captain Kidd would have marooned a modern Trust magnate for conduct unworthy of a gentleman of fortune. The law every day seizes on unsuccessful scoundrels of this type and punishes them with a cruelty worse than their own, with the result that they come out of the torture house more dangerous than they went in, and renew their evil doing (nobody will employ them at anything else) until they are again seized, again tormented, and again let loose, with the same result.

But the successful scoundrel is dealt with very differently, and very Christianly. He is not only forgiven: he is idolized, respected, made much of, all but worshipped. Society returns him good for evil in the most extravagant overmeasure. And with what result? He begins to idolize himself, to respect himself, to live up to the treatment he receives. He preaches sermons; he writes books of the most edifying advice to young men, and actually persuades himself that he got on by taking his own advice; he endows educational institutions; he supports charities; he dies finally in the odor of sanctity, leaving a will which is a monument of public spirit and bounty. And all this without any change in his character. The spots of the leopard and the stripes of the tiger are as brilliant as ever; but the conduct of the world towards him has changed; and his conduct has changed accordingly. You have only to reverse your attitude towards him — to lay hands on his property, revile him, assault him, and he will be a brigand again in a moment, as ready to crush you as you are to crush him, and quite as full of pretentious moral reasons for doing it.

In short, when Major Barbara says that there are no scoundrels, she is right: there are no absolute scoundrels, though there are impracticable people of whom I shall treat presently. Every reasonable man (and woman) is a potential scoundrel and a potential good citizen. What a man is depends on his character; but what he does, and what we think of what he does, depends on his circumstances. The characteristics that ruin a man in one class make him eminent in another. The characters that behave differently in different circumstances behave alike in similar circumstances. Take a common English character like that of Bill Walker. We meet Bill everywhere: on the judicial bench, on the episcopal bench, in the Privy Council, at the War Office and Admiralty, as well as in the Old Bailey dock or in the ranks of casual unskilled labor. And the morality of Bill's characteristics varies with these various circumstances. The faults of the burglar are the qualities of the financier: the manners and habits of a duke would cost a city clerk his situation. In short, though character is independent of circumstances, conduct is not; and our moral judgments of character are not: both are circumstantial. Take any condition of life in which the circumstances are for a mass of men practically alike: felony, the House of Lords, the factory, the stables, the gipsy encampment or where you please! In spite of diversity of character and temperament, the conduct and morals of the individuals in each group are as predictable and as alike in the main as if they were a flock of sheep, morals being mostly only social habits and circumstantial necessities. Strong people know this and count upon it. In nothing have the master-minds of the world been distinguished from the ordinary suburban season-ticket holder more than in their straightforward perception of the fact that mankind is practically a single species, and not a menagerie of gentlemen and bounders, villains and heroes, cowards and daredevils, peers and peasants, grocers and aristocrats, artisans and laborers, washerwomen and duchesses, in which all the grades of income and caste represent distinct animals who must not be introduced to one another or intermarry. Napoleon constructing a galaxy of generals and courtiers, and even of monarchs, out of his collection of social nobodies; Julius Caesar appointing as governor of Egypt the son of a freedman — one who but a short time before would have been legally disqualified for the post even of a private soldier in the Roman army; Louis XI making his barber his privy councillor: all these had in their different ways a firm hold of the scientific fact of human equality, expressed by Barbara in the Christian formula that all men are children of one father. A man who believes that men are naturally divided into upper and lower and middle classes morally is making exactly the same mistake as the man who believes that they are naturally divided in the same way socially. And just as our persistent attempts to found political institutions on a basis of social inequality have always produced long periods of destructive friction relieved from time to time by violent explosions of revolution; so the attempt — will Americans please note — to found moral institutions on a basis of moral inequality can lead to nothing but unnatural Reigns of the Saints relieved by licentious Restorations; to Americans who have made divorce a public institution turning the face of Europe into one huge sardonic smile by refusing to stay in the same hotel with a Russian man of genius who has changed wives without the sanction of South Dakota; to grotesque hypocrisy, cruel persecution, and final utter confusion of conventions and compliances with benevolence and respectability. It is quite useless to declare that all men are born free if you deny that they are born good. Guarantee a man's goodness and his liberty will take care of itself. To guarantee his freedom on condition that you approve of his moral character is formally to abolish all freedom whatsoever, as every man's liberty is at the mercy of a moral indictment which any fool can trump up against everyone who violates custom, whether as a prophet or as a rascal. This is the lesson Democracy has to learn before it can become anything but the most oppressive of all the priesthoods.

Let us now return to Bill Walker and his case of conscience against the Salvation Army. Major Barbara, not being a modern Tetzel, or the treasurer of a hospital, refuses to sell absolution to Bill for a sovereign. Unfortunately, what the Army can afford to refuse in the case of Bill Walker, it cannot refuse in the case of Bodger. Bodger is master of the situation because he holds the purse strings. "Strive as you will," says Bodger, in effect: "me you cannot do without. You cannot save Bill Walker without my money." And the Army answers, quite rightly under the circumstances, "We will take money from the devil himself sooner than abandon the work of Salvation." So Bodger pays his conscience-money and gets the absolution that is refused to Bill. In real life Bill would perhaps never know this. But I, the dramatist whose business it is to shew the connexion between things that seem apart and unrelated in the haphazard order of events in real life, have contrived to make it known to Bill, with the result that the Salvation Army loses its hold of him at once.

But Bill may not be lost, for all that. He is still in the grip of the facts and of his own conscience, and may find his taste for blackguardism permanently spoiled. Still, I cannot guarantee that happy ending. Walk through the poorer quarters of our cities on Sunday when the men are not working, but resting and chewing the cud of their reflections. You will find one expression common to every mature face: the expression of cynicism. The discovery made by Bill Walker about the Salvation Army has been made by everyone there. They have found that every man has his price; and they have been foolishly or corruptly taught to mistrust and despise him for that necessary and salutary condition of social existence. When they learn that General Booth, too, has his price, they do not admire him because it is a high one, and admit the need of organizing society so that he shall get it in an honorable way: they conclude that his character is unsound and that all religious men are hypocrites and allies of their sweaters and oppressors. They know that the large subscriptions which help to support the Army are endowments, not of religion, but of the wicked doctrine of docility in poverty and humility under oppression; and they are rent by the most agonizing of all the doubts of the soul, the doubt whether their true salvation must not come from their most abhorrent passions, from murder, envy, greed, stubbornness, rage, and terrorism, rather than from public spirit, reasonableness, humanity, generosity, tenderness, delicacy, pity and kindness. The confirmation of that doubt, at which our newspapers have been working so hard for years past, is the morality of militarism; and the justification of militarism is that circumstances may at any time make it the true morality of the moment. It is by producing such moments that we produce violent and sanguinary revolutions, such as the one now in progress in Russia and the one which Capitalism in England and America is daily and diligently provoking.

At such moments it becomes the duty of the Churches to evoke all the powers of destruction against the existing order. But if they do this, the existing order must forcibly suppress them. Churches are suffered to exist only on condition that they preach submission to the State as at present capitalistically organized. The Church of England itself is compelled to add to the thirtysix articles in which it formulates its religious tenets, three more in which it apologetically protests that the moment any of these articles comes in conflict with the State it is to be entirely renounced, abjured, violated, abrogated and abhorred, the policeman being a much more important person than any of the Persons of the Trinity. And this is why no tolerated Church nor Salvation Army can ever win the entire confidence of the poor. It must be on the side of the police and the military, no matter what it believes or disbelieves; and as the police and the military are the instruments by which the rich rob and oppress the poor (on legal and moral principles made for the purpose), it is not possible to be on the side of the poor and of the police at the same time. Indeed the religious bodies, as the almoners of the rich, become a sort of auxiliary police, taking off the insurrectionary edge of poverty with coals and blankets, bread and treacle, and soothing and cheering the victims with hopes of immense and inexpensive happiness in another world when the process of working them to premature death in the service of the rich is complete in this.

CHRISTIANITY AND ANARCHISM

Such is the false position from which neither the Salvation Army nor the Church of England nor any other religious organization whatever can escape except through a reconstitution of society. Nor can they merely endure the State passively, washing their hands of its sins. The State is constantly forcing the consciences of men by violence and cruelty. Not content with exacting money from us for the maintenance of its soldiers and policemen, its gaolers and executioners, it forces us to take an active personal part in its proceedings on pain of becoming ourselves the victims of its violence. As I write these lines, a sensational example is given to the world. A royal marriage has been celebrated, first by sacrament in a cathedral, and then by a bullfight having for its main amusement the spectacle of horses gored and disembowelled by the bull, after which, when the bull is so exhausted as to be no longer dangerous, he is killed by a cautious matador. But the ironic contrast between the bullfight and the sacrament of marriage does not move anyone. Another contrast — that between the splendor, the happiness, the atmosphere of kindly admiration surrounding the young couple, and the price paid for it under our abominable social arrangements in the misery, squalor and degradation of millions of other young couples — is drawn at the same moment by a novelist, Mr Upton Sinclair, who chips a corner of the veneering from the huge meat packing industries of Chicago, and shews it to us as a sample of what is going on all over the world underneath the top layer of prosperous plutocracy. One man is sufficiently moved by that contrast to pay his own life as the price of one terrible blow at the responsible parties. His poverty has left him ignorant enough to be duped by the pretence that the innocent young bride and bridegroom, put forth and crowned by plutocracy as the heads of a State in which they have less personal power than any policeman, and less influence than any Chairman of a Trust, are responsible. At them accordingly he launches his sixpennorth of fulminate, missing his mark, but scattering the bowels of as many horses as any bull in the arena, and slaying twentythree persons, besides wounding ninetynine. And of all these, the horses alone are innocent of the guilt he is avenging: had he blown all Madrid to atoms with every adult person in it, not one could have escaped the charge of being an accessory, before, at, and after the fact, to poverty and prostitution, to such whole-sale massacre of infants as Herod never dreamt of, to plague, pestilence and fa-mine, battle, murder and lingering death — perhaps not one who had not helped, through example, precept, connivance, and even clamor, to teach the dynamiter his well-learnt gospel of hatred and vengeance, by approving every day of sentences of years of imprisonment so infernal in their unnatural stupidity and panic-stricken cruelty, that their advocates can disavow neither the dagger nor the bomb without stripping the mask of justice and humanity from themselves also.

Be it noted that at this very moment there appears the biography of one of our dukes, who, being a Scot, could argue about politics, and therefore stood out as a great brain among our aristocrats. And what, if you please, was his grace's favorite historical episode, which he declared he never read without intense satisfaction? Why, the young General Bonapart's pounding of the Paris mob to pieces in 1795, called in playful approval by our respectable classes "the whiff of grapeshot," though Napoleon, to do him justice, took a deeper view of it, and would fain have had it forgotten. And since the Duke of Argyll was not a demon, but a man of like passions with ourselves, by no means rancorous or cruel as men go, who can doubt that all over the world proletarians of the ducal kidney are now revelling in "the whiff of dynamite" (the flavor of the joke seems to evaporate a little, does it not?) because it was aimed at the class they hate even as our argute duke hated what he called the mob.

In such an atmosphere there can be only one sequel to the Madrid explosion. All Europe burns to emulate it. Vengeance! More blood! Tear "the Anarchist beast" to shreds. Drag him to the scaffold. Imprison him for life. Let all civilized States band together to drive his like off the face of the earth; and if any State refuses to join, make war on it. This time the leading London newspaper, anti-Liberal and there-fore anti-Russian in politics, does not say "Serve you right" to the victims, as it did, in effect, when Bobrikoff, and De Plehve, and Grand Duke Sergius, were in the same manner unofficially fulminated into fragments. No: fulminate our rivals in Asia by all means, ye brave Russian revolutionaries; but to aim at an English prin-cess! monstrous! hideous! hound down the wretch to his doom: and observe, please, that we are a civilized and merciful people, and, however much we may regret it, must not treat him as Ravaillac and Damiens were treated. And meanwhile, since we have not yet caught him, let us soothe our quivering nerves with the bullfight, and comment in a courtly way on the unfailing tact and good taste of the ladies of our royal houses, who, though presumably of full normal natural tenderness, have been so effectually broken in to fashionable routine that they can be taken to see the horses slaughtered as helplessly as they could no doubt be taken to a gladiator show, if that happened to be the mode just now.

Strangely enough, in the midst of this raging fire of malice, the one man who still has faith in the kindness and intelligence of human nature is the fulminator, now a hunted wretch, with nothing, apparently, to secure his triumph over all the prisons and scaffolds of infuriate Europe except the revolver in his pocket and his readiness to discharge it at a moment's notice into his own or any other head. Think of him setting out to find a gentleman and a Christian in the multitude of human wolves howling for his blood. Think also of this: that at the very first essay he finds what he seeks, a veritable grandee of Spain, a noble, high-thinking, unterrified, malice-void soul, in the guise — of all masquerades in the world! — of a modern editor. The Anarchist wolf, flying from the wolves of plutocracy, throws himself on the honor of the man. The man, not being a wolf (nor a London editor), and therefore not having enough sympathy with his exploit to be made blood-thirsty by it, does not throw him back to the pursuing wolves — gives him, instead, what help he can to escape, and sends him off acquainted at last with a force that goes deeper than dynamite, though you cannot buy so much of it for sixpence. That righteous and honorable high human deed is not wasted on Europe, let us hope, though it bene-fits the fugitive wolf only for a moment. The plutocratic wolves presently smell him out. The fugitive shoots the unlucky wolf whose nose is nearest; shoots himself; and then convinces the world, by his photograph, that he was no monstrous freak of reversion to the tiger, but a good looking young man with nothing abnormal about him except his appalling courage and resolution (that is why the terrified shriek Coward at him): one to whom murdering a happy young couple on their wedding morning would have been an unthinkably unnatural abomination under rational and kindly human circumstances.

Then comes the climax of irony and blind stupidity. The wolves, balked of their meal of fellow-wolf, turn on the man, and proceed to torture him, after their man-ner, by imprisonment, for refusing to fasten his teeth in the throat of the dyna-miter and hold him down until they came to finish him.

Thus, you see, a man may not be a gentleman nowadays even if he wishes to. As to being a Christian, he is allowed some latitude in that matter, because, I repeat, Christianity has two faces. Popular Christianity has for its emblem a gibbet, for its chief sensation a sanguinary execution after torture, for its central mystery an in-sane vengeance bought off by a trumpery expiation. But there is a nobler and pro-founder Christianity which affirms the sacred mystery of Equality, and forbids the glaring futility and folly of vengeance, often politely called punishment or justice. The gibbet part of Christianity is tolerated. The other is criminal felony. Connois-seurs in irony are well aware of the fact that the only editor in England who de-nounces punishment as radically wrong, also repudiates Christianity; calls his paper The Freethinker; and has been imprisoned for "bad taste" under the law against blasphemy.

SANE CONCLUSIONS

And now I must ask the excited reader not to lose his head on one side or the other, but to draw a sane moral from these grim absurdities. It is not good sense to propose that laws against crime should apply to principals only and not to accesso-ries whose consent, counsel, or silence may secure impunity to the principal. If you institute punishment as part of the law, you must punish people for refusing to punish. If you have a police, part of its duty must be to compel everybody to assist the police. No doubt if your laws are unjust, and your policemen agents of oppres-sion, the result will be an unbearable violation of the private consciences of citi-zens. But that cannot be helped: the remedy is, not to license everybody to thwart the law if they please, but to make laws that will command the public assent, and not to deal cruelly and stupidly with lawbreakers. Everybody disapproves of bur-glars; but the modern burglar, when caught and overpowered by a householder, usually appeals, and often, let us hope, with success, to his captor not to deliver him over to the useless horrors of penal servitude. In other cases the lawbreaker escapes because those who could give him up do not consider his breach of the law a guilty action. Sometimes, even, private tribunals are formed in opposition to the official tribunals; and these private tribunals employ assassins as executioners, as was done, for example, by Mahomet before he had established his power officially, and by the Ribbon lodges of Ireland in their long struggle with the landlords. Under such circumstances, the assassin goes free although everybody in the district knows who he is and what he has done. They do not betray him, partly because they justify him exactly as the regular Government justifies its official executioner, and partly because they would themselves be assassinated if they betrayed him: another method learnt from the official government. Given a tribunal, employing a slayer who has no personal quarrel with the slain; and there is clearly no moral difference between official and unofficial killing.

In short, all men are anarchists with regard to laws which are against their consciences, either in the preamble or in the penalty. In London our worst anarchists are the magistrates, because many of them are so old and ignorant that when they are called upon to administer any law that is based on ideas or knowledge less than half a century old, they disagree with it, and being mere ordinary homebred private Englishmen without any respect for law in the abstract, naïvely set the example of violating it. In this instance the man lags behind the law; but when the law lags behind the man, he becomes equally an anarchist. When some huge change in social conditions, such as the industrial revolution of the eighteenth and nineteenth centuries, throws our legal and industrial institutions out of date, Anarchism becomes almost a religion. The whole force of the most energetic geniuses of the time in philosophy, economics, and art, concentrates itself on demonstrations and reminders that morality and law are only conventions, fallible and continually obsolescing. Tragedies in which the heroes are bandits, and comedies in which law-abiding and conventionally moral folk are compelled to satirize themselves by outraging the conscience of the spectators every time they do their duty, appear simultaneously with economic treatises entitled "What is Property? Theft!" and with histories of "The Conflict between Religion and Science."

Now this is not a healthy state of things. The advantages of living in society are proportionate, not to the freedom of the individual from a code, but to the complexity and subtlety of the code he is prepared not only to accept but to uphold as a matter of such vital importance that a lawbreaker at large is hardly to be tolerated on any plea. Such an attitude becomes impossible when the only men who can make themselves heard and remembered throughout the world spend all their energy in raising our gorge against current law, current morality, current respectability, and legal property. The ordinary man, uneducated in social theory even when he is schooled in Latin verse, cannot be set against all the laws of his country and yet persuaded to regard law in the abstract as vitally necessary to society. Once he is brought to repudiate the laws and institutions he knows, he will repudiate the very conception of law and the very groundwork of institutions, ridiculing human rights, extolling brainless methods as "historical," and tolerating nothing except pure empiricism in conduct, with dynamite as the basis of politics and vivisection as the basis of science. That is hideous; but what is to be done? Here am I, for instance, by class a respectable man, by common sense a hater of waste and disorder, by intellectual constitution legally minded to the verge of pedantry, and by temperament apprehensive and economically disposed to the limit of old-maidishness; yet

I am, and have always been, and shall now always be, a revolutionary writer, because our laws make law impossible; our liberties destroy all freedom; our property is organized robbery; our morality is an impudent hypocrisy; our wisdom is administered by inexperienced or malexperienced dupes, our power wielded by cowards and weaklings, and our honor false in all its points. I am an enemy of the existing order for good reasons; but that does not make my attacks any less encouraging or helpful to people who are its enemies for bad reasons. The existing order may shriek that if I tell the truth about it, some foolish person may drive it to become still worse by trying to assassinate it. I cannot help that, even if I could see what worse it could do than it is already doing. And the disadvantage of that worst even from its own point of view is that society, with all its prisons and bayonets and whips and ostracisms and starvations, is powerless in the face of the Anarchist who is prepared to sacrifice his own life in the battle with it. Our natural safety from the cheap and devastating explosives which every Russian student can make, and every Russian grenadier has learnt to handle in Manchuria, lies in the fact that brave and resolute men, when they are rascals, will not risk their skins for the good of humanity, and, when they are not, are sympathetic enough to care for humanity, abhorring murder, and never committing it until their consciences are outraged beyond endurance. The remedy is, then, simply not to outrage their consciences.

Do not be afraid that they will not make allowances. All men make very large allowances indeed before they stake their own lives in a war to the death with society. Nobody demands or expects the millennium. But there are two things that must be set right, or we shall perish, like Rome, of soul atrophy disguised as empire.

The first is, that the daily ceremony of dividing the wealth of the country among its inhabitants shall be so conducted that no crumb shall, save as a criminal's ration, go to any able-bodied adults who are not producing by their personal exertions not only a full equivalent for what they take, but a surplus sufficient to provide for their superannuation and pay back the debt due for their nurture.

The second is that the deliberate infliction of malicious injuries which now goes on under the name of punishment be abandoned; so that the thief, the ruffian, the gambler, and the beggar, may without inhumanity be handed over to the law, and made to understand that a State which is too humane to punish will also be too thrifty to waste the life of honest men in watching or restraining dishonest ones. That is why we do not imprison dogs. We even take our chance of their first bite. But if a dog delights to bark and bite, it goes to the lethal chamber. That seems to me sensible. To allow the dog to expiate his bite by a period of torment, and then let him loose in a much more savage condition (for the chain makes a dog savage) to bite again and expiate again, having meanwhile spent a great deal of human life and happiness in the task of chaining and feeding and tormenting him, seems to me idiotic and superstitious. Yet that is what we do to men who bark and bite and steal. It would be far more sensible to put up with their vices, as we put up with their illnesses, until they give more trouble than they are worth, at which point we should, with many apologies and expressions of sympathy, and some generosity in complying with their last wishes, place them in the lethal chamber and get rid of them. Under no circumstances should they be allowed to expiate their misdeeds by a manufactured penalty, to subscribe to a charity, or to compensate the victims. If there is to be no punishment there can be no forgiveness. We shall never have real moral responsibility until everyone knows that his deeds are irrevocable, and that his life depends on his usefulness. Hitherto, alas! humanity has never dared face these hard facts. We frantically scatter conscience money and invent systems of conscience banking, with expiatory penalties, atonements, redemptions, salvations, hospital subscription lists and what not, to enable us to contract-out of the moral code. Not content with the old scapegoat and sacrificial lamb, we deify human saviors, and pray to miraculous virgin intercessors. We attribute mercy to the inexorable; soothe our consciences after committing murder by throwing ourselves on the bosom of divine love; and shrink even from our own gallows because we are forced to admit that it, at least, is irrevocable — as if one hour of imprisonment were not as irrevocable as any execution!

If a man cannot look evil in the face without illusion, he will never know what it really is, or combat it effectually. The few men who have been able (relatively) to do this have been called cynics, and have sometimes had an abnormal share of evil in themselves, corresponding to the abnormal strength of their minds; but they have never done mischief unless they intended to do it. That is why great scoundrels have been beneficent rulers whilst amiable and privately harmless monarchs have ruined their countries by trusting to the hocus-pocus of innocence and guilt, reward and punishment, virtuous indignation and pardon, instead of standing up to the facts without either malice or mercy. Major Barbara stands up to Bill Walker in that way, with the result that the ruffian who cannot get hated, has to hate himself. To relieve this agony he tries to get punished; but the Salvationist whom he tries to provoke is as merciless as Barbara, and only prays for him. Then he tries to pay, but can get nobody to take his money. His doom is the doom of Cain, who, failing to find either a savior, a policeman, or an almoner to help him to pretend that his brother's blood no longer cried from the ground, had to live and die a murderer. Cain took care not to commit another murder, unlike our railway shareholders (I am one) who kill and maim shunters by hundreds to save the cost of automatic couplings, and make atonement by annual subscriptions to deserving charities. Had Cain been allowed to pay off his score, he might possibly have killed Adam and Eve for the mere sake of a second luxurious reconciliation with God afterwards. Bodger, you may depend on it, will go on to the end of his life poisoning people with bad whisky, because he can always depend on the Salvation Army or the Church of England to negotiate a redemption for him in consideration of a trifling percentage of his profits.

There is a third condition too, which must be fulfilled before the great teachers of the world will cease to scoff at its religions. Creeds must become intellectually honest. At present there is not a single credible established religion in the world. That is perhaps the most stupendous fact in the whole world-situation. This play of mine, Major Barbara, is, I hope, both true and inspired; but whoever says that it all happened, and that faith in it and understanding of it consist in believing that it is a record of an actual occurrence, is, to speak according to Scripture, a fool and a liar, and is hereby solemnly denounced and cursed as such by me, the author, to all posterity.

London, June 1906.

N.B. The Euripidean verses in the second act of Major Barbara are not by me, nor even directly by Euripides. They are by Professor Gilbert Murray, whose English version of The Bacchæ came into our dramatic literature with all the impulsive power of an original work shortly before Major Barbara was begun. The play, indeed, stands indebted to him in more ways than one.

                                                              G. B. S.

CHARACTERS

ANDREW UNDERSHAFT	RUMMY MITCHENS
LADY BRITOMART	SNOBBY PRICE
STEPHEN UNDERSHAFT	PETER SHIRLEY
BARBARA UNDERSHAFT	BILL WALKER
SARAH UNDERSHAFT	JENNY HILL
ADOLPHUS CUSINS	MRS. BAINES
CHARLES LOMAX	BILTON
MORRISON	

ACT I

It is after dinner in January 1906, in the library in LADY BRITOMART UNDER-SHAFT's *house in Wilton Crescent. A large and comfortable settee is in the middle of the room, upholstered in dark leather. A person sitting on it (it is vacant at present) would have, on his right,* LADY BRITOMART's *writing table, with the lady herself busy at it; a smaller writing table behind him on his left; the door behind him on* LADY BRITOMART's *side; and a window with a window seat directly on his left. Near the window is an armchair.*

LADY BRITOMART *is a woman of fifty or thereabouts, well dressed and yet careless of her dress, well bred and quite reckless of her breeding, well mannered and yet appallingly outspoken and indifferent to the opinion of her interlocutors, amiable and yet peremptory, arbitrary, and high-tempered to the last bearable degree, and withal a very typical managing matron of the upper class, treated as a naughty child until she grew into a scolding mother, and finally settling down with plenty of practical ability and worldly experience, limited in the oddest way with domestic and class limitations, conceiving the universe exactly as if it were a large house in Wilton Crescent, though handling her corner of it very effectively on that assumption, and being quite enlightened and liberal as to the books in the library, the pictures on the walls, and the music in the portfolios, and the articles in the papers.*

Her son, STEPHEN, *comes in. He's a gravely correct young man under 25, taking himself very seriously, but still in some awe of his mother, from childish habit and bachelor shyness rather than from any weakness of character.*

STEPHEN: Whats the matter?
LADY BRITOMART: Presently, Stephen.

(STEPHEN *submissively walks to the settee and sits down. He takes up a Liberal weekly called The Speaker.*)

LADY BRITOMART: Dont begin to read, Stephen. I shall require all your attention.
STEPHEN: It was only while I was waiting —
LADY BRITOMART: Dont make excuses, Stephen. (*He puts down The Speaker.*) Now!
   (*She finishes her writing; rises; and comes to the settee.*) I have not kept you
   waiting very long, I think.
STEPHEN: Not at all, mother.
LADY BRITOMART: Bring me my cushion. (*He takes the cushion from the chair at the*

desk and arranges it for her as she sits down on the settee.) Sit down. (*He sits down and fingers his tie nervously.*) Don't fiddle with your tie, Stephen: there is nothing the matter with it.

STEPHEN: I beg your pardon. (*He fiddles with his watch chain instead.*)

LADY BRITOMART: Now are you attending to me, Stephen?

STEPHEN: Of course, mother.

LADY BRITOMART: No: it's not of course. I want something much more than your everyday matter-of-course attention. I am going to speak to you very seriously, Stephen. I wish you would let that chain alone.

STEPHEN (*hastily relinquishing the chain*): Have I done anything to annoy you, mother? If so, it was quite unintentional.

LADY BRITOMART (*astonished*): Nonsense! (*With some remorse.*) My poor boy, did you think I was angry with you?

STEPHEN: What is it, then, mother? You are making me very uneasy.

LADY BRITOMART (*squaring herself at him rather aggressively*): Stephen: may I ask how soon you intend to realize that you are a grown-up man, and that I am only a woman?

STEPHEN (*amazed*): Only a —

LADY BRITOMART: Dont repeat my words, please: it is a most aggravating habit. You must learn to face life seriously, Stephen. I really cannot bear the whole burden of our family affairs any longer. You must advise me: you must assume the responsibility.

STEPHEN: I!

LADY BRITOMART: Yes, you, of course. You were 24 last June. Youve been at Harrow and Cambridge. Youve been to India and Japan. You must know a lot of things, now; unless you have wasted your time most scandalously. Well, advise me.

STEPHEN (*much perplexed*): You know I have never interfered in the household —

LADY BRITOMART: No: I should think not. I dont want you to order the dinner.

STEPHEN: I mean in our family affairs.

LADY BRITOMART: Well, you must interfere now; for they are getting quite beyond me.

STEPHEN (*troubled*): I have thought sometimes that perhaps I ought; but really, mother, I know so little about them; and what I do know is so painful! it is so impossible to mention some things to you — (*He stops, ashamed.*)

LADY BRITOMART: I suppose you mean your father.

STEPHEN (*almost inaudibly*): Yes.

LADY BRITOMART: My dear: we cant go on all our lives not mentioning him. Of course you were quite right not to open the subject until I asked you to; but you are old enough now to be taken into my confidence, and to help me to deal with him about the girls.

STEPHEN: But the girls are all right. They are engaged.

LADY BRITOMART (*complacently*): Yes: I have made a very good match for Sarah. Charles Lomax will be a millionaire at 35. But that is ten years ahead and in the meantime his trustees cannot under the terms of his father's will allow him more than £800 a year.

STEPHEN: But the will says also that if he increases his income by his own exertions, they may double the increase.

LADY BRITOMART: Charles Lomax's exertions are much more likely to decrease his income than to increase it. Sarah will have to find at least another £800 a year for the next ten years; and even then they will be as poor as church mice. And what about Barbara? I thought Barbara was going to make the most brilliant career of all of you. And what does she do? Joins the Salvation Army; discharges her maid; lives on a pound a week; and walks in one evening with a professor of Greek whom she has picked up in the street, and who pretends to be a Salvationist, and actually plays the big drum for her in public because he has fallen head over ears in love with her.

STEPHEN: I was certainly rather taken aback when I heard they were engaged. Cusins is a very nice fellow, certainly: nobody would ever guess that he was born in Australia; but —

LADY BRITOMART: Oh, Adolphus Cusins will make a very good husband. After all, nobody can say a word against Greek: it stamps a man at once as an educated gentleman. And my family, thank Heaven, is not a pig-headed Tory one. We are Whigs, and believe in liberty. Let snobbish people say what they please: Barbara shall marry, not the man they like, but the man *I* like.

STEPHEN: Of course I was thinking only of his income. However, he is not likely to be extravagant.

LADY BRITOMART: Dont be too sure of that, Stephen. I know your quiet, simple, refined, poetic people like Adolphus: quite content with the best of everything! They cost more than your extravagant people, who are always as mean as they are second rate. No: Barbara will need at least £2000 a year. You see it means two additional households. Besides, my dear, you must marry soon. I dont approve of the present fashion of philandering bachelors and late marriages; and I am trying to arrange something for you.

STEPHEN: It's very good of you, mother; but perhaps I had better arrange that for myself.

LADY BRITOMART: Nonsense! you are much too young to begin matchmaking: you would be taken in by some pretty little nobody. Of course I dont mean that you are not to be consulted: you know that as well as I do. (STEPHEN *closes his lips and is silent*.) Now dont sulk, Stephen.

STEPHEN: I am not sulking, mother. What has all this got to do with — with — my father?

LADY BRITOMART: My dear Stephen: where is the money to come from? It is easy enough for you and the other children to live on my income as long as we are in the same house; but I cant keep four families in four separate houses. You know how poor my father is: he has barely seven thousand a year now; and really, if he were not the Earl of Stevenage, he would have to give up society. He can do nothing for us. He says, naturally enough, that it is absurd that he should be asked to provide for the children of a man who is rolling in money. You see, Stephen, your father must be fabulously wealthy, because there is always a war going on somewhere.

STEPHEN: You need not remind me of that, mother. I have hardly ever opened a newspaper in my life without seeing our name in it. The Undershaft torpedo! The Undershaft quick firers! The Undershaft ten inch! the Undershaft disappearing rampart gun! the Undershaft submarine! and now the Undershaft aerial battleship! At Harrow they called me the Woolwich Infant. At Cambridge it was the same. A little brute at King's who was always trying to get up revivals, spoilt my Bible — your first birthday present to me — by writing under my name, 'Son and heir to Undershaft and Lazarus, Death and Destruction Dealers: address Christendom and Judea.' But that was not so bad as the way I was kowtowed to everywhere because my father was making millions by selling cannons.

LADY BRITOMART: It is not only the cannons, but the war loans that Lazarus arranges under cover of giving credit for the cannons. You know, Stephen, it's perfectly scandalous. Those two men, Andrew Undershaft and Lazarus, positively have Europe under their thumbs. That is why your father is able to behave as he does. He is above the law. Do you think Bismarck or Gladstone or Disraeli could have openly defied every social and moral obligation all their lives as your father has? They simply wouldnt have dared. I asked Gladstone to take it up. I asked The Times to take it up. I asked the Lord Chamberlain to take it up. But it was just like asking them to declare war on the Sultan. They wouldnt. They said they couldnt touch him. I believe they were afraid.

STEPHEN: What could they do? He does not actually break the law.

LADY BRITOMART: Not break the law! He is always breaking the law. He broke the law when he was born: his parents were not married.

STEPHEN: Mother! Is that true?

LADY BRITOMART: Of course it's true: that was why we separated.

STEPHEN: He married without letting you know this!

LADY BRITOMART (*rather taken aback by this inference*): Oh no. To do Andrew justice, that was not the sort of thing he did. Besides, you know the Undershaft motto: Unashamed. Everybody knew.

STEPHEN: But you said that was why you separated.

LADY BRITOMART: Yes, because he was not content with being a foundling himself: he wanted to disinherit you for another foundling. That was what I couldnt stand.

STEPHEN (*ashamed*): Do you mean for — for — for —

LADY BRITOMART: Dont stammer, Stephen. Speak distinctly.

STEPHEN: But this is so frightful to me, mother. To have to speak to you about such things!

LADY BRITOMART: It's not pleasant for me, either, especially if you are still so childish that you must make it worse by a display of embarrassment. It is only in the middle classes, Stephen, that people get into a state of dumb helpless horror when they find that there are wicked people in the world. In our class, we have to decide what is to be done with wicked people; and nothing should disturb our self-possession. Now ask your question properly.

STEPHEN: Mother: have you no consideration for me? For Heaven's sake either treat me as a child, as you always do, and tell me nothing at all; or tell me everything and let me take it as best I can.

LADY BRITOMART: Treat you as a child! What do you mean? It is most unkind and ungrateful of you to say such a thing. You know I have never treated any of you as children. I have always made you my companions and friends, and allowed you perfect freedom to do and say whatever you liked, so long as you liked what I could approve of.

STEPHEN (*desperately*): I daresay we have been the very imperfect children of a very perfect mother; but I do beg you to let me alone for once, and tell me about this horrible business of my father wanting to set me aside for another son.

LADY BRITOMART (*amazed*): Another son! I never said anything of the kind. I never dreamt of such a thing. This is what comes of interrupting me.

STEPHEN: But you said —

LADY BRITOMART (*cutting him short*): Now be a good boy, Stephen, and listen to me patiently. The Undershafts are descended from a foundling in the parish of St Andrew Undershaft in the city. That was long ago, in the reign of James the First. Well this foundling was adopted by an armorer and gun-maker. In the course of time the foundling succeeded to the business; and from some notion of gratitude, or some vow or something, he adopted another foundling, and left the business to him. And that foundling did the same. Ever since that, the cannon business has always been left to an adopted foundling named Andrew Undershaft.

STEPHEN: But did they never marry? Were there no legitimate sons?

LADY BRITOMART: Oh yes: they married just as your father did; and they were rich enough to buy land for their own children and leave them well provided for. But they always adopted and trained some foundling to succeed them in the business; and of course they always quarreled with their wives furiously over it. Your father was adopted in that way; and he pretends to consider himself bound to keep up the tradition and adopt somebody to leave the business to. Of course I was not going to stand that. There may have been some reason for it when the Undershafts could only marry women in their own class, whose sons were not fit to govern great estates. But there could be no excuse for passing over my son.

STEPHEN (*dubiously*): I am afraid I should make a poor hand of managing a cannon foundry.

LADY BRITOMART: Nonsense! you could easily get a manager and pay him a salary.

STEPHEN: My father evidently had no great opinion of my capacity.

LADY BRITOMART: Stuff, child! you were only a baby: it had nothing to do with your capacity. Andrew did it on principle, just as he did every perverse and wicked thing on principle. When my father remonstrated, Andrew actually told him to his face that history tells us of only two successful institutions: one the Undershaft firm, and the other the Roman Empire under the Antonines. That was because the Antonine emperors all adopted their successors. Such rubbish! The Stevenages are as good as the Antonines, I hope; and you are a Stevenage. But that was Andrew all over. There you have the man! Always clever and unanswerable when he was defending nonsense and wickedness: always awkward and sullen when he had to behave sensibly and decently!

STEPHEN: Then it was on my account that your home life was broken up, mother. I am sorry.

LADY BRITOMART: Well, dear, there were other differences. I really cannot bear an immoral man. I am not a Pharisee, I hope; and I should not have minded his merely doing wrong things: we are none of us perfect. But your father didnt exactly do wrong things: he said them and thought them: that was what was so dreadful. He really had a sort of religion of wrongness. Just as one doesnt mind men practising immorality so long as they own that they are in the wrong by preaching morality; so I couldn't forgive Andrew for preaching immorality while he practised morality. You would all have grown up without principles, without any knowledge of right and wrong, if he had been in the house. You know, my dear, your father was a very attractive man in some ways. Children did not dislike him; and he took advantage of it to put the wickedest ideas into their heads, and make them quite unmanageable. I did not dislike him myself: very far from it; but nothing can bridge over moral disagreement.

STEPHEN: All this simply bewilders me, mother. People may differ about matters of opinion, or even about religion; but how can they differ about right and wrong? Right is right; and wrong is wrong; and if a man cannot distinguish them properly, he is either a fool or a rascal: thats all.

LADY BRITOMART (*touched*): Thats my own boy (*she pats his cheek*)! Your father never could answer that: he used to laugh and get out of it under cover of some affectionate nonsense. And now that you understand the situation, what do you advise me to do?

STEPHEN: Well, what *can* you do?

LADY BRITOMART: I must get the money somehow.

STEPHEN: We cannot take money from him. I had rather go and live in some cheap place like Bedford Square or even Hampstead than take a farthing of his money.

LADY BRITOMART: But after all, Stephen, our present income comes from Andrew.

STEPHEN (*shocked*): I never knew that.

LADY BRITOMART: Well, you surely didnt suppose your grandfather had anything to give me. The Stevenages could not do everything for you. We gave you social position. Andrew had to contribute something. He had a very good bargain, I think.

STEPHEN (*bitterly*): We are utterly dependent on him and his cannons, then?

LADY BRITOMART: Certainly not: the money is settled. But he provided it. So you see it is not a question of taking money from him or not: it is simply a question of how much. I dont want any more for myself.

STEPHEN: Nor do I.

LADY BRITOMART: But Sarah does; and Barbara does. That is, Charles Lomax and Adolphus Cusins will cost them more. So I must put my pride in my pocket and ask for it, I suppose. That is your advice, Stephen, is it not?

STEPHEN: No.

LADY BRITOMART (*sharply*): Stephen!

STEPHEN: Of course if you are determined —

LADY BRITOMART: I am not determined: I ask your advice; and I am waiting for it. I will not have all the responsibility thrown on my shoulders.

STEPHEN (*obstinately*): I would die sooner than ask him for another penny.

LADY BRITOMART (*resignedly*): You mean that *I* must ask him. Very well, Stephen: it shall be as you wish. You will be glad to know that your grandfather concurs. But he thinks I ought to ask Andrew to come here and see the girls. After all, he must have some natural affection for them.

STEPHEN: Ask him here!!!

LADY BRITOMART: Do not repeat my words, Stephen. Where else can I ask him?

STEPHEN: I never expected you to ask him at all.

LADY BRITOMART: Now dont tease, Stephen. Come! you see that it is necessary that he should pay us a visit, dont you?

STEPHEN (*reluctantly*): I suppose so, if the girls cannot do without his money.

LADY BRITOMART: Thank you, Stephen: I knew you would give me the right advice when it was properly explained to you. I have asked your father to come this evening. (STEPHEN *bounds from his seat*.) Dont jump, Stephen: it fidgets me.

STEPHEN (*in utter consternation*): Do you mean to say that my father is coming here tonight — that he may be here at any moment?

LADY BRITOMART (*looking at her watch*): I said nine. (*He gasps. She rises.*) Ring the bell, please. (STEPHEN *goes to the smaller writing table; presses a button on it; and sits at it with his elbows on the table and his head in his hands, outwitted and overwhelmed*.) It is ten minutes to nine yet; and I have to prepare the girls. I asked Charles Lomax and Adolphus to dinner on purpose that they might be here. Andrew had better see them in case he should cherish any delusions as to their being capable of supporting their wives. (*The butler enters:* LADY BRITOMART *goes behind the settee to speak to him*.) Morrison: go up to the drawing room and tell everybody to come down here at once. (MORRISON *withdraws*. LADY BRITO-MART *turns to* STEPHEN.) Now remember, Stephen: I shall need all your counte-nance and authority. (*He rises and tries to recover some vestige of these attributes*.) Give me a chair, dear. (*He pushes a chair forward from the wall to where she stands, near the smaller writing table. She sits down; and he goes to the armchair, into which he throws himself*.) I dont know how Barbara will take it. Ever since they made her a major in the Salvation Army she has developed a propensity to have her own way and order people about which quite cows me sometimes. It's not ladylike: I'm sure I dont know where she picked it up. Any-how, Barbara shant bully me; but still it's just as well that your father should be here before she has time to refuse to meet him or make a fuss. Dont look ner-vous, Stephen: it will only encourage Barbara to make difficulties. *I* am nervous enough, goodness knows; but I dont shew it.

(SARAH *and* BARBARA *come in with their respective young men,* CHARLES LOMAX *and* ADOLPHUS CUSINS. SARAH *is slender, bored, and mundane.* BARBARA *is ro-buster, jollier, much more energetic.* SARAH *is fashionably dressed:* BARBARA *is in Salvation Army uniform.* LOMAX, *a young man about town, is like many other young men about town. He is afflicted with a frivolous sense of humor which plunges him at the most inopportune moments into paroxysms of imperfectly suppressed laughter.* CUSINS *is a spectacled student, slight, thin haired, and sweet voiced, with a more complex form of* LOMAX's *complaint. His sense of humor is intellectual and subtle, and is complicated by an appalling temper. The lifelong struggle of a benevolent temperament and a high conscience against impulses of inhuman ridicule and fierce impatience has set up a chronic strain which has visibly wrecked his constitution. He is a most implacable, determined, tenacious, intolerant person who by mere force of character presents himself as — and indeed actually is — considerate, gentle, explanatory, even mild and apologetic, capable possibly of murder, but not of cruelty or coarse-ness. By the operation of some instinct which is not merciful enough to blind him with the illusions of love, he is obstinately bent on marrying* BARBARA. LOMAX *likes* SARAH *and thinks it will be rather a lark to marry her. Consequently he has not attempted to resist* LADY BRITOMART's *arrangements to that end.*

  All four look as if they had been having a good deal of fun in the drawing room. The girls enter first, leaving the swains outside. SARAH *comes to the set-tee.* BARBARA *comes in after her and stops at the door*.)

BARBARA: Are Cholly and Dolly to come in?

LADY BRITOMART (*forcibly*): Barbara: I will not have Charles called Cholly: the vul-garity of it positively makes me ill.

BARBARA: It's all right, mother: Cholly is quite correct nowadays. Are they to come in?

LADY BRITOMART: Yes, if they will behave themselves.

BARBARA (*through the door*): Come in, Dolly; and behave yourself.

(BARBARA *comes to her mother's writing table.* CUSINS *enters smiling, and wanders towards* LADY BRITOMART.)

SARAH (*calling*): Come in, Cholly. (LOMAX *enters, controlling his features very imperfectly, and places himself vaguely between* SARAH *and* BARBARA.)

LADY BRITOMART (*peremptorily*): Sit down, all of you. (*They sit.* CUSINS *crosses to the window and seats himself there.* LOMAX *takes a chair.* BARBARA *sits at the writing table and* SARAH *on the settee.*) I dont in the least know what you are laughing at, Adolphus. I am surprised at you, though I expected nothing better from Charles Lomax.

CUSINS (*in a remarkably gentle voice*): Barbara has been trying to teach me the West Ham Salvation March.

LADY BRITOMART: I see nothing to laugh at in that; nor should you if you are really converted.

CUSINS (*sweetly*): You were not present. It was really funny, I believe.

LOMAX: Ripping.

LADY BRITOMART: Be quiet, Charles. Now listen to me, children. Your father is coming here this evening.

(*General stupefaction.* LOMAX, SARAH, *and* BARBARA *rise:* SARAH *scared, and* BARBARA *amused and expectant.*)

LOMAX (*remonstrating*): Oh I say!

LADY BRITOMART: You are not called on to say anything, Charles.

SARAH: Are you serious, mother?

LADY BRITOMART: Of course I am serious. It is on your account, Sarah, and also on Charles's. (*Silence.* SARAH *sits, with a shrug.* CHARLES *looks painfully unworthy.*) I hope you are not going to object, Barbara.

BARBARA: I! why should I? My father has a soul to be saved like anybody else. He's quite welcome as far as I am concerned. (*She sits on the table, and softly whistles 'Onward, Christian Soldiers.'*)

LOMAX (*still remonstrant*): But really, dont you know! Oh I say!

LADY BRITOMART (*frigidly*): What do you wish to convey, Charles?

LOMAX: Well, you must admit that this is a bit thick.

LADY BRITOMART (*turning with ominous suavity to* CUSINS): Adolphus: you are a professor of Greek. Can you translate Charles Lomax's remarks into reputable English for us?

CUSINS (*cautiously*): If I may say so, Lady Brit, I think Charles has rather happily expressed what we all feel. Homer, speaking of Autolycus, uses the same phrase. πυχινὸν δόμον ἐλθεῖν means a bit thick.

LOMAX (*handsomely*): Not that I mind, you know, if Sarah dont. (*He sits.*)

LADY BRITOMART (*crushingly*): Thank you. Have I your permission, Adolphus, to invite my own husband to my own house?

CUSINS (*gallantly*): You have my unhesitating support in everything you do.

LADY BRITOMART: Tush! Sarah: have you nothing to say?

SARAH: Do you mean that he is coming regularly to live here?

LADY BRITOMART: Certainly not. The spare room is ready for him if he likes to stay for a day or two and see a little more of you; but there are limits.

SARAH: Well, he cant eat us, I suppose. *I* dont mind.

LOMAX (*chuckling*): I wonder how the old man will take it.

LADY BRITOMART: Much as the old woman will, no doubt, Charles.

LOMAX (*abashed*): I didnt mean — at least —

LADY BRITOMART: You didnt think, Charles. You never do; and the result is, you never mean anything. And now please attend to me, children. Your father will be quite a stranger to us.

LOMAX: I suppose he hasnt seen Sarah since she was a little kid.

LADY BRITOMART: Not since she was a little kid, Charles, as you express it with that elegance of diction and refinement of thought that seem never to desert you. Accordingly — er — (*Impatiently.*) Now I have forgotten what I was going to say. That comes of your provoking me to be sarcastic, Charles. Adolphus: will you kindly tell me where I was.

CUSINS (*sweetly*): You were saying that as Mr Undershaft has not seen his children since they were babies, he will form his opinion of the way you have brought them up from their behavior tonight, and that therefore you wish us all to be particularly careful to conduct ourselves well, especially Charles.

LADY BRITOMART (*with emphatic approval*): Precisely.

LOMAX: Look here, Dolly: Lady Brit didnt say that.

LADY BRITOMART (*vehemently*): I did, Charles. Adolphus's recollection is perfectly correct. It is most important that you should be good; and I do beg you for once not to pair off into opposite corners and giggle and whisper while I am speaking to your father.

BARBARA: All right, mother. We'll do you credit. (*She comes off the table, and sits in her chair with ladylike elegance.*)

LADY BRITOMART: Remember, Charles, that Sarah will want to feel proud of you instead of ashamed of you.

LOMAX: Oh I say! theres nothing to be exactly proud of, dont you know.

LADY BRITOMART: Well, try and look as if there was.

(MORRISON, *pale and dismayed, breaks into the room in unconcealed disorder.*)

MORRISON: Might I speak a word to you, my lady?

LADY BRITOMART: Nonsense! Shew him up.

MORRISON: Yes, my lady. (*He goes.*)

LOMAX: Does Morrison know who it is?

LADY BRITOMART: Of course. Morrison has always been with us.

LOMAX: It must be a regular corker for him, dont you know.

LADY BRITOMART: Is this a moment to get on my nerves, Charles, with your outrageous expressions?

LOMAX: But this is something out of the ordinary, really —

MORRISON (*at the door*): The — er — Mr Undershaft. (*He retreats in confusion.*)

ANDREW UNDERSHAFT *comes in. All rise.* LADY BRITOMART *meets him in the middle of the room behind the settee.*

ANDREW *is, on the surface, a stoutish, easy-going elderly man, with kindly patient manners, and an engaging simplicity of character. But he has a watchful, deliberate, waiting, listening face, and formidable reserves of power, both bodily and mental, in his capacious chest and long head. His gentleness is partly that of a strong man who has learnt by experience that his natural grip hurts ordinary people unless he handles them very carefully, and partly the mellowness of age and success. He is also a little shy in his present very delicate situation.*)

LADY BRITOMART: Good evening, Andrew.

UNDERSHAFT: How d'ye do, my dear.

LADY BRITOMART: You look a good deal older.

UNDERSHAFT (*apologetically*): I *am* somewhat older. (*Taking her hand with a touch of courtship.*) Time has stood still with you.

LADY BRITOMART (*throwing away his hand*): Rubbish! This is your family.

UNDERSHAFT (*surprised*): Is it so large? I am sorry to say my memory is failing very badly in some things. (*He offers his hand with paternal kindness to* LOMAX.)

LOMAX (*jerkily shaking his hand*): Ahdedoo.

UNDERSHAFT: I can see you are my eldest. I am very glad to meet you again, my boy.

LOMAX (*remonstrating*): No, but look here dont you know — (*Overcome.*) Oh I say!

LADY BRITOMART (*recovering from momentary speechlessness*): Andrew: do you mean to say that you dont remember how many children you have?

UNDERSHAFT: Well, I am afraid I — . They have grown so much — er. Am I making any ridiculous mistake? I may as well confess: I recollect only one son. But so many things have happened since, of course — er —

LADY BRITOMART (*decisively*): Andrew: you are talking nonsense. Of course you have only one son.

UNDERSHAFT: Perhaps you will be good enough to introduce me, my dear.

LADY BRITOMART: That is Charles Lomax, who is engaged to Sarah.

UNDERSHAFT: My dear sir, I beg your pardon.

LOMAX: Notatall. Delighted, I assure you.

LADY BRITOMART: This is Stephen.

UNDERSHAFT (*bowing*): Happy to make your acquaintance, Mr Stephen. Then (*going to* CUSINS) you must be my son. (*Taking* CUSINS' *hands in his.*) How are you, my young friend! (*To* LADY BRITOMART.) He is very like you, my love.

CUSINS: You flatter me, Mr Undershaft. My name is Cusins: engaged to Barbara. (*Very explicitly.*) That is Major Barbara Undershaft, of the Salvation Army. That is Sarah, your second daughter. This is Stephen Undershaft, your son.

UNDERSHAFT: My dear Stephen, I beg your pardon.

STEPHEN: Not at all.

UNDERSHAFT: Mr Cusins: I am much indebted to you for explaining so precisely. (*Turning to* SARAH.) Barbara, my dear —

SARAH (*prompting him*): Sarah.

UNDERSHAFT: Sarah, of course. (*They shake hands. He goes over to* BARBARA.) Barbara — I am right this time, I hope?

BARBARA: Quite right! (*They shake hands.*)

LADY BRITOMART (*resuming command*): Sit down, all of you. Sit down, Andrew. (*She comes forward and sits on the settee.* CUSINS *also brings his chair forward on her left.* BARBARA *and* STEPHEN *resume their seats.* LOMAX *gives his chair to* SARAH *and goes for another.*)

UNDERSHAFT: Thank you, my love.

LOMAX (*conversationally, as he brings a chair forward between the writing table and the settee, and offers it to* UNDERSHAFT): Takes you some time to find out exactly where you are, dont it?

UNDERSHAFT (*accepting the chair, but remaining standing*): That is not what embarrasses me, Mr Lomax. My difficulty is that if I play the part of a father, I shall produce the effect of an intrusive stranger; and if I play the part of a discreet stranger, I may appear a callous father.

LADY BRITOMART: There is no need for you to play any part at all, Andrew. You had much better be sincere and natural.

UNDERSHAFT (*submissively*): Yes, my dear: I daresay that will be best. (*He sits down comfortably.*) Well, here I am. Now what can I do for you all?

LADY BRITOMART: You need not do anything, Andrew. You are one of the family. You can sit with us and enjoy yourself.

(*A painfully conscious pause.* BARBARA *makes a face at* LOMAX, *whose too long suppressed mirth immediately explodes in agonized neighings.*)

LADY BRITOMART (*outraged*): Charles Lomax: if you can behave yourself, behave yourself. If not, leave the room.

LOMAX: I'm awfully sorry, Lady Brit; but really you know, upon my soul! (*He sits on the settee between* LADY BRITOMART *and* UNDERSHAFT, *quite ovecome.*)

BARBARA: Why dont you laugh if you want to, Cholly? It's good for your inside.

LADY BRITOMART: Barbara: you have had the education of a lady. Please let your father see that; and dont talk like a street girl.

UNDERSHAFT: Never mind me, my dear. As you know, I am not a gentleman; and I was never educated.

LOMAX (*encouragingly*): Nobody'd know it, I assure you. You look all right, you know.

CUSINS: Let me advise you to study Greek, Mr Undershaft. Greek scholars are privileged men. Few of them know Greek; and none of them know anything else; but their position is unchallengeable. Other languages are the qualifications of waiters and commercial travellers: Greek is to a man of position what the hallmark is to silver.

BARBARA: Dolly: dont be insincere. Cholly: fetch your concertina and play something for us.

LOMAX (*jumps up eagerly, but checks himself to remark doubtfully to* UNDERSHAFT): Perhaps that sort of thing isnt in your line, eh?

UNDERSHAFT: I am particularly fond of music.

LOMAX (*delighted*): Are you? Then I'll get it. (*He goes upstairs for the instrument.*)

UNDERSHAFT: Do you play, Barbara?

BARBARA: Only the tambourine. But Cholly's teaching me the concertina.

UNDERSHAFT: Is Cholly also a member of the Salvation Army?

BARBARA: No: he says it's bad form to be a dissenter. But I dont despair of Cholly. I made him come yesterday to a meeting at the dock gates, and take the collection in his hat.

UNDERSHAFT (*looks whimsically at his wife*): !!

LADY BRITOMART: It is not my doing, Andrew. Barbara is old enough to take her own way. She has no father to advise her.

BARBARA: Oh yes she has. There are no orphans in the Salvation Army.

UNDERSHAFT: Your father there has a great many children and plenty of experience, eh?

BARBARA (*looking at him with quick interest and nodding*): Just so. How did you come to understand that? (LOMAX *is heard at the door trying the concertina.*)

LADY BRITOMART: Come in, Charles. Play us something at once.

LOMAX: Righto! (*He sits down in his former place, and preludes.*)

UNDERSHAFT: One moment, Mr. Lomax. I am rather interested in the Salvation Army. Its motto might be my own: Blood and Fire.

LOMAX (*shocked*): But not your sort of blood and fire, you know.

UNDERSHAFT: My sort of blood cleanses: my sort of fire purifies.

BARBARA: So do ours. Come down tomorrow to my shelter — the West Ham shelter — and see what we're doing. We're going to march to a great meeting in the Assembly Hall at Mile End. Come and see the shelter and then march with us: it will do you a lot of good. Can you play anything?

UNDERSHAFT: In my youth I earned pennies, and even shillings occasionally, in the streets and in public house parlors by my natural talent for stepdancing. Later on, I became a member of the Undershaft orchestral society, and performed passably on the tenor trombone.

LOMAX (*scandalized — putting down the concertina*): Oh I say!

BARBARA: Many a sinner has played himself into heaven on the trombone, thanks to the Army.

LOMAX (*to* BARBARA, *still rather shocked*): Yes; but what about the cannon business, dont you know? (*To* UNDERSHAFT.) Getting into heaven is not exactly in your line, is it?

LADY BRITOMART: Charles!!!

LOMAX: Well; but it stands to reason, dont it? The cannon business may be necessary and all that: we cant get on without cannons; but it isnt right, you know. On the other hand, there may be a certain amount of tosh about the Salvation Army — I belong to the Established Church myself — but still you cant deny that it's religion; and you cant go against religion, can you? At least unless youre downright immoral, dont you know.

UNDERSHAFT: You hardly appreciate my position, Mr Lomax —

LOMAX (*hastily*): I'm not saying anything against you personally —

UNDERSHAFT: Quite so, quite so. But consider for a moment. Here I am, a profiteer in mutilation and murder. I find myself in a specially amiable humor just now because, this morning, down at the foundry, we blew twenty-seven dummy soldiers into fragments with a gun which formerly destroyed only thirteen.

LOMAX (*leniently*): Well, the more destructive war becomes, the sooner it will be abolished, eh?

UNDERSHAFT: Not at all. The more destructive war becomes the more fascinating we find it. No, Mr Lomax: I am obliged to you for making the usual excuse for my trade; but I am not ashamed of it. I am not one of those men who keep their morals and their business in watertight compartments. All the spare money my trade rivals spend on hospitals, cathedrals, and other receptacles for conscience money, I devote to experiments and researches in improved methods of destroying life and property. I have always done so; and I always shall. Therefore your Christmas card moralities of peace on earth and goodwill among men are of no use to me. Your Christianity, which enjoins you to resist not evil, and to turn the other cheek, would make me a bankrupt. My morality — my religion — must have a place for cannons and torpedoes in it.

STEPHEN (*coldly — almost sullenly*): You speak as if there were half a dozen moralities and religions to choose from, instead of one true morality and one true religion.

UNDERSHAFT: For me there is only one true morality; but it might not fit you, as you do not manufacture aerial battleships. There is only one true morality for every man; but every man has not the same true morality.

LOMAX (*overtaxed*): Would you mind saying that again? I didnt quite follow it.

CUSINS: It's quite simple. As Euripides says, one man's meat is another man's poison morally as well as physically.

UNDERSHAFT: Precisely.

LOMAX: Oh, that! Yes, yes, yes. True. True.

STEPHEN: In other words, some men are honest and some are scoundrels.

BARBARA: Bosh! There are no scoundrels.

UNDERSHAFT: Indeed? Are there any good men?

BARBARA: No. Not one. There are neither good men nor scoundrels: there are just children of one Father; and the sooner they stop calling one another names the better. You neednt talk to me: I know them. Ive had scores of them through my hands: scoundrels, criminals, infidels, philanthropists, missionaries, county councillors, all sorts. Theyre all just the same sort of sinner; and theres the same salvation ready for them all.

UNDERSHAFT: May I ask have you ever saved a maker of cannons?

BARBARA: No. Will you let me try?

UNDERSHAFT: Well, I will make a bargain with you. If I go to see you tomorrow in your Salvation Shelter, will you come the day after to see me in my cannon works?

BARBARA: Take care. It may end in your giving up the cannons for the sake of the Salvation Army.

UNDERSHAFT: Are you sure it will not end in your giving up the Salvation Army for the sake of the cannons?

BARBARA: I will take my chance of that.

UNDERSHAFT: And I will take my chance of the other. (*They shake hands on it.*) Where is your shelter?

BARBARA: In West Ham. At the sign of the cross. Ask anybody in Canning Town. Where are your works?

UNDERSHAFT: In Perivale St Andrews. At the sign of the sword. Ask anybody in Europe.

LOMAX: Hadnt I better play something?

BARBARA: Yes. Give us Onward, Christian Soldiers.

LOMAX: Well, thats rather a strong order to begin with, dont you know. Suppose I sing Thourt passing hence, my brother. It's much the same tune.

BARBARA: It's too melancholy. You get saved, Cholly; and youll pass hence, my brother, without making such a fuss about it.

LADY BRITOMART: Really, Barbara, you go on as if religion were a pleasant subject. Do have some sense of propriety.

UNDERSHAFT: I do not find it an unpleasant subject, my dear. It is the only one that capable people really care for.

LADY BRITOMART (*looking at her watch*): Well, if you are determined to have it, I insist on having it in a proper and respectable way. Charles: ring for prayers.

(*General amazement.* STEPHEN *rises in dismay.*)

LOMAX (*rising*): Oh I say!

UNDERSHAFT (*rising*): I am afraid I must be going.

LADY BRITOMART: You cannot go now, Andrew: it would be most improper. Sit down. What will the servants think?

UNDERSHAFT: My dear: I have conscientious scruples. May I suggest a compromise? If Barbara will conduct a little service in the drawing room, with Mr Lomax as organist, I will attend it willingly. I will even take part, if a trombone can be procured.

LADY BRITOMART: Dont mock, Andrew.

UNDERSHAFT (*shocked — to* BARBARA): You dont think I am mocking, my love, I hope.

BARBARA: No, of course not; and it wouldnt matter if you were: half the Army came to their first meeting for a lark. (*Rising.*) Come along. (*She throws her arm round her father and sweeps him out, calling to the others from the threshold.*) Come, Dolly. Come, Cholly.

(CUSINS *rises.*)

LADY BRITOMART: I will not be disobeyed by everybody. Adolphus: sit down. (*He does not.*) Charles: you may go. You are not fit for prayers: you cannot keep your countenance.

LOMAX: Oh I say! (*He goes out.*)

LADY BRITOMART (*continuing*): But you, Adolphus, can behave yourself if you choose to. I insist on your staying.

CUSINS: My dear Lady Brit: there are things in the family prayer book that I couldn't bear to hear you say.

LADY BRITOMART: What things, pray?

CUSINS: Well, you would have to say before all the servants that we have done things we ought not to have done, and left undone things we ought to have done, and that there is no health in us. I cannot bear to hear you doing yourself such an injustice, and Barbara such an injustice. As for myself, I flatly deny it: I have done my best. I shouldn't dare to marry Barbara — I couldn't look you in the face — if it were true. So I must go to the drawing room.

LADY BRITOMART (*offended*): Well, go. (*He starts for the door.*) And remember this, Adolphus (*he turns to listen*): I have a very strong suspicion that you went to the Salvation Army to worship Barbara and nothing else. And I quite appreciate the very clever way in which you systematically humbug me. I have found you out. Take care Barbara doesnt. Thats all.

CUSINS (*with unruffled sweetness*): Dont tell on me. (*He steals out.*)

LADY BRITOMART: Sarah: if you want to go, go. Anything's better than to sit there as if you wished you were a thousand miles away.

SARAH (*languidly*): Very well, mamma. (*She goes.*)

(LADY BRITOMART, *with a sudden flounce, gives way to a little gust of tears.*)

STEPHEN (*going to her*): Mother: whats the matter?

LADY BRITOMART (*swishing away her tears with her handkerchief*): Nothing. Foolishness. You can go with him, too, if you like, and leave me with the servants.

STEPHEN: Oh, you mustnt think that, mother. I — I dont like him.

LADY BRITOMART: The others do. That is the injustice of a woman's lot. A woman has to bring up her children; and that means to restrain them, to deny them things they want, to set them tasks, to punish them when they do wrong, to do all the unpleasant things. And then the father, who has nothing to do but pet them and spoil them, comes in when all her work is done and steals their affection from her.

STEPHEN: He has not stolen our affection from you. It is only curiosity.

LADY BRITOMART (*violently*): I wont be consoled, Stephen. There is nothing the matter with me. (*She rises and goes towards the door.*)

STEPHEN: Where are you going, mother?

LADY BRITOMART: To the drawing room, of course. (*She goes out. Onward, Christian Soldiers, on the concertina, with tambourine accompaniment, is heard when the door opens.*) Are you coming, Stephen?

STEPHEN: No. Certainly not. (*She goes. He sits down on the settee, with compressed lips and an expression of strong dislike.*)

ACT II

The yard of the West Ham shelter of the Salvation Army is a cold place on a January morning. The building itself, an old warehouse, is newly whitewashed. Its gabled end projects into the yard in the middle, with a door on the ground floor, and another in the loft above it without any balcony or ladder, but with a pulley rigged over it for hoisting sacks. Those who come from this central gable end into the yard have the gateway leading to the street on their left, with a stone horse-trough just beyond it, and, on the right, a penthouse shielding a table from the weather. There are forms at the table; and on them are seated a man and a woman, both much down on their luck, finishing a meal of bread (one thick slice each, with margarine and golden syrup) and diluted milk.

The man, a workman out of employment, is young, agile, a talker, a poser, sharp enough to be capable of anything in reason except honesty or altruistic considerations of any kind. The woman is a commonplace old bundle of poverty and hard-worn humanity. She looks sixty and probably is forty-five. If they were rich people, gloved and muffed and well wrapped up in furs and overcoats, they would be numbed and miserable; for it is a grindingly cold raw January day; and a glance at the background of grimy warehouses and leaden sky visible over the white-washed walls of the yard would drive any idle rich person straight to the Mediterranean. But these two, being no more troubled with visions of the Mediterranean than of the moon, and being compelled to keep more of their clothes in the pawnshop, and less on their persons, in winter than in summer, are not depressed by the cold: rather are they stung into vivacity, to which their meal has just now given an almost jolly turn. The man takes a pull at his mug, and then gets up and moves about the yard with his hands deep in his pockets, occasionally breaking into a stepdance.

THE WOMAN: Feel better arter your meal, sir?

THE MAN: No. Call that a meal! Good enough for you, praps; but wot is it to me, an intelligent workin man.

THE WOMAN: Workin man! Wot are you?

THE MAN: Painter.

THE WOMAN (*sceptically*): Yus, I dessay.

THE MAN: Yus, you dessay! I know. Every loafer that cant do nothink calls isself a painter. Well, I'm a real painter: grainer, finisher, thirty-eight bob a week when I can get it.

THE WOMAN: Then why dont you go and get it?

THE MAN: I'll tell you why. Fust: I'm intelligent — fffff! it's rotten cold here (*he dances a step or two*) — yes: intelligent beyond the station o life into which it has pleased the capitalists to call me; and they dont like a man that sees through em. Second, an intelligent bein needs a doo share of appiness; so I drink somethink cruel when I get the chawnce. Third, I stand by my class and do as little as I can so's to leave arf the job for me fellow workers. Fourth, I'm fly enough to know wots inside the law and wots outside it; and inside it I do as the capitalists do: pinch wot I can lay me ands on. In a proper state of society I am sober, industrious and honest: in Rome, so to speak, I do as the Romans do. Wots the consequence? When trade is bad — and it's rotten bad just now — and the employers az to sack arf their men, they generally start on me.

THE WOMAN: Whats your name?

THE MAN: Price. Bronterre O'Brien Price. Usually called Snobby Price, for short.

THE WOMAN: Snobby's a carpenter, aint it? You said you was a painter.

PRICE: Not that kind of snob, but the genteel sort. I'm too uppish, owing to my intelligence, and my father being a Chartist and a reading, thinking man: a stationer, too. I'm none of your common hewers of wood and drawers of water; and dont you forget it. (*He returns to his seat at the table, and takes up his mug.*) Wots your name?

THE WOMAN: Rummy Mitchens, sir.

PRICE (*quaffing the remains of his milk to her*): Your elth, Miss Mitchens.

RUMMY (*correcting him*): Missis Mitchens.

PRICE: Wot! Oh Rummy, Rummy! Respectable married woman, Rummy, gittin rescued by the Salvation Army by pretendin to be a bad un. Same old game!

RUMMY: What am I to do? I cant starve. Them Salvation lasses is dear good girls; but the better you are, the worse they likes to think you were before they rescued you. Why shouldnt they av a bit o credit, poor loves? theyre worn to rags by their work. And where would they get the money to rescue us if we was to let on we're no worse than other people? You know what ladies and gentlemen are.

PRICE: Thievin swine! Wish I ad their job, Rummy, all the same. Wot does Rummy stand for? Pet name praps?

RUMMY: Short for Romola.

PRICE: For wot!?

RUMMY: Romola. It was out of a new book. Somebody me mother wanted me to grow up like.

PRICE: We're companions in misfortune, Rummy. Both on us got names that nobody cawnt pronounce. Consequently I'm Snobby and youre Rummy because Bill and Sally wasnt good enough for our parents. Such is life!

RUMMY: Who saved you, Mr Price? Was it Major Barbara?

PRICE: No: I come here on my own. I'm going to be Bronterre O'Brien Price, the converted painter. I know wot they like. I'll tell em how I blasphemed and gambled and wopped my poor old mother —

RUMMY (*shocked*): Used you to beat your mother?

PRICE: Not likely. She used to beat me. No matter: you come and listen to the converted painter, and youll hear how she was a pious woman that taught me me prayers at er knee, an how I used to come home drunk and drag her out o bed be er snow white airs, an lam into er with the poker.

RUMMY: Thats whats so unfair to us women. Your confessions is just as big lies as ours: you dont tell what you really done no more than us; but you men can tell your lies right out at the meetins and be made much of for it; while the sort o confessions we az to make az to be wispered to one lady at a time. It ain't right, spite of all their piety.

PRICE: Right! Do you spose the Army'd be allowed if it went and did right? Not much. It combs our air and makes us good little blokes to be robbed and put upon. But I'll play the game as good as any of em. I'll see somebody struck by lightnin, or hear a voice saying 'Snobby Price: where will you spend eternity?' I'll av a time of it, I tell you.

RUMMY: You wont be let drink, though.

PRICE: I'll take it out in gorspellin, then. I dont want to drink if I can get fun enough any other way.

(JENNY HILL, *a pale, overwrought, pretty Salvation lass of 18, comes in through the yard gate, leading* PETER SHIRLEY, *a half hardened, half worn-out elderly man, weak with hunger.*)

JENNY (*supporting him*): Come! pluck up. I'll get you something to eat. Youll be all right then.

PRICE (*rising and hurrying officiously to take the old man off* JENNY's *hands*): Poor old man! Cheer up, brother: youll find rest and peace and appiness ere. Hurry up with the food, miss: e's fair done. (JENNY *hurries into the shelter.*) Ere, buck up, daddy! she's fetchin y'a thick slice o breadn treacle, an a mug of skyblue. (*He seats him at the corner of the table.*)

RUMMY (*gaily*): Keep up your old art! Never say die!

SHIRLEY: I'm not an old man. I'm only 46. I'm as good as ever I was. The grey patch come in my hair before I was thirty. All it wants is three pennorth o hair dye: am I to be turned on the streets to starve for it? Holy God! Ive worked ten to twelve hours a day since I was thirteen, and paid my way all through; and now am I to be thrown into the gutter and my job given to a young man that can do it no better than me because Ive black hair that goes white at the first change?

PRICE (*cheerfully*): No good jawrin about it. Youre ony a jumped-up, jerked-off, orspittle-turned-out incurable of an ole workin man: who cares about you? Eh? Make the thievin swine give you a meal: theyve stole many a one from you. Get a bit o your own back. (JENNY *returns with the usual meal.*) There you are, brother, Awsk a blessin an tuck that into you.

SHIRLEY (*looking at it ravenously but not touching it, and crying like a child*): I never took anything before.

JENNY (*petting him*): Come, come! the Lord sends it to you: he wasnt above taking bread from his friends; and why should you be? Besides, when we find you a job you can pay us for it if you like.

SHIRLEY (*eagerly*): Yes, yes: thats true. I can pay you back: it's only a loan. (*Shivering.*) Oh Lord! oh Lord! (*He turns to the table and attacks the meal ravenously.*)

JENNY: Well, Rummy, are you more comfortable now?

RUMMY: God bless you, lovely! youve fed my body and saved my soul, havnt you? (JENNY, *touched, kisses her.*) Sit down and rest a bit: you must be ready to drop.

JENNY: Ive been going hard since morning. But theres more work than we can do. I mustnt stop.

RUMMY: Try a prayer for just two minutes. Youll work all the better after.

JENNY (*her eyes lighting up*): Oh isnt it wonderful how a few minutes prayer revives you! I was quite lightheaded at twelve o'clock, I was so tired; but Major Barbara just sent me to pray for five minutes; and I was able to go on as if I had only just begun. (*To* PRICE.) Did you have a piece of bread?

PRICE (*with unction*): Yes, miss; but Ive got the piece that I value more; and thats the peace that passeth hall hannerstennin.

RUMMY (*fervently*): Glory Hallelujah!

(BILL WALKER, *a rough customer of about 25, appears at the yard gate and looks malevolently at* JENNY.)

JENNY: That makes me so happy. When you say that, I feel wicked for loitering here. I must get to work again.

(*She is hurrying to the shelter, when the new-comer moves quickly up to the door and intercepts her. His manner is so threatening that she retreats as he comes at her truculently, driving her down the yard.*)

BILL: Aw knaow you. Youre the one that took awy maw girl. Youre the one that set er agen me. Well, I'm gowin to ev er aht. Not that Aw care a carse for er or you: see? Bat Aw'll let er knaow; and Aw'll let you knaow. Aw'm gowing to give her a doin thatll teach er to cat away from me. Nah in wiv you and tell er to cam aht afore Aw cam in and kick er aht. Tell er Bill Walker wants er. She'll knaow wot thet means; and if she keeps me witin itll be worse. You stop to jawr beck at me; and Aw'll stawt on you: d'ye eah? Theres your wy. In you gow. (*He takes her by the arm and slings her towards the door of the shelter. She falls on her hand and knee.* RUMMY *helps her up again.*)[1]

PRICE (*rising, and venturing irresolutely towards* BILL): Easy there, mate. She aint doin you no arm.

BILL: Oo are you callin mite? (*Standing over him threateningly.*) Youre gowing to stend ap for er, aw yer? Put ap your ends.

RUMMY (*running indignantly to him to scold him*): Oh, you great brute — (*He instantly swings his left hand back against her face. She screams and reels back to the trough, where she sits down, covering her bruised face with her hands and rocking herself and moaning with pain.*)

[1] Shaw's practice of rendering lower-class pronunciation in unconventional spelling is a rather tiresome and quite unnecessary aspect of his realism. He does the same thing with Eliza Doolittle's first two speeches in *Pygmalion* but then abandons the effort, and there, at least, he has the excuse that the play is *about* phonetics. Here in *Major Barbara* Bill Walker speaks an extreme form of cockney (lower-class East London dialect). Rummy Mitchens and Snobby Price speak moderate cockney. Since many readers are likely to find it hard to trans-literate Shaw's spellings of Bill Walker's speech into conventional spelling, I give a "transla-tion" of Bill's first speech. Most of the difficult spellings appear in it, and with it as a guide the reader should be able to make sense out of Bill's later speeches.

I know you. You're the one that took away my girl. You're the one that set her against me. Well, I am going to have her out. Not that I care a curse for her or you: see? But I'll let her know; and I'll let you know. I'm going to give her a doing that'll teach her to cut away from me. Now in with you and tell her to come out before I come in and kick her out. Tell her Bill Walker wants her. She'll know what that means; and if she keeps me waiting it'll be worse. You stop to jaw ["talk"] back at me; and I'll start on you: do you hear? There's your way. In you go.

Other difficult spellings in Bill's later speeches include (in alphabetical order): "arf" (= "half"), "arter" (= "after"), "dan" (= "done"), "ends" (= "hands"), "fahnd" (= "found"), "loy" (= "lie"), "mite" (= "mate"), "pryin" (= "praying"), "sathink" (= "something"), and "urtin" (= "hurting").

JENNY (*going to her*): Oh, God forgive you! How could you strike an old woman like that?

BILL (*seizing her by the hair so violently that she also screams, and tearing her away from the old woman*): You Gawd forgimme again an Aw'll Gawd forgive you one on the jawr thetll stop you pryin for a week. (*Holding her and turning fiercely on* PRICE.) Ev you ennything to sy agen it?

PRICE (*intimidated*): No, matey: she aint anything to do with me.

BILL: Good job for you! Aw'd pat two meals into you and fawt you with one finger arter, you stawved cur. (*To* JENNY.) Nah are you gowin to fetch aht Mog Ebbijem; or em Aw to knock your fice off you and fetch her meself?

JENNY (*writhing in his grasp*): Oh please someone go in and tell Major Barbara — (*She screams again as he wrenches her head down; and* PRICE *and* RUMMY *flee into the shelter.*)

BILL: You want to gow in and tell your Mijor of me, do you?

JENNY: Oh please dont drag my hair. Let me go.

BILL: Do you or downt you? (*She stifles a scream.*) Yus or nao?

JENNY: God give me strength —

BILL (*striking her with his fist in the face*): Gow an shaow her thet, and tell her if she wants one lawk it to cam and interfere with me. (JENNY, *crying with pain, goes into the shed. He goes to the form and addresses the old man.*) Eah: finish your mess; an git aht o maw wy.

SHIRLEY (*springing up and facing him fiercely, with the mug in his hand*): You take a liberty with me, and I'll smash you over the face with the mug and cut your eye out. Aint you satisfied — young whelps like you — with takin the bread out o the mouths of your elders that have brought you up and slaved for you, but you must come shovin and cheekin and bullyin in here, where the bread o charity is sickenin in our stummicks?

BILL (*contemptuously, but backing a little*): Wot good are you, you aold palsy mag? Wot good are you?

SHIRLEY: As good as you and better. I'll do a day's work agen you or any fat young soaker of your age. Go and take my job at Horrockses, where I worked for ten year. They want young men there: they cant afford to keep men over forty-five. Theyre very sorry — give you a character and happy to help you to get anything suited to your years — sure a steady man wont be long out of a job. Well, let em try you. Theyll find the differ. What do you know? Not as much as how to beeyave yourself — laying your dirty fist across the mouth of a respectable woman!

BILL: Downt provowk me to ly it acrost yours: d'ye eah?

SHIRLEY (*with blighting contempt*): Yes: you like an old man to hit, dont you, when youve finished with the women. I aint seen you a hit a young one yet.

BILL (*stung*): You loy, you aold soupkitchener, you. There was a yang menn eah. Did Aw offer to itt him or did Aw not?

SHIRLEY: Was he starvin or was he not? Was he a man or only a crosseyed thief an a loafer? Would you hit my son-in-law's brother?

BILL: Oo's ee?

SHIRLEY: Todger Fairmile o Balls Pond. Him that won £20 off the Japanese wrastler at the music hall by standin out 17 minutes 4 seconds agen him.

BILL (*sullenly*): Aw'm nao music awl wrastler. Ken he box?

SHIRLEY: Yes: an you cant.

BILL: Wot! Aw cawnt, cawnt Aw? Wots thet you sy (*threatening him*)?

SHIRLEY (*not budging an inch*): Will you box Todger Fairmile if I put him on to you? Say the word.

BILL (*subsiding with a slouch*): Aw'll stend ap to enny menn alawy, if he was ten Todger Fairmawls. But Aw dont set ap to be a perfeshnal.

SHIRLEY (*looking down on him with unfathomable disdain*): You box! Slap an old woman with the back o your hand! You hadnt even the sense to hit her where a magistrate couldnt see the mark of it, you silly young lump of conceit and ignorance. Hit a girl in the jaw and ony make her cry! If Todger Fairmile'd done it, she wouldnt a got up inside o ten minutes, no more than you would if he got on to you. Yah! I'd set about you myself if I had a week's feedin in me instead o two months' starvation. (*He turns his back on him and sits down moodily at the table.*)

BILL (*following him and stooping over him to drive the taunt in*): You loy! youve the bread and treacle in you that you cam eah to beg.

SHIRLEY (*bursting into tears*): Oh God! it's true: I'm only an old pauper on the scrap heap. (*Furiously.*) But youll come to it yourself; and then youll know. Youll come to it sooner than a teetotaller like me, fillin yourself with gin at this hour o the mornin!

BILL: Aw'm nao gin drinker, you oald lawr; bat wen Aw want to give my girl a bloomin good awdin Aw lawk to ev a bit o devil in me: see? An eah Aw emm, talkin to a rotten aold blawter like you sted o givin her wot for. (*Working himself into a rage.*) Aw'm gowin in there to fetch her aht. (*He makes vengefully for the shelter door.*)

SHIRLEY: Youre going to the station on a stretcher, more likely; and theyll take the gin and the devil out of you there when they get you inside. You mind what youre about: the major here is the Earl o Stevenage's granddaughter.

BILL (*checked*): Garn!

SHIRLEY: Youll see.

BILL (*his resolution oozing*): Well, Aw aint dan nathin to er.

SHIRLEY: Spose she said you did! who'd believe you?

BILL (*very uneasy, skulking back to the corner of the penthouse*): Gawd! theres no jastice in this cantry. To think wot them people can do! Aw'm as good as er.

SHIRLEY: Tell her so. It's just what a fool like you would do.

(BARBARA, *brisk and businesslike, comes from the shelter with a note book, and addresses herself to* SHIRLEY. BILL, *cowed, sits down in the corner of a form, and turns his back on them.*)

BARBARA: Good morning.

SHIRLEY (*standing up and taking off his hat*): Good morning, miss.

BARBARA: Sit down: make yourself at home. (*He hesitates; but she puts a friendly hand on his shoulder and makes him obey.*) Now then! since youve made friends with us, we want to know all about you. Names and addresses and trades.

SHIRLEY: Peter Shirley. Fitter. Chucked out two months ago because I was too old.

BARBARA (*not at all surprised*): Youd pass still. Why didnt you dye your hair?

SHIRLEY: I did. Me age come out at a coroner's inquest on me daughter.

BARBARA: Steady?

SHIRLEY: Teetotaller. Never out of a job before. Good worker. And sent to the knackers like an old horse!

BARBARA: No matter: if you did your part God will do his.

SHIRLEY (*suddenly stubborn*): My religion's no concern of anybody but myself.

BARBARA (*guessing*): I know. Secularist?

SHIRLEY (*hotly*): Did I offer to deny it?

BARBARA: Why should you? My own father's a Secularist, I think. Our Father — yours and mine — fulfills himself in many ways; and I daresay he knew what he was about when he made a Secularist of you. So buck up, Peter! we can always find a job for a steady man like you. (SHIRLEY, *disarmed and a little bewildered, touches his hat. She turns from him to* BILL.) Whats your name?

BILL (*insolently*): Wots thet to you?

BARBARA (*calmly making a note*): Afraid to give his name. Any trade?

BILL: Oo's afride to give is nime? (*Doggedly, with a sense of heroically defying the House of Lords in the person of Lord Stevenage.*) If you want to bring a chawge agen me, bring it. (*She waits, unruffled.*) Moy nime's Bill Walker.

BARBARA (*as if the name were familiar: trying to remember how*): Bill Walker? (*Recollecting.*) Oh, I know: youre the man that Jenny Hill was praying for inside just now. (*She enters his name in her note book.*)

BILL: Oo's Jenny Ill? And wot call as she to pry for me?

BARBARA: I dont know. Perhaps it was you that cut her lip.

BILL (*defiantly*): Yus, it was me that cat her lip. Aw aint afride o you.

BARBARA: How could you be, since youre not afraid of God? Youre a brave man, Mr Walker. It takes some pluck to do our work here; but none of us dare lift our hand against a girl like that, for fear of her father in heaven.

BILL (*sullenly*): I want nan o your kentin jawr. I spowse you think Aw cam eah to beg from you, like this demmiged lot eah. Not me. Aw downt want your bread and scripe and ketlep. Aw dont believe in your Gawd, no more than you do yourself.

BARBARA (*sunnily apologetic and ladylike, as on a new footing with him*): Oh, I beg your pardon for putting your name down, Mr Walker. I didnt understand. I'll strike it out.

BILL (*taking this as a slight, and deeply wounded by it*): Eah! you let maw nime alown. Aint it good enaff to be in your book?

BARBARA (*considering*): Well, you see, theres no use putting down your name unless I can do something for you, is there? Whats your trade?

BILL (*still smarting*): Thets nao concern o yours.

BARBARA: Just so. (*Very businesslike.*) I'll put you down as (*writing*) the man who — struck — poor little Jenny Hill — in the mouth.

BILL (*rising threateningly*): See eah. Awve ed enaff o this.

BARBARA (*quite sunny and fearless*): What did you come to us for?

BILL: Aw cam for maw gel, see? Aw cam to tike her aht o this and to brike er jawr for er.

BARBARA (*complacently*): You see I was right about your trade. (BILL, *on the point of retorting furiously, finds himself, to his great shame and terror, in danger of crying instead. He sits down again suddenly.*) Whats her name?

BILL (*dogged*): Er nime's Mog Ebbijem: thets wot her nime is.

BARBARA: Mog Habbijam! Oh, she's gone to Canning Town, to our barracks there.

BILL (*fortified by his resentment of Mog's perfidy*): Is she? (*Vindictively.*) Then Aw'm gowing to Kennintahn arter her. (*He crosses to the gate; hesitates; finally comes back at* BARBARA.) Are you loyin to me to git shat o me?

BARBARA: I dont want to get shut of you. I want to keep you here and save your soul. Youd better stay: youre going to have a bad time today, Bill.

BILL: Oo's gowing to give it to me? You, preps?

BARBARA: Someone you dont believe in. But youll be glad afterwards.

BILL (*slinking off*): Aw'll gow to Kennintahn to be aht o reach o your tangue. (*Suddenly turning on her with intense malice.*) And if Aw downt fawnd Mog there, Aw'll cam beck and do two years for you, selp me Gawd if Aw downt!

BARBARA (*a shade kindlier, if possible*): It's no use, Bill. She's got another bloke.

BILL: Wot!

BARBARA: One of her own converts. He fell in love with her when he saw her with her soul saved, and her face clean, and her hair washed.

BILL (*surprised*): Wottud she wash it for, the carroty slat? It's red.

BARBARA: It's quite lovely now, because she wears a new look in her eyes with it. It's a pity youre too late. The new bloke has put your nose out of joint, Bill.

BILL: Aw'll put his nowse aht o joint for him. Not that Aw care a carse for er, mawnd thet. But Aw'll teach her to drop me as if Aw was dirt. And Aw'll teach him to meddle with maw judy. Wots iz bleedin nime?

BARBARA: Sergeant Todger Fairmile.

SHIRLEY (*rising with grim joy*): I'll go with him, miss. I want to see them two meet. I'll take him to the infirmary when it's over.

BILL (*to* SHIRLEY, *with undissembled misgiving*): Is thet im you was speakin on?

SHIRLEY: Thats him.

BILL: Im that wrastled in the music awl?

SHIRLEY: The competitions at the National Sportin Club was worth nigh a hundred a year to him. He's gev em up now for religion; so he's a bit fresh for want of the exercise he was accustomed to. He'll be glad to see you. Come along.

BILL: Wots is wight?

SHIRLEY: Thirteen four. (BILL's *last hope expires.*)

BARBARA: Go and talk to him, Bill. He'll convert you.

SHIRLEY: He'll convert your head into a mashed potato.

BILL (*sullenly*): Aw aint afride of im. Aw aint afride of ennybody. Bat e can lick me. She's dan me. (*He sits down moodily on the edge of the horse trough.*)

SHIRLEY: You aint going. I thought not. (*He resumes his seat.*)

BARBARA (*calling*): Jenny!

JENNY (*appearing at the shelter door with a plaster on the corner of her mouth*): Yes, Major.

BARBARA: Send Rummy Mitchens out to clear away here.

JENNY: I think she's afraid.

BARBARA (*her resemblance to her mother flashing out for a moment*): Nonsense! she must do as she's told.

JENNY (*calling into the shelter*): Rummy: the Major says you must come.

(JENNY *comes to* BARBARA, *purposely keeping on the side next* BILL, *lest he should suppose that she shrank from him or bore malice.*)

BARBARA: Poor little Jenny! Are you tired? (*Looking at the wounded cheek.*) Does it hurt?

JENNY: No: it's all right now. It was nothing.

BARBARA (*critically*): It was as hard as he could hit, I expect. Poor Bill! You dont feel angry with him, do you?

JENNY: Oh no, no, no: indeed I dont, Major, bless his poor heart!

(BARBARA *kisses her; and she runs away merrily into the shelter.* BILL *writhes with an agonizing return of his new and alarming symptoms, but says nothing.* RUMMY MITCHENS *comes from the shelter.*)

BARBARA (*going to meet* RUMMY): Now Rummy, bustle. Take in those mugs and plates to be washed; and throw the crumbs about for the birds.

(RUMMY *takes the three plates and mugs; but* SHIRLEY *takes back his mug from her, as there is still some milk left in it.*)

RUMMY: There aint any crumbs. This aint a time to waste good bread on birds.

PRICE (*appearing at the shelter door*): Gentleman come to see the shelter, Major. Says he's your father.

BARBARA: All right. Coming. (SNOBBY *goes back into the shelter, followed by* BARBARA.)

RUMMY (*stealing across to* BILL *and addressing him in a subdued voice, but with intense conviction*): I'd av the lor of you, you flat eared pignosed potwalloper, if she'd let me. Youre no gentleman, to hit a lady in the face. (BILL, *with greater things moving in him, takes no notice.*)

SHIRLEY (*following her*): Here! In with you and dont get yourself into more trouble by talking.

RUMMY (*with hauteur*): I aint ad the pleasure o being hintroduced to you, as I can remember. (*She goes into the shelter with the plates.*)

SHIRLEY: Thats the —

BILL (*savagely*): Downt you talk to me, d'ye eah? You lea me alown, or Aw'll do you a mischief. Aw'm not dirt under your feet, ennywy.

SHIRLEY (*calmly*): Dont you be afeerd. You aint such prime company that you need expect to be sought after. (*He is about to go into the shelter when* BARBARA *comes out, with* UNDERSHAFT *on her right.*)

BARBARA: Oh, there you are, Mr Shirley! (*Between them.*) This is my father: I told you he was a Secularist, didn't I? Perhaps youll be able to comfort one another.

UNDERSHAFT (*startled*): A Secularist! Not the least in the world: on the contrary, a confirmed mystic.

BARBARA: Sorry, I'm sure. By the way, papa, what is your religion? in case I have to introduce you again.

UNDERSHAFT: My religion? Well, my dear, I am a Millionaire. That is my religion.

BARBARA: Then I'm afraid you and Mr Shirley wont be able to comfort one another after all. Youre not a Millionaire, are you, Peter?

SHIRLEY: No; and proud of it.

UNDERSHAFT (*gravely*): Poverty, my friend, is not a thing to be proud of.

SHIRLEY (*angrily*): Who made your millions for you? Me and my like. Whats kep us poor? Keepin you rich. I wouldnt have your conscience, not for all your income.

UNDERSHAFT: I wouldn't have your income, not for all your conscience, Mr Shirley. (*He goes to the penthouse and sits down on a form.*)

BARBARA (*stopping* SHIRLEY *adroitly as he is about to retort*): You wouldnt think he was my father, would you, Peter? Will you go into the shelter and lend the lasses a hand for a while: we're worked off our feet.

SHIRLEY (*bitterly*): Yes: I'm in their debt for a meal, aint I?

BARBARA: Oh, not because youre in their debt, but for love of them, Peter, for love of them. (*He cannot understand, and is rather scandalized.*) There! dont stare at me. In with you; and give that conscience of yours a holiday. (*Bustling him into the shelter.*)

SHIRLEY (*as he goes in*): Ah! it's a pity you never was trained to use your reason, miss. Youd have been a very taking lecturer on Secularism.

(BARBARA *turns to her father.*)

UNDERSHAFT: Never mind me, my dear. Go about your work; and let me watch it for a while.

BARBARA: All right.

UNDERSHAFT: For instance, whats the matter with that outpatient over there?

BARBARA (*looking at* BILL, *whose attitude has never changed, and whose expression of brooding wrath has deepened*): Oh, we shall cure him in no time. Just watch. (*She goes over to* BILL *and waits. He glances up at her and casts his eyes down again, uneasy, but grimmer than ever.*) It would be nice to just stamp on Mog Habbijam's face, wouldnt it, Bill?

BILL (*starting up from the trough in consternation*): It's a loy: Aw never said so. (*She shakes her head.*) Oo taold you wot was in moy mawnd?

BARBARA: Only your new friend.

BILL: Wot new friend?

BARBARA: The devil, Bill. When he gets round people they get miserable, just like you.

BILL (*with a heartbreaking attempt at devil-may-care cheerfulness*): Aw aint miserable. (*He sits down again, and stretches his legs in an attempt to seem indifferent.*)

BARBARA: Well, if youre happy, why dont you look happy, as we do?

BILL (*his legs curling back in spite of him*): Aw'm eppy enaff. Aw tell you. Woy cawnt you lea me alown? Wot ev I dan to you? Aw aint smashed your fice, ev Aw?

BARBARA (*softly: wooing his soul*): It's not me thats getting at you, Bill.

BILL: Oo else is it?

BARBARA: Somebody that doesnt intend you to smash women's faces, I suppose. Somebody or something that wants to make a man of you.

BILL (*blustering*): Mike a menn o me! Aint Aw a menn? eh? Oo sez Aw'm not a menn?

BARBARA: Theres a man in you somewhere, I suppose. But why did he let you hit poor little Jenny Hill? That wasnt very manly of him, was it?

BILL (*tormented*): Ev dan wiv it, Aw tell you. Chack it. Aw'm sick o your Jenny Ill and er silly little fice.

BARBARA: Then why do you keep thinking about it? Why does it keep coming up against you in your mind? Youre not getting converted, are you?

BILL (*with conviction*): Not ME. Not lawkly.

BARBARA: Thats right, Bill. Hold out against it. Put out your strength. Dont lets get you cheap. Todger Fairmile said he wrestled for three nights against his salvation harder than he ever wrestled with the Jap at the music hall. He gave in to the Jap when his arm was going to break. But he didnt give in to his salvation until his heart was going to break. Perhaps youll escape that. You havnt any heart, have you?

BILL: Wot d'ye mean? Woy aint Aw got a awt the sime as ennybody else?

BARBARA: A man with a heart wouldnt have bashed poor little Jenny's face, would he?

BILL (*almost crying*): Ow, will you lea me alown? Ev Aw ever offered to meddle with you, that you cam neggin and provowkin me lawk this? (*He writhes convulsively from his eyes to his toes.*)

BARBARA (*with a steady soothing hand on his arm and a gentle voice that never lets him go*): It's your soul thats hurting you, Bill, and not me. Weve been through it all ourselves. Come with us, Bill. (*He looks wildly round.*) To brave manhood on earth and eternal glory in heaven. (*He is on the point of breaking down.*) Come. (*A drum is heard in the shelter; and* BILL, *with a gasp, escapes from the spell as* BARBARA *turns quickly.* ADOLPHUS *enters from the shelter with a big drum.*) Oh! there you are, Dolly. Let me introduce a new friend of mine, Mr Bill Walker. This is my bloke, Bill: Mr Cusins. (CUSINS *salutes with his drumstick.*)

BILL: Gowin to merry im?

BARBARA: Yes.

BILL (*fervently*): Gawd elp im! Gaw-aw-aw-awd elp im!

BARBARA: Why? Do you think he wont be happy with me?

BILL: Awve aony ed to stend it for a mawnin: e'll ev to stend it for a lawftawm.

CUSINS: That is a frightful reflection, Mr Walker. But I cant tear myself away from her.

BILL: Well, Aw ken. (*To* BARBARA.) Eah! do you knaow where Aw'm gowin to, and wot Aw'm gowin to do?

BARBARA: Yes: youre going to heaven; and youre coming back here before the week's out to tell me so.

BILL: You loy. Aw'm gowin to Kennintahn, to spit in Todger Fairmawl's eye. Aw beshed Jenny Ill's fice; and nar Aw'll git me aown fice beshed and cam beck and shaow it to er. Ee'll itt me ardern Aw itt her. Thatll mike us square. (*To* ADOLPHUS.) Is thet fair or is it not? Youre a genlmn: you oughter knaow.

BARBARA: Two black eyes wont make one white one, Bill.

BILL: Aw didnt awst you. Cawnt you never keep your mahth shat? Oy awst the genlmn.

CUSINS (*reflectively*): Yes: I think youre right, Mr Walker. Yes: I should do it. It's curious: it's exactly what an ancient Greek would have done.

BARBARA: But what good will it do?

CUSINS: Well, it will give Mr. Fairmile some exercise; and it will satisfy Mr Walker's soul.

BILL: Rot! there aint nao sach a thing as a saoul. Ah kin you tell wevver Awve a saoul or not? You never seen it.

BARBARA: Ive seen it hurting you when you went against it.

BILL (*with compressed aggravation*): If you was maw gel and took the word aht o me mahth lawk thet, Aw'd give you sathink youd feel urtin, Aw would. (*To* ADOLPHUS.) You tike maw tip, mite. Stop er jawr; or youll doy afoah your tawm (*With intense expression.*) Wore aht: thets wot youll be: wore aht. (*He goes away through the gate.*)

CUSINS (*looking after him*): I wonder!

BARBARA: Dolly! (*indignant, in her mother's manner*).

CUSINS: Yes, my dear, it's very wearing to be in love with you. If it lasts, I quite think I shall die young.

BARBARA: Should you mind?

CUSINS: Not at all. (*He is suddenly softened, and kisses her over the drum, evidently not for the first time, as people cannot kiss over a big drum without practice.* UNDERSHAFT *coughs.*)

BARBARA: It's all right, papa, weve not forgotten you. Dolly: explain the place to papa: I havent time. (*She goes busily into the shelter.*)

(UNDERSHAFT *and* ADOLPHUS *now have the yard to themselves.* UNDERSHAFT, *seated on a form, and still keenly attentive, looks hard at* ADOLPHUS. ADOL-PHUS *looks hard at him.*)

UNDERSHAFT: I fancy you guess something of what is in my mind, Mr Cusins. (CUSINS *flourishes his drumsticks as if in the act of beating a lively rataplan, but makes no sound.*) Exactly so. But suppose Barbara finds you out!

CUSINS: You know, I do not admit that I am imposing on Barbara. I am quite genuinely interested in the views of the Salvation Army. The fact is, I am a sort of collector of religions; and the curious thing is that I find I can believe them all. By the way, have you any religion?

UNDERSHAFT: Yes.

CUSINS: Anything out of the common?

UNDERSHAFT: Only that there are two things necessary to Salvation.

CUSINS (*disappointed, but polite*): Ah, the Church Catechism. Charles Lomax also belongs to the Established Church.

UNDERSHAFT: The two things are —

CUSINS: Baptism and —

UNDERSHAFT: No. Money and gunpowder.

CUSINS (*surprised, but interested*): That is the general opinion of our governing classes. The novelty is in hearing any man confess it.

UNDERSHAFT: Just so.

CUSINS: Excuse me: is there any place in your religion for honor, justice, truth, love, mercy and so forth?

UNDERSHAFT: Yes: they are the graces and luxuries of a rich, strong, and safe life.

CUSINS: Suppose one is forced to choose between them and money or gunpowder?

UNDERSHAFT: Choose money and gunpowder; for without enough of both you cannot afford the others.

CUSINS: That is your religion?

UNDERSHAFT: Yes.

(*The cadence of this reply makes a full close in the conversation.* CUSINS *twists his face dubiously and contemplates* UNDERSHAFT. UNDERSHAFT *contemplates him.*)

CUSINS: Barbara wont stand that. You will have to choose between your religion and Barbara.

UNDERSHAFT: So will you, my friend. She will find out that that drum of yours is hollow.

CUSINS: Father Undershaft: you are mistaken: I am a sincere Salvationist. You do not understand the Salvation Army. It is the army of joy, of love, of courage: it has banished the fear and remorse and despair of the old hell-ridden evangelical sects: it marches to fight the devil with trumpet and drum, with music and dancing, with banner and palm, as becomes a sally from heaven by its happy garrison. It picks the waster out of the public house and makes a man of him: it finds a worm wriggling in a back kitchen, and lo! a woman! Men and women of rank too, sons and daughters of the Highest. It takes the poor professor of Greek, the most artificial and self-suppressed of human creatures, from his meal of roots, and lets loose the rhapsodist in him; reveals the true worship of Dionysos to him; sends him down the public street drumming dithyrambs. (*He plays a thundering flourish on the drum.*)

UNDERSHAFT: You will alarm the shelter.

CUSINS: Oh, they are accustomed to these sudden ecstasies. However, if the drum worries you — (*He pockets the drumsticks; unhooks the drum; and stands it on the ground opposite the gateway.*)

UNDERSHAFT: Thank you.

CUSINS: You remember what Euripides says about your money and gunpowder?

UNDERSHAFT: No.

CUSINS (*declaiming*):

One and another
In money and guns may outpass his brother;
And men in their millions float and flow
And seethe with a million hopes as leaven;
And they win their will; or they miss their will;
And their hopes are dead or are pined for still;
    But who'er can know
    As the long days go
That to live is happy, has found his heaven.

My translation: what do you think of it?

UNDERSHAFT: I think, my friend, that if you wish to know, as the long days go, that to live is happy, you must first acquire money enough for a decent life, and power enough to be your own master.

CUSINS: You are damnably discouraging. (*He resumes his declamation.*)

    Is it so hard a thing to see
    That the spirit of God — whate'er it be —
The law that abides and changes not, ages long,
The Eternal and Nature-born: these things be strong?
What else is Wisdom? What of Man's endeavor,
Or God's high grace so lovely and so great?
To stand from fear set free? to breathe and wait?
To hold a hand uplifted over Fate?
And shall not Barbara be loved for ever?

UNDERSHAFT: Euripides mentions Barbara, does he?

CUSINS: It is a fair translation. The word means Loveliness.

UNDERSHAFT: May I ask — as Barbara's father — how much a year she is to be loved for ever on?

CUSINS: As for Barbara's father, that is more your affair than mine. I can feed her by teaching Greek: that is about all.

UNDERSHAFT: Do you consider it a good match for her?

CUSINS (*with polite obstinacy*): Mr. Undershaft: I am in many ways a weak, timid, ineffectual person; and my health is far from satisfactory. But whenever I feel that I must have anything, I get it, sooner or later. I feel that way about Barbara. I dont like marriage: I feel intensely afraid of it; and I dont know what I shall do with Barbara or what she will do with me. But I feel that I and nobody else must marry her. Please regard that as settled. — Not that I wish to be arbitrary; but why should I waste your time in discussing what is inevitable?

UNDERSHAFT: You mean that you will stick at nothing; not even the conversion of the Salvation Army to the worship of Dionysos.

CUSINS: The business of the Salvation Army is to save, not to wrangle about the name of the pathfinder. Dionysos or another: what does it matter?

UNDERSHAFT (*rising and approaching him*): Professor Cusins: you are a young man after my own heart.

CUSINS: Mr Undershaft: you are, as far as I am able to gather, a most infernal old rascal: but you appeal very strongly to my sense of ironic humor.

(UNDERSHAFT *mutely offers his hand. They shake.*)

UNDERSHAFT (*suddenly concentrating himself*): And now to business.

CUSINS: Pardon me. We are discussing religion. Why go back to such an uninteresting and unimportant subject as business?

UNDERSHAFT: Religion is our business at present, because it is through religion alone that we can win Barbara.

CUSINS: Have you, too, fallen in love with Barbara?

UNDERSHAFT: Yes, with a father's love.

CUSINS: A father's love for a grown-up daughter is the most dangerous of all infatuations. I apologize for mentioning my own pale, coy, mistrustful fancy in the same breath with it.

UNDERSHAFT: Keep to the point. We have to win her; and we are neither of us Methodists.

CUSINS: That doesnt matter. The power Barbara wields here — the power that wields Barbara herself — is not Calvinism, not Presbyterianism, not Methodism —

UNDERSHAFT: Not Greek Paganism either, eh?

CUSINS: I admit that. Barbara is quite original in her religion.

UNDERSHAFT (*triumphantly*): Aha! Barbara Undershaft would be. Her inspiration comes from within herself.

CUSINS: How do you suppose it got there?

UNDERSHAFT (*in towering excitement*): It is the Undershaft inheritance. I shall hand on my torch to my daughter. She shall make my converts and preach my gospel —

CUSINS: What! Money and gunpowder!

UNDERSHAFT: Yes, money and gunpowder. Freedom and power. Command of life and command of death.

CUSINS (*urbanely: trying to bring him down to earth*): This is extremely interesting, Mr Undershaft. Of course you know that you are mad.

UNDERSHAFT (*with redoubled force*): And you?

CUSINS: Oh, mad as a hatter. You are welcome to my secret since I have discovered yours. But I am astonished. Can a madman make cannons?

UNDERSHAFT: Would anyone else than a madman make them? And now (*with surging energy*) question for question. Can a sane man translate Euripides?

CUSINS: No.

UNDERSHAFT (*seizing him by the shoulder*): Can a sane woman make a man of a waster or a woman of a worm?

CUSINS (*reeling before the storm*): Father Colossus — Mammoth Millionaire —

UNDERSHAFT (*pressing him*): Are there two mad people or three in this Salvation shelter today?

CUSINS: You mean Barbara is as mad as we are?

UNDERSHAFT (*pushing him lightly off and resuming his equanimity suddenly and completely*): Pooh, Professor! let us call things by their proper names. I am a millionaire; you are a poet: Barbara is a savior of souls. What have we three to do with the common mob of slaves and idolators? (*He sits down again with a shrug of contempt for the mob.*)

CUSINS: Take care! Barbara is in love with the common people. So am I. Have you never felt the romance of that love?

UNDERSHAFT (*cold and sardonic*): Have you ever been in love with Poverty, like St Francis? Have you ever been in love with Dirt, like St Simeon! Have you ever been in love with disease and suffering, like our nurses and philanthropists? Such passions are not virtues, but the most unnatural of all the vices. This love of the common people may please an earl's granddaughter and a university professor; but I have been a common man and a poor man; and it has no romance for me. Leave it to the poor to pretend that poverty is a blessing: leave it to the coward to make a religion of his cowardice by preaching humility: we know better than that. We three must stand together above the common people: how else can we help their children to climb up beside us? Barbara must belong to us, not to the Salvation Army.

CUSINS: Well, I can only say that if you think you will get her away from the Salvation Army by talking to her as you have been talking to me, you don't know Barbara.

UNDERSHAFT: My friend: I never ask for what I can buy.

CUSINS (*in a white fury*): Do I understand you to imply that you can buy Barbara?

UNDERSHAFT: No; but I can buy the Salvation Army.

CUSINS: Quite impossible.

UNDERSHAFT: You shall see. All religious organizations exist by selling themselves to the rich.

CUSINS: Not the Army. That is the Church of the poor.

UNDERSHAFT: All the more reason for buying it.

CUSINS: I don't think you quite know what the Army does for the poor.

UNDERSHAFT: Oh yes I do. It draws their teeth: that is enough for me as a man of business.

CUSINS: Nonsense! It makes them sober —

UNDERSHAFT: I prefer sober workmen. The profits are larger.

CUSINS: — honest —

UNDERSHAFT: Honest workmen are the most economical.

CUSINS: — attached to their homes —

UNDERSHAFT: So much the better: they will put up with anything sooner than change their shop.

CUSINS: — happy —

UNDERSHAFT: An invaluable safeguard against revolution.

CUSINS: — unselfish —

UNDERSHAFT: Indifferent to their own interests, which suits me exactly.

CUSINS: — with their thoughts on heavenly things —

UNDERSHAFT (*rising*): And not on Trade Unionism nor Socialism. Excellent.

CUSINS (*revolted*): You really are an infernal old rascal.

UNDERSHAFT (*indicating* PETER SHIRLEY, *who has just come from the shelter and strolled dejectedly down the yard between them*): And this is an honest man!

SHIRLEY: Yes: and what av I got by it? (*He passes on bitterly and sits on the form, in the corner of the penthouse.*)

(SNOBBY PRICE, *beaming sactimoniously, and* JENNY HILL, *with a tambourine full of coppers, come from the shelter and go to the drum, on which* JENNY *begins to count the money.*)

UNDERSHAFT (*replying to* SHIRLEY): Oh, your employers must have got a good deal by it from first to last. (*He sits on the table, with one foot on the side form.* CUSINS, *overwhelmed, sits down on the same form nearer the shelter.* BARBARA *comes from the shelter to the middle of the yard. She is excited and a little over-wrought.*)

BARBARA: Weve just had a splendid experience meeting at the other gate in Cripps's lane. I've hardly ever seen them so much moved as they were by your confession, Mr Price.

PRICE: I could almost be glad of my past wickedness if I could believe that it would elp to keep hathers stright.

BARBARA: So it will, Snobby. How much, Jenny?

JENNY: Four and tenpence, Major.

BARBARA: Oh Snobby, if you had given your poor mother just one more kick, we should have got the whole five shillings!

PRICE: If she heard you say that, miss, she'd be sorry I didnt. But I'm glad. Oh what a joy it will be to her when she hears I'm saved!

UNDERSHAFT: Shall I contribute the odd twopence, Barbara? The millionaire's mite, eh? (*He takes a couple of pennies from his pocket.*)

BARBARA: How did you make that twopence?

UNDERSHAFT: As usual. By selling cannons, torpedoes, submarines, and my new patent Grand Duke hand grenade.

BARBARA: Put it back in your pocket. You cant buy your salvation here for twopence: you must work it out.

UNDERSHAFT: Is twopence not enough? I can afford a little more, if you press me.

BARBARA: Two million millions would not be enough. There is bad blood on your hands; and nothing but good blood can cleanse them. Money is no use. Take it away. (*She turns to* CUSINS.) Dolly: you must write another letter for me to the papers. (*He makes a wry face.*) Yes: I know you dont like it; but it must be done. The starvation this winter is beating us: everybody is unemployed. The General says we must close this shelter if we cant get more money. I force the collections at the meetings until I am ashamed: dont I, Snobby?

PRICE: It's a fair treat to see you work it, miss. The way you got them up from three-and-six to four-and-ten with that hymn, penny by penny and verse by verse, was a caution. Not a Cheap Jack on Mile End Waste could touch you at it.

BARBARA: Yes; but I wish we could do without it. I am getting at last to think more of the collection than of the people's souls. And what are those hatfuls of pence and halfpence? We want thousands! tens of thousands! hundreds of thousands! I want to convert people, not to be always begging for the Army in a way I'd die sooner than beg for myself.

UNDERSHAFT (*in profound irony*): Genuine unselfishness is capable of anything, my dear.

BARBARA (*unsuspectingly, as she turns away to take the money from the drum and put it in a cash bag she carries*): Yes, isnt it? (UNDERSHAFT *looks sardonically at* CUSINS.)

CUSINS (*aside to* UNDERSHAFT): Mephistopheles! Machiavelli!

BARBARA (*tears coming into her eyes as she ties the bag and pockets it*): How are we to feed them? I cant talk religion to a man with bodily hunger in his eyes. (*Almost breaking down.*) It's frightful.

JENNY (*running to her*): Major, dear —

BARBARA (*rebounding*): No: dont comfort me. It will be all right. We shall get the money.

UNDERSHAFT: How?

JENNY: By praying for it, of course. Mrs Baines says she prayed for it last night; and she has never prayed for it in vain: never once. (*She goes to the gate and looks out into the street.*)

BARBARA (*who has dried her eyes and regained her composure*): By the way, dad, Mrs Baines has come to march with us to our big meeting this afternoon; and she is very anxious to meet you, for some reason or other. Perhaps she'll convert you.

UNDERSHAFT: I shall be delighted, my dear.

JENNY (*at the gate: excitedly*): Major! Major! heres that man back again.

BARBARA: What man?

JENNY: The man that hit me. Oh, I hope he's coming back to join us.

(BILL WALKER, *with frost on his jacket, comes through the gate, his hands deep in his pockets and his chin sunk between his shoulders, like a cleaned-out gambler. He halts between* BARBARA *and the drum.*)

BARBARA: Hullo, Bill! Back already!

BILL (*nagging at her*): Bin talkin ever sence, ev you?

BARBARA: Pretty nearly. Well, has Todger paid you out for poor Jenny's jaw?

BILL: Nao e aint.

BARBARA: I thought your jacket looked a bit snowy.

BILL: Sao it is snaowy. You want to knaow where the snow cam from, downt you?

BARBARA: Yes.

BILL: Well, it cam from orf the grahnd in Pawkinses Corner in Kennintahn. It got rabbed orf be maw shaoulders: see?

BARBARA: Pity you didnt rub some off with your knees, Bill! That would have done you a lot of good.

BILL (*with sour mirthless humor*): Aw was sivin anather menn's knees at the tawm. E was kneelin on moy ed, e was.

JENNY: Who was kneeling on your head?

BILL: Todger was. E was pryin for me: pryin camfortable wiv me as a cawpet. Sow was Mog. Sao was the aol bloomin meetin. Mog she sez 'Ow Lawd brike is stabborn sperrit: bat downt urt is dear art.' Thet was wot she said. 'Downt urt is dear art'! An er blowk — thirteen stun four! — kneelin wiv all is wight on me. Fanny, aint it?

JENNY: Oh no. We're so sorry, Mr Walker.

BARBARA (*enjoying it frankly*): Nonsense! of course it's funny. Served you right, Bill! You must have done something to him first.

BILL (*doggedly*): Aw did wot Aw said Aw'd do. Aw spit in is eye. E looks ap at the skoy and sez, 'Ow that Aw should be fahnd worthy to be spit upon for the gospel's sike!' e sez; an Mog sez 'Glaory Allelloolier!'; an then e called me brad-dher, an dahned me as if Aw was a kid and e was me mather worshin me a Setterda nawt. Aw ednt jast nao shaow wiv im at all. Arf the street pryed; an the tather arf larfed fit to split theirselves. (*To* BARBARA.) There! are you settisfawd nah?

BARBARA (*her eyes dancing*): Wish I'd been there, Bill.

BILL: Yus: youd a got in a hextra bit o talk on me, wouldnt you?

JENNY: I'm so sorry, Mr Walker.

BILL (*fiercely*): Downt you gow being sorry for me: youve no call. Listen eah. Aw browk your jawr.

JENNY: No, it didn't hurt me: indeed it didnt, except for a moment. It was only that I was frightened.

BILL: Aw downt want to be forgive be you, or be ennybody. Wot Aw did Aw'll py for. Aw trawd to gat me aown jawr browk to settisfaw you —

JENNY (*distressed*): Oh no —

BILL (*impatiently*): Tell y' Aw did: cawnt you listen to wots bein taold you? All Aw got be it was bein mide a sawt of in the pablic street for me pines. Well, if Aw cawnt settisfaw you one way, Aw ken anather. Listen eah! Aw ed two quid sived agen the frost; an Awve a pahnd of it left. A mite o mawn last week ed words with the judy e's gowing to merry. E give er wot-for; an e's bin fawnd fifteen bob. E ed a rawt to itt er cause they was gowin to be merrid; but Aw ednt nao rawt to itt you! sao put anather fawv bob on an call it a pahnd's worth. (*He produces a sovereign*.) Eahs the manney. Tike it; and lets ev no more o your forgivin an prying and your Mijor jawrin me. Let wot Aw dan be dan an pide for; and let there be a end of it.

JENNY: Oh, I couldnt take it, Mr Walker. But if you would give a shilling or two to poor Rummy Mitchens! you really did hurt her; and she's old.

BILL (*contemptuously*): Not lawkly. Aw'd give her anather as soon as look at er. Let her ev the lawr o me as she threatened! She aint forgiven me: not mach. Wot Aw dan to er is not on me mawnd — wot she (*indicating* BARBARA) mawt call on me conscience — no more than stickin a pig. It's this Christian gime o yours that Aw wownt ev plyed agen me: this bloomin forgivin an neggin an jawrin that mikes a menn thet sore that iz lawf's a burdn to im. Aw wownt ev it, Aw tell you; sao tike your manney and stop thraowin your silly beshed fice hap agen me.

JENNY: Major: may I take a little of it for the Army?

BARBARA: No: the Army is not to be bought. We want your soul, Bill; and we'll take nothing less.

BILL (*bitterly*): Aw knaow. Me an maw few shillins is not good enaff for you. Youre a earl's grendorter, you are. Nathink less than a andered pahnd for you.

UNDERSHAFT: Come Barbara! you could do a great deal of good with a hundred pounds. If you will set this gentleman's mind at ease by taking his pound, I will give the other ninety-nine.

(BILL, *dazed by such opulence, instinctively touches his cap*.)

BARBARA: Oh, youre too extravagant, papa. Bill offers twenty pieces of silver. All you need offer is the other ten. That will make the standard price to buy anybody who's for sale. I'm not; and the Army's not. (*To* BILL.) Youll never have another quiet moment, Bill, until you come round to us. You cant stand out against your salvation.

BILL (*sullenly*): Aw cawnt stend aht agen music awl wrastlers and awtful tangued women. Awve offered to py. Aw can do no more. Tike it or leave it. There it is. (*He throws the sovereign on the drum, and sits down on the horse-trough. The coin fascinates* SNOBBY PRICE, *who takes an early opportunity of dropping his cap on it.*)

(MRS BAINES *comes from the shelter. She is dressed as a Salvation Army Commissioner. She is an earnest looking woman of about 40, with a caressing urgent voice, and an appealing manner.*)

BARBARA: This is my father, Mrs Baines. (UNDERSHAFT *comes from the table, taking his hat off with marked civility.*) Try what you can do with him. He wont listen to me, because he remembers what a fool I was when I was a baby. (*She leaves them together and chats with* JENNY.)

MRS BAINES: Have you been shewn over the shelter, Mr Undershaft? You know the work we're doing, of course.

UNDERSHAFT (*very civilly*): The whole nation knows it, Mrs Baines.

MRS BAINES: No, sir: the whole nation does not know it, or we should not be crippled as we are for want of money to carry our work through the length and breadth of the land. Let me tell you that there would have been rioting this winter in London but for us.

UNDERSHAFT: You really think so?

MRS BAINES: I know it. I remember 1886, when you rich gentlemen hardened your hearts against the cry of the poor. They broke the windows of your clubs in Pall Mall.

UNDERSHAFT (*gleaming with approval of their method*): And the Mansion House Fund went up next day from thirty thousand pounds to seventy-nine thousand! I remember quite well.

MRS BAINES: Well, wont you help me to get at the people? They wont break windows then. Come here, Price. Let me shew you to this gentleman. (*Price comes to be inspected.*) Do you remember the window breaking?

PRICE: My ole father thought it was the revolution, maam.

MRS BAINES: Would you break windows now?

PRICE: Oh no, maam. The windows of eaven av bin opened to me. I know now that the rich man is a sinner like myself.

RUMMY (*appearing above at the loft door*): Snobby Price!

SNOBBY: Wot is it?

RUMMY: Your mother's askin for you at the other gate in Cripps's Lane. She's heard about your confession. (PRICE *turns pale.*)

MRS BAINES: Go, Mr Price; and pray with her.

JENNY: You can go through the shelter, Snobby.

PRICE (*to* MRS BAINES): I couldnt face her now, maam, with all the weight of my sins fresh on me. Tell her she'll find her son at ome, waitin for her in prayer. (*He skulks off through the gate, incidentally stealing the sovereign on his way out by picking up his cap from the drum.*)

MRS BAINES (*with swimming eyes*): You see how we take the anger and the bitterness against you out of their hearts, Mr Undershaft.

UNDERSHAFT: It is certainly most convenient and gratifying to all large employers of labor, Mrs Baines.

MRS BAINES: Barbara: Jenny: I have good news: most wonderful news. (JENNY *runs to her*.) My prayers have been answered. I told you they would, Jenny, didnt I?

JENNY: Yes, yes.

BARBARA (*moving nearer to the drum*): Have we got money enough to keep the shelter open?

MRS BAINES: I hope we shall have enough to keep all the shelters open. Lord Saxmundham has promised us five thousand pounds —

BARBARA: Hooray!

JENNY: Glory!

MRS BAINES: — if —

BARBARA: 'If!' If what?

MRS BAINES: — if five other gentlemen will give a thousand each to make it up to ten thousand.

BARBARA: Who is Lord Saxmundham? I never heard of him.

UNDERSHAFT (*who has pricked up his ears at the peer's name, and is now watching* BARBARA *curiously*): A new creation, my dear. You have heard of Sir Horace Bodger?

BARBARA: Bodger! Do you mean the distiller? Bodger's whisky!

UNDERSHAFT: That is the man. He is one of the greatest of our public benefactors. He restored the cathedral at Hakington. They made him a baronet for that. He gave half a million to the funds of his party: they made him a baron for that.

SHIRLEY: What will they give him for the five thousand?

UNDERSHAFT: There is nothing left to give him. So the five thousand, I should think, is to save his soul.

MRS BAINES: Heaven grant it may! O Mr Undershaft, you have some very rich friends. Cant you help us towards the other five thousand? We are going to hold a great meeting this afternoon at the Assembly Hall in the Mile End Road. If I could only announce that one gentleman had come forward to support Lord Saxmundham, others would follow. Dont you know somebody? couldnt you? wouldn't you? (*her eyes fill with tears*) oh, think of those poor people, Mr Undershaft: think of how much it means to them, and how little to a great man like you.

UNDERSHAFT (*sardonically gallant*): Mrs Baines: you are irresistible. I cant disappoint you; and I cant deny myself the satisfaction of making Bodger pay up. You shall have your five thousand pounds.

MRS BAINES: Thank God!

UNDERSHAFT: You dont thank me?

MRS BAINES: Oh sir, dont try to be cynical: dont be ashamed of being a good man. The Lord will bless you abundantly; and our prayers will be like a strong fortification round you all the days of your life. (*With a touch of caution*.) You will let me have the cheque to shew at the meeting, wont you? Jenny: go in and fetch a pen and ink. (JENNY *runs to the shelter door*.)

UNDERSHAFT: Do not disturb Miss Hill: I have a fountain pen (JENNY *halts. He sits at the table and writes the cheque.* CUSINS *rises to make room for him. They all watch him silently.*)

BILL (*cynically aside to* BARBARA, *his voice and accent horribly debased*): Wot prawce selvytion nah?

BARBARA: Stop. (UNDERSHAFT *stops writing: they all turn to her in surprise.*) Mrs Baines: are you really going to take this money?

MRS BAINES (*astonished*): Why not, dear?

BARBARA: Why not! Do you know what my father is? Have you forgotten that Lord
    Saxmundham is Bodger the whisky man? do you remember how we implored the
    County Council to stop him from writing Bodger's Whisky in letters of fire
    against the sky; so that the poor drink-ruined creatures on the Embankment
    could not wake up from their snatches of sleep without being reminded of their
    deadly thirst by that wicked sky sign? Do you know that the worst thing I have
    had to fight here is not the devil, but Bodger, Bodger, Bodger, with his whisky,
    his distilleries, and his tied houses? Are you going to make our shelter another
    tied house for him, and ask me to keep it?

BILL: Rotten dranken whisky it is too.

MRS BAINES: Dear Barbara: Lord Saxmundham has a soul to be saved like any of us.
    If heaven has found the way to make a good use of his money, are we to set
    ourselves up against the answer to our prayers?

BARBARA: I know he has a soul to be saved. Let him come down here; and I'll do my
    best to help him to his salvation. But he wants to send his cheque down to buy
    us, and go on being as wicked as ever.

UNDERSHAFT (*with a reasonableness which* CUSINS *alone perceives to be ironical*):
    My dear Barbara: alcohol is a very necessary article. It heals the sick —

BARBARA: It does nothing of the sort.

UNDERSHAFT: Well, it assists the doctor: that is perhaps a less questionable way of
    putting it. It makes life bearable to millions of people who could not endure their
    existence if they were quite sober. It enables Parliament to do things at eleven at
    night that no sane person would do at eleven in the morning. Is it Bodger's fault
    that this inestimable gift is deplorably abused by less than one per cent of the
    poor? (*He turns again to the table; signs the cheque; and crosses it.*)

MRS BAINES: Barbara: will there be less drinking or more if all those poor souls we
    are saving come tomorrow and find the doors of our shelters shut in their faces?
    Lord Saxmundham gives us the money to stop drinking — to take his own busi-
    ness from him.

CUSINS (*impishly*): Pure self-sacrifice on Bodger's part, clearly! Bless dear Bodger!
    (BARBARA *almost breaks down as* ADOLPHUS, *too, fails her.*)

UNDERSHAFT (*tearing the cheque and pocketing the book as he rises and goes past*
    CUSINS *to* MRS BAINES): I also, Mrs Baines, may claim a little disinterestedness.
    Think of my business! think of the widows and orphans! the men and lads torn to
    pieces with shrapnel and poisoned with lyddite! (MRS BAINES *shrinks; but he goes
    on remorselessly*) the oceans of blood, not one drop of which is shed in a really
    just cause! the ravaged crops! the peaceful peasants forced, women and men, to
    till their fields under the fire of opposing armies on pain of starvation! the bad
    blood of the fierce little cowards at home who egg on others to fight for the
    gratification of their national vanity! All this makes money for me: I am never
    richer, never busier than when the papers are full of it. Well, it is your work to
    preach peace on earth and good will to men. (MRS BAINES's *face lights up again.*)
    Every convert you make is a vote against war. (*Her lips move in prayer.*) Yet I
    give you this money to help you to hasten my own commercial ruin. (*He gives her
    the cheque.*)

CUSINS (*mounting the form in an ecstasy of mischief*): The millennium will be inau-
    gurated by the unselfishness of Undershaft and Bodger. Oh be joyful! (*He takes
    the drumsticks from his pocket and flourishes them.*)

MRS BAINES (*taking the cheque*): The longer I live the more proof I see that there is an Infinite Goodness that turns everything to the work of salvation sooner or later. Who would have thought that any good could have come out of war and drink? And yet their profits are brought today to the feet of salvation to do its blessed work. (*She is affected to tears.*)

JENNY (*running to* MRS BAINES *and throwing her arms around her*): Oh dear! how blessed, how glorious it all is!

CUSINS (*in a convulsion of irony*): Let us seize this unspeakable moment. Let us march to the great meeting at once. Excuse me just an instant. (*He rushes into the shelter.* JENNY *takes her tambourine from the drum head.*)

MRS BAINES: Mr Undershaft: have you ever seen a thousand people fall on their knees with one impulse and pray? Come with us to the meeting. Barbara shall tell them that the Army is saved, and saved through you.

CUSINS (*returning impetuously from the shelter with a flag and a trombone, and coming between* MRS BAINES *and* UNDERSHAFT): You shall carry the flag down the first street, Mrs Baines (*he gives her the flag*). Mr Undershaft is a gifted trombonist: he shall intone an Olympian diapason to the West Ham Salvation March. (*Aside to* UNDERSHAFT, *as he forces the trombone on him.*) Blow, Machiavelli, blow.

UNDERSHAFT (*aside to him, as he takes the trombone*): The trumpet in Zion! (CUSINS *rushes to the drum, which he takes up and puts on.* UNDERSHAFT *continues, aloud.*) I will do my best. I could vamp a bass if I knew the tune.

CUSINS: It is a wedding chorus from one of Donizetti's operas; but we have converted it. We convert everything to good here, including Bodger. You remember the chorus. 'For thee immense rejoicing — immenso giubilo — immenso giubilo.' (*With drum obbligato.*) Rum tum ti tum tum, tum tum ti ta —

BARBARA: Dolly: you are breaking my heart.

CUSINS: What is a broken heart more or less here? Dionysos Undershaft has descended. I am possessed.

MRS BAINES: Come, Barbara: I must have my dear Major to carry the flag with me.

JENNY: Yes, yes, Major darling.

CUSINS (*snatches the tambourine out of* JENNY's *hand and mutely offers it to* BARBARA).

BARBARA (*coming forward a little as she puts the offer behind her with a shudder, whilst* CUSINS *recklessly tosses the tambourine back to* JENNY *and goes to the gate*): I cant come.

JENNY: Not come!

MRS BAINES (*with tears in her eyes*): Barbara: do you think I am wrong to take the money?

BARBARA (*impulsively going to her and kissing her*): No, no: God help you, dear, you must: you are saving the Army. Go; and may you have a great meeting!

JENNY: But arent you coming?

BARBARA: No. (*She begins taking off the silver S brooch from her collar.*)

MRS BAINES: Barbara: what are you doing?

JENNY: Why are you taking your badge off? You cant be going to leave us, Major.

BARBARA (*quietly*): Father: come here.

UNDERSHAFT (*coming to her*): My dear! (*Seeing that she is going to pin the badge on his collar, he retreats to the penthouse in some alarm.*)

BARBARA (*following him*): Dont be frightened. (*She pins the badge on and steps back

towards the table, shewing him to the others.) There! It's not much for £5000, is
it?

MRS BAINES: Barbara: if you wont come and pray with us, promise me you will pray
for us.

BARBARA: I cant pray now. Perhaps I shall never pray again.

MRS BAINES: Barbara!

JENNY: Major!

BARBARA (*almost delirious*): I cant bear any more. Quick march!

CUSINS (*calling to the procession in the street outside*): Off we go. Play up, there!
Immenso giubilo. (*He gives the time with his drum; and the band strikes up the
march, which rapidly becomes more distant as the procession moves briskly away.*)

MRS BAINES: I must go, dear. Youre overworked: you will be all right tomorrow.
We'll never lose you. Now Jenny: step out with the old flag. Blood and Fire! (*She
marches out through the gate with her flag.*)

JENNY: Glory Hallelujah! (*flourishing her tambourine and marching*).

UNDERSHAFT (*to* CUSINS, *as he marches out past him easing the slide of his trombone*): 'My ducats and my daughter'!

CUSINS (*following him out*): Money and gunpowder!

BARBARA: Drunkenness and Murder! My God: why hast thou forsaken me?

(*She sinks on the form with her face buried in her hands. The march passes away
into silence.* BILL WALKER *steals across to her.*)

BILL (*taunting*): Wot prawce selvytion nah?

SHIRLEY: Dont you hit her when she's down.

BILL: She itt me wen aw wiz dahn. Waw shouldnt Aw git a bit o me aown beck?

BARBARA (*raising her head*): I didn't take your money, Bill.

(*She crosses the yard to the gate and turns her back on the two men to hide her
face from them.*)

BILL (*sneering after her*): Naow, it warnt enaff for you. (*Turning to the drum, he
misses the money.*) Ellow! If you aint took it sammun else ez. Weres it gorn? Bly
me if Jenny Ill didnt tike it arter all!

RUMMY (*screaming at him from the loft*): You lie, you dirty blackguard! Snobby
Price pinched it off the drum when he took up his cap. I was up here all the time
an see im do it.

BILL: Wot! Stowl maw manney! Waw didnt you call thief on him, you silly aold
macker you?

RUMMY: To serve you aht for ittin me acrost the fice. It's cost y'pahnd, that az.
(*Raising a pœan of squalid triumph.*) I done you. I'm even with you. Uve ad it
aht o y — (BILL *snatches up* SHIRLEY's *mug and hurls it at her. She slams the loft
door and vanishes. The mug smashes against the door and falls in fragments.*)

BILL (*beginning to chuckle*): Tell us, aol menn, wot o'clock this mawnin was it wen
im as they call Snobby Prawce was sived?

BARBARA (*turning to him more composedly, and with unspoiled sweetness*): About
half past twelve, Bill. And he pinched your pound at a quarter to two. I know.
Well, you cant afford to lose it. I'll send it to you.

BILL (*his voice and accent suddenly improving*): Not if Aw wiz to stawve for it. Aw
aint to be bought.

SHIRLEY: Aint you? Youd sell yourself to the devil for a pint o beer; only there aint no devil to make the offer.

BILL (*unashamed*): Sao. Aw would, mite, and often ev, cheerful. But she cawnt baw me. (*Approaching* BARBARA.) You wanted maw saoul, did you? Well, you aint got it.

BARBARA: I nearly got it, Bill. But weve sold it back to you for ten thousand pounds.

SHIRLEY: And dear at the money!

BARBARA: No, Peter: it was worth more than money.

BILL (*salvationproof*): It's nao good: you cawnt get rahnd me nah. Aw downt blieve in it; and Awve seen tody that Aw was rawt. (*Going.*) Sao long, aol soupkitchener! Ta, ta, Mijor Earl's Grendorter! (*Turning at the gate.*) Wot prawce selvytion nah? Snobby Prawce! Ha! Ha!

BARBARA (*offering her hand*): Goodbye, Bill.

BILL (*taken aback, half plucks his cap off; then shoves it on again defiantly*): Git aht. (BARBARA *drops her hand, discouraged. He has a twinge of remorse.*) But thets aw rawt, you knaow. Nathink pasnl. Naow mellice. Sao long, Judy. (*He goes.*)

BARBARA: No malice. So long, Bill.

SHIRLEY (*shaking his head*): You make too much of him, miss, in your innocence.

BARBARA (*going to him*): Peter: I'm like you now. Cleaned out, and lost my job.

SHIRLEY: Youve youth an hope. Thats two better than me.

BARBARA: I'll get you a job, Peter. Thats hope for you: the youth will have to be enough for me. (*She counts her money.*) I have just enough left for two teas at Lockharts, a Rowton doss for you, and my tram and bus home. (*He frowns and rises with offended pride. She takes his arm.*) Dont be proud, Peter: it's sharing between friends. And promise me youll talk to me and not let me cry. (*She draws him towards the gate.*)

SHIRLEY: Well, I'm not accustomed to talk to the like of you —

BARBARA (*urgently*): Yes, yes: you must talk to me. Tell me about Tom Paine's books and Bradlaugh's lectures. Come along.

SHIRLEY: Ah, if you would only read Tom Paine in the proper spirit, miss! (*They go out through the gate together.*)

ACT III

Next day after lunch LADY BRITOMART *is writing in the library in Wilton Crescent.* SARAH *is reading in the armchair near the window.* BARBARA, *in ordinary fashionable dress, pale and brooding, is on the settee.* CHARLES LOMAX *enters. He starts on seeing* BARBARA *fashionably attired and in low spirits.*

LOMAX: Youve left off your uniform!

(BARBARA *says nothing; but an expression of pain passes over her face.*)

LADY BRITOMART (*warning him in low tones to be careful*): Charles!

LOMAX (*much concerned, coming behind the settee and bending sympathetically over* BARBARA): I'm awfully sorry, Barbara. You know I helped you all I could with the concertina and so forth. (*Momentously.*) Still, I have never shut my eyes to the fact that there is a certain amount of tosh about the Salvation Army. Now the claims of the Church of England —

LADY BRITOMART: Thats enough, Charles. Speak of something suited to your mental capacity.

LOMAX: But surely the Church of England is suited to all our capacities.

BARBARA (*pressing his hand*): Thank you for your sympathy, Cholly. Now go and spoon with Sarah.

LOMAX (*dragging a chair from the writing table and seating himself affectionately by* SARAH'*s side*): How is my ownest today?

SARAH: I wish you wouldnt tell Cholly to do things, Barbara. He always comes straight and does them. Cholly: we're going to the works this afternoon.

LOMAX: What works?

SARAH: The cannon works.

LOMAX: What? your governor's shop!

SARAH: Yes.

LOMAX: Oh I say!

(CUSINS *enters in poor condition. He also starts visibly when he sees* BARBARA *without her uniform.*)

BARBARA: I expected you this morning, Dolly. Didnt you guess that?

CUSINS (*sitting down beside her*): I'm sorry. I have only just breakfasted.

SARAH: But weve just finished lunch.

BARBARA: Have you had one of your bad nights?

CUSINS: No: I had rather a good night: in fact, one of the most remarkable nights I have ever passed.

BARBARA: The meeting?

CUSINS: No: after the meeting.

LADY BRITOMART: You should have gone to bed after the meeting. What were you doing?

CUSINS: Drinking.

LADY BRITOMART:	Adolphus!
SARAH:	Dolly!
BARBARA:	Dolly!
LOMAX:	Oh I say!

LADY BRITOMART: What were you drinking, may I ask?

CUSINS: A most devilish kind of Spanish burgundy, warranted free from added alcohol: a Temperance burgundy in fact. Its richness in natural alcohol made any addition superfluous.

BARBARA: Are you joking, Dolly?

CUSINS (*patiently*): No. I have been making a night of it with the nominal head of this household: that is all.

LADY BRITOMART: Andrew made you drunk!

CUSINS: No: he only provided the wine. I think it was Dionysos who made me drunk. (*To* BARBARA.) I told you I was possessed.

LADY BRITOMART: Youre not sober yet. Go home to bed at once.

CUSINS: I have never before ventured to reproach you, Lady Brit; but how could you marry the Prince of Darkness?

LADY BRITOMART: It was much more excusable to marry him than to get drunk with him. That is a new accomplishment of Andrew's, by the way. He usent to drink.

CUSINS: He doesnt now. He only sat there and completed the wreck of my moral basis, the rout of my convictions, the purchase of my soul. He cares for you, Barbara. That is what makes him so dangerous to me.

BARBARA: That has nothing to do with it, Dolly. There are larger loves and diviner dreams than the fireside ones. You know that, dont you?

CUSINS: Yes: that is our understanding. I know it. I hold to it. Unless he can win me on that holier ground he may amuse me for a while; but he can get no deeper hold, strong as he is.

BARBARA: Keep to that; and the end will be right. Now tell me what happened at the meeting?

CUSINS: It was an amazing meeting. Mrs Baines almost died of emotion. Jenny Hill simply gibbered with hysteria. The Prince of Darkness played his trombone like a madman: its brazen roarings were like the laughter of the damned. 117 conversions took place then and there. They prayed with the most touching sincerity and gratitude for Bodger, and for the anonymous donor of the £5000. Your father would not let his name be given.

LOMAX: That was rather fine of the old man, you know. Most chaps would have wanted the advertisement.

CUSINS: He said all the charitable institutions would be down on him like kites on a battle-field if he gave his name.

LADY BRITOMART: Thats Andrew all over. He never does a proper thing without giving an improper reason for it.

CUSINS: He convinced me that I have all my life been doing improper things for proper reasons.

LADY BRITOMART: Adolphus: now that Barbara has left the Salvation Army, you had better leave it too. I will not have you playing that drum in the streets.

CUSINS: Your orders are already obeyed, Lady Brit.

BARBARA: Dolly: were you ever really in earnest about it? Would you have joined if you had never seen me?

CUSINS (*disingenuously*): Well — er — well, possibly, as a collector of religious —

LOMAX (*cunningly*): Not as a drummer, though, you know. You are a very clear-headed brainy chap, Dolly; and it must have been apparent to you that there is a certain amount of tosh about —

LADY BRITOMART: Charles: if you must drivel, drivel like a grown-up man and not like a schoolboy.

LOMAX (*out of countenance*): Well, drivel is drivel, dont you know, whatever a man's age.

LADY BRITOMART: In good society in England, Charles, men drivel at all ages by repeating silly formulas with an air of wisdom. Schoolboys make their own formulas out of slang, like you. When they reach your age, and get political private secretaryships and things of that sort, they drop slang and get their formulas out of The Spectator or The Times. You had better confine yourself to The Times. You will find that there is a certain amount of tosh about The Times; but at least its language is reputable.

LOMAX (*overwhelmed*): You are so awfully strong-minded, Lady Brit —

LADY BRITOMART: Rubbish! (MORRISON *comes in.*) What is it?

MORRISON: If you please, my lady, Mr Undershaft has just drove up to the door.

LADY BRITOMART: Well, let him in. (MORRISON *hesitates.*) Whats the matter with you?

MORRISON: Shall I announce him, my lady; or is he at home here, so to speak, my lady?

LADY BRITOMART: Announce him.

MORRISON: Thank you, my lady. You wont mind my asking, I hope. The occasion is in a manner of speaking new to me.

LADY BRITOMART: Quite right. Go and let him in.

MORRISON: Thank you, my lady. (*He withdraws.*)

LADY BRITOMART: Children: go and get ready. (SARAH *and* BARBARA *go upstairs for their out-of-door wraps.*) Charles: go and tell Stephen to come down here in five minutes: you will find him in the drawing room. (CHARLES *goes.*) Adolphus: tell them to send round the carriage in about fifteen minutes. (ADOLPHUS *goes.*)

MORRISON (*at the door*): Mr Undershaft.

(UNDERSHAFT *comes in.* MORRISON *goes out.*)

UNDERSHAFT: Alone! How fortunate!

LADY BRITOMART (*rising*): Dont be sentimental, Andrew. Sit down. (*She sits on the settee: he sits beside her, on her left. She comes to the point before he has time to breathe.*) Sarah must have £800 a year until Charles Lomax comes into his property. Barbara will need more, and need it permanently, because Adolphus hasnt any property.

UNDERSHAFT (*resignedly*): Yes, my dear: I will see to it. Anything else? for yourself, for instance?

LADY BRITOMART: I want to talk to you about Stephen.

UNDERSHAFT (*rather wearily*): Dont, my dear. Stephen doesnt interest me.

LADY BRITOMART: He does interest me. He is our son.

UNDERSHAFT: Do you really think so? He has induced us to bring him into the world; but he chose his parents very incongruously, I think. I see nothing of myself in him, and less of you.

LADY BRITOMART: Andrew: Stephen is an excellent son, and a most steady, capable, highminded young man. You are simply trying to find an excuse for disinheriting him.

UNDERSHAFT: My dear Biddy: the Undershaft tradition disinherits him. It would be dishonest of me to leave the cannon foundry to my son.

LADY BRITOMART: It would be most unnatural and improper of you to leave it to anyone else, Andrew. Do you suppose this wicked and immoral tradition can be kept up for ever? Do you pretend that Stephen could not carry on the foundry just as well as all the other sons of the big business houses?

UNDERSHAFT: Yes: he could learn the office routine without understanding the business, like all the other sons; and the firm would go on by its own momentum until the real Undershaft — probably an Italian or a German — would invent a new method and cut him out.

LADY BRITOMART: There is nothing that any Italian or German could do that Stephen could not do. And Stephen at least has breeding.

UNDERSHAFT: The son of a foundling! Nonsense!

LADY BRITOMART: My son, Andrew! and even you may have good blood in your veins for all you know.

UNDERSHAFT: True. Probably I have. That is another argument in favor of a foundling.

LADY BRITOMART: Andrew: dont be aggravating. And dont be wicked. At present you are both.

UNDERSHAFT: This conversation is part of the Undershaft tradition, Biddy. Every Undershaft's wife has treated him to it ever since the house was founded. It is mere waste of breath. If the tradition be ever broken it will be for an abler man than Stephen.

LADY BRITOMART (*pouting*): Then go away.

UNDERSHAFT (*deprecatory*): Go away!

LADY BRITOMART: Yes: Go away. If you will do nothing for Stephen, you are not wanted here. Go to your foundling, whoever he is; and look after him.

UNDERSHAFT: The fact is, Biddy —

LADY BRITOMART: Dont call me Biddy. I dont call you Andy.

UNDERSHAFT: I will not call my wife Britomart: it is not good sense. Seriously, my love, the Undershaft tradition has landed me in a difficulty. I am getting on in years; and my partner Lazarus has at last made a stand and insisted that the succession must be settled one way or the other; and of course he is quite right. You see, I havent found a fit successor yet.

LADY BRITOMART (*obstinately*): There is Stephen.

UNDERSHAFT: Thats just it: all the foundlings I can find are exactly like Stephen.

LADY BRITOMART: Andrew!

UNDERSHAFT: I want a man with no relations and no schooling: that is, a man who would be out of the running altogether if he were not a strong man. And I cant find him. Every blessed foundling nowadays is snapped up in his infancy by Barnardo homes, or School Board officers, or Boards of Guardians; and if he shews the least ability he is fastened on by schoolmasters; trained to win scholarships like a racehorse; crammed with secondhand ideas; drilled and disciplined in docility and what they call good taste; and lamed for life so that he is fit for nothing but teaching. If you want to keep the foundry in the family, you had better find an eligible foundling and marry him to Barbara.

LADY BRITOMART: Ah! Barbara! Your pet! You would sacrifice Stephen to Barbara.

UNDERSHAFT: Cheerfully. And you, my dear, would boil Barbara to make soup for Stephen.

LADY BRITOMART: Andrew: this is not a question of our likings and dislikings: it is a question of duty. It is your duty to make Stephen your successor.

UNDERSHAFT: Just as much as it is your duty to submit to your husband. Come, Biddy! these tricks of the governing class are of no use with me. I am one of the governing class myself; and it is waste of time giving tracts to a missionary. I have the power in this matter; and I am not to be humbugged into using it for your purposes.

LADY BRITOMART: Andrew: you can talk my head off; but you cant change wrong into right. And your tie is all on one side. Put it straight.

UNDERSHAFT (*disconcerted*): It wont stay unless it's pinned (*he fumbles at it with childish grimaces*) —

(STEPHEN *comes in.*)

STEPHEN (*at the door*): I beg your pardon (*about to retire*).

LADY BRITOMART: No: come in, Stephen. (STEPHEN *comes forward to his mother's writing table.*)

UNDERSHAFT (*not very cordially*): Good afternoon.

STEPHEN (*coldly*): Good afternoon.

UNDERSHAFT (*to* LADY BRITOMART): He knows all about the tradition, I suppose?

LADY BRITOMART: Yes. (*To* STEPHEN.) It is what I told you last night, Stephen.

UNDERSHAFT (*sulkily*): I understand you want to come into the cannon business.

STEPHEN: I go into the trade! Certainly not.

UNDERSHAFT (*opening his eyes, greatly eased in mind and manner*): Oh! in that case —

LADY BRITOMART: Cannons are not trade, Stephen. They are enterprise.

STEPHEN: I have no intention of becoming a man of business in any sense. I have no capacity for business and no taste for it. I intend to devote myself to politics.

UNDERSHAFT (*rising*): My dear boy: this is an immense relief to me. And I trust it may prove an equally good thing for the country. I was afraid you would consider yourself disparaged and slighted. (*He moves toward* STEPHEN *as if to shake hands with him.*)

LADY BRITOMART (*rising and interposing*): Stephen: I cannot allow you to throw away an enormous property like this.

STEPHEN (*stiffly*): Mother: there must be an end of treating me as a child, if you please. (LADY BRITOMART *recoils, deeply wounded by his tone.*) Until last night I did not take your attitude seriously, because I did not think you meant it seriously. But I find now that you left me in the dark as to matters which you should have explained to me years ago. I am extremely hurt and offended. Any further discussion of my intentions had better take place with my father, as between one man and another.

LADY BRITOMART: Stephen! (*She sits down again, her eyes filling with tears.*)

UNDERSHAFT (*with grave compassion*): You see, my dear, it is only the big men who can be treated as children.

STEPHEN: I am sorry, mother, that you have forced me —

UNDERSHAFT (*stopping him*): Yes, yes, yes, yes: thats all right, Stephen. She wont interfere with you any more: your independence is achieved: you have won your latchkey. Dont rub it in; and above all, dont apologize. (*He resumes his seat.*) Now what about your future, as between one man and another — I beg your pardon, Biddy: as between two men and a woman.

LADY BRITOMART (*who has pulled herself together strongly*): I quite understand, Stephen. By all means go your own way if you feel strong enough. (STEPHEN *sits down magisterially in the chair at the writing table with an air of affirming his majority.*)

UNDERSHAFT: It is settled that you do not ask for the succession to the cannon business.

STEPHEN: I hope it is settled that I repudiate the cannon business.

UNDERSHAFT: Come, come! dont be so devilishly sulky: it's boyish. Freedom should be generous. Besides, I owe you a fair start in life in exchange for disinheriting you. You cant become prime minister all at once. Havnt you a turn for something? What about literature, art, and so forth?

STEPHEN: I have nothing of the artist about me, either in faculty or character, thank Heaven!

UNDERSHAFT: A philosopher, perhaps? Eh?

STEPHEN: I make no such ridiculous pretension.

UNDERSHAFT: Just so. Well, there is the army, the navy, the Church, the Bar. The Bar requires some ability. What about the Bar?

STEPHEN: I have not studied law. And I am afraid I have not the necessary push — I believe that is the name barristers give to their vulgarity — for success in pleading.

UNDERSHAFT: Rather a difficult case, Stephen. Hardly anything left but the stage, is there? (STEPHEN *makes an impatient movement.*) Well, come! is there anything you know or care for?

STEPHEN (*rising and looking at him steadily*): I know the difference between right and wrong.

UNDERSHAFT (*hugely tickled*): You dont say so! What! no capacity for business, no knowledge of law, no sympathy with art, no pretension to philosophy; only a simple knowledge of the secret that has puzzled all the philosophers, baffled all the lawyers, muddled all the men of business, and ruined most of the artists: the secret of right and wrong. Why, man, youre a genius, a master of masters, a god! At twentyfour, too!

STEPHEN (*keeping his temper with difficulty*): You are pleased to be facetious. I pretend to nothing more than any honorable English gentleman claims as his birthright (*he sits down angrily*).

UNDERSHAFT: Oh, thats everybody's birthright. Look at poor little Jenny Hill, the Salvation lassie! she would think you were laughing at her if you asked her to stand up in the street and teach grammar or geography or mathematics or even drawing room dancing; but it never occurs to her to doubt that she can teach morals and religion. You are all alike, you respectable people. You cant tell me the bursting strain of a ten-inch gun, which is a very simple matter; but you all think you can tell me the bursting strain of a man under temptation. You darent handle high explosives; but youre all ready to handle honesty and truth and justice and the whole duty of man, and kill one another at that game. What a country! What a world!

LADY BRITOMART (*uneasily*): What do you think he had better do, Andrew?

UNDERSHAFT: Oh, just what he wants to do. He knows nothing and he thinks he knows everything. That points clearly to a political career. Get him a private secretaryship to someone who can get him an Under Secretaryship; and then leave him alone. He will find his natural and proper place in the end on the Treasury Bench.

STEPHEN (*springing up again*): I am sorry, sir, that you force me to forget the respect due to you as my father. I am an Englishman and I will not hear the Government of my country insulted. (*He thrusts his hands in his pockets, and walks angrily across to the window.*)

UNDERSHAFT (*with a touch of brutality*): The government of your country! I am the government of your country: I, and Lazarus. Do you suppose that you and half a dozen amateurs like you, sitting in a row in that foolish gabble shop, can govern Undershaft and Lazarus? No, my friend: you will do what pays us. You will make war when it suits us, and keep peace when it doesnt. You will find out that trade requires certain measures when we have decided on those measures. When I want anything to keep my dividends up, you will discover that my want is a national need. When other people want something to keep my dividends down, you will call out the police and military. And in return you shall have the support and applause of my newspapers, and the delight of imagining that you are a great statesman. Government of your country! Be off with you, my boy, and play with your caucuses and leading articles and historical parties and great leaders and burning questions and the rest of your toys. I am going back to my counting-house to pay the piper and call the tune.

STEPHEN (*actually smiling, and putting his hand on his father's shoulder with indulgent patronage*): Really, my dear father, it is impossible to be angry with you.

You dont know how absurd all this sounds to me. You are very properly proud of having been industrious enough to make money; and it is greatly to your credit that you have made so much of it. But it has kept you in circles where you are valued for your money and deferred to for it, instead of in the doubtless very old-fashioned and behind-the-times public school and university where I formed my habits of mind. It is natural for you to think that money governs England; but you must allow me to think I know better.

UNDERSHAFT: And what does govern England, pray?

STEPHEN: Character, father, character.

UNDERSHAFT: Whose character? Yours or mine?

STEPHEN: Neither yours nor mine, father, but the best elements in the English national character.

UNDERSHAFT: Stephen: Ive found your profession for you. Youre a born journalist. I'll start you with a high-toned weekly review. There!

(*Before* STEPHEN *can reply* SARAH, BARBARA, LOMAX, *and* CUSINS *come in ready for walking.* BARBARA *crosses the room to the window and looks out.* CUSINS *drifts amiably to the armchair.* LOMAX *remains near the door, whilst* SARAH *comes to her mother.*

STEPHEN *goes to the smaller writing table and busies himself with his letters.*)

SARAH: Go and get ready, mamma: the carriage is waiting. (LADY BRITOMART *leaves the room.*)

UNDERSHAFT (*to* SARAH): Good day, my dear. Good afternoon, Mr Lomax.

LOMAX (*vaguely*): Ahdedoo.

UNDERSHAFT (*to* CUSINS): Quite well after last night, Euripides, eh?

CUSINS: As well as can be expected.

UNDERSHAFT: Thats right. (*To* BARBARA.) So you are coming to see my death and devastation factory, Barbara?

BARBARA (*at the window*): You came yesterday to see my salvation factory. I promised you a return visit.

LOMAX (*coming forward between* SARAH *and* UNDERSHAFT): Youll find it awfully interesting. Ive been through the Woolwich Arsenal; and it gives you a ripping feeling of security, you know, to think of the lot of beggars we could kill if it came to fighting. (*To* UNDERSHAFT, *with sudden solemnity*.) Still, it must be rather an awful reflection for you, from the religious point of view as it were. Youre getting on, you know, and all that.

SARAH: You dont mind Cholly's imbecility, papa, do you?

LOMAX (*much taken aback*): Oh I say!

UNDERSHAFT: Mr Lomax looks at the matter in a very proper spirit, my dear.

LOMAX: Just so. Thats all I meant, I assure you.

SARAH: Are you coming, Stephen?

STEPHEN: Well, I am rather busy — er — (*Magnanimously*.) Oh well, yes: I'll come. That is, if there is room for me.

UNDERSHAFT: I can take two with me in a little motor I am experimenting with for field use. You wont mind its being rather unfashionable. It's not painted yet; but it's bullet proof.

LOMAX (*appalled at the prospect of confronting Wilton Crescent in an unpainted motor*): Oh I say!

SARAH: The carriage for me, thank you. Barbara doesnt mind what she's seen in.

LOMAX: I say, Dolly, old chap: do you really mind the car being a guy? Because of course if you do I'll go in it. Still —

CUSINS: I prefer it.

LOMAX: Thanks awfully, old man. Come, my ownest. (*He hurries out to secure his seat in the carriage.* SARAH *follows him.*)

CUSINS (*moodily walking across to* LADY BRITOMART's *writing table*): Why are we two coming to this Works Department of Hell? that is what I ask myself.

BARBARA: I have always thought of it as a sort of pit where lost creatures with blackened faces stirred up smoky fires and were driven and tormented by my father. Is it like that, dad?

UNDERSHAFT (*scandalized*): My dear! It is a spotlessly clean and beautiful hillside town.

CUSINS: With a Methodist chapel? Oh do say theres a Methodist chapel?

UNDERSHAFT: There are two: a Primitive one and a sophisticated one. There is even an Ethical Society; but it is not much patronized, as my men are all strongly religious. In the High Explosives Sheds they object to the presence of Agnostics as unsafe.

CUSINS: And yet they dont object to you!

BARBARA: Do they obey all your orders?

UNDERSHAFT: I never give them any orders. When I speak to one of them it is 'Well, Jones, is the baby doing well? and has Mrs Jones made a good recovery?' 'Nicely, thank you, sir.' And thats all.

CUSINS: But Jones has to be kept in order. How do you maintain discipline among your men?

UNDERSHAFT: I dont. They do. You see, the one thing Jones wont stand is any rebellion from the man under him, or any assertion of social equality between the wife of the man with 4 shillings a week less than himself, and Mrs Jones! Of course they all rebel against me, theoretically. Practically, every man of them keeps the man just below him in his place. I never meddle with them. I never bully them. I dont even bully Lazarus. I say that certain things are to be done: but I dont order anybody to do them. I dont say, mind you, that there is no ordering about and snubbing and even bullying. The men snub the boys and order them about; the carmen snub the sweepers; the artisans snub the unskilled laborers; the foremen drive and bully both the laborers and artisans; the assistant engineers find fault with the foremen; the chief engineers drop on the assistants; the departmental managers worry the chiefs; and the clerks have tall hats and hymnbooks and keep up the social tone by refusing to associate on equal terms with anybody. The result is a colossal profit, which comes to me.

CUSINS (*revolted*): You really are a — well, what I was saying yesterday.

BARBARA: What was he saying yesterday?

UNDERSHAFT: Never mind, my dear. He thinks I have made you unhappy. Have I?

BARBARA: Do you think I can be happy in this vulgar silly dress? I! who have worn the uniform. Do you understand what you have done to me? Yesterday I had a man's soul in my hand. I set him in the way of life with his face to salvation. But when we took your money he turned back to drunkenness and derision. (*With intense conviction.*) I will never forgive you that. If I had a child, and you destroyed its body with your explosives — if you murdered Dolly with your horrible guns — I could forgive you if my forgiveness would open the gates of heaven to you. But to take a human soul from me, and turn it into the soul of a wolf! that is worse than any murder.

UNDERSHAFT: Does my daughter despair so easily? Can you strike a man to the heart and leave no mark on him?

BARBARA (*her face lighting up*): Oh, you are right: he can never be lost now: where was my faith?

CUSINS: Oh, clever clever devil!

BARBARA: You may be a devil; but God speaks through you sometimes. (*She takes her father's hands and kisses them.*) You have given me back my happiness: I feel it deep down now, though my spirit is troubled.

UNDERSHAFT: You have learnt something. That always feels at first as if you had lost something.

BARBARA: Well, take me to the factory of death; and let me learn something more. There must be some truth or other behind all this frightful irony. Come, Dolly. (*She goes out.*)

CUSINS: My guardian angel! (*To* UNDERSHAFT.) Avaunt! (*He follows* BARBARA.)

STEPHEN (*quietly, at the writing table*): You must not mind Cusins, father. He is a very amiable good fellow; but he is a Greek scholar and naturally a little eccentric.

UNDERSHAFT: Ah, quite so. Thank you, Stephen. Thank you. (*He goes out.*)

(STEPHEN *smiles patronizingly; buttons his coat responsibly; and crosses the room to the door.* LADY BRITOMART, *dressed for out-of-doors, opens it before he reaches it. She looks round for others; looks at* STEPHEN; *and turns to go without a word.*)

STEPHEN (*embarrassed*): Mother —

LADY BRITOMART: Dont be apologetic, Stephen. And dont forget that you have outgrown your mother. (*She goes out.*)

(*Perivale St Andrews lies between two Middlesex hills, half climbing the northern one. It is an almost smokeless town of white walls, roofs of narrow green slates or red tiles, tall trees, domes, campaniles, and slender chimney shafts, beautifully situated and beautiful in itself. The best view of it is obtained from the crest of a slope about half a mile to the east, where the high explosives are dealt with. The foundry lies hidden in the depths between, the tops of its chimneys sprouting like huge skittles into the middle distance. Across the crest runs an emplacement of concrete, with a firestep, and a parapet which suggests a fortification, because there is a huge cannon of the obsolete Woolwich Infant pattern peering across it at the town. The cannon is mounted on an experimental gun carriage: possibly the original model of the Undershaft disappearing rampart gun alluded to by* STEPHEN. *The firestep, being a convenient place to sit, is furnished here and there with straw disc cushions; and at one place there is the additional luxury of a fur rug.*

BARBARA *is standing on the firestep, looking over the parapet towards the town. On her right is the cannon; on her left the end of a shed raised on piles, with a ladder of three or four steps up to the door, which opens outwards and has a little wooden landing at the threshold, with a fire bucket in the corner of the landing. Several dummy soldiers more or less mutilated, with straw protruding from their gashes, have been shoved out of the way under the landing. A few others are nearly upright against the shed; and one has fallen forward and lies, like a grotesque corpse, on the emplacement. The parapet stops short of the shed, leaving a gap which is the beginning of the path down the hill through the foundry to the town. The rug is on the firestep near this gap. Down on the emplacement behind the cannon is a trolley carrying a huge conical bombshell with a red band painted on it. Further to the right is the door of an office, which, like the sheds, is of the lightest possible construction.*

CUSINS *arrives by the path from the town.*)

BARBARA: Well?

CUSINS: Not a ray of hope. Everything perfect! wonderful! real! It only needs a cathedral to be a heavenly city instead of a hellish one.

BARBARA: Have you found out whether they have done anything for old Peter Shirley?

CUSINS: They have found him a job as gatekeeper and timekeeper. He's frightfully miserable. He calls the time-keeping brainwork, and says he isnt used to it; and his gate lodge is so splendid that he's ashamed to use the rooms, and skulks in the scullery.

BARBARA: Poor Peter!

(STEPHEN *arrives from the town. He carries a fieldglass.*)

STEPHEN (*enthusiastically*): Have you two seen the place? Why did you leave us?

CUSINS: I wanted to see everything I was not intended to see; and Barbara wanted to make the men talk.

STEPHEN: Have you found anything discreditable?

CUSINS: No. They call him Dandy Andy and are proud of his being a cunning old rascal; but it's all horribly, frightfully, immorally, unanswerably perfect.

(SARAH *arrives.*)

SARAH: Heavens! what a place! (*She crosses to the trolley.*) Did you see the nursing home!? (*She sits down on the shell.*)

STEPHEN: Did you see the libraries and schools!?

SARAH: Did you see the ball room and the banqueting chamber in the Town Hall!?

STEPHEN: Have you gone into the insurance fund, the pension fund, the building society, the various applications of cooperation!?

(UNDERSHAFT *comes from the office, with a sheaf of telegrams in his hand.*)

UNDERSHAFT: Well, have you seen everything? I'm sorry I was called away. (*Indicating the telegrams.*) Good news from Manchuria.

STEPHEN: Another Japanese victory?

UNDERSHAFT: Oh, I don't know. Which side wins does not concern us here. No: the good news is that the aerial battleship is a tremendous success. At the first trial it has wiped out a fort with three hundred soldiers in it.

CUSINS (*from the platform*): Dummy soldiers?

UNDERSHAFT (*striding across to* STEPHEN *and kicking the prostrate dummy brutally out of his way*): No: the real thing.

(CUSINS *and* BARBARA *exchange glances. Then* CUSINS *sits on the step and buries his face in his hands.* BARBARA *gravely lays her hand on his shoulder. He looks up at her in whimsical desperation.*)

UNDERSHAFT: Well, Stephen, what do you think of the place?

STEPHEN: Oh, magnificent. A perfect triumph of modern industry. Frankly, my dear father, I have been a fool: I had no idea of what it all meant: of the wonderful forethought, the power of organization, the administrative capacity, the financial genius, the colossal capital it represents. I have been repeating to myself as I came through your streets 'Peace hath her victories no less renowned than War.' I have only one misgiving about it all.

UNDERSHAFT: Out with it.

STEPHEN: Well, I cannot help thinking that all this provision for every want of your workmen may sap their independence and weaken their sense of responsibility. And greatly as we enjoyed our tea at that splendid restaurant — how they gave us all that luxury and cake and jam and cream for threepence I really cannot imagine! — still you must remember that restaurants break up home life. Look at the continent, for instance! Are you sure so much pampering is really good for the men's characters?

UNDERSHAFT: Well you see, my dear boy, when you are organizing civilization you have to make up your mind whether trouble and anxiety are good things or not. If you decide that they are, then, I take it, you simply dont organize civilization; and there you are, with trouble and anxiety enough to make us all angels! But if you decide the other way, you may as well go through with it. However, Stephen, our characters are safe here. A sufficient dose of anxiety is always provided by the fact that we may be blown to smithereens at any moment.

SARAH: By the way, papa, where do you make the explosives?

UNDERSHAFT: In separate little sheds, like that one. When one of them blows up, it costs very little; and only the people quite close to it are killed.

(STEPHEN, *who is quite close to it, looks at it rather scaredly, and moves away quickly to the cannon. At the same moment the door of the shed is thrown abruptly open; and a foreman in overalls and list slippers comes out on the little landing and holds the door for* LOMAX, *who appears in the doorway.*)

LOMAX (*with studied coolness*): My good fellow: you neednt get into a state of nerves. Nothing's going to happen to you; and I suppose it wouldnt be the end of the world if anything did. A little bit of British pluck is what you want, old chap. (*He descends and strolls across to* SARAH.)

UNDERSHAFT (*to the foreman*): Anything wrong, Bilton?

BILTON (*with ironic calm*): Gentleman walked into the high explosives shed and lit a cigaret, sir: thats all.

UNDERSHAFT: Ah, quite so. (*Going over to* LOMAX.) Do you happen to remember what you did with the match?

LOMAX: Oh come! I'm not a fool. I took jolly good care to blow it out before I chucked it away.

BILTON: The top of it was red hot inside, sir.

LOMAX: Well, suppose it was! I didnt chuck it into any of your messes.

UNDERSHAFT: Think no more of it, Mr Lomax. By the way, would you mind lending me your matches.

LOMAX (*offering his box*): Certainly.

UNDERSHAFT: Thanks. (*He pockets the matches.*)

LOMAX (*lecturing to the company generally*): You know, these high explosives dont go off like gunpowder, except when theyre in a gun. When theyre spread loose, you can put a match to them without the least risk; they just burn quietly like a bit of paper. (*Warming to the scientific interest of the subject.*) Did you know that, Undershaft? Have you ever tried?

UNDERSHAFT: Not on a large scale, Mr Lomax. Bilton will give you a sample of gun cotton when you are leaving if you ask him. You can experiment with it at home. (BILTON *looks puzzled.*)

SARAH: Bilton will do nothing of the sort, papa. I suppose it's your business to blow up the Russians and Japs; but you might really stop short of blowing up poor Cholly. (BILTON *gives it up and retires into the shed.*)

LOMAX: My ownest, there is no danger. (*He sits beside her on the shell.*)

(LADY BRITOMART *arrives from the town with a bouquet.*)

LADY BRITOMART (*impetuously*): Andrew: you shouldnt have let me see this place.

UNDERSHAFT: Why, my dear?

LADY BRITOMART: Never mind why: you shouldnt have: thats all. To think of all that (*indicating the town*) being yours! and that you have kept it to yourself all these years!

UNDERSHAFT: It does not belong to me. I belong to it. It is the Undershaft inheritance.

LADY BRITOMART: It is not. Your ridiculous cannons and that noisy banging foundry may be the Undershaft inheritance; but all that plate and linen, all that furniture and those houses and orchards and gardens belong to us. They belong to me: they are not a man's business. I wont give them up. You must be out of your senses to throw them all away; and if you persist in such folly, I will call in a doctor.

UNDERSHAFT (*stooping to smell the bouquet*): Where did you get the flowers, my dear?

LADY BRITOMART: Your men presented them to me in your William Morris Labor Church.

CUSINS: Oh! It needed only that. A Labor Church! (*He mounts the firestep distractedly, and leans with his elbows on the parapet, turning his back to them.*)

LADY BRITOMART: Yes, with Morris's words in mosaic letters ten feet high round the dome. NO MAN IS GOOD ENOUGH TO BE ANOTHER MAN'S MASTER. The cynicism of it!

UNDERSHAFT: It shocked the men at first, I am afraid. But now they take no more notice of it than of the ten commandments in church.

LADY BRITOMART: Andrew: you are trying to put me off the subject of the inheritance by profane jokes. Well, you shant. I dont ask it any longer for Stephen: he has inherited far too much of your perversity to be fit for it. But Barbara has rights as well as Stephen. Why should not Adolphus succeed to the inheritance? I could manage the town for him: and he can look after the cannons, if they are really necessary.

UNDERSHAFT: I should ask nothing better if Adolphus were a foundling. He is exactly the sort of new blood that is wanted in English business. But he's not a foundling; and theres an end of it. (*He makes for the office door.*)

CUSINS (*turning to them*): Not quite. (*They all turn and stare at him.*) I think — Mind! I am not committing myself in any way as to my future course — but I think the foundling difficulty can be got over. (*He jumps down to the emplacement.*)

UNDERSHAFT (*coming back to him*): What do you mean?

CUSINS: Well, I have something to say which is in the nature of a confession.

SARAH:
LADY BRITOMART: } Confession!
BARBARA:
STEPHEN:

LOMAX: Oh I say!

CUSINS: Yes, a confession. Listen, all. Until I met Barbara I thought myself in the main an honorable, truthful man, because I wanted the approval of my conscience more than I wanted anything else. But the moment I saw Barbara, I wanted her far more than the approval of my conscience.

LADY BRITOMART: Adolphus!

CUSINS: It is true. You accused me yourself, Lady Brit, of joining the Army to worship Barbara; and so I did. She bought my soul like a flower at a street corner; but she bought it for herself.

UNDERSHAFT: What! Not for Dionysos or another?

CUSINS: Dionysos and all the others are in herself. I adored what was divine in her, and was therefore a true worshipper. But I was romantic about her too. I thought she was a woman of the people, and that a marriage with a professor of Greek would be far beyond the wildest social ambitions of her rank.

LADY BRITOMART: Adolphus!!

LOMAX: Oh I say!!!

CUSINS: When I learnt the horrible truth —

LADY BRITOMART: What do you mean by the horrible truth, pray?

CUSINS: That she was enormously rich; that her grandfather was an earl; that her father was the Prince of Darkness —

UNDERSHAFT: Chut!

CUSINS: — and that I was only an adventurer trying to catch a rich wife, then I stooped to deceive her about my birth.

BARBARA (*rising*): Dolly!

LADY BRITOMART: Your birth! Now Adolphus, dont dare to make up a wicked story for the sake of these wretched cannons. Remember: I have seen photographs of your parents; and the Agent General for South Western Australia knows them personally and has assured me that they are most respectable married people.

CUSINS: So they are in Australia; but here they are outcasts. Their marriage is legal in Australia, but not in England. My mother is my father's deceased wife's sister; and in this island I am consequently a foundling. (*Sensation.*)

BARBARA: Silly! (*She climbs to the cannon, and leans, listening, in the angle it makes with the parapet.*)

CUSINS: Is the subterfuge good enough, Machiavelli?

UNDERSHAFT (*thoughtfully*): Biddy: this may be a way out of the difficulty.

LADY BRITOMART: Stuff! A man cant make cannons any the better for being his own cousin instead of his proper self. (*She sits down on the rug with a bounce that expresses her downright contempt for their casuistry.*)

UNDERSHAFT (*to* CUSINS): Your are an educated man. That is against the tradition.

CUSINS: Once in ten thousand times it happens that the schoolboy is a born master of what they try to teach him. Greek has not destroyed my mind: it has nourished it. Besides, I did not learn it at an English public school.

UNDERSHAFT: Hm! Well, I cannot afford to be too particular: you have cornered the foundling market. Let it pass. You are eligible, Euripides: you are eligible.

BARBARA: Dolly: yesterday morning, when Stephen told us all about the tradition, you became very silent; and you have been strange and excited ever since. Were you thinking of your birth then?

CUSINS: When the finger of Destiny suddenly points at a man in the middle of his breakfast, it makes him thoughtful.

UNDERSHAFT: Aha! You have had your eye on the business, my young friend, have you?

CUSINS: Take care! There is an abyss of moral horror between me and your accursed aerial battleships.

UNDERSHAFT: Never mind the abyss for the present. Let us settle the practical details and leave your final decision open. You know that you will have to change your name. Do you object to that?

CUSINS: Would any man named Adolphus — any man called Dolly! — object to be called something else?

UNDERSHAFT: Good. Now, as to money! I propose to treat you handsomely from the beginning. You shall start at a thousand a year.

CUSINS (*with sudden heat, his spectacles twinkling with mischief*): A thousand! You dare offer a miserable thousand to the son-in-law of a millionaire! No, by Heavens, Machiavelli! you shall not cheat me. You cannot do without me; and I can do without you. I must have two thousand five hundred a year for two years. At the end of that time, if I am a failure, I go. But if I am a success, and stay on, you must give me the other five thousand.

UNDERSHAFT: What other five thousand?

CUSINS: To make the two years up to five thousand a year. The two thousand five hundred is only half pay in case I should turn out a failure. The third year I must have ten per cent on the profits.

UNDERSHAFT (*taken aback*): Ten per cent! Why, man, do you know what my profits are?

CUSINS: Enormous, I hope: otherwise I shall require twenty-five per cent.

UNDERSHAFT: But, Mr Cusins, this is a serious matter of business. You are not bringing any capital into the concern.

CUSINS: What! no capital! Is my mastery of Greek no capital? Is my access to the subtlest thought, the loftiest poetry yet attained by humanity, no capital? My character! my intellect! my life! my career! what Barbara calls my soul! are these no capital? Say another word; and I double my salary.

UNDERSHAFT: Be reasonable —

CUSINS (*peremptorily*): Mr Undershaft: you have my terms. Take them or leave them.

UNDERSHAFT (*recovering himself*): Very well, I note your terms; and I offer you half.

CUSINS (*disgusted*): Half!

UNDERSHAFT (*firmly*): Half.

CUSINS: You call yourself a gentleman; and you offer me half!!

UNDERSHAFT: I do not call myself a gentleman; but I offer you half.

CUSINS: This to your future partner! your successor! your son-in-law!

BARBARA: You are selling your own soul, Dolly, not mine. Leave me out of the bargain, please.

UNDERSHAFT: Come! I will go a step further for Barbara's sake. I will give you three fifths; but that is my last word.

CUSINS: Done!

LOMAX: Done in the eye! Why, *I* get only eight hundred, you know.

CUSINS: By the way, Mac, I am a classical scholar, not an arithmetical one. Is three fifths more than half or less?

UNDERSHAFT: More, of course.

CUSINS: I would have taken two hundred and fifty. How you can succeed in business when you are willing to pay all that money to a University don who is obviously not worth a junior clerk's wages! — well! What will Lazarus say?

UNDERSHAFT: Lazarus is a gentle romantic Jew who cares for nothing but string quartets and stalls at fashionable theatres. He will be blamed for your rapacity in money matters, poor fellow! as he has hitherto been blamed for mine. You are a shark of the first order, Euripides. So much the better for the firm!

BARBARA: Is the bargain closed, Dolly? Does your soul belong to him now?

CUSINS: No: the price is settled: that is all. The real tug of war is still to come. What about the moral question?

LADY BRITOMART: There is no moral question in the matter at all, Adolphus. You must simply sell cannons and weapons to people whose cause is right and just, and refuse them to foreigners and criminals.

UNDERSHAFT (*determined*): No: None of that. You must keep the true faith of an Armorer, or you dont come in here.

CUSINS: What on earth is the true faith of an Armorer?

UNDERSHAFT: To give arms to all men who offer an honest price for them, without respect of persons or principles: to aristocrat and republican, to Nihilist and Tsar, to Capitalist and Socialist, to Protestant and Catholic, to burglar and policeman, to black man, white man and yellow man, to all sorts and conditions, all nationalities, all faiths, all follies, all causes and all crimes. The first Undershaft wrote up in his shop, IF GOD GAVE THE HAND, LET NOT MAN WITHHOLD THE SWORD. The second wrote up, ALL HAVE THE RIGHT TO FIGHT: NONE HAVE THE RIGHT TO JUDGE. The third wrote up, TO MAN THE WEAPON: TO HEAVEN THE VICTORY. The fourth had no literary turn; so he did not write up anything; but he sold cannons to Napoleon under the nose of George the Third. The fifth wrote up, PEACE SHALL NOT PREVAIL SAVE WITH A SWORD IN HER HAND. The sixth, my master, was the best of all. He wrote up, NOTHING IS EVER DONE IN THIS WORLD UNTIL MEN ARE PREPARED TO KILL ONE ANOTHER IF IT IS NOT DONE. After that, there was nothing left for the seventh to say. So he wrote up, simply, UNASHAMED.

CUSINS: My good Machiavelli, I shall certainly write something up on the wall; only, as I shall write it in Greek, you wont be able to read it. But as to your Armorer's faith, if I take my neck out of the noose of my own morality I am not going to put it into the noose of yours. I shall sell cannons to whom I please and refuse them to whom I please. So there!

UNDERSHAFT: From the moment when you become Andrew Undershaft, you will never do as you please again. Dont come here lusting for power, young man.

CUSINS: If power were my aim I should not come here for it. You have no power.

UNDERSHAFT: None of my own, certainly.

CUSINS: I have more power than you, more will. You do not drive this place: it drives you. And what drives the place?

UNDERSHAFT (*enigmatically*): A will of which I am a part.

BARBARA (*startled*): Father! Do you know what you are saying; or are you laying a snare for my soul?

CUSINS: Dont listen to his metaphysics, Barbara. The place is driven by the most rascally part of society, the money hunters, the pleasure hunters, the military promotion hunters; and he is their slave.

UNDERSHAFT: Not necessarily. Remember the Armorer's Faith. I will take an order from a good man as cheerfully as from a bad one. If you good people prefer preaching and shirking to buying my weapons and fighting the rascals, dont blame me. I can make cannons: I cannot make courage and conviction. Bah! you tire me, Euripides, with your morality mongering. Ask Barbara: *she* understands. (*He suddenly reaches up and takes* BARBARA's *hands, looking powerfully into her eyes.*) Tell him, my love, what power really means.

BARBARA (*hypnotized*): Before I joined the Salvation Army, I was in my own power; and the consequence was that I never knew what to do with myself. When I joined it, I had not time enough for all the things I had to do.

UNDERSHAFT (*approvingly*): Just so. And why was that, do you suppose?

BARBARA: Yesterday I should have said, because I was in the power of God. (*She resumes her self-possession, withdrawing her hands from his with a power equal to his own.*) But you came and shewed me that I was in the power of Bodger and Undershaft. Today I feel — oh! how can I put it into words? Sarah: do you remember the earthquake at Cannes, when we were little children? — how little the surprise of the first shock mattered compared to the dread and horror of waiting for the second? That is how I feel in this place today. I stood on the rock I thought eternal; and without a word of warning it reeled and crumbled under me. I was safe with an infinite wisdom watching me, an army marching to Salvation with me; and in a moment, at a stroke of your pen in a cheque book, I stood alone; and the heavens were empty. That was the first shock of the earthquake: I am waiting for the second.

UNDERSHAFT: Come, come, my daughter! dont make too much of your tinpot tragedy. What do we do here when we spend years of work and thought and thousands of pounds of solid cash on a new gun or an aerial battleship that turns out just a hairsbreadth wrong after all? Scrap it. Scrap it without wasting another hour or another pound on it. Well, you have made for yourself something that you call a morality or a religion or what not. It doesn't fit the facts. Well, scrap it. Scrap it and get one that does fit. That is what is wrong with the world at present. It scraps its obsolete steam engines and dynamos; but it wont scrap its old prejudices and its old moralities and its old religions and its old political constitutions. Whats the result? In machinery it does very well; but in morals and religion and politics it is working at a loss that brings it nearer bankruptcy every year. Dont persist in that folly. If your old religion broke down yesterday, get a newer and a better one for tomorrow.

BARBARA: Oh how gladly I would take a better one to my soul! But you offer me a worse one. (*Turning on him with sudden vehemence.*) Justify yourself: shew me some light through the darkness of this dreadful place, with its beautifully clean workshops, and respectable workmen, and model homes.

UNDERSHAFT: Cleanliness and respectability do not need justification, Barbara: they justify themselves. I see no darkness here, no dreadfulness. In your Salvation shelter I saw poverty, misery, cold and hunger. You gave them bread and treacle and dreams of heaven. I give from thirty shillings a week to twelve thousand a year. They find their own dreams; but I look after the drainage.

BARBARA: And their souls?

UNDERSHAFT: I save their souls just as I saved yours.

BARBARA (*revolted*): You saved my soul! What do you mean?

UNDERSHAFT: I fed you and clothed you and housed you. I took care that you should have money enough to live handsomely — more than enough; so that you could be wasteful, careless, generous. That saved your soul from the seven deadly sins.

BARBARA (*bewildered*): The seven deadly sins!

UNDERSHAFT: Yes, the deadly seven. (*Counting on his fingers.*) Food, clothing, firing, rent, taxes, respectability and children. Nothing can lift those seven millstones from Man's neck but money; and the spirit cannot soar until the millstones are lifted. I lifted them from your spirit. I enabled Barbara to become Major Barbara; and I saved her from the crime of poverty.

CUSINS: Do you call poverty a crime?

UNDERSHAFT: The worst of crimes. All the other crimes are virtues beside it: all the other dishonors are chivalry itself by comparison. Poverty blights whole cities; spreads horrible pestilences; strikes dead the very souls of all who come within sight, sound, or smell of it. What you call crime is nothing: a murder here and a theft there, a blow now and a curse then: what do they matter? they are only the accidents and illnesses of life: there are not fifty genuine professional criminals in London. But there are millions of poor people, abject people, dirty people, ill fed, ill clothed people. They poison us morally and physically: they kill the happiness of society: they force us to do away with our own liberties and to organize unnatural cruelties for fear they should rise against us and drag us down into their abyss. Only fools fear crime: we all fear poverty. Pah! (*turning on* BARBARA) you talk of your half-saved ruffian in West Ham: you accuse me of dragging his soul back to perdition. Well, bring him to me here; and I will drag his soul back again to salvation for you. Not by words and dreams; but by thirtyeight shillings a week, a sound house in a handsome street, and a permanent job. In three weeks he will have a fancy waistcoat; in three months a tall hat and a chapel sitting; before the end of the year he will shake hands with a duchess at a Primrose League meeting, and join the Conservative Party.

BARBARA: And will he be the better for that?

UNDERSHAFT: You know he will. Dont be a hypocrite, Barbara. He will be better fed, better housed, better clothed, better behaved; and his children will be pounds heavier and bigger. That will be better than an American cloth mattress in a shelter, chopping firewood, eating bread and treacle, and being forced to kneel down from time to time to thank heaven for it: knee drill, I think you call it. It is cheap work converting starving men with a Bible in one hand and a slice of bread in the other. I will undertake to convert West Ham to Mahometanism on the same terms. Try your hand on my men: their souls are hungry because their bodies are full.

BARBARA: And leave the east end to starve?

UNDERSHAFT (*his energetic tone dropping into one of bitter and brooding remembrance*): I was an east ender. I moralized and starved until one day I swore that I would be a full-fed free man at all costs; that nothing should stop me except a bullet, neither reason nor morals nor the lives of other men. I said 'Thou shalt starve ere I starve'; and with that word I became free and great. I was a dangerous man until I had my will: now I am a useful, beneficent, kindly person. That is the history of most self-made millionaires, I fancy. When it is the history of every Englishman we shall have an England worth living in.

LADY BRITOMART: Stop making speeches, Andrew. This is not the place for them.

UNDERSHAFT (*punctured*): My dear: I have no other means of conveying my ideas.

LADY BRITOMART: Your ideas are nonsense. You got on because you were selfish and unscrupulous.

UNDERSHAFT: Not at all. I had the strongest scruples about poverty and starvation. Your moralists are quite unscrupulous about both: they make virtues of them. I had rather be a thief than a pauper. I had rather be a murderer than a slave. I dont want to be either; but if you force the alternative on me, then, by Heaven, I'll choose the braver and more moral one. I hate poverty and slavery worse than any other crimes whatsoever. And let me tell you this. Poverty and slavery have stood up for centuries to your sermons and leading articles: they will not stand up to my machine guns. Dont preach at them: dont reason with them. Kill them.

BARBARA: Killing. Is that your remedy for everything?

UNDERSHAFT: It is the final test of conviction, the only lever strong enough to overturn a social system, the only way of saying Must. Let six hundred and seventy fools loose in the streets; and three policemen can scatter them. But huddle them together in a certain house in Westminster; and let them go through certain ceremonies and call themselves certain names until at last they get the courage to kill: and your six hundred and seventy fools become a government. Your pious mob fills up ballot papers and imagines it is governing its masters; but the ballot paper that really governs is the paper that has a bullet wrapped up in it.

CUSINS: That is perhaps why, like most intelligent people, I never vote.

UNDERSHAFT: Vote! Bah! When you vote, you only change the names of the cabinet. When you shoot, you pull down governments, inaugurate new epochs, abolish old orders and set up new. Is that historically true, Mr Learned Man, or is it not?

CUSINS: It is historically true. I loathe having to admit it. I repudiate your sentiments. I abhor your nature. I defy you in every possible way. Still, it is true. But it ought not to be true.

UNDERSHAFT: Ought! ought! ought! ought! ought! Are you going to spend your life saying ought, like the rest of our moralists? Turn your oughts into shalls, man. Come and make explosives with me. Whatever can blow men up can blow society up. The history of the world is the history of those who had courage enough to embrace this truth. Have you the courage to embrace it, Barbara?

LADY BRITOMART: Barbara: I positively forbid you to listen to your father's abominable wickedness. And you, Adolphus, ought to know better than to go about saying that wrong things are true. What does it matter whether they are true if they are wrong?

UNDERSHAFT: What does it matter whether they are wrong if they are true?

LADY BRITOMART (*rising*): Children: come home instantly. Andrew: I am exceedingly sorry I allowed you to call on us. You are wickeder than ever. Come at once.

BARBARA (*shaking her head*): It's no use running away from wicked people, mamma.

LADY BRITOMART: It is every use. It shews your disapprobation of them.

BARBARA: It does not save them.

LADY BRITOMART: I can see that you are going to disobey me, Sarah: are you coming home or are you not?

SARAH: I daresay it's very wicked of papa to make cannons; but I dont think I shall cut him on that account.

LOMAX (*pouring oil on the troubled waters*): The fact is, you know, there is a certain amount of tosh about this notion of wickedness. It doesnt work. You must look at facts. Not that I would say a word in favor of anything wrong; but then, you see, all sorts of chaps are always doing all sorts of things; and we have to fit them in somehow, dont you know. What I mean is that you cant go cutting everybody; and thats about what it comes to. (*Their rapt attention to his eloquence makes him nervous.*) Perhaps I dont make myself clear.

LADY BRITOMART: You are lucidity itself, Charles. Because Andrew is successful and has plenty of money to give to Sarah, you will flatter him and encourage him in his wickedness.

LOMAX (*unruffled*): Well, where the carcase is, there will the eagles be gathered, dont you know. (*To* UNDERSHAFT.) Eh? What?

UNDERSHAFT: Precisely. By the way, may I call you Charles?

LOMAX: Delighted. Cholly is the usual ticket.

UNDERSHAFT (*to* LADY BRITOMART): Biddy —

LADY BRITOMART (*violently*): Dont dare call me Biddy. Charles Lomax: you are a fool. Adolphus Cusins: you are a Jesuit. Stephen: you are a prig. Barbara: you are a lunatic. Andrew: you are a vulgar tradesman. Now you all know my opinion; and my conscience is clear, at all events. (*She sits down with a vehemence that the rug fortunately softens.*)

UNDERSHAFT: My dear: you are the incarnation of morality. (*She snorts.*) Your conscience is clear and your duty done when you have called everybody names. Come, Euripides! It is getting late; and we all want to go home. Make up your mind.

CUSINS: Understand this, you old demon —

LADY BRITOMART: Adolphus!

UNDERSHAFT: Let him alone, Biddy. Proceed, Euripides.

CUSINS: You have me in a horrible dilemma. I want Barbara.

UNDERSHAFT: Like all young men, you greatly exaggerate the difference between one young woman and another.

BARBARA: Quite true, Dolly.

CUSINS: I also want to avoid being a rascal.

UNDERSHAFT (*with biting contempt*): You lust for personal righteousness, for self-approval, for what you call a good conscience, for what Barbara calls salvation, for what I call patronizing people who are not so lucky as yourself.

CUSINS: I do not: all the poet in me recoils from being a good man. But there are things in me that I must reckon with. Pity —

UNDERSHAFT: Pity! The scavenger of misery.

CUSINS: Well, love.

UNDERSHAFT: I know. You love the needy and the outcast: you love the oppressed races, the negro, the Indian ryot, the underdog everywhere. Do you love the Japanese? Do you love the English?

CUSINS: No. Every true Englishman detests the English. We are the wickedest nation on earth; and our success is a moral horror.

UNDERSHAFT: That is what comes of your gospel of love, is it?

CUSINS: May I not love even my father-in-law?

UNDERSHAFT: Who wants your love, man? By what right do you take the liberty of offering it to me? I will have your due heed and respect, or I will kill you. But your love! Damn your impertinence!

CUSINS (*grinning*): I may not be able to control my affections, Mac.

UNDERSHAFT: You are fencing, Euripides. You are weakening: your grip is slipping. Come! try your last weapon. Pity and love have broken in your hand: forgiveness is still left.

CUSINS: No: forgiveness is a beggar's refuge. I am with you there: we must pay our debts.

UNDERSHAFT: Well said. Come! you will suit me. Remember the words of Plato.

CUSINS (*starting*): Plato! You dare quote Plato to me!

UNDERSHAFT: Plato says, my friend, that society cannot be saved until either the Professors of Greek take to making gunpowder, or else the makers of gunpowder become Professors of Greek.

CUSINS: Oh, tempter, cunning tempter!

UNDERSHAFT: Come! choose, man, choose.

CUSINS: But perhaps Barbara will not marry me if I make the wrong choice.

BARBARA: Perhaps not.

CUSINS (*desperately perplexed*): You hear!

BARBARA: Father: do you love nobody?

UNDERSHAFT: I love my best friend.

LADY BRITOMART: And who is that, pray?

UNDERSHAFT: My bravest enemy. That is the man who keeps me up to the mark.

CUSINS: You know, the creature is really a sort of poet in his way. Suppose he is a great man, after all!

UNDERSHAFT: Suppose you stop talking and make up your mind, my young friend.

CUSINS: But you are driving me against my nature. I hate war.

UNDERSHAFT: Hatred is the coward's revenge for being intimidated. Dare you make war on war? Here are the means: my friend Mr Lomax is sitting on them.

LOMAX (*springing up*): Oh I say! You dont mean that this thing is loaded, do you? My ownest: come off it.

SARAH (*sitting placidly on the shell*): If I am to be blown up, the more thoroughly it is done the better. Dont fuss, Cholly.

LOMAX (*to* UNDERSHAFT, *strongly remonstrant*): Your own daughter, you know!

UNDERSHAFT: So I see. (*To* CUSINS.) Well, my friend, may we expect you here at six tomorrow morning?

CUSINS (*firmly*): Not on any account. I will see the whole establishment blown up with its own dynamite before I will get up at five. My hours are healthy, rational hours: eleven to five.

UNDERSHAFT: Come when you please: before a week you will come at six and stay until I turn you out for the sake of your health. (*Calling.*) Bilton! (*He turns to* LADY BRITOMART, *who rises.*) My dear: let us leave these two young people to themselves for a moment. (BILTON *comes from the shed.*) I am going to take you through the gun cotton shed.

BILTON (*barring the way*): You cant take anything explosive in here, sir.

LADY BRITOMART: What do you mean? Are you alluding to me?

BILTON (*unmoved*): No, maam. Mr Undershaft has the other gentleman's matches in his pocket.

LADY BRITOMART (*abruptly*): Oh! I beg your pardon. (*She goes into the shed.*)

UNDERSHAFT: Quite right, Bilton, quite right: here you are. (*He gives* BILTON *the box of matches.*) Come, Stephen. Come, Charles. Bring Sarah. (*He passes into the shed.*)

(BILTON *opens the box and deliberately drops the matches into the fire-bucket.*)

LOMAX: Oh! I say. (BILTON *stolidly hands him the empty box.*) Infernal nonsense! Pure scientific ignorance! (*He goes in.*)

SARAH: Am I all right, Bilton?

BILTON: Youll have to put on list slippers, miss: thats all. Weve got em inside. (*She goes in.*)

STEPHEN (*very seriously to* CUSINS): Dolly, old fellow, think. Think before you decide. Do you feel that you are a sufficiently practical man? It is a huge undertaking, an enormous responsibility. All this mass of business will be Greek to you.

CUSINS: Oh, I think it will be much less difficult than Greek.

STEPHEN: Well, I just want to say this before I leave you to yourselves. Dont let anything I have said about right and wrong prejudice you against this great chance in life. I have satisfied myself that the business is one of the highest character and a credit to our country. (*Emotionally.*) I am very proud of my father. I — (*Unable to proceed, he presses* CUSINS' *hand and goes hastily into the shed, followed by* BILTON.)

(BARBARA *and* CUSINS, *left alone together, look at one another silently.*)

CUSINS: Barbara: I am going to accept this offer.

BARBARA: I thought you would.

CUSINS: You understand, dont you, that I had to decide without consulting you. If I had thrown the burden of the choice on you, you would sooner or later have despised me for it.

BARBARA: Yes: I did not want you to sell your soul for me any more than for this inheritance.

CUSINS: It is not the sale of my soul that troubles me: I have sold it too often to care about that. I have sold it for a professorship. I have sold it for an income. I have sold it to escape being imprisoned for refusing to pay taxes for hangmen's ropes and unjust wars and things that I abhor. What is all human conduct but the daily and hourly sale of our souls for trifles? What I am now selling it for is neither money nor position nor comfort, but for reality and for power.

BARBARA: You know that you will have no power, and that he has none.

CUSINS: I know. It is not for myself alone. I want to make power for the world.

BARBARA: I want to make power for the world too; but it must be spiritual power.

CUSINS: I think all power is spiritual: these cannons will not go off by themselves. I have tried to make spiritual power by teaching Greek. But the world can never be really touched by a dead language and a dead civilization. The people must have power; and the people cannot have Greek. Now the power that is made here can be wielded by all men.

BARBARA: Power to burn women's houses down and kill their sons and tear their husbands to pieces.

CUSINS: You cannot have power for good without having power for evil too. Even mother's milk nourishes murderers as well as heroes. This power which only tears men's bodies to pieces has never been so horribly abused as the intellectual power, the imaginative power, the poetic, religious power that can enslave men's souls. As a teacher of Greek I gave the intellectual man weapons against the common man. I now want to give the common man weapons against the intellectual man. I love the common people. I want to arm them against the lawyers, the doctors, the priests, the literary men, the professors, the artists, and the politicians, who, once in authority, are more disastrous and tyrannical than all the fools, rascals, and impostors. I want a power simple enough for common men to use, yet strong enough to force the intellectual oligarchy to use its genius for the general good.

BARBARA: Is there no higher power than that (*pointing to the shell*)?

CUSINS: Yes; but that power can destroy the higher powers just as a tiger can destroy a man: therefore Man must master that power first. I admitted this when the Turks and Greeks were last at war. My best pupil went out to fight for Hellas. My parting gift to him was not a copy of Plato's Republic, but a revolver and a hundred Undershaft cartridges. The blood of every Turk he shot — if he shot any — is on my head as well as on Undershaft's. That act committed me to this place for ever. Your father's challenge has beaten me. Dare I make war on war? I must. I will. And now, is it all over between us?

BARBARA (*touched by his evident dread of her answer*): Silly baby Dolly! How could it be!

CUSINS (*overjoyed*): Then you — you — you — Oh for my drum! (*He flourishes imaginary drumsticks.*)

BARBARA (*angered by his levity*): Take care, Dolly, take care. Oh, if only I could get away from you and from father and from it all! if I could have the wings of a dove and fly away to heaven!

CUSINS: And leave *me*!

BARBARA: Yes, you, and all the other naughty mischievous children of men. But I cant. I was happy in the Salvation Army for a moment. I escaped from the world into a paradise of enthusiasm and prayer and soul saving; but the moment our money ran short, it all came back to Bodger: it was he who saved our people: he, and the Prince of Darkness, my papa. Undershaft and Bodger: their hands stretch everywhere: when we feed a starving fellow creature, it is with their bread, because there is no other bread; when we tend the sick, it is in the hospitals they endow; if we turn from the churches they build, we must kneel on the stones of the streets they pave. As long as that lasts, there is no getting away from them. Turning our backs on Bodger and Undershaft is turning our backs on life.

CUSINS: I thought you were determined to turn your back on the wicked side of life.

BARBARA: There is no wicked side: life is all one. And I never wanted to shirk my share in whatever evil must be endured, whether it be sin or suffering. I wish I could cure you of middle-class ideas, Dolly.

CUSINS (*gasping*): Middle cl — ! A snub! A social snub to me! from the daughter of a foundling!

BARBARA: That is why I have no class, Dolly: I come straight out of the heart of the whole people. If I were middle-class I should turn my back on my father's business; and we should both live in an artistic drawing room, with you reading the reviews in one corner, and I in the other at the piano, playing Schumann: both very superior persons, and neither of us a bit of use. Sooner than that, I would sweep out the guncotton shed, or be one of Bodger's barmaids. Do you know what would have happened if you had refused papa's offer?

CUSINS: I wonder!

BARBARA: I should have given you up and married the man who accepted it. After all, my dear old mother has more sense than any of you. I felt like her when I saw this place — felt that I must have it — that never, never, never could I let it go; only she thought it was the houses and the kitchen ranges and the linen and

china, when it was really all the human souls to be saved: not weak souls in
starved bodies, sobbing with gratitude for a scrap of bread and treacle, but
fullfed, quarrelsome, snobbish, uppish creatures, all standing on their little rights
and dignities, and thinking that my father ought to be greatly obliged to them for
making so much money for him — and so he ought. That is where salvation is
really wanted. My father shall never throw it in my teeth again that my converts
were bribed with bread. (*She is transfigured.*) I have got rid of the bribe of bread.
I have got rid of the bribe of heaven. Let God's work be done for its own sake:
the work he had to create us to do because it cannot be done except by living
men and women. When I die, let him be in my debt, not I in his; and let me
forgive him as becomes a woman of my rank.

CUSINS: Then the way of life lies through the factory of death?

BARBARA: Yes, through the raising of hell to heaven and of man to God, through
the unveiling of an eternal light in the Valley of The Shadow. (*Seizing him with
both hands.*) Oh, did you think my courage would never come back? did you
believe that I was a deserter? that I, who have stood in the streets, and taken my
people to my heart, and talked of the holiest and greatest things with them, could
ever turn back and chatter foolishly to fashionable people about nothing in a
drawing room? Never, never, never, never: Major Barbara will die with the colors. Oh! and I have my dear little Dolly boy still; and he has found me my place
and my work. Glory Hallelujah! (*She kisses him.*)

CUSINS: My dearest: consider my delicate health. I cannot stand as much happiness
as you can.

BARBARA: Yes: it is not easy work being in love with me, is it? But it's good for you.
(*She runs to the shed, and calls, childlike.*) Mamma! Mamma! (BILTON *comes out
of the shed, followed by* UNDERSHAFT.) I want Mamma.

UNDERSHAFT: She is taking off her list slippers, dear. (*He passes on to* CUSINS.)
Well? What does she say?

CUSINS: She has gone right up into the skies.

LADY BRITOMART (*coming from the shed and stopping on the steps, obstructing*
SARAH, *who follows with* LOMAX. BARBARA *clutches like a baby at her mother's
skirt*): Barbara: when will you learn to be independent and to act and think for
yourself? I know as well as possible what that cry of 'Mamma, Mamma,' means.
Always running to me!

SARAH (*touching* LADY BRITOMART'S *ribs with her finger tips and imitating a bicycle
horn*): Pip! pip!

LADY BRITOMART (*highly indignant*): How dare you say Pip! pip! to me, Sarah? You
are both very naughty children. What do you want, Barbara?

BARBARA: I want a house in the village to live in with Dolly. (*Dragging at the skirt.*)
Come and tell me which one to take.

UNDERSHAFT (*to* CUSINS): Six o'clock tomorrow morning, Euripides.

THE END

AFTERWORD

We are so used to not taking Shaw quite seriously that we may fail to see
what a disturbing play *Major Barbara* is — how full of dark ironies and un-

resolved paradoxes beneath the surface intellectual farce. A case could be made for calling it a cynical, blasphemous, and amoral play, an expression of materialistic philosophy and totalitarian politics. Truth, says Andrew Undershaft, is more important than Right, Is than Ought, power than principle. Poverty is the worst of all crimes, and charity is its accessory. A good income is better than a good conscience. Morals are relative. Some things are worth killing for. Turning away from evil is turning away from life. All money is tainted, which means that none is. The Lord of War serves the Prince of Peace, and the Prince of Darkness is a bringer of light. Only capitalists can afford to build a socialist state, and only capitalists with guns can keep it safe.

But is the *play* saying all this? Isn't it just Shaw-as-Undershaft up to his old tricks, the court jester of the establishment juggling paradoxes for our amusement? Perhaps, but nothing in the play suggests that Undershaft is either wrong or frivolous. The play's central character is his daughter Barbara, an exuberant Salvation Army officer, for whose soul he and the Army contend. He wins, converting the converter, and it is really *his* play rather than Barbara's. At the end, she and her fiancé Cusins, a professor of Greek with a gift for poetry, join Undershaft in the running of his munitions-making business. This would seem less unsettling if all three weren't such thoughtful, vital, and attractive people, or if the name 'Undershaft' didn't sound like an indispensable piece of machinery. In the loving, death indus-try partnership of millionaire, scholar-poet, and savior of souls there is a hint of a chilling allegory.

Consider the plot resolution. Two issues are pending: whether Barbara and Cusins will marry, and what is to become of the Undershaft inheri-tance. The issues are resolved together. The romantic ending in most com-edies carries an implicit promise of new birth, but if the ending here cele-brates life, it also celebrates death. After Cusins accepts the inheritance and Barbara accepts him, they kiss — with a cannon on one side of them and scattered dummies of mutilated human bodies on the other. They'll make love *and* war. And the only births here are symbolic, second births: Barbara's into her father's "armorer's faith" and Cusins's out of his old identity as Euripides and into his new as Andrew Undershaft VIII.

Making a culture hero of an arms manufacturer strikes us as grim irony — grimmer, perhaps, than Shaw intended. He is supposed to have got the idea for Undershaft from the career of the Swedish inventor and philan-thropist Alfred Nobel. Nobel made an enormous fortune from his commer-cial development of the high-explosive compound nitroglycerine and from his invention of dynamite. He used the bulk of that fortune to establish the Nobel Prizes, including a prize for peace. The moral paradox appealed to Shaw, and the result was Undershaft, the death-dealing capitalist with a socialist's vision of a world without war and poverty. But this was in 1905, nine years before the outbreak of the war that shattered the comfortable conviction among western people that social progress was as inevitable as further technological progress. The idea of war among the so-called civilized nations was, despite an occasional international "episode," unthinkable. And Shaw neither predicts the coming catastrophe nor diagnoses the mentality that caused it. What he does do is debate some of the ideological contradictions in his society — mainly that between its official Christian morality and the principles affirmed and the practices followed in its business and politics.

Even before Shaw's death at 94 in 1950 there was a general feeling that the violent changes in the world after 1914 had left his ideas far behind — wars, revolutions, depressions, new developments in science, philosophy, and art. Shaw, by his own admission and general reputation, was nothing if not a playwright of ideas, and he came to seem increasingly old-fashioned. Today we condescend to him. We respect the sincerity of his reformative zeal but not its premises. We acknowledge the keenness of his intellect but question its depth. We admire his articulateness but suspect its facility. We find his faith in reason naive, his confidence in his own sensible solutions irritating, his brisk utilitarianism crude. We are tired of having our heads cheerfully thumped because we won't learn his perfectly simple lessons in good citizenship. The fireworks of his wit have fizzled; only the talkativeness remains. We admit his dramatic gifts but regret that he channeled them into polemics and wrote plays that are arguments rather than actions and characters who are opinions rather than people. We say he wasn't multi-minded enough, and we think of him as a remarkably busy publicist who had excellent intentions, rather than as a great dramatist. We prefer *My Fair Lady* to *Pygmalion*.

We find him oddly inconsistent. As a radical critic of society he thought of himself as Ibsen's heir, but he completely missed Ibsen's tragic concept of character. Obsessed with wrongs, he had no sense of evil as an inexplicable malignity in the soul. He prided himself on doing away with melodrama's distinction between good and bad characters, but he substituted for it a dramatically less useful distinction between characters who further what he called "the purpose of the universe" and characters who do not. The related, semimystical notions about "the Life Force," the agent of "Creative Evolution" — a process partly metaphysical and partly biological, by which the human race gradually approaches a state of pure intelligence — clog some of the dialogues in his plays of social realism. His long prefaces to his plays suggest a distrust of the dramatic medium. He considered himself a teacher-preacher-reformer but didn't appreciably change his society. He detested art for art's sake, but those of his plays that are still being performed are staged as commercially successful pieces of theater entertainment.

Much in this image distorts the real Shaw or doesn't touch his real achievement as a dramatist. He was more than a clever ventriloquist. His best characters are lively and distinct and capture the imagination. But it is true that they generally define themselves by what they think rather than by what they are. The problem was that Shaw genuinely thought that people are what they think. And he was such a thinking playwright that he sometimes seems to have forgotten that drama doesn't mean by words alone. A telling little example is in the opening of the first scene of Act III of *Major Barbara* (after lunch at Lady Britomart's). The stage direction tells us that Barbara is no longer wearing her uniform. In performance our eyes would instantly take in the significance of this. But Shaw, as if not trusting us to use our eyes — or to imagine using them — spoils much of his effect and our fun by having Lomax call attention to the change in his first speech. But *Major Barbara* can also serve to show up what is not true or fair, or not wholly true and fair, in the current image of Shaw, and show as well what the image misses. For there is nothing stale about its thought, and not all its paradoxes have been safely defused.

Shaw subtitled *Major Barbara* "A Discussion in Three Acts" — an apt enough label but also an instance of the way he himself contributed to the critical stereotype. The play isn't *all* discussion. The opening scene is light comedy of manners. In Charles Lomax it approaches Oscar Wilde's farcical, mock-serious fluff about vacuous well-breds. The play of ideas begins only after the funny business of Undershaft's introduction to his children. Also, Cusins's disclosure of the circumstance of his parents' marriage that by English law qualifies him as a foundling solves the problem of the Undershaft succession by the kind of sudden plot contrivance that used to resolve the deadlocked plots of Victorian melodrama. Shaw, of course, uses the *deus ex machina* device tongue in cheek; his drama is not in well-made-ness. But the point is that he has deliberately grafted two forms of the light popular drama of his time on to his serious discussion play.

The play's dialectical scheme is manifest in the main dramatic movement. The bargain Undershaft and Barbara strike in Act I, each promising to visit the other's place of work, determines setting and action in the two acts that follow: The contest for Barbara's soul is between the Salvation Army shelter and Undershaft's factory town. The three acts make up one whole, but each retains a degree of autonomy as a separate debate. They are related more like movements in a symphony than like episodes in a connected plot; it is the ideological conflict that provides the dramatic momentum. In Act I, Barbara's religious idealism and Undershaft's business realism are aligned against Lady Britomart's philistinism. In Act II, the allies have become rivals. When her father's accepted bribe of money pries Barbara loose from the Salvation Army and when Cusins, who in Act I was little more than her arch adjunct, goes off with Undershaft to the Army meeting, she is left triply deserted: by father, lover, and God. In Act III, Barbara and Cusins do what the Army did in Act II: Reconcile their scruples with the taking of Undershaft's blood money. They do so because Undershaft convinces them that society won't be saved till professors of Greek become makers of gunpowder or makers of gunpowder become professors of Greek. The idea behind this is that of Plato's philosopher-king, the wise man in power.

We see how integral the story of Barbara's soul is to this dialectical play when we think of the three acts as forming a parabola, ends high and curve low, graphing both dramatic movements. Act I shows us the affluence of the upper class under the capitalist system, Act II the slums on the system's underside, and Act III the equitable distribution of wealth under industrial socialism. The movement is from one kind of economic high via a low to another kind of high. Barbara, similarly, is happy in her Salvationist faith in Act I, plummets to disillusion and despair in Act II, and rises to a new kind of religious ecstasy and a new kind of philanthropic dedication in Act III. Her development is like that of some of Shaw's other heroines (Raina in *Arms and the Man*, Cleopatra in *Caesar and Cleopatra*, Eliza Doolittle in *Pygmalion*). They all move from vulnerable idealism through a dark vale of disillusion to new faith, stronger than the old for being founded on facts and reality. Innocence gains experience through pain.

The parallel in structure between the socioeconomic drama of ideas and the drama about Barbara suggests a connection between salvation work and what Lomax calls "the cannon business." Considering that Barbara pretty much ends up being what she was at the beginning, only more so, there doesn't even seem to be very much to choose between the two. Another piece of evidence for this is Undershaft's claim to be in the salvation business himself. He saves his workers' souls, he says, by providing them with good jobs and good housing. Barbara, still keeping body and soul separate and putting soul over body, wonders if a man will "be the better for that."

UNDERSHAFT: You know he will. Dont be a hypocrite, Barbara. . . . It is cheap work converting starving men with a Bible in one hand and a slice of bread in the other. . . . Try your hand on my men: their souls are hungry because their bodies are full.

Thus "The Gospel of St. Andrews," which is the title for one of the sections of Shaw's Preface.

It is harder to accept Undershaft's corollary proposition: Because a man's body must be fed and housed before he can call his soul his own, poverty is the worst of all crimes. An evil, certainly, but a crime? The idea offends because it ignores victimization. Saying that society carries a collective guilt for causing and allowing poverty makes sense; saying that the individual pauper is a criminal *because* he is poor does not. As Lomax might say, there is "a certain amount of tosh" in Undershaft's notion about poverty. Or Shaw is pointing the paradox to rouse an argument.

Undershaft's general point, of course, is that anyone who puts up with a system that tolerates poverty shares responsibility for it. This is his charge against the Salvation Army. Either the Army turns clients like Rummy Mitchens and Snobby Price into hypocrites who confess faked sins to please their helpers, or it affronts the personal dignity of proud people like Peter Shirley and Bill Walker. And by keeping the victims of capitalism from starving and freezing with "the bribe of bread" and feeding their hopes with "the bribe of Heaven," it diverts proletarian energies that might have fueled a revolution. The ethic of humility and endurance and the pious lie that poor people are good and rich people bad only perpetuate poverty. The softer Christian virtues, like pity and love, Undershaft tells Cusins, are parasites on human misery and subterfuges for particularly insidious forms of egoism.

So on the level of polemics money is what the play is about. The action begins with Lady Britomart's summons of Undershaft to make financial settlements for their children. She points up the contrast between Barbara's joyous and useful life in the Salvation Army and the empty and useless life of high society when she blandly notes that Barbara is able to live on "a pound a week" but that Sarah and Charles Lomax will be "poor as church mice" on 1,600 pounds a year. She is as practical and as venal as Mrs. Baines in the Army. That the Army refuses Bill Walker's sovereign (a gold coin worth one pound, 20 shillings) and accepts Undershaft's 5,000 pounds raises no problem about its integrity for Mrs. Baines. She justifies the refusal on the grounds that the Army wants people's souls, not their money, and she justifies the acceptance on the grounds that the shelters must be kept open lest the poor suffer. The generous Barbara isn't angry with her, but she has no answer to Bill Walker's "Wot prawce selvytion nah?" ("What price salvation now?"). What Shaw wants us to see is that Bill doesn't have enough money to buy himself a piece of quiet conscience but that Undershaft has enough to buy the apostasy of one of the Army's own officers. "Money," he says, without a hint of levity or sarcasm, "is the most important thing in the world." Everything in the play shows that he is right. Money wins over Lady Britomart, Stephen, and Sarah at the end, and Cusins stipulates a certain percentage of the profits before he is willing even to consider Undershaft's offer of a partnership in the business.

If money is the main topic of the discussion in *Major Barbara*, religious allusions are Shaw's main device for charging the discussion with irony. Undershaft is rich, but so is his partner Lazarus. But Lazarus is named after the Poor Man in Christ's parable (Luke 16:19–31), who suffered on Earth but in Paradise reclines "in Abraham's bosom," while the Rich Man (Dives), who had his rewards on Earth, suffers in Hell. And in no way can either of them cross the chasm that separates them. Cusins calls Undershaft "Mephistopheles," Satan's agent and Faust's tempter in the old legend about Dr. Faust, who sold his soul for worldly power and pleasure. But though Barbara and Cusins make their compact with Mephistopheles-Undershaft, they do not suffer damnation like the Rich Man in the Bible or like Faust in the legend and in Christopher Marlowe's play. They go to Hell in *this* life — or at least think they do. Before their trip to Perivale St. Andrews, Cusins refers to it as the "Works Department of Hell," and Barbara has had visions of it as "a sort of pit where lost creatures with blackened faces stirred up smoky fires and were driven and tormented by my father." Instead they find a secular paradise, where every material, intellectual, and spiritual need of the workers and their families is taken care of by the management. Barbara lost her faith when she discovered that the Salvation Army's good work in the West Ham shelter was paid for with Bodger's and Undershaft's evil money — with whisky and guns, "drunkenness and murder." She gets herself a new faith when she discovers that some of the same evil money pays for the good life at Perivale St. Andrews. Of the two places, Undershaft's is obviously preferable. More souls are saved there, and saved more honestly, than at the shelter. Barbara does what Mrs Baines did before. She resists a small temptation but falls for a big one, without realizing that there is a question of a "fall" at all.

The associations of religion with the Undershaft enterprise may seem to mute the irony of this. Actually, they make it more sardonic. They bear out Barbara's insight that "Life is all one," that you not only don't have to but that you can't turn your back on "Bodger and Undershaft," even if you are in the salvation business. As her father is "unashamed" of his armorer's trade, so is she of her Salvation Army uniform. "Blood and Fire" are fit emblems for what each is working with. Barbara's "sign of the cross" is the same shape as Undershaft's "sign of the sword." Undershaft, denying that he is a "secularist" like Peter Shirley, calls himself "a confirmed mystic" and adds, ". . . I am a Millionaire. That is my religion." What he means becomes clearer in an exchange near the end of the play.

CUSINS: . . . . You do not drive this place: it drives you. And what drives the place?
UNDERSHAFT (*enigmatically*): A will of which I am a part.
BARBARA (*startled*): Father! Do you know what you are saying; or are you laying a snare for my soul?
CUSINS: Dont listen to his metaphysics, Barbara. . . .

Undershaft isn't really being all that "enigmatic" here. For those who know their Shaw, the "will" he claims to be a part of is the World Will or the Life Force. As the world's armorer, making war on the obscene outrage that poverty is, Undershaft is an agent of the cosmic teleology. Barbara's fear that his words are a "snare" for her soul shows how strong an appeal the mystic side of the Undershaftian creed makes to her religious feelings, but it also makes Undershaft something of a satanic tempter. Cusins's warning that she not listen to her father's "metaphysics" shows that he too is aware of what is at stake.

Cusins, in fact, is the main authority in the play for linking Undershaft and his trade with a religion that rivals Barbara's Christianity. As he marches off in the Salvation Army procession at the end of Act II, he intones, drum booming: "Dionysos Undershaft has descended. I am possessed." That night he does indeed get drunk on the new god's wine. He compares the joy of the marching, singing Salvationists to the sensuous joy of the Dionysian celebrants in ancient Greece. A crucial passage of dialogue follows.

MRS BAINES: . . . Now Jenny: step out with the old flag. Blood and Fire! (*She marches out through the gate with her flag.*)

JENNY: Glory hallelujah! (*flourishing her tambourine and marching*).

UNDERSHAFT (*to* CUSINS, *as he marches out past him easing the slide of his trombone*): "My ducats and my daughter"!

CUSINS (*following him out*): Money and gunpowder!

BARBARA: Drunkenness and Murder! My God: why hast thou forsaken me?

. . .

BILL (*taunting*): Wot prawce selvytion nah?

It looks as if Shaw intends the passage as a gathering of attitudes towards the sale of the Salvation Army; there are six different speakers of as many speeches. First, the untroubled affirmation of faith by the two Salvationists, then the wry mockery of the two pseudo-converts, then the apostate Barbara's despair, and finally Bill Walker's cynical revenge for his humiliation. This is good theater, but it is also a moving human action and a crisp drama of ideas.

Two of the allusions call for comment. Undershaft's "My ducats and my daughter!" is the Jew Shylock's cry in Shakespeare's *Merchant of Venice* when he discovers that his daughter Jessica has run off with one of his Christian enemies and has taken his money with her. Like Shylock, Undershaft has lost both money (the gift check to the Army) and daughter (Barbara rejects both the bribed Army and him, the briber). But since Undershaft's gift was part of his campaign to win Barbara away from the Army and since his strategy is obviously working, his grief here is hardly genuine. It is, however, another irony. Like Shylock, Undershaft is a business man, and he and his Jewish partner have become rich by selling arms to Christians and non-Christians alike.

Forsaken (as she thinks) by both her Father in Heaven and her natural father, Barbara echoes Christ's words on the cross. Her desolation, however, is only a brief prelude to her conversion to the faith of a man who, by Cusins's repeated allusions, represents, from a Christian point of view, the unholy trinity of Dionysos, Mephistopheles, and Machiavelli. Each imputed name fits Undershaft. Like Dionysos he is joyous and brutal, like Mephistopheles he is seductive and demonic, like Machiavelli he is cunning and practical. His religion unites pagan hedonism, temptation of good Christians by black magic, and unscrupulous power politics. That Barbara after her conversion will become mistress of a place named after a saint, Perivale *St. Andrews*, is another irony. "Heavens! What a place!" exclaims her sister Sarah when she sees it (it is the only one of her speeches in the play that matters). "Angered" by the "levity" of mere romance, Barbara wishes she "could have the wings of a dove and fly away to heaven!" She gets her wish. She is "transfigured" as she contemplates the joys of coming soul-saving, and when Cusins accepts the Undershaft inheritance, she shouts "Glory Hallelujah!" like Rummy Mitchens and Jenny Hill before her, and goes, like another saint (and unlike them), "right up into the skies." We cannot miss the ambiguous religious implications of her and Cusins's succession to the Undershaft enterprise and all it stands for, practically and morally.

Before setting off for Perivale St. Andrews, Barbara hopes she will learn there "some truth or other behind all this frightful irony," and so, of course, she does. But we may well feel that the truth she learns is only a part of a larger and yet more frightful irony.

The irony is that the play's most obvious candidate for the villain's part is actually its hero. Undershaft's trade is abominable, his philosophy ruthlessly pragmatic, his religion money and facts, and his politics a socialist dictatorship that is only conditionally benevolent. When the kindly Lomax tries to excuse the nature of his business by suggesting that he develops more and more horrible means of destruction only as deterrents to war, Undershaft brusquely rejects the argument. Presumably, then, when he speaks to Cusins about "making war on war," he does not have in mind anything like a 1905 equivalent of what we call nuclear stalemate. And he doesn't explain how putting an end to war and the threat of war will keep the armorer in business and support his model economy. Undershaft, in short, seems to be the ogre of the liberal imagination: the callous exploiter of human corruption, the manipulative, power-hungry capitalist war-monger and war profiteer, an affront to the whole tradition of classical and Christian humanism.

But Shaw has transvalued ideological melodrama. The villains of his play are Barbara's sentimental charity and Christian evangelism and Cusins's gentle humanistic ethic and refined poetic sensibility, which for some two thousand years have failed to do away with either poverty or war. Undershaft represents a new, pragmatic set of values that will do just that. Barbara's conversion to her father's faith turns a *major* in an *army* into one of the controllers of the war industry. Even Lomax (who functions as a chorus figure at important points of the developing dialectic) gets Undershaft's point: "The fact is, you know, there is a certain amount of tosh about this notion of wickedness. It doesn't work. You must look at facts." With the transvaluation goes a reversal of the usual comedic pattern. Instead of a viable society winning its conflict with a deviant individual, a viable individual here wins his conflict with a deviant society — deviant, that is, by the standards of a socialist Utopia.

It may be that Shaw, writing in the comparatively innocent days before World War I, didn't see all the ambiguities in his fable that we see. His Preface suggests that he wrote his play as an attack on a rich society that allows poverty. But that doesn't mean that the ending, with Barbara and Cusins vindicating Undershaft, is either cynical or frivolous. Francis Fergusson finds it frivolous. *Major Barbara*, he writes, "is a parlor-game, based upon the freedom of the mind to name and then to rationalize anything, without ever deviating from the concept to the thing — the British Empire and Original Sin as light and portable as the blueprints of the social plan-ners and human engineers"* — in short, a piece of Shavian clowning with ideas.

But the old cliché that Shaw was all head and no heart, all bright brittleness and no substance, is not supported by *Major Barbara*. There was a puritan in Shaw who insisted that the only passion that matters is moral passion. His most heroic — and most Shavian — characters make moral commitments not to a cause or to another person but to an idea so large and vital and compelling that it transcends all other commitments. Such characters are Caesar, John Tanner in *Man and Superman*, Saint Joan, the Ancients in *Back to Methuselah* — and Andrew Undershaft. And there was an esthete in Shaw as well, who would not tolerate the confusion and imprecision and biases of ordinary thought and feeling. Sometimes in his plays the puritan and the esthete don't just collaborate but trade functions: The purging of the passions becomes an act of art, the perfection of the forms of the intellect an act of moral virtue. The questions we should ask of *Major Barbara* are not whether Undershaft's reorganizaton of our social economics will work, or whether Shaw thought it would, but what the paradoxes that Undershaft poses can tell us about ourselves and our society. The play *is* disturbing. Its ironies are uncomfortable; they are meant to be. Only when Utopia is realized, will *Major Barbara* have become a historical document from a dark age.

---

* *The Idea of a Theater* (Princeton, N.J.: Princeton University Press, 1949), p. 181.

August Strindberg

THE GHOST SONATA

Translated by Elizabeth Sprigge

FOREWORD

Strindberg was another Scandinavian dramatist who infused a new burst of vitality into the theater, though his influence was less rapidly felt than Ibsen's. Several of his works did not achieve English translation until the 1930s, and even now the complex demands of his longer plays are beyond the resources of all but the largest theaters. Though he began as a realistic playwright, he later wrote what are now considered early examples of the expressionist movement in drama. Expressionism implies the distortion of objective reality to stress the essence of a character, scene, or relationship. Characters are exaggerated or dehumanized, time sequences are jumbled, the conventional script is dismembered. The effect on stage production, in which Strindberg was keenly interested, was comparable — the realistic setting was fragmented and distorted. Sets became harsh and angular. Walls leant inward to suggest oppression or confinement. Actors substituted painted masks for realistic makeup, turning themselves into grotesques, abstractions, cartoon figures. Strindberg was of course limited to the resources primarily developed for the realistic theater of his time, and because of the difficulty of staging some of his works one often feels that he was anticipating a cinema technology still in the future. Indeed, the best place to study theatrical expressionism now is in the surviving works of the early German cinema. The fluidity of film offered a perfect medium for the nightmare world that expressionism conveys.

CHARACTERS

THE OLD MAN, Hummel, a Company Di-
  rector
THE STUDENT, Arkenholtz
THE MILKMAID, an apparition
THE CARETAKER'S WIFE
THE CARETAKER
THE LADY IN BLACK, the daughter of the
  Caretaker's Wife and the Dead Man.
  Also referred to as the Dark Lady
THE COLONEL
THE MUMMY, the Colonel's wife

THE GIRL, the Colonel's daughter, ac-
  tually the daughter of the Old Man
THE ARISTOCRAT, Baron Skanskorg. En-
  gaged to the Lady in Black
JOHANSSON, the Old Man's servant
BENGTSSON, the Colonel's servant
THE FIANCÉE, a white-haired old woman,
  once betrothed to the Old Man
THE COOK
A MAIDSERVANT
BEGGARS

SCENE I

*Outside the house. The corner of the façade of a modern house, showing the
ground floor above, and the street in front. The ground floor terminates on the
right in the Round Room, above which, on the first floor, is a balcony with a
flagstaff. The windows of the Round Room face the street in front of the house,
and at the corner look on to the suggestion of a side-street running toward the
back. At the beginning of the scene the blinds of the Round Room are down.
When, later, they are raised, the white marble statue of a young woman can be
seen, surrounded with palms and brightly lighted by rays of sunshine.*

*To the left of the Round Room is the Hyacinth Room; its window filled with
pots of hyacinths, blue, white and pink. Further left, at the back, is an imposing double front door with laurels in tubs on either side of it. The doors are wide
open, showing a staircase of white marble with a banister of mahogany and
brass. To the left of the front door is another ground-floor window, with a window-mirror.[1] On the balcony rail in the corner above the Round Room are a blue
silk quilt and two white pillows. The windows to the left of this are hung with
white sheets.[2]*

*In the foreground, in front of the house, is a green bench; to the right a street
drinking-fountain, to the left an advertisement column.*

*It is a bright Sunday morning, and as the curtain rises the bells of several
churches, some near, some far away, are ringing.*

On the staircase the LADY IN BLACK *stands motionless.*

The CARETAKER'S WIFE *sweeps the doorstep, then polishes the brass on the
door and waters the laurels.*

In a wheelchair by the advertisement column sits the OLD MAN, *reading a
newspaper. His hair and beard are white and he wears spectacles.*

The Ghost Sonata by Strindberg, translated by Elizabeth Sprigge. Copyright © 1955, 1960,
1962 by Elizabeth Sprigge. Reprinted by permission of Curtis Brown, Ltd.
    [1] Set at an angle inside the window, so as to show what is going on in the street. [Sprigge's
note.]
    [2] Sign of mourning. [Sprigge's note.]

The MILKMAID *comes round the corner on the right, carrying milk bottles in a wire basket. She is wearing a summer dress with brown shoes, black stockings and a white cap. She takes off her cap and hangs it on the fountain, wipes the perspiration from her forehead, washes her hands and arranges her hair, using the water as a mirror.*

A steamship bell is heard, and now and then the silence is broken by the deep notes of an organ in a nearby church.

After a few moments, when all is silent and the MILKMAID *has finished her toilet, the* STUDENT *enters from the left. He has had a sleepless night and is unshaven. He goes straight up to the fountain. There is a pause before he speaks.*

STUDENT: *May I have the cup?*

(The MILKMAID *clutches the cup to her.)*

Haven't you finished yet?

(The MILKMAID *looks at him with horror.)*

OLD MAN *(to himself)*: Who's he talking to? I don't see anybody. Is he crazy? *(He goes on watching them in great astonishment.)*
STUDENT *(to the* MILKMAID*)*: What are you staring at? Do I look so terrible? Well, I've had no sleep, and of course you think I've been making a night of it . . .

(The MILKMAID *stays just as she is.)*

You think I've been drinking, eh? Do I smell of liquor?

(The MILKMAID *does not change.)*

I haven't shaved, I know. Give me a drink of water, girl. I've earned it. *(Pause.)* Oh well, I suppose I'll have to tell you. I spent the whole night dressing wounds and looking after the injured. You see, I was there when that house collapsed last night. Now you know.

(The MILKMAID *rinses the cup and gives him a drink.)*

Thanks.

(The MILKMAID *stands motionless. Slowly.)*

Will you do me a great favor? *(Pause.)* The thing is, my eyes, as you can see, are inflamed, but my hands have been touching wounds and corpses, so it would be dangerous to put them near my eyes. Will you take my handkerchief — it's quite clean — and dip it in the fresh water and bathe my eyes? Will you do this? Will you play the good Samaritan?

(The MILKMAID *hesitates, but does as he bids.)*

Thank you, my dear. *(He takes out his purse. She makes a gesture of refusal.)* Forgive my stupidity, but I'm only half-awake. . . .

(The MILKMAID *disappears.)*

OLD MAN (*to the* STUDENT): Excuse me speaking to you, but I heard you say you were at the scene of the accident last night. I was just reading about it in the paper.

STUDENT: Is it in the paper already?

OLD MAN: The whole thing, including your portrait. But they regret that they have been unable to find out the name of the splendid young student. . . .

STUDENT: Really? (*Glances at the paper*.) Yes, that's me. Well I never!

OLD MAN: Who was it you were talking to just now?

STUDENT: Didn't you see? (*Pause*.)

OLD MAN: Would it be impertinent to inquire — what in fact your name is?

STUDENT: What would be the point? I don't care for publicity. If you get any praise, there's always disapproval too. The art of running people down has been developed to such a pitch. . . . Besides, I don't want any reward.

OLD MAN: You're well off, perhaps.

STUDENT: No, indeed. On the contrary, I'm very poor.

OLD MAN: Do you know, it seems to me I've heard your voice before. When I was young I had a friend who pronounced certain words just as you do. I've never met anyone else with quite that pronunciation. Only him — and you. Are you by any chance related to Mr. Arkenholtz, the merchant?

STUDENT: He was my father.

OLD MAN: Strange are the paths of fate. I saw you when you were an infant, under very painful circumstances.

STUDENT: Yes, I understand I came into the world in the middle of a bankruptcy.

OLD MAN: Just that.

STUDENT: Perhaps I might ask your name.

OLD MAN: I am Mr. Hummel.

STUDENT: Are you the? . . . I remember that . . .

OLD MAN: Have you often heard my name mentioned in your family?

STUDENT: Yes.

OLD MAN: And mentioned perhaps with a certain aversion?

(*The* STUDENT *is silent*.)

Yes, I can imagine it. You were told, I suppose, that I was the man who ruined your father? All who ruin themselves through foolish speculations consider they were ruined by those they couldn't fool. (*Pause*.) Now these are the facts. Your father robbed me of seventeen thousand crowns — the whole of my savings at that time.

STUDENT: It's queer that the same story can be told in two such different ways.

OLD MAN: You surely don't believe I'm telling you what isn't true?

STUDENT: What am I to believe? My father didn't lie.

OLD MAN: That is so true. A father never lies. But I too am a father, and so it follows . . .

STUDENT: What are you driving at?

OLD MAN: I saved your father from disaster, and he repaid me with all the frightful hatred that is born of an obligation to be grateful. He taught his family to speak ill of me.

STUDENT: Perhaps you made him ungrateful by poisoning your help with unnecessary humiliation.

OLD MAN: All help is humiliating, sir.

STUDENT: What do you want from me?

OLD MAN: I'm not asking for the money, but if you will render me a few small services, I shall consider myself well paid. You see that I am a cripple. Some say it is my own fault; others lay the blame on my parents. I prefer to blame life itself, with its pitfalls. For if you escape one snare, you fall headlong into another. In any case, I am unable to climb stairs or ring doorbells, and that is why I am asking you to help me.

STUDENT: What can I do?

OLD MAN: To begin with, push my chair so that I can read those playbills. I want to see what is on tonight.

STUDENT (*pushing the chair*): Haven't you got an attendant?

OLD MAN: Yes, but he has gone on an errand. He'll be back soon. Are you a medical student?

STUDENT: No, I am studying languages, but I don't know at all what I'm going to do.

OLD MAN: Aha! Are you good at mathematics?

STUDENT: Yes, fairly.

OLD MAN: Good. Perhaps you would like a job.

STUDENT: Yes, why not?

OLD MAN: Splendid. (*He studies the playbills.*) They are doing *The Valkyrie* for the matinée. That means the Colonel will be there with his daughter, and as he always sits at the end of the sixth row, I'll put you next to him. Go to that telephone kiosk please and order a ticket for seat eighty-two in the sixth row.

STUDENT: Am I to go to the Opera in the middle of the day?

OLD MAN: Yes. Do as I tell you and things will go well with you. I want to see you happy, rich and honored. Your début last night as the brave rescuer will make you famous by tomorrow and then your name will be worth something.

STUDENT (*going to the telephone kiosk*): What an odd adventure!

OLD MAN: Are you a gambler?

STUDENT: Yes, unfortunately.

OLD MAN: We'll make it fortunately. Go on now, telephone.

(*The* STUDENT *goes. The* OLD MAN *reads his paper. The* LADY IN BLACK *comes out on to the pavement and talks to the* CARETAKER'S WIFE. *The* OLD MAN *listens, but the audience hears nothing. The* STUDENT *returns.*)

Did you fix it up?

STUDENT: It's done.

OLD MAN: You see that house?

STUDENT: Yes, I've been looking at it a lot. I passed it yesterday when the sun was shining on the windowpanes, and I imagined all the beauty and elegance there must be inside. I said to my companion: "Think of living up there in the top flat, with a beautiful young wife, two pretty little children and an income of twenty thousand crowns a year."

OLD MAN: So that's what you said. That's what you said. Well, well! I too am very fond of this house.

STUDENT: Do you speculate in houses?

OLD MAN: Mm — yes. But not in the way you mean.

STUDENT: Do you know the people who live here?

OLD MAN: Every one of them. At my age one knows everybody, and their parents and grandparents too, and one's always related to them in some way or other. I am just eighty, but no one knows me — not really. I take an interest in human destiny.

(The blinds of the Round Room are drawn up. The COLONEL *is seen, wearing mufti. He looks at the thermometer outside one of the windows, then turns back into the room and stands in front of the marble statue.)*

Look, that's the Colonel, whom you will sit next to this afternoon.

STUDENT: Is he — the Colonel? I don't understand any of this, but it's like a fairy story.

OLD MAN: My whole life's like a book a fairy stories, sir. And although the stories are different, they are held together by one thread, and the main theme constantly recurs.

STUDENT: Who is that marble statue of?

OLD MAN: That, naturally, is his wife.

STUDENT: Was she such a wonderful person?

OLD MAN: Er . . . yes.

STUDENT: Tell me.

OLD MAN: We can't judge people, young man. If I were to tell you that she left him, that he beat her, that she returned to him and married him a second time, and that now she is sitting inside there like a mummy, worshipping her own statue — then you would think me crazy.

STUDENT: I don't understand.

OLD MAN: I didn't think you would. Well, then we have the window with the hyacinths. His daughter lives there. She has gone out for a ride, but she will be home soon.

STUDENT: And who is the dark lady talking to the caretaker?

OLD MAN: Well, that's a bit complicated, but it is connected with the dead man, up there where you see the white sheets.

STUDENT: Why, who was he?

OLD MAN: A human being like you or me, but the most conspicuous thing about him was his vanity. If you were a Sunday child, you would see him presently come out of that door to look at the Consulate flag flying at half-mast. He was, you understand, a Consul, and he reveled in coronets and lions and plumed hats and colored ribbons.

STUDENT: Sunday child, you say? I'm told I was born on a Sunday.

OLD MAN: No, were you really? I might have known it. I saw it from the color of your eyes. Then you can see what others can't. Have you noticed that?

STUDENT: I don't know what others do see, but at times. . . . Oh, but one doesn't talk of such things!

OLD MAN: I was almost sure of it. But you can talk to me, because I understand such things.

STUDENT: Yesterday, for instance . . . I was drawn to that obscure little street where later on the house collapsed. I went there and stopped in front of that building which I had never seen before. Then I noticed a crack in the wall. . . . I heard the floor boards snapping. . . . I dashed over and picked up a child that was passing under the wall. . . . The next moment the house collapsed. I was saved, but in my arms, which I thought held the child, was nothing at all.

OLD MAN: Yes, yes, just as I thought. Tell me something. Why were you gesticulat-
ing that way just now by the fountain? And why were you talking to yourself?
STUDENT: Didn't you see the milkmaid I was talking to?
OLD MAN (*in horror*): Milkmaid?
STUDENT: Surely. The girl who handed me the cup.
OLD MAN: Really? So that's what was going on. Ah well, I haven't second sight, but
there are things I can do.

(THE FIANCÉE *is now seen to sit down by the window which has the window-mirror.*)

Look at that old woman in the window. Do you see her? Well, she was my
fiancée once, sixty years ago. I was twenty. Don't be alarmed. She doesn't recognize me. We see one another every day, and it makes no impression on me,
although once we vowed to love one another eternally. Eternally!
STUDENT: How foolish you were in those days! We never talk to our girls like that.
OLD MAN: Forgive us, young man. We didn't know any better. But can you see that
that old woman was once young and beautiful?
STUDENT: It doesn't show. And yet there's some charm in her looks. I can't see her
eyes.

(*The* CARETAKER'S WIFE *comes out with a basket of chopped fir branches.*[3])

OLD MAN: Ah, the caretaker's wife! That dark lady is her daughter by the dead man.
That's why her husband was given the job of caretaker. But the dark lady has a
suitor, who is an aristocrat with great expectations. He is in the process of getting
a divorce — from his present wife, you understand. She's presenting him with a
stone mansion in order to be rid of him. This aristocratic suitor is the son-in-law
of the dead man, and you can see his bedclothes being aired on the balcony
upstairs. It is complicated, I must say.
STUDENT: It's fearfully complicated.
OLD MAN: Yes, that it is, internally and externally, although it looks quite simple.
STUDENT: But then who was the dead man?
OLD MAN: You asked me that just now, and I answered. If you were to look round
the corner, where the tradesmen's entrance is, you would see a lot of poor people
whom he used to help — when it suited him.
STUDENT: He was a kind man then.
OLD MAN: Yes — sometimes.
STUDENT: Not always?
OLD MAN: No-o. That's the way of people. Now, sir, will you push my chair a little,
so that it gets into the sun. I'm horribly cold. When you're never able to move
about, the blood congeals. I'm going to die soon, I know that, but I have a few
things to do first. Take my hand and feel how cold I am.
STUDENT (*taking it*): Yes, inconceivably. (*He shrinks back, trying in vain to free his
hand.*)
OLD MAN: Don't leave me. I am tired now and lonely, but I haven't always been like
this, you know. I have an enormously long life behind me, enormously long. I
have made people unhappy and people have made me unhappy — the one can-

---

[3] It was customary in Sweden to strew the ground with these for a funeral. [Sprigge's note.]

cels out the other — but before I die I want to see you happy. Our fates are entwined through your father — and other things.

STUDENT: Let go of my hand. You are taking all my strength. You are freezing me. What do you want with me?

OLD MAN (*letting go*): Be patient and you shall see and understand. Here comes the young lady.

(*They watch the* GIRL *approaching, though the audience cannot yet see her.*)

STUDENT: The Colonel's daughter?

OLD MAN: His daughter — yes. Look at her. Have you ever seen such a masterpiece?

STUDENT: She is like the marble statue in there.

OLD MAN: That's her mother, you know.

STUDENT: You are right. Never have I seen such a woman of woman born. Happy the man who may lead her to the altar and his home.

OLD MAN: You can see it. Not everyone recognizes her beauty. So, then, it is written.

(*The* GIRL *enters, wearing an English riding habit. Without noticing anyone she walks slowly to the door, where she stops to say a few words to the* CARETAKER'S WIFE. *Then she goes into the house. The* STUDENT *covers his eyes with his hand.*)

OLD MAN: Are you weeping?

STUDENT: In the face of what's hopeless there can be nothing but despair.

OLD MAN: I can open doors and hearts, if only I find an arm to do my will. Serve me and you shall have power.

STUDENT: Is it a bargain? Am I to sell my soul?

OLD MAN: Sell nothing. Listen. All my life I have *taken*. Now I have a craving to give — give. But no one will accept. I am rich, very rich, but I have no heirs, except for a good-for-nothing who torments the life out of me. Become my son. Inherit me while I am still alive. Enjoy life so that I can watch, at least from a distance.

STUDENT: What am I to do?

OLD MAN: First go to *The Valkyrie*.

STUDENT: That's settled. What else?

OLD MAN: This evening you must be in there — in the Round Room.

STUDENT: How am I to get there?

OLD MAN: By way of *The Valkyrie*.

STUDENT: Why have you chosen me as your medium? Did you know me before?

OLD MAN: Yes, of course. I have had my eye on you for a long time. But now look up there at the balcony. The maid is hoisting the flag to half-mast for the Consul. And now she is turning the bedclothes. Do you see that blue quilt? It was made for two to sleep under, but now it covers only one.

(*The* GIRL, *having changed her dress, appears in the window and waters the hyacinths.*)

There is my little girl. Look at her, look! She is talking to the flowers. Is she not like that blue hyacinth herself? She gives them drink — nothing but pure water, and they transform the water into color and fragrance. Now here comes the Colonel with the newspaper. He is showing her the bit about the house that collapsed. Now he's pointing to your portrait. She's not indifferent. She's reading of your brave deed. . . .

I believe it's clouding over. If it turns to rain I shall be in a pretty fix, unless Johansson comes back soon.

(*It grows cloudy and dark. The* FIANCÉE *at the window-mirror closes her window*.)

Now my fiancée is closing the window. Seventy-nine years old. The window-mirror is the only mirror she uses, because in it she sees not herself, but the world outside — in two directions. But the world can see her; she hasn't thought of that. Anyhow she's a handsome old woman.

(*Now the* DEAD MAN, *wrapped in a winding sheet, comes out of the door*.)

STUDENT: Good God, what do I see?

OLD MAN: What do you see?

STUDENT: Don't *you* see? There, in the doorway, the dead man?

OLD MAN: I see nothing, but I expected this. Tell me.

STUDENT: He is coming out into the street. (*Pause*.) Now he is turning his head and looking up at the flag.

OLD MAN: What did I tell you? You may be sure he'll count the wreaths and read the visiting cards. Woe to him who's missing.

STUDENT: Now he's turning the corner.

OLD MAN: He's gone to count the poor at the back door. The poor are in the nature of a decoration, you see. "Followed by the blessings of many." Well, he's not going to have my blessing. Between ourselves he was a great scoundrel.

STUDENT: But charitable.

OLD MAN: A charitable scoundrel, always thinking of his grand funeral. When he knew his end was near, he cheated the State out of fifty thousand crowns. Now his daughter has relations with another woman's husband and is wondering about the Will. Yes, the scoundrel can hear every word we're saying, and he's welcome to it. Ah, here comes Johansson!

(JOHANSSON *enters*.)

Report!

(JOHANSSON *speaks, but the audience does not hear*.)

Not at home, eh? You are an ass. And the telegram? Nothing? Go on. . . . At six this evening? That's good. Special edition, you say? With his name in full. Arken- holtz, a student, born . . . parents . . . That's splendid. . . . I think it's beginning to rain. . . . What did he say about it? So — so. He wouldn't? Well, he must. Here comes the aristocrat. Push me round the corner, Johansson, so I can hear what the poor are saying. And, Arkenholtz, you wait for me here. Understand? (*To* JOHANSSON.) Hurry up now, hurry up.

(JOHANSSON *wheels the chair round the corner. The* STUDENT *remains watching the* GIRL, *who is now loosening the earth round the hyacinths. The* ARISTOCRAT, *wearing mourning, comes in and speaks to the* DARK LADY, *who has been walk- ing to and fro on the pavement*.)

ARISTOCRAT: But what can we do about it? We shall have to wait.

LADY: I can't wait.

ARISTOCRAT: You can't? Well then, go into the country.

LADY: I don't want to do that.

ARISTOCRAT: Come over here or they will hear what we are saying.

(*They move toward the advertisement column and continue their conversation inaudibly.* JOHANSSON *returns.*)

JOHANSSON (*to the* STUDENT): My master asks you not to forget that other thing, sir.

STUDENT (*hesitating*): Look here . . . first of all tell me . . . who is your master?

JOHANSSON: Well, he's so many things, and he has been everything.

STUDENT: Is he a wise man?

JOHANSSON: Depends what that is. He says all his life he's been looking for a Sunday child, but that may not be true.

STUDENT: What does he want? He's grasping, isn't he?

JOHANSSON: It's power he wants. The whole day long he rides round in his chariot like the god Thor himself. He looks at houses, pulls them down, opens up new streets, builds squares. . . . But he breaks into houses too, sneaks through windows, plays havoc with human destinies, kills his enemies — and never forgives. Can you imagine it, sir? This miserable cripple was once a Don Juan — although he always lost his women.

STUDENT: How do you account for that?

JOHANSSON: You see he's so cunning he makes the women leave him when he's tired of them. But what he's most like now is a horse thief in the human market. He steals human beings in all sorts of different ways. He literally stole me out of the hands of the law. Well, as a matter of fact I'd made a slip — hm, yes — and only he knew about it. Instead of getting me put in gaol, he turned me into a slave. I slave — for my food alone, and that's none of the best.

STUDENT: Then what is it he means to do in this house?

JOHANSSON: I'm not going to talk about that. It's too complicated.

STUDENT: I think I'd better get away from it all.

(*The* GIRL *drops a bracelet out the window.*)

JOHANSSON: Look! The young lady has dropped her bracelet out of the window.

(*The* STUDENT *goes slowly over, picks up the bracelet and returns it to the* GIRL, *who thanks him stiffly. The* STUDENT *goes back to* JOHANSSON.)

So you mean to get away. That's not so easy as you think, once he's got you in his net. And he's afraid of nothing between heaven and earth — yes, of one thing he is — of one person rather. . . .

STUDENT: Don't tell me. I think perhaps I know.

JOHANSSON: How can you know?

STUDENT: I'm guessing. Is it a little milkmaid he's afraid of?

JOHANSSON: He turns his head the other way whenever he meets a milk cart. Besides, he talks in his sleep. It seems he was once in Hamburg. . . .

STUDENT: Can one trust this man?

JOHANSSON: You can trust him — to do anything.

STUDENT: What's he doing now round the corner?

JOHANSSON: Listening to the poor. Sowing a little word, loosening one stone at a time, till the house falls down — metaphorically speaking. You see I'm an educated man. I was once a book-seller. . . . Do you still mean to go away?

STUDENT: I don't like to be ungrateful. He saved my father once, and now he only asks a small service in return.

JOHANSSON: What is that?

STUDENT: I am to go to *The Valkyrie*.

JOHANSSON: That's beyond me. But he's always up to new tricks. Look at him now, talking to that policeman. He is always thick with the police. He uses them, gets them involved in his interests, holds them with false promises and expectations, while all the time he's pumping them. You'll see that before the day is over he'll be received in the Round Room.

STUDENT: What does he want there? What connection has he with the Colonel?

JOHANSSON: I think I can guess, but I'm not sure. You'll see for yourself once you're in there.

STUDENT: I shall never be in there.

JOHANSSON: That depends on yourself. Go to *The Valkyrie*.

STUDENT: Is that the way?

JOHANSSON: Yes, if he said so. Look. Look at him in his war chariot, drawn in triumph by the beggars, who get nothing for their pains but the hint of a treat at his funeral.

(*The* OLD MAN *appears standing up in his wheel-chair, drawn by one of the beggars and followed by the rest.*)

OLD MAN: Hail the noble youth who, at the risk of his own life, saved so many others in yesterday's accident. Three cheers for Arkenholtz!

(*The* BEGGARS *bare their heads but do not cheer. The* GIRL *at the window waves her handkerchief. The* COLONEL *gazes from the window of the Round Room. The* OLD WOMAN *rises at her window. The* MAID *on the balcony hoists the flag to the top.*)

Clap your hands, citizens. True, it is Sunday, but the ass in the pit and the ear in the corn field will absolve us. And although I am not a Sunday child, I have the gift of prophecy and also that of healing. Once I brought a drowned person back to life. That was in Hamburg on a Sunday morning just like this. . . .

(*The* MILKMAID *enters, seen only by the* STUDENT *and the* OLD MAN. *She raises her arms like one who is drowning and gazes fixedly at the* OLD MAN. *He sits down, then crumples up, stricken with horror.*)

Johansson! Take me away! Quick!. . . . Arkenholtz, don't forget *The Valkyrie*.

STUDENT: What is all this?

JOHANSSON: We shall see. We shall see.

SCENE II

Inside the Round Room. At the back is a white porcelain stove. On either side of it are a mirror, a pendulum clock and candelabra. On the right of the stove is the entrance to the hall beyond which is a glimpse of a room furnished in green and mahogany. On the left of the stove is the door to a cupboard, papered like the wall. The statue, shaded by palms, has a curtain which can be drawn to conceal it.

A door on the left leads into the Hyacinth Room, where the GIRL *sits reading.*

The back of the COLONEL *can be seen, as he sits in the Green Room, writing.*
BENGTSSON, *the Colonel's servant, comes in from the hall. He is wearing livery, and is followed by* JOHANSSON, *dressed as a waiter.*

BENGTSSON: Now you'll have to serve the tea, Johansson, while I take the coats. Have you ever done it before?

JOHANSSON: It's true I push a war chariot in the daytime, as you know, but in the evenings I go as a waiter to receptions and so forth. It's always been my dream to get into this house. They're queer people here, aren't they?

BENGTSSON: Ye-es. A bit out of the ordinary anyhow.

JOHANSSON: Is it to be a musical party or what?

BENGTSSON: The usual ghost supper, as we call it. They drink tea and don't say a word — or else the Colonel does all the talking. And they crunch their biscuits, all at the same time. It sounds like rats in an attic.

JOHANSSON: Why do you call it the ghost supper?

BENGTSSON: They look like ghosts. And they've kept this up for twenty years, always the same people saying the same things or saying nothing at all for fear of being found out.

JOHANSSON: Isn't there a mistress of the house?

BENGTSSON: Oh yes, but she's crazy. She sits in a cupboard because her eyes can't bear the light. (*He points to the papered door.*) She sits in there.

JOHANSSON: In there?

BENGTSSON: Well, I told you they were a bit out of the ordinary.

JOHANSSON: But then — what does she look like?

BENGTSSON: Like a mummy. Do you want to have a look at her? (*He opens the door.*) There she is.

(*The figure of the* COLONEL'S WIFE *is seen, white and shrivelled into a* MUMMY.)

JOHANSSON: Oh my God!

MUMMY (*babbling*): Why do you open the door? Haven't I told you to keep it closed?

BENGTSSON (*in a wheedling tone*): Ta, ta, ta, ta. Be a good girl now, then you'll get something nice. Pretty Polly.

MUMMY (*parrot-like*): Pretty Polly. Are you there, Jacob? Currrrr!

BENGTSSON: She thinks she's a parrot, and maybe she's right. (*To the* MUMMY.) Whistle for us, Polly.

(*The* MUMMY *whistles.*)

JOHANSSON: Well, I've seen a few things in my day, but this beats everything.

BENGTSSON: You see, when a house gets old, it grows moldy, and when people stay a long time together and torment each other they go mad. The mistress of the house — shut up, Polly! — that mummy there, has been living here for forty years — same husband, same furniture, same relatives, same friends. (*He closes the papered door.*) And the goings-on in this house — well, they're beyond me. Look at that statue — that's her when she was young.

JOHANSSON: Good Lord! Is that the mummy?

BENGTSSON: Yes. It's enough to make you weep. And somehow, carried away by her own imagination or something, she's got to be a bit like a parrot — the way she talks and the way she can't stand cripples or sick people. She can't stand the sight of her own daughter, because she's sick.

JOHANSSON: Is the young lady sick?

BENGTSSON: Didn't you know that?

JOHANSSON: No. And the Colonel, who is he?

BENGTSSON: You'll see.

JOHANSSON (*looking at the statue*): It's horrible to think that . . . How old is she now?

BENGTSSON: Nobody knows. But it's said that when she was thirty-five she looked nineteen, and that's what she made the Colonel believe she was — here in this very house. Do you know what that black Japanese screen by the couch is for? They call it the death-screen, and when someone's going to die, they put it round — same as in a hospital.

JOHANSSON: What a horrible house! And the student was longing to get in, as if it were paradise.

BENGTSSON: What student? Oh, I know. The one who's coming here this evening. The Colonel and the young lady happened to meet him at the Opera, and both of them took a fancy to him. Hm. Now it's my turn to ask questions. Who is your master — the man in the wheelchair?

JOHANSSON: Well, he . . . er . . . Is he coming here too?

BENGTSSON: He hasn't been invited.

JOHANSSON: He'll come uninvited — if need be.

(*The* OLD MAN *appears in the hall on crutches, wearing a frock-coat and top-hat. He steals forward and listens.*)

BENGTSSON: He's a regular old devil, isn't he?

JOHANSSON: Up to the ears.

BENGTSSON: He looks like old Nick himself.

JOHANSSON: And he must be a wizard too, for he goes through locked doors.

(*The* OLD MAN *comes forward and takes hold of* JOHANSSON *by the ear.*)

OLD MAN: Rascal — take care! (*To* BENGTSSON.) Tell the Colonel I am here.

BENGTSSON: But we are expecting guests.

OLD MAN: I know. But my visit is as good as expected, if not exactly looked forward to.

BENGTSSON: I see. What name shall I say? Mr. Hummel?

OLD MAN: Exactly. Yes.

(BENGTSSON *crosses the hall to the Green Room, the door of which he closes behind him.*)

(*To* JOHANSSON.) Get out!

(JOHANSSON *hesitates.*)

Get out!

(JOHANSSON *disappears into the hall. The* OLD MAN *inspects the room and stops in front of the statue in much astonishment.*)

Amelia! It is she — she!

MUMMY (*from the cupboard*): Prrr-etty Polly.

(*The* OLD MAN *starts.*)

OLD MAN: What was that? Is there a parrot in the room? I don't see it.

MUMMY: Are you there, Jacob?

OLD MAN: The house is haunted.

MUMMY: Jacob!

OLD MAN: I'm scared. So these are the kind of secrets they guard in this house. (*With his back turned to the cupboard he stands looking at a portrait.*) There he is — he!

(*The* MUMMY *comes out behind the* OLD MAN *and gives a pull at his wig.*)

MUMMY: Currrrr! Is it . . . ? Currrrr!

OLD MAN (*jumping out of his skin*): God in heaven! Who is it?

MUMMY (*in a natural voice*): Is it Jacob?

OLD MAN: Yes, my name is Jacob.

MUMMY (*with emotion*): And my name is Amelia.

OLD MAN: No, no, no . . . Oh my God!

MUMMY: That's how I look. Yes. (*Pointing to the statue.*) And that's how I *did* look. Life opens one's eyes, does it not? I live mostly in the cupboard to avoid seeing and being seen. . . . But, Jacob, what do you want here?

OLD MAN: My child. Our child.

MUMMY: There she is.

OLD MAN: Where?

MUMMY: There — in the Hyacinth Room.

OLD MAN (*looking at the* GIRL): Yes, that is she. (*Pause.*) And what about her father — the Colonel, I mean — your husband?

MUMMY: Once, when I was angry with him, I told him everything.

OLD MAN: Well . . . ?

MUMMY: He didn't believe me. He just said: "That's what all wives say when they want to murder their husbands." It was a terrible crime none the less. It has falsified his whole life — his family tree too. Sometimes I take a look in the Peerage, and then I say to myself: Here she is, going about with a false birth certificate like some servant girl, and for such things people are sent to the reformatory.

OLD MAN: Many do it. I seem to remember your own date of birth was given incorrectly.

MUMMY: My mother made me do that. I was not to blame. And in our crime, *you* played the biggest part.

OLD MAN: No. Your husband caused that crime, when he took my fiancée from me. I was born one who cannot forgive until he has punished. That was to me an imperative duty — and is so still.

MUMMY: What are you expecting to find in this house? What do you want? How did you get in? Is it to do with my daughter? If you touch her, you shall die.

OLD MAN: I mean well by her.

MUMMY: Then you must spare her father.

OLD MAN: No.

MUMMY: Then you shall die. In this room, behind that screen.

OLD MAN: That may be. But I can't let go once I've got my teeth into a thing.

MUMMY: You want to marry her to that student. Why? He is nothing and has nothing.

OLD MAN: He will be rich, through me.

MUMMY: Have you been invited here tonight?

OLD MAN: No, but I propose to get myself an invitation to this ghost supper.

MUMMY: Do you know who is coming?

OLD MAN: Not exactly.

MUMMY: The Baron. The man who lives up above — whose father-in-law was buried this afternoon.

OLD MAN: The man who is getting a divorce in order to marry the daughter of the Caretaker's wife . . . The man who used to be — your lover.

MUMMY: Another guest will be your former fiancée, who was seduced by my husband.

OLD MAN: A select gathering.

MUMMY: Oh God, if only we might die, might die!

OLD MAN: Then why have you stayed together?

MUMMY: Crime and secrets and guilt bind us together. We have broken our bonds and gone our own ways, times without number, but we are always drawn together again.

OLD MAN: I think the Colonel is coming.

MUMMY: Then I will go in to Adèle. (*Pause.*) Jacob, mind what you do. Spare him. (*Pause. She goes into the Hyacinth Room and disappears.*)

(*The* COLONEL *enters, cold and reserved, with a letter in his hand.*)

COLONEL: Be seated, please.

(*Slowly the* OLD MAN *sits down. Pause. The* COLONEL *stares at him.*)

You wrote this letter, sir?

OLD MAN: I did.

COLONEL: Your name is Hummel?

OLD MAN: It is. (*Pause.*)

COLONEL: As I understand, you have bought in all my unpaid promissory notes. I can only conclude that I am in your hands. What do you want?

OLD MAN: I want payment, in one way or another.

COLONEL: In what way?

OLD MAN: A very simple one. Let us not mention the money. Just bear with me in your house as a guest.

COLONEL: If so little will satisfy you . . .

OLD MAN: Thank you.

COLONEL: What else?

OLD MAN: Dismiss Bengtsson.

COLONEL: Why should I do that? My devoted servant, who has been with me a lifetime, who has the national medal for long and faithful service — why should I do that?

OLD MAN: That's how you see him — full of excellent qualities. He is not the man he appears to be.

COLONEL: Who is?

OLD MAN (*taken aback*): True. But Bengtsson must go.

COLONEL: Are you going to run my house?

OLD MAN: Yes. Since everything here belongs to me — furniture, curtains, dinner service, linen . . . and more too.

COLONEL: How do you mean — more?

OLD MAN: Everything. I own everything here. It is mine.

COLONEL: Very well, it is yours. But my family escutcheon and my good name remain my own.

OLD MAN: No, not even those. (*Pause.*) You are not a nobleman.

COLONEL: How dare you!

OLD MAN (*producing a document*): If you read this extract from *The Armorial Gazette,* you will see that the family whose name you are using has been extinct for a hundred years.

COLONEL: I have heard rumors to this effect, but I inherited the name from my father. (*Reads.*) It is true. You are right. I am not a nobleman. Then I must take off my signet ring. It is true, it belongs to you. (*Gives it to him.*) There you are.

OLD MAN (*pocketing the ring*): Now we will continue. You are not a Colonel either.

COLONEL: I am not . . . ?

OLD MAN: No. You once held the temporary rank of Colonel in the American Volunteer Force, but after the war in Cuba and the reorganization of the Army, all such titles were abolished.

COLONEL: Is this true?

OLD MAN (*indicating his pocket*): Do you want to read it?

COLONEL: No, that's not necessary. Who are you, and what right have you to sit there stripping me in this fashion?

OLD MAN: You will see. But as far as stripping you goes . . . do you know who you are?

COLONEL: How dare you?

OLD MAN: Take off that wig and have a look at yourself in the mirror. But take your teeth out at the same time and shave off your moustache. Let Bengtsson unlace your metal stays and perhaps a certain X.Y.Z., a lackey, will recognize himself. The fellow who was a cupboard lover in a certain kitchen . . .

(*The* COLONEL *reaches for the bell on the table, but* HUMMEL *checks him.*)

Don't touch that bell, and don't call Bengtsson. If you do, I'll have him arrested. (*Pause.*) And now the guests are beginning to arrive. Keep your composure and we will continue to play our old parts for a while.

COLONEL: Who are you? I recognize your voice and eyes.

OLD MAN: Don't try to find out. Keep silent and obey.

(*The* STUDENT *enters and bows to the* COLONEL.)

STUDENT: How do you do, sir.

COLONEL: Welcome to my house, young man. Your splendid behavior at that great disaster has brought your name to everybody's lips, and I count it an honor to receive you in my home.

STUDENT: My humble descent, sir . . . Your illustrious name and noble birth. . . .

COLONEL: May I introduce Mr. Arkenholtz — Mr. Hummel. If you will join the ladies in here, Mr. Arkenholtz — I must conclude my conversation with Mr. Hummel.

(*He shows the* STUDENT *into the Hyacinth Room, where he remains visible, talking shyly to the* GIRL.)

A splendid young man, musical, sings, writes poetry. If he only had blue blood in him, if he were of the same station, I don't think I should object . . .

OLD MAN: To what?

COLONEL: To my daughter . . .

OLD MAN: *Your* daughter! But apropos of that, why does she spend all her time in there?

COLONEL: She insists on being in the Hyacinth Room except when she is out-of-doors. It's a peculiarity of hers. Ah, here comes Miss Beatrice von Holsteinkrona — a charming woman, a pillar of the Church, with just enough money of her own to suit her birth and position.

OLD MAN (*to himself*): My fiancée.

(*The* FIANCÉE *enters, looking a little crazy.*)

COLONEL: Miss Holsteinkrona — Mr. Hummel.

(*The* FIANCÉE *curtseys and takes a seat. The* ARISTOCRAT *enters and seats himself. He wears mourning and looks mysterious.*)

Baron Skanskorg . . .

OLD MAN (*aside, without rising*): That's the jewel-thief, I think. (*To the* COLONEL.) If you bring in the Mummy, the party will be complete.

COLONEL (*at the door of the Hyacinth Room*): Polly!

MUMMY (*entering*): Currrrr . . . !

COLONEL: Are the young people to come in too?

OLD MAN: No, not the young people. They shall be spared.

(*They all sit silent in a circle.*)

COLONEL: Shall we have the tea brought in?

OLD MAN: What's the use? No one wants tea. Why should we pretend about it?

COLONEL: Then shall we talk?

OLD MAN: Talk of the weather, which we know? Inquire about each other's health, which we know just as well? I prefer silence — then one can hear thoughts and see the past. Silence cannot hide anything — but words can. I read the other day that differences of language originated among savages for the purpose of keeping one tribe's secrets hidden from another. Every language therefore is a code, and he who finds the key can understand every language in the world. But this does not prevent secrets from being exposed without a key, specially when there is a question of paternity to be proved. Proof in a Court of Law is another matter. Two false witnesses suffice to prove anything about which they are agreed, but one does not take witnesses along on the kind of explorations I have in mind. Nature herself has instilled in human beings a sense of modesty which tries to hide what should be hidden, but we slip into situations unintentionally, and by chance sometimes the deepest secret is divulged — the mask torn from the impostor, the villain exposed. . . .

(*Pause. All look at each other in silence.*)

What a silence there is now!

(*Long silence.*)

Here, for instance, in this honorable house, in this elegant home, where beauty, wealth and culture are united. . . .

(*Long silence.*)

All of us now sitting here know who we are — do we not? There's no need for me to tell you. And you know me, although you pretend ignorance. (*He indicates the Hyacinth Room.*) In there is my daughter. *Mine* — you know that too. She had lost the desire to live, without knowing why. The fact is she was withering away in this air charged with crime and deceit and falseness of every kind. That is why I looked for a friend for her in whose company she might enjoy the light and warmth of noble deeds.

(*Long silence.*)

That was my mission in this house: to pull up the weeds, to expose the crimes, to settle all accounts, so that those young people might start afresh in this home, which is my gift to them.

(*Long silence.*)

Now I am going to grant safe-conduct, to each of you in his and her proper time and turn. Whoever stays I shall have arrested.

(*Long silence.*)

Do you hear the clock ticking like a death-watch beetle in the wall? Do you hear what it says? "It's time, it's time, it's time." When it strikes, in a few moments, your time will be up. Then you can go, but not before. It's raising its arm against you before it strikes. Listen! It is warning you. "The clock can strike." And I can strike too. (*He strikes the table with one of his crutches.*) Do you hear?

(*Silence. The* MUMMY *goes up to the clock and stops it, then speaks in a normal and serious voice.*)

MUMMY: But I can stop time in its course. I can wipe out the past and undo what is done. But not with bribes, not with threats — only through suffering and repentance. (*She goes up to the* OLD MAN.) We are miserable human beings, that we know. We have erred and we have sinned, we like all the rest. We are not what we seem, because at bottom we are better than ourselves, since we detest our sins. But when you, Jacob Hummel, with your false name, choose to sit in judgment over us, you prove yourself worse than us miserable sinners. For you are not the one you appear to be. You are a thief of human souls. You stole me once with false promises. You murdered the Consul who was buried today; you strangled him with debts. You have stolen the student, binding him by the pretence of a claim on his father, who never owed you a farthing.

(*Having tried to rise and speak, the* OLD MAN *sinks back in his chair and crumples up more and more as she goes on.*)

But there is one dark spot in your life which I am not quite sure about, although I have my suspicions. I think Bengtsson knows. (*She rings the bell on the table.*)
OLD MAN: No, not Bengtsson, not him.
MUMMY: So he does know. (*She rings again.*)

(*The* MILKMAID *appears in the hallway door, unseen by all but the* OLD MAN, *who shrinks back in horror. The* MILKMAID *vanishes as* BENGTSSON *enters.*)

Do you know this man, Bengtsson?

BENGTSSON: Yes, I know him and he knows me. Life, as you are aware, has its ups and downs. I have been in his service; another time he was in mine. For two whole years he was a sponger in my kitchen. As he had to be away by three, the dinner was got ready at two, and the family had to eat the warmed-up leavings of that brute. He drank the soup stock, which the cook then filled up with water. He sat out there like a vampire, sucking the marrow out of the house, so that we became like skeletons. And he nearly got us put in prison when we called the cook a thief. Later I met this man in Hamburg under another name. He was a usurer then, a blood-sucker. But while he was there he was charged with having lured a young girl out on to the ice so as to drown her, because she had seen him commit a crime he was afraid would be discovered. . . .

(*The* MUMMY *passes her hand over the* OLD MAN's *face.*)

MUMMY: *This* is you. Now give up the notes and the Will.

(JOHANSSON *appears in the hallway door and watches the scene with great interest, knowing he is now to be freed from slavery. The* OLD MAN *produces a bundle of papers and throws it on the table. The* MUMMY *goes over and strokes his back.*)

Parrot. Are you there, Jacob?

OLD MAN (*like a parrot*): Jacob is here. Pretty Polly. Currrrr!

MUMMY: May the clock strike?

OLD MAN (*with a clucking sound*): The clock may strike. (*Imitating a cuckoo clock.*) Cuckoo, cuckoo, cuckoo. . . .

(*The* MUMMY *opens the cupboard door.*)

MUMMY: Now the clock has struck. Rise, and enter the cupboard where I have spent twenty years repenting our crime. A rope is hanging there, which you can take as the one with which you strangled the Consul, and with which you meant to strangle your benefactor. . . . Go!

(*The* OLD MAN *goes in to the cupboard. The* MUMMY *closes the door.*)

Bengtsson! Put up the screen — the death-screen.

(BENGTSSON *places the screen in front of the door.*)

It is finished. God have mercy on his soul.

ALL: Amen. (*Long silence.*)

(*The* GIRL *and the* STUDENT *appear in the Hyacinth Room. She has a harp, on which she plays a prelude, and then accompanies the* STUDENT's *recitation.*)

STUDENT: *I saw the sun. To me it seemed*
                      that I beheld the Hidden.
                      Men must reap what they have sown;
                      blest is he whose deeds are good.
                      Deeds which you have wrought in fury,
                      cannot in evil find redress.
                      Comfort him you have distressed
                      with loving-kindness — this will heal.
                      No fear has he who does no ill.
                      Sweet is innocence.

SCENE III

*Inside the Hyacinth Room. The general effect of the room is exotic and oriental.
There are hyacinths everywhere, of every color, some in pots, some with the
bulbs in glass vases and the roots going down into the water.*

*On top of the tiled stove is a large seated Buddha, in whose lap rests a bulb
from which rises the stem of a shallot* (Allium ascalonicum), *bearing its globular
cluster of white, starlike flowers.*

On the right is an open door, leading into the Round Room, where the COLO-
NEL *and the* MUMMY *are seated, inactive and silent. A part of the death-screen
is also visible.*

On the left is a door to the pantry and kitchen.

The STUDENT *and the* GIRL (Adèle) *are beside the table; he standing, she
seated with her harp.*

GIRL: Now sing to my flowers.

STUDENT: Is this the flower of your soul?

GIRL: The one and only. Do you too love the hyacinth?

STUDENT: I love it above all other flowers — its virginal shape rising straight and
slender out of the bulb, resting on the water and sending its pure white roots
down into the colorless fluid. I love its colors: the snow-white, pure as innocence,
the yellow honey-sweet, the youthful pink, the ripe red, but best of all the blue —
the dewy blue, deep-eyed and full of faith. I love them all, more than gold or
pearls. I have loved them ever since I was a child, have worshipped them because
they have all the fine qualities I lack. . . . And yet . . .

GIRL: Go on.

STUDENT: My love is not returned, for these beautiful blossoms hate me.

GIRL: How do you mean?

STUDENT: Their fragrance, strong and pure as the early winds of spring which have
passed over melting snows, confuses my senses, deafens me, blinds me, thrusts
me out of the room, bombards me with poisoned arrows that wound my heart
and set my head on fire. Do you know the legend of that flower?

GIRL: Tell it to me.

STUDENT: First its meaning. The bulb is the earth, resting on the water or buried in
the soil. Then the stalk rises, straight as the axis of the world, and at the top are
the six-pointed star-flowers.

GIRL: Above the earth — the stars. Oh, that is wonderful! Where did you learn this?
How did you find it out?

STUDENT: Let me think . . . In your eyes. And so, you see, it is an image of the
Cosmos. This is why Buddha sits holding the earth-bulb, his eyes brooding as he
watches it grow, outward and upward, transforming itself into a heaven. This
poor earth will become a heaven. It is for this that Buddha waits.

GIRL: I see it now. Is not the snowflake six-pointed too like the hyacinth flower?

STUDENT: You are right. The snowflakes must be falling stars.

GIRL: And the snowdrop is a snow-star, grown out of snow.

STUDENT: But the largest and most beautiful of all the stars in the firmament, the
golden-red Sirius, is the narcissus with its gold and red chalice and its six white
rays.

GIRL: Have you seen the shallot in bloom?

STUDENT: Indeed I have. It bears its blossoms within a ball, a globe like the celestial one, strewn with white stars.

GIRL: Oh how glorious! Whose thought was that?

STUDENT: Yours.

GIRL: Yours.

STUDENT: Ours. We have given birth to it together. We are wedded.

GIRL: Not yet.

STUDENT: What's still to do?

GIRL: Waiting, ordeals, patience.

STUDENT: Very well. Put me to the test. (*Pause.*) Tell me. Why do your parents sit in there so silently, not saying a single word?

GIRL: Because they have nothing to say to each other, and because neither believes what the other says. This is how my father puts it: What's the point of talking, when neither of us can fool the other?

STUDENT: What a horrible thing to hear!

GIRL: Here comes the Cook. Look at her, how big and fat she is.

(*They watch the* COOK, *although the audience cannot yet see her.*)

STUDENT: What does she want?

GIRL: To ask me about the dinner. I have to do the housekeeping as my mother's ill.

STUDENT: What have we to do with the kitchen?

GIRL: We must eat. Look at the Cook. I can't bear the sight of her.

STUDENT: Who is that ogress?

GIRL: She belongs to the Hummel family of vampires. She is eating us.

STUDENT: Why don't you dismiss her?

GIRL: She won't go. We have no control over her. We've got her for our sins. Can't you see that we are pining and wasting away?

STUDENT: Don't you get enough to eat?

GIRL: Yes, we get many dishes, but all the strength has gone. She boils the nourishment out of the meat and gives us the fibre and water, while she drinks the stock herself. And when there's a roast, she first boils out the marrow, eats the gravy and drinks the juices herself. Everything she touches loses its savor. It's as if she sucked with her eyes. We get the grounds when she has drunk the coffee. She drinks the wine and fills the bottles up with water.

STUDENT: Send her packing.

GIRL: We can't.

STUDENT: Why not?

GIRL: We don't know. She won't go. No one has any control over her. She has taken all our strength from us.

STUDENT: May I get rid of her?

GIRL: No. It must be as it is. Here she is. She will ask me what is to be for dinner. I shall tell her. She will make objections and get her own way.

STUDENT: Let her do the ordering herself then.

GIRL: She won't do that.

STUDENT: What an extraordinary house! It is bewitched.

GIRL: Yes. But now she is turning back, because she has seen you.

COOK (*in the doorway*): No, that wasn't the reason. (*She grins, showing all her teeth.*)

STUDENT: Get out!

COOK: When it suits me. (*Pause.*) It does suit me now. (*She disappears.*)

GIRL: Don't lose your temper. Practice patience. She is one of the ordeals we have to go through in this house. You see, we have a housemaid too, whom we have to clean up after.

STUDENT: I am done for. *Cor in æthere.* Music!

GIRL: Wait.

STUDENT: Music!

GIRL: Patience. This room is called the room of ordeals. It looks beautiful, but it is full of defects.

STUDENT: Really? Well, such things must be seen to. It is very beautiful, but a little cold. Why don't you have a fire?

GIRL: Because it smokes.

STUDENT: Can't you have the chimney swept?

GIRL: It doesn't help. You see that writing-desk there?

STUDENT: An unusually fine piece.

GIRL: But it wobbles. Every day I put a piece of cork under that leg, and every day the housemaid takes it away when she sweeps and I have to cut a new piece. The penholder is covered with ink every morning and so is the inkstand. I have to clean them up every morning after that woman, as sure as the sun rises. (*Pause.*) What's the worst job you can think of?

STUDENT: To count the washing. Ugh!

GIRL: That I have to do. Ugh!

STUDENT: What else?

GIRL: To be waked in the middle of the night and have to get up and see to the window, which the housemaid has left banging.

STUDENT: What else?

GIRL: To get up on a ladder and tie the cord on the damper[4] which the housemaid has torn off.

STUDENT: What else?

GIRL: To sweep after her, to dust after her, to light the fire in the stove when all she's done is throw in some wood. To see to the damper, to wipe the glasses, to lay the table over again, to open the bottles, to see that the rooms are aired, to remake my bed, to rinse the water-bottle when it's green with sediment, to buy matches and soap which are always lacking, to wipe the chimneys and trim the wicks to keep the lamps from smoking — and so that they don't go out when we have company, I have to fill them myself. . . .

STUDENT: Music!

GIRL: Wait. The labor comes first. The labor of keeping the dirt of life at a distance.

STUDENT: But you are wealthy and have two servants.

GIRL: It doesn't help. Even if we had three. Living is hard work, and sometimes I grow tired. (*Pause.*) Think then if there were a nursery as well.

STUDENT: The greatest of joys.

GIRL: And the costliest. Is life worth so much hardship?

STUDENT: That must depend on the reward you expect for your labors. I would not shrink from anything to win your hand.

GIRL: Don't say that. You can never have me.

---

[4] Damper to the big stove. [Sprigge's note.]

STUDENT: Why not?

GIRL: You mustn't ask. (*Pause.*)

STUDENT: You dropped your bracelet out of the window. . . .

GIRL: Because my hand has grown so thin. (*Pause.*)

(*The* COOK *appears with a Japanese bottle in her hand.*)

There she is — the one who devours me and all of us.

STUDENT: What has she in her hand?

GIRL: It is the bottle of coloring matter that has letters like scorpions on it. It is the soy which turns water into soup and takes the place of gravy. She makes cabbage soup with it — and mock-turtle soup too.

STUDENT (*to* COOK): Get out!

COOK: You drain us of sap, and we drain you. We take the blood and leave you the water, but colored . . . colored. I am going now, but all the same I shall stay, as long as I please. (*She goes out.*)

STUDENT: Why did Bengtsson get a medal?

GIRL: For his great merits.

STUDENT: Has he no defects?

GIRL: Yes, great ones. But you don't get a medal for them.

(*They smile.*)

STUDENT: You have many secrets in this house.

GIRL: As in all others. Permit us to keep ours.

STUDENT: Don't you approve of candor?

GIRL: Yes — within reason.

STUDENT: Sometimes I'm seized with a raging desire to say all I think. But I know the world would go to pieces if one were completely candid. (*Pause.*) I went to a funeral the other day . . . in church. It was very solemn and beautiful.

GIRL: Was it Mr. Hummel's?

STUDENT: My false benefactor's — yes. At the head of the coffin stood an old friend of the deceased. He carried the mace. I was deeply impressed by the dignified manner and moving words of the clergyman. I cried. We all cried. Afterwards we went to a tavern, and there I learned that the man with the mace had been in love with the dead man's son. . . .

(*The* GIRL *stares at him, trying to understand.*)

And that the dead man had borrowed money from his son's admirer. (*Pause.*) Next day the clergyman was arrested for embezzling the church funds. A pretty story.

GIRL: Oh . . . ! (*Pause.*)

STUDENT: Do you know how I am thinking about you now?

GIRL: Don't tell me, or I shall die.

STUDENT: I must, or I shall die.

GIRL: It is in asylums that people say everything they think.

STUDENT: Exactly. My father finished up in an asylum.

GIRL: Was he ill?

STUDENT: No, he was well, but he was mad. You see, he broke out once — in these circumstances. Like all of us, he was surrounded with a circle of acquaintances; he called them friends for short. They were a lot of rotters, of course, as most people are, but he had to have some society — he couldn't get on all alone. Well, as you know, in everyday life no one tells people what he thinks of them, and he didn't either. He knew perfectly well what frauds they were — he'd sounded the depths of their deceit — but as he was a wise and well-bred man, he was always courteous to them. Then one day he gave a big party. It was in the evening and he was tired by the day's work and by the strain of holding his tongue and at the same time talking rubbish with his guests. . . .

(The GIRL is frightened.)

Well, at the dinner table he rapped for silence, raised his glass, and began to speak. Then something loosed the trigger. He made an enormous speech in which he stripped the whole company naked, one after the other, and told them of all their treachery. Then, tired out, he sat down on the table and told them all to go to hell.

GIRL: Oh!

STUDENT: I was there, and I shall never forget what happened then. Father and Mother came to blows, the guests rushed for the door . . . and my father was taken to a madhouse, where he died. (Pause.) Water that is still too long stagnates, and so it is in this house too. There is something stagnating here. And yet I thought it was paradise itself that first time I saw you coming in here. There I stood that Sunday morning, gazing in. I saw a Colonel who was no Colonel. I had a benefactor who was a thief and had to hang himself. I saw a mummy who was not a mummy and an old maid — what of the maidenhood, by the way? Where is beauty to be found? In nature, and in my own mind, when it is in its Sunday clothes. Where are honor and faith? In fairy-tales and children's fancies. Where is anything that fulfills its promise? In my imagination. Now your flowers have poisoned me and I have given the poison back to you. I asked you to become my wife in a home full of poetry and song and music. Then the Cook came. . . . Sursum Corda! Try once more to strike fire and glory out of the golden harp. Try, I beg you, I implore you on my knees. (Pause.) Then I will do it myself. (He picks up the harp, but the strings give no sound.) It is dumb and deaf. To think that the most beautiful flowers are so poisonous, are the most poisonous. The curse lies over the whole of creation, over life itself. Why will you not be my bride? Because the very life-spring within you is sick . . . now I can feel that vampire in the kitchen beginning to suck me. I believe she is a Lamia, one of those that suck the blood of children. It is always in the kitchen quarters that the seed-leaves of the children are nipped, if it has not already happened in the bedroom. There are poisons that destroy the sight and poisons that open the eyes. I seem to have been born with the latter kind, for I cannot see what is ugly as beautiful, nor call evil good. I cannot. Jesus Christ descended into hell. That was His pilgrimage on earth — to this madhouse, this prison, this charnel-house, this earth. And the madmen killed Him when He wanted to set them free; but the robber they let go. The robber always gets the sympathy. Woe! Woe to us all. Saviour of the world, save us! We perish.

(And now the GIRL has drooped, and it is seen that she is dying. She rings. BENGTSSON enters.)

GIRL: Bring the screen. Quick. I am dying.

(BENGTSSON *comes back with the screen, opens it and arranges it in front of the* GIRL.)

STUDENT: The Liberator is coming. Welcome, pale and gentle one. Sleep, you lovely, innocent, doomed creature, suffering for no fault of your own. Sleep without dreaming, and when you wake again . . . may you be greeted by a sun that does not burn, in a home without dust, by friends without stain, by a love without flaw. You wise and gentle Buddha, sitting there waiting for a Heaven to sprout from the earth, grant us patience in our ordeal and purity of will, so that this hope may not be confounded.

(*The strings of the harp hum softly and a white light fills the room.*)

> I saw the sun. To me it seemed
> that I beheld the Hidden.
> Men must reap what they have sown;
> blest is he whose deeds are good.
> Deeds which you have wrought in fury,
> cannot in evil find redress.
> Comfort him you have distressed
> with loving-kindness — this will heal.
> No fear has he who does no ill.
> Sweet is innocence.

(A *faint moaning is heard behind the screen.*)

You poor little child, child of this world of illusion, guilt, suffering, and death, this world of endless change, disappointment, and pain. May the Lord of Heaven be merciful to you upon your journey.

(*The room disappears. Böcklin's picture* The Island of the Dead *is seen in the distance, and from the island comes music, soft, sweet, and melancholy.*)

AFTERWORD

When Strindberg wrote *The Ghost Sonata* (in 1907) his Intimate Theater in Stockholm had just opened and he was worried about its success, his domestic arrangements were made trying by problems with servants (one reason, perhaps, for the prominent "kitchen imagery" in the play, which obtuse critics used to ridicule), and he suffered from a severe attack of psoriasis (a painful skin disease) of the hands. *The Ghost Sonata*, he wrote to his German translator, had been written "with bleeding hands."

The difficulties one experiences with *The Ghost Sonata* could be due to something we might call the inertia of literary taste. Perhaps the play baffles because it seems so unlike the kind of plays with which we are familiar, plays like *The Wild Duck* and *The Cherry Orchard*, in which people much like ourselves suffer and triumph, are good and evil, sick and sane, noble and ignoble, act or fail to act, in a world much like our own. But if we get past our initial sense of being lost among incoherent and inexplicable events, we may begin to recognize familiar themes. Strindberg, too, looks behind the façade of middle-class life and uncovers its moral iniquities. Like Ibsen's, his characters are guilt-haunted captives of their past. And his picture of life stagnating and rotting in a petty and sordid everyday existence, in which people torture one another with silences and "the labor of keeping the dirt of life at a distance" saps the good and the young, is close to Chekhov's.

Still, the differences between *The Ghost Sonata* and naturalistic plays are obvious. Strindberg's play is not an authentic image of what actual life appears to be. It deals with the irrational, the mystical, in human life; it is scarcely a coincidence that the play is roughly contemporary with the birth of psychoanalysis. Strindberg's stage is more than a setting for the action. It is plastic and fluid, responsive to the playwright's shifting phantasmagoria, an integral part of the play. To move from *The Cherry Orchard* to *The Ghost Sonata* is to leave the familiar living room, drab, perhaps, and stifling, but safely *real*, and to enter a nightmare where ordinary realities appear in new and changing shapes and grotesque combinations, all the more disturbing for being recognizable as their ordinary selves behind the distortions. Clocks and screens and a bottle of soy sauce loom larger than life in Strindberg's ghostly dream. And yet, they are not symbols. They are nothing but themselves, only, somehow, more frighteningly so than in real life; they are solidly there, as things, but imbued with more than thinglike power. And *as* things they will not allow us to think the nightmare unreal. Here horror is a commonplace, normality a dread beyond comprehension and remedy. It is the essence of Strindberg's art that his ultimate "ghost" is a lazy and impudent cook. The ordinary is both ordinary and supernatural, both tiresome and terrifying.

The reader who still feels that the play "doesn't make sense" may take the dream metaphor a step further. If in Ibsen's and Chekhov's plays our position as audience is that of an unobserved observer, a fly on the living room wall, in *The Ghost Sonata* it may be thought of as that of a troubled dreamer. And dreams are not required to make sense. That they do not is often what makes them most compelling.

The Ghost Sonata has come to be regarded as a pioneer specimen of a kind of drama that has been given the name *expressionistic*. The term is not Strindberg's — it is unlikely that he ever heard it applied to his plays — but it is as meaningful as such labels ever are. Expressionists do not try to copy nature, don't care to make a cow look like a cow. They express themselves, turn reality inside out, fragmentize it, bring its meaning (as they see it) to the surface, record the feel of experience in bone and nerve. They claim for their subjectivity as much reality as does the scientist for his objectivity. Suppose you don't like liver or colonial furniture (the expressionist may say). What is for you the truer statement about these things: that liver has a certain color, taste, texture, chemical composition, nutritional value, price per pound? Or that it makes you sick? That American colonial is characterized by certain lines and shapes and finishes, a certain use of maple wood? Or that it is ugly? Isn't the second statement in each case as true as the first? Isn't it as important, since it takes account of your feelings? Isn't it at any rate worth expressing?

The distortions of objective reality in this art — sometimes to the point of the unrecognizability of pure abstractionism — serve to universalize it. The emphasis is on the feeling rather than on the real-life object that occasions the feeling. "Abstractionism," says a modern practitioner, "can touch many springs in the human spirit, whereas reality can touch only one." The same premise underlies expressionism — though it is surrealistic rather than nonrealistic, like abstractionism. In expressing himself or herself the artist expresses everyone's subjectivity, articulates the inarticulate, helps us for the moment exercise our human potential. The artist's work is evocative rather than representational; it intimates experience and does not try to recreate it or account for it or argue about it. "We don't live in reality," says Strindberg, "but in what we take reality to be." Perhaps the theory of expressionism is best summed up in the answer a painter acquaintance of Strindberg's gave to a technology-minded friend's suggestion that in an age of photography paint and brush were old-fashioned and inaccurate tools for recording truth: "As long as the camera can't enter heaven and hell," said Edvard Munch, "people will keep on painting and other people keep on looking at what they paint." In *The Ghost Sonata* Strindberg enters hell.

This hell is a state of mind, a climate of the soul, something experienced rather than understood. The musical term "sonata" in the title suggests a work that calls for a sensory and emotional response to its evocation of evil, not for explanation; and Strindberg's use of fairy-tale archetypes (the Old Man is a male equivalent of the fairy godmother, the Student the poor but good and plucky young man with supernatural helpers, and the Girl the beautiful princess in the enchanted castle) contributes to the quality of timeless fable in the play and reinforces its dark meaning by inverting the happy ending of the romantic folk tale. The play's theme is the universality of evil, the suffering of the innocent, the ambiguity of human motives. By the time he leaves the stage, the Old Man has come to seem like a satanic figure — the Mummy calls him "A thief of human souls" — but we cannot really be sure that he is not also the would-be redeemer of his natural daughter and the benefactor of the young man whose father he once wronged (or did he?) that he seemed to be in the beginning of the play. The anguish of sin and shame that constitutes the human condition in this most mercilessly dark of all Strindberg's plays is expressed in personal relationships seen as a vast and complicated network of mutual guilt and recrimination.* This is the master image of the play, and it explains why

* It may be as well to clarify those relationships here. To do so is not to "get" the play; it is not even a necessary step toward adequate response. But the relationships are so involved and so implausible (as realism) that they are likely to be obstacles to enjoyment if left unclarified. There are two sets of relationships, both adulterous and both involving an illegitimate

some of the structurally most important characters are little more than names. Their function is to be strands in the web of universal sin. Their anonymity furthers that function.

The play's world is a world of deceptions. Scene I begins in hope and promise as a penniless young hero is befriended by a wealthy old man on a bright Sunday morning. But the sun disappears, the kindly benefactor appears as a stricken Thor, the blustering heathen god of wrath and war, and the blessing of being a Sunday child amounts only to seeing ghosts from the Old Man's evil past. The second "movement" of the sonata marks the seeming fulfillment of the Student's hopes. He enters the elegant apartment house and meets his beloved. But the remainder of the scene disillusions hope in a sequence of disclosure and counterdisclosure. The Old Man's exposure of his victims and the purgation of his sinful past are frustrated at their moment of apparent fruition in a dramatization of something close to Christ's "Judge not, that ye be not judged." Acting outside of time, the insane Mummy suddenly turns sane savior, and the wise benefactor hangs himself — the unmasker unmasked. But the company stands revealed: a seduced virgin; a jewel thief turned baron about to enter a mésalliance; a host who is fake father, fake officer, fake nobleman, and whose very appearance is faked by means of wig, false teeth, and iron corset; an adulterous wife; a master who once was servant; and a servant who once was master.

In the third movement, the house of promised happiness has shrunk to a room of desperate but passive suffering, the Hyacinth Room of ordeals, beautiful but fatal, where the mysterious poetry of love decays to complaints about servants and housekeeping, where flowers sicken and the Girl dies. Here rules the same vampire evil that had seemed to die with the Old Man, and the suffering of the beautiful and the innocent is presided over by a statue of Buddha, incarnating that infinite patience with which weary mankind must await the miraculous liberation from the curse of life.

Anticipation, disillusionment, suffering — these are the phases of life. Existence, poisoned at the roots, is paralysis in the contemplation of one's own damnation or slow dystrophy in the endless execution of small and distasteful domestic tasks. The kitchen is in the charge of a giant, undismissible slattern, whose actions contradict her calling: She grows fat on the food she should serve others. There is no restoration of the ruined house,

---

daughter. (1) The Caretaker's Wife is the mother of the Dark Lady by the Dead Man (the Consul). The Dark Lady is engaged to be married to Baron Skanskorg (the Aristocrat) and is apparently pregnant with his child. The Baron is getting a divorce from another daughter (presumably legitimate) of the Dead Man. (2) The Mummy is the wife of the Colonel and the mother of the Girl by the Old Man (Hummel). The Old Man seduced the Mummy in revenge for the Colonel's seduction of the Old Man's Fiancée. The two sets of relationships are linked by still another illicit affair: that between the Mummy and the Baron. The Old Man's relationships with the Student and the Student's father, with Johansson and Bengtsson, and with the Milkmaid, while part of the general mesh of past and hidden crimes, do not concern these love entanglements.

no atonement for the Old Man, the Mummy, or the Colonel. Salvation is hardly more than a pious hope and a prayer set to soft music before a sentimental picture. The action does not include the Christian redemption the ending hints at. The burden of life is too heavy to bear; blessed are those who, like the Girl, find release in death. "Oh God, if only we might die, might die!" cries the Mummy. But the sleep of death is denied these tormented souls. They are ghosts, miserably, hopelessly immortal.

Philosophically, the pervasive gloom of *The Ghost Sonata* may not survive scrutiny. The play is not, as far as reader or spectator can discover, based on any rational, coherent system of thought. It asserts, or, rather, it shows — it does not prove. On the other hand, that Strindberg has not philosophized his vision renders it immune to rational criticism. It does not presume to conform to its tenets and can refuse to be judged on its terms. That may be its strength. Its sense-defying manipulation of fragments of reality weaves a spell for those who once have shared, if only in a dream, the awareness of evil at the very core of human existence. It haunts our imagination long after our daylight minds have assented or refused assent to its ghastly judgment.

John Millington Synge

RIDERS TO THE SEA

FOREWORD

In the ferment of Irish politics that began in the late nineteenth century and erupted in the twentieth into militant demands for independence whose repercussions have not yet ceased, the theater came to the fore as an expression of popular feeling. Both Yeats and Synge were vitally involved in this movement for cultural separatism. W. B. Yeats saw the arts in his country as a growth that had been deformed by the prevailing wind from England, and considered it his patriotic duty to foster native forms of expression. Much of this work, as we know from his letters, was tedious to him, and took time from his own poetic writing. He was uneasy with the practical aspects of theater, and found himself too often forced to waste enthusiasm on well-meaning amateurs who substituted patriotism for talent. Nevertheless, he recognized the power of theater as a public voice, and a great deal emerged from the movement that was genuinely admirable. Some plays were frankly propagandistic, hailing the contemporary revolutionary movements and heaping odium on the English oppressor. Others sought to instill a sense of Irish individuality by turning to native myth and folkways. Synge in particular sought inspiration from his explorations of the remoter Irish countryside, offering a view of the harsh realities of peasant life that his urban audiences sometimes resented. The Abbey

This Foreword on the Irish theater pertains to both *Riders to the Sea* and *Purgatory*, the next play in this volume.

Theater, founded in Dublin in 1904, served as a focus for these ventures, though its internal politics were often as stormy as those of the country it represented and though, with typical Irish paradox, it was susceptible to a good deal of English influence. Yeats, who, like Synge, served on the board of directors, found that one of his greatest obstacles was the prudishness and conservatism of the Abbey audience, who often found the sentiments and language of the more liberated dramatists offensive. His onstage harangues in defense of controversial works became famous, just as the Abbey audience gained notoriety as one of the most unruly in the world. The Abbey, though muted, is still with us, and several plays from its tempestuous beginnings have become part of the world repertory.

CHARACTERS

MAURYA, an old woman   NORA, a younger daughter
BARTLEY, her son   MEN and WOMEN
CATHLEEN, her daughter

Scene: An Island off the West of Ireland.

Cottage kitchen, with nets, oilskins, spinning-wheel, some new boards standing by the wall, etc. CATHLEEN, *a girl of about twenty, finishes kneading cake, and puts it down in the pot-oven by the fire; then wipes her hands, and begins to spin at the wheel.* NORA, *a young girl, puts her head in at the door.*

NORA (*in a low voice*): Where is she?
CATHLEEN: She's lying down, God help her, and maybe sleeping, if she's able.

(NORA *comes in softly, and takes a bundle from under her shawl.*)

CATHLEEN (*spinning the wheel rapidly*): What is it you have?
NORA: The young priest is after bringing[1] them. It's a shirt and a plain stocking were got off a drowned man in Donegal.

(CATHLEEN *stops her wheel with a sudden movement, and leans out to listen.*)

NORA: We're to find out if it's Michael's they are, some time herself[2] will be down looking by the sea.
CATHLEEN: How would they be Michael's, Nora? How would he go the length of that way to the far north?
NORA: The young priest says he's known the like of it. "If it's Michael's they are," says he, "you can tell herself he's got a clean burial by the grace of God, and if they're not his, let no one say a word about them, for she'll be getting her death," says he, "with crying and lamenting."

From *The Complete Works of John M. Synge* (Random House).
  [1] has just brought
  [2] i.e., Maurya, the head of the household

(*The door which* NORA *half closed is blown open by a gust of wind.*)

CATHLEEN (*looking out anxiously*): Did you ask him would he stop Bartley going this day with the horses to the Galway fair?

NORA: "I won't stop him," says he, "but let you not be afraid. Herself does be saying prayers half through the night, and the Almighty God won't leave her destitute," says he, "with no son living."

CATHLEEN: Is the sea bad by the white rocks, Nora?

NORA: Middling bad, God help us. There's a great roaring in the west, and it's worse it'll be getting when the tide's turned to the wind. (*She goes over to the table with the bundle.*) Shall I open it now?

CATHLEEN: Maybe she'd wake up on us, and come in before we'd done. (*Coming to the table.*) It's a long time we'll be, and the two of us crying.

NORA (*goes to the inner door and listens*): She's moving about on the bed. She'll be coming in a minute.

CATHLEEN: Give me the ladder, and I'll put them up in the turf-loft, the way[3] she won't know of them at all, and maybe when the tide turns she'll be going down to see would he be floating from the east.

(*They put the ladder against the gable of the chimney;* CATHLEEN *goes up a few steps and hides the bundle in the turf-loft.* MAURYA *comes from the inner room.*)

MAURYA (*looking up at* CATHLEEN *and speaking querulously*): Isn't it turf enough you have for this day and evening?

CATHLEEN: There's a cake baking at the fire for a short space (*throwing down the turf*), and Bartley will want it when the tide turns if he goes to Connemara.

(NORA *picks up the turf and puts it round the pot-oven.*)

MAURYA (*sitting down on a stool at the fire*): He won't go this day with the wind rising from the south and west. He won't go this day, for the young priest will stop him surely.

NORA: He'll not stop him, mother, and I heard Eamon Simon and Stephen Pheety and Colum Shawn saying he would go.

MAURYA: Where is he itself?

NORA: He went down to see would there be another boat sailing in the week, and I'm thinking it won't be long till he's here now, for the tide's turning at the green head, and the hooker's[4] tacking from the east.

CATHLEEN: I hear some one passing the big stones.

NORA (*looking out*): He's coming now, and he in a hurry.

BARTLEY (*comes in and looks round the room. Speaking sadly and quietly*): Where is the bit of new rope, Cathleen, was bought in Connemara?

CATHLEEN (*coming down*): Give it to him, Nora; it's on a nail by the white boards. I hung it up this morning, for the pig with the black feet was eating it.

NORA (*giving him a rope*): Is that it, Bartley?

MAURYA: You'd do right to leave that rope, Bartley, hanging by the boards. (BARTLEY *takes the rope.*) It will be wanting in this place, I'm telling you, if Mi-

---

[3] so that
[4] a one-masted fishing vessel

chael is washed up to-morrow morning, or the next morning, or any morning in the week, for it's a deep grave we'll make him by the grace of God.

BARTLEY (*beginning to work with the rope*): I've no halter the way I can ride down on the mare, and I must go now quickly. This is the one boat going for two weeks or beyond it, and the fair will be a good fair for horses I heard them saying below.

MAURYA: It's a hard thing they'll be saying below if the body is washed up and there's no man in it[5] to make the coffin, and I after giving a big price for the finest white boards you'd find in Connemara.

(*She looks round at the boards.*)

BARTLEY: How would it be washed up, and we after looking[6] each day for nine days, and a strong wind blowing a while back from the west and south?

MAURYA: If it isn't found itself,[7] that wind is raising the sea, and there was a star up against the moon, and it rising in the night. If it was a hundred horses, or a thousand horses you had itself, what is the price of a thousand horses against a son where there is one son only?

BARTLEY (*working at the halter, to* CATHLEEN): Let you go down each day, and see the sheep aren't jumping in on the rye, and if the jobber comes you can sell the pig with the black feet if there is a good price going.

MAURYA: How would the like of her get a good price for a pig?

BARTLEY (*to* CATHLEEN): If the west wind holds with the last bit of the moon let you and Nora get up weed[8] enough for another cock[9] for the kelp.[10] It's hard set we'll be from this day with no one in it but one man to work.

MAURYA: It's hard set we'll be surely the day you're drownd'd with the rest. What way will I live and the girls with me, and I an old woman looking for the grave?

(BARTLEY *lays down the halter, takes off his old coat, and puts on a newer one of the same flannel.*)

BARTLEY (*to* NORA): Is she coming to the pier?

NORA (*looking out*): She's passing the green head and letting fall her sails.

BARTLEY (*getting his purse and tobacco*): I'll have half an hour to go down, and you'll see me coming again in two days, or in three days, or maybe in four days if the wind is bad.

MAURYA (*turning round to the fire, and putting her shawl over her head*): Isn't it a hard and cruel man won't hear a word from an old woman, and she holding him from the sea?

CATHLEEN: It's the life of a young man to be going on the sea, and who would listen to an old woman with one thing and she saying it over?

BARTLEY (*taking the halter*): I must go now quickly. I'll ride down on the red mare, and the gray pony'll run behind me. . . . . The blessing of God on you.

(*He goes out.*)

---

[5] i.e., the house
[6] when we have been looking
[7] even if it isn't found
[8] seaweed
[9] conical rick
[10] ashes of seaweed, from which iodine is obtained

MAURYA (*crying out as he is in the door*): He's gone now, God spare us, and we'll not see him again. He's gone now, and when the black night is falling I'll have no son left me in the world.

CATHLEEN: Why wouldn't you give him your blessing and he looking round in the door? Isn't it sorrow enough is on every one in this house without your sending him out with an unlucky word behind him, and a hard word in his ear?

(MAURYA *takes up the tongs and begins raking the fire aimlessly without looking round.*)

NORA (*turning towards her*): You're taking away the turf from the cake.

CATHLEEN (*crying out*): The Son of God forgive us, Nora, we're after forgetting his bit of bread.

(*She comes over to the fire.*)

NORA: And it's destroyed[11] he'll be going till dark night, and he after eating nothing since the sun went up.

CATHLEEN (*turning the cake out of the oven*): It's destroyed he'll be, surely. There's no sense left on any person in a house where an old woman will be talking for ever.

(MAURYA *sways herself on her stool.*)

CATHLEEN (*cutting off some of the bread and rolling it in a cloth; to* MAURYA): Let you go down now to the spring well and give him this and he passing. You'll see him then and the dark word will be broken, and you can say "God speed you," the way he'll be easy in his mind.

MAURYA (*taking the bread*): Will I be in it[12] as soon as himself?

CATHLEEN: If you go now quickly.

MAURYA (*standing up unsteadily*): It's hard set I am to walk.

CATHLEEN (*looking at her anxiously*): Give her the stick, Nora, or maybe she'll slip on the big stones.

NORA: What stick?

CATHLEEN: The stick Michael brought from Connemara.

MAURYA (*taking a stick* NORA *gives her*): In the big world the old people do be leaving things after them for their sons and children, but in this place it is the young men do be leaving things behind for them that do be old.

(*She goes out slowly.* NORA *goes over to the ladder.*)

CATHLEEN: Wait, Nora, maybe she'd turn back quickly. She's that sorry, God help her, you wouldn't know the thing she'd do.

NORA: Is she gone round by the bush?

CATHLEEN (*looking out*): She's gone now. Throw it down quickly, for the Lord knows when she'll be out of it again.

NORA (*getting the bundle from the loft*): The young priest said he'd be passing tomorrow, and we might go down and speak to him below if it's Michael's they are surely.

CATHLEEN (*taking the bundle*): Did he say what way they were found?

[11] i.e., with hunger and fatigue
[12] there

NORA (*coming down*): "There were two men," says he, "and they rowing round with poteen[13] before the cocks crowed, and the oar of one of them caught the body, and they passing the black cliffs of the north."

CATHLEEN (*trying to open the bundle*): Give me a knife, Nora, the string's perished with the salt water, and there's a black knot on it you wouldn't loosen in a week.

NORA (*giving her a knife*): I've heard tell it was a long way to Donegal.

CATHLEEN (*cutting the string*): It is surely. There was a man here a while ago — the man sold us that knife — and he said if you set off walking from the rocks beyond, it would be in seven days you'd be in Donegal.

NORA: And what time would a man take, and he floating?

(CATHLEEN *opens the bundle and takes out a bit of a stocking. They look at them eagerly.*)

CATHLEEN (*in a low voice*): The Lord spare us, Nora! isn't it a queer hard thing to say if it's his they are surely?

NORA: I'll get his shirt off the hook the way we can put the one flannel on the other. (*She looks through some clothes hanging in the corner.*) It's not with them, Cathleen, and where will it be?

CATHLEEN: I'm thinking Bartley put it on him in the morning, for his own shirt was heavy with the salt in it. (*Pointing to the corner.*) There's a bit of a sleeve was of the same stuff. Give me that and it will do.

(NORA *brings it to her and they compare the flannel.*)

CATHLEEN: It's the same stuff, Nora; but if it is itself aren't there great rolls of it in the shops of Galway, and isn't it many another man may have a shirt of it as well as Michael himself?

NORA (*who has taken up the stocking and counted the stitches, crying out*): It's Michael, Cathleen, it's Michael; God spare his soul, and what will herself say when she hears this story, and Bartley on the sea?

CATHLEEN (*taking the stocking*): It's a plain stocking.

NORA: It's the second one of the third pair I knitted, and I put up three score stitches, and I dropped four of them.

CATHLEEN (*counts the stitches*): It's that number is in it. (*Crying out.*) Ah, Nora, isn't it a bitter thing to think of him floating that way to the far north, and no one to keen him but the black hags that do be flying on the sea?

NORA (*swinging herself half round, and throwing out her arms on the clothes*): And isn't it a pitiful thing when there is nothing left of a man who was a great rower and fisher, but a bit of an old shirt and a plain stocking?

CATHLEEN (*after an instant*): Tell me is herself coming, Nora? I hear a little sound on the path.

NORA (*looking out*): She is, Cathleen. She's coming up to the door.

CATHLEEN: Put these things away before she'll come in. Maybe it's easier she'll be after giving her blessing to Bartley, and we won't let on we've heard anything the time he's on the sea.

NORA (*helping* CATHLEEN *to close the bundle*): We'll put them here in the corner.

(*They put them into a hole in the chimney corner.* CATHLEEN *goes back to the spinning-wheel.*)

---

[13] moonshine whisky

NORA: Will she see it was crying I was?

CATHLEEN: Keep your back to the door the way the light'll not be on you.

(NORA *sits down at the chimney corner, with her back to the door.* MAURYA *comes in very slowly, without looking at the girls, and goes over to her stool at the other side of the fire. The cloth with the bread is still in her hand. The girls look at each other, and* NORA *points to the bundle of bread.*)

CATHLEEN (*after spinning for a moment*): You didn't give him his bit of bread?

(MAURYA *begins to keen softly, without turning round.*)

CATHLEEN: Did you see him riding down?

(MAURYA *goes on keening.*)

CATHLEEN (*a little impatiently*): God forgive you; isn't it a better thing to raise your voice and tell what you seen, than to be making lamentation for a thing that's done? Did you see Bartley, I'm saying to you.

MAURYA (*with a weak voice*): My heart's broken from this day.

CATHLEEN (*as before*): Did you see Bartley?

MAURYA: I seen the fearfulest thing.

CATHLEEN (*leaves her wheel and looks out*): God forgive you; he's riding the mare now over the green head, and the gray pony behind him.

MAURYA (*starts, so that her shawl falls back from her head and shows her white tossed hair. With a frightened voice*): The gray pony behind him. . . .

CATHLEEN (*coming to the fire*): What is it ails you, at all?

MAURYA (*speaking very slowly*): I've seen the fearfulest thing any person has seen, since the day Bride Dara seen the dead man with the child in his arms.

CATHLEEN and NORA: Uah.

(*They crouch down in front of the old woman at the fire.*)

NORA: Tell us what it is you seen.

MAURYA: I went down to the spring well, and I stood there saying a prayer to myself. Then Bartley came along, and he riding on the red mare with the gray pony behind him. (*She puts up her hands, as if to hide something from her eyes.*) The Son of God spare us, Nora!

CATHLEEN: What is it you seen?

MAURYA: I seen Michael himself.

CATHLEEN (*speaking softly*): You did not, mother. It wasn't Michael you seen, for his body is after being found in the far north, and he's got a clean burial by the grace of God.

MAURYA (*a little defiantly*): I'm after seeing him this day, and he riding and galloping. Bartley came first on the red mare; and I tried to say "God speed you," but something choked the words in my throat. He went by quickly; and "the blessing of God on you," says he, and I could say nothing. I looked up then, and I crying, at the gray pony, and there was Michael upon it — with fine clothes on him, and new shoes on his feet.

CATHLEEN (*begins to keen*): It's destroyed we are from this day. It's destroyed, surely.

NORA: Didn't the young priest say the Almighty God won't leave her destitute with no son living?

MAURYA (*in a low voice, but clearly*): It's little the like of him knows of the sea. . . . Bartley will be lost now, and let you call in Eamon and make me a good coffin out of the white boards, for I won't live after them. I've had a husband, and a husband's father, and six sons in this house — six fine men, though it was a hard birth I had with every one of them and they coming to the world — and some of them were found and some of them were not found, but they're gone now the lot of them. . . . There were Stephen, and Shawn, were lost in the great wind, and found after in the Bay of Gregory of the Golden Mouth, and carried up the two of them on one plank, and in by that door.

(*She pauses for a moment, the girls start as if they heard something through the door that is half open behind them.*)

NORA (*in a whisper*): Did you hear that, Cathleen? Did you hear a noise in the north-east?

CATHLEEN (*in a whisper*): There's some one after crying out by the seashore.

MAURYA (*continues without hearing anything*): There was Sheamus and his father, and his own father again, were lost in a dark night, and not a stick or sign was seen of them when the sun went up. There was Patch after was drowned out of a curragh[14] that turned over. I was sitting here with Bartley, and he a baby, lying on my two knees, and I seen two women, and three women, and four women coming in, and they crossing themselves, and not saying a word. I looked out then, and there were men coming after them, and they holding a thing in the half of a red sail, and water dripping out of it — it was a dry day, Nora — and leaving a track to the door.

(*She pauses again with her hand stretched out towards the door. It opens softly and old women begin to come in, crossing themselves on the threshold, and kneeling down in front of the stage with their backs to the people, and the white waist-bands of the red petticoats they wear over their heads just seen from behind.*)

MAURYA (*half in a dream, to* CATHLEEN): Is it Patch, or Michael, or what is it at all?

CATHLEEN: Michael is after being found in the far north, and when he is found there how could he be here in this place?

MAURYA: There does be a power of young men floating round in the sea, and what way would they know if it was Michael they had, or another man like him, for when a man is nine days in the sea, and the wind blowing, it's hard set his own mother would be to say what man was in it.

CATHLEEN: It's Michael, God spare him, for they're after sending us a bit of his clothes from the far north.

(*She reaches out and hands* MAURYA *the clothes that belonged to Michael.* MAURYA *stands up slowly, and takes them in her hands.* NORA *looks out.*)

NORA: They're carrying a thing among them and there's water dripping out of it and leaving a track by the big stones.

CATHLEEN (*in a whisper to the women who have come in*): Is it Bartley it is?

ONE OF THE WOMEN: It is surely, God rest his soul.

---

[14] a light, open boat

(*Two younger women come in and pull out the table. Then men carry in the body of* BARTLEY, *laid on a plank, with a bit of a sail over it, and lay it on the table.*)

CATHLEEN (*to the women, as they are doing so*): What way was he drowned?

ONE OF THE WOMEN: The gray pony knocked him over into the sea, and he was washed out where there is a great surf on the white rocks.

(MAURYA *has gone over and knelt down at the head of the table. The women are keening softly and swaying themselves with a slow movement.* CATHLEEN *and* NORA *kneel at the other end of the table. The men kneel near the door.*)

MAURYA (*raising her head and speaking as if she did not see the people around her*): They're all gone now, and there isn't anything more the sea can do to me. . . . I'll have no call now to be up crying and praying when the wind breaks from the south, and you can hear the surf is in the east, and the surf is in the west, making a great stir with the two noises, and they hitting one on the other. I'll have no call now to be going down and getting Holy Water in the dark nights after Samhain,[15] and I won't care what way the sea is when the other women will be keening. (*To* NORA.) Give me the Holy Water, Nora, there's a small cup still on the dresser.

(NORA *gives it to her.*)

MAURYA (*drops Michael's clothes across* BARTLEY'*s feet, and sprinkles the Holy Water over him*): It isn't that I haven't prayed for you, Bartley, to the Almighty God. It isn't that I haven't said prayers in the dark night till you wouldn't know what I'd be saying; but it's a great rest I'll have now, and it's time surely. It's a great rest I'll have now, and great sleeping in the long nights after Samhain, if it's only a bit of wet flour we do have to eat, and maybe a fish that would be stinking.

(*She kneels down again, crossing herself, and saying prayers under her breath.*)

CATHLEEN (*to an* OLD MAN): Maybe yourself and Eamon would make a coffin when the sun rises. We have fine white boards herself bought, God help her, thinking Michael would be found, and I have a new cake you can eat while you'll be working.

THE OLD MAN (*looking at the boards*): Are there nails with them?

CATHLEEN: There are not, Colum; we didn't think of the nails.

ANOTHER MAN: It's a great wonder she wouldn't think of the nails, and all the coffins she's seen made already.

CATHLEEN: It's getting old she is, and broken.

(MAURYA *stands up again very slowly and spreads out the pieces of Michael's clothes beside the body, sprinkling them with the last of the Holy Water.*)

NORA (*in a whisper to* CATHLEEN): She's quiet now and easy; but the day Michael was drowned you could hear her crying out from this to the spring well. It's fonder she was of Michael, and would any one have thought that?

CATHLEEN (*slowly and clearly*): An old woman will be soon tired with anything she

[15] All Souls' Day, November 1

will do, and isn't it nine days herself is after crying and keening, and making great sorrow in the house?

MAURYA (*puts the empty cup mouth downwards on the table, and lays her hands together on* BARTLEY's *feet*): They're all together this time, and the end is come. May the Almighty God have mercy on Bartley's soul, and on Michael's soul, and on the souls of Sheamus and Patch, and Stephen and Shawn (*bending her head*); and may He have mercy on my soul, Nora, and on the soul of every one is left living in the world.

(*She pauses, and the keen rises a little more loudly from the women, then sinks away.*)

MAURYA (*continuing*): Michael has a clean burial in the far north, by the grace of the Almighty God. Bartley will have a fine coffin out of the white boards, and a deep grave surely. What more can we want than that? No man at all can be living for ever, and we must be satisfied.

(*She kneels down again and the curtain falls slowly.*)

AFTERWORD

By 1896 Synge had abandoned his plan to become a professional musician and was living in Paris, studying language and literature at the Sorbonne, and trying, without much success, to be a poet. There, in December, he met W. B. Yeats. Yeats, six years older than Synge and already actively promoting a national Irish literature, urged him to give up both his studies and his conventional poetry and to find his own subject matter and voice in the unspoiled folk life of his native country. "Go to the Aran Islands," he told him. "Live there as if you were one of the people themselves; express a life that has never found expression."

Their meeting set Synge on the course that was to take him to his brief literary fulfillment. Beginning in 1898 and for five successive years he spent a total of almost five months on the Arans, three small limestone islands, windswept, seaweed-ringed, and fog-bound, lying at the mouth of Galway Bay on the Irish west coast. The first year, he was there in May and June; his later visits were all in early fall. He spent most of his time on Inishmaan, the middle island, among a few hundred people making their living by fishing, burning kelp, turf-cutting, and growing a few, sparse crops. The daily struggle with sea and soil within the larger seasonal cycle gave a natural rhythm to a life that was harsh and simple but not joyless or without beauty and sturdy dignity. In this small community on a bleak Atlantic island Synge found what had eluded him in the cultural capital of Europe. He discovered a way to reconcile his commitment to social fact with escape from the "pallid words" that were all he heard in the middle-class

living rooms on the Ibsenite stage. The elemental quality of island life became the pastoral mode of his plays.

Synge had little interest in reworking the traditional stock of native Irish
folklore and myth, which Yeats and many others in the national movement considered a main aspect of the Irish literary revival. What fascinated
him were actual people and the poetic resources in peasant speech, not the
romantic patriotism of the nationalist writers. His literary sensibility delighted in the lilting rhythms of the islanders' spoken English and in its
quaint blend of formality and directness — a product, perhaps, of their
bilingualism — but it was offended by what he called "the incoherent
twaddle that is passed off as Irish by the Gaelic League." He regarded the
League's effort to establish the ancient Gaelic tongue as the national language of Ireland as vulgar and sentimental archaism that would either
prove abortive or else serve only to further isolate the Irish from the rest of
Europe. The distinctive language of Synge's own plays is in no strict sense
a dialect. Their Irishness and rural flavor are intense and pervasive, but
they do the errand of no social or political or cultural cause. If some of
them caused controversy — most notably in the case of the riots at the
opening run of *The Playboy of the Western World* in 1907 — it was because
chauvinists and moralists were scandalized by his unsentimental presentation of Irish peasantry and mistook his artistic disinterestedness for callous
condescension to primitives.

Yeats's prediction that the Aran Islands would make a poet of Synge first
came true in the summer of 1902 when Synge wrote *In the Shadow of the
Glen* and *Riders to the Sea*, the first two of his six plays. Both are set in
western Ireland, but only *Riders to the Sea* is based directly on Synge's
island experience. Its language is the Aran idiom carefully cadenced and its
subject matter the stern physical and emotional facts of Aran life. The play
was first performed by the Irish National Theater Society on February 25,
1904, in Molesworth Hall in Dublin. (It was only in December of that year
the company moved into its new permanent home in Abbey Street.) The
audience seems to have received it with indifference.

In *The Aran Islands*, an autobiographical account of his first four visits,
which he published in 1907, Synge notes "the reverence for life and the sea
that is inevitable in this place" — a good description of the sustaining emotion of *Riders to the Sea*. Synge's book shows that his play is an authentic
picture of Aran life in its specifics as well. Landscape and weather and the
bitter island economics, food and dress and implements, the circumstances
of Michael's and Bartley's deaths, even some actual speeches, have their
counterparts in *The Aran Islands*. "Isn't it great danger and sorrow is on
everyone on this island?" an old woman asks Synge when the body of a
young man is recovered after three weeks in the sea. "On these islands,"
writes Synge, "the women live only for their children. . . . The maternal
feeling is so powerful . . . that it gives a life of torment to the women."
When they bewail their dead in the traditional keen, half spontaneous, half

ritual, he thinks he hears "the plaintive intonation of an old race that is worn with sorrow." There is no better gloss on *Riders to the Sea* than the following:

This grief of the keen is no personal complaint . . . but seems to contain the whole passionate rage that lurks somewhere in every native of the island. In this cry of pain the inner consciousness of the people seems to lay itself bare for an instant, and to reveal the mood of beings who feel their isolation in the face of a universe that wars on them with winds and seas.

To the people of Aran, the educated and cosmopolitan Synge can hardly have been more than a likable outsider, but this was not a handicap to his writing about them. His detachment kept his intuitive sympathy with those who lost friends and kin at sea from subverting the objectivity of his perceptions, and he had the philosophical sophistication and the right words to express the timeless, placeless quality of their grief. In *Riders to the Sea*, art has invested the realistic particulars of local conditions with larger significance without burying them in generalization. The setting of the play on "an island off the west of Ireland" rather than on "the Aran Islands" strikes just the right balance between the specific and the archetypal, between the allegorist's universal "anywhere" and the sociologist's documented "there." It is the same kind of artistic tact that spares us the details of what happens to a body that floats in rough seas for nine days. What is acceptable as a bit of gruesome hearsay in the corresponding incident in *The Aran Islands* would in the play have been a ghoulish intrusion into the self-absorbed lyricism of Maurya's lament. The grim fact remains only as a hint of strange but not ugly sea-change in one of Maurya's speeches after she knows the sea has done its worst and can hurt her no more.

To say that *Riders to the Sea* transcends the limitations of its particulars because the particulars have been so intensely realized sounds like a paradox, but it is only an illustration of the old truism that it takes an individual to be a type, a story to be an allegory, and something concrete to be a symbol. The girls' knitting and the black knot that has to be cut are facts of life in Maurya's cottage, immediate and plausible, but they also resonate with the old mythology of female figures of fate who weave and cut the web of men's lives. The black pig eating the white rope and Bartley's wearing Michael's shirt because his own is water-soaked are portents of death. Basic colors suggest a vivid, unchanging world of primal values: white rocks, gray sea, black hags, black pig, black knot, gray pony, red mare, red sail, red petticoats, green head of land — life against death, land against sea. The stinking fish that Maurya and her daughters will be eating now that all their men are dead, the neighbor's grumble over Maurya's failure to get nails for the coffin boards, and Cathleen's attributing her mother's final calm to physical and emotional exhaustion keep the mythic image of man's frailty in a hostile environment and his spiritual nobility in physical defeat embedded in small, sad actuality. The play achieves its transcendent meaning because island life is life stripped to its essentials and because it is rendered through an accumulation of honest detail. Maurya's fate speaks to us of primal fears, hard necessity, suffering, hope, courage, and endurance, and her cottage represents all the shelters that man vainly erects between himself and the destructive forces of nature. All we see on the stage is the human world; the antagonist remains ironically invisible, except when Bartley's dripping corpse brings the sea into the cottage in a symbolic climactic action. In *The Aran Islands*, Synge says after talking with some fishermen, "I could not help feeling that I was talking to men under judgment of death." So, of course, are we all, and it is because in *Riders to the Sea* sudden death is such a continuously imminent actuality that the whole play is a symbol of all human life as a brief, embattled stay on a small island in the midst of an implacable sea. We are all, as one critic puts it, riders to the sea.

That so short a play can achieve such large meaning is all the more astonishing in view of its small range of feeling. Its main event is the death of men at sea, but it is about the surviving women. There are only three male characters, and two of them are part of the choric group at the end and have only one speech each. Bartley's part is larger, but he is less a character with an inner life — almost all he says concerns small, practical matters — than the occasion for Maurya's long years of grief and anxiety to come to a climax and an end. His sole function in the play is to be her last son who goes out and dies. Moreover, the womanly feeling on which the play concentrates is almost exclusively maternal feeling. Maurya is more mother than wife or widow, and her daughters worry more about her feelings than about their own. As a result, she is the main character even before she appears. But small focus gives depth and sharpness of vision. Within its half an hour on stage Synge's play compresses a lifetime of bereavement, a story of a mother's grief finally set free.

The economy of the play is also the result of the way a number of key speeches seem to reach out for the kind of general folk wisdom that is distilled in proverbs: "What is the price of a thousand horses against a son where there is one son only?" "There's no sense left on any person in a house where an old woman will be talking forever." "In the big world the old people do be leaving things after them for their sons and children, but in this place it is the young men do be leaving things behind for them that do be old." "Isn't it a pitiful thing when there is nothing left of a man who was a great rower and fisher, but a bit of an old shirt and a plain stocking?" "There does be a power of young men floating round in the sea." "An old woman will be soon tired with anything she will do." Because the momentum of feeling in such speeches is away from the individual toward the communal, a kind of inertia of psychic dynamics begins to operate in the reader or spectator, pushing the communal feeling in the direction of the universal: "It's the life of a young man to be going on the sea, and who would listen to an old woman with one thing and she saying it over?"

James Joyce said that *Riders to the Sea* was "un-Aristotelian" and meant by that to call attention to a shortcoming.* What exactly he found wanting in the play by the norms of the Aristotelian poetic of tragedy he didn't say, but we can guess. The play deals with a situation rather than with an action, and it can therefore be argued that it has no distinct beginning, middle, and end. Since local conditions of climate and topography determine events and since a particular way of island life determines responses to the events, the real protagonist could be said to be the communal ethos rather than an individual. The proverbial thrust of so many speeches contributes to this impression. In this sense, the play is both a naturalistic and a folk or group play, and Maurya has archetypal dimensions largely because she represents feelings and attitudes common to all island mothers. It is not a play of ideas; there is in it no open or hidden theme of social or metaphysical protest. Events prove the young priest wrong when he reassures Nora that God surely will spare Maurya's last son, but the point of his misplaced faith is not anticlerical satire, atheism, or human indictment of divine severity. Maurya's comment, "It's little the like of him knows of the sea," is only a stoic recognition of the cruel indifference of a power alien to a tidy theological scheme. There is no character whose soul is divided by clashing imperatives. Bartley does not resent the necessity that sends him out to sea when "there's a great roaring in the west, and it's worse it'll be getting when the tide's turned to the wind"; Maurya's states of mind and feeling are successive, not conflicting; and Nora and Cathleen control their grief by busying themselves with practical concerns — the level of their feelings hardly ever changes. Most important, what happens has no moral significance since the human sufferer is necessarily passive under the catastrophe and the destructive agent is an amoral, mindless force built into the physical universe. The world of the play is ruthless but not evil. These are good reasons for challenging not just the usual view that *Riders to the Sea* is one of the greatest one-act tragedies in the language but that it is a tragedy at all.

Labeling literary works is pointless pedantry unless the labels help us better understand what they label. The point in raising the issue of whether or not *Riders to the Sea* is a tragedy is neither to grant it nor to withhold from it the ultimate critical tribute ("tragedy," unfortunately, having become an honorific rather than simply a descriptive term), but to try to account for a common response to the play that is akin to our response to traditional tragedies but one for which there may seem to be no assignable cause in Synge's play.

Joyce cannot have meant that the play is without its moment of Aristotelian peripety. It comes in Maurya's vision of the dead Michael "with fine clothes on him, and new shoes on his feet," riding the gray pony behind

---

* Joyce later admired the play, though this does not necessarily mean that he found it a true tragedy by Aristotelian criteria.

his still living brother on the red mare. Her vision brings about a change in her, which, if it does not constitute an Aristotelian plot, does represent a significant human action; the main character is not static. Before her vision Maurya is a fretful old woman, petulantly and — in terms of the circumstances — unreasonably trying to keep Bartley from doing what he must do. After her vision, she accepts Bartley's death as a certainty, even before it has actually occurred. In commenting in *The Aran Islands* on the actual incident on which he based this detail in his play, Synge writes, "These people make no distinction between the natural and the supernatural." This is clearly Maurya's case, but Synge has transmuted island superstition into a dramatic image that achieves an effect of catharsis, Aristotle's term for the final release of the spectator's feelings of pity and fear at the end of the tragic action. Bartley's body is carried in just as Maurya is telling Cathleen and Nora how the men brought Patch in many years ago, wrapped in "the half of a red sail." The room in which she is lost in memory is the same as it was then, and the distinction between naturalism and the supernatural disappears, as reality and imagination, past and present, become one in the spectacle that stages the past she is narrating. In the crowding scene, Maurya's maternal sorrow is lifted to some timeless dimension of resignation and acceptance, beyond the immediate realism of drowned man and keening women. The scene ritualizes her last loss, and the ritual releases the coiled spring of an anguish that has been gathering through a lifetime of human losses. The dead brothers are together, wearing fine clothes and new shoes. The sea has taken her last son, and she triumphs in her invulnerability after her ultimate bereavement:

. . . there isn't anything more the sea can do to me. . . . I'll have no call now to be up crying and praying when the wind breaks from the south, and you can hear the surf is in the east. . . . It's a great rest I'll have now, and it's time surely. It's a great rest I'll have now, and great sleeping in the long nights after Samhain. . . .

If there is no *moral* victory in Maurya's final serenity and peace, if she is only a woman to whom things have happened, she nevertheless speaks from an awareness for which mere exhaustion is an inadequate as well as an irrelevant explanation. She has gained recognition and she accepts her destiny: "No man at all can be living for ever, and we must be satisfied." There is nothing in her final calm that does not meet the Aristotelian requirements of character (*ethos*) and thought (*dianoia*) proper to tragedy.

W. B. Yeats

PURGATORY

FOREWORD

See the Foreword preceding *Riders to the Sea* (p. 711).

CHARACTERS

A BOY
AN OLD MAN

Scene: A ruined house and a bare tree in the background.

BOY: Half-door, hall door,
   Hither and thither day and night,
   Hill or hollow, shouldering his pack,
   Hearing you talk.
OLD MAN: Study that house.
   I think about its jokes and stories;
   I try to remember what the butler
   Said to a drunken gamekeeper
   In mid-October, but I cannot.

5

If I cannot, none living can.
Where are the jokes and stories of a house,   10
Its threshold gone to patch a pig-sty?
BOY: So you have come this path before?
OLD MAN: The moonlight falls upon the path,
The shadow of a cloud upon the house,
And that's symbolical; study that tree,   15
What is it like?
BOY: A silly old man.
OLD MAN: It's like — no matter what it's like.
I saw it a year ago stripped bare as now,
So I chose a better trade.
I saw it fifty years ago   20
Before the thunderbolt had riven it,
Green leaves, ripe leaves, leaves thick as butter,
Fat, greasy life. Stand there and look,
Because there is somebody in that house.

(*The* BOY *puts down pack and stands in the doorway.*)

BOY: There's nobody here.
OLD MAN: There's somebody there.   25
BOY: The floor is gone, the window's gone,
And where there should be roof there's sky,
And here's a bit of an egg-shell thrown
Out of a jackdaw's nest.
OLD MAN: But there are some
That do not care what's gone, what's left: 30
The souls of Purgatory that come back
To habitations and familiar spots.
BOY: Your wits are out again.
OLD MAN: Re-live
Their transgressions, and that not once
But many times; they know at last   35
The consequence of those transgressions
Whether upon others or upon themselves;
Upon others, others may bring help,
For when the consequence is at an end
The dream must end; if upon themselves,   40
There is no help but in themselves
And in the mercy of God.
BOY: I have had enough!
Talk to the jackdaws, if talk you must.
OLD MAN: Stop! Sit there upon that stone.
That is the house where I was born.   45
BOY: The big old house that was burnt down?
OLD MAN: My mother that was your grand-dam owned it,
This scenery and this countryside,
Kennel and stable, horse and hound —
She had a horse at the Curragh, and there met   50

My father, a groom in the training stable,
Looked at him and married him.
Her mother never spoke to her again,
  And she did right.
BOY: What's right and wrong?
  My grand-dad got the girl and the money.   55
OLD MAN: Looked at him and married him,
  And he squandered everything she had.
  She never knew the worst, because
  She died in giving birth to me,
  But now she knows it all, being dead.   60
  Great people lived and died in this house;
  Magistrates, colonels, members of Parliament,
  Captains and Governors, and long ago
  Men that had fought at Aughrim and the Boyne.
  Some that had gone on government work   65
  To London or to India came home to die,
  Or came from London every spring
  To look at the may-blossom in the park.
  They had loved the trees that he cut down
  To pay what he had lost at cards   70
  Or spent on horses, drink, and women;
  Had loved the house, had loved all
  The intricate passages of the house,
  But he killed the house; to kill a house
  Where great men grew up, married, died,   75
  I here declare a capital offence.
BOY: My God, but you had luck! Grand clothes,
  And maybe a grand horse to ride.
OLD MAN: That he might keep me upon his level
  He never sent me to school, but some   80
  Half-loved me for my half of her:
  A gamekeeper's wife taught me to read,
  A Catholic curate taught me Latin.
  There were old books and books made fine
  By eighteenth-century French binding, books   85
  Modern and ancient, books by the ton.
BOY: What education have you given me?
OLD MAN: I gave the education that befits
  A bastard that a pedlar got
  Upon a tinker's daughter in a ditch.   90
  When I had come to sixteen years old
  My father burned down the house when drunk.
BOY: But that is my age, sixteen years old,
  At the Puck Fair.
OLD MAN: And everything was burnt;
  Books, library, all were burnt.   95
BOY: Is what I have heard upon the road the truth,
  That you killed him in the burning house?

OLD MAN: There's nobody here but our two selves?
BOY: Nobody, Father.
OLD MAN: I stuck him with a knife,
  That knife that cuts my dinner now, 100
  And after that I left him in the fire.
  They dragged him out, somebody saw
  The knife wound but could not be certain
  Because the body was all black and charred.
  Then some that were his drunken friends 105
  Swore they would put me upon trial,
  Spoke of quarrels, a threat I had made.
  The gamekeeper gave me some old clothes,
  I ran away, worked here and there
  Till I became a pedlar on the roads, 110
  No good trade, but good enough
  Because I am my father's son,
  Because of what I did or may do.
  Listen to the hoof-beats! Listen, listen!
BOY: I cannot hear a sound.
OLD MAN: Beat! Beat! 115
  This night is the anniversary
  Of my mother's wedding night,
  Or of the night wherein I was begotten.
  My father is riding from the public-house,
  A whiskey-bottle under his arm. 120

(A *window is lit showing a young girl.*)

  Look at the window; she stands there
  Listening, the servants are all in bed,
  She is alone, he has stayed late
  Bragging and drinking in the public-house.
BOY: There's nothing but an empty gap in the wall. 125
  You have made it up. No, you are mad!
  You are getting madder every day.
OLD MAN: Its louder now because he rides
  Upon a gravelled avenue
  All grass today. The hoof-beat stops, 130
  He has gone to the other side of the house,
  Gone to the stable, put the horse up.
  She has gone down to open the door.
  This night she is no better than her man
  And does not mind that he is half drunk, 135
  She is mad about him. They mount the stairs,
  She brings him into her own chamber.
  And that is the marriage-chamber now.

(*The window is dimly lit again.*)

  Do not let him touch you! It is not true
  That drunken men cannot beget, 140

And if he touch he must beget
And you must bear his murderer.
Deaf! Both deaf! If I should throw
A stick or a stone they would not hear;
And that's a proof my wits are out.   145
But there's a problem: she must live
Through everything in exact detail,
Driven to it by remorse, and yet
Can she renew the sexual act
And find no pleasure in it, and if not,   150
If pleasure and remorse must both be there,
Which is the greater?
      I lack schooling.
Go fetch Tertullian; he and I
Will ravel all that problem out
Whilst those two lie upon the mattress   155
Begetting me.
    Come back! Come back!
And so you thought to slip away,
My bag of money between your fingers,
And that I could not talk and see!
You have been rummaging in the pack.   160

(The light in the window has faded out.)

BOY: You never gave me my right share.
OLD MAN: And had I given it, young as you are,
 You would have spent it upon drink.
BOY: What if I did? I had a right
 To get it and spend it as I chose.   165
OLD MAN: Give me that bag and no more words.
BOY: I will not.
OLD MAN: I will break your fingers.

*(They struggle for the bag. In the struggle it drops, scattering the money. The
OLD MAN staggers but does not fall. They stand looking at each other. The
window is lit up. A man is seen pouring whiskey into a glass.)*

BOY: What if I killed you? You killed my grand-dad,
 Because you were young and he was old.
 Now I am young and you are old.   170
OLD MAN *(staring at window)*: Better-looking, those sixteen years ——
BOY: What are you muttering?
OLD MAN: Younger — and yet
 She should have known he was not her kind.
BOY: What are you saying? Out with it!

(OLD MAN points to window.)

My God! The window is lit up   175
And somebody stands there, although
The floorboards are all burnt away.

OLD MAN: The window is lit up because my father
   Has come to find a glass for his whiskey.
   He leans there like some tired beast.   180
BOY: A dead, living, murdered man!
OLD MAN: "Then the bride-sleep fell upon Adam":
   Where did I read those words?
                    And yet
   There's nothing leaning in the window
   But the impression upon my mother's mind;   185
   Being dead she is alone in her remorse.
BOY: A body that was a bundle of old bones
   Before I was born, Horrible! Horrible!

(He covers his eyes.)

OLD MAN: That beast there would know nothing, being nothing,
   If I should kill a man under the window
   He would not even turn his head.   190

(He stabs the BOY.)

My father and my son on the same jack-knife!
That finishes — there — there — there —

(He stabs again and again. The window grows dark.)

"Hush-a-bye baby, thy father's a knight,
Thy mother a lady, lovely and bright."   195
No, that is something that I read in a book,
And if I sing it must be to my mother,
And I lack rhyme.

(The stage has grown dark except where the tree stands in white light.)

               Study that tree.
It stands there like a purified soul,
All cold, sweet, glistening light.   200
Dear mother, the window is dark again,
But you are in the light because
I finished all that consequence.
I killed that lad because had he grown up
He would have struck a woman's fancy,   205
Begot, and passed pollution on.

I am a wretched foul old man
And therefore harmless. When I have stuck
This old jack-knife into a sod
And pulled it out all bright again,   210
And picked up all the money that he dropped,
I'll to a distant place, and there
Tell my old jokes among new men.

(He cleans the knife and begins to pick up money.)

Hoof-beats! Dear God,
How quickly it returns — beat — beat — !   215

Her mind cannot hold up that dream.
Twice a murderer and all for nothing,
And she must animate that dead night
Not once but many times!
                    O God,
Release my mother's soul from its dream!   220
Mankind can do no more. Appease
The misery of the living and the remorse of the dead.

AFTERWORD

In the general introduction, we suggested that there is an obvious contrast between the public voice of the playwright and the quieter, more private voice of the novelist or lyric poet. In the work of Yeats, this disparity becomes particularly obvious. As we have already noted, he was primarily a poet and uneasy with the practical aspects of the commercial theater — some of his suggestions for solving practical production problems were bizarre in the extreme. But he was well aware of this and, as well as writing more conventionally constructed plays, tried to find alternative forms of theater in which the lyric voice could speak simply and clearly, without unnecessary encumbrance. In doing so, he was showing himself responsive to the theater movements of his time. Around the beginning of the twentieth century, writers and directors in many countries were beginning to profess dissatisfaction with contemporary stage "realism" and to experiment with other forms of expression that substituted suggestion and symbol for the literal depiction of actuality. This led them to look with new eyes at the dramatic forms of other, earlier cultures and at the devices that the realistic theater had long discarded: the mask, formal verse, the evocative power of dance, and the stylized gestures that belonged to a more ritualistic concept of acting.

For all his love of Ireland, Yeats himself could not escape being influenced by other cultures. He was seized by the simplicity of Greek tragedy, and its ability to make enormously powerful statements with the minimum of technical means. One of his own most powerful writings is a translation of *Oedipus the King*, employing an austere style that matches the simplicity of Sophocles' own and is still effective in the theater. An even stronger influence was the religious dance-drama of Japan, which, after centuries of that country's self-imposed isolation, was finally becoming known to western audiences and readers. In medieval times, Japan had developed a form of sacred theater called the Nō play, designed originally to expound Buddhist philosophy. This kind of theater was in many respects similar to the Greek. It used a chanting chorus, which could speak sometimes for, and sometimes about, the principal characters; a minimum of physical action, reduced to a rhythmic pattern of symbolic gestures, and moving, at the climactic moment, into dance; rarely more than two principal characters, with the dominant actor wearing a mask; and, except for certain traditional decorative elements, a virtually bare stage, which, as in the Greek theater, left the setting to be created in the audience's imagination. Yeats found this combination of rich language and technical simplicity appealing. Assisted by friends who had personal contact with this newly discovered medium, he constructed a series of plays adapting Japanese forms to his native Irish themes, one of the most extraordinary, and most productive, examples of cross-fertilization in the whole history of drama. Yeats revitalized the age-old devices of mask and chorus, and reduced the setting to a few symbolic elements. But the style seemed so strange that even the actors, some of them drawn from the Abbey, did not always understand what Yeats was asking them to do, and the plays were never popular. However, they were not meant to be: the plays were designed to be played not in the commercial theater but in private houses, for a select and initiated audience.

By 1938 these early experiments had been fully assimilated into Yeats's artistic consciousness. In *Purgatory* we have a play that is a model of structural simplicity and thematic profundity. Though short — its playing time is a mere twenty minutes — it has the power of Greek tragedy to suggest vast actions, superplots, of which the momentary, visible drama is but a tiny part. Some of *Purgatory*'s associations are clearly local. On the most immediate level, it is a vision of the decay of Ireland that Yeats knew and mourned. His audience was all too familiar with the gaunt skeletons of great houses, relics of a more serene and gracious age, which dotted the Irish landscape, and with the families that, like their mansions, had fallen from dignity to squalor. In the play, Yeats clearly uses the ruined mansion as a symbol of Ireland itself, once given a gaiety and a hectic stimulus as a second home for the governing classes, now succumbing to slovenliness and inertia. So too with the history of the owning family, losing its pride, making disastrous matches, dissipating its resources, and, finally, destroying its own proud heritage.

But the play has a broader significance. In its technical resources it is demonstrably influenced by the Japanese. For all practical purposes, this is a two-actor play; it does not matter whether we see the shadows at the window, as long as we are clear that the old man and his son see them, and, as in Nō drama, the principal characters divide the functions of expounder and inquirer. The old tree, which looms so large in the setting and in the old man's memories, is reminiscent of the gnarled pine tree that, painted in stylized form on the back wall, is the characteristic decorative feature of the Nō stage. And, with the Japanese theater as well as with the Greek, *Purgatory* shares the ability to construct a world in which the normal laws of time and space are suspended; to disassociate itself from immediate reality and, by reference and allusion, allow the past to coexist with the present. The reader may compare *Purgatory* with *Oedipus the King* and see how similar, in this respect, they are. In Sophocles' play the past is always on stage. In *Purgatory* the re-creation of the old man's childhood becomes so strong that it assumes audible, visible form in hoofbeats, lights, and shadows. Greek, too, is the sense of a family curse, an inevitable murder that must still be expiated by another death, a doomed family that cannot be permitted to survive. Yeats has performed a powerful feat in taking the dramatic means and themes of other eras and molding them to suit his own time; he also gives an object lesson in how little the theater needs to make a forceful statement, and how the range of the drama is increased when the boundaries of conventional realism are removed.

Luigi Pirandello

SIX CHARACTERS IN SEARCH OF AN AUTHOR

A Comedy in the Making

English Version by Edward Storer

FOREWORD

In the general introduction we drew attention to certain paradoxes inherent in theatrical production. How much is reality and how much is artifice? Is the audience conscious of watching a staged performance, or does it believe that it is watching a slice of real life? *Oedipus the King* stands at one pole, *The Cherry Orchard* at another. The movement away from realism at the end of the nineteenth century and the beginning of the twentieth reopened the debate. Actors were more frequently asked to reveal themselves to the audience by purely theatrical means: by mime, gymnastics, tumbling. Pirandello elevates this distinction between art and reality to a metaphysical level. The question "What is the actor's reality?" becomes "What is reality?"

One word of warning. Directors often take the easy approach to *Six Characters* by turning the "actors" into buffoons and incompetents, as contrasted with the "real" characters. But the play is not about the difference between *bad* acting and reality. It is about the difference between acting and reality; between different visions of reality.

CHARACTERS OF THE COMEDY IN THE MAKING

THE FATHER	THE BOY
THE MOTHER	THE CHILD
THE STEPDAUGHTER	(The last two do not speak.)
THE SON	MADAME PACE

ACTORS OF THE COMPANY

THE MANAGER	OTHER ACTORS AND ACTRESSES
LEADING LADY	PROPERTY MAN
LEADING MAN	PROMPTER
SECOND LADY LEAD	MACHINST
L'INGÉNUE	MANAGER'S SECRETARY
JUVENILE LEAD	DOOR-KEEPER
	SCENE-SHIFTERS

Scene: Daytime. The stage of a theater.

N.B. *The Comedy is without acts or scenes. The performance is interrupted once, without the curtain being lowered, when the* MANAGER *and the chief characters withdraw to arrange a scenario. A second interruption of the action takes place when, by mistake, the stage hands let the curtain down.*

ACT I

The spectators will find the curtain raised and the stage as it usually is during the day time. It will be half dark, and empty, so that from the beginning the public may have the impression of an impromptu performance.

PROMPTER's box and a small table and chair for the MANAGER.

Two other small tables and several chairs scattered about as during rehearsals.

The ACTORS *and* ACTRESSES *of the company enter from the back of the stage: first one, then another, then two together; nine or ten in all. They are about to rehearse a Pirandello play:* Mixing It Up.[1] *Some of the company move off towards their dressing rooms. The* PROMPTER, *who has the "book" under his arm, is waiting for the* MANAGER *in order to begin the rehearsal.*

The ACTORS *and* ACTRESSES, *some standing, some sitting, chat and smoke. One perhaps reads a paper; another cons his part.*

Finally, the MANAGER *enters and goes to the table prepared for him. His* SECRETARY *brings him his mail, through which he glances. The* PROMPTER *takes his seat, turns on a light, and opens the "book."*

From the book *Naked Masks: Five Plays* by Luigi Pirandello. Edited by Eric Bentley. Copyright, 1922, 1952 by E. P. Dutton & Co., Inc.; renewal, 1950, in the names of Stefano, Fausto and Lietta Pirandello. Reprinted by permission of the publishers, E. P. Dutton.

[1] "Il giuoco delle parti."

THE MANAGER (*throwing a letter down on the table*): I can't see. (*To* PROPERTY MAN.)
   Let's have a little light, please!

PROPERTY MAN: Yes, sir, yes, at once. (*A light comes down on to the stage.*)

THE MANAGER (*clapping his hands*): Come along! Come along! Second act of "Mixing It Up." (*Sits down.*)

   (*The* ACTORS *and* ACTRESSES *go from the front of the stage to the wings, all
   except the three who are to begin the rehearsal.*)

THE PROMPTER (*reading the "book"*): "Leo Gala's house. A curious room serving as
   dining-room and study."

THE MANAGER (*to* PROPERTY MAN): Fix up the old red room.

PROPERTY MAN (*noting it down*): Red set. All right!

THE PROMPTER (*continuing to read from the "book"*): "Table already laid and writing
   desk with books and papers. Book-shelves. Exit rear to Leo's bedroom. Exit left
   to kitchen. Principal exit to right."

THE MANAGER (*energetically*): Well, you understand: The principal exit over there;
   here, the kitchen. (*Turning to actor who is to play the part of* SOCRATES.) You
   make your entrances and exits here. (*To* PROPERTY MAN.) The baize doors at the
   rear, and curtains.

PROPERTY MAN (*noting it down*): Right!

PROMPTER (*reading as before*): "When the curtain rises, Leo Gala, dressed in cook's
   cap and apron, is busy beating an egg in a cup. Philip, also dressed as a cook, is
   beating another egg. Guidi Venanzi is seated and listening."

LEADING MAN (*to* MANAGER): Excuse me, but must I absolutely wear a cook's cap?

THE MANAGER (*annoyed*): I imagine so. It says so there anyway. (*Pointing to the
   "book."*)

LEADING MAN: But it's ridiculous!

THE MANAGER (*jumping up in a rage*): Ridiculous? Ridiculous? Is it my fault if
   France won't send us any more good comedies, and we are reduced to putting on
   Pirandello's works, where nobody understands anything, and where the author
   plays the fool with us all? (*The* ACTORS *grin. The* MANAGER *goes to* LEADING MAN
   and shouts.) Yes sir, you put on the cook's cap and beat eggs. Do you suppose
   that with all this egg-beating business you are on an ordinary stage? Get that out
   of your head. You represent the shell of the eggs you are beating! (*Laughter and
   comments among the* ACTORS.) Silence! and listen to my explanations, please! (*To
   LEADING MAN.*) "The empty form of reason without the fullness of instinct, which
   is blind." — You stand for reason, your wife is instinct. It's a mixing up of the
   parts, according to which you who act your own part become the puppet of
   yourself. Do you understand?

LEADING MAN: I'm hanged if I do.

THE MANAGER: Neither do I. But let's get on with it. It's sure to be a glorious failure
   anyway. (*Confidentially.*) But I say, please face three-quarters. Otherwise, what
   with the abstruseness of the dialogue, and the public that won't be able to hear
   you, the whole thing will go to hell. Come on! come on!

PROMPTER: Pardon sir, may I get into my box? There's a bit of a draught.

THE MANAGER: Yes, yes, of course!

   (*At this point, the* DOOR-KEEPER *has entered from the stage door and advances
   towards the* MANAGER's *table, taking off his braided cap. During this maneuver,*

the SIX CHARACTERS *enter, and stop by the door at back of stage, so that when the* DOOR-KEEPER *is about to announce their coming to the* MANAGER, *they are already on the stage. A tenuous light surrounds them, almost as if irradiated by them — the faint breath of their fantastic reality.*

This light will disappear when they come forward towards the actors. They preserve, however, something of the dream lightness in which they seem almost suspended; but this does not detract from the essential reality of their forms and expressions.

He who is known as THE FATHER *is a man of about 50: hair, reddish in color, thin at the temples; he is not bald, however; thick moustaches, falling over his still fresh mouth, which often opens in an empty and uncertain smile. He is fattish, pale; with an especially wide forehead. He has blue, oval-shaped eyes, very clear and piercing. Wears light trousers and a dark jacket. He is alternatively mellifluous and violent in his manner.*

THE MOTHER *seems crushed and terrified as if by an intolerable weight of shame and abasement. She is dressed in modest black and wears a thick widow's veil of crêpe. When she lifts this, she reveals a wax-like face. She always keeps her eyes downcast.*

THE STEPDAUGHTER *is dashing, almost impudent, beautiful. She wears mourning too, but with great elegance. She shows contempt for the timid half-frightened manner of the wretched* BOY *(14 years old, and also dressed in black): on the other hand, she displays a lively tenderness for her little sister,* THE CHILD *(about four), who is dressed in white, with a black silk sash at the waist.*

THE SON *(22) is tall, severe in his attitude of contempt for* THE FATHER, *supercilious and indifferent to* THE MOTHER. *He looks as if he had come on the stage against his will.)*

DOOR-KEEPER (*cap in hand*): Excuse me, sir . . .

THE MANAGER (*rudely*): Eh? What is it?

DOOR-KEEPER (*timidly*): These people are asking for you, sir.

THE MANAGER (*furious*): I am rehearsing, and you know perfectly well no one's allowed to come in during rehearsals! (*Turning to the* CHARACTERS.) Who are you, please? What do you want?

THE FATHER (*coming forward a little, followed by the others who seem embarrassed*): As a matter of fact . . . we have come here in search of an author . . .

THE MANAGER (*half angry, half amazed*): An author? What author?

THE FATHER: Any author, sir.

THE MANAGER: But there's no author here. We are not rehearsing a new piece.

THE STEPDAUGHTER (*vivaciously*): So much the better, so much the better! We can be your new piece.

AN ACTOR (*coming forward from the others*): Oh, do you hear that?

THE FATHER (*to* STEPDAUGHTER): Yes, but if the author isn't here . . . (*to* MANAGER) unless you would be willing . . .

THE MANAGER: You are trying to be funny.

THE FATHER: No, for Heaven's sake, what are you saying? We bring you a drama, sir.

THE STEPDAUGHTER: We may be your fortune.

THE MANAGER: Will you oblige me by going away? We haven't time to waste with mad people.

THE FATHER (*mellifluously*): Oh sir, you know well that life is full of infinite absurdities, which, strangely enough, do not even need to appear plausible, since they are true.

THE MANAGER: What the devil is he talking about?

THE FATHER: I say that to reverse the ordinary process may well be considered a madness: that is, to create credible situations, in order that they may appear true. But permit me to observe that if this be madness, it is the sole *raison d'être*[2] of your profession, gentlemen. (*The* ACTORS *look hurt and perplexed.*)

THE MANAGER (*getting up and looking at him*): So our profession seems to you one worthy of madmen then?

THE FATHER: Well, to make seem true that which isn't true . . . without any need . . . for a joke as it were . . . Isn't that your mission, gentlemen: to give life to fantastic characters on the stage?

THE MANAGER (*interpreting the rising anger of the* COMPANY): But I would beg you believe, my dear sir, that the profession of the comedian is a noble one. If today, as things go, the playwrights give us stupid comedies to play and puppets to represent instead of men, remember we are proud to have given life to immortal works here on these very boards! (*The* ACTORS, *satisfied, applaud their* MANAGER.)

THE FATHER (*interrupting furiously*): Exactly, perfectly, to living beings more alive than those who breathe and wear clothes: beings less real perhaps, but truer! I agree with you entirely. (*The* ACTORS *look at one another in amazement.*)

THE MANAGER: But what do you mean? Before, you said . . .

THE FATHER: No, excuse me, I meant it for you, sir, who were crying out that you had no time to lose with madmen, while no one better than yourself knows that nature uses the instrument of human fantasy in order to pursue her high creative purpose.

THE MANAGER: Very well, — but where does all this take us?

THE FATHER: Nowhere! It is merely to show you that one is born to life in many forms, in many shapes, as tree, or as stone, as water, as butterfly, or as woman. So one may also be born a character in a play.

THE MANAGER (*with feigned comic dismay*): So you and these other friends of yours have been born characters?

THE FATHER: Exactly, and alive as you see! (MANAGER *and* ACTORS *burst out laughing.*)

THE FATHER (*hurt*): I am sorry you laugh, because we carry in us a drama, as you can guess from this woman here veiled in black.

THE MANAGER (*losing patience at last and almost indignant*): Oh, chuck it! Get away please! Clear out of here! (*To* PROPERTY MAN.) For Heaven's sake, turn them out!

THE FATHER (*resisting*): No, no, look here, we . . .

THE MANAGER (*roaring*): We come here to work, you know.

LEADING ACTOR: One cannot let oneself be made such a fool of.

THE FATHER (*determined, coming forward*): I marvel at your incredulity, gentlemen. Are you not accustomed to see the characters created by an author spring to life in yourselves and face each other? Just because there is no "book" (*pointing to the* PROMPTER's *box*) which contains us, you refuse to believe . . .

THE STEPDAUGHTER (*advances towards* MANAGER, *smiling and coquettish*): Believe me, we are really six most interesting characters, sir; side-tracked however.

THE FATHER: Yes, that is the word! (*To* MANAGER *all at once.*) In the sense, that is,

[2] French, "reason to exist."

that the author who created us alive no longer wished, or was no longer able, materially to put us into a work of art. And this was a real crime, sir; because he who has had the luck to be born a character can laugh even at death. He cannot die. The man, the writer, the instrument of the creation will die, but his creation does not die. And to live for ever, it does not need to have extraordinary gifts or to be able to work wonders. Who was Sancho Panza? Who was Don Abbondio?[3] Yet they live eternally because — live germs as they were — they had the fortune to find a fecundating matrix, a fantasy which could raise and nourish them: make them live for ever!

THE MANAGER: That is quite all right. But what do you want here, all of you?

THE FATHER: We want to live.

THE MANAGER (*ironically*): For Eternity?

THE FATHER: No, sir, only for a moment . . . in you.

AN ACTOR: Just listen to him!

LEADING LADY: They want to live, in us . . . !

JUVENILE LEAD (*pointing to the* STEPDAUGHTER): I've no objection, as far as that one is concerned!

THE FATHER: Look here! look here! The comedy has to be made. (*To the* MANAGER.) But if you and your actors are willing, we can soon concert it among ourselves.

THE MANAGER (*annoyed*): But what do you want to concert? We don't go in for concerts here. Here we play dramas and comedies!

THE FATHER: Exactly! That is just why we have come to you.

THE MANAGER: And where is the "book"?

THE FATHER: It is in us! (*The* ACTORS *laugh*.) The drama is in us, and we are the drama. We are impatient to play it. Our inner passion drives us on to this.

THE STEPDAUGHTER (*disdainful, alluring, treacherous, full of impudence*): My passion, sir! Ah, if you only knew! My passion for him! (*Points to the* FATHER *and makes a pretense of embracing him. Then she breaks out into a loud laugh*.)

THE FATHER (*angrily*): Behave yourself! And please don't laugh in that fashion.

THE STEPDAUGHTER: With your permission, gentlemen, I, who am a two months' orphan, will show you how I can dance and sing. (*Sings and then dances* Prenez garde à Tchou-Tchin-Tchou.[4])

> Les chinois sont un peuple malin,
> De Shangaî à Pékin,
> Ils ont mis des écriteaux partout:
> Prenez garde à Tchou-Tchin-Tchou.

ACTORS AND ACTRESSES: Bravo! Well done! Tip-top!

THE MANAGER: Silence! This isn't a café concert, you know! (*Turning to the* FATHER *in consternation*.) Is she mad?

THE FATHER: Mad? No, she's worse than mad.

THE STEPDAUGHTER (*to* MANAGER): Worse? Worse? Listen! Stage this drama for us at once! Then you will see that at a certain moment I . . . when this little darling

---

[3] memorable characters in novels: squire in Cervantes' *Don Quixote* and priest in Manzoni's *I Promessi Sposi* (The Betrothed).

[4] This French popular song is an adaptation of "Chu-Chin-Chow," an old Broadway show tune. Translation: "The Chinese are a sly people; / From Shanghai to Peking, / They've stuck up warning signs: / Beware of Tchou-Tchin-Tchou." (This is funnier in French: *chou* means "cabbage.")

here. . . . (*Takes the* CHILD *by the hand and leads her to the* MANAGER.) Isn't she a dear? (*Takes her up and kisses her.*) Darling! Darling! (*Puts her down again and adds feelingly.*) Well, when God suddenly takes this dear little child away from that poor mother there; and this imbecile here (*seizing hold of the* BOY *roughly and pushing him forward*) does the stupidest things, like the fool he is, you will see me run away. Yes, gentlemen, I shall be off. But the moment hasn't arrived yet. After what has taken place between him and me (*indicates the* FATHER *with a horrible wink*) I can't remain any longer in this society, to have to witness the anguish of this mother here for that fool. . . . (*Indicates the* SON.) Look at him! Look at him! See how indifferent, how frigid he is, because he is the legitimate son. He despises me, despises him (*pointing to the* BOY), despises this baby here; because . . . we are bastards. (*Goes to the* MOTHER *and embraces her.*) And he doesn't want to recognize her as his mother — she who is the common mother of us all. He looks down upon her as if she were only the mother of us three bastards. Wretch! (*She says all this very rapidly, excitedly. At the word "bastards" she raises her voice, and almost spits out the final "Wretch!"*)

THE MOTHER (*to the* MANAGER, *in anguish*): In the name of these two little children, I beg you. . . .(*She grows faint and is about to fall.*) Oh God!

THE FATHER (*coming forward to support her as do some of the* ACTORS): Quick, a chair, a chair for this poor widow!

THE ACTORS: Is it true? Has she really fainted?

THE MANAGER: Quick, a chair! Here!

(*One of the* ACTORS *brings a chair, the others proffer assistance. The* MOTHER *tries to prevent the* FATHER *from lifting the veil which covers her face.*)

THE FATHER: Look at her! Look at her!

THE MOTHER: No, no; stop it please!

THE FATHER (*raising her veil*): Let them see you!

THE MOTHER (*rising and covering her face with her hands, in desperation*): I beg you, sir, to prevent this man from carrying out his plan which is loathsome to me.

THE MANAGER (*dumbfounded*): I don't understand at all. What is the situation? (*To the* FATHER.) Is this lady your wife?

THE FATHER: Yes, gentlemen: my wife!

THE MANAGER: But how can she be a widow if you are alive? (*The* ACTORS *find relief for their astonishment in a loud laugh.*)

THE FATHER: Don't laugh! Don't laugh like that, for Heaven's sake. Her drama lies just here in this: she has had a lover, a man who ought to be here.

THE MOTHER (*with a cry*): No! No!

THE STEPDAUGHTER: Fortunately for her, he is dead. Two months ago as I said. We are in mourning, as you see.

THE FATHER: He isn't here, you see, not because he is dead. He isn't here — look at her a moment and you will understand — because her drama isn't a drama of the love of two men for whom she was incapable of feeling anything except possibly a little gratitude — not for me but for the other. She isn't a woman, she is a mother, and her drama — powerful, sir, I assure you — lies, as a matter of fact, all in these four children she has had by two men.

THE MOTHER: I had them? Have you got the courage to say that I wanted them? (*To the* COMPANY.) It was his doing. It was he who gave me that other man, who forced me to go away with him.

THE STEPDAUGHTER: It isn't true.

THE MOTHER (*startled*): Not true, isn't it?

THE STEPDAUGHTER: No, it isn't true, it just isn't true.

THE MOTHER: And what can you know about it?

THE STEPDAUGHTER: It isn't true. Don't believe it. (*To* MANAGER.) Do you know why she says so? For that fellow there. (*Indicates the* SON.) She tortures herself, destroys herself on account of the neglect of that son there; and she wants him to believe that if she abandoned him when he was only two years old, it was because he (*indicates the* FATHER) made her do so.

THE MOTHER (*vigorously*): He forced me to it, and I call God to witness it. (*To the* MANAGER.) Ask him (*indicates* HUSBAND) if it isn't true. Let him speak. You (*to* DAUGHTER) are not in a position to know anything about it.

THE STEPDAUGHTER: I know you lived in peace and happiness with my father while he lived. Can you deny it?

THE MOTHER: No, I don't deny it. . . .

THE STEPDAUGHTER: He was always full of affection and kindness for you. (*To the* BOY, *angrily*.) It's true, isn't it? Tell them! Why don't you speak, you little fool?

THE MOTHER: Leave the poor boy alone. Why do you want to make me appear ungrateful, daughter? I don't want to offend your father. I have answered him that I didn't abandon my house and my son through any fault of mine, nor from any wilful passion.

THE FATHER: It is true. It was my doing.

LEADING MAN (*to the* COMPANY): What a spectacle!

LEADING LADY: We are the audience this time.

JUVENILE LEAD: For once, in a way.

THE MANAGER (*beginning to get really interested*): Let's hear them out. Listen!

THE SON: Oh yes, you're going to hear a fine bit now. He will talk to you of the Demon of Experiment.

THE FATHER: You are a cynical imbecile. I've told you so already a hundred times. (*To the* MANAGER.) He tries to make fun of me on account of this expression which I have found to excuse myself with.

THE SON (*with disgust*): Yes, phrases! phrases!

THE FATHER: Phrases! Isn't everyone consoled when faced with a trouble or fact he doesn't understand, by a word, some simple word, which tells us nothing and yet calms us?

THE STEPDAUGHTER: Even in the case of remorse. In fact, especially then.

THE FATHER: Remorse? No, that isn't true. I've done more than use words to quiet the remorse in me.

THE STEPDAUGHTER: Yes, there was a bit of money too. Yes, yes, a bit of money. There were the hundred lire he was about to offer me in payment, gentlemen. . . . (*Sensation of horror among the* ACTORS.)

THE SON (*to the* STEPDAUGHTER): This is vile.

THE STEPDAUGHTER: Vile? There they were in a pale blue envelope on a little mahogany table in the back of Madame Pace's shop. You know Madame Pace — one of those ladies who attract poor girls of good family into their ateliers, under the pretext of their selling *robes et manteaux*.[5]

THE SON: And he thinks he has bought the right to tyrannize over us all with those hundred lire he was going to pay; but which, fortunately — note this, gentlemen — he had no chance of paying.

[5] French, "dresses and capes."

THE STEPDAUGHTER: It was a near thing, though, you know! (*Laughs ironically.*)

THE MOTHER (*protesting*): Shame, my daughter, shame!

THE STEPDAUGHTER: Shame indeed! This is my revenge! I am dying to live that scene . . . The room . . . I see it . . . Here is the window with the mantles exposed, there the divan, the looking-glass, a screen, there in front of the window the little mahogany table with the blue envelope containing one hundred lire. I see it. I see it. I could take hold of it. . . . But you, gentlemen, you ought to turn your backs now: I am almost nude, you know. But I don't blush: I leave that to him. (*Indicating* FATHER.)

THE MANAGER: I don't understand this at all.

THE FATHER: Naturally enough. I would ask you, sir, to exercise your authority a little here, and let me speak before you believe all she is trying to blame me with. Let me explain.

THE STEPDAUGHTER: Ah yes, explain it in your own way.

THE FATHER: But don't you see that the whole trouble lies here? In words, words. Each one of us has within him a whole world of things, each man of us his own special world. And how can we ever come to an understanding if I put in the words I utter the sense and value of things as I see them; while you who listen to me must inevitably translate them according to the conception of things each one of you has within himself. We think we understand each other, but we never really do. Look here! This woman (*indicating the* MOTHER) takes all my pity for her as a specially ferocious form of cruelty.

THE MOTHER: But you drove me away.

THE FATHER: Do you hear her? I drove her away! She believes I really sent her away.

THE MOTHER: You know how to talk, and I don't; but, believe me, sir (*to* MANAGER), after he had married me . . . who knows why? . . . I was a poor insignificant woman. . . .

THE FATHER: But, good Heavens! it was just for your humility that I married you. I loved this simplicity in you. (*He stops when he sees she makes signs to contradict him, opens his arms wide in sign of desperation, seeing how hopeless it is to make himself understood.*) You see she denies it. Her mental deafness, believe me, is phenomenal, the limit: (*touches his forehead*) deaf, deaf, mentally deaf! She has plenty of feeling. Oh yes, a good heart for the children; but the brain — deaf, to the point of desperation — !

THE STEPDAUGHTER: Yes, but ask him how his intelligence has helped us.

THE FATHER: If we could see all the evil that may spring from good, what should we do? (*At this point the* LEADING LADY, *who is biting her lips, with rage at seeing the* LEADING MAN *flirting with the* STEPDAUGHTER, *comes forward and speaks to the* MANAGER.)

LEADING LADY: Excuse me, but are we going to rehearse today?

MANAGER: Of course, of course; but let's hear them out.

JUVENILE LEAD: This is something quite new.

L'INGÉNUE: Most interesting!

LEADING LADY: Yes, for the people who like that kind of thing. (*Casts a glance at* LEADING MAN.)

THE MANAGER (*to* FATHER): You must please explain yourself quite clearly. (*Sits down.*)

THE FATHER: Very well then: listen! I had in my service a poor man, a clerk, a secretary of mine, full of devotion, who became friends with her. (*Indicating the*

MOTHER.) They understood one another, were kindred souls in fact, without, however, the least suspicion of any evil existing. They were incapable even of thinking of it.

THE STEPDAUGHTER: So he thought of it — for them!

THE FATHER: That's not true. I meant to do good to them — and to myself, I confess, at the same time. Things had come to the point that I could not say a word to either of them without their making a mute appeal, one to the other, with their eyes. I could see them silently asking each other how I was to be kept in countenance, how I was to be kept quiet. And this, believe me, was just about enough of itself to keep me in a constant rage, to exasperate me beyond measure.

THE MANAGER: And why didn't you send him away then — this secretary of yours?

THE FATHER: Precisely what I did, sir. And then I had to watch this poor woman drifting forlornly about the house like an animal without a master, like an animal one has taken in out of pity.

THE MOTHER: Ah yes . . . !

THE FATHER (suddenly turning to the MOTHER): It's true about the son anyway, isn't it?

THE MOTHER: He took my son away from me first of all.

THE FATHER: But not from cruelty. I did it so that he should grow up healthy and strong by living in the country.

THE STEPDAUGHTER (pointing to him ironically): As one can see.

THE FATHER (quickly): Is it my fault if he has grown up like this? I sent him to a wet nurse in the country, a peasant, as she did not seem to me strong enough, though she is of humble origin. That was, anyway, the reason I married her. Unpleasant all this may be, but how can it be helped? My mistake possibly, but there we are! All my life I have had these confounded aspirations towards a certain moral sanity. (At this point the STEPDAUGHTER bursts into a noisy laugh.) Oh, stop it! Stop it! I can't stand it.

THE MANAGER: Yes, please stop it, for Heaven's sake.

THE STEPDAUGHTER: But imagine moral sanity from him, if you please — the client of certain ateliers like that of Madame Pace!

THE FATHER: Fool! That is the proof that I am a man! This seeming contradiction, gentlemen, is the strongest proof that I stand here a live man before you. Why, it is just for this very incongruity in my nature that I have had to suffer what I have. I could not live by the side of that woman (indicating the MOTHER) any longer; but not so much for the boredom she inspired me with as for the pity I felt for her.

THE MOTHER: And so he turned me out —.

THE FATHER: — well provided for! Yes, I sent her to that man, gentlemen . . . to let her go free of me.

THE MOTHER: And to free himself.

THE FATHER: Yes, I admit it. It was also a liberation for me. But great evil has come of it. I meant well when I did it; and I did it more for her sake than mine. I swear it. (Crosses his arms on his chest; then turns suddenly to the MOTHER.) Did I ever lose sight of you until that other man carried you off to another town, like the angry fool he was? And on account of my pure interest in you . . . my pure interest, I repeat, that had no base motive in it . . . I watched with the tenderest concern the new family that grew up around her. She can bear witness to this. (Points to the STEPDAUGHTER.)

THE STEPDAUGHTER: Oh yes, that's true enough. When I was a kiddie, so so high, you know, with plaits over my shoulders and knickers longer than my skirts, I used to see him waiting outside the school for me to come out. He came to see how I was growing up.

THE FATHER: This is infamous, shameful!

THE STEPDAUGHTER: No. Why?

THE FATHER: Infamous! infamous! (*Then excitedly to* MANAGER, *explaining*.) After she (*indicating the* MOTHER) went away, my house seemed suddenly empty. She was my incubus, but she filled my house. I was like a dazed fly alone in the empty rooms. This boy here (*indicating the* SON) was educated away from home, and when he came back, he seemed to me to be no more mine. With no mother to stand between him and me, he grew up entirely for himself, on his own, apart, with no tie of intellect or affection binding him to me. And then — strange but true — I was driven, by curiosity at first and then by some tender sentiment, towards her family, which had come into being through my will. The thought of her began gradually to fill up the emptiness I felt all around me. I wanted to know if she were happy in living out the simple daily duties of life. I wanted to think of her as fortunate and happy because far away from the complicated torments of my spirit. And so, to have proof of this, I used to watch that child coming out of school.

THE STEPDAUGHTER: Yes, yes. True. He used to follow me in the street and smiled at me, waved his hand, like this. I would look at him with interest, wondering who he might be. I told my mother, who guessed at once. (*The* MOTHER *agrees with a nod*.) Then she didn't want to send me to school for some days; and when I finally went back, there he was again — looking so ridiculous — with a paper parcel in his hands. He came close to me, caressed me, and drew out a fine straw hat from the parcel, with a bouquet of flowers — all for me!

THE MANAGER: A bit discursive this, you know!

THE SON (*contemptuously*): Literature! Literature!

THE FATHER: Literature indeed! This is life, this is passion!

THE MANAGER: It may be, but it won't act.

THE FATHER: I agree. This is only the part leading up. I don't suggest this should be staged. She (*pointing to the* STEPDAUGHTER), as you see, is no longer the flapper with plaits down her back —

THE STEPDAUGHTER: — and knickers showing below the skirt!

THE FATHER: The drama is coming now, sir; something new, complex, most interesting.

THE STEPDAUGHTER: As soon as my father died . . .

THE FATHER: — there was absolute misery for them. They came back here, unknown to me. Through her stupidity! (*Pointing to the* MOTHER.) It is true she can barely write her own name; but she could anyhow have got her daughter to write to me that they were in need . . .

THE MOTHER: And how was I to divine all this sentiment in him?

THE FATHER: That is exactly your mistake, never to have guessed any of my sentiments.

THE MOTHER: After so many years apart, and all that had happened . . .

THE FATHER: Was it my fault if that fellow carried you away? It happened quite suddenly; for after he had obtained some job or other, I could find no trace of them; and so, not unnaturally, my interest in them dwindled. But the drama culminated unforeseen and violent on their return, when I was impelled by my miserable flesh that still lives. . . .Ah! what misery, what wretchedness is that of the man who is alone and disdains debasing *liaisons!* Not old enough to do without women, and not young enough to go and look for one without shame. Misery? It's worse than misery; it's a horror; for no woman can any longer give him love; and when a man feels this. . . . One ought to do without, you say? Yes, yes, I know. Each of us when he appears before his fellows is clothed in a certain dignity. But every man knows what unconfessable things pass within the secrecy of his own heart. One gives way to the temptation, only to rise from it again, afterwards, with a great eagerness to re-establish one's dignity, as if it were a tombstone to place on the grave of one's shame, and a monument to hide and sign the memory of our weaknesses. Everybody's in the same case. Some folks haven't the courage to say certain things, that's all!

THE STEPDAUGHTER: All appear to have the courage to do them though.

THE FATHER: Yes, but in secret. Therefore, you want more courage to say these things. Let a man but speak these things out, and folks at once label him a cynic. But it isn't true. He is like all the others, better indeed, because he isn't afraid to reveal with the light of the intelligence the red shame of human bestiality on which most men close their eyes so as not to see it. Woman — for example, look at her case! She turns tantalizing inviting glances on you. You seize her. No sooner does she feel herself in your grasp than she closes her eyes. It is the sign of her mission, the sign by which she says to man: "Blind yourself, for I am blind."

THE STEPDAUGHTER: Sometimes she can close them no more: when she no longer feels the need of hiding her shame to herself, but dry-eyed and dispassionately, sees only that of the man who has blinded himself without love. Oh, all these intellectual complications make me sick, disgust me — all this philosophy that uncovers the beast in man, and then seeks to save him, excuse him . . . I can't stand it, sir. When a man seeks to "simplify" life bestially, throwing aside every relic of humanity, every chaste aspiration, every pure feeling, all sense of ideality, duty, modesty, shame . . . then nothing is more revolting and nauseous than a certain kind of remorse — crocodiles' tears, that's what it is.

THE MANAGER: Let's come to the point. This is only discussion.

THE FATHER: Very good, sir! But a fact is like a sack which won't stand up when it's empty. In order that it may stand up, one has to put into it the reason and sentiment which have caused it to exist. I couldn't possibly know that after the death of that man, they had decided to return here, that they were in misery, and that she (*pointing to the* MOTHER) had gone to work as a modiste, and at a shop of the type of that of Madame Pace.

THE STEPDAUGHTER: A real high-class modiste, you must know, gentlemen. In appearance, she works for the leaders of the best society; but she arranges matters so that these elegant ladies serve her purpose . . . without prejudice to other ladies who are . . . well . . . only so so.

THE MOTHER: You will believe me, gentlemen, that it never entered my mind that the old hag offered me work because she had her eye on my daughter.

THE STEPDAUGHTER: Poor mamma! Do you know, sir, what that woman did when I brought her back the work my mother had finished? She would point out to me that I had torn one of my frocks, and she would give it back to my mother to mend. It was I who paid for it, always I; while this poor creature here believed she was sacrificing herself for me and these two children here, sitting up at night sewing Madame Pace's robes.

THE MANAGER: And one day you met there . . .

THE STEPDAUGHTER: Him, him. Yes sir, an old client. There's a scene for you to play! Superb!

THE FATHER: She, the Mother arrived just then . . .

THE STEPDAUGHTER (*treacherously*): Almost in time!

THE FATHER (*crying out*): No, in time! in time! Fortunately I recognized her . . . in time. And I took them back home with me to my house. You can imagine now her position and mine; she, as you see her; and I who cannot look her in the face.

THE STEPDAUGHTER: Absurd! How can I possibly be expected — after that — to be a modest young miss, a fit person to go with his confounded aspirations for "a solid moral sanity"?

THE FATHER: For the drama lies all in this — in the conscience that I have, that each one of us has. We believe this conscience to be a single thing, but it is many-sided. There is one for this person, and another for that. Diverse consciences. So we have this illusion of being one person for all, of having a personality that is unique in all our acts. But it isn't true. We perceive this when, tragically perhaps, in something we do, we are as it were, suspended, caught up in the air on a kind of hook. Then we perceive that all of us was not in that act, and that it would be an atrocious injustice to judge us by that action alone, as if all our existence were summed up in that one deed. Now do you understand the perfidy of this girl? She surprised me in a place, where she ought not to have known me, just as I could not exist for her; and she now seeks to attach to me a reality such as I could never suppose I should have to assume for her in a shameful and fleeting moment of my life. I feel this above all else. And the drama, you will see, acquires a tremendous value from this point. Then there is the position of the others . . . his. . . . (*Indicating the* SON.)

THE SON (*shrugging his shoulders scornfully*): Leave me alone! I don't come into this.

THE FATHER: What? You don't come into this?

THE SON: I've got nothing to do with it, and don't want to have; because you know well enough I wasn't made to be mixed up in all this with the rest of you.

THE STEPDAUGHTER: We are only vulgar folk! He is the fine gentleman. You may have noticed, Mr. Manager, that I fix him now and again with a look of scorn while he lowers his eyes — for he knows the evil he has done me.

THE SON (*scarcely looking at her*): I?

THE STEPDAUGHTER: You! you! I owe my life on the streets to you. Did you or did you not deny us, with your behavior, I won't say the intimacy of home, but even that mere hospitality which makes guests feel at their ease? We were intruders who had come to disturb the kingdom of your legitimacy. I should like to have you witness, Mr. Manager, certain scenes between him and me. He says I have tyrannized over everyone. But it was just his behavior which made me insist on the reason for which I had come into the house, — this reason he calls "vile" — into his house, with my mother who is his mother too. And I came as mistress of the house.

THE SON: It's easy for them to put me always in the wrong. But imagine, gentlemen, the position of a son, whose fate it is to see arrive one day at his home a young woman of impudent bearing, a young woman who inquires for his father, with whom who knows what business she has. This young man has then to witness her return bolder than ever, accompanied by that child there. He is obliged to watch her treat his father in an equivocal and confidential manner. She asks for money of him in a way that lets one suppose he must give it to her, *must*, do you understand, because he has every obligation to do so.

THE FATHER: But I have, as a matter of fact, this obligation. I owe it to your mother.

THE SON: How should I know? When had I ever seen or heard of her? One day there arrive with her (*indicating* STEPDAUGHTER) that lad and this baby here. I am told: "This is *your* mother too, you know." I divine from her manner (*indicating* STEPDAUGHTER *again*) why it is they have come home. I had rather not say what I feel and think about it. I shouldn't even care to confess to myself. No action can therfore be hoped for from me in this affair. Believe me, Mr. Manager, I am an "unrealized" character, dramatically speaking; and I find myself not at all at ease in their company. Leave me out of it, I beg you.

THE FATHER: What? It is just because you are so that . . .

THE SON: How do you know what I am like? When did you ever bother your head about me?

THE FATHER: I admit it. I admit it. But isn't that a situation in itself? This aloofness of yours which is so cruel to me and to your mother, who returns home and sees you almost for the first time grown up, who doesn't recognize you but knows you are her son. . . . (*Pointing out the* MOTHER *to the* MANAGER.) See, she's crying!

THE STEPDAUGHTER (*angrily, stamping her foot*): Like a fool!

THE FATHER (*indicating* STEPDAUGHTER): She can't stand him, you know. (*Then referring again to the* SON.) He says he doesn't come into the affair, whereas he is really the hinge of the whole action. Look at that lad who is always clinging to his mother, frightened and humiliated. It is on account of this fellow here. Possibly his situation is the most painful of all. He feels himself a stranger more than the others. The poor little chap feels mortified, humiliated at being brought into a home out of charity as it were. (*In confidence.*) He is the image of his father. Hardly talks at all. Humble and quiet.

THE MANAGER: Oh, we'll cut him out. You've no notion what a nuisance boys are on the stage. . . .

THE FATHER: He disappears soon, you know. And the baby too. She is the first to vanish from the scene. The drama consists finally in this: when that mother re-enters my house, her family born outside of it, and shall we say superimposed on the original, ends with the death of the little girl, the tragedy of the boy and the flight of the elder daughter. It cannot go on, because it is foreign to its surround-ings. So after much torment, we three remain: I, the mother, that son. Then, owing to the disappearance of that extraneous family, we too find ourselves strange to one another. We find we are living in an atmosphere of mortal desola-tion which is the revenge, as he (*indicating* SON) scornfully said of the Demon of Experiment, that unfortunately hides in me. Thus, sir, you see when faith is lacking, it becomes impossible to create certain states of happiness, for we lack the necessary humility. Vaingloriously, we try to substitute ourselves for this faith, creating thus for the rest of the world a reality which we believe after their fashion, while, actually, it doesn't exist. For each one of us has his own reality to be respected before God, even when it is harmful to one's very self.

THE MANAGER: There is something in what you say. I assure you all this interests me very much. I begin to think there's the stuff for a drama in all this, and not a bad drama either.

THE STEPDAUGHTER (*coming forward*): When you've got a character like me . . .

THE FATHER (*shutting her up, all excited to learn the decision of the* MANAGER): You be quiet!

THE MANAGER (*reflecting, heedless of interruption*): It's new . . . hem . . . yes. . . .

THE FATHER: Absolutely new!

THE MANAGER: You've got a nerve though, I must say, to come here and fling it at me like this . . .

THE FATHER: You will understand, sir, born as we are for the stage . . .

THE MANAGER: Are you amateur actors then?

THE FATHER: No, I say born for the stage, because . . .

THE MANAGER: Oh, nonsense. You're an old hand, you know.

THE FATHER: No sir, no. We act that rôle for which we have been cast, that rôle which we are given in life. And in my own case, passion itself, as usually happens, becomes a trifle theatrical when it is exalted.

THE MANAGER: Well, well, that will do. But you see, without an author. . . . I could give you the address of an author if you like . . .

THE FATHER: No, no. Look here! You must be the author.

THE MANAGER: I? What are you talking about?

THE FATHER: Yes, you, you! Why not?

THE MANAGER: Because I have never been an author: that's why.

THE FATHER: Then why not turn author now? Everybody does it. You don't want any special qualities. Your task is made much easier by the fact that we are all here alive before you. . . .

THE MANAGER: It won't do.

THE FATHER: What? When you see us live our drama. . . .

THE MANAGER: Yes, that's all right. But you want someone to write it.

THE FATHER: No, no. Someone to take it down, possibly, while we play it, scene by scene! It will be enough to sketch it out at first, and then try it over.

THE MANAGER: Well . . . I am almost tempted. It's a bit of an idea. One might have a shot at it.

THE FATHER: Of course. You'll see what scenes will come out of it. I can give you one, at once . . .

THE MANAGER: By Jove, it tempts me. I'd like to have a go at it. Let's try it out. Come with me to my office. (*Turning to the* ACTORS.) You are at liberty for a bit, but don't step out of the theatre for long. In a quarter of an hour, twenty minutes, all back here again! (*To the* FATHER.) We'll see what can be done. Who knows if we don't get something really extraordinary out of it?

THE FATHER: There's no doubt about it. They (*indicating the* CHARACTERS) had better come with us too, hadn't they?

THE MANAGER: Yes, yes. Come on! come on! (*Moves away and then turning to the* ACTORS.) Be punctual, please! (MANAGER *and the* SIX CHARACTERS *cross the stage and go off. The other* ACTORS *remain, looking at one another in astonishment.*)

LEADING MAN: Is he serious? What the devil does he want to do?

JUVENILE LEAD: This is rank madness.

THIRD ACTOR: Does he expect to knock up a drama in five minutes?

JUVENILE LEAD: Like the improvisers!

LEADING LADY: If he thinks I'm going to take part in a joke like this. . . .

JUVENILE LEAD: I'm out of it anyway.

FOURTH ACTOR: I should like to know who they are. (*Alludes to* CHARACTERS.)

THIRD ACTOR: What do you suppose? Madmen or rascals!

JUVENILE LEAD: And he takes them seriously!

L'INGÉNUE: Vanity! He fancies himself as an author now.

LEADING MAN: It's absolutely unheard of. If the stage has come to this . . . well I'm . . .

FIFTH ACTOR: It's rather a joke.

THIRD ACTOR: Well, we'll see what's going to happen next.

(*Thus talking, the* ACTORS *leave the stage; some going out by the little door at the back; others retiring to their dressing-rooms.*
The curtain remains up.
The action of the play is suspended for twenty minutes.)

ACT II

The stage call-bells ring to warn the company that the play is about to begin again.

The STEPDAUGHTER *comes out of the* MANAGER's *office along with the* CHILD *and the* BOY. *As she comes out of the office, she cries:* —

Nonsense! nonsense! Do it yourselves! I'm not going to mix myself up in this mess. (*Turning to the* CHILD *and coming quickly with her on to the stage.*) Come on, Rosetta, let's run!

(*The* BOY *follows them slowly, remaining a little behind and seeming perplexed.*)

THE STEPDAUGHTER (*stops, bends over the* CHILD *and takes the latter's face between her hands*): My little darling! You're frightened, aren't you? You don't know where we are, do you? (*Pretending to reply to a question of the* CHILD.) What is the stage? It's a place, baby, you know, where people play at being serious, a place where they act comedies. We've got to act a comedy now, dead serious, you know; and you're in it also, little one. (*Embraces her, pressing the little head to her breast, and rocking the* CHILD *for a moment.*) Oh darling, darling, what a horrid comedy you've got to play! What a wretched part they've found for you! A garden . . . a fountain . . . look . . . just suppose, kiddie, it's here. Where, you say? Why, right here in the middle. It's all pretense you know. That's the trouble, my pet: it's all make-believe here. It's better to imagine it, though, because if they fix it up for you, it'll only be painted cardboard, painted cardboard for the rockery, the water, the plants. . . . Ah, but I think a baby like this one would sooner have a make-believe fountain than a real one, so she could play with it. What a joke it'll be for the others! But for you, alas! not quite such a joke: you who are real, baby dear, and really play by a real fountain that is big and green and beautiful, with ever so many bamboos around it that are reflected in the water, and a whole lot of little ducks swimming about. . . . No, Rosetta, no, your mother doesn't bother about you on account of that wretch of a son there. I'm in the devil of a temper, and as for that lad. . . . (*Seizes* BOY *by the arm to force him to take one of his hands out of his pockets.*) What have you got there? What are you hiding? (*Pulls his hand out of his pocket, looks into it and catches the glint of a revolver.*) Ah! where did you get this?

(*The* BOY, *very pale in the face, looks at her, but does not answer.*) Idiot! If I'd been in your place, instead of killing myself, I'd have shot one of those two, or both of them: father and son.

(*The* FATHER *enters from the office, all excited from his work. The* MANAGER *follows him.*)

THE FATHER: Come on, come on dear! Come here for a minute! We've arranged everything. It's all fixed up.

THE MANAGER (*also excited*): If you please, young lady, there are one or two points to settle still. Will you come along?

THE STEPDAUGHTER (*following him towards the office*): Ouff! what's the good, if you've arranged everything.

(*The* FATHER, MANAGER *and* STEPDAUGHTER *go back into the office again [off] for a moment. At the same time, the* SON, *followed by the* MOTHER, *comes out.*)

THE SON (*looking at the three entering office*): Oh this is fine, fine! And to think I can't even get away!

(*The* MOTHER *attempts to look at him, but lowers her eyes immediately when he turns away from her. She then sits down. The* BOY *and the* CHILD *approach her. She casts a glance again at the* SON, *and speaks with humble tones, trying to draw him into conversation.*

THE MOTHER: And isn't my punishment the worst of all? (*Then seeing from the* SON's *manner that he will not bother himself about her.*) My God! Why are you so cruel? Isn't it enough for one person to support all this torment? Must you then insist on others seeing it also?

THE SON (*half to himself, meaning the* MOTHER *to hear, however*): And they want to put it on the stage! If there was at least a reason for it! He thinks he has got at the meaning of it all. Just as if each one of us in every circumstance of life couldn't find his own explanation of it! (*Pauses.*) He complains he was discovered in a place where he ought not to have been seen, in a moment of his life which ought to have remained hidden and kept out of the reach of that convention which he has to maintain for other people. And what about my case? Haven't I had to reveal what no son ought ever to reveal: how father and mother live and are man and wife for themselves quite apart from that idea of father and mother which we give them? When this idea is revealed, our life is then linked at one point only to that man and that woman; and as such it should shame them, shouldn't it?

(*The* MOTHER *hides her face in her hands. From the dressing-rooms and the little door at the back of the stage the* ACTORS *and* STAGE MANAGER *return, followed by the* PROPERTY MAN, *and the* PROMPTER. *At the same moment, the* MANAGER *comes out of his office, accompanied by the* FATHER *and the* STEPDAUGHTER.)

THE MANAGER: Come on, come on, ladies and gentlemen! Heh! you there, machinist!

MACHINIST: Yes sir?

THE MANAGER: Fix up the parlor with the floral decorations. Two wings and a drop with a door will do. Hurry up!

(*The* MACHINIST *runs off at once to prepare the scene, and arranges it while the* MANAGER *talks with the* STAGE MANAGER, *the* PROPERTY MAN, *and the* PROMPTER *on matters of detail.*)

THE MANAGER (*to* PROPERTY MAN): Just have a look, and see if there isn't a sofa or a divan in the wardrobe . . .

PROPERTY MAN: There's the green one.

THE STEPDAUGHTER: No no! Green won't do. It was yellow, ornamented with flowers — very large! and most comfortable!

PROPERTY MAN: There isn't one like that.

THE MANAGER: It doesn't matter. Use the one we've got.

THE STEPDAUGHTER: Doesn't matter? It's most important!

THE MANAGER: We're only trying it now. Please don't interfere. (*To* PROPERTY MAN.) See if we've got a shop window — long and narrowish.

THE STEPDAUGHTER: And the little table! The little mahogany table for the pale blue envelope!

PROPERTY MAN (*to* MANAGER): There's that little gilt one.

THE MANAGER: That'll do fine.

THE FATHER: A mirror.

THE STEPDAUGHTER: And the screen! We must have a screen. Otherwise how can I manage?

PROPERTY MAN: That's all right, Miss. We've got any amount of them.

THE MANAGER (*to the* STEPDAUGHTER): We want some clothes pegs too, don't we?

THE STEPDAUGHTER: Yes, several, several!

THE MANAGER: See how many we've got and bring them all.

PROPERTY MAN: All right!

(*The* PROPERTY MAN *hurries off to obey his orders. While he is putting the things in their places, the* MANAGER *talks to the* PROMPTER *and then with the* CHARACTERS *and the* ACTORS.)

THE MANAGER (*to* PROMPTER): Take your seat. Look here: this is the outline of the scenes, act by act. (*Hands him some sheets of paper.*) And now I'm going to ask you to do something out of the ordinary.

PROMPTER: Take it down in shorthand?

THE MANAGER (*pleasantly surprised*): Exactly! Can you do shorthand?

PROMPTER: Yes, a little.

THE MANAGER: Good! (*Turning to a* STAGE HAND.) Go and get some paper from my office, plenty, as much as you can find.

(*The* STAGE HAND *goes off, and soon returns with a handful of paper which he gives to the* PROMPTER.)

THE MANAGER (*to* PROMPTER): You follow the scenes as we play them, and try and get the points down, at any rate the most important ones. (*Then addressing the* ACTORS.) Clear the stage, ladies and gentlemen! Come over here (*pointing to the left*) and listen attentively.

LEADING LADY: But, excuse me, we . . .

THE MANAGER (*guessing her thought*): Don't worry! You won't have to improvise.

LEADING MAN: What have we to do then?

THE MANAGER: Nothing. For the moment you just watch and listen. Everybody will get his part written out afterwards. At present we're going to try the thing as best we can. They're going to act now.

THE FATHER (*as if fallen from the clouds into the confusion of the stage*): We? What do you mean, if you please, by a rehearsal?

THE MANAGER: A rehearsal for them. (*Points to the* ACTORS.)

THE FATHER: But since we are the characters . . .

THE MANAGER: All right: "characters" then, if you insist on calling yourselves such. But here, my dear sir, the characters don't act. Here the actors do the acting. The characters are there, in the "book" (*pointing towards* PROMPTER'S *box*) — when there is a "book"!

THE FATHER: I won't contradict you; but excuse me, the actors aren't the characters. They want to be, they pretend to be, don't they? Now if these gentlemen here are fortunate enough to have us alive before them . . .

THE MANAGER: Oh, this is grand! You want to come before the public yourselves then?

THE FATHER: As we are. . . .

THE MANAGER: I can assure you it would be a magnificent spectacle!

LEADING MAN: What's the use of us here anyway then?

THE MANAGER: You're not going to pretend that you can act? It makes me laugh! (*The* ACTORS *laugh*.) There, you see, they are laughing at the notion. But, by the way, I must cast the parts. That won't be difficult. They cast themselves. (*To the* SECOND LADY LEAD.) You play the Mother. (*To the* FATHER.) We must find her a name.

THE FATHER: Amalia, sir.

THE MANAGER: But that is the real name of your wife. We don't want to call her by her real name.

THE FATHER: Why ever not, if it is her name? . . . Still, perhaps, if that lady must . . . (*Makes a slight motion of the hand to indicate the* SECOND LADY LEAD.) I see this woman here (*means the* MOTHER) as Amalia. But do as you like. (*Gets more and more confused.*) I don't know what to say to you. Already, I begin to hear my own words ring false, as if they had another sound . . .

THE MANAGER: Don't you worry about it. It'll be our job to find the right tones. And as for her name, if you want her Amalia, Amalia it shall be; and if you don't like it, we'll find another! For the moment though, we'll call the characters in this way: (*To* JUVENILE LEAD.) You are the Son. (*To the* LEADING LADY.) You naturally are the Stepdaughter. . . .

THE STEPDAUGHTER (*excitedly*): What? what? I, that woman there? (*Bursts out laughing.*)

THE MANAGER (*angry*): What is there to laugh at?

LEADING LADY (*indignant*): Nobody has ever dared to laugh at me. I insist on being treated with respect; otherwise I go away.

THE STEPDAUGHTER: No, no, excuse me . . . I am not laughing at you. . . .

THE MANAGER (*to* STEPDAUGHTER): You ought to feel honored to be played by . . .

LEADING LADY (*at once, contemptuously*): "That woman there" . . .

THE STEPDAUGHTER: But I wasn't speaking of you, you know. I was speaking of myself — whom I can't see at all in you! That is all. I don't know . . . but . . . you . . . aren't in the least like me. . . .

THE FATHER: True: Here's the point. Look here, sir, our temperaments, our souls. . . .

THE MANAGER: Temperament, soul, be hanged! Do you suppose the spirit of the piece is in you? Nothing of the kind!

THE FATHER: What, haven't we our own temperaments, our own souls?

THE MANAGER: Not at all. Your soul or whatever you like to call it takes shape here. The actors give body and form to it, voice and gesture. And my actors — I may tell you — have given expression to much more lofty material than this little drama of yours, which may or may not hold up on the stage. But if it does, the merit of it, believe me, will be due to my actors.

THE FATHER: I don't dare contradict you, sir; but, believe me, it is a terrible suffering for us who are as we are, with these bodies of ours, these features to see. . . .

THE MANAGER (*cutting him short and out of patience*): Good heavens! The make-up will remedy all that, man, the make-up. . . .

THE FATHER: Maybe. But the voice, the gestures . . .

THE MANAGER: Now, look here! On the stage, you as yourself, cannot exist. The actor here acts you, and that's an end to it!

THE FATHER: I understand. And now I think I see why our author who conceived us as we are, all alive, didn't want to put us on the stage after all. I haven't the least desire to offend your actors. Far from it! But when I think that I am to be acted by . . . I don't know by whom. . . .

LEADING MAN (*on his dignity*): By me, if you've no objection!

THE FATHER (*humbly, mellifluously*): Honored, I assure you, sir. (*Bows.*) Still, I must say that try as this gentleman may, with all his good will and wonderful art, to absorb me into himself. . . .

LEADING MAN: Oh chuck it! "Wonderful art!" Withdraw that, please!

THE FATHER: The performance he will give, even doing his best with make-up to look like me. . . .

LEADING MAN: It will certainly be a bit difficult! (*The* ACTORS *laugh.*)

THE FATHER: Exactly! It will be difficult to act me as I really am. The effect will be rather — apart from the make-up — according as to how he supposes I am, as he senses me — if he does sense me — and not as I inside of myself feel myself to be. It seems to me then that account should be taken of this by everyone whose duty it may become to criticize us. . . .

THE MANAGER: Heavens! The man's starting to think about the critics now! Let them say what they like. It's up to us to put on the play if we can. (*Looking around.*) Come on! come on! Is the stage set? (*To the* ACTORS *and* CHARACTERS.) Stand back — stand back! Let me see, and don't let's lose any more time! (*To the* STEPDAUGHTER.) Is it all right as it is now?

THE STEPDAUGHTER: Well, to tell the truth, I don't recognize the scene.

THE MANAGER: My dear lady, you can't possibly suppose that we can construct that shop of Madame Pace piece by piece here? (*To the* FATHER.) You said a white room with flowered wall paper, didn't you?

THE FATHER: Yes.

THE MANAGER: Well then. We've got the furniture right more or less. Bring that little table a bit further forward. (*The* STAGE HANDS *obey the order. To* PROPERTY MAN.) You go and find an envelope, if possible, a pale blue one; and give it to that gentleman. (*Indicates* FATHER.)

PROPERTY MAN: An ordinary envelope?

MANAGER AND FATHER: Yes, yes, an ordinary envelope.

PROPERTY MAN: At once, sir. (*Exit.*)

THE MANAGER: Ready, everyone! First scene — the Young Lady. (*The* LEADING LADY *comes forward.*) No, no, you must wait. I meant her. (*Indicating the* STEP-DAUGHTER.) You just watch —

THE STEPDAUGHTER (*adding at once*): How I shall play it, how I shall live it! . . .

LEADING LADY (*offended*): I shall live it also, you may be sure, as soon as I begin!

THE MANAGER (*with his hands to his head*): Ladies and gentlemen, if you please! No more useless discussions! Scene I: the Young Lady with Madame Pace: Oh! (*Looks around as if lost.*) And this Madame Pace, where is she?

THE FATHER: She isn't with us, sir.

THE MANAGER: Then what the devil's to be done?

THE FATHER: But she is alive too.

THE MANAGER: Yes, but where is she?

THE FATHER: One minute. Let me speak! (*Turning to the* ACTRESSES.) If these ladies would be so good as to give me their hats for a moment. . . .

THE ACTRESSES (*half surprised, half laughing, in chorus*): What? Why? Our hats? What does he say?

THE MANAGER: What are you going to do with the ladies' hats? (*The* ACTORS *laugh.*)

THE FATHER: Oh nothing. I just want to put them on these pegs for a moment. And one of the ladies will be so kind as to take off her mantle. . . .

THE ACTORS: Oh, what d'you think of that? Only the mantle? He must be mad.

SOME ACTRESSES: But why? Mantles as well?

THE FATHER: To hang them up here for a moment. Please be so kind, will you?

THE ACTRESSES (*taking off their hats, one or two also their cloaks, and going to hang them on the racks*): After all, why not? There you are! This is really funny. We've got to put them on show.

THE FATHER: Exactly; just like that, on show.

THE MANAGER: May we know why?

THE FATHER: I'll tell you. Who knows if, by arranging the stage for her, she does not come here herself, attracted by the very articles of her trade? (*Inviting the* AC-TORS *to look towards the exit at back of stage.*) Look! Look!

(*The door at the back of stage opens and* MADAME PACE *enters and takes a few steps forward. She is a fat, oldish woman with puffy oxygenated hair. She is rouged and powdered, dressed with a comical elegance in black silk. Round her waist is a long silver chain from which hangs a pair of scissors. The* STEPDAUGH-TER *runs over to her at once amid the stupor of the* ACTORS.)

THE STEPDAUGHTER (*turning towards her*): There she is! There she is!

THE FATHER (*radiant*): It's she! I said so, didn't I! There she is!

THE MANAGER (*conquering his surprise, and then becoming indignant*): What sort of a trick is this?

LEADING MAN (*almost at the same time*): What's going to happen next?

JUVENILE LEAD: Where does *she* come from?

L'INGÉNUE: They've been holding her in reserve, I guess.

THE LEADING LADY: A vulgar trick!

THE FATHER (*dominating the protests*): Excuse me, all of you! Why are you so anxious to destroy in the name of a vulgar, commonplace sense of truth, this reality which comes to birth attracted and formed by the magic of the stage itself, which has indeed more right to live here than you, since it is much truer than you — if you don't mind my saying so? Which is the actress among you who is to play

Madame Pace? Well, here is Madame Pace herself. And you will allow, I fancy, that the actress who acts her will be less true than this woman here, who is herself in person. You see my daughter recognized her and went over to her at once. Now you're going to witness the scene!

(*But the scene between the* STEPDAUGHTER *and* MADAME PACE *has already begun despite the protest of the* ACTORS *and the reply of the* FATHER. *It has begun quietly, naturally, in a manner impossible for the stage. So when the* ACTORS, *called to attention by the* FATHER, *turn round and see* MADAME PACE, *who has placed one hand under the* STEPDAUGHTER's *chin to raise her head, they observe her at first with great attention, but hearing her speak in an unintelligible manner their interest begins to wane.*)

THE MANAGER: Well? well?

LEADING MAN: What does she say?

LEADING LADY: One can't hear a word.

JUVENILE LEAD: Louder! Louder please!

THE STEPDAUGHTER (*leaving* MADAME PACE, *who smiles a Sphinx-like smile, and advancing towards the* ACTORS): Louder? Louder? What are you talking about? These aren't matters which can be shouted at the top of one's voice. If I have spoken them out loud, it was to shame him and have my revenge. (*Indicates* FATHER.) But for Madame it's quite a different matter.

THE MANAGER: Indeed? indeed? But here, you know, people have got to make themselves heard, my dear. Even we who are on the stage can't hear you. What will it be when the public's in the theatre? And anyway, you can very well speak up now among yourselves, since we shan't be present to listen to you as we are now. You've got to pretend to be alone in a room at the back of a shop where no one can hear you.

(*The* STEPDAUGHTER *coquettishly and with a touch of malice makes a sign of disagreement two or three times with her finger.*)

THE MANAGER: What do you mean by no?

THE STEPDAUGHTER (*sotto voce, mysteriously*): There's someone who will hear us if she (*indicating* MADAME PACE) speaks out loud.

THE MANAGER (*in consternation*): What? Have you got someone else to spring on us now? (*The* ACTORS *burst out laughing.*)

THE FATHER: No, no sir. She is alluding to me. I've got to be here — there behind that door, in waiting; and Madame Pace knows it. In fact, if you will allow me, I'll go there at once, so I can be ready. (*Moves away.*)

THE MANAGER (*stopping him*): No! Wait! wait! We must observe the conventions of the theatre. Before you are ready. . . .

THE STEPDAUGHTER (*interrupting him*): No, get on with it at once! I'm just dying, I tell you, to act this scene. If he's ready, I'm more than ready.

THE MANAGER (*shouting*): But, my dear young lady, first of all, we must have the scene between you and this lady. . . . (*Indicates* MADAME PACE.) Do you understand? . . .

THE STEPDAUGHTER: Good Heavens! She's been telling me what you know already: that mama's work is badly done again, that the material's ruined; and that if I want her to continue to help us in our misery I must be patient. . . .

MADAME PACE (*coming forward with an air of great importance*): Yes indeed, sir, I no wanta take advantage of her, I no wanta be hard. . . .

(*Note:* MADAME PACE *is supposed to talk in a jargon half Italian, half English.*)

THE MANAGER (*alarmed*): What? What? She talks like that? (*The* ACTORS *burst out laughing again.*)

THE STEPDAUGHTER (*also laughing*): Yes yes, that's the way she talks, half English, half Italian! Most comical it is!

MADAME PACE: Itta seem not verra polite gentlemen laugha atta me eeff I trya best speaka English.

THE MANAGER: *Diamine!*[1] Of course! Of course! Let her talk like that! Just what we want. Talk just like that, Madame, if you please! The effect will be certain. Exactly what was wanted to put a little comic relief into the crudity of the situation. Of course she talks like that! Magnificent!

THE STEPDAUGHTER: Magnificent? Certainly! When certain suggestions are made to one in language of that kind, the effect is certain, since it seems almost a joke. One feels inclined to laugh when one hears her talk about an "old signore" "who wanta talka nicely with you." Nice old signore, eh, Madame?

MADAME PACE: Not so old my dear, not so old! And even if you no lika him, he won't make any scandal!

THE MOTHER (*jumping up amid the amazement and consternation of the* ACTORS, *who had not been noticing her. They move to restrain her.*): You old devil! You murderess!

THE STEPDAUGHTER (*running over to calm her* MOTHER): Calm yourself, Mother, calm yourself! Please don't. . . .

THE FATHER (*going to her also at the same time*): Calm yourself! Don't get excited! Sit down now!

THE MOTHER: Well then, take that woman away out of my sight!

THE STEPDAUGHTER (*to* MANAGER): It is impossible for my mother to remain here.

THE FATHER (*to* MANAGER): They can't be here together. And for this reason, you see: that woman there was not with us when we came. . . . If they are on together, the whole thing is given away inevitably, as you see.

THE MANAGER: It doesn't matter. This is only a first rough sketch — just to get an idea of the various points of the scene, even confusedly. . . . (*Turning to the* MOTHER *and leading her to her chair.*) Come along, my dear lady, sit down now, and let's get on with the scene. . . .

Meanwhile, the STEPDAUGHTER, *coming forward again, turns to* MADAME PACE.

THE STEPDAUGHTER: Come on, Madame, come on!

MADAME PACE (*offended*): No, no, *grazie.* I do not do anything witha your mother present.

THE STEPDAUGHTER: Nonsense! Introduce this "old signore" who wants to talk nicely to me. (*Addressing the* COMPANY *imperiously.*) We've got to do this scene one way or another, haven't we? Come on! (*To* MADAME PACE.) You can go!

MADAME PACE: Ah yes! I go'way! I go'way! Certainly! (*Exits furious.*)

THE STEPDAUGHTER (*to the* FATHER): Now you make your entry. No, you needn't go over there. Come here. Let's suppose you've already come in. Like that, yes! I'm

---

[1] Italian, "Well I'll be damned!"

here with bowed head, modest like. Come on! Out with your voice! Say "Good morning, Miss" in that peculiar tone, that special tone. . . .

THE MANAGER: Excuse me, but are you the Manager, or am I? (*To the* FATHER *who looks undecided and perplexed.*) Get on with it, man! Go down there to the back of the stage. You needn't go off. Then come right forward here.

(*The* FATHER *does as he is told, looking troubled and perplexed at first. But as soon as he begins to move, the reality of the action affects him, and he begins to smile and to be more natural. The* ACTORS *watch intently.*)

THE MANAGER (*sotto voce, quickly to the* PROMPTER *in his box*): Ready! ready! Get ready to write now.

THE FATHER (*coming forward and speaking in a different tone*): Good afternoon, Miss!

THE STEPDAUGHTER (*head bowed down slightly, with restrained disgust*): Good afternoon!

THE FATHER (*looks under her hat which partly covers her face. Perceiving she is very young, he makes an exclamation, partly of surprise, partly of fear lest he compromise himself in a risky adventure*): Ah . . . but . . . ah . . . I say . . . this is not the first time that you have come here, is it?

THE STEPDAUGHTER (*modestly*): No sir.

THE FATHER: You've been here before, eh? (*Then seeing her nod agreement.*) More than once? (*Waits for her to answer, looks under her hat, smiles, and then says:*) Well then, there's no need to be so shy, is there? May I take off your hat?

THE STEPDAUGHTER (*anticipating him and with veiled disgust*): No sir . . . I'll do it myself. (*Takes it off quickly.*)

(*The* MOTHER, *who watches the progress of the scene with the* SON *and the other two children who cling to her, is on thorns; and follows with varying expressions of sorrow, indignation, anxiety, and horror the words and actions of the other two. From time to time she hides her face in her hands and sobs.*)

THE MOTHER: Oh, my God, my God!

THE FATHER (*playing his part with a touch of gallantry*): Give it to me! I'll put it down. (*Takes hat from her hands.*) But a dear little head like yours ought to have a smarter hat. Come and help me choose one from the stock, won't you?

L'INGÉNUE (*interrupting*): I say . . . those are our hats you know.

THE MANAGER (*furious*): Silence! silence! Don't try and be funny, if you please. . . . We're playing the scene now, I'd have you notice. (*To the* STEPDAUGHTER.) Begin again, please!

THE STEPDAUGHTER (*continuing*): No thank you, sir.

THE FATHER: Oh, come now. Don't talk like that. You must take it. I shall be upset if you don't. There are some lovely little hats here; and then — Madame will be pleased. She expects it, anyway, you know.

THE STEPDAUGHTER: No, no! I couldn't wear it!

THE FATHER: Oh, you're thinking about what they'd say at home if they saw you come in with a new hat? My dear girl, there's always a way round these little matters, you know.

THE STEPDAUGHTER (*all keyed up*): No, it's not that. I couldn't wear it because I am . . . as you see . . . you might have noticed . . .

(*Showing her black dress.*)

THE FATHER: . . . in mourning! Of course: I beg your pardon: I'm frightfully sorry. . . .

THE STEPDAUGHTER (*forcing herself to conquer her indignation and nausea*): Stop! Stop! It's I who must thank you. There's no need for you to feel mortified or specially sorry. Don't think any more of what I've said. (*Tries to smile.*) I must forget that I am dressed so. . . .

THE MANAGER (*interrupting and turning to the* PROMPTER: Stop a minute! Stop! Don't write that down. Cut out that last bit. (*Then to the* FATHER *and* STEPDAUGHTER.) Fine! it's going fine! (*To the* FATHER *only.*) And now you can go on as we arranged. (*To the* ACTORS.) Pretty good that scene, where he offers her the hat, eh?

THE STEPDAUGHTER: The best's coming now. Why can't we go on?

THE MANAGER: Have a little patience! (*To the* ACTORS.) Of course, it must be treated rather lightly.

LEADING MAN: Still, with a bit of go in it!

LEADING LADY: Of course! It's easy enough! (*To* LEADING MAN.) Shall you and I try it now?

LEADING MAN: Why, yes! I'll prepare my entrance. (*Exit in order to make his entrance.*)

THE MANAGER (*to* LEADING LADY): See here! The scene between you and Madame Pace is finished. I'll have it written out properly after. You remain here . . . oh, where are you going?

LEADING LADY: One minute. I want to put my hat on again. (*Goes over to hat-rack and puts her hat on her head.*)

THE MANAGER: Good! You stay here with your head bowed down a bit.

THE STEPDAUGHTER: But she isn't dressed in black.

LEADING LADY: But I shall be, and much more effectively than you.

THE MANAGER (*to* STEPDAUGHTER): Be quiet please, and watch! You'll be able to learn something. (*Clapping his hands.*) Come on! come on! Entrance, please!

(*The door at rear of stage opens, and the* LEADING MAN *enters with the lively manner of an old gallant. The rendering of the scene by the* ACTORS *from the very first words is seen to be quite a different thing, though it has not in any way the air of a parody. Naturally, the* STEPDAUGHTER *and the* FATHER, *not being able to recognize themselves in the* LEADING LADY *and the* LEADING MAN, *who deliver their words in different tones and with a different psychology, express, sometimes with smiles, sometimes with gestures, the impression they receive.*)

LEADING MAN: Good afternoon, Miss. . . .

THE FATHER (*at once unable to contain himself*): No!

(*The* STEPDAUGHTER, *noticing the way the* LEADING MAN *enters, bursts out laughing.*)

THE MANAGER (*furious*): Silence! and you please just stop that laughing. If we go on like this, we shall never finish.

THE STEPDAUGHTER: Forgive me, sir, but it's natural enough. This lady (*indicating* LEADING LADY) stands there still; but if she is supposed to be me, I can assure you that if I heard anyone say "Good afternoon" in that manner and in that tone, I should burst out laughing as I did.

THE FATHER: Yes, yes; the manner, the tone. . . .

THE MANAGER: Nonsense! Rubbish! Stand aside and let me see the action.

LEADING MAN: If I've got to represent an old fellow who's coming into a house of an equivocal character. . . .

THE MANAGER: Don't listen to them, for Heaven's sake! Do it again! It goes fine. (*Waiting for the* ACTORS *to begin again*.) Well?

LEADING MAN: Good afternoon, Miss.

LEADING LADY: Good afternoon.

LEADING MAN (*imitating the gesture of the* FATHER *when he looked under the hat, and then expressing quite clearly first satisfaction and then fear*): Ah, but . . . I say . . . this is not the first time that you have come here, is it?

THE MANAGER: Good, but not quite so heavily. Like this. (*Acts himself*.) "This isn't the first time you have come here" . . . (*To* LEADING LADY.) And you say: "No sir."

LEADING LADY: No, sir.

LEADING MAN: You've been here before, more than once.

THE MANAGER: No, no, stop! Let her nod "yes" first. "You've been here before, eh?" (*The* LEADING LADY *lifts up her head slightly and closes her eyes as though in disgust. Then she inclines her head twice*.)

THE STEPDAUGHTER (*unable to contain herself*): Oh my God! (*Puts a hand to her mouth to prevent herself from laughing*.)

THE MANAGER (*turning round*): What's the matter?

THE STEPDAUGHTER: Nothing, nothing!

THE MANAGER (*to* LEADING MAN): Go on!

LEADING MAN: You've been here before, eh? Well then, there's no need to be shy, is there? May I take off your hat?

(*The* LEADING MAN *says this last speech in such a tone and with such gestures that the* STEPDAUGHTER, *though she has her hand to her mouth, cannot keep from laughing*.)

LEADING LADY (*indignant*): I'm not going to stop here to be made a fool of by that woman there.

LEADING MAN: Neither am I! I'm through with it!

THE MANAGER (*shouting to* STEPDAUGHTER): Silence! for once and all, I tell you!

THE STEPDAUGHTER: Forgive me! forgive me!

THE MANAGER: You haven't any manners: that's what it is! You go too far.

THE FATHER (*endeavoring to intervene*): Yes, it's true, but excuse her. . . .

THE MANAGER: Excuse what? It's absolutely disgusting.

THE FATHER: Yes, sir, but believe me, it has such a strange effect when . . .

THE MANAGER: Strange? Why strange? Where is it strange?

THE FATHER: No, Sir; I admire your actors — this gentleman here, this lady; but they are certainly not us!

THE MANAGER: I should hope not. Evidently they cannot be you, if they are actors.

THE FATHER: Just so: actors! Both of them act our parts exceedingly well. But, believe me, it produces quite a different effect on us. They want to be us, but they aren't, all the same.

THE MANAGER: What is it then anyway?

THE FATHER: Something that is . . . that is theirs — and no longer ours . . .

THE MANAGER: But naturally, inevitably. I've told you so already.

THE FATHER: Yes, I understand . . . I understand . . .

THE MANAGER: Well then, let's have no more of it! (*Turning to the* ACTORS.) We'll have the rehearsals by ourselves, afterwards, in the ordinary way. I never could stand rehearsing with the author present. He's never satisfied! (*Turning to* FATHER *and* STEPDAUGHTER.) Come on! Let's get on with it again; and try and see if you can't keep from laughing.

THE STEPDAUGHTER: Oh, I shan't laugh any more. There's a nice little bit coming from me now: you'll see.

THE MANAGER: Well then: when she says "Don't think any more of what I've said, I must forget, etc.," you (*addressing the* FATHER) come in sharp with "I understand"; and then you ask her . . .

THE STEPDAUGHTER (*interrupting*): What?

THE MANAGER: Why she is in mourning.

THE STEPDAUGHTER: Not at all! See here: when I told him that it was useless for me to be thinking about my wearing mourning, do you know how he answered me? "Ah well," he said, "then let's take off this little frock."

THE MANAGER: Great! Just what we want, to make a riot in the theater!

THE STEPDAUGHTER: But it's the truth!

THE MANAGER: What does that matter? Acting is our business here. Truth up to a certain point, but no further.

THE STEPDAUGHTER: What do you want to do then?

THE MANAGER: You'll see, you'll see! Leave it to me.

THE STEPDAUGHTER: No sir! What you want to do is to piece together a little romantic sentimental scene out of my disgust, out of all the reasons, each more cruel and viler than the other, why I am what I am. He is to ask me why I'm in mourning; and I'm to answer with tears in my eyes, that it is just two months since papa died. No sir, no! He's got to say to me, as he did say, "Well, let's take off this little dress at once." And I, with my two months' mourning in my heart, went there behind that screen, and with these fingers tingling with shame . . .

THE MANAGER (*running his hands through his hair*): For Heaven's sake! What are you saying?

THE STEPDAUGHTER (*crying out excitedly*): The truth! The truth!

THE MANAGER: It may be. I don't deny it, and I can understand all your horror; but you must surely see that you can't have this kind of thing on the stage. It won't go.

THE STEPDAUGHTER: Not possible, eh? Very well! I'm much obliged to you — but I'm off.

THE MANAGER: Now be reasonable! Don't lose your temper!

THE STEPDAUGHTER: I won't stop here! I won't! I can see you fixed it all up with him in your office. All this talk about what is possible for the stage . . . I understand! He wants to get at his complicated "cerebral drama," to have his famous remorses and torments acted; but I want to act my part, *my part!*

THE MANAGER (*annoyed, shaking his shoulders*): Ah! Just *your* part! But, if you will pardon me, there are other parts than yours: His (*indicating the* FATHER) and hers (*indicating the* MOTHER)! On the stage you can't have a character becoming too prominent and overshadowing all the others. The thing is to pack them all into a neat little framework and then act what is actable. I am aware of the fact that everyone has his own interior life which he wants very much to put forward. But the difficulty lies in this fact: to set out just so much as is necessary for the stage, taking the other characters into consideration, and at the same time hint at the unrevealed interior life of each. I am willing to admit, my dear young lady, that from your point of view it would be a fine idea if each character could tell the public all his troubles in a nice monologue or a regular one-hour lecture. (*Good humoredly.*) You must restrain yourself, my dear, and in your own interest, too; because this fury of yours, this exaggerated disgust you show, may make a bad impression, you know. After you have confessed to me that there were others before him at Madame Pace's and more than once . . .

THE STEPDAUGHTER (*bowing her head, impressed*): It's true. But remember those others mean him for me all the same.

THE MANAGER (*not understanding*): What? The others? What do you mean?

THE STEPDAUGHTER: For one who has gone wrong, sir, he who was responsible for the first fault is responsible for all that follow. He is responsible for my faults, was, even before I was born. Look at him, and see if it isn't true!

THE MANAGER: Well, well! And does the weight of so much responsibility seem nothing to you? Give him a chance to act it, to get it over!

THE STEPDAUGHTER: How? How can he act all his "noble remorses," all his "moral torments," if you want to spare him the horror of being discovered one day — after he had asked her what he did ask her — in the arms of her, that already fallen woman, that child, sir, that child he used to watch come out of school? (*She is moved.*)

(*The* MOTHER *at this point is overcome with emotion, and breaks out into a fit of crying. All are touched. A long pause.*)

THE STEPDAUGHTER (*as soon as the* MOTHER *becomes a little quieter, adds resolutely and gravely*): At present, we are unknown to the public. Tomorrow, you will act us as you wish, treating us in your own manner. But do you really want to see drama, do you want to see it flash out as it really did?

THE MANAGER: Of course! That's just what I do want, so I can use as much of it as is possible.

THE STEPDAUGHTER: Well then, ask that Mother there to leave us.

THE MOTHER (*changing her low plaint into a sharp cry*): No! No! Don't permit it, sir, don't permit it!

THE MANAGER: But it's only to try it.

THE MOTHER: I can't bear it. I can't.

THE MANAGER: But since it has happened already . . . I don't understand!

THE MOTHER: It's taking place now. It happens all the time. My torment isn't a pretended one. I live and feel every minute of my torture. Those two children there — have you heard them speak? They can't speak any more. They cling to me to keep my torment actual and vivid for me. But for themselves, they do not exist, they aren't any more. And she (*indicating the* STEPDAUGHTER) has run away, she has left me, and is lost. If I now see her here before me, it is only to renew for me the tortures I have suffered for her too.

THE FATHER: The eternal moment! She (*indicating the* STEPDAUGHTER) is here to catch me, fix me, and hold me eternally in the stocks for that one fleeting and shameful moment of my life. She can't give it up! And you, sir, cannot either fairly spare me it.

THE MANAGER: I never said I didn't want to act it. It will form, as a matter of fact, the nucleus of the whole first act right up to her surprise. (*Indicates the* MOTHER.)

THE FATHER: Just so! This is my punishment: the passion in all of us that must culminate in her final cry.

THE STEPDAUGHTER: I can hear it still in my ears. It's driven me mad, that cry! — You can put me on as you like; it doesn't matter. Fully dressed, if you like — provided I have at least the arm bare; because, standing like this (*she goes close to the* FATHER *and leans her head on his breast*) with my head so, and my arms round his neck, I saw a vein pulsing in my arm here; and then, as if that live vein had awakened disgust in me, I closed my eyes like this, and let my head sink on his breast. (*Turning to the* MOTHER.) Cry out, mother! Cry out! (*Buries head in* FATHER's *breast, and with her shoulders raised as if to prevent her hearing the cry, adds in tones of intense emotion:*) Cry out as you did then!

THE MOTHER (*coming forward to separate them*): No! My daughter, my daughter! (*And after having pulled her away from him.*) You brute! you brute! She is my daughter! Don't you see she's my daughter?

THE MANAGER (*walking backwards towards footlights*): Fine! fine! Damned good! And then, of course — curtain!

THE FATHER (*going towards him excitedly*): Yes, of course, because that's the way it really happened.

THE MANAGER (*convinced and pleased*): Oh, yes, no doubt about it. Curtain here, curtain!

(*At the reiterated cry of the* MANAGER, *the* MACHINIST *lets the curtain down, leaving the* MANAGER *and the* FATHER *in front of it before the footlights.*)

THE MANAGER: The darned idiot! I said "curtain" to show the act should end there, and he goes and lets it down in earnest. (*To the* FATHER, *while he pulls the curtain back to go on to the stage again.*) Yes, yes, it's all right. Effect certain! That's the right ending. I'll guarantee the first act at any rate.

ACT III

When the curtain goes up again, it is seen that the STAGE HANDS *have shifted the bit of scenery used in the last part, and have rigged up instead at the back of the stage a drop, with some trees, and one or two wings. A portion of a fountain basin is visible. The* MOTHER *is sitting on the right with the two children by her side. The* SON *is on the same side, but away from the others. He seems bored, angry, and full of shame. The* FATHER *and the* STEPDAUGHTER *are also seated towards the right front. On the other side (left) are the* ACTORS, *much in the positions they occupied before the curtain was lowered. Only the* MANAGER *is standing up in the middle of the stage, with his hand closed over his mouth in the act of meditating.*

THE MANAGER (*shaking his shoulders after a brief pause*): Ah yes: the second act! Leave it to me, leave it all to me as we arranged, and you'll see! It'll go fine!

THE STEPDAUGHTER: Our entry into his house (*indicates* FATHER) in spite of him. . . . (*Indicates the* SON.)

THE MANAGER (*out of patience*): Leave it to me, I tell you!

THE STEPDAUGHTER: Do let it be clear, at any rate, that it is in spite of my wishes.

THE MOTHER (*from her corner, shaking her head*): For all the good that's come of it. . . .

THE STEPDAUGHTER (*turning towards her quickly*): It doesn't matter. The more harm done us, the more remorse for him.

THE MANAGER (*impatiently*): I understand! Good Heavens! I understand! I'm taking it into account.

THE MOTHER (*supplicatingly*): I beg you, sir, to let it appear quite plain that for conscience' sake I did try in every way. . . .

THE STEPDAUGHTER (*interrupting indignantly and continuing for the* MOTHER): . . . to pacify me, to dissuade me from spiting him. (*To* MANAGER.) Do as she wants: satisfy her, because it is true! I enjoy it immensely. Anyhow, as you can see, the meeker she is, the more she tries to get at his heart, the more distant and aloof does he become.

THE MANAGER: Are we going to begin this second act or not?

THE STEPDAUGHTER: I'm not going to talk any more now. But I must tell you this: you can't have the whole action take place in the garden, as you suggest. It isn't possible!

THE MANAGER: Why not?

THE STEPDAUGHTER: Because he (*indicates the* SON *again*) is always shut up alone in his room. And then there's all the part of that poor dazed-looking boy there which takes place indoors.

THE MANAGER: Maybe! On the other hand, you will understand — we can't change scenes three or four times in one act.

THE LEADING MAN: They used to once.

THE MANAGER: Yes, when the public was up to the level of that child there.

THE LEADING LADY: It makes the illusion easier.

THE FATHER (*irritated*): The illusion! For Heaven's sake, don't say illusion. Please don't use that word, which is particularly painful for us.

THE MANAGER (*astounded*): And why, if you please?

THE FATHER: It's painful, cruel, really cruel; and you ought to understand that.

THE MANAGER: But why? What ought we to say then? The illusion, I tell you, sir, which we've got to create for the audience. . . .

THE LEADING MAN: With our acting.

THE MANAGER: The illusion of a reality.

THE FATHER: I understand; but you, perhaps, do not understand us. Forgive me! You see . . . here for you and your actors, the thing is only — and rightly so . . . a kind of game. . . .

THE LEADING LADY (*interrupting indignantly*): A game! We're not children here, if you please! We are serious actors.

THE FATHER: I don't deny it. What I mean is the game, or play, of your art, which has to give, as the gentleman says, a perfect illusion of reality.

THE MANAGER: Precisely — !

THE FATHER: Now, if you consider the fact that we (*indicates himself and the other five* CHARACTERS), as we are, have no other reality outside of this illusion. . . .

THE MANAGER (*astonished, looking at his* ACTORS, *who are also amazed*): And what does that mean?

THE FATHER (*after watching them for a moment with a wan smile*): As I say, sir, that which is a game of art for you is our sole reality. (*Brief pause. He goes a step or two nearer the* MANAGER *and adds:*) But not only for us, you know, by the way. Just you think it over well. (*Looks him in the eyes.*) Can you tell me who you are?

THE MANAGER (*perplexed, half smiling*): What? Who am I? I am myself.

THE FATHER: And if I were to tell you that that isn't true, because you and I . . . ?

THE MANAGER: I should say you were mad — ! (*The* ACTORS *laugh*.)

THE FATHER: You're quite right to laugh: because we are all making believe here. (*To* MANAGER.) And you can therefore object that it's only for a joke that that gentleman there (*indicates the* LEADING MAN), who naturally is himself, has to be me, who am on the contrary myself — this thing you see here. You see I've caught you in a trap! (*The* ACTORS *laugh*.)

THE MANAGER (*annoyed*): But we've had all this over once before. Do you want to begin again?

THE FATHER: No, no! That wasn't my meaning! In fact, I should like to request you to abandon this game of art (*looking at the* LEADING LADY *as if anticipating her*) which you are accustomed to play here with your actors, and to ask you seriously once again: who are you?

THE MANAGER (*astonished and irritated, turning to his* ACTORS): If this fellow here hasn't got a nerve! A man who calls himself a character comes and asks me who I am!

THE FATHER (*with dignity, but not offended*): A character, sir, may always ask a man who he is. Because a character has really a life of his own, marked with his especial characteristics; for which reason he is always "somebody." But a man — I'm not speaking of you now — may very well be "nobody."

THE MANAGER: Yes, but you are asking these questions of me, the boss, the manager! Do you understand?

THE FATHER: But only in order to know if you, as you really are now, see yourself as you once were with all the illusions that were yours then, with all the things both inside and outside of you as they seemed to you — as they were then indeed for you. Well, sir, if you think of all those illusions that mean nothing to you now, of all those things which don't even *seem* to you to exist any more, while once they *were* for you, don't you feel that — I won't say these boards — but the very earth under your feet is sinking away from you when you reflect that in the same way this *you* as you feel it today — all this present reality of yours — is fated to seem a mere illusion to you tomorrow?

THE MANAGER (*without having understood much, but astonished by the specious argument*): Well, well! And where does all this take us anyway?

THE FATHER: Oh, nowhere! It's only to show you that if we (*indicating the* CHARACTERS) have no other reality beyond the illusion, you too must not count overmuch on your reality as you feel it today, since, like that of yesterday, it may prove an illusion for you tomorrow.

THE MANAGER (*determining to make fun of him*): Ah, excellent! Then you'll be saying next that you, with this comedy of yours that you brought here to act, are truer and more real than I am.

THE FATHER (*with the greatest seriousness*): But of course; without doubt!

THE MANAGER: Ah, really?

THE FATHER: Why, I thought you'd understand that from the beginning.

THE MANAGER: More real than I?

THE FATHER: If your reality can change from one day to another. . . .

THE MANAGER: But everyone knows it can change. It is always changing, the same as anyone else's.

THE FATHER (*with a cry*): No, sir, not ours! Look here! That is the very difference! Our reality doesn't change: it can't change! It can't be other than what it is, because it is already fixed for ever. It's terrible. Ours is an immutable reality which should make you shudder when you approach us if you are really conscious of the fact that your reality is a mere transitory and fleeting illusion, taking this form today and that tomorrow, according to the conditions, according to your will, your sentiments, which in turn are controlled by an intellect that shows them to you today in one manner and tomorrow . . . who knows how? . . . Illusions of reality represented in this fatuous comedy of life that never ends, nor can ever end! Because if tomorrow it were to end . . . then why, all would be finished.

THE MANAGER: Oh for God's sake, will you *at least* finish with this philosophizing and let us try and shape this comedy which you yourself have brought me here? You argue and philosophize a bit too much, my dear sir. You know you seem to me almost, almost . . . (*Stops and looks him over from head to foot.*) Ah, by the way, I think you introduced yourself to me as a — what shall . . . we say — a "character," created by an author who did not afterward care to make a drama of his own creations.

THE FATHER: It is the simple truth, sir.

THE MANAGER: Nonsense! Cut that out, please! None of us believes it, because it isn't a thing, as you must recognize yourself, which one can believe seriously. If you want to know, it seems to me you are trying to imitate the manner of a certain author whom I heartily detest — I warn you — although I have unfortunately bound myself to put on one of his works. As a matter of fact, I was just starting to rehearse it, when you arrived. (*Turning to the* ACTORS.) And this is what we've gained — out of the frying-pan into the fire!

THE FATHER: I don't know to what author you may be alluding, but believe me I feel what I think; and I seem to be philosophizing only for those who do not think what they feel, because they blind themselves with their own sentiment. I know that for many people this self-blinding seems much more "human"; but the contrary is really true. For man never reasons so much and becomes so introspective as when he suffers; since he is anxious to get at the cause of his sufferings, to learn who has produced them, and whether it is just or unjust that he should have to bear them. On the other hand, when he is happy, he takes his happiness as it comes and doesn't analyze it, just as if happiness were his right. The animals suffer without reasoning about their sufferings. But take the case of a man who suffers and begins to reason about it. Oh no! it can't be allowed! Let him suffer like an animal, and then — ah yes, he is "human"!

THE MANAGER: Look here! Look here! You're off again, philosophizing worse than ever.

THE FATHER: Because I suffer, sir! I'm not philosophizing: I'm crying aloud the reason of my sufferings.

THE MANAGER (*makes brusque movement as he is taken with a new idea*): I should like to know if anyone has ever heard of a character who gets right out of his part and perorates and speechifies as you do. Have you ever heard of a case? I haven't.

THE FATHER: You have never met such a case, sir, because authors, as a rule, hide the labor of their creations. When the characters are really alive before their author, the latter does nothing but follow them in their action, in other words, in the situations which they suggest to him; and he has to will them the way they will themselves — for there's trouble if he doesn't. When a character is born, he acquires at once such an independence, even of his own author, that he can be imagined by everybody even in many other situations where the author never dreamed of placing him; and so he acquires for himself a meaning which the author never thought of giving him.

THE MANAGER: Yes, yes, I know this.

THE FATHER: What is there then to marvel at in us? Imagine such a misfortune for characters as I have described to you: to be born of an author's fantasy, and be denied life by him; and then answer me if these characters left alive, and yet without life, weren't right in doing what they did do and are doing now, after they have attempted everything in their power to persuade him to give them their stage life. We've all tried him in turn, I, she (*indicating the* STEPDAUGHTER) and she (*indicating the* MOTHER).

THE STEPDAUGHTER: It's true. I too have sought to tempt him, many, many times, when he has been sitting at his writing table, feeling a bit melancholy, at the twilight hour. He would sit in his armchair too lazy to switch on the light, and all the shadows that crept into his room were full of our presence coming to tempt him. (*As if she saw herself still there by the writing table, and was annoyed by the presence of the* ACTORS.) Oh, if you would only go away, go away and leave us alone — mother here with that son of hers — I with that child — that boy there always alone — and then I with him (*just hints at the* FATHER) — and then I alone, alone . . . in those shadows! (*Makes a sudden movement as if in the vision she has of herself illuminating those shadows she wanted to seize hold of herself.*) Ah! my life! my life! Oh, what scenes we proposed to him — and I tempted him more than any of the others!

THE FATHER: Maybe. But perhaps it was your fault that he refused to give us life: because you were too insistent, too troublesome.

THE STEPDAUGHTER: Nonsense! Didn't he make me so himself? (*Goes close to the* MANAGER *to tell him as if in confidence.*) In my opinion he abandoned us in a fit of depression, of disgust for the ordinary theater as the public knows it and likes it.

THE SON: Exactly what it was, sir; exactly that!

THE FATHER: Not at all! Don't believe it for a minute. Listen to me! You'll be doing quite right to modify, as you suggest, the excesses both of this girl here, who wants to do too much, and of this young man, who won't do anything at all.

THE SON: No, nothing!

THE MANAGER: You too get over the mark ocasionally, my dear sir, if I may say so.

THE FATHER: I? When? Where?

THE MANAGER: Always! Continuously! Then there's this insistence of yours in trying to make us believe you are a character. And then too, you must really argue and philosophize less, you know, much less.

THE FATHER: Well, if you want to take away from me the possibility of representing the torment of my spirit which never gives me peace, you will be suppressing me: that's all. Every true man, sir, who is a little above the level of the beasts and plants does not live for the sake of living, without knowing how to live; but he lives so as to give a meaning and a value of his own to life. For me this is *everything*. I cannot give up this, just to represent a mere fact as she (*indicating the* STEPDAUGHTER) wants. It's all very well for her, since her "vendetta" lies in the "fact." I'm not going to do it. It destroys my *raison d'être*.

THE MANAGER: Your *raison d'être*! Oh, we're going ahead fine! First she starts off, and then you jump in. At this rate, we'll never finish.

THE FATHER: Now, don't be offended! Have it your own way — provided, however, that within the limits of the parts you assign us each one's sacrifice isn't too great.

THE MANAGER: You've got to understand that you can't go on arguing at your own pleasure. Drama is action, sir, action and not confounded philosophy.

THE FATHER: All right. I'll do just as much arguing and philosophizing as everybody does when he is considering his own torments.

THE MANAGER: If the drama permits! But for Heaven's sake, man, let's get along and come to the scene.

THE STEPDAUGHTER: It seems to me we've got too much action with our coming into his house. (*Indicating* FATHER.) You said, before, you couldn't change the scene every five minutes.

THE MANAGER: Of course not. What we've got to do is to combine and group up all the facts in one simultaneous, close-knit action. We can't have it as you want, with your little brother wandering like a ghost from room to room, hiding behind doors and meditating a project which — what did you say it did to him?

THE STEPDAUGHTER: Consumes him, sir, wastes him away!

THE MANAGER: Well, it may be. And then at the same time, you want the little girl there to be playing in the garden . . . one in the house, and the other in the garden: isn't that it?

THE STEPDAUGHTER: Yes, in the sun, in the sun! That is my only pleasure: to see her happy and careless in the garden after the misery and squalor of the horrible room where we all four slept together. And I had to sleep with her — I, do you understand? — with my vile contaminated body next to hers; with her folding me fast in her loving little arms. In the garden, whenever she spied me, she would run to take me by the hand. She didn't care for the big flowers, only the little ones; and she loved to show me them and pet me.

THE MANAGER: Well then, we'll have it in the garden. Everything shall happen in the garden; and we'll group the other scenes there. (*Calls a* STAGE HAND.) Here, a backcloth with trees and something to do as a fountain basin. (*Turning round to look at the back of the stage.*) Ah, you've fixed it up. Good! (*To* STEPDAUGHTER.) This is just to give an idea, of course. The Boy, instead of hiding behind the doors, will wander about here in the garden, hiding behind the trees. But it's going to be rather difficult to find a child to do that scene with you where she shows you the flowers. (*Turning to the* BOY.) Come forward a little, will you please? Let's try it now! Come along! come along! (*Then seeing him come shyly forward, full of fear and looking lost.*) It's a nice business, this lad here. What's the matter with him? We'll have to give him a word or two to say. (*Goes close to him, puts a hand on his shoulders, and leads him behind one of the trees.*) Come on! come on! Let me see you a little! Hide here . . . yes, like that. Try and show your head just a little as if you were looking for someone. . . . (*Goes back to observe the effect, when the* BOY *at once goes through the action.*) Excellent! fine! (*Turning to* STEPDAUGHTER.) Suppose the little girl there were to surprise him as he looks round, and run over to himn, so we could give him a word or two to say?

THE STEPDAUGHTER: It's useless to hope he will speak, as long as that fellow there is here. . . . (*Indicates the* SON.) You must send him away first.

THE SON (*jumping up*): Delighted! Delighted! I don't ask for anything better. (*Begins to move away.*)

THE MANAGER (*at once stopping him*): No! No! Where are you going? Wait a bit!

(*The* MOTHER *gets up alarmed and terrified at the thought that he is really about to go away. Instinctively she lifts her arms to prevent him, without, however, leaving her seat.*)

THE SON (*to* MANAGER, *who stops him*): I've got nothing to do with this affair. Let me go, please! Let me go!

THE MANAGER: What do you mean by saying you've got nothing to do with this?

THE STEPDAUGHTER (*calmly, with irony*): Don't bother to stop him: he won't go away.

THE FATHER: He has to act the terrible scene in the garden with his mother.

THE SON (*suddenly resolute and with dignity*): I shall act nothing at all. I've said so from the very beginning. (*To the* MANAGER.) Let me go!

THE STEPDAUGHTER (*going over to the* MANAGER): Allow me? (*Puts down the* MANAGER's *arm which is restraining the* SON.) Well, go away then, if you want to! (*The* SON *looks at her with contempt and hatred. She laughs and says:*) You see, he can't, he can't go away! He is obliged to stay here, indissolubly bound to the chain. If I, who fly off when that happens which has to happen, because I can't bear him — if I am still here and support that face and expression of his, you can well imagine that he is unable to move. He has to remain here, has to stop with that nice father of his, and that mother whose only son he is. (*Turning to the* MOTHER.) Come on, mother, come along! (*Turning to* MANAGER *to indicate her.*) You see, she was getting up to keep him back. (*To the* MOTHER, *beckoning her with her hand.*) Come on! come on! (*Then to* MANAGER.) You can imagine how little she wants to show these actors of yours what she really feels; but so eager is she to get near him that. . . . There, you see? She is willing to act her part. (*And in fact, the* MOTHER *approaches him; and as soon as the* STEPDAUGHTER *has finished speaking, opens her arms to signify that she consents.*)

THE SON (*suddenly*): No! no! If I can't go away, then I'll stop here; but I repeat: I act nothing!

THE FATHER (*to* MANAGER *excitedly*): You can force him, sir.

THE SON: Nobody can force me.

THE FATHER: I can.

THE STEPDAUGHTER: Wait a minute, wait . . . First of all, the baby has to go to the fountain. . . . (*Runs to take the* CHILD *and leads her to the fountain.*)

THE MANAGER: Yes, yes of course; that's it. Both at the same time.

(*The* SECOND LADY LEAD *and the* JUVENILE LEAD *at this point separate themselves from the group of* ACTORS. *One watches the* MOTHER *attentively; the other moves about studying the movements and manner of the* SON *whom he will have to act.*)

THE SON (*to* MANAGER): What do you mean by both at the same time? It isn't right. There was no scene between me and her. (*Indicates the* MOTHER.) Ask her how it was!

THE MOTHER: Yes, it's true. I had come into his room. . . .

THE SON: Into my room, do you understand? Nothing to do with the garden.

THE MANAGER: It doesn't matter. Haven't I told you we've got to group the action?

THE SON (*observing the* JUVENILE LEAD *studying him*): What do you want?

THE JUVENILE LEAD: Nothing! I was just looking at you.

THE SON (*turning towards the* SECOND LADY LEAD): Ah! she's at it too: to re-act her part! (*Indicating the* MOTHER.)

THE MANAGER: Exactly! And it seems to me that you ought to be grateful to them for their interest.

THE SON: Yes, but haven't you yet perceived that it isn't possible to live in front of a mirror which not only freezes us with the image of ourselves, but throws our likeness back at us with a horrible grimace?

THE FATHER: That is true, absolutely true. You must see that.

THE MANAGER (*to* SECOND LADY LEAD *and* JUVENILE LEAD): He's right! Move away from them!

THE SON: Do as you like. I'm out of this!

THE MANAGER: Be quiet, you, will you? And let me hear your mother! (*To* MOTHER.) You were saying you had entered. . . .

THE MOTHER: Yes, into his room, because I couldn't stand it any longer. I went to empty my heart to him of all the anguish that tortures me. . . . But as soon as he saw me come in. . . .

THE SON: Nothing happened! There was no scene. I went away, that's all! I don't care for scenes!

THE MOTHER: It's true, true. That's how it was.

THE MANAGER: Well now, we've got to do this bit between you and him. It's indispensable.

THE MOTHER: I'm ready . . . when you are ready. If you could only find a chance for me to tell him what I feel here in my heart.

THE FATHER (*going to* SON *in a great rage*): You'll do this for your mother, for your mother, do you understand?

THE SON (*quite determined*): I do nothing!

THE FATHER (*taking hold of him and shaking him*): For God's sake, do as I tell you! Don't you hear your mother asking you for a favor? Haven't you even got the guts to be a son?

THE SON (*taking hold of the* FATHER): No! No! And for God's sake stop it, or else. . . . (*General agitation. The* MOTHER *frightened, tries to separate them*).

THE MOTHER (*pleading*): Please! please!

THE FATHER (*not leaving hold of the* SON): You've got to obey, do you hear?

THE SON (*almost crying from rage*): What does it mean, this madness you've got? (*They separate.*) Have you no decency, that you insist on showing everyone our shame? I won't do it! I won't! And I stand for the will of our author in this. He didn't want to put us on the stage, after all!

THE MANAGER: Man alive! You came here . . .

THE SON (*indicating* FATHER): He did! I didn't!

THE MANAGER: Aren't you here now?

THE SON: It was his wish, and he dragged us along with him. He's told you not only the things that did happen, but also things that have never happened at all.

THE MANAGER: Well, tell me then what did happen. You went out of your room without saying a word?

THE SON: Without a word, so as to avoid a scene!

THE MANAGER: And then what did you do?

THE SON: Nothing . . . walking in the garden. . . . (*Hesitates for a moment with expression of gloom.*)

THE MANAGER (*coming closer to him, interested by his extraordinary reserve*): Well, well . . . walking in the garden. . . .

THE SON (*exasperated*): Why on earth do you insist? It's horrible!

(*The* MOTHER *trembles, sobs, and looks towards the fountain.*)

THE MANAGER (*slowly observing the glance and turning towards the* SON *with increasing apprehension*): The baby?

THE SON: There in the fountain. . . .

THE FATHER (*pointing with tender pity to the* MOTHER): She was following him at the moment. . . .

THE MANAGER (*to the* SON *anxiously*): And then you. . . .

THE SON: I ran over to her; I was jumping in to drag her out when I saw something that froze my blood . . . the boy standing stock still, with eyes like a madman's, watching his little drowned sister, in the fountain! (*The* STEPDAUGHTER *bends over the fountain to hide the* CHILD. *She sobs.*) Then. . . . (*A revolver shot rings out behind the trees where the* BOY *is hidden.*)

THE MOTHER (*with a cry of terror runs over in that direction together with several of the* ACTORS *amid general confusion*): My son! My son! (*Then amid the cries and exclamations one hears her voice.*) Help! Help!

THE MANAGER (*pushing the* ACTORS *aside while they lift up the* BOY *and carry him off*): Is he really wounded?

SOME ACTORS: He's dead! dead!

OTHER ACTORS: No, no, it's only make-believe, it's only pretense!

THE FATHER (*with a terrible cry*): Pretense? Reality, sir, reality!

THE MANAGER: Pretense? Reality? To hell with it all! Never in my life has such a thing happened to me. I've lost a whole day over these people, a whole day!

AFTERWORD

Six Characters in Search of an Author (1921) remains in the memory as the image of the real-life theater of illusionism invaded by the "fantastic reality" of imaginative truth. Pirandello, perhaps as thinking a playwright as there ever was, subordinates philosophy to drama — the action of the six characters usurping the stage. In that action is the secret of the play's success as a play of ideas. We are looking at reflections in facing mirrors. The eye is lost, the mind reels, in the infinitely reciprocal vistas of play and reality, actors and characters, illusion and truth. Is there water in the fountain in which the little girl drowns at the end? If there is, the Manager's stage is no longer itself but the real-life garden, and he and his company are intruders into the family's tragedy, their theatrical art irrelevant to the child's real death. If there isn't, how does the child drown?

As a radical questioning of dramatic art, *Six Characters* must be just about the most subversive play ever written. It does what no play, in any convention of the theater, is supposed to do: present characters who belong neither to a world of fictional reality (like Oedipus and Hamlet and Nora Helmer) nor to the professional world of the theater (like the Manager and Brecht's Singer) but to a limbo where the distinction between drama-as-imitation and the reality it imitates disappears. The illusion cre-

ated by a character who comes on stage and announces that he is a character in a play defies definition, but we can at least single out a moment in
the play when Pirandello's method is in sharp focus. It is the scene in Act
II in which the Father and the Stepdaughter, "characters" both, observe
themselves being impersonated by the Leading Man and the Leading Lady
and find that performance all wrong. The implied lesson seems to be that a
human identity is unique and inviolable and that the whole theatrical enterprise is based on the fallacy that it is not. No actor can ever in a meaningful sense *become* the character he is acting. Pirandello here takes realism beyond realism, but exactly where he takes it *to* is an open question.
And yet, in the very act of querying the validity of the art he is practicing,
Pirandello creates compelling drama. The brilliance of his whole play is its
containment of all its riddles and paradoxes within the single image of the
invaded theater.

Not surprisingly, *Six Characters* has been provocative and controversial
ever since its first appearance. Though it established Pirandello's fame,
there were some, then as now, whom it irritated as a scoreless cerebral
game. Others, friendly or hostile, saw in it only a new way of presenting
the old middle-class domestic tragedy of past guilt and present anguish —
Ibsen with a gimmick. Such views appear inadequate to explain the fact
that *Six Characters* has been one of the most seminal plays of our time. In
America it has influenced such theatricalist pieces as O'Neill's *Great God
Brown* and *Marco Millions*, Thornton Wilder's *Our Town*, and Tennessee
Williams's *Glass Menagerie*. It has anticipated much of the mood and manner of today's "absurd" drama. It has been partly responsible for the current scorn of straightforward realism in the theater as unimaginative and
old-fashioned photographism.

But its family connections run backward, too, for even the avant-garde
has a way of slipping into place in the continuum of our dramatic tradition.
The play-within-the-play device is traditional. The play's form has been
partly suggested by that of the sixteenth- and seventeenth-century Italian
commedia dell' arte, a playful, earthy drama of dialogue improvisation with
stock characters, situations, and plots. Like expressionistic drama *Six Characters* shatters the surface of experience without abandoning the fragments
in pursuit of symbol and myth. Its immediate historical context was the
"grotesque" theater movement in Italy during and immediately after World
War I, whose leader was Luigi Chiarelli and the aim and method of which
was to mock and shock conventional sensibilities and institutions while
proclaiming universal meaninglessness. But most significant of all is the
play's relationship to the serious naturalistic drama of the previous generation.

That drama — Ibsenism and Chekhovianism rather than Ibsen's and
Chekhov's own plays — stimulated Pirandello into revolutionizing dramatic form, but he did not simply react against it. He applied to it a new
viewpoint. In a sense, what *Six Characters in Search of an Author* does is

putting on trial the reality the nineteenth century had taken for granted: the reality of positivist science, matter in motion governed by discoverable, stable laws. It does not bring in a verdict of guilt; Pirandello's thought and art are both too subtle for that. It gives a vote of no confidence. In an important preface to the play, which he wrote in 1925, Pirandello contrasts playwrights to whom it is "enough to present a man or a woman and what is special and characteristic about them simply for the pleasure of present-ing them" with those "others, who, beyond such pleasure, feel a more pro-found spiritual need on whose account they admit only figures, affairs, landscapes which have been soaked, so to speak, in a particular sense of life and acquire from it a universal value." Among these latter, "philosophi-cal," writers he includes himself. His plays suggest that the concatenation of scene, event, and character that constitutes theme or mood within the realistic convention of scenic and psychological plausibility yielded no "particular sense of life" for him. Just as Strindberg's expressionistic cham-ber plays today seem more contemporary with our own sense of life than his historical and his naturalistic plays, so is the peculiar quality of Piran-dello's modernity precisely his disaffection with the realistic theater of the first generation of modern masters. The particular sense of life that ani-mates *Six Characters* derives from Pirandello's use of the theater itself to challenge the reality his predecessors had made it their artistic end to re-cord as honestly as possible. It is as if he were telling the popular, commer-cial, Ibsenite theater of his time, "You say you want 'real life' on stage. All right, here are my six characters, bringing you their reality. Let's see how you handle it." The theater company's subsequent failure is a satirical vin-dication of Pirandello's own philosophical approach to drama.

Making playwriting conscious of itself as medium has been Pirandello's most important original contribution to modern drama. Ever since, we have been getting plays of double vision: not just (to paraphrase Francis Fergusson) the stage seen as real-life parlor, but the real-life parlor seen as stage — a shifting and multiple stage at that. It is not Pirandello's fault that much of this drama has been mere toying with cleverness. Rather, the number of imitations suggests that the theatricalist convention invites and sometimes allows expression of a reality particularly meaningful to an age haunted by disaster, space, and relativity.

Conventional analysis of the structure of *Six Characters* distinguishes three levels of action. First is the "inner" action about the bourgeois family suffering the consequences of past sexual guilt, the Father's guilt and the Mother's shame interacting with the Stepdaughter's desire for revenge. It is the kind of somber, realistic, retrospective psychological drama Ibsen used to revolutionize the nineteenth-century theater. Second is the conflict be-tween the six characters and the Manager and his company, resolved in a grotesque climax of melodrama, a kind of tragic farce, which suggests the inability of the "realistic" theater to deal with psychological realism. This is the satiric-esthetic level of the play, discussed earlier. Third is the metaphysical or existential level of meaning, carried mainly by the discussions between the Father and the Manager about the relationship between art and life, illusion and reality, and the status in the general scheme of things of someone who is "born" a character in a play. Madame Pace's unexpected appearance in Act II also involves these issues: Independent of her author, she turns up when the situation requires her presence. Of these three levels of action (the last a drama of ideas), the last two, the esthetics and the metaphysics, account for the uniqueness of Pirandello's play and make it a problem play — different in the nature of its "problem" from Ibsen's *A Doll's House* but every bit as complex and teasingly open-ended.

When the Manager, at the end of the play, complains that he has "lost a whole day," his sentiment strikes us as ironic, because our view is more inclusive than his. It is Pirandello's theatricalism that provides that more inclusive view. The Manager is interested in the play the six characters bring him only as long as he senses a hit. At the end he abandons them to the strange limbo in which their author left them. But *we* see that the aborted play-within is not the whole play. The burden of the whole is the tension and interplay between the framing and the framed action — not the family agony, but the family agony *seeking expression in the theater.* Hence, "A Comedy in the Making." The plot that unites the six characters — the web of jealousy, shame, scorn, guilt, rage, and inarticulate, childish sorrow, the demonstration that good intentions may have evil consequences — all this is neither comic nor in the making. The tragedy is rather that the script is finished and can never be changed. But the Manager's effort to reduce raw suffering to a play *is* comic, because it offers the incongruous spectacle of the irascible, confident, bustlingly effective man of the theater being defeated by a play more real, in the Platonic sense, than reality itself. Since the core of the larger play is here, the point will bear illustration.

The curtain that falls at the end of Act II falls simultaneously in two distinct plays and, falling, brings them together without reconciling them. The crude matter-of-factness of the physical stage and its personnel dispels the purer reality of the family torment. Theatrical expedience, "effective drama," interrupts the characters' "eternal moment" of agony, the terrible scene in Madame Pace's shop that is a debased version of the recognition scene in older tragedy (recognition of identity bringing about recognition of unwitting guilt in an incestuous situation). The ironies proliferate as one ponders the scene. Beings who have no life except as characters in a play are betrayed by heavy-handed theatrical technique. The Manager does not believe in the reality only his craft can bestow. He loses his temper with an underling who is only trying to translate the projected play into theatrical actuality (itself a concept of ironic paradox). The psychological and moral realities of the inner play suddenly accommodate box office demands for a thrilling act climax, with the result that everything comes to a screeching halt. Where does reality end and art begin? The characters rehearse their reality, while the real-life troupe distorts it into an actable play and finally closes the curtain on both. We witness simultaneously a play about a rehearsal and one about a husband who ceded his wife to her lover with dreadful consequences for husband, wife, lover, and both sets of children. Clearly, there is a sense in which the rehearsal of *Mixing It Up* (there is such a play, Pirandello wrote it in 1918) has not been interrupted at all! The end impression is fireworks rather than incandescence.

But the bewildering doubt, the teasing skepticism, is the play's metaphysical point. The image of the invaded theater is a dramatization of relativism. And the built-in paradox of philosophical relativism is that any assertion of its validity necessarily forgoes all claim to being considered absolutely valid. For to hold that the statement "Everything is relative" is true is also to hold that no truth is absolute, including the assertion of relativity itself. This, of course, is a sophism, and people who don't like to be made dizzy by sophisms don't like Pirandello. What they fail to see is the disturbing truth of the drama of relativity: It is humanity's doom to live with and in the metaphysical uncertainty. The passion (as distinct from the intellectualism) of a Pirandello play is our cry of protest against this condition: perched on the sharp edge of paradox.

What is more, the metaphysical sophism has an esthetic counterpart. To consider it we must begin with a point of ethics. As ethics, the play implies a radical doctrine of human irresponsibility. For if identity is discontinuous, as the Father insists, no one is accountable for his or her past. The Father refuses to be judged by the degrading moment in the dress shop, because the visitor to Madame Pace's establishment was not his "true" self. In fact, he has no true self; there is no such thing. Art (ethics becoming esthetics), says the Father, is permanence, but life is ceaseless change. It is his misfortune that as "character," a figure of literary art, he has been arrested in a single, disgraceful moment. The sordid assignation, the child in the fountain — these are forever. And like the figures on Keats's Grecian urn, only grimly so, these too do "tease us out of thought / As doth eternity." But if, as "character," the Father can rightly claim to be "less real perhaps, but truer" than the Manager and everyone else in the empirical, non-art reality of change, it follows — and this is the sophism — that the truth of art necessarily falsifies life, for when flux freezes as "eternal moment" it is no longer flux. The very essence of experience forever eludes art.

And so *Six Characters in Search of an Author* may be said to embody also the artist's unresolvable dilemma. The primary dramatic conflict between company and characters, invaded and invader, is a fable of artistic creation, with the Manager as a kind of semicomical middle man, resentful, interested, again resentful, a mocking but painful self-portrait of the author haunted by shapes he can neither give life to nor exorcise.

A statement in Pirandello's preface to the play pinpoints the startlingly original perception that was the seed from which his play grew. For a long time he tried to but couldn't find the right form for a play about the six characters who, uninvited, had taken over his imagination. Finally he abandoned them. But then, later, he found that he could, after all, "accept them" — but "accept them only as rejected." "All that lives," says Pirandello in the preface, "by the fact of living, has a form, and by the same token must die — except the work of art which lives forever in so far as it *is* form." Again paradox. His play, according to his own account, grew out of his futile search for a form for the six characters of his imagination. He made living art out of his inability to do so.

Eugene O'Neill

AH, WILDERNESS!

FOREWORD

Although the American colonies declared their freedom from Great Britain in 1776, theatrical independence took considerably longer to achieve. For the greater part of the nineteenth century, British influences still dominated the American stage. British plays, or imitations of them, filled the repertories. Gilbert and Sullivan, for example, were enormous favorites, and their works, in pirated versions, played to packed houses. Visiting British star actors toured the country and rivaled Americans on their home ground; even today, Broadway is still highly receptive to British imports. Plays by native authors, dealing with indigenous subject matter, were curiously slow to appear. Even shattering national events like the Civil War inspired relatively little drama. Native influence was most readily apparent in comedy — in the emergence of the "Yankee" character, for instance, as a hardheaded, homespun philosopher, or in a spate of plays finding comedic material in whatever wave of immigrants happened to be in the news at the moment. By the early twentieth century, however, this picture had begun to change, with the emergence of a number of dramatists of stature who were seriously concerned with discussing on stage American life and values. O'Neill's generation of writers — H. L. Mencken and Sinclair Lewis among them, off the stage — wrote with irritated affection of the American way of life, critical of its mercantile smugness and nouveau-riche pomposity. O'Neill's work has achieved international renown largely from the power infused into his writing by his own brooding melancholy, and his near-tragic studies that speak with an autobiographical veracity. *Ah, Wilderness!* (1933) is an exception, an O'Neill play written in a light-hearted mood.

CHARACTERS

NAT MILLER, owner of the *Evening Globe*

ESSIE, his wife

ARTHUR
RICHARD
MILDRED } their children
TOMMY

SID DAVIS, Essie's brother

LILY MILLER, Nat's sister

DAVID McCOMBER

MURIEL McCOMBER, his daughter

WINT SELBY, a classmate of Arthur's at Yale

BELLE

NORAH

BARTENDER

SALESMAN

SCENES

ACT I

Sitting-room of the MILLER *home in a large small-town in Connecticut — early morning, July 4th, 1906.*

ACT II

Dining-room of the MILLER *home — evening of the same day.*

ACT III

Scene 1 — Back room of a bar in a small hotel — 10 o'clock the same night.

Scene 2 — Same as Act I — the sitting-room of the MILLER *home —
a little after 11 o'clock the same night.*

ACT IV

Scene 1 — The MILLER *sitting-room again — about 1 o'clock
the following afternoon.*
Scene 2 — A strip of beach along the harbor — about 9 o'clock that night.
*Scene 3 — Same as Scene 1 — the sitting-room — about 10 o'clock
the same night.*

ACT I

Scene — Sitting-room of the MILLER *home in a large small-town in Connecticut — about 7:30 in the morning of July 4th, 1906.*

The room is fairly large, homely looking and cheerful in the morning sunlight, furnished with scrupulous medium-priced tastelessness of the period. Beneath the two windows at left, front, a sofa with silk and satin cushions stands against the wall. At rear of sofa, a bookcase with glass doors, filled with cheap sets, extends along the remaining length of wall. In the rear wall, left, is a double doorway with sliding doors and portières, leading into a dark, windowless, back parlor. At right of this doorway, another bookcase, this time a small, open one, crammed with boys' and girls' books and the best-selling novels of many past years — books the family really have read. To the right of this bookcase is the mate of the double doorway at its left, with sliding doors and portières, this one leading to a well-lighted front parlor. In the right wall, rear, a screen door opens on a porch. Farther forward in this wall are two windows, with a writing desk and a chair between them. At center is a big, round table with a green-shaded reading lamp, the cord of the lamp running up to one of five sockets in the chandelier above. Five chairs are grouped about the table — three rockers at left, right, and right rear of it, two armchairs at rear and left rear. A medium-priced, inoffensive rug covers most of the floor. The walls are papered white with a cheerful, ugly blue design.

Voices are heard in a conversational tone from the dining-room beyond the back parlor, where the family are just finishing breakfast. Then MRS. MILLER'S *voice, raised commandingly, "Tommy! Come back here and finish your milk!" At the same moment* TOMMY *appears in the doorway from the back parlor — a chubby, sun-burnt boy of eleven with dark eyes, blond hair wetted and plastered down in a part, and a shiny, good-natured face, a rim of milk visible about his lips. Bursting with bottled-up energy and a longing to get started on the Fourth, he nevertheless has hesitated obediently at his mother's call.*

TOMMY (*calls back pleadingly*): Aw, I'm full, Ma. And I said excuse me and you said all right. (*His* FATHER'S *voice is heard speaking to his mother. Then she calls:* "All right, Tommy," *and* TOMMY *asks eagerly.*) Can I go out now?
MOTHER'S VOICE (*correctingly*): May I!
TOMMY (*fidgeting, but obediently*): May I, Ma?
MOTHER'S VOICE: Yes. (TOMMY *jumps for the screen door to the porch at right like a sprinter released by the starting shot.*)

FATHER'S VOICE (*shouts after him*): But you set off your crackers away from the house, remember! (*But* TOMMY *is already through the screen door, which he leaves open behind him.*)

(*A moment later the family appear from the back parlor, coming from the dining-room. First are* MILDRED *and* ARTHUR. MILDRED *is fifteen, tall and slender, with big, irregular features, resembling her father to the complete effacing of any pretense at prettiness. But her big, gray eyes are beautiful; she has vivacity and a fetching smile, and everyone thinks of her as an attractive girl. She is dressed in shirtwaist and skirt in the fashion of the period.*

ARTHUR, *the eldest of the Miller children who are still living home, is nineteen. He is tall, heavy, barrel-chested and muscular, the type of football linesman of that period, with a square, stolid face, small blue eyes and thick sandy hair. His manner is solemnly collegiate. He is dressed in the latest college fashion of that day, which has receded a bit from the extreme of preceding years, but still runs to padded shoulders and pants half pegged at the top, and so small at their wide-cuffed bottoms that they cannot be taken off with shoes on.*)

MILDRED (*as they appear — inquisitively*): Where are you going today, Art?

ARTHUR (*with superior dignity*): That's my business. (*He ostentatiously takes from his pocket a tobacco pouch with a big Y and class numerals stamped on it, and a heavy bulldog briar pipe with silver Y and numerals, and starts filling the pipe.*)

MILDRED (*teasingly*): Bet I know, just the same! Want me to tell you her initials? E.R.!

(*She laughs.* ARTHUR, *pleased by this insinuation at his lady-killing activities, yet finds it beneath his dignity to reply. He goes to the table, lights his pipe and picks up the local morning paper, and slouches back into the armchair at left rear of table, beginning to whistle "Oh, Waltz Me Around Again, Willie" as he scans the headlines.* MILDRED *sits on the sofa at left, front.*

Meanwhile, *their mother and their* AUNT LILY, *their father's sister, have appeared, following them from the back parlor.* MRS. MILLER *is around fifty, a short, stout woman with fading light-brown hair sprinkled with gray, who must have been decidedly pretty as a girl in a round-faced, cute, small-featured, wide-eyed fashion. She has big brown eyes, soft and maternal — a bustling, mother-of-a-family manner. She is dressed in shirtwaist and skirt.*

LILY MILLER, *her sister-in-law, is forty-two, tall, dark and thin. She conforms outwardly to the conventional type of old-maid school teacher, even to wearing glasses. But behind the glasses her gray eyes are gentle and tired, and her whole atmosphere is one of shy kindliness. Her voice presents the greatest contrast to her appearance — soft and full of sweetness. She, also, is dressed in a shirtwaist and skirt.*)

MRS. MILLER (*as they appear*): Getting milk down him is like — (*Suddenly she is aware of the screen door standing half open.*) Goodness, look at that door he's left open! The house will be alive with flies! (*Rushing out to shut it.*) I've told him again and again — and that's all the good it does! It's just a waste of breath. (*She slams the door shut.*)

LILY (*smiling*): Well, you can't expect a boy to remember to shut doors — on the Fourth of July. (*She goes diffidently to the straight-backed chair before the desk at right, front, leaving the comfortable chairs to the others.*)

MRS. MILLER: That's you all over, Lily — always making excuses for him. You'll have him spoiled to death in spite of me. (*She sinks in rocker at right of table.*) Phew, I'm hot, aren't you? This is going to be a scorcher. (*She picks up a magazine from the table and begins to rock, fanning herself.*)

(*Meanwhile, her husband and her brother have appeared from the back parlor, both smoking cigars. NAT MILLER is in his late fifties, a tall, dark, spare man, a little stoop-shouldered, more than a little bald, dressed with an awkward attempt at sober respectability imposed upon an innate heedlessness of clothes. His long face has large, irregular, undistinguished features, but he has fine, shrewd, humorous gray eyes.*)

(SID DAVIS, *his brother-in-law, is forty-five, short and fat, bald-headed, with the Puckish face of a Peck's Bad Boy who has never grown up. He is dressed in what had once been a very natty loud light suit but is now a shapeless and faded nondescript in cut and color.*)

SID (*as they appear*): Oh, I like the job first rate, Nat. Waterbury's a nifty old town with the lid off, when you get to know the ropes. I rang in a joke in one of my stories that tickled the folks there pink. Waterwagon — Waterbury — Waterloo!

MILLER (*grinning*): Darn good!

SID (*pleased*): I thought it was pretty fair myself. (*Goes on a bit ruefully, as if oppressed by a secret sorrow.*) Yes, you can see life in Waterbury, all right — that is, if you're looking for life in Waterbury!

MRS. MILLER: What's that about Waterbury, Sid?

SID: I was saying it's all right in its way — but there's no place like home. (*As if to punctuate this remark, there begins a series of bangs from just beyond the porch outside, as TOMMY inaugurates his celebration by setting off a package of firecrackers. The assembled family jump in their chairs.*)

MRS. MILLER: That boy! (*She rushes to the screen door and out on the porch, calling.*) Tommy! You mind what your Pa told you! You take your crackers out in the back yard, you hear me!

ARTHUR (*frowning scornfully*): Fresh kid! He did it on purpose to scare us.

MILLER (*grinning through his annoyance*): Darned youngster! He'll have the house afire before the day's out.

SID (*grins and sings*):

> "Dunno what ter call 'im
> But he's mighty like a Rose — velt."

(*They all laugh.*)

LILY: Sid, you Crazy! (SID *beams at her.* MRS. MILLER *comes back from the porch, still fuming.*)

MRS. MILLER: Well, I've made him go out back at last. Now we'll have a little peace. (*As if to contradict this, the bang of firecrackers and torpedoes begins from the rear of the house, left, and continues at intervals throughout the scene, not nearly so loud as the first explosion, but sufficiently emphatic to form a disturbing punctuation to the conversation.*)

MILLER: Well, what's on the tappee for all of you today? Sid, you're coming to the Sachem Club picnic with me, of course.

SID (*a bit embarrassedly*): You bet. I mean I'd like to, Nat — that is, if —

MRS. MILLER (*regarding her brother with smiling suspicion*): Hmm! I know what that Sachem Club picnic's always meant!

LILY (*breaks in in a forced joking tone that conceals a deep earnestness*): No, not this time, Essie. Sid's a reformed character since he's been on the paper in Waterbury. At least, that's what he swore to me last night.

SID (*avoiding her eyes, humiliated — joking it off*): Pure as the driven snow, that's me. They're running me for president of the W.C.T.U. (*They all laugh.*)

MRS. MILLER: Sid, you're a caution. You turn everything into a joke. But you be careful, you hear? We're going to have dinner in the evening tonight, you know — the best shore dinner you ever tasted and I don't want you coming home — well, not able to appreciate it.

LILY: Oh, I know he'll be careful today. Won't you, Sid?

SID (*more embarrassed than ever — joking it off melodramatically*): Lily, I swear to you if any man offers me a drink, I'll kill him — that is, if he changes his mind! (*They all laugh except* LILY, *who bites her lip and stiffens.*)

MRS. MILLER: No use talking to him, Lily. You ought to know better by this time. We can only hope for the best.

MILLER: Now, you women stop picking on Sid. It's the Fourth of July and even a downtrodden newspaperman has a right to enjoy himself when he's on his holiday.

MRS. MILLER: I wasn't thinking only of Sid.

MILLER (*with a wink at the others*): What, are you insinuating I ever — ?

MRS. MILLER: Well, to do you justice, no, not what you'd really call — But I've known you to come back from this darned Sachem Club picnic — Well, I didn't need any little bird to whisper that you'd been some place besides to the well! (*She smiles good-naturedly.* MILLER *chuckles.*)

SID (*after a furtive glance at the stiff and silent* LILY — *changes the subject abruptly by turning to* ARTHUR): How are you spending the festive Fourth, Boola-Boola? (ARTHUR *stiffens dignifiedly.*)

MILDRED (*teasingly*): I can tell you, if he won't.

MRS. MILLER (*smiling*): Off to the Rands', I suppose.

ARTHUR (*with dignity*): I and Bert Turner are taking Elsie and Ethel Rand canoeing. We're going to have a picnic lunch on Strawberry Island. And this evening I'm staying at the Rands' for dinner.

MILLER: You're accounted for, then. How about you, Mid?

MILDRED: I'm going to the beach to Anne Culver's.

ARTHUR (*sarcastically*): Of course, there won't be any boys present! Johnny Dodd, for example?

MILDRED (*giggles — then with a coquettish toss of her head*): Pooh! What do I care for him? He's not the only pebble on the beach.

MILLER: Stop your everlasting teasing, you two. How about you and Lily, Essie?

MRS. MILLER: I don't know. I haven't made any plans. Have you, Lily?

LILY (*quietly*): No. Anything you want to do.

MRS. MILLER: Well, I thought we'd just sit around and rest and talk.

MILLER: You can gossip any day. This is the Fourth. Now, I've got a better suggestion than that. What do you say to an automobile ride? I'll get out the Buick and we'll drive around town and out to the lighthouse and back. Then Sid and I will let you off here, or anywhere you say, and we'll go on to the picnic.

MRS. MILLER: I'd love it. Wouldn't you, Lily?

LILY: It would be nice.

MILLER: Then, that's all settled.

SID (*embarrassedly*): Lily, want to come with me to the fireworks display at the beach tonight?

MRS. MILLER: That's right, Sid. You take her out. Poor Lily never has any fun, always sitting home with me.

LILY (*flustered and grateful*): I — I'd like to, Sid, thank you. (*Then an apprehensive look comes over her face.*) Only not if you come home — you know.

SID (*again embarrassed and humiliated — again joking it off, solemnly*): Evil-minded, I'm afraid, Nat. I hate to say it of your sister. (*They all laugh. Even* LILY *cannot suppress a smile.*)

ARTHUR (*with heavy jocularity*): Listen, Uncle Sid. Don't let me catch you and Aunt Lily spooning on a bench tonight — or it'll be my duty to call a cop! (SID *and* LILY *both look painfully embarrassed at this, and the joke falls flat, except for* MILDRED *who can't restrain a giggle at the thought of these two ancients spooning.*)

MRS. MILLER (*rebukingly*): Arthur!

MILLER (*dryly*): That'll do you. Your education in kicking a football around Yale seems to have blunted your sense of humor.

MRS. MILLER (*suddenly — startledly*): But where's Richard? We're forgetting all about him. Why, where is that boy? I thought he came in with us from breakfast.

MILDRED: I'll bet he's off somewhere writing a poem to Muriel McComber, the silly! Or pretending to write one. I think he just copies ——

ARTHUR (*looking back toward the dining-room*): He's still in the dining-room, reading a book. (*Turning back — scornfully.*) Gosh, he's always reading now. It's not my idea of having a good time in vacation.

MILLER (*caustically*): He read his school books, too, strange as that may seem to you. That's why he came out top of his class. I'm hoping before you leave New Haven they'll find time to teach you reading is a good habit.

MRS. MILLER (*sharply*): That reminds me, Nat. I've been meaning to speak to you about those awful books Richard is reading. You've got to give him a good talking to — (*She gets up from her chair.*) I'll go up and get them right now. I found them where he'd hid them on the shelf in his wardrobe. You just wait till you see what — (*She bustles off, rear right, through the front parlor.*)

MILLER (*plainly not relishing whatever is coming — to* SID, *grumblingly*): Seems to me she might wait until the Fourth is over before bringing up — (*Then with a grin*) I know there's nothing to it, anyway. When I think of the books I used to sneak off and read when I was a kid.

SID: Me, too. I suppose Dick is deep in Nick Carter or Old Cap Collier.

MILLER: No, he passed that period long ago. Poetry's his red meat nowadays, I think — love poetry — and socialism, too, I suspect, from some dire declarations he's made. (*Then briskly.*) Well, might as well get him on the carpet. (*He calls.*) Richard. (*No answer — louder.*) Richard. (*No answer — then in a bellow.*) Richard!

ARTHUR (*shouting*): Hey, Dick, wake up! Pa's calling you.

RICHARD'S VOICE (*from the dining-room*): All right. I'm coming.

MILLER: Darn him! When he gets his nose in a book, the house could fall down and he'd never ——

(RICHARD *appears in the doorway from the back parlor, the book he has been reading in one hand, a finger marking his place. He looks a bit startled still, reluctantly called back to earth from another world.*

*He is going on seventeen, just out of high school. In appearance he is a
perfect blend of father and mother, so much so that each is convinced he is the
image of the other. He has his mother's light-brown hair, his father's gray eyes;
his features are neither large nor small; he is of medium height, neither fat nor
thin. One would not call him a handsome boy; neither is he homely. But he is
definitely different from both of his parents, too. There is something of extreme
sensitiveness added — a restless, apprehensive, defiant, shy, dreamy, self-conscious intelligence about him. In manner he is alternately plain simple boy and
a posey actor solemnly playing a role. He is dressed in prep. school reflection of
the college style of* ARTHUR.)

RICHARD: Did you want me, Pa?

MILLER: I'd hoped I'd made that plain. Come and sit down a while. (*He points to
the rocking chair at the right of table near his.*)

RICHARD (*coming forward — seizing on the opportunity to play up his preoccupation
— with apologetic superiority*): I didn't hear you, Pa. I was off in another world.
(MILDRED *slyly shoves her foot out so that he trips over it, almost falling. She
laughs gleefully. So does* ARTHUR.)

ARTHUR: Good for you, Mid! That'll wake him up!

RICHARD (*grins sheepishly — all boy now*): Darn you, Mid! I'll show you! (*He pushes
her back on the sofa and tickles her with his free hand, still holding the book in the
other. She shrieks.*)

ARTHUR: Give it to her, Dick!

MILLER: That's enough, now. No more roughhouse. You sit down here, Richard.
(RICHARD *obediently takes the chair at right of table, opposite his father.*) What
were you planning to do with yourself today? Going out to the beach with
Mildred?

RICHARD (*scornfully superior*): That silly skirt party! I should say not!

MILDRED: He's not coming because Muriel isn't. I'll bet he's got a date with her
somewheres.

RICHARD (*flushing bashfully*): You shut up! (*Then to his father.*) I thought I'd just
stay home, Pa — this morning, anyway.

MILLER: Help Tommy set off firecrackers, eh?

RICHARD (*drawing himself up — with dignity*): I should say not. (*Then frowning
portentously.*) I don't believe in this silly celebrating the Fourth of July — all this
lying talk about liberty — when there is no liberty!

MILLER (*a twinkle in his eye*): Hmm.

RICHARD (*getting warmed up*): The land of the free and the home of the brave!
Home of the slave is what they ought to call it — the wage slave ground under
the heel of the capitalist class, starving, crying for bread for his children, and all
he gets is a stone! The Fourth of July is a stupid farce!

MILLER (*putting a hand to his mouth to conceal a grin*): Hmm. Them are mighty
strong words. You'd better not repeat such sentiments outside the bosom of the
family or they'll have you in jail.

SID: And throw away the key.

RICHARD (*darkly*): Let them put me in jail. But how about the freedom of speech in
the Constitution, then? That must be a farce, too. (*Then he adds grimly.*) No,
you can celebrate your Fourth of July. I'll celebrate the day the people bring out
the guillotine again and I see Pierpont Morgan being driven by in a tumbril! (*His*

father and SID *are greatly amused;* LILY *is shocked but, taking her cue from them, smiles.* MILDRED *stares at him in puzzled wonderment, never having heard this particular line before. Only* ARTHUR *betrays the outraged reaction of a patriot.*)

ARTHUR: Aw say, you fresh kid, tie that bull outside! You ought to get a punch in the nose for talking that way on the Fourth!

MILLER (*solemnly*): Son, if I didn't know it was you talking, I'd think we had Emma Goldman with us.

ARTHUR: Never mind, Pa. Wait till we get him down to Yale. We'll take that out of him!

RICHARD (*with high scorn*): Oh, Yale! You think there's nothing in the world besides Yale. After all, what is Yale?

ARTHUR: You'll find out what!

SID (*provocatively*): Don't let them scare you, Dick. Give 'em hell!

LILY (*shocked*): Sid! You shouldn't swear before —

RICHARD: What do you think I am, Aunt Lily — a baby? I've heard worse than anything Uncle Sid says.

MILDRED: And said worse himself, I bet!

MILLER (*with a comic air of resignation*): Well, Richard, I've always found I've had to listen to at least one stump speech every Fourth. I only hope getting your extra strong one right after breakfast will let me off for the rest of the day. (*They all laugh now, taking this as a cue.*)

RICHARD (*somberly*): That's right, laugh! After you, the deluge, you think! But look out! Supposing it comes before? Why shouldn't the workers of the world unite and rise? They have nothing to lose but their chains! (*He recites threateningly.*) "The days grow hot, O Babylon! 'Tis cool beneath thy willow trees!"

MILLER: Hmm. That's good. But where's the connection, exactly? Something from that book you're reading?

RICHARD (*superior*): No. That's poetry. This is prose.

MILLER: I've heard there was a difference between 'em. What is the book?

RICHARD (*importantly*): Carlyle's French Revolution.

MILLER: Hmm. So that's where you drove the tumbril from and piled poor old Pierpont in it. (*Then seriously.*) Glad you're reading it, Richard. It's a darn fine book.

RICHARD (*with unflattering astonishment*): What, have you read it?

MILLER: Well, you see, even a newspaper owner can't get out of reading a book every now and again.

RICHARD (*abashed*): I — I didn't mean — I know you — (*Then enthusiastically.*) Say, isn't it a great book, though — that part about Mirabeau — and about Marat and Robespierre —

MRS. MILLER (*appears from the front parlor in a great state of flushed annoyance*): Never you mind Robespierre, young man! You tell me this minute where you've hidden those books! They were on the shelf in your wardrobe and now you've gone and hid them somewheres else. You go right up and bring them to your father! (RICHARD, *for a second, looks suddenly guilty and crushed. Then he bristles defensively.*)

MILLER (*after a quick understanding glance at him*): Never mind his getting them now. We'll waste the whole morning over those darned books. And anyway, he has a right to keep his library to himself — that is, if they're not too — What books are they, Richard?

RICHARD (*self-consciously*): Well — there's —

MRS. MILLER: I'll tell you, if he won't — and you give him a good talking to. (*Then, after a glance at Richard, mollifiedly.*) Not that I blame Richard. There must be some boy he knows who's trying to show off as advanced and wicked, and he told him about —

RICHARD: No! I read about them myself, in the papers and in other books.

MRS. MILLER: Well, no matter how, there they were on his shelf. Two by that awful Oscar Wilde they put in jail for heaven knows what wickedness.

ARTHUR (*suddenly — solemnly authoritative*): He committed bigamy. (*Then as* SID *smothers a burst of ribald laughter.*) What are you laughing at? I guess I ought to know. A fellow at college told me. His father was in England when this Wilde was pinched — and he said he remembered once his mother asked his father about it and he told her he's committed bigamy.

MILLER (*hiding a smile behind his hand*): Well then, that must be right, Arthur.

MRS. MILLER: I wouldn't put it past him, nor anything else. One book was called the Picture of something or other.

RICHARD: The Picture of Dorian Gray. It's one of the greatest novels ever written!

MRS. MILLER: Looked to me like cheap trash. And the second book was poetry. The Ballad of I forget what.

RICHARD: The Ballad of Reading Gaol, one of the greatest poems ever written. (*He pronounces it Reading Goal [as in goalpost].*)

MRS. MILLER: All about someone who murdered his wife and got hung, as he richly deserved, as far as I could make out. And then there were two books by that Bernard Shaw —

RICHARD: The greatest playwright alive today!

MRS. MILLER: To hear him tell it, maybe! You know, Nat, the one who wrote a play about — well, never mind — that was so vile they wouldn't even let it play in New York!

MILLER: Hmm. I remember.

MRS. MILLER: One was a book of his plays and the other had a long title I couldn't make head or tail of, only it wasn't a play.

RICHARD (*proudly*): The Quintessence of Ibsenism.

MILDRED: Phew! Good gracious, what a name! What does it mean, Dick? I'll bet he doesn't know.

RICHARD (*outraged*): I do, too, know! It's about Ibsen, the greatest playwright since Shakespeare!

MRS. MILLER: Yes, there was a book of plays by that Ibsen there, too! And poems by Swin something —

RICHARD: Poems and Ballads by Swinburne, Ma. The greatest poet since Shelley! He tells the truth about real love!

MRS. MILLER: Love! Well, all I can say is, from reading here and there, that if he wasn't flung in jail along with Wilde, he should have been. Some of the things I simply couldn't read, they were so indecent — All about — well, I can't tell you before Lily and Mildred.

SID (*with a wink at* RICHARD — *jokingly*): Remember, I'm next on that one, Dick. I feel the need of a little poetical education.

LILY (*scandalized, but laughing*): Sid! Aren't you ashamed?

MRS. MILLER: This is no laughing matter. And then there was Kipling — but I suppose he's not so bad. And last there was a poem — a long one — the Rubay — What is it, Richard?

RICHARD: The Rubaiyat of Omar Khayyam. That's the best of all!

MILLER: Oh, I've read that, Essie — got a copy down at the office.

SID (*enthusiastically*): So have I. It's a pippin!

LILY (*with shy excitement*): I — I've read it, too — at the library. I like — some parts of it.

MRS. MILLER (*scandalized*): Why, Lily!

MILLER: Everybody's reading that now, Essie — and it don't seem to do them any harm. There's fine things in it, seems to me — true things.

MRS. MILLER (*a bit bewildered and uncertain now*): Why, Nat, I don't see how you — It looked terrible blasphemous — parts I read.

SID: Remember this one: (*He quotes rhetorically*) "Oh Thou, who didst with pitfall and gin beset the path I was to wander in — " Now, I've always noticed how beset my path was with gin — in the past, you understand! (*He casts a joking side glance at* LILY. *The others laugh. But* LILY *is in a melancholy dream and hasn't heard him.*)

MRS. MILLER (*tartly, but evidently suppressing her usual smile where he is concerned*): You would pick out the ones with liquor in them!

LILY (*suddenly — with a sad pathos, quotes awkwardly and shyly*): I like — because it's true:

> "The Moving Finger writes, and having writ,
> Moves on: nor all your Piety nor Wit
> Shall lure it back to cancel half a Line,
> Nor all your Tears wash out a Word of it."

MRS. MILLER (*astonished, as are all the others*): Why, Lily, I never knew you to recite poetry before!

LILY (*immediately guilty and apologetic*): I — it just stuck in my memory somehow.

RICHARD (*looking at her as if he had never seen her before*): Good for you, Aunt Lily! (*Then enthusiastically.*) But that isn't the best. The best is:

> "A Book of Verses underneath the Bough,
> A Jug of Wine, A Loaf of Bread — and Thou
> Beside me singing in the Wilderness — "

ARTHUR (*who, bored to death by all this poetry quoting, has wandered over to the window at rear of desk, right*): Hey! Look who's coming up the walk — Old Man McComber!

MILLER (*irritably*): Dave? Now what in thunder does that damned old — Sid, I can see where we never are going to get to that picnic.

MRS. MILLER (*vexatiously*): He'll know we're in this early, too. No use lying. (*Then appalled by another thought.*) That Norah — she's that thick, she never can answer the front door right unless I tell her each time. Nat, you've got to talk to Dave. I'll have her show him in here. Lily, you run up the back stairs and get your things on. I'll be up in a second. Nat, you get rid of him the first second you can! Whatever can the old fool want — (*She and* LILY *hurry out through the back parlor.*)

ARTHUR: I'm going to beat it — just time to catch the eight-twenty trolley.

MILDRED: I've got to catch that, too. Wait till I get my hat, Art! (*She rushes into the back parlor.*)

ARTHUR (*shouts after her*): I can't wait. You can catch up with me if you hurry. (*He turns at the back-parlor door — with a grin.*) McComber may be coming to see if your intentions toward his daughter are dishonorable, Dick! You'd better beat it while your shoes are good! (*He disappears through the back-parlor door, laughing.*)

RICHARD (*a bit shaken, but putting on a brave front*): Think I'm scared of him?

MILLER (*gazing at him — frowning*): Can't imagine what — But it's to complain about something, I know that. I only wish I didn't have to be pleasant with the old buzzard — but he's about the most valuable advertiser I've got.

SID (*sympathetically*): I know. But tell him to go to hell, anyway. He needs that ad more than you.

(*The sound of the bell comes from the rear of the house, off left from back parlor.*)

MILLER: There he is. You clear out, Dick — but come right back as soon as he's gone, you hear? I'm not through with you, yet.

RICHARD: Yes, Pa.

MILLER: You better clear out, too, Sid. You know Dave doesn't approve jokes.

SID: And loves me like poison! Come on, Dick, we'll go out and help Tommy celebrate. (*He takes* RICHARD's *arm and they also disappear through the back-parlor door.* MILLER *glances through the front parlor toward the front door, then calls in a tone of strained heartiness.*)

MILLER: Hello, Dave. Come right in here. What good wind blows you around on this glorious Fourth?

(*A flat, brittle voice answers him:* "Good morning," *and a moment later* DAVID MCCOMBER *appears in the doorway from the front parlor. He is a thin, dried-up little man with a head too large for his body perched on a scrawny neck, and a long solemn horse face with deep-set little black eyes, a blunt formless nose and a tiny slit of a mouth. He is about the same age as* MILLER *but is entirely bald, and looks ten years older. He is dressed with a prim neatness in shiny old black clothes.*)

MILLER: Here, sit down and make yourself comfortable. (*Holding out the cigar box.*) Have a cigar?

MCCOMBER (*sitting down in the chair at the right of table — acidly*): You're forgetting. I never smoke.

MILLER (*forcing a laugh at himself*): That's so. So I was. Well, I'll smoke alone then. (*He bites off the end of the cigar viciously, as if he wished it were* MCCOMBER's *head, and sits down opposite him.*)

MCCOMBER: You asked me what brings me here, so I'll come to the point at once. I regret to say it's something disagreeable — disgraceful would be nearer the truth — and it concerns your son, Richard!

MILLER (*beginning to bristle — but calmly*): Oh, come now, Dave, I'm sure Richard hasn't —

MCCOMBER (*sharply*): And I'm positive he has. You're not accusing me of being a liar, I hope.

MILLER: No one said anything about liar. I only meant you're surely mistaken if you think —

MCCOMBER: I'm not mistaken. I have proof of everything in his own handwriting!

MILLER (*sharply*): Let's get down to brass tacks. Just what is it you're charging him with?

MCCOMBER: With being dissolute and blasphemous — with deliberately attempting to corrupt the morals of my young daughter, Muriel.

MILLER: Then I'm afraid I will have to call you a liar, Dave!

MCCOMBER (*without taking offense — in the same flat, brittle voice*): I thought you'd get around to that, so I brought some of the proofs with me. I've a lot more of 'em at home. (*He takes a wallet from his inside coat pocket, selects five or six slips of paper, and holds them out to* MILLER.) These are good samples of the rest. My wife discovered them in one of Muriel's bureau drawers hidden under the underwear. They're all in his handwriting, you can't deny it. Anyway, Muriel's confessed to me he wrote them. You read them and then say I'm a liar. (MILLER *has taken the slips and is reading them frowningly.* MCCOMBER *talks on.*) Evidently you've been too busy to take the right care about Richard's bringing up or what he's allowed to read — though I can't see why his mother failed in her duty. But that's your misfortune, and none of my business. But Muriel is my business and I can't and I won't have her innocence exposed to the contamination of a young man whose mind, judging from his choice of reading matter, is as foul —

MILLER (*making a tremendous effort to control his temper*): Why, you damned old fool! Can't you see Richard's only a fool kid who's just at the stage when he's out to rebel against all authority, and so he grabs at everything radical to read and wants to pass it on to his elders and his girl and boy friends to show off what a young hellion he is! Why, at heart you'd find Richard is just as innocent and as big a kid as Muriel is! (*He pushes the slips of paper across the table contemptuously.*) This stuff doesn't mean anything to me — that is, nothing of what you think it means. If you believe this would corrupt Muriel, then you must believe she's easily corrupted! But I'll bet you'd find she knows a lot more about life than you give her credit for — and can guess a stork didn't bring her down your chimney!

MCCOMBER: Now you're insulting my daughter. I won't forget that.

MILLER: I'm not insulting her. I think Muriel is a darn nice girl. That's why I'm giving her credit for ordinary good sense. I'd say the same about my own Mildred, who's the same age.

MCCOMBER: I know nothing about your Mildred except that she's known all over as a flirt. (*Then more sharply.*) Well, I knew you'd prove obstinate, but I certainly never dreamed you'd have the impudence, after reading those papers, to claim your son was innocent of all wrongdoing!

MILLER: And what did you dream I'd do?

MCCOMBER: Do what it's your plain duty to do as a citizen to protect other people's children! Take and give him a hiding he'd remember to the last day of his life! You'd ought to do it for his sake, if you had any sense — unless you want him to end up in jail!

MILLER (*his fists clenched, leans across the table*): Dave, I've stood all I can stand from you! You get out! And get out quick, if you don't want a kick in the rear to help you!

MCCOMBER (*again in his flat, brittle voice, slowly getting to his feet*): You needn't lose your temper. I'm only demanding you do your duty by your own as I've already done by mine. I'm punishing Muriel. She's not to be allowed out of the house for a month and she's to be in bed every night by eight sharp. And yet she's blameless, compared to that —

MILLER: I said I'd had enough out of you, Dave! (*He makes a threatening movement.*)

MCCOMBER: You needn't lay hands on me. I'm going. But there's one thing more. (*He takes a letter from his wallet.*) Here's a letter from Muriel for your son. (*Puts it on the table.*) It makes clear, I think, how she's come to think about him, now that her eyes have been opened. I hope he heeds what's inside — for his own good and yours — because if I ever catch him hanging about my place again I'll have him arrested! And don't think I'm not going to make you regret the insults you've heaped on me. I'm taking the advertisement for my store out of your paper — and it won't go in again, I tell you, not unless you apologize in writing and promise to punish —

MILLER: I'll see you in hell first! As for your damned old ad, take it out and go to hell!

MCCOMBER: That's plain bluff. You know how badly you need it. So do I. (*He starts stiffly for the door.*)

MILLER: Here! Listen a minute! I'm just going to call *your* bluff and tell you that, whether you want to reconsider your decision or not, I'm going to refuse to print your damned ad after tomorrow! Put that in your pipe and smoke it! Furthermore, I'll start a campaign to encourage outside capital to open a dry-goods store in opposition to you that won't be the public swindle I can prove yours is!

MCCOMBER (*a bit shaken by this threat — but in the same flat tone*): I'll sue you for libel.

MILLER: When I get through, there won't be a person in town will buy a dishrag in your place!

MCCOMBER (*more shaken, his eyes shifting about furtively*): That's all bluff. You wouldn't dare — (*Then finally he says uncertainly.*) Well, good day. (*And turns and goes out. NAT stands looking after him. Slowly the anger drains from his face and leaves him looking a bit sick and disgusted. SID appears from the back parlor. He is nursing a burn on his right hand, but his face is one broad grin of satisfaction.*)

SID: I burned my hand with one of Tommy's damned firecrackers and came in to get some vaseline. I was listening to the last of your scrap. Good for you, Nat! You sure gave him hell!

MILLER (*dully*): Much good it'll do. He knows it was all talk.

SID: That's just what he don't know, Nat. The old skinflint has a guilty conscience.

MILLER: Well, anyone who knows me knows I wouldn't use my paper for a dirty, spiteful trick like that — no matter what he did to me.

SID: Yes, everyone knows you're an old sucker, Nat, too decent for your own good. But McComber never saw you like this before. I tell you you scared the pants off him. (*He chuckles.*)

MILLER (*still dejectedly*): I don't know what made me let go like that. The hell of skunks like McComber is that after being with them ten minutes you become as big skunks as they are.

SID (*notices the slips of paper on the table*): What's this? Something he brought? (*He picks them up and starts to read.*)

MILLER (*grimly*): Samples of the new freedom — from those books Essie found — that Richard's been passing on to Muriel to educate her. They're what started the rumpus. (*Then frowning.*) I've got to do something about that young anarchist or he'll be getting me, and himself, in a peck of trouble. (*Then pathetically helpless.*) But what can I do? Putting the curb bit on would make him worse. Then he'd have a harsh tyrant to defy. He'd love that, darn him!

SID (*has been reading the slips, a broad grin on his face — suddenly he whistles*): Phew! This is a warm lulu for fair! (*He recites with a joking intensity.*)

> "My life is bitter with thy love; thine eyes
> Blind me, thy tresses burn me, thy sharp sighs
> Divide my flesh and spirit with soft sound — "

MILLER (*with a grim smile*): Hmm. I missed that one. That must be Mr. Swinburne's copy. I've never read him, but I've heard something like that was the matter with him.

SID: Yes, it's labelled Swinburne — "Anactoria." Whatever that is. But wait, watch and listen! The worst is yet to come! (*He recites with added comic intensity.*)

> "That I could drink thy veins as wine, and eat
> Thy breasts like honey, that from face to feet
> Thy body were abolished and consumed,
> And in my flesh thy very flesh entombed!"

MILLER (*an irrepressible boyish grin coming to his face*): Hell and hallelujah! Just picture old Dave digesting that for the first time! Gosh, I'd give a lot to have seen his face! (*Then a trace of shocked reproof showing in his voice.*) But it's no joking matter. That stuff *is* warm — too damned warm, if you ask me! I don't like this a damned bit, Sid. That's no kind of thing to be sending a decent girl. (*More worriedly.*) I thought he was really stuck on her — as one gets stuck on a decent girl at his age — all moonshine and holding hands and a kiss now and again. But this looks — I wonder if he is hanging around her to see what he can get? (*Angrily.*) By God, if that's true, he deserves that licking McComber says it's my duty to give him! I've got to draw the line somewhere!

SID: Yes, it won't do to have him getting any decent girl in trouble.

MILLER: The only thing I can do is put it up to him straight. (*With pride.*) Richard'll stand up to his guns, no matter what. I've never known him to lie to me.

SID (*at a noise from the back parlor, looks that way — in a whisper*): Then now's your chance. I'll beat it and leave you alone — see if the women folks are ready upstairs. We ought to get started soon — if we're ever going to make that picnic. (*He is halfway to the entrance to the front parlor as* RICHARD *enters from the back parlor, very evidently nervous about* MCCOMBER'S *call.*)

RICHARD (*adopting a forced, innocent tone*): How's your hand, Uncle Sid?

SID: All right, Dick, thanks — only hurts a little. (*He disappears.* MILLER *watches his son frowningly.* RICHARD *gives him a quick side glance and grows more guiltily self-conscious.*)

RICHARD (*forcing a snicker*): Gee, Pa, Uncle Sid's a bigger kid than Tommy is. He was throwing firecrackers in the air and catching them on the back of his hand and throwing 'em off again just before they went off — and one came and he wasn't quick enough, and it went off almost on top of —

MILLER: Never mind that. I've got something else to talk to you about besides firecrackers.

RICHARD (*apprehensively*): What, Pa?

MILLER (*suddenly puts both hands on his shoulders — quietly*): Look here, Son. I'm going to ask you a question, and I want an honest answer. I warn you beforehand if the answer is "yes" I'm going to punish you and punish you hard because you'll have done something no boy of mine ought to do. But you've never lied to me before, I know, and I don't believe, even to save yourself punishment, you'd lie to me now, would you?

RICHARD (*impressed — with dignity*): I won't lie, Pa.

MILLER: Have you been trying to have something to do with Muriel — something you shouldn't — you know what I mean.

RICHARD (*stares at him for a moment, as if he couldn't comprehend — then, as he does, a look of shocked indignation comes over his face*): No! What do you think I am, Pa? I never would! She's not that kind! Why, I — I love her! I'm going to marry her — after I get out of college! She's said she would! We're engaged!

MILLER (*with great relief*): All right. That's all I wanted to know. We won't talk any more about it. (*He gives him an approving pat on the back.*)

RICHARD: I don't see how you could think — Did that old idiot McComber say that about me?

MILLER (*joking now*): Shouldn't call your future father-in-law names, should you? 'Taint respectful. (*Then after a glance at* RICHARD's *indignant face — points to the slips of paper on the table.*) Well, you can't exactly blame old Dave, can you, when you read through that literature you wished on his innocent daughter?

RICHARD (*sees the slips for the first time and is overcome by embarrassment, which he immediately tries to cover up with a superior carelessness*): Oh, so that's why. He found those, did he? I told her to be careful — Well, it'll do him good to read the truth about life for once and get rid of his old-fogy ideas.

MILLER: I'm afraid I've got to agree with him, though, that they're hardly fit reading for a young girl. (*Then with subtle flattery.*) They're all well enough, in their way, for you who're a man, but — Think it over, and see if you don't agree with me.

RICHARD (*embarrassedly*): Aw, I only did it because I liked them — and I wanted her to face life as it is. She's so darned afraid of life — afraid of her Old Man — afraid of people saying this or that about her — afraid of being in love — afraid of everything. She's even afraid to let me kiss her. I thought, maybe, reading those things — they're beautiful, aren't they, Pa? — I thought they would give her the spunk to lead her own life, and not be — always thinking of being afraid.

MILLER: I see. Well, I'm afraid she's still afraid. (*He takes the letter from the table.*) Here's a letter from her he said to give you. (RICHARD *takes the letter from him uncertainly, his expression changing to one of apprehension.* MILLER *adds with a kindly smile.*) You better be prepared for a bit of a blow. But never mind. There's lots of other fish in the sea. (RICHARD *is not listening to him, but staring at the letter with a sort of fascinated dread.* MILLER *looks into his son's face a second, then turns away, troubled and embarrassed.*) Darn it! I better go upstairs and get rigged out or I never will get to that picnic. (*He moves awkwardly and self-consciously off through the front parlor.* RICHARD *continues to stare at the letter for a moment — then girds up his courage and tears it open and begins to read swiftly. As he reads his face grows more and more wounded and tragic, until at the end his mouth draws down at the corners, as if he were about to break into tears. With an effort he forces them back and his face grows flushed with humiliation and wronged anger.*)

RICHARD (*blurts out to himself*): The little coward! I hate her! She can't treat me like that! I'll show her! (*At the sound of voices from the front parlor, he quickly shoves the letter into the inside pocket of his coat and does his best to appear calm and indifferent, even attempting to whistle "Waiting at the Church." But the whistle peters out miserably as his mother,* LILY *and* SID *enter from the front parlor. They*

*are dressed in all the elaborate paraphernalia of motoring at that period — linen
dusters, veils, goggles,* SID *in a snappy cap.*)

MRS. MILLER: Well, we're about ready to start at last, thank goodness! Let's hope no
more callers are on the way. What did that McComber want, Richard, do you
know? Sid couldn't tell us.

RICHARD: You can search me. Ask Pa.

MRS. MILLER (*immediately sensing something "down" in his manner — going to
him worriedly*): Why, whatever's the matter with you, Richard? You sound as if
you'd lost your last friend! What is it?

RICHARD (*desperately*): I — I don't feel so well — my stomach's sick.

MRS. MILLER (*immediately all sympathy — smoothing his hair back from his forehead*): You poor boy! What a shame — on the Fourth, too, of all days! (*Turning
to the others.*) Maybe I better stay home with him, if he's sick.

LILY: Yes, I'll stay, too.

RICHARD (*more desperately*): No! You go, Ma! I'm not really sick. I'll be all right.
You go. I want to be alone! (*Then, as a louder bang comes from in back as* TOMMY
sets off a cannon cracker, he jumps to his feet.) Darn Tommy and his darned
firecrackers! You can't get any peace in this house with that darned kid around!
Darn the Fourth of July, anyway! I wish we still belonged to England! (*He strides
off in an indignant fury of misery through the front parlor.*)

MRS. MILLER (*stares after him worriedly — then sighs philosophically*): Well, I guess
he can't be so very sick — after that. (*She shakes her head.*) He's a queer boy.
Sometimes I can't make head or tail of him.

MILLER (*calls from the front door beyond the back parlor*): Come along, folks. Let's
get started.

SID: We're coming, Nat. (*He and the two women move off through the front parlor.*)

CURTAIN

ACT II

Scene — Dining-room of the MILLER *home — a little after 6 o'clock in the evening of the same day.*

    *The room is much too small for the medium-priced, formidable dining-room
set, especially now when all the leaves of the table are in. At left, toward rear, is
a double doorway with sliding doors and portières leading into the back parlor.
In the rear wall, left, is the door to the pantry. At the right of door is the china
closet with its display of the family cut glass and fancy china. In the right wall
are two windows looking out on a side lawn. In front of the windows is a heavy,
ugly sideboard with three pieces of old silver on its top. In the left wall, extreme
front, is a screen door opening on a side porch. A dark rug covers most of the
floor. The table, with a chair at each end, left and right, three chairs on the far
side, facing front, and two on the near side, their backs to front, takes up most
of the available space. The walls are papered in a somber brown and dark-red
design.*

    MRS. MILLER *is supervising and helping the Second Girl,* NORAH, *in the set-
ting of the table.* NORAH *is a clumsy, heavy-handed, heavy-footed, long-jawed,
beamingly good-natured young Irish girl — a "greenhorn."*

MRS. MILLER: I really think you better put on the lights, Norah. It's getting so cloudy out, and this pesky room is so dark, anyway.

NORAH: Yes, Mum. (*She stretches awkwardly over the table to reach the chandelier that is suspended from the middle of the ceiling and manages to turn one light on — scornfully.*) Arrah, the contraption!

MRS. MILLER (*worriedly*): Careful!

NORAH: Careful as can be, Mum. (*But in moving around to reach the next bulb she jars heavily against the table.*)

MRS. MILLER: There! I knew it! I do wish you'd watch — !

NORAH (*a flustered appeal in her voice*): Arrah, what have I done wrong now?

MRS. MILLER (*draws a deep breath — then sighs helplessly*): Oh, nothing. Never mind the rest of the lights. You might as well go out in the kitchen and wait until I ring.

NORAH (*relieved and cheerful again*): Yes, Mum. (*She starts for the pantry.*)

MRS. MILLER: But there's one thing — (NORAH *turns apprehensively.*) No, two things — things I've told you over and over, but you always forget. Don't pass the plates on the wrong side at dinner tonight, and do be careful not to let that pantry door slam behind you. Now you will try to remember, won't you?

NORAH: Yes, Mum. (*She goes into the pantry and shuts the door behind her with exaggerated care as* MRS. MILLER *watches her apprehensively.* MRS. MILLER *sighs and reaches up with difficulty and turns on another of the four lights in the chandelier. As she is doing so,* LILY *enters from the back parlor.*)

LILY: Here, let me do that, Essie. I'm taller. You'll only strain yourself. (*She quickly lights the other two bulbs.*)

MRS. MILLER (*gratefully*): Thank you, Lily. It's a stretch for me, I'm getting so fat.

LILY: But where's Norah? Why didn't she — ?

MRS. MILLER (*exasperatedly*): Oh, that girl! Don't talk about her! She'll be the death of me! She's that thick, you honestly wouldn't believe it possible.

LILY (*smiling*): Why, what did she do now?

MRS. MILLER: Oh, nothing. She means all right.

LILY: Anything else I can do, Essie?

MRS. MILLER: Well, she's got the table all wrong. We'll have to reset it. But you're always helping me. It isn't fair to ask you — in your vacation. You need your rest after teaching a pack of wild Indians of kids all year.

LILY (*beginning to help with the table*): You know I love to help. It makes me feel I'm some use in this house instead of just sponging —

MRS. MILLER (*indignantly*): Sponging! You pay, don't you?

LILY: Almost nothing. And you and Nat only take that little to make me feel better about living with you. (*Forcing a smile.*) I don't see how you stand me — having a cranky old maid around all the time.

MRS. MILLER: What nonsense you talk! As if Nat and I weren't only too tickled to death to have you! Lily Miller, I've no patience with you when you go on like that. We've been over this a thousand times before, and still you go on! Crazy, that's what it is! (*She changes the subject abruptly.*) What time's it getting to be?

LILY (*looking at her watch*): Quarter past six.

MRS. MILLER: I do hope those men folks aren't going to be late for dinner. (*She sighs.*) But I suppose with that darned Sachem Club picnic it's more likely than not. (LILY *looks worried, and sighs.* MRS. MILLER *gives her a quick side glance.*) I see you've got your new dress on.

LILY (*embarrassedly*): Yes, I thought — if Sid's taking me to the fireworks — I ought to spruce up a little.

MRS. MILLER (*looking away*): Hmm. (*A pause — then she says with an effort to be casual.*) You mustn't mind if Sid comes home feeling a bit — gay. I expect Nat to — and we'll have to listen to all those old stories of his about when he was a boy. You know what those picnics are, and Sid'd be running into all his old friends.

LILY (*agitatedly*): I don't think he will — this time — not after his promise.

MRS. MILLER (*avoiding looking at her*): I know. But men are weak. (*Then quickly.*) That was a good notion of Nat's, getting Sid the job on the Waterbury *Standard*. All he ever needed was to get away from the rut he was in here. He's the kind that's the victim of his friends. He's easily led — but there's no real harm in him, you know that. (LILY *keeps silent, her eyes downcast.* MRS. MILLER *goes on meaningly.*) He's making good money in Waterbury, too — thirty-five a week. He's in a better position to get married than he ever was.

LILY (*stiffly*): Well, I hope he finds a woman who's willing — though after he's through with his betting on horse races, and dice, and playing Kelly pool, there won't be much left for a wife — even if there was nothing else he spent his money on.

MRS. MILLER: Oh, he'd give up all that — for the right woman. (*Suddenly she comes directly to the point.*) Lily, why don't you change your mind and marry Sid and reform him? You love him and always have —

LILY (*stiffly*): I can't love a man who drinks.

MRS. MILLER: You can't fool me. I know darned well you love him. And he loves you and always has.

LILY: Never enough to stop drinking for. (*Cutting off* MRS. MILLER's *reply.*) No, it's no good in your talking, Essie. We've been over this a thousand times before and I'll always feel the same as long as Sid's the same. If he gave me proof he'd — but even then I don't believe I could. It's sixteen years since I broke off our engagement, but what made me break it off is as clear to me today as it was then. It was what he'd be liable to do now to anyone who married him — his taking up with bad women.

MRS. MILLER (*protests half-heartedly*): But he's always sworn he got raked into that party and never had anything to do with those harlots.

LILY: Well, I don't believe him — didn't then and don't now. I do believe he didn't deliberately plan to, but — Oh, it's no good talking, Essie. What's done is done. But you know how much I like Sid — in spite of everything. I know he was just born to be what he is — irresponsible, never meaning to harm but harming in spite of himself. But don't talk to me about marrying him — because I never could.

MRS. MILLER (*angrily*): He's a dumb fool — a stupid dumb fool, that's what he is!

LILY (*quietly*): No. He's just Sid.

MRS. MILLER: It's a shame for you — a measly shame — you that would have made such a wonderful wife for any man — that ought to have your own home and children!

LILY (*winces but puts her arm around her affectionately — gently*): Now don't you go feeling sorry for me. I won't have that. Here I am, thanks to your and Nat's kindness, with the best home in the world; and as for the children, I feel the same love for yours as if they were mine, and I didn't have the pain of bearing them. And then there are all the boys and girls I teach every year. I like to feel

I'm a sort of second mother to them and helping them to grow up to be good men and women. So I don't feel such a useless old maid, after all.

MRS. MILLER (*kisses her impulsively — her voice husky*): You're a good woman, Lily — too good for the rest of us. (*She turns away, wiping a tear furtively — then abruptly changing the subject.*) Good gracious, if I'm not forgetting one of the most important things! I've got to warn that Tommy against giving me away to Nat about the fish. He knows, because I had to send him to market for it, and he's liable to burst out laughing —

LILY: Laughing about what?

MRS. MILLER (*guiltily*): Well, I've never told you, because it seemed sort of a sneaking trick, but you know how Nat carries on about not being able to eat bluefish.

LILY: I know he says there's a certain oil in it that poisons him.

MRS. MILLER (*chuckling*): Poisons him, nothing! He's been eating bluefish for years — only I tell him each time it's weakfish. We're having it tonight — and I've got to warn that young imp to keep his face straight.

LILY (*laughing*): Aren't you ashamed, Essie!

MRS. MILLER: Not much, I'm not! I like bluefish! (*She laughs.*) Where is Tommy? In the sitting-room?

LILY: No, Richard's there alone. I think Tommy's out on the piazza with Mildred. (MRS. MILLER *bustles out through the back parlor. As soon as she is gone, the smile fades from* LILY's *lips. Her face grows sad and she again glances nervously at her watch.* RICHARD *appears from the back parlor, moving in an aimless way. His face wears a set expression of bitter gloom; he exudes tragedy. For* RICHARD, *after his first outburst of grief and humiliation, has begun to take a masochistic satisfaction in his great sorrow, especially in the concern which it arouses in the family circle. On seeing his aunt, he gives her a dark look and turns and is about to stalk back toward the sitting-room when she speaks to him pityingly.*) Feel any better, Richard?

RICHARD (*somberly*): I'm all right, Aunt Lily. You mustn't worry about me.

LILY (*going to him*): But I do worry about you. I hate to see you so upset.

RICHARD: It doesn't matter. Nothing matters.

LILY (*puts her arm around him sympathetically*): You really mustn't let yourself take it so seriously. You know, something happens and things like that come up, and we think there's no hope —

RICHARD: Things like what come up?

LILY: What's happened between you and Muriel.

RICHARD (*with disdain*): Oh, her! I wasn't even thinking about her. I was thinking about life.

LILY: But then — if we really, *really* love — why, then something else is bound to happen soon that changes everything again, and it's all as it was before the misunderstanding, and everything works out all right in the end. That's the way it is with life.

RICHARD (*with a tragic sneer*): Life! Life is a joke! And everything comes out all wrong in the end!

LILY (*a little shocked*): You mustn't talk that way. But I know you don't mean it.

RICHARD: I do too mean it! You can have your silly optimism, if you like, Aunt Lily. But don't ask me to be so blind. I'm a pessimist! (*Then with an air of cruel cynicism.*) As for Muriel, that's all dead and past. I was only kidding her, anyway, just to have a little fun, and she took it seriously, like a fool. (*He forces a cruel smile to his lips.*) You know what they say about women and trolley cars, Aunt Lily: there's always another one along in a minute.

LILY (*really shocked this time*): I don't like you when you say such horrible, cynical things. It isn't nice.

RICHARD: Nice! That's all you women think of! I'm proud to be a cynic. It's the only thing you can be when you really face life. I suppose you think I ought to be heart-broken about Muriel — a little coward that's afraid to say her soul's her own, and keeps tied to her father's apron strings! Well, not for mine! There's plenty of other fish in the sea! (*As he is finishing, his mother comes back through the back parlor.*)

MRS. MILLER: Why, hello. You here, Richard? Getting hungry, I suppose?

RICHARD (*indignantly*): I'm not hungry a bit! That's all you think of, Ma — food!

MRS. MILLER: Well, I must say I've never noticed you to hang back at meal times. (*To LILY.*) What's that he was saying about fish in the sea?

LILY (*smiling*): He says he's through with Muriel now.

MRS. MILLER (*tartly — giving her son a rebuking look*): She's through with him, he means! The idea of your sending a nice girl like her things out of those indecent books! (*Deeply offended,* RICHARD *disdains to reply but stalks woundedly to the screen door at left, front, and puts a hand on the knob.*) Where are you going?

RICHARD (*quotes from "Candida" in a hollow voice*): "Out, then, into the night with me!" (*He stalks out, slamming the door behind him.*)

MRS. MILLER (*calls*): Well, don't you go far, 'cause dinner'll be ready in a minute, and I'm not coming running after you! (*She turns to* LILY *with a chuckle.*) Goodness, that boy! He ought to be on the stage! (*She mimics.*) "Out — into the night" — and it isn't even dark yet! He got that out of one of those books, I suppose. Do you know, I'm actually grateful to old Dave McComber for putting an end to his nonsense with Muriel. I never did approve of Richard getting so interested in girls. He's not old enough for such silliness. Why, seems to me it was only yesterday he was still a baby. (*She sighs — then matter-of-factly.*) Well, nothing to do now till those men turn up. No use standing here like gawks. We might as well go in the sitting-room and be comfortable.

LILY (*the nervous, worried note in her voice again*): Yes, we might as well. (*They go out through the back parlor. They have no sooner disappeared than the screen door is opened cautiously and* RICHARD *comes back in the room.*)

RICHARD (*stands inside the door, looking after them — quotes bitterly*): "They do not know the secret in the poet's heart." (*He comes nearer the table and surveys it, especially the cut-glass dish containing olives, with contempt and mutters disdainfully.*) Food! (*But the dish of olives seems to fascinate him and presently he has approached nearer, and stealthily lifts a couple and crams them into his mouth. He is just reaching out for more when the pantry door is opened slightly and* NORAH *peers in.*)

NORAH: Mister Dick, you thief, lave them olives alone, or the missus'll be swearing it was me at them!

RICHARD (*draws back his hand as if he had been stung — too flustered to be anything but guilty boy for a second*): I — I wasn't eating —

NORAH: Oho, no, of course not, divil fear you, you was only feeling their pulse! (*Then warningly.*) Mind what I'm saying now, or I'll have to tell on you to protect me good name! (*She draws back into the pantry, closing the door.* RICHARD *stands, a prey to feelings of bitterest humiliation and seething revolt against everyone and everything. A low whistle comes from just outside the porch door. He starts. Then a masculine voice calls: "Hey, Dick." He goes over to the screen door grumpily — then as he recognizes the owner of the voice, his own as he answers becomes respectful and admiring.*)

RICHARD: Oh, hello, Wint. Come on in. (*He opens the door and* WINT SELBY *enters and stands just inside the door.* SELBY *is nineteen, a classmate of* ARTHUR'S *at Yale. He is a typical, good-looking college boy of the period, not the athletic but the hell-raising sport type. He is tall, blond, dressed in extreme collegiate cut.*)

WINT (*as he enters — warningly, in a low tone*): Keep it quiet, Kid. I don't want the folks to know I'm here. Tell Art I want to see him a second — on the Q.T.

RICHARD: Can't. He's up at the Rands' — won't be home before ten, anyway.

WINT (*irritably*): Damn, I thought he'd be here for dinner. (*More irritably.*) Hell, that gums the works for fair!

RICHARD (*ingratiatingly*): What is it, Wint? Can't I help?

WINT (*gives him an appraising glance*): I might tell you, if you can keep your face shut.

RICHARD: I can.

WINT: Well, I ran into a couple of swift babies from New Haven this after, and I dated them up for tonight, thinking I could catch Art. But now it's too late to get anyone else and I'll have to pass it up. I'm nearly broke and I can't afford to blow them both to drinks.

RICHARD (*with shy eagerness*): I've got eleven dollars saved up. I could loan you some.

WINT (*surveys him appreciatively*): Say, you're a good sport. (*Then shaking his head.*) Nix, Kid, I don't want to borrow your money. (*Then getting an idea.*) But say, have you got anything on for tonight?

RICHARD: No.

WINT: Want to come along with me? (*Then quickly.*) I'm not trying to lead you astray, understand. But it'll be a help if you would just sit around with Belle and feed her a few drinks while I'm off with Edith. (*He winks.*) See what I mean? You don't have to do anything, not even take a glass of beer — unless you want to.

RICHARD (*boastfully*): Aw, what do you think I am — a rube?

WINT: You mean you're game for anything that's doing?

RICHARD: Sure I am!

WINT: Ever been out with any girls — I mean, real swift ones that there's something doing with, not these dead Janes around here?

RICHARD (*lies boldly*): Aw, what do you think? Sure I have!

WINT: Ever drink anything besides sodas?

RICHARD: Sure. Lots of times. Beer and sloe-gin fizz and — Manhattans.

WINT (*impressed*): Hell, you know more than I thought. (*Then considering.*) Can you fix it so your folks won't get wise? I don't want your old man coming after me. You can get back by half-past ten or eleven, though, all right. Think you can cook up some lie to cover that? (*As Richard hesitates — encouraging him.*) Ought to be easy — on the Fourth.

RICHARD: Sure. Don't worry about that.

WINT: But you've got to keep your face closed about this, you hear? — to Art and everybody else. I tell you straight, I wouldn't ask you to come if I wasn't in a hole — and if I didn't know you were coming down to Yale next year, and didn't think you're giving me the straight goods about having been around before. I don't want to lead you astray.

RICHARD (*scornfully*): Aw, I told you that was silly.

WINT: Well, you be at the Pleasant Beach Hotel at half-past nine then. Come in the back room. And don't forget to grab some cloves to take the booze off your breath.

RICHARD: Aw, I know what to do.

WINT: See you later, then. (*He starts out and is just about to close the door when he thinks of something.*) And say, I'll say you're a Harvard freshman, and you back me up. They don't know a damn thing about Harvard. I don't want them thinking I'm travelling around with any high-school kid.

RICHARD: Sure. That's easy.

WINT: So long, then. You better beat it right after your dinner while you've got a chance, and hang around until it's time. Watch your step, Kid.

RICHARD: So long. (*The door closes behind* WINT. RICHARD *stands for a moment, a look of bitter, defiant rebellion coming over his face, and mutters to himself.*) I'll show her she can't treat me the way she's done! I'll show them all! (*Then the front door is heard slamming, and a moment later* TOMMY *rushes in from the back parlor.*)

TOMMY: Where's Ma?

RICHARD (*surlily*): In the sitting-room. Where did you think, Bonehead?

TOMMY: Pa and Uncle Sid are coming. Mid and I saw them from the front piazza. Gee, I'm glad. I'm awful hungry, ain't you? (*He rushes out through the back parlor, calling.*) Ma! They're coming! Let's have dinner quick! (*A moment later* MRS. MILLER *appears from the back parlor accompanied by* TOMMY, *who keeps insisting urgently.*) Gee, but I'm awful hungry, Ma!

MRS. MILLER: I know. You always are. You've got a tapeworm, that's what I think.

TOMMY: Have we got lobsters, Ma? Gee, I love lobsters.

MRS. MILLER: Yes, we've got lobsters. And fish. You remember what I told you about that fish. (*He snickers.*) Now, do be quiet, Tommy! (*Then with a teasing smile at* RICHARD.) Well, I'm glad to see you've got back out of the night, Richard. (*He scowls and turns his back on her.* LILY *appears through the back parlor, nervous and apprehensive. As she does so, from the front yard* SID's *voice is heard singing "Poor John!"* MRS. MILLER *shakes her head forebodingly — but, so great is the comic spell for her even in her brother's voice, a humorous smile hovers at the corners of her lips.*) Mmm! Mmm! Lily, I'm afraid —

LILY (*bitterly*): Yes, I might have known. (MILDRED *runs in through the back parlor. She is laughing to herself a bit shamefacedly. She rushes to her mother.*)

MILDRED: Ma, Uncle Sid's — (*She whispers in her ear.*)

MRS. MILLER: Never mind! You shouldn't notice such things — at your age! And don't you encourage him by laughing at his foolishness, you hear!

TOMMY: You needn't whisper, Mid. Think I don't know? Uncle Sid's soused again.

MRS. MILLER (*shakes him by the arm indignantly*): You be quiet! Did I ever! You're getting too smart! (*Gives him a push.*) Go to your place and sit right down and not another word out of you!

TOMMY (*aggrieved — rubbing his arm as he goes to his place*): Aw, Ma!

MRS. MILLER: And you sit down, Richard and Mildred. You better, too, Lily. We'll get him right in here and get some food in him. He'll be all right then. (RICHARD, *preserving the pose of the bitter, disillusioned pessimist, sits down in his place in the chair at right of the two whose backs face front.* MILDRED *takes the other chair facing back, at his left.* TOMMY *has already slid into the end chair at right of those at the rear of table facing front.* LILY *sits in the one of those at left, by the head of the table, leaving the middle one* [SID'S] *vacant. While they are doing this, the front screen door is heard slamming and* NAT's *and* SID's *laughing voices, raised as they come in and for a moment after, then suddenly cautiously lowered.* MRS. MILLER *goes to the entrance to the back parlor and calls peremptorily.)* You come right in here! Don't stop to wash up or anything. Dinner's coming right on the table.

MILLER'S VOICE (*jovially*): All right, Essie. Here we are! Here we are!

MRS. MILLER (*goes to pantry door, opens it and calls*): All right, Norah. You can bring in the soup. (*She comes back to the back-parlor entrance just as* MILLER *enters. He isn't drunk by any means. He is just mellow and benignly ripened. His face is one large, smiling, happy beam of utter appreciation of life. All's right with the world, so satisfyingly right that he becomes sentimentally moved even to think of it.*)

MILLER: Here we are, Essie! Right on the dot! Here we are! (*He pulls her to him and gives her a smacking kiss on the ear as she jerks her head away.* MILDRED *and* TOMMY *giggle.* RICHARD *holds rigidly aloof and disdainful, his brooding gaze fixed on his plate.* LILY *forces a smile.*)

MRS. MILLER (*pulling away — embarrassedly, almost blushing*): Don't, you Crazy! (*Then recovering herself — tartly.*) So I see, you're here! And if I didn't, you've told me four times already!

MILLER (*beamingly*): Now, Essie, don't be critical. Don't be carpingly critical. Good news can stand repeating, can't it? 'Course it can! (*He slaps her jovially on her fat buttocks.* TOMMY *and* MILDRED *roar with glee. And* NORAH, *who has just entered from the pantry with a huge tureen of soup in her hands, almost drops it as she explodes in a merry guffaw.*)

MRS. MILLER (*scandalized*): Nat! Aren't you ashamed!

MILLER: Couldn't resist it! Just simply couldn't resist it! (NORAH, *still standing with the soup tureen held out stiffly in front of her, again guffaws.*)

MRS. MILLER (*turns on her with outraged indignation*): Norah! Bring that soup here this minute! (*She stalks with stiff dignity toward her place at the foot of the table, right.*)

NORAH (*guiltily*): Yes, Mum. (*She brings the soup around the head of the table, passing* MILLER.)

MILLER (*jovially*): Why, hello, Norah!

MRS. MILLER: Nat! (*She sits down stiffly at the foot of the table.*)

NORAH (*rebuking him familiarly*): Arrah now, don't be making me laugh and getting me into trouble!

MRS. MILLER: Norah!

NORAH (*a bit resentfully*): Yes, Mum. Here I am. (*She sets the soup tureen down with a thud in front of* MRS. MILLER *and passes around the other side, squeezing with difficulty between the china closet and the backs of chairs at the rear of the table.*)

MRS. MILLER: Tommy! Stop spinning your napkin ring! How often have I got to tell you? Mildred! Sit up straight in your chair! Do you want to grow up a humpback? Richard! Take your elbows off the table!

MILLER (*coming to his place at the head of the table, rubbing his hands together genially*): Well, well, well. Well, well, well. It's good to be home again. (NORAH *exits into the pantry and lets the door slam with a bang behind her.*)

MRS. MILLER (*jumps*): Oh! (*Then exasperatedly.*) Nat, I do wish you wouldn't encourage that stupid girl by talking to her, when I'm doing my best to train —

MILLER (*beamingly*): All right, Essie. Your word is law! (*Then laughingly.*) We did have the darndest fun today! And Sid was the life of that picnic! You ought to have heard him! Honestly, he had that crowd just rolling on the ground and splitting their sides! He ought to be on the stage.

MRS. MILLER (*as* NORAH *comes back with a dish of saltines — begins ladling soup into the stack of plates before her*): He ought to be at this table eating something to sober him up, that's what he ought to be! (*She calls.*) Sid! You come right in here! (*Then to* NORAH, *handing her a soup plate.*) Here, Norah. (NORAH *begins passing soup.*) Sit down, Nat, for goodness sakes. Start eating, everybody. Don't wait for me. You know I've given up soup.

MILLER (*sits down but bends forward to call to his wife in a confidential tone*): Essie — Sid's sort of embarrassed about coming — I mean I'm afraid he's a little bit — not too much, you understand — but he met such a lot of friends and — well, you know, don't be hard on him. Fourth of July is like Christmas — comes but once a year. Don't pretend to notice, eh? And don't you kids, you hear! And don't you, Lily. He's scared of you.

LILY (*with stiff meekness*): Very well, Nat.

MILLER (*beaming again — calls*): All right, Sid. The coast's clear. (*He begins to absorb his soup ravenously.*) Good soup, Essie! Good soup! (*A moment later* SID *makes his entrance from the back parlor. He is in a condition that can best be described as blurry. His movements have a hazy uncertainty about them. His shiny fat face is one broad, blurred, Puckish, naughty-boy grin; his eyes have a blurred, wondering vagueness. As he enters he makes a solemnly intense effort to appear casual and dead, cold sober. He waves his hand aimlessly and speaks with a silly gravity.*)

SID: Good evening. (*They all answer* "Good evening," *their eyes on their plates. He makes his way vaguely toward his place, continuing his grave effort at conversation.*) Beautiful evening. I never remember seeing — more beautiful sunset. (*He bumps vaguely into* LILY's *chair as he attempts to pass behind her — immediately he is all grave politeness.*) Sorry — sorry, Lily — deeply sorry.

LILY (*her eyes on her plate — stiffly*): It's all right.

SID (*manages to get into his chair at last — mutters to himself*): Wha' was I sayin'? Oh, sunsets. But why butt in? Hasn't sun — perfect right to set? Mind y'r own business. (*He pauses thoughtfully, considering this — then looks around from face to face, fixing each with a vague, blurred, wondering look, as if some deep puzzle were confronting him. Then suddenly he grins mistily and nods with satisfaction.*) And there you are! Am I right?

MILLER (*humoring him*): Right.

SID: Right! (*He is silent, studying his soup plate, as if it were some strange enigma. Finally he looks up and regards his sister and asks with wondering amazement.*) Soup?

MRS. MILLER: Of course, it's soup. What did you think it was? And you hurry up and eat it.

SID (*again regards his soup with astonishment*): Well! (*Then suddenly.*) Well, all right then! Soup be it! (*He picks up his spoon and begins to eat, but after two tries in which he finds it difficult to locate his mouth, he addresses the spoon plaintively.*) Spoon, is this any way to treat a pal? (*Then suddenly comically angry, putting the spoon down with a bang.*) Down with spoons! (*He raises his soup plate and declaims.*) "We'll drink to the dead already, and hurrah for the next who dies." (*Bowing solemnly to right and left.*) Your good health, ladies *and* gents. (*He starts drinking the soup.* MILLER *guffaws and* MILDRED *and* TOMMY *giggle. Even* RICHARD *forgets his melancholy and snickers, and* MRS. MILLER *conceals a smile. Only* LILY *remains stiff and silent.*)

MRS. MILLER (*with forced severity*): Sid!

SID (*peers at her muzzily, lowering the soup plate a little from his lips*): Eh?

MRS. MILLER: Oh, nothing. Never mind.

SID (*solemnly offended*): Are you — publicly rebuking me before assembled — ? Isn't soup liquid? Aren't liquids drunk? (*Then considering this to himself.*) What if they are drunk? It's a good man's failing. (*He again peers mistily about at the company.*) Am I right or wrong?

MRS. MILLER: Hurry up and finish your soup, and stop talking nonsense!

SID (*turning to her — again offendedly*): Oh, no, Essie, if I ever so far forget myself as to drink a leg of lamb, then you might have some — excuse for — Just think of waste effort eating soup with spoons — fifty gruelling lifts per plate — billions of soup-eaters on globe — why, it's simply staggering! (*Then darkly to himself.*) No more spoons for me! If I want develop my biceps, I'll buy Sandow Exerciser! (*He drinks the rest of his soup in a gulp and beams around at the company, suddenly all happiness again.*) Am I right, folks?

MILLER (*who has been choking with laughter*): Haw, haw! You're right, Sid.

SID (*peers at him blurredly and shakes his head sadly*): Poor old Nat! Always wrong — but heart of gold, heart of purest gold. And drunk again, I regret to note. Sister, my heart bleeds for you and your poor fatherless chicks!

MRS. MILLER (*restraining a giggle — severely*): Sid! Do shut up for a minute! Pass me your soup plates, everybody. If we wait for that girl to take them, we'll be here all night. (*They all pass their plates, which* MRS. MILLER *stacks up and then puts on the side-board. As she is doing this,* NORAH *appears from the pantry with a platter of broiled fish. She is just about to place these before* MILLER *when* SID *catches her eye mistily and rises to his feet, making her a deep, uncertain bow.*)

SID (*raptly*): Ah, Sight for Sore Eyes, my beautiful Macushla, my star-eyed Mavourneen —

MRS. MILLER: Sid!

NORAH (*immensely pleased — gives him an arch, flirtatious glance*): Ah sure, Mister Sid, it's you that have kissed the Blarney Stone, when you've a drop taken!

MRS. MILLER (*outraged*): Norah! Put down that fish!

NORAH (*flusteredly*): Yes, Mum. (*She attempts to put the fish down hastily before* MILLER, *but her eyes are fixed nervously on* MRS. MILLER *and she gives* MILLER *a nasty swipe on the side of the head with the edge of the dish.*)

MILLER: Ouch! (*The children, even* RICHARD, *explode into laughter.*)

NORAH (*almost lets the dish fall*): Oh, glory be to God! Is it hurted you are?

MILLER (*rubbing his head — good-naturedly*): No, no harm done. Only careful, Norah, careful.

NORAH (*gratefully*): Yes, sorr. (*She thumps down the dish in front of him with a sigh of relief.*)

SID (*who is still standing — with drunken gravity*): Careful, Mavourneen, careful! You might have hit him some place besides the head. Always aim at his head, remember — so as not to worry us. (*Again the children explode. Also* NORAH. *Even* LILY *suddenly lets out an hysterical giggle and is furious with herself for doing so.*)

LILY: I'm so sorry, Nat. I didn't mean to laugh. (*Turning on* SID *furiously.*) Will you please sit down and stop making a fool of yourself! (SID *gives her a hurt, mournful look and then sinks meekly down on his chair.*)

NORAH (*grinning cheerfully, gives* LILY *a reassuring pat on the back*): Ah, Miss Lily, don't mind him. He's only under the influence. Sure, there's no harm in him at all.

MRS. MILLER: Norah! (NORAH *exits hastily into the pantry, letting the door slam with a crash behind her. There is silence for a moment as* MILLER *serves the fish and it is passed around.* NORAH *comes back with the vegetables and disappears again, and these are dished out.*)

MILLER (*is about to take his first bite — stops suddenly and asks his wife*): This isn't, by any chance, bluefish, is it, my dear?

MRS. MILLER (*with a warning glance at* TOMMY): Of course not. You know we never have bluefish, on account of you.

MILLER (*addressing the table now with the gravity of a man confessing his strange peculiarities*): Yes, I regret to say, there's a certain peculiar oil in bluefish that invariably poisons me. (*At this,* TOMMY *cannot stand it any more but explodes into laughter.* MRS. MILLER, *after a helpless glance at him, follows suit; then* LILY *goes off into uncontrollable, hysterical laughter, and* RICHARD *and* MILDRED *are caught in the contagion.* MILLER *looks around at them with a weak smile, his dignity now ruffled a bit.*) Well, I must say I don't see what's so darned funny about my being poisoned.

SID (*peers around him — then with drunken cunning*): Aha! Nat, I suspect — plot! This fish looks blue to me — very blue — in fact despondent, desperate, and — (*He points his fork dramatically at* MRS. MILLER.) See how guilty she looks — a ver — veritable Lucretia Georgia! Can it be this woman has been slowly poisoning you all these years? And how well — you've stood it! What iron constitution! Even now, when you are invariably at death's door, I can't believe — (*Everyone goes off into uncontrollable laughter.*)

MILLER (*grumpily*): Oh, give us a rest, you darned fool! A joke's a joke, but — (*He addresses his wife in a wounded tone.*) Is this true, Essie?

MRS. MILLER (*wiping the tears from her eyes — defiantly*): Yes, it is true, if you must know, and you'd never have suspected it, if it weren't for that darned Tommy, and Sid poking his nose in. You've eaten bluefish for years and thrived on it and it's all nonsense about that peculiar oil.

MILLER (*deeply offended*): Kindly allow me to know my own constitution! Now I think of it, I've felt upset afterwards every damned time we've had fish! (*He pushes his plate away from him with proud renunciation.*) I can't eat this.

MRS. MILLER (*insultingly matter-of-fact*): Well, don't then. There's lots of lobster coming and you can fill up on that. (RICHARD *suddenly bursts out laughing again.*)

MILLER (*turns to him caustically*): You seem in a merry mood, Richard. I thought you were the original of the Heart Bowed Down today.

SID (*with mock condolence*): Never mind, Dick. Let them — scoff! What can they understand about girls whose hair sizzchels, whose lips are fireworks, whose eyes are red-hot sparks —

MILDRED (*laughing*): Is that what he wrote to Muriel? (*Turning to her brother.*) You silly goat, you!

RICHARD (*surlily*): Aw, shut up, Mid. What do I care about her? I'll show all of you how much I care!

MRS. MILLER: Pass your plates as soon as you're through, everybody. I've rung for the lobster. And that's all. You don't get any dessert or tea after lobster, you know. (NORAH *appears bearing a platter of cold boiled lobsters which she sets before* MILLER, *and disappears.*)

TOMMY: Gee, I love lobster! (MILLER *puts one on each plate, and they are passed around and everyone starts in pulling the cracked shells apart.*)

MILLER (*feeling more cheerful after a couple of mouthfuls — determining to give the conversation another turn, says to his daughter*): Have a good time at the beach, Mildred?

MILDRED: Oh, fine, Pa, thanks. The water was wonderful and warm.

MILLER: Swim far?

MILDRED: Yes, for me. But that isn't so awful far.

MILLER: Well, you ought to be a good swimmer, if you take after me. I used to be a regular water rat when I was a boy. I'll have to go down to the beach with you one of these days — though I'd be rusty, not having been in in all these years. (*The reminiscent look comes into his eyes of one about to embark on an oft-told tale of childhood adventure.*) You know, speaking of swimming, I never go down to that beach but what it calls to mind the day I and Red Sisk went in swimming there and I saved his life. (*By this time the family are beginning to exchange amused, guilty glances. They all know what is coming.*)

SID (*with a sly, blurry wink around*): Ha! Now we — have it again!

MILLER (*turning on him*): Have what?

SID: Nothing — go on with your swimming — don't mind me.

MILLER (*glares at him — but immediately is overcome by the reminiscent mood again*): Red Sisk — his father kept a blacksmith shop where the Union Market is now — we kids called him Red because he had the darndest reddest crop of hair —

SID (*as if he were talking to his plate*): Remarkable! — the curious imagination — of little children.

MRS. MILLER (*as she sees* MILLER *about to explode — interposes tactfully*): Sid! Eat your lobster and shut up! Go on, Nat.

MILLER (*gives* SID *a withering look — then is off again*): Well, as I was saying, Red and I went swimming that day. Must have been — let me see — Red was fourteen, bigger and older than me, I was only twelve — forty-five years ago — wasn't a single house down there then — but there was a stake out where the whistling buoy is now, about a mile out. (TOMMY, *who has been having difficulty restraining himself, lets out a stifled giggle.* MILLER *bends a frowning gaze on him.*) One more sound out of you, young man, and you'll leave the table!

MRS. MILLER (*quickly interposing, trying to stave off the story*): Do eat your lobster, Nat. You didn't have any fish, you know.

MILLER (*not liking the reminder — pettishly*): Well, if I'm going to be interrupted every second anyway — (*He turns to his lobster and chews in silence for a moment.*)

MRS. MILLER (*trying to switch the subject*): How's Anne's mother's rheumatism, Mildred?

MILDRED: Oh, she's much better, Ma. She was in wading today. She says salt water's the only thing that really helps her bunion.

MRS. MILLER: Mildred! Where are your manners? At the table's no place to speak of —

MILLER (*fallen into the reminiscent obsession again*): Well, as I was saying, there was I and Red, and he dared me to race him out to the stake and back. Well, I didn't let anyone dare me in those days. I was a spunky kid. So I said all right and we started out. We swam and swam and were pretty evenly matched; though, as I've said, he was bigger and older than me, but finally I drew ahead. I was going along easy, with lots in reserve, not a bit tired, when suddenly I heard a sort of gasp from behind me — like this — "help." (*He imitates. Everyone's eyes are firmly fixed on their plates, except* SID's.) And I turned and there was Red, his face all pinched and white, and he says weakly: "Help, Nat! I got a cramp in my leg!" Well, I don't mind telling you I got mighty scared. I didn't know what to do. Then suddenly I thought of the pile. If I could pull him to that, I could hang on to him till someone'd notice us. But the pile was still — well, I calculate it must have been two hundred feet away.

SID: Two hundred and fifty!

MILLER (*in confusion*): What's that?

SID: Two hundred *and* fifty! I've taken down the distance every time you've saved Red's life for thirty years and the mean average to that pile is two hundred and fifty feet! (*There is a burst of laughter from around the table.* SID *continues complainingly*.) Why didn't you let that Red drown, anyway, Nat? I never knew him but I know I'd never have liked him.

MILLER (*really hurt, forces a feeble smile to his lips and pretends to be a good sport about it*): Well, guess you're right, Sid. Guess I have told that one too many times and bored everyone. But it's a good true story for kids because it illustrates the danger of being foolhardy in the water —

MRS. MILLER (*sensing the hurt in his tone, comes to his rescue*): Of course it's a good story — and you tell it whenever you've a mind to. And you, Sid, if you were in any responsible state, I'd give you a good piece of my mind for teasing Nat like that.

MILLER (*with a sad, self-pitying smile at his wife*): Getting old, I guess, Mother — getting to repeat myself. Someone ought to stop me.

MRS. MILLER: No such thing! You're as young as you ever were. (*She turns on* SID *again angrily*.) You eat your lobster and maybe it'll keep your mouth shut!

SID (*after a few chews — irrepressibly*): Lobster! Did you know, Tommy, your Uncle Sid is the man invented lobster? Fact! One day — when I was building the Pyramids — took a day off and just dashed off lobster. He was bigger'n' older than me and he had the darndest reddest crop of hair but I dashed him off just the same! Am I right, Nat? (*Then suddenly in the tones of a side-show barker*.) Ladies *and* Gents —

MRS. MILLER: Mercy sakes! Can't you shut up?

SID: In this cage you see the lobster. You will not believe me, ladies *and* gents, but it's a fact that this interesting bivalve only makes love to his mate once in every thousand years — but, dearie me, how he does enjoy it! (*The children roar,* LILY *and* MRS. MILLER *laugh in spite of themselves — then look embarrassed.* MILLER *guffaws — then suddenly grows shocked*.)

MILLER: Careful, Sid, careful. Remember you're at home.

TOMMY (*suddenly in a hoarse whisper to his mother, with an awed glance of admiration at his uncle*): Ma! Look at him! He's eating that claw, shells and all!

MRS. MILLER (*horrified*): Sid, do you want to kill yourself? Take it away from him, Lily!

SID (*with great dignity*): But I prefer the shells. All famous epicures prefer the shells — to the less delicate, coarser meat. It's the same with clams. Unless I eat the shells there is a certain, peculiar oil that invariably poisons — Am I right, Nat?

MILLER (*good-naturedly*): You seem to be getting a lot of fun kidding me. Go ahead, then. I don't mind.

MRS. MILLER: He better go right up to bed for a while, that's what he better do.

SID (*considering this owlishly*): Bed? Yes, maybe you're right. (*He gets to his feet.*) I am not at all well — in very delicate condition — we are praying for a boy. Am I right, Nat? Nat, I kept telling you all day I was in delicate condition and yet you kept forcing demon chowder on me, although you knew full well — even if you were full — that there is a certain, peculiar oil in chowder that invariably — (*They are again all laughing* — LILY, *hysterically*.)

MRS. MILLER: *Will* you get to bed, you idiot!

SID (*mutters graciously*): Immediately — if not sooner. (*He turns to pass behind* LILY, *then stops, staring down at her.*) But wait. There is still a duty I must perform. No day is complete without it. Lily, answer once and for all, will you marry me?

LILY (*with an hysterical giggle*): No, I won't — never!

SID (*nodding his head*): Right! And perhaps it's all for the best. For how could I forget the pre — preepts taught me at mother's dying knee. "Sidney," she said, "never marry a woman who drinks! Lips that touch liquor shall never touch yours!" (*Gazing at her mournfully.*) Too bad! So fine a woman once — and now such a slave to rum! (*Turning to* NAT.) What can we do to save her, Nat? (*In a hoarse, confidential whisper.*) Better put her in institution where she'll be removed from temptation! The mere smell of it seems to drive her frantic!

MRS. MILLER (*struggling with her laughter*): You leave Lily alone, and go to bed!

SID: Right! (*He comes around behind* LILY's *chair and moves toward the entrance to the back parlor — then suddenly turns and says with a bow.*) Good night, ladies — *and* gents. We will meet — bye and bye! (*He gives an imitation of a Salvation Army drum.*) Boom! Boom! Boom! Come and be saved, Brothers! (*He starts to sing the old Army hymn.*)

> "In the sweet
> Bye and bye
> We will meet on that beautiful shore."

(*He turns and marches solemnly out through the back parlor, singing.*)

> "Work and pray
> While you may.
> We will meet in the sky bye and bye."

(MILLER *and his wife and the children are all roaring with laughter.* LILY *giggles hysterically.*)

MILLER (*subsiding at last*): Haw, haw. He's a case, if ever there was one! Darned if you can help laughing at him — even when he's poking fun at you!

MRS. MILLER: Goodness, but he's a caution! Oh, my sides ache, I declare! I was trying so hard not to — but you can't help it, he's so silly! But I suppose we really shouldn't. It only encourages him. But, my lands — !

LILY (*suddenly gets up from her chair and stands rigidly, her face working — jerkily*): That's just it — you shouldn't — even I laughed — it does encourage — that's been his downfall — everyone always laughing, everyone always saying what a card he is, what a case, what a caution, so funny — and he's gone on — and we're all responsible — making it easy for him — we're all to blame — and all we do is laugh!

MILLER (*worriedly*): Now, Lily, now, you mustn't take on so. It isn't as serious as all that.

LILY (*bitterly*): Maybe — it is — to me. Or was — once. (*Then contritely.*) I'm sorry, Nat. I'm sorry, Essie. I didn't mean to — I'm not feeling myself tonight. If you'll excuse me, I'll go in the front parlor and lie down on the sofa awhile.

MRS. MILLER: Of course, Lily. You do whatever you've a mind to. (LILY *goes out.*)

MILLER (*frowning — a little shamefaced*): Hmm. I suppose she's right. Never knew Lily to come out with things that way before. Anything special happened, Essie?

MRS. MILLER: Nothing I know — except he'd promised to take her to the fireworks.

MILLER: That's so. Well, supposing I take her. I don't want her to feel disappointed.

MRS. MILLER (*shaking her head*): Wild horses couldn't drag her there now.

MILLER: Hmm. I thought she'd got completely over her foolishness about him long ago.

MRS. MILLER: She never will.

MILLER: She'd better. He's got fired out of that Waterbury job — told me at the picnic after he'd got enough Dutch courage in him.

MRS. MILLER: Oh, dear! Isn't he the fool!

MILLER: I knew something was wrong when he came home. Well, I'll find a place for him on my paper again, of course. He always was the best news-getter this town ever had. But I'll tell him he's got to stop his damn nonsense.

MRS. MILLER (*doubtfully*): Yes.

MILLER: Well, no use sitting here mourning over spilt milk. (*He gets up, and* RICHARD, MILDRED, TOMMY *and* MRS. MILLER *follow his example, the children quiet and a bit awed.*) You kids go out in the yard and try to keep quiet for a while, so's your Uncle Sid'll get to sleep and your Aunt Lily can rest.

TOMMY (*mournfully*): Ain't we going to set off the sky rockets and Roman candles, Pa?

MILLER: Later, Son, later. It isn't dark enough for them yet anyway.

MILDRED: Come on, Tommy. I'll see he keeps quiet, Pa.

MILLER: That's a good girl. (MILDRED *and* TOMMY *go out through the screen door.* RICHARD *remains standing, sunk in bitter, gloomy thoughts.* MILLER *glances at him — then irritably.*) Well, Melancholy Dane, what are you doing?

RICHARD (*darkly*): I'm going out — for a while. (*Then suddenly.*) Do you know what I think? It's Aunt Lily's fault, Uncle Sid's going to ruin. It's all because he loves her, and she keeps him dangling after her, and eggs him on and ruins his life — like all women love to ruin men's lives! I don't blame him for drinking himself to death! What does he care if he dies, after the way she's treated him! I'd do the same thing myself if I were in his boots!

MRS. MILLER (*indignantly*): Richard! You stop that talk!

RICHARD (*quotes bitterly*):

> "Drink! for you know not whence you come nor why.
> Drink! for you know not why you go nor where!"

MILLER (*losing his temper — harshly*): Listen here, young man! I've had about all I can stand of your nonsense for one day! You're growing a lot too big for your size, seems to me! You keep that damn fool talk to yourself, you hear me — or you're going to regret it! Mind, now! (*He strides angrily away through the back parlor.*)

MRS. MILLER (*still indignant*): Richard, I'm ashamed of you, that's what I am. (*She follows her husband.* RICHARD *stands for a second, bitter, humiliated, wronged, even his father turned enemy, his face growing more and more rebellious. Then he forces a scornful smile to his lips.*)

RICHARD: Aw, what the hell do I care? I'll show them! (*He turns and goes out the screen door.*)

CURTAIN

ACT III

SCENE 1

Scene — The back room of a bar in a small hotel — a small, dingy room, dimly lighted by two fly-specked globes in a fly-specked gilt chandelier suspended from the middle of the ceiling. At left, front, is the swinging door leading to the bar. At rear of door, against the wall, is a nickel-in-the-slot player-piano. In the rear wall, right, is a door leading to the "Family Entrance" and the stairway to the upstairs rooms. In the middle of the right wall is a window with closed shutters. Three tables with stained tops, four chairs around each table, are placed at center, front, at right, toward rear, and at rear, center. A brass cuspidor is on the floor by each table. The floor is unswept, littered with cigarette and cigar butts. The hideous saffron-colored wall-paper is blotched and spotted.

It is about 10 o'clock the same night. RICHARD *and* BELLE *are discovered sitting at the table at center,* BELLE *at left of it,* RICHARD *in the next chair at the middle of table, rear, facing front.*

BELLE *is twenty, a rather pretty peroxide blonde, a typical college "tart" of the period, and of the cheaper variety, dressed with tawdry flashiness. But she is a fairly recent recruit to the ranks, and is still a bit remorseful behind her make-up and defiantly careless manner.*

BELLE *has an empty gin-rickey glass before her,* RICHARD *a half-empty glass of beer. He looks horribly timid, embarrassed and guilty, but at the same time thrilled and proud of at last mingling with the pace that kills.*

The player-piano is grinding out "Bedelia." The BARTENDER, *a stocky young Irishman with a foxily cunning, stupid face and a cynically wise grin, stands just inside the bar entrance, watching them over the swinging door.*

BELLE (*with an impatient glance at her escort — rattling the ice in her empty glass*): Drink up your beer, why don't you? It's getting flat.

RICHARD (*embarrassedly*): I let it get that way on purpose. I like it better when it's flat. (*But he hastily gulps down the rest of his glass, as if it were some nasty-tasting medicine. The* BARTENDER *chuckles audibly.* BELLE *glances at him.*)

BELLE (*nodding at the player-piano scornfully*): Say, George, is "Bedelia" the latest to hit this hick burg? Well, it's only a couple of years old! You'll catch up in time! Why don't you get a new roll for that old box?

BARTENDER (*with a grin*): Complain to the boss, not me. We're not used to having Candy Kiddoes like you around — or maybe we'd get up to date.

BELLE (*with a professionally arch grin at him*): Don't kid me, please. I can't bear it. (*Then she sings to the music from the piano, her eyes now on* RICHARD.) "Bedelia, I'd like to feel yer." (*The* BARTENDER *laughs. She smirks at* RICHARD.) Ever hear those words to it, Kid?

RICHARD (*who has heard them but is shocked at hearing a girl say them — putting on a blasé air*): Sure, lots of times. That's old.

BELLE (*edging her chair closer and putting a hand over one of his*): Then why don't you act as if you knew what they were all about?

RICHARD (*terribly flustered*): Sure, I've heard that old parody lots of times. What do you think I am?

BELLE: I don't know, Kid. Honest to God, you've got me guessing.

BARTENDER (*with a mocking chuckle*): He's a hot sport, can't you tell it? I never seen such a spender. My head's dizzy bringing you in drinks!

BELLE (*laughs irritably — to* RICHARD): Don't let him kid you. You show him. Loosen up and buy another drink, what say?

RICHARD (*humiliated — manfully*): Sure. Excuse me. I was thinking of something else. Have anything you like. (*He turns to the* BARTENDER *who has entered from the bar*.) See what the lady will have — and have one on me yourself.

BARTENDER (*coming to the table — with a wink at* BELLE): That's talking! Didn't I say you were a sport? I'll take a cigar on you. (*To* BELLE.) What's yours, Kiddo — the same?

BELLE: Yes. And forget the house rules this time and remember a rickey is supposed to have gin in it.

BARTENDER (*grinning*): I'll try to — seeing it's you. (*Then to* RICHARD.) What's yours — another beer?

RICHARD (*shyly*): A small one, please. I'm not thirsty.

BELLE (*calculatedly taunting*): Say, honest, are things that slow up at Harvard? If they had you down at New Haven, they'd put you in a kindergarten! Don't be such a dead one! Filling up on beer will only make you sleepy. Have a man's drink!

RICHARD (*shamefacedly*): All right. I was going to. Bring me a sloe-gin fizz.

BELLE (*to* BARTENDER): And make it a real one.

BARTENDER (*with a wink*): I get you. Something that'll warm him up, eh? (*He goes into the bar, chuckling.*)

BELLE (*looks around the room — irritably*): Christ, what a dump! (RICHARD *is startled and shocked by this curse and looks down at the table.*) If this isn't the deadest burg I ever struck! Bet they take the sidewalks in after nine o'clock! (*Then turning on him.*) Say, honestly, Kid, does your mother know you're out?

RICHARD (*defensively*): Aw, cut it out, why don't you — trying to kid me!

BELLE (*glances at him — then resolves on a new tack — patting his hand*): All right. I didn't mean to, Dearie. Please don't get sore at me.

RICHARD: I'm not sore.

BELLE (*seductively*): You see, it's this way with me. I think you're one of the sweetest kids I've ever met — and I could like you such a lot if you'd give me half a chance — instead of acting so cold and indifferent.

RICHARD: I'm not cold and indifferent. (*Then solemnly tragic.*) It's only that I've got — a weight on my mind.

BELLE (*impatiently*): Well, get it off your mind and give something else a chance to work. (*The* BARTENDER *comes in, bringing the drinks.*)

BARTENDER (*setting them down — with a wink at* BELLE): This'll warm him for you. Forty cents, that is — with the cigar.

RICHARD (*pulls out his roll and hands a dollar bill over — with exaggerated careless-ness*): Keep the change. (BELLE *emits a gasp and seems about to protest, then thinks better of it. The* BARTENDER *cannot believe his luck for a moment — then pockets the bill hastily, as if afraid* RICHARD *will change his mind.*)

BARTENDER (*respect in his voice*): Thank you, sir.

RICHARD (*grandly*): Don't mention it.

BARTENDER: I hope you like the drink. I took special pains with it. (*The voice of the* SALESMAN, *who has just come in the bar, calls* "Hey! Anybody here?" *and a coin is rapped on the bar.*) I'm coming. (*The* BARTENDER *goes out.*)

BELLE (*remonstrating gently, a new appreciation for her escort's possibilities in her voice*): You shouldn't be so generous, Dearie. Gets him in bad habits. A dime would have been plenty.

RICHARD: Ah, that's all right. I'm no tightwad.

BELLE: That's the talk I like to hear. (*With a quick look toward the bar, she stealthily pulls up her dress — to* RICHARD's *shocked fascination — and takes a package of cheap cigarettes from her stocking.*) Keep an eye out for that bartender, Kid, and tell me if you see him coming. Girls are only allowed to smoke upstairs in the rooms, he said.

RICHARD (*embarrassedly*): All right. I'll watch.

BELLE (*having lighted her cigarette and inhaled deeply, holds the package out to him*): Have a Sweet? You smoke, don't you?

RICHARD (*taking one*): Sure! I've been smoking for the last two years — on the sly. But next year I'll be allowed — that is, pipes and cigars. (*He lights his cigarette with elaborate nonchalance, puffs, but does not inhale — then, watching her, with shocked concern.*) Say, you oughtn't to inhale like that! Smoking's awful bad for girls, anyway, even if they don't —

BELLE (*cynically amused*): Afraid it will stunt my growth? Gee, Kid, you are a scream! You'll grow up to be a minister yet! (RICHARD *looks shamefaced. She scans him impatiently — then holds up her drink.*) Well, here's how! Bottoms up, now! Show me you really know how to drink. It'll take that load off your mind. (RICH-ARD *follows her example and they both drink the whole contents of their glasses before setting them down.*) There! That's something like! Feel better?

RICHARD (*proud of himself — with a shy smile*): You bet.

BELLE: Well, you'll feel still better in a minute — and then maybe you won't be so distant and unfriendly, eh?

RICHARD: I'm not.

BELLE: Yes, you are. I think you just don't like me.

RICHARD (*more manfully*): I do too like you.

BELLE: How much? A lot?

RICHARD: Yes, a lot.

BELLE: Show me how much! (*Then as he fidgets embarrassedly.*) Want me to come sit on your lap?

RICHARD: Yes — I — (*She comes and sits on his lap. He looks desperately uncom-fortable, but the gin is rising to his head and he feels proud of himself and devil-ish, too.*)

BELLE: Why don't you put your arm around me? (*He does so awkwardly.*) No, not that dead way. Hold me tight. You needn't be afraid of hurting me. I like to be held tight, don't you?

RICHARD: Sure I do.

BELLE: 'Specially when it's by a nice handsome kid like you. (*Ruffling his hair.*) Gee, you've got pretty hair, do you know it? Honest, I'm awfully strong for you! Why can't you be about me? I'm not so awfully ugly, am I?

RICHARD: No, you're — you're pretty.

BELLE: You don't say it as if you meant it.

RICHARD: I do mean it — honest.

BELLE: Then why don't you kiss me? (*She bends down her lips toward his. He hesitates, then kisses her and at once shrinks back.*) Call that kissing? Here. (*She holds his head and fastens her lips on his and holds them there. He starts and struggles. She laughs.*) What's the matter, Honey Boy? Haven't you ever kissed like that before?

RICHARD: Sure. Lots of times.

BELLE: Then why did you jump as if I'd bitten you? (*Squirming around on his lap.*) Gee, I'm getting just crazy about you! What shall we do about it, eh? Tell me.

RICHARD: I — don't know. (*Then boldly.*) I — I'm crazy about you, too.

BELLE (*kissing him again*): Just think of the wonderful time Edith and your friend, Wint, are having upstairs — while we sit down here like two dead ones. A room only costs two dollars. And, seeing I like you so much, I'd only take five dollars — from you. I'd do it for nothing — for you — only I've got to live and I owe my room rent in New Haven — and you know how it is. I get ten dollars from everyone else. Honest! (*She kisses him again, then gets up from his lap — briskly.*) Come on. Go out and tell the bartender you want a room. And hurry. Honest, I'm so strong for you I can hardly wait to get you upstairs!

RICHARD (*starts automatically for the door to the bar — then hesitates, a great struggle going on in his mind — timidity, disgust at the money element, shocked modesty, and the guilty thought of MURIEL, fighting it out with the growing tipsiness that makes him want to be a hell of a fellow and go in for all forbidden fruit, and makes this tart a romantic, evil vampire in his eyes. Finally, he stops and mutters in confusion.*) I can't.

BELLE: What, are you too bashful to ask for a room? Let me do it, then. (*She starts for the door.*)

RICHARD (*desperately*): No — I don't want you to — I don't want to.

BELLE (*surveying him, anger coming into her eyes*): Well, if you aren't the lousiest cheap skate!

RICHARD: I'm not a cheap skate!

BELLE: Keep me around here all night fooling with you when I might be out with some real live one — if there is such a thing in this burg! — and now you quit on me! Don't be such a piker! You've got five dollars! I seen it when you paid for the drinks, so don't hand me any lies!

RICHARD: I — Who said I hadn't? And I'm not a piker. If you need the five dollars so bad — for your room rent — you can have it without — I mean, I'll be glad to give — (*He has been fumbling in his pocket and pulls out his nine-dollar roll and holds out the five to her.*)

BELLE (*hardly able to believe her eyes, almost snatches it from his hand — then laughs and immediately becomes sentimentally grateful*): Thanks, Kid. Gee —

oh, thanks — Gee, forgive me for losing my temper and bawling you out, will you? Gee, you're a regular peach! You're the nicest kid I've ever met! (*She kisses him and he grins proudly, a hero to himself now on many counts.*) Gee, you're a peach! Thanks, again!

RICHARD (*grandly — and quite tipsily*): It's — nothing — only too glad. (*Then boldly.*) Here — give me another kiss, and that'll pay me back.

BELLE (*kissing him*): I'll give you a thousand, if you want 'em. Come on, let's sit down, and we'll have another drink — and this time I'll blow you just to show my appreciation. (*She calls.*) Hey, George! Bring us another round — the same!

RICHARD (*a remnant of caution coming to him*): I don't know as I ought to —

BELLE: Oh, another won't hurt you. And I want to blow you, see. (*They sit down in their former places.*)

RICHARD (*boldly draws his chair closer and puts an arm around her — tipsily*): I like you a lot — now I'm getting to know you. You're a darned nice girl.

BELLE: Nice is good! Tell me another. Well, if I'm so nice, why didn't you want to take me upstairs? That's what I don't get.

RICHARD (*lying boldly*): I did want to — only I — (*Then he adds solemnly.*) I've sworn off. (*The* BARTENDER *enters with the drinks.*)

BARTENDER (*setting them on the table*): Here's your pleasure. (*Then regarding* RICHARD's *arm about her waist.*) Ho-ho, we're coming on, I see. (RICHARD *grins at him muzzily.*)

BELLE (*digs into her stocking and gives him a dollar*): Here. This is mine. (*He gives her change and she tips him a dime, and he goes out. She puts the five* RICHARD *had given her in her stocking and picks up her glass.*) Here's how — and thanks again. (*She sips.*)

RICHARD (*boisterously*): Bottoms up! Bottoms up! (*He drinks all of his down and sighs with exaggerated satisfaction.*) Gee, that's good stuff, all right. (*Hugging her.*) Give me another kiss, Belle.

BELLE (*kisses him*): What did you mean a minute ago when you said you'd sworn off?

RICHARD (*solemnly*): I took an oath I'd be faithful.

BELLE (*cynically*): Till death do us part, eh? Who's the girl?

RICHARD (*shortly*): Never mind.

BELLE (*bristling*): I'm not good enough to talk about her, I suppose?

RICHARD: I didn't — mean that. You're all right. (*Then with tipsy gravity.*) Only you oughtn't to lead this kind of life. It isn't right — for a nice girl like you. Why don't you reform?

BELLE (*sharply*): Nix on that line of talk! Can it, you hear! You can do a lot with me for five dollars — but you can't reform me, see. Mind your own business, Kid, and don't butt in where you're not wanted!

RICHARD: I — I didn't mean to hurt your feelings.

BELLE: I know you didn't mean. You're only like a lot of people who mean well, to hear them tell it. (*Changing the subject.*) So you're faithful to your one love, eh? (*With an ugly sneer.*) And how about her? Bet you she's out with a guy under some bush this minute, giving him all he wants. Don't be a sucker, Kid! Even the little flies do it!

RICHARD (*starting up in his chair — angrily*): Don't you say that! Don't you dare!

BELLE (*unimpressed — with a cynical shrug of her shoulders*): All right. Have it your own way and be a sucker! It cuts no ice with me.

RICHARD: You don't know her or —

BELLE: And don't want to. Shut up about her, can't you?

(*She stares before her bitterly.* RICHARD *subsides into scowling gloom. He is becoming perceptibly more intoxicated with each moment now. The* BARTENDER *and the* SALESMAN *appear just inside the swinging door. The* BARTENDER *nods toward* BELLE, *giving the* SALESMAN *a wink. The* SALESMAN *grins and comes into the room, carrying his highball in his hand. He is a stout, jowly-faced man in his late thirties, dressed with cheap nattiness, with the professional breeziness and jocular, kid-'em-along manner of his kind.* BELLE *looks up as he enters and he and she exchange a glance of complete recognition. She knows his type by heart and he knows hers.*)

SALESMAN (*passes by her to the table at right — grinning genially*): Good evening.

BELLE: Good evening.

SALESMAN (*sitting down*): Hope I'm not butting in on your party — but my dogs were giving out standing at that bar.

BELLE: All right with me. (*Giving* RICHARD *a rather contemptuous look.*) I've got no party on.

SALESMAN: That sounds hopeful.

RICHARD (*suddenly recites sentimentally*):

> "But I wouldn't do such, 'cause I loved her too much,
> But I learned about women from her."

(*Turns to scowl at the* SALESMAN *— then to* BELLE.) Let's have 'nother drink!

BELLE: You've had enough. (RICHARD *subsides, muttering to himself.*)

SALESMAN: What is it — a child poet or a child actor?

BELLE: Don't know. Got me guessing.

SALESMAN: Well, if you could shake the cradle-robbing act, maybe we could do a little business.

BELLE: That's easy. I just pull my freight. (*She shakes* RICHARD *by the arm*) Listen, Kid. Here's an old friend of mine, Mr. Smith of New Haven, just come in. I'm going over and sit at his table for a while, see. And you better go home.

RICHARD (*blinking at her and scowling*): I'm never going home! I'll show them!

BELLE: Have it your own way — only let me up. (*She takes his arm from around her and goes to sit by the* SALESMAN. RICHARD *stares after her offendedly.*)

RICHARD: Go on. What do I care what you do? (*He recites scornfully.*) "For a woman's only a woman, but a good cigar's a smoke."

SALESMAN (*as* BELLE *sits beside him*): Well, what kind of beer will you have, Sister?

BELLE: Mine's a gin rickey.

SALESMAN: You've got extravagant tastes, I'm sorry to see.

RICHARD (*begins to recite sepulchrally*):

> "Yet each man kills the thing he loves,
> By each let this be heard."

SALESMAN (*grinning*): Say, this is rich! (*He calls encouragement.*) That's swell dope, young feller. Give us some more.

RICHARD (*ignoring him — goes on more rhetorically*):

> "Some do it with a bitter look,
> Some with a flattering word,

The coward does it with a kiss,
The brave man with a sword!"

(*He stares at* BELLE *gloomily and mutters tragically*.) I did it with a kiss! I'm a coward.

SALESMAN: That's the old stuff, Kid. You've got something on the ball, all right, all right! Give us another — right over the old pan, now!

BELLE (*with a laugh*): Get the hook!

RICHARD (*glowering at her — tragically*):

" 'Oho,' they cried, 'the whole world is wide,
But fettered limbs go lame!
And once, or twice, to throw the dice
Is a gentlemanly game,
But he does not win who plays with Sin
In the secret House of Shame!' "

BELLE (*angrily*): Aw, can it! Give us a rest from that bunk!

SALESMAN (*mockingly*): This gal of yours don't appreciate poetry. She's a lowbrow. But I'm the kid that eats it up. My middle name is Kelly and Sheets! Give us some more of the same! Do you know "The Lobster and the Wise Guy"? (*Turns to* BELLE *seriously*.) No kidding, that's a peacherino. I heard a guy recite it at Poli's. Maybe this nut knows it. Do you, Kid? (*But* RICHARD *only glowers at him gloomily without answering*.)

BELLE (*surveying* RICHARD *contemptuously*): He's copped a fine skinful — and gee, he's hardly had anything.

RICHARD (*suddenly — with a dire emphasis*): "And then — at ten o'clock — Eilert Lovborg will come — with vine leaves in his hair!"

BELLE: And bats in his belfry, if he's you!

RICHARD (*regards her bitterly — then starts to his feet bellicosely — to the* SALES-MAN): I don't believe you ever knew her in New Haven at all! You just picked her up now! You leave her alone, you hear! You won't do anything to her — not while I'm here to protect her!

BELLE (*laughing*): Oh, my God! Listen to it!

SALESMAN: Ssshh! This is a scream! Wait! (*He addresses* RICHARD *in tones of exaggerated melodrama*.) Curse you, Jack Dalton, if I won't unhand her, what then?

RICHARD (*threateningly*): I'll give you a good punch in the snoot, that's what! (*He moves toward their table*.)

SALESMAN (*with mock terror — screams in falsetto*): Help! Help! (*The* BARTENDER *comes in irritably*.)

BARTENDER: Hey. Cut out the noise. What the hell's up with you?

RICHARD (*tipsily*): He's too — damn fresh!

SALESMAN (*with a wink*): He's going to murder me. (*Then gets a bright idea for eliminating* RICHARD — *seriously to the* BARTENDER.) It's none of my business, Brother, but if I were in your boots I'd give this young souse the gate. He's under age; any fool can see that.

BARTENDER (*guiltily*): He told me he was over eighteen.

SALESMAN: Yes, and I tell you I'm the Pope — but you don't have to believe me. If you're not looking for trouble, I'd advise you to get him started for some other gin mill and let them do the lying, if anything comes up.

BARTENDER: Hmm. (*He turns to* RICHARD *angrily and gives him a push.*) Come on, now. On your way! You'll start no trouble in here! Beat it now!

RICHARD: I will not beat it!

BARTENDER: Oho, won't you? (*He gives him another push that almost sends him sprawling.*)

BELLE (*callously*): Give him the bum's rush! I'm sick of his bull! (RICHARD *turns furiously and tries to punch the* BARTENDER.)

BARTENDER (*avoids the punch*): Oho, you would, would you!

(*He grabs* RICHARD *by the back of the neck and the seat of the pants and marches him ignominiously toward the swinging door.*)

RICHARD: Leggo of me, you dirty coward!

BARTENDER: Quiet now — or I'll pin a Mary Ann on your jaw that'll quiet you! (*He rushes him through the screen door and a moment later the outer doors are heard swinging back and forth.*)

SALESMAN (*with a chuckle*): Hand it to me, Kid. How was that for a slick way of getting rid of him?

BELLE (*suddenly sentimental*): Poor kid. I hope he makes home all right. I liked him — before he got soused.

SALESMAN: Who is he?

BELLE: The boy who's upstairs with my friend told me, but I didn't pay much attention. Name's Miller. His old man runs a paper in this one-horse burg, I think he said.

SALESMAN (*with a whistle*): Phew! He must be Nat Miller's kid, then.

BARTENDER (*coming back from the bar*): Well, he's on his way — with a good boot in the tail to help him!

SALESMAN (*with a malicious chuckle*): Yes? Well, maybe that boot will cost you a job, Brother. Know Nat Miller who runs the *Globe*? That's his kid.

BARTENDER (*his face falling*): The hell he is! Who said so?

SALESMAN: This baby doll. (*Getting up.*) Say, I'll go keep cases on him — see he gets on the trolley all right, anyway. Nat Miller's a good scout. (*He hurries out.*)

BARTENDER (*viciously*): God damn the luck! If he ever finds out I served his kid, he'll run me out of town. (*He turns on* BELLE *furiously.*) Why didn't you put me wise, you lousy tramp, you!

BELLE: Hey! I don't stand for that kind of talk — not from no hick beer-squirter like you, see!

BARTENDER (*furiously*): You don't, don't you! Who was it but you told me to hand him dynamite in that fizz? (*He gives her chair a push that almost throws her to the floor.*) Beat it, you — and beat it quick — or I'll call Sullivan from the corner and have you run in for street-walking! (*He gives her a push that lands her against the family-entrance door.*) Get the hell out of here — and no long waits!

BELLE (*opens the door and goes out — turns and calls back viciously*): I'll fix you for this, you thick Mick, if I have to go to jail for it. (*She goes out and slams the door.*)

BARTENDER (*looks after her worriedly for a second — then shrugs his shoulders*): That's only her bull. (*Then with a sigh as he returns to the bar.*) Them lousy tramps is always getting this dump in Dutch!

CURTAIN

SCENE 2

Scene — Same as Act I — Sitting-room of the MILLER *home — about 11 o'clock the same night.*

MILLER *is sitting in his favorite rocking-chair at left of table, front. He has discarded collar and tie, coat and shoes, and wears an old, worn, brown dressing-gown and disreputable-looking carpet slippers. He has his reading specs on and is running over items in a newspaper. But his mind is plainly preoccupied and worried, and he is not paying much attention to what he reads.*

MRS. MILLER *sits by the table at right, front. She also has on her specs. A sewing basket is on her lap and she is trying hard to keep her attention fixed on the doily she is doing. But, as in the case of her husband, but much more apparently, her mind is preoccupied, and she is obviously on tenterhooks of nervous uneasiness.*

LILY *is sitting in the armchair by the table at rear, facing right. She is pretending to read a novel, but her attention wanders, too, and her expression is sad, although now it has lost all its bitterness and become submissive and resigned again.*

MILDRED *sits at the desk at right, front, writing two words over and over again, stopping each time to survey the result critically, biting her tongue, intensely concentrated on her work.*

TOMMY *sits on the sofa at left, front. He has had a hard day and is terribly sleepy but will not acknowledge it. His eyes blink shut on him, his head begins to nod, but he isn't giving up, and every time he senses any of the family glancing in his direction, he goads himself into a bright-eyed wakefulness.*

MILDRED (*finally surveys the two words she has been writing and is satisfied with them*): There. (*She takes the paper over to her mother.*) Look, Ma. I've been practising a new way of writing my name. Don't look at the others, only the last one. Don't you think it's the real goods?

MRS. MILLER (*pulled out of her preoccupation*): Don't talk that horrible slang. It's bad enough for boys, but for a young girl supposed to have manners — my goodness, when I was your age, if my mother'd ever heard me —

MILDRED: Well, don't you think it's nice, then?

MRS. MILLER (*sinks back into preoccupation — scanning the paper — vaguely*): Yes, very nice, Mildred — very nice, indeed. (*Hands the paper back mechanically.*)

MILDRED (*is a little piqued, but smiles*): Absent-minded! I don't believe you even saw it. (*She passes around the table to show her* AUNT LILY. MILLER *gives an uneasy glance at his wife and then, as if afraid of meeting her eye, looks quickly back at his paper again.*)

MRS. MILLER (*staring before her — sighs worriedly*): Oh, I do wish Richard would come home!

MILLER: There now, Essie. He'll be in any minute now. Don't you worry about him.

MRS. MILLER: But I do worry about him!

LILY (*surveying* MILDRED's *handiwork — smiling*): This is fine, Mildred. Your penmanship is improving wonderfully. But don't you think that maybe you've got a little too many flourishes?

MILDRED (*disappointedly*): But, Aunt Lily, that's just what I was practising hardest on.

MRS. MILLER (*with another sigh*): What time is it now, Nat?

MILLER (*adopting a joking tone*): I'm going to buy a clock for in here. You have me reaching for my watch every couple of minutes. (*He has pulled his watch out of his vest pocket — with forced carelessness.*) Only a little past ten.

MRS. MILLER: Why, you said it was that an hour ago! Nat Miller, you're telling me a fib, so's not to worry me. You let me see that watch!

MILLER (*guiltily*): Well, it's quarter to eleven — but that's not so late — when you remember it's Fourth of July.

MRS. MILLER: If you don't stop talking Fourth of July — ! To hear you go on, you'd think that was an excuse for anything from murder to picking pockets!

MILDRED (*has brought her paper around to her father and now shoves it under his nose*): Look, Pa.

MILLER (*seizes on this interruption with relief*): Let's see. Hmm. Seems to me you've been inventing a new signature every week lately. What are you in training for — writing checks? You must be planning to catch a rich husband.

MILDRED (*with an arch toss of her head*): No wedding bells for me! But how do you like it, Pa?

MILLER: It's overpowering — no other word for it, overpowering! You could put it on the Declaration of Independence and not feel ashamed.

MRS. MILLER (*desolately, almost on the verge of tears*): It's all right for you to laugh and joke with Mildred! I'm the only one in this house seems to care — (*Her lips tremble.*)

MILDRED (*a bit disgustedly*): Ah, Ma, Dick only sneaked off to the fireworks at the beach, you wait and see.

MRS. MILLER: Those fireworks were over long ago. If he had, he'd be home.

LILY (*soothingly*): He probably couldn't get a seat, the trolleys are so jammed, and he had to walk home.

MILLER (*seizing on this with relief*): Yes, I never thought of that, but I'll bet that's it.

MILDRED: Ah, don't let him worry you, Ma. He just wants to show off he's heart-broken about that silly Muriel — and get everyone fussing over him and wondering if he hasn't drowned himself or something.

MRS. MILLER (*snappily*): You be quiet! The way you talk at times, I really believe you're that hard-hearted you haven't got a heart in you! (*With an accusing glance at her husband.*) One thing I know, you don't get that from me! (*He meets her eye and avoids it guiltily. She sniffs and looks away from him around the room. TOMMY, who is nodding and blinking, is afraid her eye is on him. He straightens alertly and speaks in a voice that, in spite of his effort, is dripping with drowsiness.*)

TOMMY: Let me see what you wrote, Mid.

MILDRED (*cruelly mocking*): You? You're so sleepy you couldn't see it!

TOMMY (*valiantly*): I am not sleepy!

MRS. MILLER (*has fixed her eye on him*): My gracious, I was forgetting you were still up! You run up to bed this minute! It's hours past your bedtime!

TOMMY: But it's the Fourth of July. Ain't it, Pa?

MRS. MILLER (*gives her husband an accusing stare*): There! You see what you've done? You might know he'd copy your excuses! (*Then sharply to TOMMY.*) You heard what I said, Young Man!

TOMMY: Aw, Ma, can't I stay up a *little* longer?

MRS. MILLER: I said, no! You obey me and no more arguing about it!

TOMMY (*drags himself to his feet*): Aw! I should think I could stay up till Dick —

MILLER (*kindly but firmly*): You heard your ma say no more arguing. When she says git, you better git. (TOMMY *accepts his fate resignedly and starts around kissing them all good night*.)

TOMMY (*kissing her*): Good night, Aunt Lily.

LILY: Good night, Dear. Sleep well.

TOMMY (*pecking at* MILDRED): Good night, you.

MILDRED: Good night, you.

TOMMY (*kissing him*): Good night, Pa.

MILLER: Good night, Son. Sleep tight.

TOMMY (*kissing her*): Good night, Ma.

MRS. MILLER: Good night. Here! You look feverish. Let me feel of your head. No, you're all right. Hurry up, now. And don't forget your prayers.

(TOMMY *goes slowly to the doorway — then turns suddenly, the discovery of another excuse lighting up his face*.)

TOMMY: Here's another thing, Ma. When I was up to the water closet last —

MRS. MILLER (*sharply*): When you were *where?*

TOMMY: The bathroom.

MRS. MILLER: That's better.

TOMMY: Uncle Sid was snoring like a fog horn — and he's right next to my room. How can I ever get to sleep while he's — (*He is overcome by a jaw-cracking yawn*.)

MRS. MILLER: I guess you'd get to sleep all right if you were inside a fog horn. You run along now. (TOMMY *gives up, grins sleepily, and moves off to bed. As soon as he is off her mind, all her former uneasiness comes back on* MRS. MILLER *tenfold. She sighs, moves restlessly, then finally asks*.) What time is it now, Nat?

MILLER: Now, Essie, I just told you a minute ago.

MRS. MILLER (*resentfully*): I don't see how you can take it so calm! Here it's midnight, you might say, and our Richard still out, and we don't even know where he is.

MILDRED: I hear someone on the piazza. Bet that's him now, Ma.

MRS. MILLER (*her anxiety immediately turning to relieved anger*): You give him a good piece of your mind, Nat, you hear me! You're too easy with him, that's the whole trouble! The idea of him daring to stay out like this! (*The front door is heard being opened and shut, and someone whistling "Waltz Me Around Again, Willie."*)

MILDRED: No, that isn't Dick. It's Art.

MRS. MILLER (*her face falling*): Oh. (*A moment later* ARTHUR *enters through the front parlor, whistling softly, half under his breath, looking complacently pleased with himself*.)

MILLER (*surveys him over his glasses, not with enthusiasm — shortly*): So you're back, eh? We thought it was Richard.

ARTHUR: Is he still out? Where'd he go to?

MILLER: That's just what we'd like to know. You didn't run into him anywhere, did you?

ARTHUR: No. I've been at the Rands' ever since dinner. (*He sits down in the armchair at left of table, rear*.) I suppose he sneaked off to the beach to watch the fireworks.

MILLER (*pretending an assurance he is far from feeling*): Of course. That's what we've been trying to tell your mother, but she insists on worrying her head off.

MRS. MILLER: But if he was going to the fireworks, why wouldn't he say so? He knew we'd let him.

ARTHUR (*with calm wisdom*): That's easy, Ma. (*He grins superiorly.*) Didn't you hear him this morning showing off bawling out the Fourth like an anarchist? He wouldn't want to renege on that to you — but he'd want to see the old fireworks just the same. (*He adds complacently.*) I know. He's at the foolish age.

MILLER (*stares at* ARTHUR *with ill-concealed astonishment, then grins*): Well, Arthur, by gosh, you make me feel as if I owed you an apology when you talk horse sense like that. (*He turns to his wife, greatly relieved.*) Arthur's hit the nail right on the head, I think, Essie. That was what I couldn't figure out — why he — but now it's clear as day.

MRS. MILLER (*with a sigh*): Well, I hope you're right. But I wish he was home.

ARTHUR (*takes out his pipe and fills and lights it with solemn gravity*): He oughtn't to be allowed out this late at his age. I wasn't, Fourth or no Fourth — if I remember.

MILLER (*a twinkle in his eyes*): Don't tax your memory trying to recall those ancient days of your youth. (MILDRED *laughs and* ARTHUR *looks sheepish. But he soon regains his aplomb.*)

ARTHUR (*importantly*): We had a corking dinner at the Rands'. We had sweetbreads on toast.

MRS. MILLER (*arising momentarily from her depression*): Just like the Rands to put on airs before you! I never could see anything to sweetbreads. Always taste like soap to me. And no real nourishment to them. I wouldn't have the pesky things on my table! (ARTHUR *again feels sat upon.*)

MILDRED (*teasingly*): Did you kiss Elsie good night?

ARTHUR: Stop trying to be so darn funny all the time! You give me a pain in the ear!

MILDRED: And that's where she gives me a pain, the stuck-up thing! — thinks she's the whole cheese!

MILLER (*irritably*): And it's where your everlasting wrangling gives me a pain, you two! Give us a rest! (*There is silence for a moment.*)

MRS. MILLER (*sighs worriedly again*): I do wish that boy would get home!

MILLER (*glances at her uneasily, peeks surreptitiously at his watch — then has an inspiration and turns to* ARTHUR): Arthur, what's this I hear about your having such a good singing voice? Rand was telling me he liked nothing better than to hear you sing — said you did every night you were up there. Why don't you ever give us folks at home here a treat?

ARTHUR (*pleased, but still nursing wounded dignity*): I thought you'd only sit on me.

MRS. MILLER (*perking up — proudly*): Arthur has a real nice voice. He practices when you're not at home. I didn't know you cared for singing, Nat.

MILLER: Well, I do — nothing better — and when I was a boy I had a fine voice myself and folks used to say I'd ought — (*Then abruptly, mindful of his painful experience with reminiscence at dinner, looking about him guiltily.*) Hmm. But don't hide your light under a bushel, Arthur. Why not give us a song or two now? You can play for him, can't you, Mildred?

MILDRED (*with a toss of her head*): I can play as well as Elsie Rand, at least!

ARTHUR (*ignoring her — clearing his throat importantly*): I've been singing a lot tonight. I don't know if my voice —

MILDRED (*forgetting her grudge, grabs her brother's hand and tugs at it*): Come on. Don't play modest. You know you're just dying to show off. (*This puts* ARTHUR *off it at once. He snatches his hand away from her angrily.*)

ARTHUR: Let go of me, you! (*Then with surly dignity.*) I don't feel like singing tonight, Pa. I will some other time.

MILLER: You let him alone, Mildred! (*He winks at* ARTHUR, *indicating with his eyes and a nod of his head* MRS. MILLER, *who has again sunk into worried brooding. He makes it plain by this pantomime that he wants him to sing to distract his mother's mind.*)

ARTHUR (*puts aside his pipe and gets up promptly*): Oh — sure, I'll do the best I can. (*He follows* MILDRED *into the front parlor, where he switches on the lights.*)

MILLER (*to his wife*): It won't keep Tommy awake. Nothing could. And Sid, he'd sleep through an earthquake. (*Then suddenly, looking through the front parlor — grumpily.*) Darn it, speak of the devil, here he comes. Well, he's had a good sleep and he'd ought to be sobered up. (LILY *gets up from her chair and looks around her huntedly, as if for a place to hide.* MILLER *says soothingly.*) Lily, you just sit down and read your book and don't pay any attention to him. (*She sits down again and bends over her book tensely. From the front parlor comes the tinkling of a piano as* MILDRED *runs over the scales. In the midst of this,* SID *enters through the front parlor. All the effervescence of his jag has worn off and he is now suffering from a bad case of hangover — nervous, sick, a prey to gloomy remorse and bitter feelings of self-loathing and self-pity. His eyes are bloodshot and puffed, his face bloated, the fringe of hair around his baldness tousled and tufty. He sidles into the room guiltily, his eyes shifting about, avoiding looking at anyone.*)

SID (*forcing a sickly, twitching smile*): Hello.

MILLER (*considerately casual*): Hello, Sid. Had a good nap? (*Then, as* SID *swallows hard and is about to break into further speech,* MILDRED's *voice comes from the front parlor,* "I haven't played that in ever so long, but I'll try," *and she starts an accompaniment.* MILLER *motions* SID *to be quiet.*) Ssshh! Arthur's going to sing for us. (SID *flattens himself against the edge of the bookcase at center, rear, miserably self-conscious and ill-at-ease there but nervously afraid to move anywhere else.* ARTHUR *begins to sing. He has a fairly decent voice but his method is untrained sentimentality to a dripping degree. He sings that old sentimental favorite,* "Then You'll Remember Me." *The effect on his audience is instant.* MILLER *gazes before him with a ruminating melancholy, his face seeming to become gently sorrowful and old.* MRS. MILLER *stares before her, her expression becoming more and more doleful.* LILY *forgets to pretend to read her book but looks over it, her face growing tragically sad. As for* SID, *he is moved to his remorseful, guilt-stricken depths. His mouth pulls down at the corners and he seems about to cry. The song comes to an end.* MILLER *starts, then claps his hands enthusiastically and calls.*) Well done, Arthur — well done! Why, you've got a splendid voice! Give us some more! You liked that, didn't you, Essie?

MRS. MILLER (*dolefully*): Yes — but it's sad — terrible sad.

SID (*after swallowing hard, suddenly blurts out*): Nat and Essie — and Lily — I — I want to apologize — for coming home — the way I did — there's no excuse — but I didn't mean —

MILLER (*sympathetically*): Of course, Sid. It's all forgotten.

MRS. MILLER (*rousing herself — affectionately pitying*): Don't be a goose, Sid. We know how it is with picnics. You forget it. (*His face lights up a bit but his gaze shifts to* LILY *with a mute appeal, hoping for a word from her which is not forth-coming. Her eyes are fixed on her book, her body tense and rigid.*)

SID (*finally blurts out desperately*): Lily — I'm sorry — about the fireworks. Can you — forgive me? (*But* LILY *remains implacably silent. A stricken look comes over* SID's *face. In the front parlor* MILDRED *is heard saying* "But I only know the chorus" — *and she starts another accompaniment.*)

MILLER (*comes to* SID's *rescue*): Ssshh! We're going to have another song. Sit down, Sid. (SID, *hanging his head, flees to the farthest corner, left, front, and sits at the end of the sofa, facing front, hunched up, elbows on knees, face in hands, his round eyes childishly wounded and woe-begone.* ARTHUR *sings the popular* "Dearie," *playing up its sentimental values for all he is worth. The effect on his audience is that of the previous song, intensified — especially upon* SID. *As he finishes,* MILLER *again starts and applauds.*) Mighty fine, Arthur! You sang that darned well! Didn't he, Essie?

MRS. MILLER (*dolefully*): Yes — but I wish he wouldn't sing such sad songs. (*Then, her lips trembling.*) Richard's always whistling that.

MILLER (*hastily — calls*): Give us something cheery, next one, Arthur. You know, just for variety's sake.

SID (*suddenly turns toward* LILY — *his voice choked with tears — in a passion of self-denunciation*): You're right, Lily! — right not to forgive me! — I'm no good and never will be! — I'm a no-good drunken bum! — you shouldn't even wipe your feet on me! — I'm a dirty, rotten drunk! — no good to myself or anybody else! — if I had any guts I'd kill myself, and good riddance! — but I haven't! — I'm yellow, too! — a yellow, drunken bum! (*He hides his face in his hands and begins to sob like a sick little boy. This is too much for* LILY. *All her bitter hurt and steely resolve to ignore and punish him vanish in a flash, swamped by a pitying love for him. She runs and puts her arm around him — even kisses him tenderly and impulsively on his bald head, and soothes him as if he were a little boy.* MRS. MILLER, *almost equally moved, has half risen to go to her brother, too, but* MILLER *winks and shakes his head vigorously and motions her to sit down.*)

LILY: There! Don't cry, Sid! I can't bear it! Of course, I forgive you! Haven't I always forgiven you? I know you're not to blame — So don't, Sid!

SID (*lifts a tearful, humbly grateful, pathetic face to her — but a face that the dawn of a cleansed conscience is already beginning to restore to its natural Puckish expression*): Do you really forgive me — I know I don't deserve it — can you really — ?

LILY (*gently*): I told you I did, Sid — and I do.

SID (*kisses her hand humbly, like a big puppy licking it*): Thanks, Lily. I can't tell you — (*In the front parlor,* ARTHUR *begins to sing rollickingly* "Waiting at the Church," *and after the first line or two* MILDRED *joins in.* SID's *face lights up with appreciation and, automatically, he begins to tap one foot in time, still holding fast to* LILY's *hand. When they come to* "sent around a note, this is what she wrote," *he can no longer resist, but joins in a shaky bawl.*) "Can't get away to marry you today, My wife won't let me!" (*As the song finishes, the two in the other room laugh.* MILLER *and* SID *laugh.* LILY *smiles at* SID's *laughter. Only* MRS. MILLER *remains dolefully preoccupied, as if she hadn't heard.*)

MILLER: That's fine, Arthur and Mildred. That's darned good.

SID (*turning to* LILY *enthusiastically*): You ought to hear Vesta Victoria sing that!

Gosh, she's great! I heard her at Hammerstein's Victoria — you remember, that trip I made to New York.

LILY (*her face suddenly tired and sad again — for her memory of certain aspects of that trip is the opposite from what he would like her to recall at this moment — gently disengaging her hand from his — with a hopeless sigh*): Yes, I remember, Sid. (*He is overcome momentarily by guilty confusion. She goes quietly and sits down in her chair again. In the front parlor, from now on,* MILDRED *keeps starting to run over popular tunes but always gets stuck and turns to another.*)

MRS. MILLER (*suddenly*): What time is it now, Nat? (*Then without giving him a chance to answer.*) Oh, I'm getting worried something dreadful, Nat! You don't know what might have happened to Richard! You read in the papers every day about boys getting run over by automobiles.

LILY: Oh, don't say that, Essie!

MILLER (*sharply, to conceal his own reawakened apprehension*): Don't get to imagining things, now!

MRS. MILLER: Well, why couldn't it happen, with everyone that owns one out tonight, and lots of those driving, drunk? Or he might have gone down to the beach dock and fallen overboard! (*On the verge of hysteria.*) Oh, I know something dreadful's happened! And you can sit there listening to songs and laughing as if — Why don't you do something? Why don't you go out and find him? (*She bursts into tears.*)

LILY (*comes to her quickly and puts her arm around her*): Essie, you mustn't worry so! You'll make yourself sick! Richard's all right. I've got a feeling in my bones he's all right.

MILDRED (*comes hurrying in from the front parlor*): What's the trouble? (ARTHUR *appears in the doorway beside her. She goes to her mother and also puts an arm around her.*) Ah, don't cry, Ma! Dick'll turn up in a minute or two, wait and see!

ARTHUR: Sure, he will!

MILLER (*has gotten to his feet, frowning — soberly*): I was going out to look — if he wasn't back by twelve sharp. That'd be the time it'd take him to walk from the beach if he left after the last car. But I'll go now, if it'll ease your mind. I'll take the auto and drive out the beach road — and likely pick him up on the way. (*He has taken his collar and tie from where they hang from one corner of the bookcase at rear, center, and is starting to put them on.*) You better come with me, Arthur.

ARTHUR: Sure thing, Pa. (*Suddenly he listens and says.*) Ssshh! There's someone on the piazza now — coming around to this door, too. That must be him. No one else would —

MRS. MILLER: Oh, thank God, thank God!

MILLER (*with a sheepish smile*): Darn him! I've a notion to give him hell for worrying us all like this. (*The screen door is pushed violently open and* RICHARD *lurches in and stands swaying a little, blinking his eyes in the light. His face is a pasty pallor, shining with perspiration, and his eyes are glassy. The knees of his trousers are dirty, one of them torn from the sprawl on the sidewalk he had taken, following the* BARTENDER's *kick. They all gape at him, too paralyzed for a moment to say anything.*)

MRS. MILLER: Oh God, what's happened to him! He's gone crazy! Richard!

SID (*the first to regain presence of mind — with a grin*): Crazy, nothing. He's only soused!

ARTHUR: He's drunk, that's what! (*Then shocked and condemning.*) You've got your nerve! You fresh kid! We'll take that out of you when we get you down to Yale!

RICHARD (*with a wild gesture of defiance — maudlinly dramatic*):

> "Yesterday this Day's Madness did prepare
> Tomorrow's Silence, Triumph, or Despair.
> Drink! for — "

MILLER (*his face grown stern and angry, takes a threatening step toward him*): Richard! How dare — !

MRS. MILLER (*hysterically*): Don't you strike him, Nat! Don't you — !

SID (*grabbing his arm*): Steady, Nat! Keep your temper! No good bawling him out now! He don't know what he's doing!

MILLER (*controlling himself and looking a bit ashamed*): All right — you're right, Sid.

RICHARD (*drunkenly glorying in the sensation he is creating — recites with dramatic emphasis*): "And then — I will come — with vine leaves in my hair!" (*He laughs with a double-dyed sardonicism.*)

MRS. MILLER (*staring at him as if she couldn't believe her eyes*): Richard! You're intoxicated! — you bad, wicked boy, you!

RICHARD (*forces a wicked leer to his lips and quotes with ponderous mockery*): "Fancy that, Hedda!" (*Then suddenly his whole expression changes, his pallor takes on a greenish, sea-sick tinge, his eyes seem to be turned inward uneasily — and, all pose gone, he calls to his mother appealingly, like a sick little boy.*) Ma! I feel — rotten! (MRS. MILLER *gives a cry and starts to go to him, but* SID *steps in her way.*)

SID: You let me take care of him, Essie. I know this game backwards.

MILLER (*putting his arm around his wife*): Yes, you leave him to Sid.

SID (*his arm around* RICHARD — *leading him off through the front parlor*): Come on, Old Sport! Upstairs we go! Your old Uncle Sid'll fix you up. He's the kid that wrote the book!

MRS. MILLER (*staring after them — still aghast*): Oh, it's too terrible! Imagine our Richard! And did you hear him talking about some Hedda? Oh, I know he's been with one of those bad women, I know he has — my Richard! (*She hides her face on* MILLER's *shoulder and sobs heart-brokenly.*)

MILLER (*a tired, harassed, deeply worried look on his face — soothing her*): Now, now, you mustn't get to imagining such things! You mustn't, Essie! (LILY *and* MILDRED *and* ARTHUR *are standing about awkwardly with awed, shocked faces.*)

CURTAIN

ACT IV

SCENE 1

Scene — The same — Sitting-room of the MILLER *house — about 1 o'clock in the afternoon of the following day.*

    As the curtain rises, the family, with the exception of RICHARD, *are discovered coming in through the back parlor from dinner in the dining-room.* MILLER *and his wife come first. His face is set in an expression of frowning severity.* MRS. MILLER's *face is drawn and worried. She has evidently had no rest yet from a sleepless, tearful night.* SID *is himself again, his expression as innocent as if nothing had occurred the previous day that remotely concerned him. And, outside of eyes that are blood-shot and nerves that are shaky, he shows no aftereffects except that he is terribly sleepy.* LILY *is gently sad and depressed.* AR-THUR *is self-consciously a virtuous young man against whom nothing can be said.* MILDRED *and* TOMMY *are subdued, covertly watching their father.*

They file into the sitting-room in silence and then stand around uncertainly, as if each were afraid to be the first to sit down. The atmosphere is as stiltedly. grave as if they were attending a funeral service. Their eyes keep fixed on the head of the house, who has gone to the window at right and is staring out frowningly, savagely chewing a toothpick.

MILLER (*finally — irritably*): Damn it, I'd ought to be back at the office putting in some good licks! I've a whole pile of things that have got to be done today!

MRS. MILLER (*accusingly*): You don't mean to tell me you're going back without seeing him? It's your duty — !

MILLER (*exasperatedly*): 'Course I'm not! I wish you'd stop jumping to conclusions! What else did I come home for, I'd like to know? Do I usually come way back here for dinner on a busy day? I was only wishing this hadn't come up — just at this particular time. (*He ends up very lamely and is irritably conscious of the fact.*)

TOMMY (*who has been fidgeting restlessly — unable to bear the suspense a moment longer*): What is it Dick done? Why is everyone scared to tell me?

MILLER (*seizes this as an escape valve — turns and fixes his youngest son with a stern forbidding eye*): Young man, I've never spanked you yet, but that don't mean I never will! Seems to me that you've been just itching for it lately! You keep your mouth shut till you're spoken to — or I warn you something's going to happen!

MRS. MILLER: Yes, Tommy, you keep still and don't bother your pa. (*Then warningly to her husband.*) Careful what you say, Nat. Little pitchers have big ears.

MILLER (*peremptorily*): You kids skedaddle — all of you. Why are you always hanging around the house? Go out and play in the yard, or take a walk, and get some fresh air. (MILDRED *takes* TOMMY's *hand and leads him out through the front parlor.* ARTHUR *hangs back, as if the designation "kids" couldn't possibly apply to him. His father notices this — impatiently.*) You, too, Arthur. (ARTHUR *goes out with a stiff, wounded dignity.*)

LILY (*tactfully*): I think I'll go for a walk, too. (*She goes out through the front parlor.* SID *makes a movement as if to follow her.*)

MILLER: I'd like you to stay, Sid — for a while, anyway.

SID: Sure. (*He sits down in the rocking-chair at right, rear, of table and immediately yawns.*) Gosh, I'm dead. Don't know what's the matter with me today. Can't seem to keep awake.

MILLER (*with caustic sarcasm*): Maybe that demon chowder you drank at the picnic poisoned you! (SID *looks sheepish and forces a grin. Then* MILLER *turns to his wife with the air of one who determinedly faces the unpleasant.*) Where is Richard?

MRS. MILLER (*flusteredly*): He's still in bed. I made him stay in bed to punish him — and I thought he ought to, anyway, after being so sick. But he says he feels all right.

SID (*with another yawn*): 'Course he does. When you're young you can stand anything without it fazing you. Why, I remember when I could come down on the morning after, fresh as a daisy, and eat a breakfast of pork chops and fried onions and — (*He stops guiltily.*)

MILLER (*bitingly*): I suppose that was before eating lobster shells had ruined your iron constitution!

MRS. MILLER (*regards her brother severely*): If I was in your shoes, I'd keep still! (*Then turning to her husband.*) Richard must be feeling better. He ate all the dinner I sent up, Norah says.

MILLER: I thought you weren't going to give him any dinner — to punish him.

MRS. MILLER (*guiltily*): Well — in his weakened condition — I thought it best — (*Then defensively.*) But you needn't think I haven't punished him. I've given him pieces of my mind he won't forget in a hurry. And I've kept reminding him his real punishment was still to come — that you were coming home to dinner on purpose — and then he'd learn that you could be terrible stern when he did such awful things.

MILLER (*stirs uncomfortably*): Hmm!

MRS. MILLER: And that's just what it's your duty to do — punish him good and hard! The idea of him daring — (*Then hastily.*) But you be careful how you go about it, Nat. Remember he's like you inside — too sensitive for his own good. And he never would have done it, I know, if it hadn't been for that darned little dunce, Muriel, and her numbskull father — and then all of us teasing him and hurting his feelings all day — and then you lost your temper and were so sharp with him right after dinner before he went out.

MILLER (*resentfully*): I see this is going to work round to where it's all my fault!

MRS. MILLER: Now, I didn't say that, did I? Don't go losing your temper again. And here's another thing. You know as well as I, Richard would never have done such a thing alone. Why, he wouldn't know how! He must have been influenced and led by someone.

MILLER: Yes, I believe that. Did you worm out of him who it was? (*Then angrily.*) By God, I'll make whoever it was regret it!

MRS. MILLER: No, he wouldn't admit there was anyone. (*Then triumphantly.*) But there is one thing I did worm out of him — and I can tell you it relieved my mind more'n anything. You know, I was afraid he'd been with one of those bad women. Well, turns out there wasn't any Hedda. She was just out of those books he's been reading. He swears he's never known a Hedda in his life. And I believe him. Why, he seemed disgusted with me for having such a notion. (*Then lamely.*) So somehow — I can't kind of feel it's all as bad as I thought it was. (*Then quickly and indignantly.*) But it's bad enough, goodness knows — and you punish him good just the same. The idea of a boy of his age — ! Shall I go up and tell him to get dressed, you want to see him?

MILLER (*helplessly — and irritably*): Yes! I can't waste all day listening to you!

MRS. MILLER (*worriedly*): Now you keep your temper, Nat, remember! (*She goes out through the front parlor.*)

MILLER: Darn women, anyway! They always get you mixed up. Their minds simply don't know what logic is! (*Then he notices that* SID *is dozing — sharply.*) Sid!

SID (*blinking — mechanically*): I'll take the same. (*Then hurriedly.*) What'd you say, Nat?

MILLER (*caustically*): What I didn't say was what'll you have. (*Irritably.*) Do you want to be of some help, or don't you? Then keep awake and try and use your brains! This is a damned sight more serious than Essie has any idea! She thinks there weren't any girls mixed up with Richard's spree last night — but I happen to know there were! (*He takes a letter from his pocket.*) Here's a note a woman left with one of the boys downstairs at the office this morning — didn't ask to see me, just said give me this. He'd never seen her before — said she looked like a tart. (*He has opened the letter and reads.*) "Your son got the booze he drank last night at the Pleasant Beach House. The bartender there knew he was under age but served him just the same. He thought it was a good joke to get him soused. If you have any guts you will run that bastard out of town." Well, what do you think of that? It's a woman's handwriting — not signed, of course.

SID: She's one of the babies, all right — judging from her elegant language.

MILLER: See if you recognize the handwriting.

SID (*with a reproachful look*): Nat, I resent the implication that I correspond with all the tramps around this town. (*Looking at the letter.*) No, I don't know who this one could be. (*Handing the letter back.*) But I deduce that the lady had a run-in with the barkeep and wants revenge.

MILLER (*grimly*): And I deduce that before that she must have picked up Richard — or how would she know who he was? — and took him to this dive.

SID: Maybe. The Pleasant Beach House is nothing but a bed house — (*Quickly.*) At least, so I've been told.

MILLER: That's just the sort of damned fool thing he might do to spite Muriel, in the state of mind he was in — pick up some tart. And she'd try to get him drunk so —

SID: Yes, it might have happened like that — and it might not. How're we ever going to prove it? Everyone at the Pleasant Beach will lie their heads off.

MILLER (*simply and proudly*): Richard won't lie.

SID: Well, don't blame him if he don't remember everything that happened last night. (*Then sincerely concerned.*) I hope you're wrong, Nat. That kind of baby is dangerous for a kid like Dick — in more ways than one. You know what I mean.

MILLER (*frowningly*): Yep — and that's just what's got me worried. Damn it, I've got to have a straight talk with him — about women and all those things. I ought to have long ago.

SID: Yes. You ought.

MILLER: I've tried to a couple of times. I did it all right with Wilbur and Lawrence and Arthur, when it came time — but, hell, with Richard I always get sort of ashamed of myself and can't get started right. You feel, in spite of all his bold talk out of books, that he's so darned innocent inside.

SID: I know. I wouldn't like the job. (*Then after a pause — curiously.*) How were you figuring to punish him for his sins?

MILLER (*frowning*): To be honest with you, Sid, I'm damned if I know. All depends on what I feel about what he feels when I first size him up — and then it'll be like shooting in the dark.

SID: If I didn't know you so well, I'd say don't be too hard on him. (*He smiles a little bitterly.*) If you remember, I was always getting punished — and see what a lot of good it did me!

MILLER (*kindly*): Oh, there's lots worse than you around, so don't take to boasting. (*Then, at a sound from the front parlor — with a sigh.*) Well, here comes the Bad Man, I guess.

SID (*getting up*): I'll beat it. (*But it is* MRS. MILLER *who appears in the doorway, looking guilty and defensive.* SID *sits down again.*)

MRS. MILLER: I'm sorry, Nat — but he was sound asleep and I didn't have the heart to wake him. I waited for him to wake up but he didn't.

MILLER (*concealing a relief of which he is ashamed — exasperatedly*): Well, I'll be double damned! If you're not the —

MRS. MILLER (*defensively aggressive*): Now don't lose your temper at me, Nat Miller! You know as well as I do he needs all the sleep he can get today — after last night's ructions! Do you want him to be taken down sick? And what difference does it make to you, anyway? You can see him when you come home for supper, can't you? My goodness, I never saw you so savage-tempered! You'd think you couldn't bear waiting to punish him!

MILLER (*outraged*): Well, I'll be eternally — (*Then suddenly he laughs.*) No use talking, you certainly take the cake! But you know darned well I told you I'm not coming home to supper tonight. I've got a date with Jack Lawson that may mean a lot of new advertising and it's important.

MRS. MILLER: Then you can see him when you do come home.

MILLER (*covering his evident relief at this respite with a fuming manner*): All right! All right! I give up! I'm going back to the office. (*He starts for the front parlor.*) Bring a man all the way back here on a busy day and then you — No consideration — (*He disappears, and a moment later the front door is heard shutting behind him.*)

MRS. MILLER: Well! I never saw Nat so bad-tempered.

SID (*with a chuckle*): Bad temper, nothing. He's so tickled to get out of it for a while he can't see straight!

MRS. MILLER (*with a sniff*): I hope I know him better than you. (*Then fussing about the room, setting this and that in place, while* SID *yawns drowsily and blinks his eyes.*) Sleeping like a baby — so innocent-looking. You'd think butter wouldn't melt in his mouth. It all goes to show you never can tell by appearances — not even when it's your own child. The idea!

SID (*drowsily*): Oh, Dick's all right, Essie. Stop worrying.

MRS. MILLER (*with a sniff*): Of course, you'd say that. I suppose you'll have him out with you painting the town red the next thing! (*As she is talking,* RICHARD *appears in the doorway from the sitting-room. He shows no ill effects from his experience the night before. In fact, he looks surprisingly healthy. He is dressed in old clothes that look as if they had been hurriedly flung on. His expression is one of hang-dog guilt mingled with a defensive defiance.*)

RICHARD (*with self-conscious unconcern, ignoring his mother*): Hello, Sid.

MRS. MILLER (*whirls on him*): What are you doing here, Young Man? I thought you were asleep! Seems to me you woke up pretty quick — just after your pa left the house!

RICHARD (*sulkily*): I wasn't asleep. I heard you in the room.

MRS. MILLER (*outraged*): Do you mean to say you were deliberately deceiving —

RICHARD: I wasn't deceiving. You didn't ask if I was asleep.

MRS. MILLER: It amounts to the same thing and you know it! It isn't enough your wickedness last night, but now you have to take to lying!

RICHARD: I wasn't lying, Ma. If you'd asked if I was asleep I'd have said no.

MRS. MILLER: I've a good mind to send you straight back to bed and make you stay there!

RICHARD: Ah, what for, Ma? It was only giving me a headache, lying there.

MRS. MILLER: If you've got a headache, I guess you know it doesn't come from that! And imagine me standing there, and feeling sorry for you, like a fool — even having a run-in with your pa because — But you wait till he comes back tonight! If you don't catch it!

RICHARD (*sulkily*): I don't care.

MRS. MILLER: You don't care? You talk as if you weren't sorry for what you did last night!

RICHARD (*defiantly*): I'm not sorry.

MRS. MILLER: Richard! You ought to be ashamed! I'm beginning to think you're hardened in wickedness, that's what!

RICHARD (*with bitter despondency*): I'm not sorry because I don't care a darn what I did, or what's done to me, or anything about anything! I won't do it again —

MRS. MILLER (*seizing on this to relent a bit*): Well, I'm glad to hear you say that, anyway!

RICHARD: But that's not because I think it was wicked or any such old-fogy moral notion, but because it wasn't any fun. It didn't make me happy and funny like it does Uncle Sid —

SID (*drowsily*): What's that? Who's funny?

RICHARD (*ignoring him*): It only made me sadder — and sick — so I don't see any sense in it.

MRS. MILLER: Now you're talking sense! That's a good boy.

RICHARD: But I'm not sorry I tried it once — curing the soul by means of the senses, as Oscar Wilde says. (*Then with despairing pessimism.*) But what does it matter what I do or don't do? Life is all a stupid farce! I'm through with it! (*With a sinister smile.*) It's lucky there aren't any of General Gabler's pistols around — or you'd see if I'd stand it much longer!

MRS. MILLER (*worriedly impressed by this threat — but pretending scorn*): I don't know anything about General Gabler — I suppose that's more of those darned books — but you're a silly gabbler yourself when you talk that way!

RICHARD (*darkly*): That's how little you know about me.

MRS. MILLER (*giving in to her worry*): I wish you wouldn't say those terrible things — about life and pistols! You don't want to worry me to death, do you?

RICHARD (*reassuringly stoical now*): You needn't worry, Ma. It was only my despair talking. But I'm not a coward. I'll face — my fate.

MRS. MILLER (*stands looking at him puzzledly — then gives it up with a sigh*): Well, all I can say is you're the queerest boy I ever did hear of! (*Then solicitously, putting her hand on his forehead.*) How's your headache? Do you want me to get you some Bromo Seltzer?

RICHARD (*taken down — disgustedly*): No, I don't! Aw, Ma, you don't understand anything!

MRS. MILLER: Well, I understand this much: It's your liver, that's what! You'll take a good dose of salts tomorrow morning, and no nonsense about it! (*Then suddenly.*) My goodness, I wonder what time it's getting to be. I've got to go upstreet. (*She goes to the front-parlor doorway — then turns.*) You stay here, Richard, you hear? Remember you're not allowed out today — for a punishment. (*She hurries away.* RICHARD *sits in tragic gloom.* SID, *without opening his eyes, speaks to him drowsily.*)

SID: Well, how's my fellow Rum Pot, as good old Dowie calls us? Got a head?

RICHARD (*startled — sheepishly*): Aw, don't go dragging that up, Uncle Sid. I'm never going to be such a fool again, I tell you.

SID (*with drowsy cynicism — not unmixed with bitterness at the end*): Seems to me I've heard someone say that before. Who could it have been, I wonder? Why, if it wasn't Sid Davis! Yes, sir, I've heard him say that very thing a thousand times, must be. But then he's always fooling; you can't take a word he says seriously; he's a card, that Sid is!

RICHARD (*darkly*): I was desperate, Uncle — even if she wasn't worth it. I was wounded to the heart.

SID: I like "to the quick" better myself — more stylish. (*Then sadly.*) But you're right. Love is hell on a poor sucker. Don't I know it? (RICHARD *is disgusted and disdains to reply.* SID's *chin sinks on his chest and he begins to breathe noisily, fast asleep.* RICHARD *glances at him with aversion. There is a sound of someone on the porch and the screen door is opened and* MILDRED *enters. She smiles on seeing her uncle, then gives a start on seeing* RICHARD.)

MILDRED: Hello! Are you allowed up?

RICHARD: Of course, I'm allowed up.

MILDRED (*comes and sits in her father's chair at right, front, of table*): How did Pa punish you?

RICHARD: He didn't. He went back to the office without seeing me.

MILDRED: Well, you'll catch it later. (*Then rebukingly.*) And you ought to. If you'd ever seen how awful you looked last night!

RICHARD: Ah, forget it, can't you?

MILDRED: Well, are you ever going to do it again, that's what I want to know.

RICHARD: What's that to you?

MILDRED (*with suppressed excitement*): Well, if you don't solemnly swear you won't — then I won't give you something I've got for you.

RICHARD: Don't try to kid me. You haven't got anything.

MILDRED: I have, too.

RICHARD: What?

MILDRED: Wouldn't you like to know! I'll give you three guesses.

RICHARD (*with disdainful dignity*): Don't bother me. I'm in no mood to play riddles with kids!

MILDRED: Oh, well, if you're going to get snippy! Anyway, you haven't promised yet.

RICHARD (*a prey to keen curiosity now*): I promise. What is it?

MILDRED: What would you like best in the world?

RICHARD: I don't know. What?

MILDRED: And you pretend to be in love! If I told Muriel that!

RICHARD (*breathlessly*): Is it — from her?

MILDRED (*laughing*): Well, I guess it's a shame to keep you guessing. Yes. It is from her. I was walking past her place just now when I saw her waving from their parlor window, and I went up and she said give this to Dick, and she didn't have a chance to say anything else because her mother called her and said she wasn't allowed to have company. So I took it — and here it is. (*She gives him a letter folded many times into a tiny square.* RICHARD *opens it with a trembling eagerness and reads.* MILDRED *watches him curiously — then sighs affectedly.*) Gee, it must be nice to be in love like you are — all with one person.

RICHARD (*his eyes shining*): Gee, Mid, do you know what she says — that she didn't mean a word in that other letter. Her old man made her write it. And she loves me and only me and always will, no matter how they punish her!

MILDRED: My! I'd never think she had that much spunk.

RICHARD: Huh! You don't know her! Think I could fall in love with a girl that was afraid to say her soul's her own? I should say not! (*Then more gleefully still.*) And she's going to try and sneak out and meet me tonight. She says she thinks she can do it. (*Then suddenly feeling this enthusiasm before* MILDRED *is entirely the wrong note for a cynical pessimist — with an affected bitter laugh.*) Ha! I knew darned well she couldn't hold out — that she'd ask to see me again. (*He misquotes cynically.*) "Women never know when the curtain has fallen. They always want another act."

MILDRED: Is that so, Smarty?

RICHARD (*as if he were weighing the matter*): I don't know whether I'll consent to keep this date or not.

MILDRED: Well, I know! You're not allowed out, you silly! So you can't!

RICHARD (*dropping all pretense — defiantly*): Can't I, though! You wait and see if I can't! I'll see her tonight if it's the last thing I ever do! I don't care how I'm punished after!

MILDRED (*admiringly*): Goodness! I never thought you had such nerve!

RICHARD: You promise to keep your face shut, Mid — until after I've left — then you can tell Pa and Ma where I've gone — I mean, if they're worrying I'm off like last night.

MILDRED: All right. Only you've got to do something for me when I ask.

RICHARD: 'Course I will. (*Then excitedly.*) And say, Mid! Right now's the best chance for me to get away — while everyone's out! Ma'll be coming back soon and she'll keep watching me like a cat — (*He starts for the back parlor.*) I'm going. I'll sneak out the back.

MILDRED (*excitedly*): But what'll you do till nighttime? It's ages to wait.

RICHARD: What do I care how long I wait! (*Intensely sincere now.*) I'll think of her — and dream! I'd wait a million years and never mind it — for her! (*He gives his sister a superior scornful glance.*) The trouble with you is, you don't understand what love means! (*He disappears through the back parlor.* MILDRED *looks after him admiringly.* SID *puffs and begins to snore peacefully.*)

CURTAIN

SCENE 2

Scene — A strip of beach along the harbor. At left, a bank of dark earth, running half-diagonally back along the beach, marking the line where the sand of the beach ends and fertile land begins. The top of the bank is grassy and the trailing boughs of willow trees extend out over it and over a part of the beach. At left, front, is a path leading up the bank, between the willows. On the beach, at center, front, a white, flat-bottomed rowboat is drawn up, its bow about touching the bank, the painter trailing up the bank, evidently made fast to the trunk of a willow. Halfway down the sky, at rear, left, the crescent of the new moon casts a soft, mysterious, caressing light over everything. The sand of the beach shimmers palely. The forward half (left of center) of the rowboat is in the deep shadow cast by the willow, the stern section is in moonlight. In the distance, the orchestra of a summer hotel can be heard very faintly at intervals.

RICHARD *is discovered sitting sideways on the gunwale of the rowboat near the stern. He is facing left, watching the path. He is in a great state of anxious expectancy, squirming about uncomfortably on the narrow gunwale, kicking at the sand restlessly, twirling his straw hat, with a bright-colored band in stripes, around on his finger.*

RICHARD (*thinking aloud*): Must be nearly nine. . . . I can hear the Town Hall clock strike, it's so still tonight . . . Gee, I'll bet Ma had a fit when she found out I'd sneaked out . . . I'll catch hell when I get back, but it'll be worth it . . . if only Muriel turns up . . . she didn't say for certain she could . . . gosh, I wish she'd come! . . . am I sure she wrote nine? . . . (*He puts the straw hat on the seat amidships and pulls the folded letter out of his pocket and peers at it in the moonlight.*) Yes, it's nine, all right. (*He starts to put the note back in his pocket, then stops and kisses it — then shoves it away hastily, sheepish, looking around him shamefacedly, as if afraid he were being observed.*) Aw, that's silly . . . no, it isn't either . . . not when you're really in love. . . . (*He jumps to his feet restlessly.*) Darn it, I wish she'd show up! . . . think of something else . . . that'll make the time pass quicker . . . where was I this time last night? . . . waiting outside the Pleasant Beach House . . . Belle . . . ah, forget her! . . . now, when Muriel's coming . . . that's a fine time to think of — ! . . . but you hugged and kissed her . . . not until I was drunk, I didn't . . . and then it was all showing off . . . darned fool! . . . and I didn't go upstairs with her . . . even if she was pretty . . . aw, she wasn't pretty . . . she was all painted up . . . she was just a whore . . . she was everything dirty . . . Muriel's a million times prettier anyway . . . Muriel and I will go upstairs . . . when we're married . . . but that will be beautiful . . . but I oughtn't even to think of that yet . . . it's not right . . . I'd never — now . . . and she'd never . . . she's a decent girl . . . I couldn't love her if she wasn't . . . but after we're married. . . . (*He gives a little shiver of passionate longing — then resolutely turns his mind away from these improper, almost desecrating thoughts.*) That damned barkeep kicking me . . . I'll bet you if I hadn't been drunk I'd have given him one good punch in the nose, even if he could have licked me after! . . . (*Then with a shiver of shamefaced revulsion and self-disgust.*) Aw, you deserved a kick in the pants . . . making such a darned slob of yourself . . . reciting the Ballad of Reading Gaol to those lowbrows! . . . you must have been a fine sight when you got home! . . . having to be put to bed and getting sick! . . . Phaw! . . . (*He squirms disgustedly.*) Think of something else, can't you? . . . recite something . . . see if you remember . . .

> "Nay, let us walk from fire unto fire
> From passionate pain to deadlier delight —
> I am too young to live without desire,
> Too young art thou to waste this summernight — "

. . . gee, that's a peach! . . . I'll have to memorize the rest and recite it to Muriel the next time. . . . I wish I could write poetry . . . about her and me. . . . (*He sighs and stares around him at the night.*) Gee, it's beautiful tonight . . . as if it was a special night . . . for me and Muriel. . . . Gee, I love tonight. . . . I love the sand, and the trees, and the grass, and the water and the sky, and the moon

. . . it's all in me and I'm in it . . . God, it's so beautiful! (*He stands staring at the moon with a rapt face. From the distance the Town Hall clock begins to strike. This brings him back to earth with a start.*) There's nine now. . . . (*He peers at the path apprehensively.*) I don't see her . . . she must have got caught. . . . (*Almost tearfully.*) Gee, I hate to go home and catch hell . . . without having seen her! . . . (*Then calling a manly cynicism to his aid.*) Aw, who ever heard of a woman ever being on time. . . . I ought to know enough about life by this time not to expect . . . (*Then with sudden excitement.*) There she comes now. . . . Gosh! (*He heaves a huge sigh of relief — then recites dramatically to himself, his eyes on the approaching figure.*)

> "And lo my love, mine own soul's heart, more dear
> Than mine own soul, more beautiful than God,
> Who hath my being between the hands of her — "

(*Then hastily.*) Mustn't let her know I'm so tickled. . . . I ought to be about that first letter, anyway . . . if women are too sure of you, they treat you like slaves . . . let her suffer, for a change. . . . (*He starts to stroll around with exaggerated carelessness, turning his back on the path, hands in pockets, whistling with insouciance "Waiting at the Church."*)

(MURIEL MCCOMBER *enters from down the path, left front. She is fifteen, going on sixteen. She is a pretty girl with a plump, graceful little figure, fluffy, light-brown hair, big naïve wondering dark eyes, a round, dimpled face, a melting drawly voice. Just now she is in a great thrilled state of timid adventurousness. She hesitates in the shadow at the foot of the path, waiting for* RICHARD *to see her; but he resolutely goes on whistling with back turned, and she has to call him.*)

MURIEL: Oh, Dick.

RICHARD (*turns around with an elaborate simulation of being disturbed in the midst of profound meditation*): Oh, hello. Is it nine already? Gosh, time passes — when you're thinking.

MURIEL (*coming toward him as far as the edge of the shadow — disappointedly*): I thought you'd be waiting right here at the end of the path. I'll bet you'd forgotten I was even coming.

RICHARD (*strolling a little toward her but not too far — carelessly*): No, I hadn't forgotten, honest. But I got to thinking about life.

MURIEL: You might think of me for a change, after all the risk I've run to see you! (*Hesitating timidly on the edge of the shadow.*) Dick! You come here to me. I'm afraid to go out in that bright moonlight where anyone might see me.

RICHARD (*coming toward her — scornfully*): Aw, there you go again — always scared of life!

MURIEL (*indignantly*): Dick Miller, I do think you've got an awful nerve to say that after all the risks I've run making this date and then sneaking out! You didn't take the trouble to sneak any letter to me, I notice!

RICHARD: No, because after your first letter, I thought everything was dead and past between us.

MURIEL: And I'll bet you didn't care one little bit! (*On the verge of humiliated tears.*) Oh, I was a fool ever to come here! I've got a good notion to go right home and never speak to you again! (*She half turns back toward the path.*)

RICHARD (*frightened — immediately becomes terribly sincere — grabbing her hand*):

Aw, don't go, Muriel! Please! I didn't mean anything like that, honest I didn't! Gee, if you knew how broken-hearted I was by that first letter, and how darned happy your second letter made me — !

MURIEL (*happily relieved — but appreciates she has the upper hand now and doesn't relent at once*): I don't believe you.

RICHARD: You ask Mid how happy I was. She can prove it.

MURIEL: She'd say anything you told her to. I don't care anything about what she'd say. It's you. You've got to swear to me —

RICHARD: I swear!

MURIEL (*demurely*): Well then, all right, I'll believe you.

RICHARD (*his eyes on her face lovingly — genuine adoration in his voice*): Gosh, you're pretty tonight, Muriel! It seems ages since we've been together! If you knew how I've suffered — !

MURIEL: I did, too.

RICHARD (*unable to resist falling into his tragic literary pose for a moment*): The despair in my soul — (*He recites dramatically.*) "Something was dead in each of us, And what was dead was Hope!" That was me! My hope of happiness was dead! (*Then with sincere boyish fervor.*) Gosh, Muriel, it sure is wonderful to be with you again! (*He puts a timid arm around her awkwardly.*)

MURIEL (*shyly*): I'm glad — it makes you happy. I'm happy, too.

RICHARD: Can't I — won't you let me kiss you — now? Please! (*He bends his face toward hers.*)

MURIEL (*ducking her head away — timidly*): No. You mustn't. Don't —

RICHARD: Aw, why can't I?

MURIEL: Because — I'm afraid.

RICHARD (*discomfited — taking his arm from around her — a bit sulky and impatient with her*): Aw, that's what you always say! You're always so afraid! Aren't you ever going to let me?

MURIEL: I will — sometime.

RICHARD: When?

MURIEL: Soon, maybe.

RICHARD: Tonight, will you?

MURIEL (*coyly*): I'll see.

RICHARD: Promise?

MURIEL: I promise — maybe.

RICHARD: All right. You remember you've promised. (*Then coaxingly.*) Aw, don't let's stand here. Come on out and we can sit down in the boat.

MURIEL (*hesitantly*): It's so bright out there.

RICHARD: No one'll see. You know there's never anyone around here at night.

MURIEL (*illogically*): I know there isn't. That's why I thought it would be the best place. But there might be someone.

RICHARD (*taking her hand and tugging at it gently*): There isn't a soul. (MURIEL *steps out a little and looks up and down fearfully.* RICHARD *goes on insistently.*) Aw, what's the use of a moon if you can't see it!

MURIEL: But it's only a new moon. That's not much to look at.

RICHARD: But I want to see you. I can't here in the shadow. I want to — drink in — all your beauty.

MURIEL (*can't resist this*): Well, all right — only I can't stay only a few minutes. (*She lets him lead her toward the stern of the boat.*)

RICHARD (*pleadingly*): Aw, you can stay a little while, can't you? Please! (*He helps her in and she settles herself in the stern seat of the boat, facing diagonally left front.)*

MURIEL: A little while. (*He sits beside her.*) But I've got to be home in bed again pretending to be asleep by ten o'clock. That's the time Pa and Ma come up to bed, as regular as clock work, and Ma always looks into my room.

RICHARD: But you'll have oodles of time to do that.

MURIEL (*excitedly*): Dick, you have no idea what I went through to get here tonight! My, but it was exciting! You know Pa's punishing me by sending me to bed at eight sharp, and I had to get all undressed and into bed 'cause at half-past he sends Ma up to make sure I've obeyed, and she came up, and I pretended to be asleep, and she went down again, and I got up and dressed in such a hurry — I must look a sight, don't I?

RICHARD: You do not! You look wonderful!

MURIEL: And then I sneaked down the back stairs. And the pesky old stairs squeaked, and my heart was in my mouth, I was so scared, and then I sneaked out through the back yard, keeping in the dark under the trees, and — My, but it was exciting! Dick, you don't realize how I've been punished for your sake. Pa's been so mean and nasty, I've almost hated him!

RICHARD: And you don't realize what I've been through for you — and what I'm in for — for sneaking out — (*Then darkly.*) And for what I did last night — what your letter made me do!

MURIEL (*made terribly curious by his ominous tone*): What did my letter make you do?

RICHARD (*beginning to glory in this*): It's too long a story — and let the dead past bury its dead. (*Then with real feeling.*) Only it isn't past, I can tell you! What I'll catch when Pa gets hold of me!

MURIEL: Tell me, Dick! Begin at the beginning and tell me!

RICHARD (*tragically*): Well, after your old — your father left our place I caught holy hell from Pa.

MURIEL: Dick! You mustn't swear!

RICHARD (*somberly*): Hell is the only word that can describe it. And on top of that, to torture me more, he gave me your letter. After I'd read that I didn't want to live any more. Life seemed like a tragic farce.

MURIEL: I'm so awful sorry, Dick — honest I am! But you might have known I'd never write that unless —

RICHARD: I thought your love for me was dead. I thought you'd never loved me, that you'd only been cruelly mocking me — to torture me!

MURIEL: Dick! I'd never! You know I'd never!

RICHARD: I wanted to die. I sat and brooded about death. Finally I made up my mind I'd kill myself.

MURIEL (*excitedly*): Dick! You didn't!

RICHARD: I did, too! If there'd been one of Hedda Gabler's pistols around, you'd have seen if I wouldn't have done it beautifully! I thought, when I'm dead, she'll be sorry she ruined my life!

MURIEL (*cuddling up a little to him*): If you ever had! I'd have died, too! Honest, I would!

RICHARD: But suicide is the act of a coward. That's what stopped me. (*Then with a bitter change of tone.*) And anyway, I thought to myself, she isn't worth it.

MURIEL (*huffily*): That's a nice thing to say!

RICHARD: Well, if you meant what was in that letter, you wouldn't have been worth it, would you?

MURIEL: But I've told you Pa —

RICHARD: So I said to myself, I'm through with women; they're all alike!

MURIEL: I'm not.

RICHARD: And I thought, what difference does it make what I do now? I might as well forget her and lead the pace that kills, and drown my sorrows! You know I had eleven dollars saved up to buy you something for your birthday, but I thought, she's dead to me now and why shouldn't I throw it away? (*Then hastily.*) I've still got almost five left, Muriel, and I can get you something nice with that.

MURIEL (*excitedly*): What do I care about your old presents? You tell me what you did!

RICHARD (*darkly again*): After it was dark, I sneaked out and went to a low dive I know about.

MURIEL: Dick Miller, I don't believe you ever!

RICHARD: You ask them at the Pleasant Beach House if I didn't! They won't forget me in a hurry!

MURIEL (*impressed and horrified*): You went there? Why, that's a terrible place! Pa says it ought to be closed by the police!

RICHARD (*darkly*): I said it was a dive, didn't I? It's a "secret house of shame." And they let me into a secret room behind the barroom. There wasn't anyone there but a Princeton Senior I know — he belongs to Tiger Inn and he's fullback on the football team — and he had two chorus girls from New York with him, and they were all drinking champagne.

MURIEL (*disturbed by the entrance of the chorus girls*): Dick Miller! I hope you didn't notice —

RICHARD (*carelessly*): I had a highball by myself and then I noticed one of the girls — the one that wasn't with the fullback — looking at me. She had strange-looking eyes. And then she asked me if I wouldn't drink champagne with them and come and sit with her.

MURIEL: She must have been a nice thing! (*Then a bit falteringly.*) And did — you?

RICHARD (*with tragic bitterness*): Why shouldn't I, when you'd told me in that letter you'd never see me again?

MURIEL (*almost tearfully*): But you ought to have known Pa made me —

RICHARD: I didn't know that then. (*Then rubbing it in.*) Her name was Belle. She had yellow hair — the kind that burns and stings you!

MURIEL: I'll bet it was dyed!

RICHARD: She kept smoking one cigarette after another — but that's nothing for a chorus girl.

MURIEL (*indignantly*): She was low and bad, that's what she was or she couldn't be a chorus girl, and her smoking cigarettes proves it! (*Then falteringly again.*) And then what happened?

RICHARD (*carelessly*): Oh, we just kept drinking champagne — I bought a round — and then I had a fight with the barkeep and knocked him down because he'd insulted her. He was a great big thug but —

MURIEL (*huffily*): I don't see how he could — insult that kind! And why did you fight for her? Why didn't the Princeton fullback who'd brought them there? He must have been bigger than you.

RICHARD (*stopped for a moment — then quickly*): He was too drunk by that time.

MURIEL: And were you drunk?

RICHARD: Only a little then. I was worse later. (*Proudly.*) You ought to have seen me when I got home! I was on the verge of delirium tremens!

MURIEL: I'm glad I didn't see you. You must have been awful. I hate people who get drunk. I'd have hated you!

RICHARD: Well, it was all your fault, wasn't it? If you hadn't written that letter —

MURIEL: But I've told you I didn't mean — (*Then faltering but fascinated.*) But what happened with that Belle — after — before you went home?

RICHARD: Oh, we kept drinking champagne and she said she'd fallen in love with me at first sight and she came and sat on my lap and kissed me.

MURIEL (*stiffening*): Oh!

RICHARD (*quickly, afraid he has gone too far*): But it was only all in fun, and then we just kept on drinking champagne, and finally I said good night and came home.

MURIEL: And did you kiss her?

RICHARD: No, I didn't.

MURIEL (*distractedly*): You did, too! You're lying and you know it. You did, too! (*Then tearfully.*) And there I was right at that time lying in bed not able to sleep, wondering how I was ever going to see you again and crying my eyes out, while you — ! (*She suddenly jumps to her feet in a tearful fury.*) I hate you! I wish you were dead! I'm going home this minute! I never want to lay eyes on you again! And this time I mean it! (*She tries to jump out of the boat but he holds her back. All the pose has dropped from him now and he is in a frightened state of contrition.*)

RICHARD (*imploringly*): Muriel! Wait! Listen!

MURIEL: I don't want to listen! Let me go! If you don't I'll bite your hand!

RICHARD: I won't let you go! You've got to let me explain! I never — ! Ouch! (*For* MURIEL *has bitten his hand and it hurts, and, stung by the pain, he lets go instinctively, and she jumps quickly out of the boat and starts running toward the path.* RICHARD *calls after her with bitter despair and hurt.*) All right! Go if you want to — if you haven't the decency to let me explain! I hate you, too! I'll go and see Belle!

MURIEL (*seeing he isn't following her, stops at the foot of the path — defiantly*): Well, go and see her — if that's the kind of girl you like! What do I care? (*Then as he only stares before him broodingly, sitting dejectedly in the stern of the boat, a pathetic figure of injured grief.*) You can't explain! What can you explain? You owned up you kissed her!

RICHARD: I did not. I said she kissed me.

MURIEL (*scornfully, but drifting back a step in his direction*): And I suppose you just sat and let yourself be kissed! Tell that to the Marines!

RICHARD (*injuredly*): All right! If you're going to call me a liar every word I say —

MURIEL (*drifting back another step*): I didn't call you a liar. I only meant — it sounds fishy. Don't you know it does?

RICHARD: I don't know anything. I only know I wish I was dead!

MURIEL (*gently reproving*): You oughtn't to say that. It's wicked. (*Then after a pause.*) And I suppose you'll tell me you didn't fall in love with her?

RICHARD (*scornfully*): I should say not! Fall in love with that kind of girl! What do you take me for?

MURIEL (*practically*): How do you know what you did if you drank so much champagne?

RICHARD: I kept my head — with her. I'm not a sucker, no matter what you think!

MURIEL (*drifting nearer*): Then you didn't — love her?

RICHARD: I hated her! She wasn't even pretty! And I had a fight with her before I left, she got so fresh. I told her I loved you and never could love anyone else, and for her to leave me alone.

MURIEL: But you said just now you were going to see her —

RICHARD: That was only bluff. I wouldn't — unless you left me. Then I wouldn't care what I did — any more than I did last night. (*Then suddenly defiant.*) And what if I did kiss her once or twice? I only did it to get back at you!

MURIEL: Dick!

RICHARD: You're a fine one to blame me — when it was all your fault! Why can't you be fair? Didn't I think you were out of my life forever? Hadn't you written me you were? Answer me that!

MURIEL: But I've told you a million times that Pa —

RICHARD: Why didn't you have more sense than to let him make you write it? Was it my fault you didn't?

MURIEL: It was your fault for being so stupid! You ought to have known he stood right over me and told me each word to write. If I'd refused, it would only have made everything worse. I had to pretend, so I'd get a chance to see you. Don't you see, Silly? And I had sand enough to sneak out to meet you tonight, didn't I? (*He doesn't answer. She moves nearer.*) Still I can see how you felt the way you did — and maybe I am to blame for that. So I'll forgive and forget, Dick — if you'll swear to me you didn't even think of loving that —

RICHARD (*eagerly*): I didn't! I swear, Muriel. I couldn't. I love you!

MURIEL: Well, then — I still love you.

RICHARD: Then come back here, why don't you?

MURIEL (*coyly*): It's getting late.

RICHARD: It's not near half-past yet.

MURIEL (*comes back and sits down by him shyly*): All right — only I'll have to go soon, Dick. (*He puts his arm around her. She cuddles up close to him.*) I'm sorry — I hurt your hand.

RICHARD: That was nothing. It felt wonderful — even to have you bite!

MURIEL (*impulsively takes his hand and kisses it*): There! That'll cure it. (*She is overcome by confusion at her boldness.*)

RICHARD: You shouldn't — waste that — on my hand. (*Then tremblingly.*) You said — you'd let me —

MURIEL: I said, maybe.

RICHARD: Please, Muriel. You know — I want it so!

MURIEL: Will it wash off — her kisses — make you forget you ever — for always?

RICHARD: I should say so! I'd never remember — anything but it — never want anything but it — ever again.

MURIEL (*shyly lifting her lips*): Then — all right — Dick. (*He kisses her tremblingly and for a moment their lips remain together. Then she lets her head sink on his shoulder and sighs softly.*) The moon *is* beautiful, isn't it?

RICHARD (*kissing her hair*): Not as beautiful as you! Nothing is! (*Then after a pause.*) Won't it be wonderful when we're married?

MURIEL: Yes — but it's so long to wait.

RICHARD: Perhaps I needn't go to Yale. Perhaps Pa will give me a job. Then I'd soon be making enough to —

MURIEL: You better do what your pa thinks best — and I'd like you to be at Yale. (*Then patting his face.*) Poor you! Do you think he'll punish you awful?

RICHARD (*intensely*): I don't know and I don't care! Nothing would have kept me from seeing you tonight — not if I'd had to crawl over red-hot coals! (*Then falling back on Swinburne — but with passionate sincerity.*) You have my being between the hands of you! You are "my love, mine own soul's heart, more dear than mine own soul, more beautiful than God!"

MURIEL (*shocked and delighted*): Ssshh! It's wrong to say that.

RICHARD (*adoringly*): Gosh, but I love you! Gosh, I love you — Darling!

MURIEL: I love you, too — Sweetheart! (*They kiss. Then she lets her head sink on his shoulder again and they both sit in a rapt trance, staring at the moon. After a pause — dreamily.*) Where'll we go on our honeymoon, Dick? To Niagara Falls?

RICHARD (*scornfully*): That dump where all the silly fools go? I should say not! (*With passionate romanticism.*) No, we'll go to some far-off wonderful place! (*He calls on Kipling to help him.*) Somewhere out on the Long Trail — the trail that is always new — on the road to Mandalay! We'll watch the dawn come up like thunder out of China!

MURIEL (*hazily but happily*): That'll be wonderful, won't it?

CURTAIN

SCENE 3

Scene — The sitting-room of the MILLER *house again — about 10 o'clock the same night.* MILLER *is sitting in his rocker at left, front, of table, his wife in the rocker at right, front, of table. Moonlight shines through the screen door at right, rear. Only the green-shaded reading lamp is lit and by its light* MILLER, *his specs on, is reading a book while his wife, sewing basket in lap, is working industriously on a doily.* MRS. MILLER's *face wears an expression of unworried content.* MILLER's *face has also lost its look of harassed preoccupation, although he still is a prey to certain misgivings, when he allows himself to think of them. Several books are piled on the table by his elbow, the books that have been confiscated from* RICHARD.

MILLER (*chuckles at something he reads — then closes the book and puts it on the table.* MRS. MILLER *looks up from her sewing*): This Shaw's a comical cuss — even if his ideas are so crazy they oughtn't to allow them to be printed. And that Swinburne's got a fine swing to his poetry — if he'd only choose some other subjects besides loose women.

MRS. MILLER (*smiling teasingly*): I can see where you're becoming corrupted by those books, too — pretending to read them out of duty to Richard, when your nose has been glued to the page!

MILLER: No, no — but I've got to be honest. There's something to them. That Rubaiyat of Omar Khayyam, now. I read that over again and liked it even better than I had before — parts of it, that is, where it isn't all about boozing.

MRS. MILLER (*has been busy with her own thoughts during this last — with a deep sigh of relief*): My, but I'm glad Mildred told me where Richard went off to. I'd have worried my heart out if she hadn't. But now, it's all right.

MILLER (*frowning a little*): I'd hardly go so far as to say that. Just because we know he's all right tonight doesn't mean last night is wiped out. He's still got to be punished for that.

MRS. MILLER (*defensively*): Well, if you ask me, I think after the way I punished him all day, and the way I know he's punished himself, he's had about all he deserves. I've told you how sorry he was, and how he said he'd never touch liquor again. It didn't make him feel happy like Sid, but only sad and sick, so he didn't see anything in it for him.

MILLER: Well, if he's really got that view of it driven into his skull, I don't know but I'm glad it all happened. That'll protect him more than a thousand lectures — just horse sense about himself. (*Then frowning again.*) Still, I can't let him do such things and go scot-free. And then, besides, there's another side to it — (*He stops abruptly.*)

MRS. MILLER (*uneasily*): What do you mean, another side?

MILLER (*hastily*): I mean, discipline. There's got to be some discipline in a family. I don't want him to get the idea he's got a stuffed shirt at the head of the table. No, he's got to be punished, if only to make the lesson stick in his mind, and I'm going to tell him he can't go to Yale, seeing he's so undependable.

MRS. MILLER (*up in arms at once*): Not go to Yale! I guess he can go to Yale! Every man of your means in town is sending his boys to college! What would folks think of you? You let Wilbur go, and you'd have let Lawrence, only he didn't want to, and you're letting Arthur! If our other children can get the benefit of a college education, you're not going to pick on Richard —

MILLER: Hush up, for God's sake! If you'd let me finish what I started to say! I said I'd *tell* him that now — bluff — then later on I'll change my mind, if he behaves himself.

MRS. MILLER: Oh well, if that's all — (*Then defensively again.*) But it's your duty to give him every benefit. He's got an exceptional brain, that boy has! He's proved it by the way he likes to read all those deep plays and books and poetry.

MILLER: But I thought you — (*He stops, grinning helplessly.*)

MRS. MILLER: You thought I what?

MILLER: Never mind.

MRS. MILLER (*sniffs, but thinks it better to let this pass*): You mark my words, that boy's going to turn out to be a great lawyer, or a great doctor, or a great writer, or —

MILLER (*grinning*): You agree he's going to be great, anyway.

MRS. MILLER: Yes, I most certainly have a lot of faith in Richard.

MILLER: Well, so have I, as far as that goes.

MRS. MILLER (*after a pause — judicially*): And as for his being in love with Muriel, I don't see but what it might work out real well. Richard could do worse.

MILLER: But I thought you had no use for her, thought she was stupid.

MRS. MILLER: Well, so I did, but if she's good for Richard and he wants her — (*Then inconsequentially.*) Ma used to say you weren't overbright, but she changed her mind when she saw I didn't care if you were or not.

MILLER (*not exactly pleased by this*): Well, I've been bright enough to —

MRS. MILLER (*going on as if he had not spoken*): And Muriel's real cute-looking, I have to admit that. Takes after her mother. Alice Briggs was the prettiest girl before she married.

MILLER: Yes, and Muriel will get big as a house after she's married, the same as her

mother did. That's the trouble. A man never can tell what he's letting himself in
for — (*He stops, feeling his wife's eyes fixed on him with indignant suspicion.*)

MRS. MILLER (*sharply*): I'm not too fat and don't you say it!

MILLER: Who was talking about you?

MRS. MILLER: And I'd rather have some flesh on my bones than be built like a string
bean and bore a hole in a chair every time I sat down — like some people!

MILLER (*ignoring the insult — flatteringly*): Why, no one'd ever call you fat, Essie.
You're only plump, like a good figure ought to be.

MRS. MILLER (*childishly pleased — gratefully giving tit for tat*): Well, you're not
skinny, either — only slender — and I think you've been putting on weight
lately, too. (*Having thus squared matters she takes up her sewing again. A pause.
Then* MILLER *asks incredulously.*)

MILLER: You don't mean to tell me you're actually taking this Muriel crush of Richard's seriously, do you? I know it's a good thing to encourage right now but —
pshaw, why, Richard'll probably forget all about her before he's away six months,
and she'll have forgotten him.

MRS. MILLER: Don't be so cynical. (*Then, after a pause, thoughtfully.*) Well, anyway, he'll always have it to remember — no matter what happens after — and
that's something.

MILLER: You bet that's something. (*Then with a grin.*) You surprise me at times with
your deep wisdom.

MRS. MILLER: You don't give me credit for ever having common sense, that's why.
(*She goes back to her sewing.*)

MILLER (*after a pause*): Where'd you say Sid and Lily had gone off to?

MRS. MILLER: To the beach to listen to the band. (*She sighs sympathetically.*) Poor
Lily! Sid'll never change, and she'll never marry him. But she seems to get some
queer satisfaction out of fussing over him like a hen that's hatched a duck —
though Lord knows I wouldn't in her shoes!

MILLER: Arthur's up with Elsie Rand, I suppose?

MRS. MILLER: Of course.

MILLER: Where's Mildred?

MRS. MILLER: Out walking with her latest. I've forgotten who it is. I can't keep track
of them. (*She smiles.*)

MILLER (*smiling*): Then, from all reports, we seem to be completely surrounded by
love!

MRS. MILLER: Well, we've had our share, haven't we? We don't have to begrudge it
to our children. (*Then has a sudden thought.*) But I've done all this talking about
Muriel and Richard and clean forgot how wild old McComber was against it. But
he'll get over that, I suppose.

MILLER (*with a chuckle*): He has already. I ran into him upstreet this afternoon and
he was meek as pie. He backed water and said he guessed I was right. Richard
had just copied stuff out of books, and kids would be kids, and so on. So I came
off my high horse a bit — but not too far — and I guess all that won't bother
anyone any more. (*Then rubbing his hands together — with a boyish grin of pleasure.*) And I told you about getting that business from Lawson, didn't I? It's been
a good day, Essie — a darned good day! (*From the hall beyond the front parlor
the sound of the front door being opened and shut is heard.* MRS. MILLER *leans
forward to look, pushing her specs up.*)

MRS. MILLER (*in a whisper*): It's Richard.

MILLER (*immediately assuming an expression of becoming gravity*): Hmm. (*He takes off his spectacles and puts them back in their case and straightens himself in his chair.* RICHARD *comes slowly in from the front parlor. He walks like one in a trance, his eyes shining with a dreamy happiness, his spirit still too exalted to be conscious of his surroundings, or to remember the threatened punishment. He carries his straw hat dangling in his hand, quite unaware of its existence.*)

RICHARD (*dreamily, like a ghost addressing fellow shades*): Hello.

MRS. MILLER (*staring at him worriedly*): Hello, Richard.

MILLER (*sizing him up shrewdly*): Hello, Son.

(RICHARD *moves past his mother and comes to the far corner, left front, where the light is dimmest, and sits down on the sofa, and stares before him, his hat dangling in his hand.*)

MRS. MILLER (*with frightened suspicion now*): Goodness, he acts queer! Nat, you don't suppose he's been — ?

MILLER (*with a reassuring smile*): No. It's love, not liquor, this time.

MRS. MILLER (*only partly reassured — sharply*): Richard! What's the matter with you? (*He comes to himself with a start. She goes on scoldingly.*) How many times have I told you to hang up your hat in the hall when you come in! (*He looks at his hat as if he were surprised at its existence. She gets up fussily and goes to him.*) Here. Give it to me. I'll hang it up for you this once. And what are you sitting over here in the dark for? Don't forget your father's been waiting to talk to you! (*She comes back to the table and he follows her, still half in a dream, and stands by his father's chair.* MRS. MILLER *starts for the hall with his hat.*)

MILLER (*quietly but firmly now*): You better leave Richard and me alone for a while, Essie.

MRS. MILLER (*turns to stare at him apprehensively*): Well — all right. I'll go sit on the piazza. Call me if you want me. (*Then a bit pleadingly.*) But you'll remember all I've said, Nat, won't you? (MILLER *nods reassuringly. She disappears through the front parlor.* RICHARD, *keenly conscious of himself as the about-to-be-sentenced criminal by this time, looks guilty and a bit defiant, searches his father's expressionless face with uneasy side glances, and steels himself for what is coming.*)

MILLER (*casually, indicating* MRS. MILLER's *rocker*): Sit down, Richard. (RICHARD *slumps awkwardly into the chair and sits in a self-conscious, unnatural position.* MILLER *sizes him up keenly — then suddenly smiles and asks with quiet mockery.*) Well, how are the vine leaves in your hair this evening?

RICHARD (*totally unprepared for this approach — shamefacedly mutters*): I don't know, Pa.

MILLER: Turned out to be poison ivy, didn't they? (*Then kindly.*) But you needn't look so alarmed. I'm not going to read you any temperance lecture. That'd bore me more than it would you. And, in spite of your damn foolishness last night, I'm still giving you credit for having brains. So I'm pretty sure anything I could say to you you've already said to yourself.

RICHARD (*his head down — humbly*): I know I was a darned fool.

MILLER (*thinking it well to rub in this aspect — disgustedly*): You sure were — not only a fool but a downright, stupid, disgusting fool! (RICHARD *squirms, his head still lower.*) It was bad enough for you to let me and Arthur see you, but to appear like that before your mother and Mildred — ! And I wonder if Muriel would think you were so fine if she ever saw you as you looked and acted then. I think she'd give you your walking papers for keeps. And you couldn't blame her. No nice girl wants to give her love to a stupid drunk!

RICHARD (*writhing*): I know, Pa.

MILLER (*after a pause — quietly*): All right. Then that settles — the booze end of it. (*He sizes* RICHARD *up searchingly — then suddenly speaks sharply*.) But there is another thing that's more serious. How about that tart you went to bed with at the Pleasant Beach House?

RICHARD (*flabbergasted — stammers*): You know — ? But I didn't! If they've told you about her down there, they must have told you I didn't! She wanted me to — but I wouldn't. I gave her the five dollars just so she'd let me out of it. Honest, Pa, I didn't! She made everything seem rotten and dirty — and — I didn't want to do a thing like that to Muriel — no matter how bad I thought she'd treated me — even after I felt drunk, I didn't. Honest!

MILLER: How'd you happen to meet this lady, anyway?

RICHARD: I can't tell that, Pa. I'd have to snitch on someone — and you wouldn't want me to do that.

MILLER (*a bit taken aback*): No. I suppose I wouldn't. Hmm. Well, I believe you — and I guess that settles that. (*Then, after a quick, furtive glance at* RICHARD, *he nerves himself for the ordeal and begins with a shamefaced, self-conscious solemnity*.) But listen here, Richard, it's about time you and I had a serious talk about — hmm — certain matters pertaining to — and now that the subject's come up of its own accord, it's a good time — I mean, there's no use in procrastinating further — so, here goes. (*But it doesn't go smoothly and as he goes on he becomes more and more guiltily embarrassed and self-conscious and his expressions more stilted.* RICHARD *sedulously avoids even glancing at him, his own embarrassment made tenfold more painful by his father's*.) Richard, you have now come to the age when — Well, you're a fully developed man, in a way, and it's only natural for you to have certain desires of the flesh, to put it that way — I mean, pertaining to the opposite sex — certain natural feelings and temptations — that'll want to be gratified — and you'll want to gratify them. Hmm — well, human society being organized as it is, there's only one outlet for — unless you're a scoundrel and go around ruining decent girls — which you're not, of course. Well, there are a certain class of women — always have been and always will be as long as human nature is what it is — It's wrong, maybe, but what can you do about it? I mean, girls like that one you — girls there's something doing with — and lots of 'em are pretty, and it's human nature if you — But that doesn't mean to ever get mixed up with them seriously! You just have what you want and pay 'em and forget it. I know that sounds hard and unfeeling, but we're talking facts and — But don't think I'm encouraging you to — If you can stay away from 'em, all the better — but if — why — hmm — Here's what I'm driving at, Richard. They're apt to be whited sepulchres — I mean, your whole life might be ruined if — so, darn it, you've got to know how to — I mean, there are ways and means — (*Suddenly he can go no farther and winds up helplessly*.) But, hell, I suppose you boys talk all this over among yourselves and you know more about it than I do. I'll admit I'm no authority. I never had anything to do with such women, and it'll be a hell of a lot better for you if you never do!

RICHARD (*without looking at him*): I'm never going to, Pa. (*Then shocked indignation coming into his voice*.) I don't see how you could think I could — now — when you know I love Muriel and am going to marry her. I'd die before I'd — !

MILLER (*immensely relieved — enthusiastically*): That's the talk! By God, I'm proud of you when you talk like that! (*Then hastily.*) And now that's all of that. There's nothing more to say and we'll forget it, eh?

RICHARD (*after a pause*): How are you going to punish me, Pa?

MILLER: I *was* sort of forgetting that, wasn't I? Well, I'd thought of telling you you couldn't go to Yale —

RICHARD (*eagerly*): Don't I have to go? Gee, that's great! Muriel thought you'd want me to. I was telling her I'd rather you gave me a job on the paper because then she and I could get married sooner. (*Then with a boyish grin.*) Gee, Pa, you picked a lemon. That isn't any punishment. You'll have to do something besides that.

MILLER (*grimly — but only half concealing an answering grin*): Then you'll go to Yale and you'll stay there till you graduate, that's the answer to that! Muriel's got good sense and you haven't! (RICHARD *accepts this philosophically.*) And now we're finished, you better call your mother. (RICHARD *opens the screen door and calls "Ma," and a moment later she comes in. She glances quickly from son to husband and immediately knows that all is well and tactfully refrains from all questions.*)

MRS. MILLER: My, it's a beautiful night. The moon's way down low — almost setting. (*She sits in her chair and sighs contentedly.* RICHARD *remains standing by the door, staring out at the moon, his face pale in the moonlight.*)

MILLER (*with a nod at* RICHARD, *winking at his wife*): Yes, I don't believe I've hardly ever seen such a beautiful night — with such a wonderful moon. Have you, Richard?

RICHARD (*turning to them — enthusiastically*): No! It was wonderful — down at the beach — (*He stops abruptly, smiling shyly.*)

MILLER (*watching his son — after a pause — quietly*): I can only remember a few nights that were as beautiful as this — and they were long ago, when your mother and I were young and planning to get married.

RICHARD (*stares at him wonderingly for a moment, then quickly from his father to his mother and back again, strangely, as if he'd never seen them before — then he looks almost disgusted and swallows as if an acrid taste had come into his mouth — but then suddenly his face is transfigured by a smile of shy understanding and sympathy. He speaks shyly*): Yes, I'll bet those must have been wonderful nights, too. You sort of forget the moon was the same way back then — and everything.

MILLER (*huskily*): You're all right, Richard. (*He gets up and blows his nose.*)

MRS. MILLER (*fondly*): You're a good boy, Richard. (RICHARD *looks dreadfully shy and embarrassed at this. His father comes to his rescue.*)

MILLER: Better get to bed early tonight, Son, hadn't you?

RICHARD: I couldn't sleep. Can't I go out on the piazza and sit for a while — until the moon sets?

MILLER: All right. Then you better say good night now. I don't know about your mother, but I'm going to bed right away. I'm dead tired.

MRS. MILLER: So am I.

RICHARD (*goes to her and kisses her*): Good night, Ma.

MRS. MILLER: Good night. Don't you stay up till all hours now.

RICHARD (*comes to his father and stands awkwardly before him*): Good night, Pa.

MILLER (*puts his arm around him and gives him a hug*): Good night, Richard. (RICHARD *turns impulsively and kisses him — then hurries out the screen door.* MILLER *stares after him — then says huskily*): First time he's done that in years. I don't

believe in kissing between fathers and sons after a certain age — seems mushy
and silly — but that meant something! And I don't think we'll ever have to worry
about his being safe — from himself — again. And I guess no matter what life
will do to him, he can take care of it now. (*He sighs with satisfaction and, sitting
down in his chair, begins to unlace his shoes.*) My darned feet are giving me fits!
MRS. MILLER (*laughing*): Why do you bother unlacing your shoes now, you big goose
— when we're going right up to bed?
MILLER (*as if he hadn't thought of that before, stops*): Guess you're right. (*Then
getting to his feet — with a grin.*) Mind if I don't say my prayers tonight, Essie?
I'm certain God knows I'm too darned tired.
MRS. MILLER: Don't talk that way. It's real sinful. (*She gets up — then laughing
fondly.*) If that isn't you all over! Always looking for an excuse to — You're worse
than Tommy! But all right. I suppose tonight you needn't. You've had a hard
day. (*She puts her hand on the reading-lamp switch.*) I'm going to turn out the
light. All ready?
MILLER: Yep. Let her go, Gallagher. (*She turns out the lamp. In the ensuing darkness the faint moonlight shines full in through the screen door. Walking together
toward the front parlor they stand full in it for a moment, looking out.* MILLER
puts his arm around her. He says in a low voice.) There he is — like a statue of
Love's Young Dream. (*Then he sighs and speaks with a gentle nostalgic melancholy.*) What's it that Rubaiyat says:

> "Yet Ah, that Spring should vanish with the Rose!
> That Youth's sweet-scented manuscript should close!"

(*Then throwing off his melancholy, with a loving smile at her.*) Well, Spring isn't
everything, is it, Essie? There's a lot to be said for Autumn. That's got beauty,
too. And Winter — if you're together.
MRS. MILLER (*simply*): Yes, Nat. (*She kisses him and they move quietly out of the
moonlight, back into the darkness of the front parlor.*)

CURTAIN

AFTERWORD

In an anthology such as this, it is hard to avoid giving a distorted view of
the main currents of the theater. The plays selected are those that stand
head and shoulders above the others of their time, and by virtue of some
particular genius, by the universality of their statement, transcend their
own age and demand attention from posterity. It is not always easy to
remember that, for every masterpiece, a hundred other plays were considered amply satisfactory by the audiences who watched them, and indeed
represent the level of contemporary theatrical art more accurately than the
Hamlets or the *Phaedras*. Often the selective processes of history have
forced a choice on us. Virtually all the surviving Greek plays were regarded
as outstanding in their own time. The runners-up, those works that failed
to win the prizes or endear themselves to scholars, have been lost to sight

forever. For the Elizabethans, although we have a number of second-best plays and some remarkably bad ones, we still do not have anything like a complete view of the average London season, or what "going to the theatre" would have meant to the mass of the audience. We need to remind ourselves that a dramatist canonized as "great" by posterity may well have been a generation ahead of his time, misunderstood, even derided, by his immediate public. *Ah, Wilderness!* gives evidence of this recurrent phenomenon. The play is set in 1906. When the family nervously considers Richard's reading matter, Ibsen is stigmatized as a subversive, possibly dangerous figure of the avant-garde, and Shaw is dismissed as a writer of "dirty" plays. (In Sinclair Lewis's *Main Street*, the amateur dramatic society rejects Shaw as too shocking, and settles on a harmless farce.) Reading drama of conventional values thus becomes a useful corrective exercise.

If the above sounds condescending, it is not meant to be. *Ah, Wilderness!* is an excellent piece of dramatized Americana. It delighted audiences when it was first written and continues to survive as a repertory piece; a few years ago, it achieved the ultimate award of the modern American theater, transformation into a musical. Nor was O'Neill, by any standards, a mediocre or uninventive dramatist. He was fully alive to the most advanced dramatic thought of his time, and his more serious plays show the influence of the new theatricalism that was permeating Europe. He experimented with masks, music and choruses; he sought to reveal the private thoughts of his characters by the use of the "inner monologue," which was really an extension of the old conventional stage aside. In *Ah, Wilderness!*, however, he eschews experiment for the careful realism that had become the staple of most American drama, and shows himself a master at it.

Earlier plays in this volume have been classed as "realistic": *A Doll's House*, *The Cherry Orchard*. These share the aim of reproducing a small segment of the actual world as accurately as possible. But they have a further purpose: Ibsen's play is a polemic that would lose force were it not rooted in a familiar and believable life-style; *The Cherry Orchard* has reverberations that extend far beyond the small world of the immediate action, and the scrupulous exactitude of depiction asks us to think not merely of a few individual lives but of a whole way of life threatened by external forces. *Ah, Wilderness!* makes no such pretensions, but simply shows things as they are. It is a play about family life and relationships in the United States, about adolescence taking its first uncertain steps towards maturity. It draws no morals and makes no profound statements. Its counterpart in art would be the genre painting, the still life, the appeal of which lies in the artist's ability to arrange the textures and colors of familiar objects into a pleasing composition that we may look at and say, "Yes, that is how it is; and how well it is rendered."

Few plays can escape a hint of autobiography. O'Neill's own family background reveals itself slightly here, just as it did, in more important ways, in his major works. Drunkenness in the family, an occasion for mild amusement here, is a tragic theme for O'Neill elsewhere. (One critic has called *Ah, Wilderness!* a play about O'Neill's youth written on a good day.) The scene between Richard and Muriel is set, almost inevitably, in an old boat by the water's edge. For O'Neill, the sea had a mystic fascination; he had gone seafaring in his early days, and extracted some of his first plays from the experience. In *Ah, Wilderness!* all the restless emotional yearnings of the boy are focused on the water. This, however, is the limit of autobiography. *Ah, Wilderness!* is a play of general statements about everybody's adolescence, everybody's growing up, and it is all there as we remember it — the half-formulated ideas of rebellion, the conviction of one's own intellectual superiority, the first intoxication, the first love affair. "Yes," we say, "that is how it is — or how it was." The play asks no more of us than this simple recognition.

To achieve its aim the play must be as realistic as possible. Notice how careful the playwright has been to catch the nuances of family life, how all the relevant details are noted down and how much appears, not in the script, but in the stage directions. This sort of play sets itself against fine writing. In ordinary life we do not orate at each other, or make elaborate statements of our feelings and intentions. These are revealed in less verbal ways, by looks, by frowns, by reactions. The actor no longer needs to be an orator. There is more need now for the performer's self-identification with the role, for much that is important happens between the lines, in what actors call the subtext. External, physical details are important. The audience absorbs more through the eye than through the ear. Two years before this play was written the American theater had lost its great apostle of stage realism, David Belasco, who had become famous for the scrupulously exact sets in which he dressed his often inferior plays. Belasco spent countless painstaking hours reproducing actual environments, virtually brick by brick, with the natural lighting conditions faithfully copied. *Ah, Wilderness!* and many other plays testify to the influence of Belasco's school of thought on the American theater. It also belongs to a time when set construction was still cheap and union demands had not yet made the one-set play virtually obligatory. Two full sets are used to show the Miller household — sitting-room and dining-room; we also have the scene in the barroom and at the seashore. Realism could still afford to be expansive. In modern revivals the Millers usually eat in their living-room, and the scenes outside the house are reduced to small insets.

Everything in the play is carefully plotted to carry conviction; the way the plates are stacked, where Tommy lets off his firecrackers, what kind of songs the family sing, and how they sing them. Character relationships are worked out with the same care. In the general introduction we pointed out that, in this kind of play, essential information cannot be handed to the audience directly, as in *Oedipus the King*. The presumption that the play is a slice of real life forbids it. Information must therefore be conveyed indirectly, through the medium of ordinary conversation, and the measure of the playwright's skill is how well he can do this without allowing the process to become obtrusive. It's because O'Neill does it very well that it seems so unnecessary for him constantly to explain how his characters feel by adding descriptive tags to their speeches in stage directions: "excitedly," "huffily," "darkly," "impressed and horrified," and so forth. For the reader, they are irritating, unsubtle intrusions into the drama. It is as if O'Neill had no confidence in the expressive power of his dialogue. He was wrong. The listener in the theater, who is spared the tags, never misses them. Note how subtly O'Neill builds up the picture of the past and present relationship between Sid and Lily. We are never told outright, but enough hints are dropped to make the reconstruction possible; and these hints more often than not take the form of winks, looks, changes of expression, noted in the stage directions. *Ah, Wilderness!* emphasizes what a visual experience the theater has now become, under the influence of film and with the aid of more elaborate lighting conditions.

Notice too where the illusion partly breaks down, and where the necessary information is given to us too blatantly, so that it seems contrived. Most obviously, this happens in the sea-shore scene, with Richard's opening soliloquy. In real life, we do not normally talk to ourselves at such great length. In the play Richard has to because there is no other way of making his thoughts known. It jars, not so much because the soliloquy device is unlifelike in itself, as because it is out of key. The rest of the play is so very lifelike that this departure seems particularly obtrusive.

One of the most useful things the student can learn from *Ah, Wilderness!* is to understand why the soliloquy seems so unnatural here, when in *Everyman* and *Hamlet* it appears perfectly logical and proper.

Bertolt Brecht

THE CAUCASIAN CHALK CIRCLE

Translated by Eric Bentley

FOREWORD

It might be argued that the theater never discovers, only rediscovers.
The "innovations" of the twentieth century are often reversions to devices
commonplace in other eras. So it is with Brecht. For years he was regarded, and often derided, as an experimenter on the outer fringes of theater practice. With his acceptance has come a realization that his techniques are firmly rooted in the theater's ancient history. His habit of
punctuating the action with song or choral narrative was partly derived
from the Berlin cabaret-theaters, but was also familiar to the Greeks.
Brechtian acting theory owes much to the traditional theaters of the Orient. His episodic structure and fluid use of stage space recall *Everyman*.

Pirandello set art against life, the actor against the "real." Brecht attempts a more intricate combination. His stage is open and undefined, but
may, for the purposes of a particular scene, contain highly realistic objects.
He uses purely theatrical devices, like turntables, projections, and hanging
subtitles, side by side with properties made with loving care as if for real
use. He asks his actors both to identify with their characters and to stand
outside them, commenting on them. He asks his audience to accept the
reality of what they see and at the same time to be aware that it is a theatrical presentation. The spectator is expected not only to be moved, but to
think about why he or she is moved.

What the Moscow Art Theater has been for Chekhov, the Berliner Ensemble has been for Brecht. By its continued existence, and particularly by

its visits abroad, it has fostered Brechtian influence, sometimes in the most unlikely places — for example, in John Osborne's *The Entertainer*, a study of a fading vaudeville star, and in the stage and film musical *Cabaret*.

CHARACTERS

OLD MAN on the right
PEASANT WOMAN on the right
YOUNG PEASANT
A VERY YOUNG WORKER
OLD MAN on the left
PEASANT WOMAN on the left
AGRICULTURIST KATO
GIRL TRACTORIST
WOUNDED SOLDIER
THE DELEGATE from the capital
THE SINGER
GEORGI ABASHWILI, the Governor
NATELLA, the Governor's wife
MICHAEL, their son
SHALVA, an adjutant
ARSEN KAZBEKI, a fat prince
MESSENGER from the capital
NIKO MIKADZE and MIKA LOLADZE,
   doctors
SIMON SHASHAVA, a soldier
GRUSHA VASHNADZE, a kitchen maid
OLD PEASANT with the milk
CORPORAL and PRIVATE

PEASANT and his wife
LAVRENTI VASHNADZE, Grusha's brother
ANIKO, his wife
PEASANT WOMAN, for a while Grusha's
   mother-in-law
JUSSUP, her son
MONK
AZDAK, village recorder
SHAUWA, a policeman
GRAND DUKE
DOCTOR
INVALID
LIMPING MAN
BLACKMAILER
LUDOVICA
INNKEEPER, her father-in-law
STABLEMAN
POOR OLD PEASANT WOMAN
IRAKLI, her brother-in-law, a bandit
THREE WEALTHY FARMERS
ILLO SHUBOLADZE and SANDRO
   OBOLADZE, lawyers
OLD MARRIED COUPLE

SOLDIERS, SERVANTS, PEASANTS, BEGGARS, MUSICIANS,
MERCHANTS, NOBLES, ARCHITECTS

The time and the place: After a prologue, set in 1945, we move back perhaps 1000 years.

The action of The Caucasian Chalk Circle *centers on Nuka (or Nukha), a town in Azerbaijan. However, the capital referred to in the prologue is not Baku (capital of Soviet Azerbaijan) but Tiflis (or Tbilisi), capital of Georgia. When Azdak, later, refers to "the capital" he means Nuka itself, though whether Nuka was ever capital of Georgia I do not know: in what reading I have done on the subject I have only found Nuka to be the capital of a Nuka Khanate.*

The word "Georgia" has not been used in this English version because of its American associations; instead, the alternative name "Grusinia" (in Russian, Gruziya) has been used.

The reasons for resettling the old Chinese story in Transcaucasia are not far to seek. The play was written when the Soviet chief of state, Joseph Stalin, was a Georgian, as was his favorite poet, cited in the Prologue, Mayakovsky. And surely there is a point in having this story acted out at the place where Europe and Asia meet, a place incomparably rich in legend and history. Here Jason found the Golden Fleece. Here Noah's Ark touched ground. Here the armies of both Genghis Khan and Tamerlane wrought havoc.

—E.B.

PROLOGUE

Summer, 1945.

Among the ruins of a war-ravaged Caucasian village the members of two Kolkhoz villages, mostly WOMEN *and* OLDER MEN, *are sitting in a circle, smoking and drinking wine. With them is a* DELEGATE *of the the State Reconstruction Commission from Nuka.*

PEASANT WOMAN (*left, pointing*): In those hills over there we stopped three Nazi tanks, but the apple orchard was already destroyed.

OLD MAN (*right*): Our beautiful dairy farm: a ruin.

GIRL TRACTORIST: I laid the fire, Comrade.

(*Pause.*)

DELEGATE: Nuka, Azerbaijan S.S.R. Delegation received from the goat-breeding Kolkhoz "Rosa Luxemburg." This is a collective farm which moved eastwards on orders from the authorities at the approach of Hitler's armies. They are now planning to return. Their delegates have looked at the village and the land and found a lot of destruction. (DELEGATES *on the right nod.*) But the neighboring fruit farm — Kolkhoz (*to the left*) "Galinsk" — proposes to use the former grazing land of Kolkhoz "Rosa Luxemburg" for orchards and vineyards. This land lies in a valley where grass doesn't grow very well. As a delegate of the Reconstruction Commission in Nuka I request that the two Kolkhoz villages decide between themselves whether Kolkhoz "Rosa Luxemburg" shall return or not.

OLD MAN (*right*): First of all, I want to protest against the time limit on discussion. We of Kolkhoz "Rosa Luxemburg" have spent three days and three nights getting here. And now discussion is limited to half a day.

WOUNDED SOLDIER (*left*): Comrade, we haven't as many villages as we used to have. We haven't as many hands. We haven't as much time.

GIRL TRACTORIST: All pleasures have to be rationed. Tobacco is rationed, and wine. Discussion should be rationed.

OLD MAN (*right, sighing*): Death to the fascists! But I will come to the point and explain why we want our valley back. There are a great many reasons, but I'll begin with one of the simplest. Makinä Abakidze, unpack the goat cheese. (A

PEASANT WOMAN *from right takes from a basket an enormous cheese wrapped in a cloth. Applause and laughter.*) Help yourselves, Comrades, start in!

OLD MAN (*left, suspiciously*): Is this a way of influencing us?

OLD MAN (*right, amid laughter*): How could it be a way of influencing you, Surab, you valley-thief? Everyone knows you'll take the cheese and the valley, too. (*Laughter.*) All I expect from you is an honest answer. Do you like the cheese?

OLD MAN (*left*): The answer is: yes.

OLD MAN (*right*): Really. (*Bitterly.*) I ought to have known you know nothing about cheese.

OLD MAN (*left*): Why not? When I tell you I like it?

OLD MAN (*right*): Because you can't like it. Because it's not what it was in the old days. And why not? Because our goats don't like the new grass as they did the old. Cheese is not cheese because grass is not grass, that's the thing. Please put that in your report.

OLD MAN (*left*): But your cheese is excellent.

OLD MAN (*right*): It isn't excellent. It's just passable. The new grazing land is no good, whatever the young people may say. One can't live there. It doesn't even smell of morning in the morning. (*Several people laugh.*)

DELEGATE: Don't mind their laughing: they understand you. Comrades, why does one love one's country? Because the bread tastes better there, the air smells better, voices sound stronger, the sky is higher, the ground is easier to walk on. Isn't that so?

OLD MAN (*right*): The valley has belonged to us from all eternity.

SOLDIER (*left*): What does *that* mean — from all eternity? Nothing belongs to anyone from all eternity. When you were young you didn't even belong to yourself. You belonged to the Kazbeki princes.

OLD MAN (*right*): Doesn't it make a difference, though, what kind of trees stand next to the house you are born in? Or what kind of neighbors you have? Doesn't that make a difference? We want to go back just to have you as our neighbors, valley-thieves! Now you can all laugh again.

OLD MAN (*left, laughing*): Then why don't you listen to what your neighbor, Kato Wachtang, our agriculturist, has to say about the valley?

PEASANT WOMAN (*right*): We've not said all we have to say about our valley. By no means. Not all the houses are destroyed. As for the dairy farm, at the least the foundation wall is still standing.

DELEGATE: You can claim State support — here and there — you know that. I have suggestions here in my pocket.

PEASANT WOMAN (*right*): Comrade Specialist, we haven't come here to haggle. I can't take your cap and hand you another, and say "This one's better." The other one might *be* better, but you *like* yours better.

GIRL TRACTORIST: A piece of land is not a cap — not in our country, Comrade.

DELEGATE: Don't get mad. It's true we have to consider a piece of land as a tool to produce something useful, but it's also true that we must recognize love for a particular piece of land. As far as I'm concerned, I'd like to find out more exactly what you (*to those on the left*) want to do with the valley.

OTHERS: Yes, let Kato speak.

KATO (*rising; she's in military uniform*): Comrades, last winter, while we were fighting in these hills here as Partisans, we discussed how, once the Germans were expelled, we could build up our fruit culture to ten times its original size. I've

prepared a plan for an irrigation project. By means of a cofferdam on our mountain lake, 300 hectares of unfertile land can be irrigated. Our Kolkhoz could not
only cultivate more fruit, but also have vineyards. The project, however, would
pay only if the disputed valley of Kolkhoz "Rosa Luxemburg" were also included.
Here are the calculations. (*She hands* DELEGATE *a briefcase.*)

OLD MAN (*right*): Write into the report that our Kolkhoz plans to start a new stud
farm.

GIRL TRACTORIST: Comrades, the project was conceived during days and nights
when we had to take cover in the mountains. We were often without ammunition
for our half-dozen rifles. Even finding a pencil was difficult. (*Applause from both
sides.*)

OLD MAN (*right*): Our thanks to the Comrades of Kolkhoz "Galinsk" and all those
who've defended our country!

(*They shake hands and embrace.*)

PEASANT WOMAN (*left*): In doing this our thought was that our soldiers — both your
men and our men — should return to a still more productive homeland.

GIRL TRACTORIST: As the poet Mayakovsky said: "The home of the Soviet people
shall also be the home of Reason"!

(*The* DELEGATES *excluding the* OLD MAN *have got up, and with the* DELEGATE
specified proceed to study the Agriculturist's drawings. Exclamations such as:)

"Why is the altitude of fall 22 meters?" — "This rock will have to be blown up" —
"Actually, all they need is cement and dynamite" — "They force the water to
come down here, that's clever!"

A VERY YOUNG WORKER (*right, to* OLD MAN, *right*): They're going to irrigate all the
fields between the hills, look at that, Aleko!

OLD MAN (*right*): I'm not going to look. I knew the project would be good. I won't
have a pistol pointed at me!

DELEGATE: But they only want to point a pencil at you!

(*Laughter.*)

OLD MAN (*right, gets up gloomily, and walks over to look at the drawings*): These
valley-thieves know only too well that we in this country are suckers for machines
and projects.

PEASANT WOMAN (*right*): Aleko Bereshwili, you have a weakness for new projects.
That's well known.

DELEGATE: What about my report? May I write that you will all support the cession
of your old valley in the interests of this project when you get back to your
Kolkhoz?

PEASANT WOMAN (*right*): I will. What about you, Aleko?

OLD MAN (*right, bent over drawings*): I suggest that you give us copies of the drawings to take along.

PEASANT WOMAN (*right*): Then we can sit down and eat. Once he has the drawings
and he's ready to discuss them, the matter is settled. I know him. And it will be
the same with the rest of us.

(DELEGATES *laughingly embrace again.*)

OLD MAN (*left*): Long live the Kolkhoz "Rosa Luxemburg" and much luck to your horse-breeding project!

PEASANT WOMAN (*left*): In honor of the visit of the delegates from Kolkhoz "Rosa Luxemburg" and of the Specialist, the plan is that we all hear a presentation of the Singer Arkadi Tscheidse.

(*Applause.* GIRL TRACTORIST *has gone off to bring the* SINGER.)

PEASANT WOMAN (*right*): Comrades, your entertainment had better be good. It's going to cost us a valley.

PEASANT WOMAN (*left*): Arkadi Tscheidse knows about our discussion. He's promised to perform something that has a bearing on the problem.

KATO: We wired Tiflis three times. The whole thing nearly fell through at the last minute because his driver had a cold.

PEASANT WOMAN (*left*): Arkadi Tscheidse knows 21,000 lines of verse.

OLD MAN (*left*): He's hard to get. You and the Planning Commission should persuade him to come north more often, Comrade.

DELEGATE: We are more interested in economics, I'm afraid.

OLD MAN (*left, smiling*): You arrange the redistribution of vines and tractors, why not songs?

(*Enter the* SINGER *Arkadi Tscheidse, led by* GIRL TRACTORIST. *He is a well-built man of simple manners, accompanied by* FOUR MUSICIANS *with their instruments. The artists are greeted with applause.*)

GIRL TRACTORIST: This is the Comrade Specialist, Arkadi.

(*The* SINGER *greets them all.*)

DELEGATE: Honored to make your acquaintance. I heard about your songs when I was a boy at school. Will it be one of the old legends?

SINGER: A very old one. It's called "The Chalk Circle" and comes from the Chinese. But we'll do it, of course, in a changed version. Comrades, it's an honor for me to entertain you after a difficult debate. We hope you will find that the voice of the old poet also sounds well in the shadow of Soviet tractors. It may be a mistake to mix different wines, but old and new wisdom mix admirably. Now I hope we'll get something to eat before the performance begins — it would certainly help.

VOICES: Surely. Everyone into the Club House!

(*While everyone begins to move,* DELEGATE *turns to* GIRL TRACTORIST.)

DELEGATE: I hope it won't take long. I've got to get back tonight.

GIRL TRACTORIST: How long will it last, Arkadi? The Comrade Specialist must get back to Tiflis tonight.

SINGER (*casually*): It's actually two stories. An hour or two.

GIRL TRACTORIST (*confidentially*): Couldn't you make it shorter?

SINGER: No.

VOICE: Arkadi Tscheidse's performance will take place here in the square after the meal.

(*And they all go happily to eat.*)

I. THE NOBLE CHILD

As the lights go up, the SINGER *is seen sitting on the floor, a black sheepskin cloak round his shoulders, and a little, well-thumbed notebook in his hand. A small group of listeners — the* CHORUS *— sits with him. The manner of his recitation makes it clear that he has told his story over and over again. He mechanically fingers the pages, seldom looking at them. With appropriate gestures, he gives the signal for each scene to begin.*

SINGER: In olden times, in a bloody time,
There ruled in a Caucasian city —
Men called it City of the Damned —
A Governor.
His name was Georgi Abashwili.
He was rich as Croesus
He had a beautiful wife
He had a healthy baby.
No other governor in Grusinia
Had so many horses in his stable
So many beggars on his doorstep
So many soldiers in his service
So many petitioners in his courtyard.
Georgi Abashwili — how shall I describe him to you?
He enjoyed his life.
On the morning of Easter Sunday
The Governor and his family went to church.

(*At the left a large doorway, at the right an even larger gateway.* BEGGARS *and* PETITIONERS *pour from the gateway, holding up thin* CHILDREN, *crutches, and petitions. They are followed by* IRONSHIRTS, *and then, expensively dressed, the* GOVERNOR'S FAMILY.)

BEGGARS AND PETITIONERS: — Mercy! Mercy, Your Grace! The taxes are too high.
— I lost my leg in the Persian War, where can I get . . .
— My brother is innocent, Your Grace, a misunderstanding . . .
— The child is starving in my arms!
— Our petition is for our son's discharge from the army, our last remaining son!
— Please, Your Grace, the water inspector takes bribes.

(*One* SERVANT *collects the petitions. Another distributes coins from a purse.* SOLDIERS *push the crowd back, lashing at them with thick leather whips.*)

SOLDIER: Get back! Clear the church door!

(*Behind the* GOVERNOR, *his* WIFE, *and the* ADJUTANT, *the* GOVERNOR'S CHILD *is brought through the gateway in an ornate carriage.*)

CROWD: — The baby!
— I can't see it, don't shove so hard!
— God bless the child, Your Grace!
SINGER (*while the* CROWD *is driven back with whips*): For the first time on that Easter Sunday, the people saw the Governor's heir.

Two doctors never moved from the noble child, apple of the Governor's eye.
Even the mighty Prince Kazbeki bows before him at the church door.

(*The* FAT PRINCE *steps forward and greets the* FAMILY.)

FAT PRINCE: Happy Easter, Natella Abashwili! What a day! When it was raining last
night, I thought to myself, gloomy holidays! But this morning the sky was gay. I
love a gay sky, a simple heart, Natella Abashwili. And little Michael is a governor
from head to foot! Tititi! (*He tickles the* CHILD.)

GOVERNOR'S WIFE: What do you think, Arsen, at last Georgi has decided to start
building the east wing. All those wretched slums are to be torn down to make
room for the garden.

FAT PRINCE: Good news after so much bad! What's the latest on the war, Brother
Georgi? (*The* GOVERNOR *indicates a lack of interest.*) Strategical retreat, I hear.
Well, minor reverses are to be expected. Sometimes things go well, sometimes
not. Such is war. Doesn't mean a thing, does it?

GOVERNOR'S WIFE: He's coughing. Georgi, did you hear? (*She speaks sharply to the*
DOCTORS, *two dignified men standing close to the little carriage.*) He's coughing!

FIRST DOCTOR (*to the* SECOND): May I remind you, Niko Mikadze, that I was against
the lukewarm bath? (*To the* GOVERNOR'S WIFE.) There's been a little error over
warming the bath water, Your Grace.

SECOND DOCTOR (*equally polite*): Mika Loladze, I'm afraid I can't agree with you.
The temperature of the bath water was exactly what our great, beloved Mishiko
Oboladze prescribed. More likely a slight draft during the night, Your Grace.

GOVERNOR'S WIFE: But do pay more attention to him. He looks feverish, Georgi.

FIRST DOCTOR (*bending over the* CHILD): No cause for alarm, Your Grace. The bath
water will be warmer. It won't occur again.

SECOND DOCTOR (*with a venomous glance at the* FIRST): I won't forget that, my dear
Mika Loladze. No cause for concern, Your Grace.

FAT PRINCE: Well, well, well! I always say: "A pain in my liver? Then the doctor gets
fifty strokes on the soles of his feet." We live in a decadent age. In the old days
one said: "Off with his head!"

GOVERNOR'S WIFE: Let's go into church. Very likely it's the draft here.

(*The procession of* FAMILY *and* SERVANTS *turns into the doorway. The* FAT
PRINCE *follows, but the* GOVERNOR *is kept back by the* ADJUTANT, *a handsome
young man. When the crowd of* PETITIONERS *has been driven off, a young dust-
stained* RIDER, *his arm in a sling, remains behind.*)

ADJUTANT (*pointing at the* RIDER, *who steps forward*): Won't you hear the messenger from the capital, Your Excellency? He arrived this morning. With confidential papers.

GOVERNOR: Not before Service, Shalva. But did you hear Brother Kazbeki wish me
a happy Easter? Which is all very well, but I don't believe it did rain last night.

ADJUTANT (*nodding*): We must investigate.

GOVERNOR: Yes, at once. Tomorrow.

(*They pass through the doorway. The* RIDER, *who has waited in vain for an
audience, turns sharply round and, muttering a curse, goes off. Only one of the
palace guards —* SIMON SHASHAVA *— remains at the door.*)

SINGER: The city is still.
Pigeons strut in the church square.
A soldier of the Palace Guard
Is joking with a kitchen maid
As she comes up from the river with a bundle.

(A girl — GRUSHA VASHNADZE — comes through the gateway with a bundle made of large green leaves under her arm.)

SIMON: What, the young lady is not in church? Shirking?

GRUSHA: I was dressed to go. But they needed another goose for the banquet. And they asked me to get it. I know about geese.

SIMON: A goose? (He feigns suspicion.) I'd like to see that goose. (GRUSHA does not understand.) One must be on one's guard with women. "I only went for a fish," they tell you, but it turns out to be something else.

GRUSHA (walking resolutely toward him and showing him the goose): There! If it isn't a fifteen-pound goose stuffed full of corn, I'll eat the feathers.

SIMON: A queen of a goose! The Governor himself will eat it. So the young lady has been down to the river again?

GRUSHA: Yes, at the poultry farm.

SIMON: Really? At the poultry farm, down by the river . . . not higher up maybe? Near those willows?

GRUSHA: I only go to the willows to wash the linen.

SIMON (insinuatingly): Exactly.

GRUSHA: Exactly what?

SIMON (winking): Exactly that.

GRUSHA: Why shouldn't I wash the linen by the willows?

SIMON (with exaggerated laughter): "Why shouldn't I wash the linen by the willows!" That's good, really good!

GRUSHA: I don't understand the soldier. What's so good about it?

SIMON (slyly): "If something I know someone learns, she'll grow hot and cold by turns!"

GRUSHA: I don't know what I could learn about those willows.

SIMON: Not even if there was a bush opposite? That one could see everything from? Everything that goes on there when a certain person is — "washing linen"?

GRUSHA: What does go on? Won't the soldier say what he means and have done?

SIMON: Something goes on. Something can be seen.

GRUSHA: Could the soldier mean I dip my toes in the water when it's hot? There's nothing else.

SIMON: There's more. Your toes. And more.

GRUSHA: More what? At most my foot?

SIMON: Your foot. And a little more. (He laughs heartily.)

GRUSHA (angrily): Simon Shashava, you ought to be ashamed of yourself! To sit in a bush on a hot day and wait till a girl comes and dips her legs in the river! And I bet you bring a friend along too! (She runs off.)

SIMON (shouting after her): I didn't bring any friend along!

(As the SINGER resumes his tale, the SOLDIER steps into the doorway as though to listen to the service.)

SINGER: The city lies still

But why are there armed men?
The Governor's palace is at peace
But why is it a fortress?
And the Governor returned to his palace
And the fortress was a trap
And the goose was plucked and roasted
But the goose was not eaten this time
And noon was no longer the hour to eat:
Noon was the hour to die.

(*From the doorway at the left the* FAT PRINCE *quickly appears, stands still, looks around. Before the gateway at the right two* IRONSHIRTS *are squatting and playing dice. The* FAT PRINCE *sees them, walks slowly past, making a sign to them. They rise: one goes through the gateway, the other goes off at the right. Muffled voices are heard from various directions in the rear:* "To your posts!" *The palace is surrounded. The* FAT PRINCE *quickly goes off. Church bells in the distance. Enter, through the doorway, the* GOVERNOR'S FAMILY *and procession, returning from church.*)

GOVERNOR'S WIFE (*passing the* ADJUTANT): It's impossible to live in such a slum. But Georgi, of course, will only build for his little Michael. Never for me! Michael is all! All for Michael!

(*The procession turns into the gateway. Again the* ADJUTANT *lingers behind. He waits. Enter the wounded* RIDER *from the doorway. Two* IRONSHIRTS *of the Palace Guard have taken up positions by the gateway.*)

ADJUTANT (*to the* RIDER): The Governor does not wish to receive military news before dinner — especially if it's depressing, as I assume. In the afternoon His Excellency will confer with prominent architects. They're coming to dinner too. And here they are! (*Enter three* GENTLEMEN *through the doorway.*) Go to the kitchen and eat, my friend. (*As the* RIDER *goes, the* ADJUTANT *greets the* ARCHITECTS.) Gentlemen, His Excellency expects you at dinner. He will devote all his time to you and your great new plans. Come!

ONE OF THE ARCHITECTS: We marvel that His Excellency intends to build. There are disquieting rumors that the war in Persia has taken a turn for the worse.

ADJUTANT: All the more reason to build! There's nothing to those rumors anyway. Persia is a long way off, and the garrison here would let itself be hacked to bits for its Governor. (*Noise from the palace. The shrill scream of a woman. Someone is shouting orders. Dumbfounded, the* ADJUTANT *moves toward the gateway. An* IRONSHIRT *steps out, points his lance at him.*) What's this? Put down that lance, you dog.

ONE OF THE ARCHITECTS: It's the Princes! Don't you know the Princes met last night in the capital? And they're against the Grand Duke and his Governors? Gentlemen, we'd better make ourselves scarce. (*They rush off. The* ADJUTANT *remains helplessly behind.*)

ADJUTANT (*furiously to the Palace Guard*): Down with those lances! Don't you see the Governor's life is threatened?

(*The* IRONSHIRTS *of the Palace Guard refuse to obey. They stare coldly and indifferently at the* ADJUTANT *and follow the next events without interest.*)

SINGER: O blindness of the great!
  They go their way like gods,
  Great over bent backs,
  Sure of hired fists,
  Trusting in the power
  Which has lasted so long.
  But long is not forever.
  O change from age to age!
  Thou hope of the people!

(*Enter the* GOVERNOR, *through the gateway, between two* SOLDIERS *armed to the teeth. He is in chains. His face is gray.*)

  Up, great sir, deign to walk upright!
  From your palace the eyes of many foes follow you!
  And now you don't need an architect, a carpenter will do.
  You won't be moving into a new palace
  But into a little hole in the ground.
  Look about you once more, blind man!

(*The arrested man looks round.*)

  Does all you had please you?
  Between the Easter Mass and the Easter meal
  You are walking to a place whence no one returns.

(*The* GOVERNOR *is led off. A horn sounds an alarm. Noise behind the gateway.*)

  When the house of a great one collapses
  Many little ones are slain.
  Those who had no share in the *good* fortunes of the mighty
  Often have a share in their *mis*fortunes.
  The plunging wagon
  Drags the sweating oxen down with it
  Into the abyss.

(*The* SERVANTS *come rushing through the gateway in panic.*)

SERVANTS (*among themselves*): — The baskets!
  — Take them all into the third courtyard! Food for five days!
  — The mistress has fainted! Someone must carry her down.
  — She must get away.
  — What about us? We'll be slaughtered like chickens, as always.
  — Goodness, what'll happen? There's bloodshed already in the city, they say.
  — Nonsense, the Governor has just been asked to appear at a Princes' meeting. All very correct. Everything'll be ironed out. I heard this on the best authority . . .

(*The two* DOCTORS *rush into the courtyard.*)

FIRST DOCTOR (*trying to restrain the other*): Niko Mikadze, it is your duty as a doctor to attend Natella Abashwili.
SECOND DOCTOR: My duty! It's yours!

FIRST DOCTOR: Whose turn is it to look after the child today, Niko Mikadze, yours or mine?

SECOND DOCTOR: Do you really think, Mika Loladze, I'm going to stay a minute longer in this accursed house on that little brat's account? (*They start fighting. All one hears is:* "You neglect your duty!" *and* "Duty, my foot!" *Then the* SECOND DOCTOR *knocks the* FIRST *down*.) Go to hell! (*Exit.*)

(*Enter the soldier,* SIMON SHASHAVA. *He searches in the crowd for* GRUSHA.)

SIMON: Grusha! There you are at last! What are you going to do?

GRUSHA: Nothing. If worst comes to worst, I've a brother in the mountains. How about you?

SIMON: Forget about me. (*Formally again*.) Grusha Vashnadze, your wish to know my plans fills me with satisfaction. I've been ordered to accompany Madam Abashwili as her guard.

GRUSHA: But hasn't the Palace Guard mutinied?

SIMON (*seriously*): That's a fact.

GRUSHA: Isn't it dangerous to go with her?

SIMON: In Tiflis, they say: Isn't the stabbing dangerous for the knife?

GRUSHA: You're not a knife, you're a man, Simon Shashava, what has that woman to do with you?

SIMON: That woman has nothing to do with me. I have my orders, and I go.

GRUSHA: The soldier is pigheaded: he is running into danger for nothing — nothing at all. I must get into the third courtyard, I'm in a hurry.

SIMON: Since we're both in a hurry we shouldn't quarrel. You need time for a good quarrel. May I ask if the young lady still has parents?

GRUSHA: No, just a brother.

SIMON: As time is short — my second question is this: Is the young lady as healthy as a fish in water?

GRUSHA: I may have a pain in the right shoulder once in a while. Otherwise I'm strong enough for my job. No one has complained. So far.

SIMON: That's well known. When it's Easter Sunday, and the question arises who'll run for the goose all the same, she'll be the one. My third question is this: Is the young lady impatient? Does she want apples in winter?

GRUSHA: Impatient? No. But if a man goes to war without any reason and then no message comes — that's bad.

SIMON: A message will come. And now my final question . . .

GRUSHA: Simon Shashava, I must get to the third courtyard at once. My answer is yes.

SIMON (*very embarrassed*): Haste, they say, is the wind that blows down the scaffolding. But they also say: The rich don't know what haste is. I'm from . . .

GRUSHA: Kutsk . . .

SIMON: The young lady has been inquiring about me? I'm healthy, I have no dependents, I make ten piasters a month, as paymaster twenty piasters, and I'm asking — very sincerely — for your hand.

GRUSHA: Simon Shashava, it suits me well.

SIMON (*taking from his neck a thin chain with a little cross on it*): My mother gave me this cross, Grusha Vashnadze. The chain is silver. Please wear it.

GRUSHA: Many thanks, Simon.

SIMON (*hangs it round her neck*): It would be better to go to the third courtyard now.

Or there'll be difficulties. Anyway, I must harness the horses. The young lady will understand?

GRUSHA: Yes, Simon.

(*They stand undecided.*)

SIMON: I'll just take the mistress to the troops that have stayed loyal. When the war's over, I'll be back. In two weeks. Or three. I hope my intended won't get tired, awaiting my return.

GRUSHA: Simon Shashava, I shall wait for you.
Go calmly into battle, soldier
The bloody battle, the bitter battle
From which not everyone returns:
When you return I shall be there.
I shall be waiting for you under the green elm
I shall be waiting for you under the bare elm
I shall wait until the last soldier has returned
And longer
When you come back from the battle
No boots will stand at my door
The pillow beside mine will be empty
And my mouth will be unkissed.
When you return, when you return
You will be able to say: It is just as it was.

SIMON: I thank you, Grusha Vashnadze. And good-bye!

(*He bows low before her. She does the same before him. Then she runs quickly off without looking round. Enter the* ADJUTANT *from the gateway.*)

ADJUTANT (*harshly*): Harness the horses to the carriage! Don't stand there doing nothing, scum!

(SIMON SHASHAVA *stands to attention and goes off. Two* SERVANTS *crowd from the gateway, bent low under huge trunks. Behind them, supported by her women, stumbles* NATELLA ABASHWILI. *She is followed by a* WOMAN *carrying the* CHILD.)

GOVERNOR'S WIFE: I hardly know if my head's still on. Where's Michael? Don't hold him so clumsily. Pile the trunks onto the carriage. No news from the city, Shalva?

ADJUTANT: None. All's quiet so far, but there's not a minute to lose. No room for all those trunks in the carriage. Pick out what you need. (*Exit quickly.*)

GOVERNOR'S WIFE: Only essentials! Quick, open the trunks! I'll tell you what I need. (*The trunks are lowered and opened. She points at some brocade dresses.*) The green one! And, of course, the one with the fur trimming. Where are Niko Mikadze and Mika Loladze? I've suddenly got the most terrible migraine again. It always starts in the temples. (*Enter* GRUSHA.) Taking your time, eh? Go and get the hot water bottles this minute! (GRUSHA *runs off, returns later with hot water bottles; the* GOVERNOR'S WIFE *orders her about by signs.*) Don't tear the sleeves.

A YOUNG WOMAN: Pardon, madam, no harm has come to the dress.

GOVERNOR'S WIFE: Because I stopped you. I've been watching you for a long time.

Nothing in your head but making eyes at Shalva Tzereteli. I'll kill you, you bitch! (*She beats the* YOUNG WOMAN.)

ADJUTANT (*appearing in the gateway*): Please make haste, Natella Abashwili. Firing has broken out in the city. (*Exit.*)

GOVERNOR'S WIFE (*letting go of the* YOUNG WOMAN): Oh dear, do you think they'll lay hands on us? Why should they? Why? (*She herself begins to rummage in the trunks.*) How's Michael? Asleep?

WOMAN WITH THE CHILD: Yes, madam.

GOVERNOR'S WIFE: Then put him down a moment and get my little saffron-colored boots from the bedroom. I need them for the green dress. (*The* WOMAN *puts down the* CHILD *and goes off.*) Just look how these things have been packed! No love! No understanding! If you don't give them every order yourself . . . At such moments you realize what kind of servants you have! They gorge themselves at your expense, and never a word of gratitude! I'll remember this.

ADJUTANT (*entering, very excited*): Natella, you must leave at once!

GOVERNOR'S WIFE: Why? I've got to take this silver dress — it cost a thousand piasters. And that one there, and where's the wine-colored one?

ADJUTANT (*trying to pull her away*): Riots have broken out! We must leave at once. Where's the baby?

GOVERNOR'S WIFE (*calling to the* YOUNG WOMAN *who was holding the baby*): Maro, get the baby ready! Where on earth are you?

ADJUTANT (*leaving*): We'll probably have to leave the carriage behind and go ahead on horseback.

(*The* GOVERNOR'S WIFE *rummages again among her dresses, throws some onto the heap of chosen clothes, then takes them off again. Noises, drums are heard. The* YOUNG WOMAN *who was beaten creeps away. The sky begins to grow red.*)

GOVERNOR'S WIFE (*rummaging desperately*): I simply cannot find the wine-colored dress. Take the whole pile to the carriage. Where's Asja? And why hasn't Maro come back? Have you all gone crazy?

ADJUTANT (*returning*): Quick! Quick!

GOVERNOR'S WIFE (*to the* FIRST WOMAN): Run! Just throw them into the carriage!

ADJUTANT: We're not taking the carriage. And if you don't come now, I'll ride off on my own.

GOVERNOR'S WIFE (*as the* FIRST WOMAN *can't carry everything*): Where's that bitch Asja? (*The* ADJUTANT *pulls her away.*) Maro, bring the baby! (*To the* FIRST WOMAN.) Go and look for Masha. No, first take the dresses to the carriage. Such nonsense! I wouldn't dream of going on horseback!

(*Turning round, she sees the red sky, and starts back rigid. The fire burns. She is pulled out by the* ADJUTANT. *Shaking, the* FIRST WOMAN *follows with the dresses.*)

MARO (*from the doorway with the boots*): Madam! (*She sees the trunks and dresses and runs toward the* CHILD, *picks it up, and holds it a moment.*) They left it behind, the beasts. (*She hands it to* GRUSHA.) Hold it a moment. (*She runs off, following the* GOVERNOR'S WIFE.)

(*Enter* SERVANTS *from the gateway.*)

COOK: Well, so they've actually gone. Without the food wagons, and not a minute too early. It's time for us to clear out.

GROOM: This'll be an unhealthy neighborhood for quite a while. (*To one of the* WOMEN.) Suliko, take a few blankets and wait for me in the foal stables.

GRUSHA: What have they done with the Governor?

GROOM (*gesturing throat cutting*): Ffffft.

A FAT WOMAN (*seeing the gesture and becoming hysterical*): Oh dear, oh dear, oh dear, oh dear! Our master Georgi Abashwili! A picture of health he was, at the morning Mass — and now! Oh, take me away, we're all lost, we must die in sin like our master, Georgi Abashwili!

OTHER WOMAN (*soothing her*): Calm down, Nina! You'll be taken to safety. You've never hurt a fly.

FAT WOMAN (*being led out*): Oh dear, oh dear, oh dear! Quick! Let's all get out before they come, before they come!

A YOUNG WOMAN: Nina takes it more to heart than the mistress, that's a fact. They even have to have their weeping done for them.

COOK: We'd better get out, all of us.

ANOTHER WOMAN (*glancing back*): That must be the East Gate burning.

YOUNG WOMAN (*seeing the* CHILD *in* GRUSHA's *arms*): The baby! What are you doing with it?

GRUSHA: It got left behind.

YOUNG WOMAN: She simply left it there. Michael, who was kept out of all the drafts!

(*The* SERVANTS *gather round the* CHILD.)

GRUSHA: He's waking up.

GROOM: Better put him down, I tell you. I'd rather not think what'd happen to anybody who was found with that baby.

COOK: That's right. Once they get started, they'll kill each other off, whole families at a time. Let's go.

(*Exeunt all but* GRUSHA, *with the* CHILD *on her arm, and* TWO WOMEN.)

TWO WOMEN: Didn't you hear? Better put him down.

GRUSHA: The nurse asked me to hold him a moment.

OLDER WOMAN: She's not coming back, you simpleton.

YOUNGER WOMAN: Keep your hands off it.

OLDER WOMAN (*amiably*): Grusha, you're a good soul, but you're not very bright, and you know it. I tell you, if he had the plague he couldn't be more dangerous.

GRUSHA (*stubbornly*): He hasn't got the plague. He looks at me! He's human!

OLDER WOMAN: Don't look at *him*. You're a fool — the kind that always gets put upon. A person need only say, "Run for the salad, you have the longest legs," and you run. My husband has an ox cart — you can come with us if you hurry! Lord, by now the whole neighborhood must be in flames.

(*Both* WOMEN *leave, sighing. After some hesitation,* GRUSHA *puts the sleeping* CHILD *down, looks at it for a moment, then takes a brocade blanket from the heap of clothes and covers it. Then both* WOMEN *return, dragging bundles.* GRUSHA *starts guiltily away from the* CHILD *and walks a few steps to one side.*)

YOUNGER WOMAN: Haven't you packed anything yet? There isn't much time, you know. The Ironshirts will be here from the barracks.

GRUSHA: Coming!

(She runs through the doorway. Both WOMEN *go to the gateway and wait. The sound of horses is heard. They flee, screaming. Enter the* FAT PRINCE *with drunken* IRONSHIRTS. *One of them carries the* GOVERNOR's *head on a lance.)*

FAT PRINCE: Here! In the middle! *(One* SOLDIER *climbs onto the other's back, takes the head, holds it tentatively over the door.)* That's not the middle. Farther to the right. That's it. What I do, my friends, I do well. *(While with hammer and nail, the* SOLDIER *fastens the head to the wall by its hair:)* This morning at the church door I said to Georgi Abashwili: "I love a gay sky." Actually, I prefer the lightning that comes out of a gay sky. Yes, indeed. It's a pity they took the brat along, though, I need him, urgently.

(Exit with IRONSHIRTS *through the gateway. Trampling of horses again. Enter* GRUSHA *through the doorway looking cautiously about her. Clearly she has waited for the* IRONSHIRTS *to go. Carrying a bundle, she walks toward the gateway. At the last moment, she turns to see if the* CHILD *is still there. Catching sight of the head over the doorway, she screams. Horrified, she picks up her bundle again, and is about to leave when the* SINGER *starts to speak. She stands rooted to the spot.)*

SINGER: As she was standing between courtyard and gate,
She heard or she thought she heard a low voice calling.
The child called to her,
Not whining, but calling quite sensibly,
Or so it seemed to her.
"Woman," it said, "help me."
And it went on, not whining, but saying quite sensibly:
"Know, woman, he who hears not a cry for help
But passes by with troubled ears will never hear
The gentle call of a lover nor the blackbird at dawn
Nor the happy sigh of the tired grape-picker as the Angelus rings."

(She walks a few steps toward the CHILD *and bends over it.)*

Hearing this she went back for one more look at the child:
Only to sit with him for a moment or two,
Only till someone should come,
His mother, or anyone.

(Leaning on a trunk, she sits facing the CHILD.)*

Only till she would have to leave, for the danger was too great,
The city was full of flame and crying.

(The light grows dimmer, as though evening and night were coming on.)

Fearful is the seductive power of goodness!

(GRUSHA now settles down to watch over the CHILD *through the night. Once, she lights a small lamp to look at it. Once, she tucks it in with a coat. From time to time she listens and looks to see whether someone is coming.)*

And she sat with the child a long time,
Till evening came, till night came, till dawn came.

She sat too long, too long she saw
The soft breathing, the small clenched fists,
Till toward morning the seduction was complete
And she rose, and bent down and, sighing, took the child
And carried it away.

(*She does what the* SINGER *says as he describes it.*)

As if it was stolen goods she picked it up.
As if she was a thief she crept away.

II. THE FLIGHT INTO THE NORTHERN MOUNTAINS

SINGER: When Grusha Vashnadze left the city
   On the Grusinian highway
   On the way to the Northern Mountains
   She sang a song, she bought some milk.
CHORUS: How will this human child escape
   The bloodhounds, the trap-setters?
   Into the deserted mountains she journeyed
   Along the Grusinian highway she journeyed
   She sang a song, she bought some milk.

(GRUSHA VASHNADZE *walks on. On her back she carries the* CHILD *in a sack, in one hand is a large stick, in the other a bundle. She sings.*)

The Song of the Four Generals

   Four generals
   Set out for Iran.
   With the first one, war did not agree.
   The second never won a victory.
   For the third the weather never was right.
   For the fourth the men would never fight.
   Four generals
   And not a single man!

   Sosso Robakidse
   Went marching to Iran
   With him the war did so agree
   He soon had won a victory.
   For him the weather was always right.
   For him the men would always fight.

   Sosso Robakidse,
   He is our man!

(A PEASANT's *cottage appears.*)

GRUSHA (*to the* CHILD): Noontime is meal time. Now we'll sit hopefully in the grass, while the good Grusha goes and buys a little pitcher of milk. (*She lays the* CHILD *down and knocks at the cottage door. An* OLD MAN *opens it.*) Grandfather, could I have a little pitcher of milk? And a corn cake, maybe?

OLD MAN: Milk? We have no milk. The soldiers from the city have our goats. Go to the soldiers if you want milk.

GRUSHA: But grandfather, you must have a little pitcher of milk for a baby?

OLD MAN: And for a God-bless-you, eh?

GRUSHA: Who said anything about a God-bless-you? (*She shows her purse.*) We'll pay like princes. "Head in the clouds, backside in the water." (*The* PEASANT *goes off, grumbling, for milk.*) How much for the milk?

OLD MAN: Three piasters. Milk has gone up.

GRUSHA: Three piasters for this little drop? (*Without a word the* OLD MAN *shuts the door in her face.*) Michael, did you hear that? Three piasters! We can't afford it! (*She goes back, sits down again, and gives the* CHILD *her breast.*) Suck. Think of the three piasters. There's nothing there, but you *think* you're drinking, and that's something. (*Shaking her head, she sees that the* CHILD *isn't sucking any more. She gets up, walks back to the door, and knocks again.*) Open, grandfather, we'll pay. (*Softly.*) May lightning strike you! (*When the* OLD MAN *appears.*) I thought it would be half a piaster. But the baby must be fed. How about one piaster for that little drop?

OLD MAN: Two.

GRUSHA: Don't shut the door again. (*She fishes a long time in her bag.*) Here are two piasters. The milk better be good. I still have two days' journey ahead of me. It's a murderous business you have here — and sinful, too!

OLD MAN: Kill the soldiers if you want milk.

GRUSHA (*giving the* CHILD *some milk*): This is an expensive joke. Take a sip, Michael, it's a week's pay. Around here they think we earned our money just sitting on our behinds. Oh, Michael, Michael, you're a nice little load for a girl to take on! (*Uneasy, she gets up, puts the* CHILD *on her back, and walks on. The* OLD MAN, *grumbling, picks up the pitcher and looks after her unmoved.*)

SINGER: As Grusha Vashnadze went northward
    The Princes' Ironshirts went after her.

CHORUS: How will the barefoot girl escape the Ironshirts,
    The bloodhounds, the trap-setters?
    They hunt even by night.
    Pursuers never tire.
    Butchers sleep little.

(*Two* IRONSHIRTS *are trudging along the highway.*)

CORPORAL: You'll never amount to anything, blockhead, your heart's not in it. Your senior officer sees this in little things. Yesterday, when I made the fat gal, yes, you grabbed her husband as I commanded, and you did kick him in the belly, at my request, but did you *enjoy* it, like a loyal Private, or were you just doing your duty? I've kept an eye on you, blockhead, you're a hollow reed and a tinkling cymbal, you won't get promoted. (*They walk a while in silence.*) Don't think I've forgotten how insubordinate you are, either. Stop limping! I forbid you to limp! You limp because I sold the horses, and I sold the horses because I'd never have got that price again. You limp to show me you don't like marching. I know you. It won't help. You wait. Sing!

TWO IRONSHIRTS (*singing*): Sadly to war I went my way
    Leaving my loved one at her door.

My friends will keep her honor safe
Till from the war I'm back once more.

CORPORAL: Louder!

TWO IRONSHIRTS (*singing*): When 'neath a headstone I shall be
My love a little earth will bring:
"Here rest the feet that oft would run to me
And here the arms that oft to me would cling."

(*They begin to walk again in silence.*)

CORPORAL: A good soldier has his heart and soul in it. When he receives an order, he gets a hard-on, and when he drives his lance into the enemy's guts, he comes. (*He shouts for joy.*) He lets himself be torn to bits for his superior officer, and as he lies dying he takes note that his corporal is nodding approval, and that is reward enough, it's his dearest wish. You won't get any nod of approval, but you'll croak all right. Christ, how'm I to get my hands on the Governor's bastard with the help of a fool like you! (*They stay on stage behind.*)

SINGER: When Grusha Vashnadze came to the River Sirra
Flight grew too much for her, the helpless child too heavy.
In the cornfields the rosy dawn
Is cold to the sleepless one, only cold.
The gay clatter of the milk cans in the farmyard where the smoke rises
Is only a threat to the fugitive.
She who carries the child feels its weight and little more.

(GRUSHA *stops in front of a farm. A fat* PEASANT WOMAN *is carrying a milk can through the door.* GRUSHA *waits until she has gone in, then approaches the house cautiously.*)

GRUSHA (*to the* CHILD): Now you've wet yourself again, and you know I've no linen. Michael, this is where we part company. It's far enough from the city. They wouldn't want you so much that they'd follow you all *this* way, little good-for-nothing. The peasant woman is kind, and can't you just smell the milk? (*She bends down to lay the* CHILD *on the threshold.*) So farewell, Michael, I'll forget how you kicked me in the back all night to make me walk faster. And you can forget the meager fare — it was meant well. I'd like to have kept you — your nose is so tiny — but it can't be. I'd have shown you your first rabbit, I'd have trained you to keep dry, but now I must turn around. My sweetheart the soldier might be back soon, and suppose he didn't find me? You can't ask that, can you? (*She creeps up to the door and lays the* CHILD *on the threshold. Then, hiding behind a tree, she waits until the* PEASANT WOMAN *opens the door and sees the bundle.*)

PEASANT WOMAN: Good heavens, what's this? Husband!

PEASANT: What is it? Let me finish my soup.

PEASANT WOMAN (*to the* CHILD): Where's your mother then? Haven't you got one? It's a boy. Fine linen. He's from a good family, you can see that. And they just leave him on our doorstep. Oh, these are times!

PEASANT: If they think we're going to feed it, they're wrong. You can take it to the priest in the village. That's the best we can do.

PEASANT WOMAN: What'll the priest do with him? He needs a mother. There, he's waking up. Don't you think we could keep him, though?

PEASANT (*shouting*): No!

PEASANT WOMAN: I could lay him in the corner by the armchair. All I need is a crib. I can take him into the fields with me. See him laughing? Husband, we have a roof over our heads. We can do it. Not another word out of you!

(*She carries the* CHILD *into the house. The* PEASANT *follows protesting.* GRUSHA *steps out from behind the tree, laughs, and hurries off in the opposite direction.*)

SINGER: Why so cheerful, making for home?
CHORUS: Because the child has won new parents with a laugh,
  Because I'm rid of the little one, I'm cheerful.
SINGER: And why so sad?
CHORUS: Because I'm single and free, I'm sad
  Like someone who's been robbed
  Someone who's newly poor.

(*She walks for a short while, then meets the two* IRONSHIRTS *who point their lances at her.*)

CORPORAL: Lady, you are running straight into the arms of the Armed Forces. Where are you coming from? And when? Are you having illicit relations with the enemy? Where is he hiding? What movements is he making in your rear? How about the hills? How about the valleys? How are your stockings held in position? (GRUSHA *stands there frightened.*) Don't be scared, we always withdraw, if necessary . . . what, blockhead? I always withdraw. In that respect at least, I can be relied on. Why are you staring like that at my lance? In the field no soldier drops his lance, that's a rule. Learn it by heart, blockhead. Now, lady, where are you headed?

GRUSHA: To meet my intended, one Simon Shashava, of the Palace Guard in Nuka.

CORPORAL: Simon Shashava? Sure, I know him. He gave me the key so I could look you up once in a while. Blockhead, we are getting to be unpopular. We must make her realize we have honorable intentions. Lady, behind apparent frivolity I conceal a serious nature, so let me tell you officially: I want a child from you. (GRUSHA *utters a little scream.*) Blockhead, she understands me. Uh-huh, isn't it a sweet shock? "Then first I must take the noodles out of the oven, Officer. Then first I must change my torn shirt, Colonel." But away with jokes, away with my lance! We are looking for a baby. A baby from a good family. Have you heard of such a baby, from the city, dressed in fine linen, and suddenly turning up here?

GRUSHA: No, I haven't heard a thing. (*Suddenly she turns around and runs back, panic-stricken. The* IRONSHIRTS *glance at each other, then follow her, cursing.*)

SINGER: Run, kind girl! The killers are coming!
  Help the helpless babe, helpless girl!
  And so she runs!
CHORUS: In the bloodiest times
  There are kind people.

(*As* GRUSHA *rushes into the cottage, the* PEASANT WOMAN *is bending over the* CHILD's *crib.*)

GRUSHA: Hide him. Quick! The Ironshirts are coming! I laid him on your doorstep. But he isn't mine. He's from a good family.

PEASANT WOMAN: Who's coming? What Ironshirts?

GRUSHA: Don't ask questions. The Ironshirts that are looking for it.

PEASANT WOMAN: They've no business in my house. But I must have a little talk with you, it seems.

GRUSHA: Take off the fine linen. It'll give us away.

PEASANT WOMAN: Linen, my foot! In this house I make the decisions! "You can't vomit in *my* room!" Why did you abandon it? It's a sin.

GRUSHA (*looking out of the window*): Look, they're coming out from behind those trees! I shouldn't have run away, it made them angry. Oh, what shall I do?

PEASANT WOMAN (*looking out of the window and suddenly starting with fear*): Gracious! Ironshirts!

GRUSHA: They're after the baby.

PEASANT WOMAN: Suppose they come in!

GRUSHA: You mustn't give him to them. Say he's yours.

PEASANT WOMAN: Yes.

GRUSHA: They'll run him through if you hand him over.

PEASANT WOMAN: But suppose they ask for it? The silver for the harvest is in the house.

GRUSHA: If you let them have him, they'll run him through, right here in this room! You've got to say he's yours!

PEASANT WOMAN: Yes. But what if they don't believe me?

GRUSHA: You must be firm.

PEASANT WOMAN: They'll burn the roof over our heads.

GRUSHA: That's why you must say he's yours. His name's Michael. But I shouldn't have told you. (*The* PEASANT WOMAN *nods.*) Don't nod like that. And don't tremble — they'll notice.

PEASANT WOMAN: Yes.

GRUSHA: And stop saying yes, I can't stand it. (*She shakes the* WOMAN.) Don't you have any children?

PEASANT WOMAN (*muttering*): He's in the war.

GRUSHA: Then maybe *he's* an Ironshirt? Do you want *him* to run children through with a lance? You'd bawl him out. "No fooling with lances in my house!" you'd shout, "is that what I've reared you for? Wash your neck before you speak to your mother!"

PEASANT WOMAN: That's true, he couldn't get away with anything around here!

GRUSHA: So you'll say he's yours?

PEASANT WOMAN: Yes.

GRUSHA: Look! They're coming!

(*There is a knocking at the door. The* WOMEN *don't answer. Enter* IRONSHIRTS. *The* PEASANT WOMAN *bows low.*)

CORPORAL: Well, here she is. What did I tell you? What a nose I have! I *smelt* her. Lady, I have a question for you. Why did you run away? What did you think I would do to you? I'll bet it was something unchaste. Confess!

GRUSHA (*while the* PEASANT WOMAN *bows again and again*): I'd left some milk on the stove, and I suddenly remembered it.

CORPORAL: Or maybe you imagined I looked at you unchastely? Like there could be something between us? A carnal glance, know what I mean?

GRUSHA: I didn't see it.

CORPORAL: But it's possible, huh? You admit that much. After all, I might be a pig.

I'll be frank with you: I could think of all sorts of things if we were alone. (*To the* PEASANT WOMAN.) Shouldn't you be busy in the yard? Feeding the hens?

PEASANT WOMAN (*falling suddenly to her knees*): Soldier, I didn't know a thing about it. Please don't burn the roof over our heads.

CORPORAL: What are you talking about?

PEASANT WOMAN: I had nothing to do with it. She left it on my doorstep, I swear it!

CORPORAL (*suddenly seeing the* CHILD *and whistling*): Ah, so there's a little something in the crib! Blockhead, I smell a thousand piasters. Take the old girl outside and hold on to her. It looks like I have a little cross-examining to do. (*The* PEASANT WOMAN *lets herself be led out by the* PRIVATE, *without a word.*) So, you've got the child I wanted from you! (*He walks toward the crib.*)

GRUSHA: Officer, he's mine. He's not the one you're after.

CORPORAL: I'll just take a look. (*He bends over the crib.*)

(GRUSHA *looks round in despair.*)

GRUSHA: He's mine! He's mine!

CORPORAL: Fine linen!

(GRUSHA *dashes at him to pull him away. He throws her off and again bends over the crib. Again looking round in despair, she sees a log of wood, seizes it, and hits the* CORPORAL *over the head from behind. The* CORPORAL *collapses. She quickly picks up the* CHILD *and rushes off.*)

SINGER: And in her flight from the Ironshirts
    After twenty-two days of journeying
    At the foot of the Janga-Tu Glacier
    Grusha Vashnadze decided to adopt the child.

CHORUS: The helpless girl adopted the helpless child.

(GRUSHA *squats over a half-frozen stream to get the* CHILD *water in the hollow of her hand.*)

GRUSHA: Since no one else will take you, son,
    I must take you.
    Since no one else will take you, son,
    You must take me.
    O black day in a lean, lean year,
    The trip was long, the milk was dear,
    My legs are tired, my feet are sore:
    But I wouldn't be without you any more.
    I'll throw your silken shirt away
    And wrap you in rags and tatters.
    I'll wash you, son, and christen you in glacier water.
    We'll see it through together.

(*She has taken off the* CHILD's *fine linen and wrapped it in a rag.*)

SINGER: When Grusha Vashnadze
    Pursued by the Ironshirts
    Came to the bridge on the glacier
    Leading to the villages of the Eastern Slope

She sang the Song of the Rotten Bridge
And risked two lives.

(*A wind has risen. The bridge on the glacier is visible in the dark. One rope is broken and half the bridge is hanging down the abyss.* MERCHANTS, *two men and a woman, stand undecided before the bridge as* GRUSHA *and the* CHILD *arrive. One* MAN *is trying to catch the hanging rope with a stick.*)

FIRST MAN: Take your time, young woman. You won't get across here anyway.

GRUSHA: But I *have* to get the baby to the east side. To my brother's place.

MERCHANT WOMAN: Have to? How d'you mean, "have to"? I have to get there, too — because I have to buy carpets in Atum — carpets a woman had to sell because her husband had to die. But can *I* do what I have to? Can she? Andrei's been fishing for that rope for hours. And I ask you, how are we going to fasten it, even if he gets it up?

FIRST MAN (*listening*): Hush, I think I hear something.

GRUSHA: The bridge isn't quite rotted through. I think I'll try it.

MERCHANT WOMAN: I wouldn't — if the devil himself were after me. It's suicide.

FIRST MAN (*shouting*): Hi!

GRUSHA: Don't shout! (*To the* MERCHANT WOMAN.) Tell him not to shout.

FIRST MAN: But there's someone down there calling. Maybe they've lost their way.

MERCHANT WOMAN: Why shouldn't he shout? Is there something funny about you? Are they after you?

GRUSHA: All right, I'll tell. The Ironshirts are after me. I knocked one down.

SECOND MAN: Hide our merchandise!

(*The* WOMAN *hides a sack behind a rock.*)

FIRST MAN: Why didn't you say so right away? (*To the others.*) If they catch her they'll make mincemeat out of her!

GRUSHA: Get out of my way. I've got to cross that bridge.

SECOND MAN: You can't. The precipice is two thousand feet deep.

FIRST MAN: Even with the rope it'd be no use. We could hold it up with our hands. But then we'd have to do the same for the Ironshirts.

GRUSHA: Go away.

(*There are calls from the distance:* "Hi, up there!")

MERCHANT WOMAN: They're getting near. But you can't take the child on that bridge. It's sure to break. And look!

(GRUSHA *looks down into the abyss. The* IRONSHIRTS *are heard calling again from below.*)

SECOND MAN: Two thousand feet!

GRUSHA: But those men are worse.

FIRST MAN: You can't do it. Think of the baby. Risk your life but not a child's.

SECOND MAN: With the child she's that much heavier!

MERCHANT WOMAN: Maybe she's *really* got to get across. Give *me* the baby. I'll hide it. Cross the bridge alone!

GRUSHA: I won't. We belong together. (*To the* CHILD.) "Live together, die together." (*She sings.*)

The Song of the Rotten Bridge

> Deep is the abyss, son,
> I see the weak bridge sway
> But it's not for us, son,
> To choose the way.
>
> The way I know
> Is the one you must tread,
> And all you will eat
> Is my bit of bread.
>
> Of every four pieces
> You shall have three.
> Would that I knew
> How big they will be!

Get out of my way, I'll try it without the rope.

MERCHANT WOMAN: You are tempting God!

(*There are shouts from below.*)

GRUSHA: Please, throw that stick away, or they'll get the rope and follow me. (*Pressing the* CHILD *to her, she steps onto the swaying bridge. The* MERCHANT WOMAN *screams when it looks as though the bridge is about to collapse. But* GRUSHA *walks on and reaches the far side.*)

FIRST MAN: She made it!

MERCHANT WOMAN (*who has fallen on her knees and begun to pray, angrily*): I still think it was a sin.

(*The* IRONSHIRTS *appear; the* CORPORAL's *head is bandaged.*)

CORPORAL: Seen a woman with a child?

FIRST MAN (*while the* SECOND MAN *throws the stick into the abyss*): Yes, there! But the bridge won't carry you!

CORPORAL: You'll pay for this, blockhead!

(GRUSHA, *from the far bank, laughs and shows the* CHILD *to the* IRONSHIRTS. *She walks on. The wind blows.*)

GRUSHA (*turning to the* CHILD): You mustn't be afraid of the wind. He's a poor thing too. He has to push the clouds along and he gets quite cold doing it. (*Snow starts falling.*) And the snow isn't so bad, either, Michael. It covers the little fir trees so they won't die in winter. Let me sing you a little song. (*She sings.*)

The Song of the Child

> Your father is a bandit
> A harlot the mother who bore you.
> Yet honorable men
> Shall kneel down before you.
> Food to the baby horses
> The tiger's son will take.
> The mothers will get milk
> From the son of the snake.

III. IN THE NORTHERN MOUNTAINS

SINGER: Seven days the sister, Grusha Vashnadze,
    Journeyed across the glacier
    And down the slopes she journeyed.
    "When I enter my brother's house," she thought,
    "He will rise and embrace me."
    "Is that you, sister?" he will say,
    "I have long expected you.
    This is my dear wife,
    And this is my farm, come to me by marriage,
    With eleven horses and thirty-one cows. Sit down.
    Sit down with your child at our table and eat."
    The brother's house was in a lovely valley.
    When the sister came to the brother,
    She was ill from walking.
    The brother rose from the table.

(*A* fat peasant couple rise from the table. LAVRENTI VASHNADZE *still has a napkin round his neck, as* GRUSHA, *pale and supported by a* SERVANT, *enters with the* CHILD.)

LAVRENTI: Where've *you* come from, Grusha?
GRUSHA (*feebly*): Across the Janga-Tu Pass, Lavrenti.
SERVANT: I found her in front of the hay barn. She has a baby with her.
SISTER-IN-LAW: Go and groom the mare.

(*Exit the* SERVANT.)

LAVRENTI: This is my wife Aniko.
SISTER-IN-LAW: I thought you were in service in Nuka.
GRUSHA (*barely able to stand*): Yes, I was.
SISTER-IN-LAW: Wasn't it a good job? We were told it was.
GRUSHA: The Governor got killed.
LAVRENTI: Yes, we heard there were riots. Your aunt told us. Remember, Aniko?
SISTER-IN-LAW: Here with us, it's very quiet. City people always want something going on. (*She walks toward the door, calling.*) Sosso, Sosso, don't take the cake out of the oven yet, d'you hear? Where on earth are you? (*Exit, calling.*)
LAVRENTI (*quietly, quickly*): Is there a father? (*As she shakes her head.*) I thought not. We must think up something. She's religious.
SISTER-IN-LAW (*returning*): Those servants! (*To* GRUSHA.) You have a child.
GRUSHA: It's mine. (*She collapses.* LAVRENTI *rushes to her assistance.*)
SISTER-IN-LAW: Heavens, she's ill — what are we going to do?
LAVRENTI (*escorting her to a bench near the stove*): Sit down, sit. I think it's just weakness, Aniko.
SISTER-IN-LAW: As long as it's not scarlet fever!
LAVRENTI: She'd have spots if it was. It's only weakness. Don't worry, Aniko. (*To* GRUSHA.) Better, sitting down?
SISTER-IN-LAW: Is the child hers?
GRUSHA: Yes, mine.
LAVRENTI: She's on her way to her husband.
SISTER-IN-LAW: I see. Your meat's getting cold. (LAVRENTI *sits down and begins to*

eat.) Cold food's not good for you, the fat mustn't get cold, you know your stomach's your weak spot. (To GRUSHA.) If your husband's not in the city, where is he?

LAVRENTI: She got married on the other side of the mountain, she says.

SISTER-IN-LAW: On the other side of the mountain. I see. (She also sits down to eat.)

GRUSHA: I think I should lie down somewhere, Lavrenti.

SISTER-IN-LAW: If it's consumption we'll all get it. (She goes on cross-examining her.) Has your husband got a farm?

GRUSHA: He's a soldier.

LAVRENTI: But he's coming into a farm — a small one — from his father.

SISTER-IN-LAW: Isn't he in the war? Why not?

GRUSHA (with effort): Yes, he's in the war.

SISTER-IN-LAW: Then why d'you want to go to the farm?

LAVRENTI: When he comes back from the war, he'll return to his farm.

SISTER-IN-LAW: But you're going there now?

LAVRENTI: Yes, to wait for him.

SISTER-IN-LAW (calling shrilly): Sosso, the cake!

GRUSHA (murmuring feverishly): A farm — a soldier — waiting — sit down, eat.

SISTER-IN-LAW: It's scarlet fever.

GRUSHA (starting up): Yes, he's got a farm!

LAVRENTI: I think it's just weakness, Aniko. Would you look after the cake yourself, dear?

SISTER-IN-LAW: But when will he come back if war's broken out again as people say? (She waddles off, shouting.) Sosso! Where on earth are you? Sosso!

LAVRENTI (getting up quickly and going to GRUSHA): You'll get a bed in a minute. She has a good heart. But wait till after supper.

GRUSHA (holding out the CHILD to him): Take him.

LAVRENTI (taking it and looking around): But you can't stay here long with the child. She's religious, you see.

(GRUSHA collapses. LAVRENTI catches her.)

SINGER: The sister was so ill,
   The cowardly brother had to give her shelter.
   Summer departed, winter came.
   The winter was long, the winter was short.
   People mustn't know anything.
   Rats mustn't bite.
   Spring mustn't come.

(GRUSHA sits over the weaving loom in a workroom. She and the CHILD, who is squatting on the floor, are wrapped in blankets. She sings.)

The Song of the Center

   And the lover started to leave
   And his betrothed ran pleading after him
   Pleading and weeping, weeping and teaching:
   "Dearest mine, dearest mine
   When you go to war as now you do
   When you fight the foe as soon you will
   Don't lead with the front line

And don't push with the rear line
At the front is red fire
In the rear is red smoke
Stay in the war's center
Stay near the standard bearer
The first always die
The last are also hit
Those in the center come home."

Michael, we must be clever. If we make ourselves as small as cockroaches, the sister-in-law will forget we're in the house, and then we can stay till the snow melts.

(*Enter* LAVRENTI. *He sits down beside his sister.*)

LAVRENTI: Why are you sitting there muffled up like coachmen, you two? Is it too cold in the room?

GRUSHA (*hastily removing one shawl*): It's not too cold, Lavrenti.

LAVRENTI: If it's too cold, you shouldn't be sitting here with the child. Aniko would never forgive herself! (*Pause.*) I hope our priest didn't question you about the child?

GRUSHA: He did, but I didn't tell him anything.

LAVRENTI: That's good. I wanted to speak to you about Aniko. She has a good heart but she's very, very sensitive. People need only mention our farm and she's worried. She takes everything hard, you see. One time our milkmaid went to church with a hole in her stocking. Ever since, Aniko has worn two pairs of stockings in church. It's the old family in her. (*He listens.*) Are you sure there are no rats around? If there are rats, you couldn't live here. (*There are sounds as of dripping from the roof.*) What's that, dripping?

GRUSHA: It must be a barrel leaking.

LAVRENTI: Yes, it must be a barrel. You've been here six months, haven't you? Was I talking about Aniko? (*They listen again to the snow melting.*) You can't imagine how worried she gets about your soldier-husband. "Suppose he comes back and can't find her!" she says and lies awake. "He can't come before the spring," I tell her. The dear woman! (*The drops begin to fall faster.*) When d'you think he'll come? What do *you* think? (GRUSHA *is silent.*) Not before the spring, you agree? (GRUSHA *is silent.*) You don't believe he'll come at all? (GRUSHA *is silent.*) But when the spring comes and the snow melts here and on the passes, you can't stay on. They may come and look for you. There's already talk of an illegitimate child. (*The "glockenspiel" of the falling drops has grown faster and steadier.*) Grusha, the snow is melting on the roof. Spring is here.

GRUSHA: Yes.

LAVRENTI (*eagerly*): I'll tell you what we'll do. You need a place to go, and, because of the child (*he sighs*), you have to have a husband, so people won't talk. Now I've made cautious inquiries to see if we can find you a husband. Grusha, I *have* one. I talked to a peasant woman who has a son. Just the other side of the mountain. A small farm. And she's willing.

GRUSHA: But I *can't* marry! I must wait for Simon Shashava.

LAVRENTI: Of course. That's all been taken care of. You don't need a man in bed — you need a man on paper. And I've found you one. The son of this peasant

woman is going to die. Isn't that wonderful? He's at his last gasp. And all in line
with our story — a husband from the other side of the mountain! And when you
met him he was at the last gasp. So you're a widow. What do you say?

GRUSHA: It's true I could use a document with stamps on it for Michael.

LAVRENTI: Stamps make all the difference. Without something in writing the Shah
couldn't prove he's a Shah. And you'll have a place to live.

GRUSHA: How much does the peasant woman want?

LAVRENTI: Four hundred piasters.

GRUSHA: Where will you find it?

LAVRENTI (guiltily): Aniko's milk money.

GRUSHA: No one would know us there. I'll do it.

LAVRENTI (getting up): I'll let the peasant woman know. (Quick exit.)

GRUSHA: Michael, you make a lot of work. I came by you as the pear tree comes by
sparrows. And because a Christian bends down and picks up a crust of bread so
nothing will go to waste. Michael, it would have been better had I walked quickly
away on that Easter Sunday in Nuka in the second courtyard. Now I am a fool.

SINGER: The bridegroom was on his deathbed when the bride arrived.
   The bridegroom's mother was waiting at the door, telling her to hurry.
   The bride brought a child along.
   The witness hid it during the wedding.

(On one side the bed. Under the mosquito net lies a very sick MAN. GRUSHA is
pulled in at a run by her future mother-in-law. They are followed by LAVRENTI
and the CHILD.)

MOTHER-IN-LAW: Quick! Quick! Or he'll die on us before the wedding. (To
LAVRENTI.) I was never told she had a child already.

LAVRENTI: What difference does it make? (Pointing toward the DYING MAN.) It can't
matter to him — in his condition.

MOTHER-IN-LAW: To him? But I'll never survive the shame! We are honest people.
(She begins to weep.) My Jussup doesn't have to marry a girl with a child!

LAVRENTI: All right, make it another two hundred piasters. You'll have it in writing
that the farm will go to you: but she'll have the right to live here for two years.

MOTHER-IN-LAW (drying her tears): It'll hardly cover the funeral expenses. I hope
she'll really lend a hand with the work. And what's happened to the monk? He
must have slipped out through the kitchen window. We'll have the whole village
on our necks when they hear Jussup's end is come! Oh dear! I'll go get the monk.
But he mustn't see the child!

LAVRENTI: I'll take care he doesn't. But why only a monk? Why not a priest?

MOTHER-IN-LAW: Oh, he's just as good. I only made one mistake: I paid half his fee
in advance. Enough to send him to the tavern. I only hope . . . (She runs off.)

LAVRENTI: She saved on the priest, the wretch! Hired a cheap monk.

GRUSHA: You will send Simon Shashava to see me if he turns up after all?

LAVRENTI: Yes. (Pointing at the SICK PEASANT.) Won't you take a look at him? (GRU-
SHA, taking MICHAEL to her, shakes her head.) He's not moving an eyelid. I hope
we aren't too late.

(They listen. On the opposite side enter NEIGHBORS who look around and take
up positions against the walls, thus forming another wall near the bed, yet

leaving an opening so that the bed can be seen. They start murmuring prayers. Enter the MOTHER-IN-LAW *with a* MONK. *Showing some annoyance and surprise, she bows to the guests.*)

MOTHER-IN-LAW: I hope you won't mind waiting a few moments? My son's bride has just arrived from the city. An emergency wedding is about to be celebrated. (*To the* MONK *in the bedroom.*) I might have known you couldn't keep your trap shut. (*To* GRUSHA.) The wedding can take place at once. Here's the license. Me and the bride's brother (LAVRENTI *tries to hide in the background, after having quietly taken* MICHAEL *back from* GRUSHA. *The* MOTHER-IN-LAW *waves him away.*) are the witnesses.

(GRUSHA *has bowed to the* MONK. *They go to the bed. The* MOTHER-IN-LAW *lifts the mosquito net. The* MONK *starts reeling off the marriage ceremony in Latin. Meanwhile the* MOTHER-IN-LAW *beckons to* LAVRENTI *to get rid of the* CHILD, *but fearing that it will cry he draws its attention to the ceremony,* GRUSHA *glances once at the* CHILD, *and* LAVRENTI *waves the* CHILD'S *hand in a greeting.*)

MONK: Are you prepared to be a faithful, obedient, and good wife to this man, and to cleave to him until death you do part?
GRUSHA (*looking at the* CHILD): I am.
MONK (*to the* SICK PEASANT): Are you prepared to be a good and loving husband to your wife until death you do part? (*As the* SICK PEASANT *does not answer, the* MONK *looks inquiringly around.*)
MOTHER-IN-LAW: Of course he is! Didn't you hear him say yes?
MONK: All right. We declare the marriage contracted! How about extreme unction?
MOTHER-IN-LAW: Nothing doing! The wedding cost quite enough. Now I must take care of the mourners. (*To* LAVRENTI.) Did we say seven hundred?
LAVRENTI: Six hundred. (*He pays.*) Now I don't want to sit with the guests and get to know people. So farewell, Grusha, and if my widowed sister comes to visit me, she'll get a welcome from my wife, or I'll show my teeth. (*Nods, gives the* CHILD *to* GRUSHA, *and leaves. The* MOURNERS *glance after him without interest.*)
MONK: May one ask where this child comes from?
MOTHER-IN-LAW: Is there a child? I don't see a child. And you don't see a child either — you understand? Or it may turn out I saw all sorts of things in the tavern! Now come on.

(*After* GRUSHA *has put the* CHILD *down and told him to be quiet, they move over left.* GRUSHA *is introduced to the neighbors.*)

This is my daughter-in-law. She arrived just in time to find dear Jussup still alive.
ONE WOMAN: He's been ill now a whole year, hasn't he? When our Vassili was drafted he was there to say good-bye.
ANOTHER WOMAN: Such things are terrible for a farm. The corn all ripe and the farmer in bed! It'll really be a blessing if he doesn't suffer too long, I say.
FIRST WOMAN (*confidentially*): You know why we thought he'd taken to his bed? Because of the draft! And now his end is come!
MOTHER-IN-LAW: Sit yourselves down, please! And have some cakes!

(*She beckons to* GRUSHA *and both women go into the bedroom, where they pick up the cake pans off the floor. The* GUESTS, *among them the* MONK, *sit on the floor and begin conversing in subdued voices.*)

ONE PEASANT (*to whom the* MONK *has handed the bottle which he has taken from his soutane*): There's a child, you say! How can that have happened to Jussup?

A WOMAN: She was certainly lucky to get herself married, with him so sick!

MOTHER-IN-LAW: They're gossiping already. And wolfing down the funeral cakes at the same time! If he doesn't die today, I'll have to bake some more tomorrow!

GRUSHA: I'll bake them for you.

MOTHER-IN-LAW: Yesterday some horsemen rode by, and I went out to see who it was. When I came in again he was lying there like a corpse! So I sent for you. It can't take much longer. (*She listens.*)

MONK: Dear wedding and funeral guests! Deeply touched, we stand before a bed of death and marriage. The bride gets a veil; the groom, a shroud: how varied, my children, are the fates of men! Alas! One man dies and has a roof over his head, and the other is married and the flesh turns to dust from which it was made. Amen.

MOTHER-IN-LAW: He's getting his own back. I shouldn't have hired such a cheap one. It's what you'd expect. A more expensive monk would behave himself. In Sura there's one with a real air of sanctity about him, but of course he charges a fortune. A fifty piaster monk like that has no dignity, and as for piety, just fifty piasters' worth and no more! When I came to get him in the tavern he'd just made a speech, and he was shouting: "The war is over, beware of the peace!" We must go in.

GRUSHA (*giving* MICHAEL *a cake*): Eat this cake, and keep nice and still, Michael.

(*The* TWO WOMEN *offer cakes to the guests. The* DYING MAN *sits up in bed. He puts his head out from under the mosquito net, stares at the* TWO WOMEN, *then sinks back again. The* MONK *takes two bottles from his soutane and offers them to the* PEASANT *beside him. Enter three* MUSICIANS *who are greeted with a sly wink by the* MONK.)

MOTHER-IN-LAW (*to the* MUSICIANS): What are you doing here? With instruments?

ONE MUSICIAN: Brother Anastasius here (*pointing at the* MONK) told us there was a wedding on.

MOTHER-IN-LAW: What? You brought them? Three more on my neck! Don't you know there's a dying man in the next room?

MONK: A very tempting assignment for a musician: something that could be either a subdued Wedding March or a spirited Funeral Dance.

MOTHER-IN-LAW: Well, you might as well play. Nobody can stop you eating in any case.

(*The* MUSICIANS *play a potpourri. The* WOMEN *serve cakes.*)

MONK: The trumpet sounds like a whining baby. And you, little drum, what have you got to tell the world?

DRUNKEN PEASANT (*beside the* MONK, *sings*): There was a young woman who said:
  I thought I'd be happier, wed.
  But my husband is old
  And remarkably cold
  So I sleep with a candle instead.

(*The* MOTHER-IN-LAW *throws the* DRUNKEN PEASANT *out. The music stops. The* GUESTS *are embarrassed.*)

GUESTS (loudly): — Have you heard? The Grand Duke is back! But the Princes are against him.

— They say the Shah of Persia has lent him a great army to restore order in Grusinia.

— But how is that possible? The Shah of Persia is the enemy . . .

— The enemy of Grusinia, you donkey, not the enemy of the Grand Duke!

— In any case, the war's over, so our soldiers are coming back.

(GRUSHA drops a cake pan. GUESTS help her pick up the cake.)

AN OLD WOMAN (to GRUSHA): Are you feeling bad? It's just excitement about dear Jussup. Sit down and rest a while, my dear. (GRUSHA staggers.)

GUESTS: Now everything'll be the way it was. Only the taxes'll go up because now we'll have to pay for the war.

GRUSHA (weakly): Did someone say the soldiers are back?

A MAN: I did.

GRUSHA: It can't be true.

FIRST MAN (to a WOMAN): Show her the shawl. We bought it from a soldier. It's from Persia.

GRUSHA (looking at the shawl): They are here. (She gets up, takes a step, kneels down in prayer, takes the silver cross and chain out of her blouse, and kisses it.)

MOTHER-IN-LAW (while the guests silently watch GRUSHA): What's the matter with you? Aren't you going to look after our guests? What's all this city nonsense got to do with us?

GUESTS (resuming conversation while GRUSHA remains in prayer): — You can buy Persian saddles from the soldiers too. Though many want crutches in exchange for them.

— The leaders on one side can win a war, the soldiers on both sides lose it.

— Anyway, the war's over. It's something they can't draft you any more.

(The DYING MAN sits bolt upright in bed. He listens.)

— What we need is two weeks of good weather.

— Our pear trees are hardly bearing a thing this year.

MOTHER-IN-LAW (offering cakes): Have some more cakes and welcome! There are more!

(The MOTHER-IN-LAW goes to the bedroom with the empty cake pans. Unaware of the DYING MAN, she is bending down to pick up another tray when he begins to talk in a hoarse voice.)

PEASANT: How many more cakes are you going to stuff down their throats? D'you think I can shit money?

(The MOTHER-IN-LAW starts, stares at him aghast, while he climbs out from behind the mosquito net.)

FIRST WOMAN (talking kindly to GRUSHA in the next room): Has the young wife got someone at the front?

A MAN: It's good news that they're on their way home, huh?

PEASANT: Don't stare at me like that! Where's this wife you've saddled me with?

(Receiving no answer, he climbs out of bed and in his nightshirt staggers into the other room. Trembling, she follows him with the cake pan.)

GUESTS (*seeing him and shrieking*): Good God! Jussup!

(*Everyone leaps up in alarm. The* WOMEN *rush to the door.* GRUSHA, *still on her knees, turns round and stares at the* MAN.)

PEASANT: A funeral supper! You'd enjoy that, wouldn't you? Get out before I throw you out! (*As the* GUESTS *stampede from the house, gloomily to* GRUSHA.) I've upset the apple cart, huh? (*Receiving no answer, he turns round and takes a cake from the pan which his mother is holding.*)

SINGER: O confusion! The wife discovers she has a husband.
By day there's the child, by night there's the husband.
The lover is on his way both day and night.
Husband and wife look at each other.
The bedroom is small.

(*Near the bed the* PEASANT *is sitting in a high wooden bathtub, naked, the* MOTHER-IN-LAW *is pouring water from a pitcher. Opposite* GRUSHA *cowers with* MICHAEL, *who is playing at mending straw mats.*)

PEASANT (*to his* MOTHER): That's her work, not yours. Where's she hiding out now?
MOTHER-IN-LAW (*calling*): Grusha! The peasant wants you!
GRUSHA (*to* MICHAEL): There are still two holes to mend.
PEASANT (*when* GRUSHA *approaches*): Scrub my back!
GRUSHA: Can't the peasant do it himself?
PEASANT: "Can't the peasant do it himself?" Get the brush! To hell with you! Are you the wife here? Or are you a visitor? (*To the* MOTHER-IN-LAW.) It's too cold!
MOTHER-IN-LAW: I'll run for hot water.
GRUSHA: Let me go.
PEASANT: You stay here. (*The* MOTHER-IN-LAW *exits.*) Rub harder. And no shirking. You've seen a naked fellow before. That child didn't come out of thin air.
GRUSHA: The child was not conceived in joy, if that's what the peasant means.
PEASANT (*turning and grinning*): You don't look the type. (GRUSHA *stops scrubbing him, starts back. Enter the* MOTHER-IN-LAW.)
PEASANT: A nice thing you've saddled me with! A simpleton for a wife!
MOTHER-IN-LAW: She just isn't cooperative.
PEASANT: Pour — but go easy! Ow! Go easy, I said. (*To* GRUSHA.) Maybe you did something wrong in the city . . . I wouldn't be surprised. Why else should you be here? But I won't talk about that. I've not said a word about the illegitimate object you brought into my house either. But my patience has limits! It's against nature. (*To the* MOTHER-IN-LAW.) More! (*To* GRUSHA.) And even if your soldier does come back, you're married.
GRUSHA: Yes.
PEASANT: But your soldier won't come back. Don't you believe it.
GRUSHA: No.
PEASANT: You're cheating me. You're my wife and you're not my wife. Where you lie, nothing lies, and yet no other woman can lie there. When I go to work in the morning I'm tired — when I lie down at night I'm awake as the devil. God has given you sex — and what d'you do? I don't have ten piasters to buy myself a woman in the city. Besides, it's a long way. Woman weeds the fields and opens up her legs, that's what our calendar says. D'you hear?

GRUSHA (*quietly*): Yes. I didn't mean to cheat you out of it.

PEASANT: She didn't mean to cheat me out of it! Pour some more water! (*The* MOTHER-IN-LAW *pours.*) Ow!

SINGER: As she sat by the stream to wash the linen
She saw his image in the water
And his face grew dimmer with the passing moons.
As she raised herself to wring the linen
She heard his voice from the murmuring maple
And his voice grew fainter with the passing moons.
Evasions and sighs grew more numerous,
Tears and sweat flowed.
With the passing moons the child grew up.

(GRUSHA *sits by a stream, dipping linen into the water. In the rear, a few* CHILDREN *are standing.*)

GRUSHA (*to* MICHAEL): You can play with them, Michael, but don't let them boss you around just because you're the littlest. (MICHAEL *nods and joins the* CHILDREN. *They start playing.*)

BIGGEST BOY: Today it's the Heads-Off Game. (*To a* FAT BOY.) You're the Prince and you laugh. (*To* MICHAEL.) You're the Governor. (*To a* GIRL.) You're the Governor's wife and you cry when his head's cut off. And I do the cutting. (*He shows his wooden sword.*) With this. First, they lead the Governor into the yard. The Prince walks in front. The Governor's wife comes last.

(*They form a procession. The* FAT BOY *is first and laughs. Then comes* MICHAEL, *then the* BIGGEST BOY, *and then the* GIRL, *who weeps.*)

MICHAEL (*standing still*): Me cut off head!

BIGGEST BOY: That's my job. You're the littlest. The Governor's the easy part. All you do is kneel down and get your head cut off — simple.

MICHAEL: Me want sword!

BIGGEST BOY: It's mine! (*He gives* MICHAEL *a kick.*)

GIRL (*shouting to* GRUSHA): He won't play his part!

GRUSHA (*laughing*): Even the little duck is a swimmer, they say.

BIGGEST BOY: You can be the Prince if you can laugh. (MICHAEL *shakes his head.*)

FAT BOY: I laugh best. Let him cut off the head just once. Then you do it, then me.

(*Reluctantly, the* BIGGEST BOY *hands* MICHAEL *the wooden sword and kneels down. The* FAT BOY *sits down, slaps his thigh, and laughs with all his might. The* GIRL *weeps loudly.* MICHAEL *swings the big sword and "cuts off" the head. In doing so, he topples over.*)

BIGGEST BOY: Hey! I'll show you how to cut heads off!

(MICHAEL *runs away. The* CHILDREN *run after him.* GRUSHA *laughs, following them with her eyes. On looking back, she sees* SIMON SHASHAVA *standing on the opposite bank. He wears a shabby uniform.*)

GRUSHA: Simon!

SIMON: Is that Grusha Vashnadze?

GRUSHA: Simon!

SIMON (*formally*): A good morning to the young lady. I hope she is well.

GRUSHA (*getting up gaily and bowing low*): A good morning to the soldier. God be thanked he has returned in good health.

SIMON: They found better fish, so they didn't eat me, said the haddock.

GRUSHA: Courage, said the kitchen boy. Good luck, said the hero.

SIMON: How are things here? Was the winter bearable? The neighbor considerate?

GRUSHA: The winter was a trifle rough, the neighbor as usual, Simon.

SIMON: May one ask if a certain person still dips her toes in the water when rinsing the linen?

GRUSHA: The answer is no. Because of the eyes in the bushes.

SIMON: The young lady is speaking of soldiers. Here stands a paymaster.

GRUSHA: A job worth twenty piasters?

SIMON: And lodgings.

GRUSHA (*with tears in her eyes*): Behind the barracks under the date trees.

SIMON: Yes, there. A certain person has kept her eyes open.

GRUSHA: She has, Simon.

SIMON: And has not forgotten? (GRUSHA *shakes her head.*) So the door is still on its hinges as they say? (GRUSHA *looks at him in silence and shakes her head again.*) What's this? Is anything not as it should be?

GRUSHA: Simon Shashava, I can never return to Nuka. Something has happened.

SIMON: What can have happened?

GRUSHA: For one thing, I knocked an Ironshirt down.

SIMON: Grusha Vashnadze must have had her reasons for that.

GRUSHA: Simon Shashava, I am no longer called what I used to be called.

SIMON (*after a pause*): I do not understand.

GRUSHA: When do women change their names, Simon? Let me explain. Nothing stands between us. Everything is just as it was. You must believe that.

SIMON: Nothing stands between us and yet there's something?

GRUSHA: How can I explain it so fast and with the stream between us? Couldn't you cross the bridge there?

SIMON: Maybe it's no longer necessary.

GRUSHA: It is very necessary. Come over on this side, Simon. Quick!

SIMON: Does the young lady wish to say someone has come too late?

(GRUSHA *looks up at him in despair, her face streaming with tears.* SIMON *stares before him. He picks up a piece of wood and starts cutting it.*)

SINGER: So many words are said, so many left unsaid.

　　The soldier has come.

　　Where he comes from, he does not say.

　　Hear what he thought and did not say:

　　"The battle began, gray at dawn, grew bloody at noon.

　　The first man fell in front of me, the second behind me, the third at my side.

　　I trod on the first, left the second behind, the third was run through by the captain.

　　One of my brothers died by steel, the other by smoke.

　　My neck caught fire, my hands froze in my gloves, my toes in my socks.

　　I fed on aspen buds, I drank maple juice, I slept on stone, in water."

SIMON: I see a cap in the grass. Is there a little one already?

GRUSHA: There is, Simon. There's no keeping *that* from you. But please don't worry, it is not mine.

SIMON: When the wind once starts to blow, they say, it blows through every cranny. The wife need say no more. (GRUSHA *looks into her lap and is silent.*)

SINGER: There was yearning but there was no waiting.
    The oath is broken. Neither could say why.
    Hear what she thought but did not say:
    "While you fought in the battle, soldier,
    The bloody battle, the bitter battle
    I found a helpless infant
    I had not the heart to destroy him
    I had to care for a creature that was lost
    I had to stoop for breadcrumbs on the floor
    I had to break myself for that which was not mine
    That which was other people's.
    Someone must help!
    For the little tree needs water
    The lamb loses its way when the shepherd is asleep
    And its cry is unheard!"

SIMON: Give me back the cross I gave you. Better still, throw it in the stream. (*He turns to go.*)

GRUSHA (*getting up*): Simon Shashava, don't go away! He isn't mine! He isn't mine! (*She hears the children calling.*) What's the matter, children?

VOICES: Soldiers! And they're taking Michael away!

(GRUSHA *stands aghast as two* IRONSHIRTS, *with* MICHAEL *between them, come toward her.*)

ONE OF THE IRONSHIRTS: Are you Grusha? (*She nods.*) Is this your child?

GRUSHA: Yes. (SIMON *goes.*) Simon!

IRONSHIRT: We have orders, in the name of the law, to take this child, found in your custody, back to the city. It is suspected that the child is Michael Abashwili, son and heir of the late Governor Georgi Abashwili, and his wife, Natella Abashwili. Here is the document and the seal. (*They lead the* CHILD *away.*)

GRUSHA (*running after them, shouting*): Leave him here. Please! He's mine!

SINGER: The Ironshirts took the child, the beloved child.
    The unhappy girl followed them to the city, the dreaded city.
    She who had borne him demanded the child.
    She who had raised him faced trial.
    Who will decide the case?
    To whom will the child be assigned?
    Who will the judge be? A good judge? A bad?
    The city was in flames.
    In the judge's seat sat Azdak.[1]

---

[1] "The name Azdak should be accented on the second syllable." [Bentley's note.]

IV. THE STORY OF THE JUDGE

SINGER: Hear the story of the judge
  How he turned judge, how he passed judgment, what kind of judge he was.
  On that Easter Sunday of the great revolt, when the Grand Duke was over-
    thrown
  And his Governor Abashwili, father of our child, lost his head
  The Village Scrivener Azdak found a fugitive in the woods and hid him in his
    hut.

(AZDAK, *in rags and slightly drunk, is helping an* OLD BEGGAR *into his cottage.*)

AZDAK: Stop snorting, you're not a horse. And it won't do you any good with the
  police to run like a snotty nose in April. Stand still, I say. (*He catches the* OLD
  MAN, *who has marched into the cottage as if he'd like to go through the walls.*) Sit
  down. Feed. Here's a hunk of cheese. (*From under some rags, in a chest, he fishes
  out some cheese, and the* OLD MAN *greedily begins to eat.*) Haven't eaten in a long
  time, huh? (*The* OLD MAN *growls.*) Why were you running like that, asshole? The
  cop wouldn't even have seen you.
OLD MAN: Had to! Had to!
AZDAK: Blue funk? (*The* OLD MAN *stares, uncomprehending.*) Cold feet? Panic? Don't
  lick your chops like a Grand Duke. Or an old sow. I can't stand it. We have to
  accept respectable stinkers as God made them, but not you! I once heard of a
  senior judge who farted at a public dinner to show an independent spirit! Watching you eat like that gives me the most awful ideas. Why don't you say something? (*Sharply.*) Show me your hand. Can't you hear? (*The* OLD MAN *slowly puts
  out his hand.*) White! So you're not a beggar at all! A fraud, a walking swindle!
  And I'm hiding you from the cops like you were an honest man! Why were you
  running like that if you're a landowner? For that's what you are. Don't deny it! I
  see it in your guilty face! (*He gets up.*) Get out! (*The* OLD MAN *looks at him
  uncertainly.*) What are you waiting for, peasant-flogger?
OLD MAN: Pursued. Need undivided attention. Make proposition . . .
AZDAK: Make what? A proposition? Well, if that isn't the height of insolence. He's
  making me a proposition! The bitten man scratches his fingers bloody, and the
  leech that's biting him makes him a proposition! Get out, I tell you!
OLD MAN: Understand point of view! Persuasion! Pay hundred thousand piasters one
  night! Yes?
AZDAK: What, you think you can buy me? For a hundred thousand piasters? Let's
  say a hundred and fifty thousand. Where are they?
OLD MAN: Have not them here. Of course. Will be sent. Hope do not doubt.
AZDAK: Doubt very much. Get out!

(*The* OLD MAN *gets up, waddles to the door. A* VOICE *is heard offstage.*)

VOICE: Azdak!

(*The* OLD MAN *turns, waddles to the opposite corner, stands still.*)

AZDAK (*calling out*): I'm not in! (*He walks to door.*) So you're sniffing around here
  again, Shauwa?
SHAUWA (*reproachfully*): You caught another rabbit, Azdak. And you'd promised
  me it wouldn't happen again!

AZDAK (*severely*): Shauwa, don't talk about things you don't understand. The rabbit is a dangerous and destructive beast. It feeds on plants, especially on the species of plants known as weeds. It must therefore be exterminated.

SHAUWA: Azdak, don't be so hard on me. I'll lose my job if I don't arrest you. I know you have a good heart.

AZDAK: I do not have a good heart! How often must I tell you I'm a man of intellect?

SHAUWA (*slyly*): I know, Azdak. You're a superior person. You say so yourself. I'm just a Christian and an ignoramus. So I ask you: When one of the Prince's rabbits is stolen, and I'm a policeman, what should I do with the offending party?

AZDAK: Shauwa, Shauwa, shame on you. You stand and ask me a question, than which nothing could be more seductive. It's like you were a woman — let's say that bad girl Nunowna, and you showed me your thigh — Nunowna's thigh, that would be — and asked me: "What shall I do with my thigh, it itches?" Is she as innocent as she pretends? Of course not. I catch a rabbit, but you catch a man. Man is made in God's image. Not so a rabbit, you know that. I'm a rabbit-eater but you're a man-eater, Shauwa. And God will pass judgment on you. Shauwa, go home and repent. No, stop, there's something . . . (*He looks at the* OLD MAN *who stands trembling in the corner.*) No, it's nothing. Go home and repent. (*He slams the door behind* SHAUWA.) Now you're surprised, huh? Surprised I didn't hand you over? I couldn't hand over a bedbug to that animal. It goes against the grain. Now don't tremble because of a cop! So old and still so scared? Finish your cheese, but eat it like a poor man, or else they'll still catch you. Must I even explain how a poor man behaves? (*He pushes him down, and then gives him back the cheese.*) That box is the table. Lay your elbows on the table. Now, encircle the cheese on the plate like it might be snatched from you at any moment — what right have you to be safe, huh? — now, hold your knife like an undersized sickle, and give your cheese a troubled look because, like all beautiful things, it's already fading away. (AZDAK *watches him.*) They're after you, which speaks in your favor, but how can we be sure they're not mistaken about you? In Tiflis one time they hanged a landowner, a Turk, who could prove he quartered his peasants instead of merely cutting them in half, as is the custom, and he squeezed twice the usual amount of taxes out of them, his zeal was above suspicion. And yet they hanged him like a common criminal — because he was a Turk — a thing he couldn't do much about. What injustice! He got onto the gallows by a sheer fluke. In short, I don't trust you.

SINGER: Thus Azdak gave the old beggar a bed,
  And learned that old beggar was the old butcher, the Grand Duke himself,
  And was ashamed.
  He denounced himself and ordered the policeman to take him to Nuka, to court,
    to be judged.

(*In the court of justice three* IRONSHIRTS *sit drinking. From a beam hangs a* MAN *in judge's robes. Enter* AZDAK, *in chains, dragging* SHAUWA *behind him.*)

AZDAK (*shouting*): I've helped the Grand Duke, the Grand Thief, the Grand Butcher, to escape! In the name of justice I ask to be severely judged in public trial!

FIRST IRONSHIRT: Who's this queer bird?

SHAUWA: That's our Village Scrivener, Azdak.

AZDAK: I am contemptible! I am a traitor! A branded criminal! Tell them, flatfoot, how I insisted on being tied up and brought to the capital. Because I sheltered the Grand Duke, the Grand Swindler, by mistake. And how I found out afterwards. See the marked man denounce himself! Tell them how I forced you to walk half the night with me to clear the whole thing up.

SHAUWA: And all by threats. That wasn't nice of you, Azdak.

AZDAK: Shut your mouth, Shauwa. You don't understand. A new age is upon us! It'll go thundering over you. You're finished. The police will be wiped out — poof! Everything will be gone into, everything will be brought into the open. The guilty will give themselves up. Why? They couldn't escape the people in any case. (*To* SHAUWA.) Tell them how I shouted all along Shoemaker Street (*with big gestures, looking at the* IRONSHIRTS.) "In my ignorance I let the Grand Swindler escape! So tear me to pieces, brothers!" I wanted to get it in first.

FIRST IRONSHIRT: And what did your brothers answer?

SHAUWA: They comforted him in Butcher Street, and they laughed themselves sick in Shoemaker Street. That's all.

AZDAK: But with you it's different. I can see you're men of iron. Brothers, where's the judge? I must be tried.

FIRST IRONSHIRT (*pointing at the* HANGED MAN): There's the judge. And please stop "brothering" us. It's rather a sore spot this evening.

AZDAK: "There's the judge." An answer never heard in Grusinia before. Townsman, where's His Excellency the Governor? (*Pointing to the ground.*) There's His Excellency, stranger. Where's the Chief Tax Collector? Where's the official Recruiting Officer? The Patriarch? The Chief of Police? There, there, there — all there. Brothers, I expected no less of you.

SECOND IRONSHIRT: What? *What* was it you expected, funny man?

AZDAK: What happened in Persia, brother, what happened in Persia?

SECOND IRONSHIRT: What did happen in Persia?

AZDAK: Everybody was hanged. Viziers, tax collectors. Everybody. Forty years ago now. My grandfather, a remarkable man by the way, saw it all. For three whole days. Everywhere.

SECOND IRONSHIRT: And who ruled when the Vizier was hanged?

AZDAK: A peasant ruled when the Vizier was hanged.

SECOND IRONSHIRT: And who commanded the army?

AZDAK: A soldier, a soldier.

SECOND IRONSHIRT: And who paid the wages?

AZDAK: A dyer. A dyer paid the wages.

SECOND IRONSHIRT: Wasn't it a weaver, maybe?

FIRST IRONSHIRT: And why did all this happen, Persian?

AZDAK: Why did all this happen? Must there be a special reason? Why do you scratch yourself, brother? War! Too long a war! And no justice! My grandfather brought back a song that tells how it was. I will sing it for you. With my friend the policeman. (*To* SHAUWA.) And hold the rope tight. It's very suitable. (*He sings, with* SHAUWA *holding the rope tight around him.*)

The Song of Injustice in Persia

Why don't our sons bleed any more? Why don't our daughters weep?
Why do only the slaughterhouse cattle have blood in their veins?

Why do only the willows shed tears on Lake Urmia?
The king must have a new province, the peasant must give up his savings.
That the roof of the world might be conquered, the roof of the cottage is torn
    down.
Our men are carried to the ends of the earth, so that great ones can eat at
    home.
The soldiers kill each other, the marshals salute each other.
They bite the widow's tax money to see if it's good, their swords break
The battle was lost, the helmets were paid for.
Refrain: Is it so? Is it so?

SHAUWA (*refrain*):
    Yes, yes, yes, yes, yes it's so.

AZDAK: Want to hear the rest of it? (*The* FIRST IRONSHIRT *nods.*)

SECOND IRONSHIRT (*to* SHAUWA): Did he teach you that song?

SHAUWA: Yes, only my voice isn't very good.

SECOND IRONSHIRT: No. (*To* AZDAK.) Go on singing.

AZDAK: The second verse is about the peace. (*He sings.*)

The offices are packed, the streets overflow with officials.
The rivers jump their banks and ravage the fields.
Those who cannot let down their own trousers rule countries.
They can't count up to four, but they devour eight courses.
The corn farmers, looking round for buyers, see only the starving.
The weavers go home from their looms in rags.
Refrain: Is it so? Is it so?

SHAUWA (*refrain*):
    Yes, yes, yes, yes, yes it's so.

AZDAK:
    That's why our sons don't bleed any more, that's why our daughters don't
      weep,
    That's why only the slaughterhouse cattle have blood in their veins,
    And only the willows shed tears by Lake Urmia toward morning.

FIRST IRONSHIRT: Are you going to sing that song here in town?

AZDAK: Sure. What's wrong with it?

FIRST IRONSHIRT: Have you noticed that the sky's getting red? (*Turning round,* AZ-
DAK *sees the sky red with fire.*) It's the people's quarters on the outskirts of town.
The carpet weavers have caught the "Persian Sickness," too. And they've been
asking if Prince Kazbeki isn't eating too many courses. This morning they strung
up the city judge. As for us we beat them to pulp. We were paid one hundred
piasters per man, you understand?

AZDAK (*after a pause*): I understand. (*He glances shyly round and, creeping away,
sits down in a corner, his head in his hands.*)

IRONSHIRTS (*to each other*): If there ever was a troublemaker it's him.

    — He must've come to the capital to fish in the troubled waters.

SHAUWA: Oh, I don't think he's a really bad character, gentlemen. Steals a few
chickens here and there. And maybe a rabbit.

SECOND IRONSHIRT (*approaching* AZDAK): Came to fish in the troubled waters, huh?

AZDAK (*looking up*): I don't know why I came.

SECOND IRONSHIRT: Are you in with the carpet weavers maybe? (AZDAK *shakes his head.*) How about that song?

AZDAK: From my grandfather. A silly and ignorant man.

SECOND IRONSHIRT: Right. And how about the dyer who paid the wages?

AZDAK (*muttering*): That was in Persia.

FIRST IRONSHIRT: And this denouncing of yourself? Because you didn't hang the Grand Duke with your own hands?

AZDAK: Didn't I tell you I let him run? (*He creeps farther away and sits on the floor.*)

SHAUWA: I can swear to that: he let him run.

(*The* IRONSHIRTS *burst out laughing and slap* SHAUWA *on the back.* AZDAK *laughs loudest. They slap* AZDAK *too, and unchain him. They all start drinking as the* FAT PRINCE *enters with a* YOUNG MAN.)

FIRST IRONSHIRT (*to* AZDAK, *pointing at the* FAT PRINCE): There's your "new age" for you! (*More laughter.*)

FAT PRINCE: Well, my friends, what is there to laugh about? Permit me a serious word. Yesterday morning the Princes of Grusinia overthrew the warmongering government of the Grand Duke and did away with his Governors. Unfortunately the Grand Duke himself escaped. In this fateful hour our carpet weavers, those eternal troublemakers, had the effrontery to stir up a rebellion and hang the universally loved city judge, our dear Illo Orbeliani. Ts — ts — ts. My friends, we need peace, peace, peace in Grusinia! And justice! So I've brought along my dear nephew Bizergan Kazbeki. He'll be the new judge, hm? A very gifted fellow. What do you say? I want your opinion. Let the people decide!

SECOND IRONSHIRT: Does this mean we elect the judge?

FAT PRINCE: Precisely. Let the people propose some very gifted fellow! Confer among yourselves, my friends. (*The* IRONSHIRTS *confer.*) Don't worry, my little fox. The job's yours. And when we catch the Grand Duke we won't have to kiss this rabble's ass any longer.

IRONSHIRTS (*among themselves*): — Very funny: they're wetting their pants because they haven't caught the Grand Duke.

— When the outlook isn't so bright, they say: "My friends!" and "Let the people decide!"

— Now he even wants justice for Grusinia! But fun is fun as long as it lasts! (*Pointing at* AZDAK.) He knows all about justice. Hey, rascal, would you like this nephew fellow to be the judge?

AZDAK: Are you asking me? You're not asking *me?!*

FIRST IRONSHIRT: Why not? Anything for a laugh!

AZDAK: You'd like to test him to the marrow, correct? Have you a criminal on hand? An experienced one? So the candidate can show what he knows?

SECOND IRONSHIRT: Let's see. We do have a couple of doctors downstairs. Let's use them.

AZDAK: Oh, no, that's no good, we can't take real criminals till we're sure the judge will be appointed. He may be dumb, but he must be appointed, or the law is violated. And the law is a sensitive organ. It's like the spleen, you mustn't hit it — that would be fatal. Of course you can hang those two without violating the law, because there was no judge in the vicinity. But judgment, when pronounced, must be pronounced with absolute gravity — it's all such nonsense. Suppose, for instance, a judge jails a woman — let's say she's stolen a corn cake to feed her child — and this judge isn't wearing his robes — or maybe he's scratching himself while passing sentence and half his body is uncovered — a man's thigh *will* itch once in a while — the sentence this judge passes is a disgrace and the law is violated. In short it would be easier for a judge's robe and a judge's hat to pass judgment than for a man with no robe and no hat. If you don't treat it with respect, the law just disappears on you. Now you don't try out a bottle of wine by offering it to a dog; you'd only lose your wine.

FIRST IRONSHIRT: Then what do you suggest, hairsplitter?

AZDAK: I'll be the defendant.

FIRST IRONSHIRT: You? (*He bursts out laughing.*)

FAT PRINCE: What have you decided?

FIRST IRONSHIRT: We've decided to stage a rehearsal. Our friend here will be the defendant. Let the candidate be the judge and sit there.

FAT PRINCE: It isn't customary, but why not? (*To the* NEPHEW.) A mere formality, my little fox. What have I taught you? Who got there first — the slow runner or the fast?

NEPHEW: The silent runner, Uncle Arsen.

(*The* NEPHEW *takes the chair. The* IRONSHIRTS *and the* FAT PRINCE *sit on the steps. Enter* AZDAK, *mimicking the gait of the* GRAND DUKE.)

AZDAK (*in the* GRAND DUKE's *accent*): Is any here knows me? Am Grand Duke.

IRONSHIRTS: — What is he?

— The Grand Duke. He knows him, too.

— Fine. So get on with the trial.

AZDAK: Listen! Am accused instigating war? Ridiculous! Am saying ridiculous! That enough? If not, have brought lawyers. Believe five hundred. (*He points behind him, pretending to be surrounded by lawyers.*) Requisition all available seats for lawyers! (*The* IRONSHIRTS *laugh; the* FAT PRINCE *joins in.*)

NEPHEW (*to the* IRONSHIRTS): You really wish me to try this case? I find it rather unusual. From the taste angle, I mean.

FIRST IRONSHIRT: Let's go!

FAT PRINCE (*smiling*): Let him have it, my little fox!

NEPHEW: All right. People of Grusinia versus Grand Duke. Defendant, what have you got to say for yourself?

AZDAK: Plenty. Naturally, have read war lost. Only started on the advice of patriots. Like Uncle Arsen Kazbeki. Call Uncle Arsen as witness.

FAT PRINCE (*to the* IRONSHIRTS, *delightedly*): What a madcap!

NEPHEW: Motion rejected. One cannot be arraigned for declaring a war, which every ruler has to do once in a while, but only for running a war badly.

AZDAK: Rubbish! Did not run it at all! Had it run! Had it run by Princes! Naturally, they messed it up.

NEPHEW: Do you by any chance deny having been commander-in-chief?

AZDAK: Not at all! Always *was* commander-in-chief. At birth shouted at wet nurse. Was trained drop turds in toilet, grew accustomed to command. Always commanded officials rob my cash box. Officers flog soldiers only on command. Landowners sleep with peasants' wives only on strictest command. Uncle Arsen here grew his belly at *my* command!

IRONSHIRTS (*clapping*): He's good! Long live the Grand Duke!

FAT PRINCE: Answer him, my little fox: I'm with you.

NEPHEW: I shall answer him according to the dignity of the law. Defendant, preserve the dignity of the law!

AZDAK: Agreed. Command you proceed with trial!

NEPHEW: It is not your place to command me. You claim that the Princes forced you to declare war. How can you claim, then, that they — er — "messed it up"?

AZDAK: Did not send enough people. Embezzled funds. Sent sick horses. During attack, drinking in whorehouse. Call Uncle Arsen as witness.

NEPHEW: Are you making the outrageous suggestion that the Princes of this country did not fight?

AZDAK: No. Princes fought. Fought for war contracts.

FAT PRINCE (*jumping up*): That's too much! This man talks like a carpet weaver!

AZDAK: Really? Told nothing but truth.

FAT PRINCE: Hang him! Hang him!

FIRST IRONSHIRT (*pulling the* PRINCE *down*): Keep quiet! Go on, Excellency!

NEPHEW: Quiet! I now render a verdict: You must be hanged! By the neck! Having lost war!

AZDAK: Young man, seriously advise not fall publicly into jerky clipped speech. Cannot be watchdog if howl like wolf. Got it? If people realize Princes speak same language as Grand Duke, may hang Grand Duke and Princes, huh? By the way, must overrule verdict. Reason? War lost, but not for Princes. Princes won their war. Got 3,863,000 piasters for horses not delivered, 8,240,000 piasters for food supplies not produced. Are therefore victors. War lost only for Grusinia, which is not present in this court.

FAT PRINCE: I think that will do, my friends. (*To* AZDAK.) You can withdraw, funny man. (*To the* IRONSHIRTS.) You may now ratify the new judge's appointment, my friends.

FIRST IRONSHIRT: Yes, we can. Take down the judge's gown. (*One* IRONSHIRT *climbs on the back of the other, pulls the gown off the hanged man*.) (*To the* NEPHEW.) Now you run away so the right ass can get on the right chair. (*To* AZDAK.) Step forward! Go to the judge's seat! Now sit in it! (AZDAK *steps up, bows, and sits down*.) The judge was always a rascal! Now the rascal shall be a judge! (*The judge's gown is placed round his shoulders, the hat on his head*.) And what a judge!

SINGER: And there was civil war in the land.
   The mighty were not safe.
   And Azdak was made a judge by the Ironshirts.
   And Azdak remained a judge for two years.

SINGER AND CHORUS: When the towns were set afire
   And rivers of blood rose higher and higher,
   Cockroaches crawled out of every crack.
   And the court was full of schemers
   And the church of foul blasphemers.
   In the judge's cassock sat Azdak.

(AZDAK *sits in the judge's chair, peeling an apple.* SHAUWA *is sweeping out the hall. On one side an* INVALID *in a wheelchair. Opposite, a* YOUNG MAN *accused of blackmail. An* IRONSHIRT *stands guard, holding the Ironshirts' banner.*)

AZDAK: In consideration of the large number of cases, the Court today will hear two cases at a time. Before I open the proceedings, a short announcement — I accept. (*He stretches out his hand. The* BLACKMAILER *is the only one to produce any money. He hands it to* AZDAK.) I reserve the right to punish one of the parties for contempt of court. (*He glances at the* INVALID.) You (*to the* DOCTOR) are a doctor, and you (*to the* INVALID) are bringing a complaint against him. Is the doctor responsible for your condition?

INVALID: Yes. I had a stroke on his account.

AZDAK: That would be professional negligence.

INVALID: Worse than negligence. I gave this man money for his studies. So far, he hasn't paid me back a cent. It was when I heard he was treating a patient free that I had my stroke.

AZDAK: Rightly. (*To a* LIMPING MAN.) And what are *you* doing here?

LIMPING MAN: I'm the patient, Your Honor.

AZDAK: He treated your leg for nothing?

LIMPING MAN: The wrong leg! My rheumatism was in the left leg, he operated on the right. That's why I limp.

AZDAK: And you were treated free?

INVALID: A five-hundred-piaster operation free! For nothing! For a God-bless-you! And I paid for this man's studies! (*To the* DOCTOR.) Did they teach you to operate free?

DOCTOR: Your Honor, it is the custom to demand the fee before the operation, as the patient is more willing to pay before an operation than after. Which is only human. In the case in question I was convinced, when I started the operation, that my servant had already received the fee. In this I was mistaken.

INVALID: He was mistaken! A good doctor doesn't make mistakes! He examines before he operates!

AZDAK: That's right. (*To* SHAUWA.) Public Prosecutor, what's the other case about?

SHAUWA (*busily sweeping*): Blackmail.

BLACKMAILER: High Court of Justice, I'm innocent. I only wanted to find out from the landowner concerned if he really *had* raped his niece. He informed me very politely that this was not the case, and gave me the money only so I could pay for my uncle's studies.

AZDAK: Hm. (*To the* DOCTOR.) You, on the other hand, can cite no extenuating circumstances for your offense, huh?

DOCTOR: Except that to err is human.

AZDAK: And you are aware that in money matters a good doctor is a highly responsible person? I once heard of a doctor who got a thousand piasters for a sprained finger by remarking that sprains have something to do with blood circulation, which after all a less good doctor might have overlooked, and who, on another occasion made a real gold mine out of a somewhat disordered gall bladder, he treated it with such loving care. You have no excuse, Doctor. The corn merchant Uxu had his son study medicine to get some knowledge of trade, our medical schools are so good. (*To the* BLACKMAILER.) What's the landowner's name?

SHAUWA: He doesn't want it mentioned.

AZDAK: In that case I will pass judgment. The Court considers the blackmail proved. And you (*to the* INVALID) are sentenced to a fine of one thousand piasters. If you have a second stroke, the doctor will have to treat you free. Even if he has to amputate. (*To the* LIMPING MAN.) As compensation, you will receive a bottle of rubbing alcohol. (*To the* BLACKMAILER.) You are sentenced to hand over half the proceeds of your deal to the Public Prosecutor to keep the landowner's name secret. You are advised, moreover, to study medicine — you seem well suited to that calling. (*To the* DOCTOR.) You have perpetrated an unpardonable error in the practice of your profession: you are acquitted. Next cases!

SINGER AND CHORUS: Men won't do much for a shilling.
For a pound they may be willing.
For twenty pounds the verdict's in the sack.
As for the many, all too many,
Those who've only got a penny —
They've one single, sole recourse: Azdak.

(*Enter* AZDAK *from the caravansary on the highroad, followed by an old bearded* INNKEEPER. *The judge's chair is carried by a* STABLEMAN *and* SHAUWA. *An* IRON-SHIRT, *with a banner, takes up his position.*)

AZDAK: Put me down. Then we'll get some air, maybe even a good stiff breeze from the lemon grove there. It does justice good to be done in the open: the wind blows her skirts up and you can see what she's got. Shauwa, we've been eating too much. These official journeys are exhausting. (*To the* INNKEEPER.) It's a question of your daughter-in-law?

INNKEEPER: Your Worship, it's a question of the family honor. I wish to bring an action on behalf of my son, who's away on business on the other side of the mountain. This is the offending stableman, and here's my daughter-in-law.

(*Enter the* DAUGHTER-IN-LAW, *a voluptuous wench. She is veiled.*)

AZDAK (*sitting down*): I accept. (*Sighing, the* INNKEEPER *hands him some money.*) Good. Now the formalities are disposed of. This is a case of rape?

INNKEEPER: Your Honor, I caught the fellow in the act. Ludovica was in the straw on the stable floor.

AZDAK: Quite right, the stable. Lovely horses! I specially liked the little roan.

INNKEEPER: The first thing I did, of course, was to question Ludovica. On my son's behalf.

AZDAK (*seriously*): I said I specially liked the little roan.

INNKEEPER (*coldly*): Really? Ludovica confessed the stableman took her against her will.

AZDAK: Take your veil off, Ludovica. (*She does so.*) Ludovica, you please the Court. Tell us how it happened.

LUDOVICA (*well schooled*): When I entered the stable to see the new foal the stableman said to me on his own accord: "It's hot today!" and laid his hand on my left breast. I said to him: "Don't do that!" But he continued to handle me indecently, which provoked my anger. Before I realized his sinful intentions, he got much closer. It was all over when my father-in-law entered and accidentally trod on me.

INNKEEPER (*explaining*): On my son's behalf.

AZDAK (*to the* STABLEMAN): You admit you started it?

STABLEMAN: Yes.

AZDAK: Ludovica, you like to eat sweet things?

LUDOVICA: Yes, sunflower seeds!

AZDAK: You like to lie a long time in the bathtub?

LUDOVICA: Half an hour or so.

AZDAK: Public Prosecutor, drop your knife — there on the ground. (SHAUWA *does so.*) Ludovica, pick up that knife. (LUDOVICA *swaying her hips, does so.*) See that? (*He points at her.*) The way it moves? The rape is now proven. By eating too much — sweet things, especially — by lying too long in warm water, by laziness and too soft a skin, you have raped that unfortunate man. Think you can run around with a behind like that and get away with it in court? This is a case of intentional assault with a dangerous weapon! You are sentenced to hand over to the Court the little roan which your father liked to ride "on his son's behalf." And now, come with me to the stables, so the Court can inspect the scene of the crime, Ludovica.

SINGER AND CHORUS: When the sharks the sharks devour
    Little fishes have their hour.
    For a while the load is off their back.
    On Grusinia's highways faring
    Fixed-up scales of justice bearing
    Strode the poor man's magistrate: Azdak.

    And he gave to the forsaken
    All that from the rich he'd taken.
    And a bodyguard of roughnecks was Azdak's.
    And our good and evil man, he
    Smiled upon Grusinia's Granny.
    His emblem was a tear in sealing wax.

    All mankind should love each other
    But when visiting your brother
    Take an ax along and hold it fast.
    Not in theory but in practice
    Miracles are wrought with axes
    And the age of miracles is not past.

(AZDAK's *judge's chair is in a tavern. Three rich* FARMERS *stand before* AZDAK. SHAUWA *brings him wine. In a corner stands an* OLD PEASANT WOMAN. *In the open doorway, and outside, stand* VILLAGERS *looking on. An* IRONSHIRT *stands guard with a banner.*)

AZDAK: The Public Prosecutor has the floor.

SHAUWA: It concerns a cow. For five weeks, the defendant has had a cow in her stable, the property of the farmer Suru. She was also found to be in possession of a stolen ham, and a number of cows belonging to Shutoff were killed after he asked the defendant to pay the rent on a piece of land.

FARMERS: — It's a matter of my ham, Your Honor.
     — It's a matter of my cow, Your Honor.
     — It's a matter of my land, Your Honor.

AZDAK: Well, Granny, what have *you* got to say to all this?

OLD WOMAN: Your Honor, one night toward morning, five weeks ago, there was a knock at my door, and outside stood a bearded man with a cow. "My dear woman," he said, "I am the miracle-working Saint Banditus and because your son has been killed in the war, I bring you this cow as a souvenir. Take good care of it."

FARMERS: — The robber, Irakli, Your Honor!

— Her brother-in-law, Your Honor!
— The cow-thief!
— The incendiary!
— He must be beheaded!

(*Outside, a* WOMAN *screams. The* CROWD *grows restless, retreats. Enter the* BAN-
DIT *Irakli with a huge ax.*)

BANDIT: A very good evening, dear friends! A glass of vodka!
FARMERS (*crossing themselves*): Irakli!
AZDAK: Public Prosecutor, a glass of vodka for our guest. And who are you?
BANDIT: I'm a wandering hermit, Your Honor. Thanks for the gracious gift. (*He
empties the glass which* SHAUWA *has brought.*) Another!
AZDAK: I am Azdak. (*He gets up and bows. The* BANDIT *also bows.*) The Court welcomes the foreign hermit. Go on with your story, Granny.
OLD WOMAN: Your Honor, that first night I didn't yet know Saint Banditus could
work miracles, it was only the cow. But one night, a few days later, the farmer's
servants came to take the cow away again. Then they turned round in front of
my door and went off without the cow. And bumps as big as a fist sprouted on
their heads. So I knew that Saint Banditus had changed their hearts and turned
them into friendly people.

(*The* BANDIT *roars with laughter.*)

FIRST FARMER: I know what changed them.
AZDAK: That's fine. You can tell us later. Continue.
OLD WOMAN: Your Honor, the next one to become a good man was the farmer
Shutoff — a devil, as everyone knows. But Saint Banditus arranged it so he let
me off the rent on the little piece of land.
SECOND FARMER: Because my cows were killed in the field.

(*The* BANDIT *laughs.*)

OLD WOMAN (*answering* AZDAK's *sign to continue*): Then one morning the ham
came flying in at my window. It hit me in the small of the back. I'm still lame,
Your Honor, look. (*She limps a few steps. The* BANDIT *laughs.*) Your Honor, was
there ever a time when a poor old woman could get a ham *without* a miracle?

(*The* BANDIT *starts sobbing.*)

AZDAK (*rising from his chair*): Granny, that's a question that strikes straight at the
Court's heart. Be so kind as to sit here. (*The* OLD WOMAN, *hesitating, sits in the
judge's chair.*)
AZDAK (*sits on the floor, glass in hand, reciting*): Granny
We could almost call you Granny Grusinia
The Woebegone
The Bereaved Mother
Whose sons have gone to war.
Receiving the present of a cow
She bursts out crying
When she is beaten
She remains hopeful.
When she's not beaten
She's surprised.

On us
Who are already damned
May you render a merciful verdict
Granny Grusinia!

(*Bellowing at the* FARMERS.) Admit you don't believe in miracles, you atheists! Each of you is sentenced to pay five hundred piasters! For godlessness! Get out! (*The* FARMERS *slink out*.) And you Granny, and you (*to the* BANDIT) pious man, empty a pitcher of wine with the Public Prosecutor and Azdak!

SINGER AND CHORUS: And he broke the rules to save them.
Broken law like bread he gave them,
Brought them to shore upon his crooked back.
At long last the poor and lowly
Had someone who was not too holy
To be bribed by empty hands: Azdak.

For two years it was his pleasure
To give the beasts of prey short measure:
He became a wolf to fight the pack.
From All Hallows to All Hallows
On his chair beside the gallows
Dispensing justice in his fashion sat Azdak.

SINGER: But the era of disorder came to an end.
The Grand Duke returned.
The Governor's wife returned.
A trial was held.
Many died.
The people's quarters burned anew.
And fear seized Azdak.

(AZDAK's *judge's chair stands again in the court of justice.* AZDAK *sits on the floor, shaving and talking to* SHAUWA. *Noises outside. In the rear the* FAT PRINCE's *head is carried by on a lance*.)

AZDAK: Shauwa, the days of your slavery are numbered, maybe even the minutes. For a long time now I have held you in the iron curb of reason, and it has torn your mouth till it bleeds. I have lashed you with reasonable arguments, I have manhandled you with logic. You are by nature a weak man, and if one slyly throws an argument in your path, you *have* to snap it up, you can't resist. It is your nature to lick the hand of some superior being. But superior beings can be of very different kinds. And now, with your liberation, you will soon be able to follow your natural inclinations, which are low. You will be able to follow your infallible instinct, which teaches you to plant your fat heel on the faces of men. Gone is the era of confusion and disorder, which I find described in the Song of Chaos. Let us now sing that song together in memory of those terrible days. Sit down and don't do violence to the music. Don't be afraid. It sounds all right. And it has a fine refrain. (*He sings*.)

The Song of Chaos

Sister, hide your face! Brother, take your knife!
The times are out of joint!

Big men are full of complaint
And small men full of joy.
The city says:
"Let us drive the mighty from our midst!"
Offices are raided. Lists of serfs are destroyed.
They have set Master's nose to the grindstone.
They who lived in the dark have seen the light.
The ebony poor box is broken.
Sesnem[2] wood is sawed up for beds.
Who had no bread have full barns.
Who begged for alms of corn now mete it out.

SHAUWA (*refrain*):
Oh, oh, oh, oh.
AZDAK (*refrain*):
Where are you, General, where are you?
Please, please, please, restore order!

The nobleman's son can no longer be recognized;
The lady's child becomes the son of her slave-girl
The councilors meet in a shed.
Once, this man was barely allowed to sleep on the wall;
Now, he stretches his limbs in a bed.
Once, this man rowed a boat; now, he owns ships.
Their owner looks for them, but they're his no longer.
Five men are sent on a journey by their master.
"Go yourself," they say, "we have arrived."

SHAUWA (*refrain*):
Oh, oh, oh, oh.
AZDAK (*refrain*):
Where are you, General, where are you?
Please, please, please, restore order!

Yes, so it might have been, had order been neglected much longer. But now the Grand Duke has returned to the capital, and the Persians have lent him an army to restore order with. The people's quarters are already aflame. Go and get me the big book I always sit on. (SHAUWA *brings the big book from the judge's chair.* AZDAK *opens it.*) This is the Statute Book and I've always used it, as you can testify. Now I'd better look in this book and see what they can do to me. I've let the down-and-outs get away with murder, and I'll have to pay for it. I helped poverty onto its skinny legs, so they'll hang me for drunkenness. I peeped into the rich man's pocket, which is bad taste. And I can't hide anywhere — everybody knows me because I've helped everybody.

SHAUWA: Someone's coming!

---

[2] "I do not know what kind of wood this is, so I have left the word exactly as it stands in the German original. The song is based on an Egyptian papyrus which Brecht cites as such in his essay, "Five Difficulties in the Writing of the Truth." I should think he must have come across it in Adolf Erman's *Die Literatur der Aegypter*, 1923, pp. 130 ff. Erman too gives the word as Sesnem. The same papyrus is quoted in Karl Jaspers' *Man in the Modern Age* (Anchor edition, pp. 18–19) but without the sentence about the Sesnem wood." [Bentley's note.]

AZDAK (*in panic, he walks trembling to the chair*): It's the end. And now they'd enjoy seeing what a Great Man I am. I'll deprive them of that pleasure. I'll beg on my knees for mercy. Spittle will slobber down my chin. The fear of death is in me.

(*Enter* NATELLA ABASHWILI, *the* GOVERNOR'S WIFE, *followed by the* ADJUTANT *and an* IRONSHIRT.)

GOVERNOR'S WIFE: What sort of a creature is that, Shalva?

AZDAK: A willing one, Your Highness, a man ready to oblige.

ADJUTANT: Natella Abashwili, wife of the late Governor, has just returned. She is looking for her two-year-old son, Michael. She has been informed that the child was carried off to the mountains by a former servant.

AZDAK: The child will be brought back, Your Highness, at your service.

ADJUTANT: They say that the person in question is passing it off as her own.

AZDAK: She will be beheaded, Your Highness, at your service.

ADJUTANT: That is all.

GOVERNOR'S WIFE (*leaving*): I don't like that man.

AZDAK (*following her to door, bowing*): At your service, Your Highness, it will all be arranged.

V. THE CHALK CIRCLE

SINGER: Hear now the story of the trial
    Concerning Governor Abashwili's child
    And the determination of the true mother
    By the famous test of the Chalk Circle.

(*Law court in Nuka.* IRONSHIRTS *lead* MICHAEL *across stage and out at the back.* IRONSHIRTS *hold* GRUSHA *back with their lances under the gateway until the* CHILD *has been led through. Then she is admitted. She is accompanied by the former* GOVERNOR'S COOK. *Distant noises and a fire-red sky.*)

GRUSHA (*trying to hide*): He's brave, he can wash himself now.

COOK: You're lucky. It's not a real judge. It's Azdak, a drunk who doesn't know what he's doing. The biggest thieves have got by through him. Because he gets everything mixed up and the rich never offer him big enough bribes, the like of us sometimes do pretty well.

GRUSHA: I *need* luck right now.

COOK: Touch wood. (*She crosses herself.*) I'd better offer up another prayer that the judge may be drunk. (*She prays with motionless lips, while* GRUSHA *looks around, in vain, for the* CHILD.) Why must you hold on to it at any price if it isn't yours? In days like these?

GRUSHA: He's mine. I brought him up.

COOK: Have you never thought what'd happen when she came back?

GRUSHA: At first I thought I'd give him to her. Then I thought she wouldn't come back.

COOK: And even a borrowed coat keeps a man warm, hm? (GRUSHA *nods.*) I'll swear to anything for you. You're a decent girl. (*She sees the soldier* SIMON SHASHAVA *approaching*.) You've done wrong by Simon, though. I've been talking with him. He just can't understand.

GRUSHA (*unaware of* SIMON's *presence*): Right now I can't be bothered whether he understands or not!

COOK: He knows the child isn't yours, but you married and not free "till death you do part" — he can't understand *that*.

(GRUSHA *sees* SIMON *and greets him*.)

SIMON (*gloomily*): I wish the lady to know I will swear I am the father of the child.

GRUSHA (*low*): Thank you, Simon.

SIMON: At the same time I wish the lady to know my hands are not tied — nor are hers.

COOK: You needn't have said that. You know she's married.

SIMON: And it needs no rubbing in.

(*Enter an* IRONSHIRT.)

IRONSHIRT: Where's the judge? Has anyone seen the judge?

ANOTHER IRONSHIRT (*stepping forward*): The judge isn't here yet. Nothing but a bed and a pitcher in the whole house!

(*Exeunt* IRONSHIRTS.)

COOK: I hope nothing has happened to him. With any other judge you'd have as much chance as a chicken has teeth.

GRUSHA (*who has turned away and covered her face*): Stand in front of me. I shouldn't have come to Nuka. If I run into the Ironshirt, the one I hit over the head . . .

(*She screams. An* IRONSHIRT *had stopped and, turning his back, had been listening to her. He now wheels around. It is the* CORPORAL, *and he has a huge scar across his face.*)

IRONSHIRT (*in the gateway*): What's the matter, Shotta? Do you know her?

CORPORAL (*after staring for some time*): No.

IRONSHIRT: She's the one who stole the Abashwili child, or so they say. If you know anything about it you can make some money, Shotta.

(*Exit the* CORPORAL, *cursing*.)

COOK: Was it him? (GRUSHA *nods*.) I think he'll keep his mouth shut, or he'd be admitting he was after the child.

GRUSHA: I'd almost forgotten him.

(*Enter the* GOVERNOR'S WIFE, *followed by the* ADJUTANT *and two* LAWYERS.)

GOVERNOR'S WIFE: At least there are no common people here, thank God. I can't stand their smell. It always gives me migraine.

FIRST LAWYER: Madam, I must ask you to be careful what you say until we have another judge.

GOVERNOR'S WIFE: But I didn't say anything, Illo Shuboladze. I love the people with their simple straightforward minds. It's only that their smell brings on my migraine.

SECOND LAWYER: There won't be many spectators. The whole population is sitting at home behind locked doors because of the riots in the people's quarters.

GOVERNOR'S WIFE (*looking at* GRUSHA): Is that the creature?

FIRST LAWYER: Please, most gracious Natella Abashwili, abstain from invective until it is certain the Grand Duke has appointed a new judge and we're rid of the present one, who's about the lowest fellow ever seen in judge's gown. Things are all set to move, you see.

(*Enter* IRONSHIRTS *from the courtyard*.)

COOK: Her Grace would pull your hair out on the spot if 'ie didn't know Azdak is for the poor. He goes by the face.

(IRONSHIRTS *begin fastening a rope to a beam*. AZDAK, *in chains, is led in, followed by* SHAUWA, *also in chains. The three* FARMERS *bring up the rear*.)

AN IRONSHIRT: Trying to run away, were you? (*He strikes* AZDAK.)

ONE FARMER: Off with his judge's gown before we string him up!

(IRONSHIRTS *and* FARMERS *tear off* AZDAK's *gown. His torn underwear is visible. Then someone kicks him*.)

AN IRONSHIRT (*pushing him into someone else*): Want a load of justice? Here it is!

(*Accompanied by shouts of* "You take it!" *and* "Let me have him, Brother!" *they throw* AZDAK *back and forth until he collapses. Then he is lifted up and dragged under the noose*.)

GOVERNOR'S WIFE (*who, during this* "ballgame," *has clapped her hands hysterically*): I disliked that man from the moment I first saw him.

AZDAK (*covered with blood, panting*): I can't see. Give me a rag.

AN IRONSHIRT: What is it you want to see?

AZDAK: You, you dogs! (*He wipes the blood out of his eyes with his shirt*.) Good morning, dogs! How goes it, dogs! How's the dog world? Does it smell good? Got another boot for me to lick? Are you back at each other's throats, dogs?

(*Accompanied by a* CORPORAL, *a dust-covered* RIDER *enters. He takes some documents from a leather case, looks at them, then interrupts*.)

RIDER: Stop! I bring a dispatch from the Grand Duke, containing the latest appointments.

CORPORAL (*bellowing*): Atten — shun!

RIDER: Of the new judge it says: "We appoint a man whom we have to thank for saving a life indispensable to the country's welfare — a certain Azdak of Nuka." Which is he?

SHAUWA (*pointing*): That's him, Your Excellency.

CORPORAL (*bellowing*): What's going on here?

AN IRONSHIRT: I beg to report that His Honor Azdak was already His Honor Azdak, but on these farmers' denunciation was pronounced the Grand Duke's enemy.

CORPORAL (*pointing at the* FARMERS): March them off! (*They are marched off. They bow all the time*.) See to it that His Honor Azdak is exposed to no more violence.

(*Exeunt* RIDER *and* CORPORAL.)

COOK (*to* SHAUWA): She clapped her hands! I hope he saw it!

FIRST LAWYER: It's a catastrophe.

(AZDAK *has fainted. Coming to, he is dressed again in judge's robes. He walks, swaying, toward the* IRONSHIRTS.)

AN IRONSHIRT: What does Your Honor desire?
AZDAK: Nothing, fellow dogs, or just an occasional boot to lick. (*To* SHAUWA.) I pardon you. (*He is unchained.*) Get me some red wine, the sweet kind. (SHAUWA *stumbles off.*) Get out of here, I've got to judge a case. (*Exeunt* IRONSHIRTS. SHAUWA *returns with a pitcher of wine.* AZDAK *gulps it down.*) Something for my backside. (SHAUWA *brings the Statute Book, puts it on the judge's chair.* AZDAK *sits on it.*) I accept.

(*The* PROSECUTORS, *among whom a worried council has been held, smile with relief. They whisper.*)

COOK: Oh dear!
SIMON: A well can't be filled with dew, they say.
LAWYERS (*approaching* AZDAK, *who stands up expectantly*): A quite ridiculous case, Your Honor. The accused has abducted a child and refuses to hand it over.
AZDAK (*stretching out his hand, glancing at* GRUSHA): A most attractive person. (*He fingers the money, then sits down, satisfied.*) I declare the proceedings open and demand the whole truth. (*To* GRUSHA.) Especially from you.
FIRST LAWYER: High Court of Justice! Blood, as the popular saying goes, is thicker than water. This old adage . . .
AZDAK (*interrupting*): The Court wants to know the lawyers' fee.
FIRST LAWYER (*surprised*): I beg your pardon? (AZDAK, *smiling, rubs his thumb and index finger.*) Oh, I see. Five hundred piasters, Your Honor, to answer the Court's somewhat unusual question.
AZDAK: Did you hear? The question is unusual. I ask it because I listen in quite a different way when I know you're good.
FIRST LAWYER (*bowing*): Thank you, Your Honor. High Court of Justice, of all ties the ties of blood are strongest. Mother and child — is there a more intimate relationship? Can one tear a child from its mother? High Court of Justice, she has conceived it in the holy ecstasies of love. She has carried it in her womb. She has fed it with her blood. She has borne it with pain. High Court of Justice, it has been observed that the wild tigress, robbed of her young, roams restless through the mountains, shrunk to a shadow. Nature herself . . .
AZDAK (*interrupting, to* GRUSHA): What's your answer to all this and anything else that lawyer might have to say?
GRUSHA: He's mine.
AZDAK: Is that all? I hope you can prove it. Why should I assign the child to you in any case?
GRUSHA: I brought him up like the priest says "according to my best knowledge and conscience." I always found him something to eat. Most of the time he had a roof over his head. And I went to such trouble for him. I had expenses too. I didn't look out for my own comfort. I brought the child up to be friendly with everyone, and from the beginning taught him to work. As well as he could, that is. He's still very little.
FIRST LAWYER: Your Honor, it is significant that the girl herself doesn't claim any tie of blood between her and the child.
AZDAK: The Court takes note of that.

FIRST LAWYER: Thank you, Your Honor. And now permit a woman bowed in sorrow
— who has already lost her husband and now has also to fear the loss of her child
— to address a few words to you. The gracious Natella Abashwili is . . .

GOVERNOR'S WIFE (*quietly*): A most cruel fate, sir, forces me to describe to you the
tortures of a bereaved mother's soul, the anxiety, the sleepless nights, the . . .

SECOND LAWYER (*bursting out*): It's outrageous the way this woman is being treated!
Her husband's palace is closed to her! The revenue of her estates is blocked, and
she is cold-bloodedly told that it's tied to the heir. She can't do a thing without
that child. She can't even pay her lawyers!! (*To the* FIRST LAWYER, *who, desperate
about this outburst, makes frantic gestures to keep him from speaking.*) Dear Illo
Shuboladze, surely it can be divulged now that the Abashwili estates are at stake?

FIRST LAWYER: Please, Honored Sandro Oboladze! We agreed . . . (*To* AZDAK.) Of
course it is correct that the trial will also decide if our noble client can take over
the Abashwili estates, which are rather extensive. I say "also" advisedly, for in the
foreground stands the human tragedy of a mother, as Natella Abashwili very
properly explained in the first words of her moving statement. Even if Michael
Abashwili were not heir to the estates, he would still be the dearly beloved child
of my client.

AZDAK: Stop! The Court is touched by the mention of estates. It's a proof of human
feeling.

SECOND LAWYER: Thanks, Your Honor. Dear Illo Shuboladze, we can prove in any
case that the woman who took the child is not the child's mother. Permit me to
lay before the Court the bare facts. High Court of Justice, by an unfortunate
chain of circumstances, Michael Abashwili was left behind on that Easter Sunday while his mother was making her escape. Grusha, a palace kitchen maid, was
seen with the baby . . .

COOK: All her mistress was thinking of was what dresses she'd take along!

SECOND LAWYER (*unmoved*): Nearly a year later Grusha turned up in a mountain
village with a baby and there entered into the state of matrimony with . . .

AZDAK: How'd you get to that mountain village?

GRUSHA: On foot, Your Honor. And he was mine.

SIMON: I'm the father, Your Honor.

COOK: I used to look after it for them, Your Honor. For five piasters.

SECOND LAWYER: This man is engaged to Grusha, High Court of Justice: his testimony is suspect.

AZDAK: Are you the man she married in the mountain village?

SIMON: No, Your Honor, she married a peasant.

AZDAK (*to* GRUSHA): Why? (*Pointing at* SIMON.) Is he no good in bed? Tell the truth.

GRUSHA: We didn't get that far. I married because of the baby. So he'd have a roof
over his head. (*Pointing at* SIMON.) He was in the war, Your Honor.

AZDAK: And now he wants you back again, huh?

SIMON: I wish to state in evidence . . .

GRUSHA (*angrily*): I am no longer free, Your Honor.

AZDAK: And the child, you claim, comes from whoring? (GRUSHA *doesn't answer.*)
I'm going to ask you a question: What kind of child is he? A ragged little bastard?
Or from a good family?

GRUSHA (*angrily*): He's an ordinary child.

AZDAK: I mean — did he have refined features from the beginning?

GRUSHA: He had a nose on his face.

AZDAK: A very significant comment! It has been said of me that I went out one time and sniffed at a rosebush before rendering a verdict — tricks like that are needed nowadays. Well, I'll make it short, and not listen to any more lies. (*To* GRUSHA.) Especially not yours. (*To all the accused.*) I can imagine what you've cooked up to cheat me! I know you people. You're swindlers.

GRUSHA (*suddenly*): I can understand your wanting to cut it short, now I've seen what you accepted!

AZDAK: Shut up! Did I accept anything from you?

GRUSHA (*while the* COOK *tries to restrain her*): I haven't got anything.

AZDAK: True. Quite true. From starvelings I never get a thing. I might just as well starve, myself. You want justice, but do you want to pay for it, hm? When you go to a butcher you know you have to pay, but you people go to a judge as if you were off to a funeral supper.

SIMON (*loudly*): When the horse was shod, the horsefly held out its leg, as the saying is.

AZDAK (*eagerly accepting the challenge*): Better a treasure in manure than a stone in a mountain stream.

SIMON: A fine day. Let's go fishing, said the angler to the worm.

AZDAK: I'm my own master, said the servant, and cut off his foot.

SIMON: I love you as a father, said the Czar to the peasants, and had the Czarevitch's head chopped off.

AZDAK: A fool's worst enemy is himself.

SIMON: However, a fart has no nose.

AZDAK: Fined ten piasters for indecent language in court! That'll teach you what justice is.

GRUSHA (*furiously*): A fine kind of justice! You play fast and loose with us because we don't talk as refined as that crowd with their lawyers.

AZDAK: That's true. You people are too dumb. It's only right you should get it in the neck.

GRUSHA: You want to hand the child over to her, and she wouldn't even know how to keep it dry, she's so "refined"! You know about as much about justice as I do!

AZDAK: There's something in that. I'm an ignorant man. Haven't even a decent pair of pants on under this gown. Look! With me, everything goes on food and drink — I was educated in a convent. Incidentally, I'll fine you ten piasters for contempt of court. And you're a very silly girl, to turn me against you, instead of making eyes at me and wiggling your backside a little to keep me in a good temper. Twenty piasters!

GRUSHA: Even if it was thirty, I'd tell you what I think of your justice, you drunken onion! (*Incoherently.*) How dare you talk to me like the cracked Isaiah on the church window? As if you were somebody? For you weren't born to this. You weren't born to rap your own mother on the knuckles if she swipes a little bowl of salt someplace. Aren't you ashamed of yourself when you see how I tremble before you? You've made yourself their servant so no one will take their houses from them — houses they had stolen! Since when have houses belonged to the bedbugs? But you're on the watch, or they couldn't drag our men into their wars! You bribetaker!

(AZDAK *half gets up, starts beaming. With his little hammer he half-heartedly knocks on the table as if to get silence. As* GRUSHA's *scolding continues, he only beats time with his hammer.*)

I've no respect for you. No more than for a thief or a bandit with a knife! You can do what you want. You can take the child away from me, a hundred against one, but I tell you one thing: only extortioners should be chosen for a profession like yours, and men who rape children! As punishment! Yes, let *them* sit in judgment on their fellow creatures. It is worse than to hang from the gallows.

AZDAK (*sitting down*): Now it'll be thirty! And I won't go on squabbling with you — we're not in a tavern. What'd happen to my dignity as a judge? Anyway, I've lost interest in your case. Where's the couple who wanted a divorce? (*To* SHAUWA.) Bring 'em in. This case is adjourned for fifteen minutes.

FIRST LAWYER (*to the* GOVERNOR'S WIFE): Even without using the rest of the evidence, Madam, we have the verdict in the bag.

COOK (*to* GRUSHA): You've gone and spoiled your chances with him. You won't get the child now.

GOVERNOR'S WIFE: Shalva, my smelling salts!

(*Enter a very* OLD COUPLE.)

AZDAK: I accept. (*The* OLD COUPLE *don't understand*.) I hear you want to be divorced. How long have you been together?

OLD WOMAN: Forty years, Your Honor.

AZDAK: And why do you want a divorce?

OLD MAN: We don't like each other, Your Honor.

AZDAK: Since when?

OLD WOMAN: Oh, from the very beginning, Your Honor.

AZDAK: I'll think about your request and render my verdict when I'm through with the other case. (SHAUWA *leads them back*.) I need the child. (*He beckons* GRUSHA *to him and bends not unkindly toward her*.) I've noticed you have a soft spot for justice. I don't believe he's your child, but if he *were* yours, woman, wouldn't you want him to be rich? You'd only have to say he wasn't yours, and he'd have a palace and many horses in his stable and many beggars on his doorstep and many soldiers in his service and many petitioners in his courtyard, wouldn't he? What do you say — don't you want him to be rich?

(GRUSHA *is silent*.)

SINGER: Hear now what the angry girl thought but did not say:

Had he golden shoes to wear
He'd be cruel as a bear
Evil would his life disgrace.
He'd laugh in my face.

Carrying a heart of flint
Is too troublesome a stint.
Being powerful and bad
Is hard on a lad.

Then let hunger be his foe!
Hungry men and women, no.
Let him fear the darksome night
But not daylight!

AZDAK: I think I understand you, woman.

GRUSHA (*suddenly and loudly*): I won't give him up. I've raised him, and he knows me.

(*Enter* SHAUWA *with the* CHILD.)

GOVERNOR'S WIFE: He's in rags!

GRUSHA: That's not true. But I wasn't given time to put his good shirt on.

GOVERNOR'S WIFE: He must have been in a pigsty.

GRUSHA (*furiously*): I'm not a pig, but there are some who are! Where did you leave your baby?

GOVERNOR'S WIFE: I'll show you, you vulgar creature! (*She is about to throw herself on* GRUSHA, *but is restrained by her* LAWYERS.) She's a criminal, she must be whipped. Immediately!

SECOND LAWYER (*holding his hand over her mouth*): Natella Abashwili, you promised . . . Your Honor, the plaintiff's nerves . . .

AZDAK: Plaintiff and defendant! The Court has listened to your case, and has come to no decision as to who the real mother is; therefore, I, the judge, am obliged to *choose* a mother for the child. I'll make a test. Shauwa, get a piece of chalk and draw a circle on the floor. (SHAUWA *does so.*) Now place the child in the center. (SHAUWA *puts* MICHAEL, *who smiles at* GRUSHA, *in the center of the circle.*) Stand near the circle, both of you. (*The* GOVERNOR'S WIFE *and* GRUSHA *step up to the circle.*) Now each of you take the child by one hand. (*They do so.*) The true mother is she who can pull the child out of the circle.

SECOND LAWYER (*quickly*): High Court of Justice, I object! The fate of the great Abashwili estates, which are tied to the child, as the heir, should not be made dependent on such a doubtful duel. In addition, my client does not command the strength of this person, who is accustomed to physical work.

AZDAK: She looks pretty well fed to me. Pull! (*The* GOVERNOR'S WIFE *pulls the* CHILD *out of the circle on her side;* GRUSHA *has let go and stands aghast.*) What's the matter with you? You didn't pull.

GRUSHA: I didn't hold on to him.

FIRST LAWYER (*congratulating the* GOVERNOR'S WIFE): What did I say! The ties of blood!

GRUSHA (*running to* AZDAK): Your Honor, I take back everything I said against you. I ask your forgiveness. But could I keep him till he can speak all the words? He knows a few.

AZDAK: Don't influence the Court. I bet you only know about twenty words yourself. All right, I'll make the test once more, just to be certain. (*The two* WOMEN *take up their positions again.*) Pull! (*Again* GRUSHA *lets go of the* CHILD.)

GRUSHA (*in despair*): I brought him up! Shall I also tear him to bits? I can't!

AZDAK (*rising*): And in this manner the Court has determined the true mother. (*To* GRUSHA.) Take your child and be off. I advise you not to stay in the city with him. (*To the* GOVERNOR'S WIFE.) And you disappear before I fine you for fraud. Your estates fall to the city. They'll be converted into a playground for the children. They need one, and I've decided it'll be called after me: Azdak's Garden.

(*The* GOVERNOR'S WIFE *has fainted and is carried out by the* LAWYERS *and the* ADJUTANT. GRUSHA *stands motionless.* SHAUWA *leads the* CHILD *toward her.*)

Now I'll take off this judge's gown — it's got too hot for me. I'm not cut out for a hero. In token of farewell I invite you all to a little dance in the meadow outside.

Oh, I'd almost forgotten something in my excitement . . . to sign the divorce decree. (*Using the judge's chair as a table, he writes something on a piece of paper, and prepares to leave. Dance music has started.*)

SHAUWA (*having read what is on the paper*): But that's not right. You've not divorced the old people. You've divorced Grusha!

AZDAK: Divorced the wrong couple? What a pity! And I never retract! If I did, how could we keep order in the land? (*To the* OLD COUPLE.) I'll invite you to my party instead. You don't mind dancing with each other, do you? (*To* GRUSHA *and* SIMON) I've got forty piasters coming from you.

SIMON (*pulling out his purse*): Cheap at the price, Your Honor. And many thanks.

AZDAK (*pocketing the cash*): I'll be needing this.

GRUSHA (*to* MICHAEL): So we'd better leave the city tonight, Michael? (*To* SIMON.) You like him?

SIMON: With my respects, I like him.

GRUSHA: Now I can tell you: I took him because on that Easter Sunday I got engaged to you. So he's a child of love. Michael, let's dance.

(*She dances with* MICHAEL, SIMON *dances with the* COOK, *the* OLD COUPLE *with each other.* AZDAK *stands lost in thought. The* DANCERS *soon hide him from view. Occasionally he is seen, but less and less as more couples join the dance.*)

SINGER: And after that evening Azdak vanished and was never seen again.
The people of Grusinia did not forget him but long remembered
The period of his judging as a brief golden age,
Almost an age of justice.

(*All the* COUPLES *dance off.* AZDAK *has disappeared.*)

But you, you who have listened to the Story of the Chalk Circle,
Take note what men of old concluded:
That what there is shall go to those who are good for it,
Children to the motherly, that they prosper,
Carts to good drivers, that they be driven well,
The valley to the waterers, that it yield fruit.

AFTERWORD

Simplicity in art, says Eric Bentley in his Introduction to *Seven Plays by Bertolt Brecht*, may be an achievement on the far side of complexity. It is an apt comment. In Brecht, we sense the design not as something innocent of or defiant of disorder but as immanent in it, and we see the artistic process as revelatory rather than creative. The parable — the term is Brecht's — emerges from the crowded bustle on the stage with the clarity and strength of a folk tale. His art is at the opposite end from modern realism. Whereas Ibsen's stage has the stability of a room, Brecht's is open and, like Shakespeare's, momentarily capable of becoming any place the imagination calls for. The inclusive dramatic form, fluid rather than unrealistic, embeds the moral scheme of the fable in the promiscuous flux of actuality, but the scheme disciplines the flux to directed movement. Parable, almost but never quite becoming abstract scheme, balanced against stage activity, almost but never quite becoming chaos, provides inner tension. The surface naiveté masks a technique that orders a vast and subtle content.

If Brecht is a difficult playwright, he has been made even more difficult by the labels of "Marxism" and "epic theater" (also his term) with which his plays are commonly tagged. The tags would do less harm if they were simply wrong; then they could be removed. They are not wrong, however, but intrusive and misleading. They stop thought and trigger stock responses. We react, not to drama, but to political system and esthetic theory. Like all fables, Brecht's concentrate large and various experience. But the narrative that embodies the general pattern is not abstract. "Marxist" points to certain consistent value orientations evident in the plays and "epic" to certain distinctive ways of using the theater. But the labels say nothing about the particulars of plot and scenic reality that the Marxist outlook and the epic form shape into the pattern of fable. The journey motif in Grusha's story is a version of epic, but it is the particulars of the human and physical obstacles she encounters and the rhythm and direction of her progress, rather than the mere fact of narrative, that turn her journey into a superb theatrical demonstration of the "terribleness" of "the seductive power of goodness." Azdak, the proletarian scamp-judge, whose moral superiority is that of the rabbit-eater over the man-eater, challenges propertied stuffiness and arrogance, legalism, and feudal tyranny. There is revolutionary sentiment in the muted anger of his "Song of Injustice in Persia" and in the triumphant sarcasm of his "Song of Chaos." The old legend could be called proto-Marxist. But as a general concept Marxism is more of a hindrance than a help in a critical account of Azdak. His cowardice, vulgarity, and greed, his old cheese, bloody rags, and dirty, drunken jokes, the tragicomical implications of his futile self-condemnation for helping the Grand Duke to escape, the ironic fickleness of fortune by which be becomes first a mock, then a real, judge, then almost loses his neck, and then is reinstated as judge — are these, as dramatic facts, "Marxist"?

The point, of course, is that a literary work does not contain ideology the way a pudding contains plums, or even the way a cake contains butter. As a theoretical materialist Brecht wanted a more equitable distribution of economic goods and potential, and he believed in man's duty to try to improve his physical environment, and hence his conditioning, to the limit of his ability and control. Having tried Hollywood, he settled in East Berlin. But the problem of Marxism-in-Brecht is not solved by biography or by anxious search for pellets of subversive doctrine. Is property good or evil in *The Caucasian Chalk Circle* (1944–45)? Almost everyone in the play who owns anything is hard-hearted, not just the feudal masters, but the peasants as well: the farmer who sells Grusha milk, Lavrenti's wife, the mother-in-law, the Invalid, the three farmers charging the old woman with theft. But then we come upon Azdak taking bribes as a matter of course and Simon Shashava being able to marry Grusha because he has been promoted to paymaster at double his earlier pay and with a house of his own. Does the play say that riches corrupt? It is less presumptuous. It says that Grusha thinks that little Michael would be corrupted if he were brought up by Natella Abashwili — a much smaller and dramatically more serviceable proposition. Is there political dynamite in Azdak's epigram, "That the roof of the world may be conquered, the roof of the cottage is torn down?" A cold-war attitude? If Azdak's awarding the child to Grusha is taken to imply an attack on property rights, doesn't "Capitalism" come to seem incompatible with kindness and common sense? Brecht gives a new twist to the old story of the Solomonic test of mother's love. The comfortable assumption used to be that none but the child's real mother would sooner give up her right to the child than cause it pain. But here the natural mother is unnatural, the foster mother truly motherly. The new version (a verse prologue Bentley has written for the play says) naggingly involves the larger question of who owns anything, "and by what right." Is this Marxism? — or political disillusionment? The whole inquiry breaks down.

We are aware, rather, of what Brecht perhaps had in mind when he once referred to Azdak's "tragic side." There is in the crude farce of his magistracy the truth that all even *his* shrewd folk wisdom achieved was *"almost* an age of justice." Does the fault lie with his justice or with the "dog's world" in which he is a judge? Isn't he a bit of a brute himself? And even if we assume that the lesson which the two kolkhozes learn from the story of Azdak is an absolute, the modern valley setting, with evidence of Nazi ravage all around, is onstage proof that events rarely follow the rule "That what there is shall go to those who are good for it." The legend of the good judge is, after all, only an old legend.

The fact that "epic theater," unlike "Marxism," raises *literary* issues only increases the risk of hiding the play behind a label. "Epic" is misleading if it is taken to imply that Brecht's plays are undramatic ("epic" denoting a genre distinct from "drama" and "lyric"). Their solidly dimensional world can be staged in its entirety, unlike the world of novels, and by the same token is not an introspected world, like that of lyrics. "Epic" is misleading also if it suggests the slow and stately pace, the richness of reference, the elevated diction, the formulas of image and rhetoric, the mythological machinery, and the magnitude of theme, of classical or Miltonic epics.

What the term *should* denote is a drama that breaks the old five- or three-act structure and proceeds by something resembling the "stations" of the guild performances of medieval mystery and miracle plays: staged episodes in discontinuous but progressive narrative sequence. The filmic elements of large and changing cast, variety of setting, brevity of scene, and use of flashback (in the early Azdak scenes) also give a kind of epic effect.

But the main reason for calling Brecht's drama epic is that it is narrated.

Like the kolkhoz farmers we are in the hands of Arkadi Tscheidse, the professional Singer from Tiflis. What we see of Grusha's and Azdak's stories are episodes selected for dramatization from a larger entertainment-with-a-purpose, which also includes choric comment and the narrator's linking synopses. The episodes are, literally, *shown*. The audience understands that it does not see the characters of the legend themselves, but their twentieth-century impersonators.

Clearly, we are dealing here with a play convention quite different from that of the realist theater. By realist convention, we are unobserved observers of real life in the process of being lived — peepers and eavesdroppers. We are invited to believe, or to pretend to believe, that the actors are not actors but husbands and wives, bankers and Salvation Army officers — that their talk is not rehearsed but spontaneous, that they are not on a stage but in an apartment. The realist convention paradoxically denies the fact of theater. As audience we get our money's worth only if we are willing to share the denial. A realist play production, we say, is successful in direct ratio to the success with which it entices us into the make-believe and keeps us there till the curtain comes down, the lights go on, and the illusion ends.

Brecht openly violates the realist convention. For him, the stage is space inside, not outside, the theater. The devices he employs to prevent illusionism ensure theatricality.

In *The Caucasian Chalk Circle* both the most obvious and the most important of these devices is the framing of the main action in a play-within-a-play form. The device is not new. Shakespeare (for example) used it in *The Taming of the Shrew* and Beaumont in *The Knight of the Burning Pestle*. After Pirandello's *Six Characters in Search of an Author* (1921), it has become something of a cliché in plays that insinuate a philosophy of relativism. However dissimilar plays using this device may be, they all have in common the effect they give of the theater being conscious of itself — an effect ambiguous, paradoxical, and elusive. Does the spectacle of art mocking art *as* art hint at a reaffirmation of the seriousness of art as true to life? Theatricalism, at any rate, produces a much subtler stage-audience relationship than does dramatic realism. In *The Chalk Circle* an audience in the theater watches an audience on stage, and both then watch — not a play of present life but a dramatization-narration of past legend.* The familiar but profound pun on the two meanings of the verb "to act" comes alive as the characters in the play-within "live" their theatrical existence.

Verfremdung (literally, "alienation" or "estrangement" but most often rendered as "distancing" or "esthetic distancing") is Brecht's term for the effect on the audience of this insistent theatricality. Its function is to keep

---

* In Bentley's 1961 production of his adaptation of the play, members of the fruit-growing "Galinsk" kolkhoz participate in the performance, thus further blurring the stage-audience distinction.

the spectator's rational faculties alert during the performance. Brecht seeks from his audience not a spellbinding imaginative projection into the illusion of life on stage, but thoughtful attention to a meaningful dramatization of fable. He wants to reach minds, not to submerge them in a wash of stage-generated empathy. "I am not," he once said, "greatly interested in anyone making an emotional investment in my plays." This does not mean that he fails whenever an audience gives Grusha and Azdak its sympathies or finds the play charming. It means that he uses emotional appeal as a strategy of persuasion — as a means to a rational end, not as an end in itself.

And yet, the ultimate effect of *Verfremdung* in *The Chalk Circle* is perhaps more complex than Brecht's deliberate aim would indicate. The ambivalent status of the stage audience tends to obscure the distinction between stage and audience. From the viewpoint of the theater audience the stage audience are characters in the outer (framing) action. From the viewpoint of the performers in the inner (framed) action they are audience. Because the theater audience recognizes its own status in one of the two functions of the stage audience, it tends to identify with it in its other function as well. At the end, outer and inner action (and present and past, theater actuality and theater imagination) merge, as the dancing couples of actors and stage audience* gradually hide Azdak from view. Then the dancers, too, disappear, and the Singer is left alone on the stage to address the epilogue-moral directly to the audience in the theater. To what extent, by now, has the latter become implicated? *Verfremdung* eliminates the possibility of mistaking the theater for reality, but it does not, like the realist theater of illusion, draw a safe line of division between them.

Sets and the use of time also add to the theatricalist effect. The outdoor scene in the distant, war-torn valley plausibly limits the Singer's use of props and scenery. The sets are crude and improvised, suggestive-symbolic rather than lifelike. In the opening scene of the inner play, a doorway marks the palace side of the stage, a gateway the town side. Place is evoked rather than represented. The whole production is stylized. The "voice" of the play shifts freely back and forth between drama, narrative, and choric comment and would only be impeded by elaborate verisimilitude.

There are shifts in time as well:

CROWD: — The baby!
— I can't see it, don't shove so hard!
— God bless the child, Your Grace!
SINGER (*while the* CROWD *is driven back with whips*): For the first time on that Easter Sunday, the people saw the Governor's heir.

---

* It has not been made explicitly clear whether or not members of the kolkhoz audience join in the final dance, but that seems to be the implication of the stage directions of the last scene. It would, at any rate, be a scenically effective conclusion, in keeping with the play-within-the-play decorum.

The Singer's comment cuts off the gathering immediacy of the crowd scene. His viewpoint is the retrospective, generalizing one of a historian. His "saw" pulls us back sharply from the crowd's "I can't see." No sooner have we begun to suspend disbelief, accepting what we see as happening *here* and *now*, than the Singer steps in to remind us that the present tense applies only to the theater situation. He is presenting a show, but it is a show of what *happened* — *then* and *there*. Time is not always rendered realistically even within a single episode. When Lavrenti tells Grusha that she and the child must leave his farm as soon as spring comes, the accelerating drip-drip from the roof marks the passing of winter and the coming of spring even as brother and sister talk. Onstage action and dialogue proceed at normal speed, while the simultaneous offstage sound of snow melting compresses days or weeks into the span of a few minutes.

The theatricalist fable subordinates character, too, to meaningful pattern. As the kolkhoz Prologue and the Singer's Epilogue frame the legend of Grusha and Azdak, so Grusha's scenes with Simon give a framework of romance to the hardships of her journey. We get a Chinese box effect, frame within frame. The mock-formal restraint of language in the lovers' dialogues suggests the blend of passion, liking, respect, and sheer sense of fun in their feelings for one another. But the point is their attractiveness as moral types rather than, simply, delightful romance or psychological complexity.

The most striking fact of structure in the play is the two-part division. The answer to the question of whose play it is, Grusha's or Azdak's, is that it belongs to both, that the two stories are complementary halves in a dramatic whole, premises in a kind of syllogism. Parallelism prepares for their final fusion. Both Grusha and Azdak perform impulsive deeds of imprudent kindness: Grusha saves Michael, Azdak the Grand Duke. Both are rewarded for their kindness (though the reward is ironic in Azdak's case, as he regrets his kindness when he learns the old man's identity). The syllogism concludes in Grusha's and Azdak's confrontation in the chalk-circle scene. The conclusion represents a multiple climax.

It releases the suspense concerning Grusha's fate, which has been accumulating while Azdak's manner of justice has been illustrated in racy anecdote. It achieves the overt meaning of the fable. Without Azdak, Grusha's story would only have proved that in violent social upheaval there are other bitter battles fought than those on the battlefield. Without Grusha, Azdak's natural justice would have lacked a morally significant context and emotive force. Only together do the two stories have what a character in the dramatic prologue calls "a bearing on the problem" of what to do with the valley. By the test of Azdak's criterion of superior yield, as applicable to use of land as to motherliness, the settlement in favor of the fruit-growing irrigators is validated.

Finally, the chalk-circle scene completes the dramatic structure. This might have been described as two converging lines, if only Grusha's movement had not been over before Azdak's even begins, and if the flashback story of Azdak ("flashback" relative to Grusha's poignant situation at the end of Section III of the play) had moved at all after he becomes judge. Dramatically, the near-hanging is an abortive episode, and the preceding collection of law-case anecdotes, though establishing Azdak's quality as an administrator of justice, is shapeless and static. A more accurate definition of the structural function of the chalk-circle scene is that it brings the dynamics of the brave and resourceful virgin mother's odyssey to rest in the stasis of Azdak's verdict and Simon Shashava's love, concluding the legend of how goodness once received justice in a Caucasian valley.

Arthur Miller

DEATH OF A SALESMAN

Certain Private Conversations in Two Acts and a Requiem

FOREWORD

In talking of European plays we have often been able to point to independent theater groups dedicated to a particular movement, or to state-supported theaters free from commercial pressures. In the United States the commercial theater system, with rare exceptions, has predominated. The theater has become an industry in which plays stand or fall by popular acceptance. This means that "mainstream" drama has been the rule, and innovation has proceeded more tentatively. *Death of a Salesman* is a case in point. It offers cautiously modified realism, and little to jar the susceptibilities of an audience brought up on plays like *Ah, Wilderness!* True, the setting and time-scheme are fluid; Willy is plunged back from the present to the traumatic scene in an anonymous hotel-room. But these flashbacks are signaled with great care (compare the rapidity with which time and space are manipulated by Strindberg and Brecht) and offer no difficulties to audiences trained to the conventions of film.

CHARACTERS

WILLY LOMAN	UNCLE BEN
LINDA	HOWARD WAGNER
BIFF	JENNY
HAPPY	STANLEY
BERNARD	MISS FORSYTHE
THE WOMAN	LETTA
CHARLEY	

Scene. The action takes place in WILLY LOMAN's *house and yard and in various places he visits in the New York and Boston of today.*

Throughout the play, in the stage directions, left and right mean stage left and stage right.

ACT I

A melody is heard, played upon a flute. It is small and fine, telling of grass and trees and the horizon. The curtain rises.

Before us is the Salesman's house. We are aware of towering, angular shapes behind it, surrounding it on all sides. Only the blue light of the sky falls upon the house and forestage; the surrounding area shows an angry glow of orange. As more light appears, we see a solid vault of apartment houses around the small, fragile-seeming home. An air of the dream clings to the place, a dream rising out of reality. The kitchen at center seems actual enough, for there is a kitchen table with three chairs, and a refrigerator. But no other fixtures are seen. At the back of the kitchen there is a draped entrance, which leads to the living-room. To the right of the kitchen, on a level raised two feet, is a bedroom furnished only with a brass bedstead and a straight chair. On a shelf over the bed a silver athletic trophy stands. A window opens onto the apartment house at the side.

Behind the kitchen, on a level raised six and a half feet, is the boys' bedroom, at present barely visible. Two beds are dimly seen, and at the back of the room a dormer window. (This bedroom is above the unseen living-room.) At the left a stairway curves up to it from the kitchen.

The entire setting is wholly or, in some places, partially transparent. The

Death of a Salesman by Arthur Miller. Copyright 1949 by Arthur Miller, © renewed 1977 by Arthur Miller. Reprinted by permission of The Viking Press.

roof-line of the house is one-dimensional; under and over it we see the apart-ment buildings. Before the house lies an apron, curving beyond the forestage into the orchestra. This forward area serves as the back yard as well as the locale of all WILLY's *imaginings and of his city scenes. Whenever the action is in the present the actors observe the imaginary wall-lines, entering the house only through its door at the left. But in the scenes of the past these boundaries are broken, and characters enter or leave a room by stepping "through" a wall onto the forestage.*

From the right, WILLY LOMAN, *the Salesman, enters, carrying two large sam-ple cases. The flute plays on. He hears but is not aware of it. He is past sixty years of age, dressed quietly. Even as he crosses the stage to the doorway of the house, his exhaustion is apparent. He unlocks the door, comes into the kitchen, and thankfully lets his burden down, feeling the soreness of his palms. A word-sigh escapes his lips — it might be "Oh, boy, oh, boy." He closes the door, then carries his cases out into the living-room, through the draped kitchen doorway.*

LINDA, *his wife, has stirred in her bed at the right. She gets out and puts on a robe, listening. Most often jovial, she has developed an iron repression of her exceptions to* WILLY's *behavior — she more than loves him, she admires him, as though his mercurial nature, his temper, his massive dreams and little cruelties, served her only as sharp reminders of the turbulent longings within him, long-ings which she shares but lacks the temperament to utter and follow to their end.*

LINDA (*hearing* WILLY *outside the bedroom, calls with some trepidation*): Willy!

WILLY: It's all right. I came back.

LINDA: Why? What happened? (*Slight pause.*) Did something happen, Willy?

WILLY: No, nothing happened.

LINDA: You didn't smash the car, did you?

WILLY (*with casual irritation*): I said nothing happened. Didn't you hear me?

LINDA: Don't you feel well?

WILLY: I am tired to the death. (*The flute has faded away. He sits on the bed beside her, a little numb.*) I couldn't make it. I just couldn't make it, Linda.

LINDA (*very carefully, delicately*): Where were you all day? You look terrible.

WILLY: I got as far as a little above Yonkers. I stopped for a cup of coffee. Maybe it was the coffee.

LINDA: What?

WILLY (*after a pause*): I suddenly couldn't drive any more. The car kept going off onto the shoulder, y'know?

LINDA (*helpfully*): Oh. Maybe it was the steering again. I don't think Angelo knows the Studebaker.

WILLY: No, it's me, it's me. Suddenly I realize I'm goin' sixty miles an hour and I don't remember the last five minutes. I'm — I can't seem to — keep my mind to it.

LINDA: Maybe it's your glasses. You never went for your new glasses.

WILLY: No, I see everything. I came back ten miles an hour. It took me nearly four hours from Yonkers.

LINDA (*resigned*): Well, you'll just have to take a rest, Willy, you can't continue this way.

WILLY: I just got back from Florida.

LINDA: But you didn't rest your mind. Your mind is overactive, and the mind is what counts, dear.

WILLY: I'll start out in the morning. Maybe I'll feel better in the morning. (*She is taking off his shoes.*) These goddam arch supports are killing me.

LINDA: Take an aspirin. Should I get you an aspirin? It'll soothe you.

WILLY (*with wonder*): I was driving along, you understand? And I was fine. I was even observing the scenery. You can imagine, me looking at scenery, on the road every week of my life. But it's so beautiful up there, Linda, the trees are so thick, and the sun is warm. I opened the windshield and just let the warm air bathe over me. And then all of a sudden I'm goin' off the road! I'm tellin' ya, I absolutely forgot I was driving. If I'd've gone the other way over the white line I might've killed somebody. So I went on again — and five minutes later I'm dreamin' again, and I nearly — (*He presses two fingers against his eyes.*) I have such thoughts, I have such strange thoughts.

LINDA: Willy, dear. Talk to them again. There's no reason why you can't work in New York.

WILLY: They don't need me in New York. I'm the New England man. I'm vital in New England.

LINDA: But you're sixty years old. They can't expect you to keep traveling every week.

WILLY: I'll have to send a wire to Portland. I'm supposed to see Brown and Morrison tomorrow morning at ten o'clock to show the line. Goddammit, I could sell them! (*He starts putting on his jacket.*)

LINDA (*taking the jacket from him*): Why don't you go down to the place tomorrow and tell Howard you've simply got to work in New York? You're too accommodating, dear.

WILLY: If old man Wagner was alive I'd a been in charge of New York now! That man was a prince, he was a masterful man. But that boy of his, that Howard, he don't appreciate. When I went north the first time, the Wagner Company didn't know where New England was!

LINDA: Why don't you tell those things to Howard, dear?

WILLY (*encouraged*): I will, I definitely will. Is there any cheese?

LINDA: I'll make you a sandwich.

WILLY: No, go to sleep. I'll take some milk. I'll be up right away. The boys in?

LINDA: They're sleeping. Happy took Biff on a date tonight.

WILLY (*interested*): That so?

LINDA: It was so nice to see them shaving together, one behind the other, in the bathroom. And going out together. You notice? The whole house smells of shaving lotion.

WILLY: Figure it out. Work a lifetime to pay off a house. You finally own it, and there's nobody to live in it.

LINDA: Well, dear, life is a casting off. It's always that way.

WILLY: No, no, some people — some people accomplish something. Did Biff say anything after I went this morning?

LINDA: You shouldn't have criticized him, Willy, especially after he just got off the train. You mustn't lose your temper with him.

WILLY: When the hell did I lose my temper? I simply asked him if he was making any money. Is that a criticism?

LINDA: But, dear, how could he make any money?

WILLY (*worried and angered*): There's such an undercurrent in him. He became a
   moody man. Did he apologize when I left this morning?

LINDA: He was crestfallen, Willy. You know how he admires you. I think if he finds
   himself, then you'll both be happier and not fight any more.

WILLY: How can he find himself on a farm? Is that a life? A farmhand? In the
   beginning, when he was young, I thought, well, a young man, it's good for him
   to tramp around, take a lot of different jobs. But it's more than ten years now and
   he has yet to make thirty-five dollars a week!

LINDA: He's finding himself, Willy.

WILLY: Not finding yourself at the age of thirty-four is a disgrace!

LINDA: Shh!

WILLY: The trouble is he's lazy, goddammit!

LINDA: Willy, please!

WILLY: Biff is a lazy bum!

LINDA: They're sleeping. Get something to eat. Go on down.

WILLY: Why did he come home? I would like to know what brought him home.

LINDA: I don't know. I think he's still lost, Willy. I think he's very lost.

WILLY: Biff Loman is lost. In the greatest country in the world a young man with
   such — personal attractiveness, gets lost. And such a hard worker. There's one
   thing about Biff — he's not lazy.

LINDA: Never.

WILLY (*with pity and resolve*): I'll see him in the morning; I'll have a nice talk with
   him. I'll get him a job selling. He could be big in no time. My God! Remember
   how they used to follow him around in high school? When he smiled at one of
   them their faces lit up. When he walked down the street . . . (*He loses himself in
   reminiscences.*)

LINDA (*trying to bring him out of it*): Willy, dear, I got a new kind of American-type
   cheese today. It's whipped.

WILLY: Why do you get American when I like Swiss?

LINDA: I just thought you'd like a change —

WILLY: I don't want a change! I want Swiss cheese. Why am I always being contra-
   dicted?

LINDA (*with a covering laugh*): I thought it would be a surprise.

WILLY: Why don't you open a window in here, for God's sake?

LINDA (*with infinite patience*): They're all open, dear.

WILLY: The way they boxed us in here. Bricks and windows, windows and bricks.

LINDA: We should've bought the land next door.

WILLY: The street is lined with cars. There's not a breath of fresh air in the neighborhood. The grass don't grow any more, you can't raise a carrot in the back
   yard. They should've had a law against apartment houses. Remember those two
   beautiful elm trees out there? When I and Biff hung the swing between them?

LINDA: Yeah, like being a million miles from the city.

WILLY: They should've arrested the builder for cutting those down. They massacred
   the neighborhood. (*Lost.*) More and more I think of those days, Linda. This time
   of year it was lilac and wisteria. And then the peonies would come out, and the
   daffodils. What fragrance in this room!

LINDA: Well, after all, people had to move somewhere.

WILLY: No, there's more people now.

LINDA: I don't think there's more people. I think —

WILLY: There's more people! That's what's ruining this country! Population is getting out of control. The competition is maddening! Smell the stink from that apartment house! And another one on the other side . . . How can they whip cheese?

(*On* WILLY's *last line,* BIFF *and* HAPPY *raise themselves up in their beds, listening.*)

LINDA: Go down, try it. And be quiet.

WILLY (*turning to* LINDA, *guiltily*): You're not worried about me, are you, sweetheart?

BIFF: What's the matter?

HAPPY: Listen!

LINDA: You've got too much on the ball to worry about.

WILLY: You're my foundation and my support, Linda.

LINDA: Just try to relax, dear. You make mountains out of molehills.

WILLY: I won't fight with him any more. If he wants to go back to Texas, let him go.

LINDA: He'll find his way.

WILLY: Sure. Certain men just don't get started till later in life. Like Thomas Edison, I think. Or B. F. Goodrich. One of them was deaf. (*He starts for the bedroom doorway.*) I'll put my money on Biff.

LINDA: And Willy — if it's warm Sunday we'll drive in the country. And we'll open the windshield, and take lunch.

WILLY: No, the windshields don't open on the new cars.

LINDA: But you opened it today.

WILLY: Me? I didn't. (*He stops.*) Now isn't that peculiar! Isn't that a remarkable — (*He breaks off in amazement and fright as the flute is heard distantly.*)

LINDA: What, darling?

WILLY: That is the most remarkable thing.

LINDA: What, dear?

WILLY: I was thinking of the Chevvy. (*Slight pause.*) Nineteen twenty-eight . . . when I had that red Chevvy — (*Breaks off.*) That funny? I coulda sworn I was driving that Chevvy today.

LINDA: Well, that's nothing. Something must've reminded you.

WILLY: Remarkable. Ts. Remember those days? The way Biff used to simonize that car? The dealer refused to believe there was eighty thousand miles on it. (*He shakes his head.*) Heh! (*To* LINDA.) Close your eyes, I'll be right up. (*He walks out of the bedroom.*)

HAPPY (*to* BIFF): Jesus, maybe he smashed up the car again!

LINDA (*calling after* WILLY): Be careful on the stairs, dear! The cheese is on the middle shelf! (*She turns, goes over to the bed, takes his jacket, and goes out of the bedroom.*)

(*Light has risen on the boys' room. Unseen,* WILLY *is heard talking to himself, "Eighty thousand miles," and a little laugh.* BIFF *gets out of bed, comes downstage a bit, and stands attentively.* BIFF *is two years older than his brother* HAPPY, *well built, but in these days bears a worn air and seems less self-assured. He has succeeded less, and his dreams are stronger and less acceptable than* HAPPY's. HAPPY *is tall, powerfully made. Sexuality is like a visible color on him, or a scent that many women have discovered. He, like his brother, is lost, but in a different way, for he has never allowed himself to turn his face toward de-*

feat and is thus more confused and hard-skinned, although seemingly more content.)

HAPPY (*getting out of bed*): He's going to get his license taken away if he keeps that up. I'm getting nervous about him, y'know, Biff?

BIFF: His eyes are going.

HAPPY: No, I've driven with him. He sees all right. He just doesn't keep his mind on it. I drove into the city with him last week. He stops at a green light and then it turns red and he goes. (*He laughs.*)

BIFF: Maybe he's color-blind.

HAPPY: Pop? Why he's got the finest eye for color in the business. You know that.

BIFF (*sitting down on his bed*): I'm going to sleep.

HAPPY: You're not still sour on Dad, are you, Biff?

BIFF: He's all right, I guess.

WILLY (*underneath them, in the living room*): Yes, sir, eighty thousand miles — eighty-two thousand!

BIFF: You smoking?

HAPPY (*holding out a pack of cigarettes*): Want one?

BIFF (*taking a cigarette*): I can never sleep when I smell it.

WILLY: What a simonizing job, heh!

HAPPY (*with deep sentiment*): Funny, Biff, y'know? Us sleeping in here again? The old beds. (*He pats his bed affectionately.*) All the talk that went across those two beds, huh? Our whole lives.

BIFF: Yeah. Lotta dreams and plans.

HAPPY (*with a deep and masculine laugh*): About five hundred women would like to know what was said in this room.

(*They share a soft laugh.*)

BIFF: Remember that big Betsy something — what the hell was her name — over on Bushwick Avenue?

HAPPY (*combing his hair*): With the collie dog!

BIFF: That's the one. I got you in there, remember?

HAPPY: Yeah, that was my first time — I think. Boy, there was a pig! (*They laugh, almost crudely.*) You taught me everything I know about women. Don't forget that.

BIFF: I bet you forgot how bashful you used to be. Especially with girls.

HAPPY: Oh, I still am, Biff.

BIFF: Oh, go on.

HAPPY: I just control it, that's all. I think I got less bashful and you got more so. What happened, Biff? Where's the old humor, the old confidence? (*He shakes BIFF's knee. BIFF gets up and moves restlessly about the room.*) What's the matter?

BIFF: Why does Dad mock me all the time?

HAPPY: He's not mocking you, he —

BIFF: Everything I say there's a twist of mockery on his face. I can't get near him.

HAPPY: He just wants you to make good, that's all. I wanted to talk to you about Dad for a long time, Biff. Something's — happening to him. He — talks to himself.

BIFF: I noticed that this morning. But he always mumbled.

HAPPY: But not so noticeable. It got so embarrassing I sent him to Florida. And you know something? Most of the time he's talking to you.

BIFF: What's he say about me?

HAPPY: I can't make it out.

BIFF: What's he say about me?

HAPPY: I think the fact that you're not settled, that you're still kind of up in the air . . .

BIFF: There's one or two other things depressing him, Happy.

HAPPY: What do you mean?

BIFF: Never mind. Just don't lay it all to me.

HAPPY: But I think if you just got started — I mean — is there any future for you out there?

BIFF: I tell ya, Hap, I don't know what the future is. I don't know — what I'm supposed to want.

HAPPY: What do you mean?

BIFF: Well, I spent six or seven years after high school trying to work myself up. Shipping clerk, salesman, business of one kind or another. And it's a measly manner of existence. To get on that subway on the hot mornings in summer. To devote your whole life to keeping stock, or making phone calls, or selling or buying. To suffer fifty weeks of the year for the sake of a two-week vacation, when all you really desire is to be outdoors, with your shirt off. And always to have to get ahead of the next fella. And still — that's how you build a future.

HAPPY: Well, you really enjoy it on a farm? Are you content out there?

BIFF (*with rising agitation*): Hap, I've had twenty or thirty different kinds of jobs since I left home before the war, and it always turns out the same. I just realized it lately. In Nebraska when I herded cattle, and the Dakotas, and Arizona, and now in Texas. It's why I came home now, I guess, because I realized it. This farm I work on, it's spring there now, see? And they've got about fifteen new colts. There's nothing more inspiring or — beautiful than the sight of a mare and a new colt. And it's cool there now, see? Texas is cool now, and it's spring. And whenever spring comes to where I am, I suddenly get the feeling, my God, I'm not gettin' anywhere! What the hell am I doing, playing around with horses, twenty-eight dollars a week! I'm thirty-four years old, I oughta be makin' my future. That's when I come running home. And now, I get here, and I don't know what to do with myself. (*After a pause.*) I've always made a point of not wasting my life, and everytime I come back here I know that all I've done is to waste my life.

HAPPY: You're a poet, you know that, Biff? You're a — you're an idealist!

BIFF: No, I'm mixed up very bad. Maybe I oughta get married. Maybe I oughta get stuck into something. Maybe that's my trouble. I'm like a boy. I'm not married, I'm not in business, I just — I'm like a boy. Are you content, Hap? You're a success, aren't you? Are you content?

HAPPY: Hell, no!

BIFF: Why? You're making money, aren't you?

HAPPY (*moving about with energy, expressiveness*): All I can do now is wait for the merchandise manager to die. And suppose I get to be merchandise manager? He's a good friend of mine, and he just built a terrific estate on Long Island. And he lived there about two months and sold it, and now he's building another one. He can't enjoy it once it's finished. And I know that's just what I would do. I don't know what the hell I'm workin' for. Sometimes I sit in my apartment — all alone. And I think of the rent I'm paying. And it's crazy. But then, it's what I always wanted. My own apartment, a car, and plenty of women. And still, god-dammit, I'm lonely.

BIFF (*with enthusiasm*): Listen, why don't you come out West with me?

HAPPY: You and I, heh?

BIFF: Sure, maybe we could buy a ranch. Raise cattle, use our muscles. Men built like we are should be working out in the open.

HAPPY (*avidly*): The Loman Brothers, heh?

BIFF (*with vast affection*): Sure, we'd be known all over the counties!

HAPPY (*enthralled*): That's what I dream about, Biff. Sometimes I want to just rip my clothes off in the middle of the store and outbox that goddam merchandise manager. I mean I can outbox, outrun, and outlift anybody in that store, and I have to take orders from those common, petty sons-of-bitches till I can't stand it any more.

BIFF: I'm tellin' you, kid, if you were with me I'd be happy out there.

HAPPY (*enthused*): See, Biff, everybody around me is so false that I'm constantly lowering my ideals . . .

BIFF: Baby, together we'd stand up for one another, we'd have someone to trust.

HAPPY: If I were around you —

BIFF: Hap, the trouble is we weren't brought up to grub for money. I don't know how to do it.

HAPPY: Neither can I!

BIFF: Then let's go!

HAPPY: The only thing is — what can you make out there?

BIFF: But look at your friend. Builds an estate and then hasn't the peace of mind to live in it.

HAPPY: Yeah, but when he walks into the store the waves part in front of him. That's fifty-two thousand dollars a year coming through the revolving door, and I got more in my pinky finger than he's got in his head.

BIFF: Yeah, but you just said —

HAPPY: I gotta show some of those pompous, self-important executives over there that Hap Loman can make the grade. I want to walk into the store the way he walks in. Then I'll go with you, Biff. We'll be together yet, I swear. But take those two we had tonight. Now weren't they gorgeous creatures?

BIFF: Yeah, yeah, most gorgeous I've had in years.

HAPPY: I get that any time I want, Biff. Whenever I feel digusted. The only trouble is, it gets like bowling or something. I just keep knockin' them over and it doesn't mean anything. You still run around a lot?

BIFF: Naa. I'd like to find a girl — steady, somebody with substance.

HAPPY: That's what I long for.

BIFF: Go on! You'd never come home.

HAPPY: I would! Somebody with character, with resistance! Like Mom, y'know? You're gonna call me a bastard when I tell you this. That girl Charlotte I was with tonight is engaged to be married in five weeks. (*He tries on his new hat.*)

BIFF: No kiddin'!

HAPPY: Sure, the guy's in line for the vice-presidency of the store. I don't know what gets into me, maybe I just have an overdeveloped sense of competition or some-thing, but I went and ruined her, and furthermore I can't get rid of her. And he's the third executive I've done that to. Isn't that a crummy characteristic? And to top it all, I go to their weddings! (*Indignantly, but laughing.*) Like I'm not supposed to take bribes. Manufacturers offer me a hundred dollar bill now and then to throw an order their way. You know how honest I am, but it's like this girl, see. I hate myself for it. Because I don't want the girl, and, still, I take it and — I love it!

BIFF: Let's go to sleep.

HAPPY: I guess we didn't settle anything, heh?

BIFF: I just got one idea that I think I'm going to try.

HAPPY: What's that?

BIFF: Remember Bill Oliver?

HAPPY: Sure, Oliver is very big now. You want to work for him again?

BIFF: No, but when I quit he said something to me. He put his arm on my shoulder, and he said, "Biff, if you ever need anything, come to me."

HAPPY: I remember that. That sounds good.

BIFF: I think I'll go to see him. If I could get ten thousand or even seven or eight thousand dollars I could buy a beautiful ranch.

HAPPY: I bet he'd back you. 'Cause he thought highly of you, Biff. I mean, they all do. You're well liked, Biff. That's why I say to come back here, and we both have the apartment. And I'm tellin' you, Biff, any babe you want . . .

BIFF: No, with a ranch I could do the work I like and still be something. I just wonder though. I wonder if Oliver still thinks I stole that carton of basketballs.

HAPPY: Oh, he probably forgot that long ago. It's almost ten years. You're too sensitive. Anyway, he didn't really fire you.

BIFF: Well, I think he was going to. I think that's why I quit. I was never sure whether he knew or not. I know he thought the world of me, though. I was the only one he'd let lock up the place.

WILLY (*below*): You gonna wash the engine, Biff?

HAPPY: Shh!

(BIFF *looks at* HAPPY, *who is gazing down, listening.* WILLY *is mumbling in the parlor.*)

HAPPY: You hear that?

(*They listen.* WILLY *laughs warmly.*)

BIFF (*growing angry*): Doesn't he know Mom can hear that?

WILLY: Don't get your sweater dirty, Biff!

(*A look of pain crosses* BIFF's *face.*)

HAPPY: Isn't that terrible? Don't leave again, will you? You'll find a job here. You gotta stick around. I don't know what to do about him, it's getting embarrassing.

WILLY: What a simonizing job!

BIFF: Mom's hearing that!

WILLY: No kiddin', Biff, you got a date? Wonderful!

HAPPY: Go on to sleep. But talk to him in the morning, will you?

BIFF (*reluctantly getting into bed*): With her in the house. Brother!

HAPPY (*getting into bed*): I wish you'd have a good talk with him.

(*The light on their room begins to fade.*)

BIFF (*to himself in bed*): That selfish, stupid . . .

HAPPY: Sh . . . Sleep, Biff.

(*Their light is out. Well before they have finished speaking,* WILLY's *form is dimly seen below in the darkened kitchen. He opens the refrigerator, searches in there, and takes out a bottle of milk. The apartment houses are fading out, and the entire house and surroundings become covered with leaves. Music insinuates itself as the leaves appear.*)

WILLY: Just wanna be careful with those girls, Biff, that's all. Don't make any promises. No promises of any kind. Because a girl, y'know, they always believe what you tell 'em, and you're very young. Biff, you're too young to be talking seriously to girls.

(*Light rises on the kitchen.* WILLY, *talking, shuts the refrigerator door and comes downstage to the kitchen table. He pours milk into a glass. He is totally immersed in himself, smiling faintly.*)

WILLY: Too young entirely, Biff. You want to watch your schooling first. Then when you're all set, there'll be plenty of girls for a boy like you. (*He smiles broadly at a kitchen chair.*) That so? The girls pay for you? (*He laughs.*) Boy, you must really be makin' a hit.

(WILLY *is gradually addressing — physically — a point offstage, speaking through the wall of the kitchen, and his voice has been rising in volume to that of a normal conversation.*)

WILLY: I been wondering why you polish the car so careful. Ha! Don't leave the hubcaps, boys. Get the chamois to the hubcaps. Happy, use newspaper on the windows, it's the easiest thing. Show him how to do it, Biff! You see, Happy? Pad it up, use it like a pad. That's it, that's it, good work. You're doin' all right, Hap. (*He pauses, then nods in approbation for a few seconds, then looks upward.*) Biff, first thing we gotta do when we get time is clip that big branch over the house. Afraid it's gonna fall in a storm and hit the roof. Tell you what. We get a rope and sling her around, and then we climb up there with a couple of saws and take her down. Soon as you finish the car, boys, I wanna see ya. I got a surprise for you, boys.
BIFF (*offstage*): Whatta ya got, Dad?
WILLY: No, you finish first. Never leave a job till you're finished — remember that. (*Looking toward the "big trees."*) Biff, up in Albany I saw a beautiful hammock. I think I'll buy it next trip, and we'll hang it right between those two elms. Wouldn't that be something? Just swingin' there under those branches. Boy, that would be . . .

(YOUNG BIFF *and* YOUNG HAPPY *appear from the direction* WILLY *was addressing.* HAPPY *carries rags and a pail of water.* BIFF, *wearing a sweater with a block* "S," *carries a football.*)

BIFF (*pointing in the direction of the car offstage*): How's that, Pop, professional?
WILLY: Terrific. Terrific job, boys. Good work, Biff.
HAPPY: Where's the surprise, Pop?
WILLY: In the back seat of the car.
HAPPY: Boy! (*He runs off.*)
BIFF: What is it, Dad? Tell me, what'd you buy?
WILLY (*laughing, cuffs him*): Never mind, something I want you to have.

BIFF (*turns and starts off*): What is it, Hap?

HAPPY (*offstage*): It's a punching bag!

BIFF: Oh, Pop!

WILLY: It's got Gene Tunney's signature on it!

(HAPPY *runs onstage with a punching bag.*)

BIFF: Gee, how'd you know we wanted a punching bag?

WILLY: Well, it's the finest thing for the timing.

HAPPY (*lies down on his back and pedals with his feet*): I'm losing weight, you notice, Pop?

WILLY (*to* HAPPY): Jumping rope is good too.

BIFF: Did you see the new football I got?

WILLY (*examining the ball*): Where'd you get a new ball?

BIFF: The coach told me to practice my passing.

WILLY: That so? And he gave you the ball, heh?

BIFF: Well, I borrowed it from the locker room. (*He laughs confidentially.*)

WILLY (*laughing with him at the theft*): I want you to return that.

HAPPY: I told you he wouldn't like it!

BIFF (*angrily*): Well, I'm bringing it back!

WILLY (*stopping the incipient argument, to* HAPPY): Sure, he's gotta practice with a regulation ball, doesn't he? (*To* BIFF.) Coach'll probably congratulate you on your initiative!

BIFF: Oh, he keeps congratulating my initiative all the time, Pop.

WILLY: That's because he likes you. If somebody else took that ball there'd be an uproar. So what's the report, boys, what's the report?

BIFF: Where'd you go this time, Dad? Gee we were lonesome for you.

WILLY (*pleased, puts an arm around each boy and they come down to the apron*): Lonesome, heh?

BIFF: Missed you every minute.

WILLY: Don't say? Tell you a secret, boys. Don't breathe it to a soul. Someday I'll have my own business, and I'll never have to leave home any more.

HAPPY: Like Uncle Charley, heh?

WILLY: Bigger than Uncle Charley! Because Charley is not — liked. He's liked, but he's not — well liked.

BIFF: Where'd you go this time, Dad?

WILLY: Well, I got on the road, and I went north to Providence. Met the Mayor.

BIFF: The Mayor of Providence!

WILLY: He was sitting in the hotel lobby.

BIFF: What'd he say?

WILLY: He said, "Morning!" And I said, "You got a fine city here, Mayor." And then he had coffee with me. And then I went to Waterbury. Waterbury is a fine city. Big clock city, the famous Waterbury clock. Sold a nice bill there. And then Boston — Boston is the cradle of the Revolution. A fine city. And a couple of other towns in Mass., and on to Portland and Bangor and straight home!

BIFF: Gee, I'd love to go with you sometime, Dad.

WILLY: Soon as summer comes.

HAPPY: Promise?

WILLY: You and Hap and I, and I'll show you all the towns. America is full of beautiful towns and fine, upstanding people. And they know me, boys, they know me up and down New England. The finest people. And when I bring you fellas up, there'll be open sesame for all of us, 'cause one thing, boys: I have friends. I can park my car in any street in New England, and the cops protect it like their own. This summer, heh?

BIFF AND HAPPY (*together*): Yeah! You bet!

WILLY: We'll take our bathing suits.

HAPPY: We'll carry your bags, Pop!

WILLY: Oh, won't that be something! Me comin' into the Boston stores with you boys carryin' my bags. What a sensation!

(BIFF *is prancing around, practicing passing the ball*.)

WILLY: You nervous, Biff, about the game?

BIFF: Not if you're gonna be there.

WILLY: What do they say about you in school, now that they made you captain?

HAPPY: There's a crowd of girls behind him everytime the classes change.

BIFF (*taking* WILLY'S *hand*): This Saturday, Pop, this Saturday — just for you, I'm going to break through for a touchdown.

HAPPY: You're supposed to pass.

BIFF: I'm takin' one play for Pop. You watch me, Pop, and when I take off my helmet, that means I'm breakin' out. Then you watch me crash through that line!

WILLY (*kisses* BIFF): Oh, wait'll I tell this in Boston!

(BERNARD *enters in knickers. He is younger than* BIFF, *earnest and loyal, a worried boy*.)

BERNARD: Biff, where are you? You're supposed to study with me today.

WILLY: Hey, looka Bernard. What're you lookin' so anemic about, Bernard?

BERNARD: He's gotta study, Uncle Willy. He's got Regents next week.

HAPPY (*tauntingly, spinning* BERNARD *around*): Let's box, Bernard!

BERNARD: Biff! (*He gets away from* HAPPY.) Listen, Biff, I heard Mr. Birnbaum say that if you don't start studyin' math he's gonna flunk you, and you won't graduate. I heard him!

WILLY: You better study with him, Biff. Go ahead now.

BERNARD: I heard him!

BIFF: Oh, Pop, you didn't see my sneakers! (*He holds up a foot for* WILLY *to look at*.)

WILLY: Hey, that's a beautiful job of printing!

BERNARD (*wiping his glasses*): Just because he printed University of Virginia on his sneakers doesn't mean they've got to graduate him, Uncle Willy!

WILLY (*angrily*): What're you talking about? With scholarships to three universities they're gonna flunk him?

BERNARD: But I heard Mr. Birnbaum say —

WILLY: Don't be a pest, Bernard! (*To his boys*.) What an anemic!

BERNARD: Okay, I'm waiting for you in my house, Biff.

(BERNARD *goes off*. THE LOMANS *laugh*.)

WILLY: Bernard is not well liked, is he?

BIFF: He's liked, but he's not well liked.

HAPPY: That's right, Pop.

WILLY: That's just what I mean. Bernard can get the best marks in school, y'understand, but when he gets out in the business world, y'understand, you are going to be five times ahead of him. That's why I thank Almighty God you're both built like Adonises. Because the man who makes an appearance in the business world, the man who creates personal interest, is the man who gets ahead. Be liked and you will never want. You take me, for instance. I never have to wait in line to see a buyer. "Willy Loman is here!" That's all they have to know, and I go right through.

BIFF: Did you knock them dead, Pop?

WILLY: Knocked 'em cold in Providence, slaughtered 'em in Boston.

HAPPY (*on his back, pedaling again*): I'm losing weight, you notice, Pop?

(LINDA *enters, as of old, a ribbon in her hair, carrying a basket of washing.*)

LINDA (*with youthful energy*): Hello, dear!

WILLY: Sweetheart!

LINDA: How'd the Chevvy run?

WILLY: Chevrolet, Linda, is the greatest car ever built. (*To the boys.*) Since when do you let your mother carry wash up the stairs?

BIFF: Grab hold there, boy!

HAPPY: Where to, Mom?

LINDA: Hang them up on the line. And you better go down to your friends, Biff. The cellar is full of boys. They don't know what to do with themselves.

BIFF: Ah, when Pop comes home they can wait!

WILLY (*laughs appreciatively*): You better go down and tell them what to do, Biff.

BIFF: I think I'll have them sweep out the furnace room.

WILLY: Good work, Biff.

BIFF (*goes through wall-line of kitchen to doorway at back and calls down*): Fellas! Everybody sweep out the furnace room! I'll be right down!

VOICES: All right! Okay, Biff.

BIFF: George and Sam and Frank, come out back! We're hangin' up the wash! Come on, Hap, on the double! (*He and* HAPPY *carry out the basket.*)

LINDA: The way they obey him!

WILLY: Well, that's training, the training. I'm tellin' you, I was sellin' thousands and thousands, but I had to come home.

LINDA: Oh, the whole block'll be at that game. Did you sell anything?

WILLY: I did five hundred gross in Providence and seven hundred gross in Boston.

LINDA: No! Wait a minute, I've got a pencil. (*She pulls pencil and paper out of her apron pocket.*) That makes your commission . . . Two hundred — my God! Two hundred and twelve dollars!

WILLY: Well, I didn't figure it yet, but . . .

LINDA: How much did you do?

WILLY: Well, I — I did — about a hundred and eighty gross in Providence. Well, no — it came to — roughly two hundred gross on the whole trip.

LINDA (*without hesitation*): Two hundred gross. That's . . . (*She figures.*)

WILLY: The trouble was that three of the stores were half closed for inventory in Boston. Otherwise I woulda broke records.

LINDA: Well, it makes seventy dollars and some pennies. That's very good.

WILLY: What do we owe?

LINDA: Well, on the first there's sixteen dollars on the refrigerator —

WILLY: Why sixteen?

LINDA: Well, the fan belt broke, so it was a dollar eighty.

WILLY: But it's brand new.

LINDA: Well, the man said that's the way it is. Till they work themselves in, y'know.

(*They move through the wall-line into the kitchen.*)

WILLY: I hope we didn't get stuck on that machine.

LINDA: They got the biggest ads of any of them!

WILLY: I know, it's a fine machine. What else?

LINDA: Well, there's nine-sixty for the washing machine. And for the vacuum cleaner there's three and a half due on the fifteenth. Then the roof, you got twenty-one dollars remaining.

WILLY: It don't leak, does it?

LINDA: No, they did a wonderful job. Then you owe Frank for the carburetor.

WILLY: I'm not going to pay that man! That goddam Chevrolet, they ought to pro-hibit the manufacture of that car!

LINDA: Well, you owe him three and a half. And odds and ends, comes to around a hundred and twenty dollars by the fifteenth.

WILLY: A hundred and twenty dollars! My God, if business don't pick up I don't know what I'm gonna do!

LINDA: Well, next week you'll do better.

WILLY: Oh, I'll knock 'em dead next week. I'll go to Hartford. I'm very well liked in Hartford. You know, the trouble is, Linda, people don't seem to take to me.

(*They move onto the forestage.*)

LINDA: Oh, don't be foolish.

WILLY: I know it when I walk in. They seem to laugh at me.

LINDA: Why? Why would they laugh at you? Don't talk that way, Willy.

(WILLY *moves to the edge of the stage.* LINDA *goes into the kitchen and starts to darn stockings.*)

WILLY: I don't know the reason for it, but they just pass me by. I'm not noticed.

LINDA: But you're doing wonderful, dear. You're making seventy to a hundred dol-lars a week.

WILLY: But I gotta be at it ten, twelve hours a day. Other men — I don't know — they do it easier. I don't know why — I can't stop myself — I talk too much. A man oughta come in with a few words. One thing about Charley. He's a man of few words, and they respect him.

LINDA: You don't talk too much, you're just lively.

WILLY (*smiling*): Well, I figure, what the hell, life is short, a couple of jokes. (*To himself.*) I joke too much! (*The smile goes.*)

LINDA: Why? You're —

WILLY: I'm fat. I'm very — foolish to look at, Linda. I didn't tell you, but Christmas time I happened to be calling on F. H. Stewarts, and a salesman I know, as I was going in to see the buyer I heard him say something about — walrus. And I — I cracked him right across the face. I won't take that. I simply will not take that. But they do laugh at me. I know that.

LINDA: Darling . . .

WILLY: I gotta overcome it. I know I gotta overcome it. I'm not dressing to advan-tage, maybe.

LINDA: Willy, darling, you're the handsomest man in the world —

WILLY: Oh, no, Linda.

LINDA: To me you are. (*Slight pause.*) The handsomest.

(From the darkness is heard the laughter of a woman. WILLY doesn't turn to it, but it continues through LINDA's lines.)

LINDA: And the boys, Willy. Few men are idolized by their children the way you are.

(Music is heard as behind a scrim, to the left of the house, THE WOMAN, dimly seen, is dressing.)

WILLY *(with great feeling)*: You're the best there is, Linda, you're a pal, you know that? On the road — on the road I want to grab you sometimes and just kiss the life outa you.

(The laughter is loud now, and he moves into a brightening area at the left, where THE WOMAN has come from behind the scrim and is standing, putting on her hat, looking into a "mirror" and laughing.)

WILLY: 'Cause I get so lonely — especially when business is bad and there's nobody to talk to. I get the feeling that I'll never sell anything again, that I won't make a living for you, or a business, a business for the boys. *(He talks through THE WOMAN's subsiding laughter; THE WOMAN primps at the "mirror.")* There's so much I want to make for —

THE WOMAN: Me? You didn't make me, Willy. I picked you.

WILLY *(pleased)*: You picked me?

THE WOMAN *(who is quite proper-looking, WILLY's age)*: I did. I've been sitting at that desk watching all the salesmen go by, day in, day out. But you've got such a sense of humor, and we do have such a good time together, don't we?

WILLY: Sure, sure. *(He takes her in his arms.)* Why do you have to go now?

THE WOMAN: It's two o'clock . . .

WILLY: No, come on in! *(He pulls her.)*

THE WOMAN: . . . my sisters'll be scandalized. When'll you be back?

WILLY: Oh, two weeks about. Will you come up again?

THE WOMAN: Sure thing. You do make me laugh. It's good for me. *(She squeezes his arm, kisses him.)* And I think you're a wonderful man.

WILLY: You picked me, heh?

THE WOMAN: Sure. Because you're so sweet. And such a kidder.

WILLY: Well, I'll see you next time I'm in Boston.

THE WOMAN: I'll put you right through to the buyers.

WILLY *(slapping her bottom)*: Right. Well, bottoms up!

THE WOMAN *(slaps him gently and laughs)*: You just kill me, Willy. *(He suddenly grabs her and kisses her roughly.)* You kill me. And thanks for the stockings. I love a lot of stockings. Well, good night.

WILLY: Good night. And keep your pores open!

THE WOMAN: Oh, Willy!

(THE WOMAN bursts out laughing, and LINDA's laughter blends in. THE WOMAN disappears into the dark. Now the area at the kitchen table brightens. LINDA is sitting where she was at the kitchen table, but now is mending a pair of her silk stockings.)

LINDA: You are, Willy. The handsomest man. You've got no reason to feel that —

WILLY *(coming out of THE WOMAN's dimming area and going over to LINDA)*: I'll make it all up to you, Linda, I'll —

LINDA: There's nothing to make up, dear. You're doing fine, better than —
WILLY (*noticing her mending*): What's that?
LINDA: Just mending my stockings. They're so expensive —
WILLY (*angrily, taking them from her*): I won't have you mending stockings in this house! Now throw them out!

(LINDA *puts the stockings in her pocket.*)

BERNARD (*entering on the run*): Where is he? If he doesn't study!
WILLY (*moving to the forestage, with great agitation*): You'll give him the answers!
BERNARD: I do, but I can't on a Regents! That's a state exam! They're liable to arrest me!
WILLY: Where is he? I'll whip him, I'll whip him!
LINDA: And he'd better give back that football, Willy, it's not nice.
WILLY: Biff! Where is he? Why is he taking everything?
LINDA: He's too rough with the girls, Willy. All the mothers are afraid of him!
WILLY: I'll whip him!
BERNARD: He's driving the car without a license!

(THE WOMAN's *laugh is heard.*)

WILLY: Shut up!
LINDA: All the mothers —
WILLY: Shut up!
BERNARD (*backing quietly away and out*): Mr. Birnbaum says he's stuck up.
WILLY: Get outa here!
BERNARD: If he doesn't buckle down he'll flunk math! (*He goes off.*)
LINDA: He's right, Willy, you've gotta —
WILLY (*exploding at her*): There's nothing the matter with him! You want him to be a worm like Bernard? He's got spirit, personality . . .

(*As he speaks,* LINDA, *almost in tears, exits into the living-room.* WILLY *is alone in the kitchen, wilting and staring. The leaves are gone. It is night again, and the apartment houses look down from behind.*)

WILLY: Loaded with it. Loaded! What is he stealing? He's giving it back, isn't he? Why is he stealing? What did I tell him? I never in my life told him anything but decent things.

(HAPPY *in pajamas has come down the stairs;* WILLY *suddenly becomes aware of* HAPPY's *presence.*)

HAPPY: Let's go now, come on.
WILLY (*sitting down at the kitchen table*): Huh! Why did she have to wax the floors herself? Everytime she waxes the floors she keels over. She knows that!
HAPPY: Shh! Take it easy. What brought you back tonight?
WILLY: I got an awful scare. Nearly hit a kid in Yonkers. God! Why didn't I go to Alaska with my brother Ben that time! Ben! That man was a genius, that man was success incarnate! What a mistake! He begged me to go.
HAPPY: Well, there's no use in —
WILLY: You guys! There was a man started with the clothes on his back and ended up with diamond mines!
HAPPY: Boy, someday I'd like to know how he did it.
WILLY: What's the mystery? The man knew what he wanted and went out and got it!

Walked into a jungle, and comes out, the age of twenty-one, and he's rich! The world is an oyster, but you don't crack it open on a mattress!

HAPPY: Pop, I told you I'm gonna retire you for life.

WILLY: You'll retire me for life on seventy goddam dollars a week? And your women and your car and your apartment, and you'll retire me for life! Christ's sake, I couldn't get past Yonkers today! Where are you guys, where are you? The woods are burning! I can't drive a car!

(CHARLEY *has appeared in the doorway. He is a large man, slow of speech, laconic, immovable. In all he says, despite what he says, there is pity, and, now, trepidation. He has a robe over pajamas, slippers on his feet. He enters the kitchen.*)

CHARLEY: Everything all right?

HAPPY: Yeah, Charley, everything's . . .

WILLY: What's the matter?

CHARLEY: I heard some noise. I thought something happened. Can't we do something about the walls? You sneeze in here, and in my house hats blow off.

HAPPY: Let's go to bed, Dad. Come on.

(CHARLEY *signals to* HAPPY *to go.*)

WILLY: You go ahead, I'm not tired at the moment.

HAPPY (*to* WILLY): Take it easy, huh? (*He exits.*)

WILLY: What're you doin' up?

CHARLEY (*sitting down at the kitchen table opposite* WILLY): Couldn't sleep good. I had a heartburn.

WILLY: Well, you don't know how to eat.

CHARLEY: I eat with my mouth.

WILLY: No, you're ignorant. You gotta know about vitamins and things like that.

CHARLEY: Come on, let's shoot. Tire you out a little.

WILLY (*hesitantly*): All right. You got cards?

CHARLEY (*taking a deck from his pocket*): Yeah, I got them. Someplace. What is it with those vitamins?

WILLY (*dealing*): They build up your bones. Chemistry.

CHARLEY: Yeah, but there's no bones in a heartburn.

WILLY: What are you talkin' about? Do you know the first thing about it?

CHARLEY: Don't get insulted.

WILLY: Don't talk about something you don't know anything about.

(*They are playing. Pause.*)

CHARLEY: What're you doin' home?

WILLY: A little trouble with the car.

CHARLEY: Oh. (*Pause.*) I'd like to take a trip to California.

WILLY: Don't say.

CHARLEY: You want a job?

WILLY: I got a job, I told you that. (*After a slight pause.*) What the hell are you offering me a job for?

CHARLEY: Don't get insulted.

WILLY: Don't insult me.

CHARLEY: I don't see no sense in it. You don't have to go on this way.

WILLY: I got a good job. (*Slight pause.*) What do you keep comin' in here for?

CHARLEY: You want me to go?

WILLY (*after a pause, withering*): I can't understand it. He's going back to Texas again. What the hell is that?

CHARLEY: Let him go.

WILLY: I got nothin' to give him, Charley, I'm clean, I'm clean.

CHARLEY: He won't starve. None a them starve. Forget about him.

WILLY: Then what have I got to remember?

CHARLEY: You take it too hard. To hell with it. When a deposit bottle is broken you don't get your nickel back.

WILLY: That's easy enough for you to say.

CHARLEY: That ain't easy for me to say.

WILLY: Did you see the ceiling I put up in the living-room?

CHARLEY: Yeah, that's a piece of work. To put up a ceiling is a mystery to me. How do you do it?

WILLY: What's the difference?

CHARLEY: Well, talk about it.

WILLY: You gonna put up a ceiling?

CHARLEY: How could I put up a ceiling?

WILLY: Then what the hell are you bothering me for?

CHARLEY: You're insulted again.

WILLY: A man who can't handle tools is not a man. You're disgusting.

CHARLEY: Don't call me disgusting, Willy.

(UNCLE BEN, *carrying a valise and an umbrella, enters the forestage from around the right corner of the house. He is a stolid man, in his sixties, with a mustache and an authoritative air. He is utterly certain of his destiny, and there is an aura of far places about him. He enters exactly as* WILLY *speaks.*)

WILLY: I'm getting awfully tired, Ben.

(BEN's *music is heard.* BEN *looks around at everything.*)

CHARLEY: Good, keep playing; you'll sleep better. Did you call me Ben?

(BEN *looks at his watch.*)

WILLY: That's funny. For a second there you reminded me of my brother Ben.

BEN: I only have a few minutes. (*He strolls, inspecting the place.* WILLY *and* CHARLEY *continue playing.*)

CHARLEY: You never heard from him again, heh? Since that time?

WILLY: Didn't Linda tell you? Couple of weeks ago we got a letter from his wife in Africa. He died.

CHARLEY: That so.

BEN (*chuckling*): So this is Brooklyn, eh?

CHARLEY: Maybe you're in for some of his money.

WILLY: Naa, he had seven sons. There's just one opportunity I had with that man . . .

BEN: I must make a train, William. There are several properties I'm looking at in Alaska.

WILLY: Sure, sure! If I'd gone with him to Alaska that time, everything would've been totally different.

CHARLEY: Go on, you'd froze to death up there.

WILLY: What're you talking about?

BEN: Opportunity is tremendous in Alaska, William. Surprised you're not up there.

WILLY: Sure, tremendous.

CHARLEY: Heh?

WILLY: There was the only man I ever met who knew the answers.

CHARLEY: Who?

BEN: How are you all?

WILLY (*taking a pot, smiling*): Fine, fine.

CHARLEY: Pretty sharp tonight.

BEN: Is Mother living with you?

WILLY: No, she died a long time ago.

CHARLEY: Who?

BEN: That's too bad. Fine specimen of a lady, Mother.

WILLY (*to* CHARLEY): Heh?

BEN: I'd hoped to see the old girl.

CHARLEY: Who died?

BEN: Heard anything from Father, have you?

WILLY (*unnerved*): What do you mean, who died?

CHARLEY (*taking a pot*): What're you talkin' about?

BEN (*looking at his watch*): William, it's half-past eight!

WILLY (*as though to dispel his confusion he angrily stops* CHARLEY's *hand*): That's my build!

CHARLEY: I put the ace —

WILLY: If you don't know how to play the game I'm not gonna throw my money away on you!

CHARLEY (*rising*): It was my ace, for God's sake!

WILLY: I'm through, I'm through!

BEN: When did Mother die?

WILLY: Long ago. Since the beginning you never knew how to play cards.

CHARLEY (*picks up the cards and goes to the door*): All right! Next time I'll bring a deck with five aces.

WILLY: I don't play that kind of game!

CHARLEY (*turning to him*): You ought to be ashamed of yourself!

WILLY: Yeah?

CHARLEY: Yeah! (*He goes out.*)

WILLY (*slamming the door after him*): Ignoramus!

BEN (*as* WILLY *comes toward him through the wall-line of the kitchen*): So you're William.

WILLY (*shaking* BEN's *hand*): Ben! I've been waiting for you so long! What's the answer? How did you do it?

BEN: Oh, there's a story in that.

(LINDA *enters the forestage, as of old, carrying the wash basket.*)

LINDA: Is this Ben?

BEN (*gallantly*): How do you do, my dear.

LINDA: Where've you been all these years? Willy's always wondered why you —

WILLY (*pulling* BEN *away from her impatiently*): Where is Dad? Didn't you follow him? How did you get started?

BEN: Well, I don't know how much you remember.

WILLY: Well, I was just a baby, of course, only three or four years old —

BEN: Three years and eleven months.

WILLY: What a memory, Ben!

BEN: I have many enterprises, William, and I have never kept books.

WILLY: I remember I was sitting under the wagon in — was it Nebraska?

BEN: It was South Dakota, and I gave you a bunch of wild flowers.

WILLY: I remember you walking away down some open road.

BEN (*laughing*): I was going to find Father in Alaska.

WILLY: Where is he?

BEN: At that age I had a very faulty view of geography, William. I discovered after a few days that I was heading due south, so instead of Alaska, I ended up in Africa.

LINDA: Africa!

WILLY: The Gold Coast!

BEN: Principally diamond mines.

LINDA: Diamond mines!

BEN: Yes, my dear. But I've only a few minutes —

WILLY: No! Boys! Boys! (YOUNG BIFF *and* HAPPY *appear*.) Listen to this. This is your Uncle Ben, a great man! Tell my boys, Ben!

BEN: Why, boys, when I was seventeen I walked into the jungle, and when I was twenty-one I walked out. (*He laughs*.) And by God I was rich.

WILLY (*to the boys*): You see what I been talking about? The greatest things can happen!

BEN (*glancing at his watch*): I have an appointment in Ketchikan Tuesday week.

WILLY: No, Ben! Please tell about Dad. I want my boys to hear. I want them to know the kind of stock they spring from. All I remember is a man with a big beard, and I was in Mamma's lap, sitting around a fire, and some kind of high music.

BEN: His flute. He played the flute.

WILLY: Sure, the flute, that's right!

(*New music is heard, a high, rollicking tune*.)

BEN: Father was a very great and a very wild-hearted man. We would start in Boston, and he'd toss the whole family into the wagon, and then he'd drive the team right across the country; through Ohio, and Indiana, Michigan, Illinois, and all the Western states. And we'd stop in the towns and sell the flutes that he'd made on the way. Great inventor, Father. With one gadget he made more in a week than a man like you could make in a lifetime.

WILLY: That's just the way I'm bringing them up, Ben — rugged, well liked, all-around.

BEN: Yeah? (*To* BIFF.) Hit that, boy — hard as you can. (*He pounds his stomach*.)

BIFF: Oh, no, sir!

BEN (*taking boxing stance*): Come on, get to me! (*He laughs*.)

WILLY: Go to it, Biff! Go ahead, show him!

BIFF: Okay! (*He cocks his fists and starts in*.)

LINDA (*to* WILLY): Why must he fight, dear?

BEN (*sparring with* BIFF): Good boy! Good boy!

WILLY: How's that, Ben, heh?

HAPPY: Give him the left, Biff!

LINDA: Why are you fighting?

BEN: Good boy! (*Suddenly comes in, trips* BIFF, *and stands over him, the point of his umbrella poised over* BIFF'*s eye.*)

LINDA: Look out, Biff!

BIFF: Gee!

BEN (*patting* BIFF'*s knee*): Never fight fair with a stranger, boy. You'll never get out of the jungle that way. (*Taking* LINDA'*s hand and bowing.*) It was an honor and a pleasure to meet you, Linda.

LINDA (*withdrawing her hand coldly, frightened*): Have a nice — trip.

BEN (*to* WILLY): And good luck with your — what do you do?

WILLY: Selling.

BEN: Yes. Well . . . (*He raises his hand in farewell to all.*)

WILLY: No, Ben, I don't want you to think . . . (*He takes* BEN'*s arm to show him.*) It's Brooklyn, I know, but we hunt too.

BEN: Really, now.

WILLY: Oh, sure, there's snakes and rabbits and — that's why I moved out here. Why, Biff can fell any one of these trees in no time! Boys! Go right over to where they're building the apartment house and get some sand. We're gonna rebuild the entire front stoop right now! Watch this, Ben!

BIFF: Yes, sir! On the double, Hap!

HAPPY (*as he and* BIFF *run off*): I lost weight, Pop, you notice?

(CHARLEY *enters in knickers, even before the boys are gone.*)

CHARLEY: Listen, if they steal any more from that building the watchman'll put the cops on them!

LINDA (*to* WILLY): Don't let Biff . . .

(BEN *laughs lustily.*)

WILLY: You shoulda seen the lumber they brought home last week. At least a dozen six-by-tens worth all kinds a money.

CHARLEY: Listen, if that watchman —

WILLY: I gave them hell, understand. But I got a couple of fearless characters there.

CHARLEY: Willy, the jails are full of fearless characters.

BEN (*clapping* WILLY *on the back, with a laugh at* CHARLEY): And the stock exchange, friend!

WILLY (*joining in* BEN'*s laughter*): Where are the rest of your pants?

CHARLEY: My wife bought them.

WILLY: Now all you need is a golf club and you can go upstairs and go to sleep. (*To* BEN.) Great athlete! Between him and his son Bernard they can't hammer a nail!

BERNARD (*rushing in*): The watchman's chasing Biff!

WILLY (*angrily*): Shut up! He's not stealing anything!

LINDA (*alarmed, hurrying off left*): Where is he? Biff, dear! (*She exits.*)

WILLY (*moving toward the left, away from* BEN): There's nothing wrong. What's the matter with you?

BEN: Nervy boy. Good!

WILLY (*laughing*): Oh, nerves of iron, that Biff!

CHARLEY: Don't know what it is. My New England man comes back and he's bleedin', they murdered him up there.

WILLY: It's contacts, Charley, I got important contacts!

CHARLEY (*sarcastically*): Glad to hear it, Willy. Come in later, we'll shoot a little casino. I'll take some of your Portland money. (*He laughs at* WILLY *and exits.*)

WILLY (*turning to* BEN): Business is bad, it's murderous. But not for me, of course.

BEN: I'll stop by on my way back to Africa.

WILLY (*longingly*): Can't you stay a few days? You're just what I need, Ben, because I — I have a fine position here, but I — well, Dad left when I was such a baby and I never had a chance to talk to him and I still feel — kind of temporary about myself.

BEN: I'll be late for my train.

(*They are at opposite ends of the stage.*)

WILLY: Ben, my boys — can't we talk? They'd go into the jaws of hell for me, see, but I —

BEN: William, you're being first-rate with your boys. Outstanding, manly chaps!

WILLY (*hanging on to his words*): Oh, Ben, that's good to hear! Because sometimes I'm afraid that I'm not teaching them the right kind of — Ben, how should I teach them?

BEN (*giving great weight to each word, and with a certain vicious audacity*): William, when I walked into the jungle, I was seventeen. When I walked out I was twenty-one. And, by God, I was rich! (*He goes off into darkness around the right corner of the house.*)

WILLY: . . . was rich! That's just the spirit I want to imbue them with! To walk into a jungle! I was right! I was right! I was right!

(BEN *is gone, but* WILLY *is still speaking to him as* LINDA, *in nightgown and robe, enters the kitchen, glances around for* WILLY, *then goes to the door of the house, looks out and sees him. Comes down to his left. He looks at her.*)

LINDA: Willy, dear? Willy?

WILLY: I was right!

LINDA: Did you have some cheese? (*He can't answer.*) It's very late, darling. Come to bed, heh?

WILLY (*looking straight up*): Gotta break your neck to see a star in this yard.

LINDA: You coming in?

WILLY: Whatever happened to that diamond watch fob? Remember? When Ben came from Africa that time? Didn't he give me a watch fob with a diamond in it?

LINDA: You pawned it, dear. Twelve, thirteen years ago. For Biff's radio correspondence course.

WILLY: Gee, that was a beautiful thing. I'll take a walk.

LINDA: But you're in your slippers.

WILLY (*starting to go around the house at the left*): I was right! I was! (*Half to* LINDA, *as he goes, shaking his head.*) What a man! There was a man worth talking to. I was right!

LINDA (*calling after* WILLY): But in your slippers, Willy!

(WILLY *is almost gone when* BIFF, *in his pajamas, comes down the stairs and enters the kitchen.*)

BIFF: What is he doing out there?

LINDA: Sh!

BIFF: God Almighty, Mom, how long has he been doing this?

LINDA: Don't, he'll hear you.

BIFF: What the hell is the matter with him?

LINDA: It'll pass by morning.

BIFF: Shouldn't we do anything?

LINDA: Oh, my dear, you should do a lot of things, but there's nothing to do, so go to sleep.

(HAPPY *comes down the stairs and sits on the steps.*)

HAPPY: I never heard him so loud, Mom.

LINDA: Well, come around more often; you'll hear him. (*She sits down at the table and mends the lining of* WILLY's *jacket.*)

BIFF: Why didn't you ever write me about this, Mom?

LINDA: How would I write to you? For over three months you had no address.

BIFF: I was on the move. But you know I thought of you all the time. You know that, don't you, pal?

LINDA: I know, dear, I know. But he likes to have a letter. Just to know that there's still a possibility for better things.

BIFF: He's not like this all the time, is he?

LINDA: It's when you come home he's always the worst.

BIFF: When I come home?

LINDA: When you write you're coming, he's all smiles, and talks about the future, and — he's just wonderful. And then the closer you seem to come, the more shaky he gets, and then, by the time you get here, he's arguing, and he seems angry at you. I think it's just that maybe he can't bring himself to — to open up to you. Why are you so hateful to each other? Why is that?

BIFF (*evasively*): I'm not hateful, Mom.

LINDA: But you no sooner come in the door than you're fighting!

BIFF: I don't know why. I mean to change. I'm tryin', Mom, you understand?

LINDA: Are you home to stay now?

BIFF: I don't know. I want to look around, see what's doin'.

LINDA: Biff, you can't look around all your life, can you?

BIFF: I just can't take hold, Mom. I can't take hold of some kind of a life.

LINDA: Biff, a man is not a bird, to come and go with the springtime.

BIFF: Your hair . . . (*He touches her hair.*) Your hair got so gray.

LINDA: Oh, it's been gray since you were in high school. I just stopped dyeing it, that's all.

BIFF: Dye it again, will ya? I don't want my pal looking old. (*He smiles.*)

LINDA: You're such a boy! You think you can go away for a year and . . . You've got to get it into your head now that one day you'll knock on this door and there'll be strange people here —

BIFF: What are you talking about? You're not even sixty, Mom.

LINDA: But what about your father?

BIFF (*lamely*): Well, I meant him too.

HAPPY: He admires Pop.

LINDA: Biff, dear, if you don't have any feeling for him, then you can't have any feeling for me.

BIFF: Sure I can, Mom.

LINDA: No. You can't just come to see me, because I love him. (*With a threat, but only a threat, of tears.*) He's the dearest man in the world to me, and I won't have anyone making him feel unwanted and low and blue. You've got to make up your mind now, darling, there's no leeway any more. Either he's your father and you pay him that respect, or else you're not to come here. I know he's not easy to get along with — nobody knows that better than me — but . . .

WILLY (*from the left, with a laugh*): Hey, hey, Biffo!

BIFF (*starting to go out after* WILLY): What the hell is the matter with him? (HAPPY *stops him.*)

LINDA: Don't — don't go near him!

BIFF: Stop making excuses for him! He always, always wiped the floor with you. Never had an ounce of respect for you.

HAPPY: He's always had respect for —

BIFF: What the hell do you know about it?

HAPPY (*surlily*): Just don't call him crazy!

BIFF: He's got no character — Charley wouldn't do this. Not in his own house — spewing out that vomit from his mind.

HAPPY: Charley never had to cope with what he's got to.

BIFF: People are worse off than Willy Loman. Believe me, I've seen them!

LINDA: Then make Charley your father, Biff. You can't do that, can you? I don't say he's a great man. Willy Loman never made a lot of money. His name was never in the paper. He's not the finest character that ever lived. But he's a human being, and a terrible thing is happening to him. So attention must be paid. He's not to be allowed to fall into his grave like an old dog. Attention, attention must be finally paid to such a person. You called him crazy —

BIFF: I didn't mean —

LINDA: No, a lot of people think he's lost his — balance. But you don't have to be very smart to know what his trouble is. The man is exhausted.

HAPPY: Sure!

LINDA: A small man can be just as exhausted as a great man. He works for a company thirty-six years this March, opens up unheard-of territories to their trademark, and now in his old age they take his salary away.

HAPPY (*indignantly*): I didn't know that, Mom.

LINDA: You never asked, my dear! Now that you get your spending money someplace else you don't trouble your mind with him.

HAPPY: But I gave you money last —

LINDA: Christmas time, fifty dollars! To fix the hot water it cost ninety-seven fifty! For five weeks he's been on straight commission, like a beginner, an unknown!

BIFF: Those ungrateful bastards!

LINDA: Are they any worse than his sons? When he brought them business, when he was young, they were glad to see him. But now his old friends, the old buyers that loved him so and always found some order to hand him in a pinch — they're all dead, retired. He used to be able to make six, seven calls a day in Boston. Now he takes his valises out of the car and puts them back and takes them out again and he's exhausted. Instead of walking he talks now. He drives seven hundred miles, and when he gets there no one knows him any more, no one welcomes him. And what goes through a man's mind, driving seven hundred miles home without having earned a cent? Why shouldn't he talk to himself? Why? When he has to go to Charley and borrow fifty dollars a week and pretend to me that it's his pay? How long can that go on? How long? You see what I'm sitting here and waiting for? And you tell me he has no character? The man who never worked a day but for your benefit? When does he get the medal for that? Is this his reward — to turn around at the age of sixty-three and find his sons, who he loved better than his life, one a philandering bum —

HAPPY: Mom!

LINDA: That's all you are, my baby! (*To* BIFF.) And you! What happened to the love you had for him? You were such pals! How you used to talk to him on the phone every night! How lonely he was till he could come home to you!

BIFF: All right, Mom, I'll live here in my room, and I'll get a job. I'll keep away from him, that's all.

LINDA: No, Biff. You can't stay here and fight all the time.

BIFF: He threw me out of this house, remember that.

LINDA: Why did he do that? I never knew why.

BIFF: Because I know he's a fake and he doesn't like anybody around who knows!

LINDA: Why a fake? In what way? What do you mean?

BIFF: Just don't lay it all at my feet. It's between me and him — that's all I have to say. I'll chip in from now on. He'll settle for half my pay check. He'll be all right. I'm going to bed. (*He starts for the stairs.*)

LINDA: He won't be all right.

BIFF (*turning on the stairs, furiously*): I hate this city and I'll stay here. Now what do you want?

LINDA: He's dying, Biff.

(HAPPY *turns quickly to her, shocked.*)

BIFF (*after a pause*): Why is he dying?

LINDA: He's been trying to kill himself.

BIFF (*with great horror*): How?

LINDA: I live from day to day.

BIFF: What're you talking about?

LINDA: Remember I wrote you that he smashed up the car again? In February?

BIFF: Well?

LINDA: The insurance inspector came. He said that they have evidence. That all these accidents in the last year — weren't — weren't — accidents.

HAPPY: How can they tell that? That's a lie.

LINDA: It seems there's a woman . . . (*She takes a breath as —*)

BIFF (*sharply but contained*): What woman?

LINDA (*simultaneously*): . . . and this woman . . .

LINDA: What?

BIFF: Nothing. Go ahead.

LINDA: What did you say?

BIFF: Nothing. I just said what woman?

HAPPY: What about her?

LINDA: Well, it seems she was walking down the road and saw his car. She says that he wasn't driving fast at all, and that he didn't skid. She says he came to that little bridge, and then deliberately smashed into the railing, and it was only the shallowness of the water that saved him.

BIFF: Oh, no, he probably just fell asleep again.

LINDA: I don't think he fell asleep.

BIFF: Why not?

LINDA: Last month . . . (*With great difficulty.*) Oh, boys, it's so hard to say a thing like this! He's just a big stupid man to you, but I tell you there's more good in him than in many other people. (*She chokes, wipes her eyes.*) I was looking for a fuse. The lights blew out, and I went down the cellar. And behind the fuse box — it happened to fall out — was a length of rubber pipe — just short.

HAPPY: No kidding?

LINDA: There's a little attachment on the end of it. I knew right away. And sure enough, on the bottom of the water heater there's a new little nipple on the gas pipe.

HAPPY (*angrily*): That — jerk.

BIFF: Did you have it taken off?

LINDA: I'm — I'm ashamed to. How can I mention it to him? Every day I go down and take away that little rubber pipe. But, when he comes home, I put it back where it was. How can I insult him that way? I don't know what to do. I live from day to day, boys. I tell you, I know every thought in his mind. It sounds so old-fashioned and silly, but I tell you he put his whole life into you and you've turned your backs on him. (*She is bent over in the chair, weeping, her face in her hands.*) Biff, I swear to God! Biff, his life is in your hands!

HAPPY (*to* BIFF): How do you like that damned fool!

BIFF (*kissing her*): All right, pal, all right. It's all settled now. I've been remiss. I know that, Mom. But now I'll stay, and I swear to you, I'll apply myself. (*Kneeling in front of her, in a fever of self-reproach.*) It's just — you see, Mom, I don't fit in business. Not that I won't try. I'll try, and I'll make good.

HAPPY: Sure you will. The trouble with you in business was you never tried to please people.

BIFF: I know, I —

HAPPY: Like when you worked for Harrison's. Bob Harrison said you were tops, and then you go and do some damn fool thing like whistling whole songs in the elevator like a comedian.

BIFF (*against* HAPPY): So what? I like to whistle sometimes.

HAPPY: You don't raise a guy to a responsible job who whistles in the elevator!

LINDA: Well, don't argue about it now.

HAPPY: Like when you'd go off and swim in the middle of the day instead of taking the line around.

BIFF (*his resentment rising*): Well, don't you run off? You take off sometimes, don't you? On a nice summer day?

HAPPY: Yeah, but I cover myself!

LINDA: Boys!

HAPPY: If I'm going to take a fade the boss can call any number where I'm supposed to be and they'll swear to him that I just left. I'll tell you something that I hate to say, Biff, but in the business world some of them think you're crazy.

BIFF (*angered*): Screw the business world!

HAPPY: All right, screw it! Great, but cover yourself!

LINDA: Hap, Hap!

BIFF: I don't care what they think! They've laughed at Dad for years, and you know why? Because we don't belong in this nut-house of a city! We should be mixing cement on some open plain, or — or carpenters. A carpenter is allowed to whistle!

(WILLY *walks in from the entrance of the house, at left.*)

WILLY: Even your grandfather was better than a carpenter. (*Pause. They watch him.*) You never grew up. Bernard does not whistle in the elevator, I assure you.

BIFF (*as though to laugh* WILLY *out of it*): Yeah, but you do, Pop.

WILLY: I never in my life whistled in an elevator! And who in the business world thinks I'm crazy?

BIFF: I didn't mean it like that, Pop. Now don't make a whole thing out of it, will ya?

WILLY: Go back to the West! Be a carpenter, a cowboy, enjoy yourself!

LINDA: Willy, he was just saying —

WILLY: I heard what he said!

HAPPY (*trying to quiet* WILLY): Hey, Pop, come on now . . .

WILLY (*continuing over* HAPPY's *line*): They laugh at me, heh? Go to Filene's, go to the Hub, go to Slattery's, Boston. Call out the name Willy Loman and see what happens! Big shot!

BIFF: All right, Pop.

WILLY: Big!

BIFF: All right!

WILLY: Why do you always insult me?

BIFF: I didn't say a word. (*To* LINDA.) Did I say a word?

LINDA: He didn't say anything, Willy.

WILLY (*going to the doorway of the living-room*): All right, good night, good night.

LINDA: Willy, dear, he just decided . . .

WILLY (*to* BIFF): If you get tired hanging around tomorrow, paint the ceiling I put up in the living-room.

BIFF: I'm leaving early tomorrow.

HAPPY: He's going to see Bill Oliver, Pop.

WILLY (*interestedly*): Oliver? For what?

BIFF (*with reserve, but trying, trying*): He always said he'd stake me. I'd like to go into business, so maybe I can take him up on it.

LINDA: Isn't that wonderful?

WILLY: Don't interrupt. What's wonderful about it? There's fifty men in the City of New York who'd stake him. (*To* BIFF.) Sporting goods?

BIFF: I guess so. I know something about it and —

WILLY: He knows something about it! You know sporting goods better than Spalding, for God's sake! How much is he giving you?

BIFF: I don't know, I didn't even see him yet, but —

WILLY: Then what're you talkin' about?

BIFF (*getting angry*): Well, all I said was I'm gonna see him, that's all!

WILLY (*turning away*): Ah, you're counting your chickens again.

BIFF (*starting left for the stairs*): Oh, Jesus, I'm going to sleep!

WILLY (*calling after him*): Don't curse in this house!

BIFF (*turning*): Since when did you get so clean?

HAPPY (*trying to stop them*): Wait a . . .

WILLY: Don't use that language to me! I won't have it!

HAPPY (*grabbing* BIFF, *shouts*): Wait a minute! I got an idea. I got a feasible idea. Come here, Biff, let's talk this over now, let's talk some sense here. When I was down in Florida last time, I thought of a great idea to sell sporting goods. It just came back to me. You and I, Biff — we have a line, the Loman Line. We train a couple of weeks, and put on a couple of exhibitions, see?

WILLY: That's an idea!

HAPPY: Wait! We form two basketball teams, see? Two water-polo teams. We play each other. It's a million dollars' worth of publicity. Two brothers, see? The Loman Brothers. Displays in the Royal Palms — all the hotels. And banners over the ring and the basketball court: "Loman Brothers." Baby, we could sell sporting goods!

WILLY: That is a one-million-dollar idea!

LINDA: Marvelous!

BIFF: I'm in great shape as far as that's concerned.

HAPPY: And the beauty of it is, Biff, it wouldn't be like a business. We'd be out playin' ball again . . .

BIFF (*enthused*): Yeah, that's . . .

WILLY: Million-dollar . . .

HAPPY: And you wouldn't get fed up with it, Biff. It'd be the family again. There'd be the old honor, and comradeship, and if you wanted to go off for a swim or somethin' — well, you'd do it! Without some smart cooky gettin' up ahead of you!

WILLY: Lick the world! You guys together could absolutely lick the civilized world.

BIFF: I'll see Oliver tomorrow. Hap, if we could work that out . . .

LINDA: Maybe things are beginning to —

WILLY (*wildly enthused, to* LINDA): Stop interrupting! (*To* BIFF.) But don't wear sport jacket and slacks when you see Oliver.

BIFF: No, I'll —

WILLY: A business suit, and talk as little as possible, and don't crack any jokes.

BIFF: He did like me. Always liked me.

LINDA: He loved you!

WILLY (*to* LINDA): Will you stop! (*To* BIFF.) Walk in very serious. You are not applying for a boy's job. Money is to pass. Be quiet, fine, and serious. Everybody likes a kidder, but nobody lends him money.

HAPPY: I'll try to get some myself, Biff. I'm sure I can.

WILLY: I see great things for you kids, I think your troubles are over. But remember, start big and you'll end big. Ask for fifteen. How much you gonna ask for?

BIFF: Gee, I don't know —

WILLY: And don't say "Gee." "Gee" is a boy's word. A man walking in for fifteen thousand dollars does not say "Gee!"

BIFF: Ten, I think, would be top though.

WILLY: Don't be so modest. You always started too low. Walk in with a big laugh. Don't look worried. Start off with a couple of your good stories to lighten things up. It's not what you say, it's how you say it — because personality always wins the day.

LINDA: Oliver always thought the highest of him —

WILLY: Will you let me talk?

BIFF: Don't yell at her, Pop, will ya?

WILLY (*angrily*): I was talking, wasn't I?

BIFF: I don't like you yelling at her all the time, and I'm tellin' you, that's all.

WILLY: What're you, takin' over this house?

LINDA: Willy —

WILLY (*turning on her*): Don't take his side all the time, goddammit!

BIFF (*furiously*): Stop yelling at her!

WILLY (*suddenly pulling on his cheek, beaten down, guilt ridden*): Give my best to Bill Oliver — he may remember me. (*He exits through the living-room doorway.*)

LINDA (*her voice subdued*): What'd you have to start that for? (BIFF *turns away.*) You see how sweet he was as soon as you talked hopefully? (*She goes over to* BIFF.) Come up and say good night to him. Don't let him go to bed that way.

HAPPY: Come on, Biff, let's buck him up.

LINDA: Please, dear. Just say good night. It takes so little to make him happy. Come.

(*She goes through the living-room doorway, calling upstairs from within the living-room.*) Your pajamas are hanging in the bathroom, Willy!

HAPPY (*looking toward where* LINDA *went out*): What a woman! They broke the mold when they made her. You know that, Biff?

BIFF: He's off salary. My God, working on commission!

HAPPY: Well, let's face it: he's no hot-shot selling man. Except that sometimes, you have to admit, he's a sweet personality.

BIFF (*deciding*): Lend me ten bucks, will ya? I want to buy some new ties.

HAPPY: I'll take you to a place I know. Beautiful stuff. Wear one of my striped shirts tomorrow.

BIFF: She got gray. Mom got awful old. Gee, I'm gonna go in to Oliver tomorrow and knock him for a —

HAPPY: Come on up. Tell that to Dad. Let's give him a whirl. Come on.

BIFF (*steamed up*): You know, with ten thousand bucks, boy!

HAPPY (*as they go into the living-room*): That's the talk, Biff, that's the first time I've heard the old confidence out of you! (*From within the living-room, fading off.*) You're gonna live with me, kid, and any babe you want just say the word . . . (*The last lines are hardly heard. They are mounting the stairs to their parents' bedroom.*)

LINDA (*entering her bedroom and addressing* WILLY, *who is in the bathroom. She is straightening the bed for him*): Can you do anything about the shower? It drips.

WILLY (*from the bathroom*): All of a sudden everything falls to pieces! Goddam plumbing, oughta be sued, those people. I hardly finished putting it in and the thing . . . (*His words rumble off.*)

LINDA: I'm just wondering if Oliver will remember him. You think he might?

WILLY (*coming out of the bathroom in his pajamas*): Remember him? What's the matter with you, you crazy? If he'd've stayed with Oliver he'd be on top by now! Wait'll Oliver gets a look at him. You don't know the average caliber any more. The average young man today — (*he is getting into bed*) — is got a caliber of zero. Greatest thing in the world for him was to bum around.

(BIFF *and* HAPPY *enter the bedroom. Slight pause.*)

WILLY (*stops short, looking at* BIFF): Glad to hear it, boy.

HAPPY: He wanted to say good night to you, sport.

WILLY (*to* BIFF): Yeah. Knock him dead, boy. What'd you want to tell me?

BIFF: Just take it easy, Pop. Good night. (*He turns to go.*)

WILLY (*unable to resist*): And if anything falls off the desk while you're talking to him — like a package or something — don't you pick it up. They have office boys for that.

LINDA: I'll make a big breakfast —

WILLY: Will you let me finish? (*To* BIFF.) Tell him you were in the business in the West. Not farm work.

BIFF: All right, Dad.

LINDA: I think everything —

WILLY (*going right through her speech*): And don't undersell yourself. No less than fifteen thousand dollars.

BIFF (*unable to bear him*): Okay. Good night, Mom. (*He starts moving.*)

WILLY: Because you got a greatness in you, Biff, remember that. You got all kinds a greatness . . . . (*He lies back, exhausted.* BIFF *walks out.*)

LINDA (*calling after* BIFF): Sleep well, darling!

HAPPY: I'm gonna get married, Mom. I wanted to tell you.

LINDA: Go to sleep, dear.

HAPPY (*going*): I just wanted to tell you.

WILLY: Keep up the good work. (HAPPY *exits*.) God . . . remember that Ebbets Field game? The championship of the city?

LINDA: Just rest. Should I sing to you?

WILLY: Yeah. Sing to me. (LINDA *hums a soft lullaby*.) When that team came out — he was the tallest, remember?

LINDA: Oh, yes. And in gold.

(BIFF *enters the darkened kitchen, takes a cigarette, and leaves the house. He comes downstage into a golden pool of light. He smokes, staring at the night*.)

WILLY: Like a young god. Hercules — something like that. And the sun, the sun all around him. Remember how he waved to me? Right up from the field, with the representatives of three colleges standing by? And the buyers I brought, and the cheers when he came out — Loman, Loman, Loman! God Almighty, he'll be great yet. A star like that, magnificent, can never really fade away!

(*The light on* WILLY *is fading. The gas heater begins to glow through the kitchen wall, near the stairs, a blue flame beneath red coils*.)

LINDA (*timidly*): Willy dear, what has he got against you?

WILLY: I'm so tired. Don't talk any more.

(BIFF *slowly returns to the kitchen. He stops, stares toward the heater*.)

LINDA: Will you ask Howard to let you work in New York?

WILLY: First thing in the morning. Everything'll be all right.

(BIFF *reaches behind the heater and draws out a length of rubber tubing. He is horrified and turns his head toward* WILLY's *room, still dimly lit, from which the strains of* LINDA's *desperate but monotonous humming rise*.)

WILLY (*staring through the window into the moonlight*): Gee, look at the moon moving between the buildings!

(BIFF *wraps the tubing around his hand and quickly goes up the stairs*.)

CURTAIN

ACT II

Music is heard, gay and bright. The curtain rises as the music fades away. WILLY, *in shirt sleeves, is sitting at the kitchen table, sipping coffee, his hat in his lap.* LINDA *is filling his cup when she can.*

WILLY: Wonderful coffee. Meal in itself.

LINDA: Can I make you some eggs?

WILLY: No. Take a breath.

LINDA: You look so rested, dear.

WILLY: I slept like a dead one. First time in months. Imagine, sleeping till ten on a Tuesday morning. Boys left nice and early, heh?

LINDA: They were out of here by eight o'clock.

WILLY: Good work!

LINDA: It was so thrilling to see them leaving together. I can't get over the shaving lotion in this house!

WILLY (*smiling*): Mmm —

LINDA: Biff was very changed this morning. His whole attitude seemed to be hopeful. He couldn't wait to get downtown to see Oliver.

WILLY: He's heading for a change. There's no question, there simply are certain men that take longer to get — solidified. How did he dress?

LINDA: His blue suit. He's so handsome in that suit. He could be a — anything in that suit!

(WILLY *gets up from the table.* LINDA *holds his jacket for him.*)

WILLY: There's no question, no question at all. Gee, on the way home tonight I'd like to buy some seeds.

LINDA (*laughing*): That'd be wonderful. But not enough sun gets back there. Nothing'll grow any more.

WILLY: You wait, kid, before it's all over we're gonna get a little place out in the country, and I'll raise some vegetables, a couple of chickens . . .

LINDA: You'll do it yet, dear.

(WILLY *walks out of his jacket.* LINDA *follows him.*)

WILLY: And they'll get married, and come for a weekend. I'd build a little guest house. 'Cause I got so many fine tools, all I'd need would be a little lumber and some peace of mind.

LINDA (*joyfully*): I sewed the lining . . .

WILLY: I could build two guest houses, so they'd both come. Did he decide how much he's going to ask Oliver for?

LINDA (*getting him into the jacket*): He didn't mention it, but I imagine ten or fifteen thousand. You going to talk to Howard today?

WILLY: Yeah. I'll put it to him straight and simple. He'll just have to take me off the road.

LINDA: And Willy, don't forget to ask for a little advance, because we've got the insurance premium. It's the grace period now.

WILLY: That's a hundred . . . ?

LINDA: A hundred and eight, sixty-eight. Because we're a little short again.

WILLY: Why are we short?

LINDA: Well, you had the motor job on the car . . .

WILLY: That goddam Studebaker!

LINDA: And you got one more payment on the refrigerator . . .

WILLY: But it just broke again!

LINDA: Well, it's old, dear.

WILLY: I told you we should've bought a well-advertised machine. Charley bought a General Electric and it's twenty years old and it's still good, that son-of-a-bitch.

LINDA: But, Willy —

WILLY: Whoever heard of a Hastings refrigerator? Once in my life I would like to own something outright before it's broken! I'm always in a race with the junkyard! I just finished paying for the car and it's on its last legs. The refrigerator consumes belts like a goddam maniac. They time those things. They time them so when you finally paid for them, they're used up.

LINDA (*buttoning up his jacket as he unbuttons it*): All told, about two hundred dollars would carry us, dear. But that includes the last payment on the mortgage. After this payment, Willy, the house belongs to us.

WILLY: It's twenty-five years!

LINDA: Biff was nine years old when we bought it.

WILLY: Well, that's a great thing. To weather a twenty-five year mortgage is —

LINDA: It's an accomplishment.

WILLY: All the cement, the lumber, the reconstruction I put in this house! There ain't a crack to be found in it any more.

LINDA: Well, it served its purpose.

WILLY: What purpose? Some stranger'll come along, move in, and that's that. If only Biff would take this house, and raise a family . . . (*He starts to go.*) Good-by, I'm late.

LINDA (*suddenly remembering*): Oh, I forgot! You're supposed to meet them for dinner.

WILLY: Me?

LINDA: At Frank's Chop House on Forty-eighth near Sixth Avenue.

WILLY: Is that so! How about you?

LINDA: No, just the three of you. They're gonna blow you to a big meal!

WILLY: Don't say! Who thought of that?

LINDA: Biff came to me this morning, Willy, and he said, "Tell Dad, we want to blow him to a big meal." Be there six o'clock. You and your two boys are going to have dinner.

WILLY: Gee whiz! That's really somethin'. I'm gonna knock Howard for a loop, kid. I'll get an advance, and I'll come home with a New York job. Goddammit, now I'm gonna do it!

LINDA: Oh, that's the spirit, Willy!

WILLY: I will never get behind a wheel the rest of my life!

LINDA: It's changing, Willy, I can feel it changing!

WILLY: Beyond a question. G'by, I'm late. (*He starts to go again.*)

LINDA (*calling after him as she runs to the kitchen table for a handkerchief*): You got your glasses?

WILLY (*feels for them, then comes back in*): Yeah, yeah, got my glasses.

LINDA (*giving him the handkerchief*): And a handkerchief.

WILLY: Yeah, handkerchief.

LINDA: And your saccharine?

WILLY: Yeah, my saccharine.

LINDA: Be careful on the subway stairs.

(*She kisses him, and a silk stocking is seen hanging from her hand.* WILLY *notices it.*)

WILLY: Will you stop mending stockings? At least while I'm in the house. It gets me nervous. I can't tell you. Please.

(LINDA *hides the stocking in her hand as she follows* WILLY *across the forestage in front of the house.*)

LINDA: Remember, Frank's Chop House.

WILLY (*passing the apron*): Maybe beets would grow out there.

LINDA (*laughing*): But you tried so many times.

WILLY: Yeah. Well, don't work hard today. (*He disappears around the right corner of the house.*)

LINDA: Be careful!

(*As* WILLY *vanishes,* LINDA *waves to him. Suddenly the phone rings. She runs across the stage and into the kitchen and lifts it.*)

LINDA: Hello? Oh, Biff! I'm so glad you called, I just . . . Yes, sure, I just told him. Yes, he'll be there for dinner at six o'clock, I didn't forget. Listen, I was just dying to tell you. You know that little rubber pipe I told you about? That he connected to the gas heater? I finally decided to go down the cellar this morning and take it away and destroy it. But it's gone! Imagine? He took it away himself, it isn't there! (*She listens.*) When? Oh, then you took it. Oh — nothing, it's just that I'd hoped he'd taken it away himself. Oh, I'm not worried, darling, because this morning he left in such high spirits, it was like the old days! I'm not afraid any more. Did Mr. Oliver see you? . . . Well, you wait there then. And make a nice impression on him, darling. Just don't perspire too much before you see him. And have a nice time with Dad. He may have big news too! . . . That's right, a New York job. And be sweet to him tonight, dear. Be loving to him. Because he's only a little boat looking for a harbor. (*She is trembling with sorrow and joy.*) Oh, that's wonderful, Biff, you'll save his life. Thanks, darling. Just put your arm around him when he comes into the restaurant. Give him a smile. That's the boy . . . Good-by, dear. . . . You got your comb? . . . That's fine. Good-by, Biff dear.

(*In the middle of her speech,* HOWARD WAGNER, *thirty-six, wheels on a small typewriter table on which is a wire-recording machine and proceeds to plug it in. This is on the left forestage. Light slowly fades on* LINDA *as it rises on* HOWARD. HOWARD *is intent on threading the machine and only glances over his shoulder as* WILLY *appears.*)

WILLY: Pst! Pst!

HOWARD: Hello, Willy, come in.

WILLY: Like to have a little talk with you, Howard.

HOWARD: Sorry to keep you waiting. I'll be with you in a minute.

WILLY: What's that, Howard?

HOWARD: Didn't you ever see one of these? Wire recorder.

WILLY: Oh. Can we talk a minute?

HOWARD: Records things. Just got delivery yesterday. Been driving me crazy, the most terrific machine I ever saw in my life. I was up all night with it.

WILLY: What do you do with it?

HOWARD: I bought it for dictation, but you can do anything with it. Listen to this. I had it home last night. Listen to what I picked up. The first one is my daughter. Get this. (*He flicks the switch and "Roll Out the Barrel" is heard being whistled.*) Listen to that kid whistle.

WILLY: That is lifelike, isn't it?

HOWARD: Seven years old. Get that tone.

WILLY: Ts, ts. Like to ask a little favor if you . . .

(The whistling breaks off, and the voice of HOWARD's DAUGHTER *is heard.)*

HIS DAUGHTER: "Now you, Daddy."

HOWARD: She's crazy for me! (*Again the same song is whistled.*) That's me! Ha! (*He winks.*)

WILLY: You're very good!

(The whistling breaks off again. The machine runs silent for a moment.)

HOWARD: Sh! Get this now, this is my son.

HIS SON: "The capital of Alabama is Montgomery; the capital of Arizona is Phoenix; the capital of Arkansas is Little Rock; the capital of California is Sacramento . . ." (*And on, and on.*)

HOWARD (*holding up five fingers*): Five years old, Willy!

WILLY: He'll make an announcer some day!

HIS SON (*continuing*): "The capital . . ."

HOWARD: Get that — alphabetical order! (*The machine breaks off suddenly.*) Wait a minute. The maid kicked the plug out.

WILLY: It certainly is a —

HOWARD: Sh, for God's sake!

HIS SON: "It's nine o'clock, Bulova watch time. So I have to go to sleep."

WILLY: That really is —

HOWARD: Wait a minute! The next is my wife.

(They wait.)

HOWARD'S VOICE: "Go on, say something." (*Pause.*) "Well, you gonna talk?"

HIS WIFE: "I can't think of anything."

HOWARD'S VOICE: "Well, talk — it's turning."

HIS WIFE (*shyly, beaten*): "Hello." (*Silence.*) "Oh, Howard, I can't talk into this . . ."

HOWARD (*snapping the machine off*): That was my wife.

WILLY: That is a wonderful machine. Can we —

HOWARD: I tell you, Willy, I'm gonna take my camera, and my bandsaw, and all my hobbies, and out they go. This is the most fascinating relaxation I ever found.

WILLY: I think I'll get one myself.

HOWARD: Sure, they're only a hundred and a half. You can't do without it. Supposing you wanna hear Jack Benny, see? But you can't be at home at that hour. So you tell the maid to turn the radio on when Jack Benny comes on, and this automatically goes on with the radio . . .

WILLY: And when you come home you . . .

HOWARD: You can come home twelve o'clock, one o'clock, any time you like, and you get yourself a Coke and sit yourself down, throw the switch, and there's Jack Benny's program in the middle of the night!

WILLY: I'm definitely going to get one. Because lots of time I'm on the road, and I think to myself, what I must be missing on the radio!

HOWARD: Don't you have a radio in the car?

WILLY: Well, yeah, but who ever thinks of turning it on?

HOWARD: Say, aren't you supposed to be in Boston?

WILLY: That's what I want to talk to you about, Howard. You got a minute? (*He draws a chair in from the wing.*)

HOWARD: What happened? What're you doing here?

WILLY: Well . . .

HOWARD: You didn't crack up again, did you?

WILLY: Oh, no. No . . .

HOWARD: Geez, you had me worried there for a minute. What's the trouble?

WILLY: Well, tell you the truth, Howard. I've come to the decision that I'd rather not travel any more.

HOWARD: Not travel! Well, what'll you do?

WILLY: Remember, Christmas time, when you had the party here? You said you'd try to think of some spot for me here in town.

HOWARD: With us?

WILLY: Well, sure.

HOWARD: Oh, yeah, yeah. I remember. Well, I couldn't think of anything for you, Willy.

WILLY: I tell ya, Howard. The kids are all grown up, y'know. I don't need much any more. If I could take home — well, sixty-five dollars a week, I could swing it.

HOWARD: Yeah, but Willy, see I —

WILLY: I tell ya why, Howard. Speaking frankly and between the two of us, y'know — I'm just a little tired.

HOWARD: Oh, I could understand that, Willy. But you're a road man, Willy, and we do a road business. We've only got a half-dozen salesmen on the floor here.

WILLY: God knows, Howard, I never asked a favor of any man. But I was with the firm when your father used to carry you in here in his arms.

HOWARD: I know that, Willy, but —

WILLY: Your father came to me the day you were born and asked me what I thought of the name of Howard, may he rest in peace.

HOWARD: I appreciate that, Willy, but there just is no spot here for you. If I had a spot I'd slam you right in, but I just don't have a single solitary spot.

(*He looks for his lighter.* WILLY *has picked it up and gives it to him. Pause.*)

WILLY (*with increasing anger*): Howard, all I need to set my table is fifty dollars a week.

HOWARD: But where am I going to put you, kid?

WILLY: Look, it isn't a question of whether I can sell merchandise, is it?

HOWARD: No, but it's a business, kid, and everybody's gotta pull his own weight.

WILLY (*desperately*): Just let me tell you a story, Howard —

HOWARD: 'Cause you gotta admit, business is business.

WILLY (*angrily*): Business is definitely business, but just listen for a minute. You don't understand this. When I was a boy — eighteen, nineteen — I was already on the road. And there was a question in my mind as to whether selling had a future for me. Because in those days I had a yearning to go to Alaska. See, there were three gold strikes in one month in Alaska, and I felt like going out. Just for the ride, you might say.

HOWARD (*barely interested*): Don't say.

WILLY: Oh, yeah, my father lived many years in Alaska. He was an adventurous man. We've got quite a little streak of self-reliance in our family. I thought I'd go out with my older brother and try to locate him, and maybe settle in the North with the old man. And I was almost decided to go, when I met a salesman in the Parker House. His name was Dave Singleman. And he was eighty-four years old, and he'd drummed merchandise in thirty-one states. And old Dave, he'd go up to his room, y'understand, put on his green velvet slippers — I'll never forget — and pick up his phone and call the buyers, and without ever leaving his room, at the age of eighty-four, he made his living. And when I saw that, I realized that selling was the greatest career a man could want. 'Cause what could be more satisfying than to be able to go, at the age of eighty-four, into twenty or thirty different cities, and pick up a phone, and be remembered and loved and helped by so many different people? Do you know? when he died — and by the way he died the death of a salesman, in his green velvet slippers in the smoker of the New York, New Haven and Hartford, going into Boston — when he died, hundreds of salesmen and buyers were at his funeral. Things were sad on a lotta trains for months after that. (*He stands up.* HOWARD *has not looked at him.*) In those days there was personality in it, Howard. There was respect, and comradeship, and gratitude in it. Today, it's all cut and dried, and there's no chance for bringing friendship to bear — or personality. You see what I mean? They don't know me any more.

HOWARD (*moving away, to the right*): That's just the thing, Willy.

WILLY: If I had forty dollars a week — that's all I'd need. Forty dollars, Howard.

HOWARD: Kid, I can't take blood from a stone, I —

WILLY (*desperation is on him now*): Howard, the year Al Smith was nominated, your father came to me and —

HOWARD (*starting to go off*): I've got to see some people, kid.

WILLY (*stopping him*): I'm talking about your father! There were promises made across this desk! You mustn't tell me you've got people to see — I put thirty-four years into this firm, Howard, and now I can't pay my insurance! You can't eat the orange and throw the peel away — a man is not a piece of fruit! (*After a pause.*) Now pay attention. Your father — in 1928 I had a big year. I averaged a hundred and seventy dollars a week in commissions.

HOWARD (*impatiently*): Now, Willy, you never averaged —

WILLY (*banging his hand on the desk*): I averaged a hundred and seventy dollars a week in the year of 1928! And your father came to me — or rather, I was in the office here — it was right over this desk — and he put his hand on my shoulder —

HOWARD (*getting up*): You'll have to excuse me, Willy, I gotta see some people. Pull yourself together. (*Going out.*) I'll be back in a little while.

(*On* HOWARD's *exit, the light on his chair grows very bright and strange.*)

WILLY: Pull myself together! What the hell did I say to him? My God, I was yelling at him! How could I! (WILLY *breaks off, staring at the light, which occupies the chair, animating it. He approaches this chair, standing across the desk from it.*) Frank, Frank, don't you remember what you told me that time? How you put your hand on my shoulder, and Frank . . . (*He leans on the desk and as he speaks the dead man's name he accidentally switches on the recorder, and instantly —*)

HOWARD'S SON: " . . . of New York is Albany. The capital of Ohio is Cincinnati, the capital of Rhode Island is . . ." (*The recitation continues.*)

WILLY (*leaping away with fright, shouting*): Ha! Howard! Howard! Howard!

HOWARD (*rushing in*): What happened?

WILLY (*pointing at the machine, which continues nasally, childishly, with the capital cities*): Shut it off! Shut if off!

HOWARD (*pulling the plug out*): Look, Willy . . .

WILLY (*pressing his hands to his eyes*): I gotta get myself some coffee. I'll get some coffee . . .

(WILLY *starts to walk out.* HOWARD *stops him.*)

HOWARD (*rolling up the cord*): Willy, look . . .

WILLY: I'll go to Boston.

HOWARD: Willy, you can't go to Boston for us.

WILLY: Why can't I go?

HOWARD: I don't want you to represent us. I've been meaning to tell you for a long time now.

WILLY: Howard, are you firing me?

HOWARD: I think you need a good long rest, Willy.

WILLY: Howard —

HOWARD: And when you feel better, come back, and we'll see if we can work something out.

WILLY: But I gotta earn money, Howard. I'm in no position to —

HOWARD: Where are your sons? Why don't your sons give you a hand?

WILLY: They're working on a very big deal.

HOWARD: This is no time for false pride, Willy. You go to your sons and you tell them that you're tired. You've got two great boys, haven't you?

WILLY: Oh, no question, no question, but in the meantime . . .

HOWARD: Then that's that, heh?

WILLY: All right, I'll go to Boston tomorrow.

HOWARD: No, no.

WILLY: I can't throw myself on my sons. I'm not a cripple!

HOWARD: Look, kid, I'm busy this morning.

WILLY (*grasping* HOWARD's *arm*): Howard, you've got to let me go to Boston!

HOWARD (*hard, keeping himself under control*): I've got a line of people to see this morning. Sit down, take five minutes, and pull yourself together, and then go home, will ya? I need the office, Willy. (*He starts to go, turns, remembering the recorder, starts to push off the table holding the recorder.*) Oh, yeah. Whenever you can this week, stop by and drop off the samples. You'll feel better, Willy, and then come back and we'll talk. Pull yourself together, kid, there's people outside.

(HOWARD *exits, pushing the table off left.* WILLY *stares into space, exhausted. Now the music is heard —* BEN's *music — first distantly, then closer, closer. As* WILLY *speaks,* BEN *enters from the right. He carries valise and umbrella.*)

WILLY: Oh, Ben, how did you do it? What is the answer? Did you wind up the Alaska deal already?

BEN: Doesn't take much time if you know what you're doing. Just a short business trip. Boarding ship in an hour. Wanted to say good-by.

WILLY: Ben, I've got to talk to you.

BEN (*glancing at his watch*): Haven't the time, William.

WILLY (*crossing the apron to* BEN): Ben, nothing's working out. I don't know what to do.

BEN: Now, look here, William. I've bought timberland in Alaska and I need a man to look after things for me.

WILLY: God, timberland! Me and my boys in those grand outdoors!

BEN: You've a new continent at your doorstep, William. Get out of these cities, they're full of talk and time payments and courts of law. Screw on your fists and you can fight for a fortune up there.

WILLY: Yes, yes! Linda, Linda!

(LINDA *enters as of old, with the wash.*)

LINDA: Oh, you're back?

BEN: I haven't much time.

WILLY: No, wait! Linda, he's got a proposition for me in Alaska.

LINDA: But you've got — (*To* BEN.) He's got a beautiful job here.

WILLY: But in Alaska, kid, I could —

LINDA: You're doing well enough, Willy!

BEN (*to* LINDA): Enough for what, my dear?

LINDA (*frightened of* BEN *and angry at him*): Don't say those things to him! Enough to be happy right here, right now. (*To* WILLY, *while* BEN *laughs.*) Why must everybody conquer the world? You're well liked, and the boys love you, and someday — (*to* BEN) — why, old man Wagner told him just the other day that if he keeps it up he'll be a member of the firm, didn't he, Willy?

WILLY: Sure, sure. I am building something with this firm, Ben, and if a man is building something he must be on the right track, mustn't he?

BEN: What are you building? Lay your hand on it. Where is it?

WILLY (*hesitantly*): That's true, Linda, there's nothing.

LINDA: Why? (*To* BEN.) There's a man eighty-four years old —

WILLY: That's right, Ben, that's right. When I look at that man I say, what is there to worry about?

BEN: Bah!

WILLY: It's true, Ben. All he has to do is go into any city, pick up the phone, and he's making his living and you know why?

BEN (*picking up his valise*): I've got to go.

WILLY (*holding* BEN *back*): Look at this boy!

(BIFF, *in his high school sweater, enters carrying suitcase.* HAPPY *carries* BIFF's *shoulder guards, gold helmet, and football pants.*)

WILLY: Without a penny to his name, three great universities are begging for him, and from there the sky's the limit, because it's not what you do, Ben. It's who you know and the smile on your face! It's contacts, Ben, contacts! The whole wealth of Alaska passes over the lunch table at the Commodore Hotel, and that's the wonder, the wonder of this country, that a man can end with diamonds here on the basis of being liked! (*He turns to* BIFF.) And that's why when you get out on that field today it's important. Because thousands of people will be rooting for you and loving you. (*To* BEN, *who has again begun to leave.*) And Ben! when he walks into a business office his name will sound out like a bell and all the doors will open to him! I've seen it, Ben, I've seen it a thousand times! You can't feel it with your hand like timber, but it's there!

BEN: Good-by, William.

WILLY: Ben, am I right? Don't you think I'm right? I value your advice.

BEN: There's a new continent at your doorstep, William. You could walk out rich. Rich! (*He is gone.*)

WILLY: We'll do it here, Ben! You hear me? We're gonna do it here!

(YOUNG BERNARD *rushes in. The gay music of the boys is heard.*)

BERNARD: Oh, gee, I was afraid you left already!

WILLY: Why? What time is it?

BERNARD: It's half-past one!

WILLY: Well, come on, everybody! Ebbets Field next stop! Where's the pennants? (*He rushes through the wall-line of the kitchen and out into the living-room.*)

LINDA (*to* BIFF): Did you pack fresh underwear?

BIFF (*who has been limbering up*): I want to go!

BERNARD: Biff, I'm carrying your helmet, ain't I?

HAPPY: No, I'm carrying the helmet.

BERNARD: Oh, Biff, you promised me.

HAPPY: I'm carrying the helmet.

BERNARD: How am I going to get in the locker room?

LINDA: Let him carry the shoulder guards. (*She puts her coat and hat on in the kitchen.*)

BERNARD: Can I, Biff? 'Cause I told everybody I'm going to be in the locker room.

HAPPY: In Ebbets Field it's the clubhouse.

BERNARD: I meant the clubhouse. Biff!

HAPPY: Biff!

BIFF (*grandly, after a slight pause*): Let him carry the shoulder guards.

HAPPY (*as he gives* BERNARD *the shoulder guards*): Stay close to us now.

(WILLY *rushes in with the pennants.*)

WILLY (*handing them out*): Everybody wave when Biff comes out on the field. (HAPPY *and* BERNARD *run off.*) You set now, boy?

(*The music has died away.*)

BIFF: Ready to go, Pop. Every muscle is ready.

WILLY (*at the edge of the apron*): You realize what this means?

BIFF: That's right, Pop.

WILLY (*feeling* BIFF's *muscles*): You're comin' home this afternoon captain of the All-Scholastic Championship Team of the City of New York.

BIFF: I got it, Pop. And remember, pal, when I take off my helmet, that touchdown is for you.

WILLY: Let's go! (*He is starting out, with his arm around* BIFF, *when* CHARLEY *enters, as of old, in knickers.*) I got no room for you, Charley.

CHARLEY: Room? For what?

WILLY: In the car.

CHARLEY: You goin' for a ride? I wanted to shoot some casino.

WILLY (*furiously*): Casino! (*Incredulously.*) Don't you realize what today is?

LINDA: Oh, he knows, Willy. He's just kidding you.

WILLY: That's nothing to kid about!

CHARLEY: No, Linda, what's goin' on?

LINDA: He's playing in Ebbets Field.

CHARLEY: Baseball in this weather?

WILLY: Don't talk to him. Come on, come on! (*He is pushing them out.*)

CHARLEY: Wait a minute, didn't you hear the news?

WILLY: What?

CHARLEY: Don't you listen to the radio? Ebbets Field just blew up.

WILLY: You go to hell! (CHARLEY *laughs. Pushing them out.*) Come on, come on! We're late.

CHARLEY (*as they go*): Knock a homer, Biff, knock a homer!

WILLY (*the last to leave, turning to* CHARLEY): I don't think that was funny, Charley. This is the greatest day of his life.

CHARLEY: Willy, when are you going to grow up?

WILLY: Yeah, heh? When this game is over, Charley, you'll be laughing out of the other side of your face. They'll be calling him another Red Grange. Twenty-five thousand a year.

CHARLEY (*kidding*): Is that so?

WILLY: Yeah, that's so.

CHARLEY: Well, then, I'm sorry, Willy. But tell me something.

WILLY: What?

CHARLEY: Who is Red Grange?

WILLY: Put up your hands. Goddam you, put up your hands!

(CHARLEY, *chuckling, shakes his head and walks away, around the left corner of the stage.* WILLY *follows him. The music rises to a mocking frenzy.*)

WILLY: Who the hell do you think you are, better than everybody else? You don't know everything, you big, ignorant, stupid . . . Put up your hands!

(*Light rises, on the right side of the forestage, on a small table in the reception room of* CHARLEY's *office. Traffic sounds are heard.* BERNARD, *now mature, sits whistling to himself. A pair of tennis rackets and an overnight bag are on the floor beside him.*)

WILLY (*offstage*): What are you walking away for? Don't walk away! If you're going to say something say it to my face! I know you laugh at me behind my back. You'll laugh out of the other side of your goddam face after this game. Touchdown! Touchdown! Eighty thousand people! Touchdown! Right between the goal posts.

(BERNARD *is a quiet, earnest, but self-assured young man.* WILLY's *voice is coming from right upstage now.* BERNARD *lowers his feet off the table and listens.* JENNY, *his father's secretary, enters.*)

JENNY (*distressed*): Say, Bernard, will you go out in the hall?

BERNARD: What is that noise? Who is it?

JENNY: Mr. Loman. He just got off the elevator.

BERNARD (*getting up*): Who's he arguing with?

JENNY: Nobody. There's nobody with him. I can't deal with him any more, and your father gets all upset everytime he comes. I've got a lot of typing to do, and your father's waiting to sign it. Will you see him?

WILLY (*entering*): Touchdown! Touch — (*He sees* JENNY.) Jenny, Jenny, good to see you. How're ya? Workin'? Or still honest?

JENNY: Fine. How've you been feeling?

WILLY: Not much any more, Jenny. Ha, ha! (*He is surprised to see the rackets.*)

BERNARD: Hello, Uncle Willy.

WILLY (*almost shocked*): Bernard! Well, look who's here! (*He comes quickly, guiltily, to* BERNARD *and warmly shakes his hand.*)

BERNARD: How are you? Good to see you.

WILLY: What are you doing here?

BERNARD: Oh, just stopped by to see Pop. Get off my feet till my train leaves. I'm going to Washington in a few minutes.

WILLY: Is he in?

BERNARD: Yes, he's in his office with the accountant. Sit down.

WILLY (*sitting down*): What're you going to do in Washington?

BERNARD: Oh, just a case I've got there, Willy.

WILLY: That so? (*Indicating the rackets.*) You going to play tennis there?

BERNARD: I'm staying with a friend who's got a court.

WILLY: Don't say. His own tennis court. Must be fine people, I bet.

BERNARD: They are, very nice. Dad tells me Biff's in town.

WILLY (*with a big smile*): Yeah, Biff's in. Working on a very big deal, Bernard.

BERNARD: What's Biff doing?

WILLY: Well, he's been doing very big things in the West. But he decided to establish himself here. Very big. We're having dinner. Did I hear your wife had a boy?

BERNARD: That's right. Our second.

WILLY: Two boys! What do you know!

BERNARD: What kind of a deal has Biff got?

WILLY: Well, Bill Oliver — very big sporting-goods man — he wants Biff very badly. Called him in from the West. Long distance, carte blanche, special deliveries. Your friends have their own private tennis court?

BERNARD: You still with the old firm, Willy?

WILLY (*after a pause*): I'm — I'm overjoyed to see how you made the grade, Bernard, overjoyed. It's an encouraging thing to see a young man really — really — Looks very good for Biff — very — (*He breaks off, then.*) Bernard — (*He is so full of emotion, he breaks off again.*)

BERNARD: What is it, Willy?

WILLY (*small and alone*): What — what's the secret?

BERNARD: What secret?

WILLY: How — how did you? Why didn't he ever catch on?

BERNARD: I wouldn't know that, Willy.

WILLY (*confidentially, desperately*): You were his friend, his boyhood friend. There's something I don't understand about it. His life ended after that Ebbets Field game. From the age of seventeen nothing good ever happened to him.

BERNARD: He never trained himself for anything.

WILLY: But he did, he did. After high school he took so many correspondence courses. Radio mechanics; television; God knows what, and never made the slightest mark.

BERNARD (*taking off his glasses*): Willy, do you want to talk candidly?

WILLY (*rising, faces* BERNARD): I regard you as a very brilliant man, Bernard. I value your advice.

BERNARD: Oh, the hell with the advice, Willy. I couldn't advise you. There's just one thing I've always wanted to ask you. When he was supposed to graduate, and the math teacher flunked him —

WILLY: Oh, that son-of-a-bitch ruined his life.

BERNARD: Yeah, but, Willy, all he had to do was go to summer school and make up that subject.

WILLY: That's right, that's right.

BERNARD: Did you tell him not to go to summer school?

WILLY: Me? I begged him to go. I ordered him to go!

BERNARD: Then why wouldn't he go?

WILLY: Why? Why! Bernard, that question has been trailing me like a ghost for the last fifteen years. He flunked the subject, and laid down and died like a hammer hit him!

BERNARD: Take it easy, kid.

WILLY: Let me talk to you — I got nobody to talk to. Bernard, Bernard, was it my fault? Y'see? It keeps going around in my mind, maybe I did something to him. I got nothing to give him.

BERNARD: Don't take it so hard.

WILLY: Why did he lay down? What is the story there? You were his friend!

BERNARD: Willy, I remember, it was June, and our grades came out. And he'd flunked math.

WILLY: That son-of-a-bitch!

BERNARD: No, it wasn't right then. Biff just got very angry, I remember, and he was ready to enroll in summer school.

WILLY (*surprised*): He was?

BERNARD: He wasn't beaten by it at all. But then, Willy, he disappeared from the block for almost a month. And I got the idea that he'd gone up to New England to see you. Did he have a talk with you then?

(WILLY *stares in silence.*)

BERNARD: Willy?

WILLY (*with a strong edge of resentment in his voice*): Yeah, he came to Boston. What about it?

BERNARD: Well, just that when he came back — I'll never forget this, it always mystifies me. Because I'd thought so well of Biff, even though he'd always taken advantage of me. I loved him, Willy, y'know? And he came back after that month and took his sneakers — remember those sneakers with "University of Virginia" printed on them? He was so proud of those, wore them every day. And he took them down in the cellar, and burned them up in the furnace. We had a fist fight. It lasted at least half an hour. Just the two of us, punching each other down the cellar, and crying right through it. I've often thought of how strange it was that I knew he'd given up his life. What happened in Boston, Willy?

(WILLY *looks at him as at an intruder.*)

BERNARD: I just bring it up because you asked me.

WILLY (*angrily*): Nothing. What do you mean, "What happened?" What's that got to do with anything?

BERNARD: Well, don't get sore.

WILLY: What are you trying to do, blame it on me? If a boy lays down is that my fault?

BERNARD: Now, Willy, don't get —

WILLY: Well, don't — don't talk to me that way! What does that mean, "What happened?"

(CHARLEY *enters. He is in his vest, and he carries a bottle of bourbon.*)

CHARLEY: Hey, you're going to miss that train. (*He waves the bottle.*)

BERNARD: Yeah, I'm going. (*He takes the bottle.*) Thanks, Pop. (*He picks up his rackets and bag*.) Good-by, Willy, and don't worry about it. You know, "If at first you don't succeed . . ."

WILLY: Yes, I believe in that.

BERNARD: But sometimes, Willy, it's better for a man just to walk away.

WILLY: Walk away?

BERNARD: That's right.

WILLY: But if you can't walk away?

BERNARD (*after a slight pause*): I guess that's when it's tough. (*Extending his hand*.) Good-by, Willy.

WILLY (*shaking* BERNARD's *hand*): Good-by, boy.

CHARLEY (*an arm on* BERNARD's *shoulder*): How do you like this kid? Gonna argue a case in front of the Supreme Court.

BERNARD (*protesting*): Pop!

WILLY (*genuinely shocked, pained, and happy*): No! The Supreme Court!

BERNARD: I gotta run. 'By, Dad!

CHARLEY: Knock 'em dead, Bernard!

(BERNARD *goes off*.)

WILLY (*as* CHARLEY *takes out his wallet*): The Supreme Court! And he didn't even mention it!

CHARLEY (*counting out money on the desk*): He don't have to — he's gonna do it.

WILLY: And you never told him what to do, did you? You never took any interest in him.

CHARLEY: My salvation is that I never took any interest in anything. There's some money — fifty dollars. I got an accountant inside.

WILLY: Charley, look . . . (*With difficulty*.) I got my insurance to pay. If you can manage it — I need a hundred and ten dollars.

(CHARLEY *doesn't reply for a moment; merely stops moving*.)

WILLY: I'd draw it from my bank but Linda would know, and I . . .

CHARLEY: Sit down, Willy.

WILLY (*moving toward the chair*): I'm keeping an account of everything, remember. I'll pay every penny back. (*He sits*.)

CHARLEY: Now listen to me, Willy.

WILLY: I want you to know I appreciate . . .

CHARLEY (*sitting down on the table*): Willy, what're you doin'? What the hell is goin' on in your head?

WILLY: Why? I'm simply . . .

CHARLEY: I offered you a job. You can make fifty dollars a week. And I won't send you on the road.

WILLY: I've got a job.

CHARLEY: Without pay? What kind of a job is a job without pay? (*He rises*.) Now, look, kid, enough is enough. I'm no genius but I know when I'm being insulted.

WILLY: Insulted!

CHARLEY: Why don't you want to work for me?

WILLY: What's the matter with you? I've got a job.

CHARLEY: Then what're you walkin' in here every week for?

WILLY (*getting up*): Well, if you don't want me to walk in here —

CHARLEY: I am offering you a job.

WILLY: I don't want your goddam job!

CHARLEY: When the hell are you going to grow up?

WILLY (*furiously*): You big ignoramus, if you say that to me again I'll rap you one! I don't care how big you are! (*He's ready to fight.*)

(*Pause.*)

CHARLEY (*kindly, going to him*): How much do you need, Willy?

WILLY: Charley, I'm strapped. I'm strapped. I don't know what to do. I was just fired.

CHARLEY: Howard fired you?

WILLY: That snotnose. Imagine that? I named him. I named him Howard.

CHARLEY: Willy, when're you gonna realize that them things don't mean anything? You named him Howard, but you can't sell that. The only thing you got in this world is what you can sell. And the funny thing is that you're a salesman, and you don't know that.

WILLY: I've always tried to think otherwise, I guess. I always felt that if a man was impressive, and well liked, that nothing —

CHARLEY: Why must everybody like you? Who liked J. P. Morgan? Was he impressive? In a Turkish bath he'd look like a butcher. But with his pockets on he was very well liked. Now listen, Willy, I know you don't like me, and nobody can say I'm in love with you, but I'll give you a job because — just for the hell of it, put it that way. Now what do you say?

WILLY: I — I just can't work for you, Charley.

CHARLEY: What're you, jealous of me?

WILLY: I can't work for you, that's all, don't ask me why.

CHARLEY (*angered, takes out more bills*): You been jealous of me all your life, you damned fool! Here, pay your insurance. (*He puts the money in* WILLY's *hand.*)

WILLY: I'm keeping strict accounts.

CHARLEY: I've got some work to do. Take care of yourself. And pay your insurance.

WILLY (*moving to the right*): Funny, y'know? After all the highways, and the trains, and the appointments, and the years, you end up worth more dead than alive.

CHARLEY: Willy, nobody's worth nothin' dead. (*After a slight pause.*) Did you hear what I said?

(WILLY *stands still, dreaming.*)

CHARLEY: Willy!

WILLY: Apologize to Bernard for me when you see him. I didn't mean to argue with him. He's a fine boy. They're all fine boys, and they'll end up big — all of them. Someday they'll all play tennis together. Wish me luck, Charley. He saw Bill Oliver today.

CHARLEY: Good luck.

WILLY (*on the verge of tears*): Charley, you're the only friend I got. Isn't that a remarkable thing? (*He goes out.*)

CHARLEY: Jesus!

(CHARLEY *stares after him a moment and follows. All light blacks out. Suddenly raucous music is heard, and a red glow rises behind the screen at right.* STANLEY, *a young waiter, appears, carrying a table, followed by* HAPPY, *who is carrying two chairs.*)

STANLEY (*putting the table down*): That's all right, Mr. Loman, I can handle it myself. (*He turns and takes the chairs from* HAPPY *and places them at the table.*)

HAPPY (*glancing around*): Oh, this is better.

STANLEY: Sure, in the front there you're in the middle of all kinds a noise. Whenever you got a party, Mr. Loman, you just tell me and I'll put you back here. Y'know, there's a lotta people they don't like it private, because when they go out they like to see a lotta action around them because they're sick and tired to stay in the house by theirself. But I know you, you ain't from Hackensack. You know what I mean?

HAPPY (*sitting down*): So how's it coming, Stanley?

STANLEY: Ah, it's a dog's life. I only wish during the war they'd a took me in the Army. I coulda been dead by now.

HAPPY: My brother's back, Stanley.

STANLEY: Oh, he come back, heh? From the Far West.

HAPPY: Yeah, big cattle man, my brother, so treat him right. And my father's coming too.

STANLEY: Oh, your father too!

HAPPY: You got a couple of nice lobsters?

STANLEY: Hundred per cent, big.

HAPPY: I want them with the claws.

STANLEY: Don't worry, I don't give you no mice. (HAPPY *laughs*.) How about some wine? It'll put a head on the meal.

HAPPY: No. You remember, Stanley, that recipe I brought you from overseas? With the champagne in it?

STANLEY: Oh, yeah, sure. I still got it tacked up yet in the kitchen. But that'll have to cost a buck apiece anyways.

HAPPY: That's all right.

STANLEY: What'd you, hit a number or somethin'?

HAPPY: No, it's a little celebration. My brother is — I think he pulled off a big deal today. I think we're going into business together.

STANLEY: Great! That's the best for you. Because a family business, you know what I mean? — that's the best.

HAPPY: That's what I think.

STANLEY: 'Cause what's the difference? Somebody steals? It's in the family. Know what I mean? (*Sotto voce*.) Like this bartender here. The boss is goin' crazy what kinda leak he's got in the cash register. You put it in but it don't come out.

HAPPY (*raising his head*): Sh!

STANLEY: What?

HAPPY: You notice I wasn't lookin' right or left, was I?

STANLEY: No.

HAPPY: And my eyes are closed.

STANLEY: So what's the — ?

HAPPY: Strudel's comin'.

STANLEY (*catching on, looks around*): Ah, no, there's no —

(*He breaks off as a furred, lavishly dressed* GIRL *enters and sits at the next table. Both follow her with their eyes.*)

STANLEY: Geez, how'd ya know?

HAPPY: I got radar or something. (*Staring directly at her profile.*) Oooooooo . . . Stanley.

STANLEY: I think that's for you, Mr. Loman.

HAPPY: Look at that mouth. Oh, God. And the binoculars.

STANLEY: Geez, you got a life, Mr. Loman.

HAPPY: Wait on her.

STANLEY (*going to* THE GIRL's *table*): Would you like a menu, ma'am?

GIRL: I'm expecting someone, but I'd like a —

HAPPY: Why don't you bring her — excuse me, miss, do you mind? I sell champagne, and I'd like you to try my brand. Bring her a champagne, Stanley.

GIRL: That's awfully nice of you.

HAPPY: Don't mention it. It's all company money. (*He laughs.*)

GIRL: That's a charming product to be selling, isn't it?

HAPPY: Oh, gets to be like everything else. Selling is selling, y'know.

GIRL: I suppose.

HAPPY: You don't happen to sell, do you?

GIRL: No, I don't sell.

HAPPY: Would you object to a compliment from a stranger? You ought to be on a magazine cover.

GIRL (*looking at him a little archly*): I have been.

(STANLEY *comes in with a glass of champagne.*)

HAPPY: What'd I say before, Stanley? You see? She's a cover girl.

STANLEY: Oh, I could see, I could see.

HAPPY (*to* THE GIRL): What magazine?

GIRL: Oh, a lot of them. (*She takes the drink.*) Thank you.

HAPPY: You know what they say in France, don't you? "Champagne is the drink of the complexion" — Hya, Biff!

(BIFF *has entered and sits with* HAPPY.)

BIFF: Hello, kid. Sorry I'm late.

HAPPY: I just got here. Uh, Miss — ?

GIRL: Forsythe.

HAPPY: Miss Forsythe, this is my brother.

BIFF: Is Dad here?

HAPPY: His name is Biff. You might've heard of him. Great football player.

GIRL: Really? What team?

HAPPY: Are you familiar with football?

GIRL: No, I'm afraid I'm not.

HAPPY: Biff is quarterback with the New York Giants.

GIRL: Well, that is nice, isn't it? (*She drinks.*)

HAPPY: Good health.

GIRL: I'm happy to meet you.

HAPPY: That's my name. Hap. It's really Harold, but at West Point they called me Happy.

GIRL (*now really impressed*): Oh, I see. How do you do? (*She turns her profile.*)

BIFF: Isn't Dad coming?

HAPPY: You want her?

BIFF: Oh, I could never make that.

HAPPY: I remember the time that idea would never come into your head. Where's the old confidence, Biff?

BIFF: I just saw Oliver —

HAPPY: Wait a minute. I've got to see that old confidence again. Do you want her? She's on call.

BIFF: Oh, no. (*He turns to look at* THE GIRL.)

HAPPY: I'm telling you. Watch this. (*Turning to* THE GIRL.) Honey? (*She turns to him.*) Are you busy?

GIRL: Well, I am . . . but I could make a phone call.

HAPPY: Do that, will you, honey? And see if you can get a friend. We'll be here for a while. Biff is one of the greatest football players in the country.

GIRL (*standing up*): Well, I'm certainly happy to meet you.

HAPPY: Come back soon.

GIRL: I'll try.

HAPPY: Don't try, honey, try hard.

(THE GIRL *exits*. STANLEY *follows, shaking his head in bewildered admiration.*)

HAPPY: Isn't that a shame now? A beautiful girl like that? That's why I can't get married. There's not a good woman in a thousand. New York is loaded with them, kid!

BIFF: Hap, look —

HAPPY: I told you she was on call!

BIFF (*strangely unnerved*): Cut it out, will ya? I want to say something to you.

HAPPY: Did you see Oliver?

BIFF: I saw him all right. Now look, I want to tell Dad a couple of things and I want you to help me.

HAPPY: What? Is he going to back you?

BIFF: Are you crazy? You're out of your goddam head, you know that?

HAPPY: Why? What happened?

BIFF (*breathlessly*): I did a terrible thing today, Hap. It's been the strangest day I ever went through. I'm all numb, I swear.

HAPPY: You mean he wouldn't see you?

BIFF: Well, I waited six hours for him, see? All day. Kept sending my name in. Even tried to date his secretary so she'd get me to him, but no soap.

HAPPY: Because you're not showin' the old confidence, Biff. He remembered you, didn't he?

BIFF (*stopping* HAPPY *with a gesture*): Finally, about five o'clock, he comes out. Didn't remember who I was or anything. I felt like such an idiot, Hap.

HAPPY: Did you tell him my Florida idea?

BIFF: He walked away. I saw him for one minute. I got so mad I could've torn the walls down! How the hell did I ever get the idea I was a salesman there? I even believed myself that I'd been a salesman for him! And then he gave me one look and — I realized what a ridiculous lie my whole life has been! We've been talking in a dream for fifteen years. I was a shipping clerk.

HAPPY: What'd you do?

BIFF (*with great tension and wonder*): Well, he left, see. And the secretary went out. I was all alone in the waiting-room. I don't know what came over me, Hap. The next thing I know I'm in his office — paneled walls, everything. I can't explain it. I — Hap, I took his fountain pen.

HAPPY: Geez, did he catch you?

BIFF: I ran out. I ran down all eleven flights. I ran and ran and ran.

HAPPY: That was an awful dumb — what'd you do that for?

BIFF (*agonized*): I don't know, I just — wanted to take something, I don't know. You gotta help me, Hap, I'm gonna tell Pop.

HAPPY: You crazy? What for?

BIFF: Hap, he's got to understand that I'm not the man somebody lends that kind of money to. He thinks I've been spiting him all these years and it's eating him up.

HAPPY: That's just it. You tell him something nice.

BIFF: I can't.

HAPPY: Say you got a lunch date with Oliver tomorrow.

BIFF: So what do I do tomorrow?

HAPPY: You leave the house tomorrow and come back at night and say Oliver is thinking it over. And he thinks it over for a couple of weeks, and gradually it fades away and nobody's the worse.

BIFF: But it'll go on forever!

HAPPY: Dad is never so happy as when he's looking forward to something!

(WILLY *enters*.)

HAPPY: Hello, scout!

WILLY: Gee, I haven't been here in years!

(STANLEY *has followed* WILLY *in and sets a chair for him.* STANLEY *starts off but* HAPPY *stops him.*)

HAPPY: Stanley!

(STANLEY *stands by, waiting for an order.*)

BIFF (*going to* WILLY *with guilt, as to an invalid*): Sit down, Pop. You want a drink?

WILLY: Sure, I don't mind.

BIFF: Let's get a load on.

WILLY: You look worried.

BIFF: N-no. (*To* STANLEY.) Scotch all around. Make it doubles.

STANLEY: Doubles, right. (*He goes.*)

WILLY: You had a couple already, didn't you?

BIFF: Just a couple, yeah.

WILLY: Well, what happened, boy? (*Nodding affirmatively, with a smile.*) Everything go all right?

BIFF (*takes a breath, then reaches out and grasps* WILLY'S *hand*): Pal . . . (*He is smiling bravely, and* WILLY *is smiling too.*) I had an experience today.

HAPPY: Terrific, Pop.

WILLY: That so? What happened?

BIFF (*high, slightly alcoholic, above the earth*): I'm going to tell you everything from first to last. It's been a strange day. (*Silence. He looks around, composes himself as best he can, but his breath keeps breaking the rhythm of his voice.*) I had to wait quite a while for him, and —

WILLY: Oliver?

BIFF: Yeah, Oliver. All day, as a matter of cold fact. And a lot of — instances — facts, Pop, facts about my life came back to me. Who was it, Pop? Who ever said I was a salesman with Oliver?

WILLY: Well, you were.

BIFF: No, Dad, I was a shipping clerk.

WILLY: But you were practically —

BIFF (*with determination*): Dad, I don't know who said it first, but I was never a salesman for Bill Oliver.

WILLY: What're you talking about?

BIFF: Let's hold on to the facts tonight, Pop. We're not going to get anywhere bullin' around. I was a shipping clerk.

WILLY (*angrily*): All right, now listen to me —

BIFF: Why don't you let me finish?

WILLY: I'm not interested in stories about the past or any crap of that kind because the woods are burning, boys, you understand? There's a big blaze going on all around. I was fired today.

BIFF (*shocked*): How could you be?

WILLY: I was fired, and I'm looking for a little good news to tell your mother, because the woman has waited and the woman has suffered. The gist of it is that I haven't got a story left in my head, Biff. So don't give me a lecture about facts and aspects. I am not interested. Now what've you got to say to me?

(STANLEY *enters with three drinks. They wait until he leaves.*)

WILLY: Did you see Oliver?

BIFF: Jesus, Dad!

WILLY: You mean you didn't go up there?

HAPPY: Sure he went up there.

BIFF: I did. I — saw him. How could they fire you?

WILLY (*on the edge of his chair*): What kind of a welcome did he give you?

BIFF: He won't even let you work on commission?

WILLY: I'm out! (*Driving.*) So tell me, he gave you a warm welcome?

HAPPY: Sure, Pop, sure!

BIFF (*driven*): Well, it was kind of —

WILLY: I was wondering if he'd remember you. (*To* HAPPY.) Imagine, man doesn't see him for ten, twelve years and gives him that kind of a welcome!

HAPPY: Damn right!

BIFF (*trying to return to the offensive*): Pop, look —

WILLY: You know why he remembered you, don't you? Because you impressed him in those days.

BIFF: Let's talk quietly and get this down to the facts, huh?

WILLY (*as though* BIFF *had been interrupting*): Well, what happened? It's great news, Biff. Did he take you into his office or'd you talk in the waiting-room?

BIFF: Well, he came in, see, and —

WILLY (*with a big smile*): What'd he say? Betcha he threw his arm around you.

BIFF: Well, he kinda —

WILLY: He's a fine man. (*To* HAPPY.) Very hard man to see, y'know.

HAPPY (*agreeing*): Oh, I know.

WILLY (*to* BIFF): Is that where you had the drinks?

BIFF: Yeah, he gave me a couple of — no, no!

HAPPY (*cutting in*): He told him my Florida idea.

WILLY: Don't interrupt. (*To* BIFF.) How'd he react to the Florida idea?

BIFF: Dad, will you give me a minute to explain?

WILLY: I've been waiting for you to explain since I sat down here! What happened? He took you into his office and what?

BIFF: Well — I talked. And — and he listened, see.

WILLY: Famous for the way he listens, y'know. What was his answer?

BIFF: His answer was — (*He breaks off, suddenly angry.*) Dad, you're not letting me tell you what I want to tell you!

WILLY (*accusing, angered*): You didn't see him, did you?

BIFF: I did see him!

WILLY: What'd you insult him or something? You insulted him, didn't you?

BIFF: Listen, will you let me out of it, will you just let me out of it!

HAPPY: What the hell!

WILLY: Tell me what happened!

BIFF (*to* HAPPY): I can't talk to him!

(*A single trumpet note jars the ear. The light of green leaves stains the house, which holds the air of night and a dream.* YOUNG BERNARD *enters and knocks on the door of the house.*)

YOUNG BERNARD (*frantically*): Mrs. Loman, Mrs. Loman!

HAPPY: Tell him what happened!

BIFF (*to* HAPPY): Shut up and leave me alone!

WILLY: No, no! You had to go and flunk math!

BIFF: What math? What're you talking about?

YOUNG BERNARD: Mrs. Loman, Mrs. Loman!

(LINDA *appears in the house, as of old.*)

WILLY (*wildly*): Math, math, math!

BIFF: Take it easy, Pop!

YOUNG BERNARD: Mrs. Loman!

WILLY (*furiously*): If you hadn't flunked you'd've been set by now!

BIFF: Now, look, I'm gonna tell you what happened, and you're going to listen to me.

YOUNG BERNARD: Mrs. Loman!

BIFF: I waited six hours —

HAPPY: What the hell are you saying?

BIFF: I kept sending in my name but he wouldn't see me. So finally he . . . (*He continues unheard as light fades low on the restaurant.*)

YOUNG BERNARD: Biff flunked math!

LINDA: No!

YOUNG BERNARD: Birnbaum flunked him! They won't graduate him!

LINDA: But they have to. He's gotta go to the university. Where is he? Biff! Biff!

YOUNG BERNARD: No, he left. He went to Grand Central.

LINDA: Grand — You mean he went to Boston!

YOUNG BERNARD: Is Uncle Willy in Boston?

LINDA: Oh, maybe Willy can talk to the teacher. Oh, the poor, poor boy!

(*Light on house area snaps out.*)

BIFF (*at the table, now audible, holding up a gold fountain pen*): . . . so I'm washed up with Oliver, you understand? Are you listening to me?

WILLY (*at a loss*): Yeah, sure. If you hadn't flunked —

BIFF: Flunked what? What're you talking about?

WILLY: Don't blame everything on me! I didn't flunk math — you did! What pen?

HAPPY: That was awful dumb, Biff, a pen like that is worth —

WILLY (*seeing the pen for the first time*): You took Oliver's pen?

BIFF (*weakening*): Dad, I just explained it to you.

WILLY: You stole Bill Oliver's fountain pen!

BIFF: I didn't exactly steal it! That's just what I've been explaining to you!

HAPPY: He had it in his hand and just then Oliver walked in, so he got nervous and stuck it in his pocket!

WILLY: My God, Biff!

BIFF: I never intended to do it, Dad!

OPERATOR'S VOICE: Standish Arms, good evening!

WILLY (*shouting*): I'm not in my room!

BIFF (*frightened*): Dad, what's the matter? (*He and* HAPPY *stand up.*)

OPERATOR: Ringing Mr. Loman for you!

WILLY: I'm not there, stop it!

BIFF (*horrified, gets down on one knee before* WILLY): Dad, I'll make good, I'll make good. (WILLY *tries to get to his feet.* BIFF *holds him down.*) Sit down now.

WILLY: No, you're no good, you're no good for anything.

BIFF: I am, Dad, I'll find something else, you understand? Now don't worry about anything. (*He holds up* WILLY's *face.*) Talk to me, Dad.

OPERATOR: Mr. Loman does not answer. Shall I page him?

WILLY (*attempting to stand, as though to rush and silence the* OPERATOR): No, no, no!

HAPPY: He'll strike something, Pop.

WILLY: No, no . . .

BIFF (*desperately, standing over* WILLY): Pop, listen! Listen to me! I'm telling you something good. Oliver talked to his partner about the Florida idea. You listening? He — he talked to his partner, and he came to me . . . I'm going to be all right, you hear? Dad, listen to me, he said it was just a question of the amount!

WILLY: Then you . . . got it?

HAPPY: He's gonna be terrific, Pop!

WILLY (*trying to stand*): Then you got it, haven't you? You got it! You got it!

BIFF (*agonized, holds* WILLY *down*): No, no. Look, Pop. I'm supposed to have lunch with them tomorrow. I'm just telling you this so you'll know that I can still make an impression, Pop. And I'll make good somewhere, but I can't go tomorrow, see?

WILLY: Why not? You simply —

BIFF: But the pen, Pop!

WILLY: You give it to him and tell him it was an oversight!

HAPPY: Sure, have lunch tomorrow!

BIFF: I can't say that —

WILLY: You were doing a crossword puzzle and accidentally used his pen!

BIFF: Listen, kid, I took those balls years ago, now I walk in with his fountain pen? That clinches it, don't you see? I can't face him like that! I'll try elsewhere.

PAGE'S VOICE: Paging Mr. Loman!

WILLY: Don't you want to be anything?

BIFF: Pop, how can I go back?

WILLY: You don't want to be anything, is that what's behind it?

BIFF (*now angry at* WILLY *for not crediting his sympathy*): Don't take it that way! You think it was easy walking into that office after what I'd done to him? A team of horses couldn't have dragged me back to Bill Oliver!

WILLY: Then why'd you go?

BIFF: Why did I go? Why did I go! Look at you! Look at what's become of you!

(*Off left*, THE WOMAN *laughs*.)

WILLY: Biff, you're going to go to that lunch tomorrow, or —

BIFF: I can't go. I've got no appointment!

HAPPY: Biff, for . . . !

WILLY: Are you spiting me?

BIFF: Don't take it that way! Goddammit!

WILLY (*strikes* BIFF *and falters away from the table*): You rotten little louse! Are you spiting me?

THE WOMAN: Someone's at the door, Willy!

BIFF: I'm no good, can't you see what I am?

HAPPY (*separating them*): Hey, you're in a restaurant! Now cut it out, both of you! (THE GIRLS *enter*.) Hello, girls, sit down.

(THE WOMAN *laughs, off left*.)

MISS FORSYTHE: I guess we might as well. This is Letta.

THE WOMAN: Willy, are you going to wake up?

BIFF (*ignoring* WILLY): How're ya, miss, sit down. What do you drink?

MISS FORSYTHE: Letta might not be able to stay long.

LETTA: I gotta get up very early tomorrow. I got jury duty. I'm so excited! Were you fellows ever on a jury?

BIFF: No, but I been in front of them! (THE GIRLS *laugh*.) This is my father.

LETTA: Isn't he cute? Sit down with us, Pop.

HAPPY: Sit him down, Biff!

BIFF (*going to him*): Come on, slugger, drink us under the table. To hell with it! Come on, sit down, pal.

(On BIFF's *last insistence*, WILLY *is about to sit*.)

THE WOMAN (*now urgently*): Willy, are you going to answer the door!

(THE WOMAN's *call pulls* WILLY *back. He starts right, befuddled*.)

BIFF: Hey, where are you going?

WILLY: Open the door.

BIFF: The door?

WILLY: The washroom . . . the door . . . where's the door?

BIFF (*leading* WILLY *to the left*): Just go straight down.

(WILLY *moves left*.)

THE WOMAN: Willy, Willy, are you going to get up, get up, get up, get up?

(WILLY *exits left*.)

LETTA: I think it's sweet you bring your daddy along.

MISS FORSYTHE: Oh, he isn't really your father!

BIFF (*at left, turning to her resentfully*): Miss Forsythe, you've just seen a prince walk by. A fine, troubled prince. A hard-working, unappreciated prince. A pal, you understand? A good companion. Always for his boys.

LETTA: That's so sweet.

HAPPY: Well, girls, what's the program? We're wasting time. Come on, Biff. Gather round. Where would you like to go?

BIFF: Why don't you do something for him?

HAPPY: Me!

BIFF: Don't you give a damn for him, Hap?

HAPPY: What're you talking about? I'm the one who —

BIFF: I sense it, you don't give a good goddam about him. (*He takes the rolled-up hose from his pocket and puts it on the table in front of* HAPPY.) Look what I found in the cellar, for Christ's sake. How can you bear to let it go on?

HAPPY: Me? Who goes away? Who runs off and —

BIFF: Yeah, but he doesn't mean anything to you. You could help him — I can't! Don't you understand what I'm talking about? He's going to kill himself, don't you know that?

HAPPY: Don't I know it! Me!

BIFF: Hap, help him! Jesus . . . help him . . . Help me, help me, I can't bear to look at his face! (*Ready to weep, he hurries out, up right*.)

HAPPY (*starting after him*): Where are you going?

MISS FORSYTHE: What's he so mad about?

HAPPY: Come on, girls, we'll catch up with him.

MISS FORSYTHE (*as* HAPPY *pushes her out*): Say, I don't like that temper of his!

HAPPY: He's just a little overstrung, he'll be all right!

WILLY (*off left, as* THE WOMAN *laughs*): Don't answer! Don't answer!

LETTA: Don't you want to tell your father —

HAPPY: No, that's not my father. He's just a guy. Come on, we'll catch Biff, and, honey, we're going to paint this town! Stanley, where's the check! Hey, Stanley!

(*They exit.* STANLEY *looks toward left*.)

STANLEY (*calling to* HAPPY *indignantly*): Mr. Loman! Mr. Loman!

(STANLEY *picks up a chair and follows them off. Knocking is heard off left.* THE WOMAN *enters, laughing.* WILLY *follows her. She is in a black slip; he is buttoning his shirt. Raw, sensuous music accompanies their speech*.)

WILLY: Will you stop laughing? Will you stop?

THE WOMAN: Aren't you going to answer the door? He'll wake the whole hotel.

WILLY: I'm not expecting anybody.

THE WOMAN: Whyn't you have another drink, honey, and stop being so damn self-centered?

WILLY: I'm so lonely.

THE WOMAN: You know you ruined me, Willy? From now on, whenever you come to the office, I'll see that you go right through to the buyers. No waiting at my desk any more, Willy. You ruined me.

WILLY: That's nice of you to say that.

THE WOMAN: Gee, you are self-centered! Why so sad? You are the saddest self-centeredest soul I ever did see-saw. (*She laughs. He kisses her*.) Come on inside, drummer boy. It's silly to be dressing in the middle of the night. (*As knocking is heard*.) Aren't you going to answer the door?

WILLY: They're knocking on the wrong door.

THE WOMAN: But I felt the knocking. And he heard us talking in here. Maybe the hotel's on fire!

WILLY (*his terror rising*): It's a mistake.

THE WOMAN: Then tell him to go away!

WILLY: There's nobody there.

THE WOMAN: It's getting on my nerves, Willy. There's somebody standing out there and it's getting on my nerves!

WILLY (*pushing her away from him*): All right, stay in the bathroom here, and don't come out. I think there's a law in Massachusetts about it, so don't come out. It may be that new room clerk. He looked very mean. So don't come out. It's a mistake, there's no fire.

(*The knocking is heard again. He takes a few steps away from her, and she vanishes into the wing. The light follows him, and now he is facing* YOUNG BIFF, *who carries a suitcase.* BIFF *steps toward him. The music is gone.*)

BIFF: Why didn't you answer?

WILLY: Biff! What are you doing in Boston?

BIFF: Why didn't you answer? I've been knocking for five minutes, I called you on the phone —

WILLY: I just heard you. I was in the bathroom and had the door shut. Did anything happen home?

BIFF: Dad — I let you down.

WILLY: What do you mean?

BIFF: Dad . . .

WILLY: Biffo, what's this about? (*Putting his arm around* BIFF.) Come on, let's go downstairs and get you a malted.

BIFF: Dad, I flunked math.

WILLY: Not for the term?

BIFF: The term. I haven't got enough credits to graduate.

WILLY: You mean to say Bernard wouldn't give you the answers?

BIFF: He did, he tried, but I only got a sixty-one.

WILLY: And they wouldn't give you four points?

BIFF: Birnbaum refused absolutely. I begged him, Pop, but he won't give me those points. You gotta talk to him before they close the school. Because if he saw the kind of man you are, and you just talked to him in your way, I'm sure he'd come through for me. The class came right before practice, see, and I didn't go enough. Would you talk to him? He'd like you, Pop. You know the way you could talk.

WILLY: You're on. We'll drive right back.

BIFF: Oh, Dad, good work! I'm sure he'll change it for you!

WILLY: Go downstairs and tell the clerk I'm checkin' out. Go right down.

BIFF: Yes, sir! See, the reason he hates me, Pop — one day he was late for class so I got up at the blackboard and imitated him. I crossed my eyes and talked with a lithp.

WILLY (*laughing*): You did? The kids like it?

BIFF: They nearly died laughing!

WILLY: Yeah? What'd you do?

BIFF: The thquare root of thixthy twee is . . . (WILLY *bursts out laughing;* BIFF *joins him.*) And in the middle of it he walked in!

(WILLY *laughs and* THE WOMAN *joins in offstage.*)

WILLY (*without hesitation*): Hurry downstairs and —
BIFF: Somebody in there?
WILLY: No, that was next door.

(THE WOMAN *laughs offstage*.)

BIFF: Somebody got in your bathroom!
WILLY: No, it's the next room, there's a party —
THE WOMAN (*enters, laughing. She lisps this*): Can I come in? There's something in the bathtub, Willy, and it's moving!

(WILLY *looks at* BIFF, *who is staring open-mouthed and horrified at* THE WOMAN.)

WILLY: Ah — you better go back to your room. They must be finished painting by now. They're painting her room so I let her take a shower here. Go back, go back . . . (*He pushes her*.)
THE WOMAN (*resisting*): But I've got to get dressed, Willy, I can't —
WILLY: Get out of here! Go back, go back . . . (*Suddenly striving for the ordinary*.) This is Miss Francis, Biff, she's a buyer. They're painting her room. Go back, Miss Francis, go back . . .
THE WOMAN: But my clothes, I can't go out naked in the hall!
WILLY (*pushing her offstage*): Get outa here! Go back, go back!

(BIFF *slowly sits down on his suitcase as the argument continues offstage*.)

THE WOMAN: Where's my stockings? You promised me stockings, Willy!
WILLY: I have no stockings here!
THE WOMAN: You had two boxes of size nine sheers for me, and I want them!
WILLY: Here, for God's sake, will you get outa here!
THE WOMAN (*enters holding a box of stockings*): I just hope there's nobody in the hall. That's all I hope. (*To* BIFF.) Are you football or baseball?
BIFF: Football.
THE WOMAN (*angry, humiliated*): That's me too. G'night. (*She snatches her clothes from* WILLY, *and walks out*.)
WILLY (*after a pause*): Well, better get going. I want to get to the school first thing in the morning. Get my suits out of the closet. I'll get my valise. (BIFF *doesn't move*.) What's the matter? (BIFF *remains motionless, tears falling*.) She's a buyer. Buys for J. H. Simmons. She lives down the hall — they're painting. You don't imagine — (*He breaks off. After a pause*.) Now listen, pal, she's just a buyer. She sees merchandise in her room and they have to keep it looking just so . . . (*Pause. Assuming command*.) All right, get my suits. (BIFF *doesn't move*.) Now stop crying and do as I say. I gave you an order. Biff, I gave you an order! Is that what you do when I give you an order? How dare you cry! (*Putting his arm around* BIFF.) Now look, Biff, when you grow up you'll understand about these things. You mustn't — you mustn't overemphasize a thing like this. I'll see Birnbaum first thing in the morning.
BIFF: Never mind.
WILLY (*getting down beside* BIFF): Never mind! He's going to give you those points. I'll see to it.
BIFF: He wouldn't listen to you.
WILLY: He certainly will listen to me. You need those points for the U. of Virginia.
BIFF: I'm not going there.

WILLY: Heh? If I can't get him to change that mark you'll make it up in summer school. You've got all summer to —

BIFF (*his weeping breaking from him*): Dad . . .

WILLY (*infected by it*): Oh, my boy . . .

BIFF: Dad . . .

WILLY: She's nothing to me, Biff. I was lonely, I was terribly lonely.

BIFF: You — you gave her Mama's stockings! (*His tears break through and he rises to go.*)

WILLY (*grabbing for* BIFF): I gave you an order!

BIFF: Don't touch me, you — liar!

WILLY: Apologize for that!

BIFF: You fake! You phony little fake! You fake! (*Overcome, he turns quickly and weeping fully goes out with his suitcase.* WILLY *is left on the floor on his knees.*)

WILLY: I gave you an order! Biff, come back here or I'll beat you! Come back here! I'll whip you!

(STANLEY *comes quickly in from the right and stands in front of* WILLY.)

WILLY (*shouts at* STANLEY): I gave you an order . . .

STANLEY: Hey, let's pick it up, pick it up, Mr. Loman. (*He helps* WILLY *to his feet.*) Your boys left with the chippies. They said they'll see you home.

(*A second waiter watches some distance away.*)

WILLY: But we were supposed to have dinner together.

(*Music is heard,* WILLY's *theme.*)

STANLEY: Can you make it?

WILLY: I'll — sure, I can make it. (*Suddenly concerned about his clothes.*) Do I — I look all right?

STANLEY: Sure, you look all right. (*He flicks a speck off* WILLY's *lapel.*)

WILLY: Here — here's a dollar.

STANLEY: Oh, your son paid me. It's all right.

WILLY (*putting it in* STANLEY's *hand*): No, take it. You're a good boy.

STANLEY: Oh, no, you don't have to . . .

WILLY: Here — here's some more, I don't need it any more. (*After a slight pause.*) Tell me — is there a seed store in the neighborhood?

STANLEY: Seeds? You mean like to plant?

(*As* WILLY *turns,* STANLEY *slips the money back into his jacket pocket.*)

WILLY: Yes. Carrots, peas . . .

STANLEY: Well, there's hardware stores on Sixth Avenue, but it may be too late now.

WILLY (*anxiously*): Oh, I'd better hurry. I've got to get some seeds. (*He starts off to the right.*) I've got to get some seeds, right away. Nothing's planted. I don't have a thing in the ground.

(WILLY *hurries out as the light goes down.* STANLEY *moves over to the right after him, watches him off. The other waiter has been staring at* WILLY.)

STANLEY (*to the waiter*): Well, whatta you looking at?

(*The waiter picks up the chairs and moves off right.* STANLEY *takes the table and follows him. The light fades on this area. There is a long pause, the sound of the flute coming over. The light gradually rises on the kitchen, which is empty.* HAPPY *appears at the door of the house, followed by* BIFF. HAPPY *is carrying a large bunch of long-stemmed roses. He enters the kitchen, looks around for* LINDA. *Not seeing her, he turns to* BIFF, *who is just outside the house door, and makes a gesture with his hands, indicating "Not here, I guess." He looks into the living-room and freezes. Inside,* LINDA, *unseen, is seated,* WILLY's *coat on her lap. She rises ominously and quietly and moves toward* HAPPY, *who backs up into the kitchen, afraid.*)

HAPPY: Hey, what're you doing up? (LINDA *says nothing but moves toward him implacably.*) Where's Pop? (*He keeps backing to the right, and now* LINDA *is in full view in the doorway to the living-room.*) Is he sleeping?

LINDA: Where were you?

HAPPY (*trying to laugh it off*): We met two girls, Mom, very fine types. Here, we brought you some flowers. (*Offering them to her.*) Put them in your room, Ma.

(*She knocks them to the floor at* BIFF's *feet. He has now come inside and closed the door behind him. She stares at* BIFF, *silent.*)

HAPPY: Now what'd you do that for? Mom, I want you to have some flowers —

LINDA (*cutting* HAPPY *off, violently to* BIFF): Don't you care whether he lives or dies?

HAPPY (*going to the stairs*): Come upstairs, Biff.

BIFF (*with a flare of disgust, to* HAPPY): Go away from me! (*To* LINDA.) What do you mean, lives or dies? Nobody's dying around here, pal.

LINDA: Get out of my sight! Get out of here!

BIFF: I wanna see the boss.

LINDA: You're not going near him!

BIFF: Where is he? (*He moves into the living-room and* LINDA *follows.*)

LINDA (*shouting after* BIFF): You invite him for dinner. He looks forward to it all day — (BIFF *appears in his parents' bedroom, looks around, and exits*) — and then you desert him there. There's no stranger you'd do that to!

HAPPY: Why? He had a swell time with us. Listen, when I — (LINDA *comes back into the kitchen*) — desert him I hope I don't outlive the day!

LINDA: Get out of here!

HAPPY: Now look, Mom . . .

LINDA: Did you have to go to women tonight? You and your lousy rotten whores!

(BIFF *re-enters the kitchen.*)

HAPPY: Mom, all we did was follow Biff around trying to cheer him up! (*To* BIFF.) Boy, what a night you gave me!

LINDA: Get out of here, both of you, and don't come back! I don't want you tormenting him any more. Go on now, get your things together! (*To* BIFF.) You can sleep in his apartment. (*She starts to pick up the flowers and stops herself.*) Pick up this stuff, I'm not your maid any more. Pick it up, you bum, you!

(HAPPY *turns his back to her in refusal.* BIFF *slowly moves over and gets down on his knees, picking up the flowers.*)

LINDA: You're a pair of animals! Not one, not another living soul would have had the cruelty to walk out on that man in a restaurant!

BIFF (*not looking at her*): Is that what he said?

LINDA: He didn't have to say anything. He was so humiliated he nearly limped when he came in.

HAPPY: But, Mom, he had a great time with us —

BIFF (*cutting him off violently*): Shut up!

(*Without another word,* HAPPY *goes upstairs.*)

LINDA: You! You didn't even go in to see if he was all right!

BIFF (*still on the floor in front of* LINDA, *the flowers in his hand; with self-loathing*): No. Didn't. Didn't do a damned thing. How do you like that, heh? Left him babbling in a toilet.

LINDA: You louse. You . . .

BIFF: Now you hit it on the nose! (*He gets up, throws the flowers in the wastebasket.*) The scum of the earth, and you're looking at him!

LINDA: Get out of here!

BIFF: I gotta talk to the boss, Mom. Where is he?

LINDA: You're not going near him. Get out of this house!

BIFF (*with absolute assurance, determination*): No. We're gonna have an abrupt conversation, him and me.

LINDA: You're not talking to him!

(*Hammering is heard from outside the house, off right.* BIFF *turns toward the noise.*)

LINDA (*suddenly pleading*): Will you please leave him alone?

BIFF: What's he doing out there?

LINDA: He's planting the garden!

BIFF (*quietly*): Now? Oh, my God!

(BIFF *moves outside,* LINDA *following. The light dies down on them and comes up on the center of the apron as* WILLY *walks into it. He is carrying a flashlight, a hoe, and a handful of seed packets. He raps the top of the hoe sharply to fix it firmly, and then moves to the left, measuring off the distance with his foot. He holds the flashlight to look at the seed packets, reading off the instructions. He is in the blue of night.*)

WILLY: Carrots . . . quarter-inch apart. Rows . . . one-foot rows. (*He measures it off.*) One foot. (*He puts down a package and measures off.*) Beets. (*He puts down another package and measures again.*) Lettuce. (*He reads the package, puts it down.*) One foot — (*He breaks off as* BEN *appears at the right and moves slowly down to him.*) What a proposition, ts, ts. Terrific, terrific. 'Cause she's suffered, Ben, the woman has suffered. You understand me? A man can't go out the way he came in, Ben, a man has got to add up to something. You can't, you can't — (BEN *moves toward him as though to interrupt.*) You gotta consider, now. Don't answer so quick. Remember, it's a guaranteed twenty-thousand-dollar proposition. Now look, Ben, I want you to go through the ins and outs of this thing with me. I've got nobody to talk to, Ben, and the woman has suffered, you hear me?

BEN (*standing still, considering*): What's the proposition?

WILLY: It's twenty thousand dollars on the barrelhead. Guaranteed, gilt-edged, you understand?

BEN: You don't want to make a fool of yourself. They might not honor the policy.

WILLY: How can they dare refuse? Didn't I work like a coolie to meet every premium
on the nose? And now they don't pay off? Impossible!

BEN: It's called a cowardly thing, William.

WILLY: Why? Does it take more guts to stand here the rest of my life ringing up a
zero?

BEN (*yielding*): That's a point, William. (*He moves, thinking, turns.*) And twenty
thousand — that *is* something one can feel with the hand, it is there.

WILLY (*now assured, with rising power*): Oh, Ben, that's the whole beauty of it! I see
it like a diamond, shining in the dark, hard and rough, that I can pick up and
touch in my hand. Not like — like an appointment! This would not be another
damned-fool appointment, Ben, and it changes all the aspects. Because he thinks
I'm nothing, see, and so he spites me. But the funeral — (*Straightening up.*)
Ben, that funeral will be massive! They'll come from Maine, Massachusetts, Ver-
mont, New Hampshire! All the old-timers with the strange license plates — that
boy will be thunder-struck, Ben, because he never realized — I am known!
Rhode Island, New York, New Jersey — I am known, Ben, and he'll see it with
his eyes once and for all. He'll see what I am, Ben! He's in for a shock, that boy!

BEN (*coming down to the edge of the garden*): He'll call you a coward.

WILLY (*suddenly fearful*): No, that would be terrible.

BEN: Yes. And a damned fool.

WILLY: No, no, he mustn't, I won't have that! (*He is broken and desperate.*)

BEN: He'll hate you, William.

(*The gay music of the boys is heard.*)

WILLY: Oh, Ben, how do we get back to all the great times? Used to be so full of
light, and comradeship, the sleigh-riding in winter, and the ruddiness on his
cheeks. And always some kind of good news coming up, always something nice
coming up ahead. And never even let me carry the valises in the house, and
simonizing, simonizing that little red car! Why, why can't I give him something
and not have him hate me?

BEN: Let me think about it. (*He glances at his watch.*) I still have a little time.
Remarkable proposition, but you've got to be sure you're not making a fool of
yourself.

(BEN *drifts off upstage and goes out of sight.* BIFF *comes down from the left.*)

WILLY (*suddenly conscious of* BIFF, *turns and looks up at him, then begins picking
up the packages of seeds in confusion*): Where the hell is that seed? (*Indignantly.*)
You can't see nothing out here! They boxed in the whole goddam neighborhood!

BIFF: There are people all around here. Don't you realize that?

WILLY: I'm busy. Don't bother me.

BIFF (*taking the hoe from* WILLY): I'm saying good-by to you, Pop. (WILLY *looks at
him, silent, unable to move.*) I'm not coming back any more.

WILLY: You're not going to see Oliver tomorrow?

BIFF: I've got no appointment, Dad.

WILLY: He put his arm around you, and you've got no appointment?

BIFF: Pop, get this now, will you? Everytime I've left it's been a fight that sent me
out of here. Today I realized something about myself and I tried to explain it to
you and I — I think I'm just not smart enough to make any sense out of it for
you. To hell with whose fault it is or anything like that. (*He takes* WILLY's *arm.*)

Let's just wrap it up, heh? Come on in, we'll tell Mom. (*He gently tries to pull* WILLY *to left.*)

WILLY (*frozen, immobile, with guilt in his voice*): No, I don't want to see her.

BIFF: Come on! (*He pulls again, and* WILLY *tries to pull away.*)

WILLY (*highly nervous*): No, no, I don't want to see her.

BIFF (*tries to look into* WILLY's *face, as if to find the answer there*): Why don't you want to see her?

WILLY (*more harshly now*): Don't bother me, will you?

BIFF: What do you mean, you don't want to see her? You don't want them calling you yellow, do you? This isn't your fault; it's me, I'm a bum. Now come inside! (WILLY *strains to get away.*) Did you hear what I said to you?

(WILLY *pulls away and quickly goes by himself into the house.* BIFF *follows.*)

LINDA (*to* WILLY): Did you plant, dear?

BIFF (*at the door, to* LINDA): All right, we had it out. I'm going and I'm not writing any more.

LINDA (*going to* WILLY *in the kitchen*): I think that's the best way, dear. 'Cause there's no use drawing it out, you'll just never get along.

(WILLY *doesn't respond.*)

BIFF: People ask where I am and what I'm doing, you don't know, and you don't care. That way it'll be off your mind and you can start brightening up again. All right? That clears it, doesn't it? (WILLY *is silent, and* BIFF *goes to him.*) You gonna wish me luck, scout? (*He extends his hand.*) What do you say?

LINDA: Shake his hand, Willy.

WILLY (*turning to her, seething with hurt*): There's no necessity to mention the pen at all, y'know.

BIFF (*gently*): I've got no appointment, Dad.

WILLY (*erupting fiercely*): He put his arm around . . . ?

BIFF: Dad, you're never going to see what I am, so what's the use of arguing? If I strike oil I'll send you a check. Meantime forget I'm alive.

WILLY (*to* LINDA): Spite, see?

BIFF: Shake hands, Dad.

WILLY: Not my hand.

BIFF: I was hoping not to go this way.

WILLY: Well, this is the way you're going. Good-by.

(BIFF *looks at him a moment, then turns sharply and goes to the stairs.*)

WILLY (*stops him with*): May you rot in hell if you leave this house!

BIFF (*turning*): Exactly what is it that you want from me?

WILLY: I want you to know, on the train, in the mountains, in the valleys, wherever you go, that you cut down your life for spite!

BIFF: No, no.

WILLY: Spite, spite, is the word of your undoing! And when you're down and out, remember what did it. When you're rotting somewhere beside the railroad tracks, remember, and don't you dare blame it on me!

BIFF: I'm not blaming it on you!

WILLY: I won't take the rap for this, you hear?

(HAPPY *comes down the stairs and stands on the bottom step, watching.*)

BIFF: That's just what I'm telling you!

WILLY (*sinking into a chair at the table, with full accusation*): You're trying to put a knife in me — don't think I don't know what you're doing!

BIFF: All right, phony! Then let's lay it on the line. (*He whips the rubber tube out of his pocket and puts it on the table.*)

HAPPY: You crazy —

LINDA: Biff! (*She moves to grab the hose, but* BIFF *holds it down with his hand.*)

BIFF: Leave it there! Don't move it!

WILLY (*not looking at it*): What is that?

BIFF: You know goddam well what that is.

WILLY (*caged, wanting to escape*): I never saw that.

BIFF: You saw it. The mice didn't bring it into the cellar! What is this supposed to do, make a hero out of you? This supposed to make me sorry for you?

WILLY: Never heard of it.

BIFF: There'll be no pity for you, you hear it? No pity!

WILLY (*to* LINDA): You hear the spite!

BIFF: No, you're going to hear the truth — what you are and what I am!

LINDA: Stop it!

WILLY: Spite!

HAPPY (*coming down toward* BIFF): You cut it now!

BIFF (*to* HAPPY): The man don't know who we are! The man is gonna know! (*To* WILLY.) We never told the truth for ten minutes in this house!

HAPPY: We always told the truth!

BIFF (*turning on him*): You big blow, are you the assistant buyer? You're one of the two assistants to the assistant, aren't you?

HAPPY: Well, I'm practically —

BIFF: You're practically full of it! We all are! And I'm through with it. (*To* WILLY.) Now hear this, Willy, this is me.

WILLY: I know you!

BIFF: You know why I had no address for three months? I stole a suit in Kansas City and I was in jail. (*To* LINDA, *who is sobbing.*) Stop crying, I'm through with it.

(LINDA *turns away from them, her hands covering her face.*)

WILLY: I suppose that's my fault!

BIFF: I stole myself out of every good job since high school!

WILLY: And whose fault is that?

BIFF: And I never got anywhere because you blew me so full of hot air I could never stand taking orders from anybody! That's whose fault it is!

WILLY: I hear that!

LINDA: Don't, Biff!

BIFF: It's goddam time you heard that! I had to be boss big shot in two weeks, and I'm through with it!

WILLY: Then hang yourself! For spite, hang yourself!

BIFF: No! Nobody's hanging himself, Willy! I ran down eleven flights with a pen in my hand today. And suddenly I stopped, you hear me? And in the middle of that office building, do you hear this? I stopped in the middle of that building and I saw — the sky, I saw the things that I love in this world. The work and the food and time to sit and smoke. And I looked at the pen and said to myself, what the hell am I grabbing this for? Why am I trying to become what I don't want to be? What am I doing in an office, making a contemptuous, begging fool of myself, when all I want is out there, waiting for me the minute I say I know who I am! Why can't I say that, Willy? (*He tries to make* WILLY *face him, but* WILLY *pulls away and moves to the left.*)

WILLY (*with hatred, threateningly*): The door of your life is wide open!

BIFF: Pop! I'm a dime a dozen, and so are you!

WILLY (*turning on him now in an uncontrolled outburst*): I am not a dime a dozen! I am Willy Loman, and you are Biff Loman!

(BIFF *starts for* WILLY, *but is blocked by* HAPPY. *In his fury,* BIFF *seems on the verge of attacking his father.*)

BIFF: I am not a leader of men, Willy, and neither are you. You were never anything but a hard-working drummer who landed in the ash can like all the rest of them! I'm one dollar an hour, Willy! I tried seven states and couldn't raise it. A buck an hour! Do you gather my meaning? I'm not bringing home any prizes any more, and you're going to stop waiting for me to bring them home!

WILLY (*directly to* BIFF): You vengeful, spiteful mutt!

(BIFF *breaks from* HAPPY. WILLY, *in fright, starts up the stairs.* BIFF *grabs him.*)

BIFF (*at the peak of his fury*): Pop, I'm nothing! I'm nothing, Pop. Can't you understand that? There's no spite in it any more. I'm just what I am, that's all.

(BIFF'*s fury has spent itself, and he breaks down, sobbing, holding on to* WILLY, *who dumbly fumbles for* BIFF'*s face.*)

WILLY (*astonished*): What're you doing? What're you doing? (*To* LINDA.) Why is he crying?

BIFF (*crying, broken*): Will you let me go, for Christ's sake? Will you take that phony dream and burn it before something happens? (*Struggling to contain himself, he pulls away and moves to the stairs.*) I'll go in the morning. Put him — put him to bed. (*Exhausted,* BIFF *moves up the stairs to his room.*)

WILLY (*after a long pause, astonished, elevated*): Isn't that — isn't that remarkable? Biff — he likes me!

LINDA: He loves you, Willy!

HAPPY (*deeply moved*): Always did, Pop.

WILLY: Oh, Biff! (*Staring wildly.*) He cried! Cried to me. (*He is choking with his love, and now cries out his promise.*) That boy — that boy is going to be magnificent!

(BEN *appears in the light just outside the kitchen.*)

BEN: Yes, outstanding, with twenty thousand behind him.

LINDA (*sensing the racing of his mind, fearfully, carefully*): Now come to bed, Willy. It's all settled now.

WILLY (*finding it difficult not to rush out of the house*): Yes, we'll sleep. Come on. Go to sleep, Hap.

BEN: And it does take a great kind of a man to crack the jungle.

(*In accents of dread,* BEN'*s idyllic music starts up.*)

HAPPY (*his arm around* LINDA): I'm getting married, Pop, don't forget it. I'm changing everything. I'm gonna run that department before the year is up. You'll see,
Mom. (*He kisses her.*)

BEN: The jungle is dark but full of diamonds, Willy.

(WILLY *turns, moves, listening to* BEN.)

LINDA: Be good. You're both good boys, just act that way, that's all.

HAPPY: 'Night, Pop. (*He goes upstairs.*)

LINDA (*to* WILLY): Come, dear.

BEN (*with greater force*): One must go in to fetch a diamond out.

WILLY (*to* LINDA, *as he moves slowly along the edge of the kitchen, toward the door*):
I just want to get settled down, Linda. Let me sit alone for a little.

LINDA (*almost uttering her fear*): I want you upstairs.

WILLY (*taking her in his arms*): In a few minutes, Linda. I couldn't sleep right now.
Go on, you look awful tired. (*He kisses her.*)

BEN: Not like an appointment at all. A diamond is rough and hard to the touch.

WILLY: Go on now. I'll be right up.

LINDA: I think this is the only way, Willy.

WILLY: Sure, it's the best thing.

BEN: Best thing!

WILLY: The only way. Everything is gonna be — go on, kid, get to bed. You look so
tired.

LINDA: Come right up.

WILLY: Two minutes.

(LINDA *goes into the living-room, then reappears in her bedroom.* WILLY *moves
just outside the kitchen door.*)

WILLY: Loves me. (*Wonderingly.*) Always loved me. Isn't that a remarkable thing?
Ben, he'll worship me for it!

BEN (*with promise*): It's dark there, but full of diamonds.

WILLY: Can you imagine that magnificence with twenty thousand dollars in his
pocket?

LINDA (*calling from her room*): Willy! Come up!

WILLY (*calling into the kitchen*): Yes! Yes. Coming! It's very smart, you realize that,
don't you, sweetheart? Even Ben sees it. I gotta go, baby. 'By! 'By! (*Going over to*
BEN, *almost dancing.*) Imagine? When the mail comes he'll be ahead of Bernard
again!

BEN: A perfect proposition all around.

WILLY: Did you see how he cried to me? Oh, if I could kiss him, Ben!

BEN: Time, William, time!

WILLY: Oh, Ben, I always knew one way or another we were gonna make it, Biff
and I!

BEN (*looking at his watch*): The boat. We'll be late. (*He moves slowly off into the
darkness.*)

WILLY (*elegiacally, turning to the house*): Now when you kick off, boy, I want a
seventy-yard boot, and get right down the field under the ball, and when you hit,
hit low and hit hard, because it's important, boy. (*He swings around and faces the
audience.*) There's all kinds of important people in the stands, and the first thing
you know . . . (*Suddenly realizing he is alone.*) Ben! Ben, where do I . . . ? (*He
makes a sudden movement of search.*) Ben, how do I . . . ?

LINDA (*calling*): Willy, you coming up?

WILLY (*uttering a gasp of fear, whirling about as if to quiet her*): Sh! (*He turns around as if to find his way; sounds, faces, voices, seem to be swarming in upon him and he flicks at them, crying.*) Sh! Sh! (*Suddenly music, faint and high, stops him. It rises in intensity, almost to an unbearable scream. He goes up and down on his toes, and rushes off around the house.*) Shhh!

LINDA: Willy?

(*There is no answer. *LINDA* waits. *BIFF* gets up off his bed. He is still in his clothes. *HAPPY* sits up. *BIFF* stands listening.*)

LINDA (*with real fear*): Willy, answer me! Willy!

(*There is the sound of a car starting and moving away at full speed.*)

LINDA: No!

BIFF (*rushing down the stairs*): Pop!

(*As the car speeds off, the music crashes down in a frenzy of sound, which becomes the soft pulsation of a single cello string. *BIFF* slowly returns to his bedroom. He and *HAPPY* gravely don their jackets. *LINDA* slowly walks out of her room. The music has developed into a dead march. The leaves of day are appearing over everything. *CHARLEY* and *BERNARD*, somberly dressed, appear and knock on the kitchen door. *BIFF* and *HAPPY* slowly descend the stairs to the kitchen as *CHARLEY* and *BERNARD* enter. All stop a moment when *LINDA*, in clothes of mourning, bearing a little bunch of roses, comes through the draped doorway into the kitchen. She goes to *CHARLEY* and takes his arm. Now all move toward the audience, through the wall-line of the kitchen. At the limit of the apron, *LINDA* lays down the flowers, kneels, and sits back on her heels. All stare down at the grave.*)

REQUIEM

CHARLEY: It's getting dark, Linda.

(*LINDA* doesn't react. She stares at the grave.*)

BIFF: How about it, Mom? Better get some rest, heh? They'll be closing the gate soon.

(*LINDA* makes no move. Pause.*)

HAPPY (*deeply angered*): He had no right to do that. There was no necessity for it. We would've helped him.

CHARLEY (*grunting*): Hmmm.

BIFF: Come along, Mom.

LINDA: Why didn't anybody come?

CHARLEY: It was a very nice funeral.

LINDA: But where are all the people he knew? Maybe they blame him.

CHARLEY: Naa. It's a rough world, Linda. They wouldn't blame him.

LINDA: I can't understand it. At this time especially. First time in thirty-five years we were just about free and clear. He only needed a little salary. He was even finished with the dentist.

CHARLEY: No man only needs a little salary.

LINDA: I can't understand it.

BIFF: There were a lot of nice days. When he'd come home from a trip; or on Sundays, making the stoop; finishing the cellar; putting on the new porch; when he built the extra bathroom; and put up the garage. You know something, Charley, there's more of him in that front stoop than in all the sales he ever made.

CHARLEY: Yeah, He was a happy man with a batch of cement.

LINDA: He was so wonderful with his hands.

BIFF: He had the wrong dreams. All, all, wrong.

HAPPY (*almost ready to fight* BIFF): Don't say that!

BIFF: He never knew who he was.

CHARLEY (*stopping* HAPPY's *movement and reply. To* BIFF): Nobody dast blame this man. You don't understand: Willy was a salesman. And for a salesman, there is no rock bottom to the life. He don't put a bolt to a nut, he don't tell you the law or give you medicine. He's a man way out there in the blue, riding on a smile and a shoeshine. And when they start not smiling back — that's an earthquake. And then you get yourself a couple of spots on your hat, and you're finished. Nobody dast blame this man. A salesman is got to dream, boy. It comes with the territory.

BIFF: Charley, the man didn't know who he was.

HAPPY (*infuriated*): Don't say that!

BIFF: Why don't you come with me, Happy?

HAPPY: I'm not licked that easily. I'm staying right in this city, and I'm gonna beat this racket! (*He looks at* BIFF, *his chin set.*) The Loman Brothers!

BIFF: I know who I am, kid.

HAPPY: All right, boy. I'm gonna show you and everybody else that Willy Loman did not die in vain. He had a good dream. It's the only dream you can have — to come out number-one man. He fought it out here, and this is where I'm gonna win it for him.

BIFF (*with a hopeless glance at* HAPPY, *bends toward his mother*): Let's go, Mom.

LINDA: I'll be with you in a minute. Go on, Charley. (*He hesitates.*) I want to, just for a minute. I never had a chance to say good-by.

(CHARLEY *moves away, followed by* HAPPY. BIFF *remains a slight distance up and left of* LINDA. *She sits there, summoning herself. The flute begins, not far away, playing behind her speech.*)

LINDA: Forgive me, dear. I can't cry. I don't know what it is, but I can't cry. I don't understand it. Why did you ever do that? Help me, Willy, I can't cry. It seems to me that you're just on another trip. I keep expecting you. Willy, dear, I can't cry. Why did you do it? I search and search and I search, and I can't understand it, Willy. I made the last payment on the house today. Today, dear. And there'll be nobody home. (*A sob rises in her throat.*) We're free and clear. (*Sobbing more fully, released.*) We're free. (BIFF *comes slowly toward her.*) We're free . . . We're free . . .

(BIFF *lifts her to her feet and moves out up right with her in his arms.* LINDA *sobs quietly.* BERNARD *and* CHARLEY *come together and follow them, followed by* HAPPY. *Only the music of the flute is left on the darkening stage as over the house the hard towers of the apartment buildings rise into sharp focus, and —*

THE CURTAIN FALLS

AFTERWORD

When the curtain rises on *Death of a Salesman*, before us is a "small, fragile-seeming home" surrounded by "towering, angular shapes . . . a solid vault of apartment houses." The setting remains the same through the whole play, and it is obviously symbolic: Like his house, Willy Loman is trapped and threatened by the big, hard city. Nothing changes on the stage except the light, and nothing changes in Willy's situation before it finally moves in on him and crushes him. We only keep learning more about him.

With the visual symbol goes an auditory one. The melody "played upon a flute, . . . small and fine, telling of grass and trees and the horizon," suggests the kind of life Willy might have had if he hadn't chosen to move to the "raw, sensuous" music of the city. The flute is heard only once again, briefly and "distantly," before the end, when it accompanies Linda's final speech. But the nature imagery it evokes in us and the values associated with that imagery are implied in at least two other scenes. One is early in Act I, when Willy complains to Linda, "There's not a breath of fresh air in the neighborhood. The grass don't grow any more, you can't raise a carrot in the back yard." The other is the restaurant scene in Act II, when Willy, conscious of his failure both as father and as salesman, tells the waiter Stanley, "I don't have a thing in the ground," and runs off to a Sixth Avenue hardware store to buy seeds.

The Loman house is symbolic in another way, too. Its transparent walls are a device for accommodating both the realistic and the expressionistic elements in the play. The way the action moves in and out of the house is analogous to the way it moves in and out of Willy's mind. The succession of scenes set in the actual world and in Willy's memory or imagination doesn't just alternate past and present; it stages the presentness of the past. Miller uses the retrospective technique more literally than Sophocles and Ibsen. Willy is shown in a kind of double exposure that catches some of the quality of the opening stage direction: "An air of the dream clings to the place, a dream rising out of reality."

All this symbolic imagery of sight and sound might have seemed like a fancy appendage to a play otherwise noted for its authentic realism, except that Willy lives in divided worlds and quite literally confuses outer and inner, actual and symbolic, past and present, experience. There is more to the juxtaposition of realism and expressionism than the slick gimmick of hard fact shoring up soft symbol and symbol turning fact into poetry. The form of the play fits its content.

Death of a Salesman is a play about a man who for years has mistaken personality for merchandise. It stages the last crisis of his life: the day he realizes he no longer has a marketable product and decides to die. His friend and neighbor Charley thinks it is "funny" that Willy, a salesman, doesn't know that "the only thing you got in this world is what you can sell." But Willy *does* know that; for him, too, salesmanship is everything. His mistake has been in thinking that the first thing he has to sell is him-

self. The only difference in this respect between him and Happy's girls is
that he is getting fat and old and tired and worried and can't find buyers
any more. Rather than a good man destroyed by a bad system, Willy is a
bad salesman who tries but fails to make it on the system's terms. That he
is not a materialist, like Charley and his brother Ben, is not an asset in the
business world. The "something" Willy once claimed he was "building"
with his firm is, as Ben said, nothing you can "lay your hand on." Charley
says the same thing in his epitaph on Willy:

> . . . for a salesman there is no rock bottom to the life. He don't put a bolt to the
> nut, he don't tell you the law or give you medicine. He's a man way out there in the
> blue, riding on a smile and a shoeshine. And when they start not smiling back —
> that's an earthquake.

Charley neither defends nor attacks the salesman; he diagnoses his case.
The same is true of the play.

Willy is both an exemplar and a victim of the tough and shabby underside of big city commercialism, and he is exemplar and victim as well of a
spiritual dividedness that is often thought of as peculiarly American. He is
a type; the indefinite article in the title suggests as much. It is perhaps a
tribute to the nation's candor about itself that one of the few classics of the
modern American theater challenges some of our most cherished national
ideals.

Faith in rugged individualism and private enterprise is not a charitable
faith. It leaves small margin for error. Every failure is a personal failure,
measured by how far it misses the accepted signs of success: money, status,
love, popularity. There is a strange and dangerous contradiction in our
system of values. We count on inner qualities like character and ambition
and intellect for our personal achievement, but we define and value the
achievement in terms of outer rewards. We'd like to think that the inner-
oriented, environment-conscious counterculture America of today is less
likely than the first post–World War II generation to fall for Willy's phony
dream. Still, whenever we watch poor, sad, lost Willy go to pieces, some
nerve end in our collective consciousness twitches in discomfort.

It probably has something to do with the shock with which we recognize
our own gritty reality on Miller's stage: the mortgage and the overdue insurance premium, the balky car and the broken refrigerator belt, the laundry and the leaky roof, the bedtime snack and the morning coffee, the
thoughtless little meannesses and vulgarities, the automatic endearments,
the casual profanities and trite jokes. And it also has to do with our realization that all this documentary matter represents the physical and social
conditions for Willy's psychological breakdown. In conjunction with the
flashback scenes, the realism is more than slices of Bronx life.

During the first, phenomenally successful, run of *Death of a Salesman*
on Broadway in 1949, Miller published an article in *The New York Times*

called "Tragedy and the Common Man." The article doesn't mention the play, but it is about it all the same — or about the theory behind it. Tragic significance and dignity, Miller argues, do not depend on the protagonist's social rank or importance or greatness or nobility of soul, but on his or her total commitment to the task of "evaluating himself justly." If the protagonist is destroyed in the course of the quest for selfhood, that is proof of "a wrong or an evil in his environment" — of some inhibiting or corrupting force that denies him or her the accomplishment of full human potential. Since this is a quest not reserved for kings and nobles, this kind of tragedy is democratic rather than aristocratic, and since the adversary is the protagonist's human environment and not an angry god or an inscrutable fate, it is social rather than metaphysical. There is a hint of defiance of traditional norms for tragedy in the title *Death of a Salesman*. It implies that a salesman's death is as worthy a subject for serious drama as the death of Antigone, Hamlet, or Phaedra. Not surprisingly, Miller is a great admirer of Ibsen's social problem plays. His article calls for, and *Death of a Salesman* is, a tragedy suitable to a secular society founded on the belief that all people are created equal.

As in Ibsen's plays, the "problem" in *Salesman* is embedded in a family drama, in which the inner spring of action is a shameful secret from the past. And, again like Ibsen's, Miller's family drama involves a larger ideological conflict, the way *A Doll's House*, according to Ibsen, actualizes the disparity between men's and women's "moral law." In *Death of a Salesman* the conflict, as we have seen, is immediately symbolized in stage setting and sound: the small and vulnerable Loman home among the looming apartment houses and the "fine" flute tune lost in the "raucous" sounds of the city. Their counterparts in dialogue and action are the antithetical relationships among the characters who surround Willy. Of these, the contrast between Biff and Happy, the two Loman sons, is the most obvious and important.

Happy is a competitive materialist. At the funeral he defends his father: "He had a good dream. It's the only dream you can have — to come out number-one man." To Happy that means a title, a good salary, a flashy car, a fancy apartment, and lots of good-looking girls. He wants very badly to make it in Howard Wagner's and Bill Oliver's world of expensive gadgets, gold fountain pens, and Long Island estates, where business is so definitely business that there is no room for loyalty or affection or compassion or simple enjoyment. It's a punching bag kind of world, though Willy himself only partly realizes the aptness of his gift to his boys. He meant to train them to be athletic and aggressive, not to pummel and be pummeled. Set against Happy's New York rat race are Biff's open spaces of wind and grass and wide horizons and graceful young colts on Texas ranges in the springtime, and clean air and empty roads, where a man is free to whistle and move about and laze in the sun and do his own work on his own time with his own two hands. Neither Happy, the good-natured seducer and chiseler, nor Biff, the tortured drifter and petty thief, has even begun to conquer his chosen world. Biff, in fact, has left his and returned to the city he hates.

But their Uncle Ben was a success in both worlds. (Or so he appears in Willy's imagination, and since he appears nowhere else, we can't determine the truth of Willy's image of him. Nor does that matter.) Uncle Ben is the most ambivalent character in the play, representing Biff's and Happy's different kinds of success and, by so doing, the dividedness of their father. He is part heroic frontiersman and part business tycoon, part rugged individualist in love with open spaces, part ruthless predator in actual and figurative jungles. There is an aura of romance about him, the glitter of diamonds and the glamor of far-off places. But he also gives off the chill of a callous entrepreneur always in a hurry — "Time, William, time!" — and of a capitalist with a killer instinct. To Willy, he is an alluringly rich and powerful authority figure. To Linda, he is a sinister threat to her and Willy's home.

Like the Biff-Happy contrast, that between Ben and Linda also takes on overtones of allegory, for each suggests an archetypal figure that represents one of the opposite abstractions that contend for Willy's soul. Ben is the rough and roaming male adventurer, Linda the gentle female homemaker. Given her role and her love of Willy, it is ironic that it is she who keeps Willy in the city that ends up destroying him by keeping him — of all things — traveling. Torn by the conflicting pulls that Ben and Linda stand for, Willy loses out both on the adventure and the wealth that going with Ben might have brought him and on the security and comfort that staying in town with wife and children could have been expected to provide him. Instead of going to Alaska that time, he has been going to New England, and it is as a traveling salesman that he has the affair with the woman in Boston that fatefully wrecks his relationship with Biff.

Other characters, too, pair off in foil relationships, suggestive of social, psychological, and moral allegory. Bernard and Biff are, respectively, the successful and the unsuccessful son, one with a good, the other with a bad, relationship to his father. Charley and Howard are both successful businessmen, one compassionate, the other unfeeling. Howard and Uncle Ben both survive life in the brutal business jungle, but Howard is an organization man and Ben a loner. Willy and Biff are at heart manual workers who make things; Charley, Howard, and Happy are businessmen who only make money. Linda is the loving and faithful wife; Happy's Miss Forsythe and Willy's Woman in Boston represent casual, commercial sex. Collectively, these character configurations serve as coordinates that define Willy and his fate.

Even so, Willy's case isn't all that easily diagnosed. Or, rather, the problem is not that there are not enough clues, but that there are too many. The critic who asks "Why did Willy fail?" comes up with several answers. The reasonable ones are grouped into three main types.

The first has the authority of Miller's *New York Times* article on its side. *Death of a Salesman* is a social problem play about an unimportant "common man," and the problem concerns the damage that a tough and competitive commercial society does to his dignity, integrity, and self-respect. Willy, the modern big-city Everyman, is degraded and finally destroyed by values that are wrong or false. In a political context, this reading of the play takes on a radical tinge. The villain of the play is the brutal business ideology of people like Howard Wagner, the boss who fires the faithful old worker when he can no longer pull his weight.

You mustn't tell me you've got people to see [says Willy to Howard] — I put thirty-four years into this firm, Howard, and now I can't pay my insurance! You can't eat the orange and throw the peel away — a man is not a piece of fruit!

Willy is nostalgic for the days of the legendary Dave Singleman, the salesman who at eighty-four sat in his hotel room in velvet slippers and made a living telephoning the buyers.

In those days there was personality in it, Howard. There was respect, and comradeship, and gratitude in it. Today, it's all cut and dried, and there's no chance for bringing friendship to bear — or personality.

His frightened perception of present reality drives him to escape into a fantasy past.

WILLY: I never have to wait in line to see a buyer. "Willy Loman is here!" That's all they have to know, and I go right through.
BIFF: Did you knock them dead, Pop?
WILLY: Knocked 'em cold in Providence, slaughtered 'em in Boston.

What matters to Willy isn't just the commission or the sales record but the reassurance he gets from big sales that he has a terrific personality — that he is, not just "liked," like Charley and Bernard, but *"well* liked." Willy's notion is pathetically naive, but there is an ugly aggressiveness about it. Personality is a vicious weapon: "Knocked 'em cold," "slaughtered 'em."

The second answer comes closer to the traditional idea that the protagonist's tragic flaw, *hamartia*, is his failure to know himself. According to this interpretation, Willy's true measure is taken by Biff at the end: "Charley, the man didn't know who he was." He should have been working with his hands as a carpenter or a building contractor. "You know something, Charley," says Biff again, "there's more of him in that front stoop than in all the sales he ever made." And Charley agrees: "Yeah. He was a happy man with a batch of cement." But Willy renounced his origin. The itinerant flutemaker's son tells *his* son, "Even your grandfather was better than a carpenter." Instead of staying out west or going to Alaska with Ben and turning his back on the stink of apartment houses that stifles the fragrance of lilac and wisteria, he sold himself on a junky dream of popularity. Good salesmanship to him is gladhanding and cracking jokes. The ironically named Happy — restless, discontented, sexually promiscuous, envious of the merchandise manager who makes enough money to buy himself a place he can't stand living in, but not vicious or even really stupid — is a crasser version of this Willy. He takes up his heritage when he wants to fight Biff because Biff says Willy's dreams were "the wrong dreams. All, all wrong." In this view of the play, the point is not attacking big business but moving our fear and our pity with the story of an unremarkable man too weak and foolish to know himself. "Character is destiny" — or at least it is so for this particular man in these particular circumstances. It is all very sad, but there is really no one to blame.

Finally, there is the psychological interpretation, which looks for the blight on Willy's life in his relationship with Biff and finds the key to the tragedy in the scene in Boston where Biff discovers his father with another woman. This is the Ibsenite pattern: The error of an hour buys a lifetime of grief. Miller's play deviates from the pattern only in the purely technical sense that the other characters never learn the dark secret from the past. Biff hints at it a couple of times, but the audience gets to know it only from its reenactment in Willy's memory.

What has gone wrong in Willy's life has to do with Biff. Willy's memory keeps returning to two episodes in the past, one happy, the other traumatic, both centering on Biff. One was that day when seventeen-year-old Biff captained his high school football team in Ebbets Field and ran a touchdown just for his father. The other, some months later, was the night in the Boston hotel, when Biff discovered his father's adultery.

Willy feels both guilt and resentment toward Biff. Guilt, because he *knows*, though he cannot admit it even to himself, that it is his fault that Biff "gave up his life" (as Bernard puts it) after that trip to Boston. Resentment, because of the heavy burden of sexual and parental guilt Biff has placed on him. It seems to Willy as if Biff is destroying both of them from sheer spite, and whether he is right or not is a moot question. There *is* a sense in which Biff is punishing his father by never amounting to anything. But Biff is as afraid to face the Boston scene all over again as Willy is. When he finally has it out with Willy, he accuses him not of unfaithfulness to Linda but of having warped his (Biff's) personality: " . . . you blew me so full of hot air I could never stand taking orders from anybody! That's whose fault it is!" The scene is the only one in the whole play where Biff calls his father "Willy" and not "Dad" or "Pop." They are equals now: They share the guilt for Biff's failures, each is aware of the other's recognition of the nature of the guilt, and they tacitly agree not to reveal its source.

Biff's punishing his father and himself and trying to account for the punishment in terms that conceal its real reason gauge the enormity of Willy's betrayal, Biff's knowledge that Willy loves him, and the depth of Biff's love for Willy. Had Biff cared less, he would hurt less. Since he does care, he wants to fail, both because he knows that nothing could hurt Willy more and because he needs to punish himself for his inability to forgive. But this is all inference and not fact, and it is easy to take this kind of inference too far. Miller has, perhaps deliberately, left the exact nature of the father-son relationship elliptical and elusive. As a result, the critic feels free to move from psychology to mythology and to see in Biff the archetypal son over-throwing his father in an assertion of his own autonomy. The ending sug-gests that Willy's death sets Biff free to "find himself."

So who, finally, *did* kill Willy Loman? Hardhearted big business? Willy's self-unawareness? His need to atone to Biff? Obviously, there is some truth in each of these answers, and we neither want to nor have to make cate-gorical choices among them. Yet there is something unsatisfactory about a compromise interpretation: "Guilt destroyed Willy. But he wouldn't have become an adulterer if he had had enough insight into himself to realize how unfulfilling he found his life as a road man for a company that didn't appreciate him." That touches too many bases. The play's focus gets blurred. Next we'll be saying that the whole sorry business wouldn't have happened if only Biff hadn't flunked senior math.

Ultimately, the exact degree of truth in the various views on Miller's play matters less than its immediate power as a drama reflecting disturbing reali-ties in American life. Those who feel that power — and they have been many — aren't likely to ask whether the subject matter of the play is socio-economics or psychology and the play itself polemics or tragedy. Neverthe-less, the critic-editor has both the right and the obligation to assess the integrity of the play — both as a criticism of the life it shows and as a work of dramatic art. When that is done, some questions arise that are not easily answered.

One concerns Bernard, Charley's son and Biff's friend. Bernard is both brainy and modest, both successful and likeable. As if to underscore his function as a foil character, Miller has given him two sons — either to suggest that there can be a happy variant of the Loman family situation, or (which seems less likely) to suggest that here we have the makings of the Lomans' misery all over again. But the critic's *difficult* problem with Ber-nard is that although his kind of success is ever so much nicer than the kind of success that Happy wants, it is still the kind that counts in Happy's materialistic and competitive society. Its signs are friends with their own private tennis court, arguing a case before the U.S. Supreme Court, and a bottle of bourbon as a going-away present from father to son. Bernard's niceness makes it difficult to find irony in his association with these con-ventional symbols of success. But if there is nothing wrong with Bernard, and if Bernard is what Willy wishes *his* sons were, in what sense is Willy's dream phony? The ambiguous Uncle Ben is a focus for the ideological issues in the play, but Bernard's ambiguousness only confuses them.

And so does the sentimental strain in some of Linda's and Charley's speeches about Willy. For one thing, their heightened rhetoric threatens the decorum of slovenly, semiarticulate, lower middle-class urban speech.

Willy Loman never made a lot of money. His name was never in the paper. He's not the finest character that ever lived. But he's a human being, and a terrible thing is happening to him. So attention must be paid. He's not to be allowed to fall into his grave like an old dog. Attention, attention must finally be paid to such a person.

But Linda's moving eloquence, asserting the dignity and pathos and larger moral significance of Willy's case, states no premise for its plea. Since part of what is pathetic about Willy is his expendability, *why* must attention be paid to him? What will happen if attention is not paid? In an age of holocausts, does Willy Loman's death matter? That, of course, is a cynic's question, and the humanist's answer is that worth is intrinsic to the human condition and not contingent, and that we therefore debase our own humanity if we fail to pay attention to someone like Willy. But the play never really makes that case. It is barely implicit even in Linda's "attention must be paid" speech, and there is no trace of it, in speech or circumstance, anywhere else.

And *is* "attention" finally being paid to Willy? And the right kind of attention? What happens does not provide definite answers. Willy rushes out to his death only half understanding what goes on in Biff's mind during their last scene together, and there is no evidence that he does not die in vain: We don't learn that the insurance money has been or will be paid. If his death allows Biff to gain his manhood, it is still a death charged with irony, and the fact that Willy dies at all makes it doubtful that "attention" of the kind Linda has in mind *has* been "paid." There is no final self-recognition in Willy. His death doesn't teach Happy anything, and it separates the two brothers. Problematic, too, is Linda's curiously limited awareness in the "Requiem." She cannot understand why Willy killed himself, since "I made the last payment on the house today. Today, dear." Wouldn't she, of all people in the play, understand that Willy could not have been saved from himself by a paid-up mortgage? Perhaps all we can say to escape the impression that she has suddenly adopted Happy's crude categories of value is that she doesn't know the cause of Willy's guilt and has never understood — or dared to understand — that part of Willy that is attached to Ben's life.

The alternative to finding Linda's final speech cynical is finding it sentimental — on balance a more plausible but scarcely a more satisfactory reading. For it means that the speech is an appeal to audience emotions that don't have to attach themselves to anything in particular; it is enough if we feel grief and compassion and have a sense of the sadness of it all. But the mere fact of unhappiness is not an occasion for awe. We are being asked to find something grand and momentous that doesn't quite qualify. The effect is a little like that of the vaguely poetic fatalism in Charley's last words on Willy: "Nobody dast blame this man. A salesman is got to dream, boy. It comes with the territory." We may be moved, but we are hardly enlightened.

Samuel Beckett

ACT WITHOUT WORDS I

A Mime for One Player

FOREWORD

"Ancient Greek tragedy," "Elizabethan drama," "the Baroque theater," and "modern dramatic realism" are terms that imply (along with much else) certain acting conventions and certain ways of using the physical playhouse. The same is not true of "the absurd theater." It uses a variety of techniques to create different kinds of stage illusion. We can no more say that its acting is always stylized (balletlike, robotlike) or always realistic or always grotesque than we can say it never is any of these things. And just as it isn't true that Stanislavsky's kind of inner-motivated acting works only for Chekhov's plays and not (say) for Shakespeare's, so it isn't true that absurdist acting and staging are limited only to the contemporary plays we call "absurd." In *The Theatre of the Absurd*, Martin Esslin has shown how many and how different are the older theater traditions that absurdism draws upon. They include Aristophanes' comedies, the Roman *mime*, the *lazzi* (or slapstick) routines of the *zannis* (clowns) of the Italian Renaissance *commedia dell'arte*, Shakespeare's grotesques, the nineteenth-century British music hall, old and new expressionism, and the golden age of silent movie comedy (the Keystone Cops, Chaplin, Keaton). The theater of the absurd thrives on diversity, but it is the consistency with which absurdist playwrights have employed the absurdist elements of older plays that marks their own work as radically new.

The diversity should not surprise us, since the philosophical premise of absurdism is that no single system or formula fits the inexplicable facts of

our condition. What plot an absurd play has is more often circular (perpetual) than resolved, and its characters are never "explained." There is no
past to account for the present, and the present cannot be counted on to
determine the future. Incoherence, improvisation, incongruity, and incon-
clusiveness define the conventions of a drama that seeks to stage a truthful
image of an existence that makes no sense. These are flaws according to
the Aristotelian rationale for drama, but to judge from the popular and
critical success of much absurdist drama, they seem to catch some of the
modern sense of human experience.

Beckett's setting for *Act Without Words I* represents only one of many
recurrent images in the absurd theater. (The image is basically the same in
Act Without Words II, in which all that happens is that two mimes, one
"slow," the other "brisk," prodded by "a goad," move themselves, their
clothes, and the sacks they live in from one end of the otherwise empty
stage to the other.) The first three words of the opening stage direction
describe "the man's" habitat as a "desert" in "dazzling light." The bare
stage becomes a symbol: a place where King Lear's "unaccommodated
man," stripped of possessions, comforts, and defenses, is alone in a malign
universe, his void a prison or a laboratory slide for the observation of the
human specimen. Instead of the crowded pageants, the lifelike rooms, and
the significant words and actions of older drama Beckett gives us mute
antics in a sparse and cruel place. He reduces the varied human scene
almost literally *ad absurdum*.

Yet, other absurdist plays (like some of Ionesco's) achieve comparable
effects of scenic symbolism by opposite means, rendering human speech as
gibberish and the human home as space where dead things proliferate and
squeeze and smother people. Obviously, illusionism in the usual sense is
not the point of these claustrophobic images; "character acting" would be
as out of place in Beckett's desert as in Ionesco's clutter. The only generalization the practices of absurdist theater permits us to make is this: In elemental stage images, verbal and nonverbal, they show us a condition that
is mysterious, painful, futile, and hopeless.

Desert. Dazzling light.

The man is flung backwards on stage from right wing. He falls, gets up immediately, dusts himself, turns aside, reflects.

Whistle from right wing.

He reflects, goes out right.

Immediately flung back on stage he falls, gets up immediately, dusts himself, turns aside, reflects.

Whistle from left wing.

He reflects, goes out left.

Immediately flung back on stage he falls, gets up immediately, dusts himself, turns aside, reflects.

Whistle from left wing.

He reflects, goes towards left wing, hesitates, thinks better of it, halts, turns aside, reflects.

A little tree descends from flies, lands. It has a single bough some three yards from ground and at its summit a meager tuft of palms casting at its foot a circle of shadow.

He continues to reflect.

Whistle from above.

He turns, sees tree, reflects, goes to it, sits down in its shadow, looks at his hands.

A pair of tailor's scissors descends from flies, comes to rest before tree, a yard from ground.

He continues to look at his hands.

Whistle from above.

He looks up, sees scissors, takes them and starts to trim his nails.

The palms close like a parasol, the shadow disappears.

He drops scissors, reflects.

A tiny carafe, to which is attached a huge label inscribed WATER, descends from flies, comes to rest some three yards from ground.

He continues to reflect.

Whistle from above.

He looks up, sees carafe, reflects, gets up, goes and stands under it, tries in vain to reach it, renounces, turns aside, reflects.

A big cube descends from flies, lands.

He continues to reflect.

Whistle from above.

He turns, sees cube, looks at it, at carafe, reflects, goes to cube, takes it up, carries it over and sets it down under carafe, tests its stability, gets up on it, tries in vain to reach carafe, renounces, gets down, carries cube back to its place, turns aside, reflects.

A second smaller cube descends from flies, lands.

He continues to reflect.

Whistle from above.

He turns, sees second cube, looks at it, at carafe, goes to second cube, takes it up,
carries it over and sets it down under carafe, tests its stability, gets up on it, tries
in vain to reach carafe, renounces, gets down, takes up second cube to carry it
back to its place, hesitates, thinks better of it, sets it down, goes to big cube, takes
it up, carries it over and puts it on small one, tests their stability, gets up on
them, the cubes collapse, he falls, gets up immediately, brushes himself, reflects.

He takes up small cube, puts it on big one, tests their stability, gets up on them and
is about to reach carafe when it is pulled up a little way and comes to rest beyond
his reach.

He gets down, reflects, carries cubes back to their place, one by one, turns aside,
reflects.

A third still smaller cube descends from flies, lands.

He continues to reflect.

Whistle from above.

He turns, sees third cube, looks at it, reflects, turns aside, reflects.

The third cube is pulled up and disappears in flies.

Beside carafe a rope descends from flies, with knots to facilitate ascent.

He continues to reflect.

Whistle from above.

He turns, sees rope, reflects, goes to it, climbs up it and is about to reach carafe
when rope is let out and deposits him back on ground.

He reflects, looks around for scissors, sees them, goes and picks them up, returns to
rope and starts to cut it with scissors.

The rope is pulled up, lifts him off ground, he hangs on, succeeds in cutting rope,
falls back on ground, drops scissors, falls, gets up again immediately, brushes
himself, reflects.

The rope is pulled up quickly and disappears in flies.

With length of rope in his possession he makes a lasso with which he tries to lasso
carafe.

The carafe is pulled up quickly and disappears in flies.

He turns aside, reflects.

He goes with lasso in his hand to tree, looks at bough, turns and looks at cubes,
looks again at bough, drops lasso, goes to cubes, takes up small one, carries it
over and sets it down under bough, goes back for big one, takes it up and carries
it over under bough, makes to put it on small one, hesitates, thinks better of it,

sets it down, takes up small one and puts it on big one, tests their stability, turns aside and stoops to pick up lasso.

The bough folds down against trunk.

He straightens up with lasso in his hand, turns and sees what has happened.

He drops lasso, turns aside, reflects.

He carries back cubes to their place, one by one, goes back for lasso, carries it over to cubes and lays it in a neat coil on small one.

He turns aside, reflects.

Whistle from right wing.

He reflects, goes out right.

Immediately flung back on stage he falls, gets up immediately, brushes himself, turns aside, reflects.

Whistle from left wing.

He does not move.

He looks at his hands, looks around for scissors, sees them, goes and picks them up, starts to trim his nails, stops, reflects, runs his finger along blade of scissors, goes and lays them on small cube, turns aside, opens his collar, frees his neck and fingers it.

The small cube is pulled up and disappears in flies, carrying away rope and scissors.

He turns to take scissors, sees what has happened.

He turns aside, reflects.

He goes and sits down on big cube.

The big cube is pulled from under him. He falls. The big cube is pulled up and disappears in flies.

He remains lying on his side, his face towards auditorium, staring before him.

The carafe descends from flies and comes to rest a few feet from his body.

He does not move.

Whistle from above.

He does not move.

The carafe descends further, dangles and plays about his face.

He does not move.

The carafe is pulled up and disappears in flies.

The bough returns to horizontal, the palms open, the shadow returns.

Whistle from above.

He does not move.

The tree is pulled up and disappears in flies.

He looks at his hands.

CURTAIN

AFTERWORD

"Absurd drama" became a highbrow fashion on the evening of January 5, 1953, when Beckett's *Waiting for Godot* opened at the Théâtre Babylone in Paris. Ever since, the label has been applied to just about every modern play that queries the human condition. Since most serious drama does that, it is no longer very useful. Even in more discriminating usage it covers plays as dissimilar as *Waiting for Godot* (a static image of a nonhappening), Eugene Ionesco's *Rhinoceros* (a busy allegory in which people turn into animals), and Harold Pinter's *Homecoming* (straight social realism about weirdly motivated people).

Absurdism is not a philosophy to be accepted or rejected, though some forms of it have affinity with that brand of existentialist thought that posits the achievement of selfhood through conscious moral choice as our only possible value in an indifferent universe. And it isn't a literary genre, defined by formal criteria, like tragedy, or ode, or novel. It doesn't argue or explain or analyze or tell stories. It suspends time and causality, but without making a principle of it. It can be quiet or violent, banal or bizarre. Its quintessential human figures are both trapped and lost in an environment that keeps affronting their dignity, frustrating their desires, and baffling their intellect. The spiritual climate is not the religious faith of older drama, nor the secular faith in social and individual enterprise of more recent times, but the cosmic cynicism and almost humorous despair that come to someone who has run out of options. Unable to account for the what and why of existence (and sometimes the where and when), people have no meaningful relationship to the past or to the future. Their present is an arrested moment, a chronic disease, a bad joke forever in the telling. "You are on Earth," says a character in Beckett's *Endgame*; "there is no cure for that." Outside is a wasteland, and both sentiment and setting are typically "absurdist." If an absurdist work allows that a supernatural agent is in charge, there is no evidence of its goodness or justice, or even its intelligence. Because there is disjunction of mind and word and of word and thing, speech is impoverished and stalled, prostituted and self-regarding — non sequiturs, nonreferents, empty rituals of human noise. Sometimes speech stops altogether. Absurdism insinuates the unreality — the unreliability, the fragility — of everything we count on to get us through our day. It is the stuff our nightmares are made of.

Whether *Act Without Words* is drama is debatable; that it is a piece of absurdist theater is not. Its brevity and wordlessness are only extreme variants of characteristics found in other absurd plays. It compresses vast complexity into a stark and simple pantomime.

"The man is flung backwards" on to a desert stage, drenched in "dazzling light." There is no sign of confinement; yet he is not allowed to leave. Implements appear, but when he wants to use them — for solace, survival, and suicide — they are withdrawn. This pattern of stimulus and frustrated response is repeated several times. Throughout, "the man" is silent and solitary. At the end, he stops responding. He no longer "reflects," and "he does not move"; he only "looks at his hands." His specifically *human* attributes, mind and hands, the agents of making and doing, are both idle. He has become inert.

What, we ask, is this but a symbolic image of human life in the absurdist view: reluctant birth (the man's violent entry is "backwards"), a succession of frustrations, the absolute nonresponse of death? And all in desolation, pain, solitude, silence, and futility. "Nothing is more real than nothing," said Beckett once. What better illustration than *Act Without Words*, the very title of which implies deprivation?

And as if to underline the desolation and deprivation, the whole mime is rendered in the idiom of the music hall: the clown's routines with the rope that breaks, the seat that's pulled away, the undignified fall, the pick-your-self-up-brush-yourself-off-and-try-it-again attitude of the plucky little man of a Chaplin pantomime. The result is a complex effect that feeds upon itself. The tragic emblematics turn tragicomical, because the victim is laughable. But the fact that he is laughable deepens the pathos, for we perceive that his pain and his grief have been denied their rightful dignity.

Or have they? To admit an alternative view of the ending of the mime would be very much in keeping with Beckett's almost fierce and certainly consistent disinclination to explicate his meanings and to make ideological commitments. Couldn't the final tableau, with "the man" lying down on his side, passive, inert, looking at his hands, signify neither mindless apathy nor abject submission nor stoical resignation, but an assertion of pride and independence? He could be making the only gesture of defiance still available to him: ignoring further stimuli as a way of saying he'll no longer play the game. If he cannot escape, at least he doesn't have to submit and accept. In a world where things don't make sense but just *are*, he still has that option. Thus he makes of his suffering some little meaning, after all.

The man's classical prototype is Tantalus, the mythical king of a small kingdom in Asia Minor, although none of the received versions of the myth about Tantalus suggests that he *defied* the intolerable condition in which he was imprisoned. He was favored by the gods but angered them by somehow abusing his privilege. They punished him by putting him in a river up to his neck. Whenever he inclines his head to drink, the water recedes. Over his head are branches laden with fruit, but whenever he reaches for one, they bend away. From Tantalus we have our verb "tantalize," more commonly used in its passive than in its active voice. "To be tantalized" means to be forever just short of attaining something that is intensely desired and is forever in sight.

It is just possible that Beckett in *Act Without Words*, though in an oblique and much smaller way, did for Tantalus what the French existentialist philosopher-novelist-playwright, Albert Camus, did for Sisyphus in *The Myth of Sisyphus*. Like Tantalus, Sisyphus was a legendary king who suffered in Hades (Hell) for incurring the wrath of the gods by some crime. His punishment is forever to roll a huge rock up a steep hill, only to see it roll down again the moment he reaches the top. Camus turns Sisyphus into a type of existentialist man, defying his destiny by making himself superior to it. One likes to think (says Camus) of Sisyphus as smiling, whenever he descends the hill to resume his toil. Nothing in *Act Without Words*, of course, validates such an inference about "the man." His unresponsiveness to further tantalization can be differently interpreted. But by the same token, nothing in his final posture proves his defeat. There are circumstances when inertia marks a moral choice. His stillness may be his "act." And at the end he has silenced the whistle.

We noted something like absurdism in certain aspects of *Hamlet* (the mysterious iniquity, the ambiguity, the wit of despair) and *The Cherry Orchard* (the hiatus between intent and act, the noncommunication, the decent people observing the erosion of their lives). Even a rationalistic, polemical play like *Major Barbara* is about absurdity in one sense. Shaw is in effect saying, "Look, this is absurd! Let's do something about it!" But it's the difference that counts. For if Beckett is "saying" anything at all, it is something like, "Look, everything is absurd. And there isn't a thing we can do about it."

Hamlet, *The Cherry Orchard*, and *Major Barbara* belong to the Aristotelian tradition of drama. The staples of this tradition are plot — a causally connected series of events leading to resolution — and character — a stable, distinctive, and in some sense predictable psychic entity. Some modern plays in this tradition have been *about* absurdism, in the sense that their dialogues and events demonstrate the bleak futility and insignificance of human life, but their philosophical point is made by means of conventional plot structures, conventional assumptions about character, and discursive and credible dialogues.

But in Beckett's mime nothing is left but the spectacle of repeated frustration. There is no plot, for plot implies purposefulness, causality, and the possibility of achievement. There is no character, for character implies continuity of identity and efficacy of will. Aristotelian drama, for all the awe and terror of some of its tragedies, takes place in a world that operates under changeless and discoverable laws. But in our century, theories of relativity and the discontinuity of time; mutually exclusive but equally provable hypotheses to account for the behavior of matter; psychoanalysis; the new ethos of irrationality; and public events have all shaken our faith in the old premises. Strindberg, with his ideas about the multiple and fragmented "soul complex" of his "characterless characters," and Pirandello, with his relativism and skepticism and blurring of the distinctions between sane and insane, real and illusionary, life and art, both made dramatic capital of our doubts. Absurdism has only carried on from where they left off, making for itself a dramatic world in which Newton's laws of mechanics, Freud's and Jung's findings, and the Preamble to the American Constitution are not the operative verities.

And yet, *Act Without Words* is, after all, a verbal construct. It can be read. True, what we read is only a handful of pages of stage directions, written in a flat, objective style, consisting entirely of simple declaratory sentences. But its very existence asserts, however wryly and tentatively, the uses of language. There is, perhaps, some small reassurance to be had from sharing with the playwright his sly little joke at his own expense as he declares the collapse of language in stageable prose.

Act Without Words was first shown, as an afterpiece to *Endgame*, at the original production of that play, in Paris, in April, 1957. In 1958, Beckett himself translated both it and *Endgame* into English.

Harold Pinter

THE DUMB WAITER

FOREWORD

We referred earlier to Beckett's and Ionesco's plays as representative of two types of absurdist stage spectacle. The absurdist quality of Pinter's scene is achieved by yet another method.

The Dumb Waiter takes place in "a basement room," sparsely furnished but not unrealistically so. Ben and Gus await the arrival of their victim in a room that is drab, not grotesque. The "serving hatch" between the two beds may seem like an unusual feature in this kind of room, but no more so than Major Barbara's Salvation Army uniform in her mother's comfortably furnished West End library in Act I of *Major Barbara*, a "realistic" play. And nothing in the slovenly, edgy conversations between the two men fails to conform to the speech manner of lower-class hired assassins that we have come to expect from the movies and from TV.

The more convincingly lifelike the two gangsters are in their stereotyped parts, the more incongruous becomes the difference between the play's surface and its undercurrent — between the overt meaning and the covert significance. The ordinariness of what they do (reading the paper, going to the john, looking for matches, fussing with the tea kettle) and of the manner of their speech (explosive grunts, monosyllabic clichés) underscore the extraordinary circumstance (by gangster movie standards) that we are not given clues to the reason for their mission. Strange things start happening among the shabby solidities on stage, building a sinister mystery that ends up enveloping the whole scene. What happens inside the room is controlled by an outside force, the "organisation," which finally manipulates the two men into a sudden tableau of violence that is unexpected only because of the identity of the victim.

In *The Dumb Waiter*, once again, we find a variety of scenic effects in counterpoint to a muted or missing dialogue. We are made to sense an incongruity between the recognizable surface world and the inscrutable and fearful but somehow quintessentially human place it turns out to be. The playwright makes kitchen realism into a violent nightmare, vulgar smalltalk into hostile confrontation, trivia into tedium and terror. Strindberg would have understood what Pinter is about.

CHARACTERS

BEN
GUS

Scene: A basement room. Two beds, flat against the back wall. A serving hatch, closed, between the beds. A door to the kitchen and lavatory, left. A door to a passage, right.

BEN *is lying on a bed, left, reading a paper.* GUS *is sitting on a bed, right, tying his shoelaces, with difficulty. Both are dressed in shirts, trousers and braces.*
   Silence.
   GUS *ties his laces, rises, yawns and begins to walk slowly to the door, left. He stops, looks down, and shakes his foot.*
   BEN *lowers his paper and watches him.* GUS *kneels and unties his shoe-lace and slowly takes off the shoe. He looks inside it and brings out a flattened matchbox. He shakes it and examines it. Their eyes meet.* BEN *rattles his paper and reads.* GUS *puts the matchbox in his pocket and bends down to put on his shoe. He ties his lace, with difficulty.* BEN *lowers his paper and watches him.* GUS *walks to the door, left, stops, and shakes the other foot. He kneels, unties his shoe-lace, and slowly takes off the shoe. He looks inside it and brings out a flattened cigarette packet. He shakes it and examines it. Their eyes meet.* BEN *rattles his paper and reads.* GUS *puts the packet in his pocket, bends down, puts on his shoe and ties the lace.*
   He wanders off, left.
   BEN *slams the paper down on the bed and glares after him. He picks up the paper and lies on his back, reading.*
   Silence.
   A lavatory chain is pulled twice off, left, but the lavatory does not flush.
   Silence.

GUS *re-enters, left, and halts at the door, scratching his head.*
BEN *slams down the paper.*

BEN: Kaw!

(*He picks up the paper.*)

What about this? Listen to this!

(*He refers to the paper.*)

A man of eighty-seven wanted to cross the road. But there was a lot of traffic, see? He couldn't see how he was going to squeeze through. So he crawled under a lorry.
GUS: He what?
BEN: He crawled under a lorry. A stationary lorry.
GUS: No?
BEN: The lorry started and ran over him.
GUS: Go on!
BEN: That's what it says here.
GUS: Get away.
BEN: It's enough to make you want to puke, isn't it?
GUS: Who advised him to do a thing like that?
BEN: A man of eighty-seven crawling under a lorry!
GUS: It's unbelievable.
BEN: It's down here in black and white.
GUS: Incredible.

(*Silence.*
GUS *shakes his head and exits.* BEN *lies back and reads.*
The lavatory chain is pulled once off left, but the lavatory does not flush.
BEN *whistles at an item in the paper.*
GUS *re-enters.*)

I want to ask you something.
BEN: What are you doing out there?
GUS: Well, I was just —
BEN: What about the tea?
GUS: I'm just going to make it.
BEN: Well, go on, make it.
GUS: Yes, I will. (*He sits in a chair. Ruminatively.*) He's laid on some very nice crockery this time, I'll say that. It's sort of striped. There's a white stripe.

(BEN *reads.*)

It's very nice. I'll say that.

(BEN *turns the page.*)

You know, sort of round the cup. Round the rim. All the rest of it's black, you see. Then the saucer's black, except for right in the middle, where the cup goes, where it's white.

(BEN *reads.*)

Then the plates are the same, you see. Only they've got a black stripe — the plates — right across the middle. Yes, I'm quite taken with the crockery.

BEN (*still reading*): What do you want plates for? You're not going to eat.

GUS: I've brought a few biscuits.

BEN: Well, you'd better eat them quick.

GUS: I always bring a few biscuits. Or a pie. You know I can't drink tea without anything to eat.

BEN: Well, make the tea then, will you? Time's getting on.

(GUS *brings out the flattened cigarette packet and examines it.*)

GUS: You got any cigarettes? I think I've run out.

(*He throws the packet high up and leans forward to catch it.*)

I hope it won't be a long job, this one.

(*Aiming carefully, he flips the packet under his bed.*)

Oh, I wanted to ask you something.

BEN (*slamming his paper down*): Kaw!

GUS: What's that?

BEN: A child of eight killed a cat!

GUS: Get away.

BEN: It's a fact. What about that, eh? A child of eight killing a cat!

GUS: How did he do it?

BEN: It was a girl.

GUS: How did she do it?

BEN: She —

(*He picks up the paper and studies it.*)

It doesn't say.

GUS: Why not?

BEN: Wait a minute. It just says — Her brother, aged eleven, viewed the incident from the toolshed.

GUS: Go on!

BEN: That's bloody ridiculous.

(*Pause.*)

GUS: I bet he did it.

BEN: Who?

GUS: The brother.

BEN: I think you're right.

(*Pause.*)

(*Slamming down the paper.*) What about that, eh? A kid of eleven killing a cat and blaming it on his little sister of eight! It's enough to —

(*He breaks off in disgust and seizes the paper.* GUS *rises.*)

GUS: What time is he getting in touch?

(BEN *reads.*)

What time is he getting in touch?

BEN: What's the matter with you? It could be any time. Any time.

GUS (*moves to the foot of* BEN'*s bed*): Well, I was going to ask you something.

BEN: What?

GUS: Have you noticed the time that tank takes to fill?

BEN: What tank?

GUS: In the lavatory.

BEN: No. Does it?

GUS: Terrible.

BEN: Well, what about it?

GUS: What do you think's the matter with it?

BEN: Nothing.

GUS: Nothing?

BEN: It's got a deficient ballcock, that's all.

GUS: A deficient what?

BEN: Ballcock.

GUS: No? Really?

BEN: That's what I should say.

GUS: Go on! That didn't occur to me.

(GUS *wanders to his bed and presses the mattress*.)

I didn't have a very restful sleep today, did you? It's not much of a bed. I could have done with another blanket too. (*He catches sight of a picture on the wall*.) Hello, what's this? (*Peering at it*.) "The First Eleven." Cricketers. You seen this, Ben?

BEN (*reading*): What?

GUS: The first eleven.

BEN: What?

GUS: There's a photo here of the first eleven.

BEN: What first eleven?

GUS (*studying the photo*): It doesn't say.

BEN: What about that tea?

GUS: They all look a bit old to me.

(GUS *wanders downstage, looks out front, then all about the room*.)

I wouldn't like to live in this dump. I wouldn't mind if you had a window, you could see what it looked like outside.

BEN: What do you want a window for?

GUS: Well, I like to have a bit of a view, Ben. It whiles away the time.

(*He walks about the room*.)

I mean, you come into a place when it's still dark, you come into a room you've never seen before, you sleep all day, you do your job, and then you go away in the night again.

(*Pause*.)

I like to get a look at the scenery. You never get the chance in this job.

BEN: You get your holidays, don't you?

GUS: Only a fortnight.

BEN (*lowering the paper*): You kill me. Anyone would think you're working every day. How often do we do a job? Once a week? What are you complaining about?

GUS: Yes, but we've got to be on tap though, haven't we? You can't move out of the house in case a call comes.

BEN: You know what your trouble is?

GUS: What?

BEN: You haven't got any interests.

GUS: I've got interests.

BEN: What? Tell me one of your interests.

(*Pause.*)

GUS: I've got interests.

BEN: Look at me. What have I got?

GUS: I don't know. What?

BEN: I've got my woodwork. I've got my model boats. Have you ever seen me idle? I'm never idle. I know how to occupy my time, to its best advantage. Then when a call comes, I'm ready.

GUS: Don't you ever get a bit fed up?

BEN: Fed up? What with?

(*Silence.*

    BEN *reads*. GUS *feels in the pocket of his jacket, which hangs on the bed.*)

GUS: You got any cigarettes? I've run out.

(*The lavatory flushes off left.*)

There she goes.

(GUS *sits on his bed.*)

No, I mean, I say the crockery's good. It is. It's very nice. But that's about all I can say for this place. It's worse than the last one. Remember that last place we were in? Last time, where was it? At least there was a wireless there. No, honest. He doesn't seem to bother much about our comfort these days.

BEN: When are you going to stop jabbering?

GUS: You'd get rheumatism in a place like this, if you stay long.

BEN: We're not staying long. Make the tea, will you? We'll be on the job in a minute.

(GUS *picks up a small bag by his bed and brings out a packet of tea. He examines it and looks up.*)

GUS: Eh, I've been meaning to ask you.

BEN: What the hell is it now?

GUS: Why did you stop the car this morning, in the middle of that road?

BEN (*lowering the paper*): I thought you were asleep.

GUS: I was, but I woke up when you stopped. You did stop, didn't you?

(*Pause.*)

In the middle of that road. It was still dark, don't you remember? I looked out. It was all misty. I thought perhaps you wanted to kip, but you were sitting up dead straight, like you were waiting for something.

BEN: I wasn't waiting for anything.

GUS: I must have fallen asleep again. What was all that about then? Why did you stop?

BEN (*picking up the paper*): We were too early.

GUS: Early? (*He rises.*) What do you mean? We got the call, didn't we, saying we were to start right away. We did. We shoved out on the dot. So how could we be too early?

BEN (*quietly*): Who took the call, me or you?

GUS: You.

BEN: We were too early.

GUS: Too early for what?

(*Pause.*)

You mean someone had to get out before we got in?

(*He examines the bedclothes.*)

I thought these sheets didn't look too bright. I thought they ponged a bit. I was too tired to notice when I got in this morning. Eh, that's taking a bit of a liberty, isn't it? I don't want to share my bed-sheets. I told you things were going down the drain. I mean, we've always had clean sheets laid on up till now. I've noticed it.

BEN: How do you know those sheets weren't clean?

GUS: What do you mean?

BEN: How do you know they weren't clean? You've spent the whole day in them, haven't you?

GUS: What, you mean it might be my pong? (*He sniffs sheets.*) Yes. (*He sits slowly on bed.*) It could be my pong, I suppose. It's difficult to tell. I don't really know what I pong like, that's the trouble.

BEN (*referring to the paper*): Kaw!

GUS: Eh, Ben.

BEN: Kaw!

GUS: Ben.

BEN: What?

GUS: What town are we in? I've forgotten.

BEN: I've told you. Birmingham.

GUS: Go on!

(*He looks with interest about the room.*)

That's in the Midlands. The second biggest city in Great Britain. I'd never have guessed.

(*He snaps his fingers.*)

Eh, it's Friday today, isn't it? It'll be Saturday tomorrow.

BEN: What about it?

GUS (*excited*): We could go and watch the Villa.

BEN: They're playing away.

GUS: No, are they? Caarr! What a pity.

BEN: Anyway, there's no time. We've got to get straight back.

GUS: Well, we have done in the past, haven't we? Stayed over and watched a game, haven't we? For a bit of relaxation.

BEN: Things have tightened up, mate. They've tightened up.

(GUS *chuckles to himself.*)

GUS: I saw the Villa get beat in a cup tie once. Who was it against now? White shirts. It was one-all at half-time. I'll never forget it. Their opponents won by a penalty. Talk about drama. Yes, it was a disputed penalty. Disputed. They got beat two–one, anyway, because of it. You were there yourself.

BEN: Not me.

GUS: Yes, you were there. Don't you remember that disputed penalty?

BEN: No.

GUS: He went down just inside the area. Then they said he was just acting. I didn't think the other bloke touched him myself. But the referee had the ball on the spot.

BEN: Didn't touch him! What are you talking about? He laid him out flat!

GUS: Not the Villa. The Villa don't play that sort of game.

BEN: Get out of it.

(*Pause.*)

GUS: Eh, that must have been here, in Birmingham.

BEN: What must?

GUS: The Villa. That must have been here.

BEN: They were playing away.

GUS: Because you know who the other team was? It was the Spurs. It was Tottenham Hotspur.

BEN: Well, what about it?

GUS: We've never done a job in Tottenham.

BEN: How do you know?

GUS: I'd remember Tottenham.

(BEN *turns on his bed to look at him.*)

BEN: Don't make me laugh, will you?

(BEN *turns back and reads.* GUS *yawns and speaks through his yawn.*)

GUS: When's he going to get in touch!

(*Pause.*)

Yes, I'd like to see another football match. I've always been an ardent football fan. Here, what about coming to see the Spurs tomorrow?

BEN (*tonelessly*): They're playing away.

GUS: Who are?

BEN: The Spurs.

GUS: Then they might be playing here.

BEN: Don't be silly.

GUS: If they're playing away they might be playing here. They might be playing the Villa.

BEN (*tonelessly*): But the Villa are playing away.

(*Pause. An envelope slides under the door, right.* GUS *sees it. He stands, looking at it.*)

GUS: Ben.
BEN: Away. They're all playing away.
GUS: Ben, look here.
BEN: What?
GUS: Look.

(BEN *turns his head and sees the envelope. He stands.*)

BEN: What's that?
GUS: I don't know.
BEN: Where did it come from?
GUS: Under the door.
BEN: Well, what is it?
GUS: I don't know.

(*They stare at it.*)

BEN: Pick it up.
GUS: What do you mean?
BEN: Pick it up!

(GUS *slowly moves towards it, bends and picks it up.*)

What is it?
GUS: An envelope.
BEN: Is there anything on it?
GUS: No.
BEN: Is it sealed?
GUS: Yes.
BEN: Open it.
GUS: What?
BEN: Open it!

(GUS *opens it and looks inside.*)

What's in it?

(GUS *empties twelve matches into his hand.*)

GUS: Matches.
BEN: Matches?
GUS: Yes.
BEN: Show it to me.

(GUS *passes the envelope.* BEN *examines it.*)

Nothing on it. Not a word.
GUS: That's funny, isn't it?
BEN: It came under the door?
GUS: Must have done.
BEN: Well, go on.
GUS: Go on where?
BEN: Open the door and see if you can catch anyone outside.
GUS: Who, me?
BEN: Go on!

(GUS *stares at him, puts the matches in his pocket, goes to his bed and brings a revolver from under the pillow. He goes to the door, opens it, looks out and shuts it.*)

GUS: No one.

(*He replaces the revolver.*)

BEN: What did you see?
GUS: Nothing.
BEN: They must have been pretty quick.

(GUS *takes the matches from pocket and looks at them.*)

GUS: Well, they'll come in handy.
BEN: Yes.
GUS: Won't they?
BEN: Yes, you're always running out, aren't you?
GUS: All the time.
BEN: Well, they'll come in handy then.
GUS: Yes.
BEN: Won't they?
GUS: Yes, I could do with them. I could do with them too.
BEN: You could, eh?
GUS: Yes.
BEN: Why?
GUS: We haven't got any.
BEN: Well, you've got some now, haven't you?
GUS: I can light the kettle now.
BEN: Yes, you're always cadging matches. How many have you got there?
GUS: About a dozen.
BEN: Well, don't lose them. Red too. You don't even need a box.

(GUS *probes his ear with a match.*)

(*Slapping his hand*). Don't waste them! Go on, go and light it.
GUS: Eh?
BEN: Go and light it.
GUS: Light what?
BEN: The kettle.
GUS: You mean the gas.
BEN: Who does?
GUS: You do.
BEN (*his eyes narrowing*): What do you mean, I mean the gas?
GUS: Well, that's what you mean, don't you? The gas.
BEN (*powerfully*): If I say go and light the kettle I mean go and light the kettle.
GUS: How can you light a kettle?
BEN: It's a figure of speech! Light the kettle. It's a figure of speech!
GUS: I've never heard it.
BEN: Light the kettle! It's common usage!
GUS: I think you've got it wrong.
BEN (*menacing*): What do you mean?

GUS: They say put on the kettle.
BEN (*taut*): Who says?

(*They stare at each other, breathing hard.*)

(*Deliberately.*) I have never in all my life heard anyone say put on the kettle.
GUS: I bet my mother used to say it.
BEN: Your mother? When did you last see your mother?
GUS: I don't know, about —
BEN: Well, what are you talking about your mother for?

(*They stare.*)

Gus, I'm not trying to be unreasonable. I'm just trying to point out something to you.
GUS: Yes, but —
BEN: Who's the senior partner here, me or you?
GUS: You.
BEN: I'm only looking after your interests, Gus. You've got to learn, mate.
GUS: Yes, but I've never heard —
BEN (*vehemently*): Nobody says light the gas! What does the gas light?
GUS: What does the gas — ?
BEN (*grabbing him with two hands by the throat, at arm's length*). THE KETTLE, YOU FOOL!

(GUS *takes the hands from his throat.*)

GUS: All right, all right.

(*Pause.*)

BEN: Well, what are you waiting for?
GUS: I want to see if they light.
BEN: What?
GUS: The matches.

(*He takes out the flattened box and tries to strike.*)

No.

(*He throws the box under the bed.*
    BEN *stares at him.*
    GUS *raises his foot.*)

Shall I try it on here?

(BEN *stares.* GUS *strikes a match on his shoe. It lights.*)

Here we are.
BEN (*wearily*): Put on the bloody kettle, for Christ's sake.

(BEN *goes to his bed, but, realising what he has said, stops and half turns. They look at each other.* GUS *slowly exits, left.* BEN *slams his paper down on the bed and sits on it, head in hands.*)

GUS (*entering*): It's going.
BEN: What?

GUS: The stove.

(GUS *goes to his bed and sits.*)

I wonder who it'll be tonight.

(*Silence.*)

Eh, I've been wanting to ask you something.
BEN (*putting his legs on the bed*): Oh, for Christ's sake.
GUS: No. I was going to ask you something.

(*He rises and sits on* BEN's *bed.*)

BEN: What are you sitting on my bed for?

(GUS *sits.*)

What's the matter with you? You're always asking me questions. What's the matter with you?
GUS: Nothing.
BEN: You never used to ask me so many damn questions. What's come over you?
GUS: No, I was just wondering.
BEN: Stop wondering. You've got a job to do. Why don't you just do it and shut up?
GUS: That's what I was wondering about.
BEN: What?
GUS: The job.
BEN: What job?
GUS (*tentatively*): I thought perhaps you might know something.

(BEN *looks at him.*)

I thought perhaps you — I mean — have you got any idea — who it's going to be tonight?
BEN: Who what's going to be?

(*They look at each other.*)

GUS (*at length*): Who it's going to be.

(*Silence.*)

BEN: Are you feeling all right?
GUS: Sure.
BEN: Go and make the tea.
GUS: Yes, sure.

(GUS *exits, left,* BEN *looks after him. He then takes his revolver from under the pillow and checks it for ammunition.* GUS *re-enters.*)

The gas has gone out.
BEN: Well, what about it?
GUS: There's a meter.
BEN: I haven't got any money.
GUS: Nor have I.
BEN: You'll have to wait.
GUS: What for?

BEN: For Wilson.
GUS: He might not come. He might just send a message. He doesn't always come.
BEN: Well, you'll have to do without it, won't you?
GUS: Blimey.
BEN: You'll have a cup of tea afterwards. What's the matter with you?
GUS: I like to have one before.

(BEN *holds the revolver up to the light and polishes it.*)

BEN: You'd better get ready anyway.
GUS: Well, I don't know, that's a bit much, you know, for my money.

(*He picks up a packet of tea from the bed and throws it into the bag.*)

I hope he's got a shilling, anyway, if he comes. He's entitled to have. After all, it's his place, he could have seen there was enough gas for a cup of tea.
BEN: What do you mean, it's his place?
GUS: Well, isn't it?
BEN: He's probably only rented it. It doesn't have to be his place.
GUS: I know it's his place. I bet the whole house is. He's not even laying on any gas now either.

(GUS *sits on his bed.*)

It's his place all right. Look at all the other places. You go to this address, there's a key there, there's a teapot, there's never a soul in sight — (*He pauses.*) Eh, nobody ever hears a thing, have you ever thought of that? We never get any complaints, do we, too much noise or anything like that? You never see a soul, do you? — except the bloke who comes. You ever noticed that? I wonder if the walls are sound-proof. (*He touches the wall above his bed.*) Can't tell. All you do is wait, eh? Half the time he doesn't even bother to put in an appearance, Wilson.
BEN: Why should he? He's a busy man.
GUS (*thoughtfully*): I find him hard to talk to, Wilson. Do you know that, Ben?
BEN: Scrub round it, will you?

(*Pause.*)

GUS: There are a number of things I want to ask him. But I can never get round to it, when I see him.

(*Pause.*)

I've been thinking about the last one.
BEN: What last one?
GUS: That girl.

(BEN *grabs the paper, which he reads.*)

(*Rising, looking down at* BEN.) How many times have you read that paper?

(BEN *slams the paper down and rises.*)

BEN (*angrily*): What do you mean?
GUS: I was just wondering how many times you'd —
BEN: What are you doing, criticising me?

GUS: No, I was just —

BEN: You'll get a swipe round your earhole if you don't watch your step.

GUS: Now look here, Ben —

BEN: I'm not looking anywhere! (*He addresses the room.*) How many times have I — ! A bloody liberty!

GUS: I didn't mean that.

BEN: You just get on with it, mate. Get on with, that's all.

(BEN *gets back on the bed.*)

GUS: I was just thinking about that girl, that's all.

(GUS *sits on his bed.*)

She wasn't much to look at, I know, but still. It was a mess though, wasn't it? What a mess. Honest, I can't remember a mess like that one. They don't seem to hold together like men, women. A looser texture, like. Didn't she spread, eh? She didn't half spread. Kaw! But I've been meaning to ask you.

(BEN *sits up and clenches his eyes.*)

Who clears up after we've gone? I'm curious about that. Who does the clearing up? Maybe they don't clear up. Maybe they just leave them there, eh? What do you think? How many jobs have we done? Blimey, I can't count them. What if they never clear anything up after we've gone.

BEN (*pityingly*): You mutt. Do you think we're the only branch of this organisation? Have a bit of common. They got departments for everything.

GUS: What cleaners and all?

BEN: You birk!

GUS: No, it was that girl made me start to think —

(*There is a loud clatter and racket in the bulge of wall between the beds, of something descending. They grab their revolvers, jump up and face the wall. The noise comes to a stop. Silence. They look at each other.* BEN *gestures sharply towards the wall.* GUS *approaches the wall slowly. He bangs it with his revolver. It is hollow.* BEN *moves to the head of his bed, his revolver cocked.* GUS *puts his revolver on his bed and pats along the bottom of the centre panel. He finds a rim. He lifts the panel. Disclosed is a serving-hatch, a "dumb waiter." A wide box is held by pulleys.* GUS *peers into the box. He brings out a piece of paper.*)

BEN: What is it?

GUS: You have a look at it.

BEN: Read it.

GUS (*reading*): Two braised steak and chips. Two sago puddings. Two teas without sugar.

BEN: Let me see that. (*He takes the paper.*)

GUS (*to himself*): Two teas without sugar.

BEN: Mmnn.

GUS: What do you think of that?

BEN: Well —

(*The box goes up.* BEN *levels his revolver.*)

GUS: Give us a chance! They're in a hurry, aren't they?

(BEN *re-reads the note.* GUS *looks over his shoulder.*)

That's a bit — that's a bit funny, isn't it?

BEN (*quickly*): No. It's not funny. It probably used to be a café here, that's all. Upstairs. These places change hands very quickly.

GUS: A café?

BEN: Yes.

GUS: What, you mean this was the kitchen, down here?

BEN: Yes, they change hands overnight, these places. Go into liquidation. The people who run it, you know, they don't find it a going concern, they move out.

GUS: You mean the people who ran this place didn't find it a going concern and moved out?

BEN: Sure.

GUS: WELL, WHO'S GOT IT NOW?

(*Silence.*)

BEN: What do you mean, who's got it now?

GUS: Who's got it now? If they moved out, who moved in?

BEN: Well, that all depends —

(*The box descends with a clatter and bang.* BEN *levels his revolver.* GUS *goes to the box and brings out a piece of paper.*)

GUS (*reading*): Soup of the day. Liver and onions. Jam tart.

(*A pause.* GUS *looks at* BEN. BEN *takes the note and reads it. He walks slowly to the hatch.* GUS *follows.* BEN *looks into the hatch but not up it.* GUS *puts his hand on* BEN's *shoulder.* BEN *throws it off.* GUS *puts his finger to his mouth. He leans on the hatch and swiftly looks up it.* BEN *flings him away in alarm.* BEN *looks at the note. He throws his revolver on the bed and speaks with decision.*)

BEN: We'd better send something up.

GUS: Eh?

BEN: We'd better send something up.

GUS: Oh! Yes. Yes. Maybe you're right.

(*They are both relieved at the decision.*)

BEN (*purposefully*): Quick! What have you got in that bag?

GUS: Not much.

(GUS *goes to the hatch and shouts up it.*)

Wait a minute!

BEN: Don't do that!

(GUS *examines the contents of the bag and brings them out, one by one.*)

GUS: Biscuits. A bar of chocolate. Half a pint of milk.

BEN: That all?

GUS: Packet of tea.

BEN: Good.

GUS: We can't send the tea. That's all the tea we've got.

BEN: Well, there's no gas. You can't do anything with it, can you?

GUS: Maybe they can send us down a bob.

BEN: What else is there?

GUS (*reaching into bag*): One Eccles cake.

BEN: One Eccles cake?

GUS: Yes.

BEN: You never told me you had an Eccles cake.

GUS: Didn't I?

BEN: Why only one? Didn't you bring one for me?

GUS: I didn't think you'd be keen.

BEN: Well, you can't send up one Eccles cake, anyway.

GUS: Why not?

BEN: Fetch one of those plates.

GUS: All right.

(GUS *goes towards the door, left, and stops.*)

Do you mean I can keep the Eccles cake then?

BEN: Keep it?

GUS: Well, they don't know we've got it, do they?

BEN: That's not the point.

GUS: Can't I keep it?

BEN: No, you can't. Get the plate.

(GUS *exits, left.* BEN *looks in the bag. He brings out a packet of crisps. Enter* GUS *with a plate.*)

(*Accusingly, holding up the crisps.*) Where did these come from?

GUS: What?

BEN: Where did these crisps come from?

GUS: Where did you find them?

BEN (*hitting him on the shoulder*): You're playing a dirty game, my lad!

GUS: I only eat those with beer!

BEN: Well, where were you going to get the beer?

GUS: I was saving them till I did.

BEN: I'll remember this. Put everything on the plate.

(*They pile everything on to the plate. The box goes up without the plate.*)

Wait a minute!

(*They stand.*)

GUS: It's gone up.

BEN: It's all your stupid fault, playing about!

GUS: What do we do now?

BEN: We'll have to wait till it comes down.

(BEN *puts the plate on the bed, puts on his shoulder holster, and starts to put on his tie.*)

You'd better get ready.

(GUS *goes to his bed, puts on his tie, and starts to fix his holster.*)

GUS: Hey, Ben.

BEN: What?

GUS: What's going on here?

(*Pause.*)

BEN: What do you mean?

GUS: How can this be a café?

BEN: It used to be a café.

GUS: Have you seen the gas stove?

BEN: What about it?

GUS: It's only got three rings.

BEN: So what?

GUS: Well, you couldn't cook much on three rings, not for a busy place like this.

BEN (*irritably*): That's why the service is slow!

(BEN *puts on his waistcoat.*)

GUS: Yes, but what happens when we're not here? What do they do then? All these menus coming down and nothing going up. It might have been going on like this for years.

(BEN *brushes his jacket.*)

What happens when we go?

(BEN *puts on his jacket.*)

They can't do much business.

(*The box descends. They turn about.* GUS *goes to the hatch and brings out a note.*)

GUS (*reading*): Macaroni Pastitsio. Ormitha Macarounada.

BEN: What was that?

GUS: Macaroni Pastitsio. Ormitha Macarounada.

BEN: Greek dishes.

GUS: No.

BEN: That's right.

GUS: That's pretty high class.

BEN: Quick before it goes up.

(GUS *puts the plate in the box.*)

GUS (*calling up the hatch*): Three McVitie and Price! One Lyons Red Label! One Smith's Crisps! One Eccles cake! One Fruit and Nut!

BEN: Cadbury's.

GUS (*up the hatch*): Cadbury's!

BEN (*handing the milk*): One bottle of milk.

GUS (*up the hatch*): One bottle of milk! Half a pint! (*He looks at the label.*) Express Dairy! (*He puts the bottle in the box.*)

(*The box goes up.*)

Just did it.

BEN: You shouldn't shout like that.

GUS: Why not?

BEN: It isn't done.

(BEN *goes to his bed*.)

Well, that should be all right, anyway, for the time being.

GUS: You think so, eh?

BEN: Get dressed, will you? It'll be any minute now.

(GUS *puts on his waistcoat*. BEN *lies down and looks up at the ceiling*.)

GUS: This is some place. No tea and no biscuits.

BEN: Eating makes you lazy, mate. You're getting lazy, you know that? You don't want to get slack on your job.

GUS: Who me?

BEN: Slack, mate, slack.

GUS: Who me? Slack?

BEN: Have you checked your gun? You haven't even checked your gun. It looks disgraceful, anyway. Why don't you ever polish it?

(GUS *rubs his revolver on the sheet*. BEN *takes out a pocket mirror and straightens his tie*.)

GUS: I wonder where the cook is. They must have had a few, to cope with that. Maybe they had a few more gas stoves. Eh! Maybe there's another kitchen along the passage.

BEN: Of course there is! Do you know what it takes to make an Ormitha Macarounada?

GUS: No, what?

BEN: An Ormitha — ! Buck your ideas up, will you?

GUS: Takes a few cooks, eh?

(GUS *puts his revolver in his holster*.)

The sooner we're out of this place the better.

(*He puts on his jacket*.)

Why doesn't he get in touch? I feel like I've been here years. (*He takes his revolver out of its holster to check the ammunition*.) We've never let him down though, have we? We've never let him down. I was thinking only the other day, Ben. We're reliable, aren't we?

(*He puts his revolver back in its holster*.)

Still, I'll be glad when it's over tonight.

(*He brushes his jacket*.)

I hope the bloke's not going to get excited tonight, or anything. I'm feeling a bit off. I've got a splitting headache.

(*Silence*.

   The box descends. BEN *jumps up*.
   GUS *collects the note*.)

(*Reading*.) One Bamboo Shoots, Water Chestnuts and Chicken. One Char Siu and Beansprouts.

BEN: Beansprouts?
GUS: Yes.
BEN: Blimey.
GUS: I wouldn't know where to begin.

(*He looks back at the box. The packet of tea is inside it. He picks it up.*)

They've sent back the tea.
BEN (*anxious*): What'd they do that for?
GUS: Maybe it isn't tea-time.

(*The box goes up. Silence.*)

BEN (*throwing the tea on the bed, and speaking urgently*): Look here. We'd better tell them.
GUS: Tell them what?
BEN: That we can't do it, we haven't got it.
GUS: All right then.
BEN: Lend us your pencil. We'll write a note.

(GUS, *turning for a pencil, suddenly discovers the speaking-tube, which hangs on the right wall of the hatch facing his bed.*)

GUS: What's this?
BEN: What?
GUS: This.
BEN (*examining it*): This? It's a speaking-tube.
GUS: How long has that been there?
BEN: Just the job. We should have used it before, instead of shouting up there.
GUS: Funny I never noticed it before.
BEN: Well, come on.
GUS: What do you do?
BEN: See that? That's a whistle.
GUS: What, this?
BEN: Yes, take it out. Pull it out.

(GUS *does so.*)

That's it.
GUS: What do we do now?
BEN: Blow into it.
GUS: Blow?
BEN: It whistles up there if you blow. Then they know you want to speak. Blow.

(GUS *blows. Silence.*)

GUS (*tube at mouth*): I can't hear a thing.
BEN: Now you speak! Speak into it!

(GUS *looks at* BEN, *then speaks into the tube.*)

GUS: The larder's bare!
BEN: Give me that!

(*He grabs the tube and puts it to his mouth.*)

(*Speaking with great deference.*) Good evening. I'm sorry to — bother you, but we just thought we'd better let you know that we haven't got anything left. We sent up all we had. There's no more food down here.

(*He brings the tube slowly to his ear.*)

What?

(*To mouth.*)

What?

(*To ear. He listens. To mouth.*)

No, all we had we sent up.

(*To ear. He listens. To mouth.*)

Oh, I'm very sorry to hear that.

(*To ear. He listens. To* GUS.)

The Eccles cake was stale.

(*He listens. To* GUS.)

The chocolate was melted.

(*He listens. To* GUS.)

The milk was sour.
GUS: What about the crisps?
BEN (*listening*): The biscuits were mouldy.

(*He glares at* GUS. *Tube to mouth.*)

Well, we're very sorry about that.

(*Tube to ear.*)

What?

(*To mouth.*)

What?

(*To ear.*)

Yes. Yes.

(*To mouth.*)

Yes certainly. Certainly. Right away.

(*To ear. The voice has ceased. He hangs up the tube.*)

(*Excitedly*). Did you hear that?
GUS: What?
BEN: You know what he said? Light the kettle! Not put on the kettle! Not light the gas! But light the kettle!
GUS: How can we light the kettle?
BEN: What do you mean?

GUS: There's no gas.

BEN (*clapping hand to head*): Now what do we do?

GUS: What did he want us to light the kettle for?

BEN: For tea. He wanted a cup of tea.

GUS: *He* wanted a cup of tea! What about me? I've been wanting a cup of tea all night!

BEN (*despairingly*): What do we do now?

GUS: What are we supposed to drink?

(BEN *sits on his bed, staring.*)

What about us?

(BEN *sits.*)

I'm thirsty too. I'm starving. And he wants a cup of tea. That beats the band, that does.

(BEN *lets his head sink on to his chest.*)

I could do with a bit of sustenance myself. What about you? You look as if you could do with something too.

(GUS *sits on his bed.*)

We send him up all we've got and he's not satisfied. No, honest, it's enough to make the cat laugh. Why did you send him up all that stuff? (*Thoughtfully.*) Why did I send it up?

(*Pause.*)

Who knows what he's got upstairs? He's probably got a salad bowl. They must have something up there. They won't get much from down here. You notice they didn't ask for any salads? They've probably got a salad bowl up there. Cold meat, radishes, cucumbers. Watercress. Roll mops.

(*Pause.*)

Hardboiled eggs.

(*Pause.*)

The lot. They've probably got a crate of beer too. Probably eating my crisps with a pint of beer now. Didn't have anything to say about those crisps, did he? They do all right, don't worry about that. You don't think they're just going to sit there and wait for stuff to come up from down here, do you? That'll get them nowhere.

(*Pause.*)

They do all right.

(*Pause.*)

And he wants a cup of tea.

(*Pause.*)

That's past a joke, in my opinion.

(*He looks over at* BEN, *rises, and goes to him.*)

What's the matter with you? You don't look too bright. I feel like an Alka-Seltzer myself.

(BEN *sits up.*)

BEN (*in a low voice*): Time's getting on.
GUS: I know. I don't like doing a job on an empty stomach.
BEN (*wearily*): Be quiet a minute. Let me give you your instructions.
GUS: What for? We always do it the same way, don't we?
BEN: Let me give you your instructions.

(GUS *sighs and sits next to* BEN *on the bed. The instructions are stated and repeated automatically.*)

When we get the call, you go over and stand behind the door.
GUS: Stand behind the door.
BEN: If there's a knock on the door you don't answer it.
GUS: If there's a knock on the door I don't answer it.
BEN: But there won't be a knock on the door.
GUS: So I won't answer it.
BEN: When the bloke comes in —
GUS: When the bloke comes in —
BEN: Shut the door behind him.
GUS: Shut the door behind him.
BEN: Without divulging your presence.
GUS: Without divulging my presence.
BEN: He'll see me and come towards me.
GUS: He'll see you and come towards you.
BEN: He won't see you.
GUS (*absently*): Eh?
BEN: He won't see you.
GUS: He won't see me.
BEN: But he'll see me.
GUS: He'll see you.
BEN: He won't know you're there.
GUS: He won't know you're there.
BEN: He won't know *you're* there.
GUS: He won't know I'm there.
BEN: I take out my gun.
GUS: You take out your gun.
BEN: He stops in his tracks.
GUS: He stops in his tracks.
BEN: If he turns round —
GUS: If he turns round —
BEN: You're there.
GUS: I'm here.

(BEN *frowns and presses his forehead.*)

You've missed something out.

BEN: I know. What?

GUS: I haven't taken my gun out, according to you.

BEN: You take your gun out —

GUS: After I've closed the door.

BEN: After you've closed the door.

GUS: You've never missed that out before, you know that?

BEN: When he sees you behind him —

GUS: Me behind him —

BEN: And me in front of him —

GUS: And you in front of him —

BEN: He'll feel uncertain —

GUS: Uneasy.

BEN: He won't know what to do.

GUS: So what will he do?

BEN: He'll look at me and he'll look at you.

GUS: We won't say a word.

BEN: We'll look at him.

GUS: He won't say a word.

BEN: He'll look at us.

GUS: And we'll look at him.

BEN: Nobody says a word.

(*Pause.*)

GUS: What do we do if it's a girl?

BEN: We do the same.

GUS: Exactly the same?

BEN: Exactly.

(*Pause.*)

GUS: We don't do anything different?

BEN: We do exactly the same.

GUS: Oh.

(GUS *rises, and shivers.*)

Excuse me.

(*He exits through the door on the left.* BEN *remains sitting on the bed, still.*
The lavatory chain is pulled once off left, but the lavatory does not flush.
Silence.
GUS *re-enters and stops inside the door, deep in thought. He looks at* BEN,
then walks slowly across to his own bed. He is troubled. He stands, thinking.
He turns and looks at BEN. *He moves a few paces towards him.*)

(*Slowly in a low, tense voice.*) Why did he send us matches if he knew there was
no gas?

(*Silence.*
BEN *stares in front of him.* GUS *crosses to the left side of* BEN, *to the foot of*
his bed, to get to his other ear.)

Ben. Why did he send us matches if he knew there was no gas?

(BEN *looks up.*)

Why did he do that?

BEN: Who?

GUS: Who sent us those matches?

BEN: What are you talking about?

(GUS *stares down at him.*)

GUS (*thickly*): Who is it upstairs?

BEN (*nervously*): What's one thing to do with another?

GUS: Who is it, though?

BEN: What's one thing to do with another?

(BEN *fumbles for his paper on the bed.*)

GUS: I asked you a question.

BEN: Enough!

GUS (*with growing agitation*): I asked you before. Who moved in? I asked you. You said the people who had it before moved out. Well, who moved in?

BEN (*hunched*): Shut up.

GUS: I told you, didn't I?

BEN (*standing*): Shut up!

GUS (*feverishly*): I told you before who owned this place, didn't I? I told you.

(BEN *hits him viciously on the shoulder.*)

I told you who ran this place, didn't I?

(BEN *hits him viciously on the shoulder.*)

(*Violently.*) Well, what's he playing all these games for? That's what I want to know. What's he doing it for?

BEN: What games?

GUS (*passionately, advancing*): What's he doing it for? We've been through our tests, haven't we? We got right through our tests, years ago, didn't we? We took them together, don't you remember, didn't we? We've proved ourselves before now, haven't we? We've always done our job. What's he doing all this for? What's the idea? What's he playing these games for?

(*The box in the shaft comes down behind them. The noise is this time accompanied by a shrill whistle, as it falls.* GUS *rushes to the hatch and seizes the note.*)

(*Reading.*) Scampi!

(*He crumples the note, picks up the tube, takes out the whistle, blows and speaks.*)

WE'VE GOT NOTHING LEFT! NOTHING! DO YOU UNDERSTAND?

(BEN *seizes the tube and flings* GUS *away. He follows* GUS *and slaps him hard, back-handed, across the chest.*)

BEN: Stop it! You maniac!

GUS: But you heard!

BEN (*savagely*): That's enough! I'm warning you!

(*Silence.*
    BEN *hangs the tube. He goes to his bed and lies down. He picks up his paper and reads.*
    Silence.
    The box goes up.
    They turn quickly, their eyes meet. BEN *turns to his paper.*
    Slowly GUS *goes back to his bed, and sits.*
    Silence.
    The hatch falls back into place.
    They turn quickly, their eyes meet. BEN *turns back to his paper.*
    Silence.
    BEN *throws his paper down.*)

BEN: Kaw!

(*He picks up the paper and looks at it.*)

Listen to this!

(*Pause.*)

What about that, eh?

(*Pause.*)

Kaw!

(*Pause.*)

Have you ever heard such a thing?
GUS (*dully*): Go on!
BEN: It's true.
GUS: Get away.
BEN: It's down here in black and white.
GUS (*very low*): Is that a fact?
BEN: Can you imagine it.
GUS: It's unbelievable.
BEN: It's enough to make you want to puke, isn't it?
GUS (*almost inaudible*): Incredible.

(BEN *shakes his head. He puts the paper down and rises. He fixes the revolver in his holster.*
    GUS *stands up. He goes towards the door on the left.*)

BEN: Where are you going?
GUS: I'm going to have a glass of water.

(*He exits.* BEN *brushes dust off his clothes and shoes. The whistle in the speaking-tube blows. He goes to it, takes the whistle out and puts the tube to his ear. He listens. He puts it to his mouth.*)

BEN: Yes.

(*To ear. He listens. To mouth.*)

Straight away. Right.

(*To ear. He listens. To mouth.*)

Sure we're ready.

(*To ear. He listens. To mouth.*)

Understood. Repeat. He has arrived and will be coming in straight away. The normal method to be employed. Understood.

(*To ear. He listens. To mouth.*)

Sure we're ready.

(*To ear. He listens. To mouth.*)

Right.

(*He hangs the tube up.*)

Gus!

(*He takes out a comb and combs his hair, adjusts his jacket to diminish the bulge of the revolver. The lavatory flushes off left. BEN goes quickly to the door, left.*)

Gus!

(*The door right opens sharply. BEN turns, his revolver levelled at the door.
GUS stumbles in.
He is stripped of his jacket, waistcoat, tie, holster and revolver.
He stops, body stooping, his arms at his sides.
He raises his head and looks at BEN.
A long silence.
They stare at each other.*)

CURTAIN

AFTERWORD

The action of *The Dumb Waiter* (1957) is both simple and strange. Two men wait in a basement room for the arrival of someone they have been hired to kill. There is a small service elevator in the wall, and suddenly it starts bringing orders from upstairs for increasingly exotic dishes. The men send up what few snacks they have but are told those won't do. They grow more and more anxious. While one of them is out of the room, the other gets the word that their victim has arrived. The door opens, and there, disarmed, is his partner.

Rather than a plot reaching resolution this is a situation coming to a crisis and then being abruptly cut off. And Ben and Gus aren't "characters" in the sense that Oedipus, Hamlet, Nora Helmer, and Willy Loman are "characters" — that is, fictive people we come to know and can believe in because we understand who and what they are and what they are up to and why. *The Dumb Waiter* disappoints just about every conventional expectation of what drama ought to be.

Yet there is nothing vague about the immediate stage action and nothing fantastic about Ben and Gus. If we are puzzled by the oddity of what goes on beyond the room, so are they. They are small hit men on a sordid mission, recognizable social types. The title of the play refers to *them* as well as to the mechanical contraption, "the serving hatch," between their beds. Both of them are "dumb waiters," waiting for their victim and trying to wait on the mysterious customers upstairs. Gus carries out a number of small, menial, and possibly dangerous tasks on Ben's order, but he worries and wonders so much about their job and about their bosses that the "organisation" they serve may have decided he's got to go. As the apparent victim at the end, Gus is the dumb-*stupid* waiter. Ben, fretfully bossy with Gus but all unquestioning submission to the organization, is the dumb-*silent* waiter. The elaborate pun defines the trap they're in.

But we never learn enough about them to feel that we get inside them. They never explain themselves. Ben has his woodwork and his boats and Gus his undefined "interests" and his smoking, but they are not fully realized characters. Their background is sparse and fragmentary and accounts for nothing. Are Ben's "boats" models or real boats? They are now in Birmingham. They deal with the organization through somebody named Wilson, they have been through "tests" and have done similar jobs before, their most recent victim was a girl, since "things have tightened up" their creature comforts on the job are not what they used to be, they sometimes go to soccer games, Gus doesn't know when he last saw his mother, he seems to be out of cigarettes. And so on.

But even the odd snippets of information we do get aren't all certified facts. Did they or did they not get clean sheets for their beds? Did Ben watch the game that Aston Villa lost 2–1 on a penalty kick, or did he not? How can *all* the teams be playing away *all* the time? What happens after the killers finish a job — is "the mess" cleaned up, and if it is, by whom? Was the cat killed by the little girl or by her brother? Even their squabble over the proper idiom for describing making tea is ambiguous. Gus thinks the phrase is either "light the gas" or "put on the kettle"; Ben thinks it is "light the kettle." But it is Gus's "I can light the kettle now" that starts the whole discussion, and it is Ben's "put on the bloody kettle" that ends it. *Is* there some kind of restaurant above? How can those who send down orders for things like "Ormitha Macarounada" and "Char Siu and Beansprouts" expect them to be filled? Why did Ben stop the car that morning, "in the middle of that road"? As Gus says, "What's going on here?" We never find out. The play is like a photograph with the foreground figures in sharp focus but without depth and set against a background of mist.

Pinter uses the same technique in other plays. We know exactly what is happening but not *why* it happens. The surface is crisp and clear. Everything else is opaque. The context that would explain it all isn't there. This is Pinter's version of the absurdist vision of life. We are, each of us, in this place, at this time. We know who we are, what we are doing, and why. But just below our knowledge lies the nameless fear that we may be aliens in an incomprehensible existence. Why *this* self, *this* body, *these* thoughts, *these* desires? Why here and now? Trapped in time, at the mercy of genes, chance, and other people, what freedom do we have, what control, what knowledge? Who's in charge? "What's going on here?"

Given the vagueness of context, we can go beyond the realist's rational interpretation of *The Dumb Waiter* ("A gangland killing. An inside job.") and make an allegory of it. Ben and Gus are dressed alike and are on the same job. That suggests they are identical. They don't like each other much and are unequal in authority. That does not. They are one, yet two: senior partner and junior partner, acceptor and questioner, killer and victim. Together they personify some basic human dualities. Gus's question "Who's upstairs?" takes on a religious meaning. Above the waiters is an implacable power, demanding the impossible, rejecting their humble gifts (except, perhaps — and inexplicably — the "crisps," [i.e., potato chips]), manipulating them into position for the final symbolic suicide-killing. The title pun reduces the human being to a thing, a self-destroying tool in the hands of an inscrutable and capriciously violent higher power. Humankind is confined to a blind, underground room. The world outside reaches the men through the verbal (the orders for food) and nonverbal (the twelve matches in an envelope, the speaking-tube whistle) communications from the organization and through the small and random news items in Ben's newspaper. Judging from those he reads aloud, that outside world is one of accidental or deliberate violence (the old man run over by the truck he crawled under, a child killing a cat) or of silence:

BEN: . . . Listen to this!

(*Pause.*)

What about that, eh?

When Gus, referring to "the place" he and Ben are in, asks "WHO'S GOT IT NOW?" we could be hearing modern humanity questioning the nature of whatever new deity has taken over from the old.

In absurdist plays the human being's existential loneliness on the social plane is commonly manifested in a breakdown of language. As in Samuel Beckett's plays, speech in *The Dumb Waiter* sometimes functions not as communication or as expression but as ritual.

BEN: He won't see you.
GUS: He won't see me.
BEN: But he'll see me.
GUS: He'll see you.
BEN: He won't know you're there.
GUS: He won't know you're there.
BEN: He won't know *you're* there.
GUS: He won't know I'm there.

They are rehearsing the job they are about to do. In repeating Ben's instructions Gus most of the time manages to make the proper pronoun changes (as in lines 2, 4, and 8, above), but once he slips (line 6). The effect is of speech poised precariously on the edge of utility, for a moment falling into empty ritual, the pattern of repetition becoming an end in itself. We see how densely organized the passage is when we realize what a heavy charge of anticipatory irony it also carries: Gus as victim will indeed not see himself as he reenters the room, but he will see Ben. A similar ironic effect is created elsewhere in the play by the repetition of apparently innocent colloquialisms, like "Get away" (he can't), "playing away" (they are), "getting in touch" (they do and they don't), and "You kill me" (he will).

Pinter is not the first modern playwright to use waiting as an image of human life. In Chekhov's *Cherry Orchard* the family makes futile plans for saving the estate, waiting for financial rescue while the auction date draws near. In Chekhov's *Three Sisters* the sisters keep announcing their intention of moving back to Moscow, but at the end they are still stuck in their dull, provincial town and still waiting for happiness, for fulfillment, and for an answer to the riddle of their fate.

What for Chekhov was a plot item for the display of his characters' fecklessness, Beckett turned into a compendious image for existence itself in *Waiting for Godot* (1953), the breakthrough play of the contemporary absurdist theater. At nightfall two tramps are waiting near a country road in a desolate landscape for someone named Godot. When he comes, he will presumably relieve their distress, though exactly how they don't know and we never learn — they speak vaguely of "promises." On two successive evenings Godot fails to keep his appointment. On both evenings the tramps decide to leave but then "do not move." When the play ends they are still waiting. We are left with a sense of lives suspended between a painful and frustrating present and an indefinite but somehow better future. It is as if Beckett had taken for his text a couplet from Alexander Pope's *Essay on Man* (1733):

> Hope springs eternal in the human breast:
> Man never Is, but always To be blest:

Like Beckett's Vladimir and Estragon, Pinter's Ben and Gus are different but complementary figures, homeless and vulnerable, waiting in a mysterious and sexless world. But Beckett's two tramps, for all the tension between their temperaments and for all their bickering, stay together in a symbiotic and oddly touching partnership. Between Pinter's two gangsters, on the other hand, there is almost constant and unpleasant friction, and at the end Ben is presumably about to kill his partner. Pinter's room is an uglier and psychologically bleaker place than Beckett's open country. It can't even provide such a small domestic amenity as a cup of tea. As symbolic setting it is more like the desert scene in Beckett's *Act Without Words*. Gus's goings and comings between the onstage room and the offstage kitchen and toilet are a little like the mime's futile attempts to escape the stage. The ominous in Pinter's play, the sense we get that something is getting ready to pounce, corresponds to the gathering sense of inescapable doom in Beckett.

A witty critic has called Pinter's plays "comedies of menace." (The punning allusion is to "comedies of manners" — plays like Etherege's *Man of Mode*, Congreve's *Way of the World*, Sheridan's *School for Scandal*, and Wilde's *The Importance of Being Earnest*.) *The Dumb Waiter* is a particularly good example of that curious mixture of the farcical-trivial and the sinister-portentous that distinguishes so many of Pinter's plays. Yet there is more "menace" than "comedy" in the play, and what is menacing isn't just the Mafia-like "organisation" but life itself.

Absurdist plays are not "plays of ideas" in the usual sense. That is, they are not, like some of Ibsen's and most of Shaw's and Brecht's, ideological dialectics, or diagnoses of social ills. No one could possibly call Ben and Gus thinkers. And when absurdist playwrights deliberately forego not just philosophical discourse but character analysis and cause-and-effect linearity of plot, as well, they are not willfully defying tradition in quest of perverse orginality but querying the rationalistic premises of traditional drama. They arrange their dramatic matter lyrically or musically rather than narratively. Their plays tend to be short for the good reason that without plots to generate audience suspense, credible and carefully motivated characters to generate audience empathy, and coherent discussions to generate audience interest in ideas, their mere image-making on stage would soon become a bore. It is for similar reasons that lyrical poems are shorter than epics and that musical compositions, unless they are dramatic, like opera, rarely last longer than an hour or so in performance.

To the absurdist, things *are* before they *mean*, and if what the playwright shows disturbs and perplexes us, so (he or she might say in self-vindication) do things in "real life." The element of bizarre mystery in these plays is a vehicle for a kind of meta-realism. We confront the essentials of our common condition; our experience has been stripped of its reassuring subterfuges and comfortable distractions. No "explanation" in terms of a philosophical or any other kind of system is forthcoming: *that* is the point. Each play is a single, sustained metaphor for a certain way of experiencing life. So beneath their blandly impermeable surfaces of objective particulars is a play of ideas, after all. They are dramatizations of varieties of modern philosophical nihilism.

That is why the trick, shock ending of *The Dumb Waiter* works. Events are arbitrary and contingent, but when they happen they are reminders that the climate we live in is one of grim irony. And that is also why we don't need to be defensive about reading *The Dumb Waiter* as metaphysical allegory. It is another variant of the general absurdist image of minimal human life. In it, claustrophobic man is being maneuvered into violence against some vital extension of his own self, by ruthless, invisible forces.

Edward Albee

WHO'S AFRAID OF
VIRGINIA WOOLF?

FOREWORD

Like *Death of a Salesman*, this play was conceived with the pressures of
the American commercial theater in mind. One might cynically compare
the scenic expansiveness of *Ah, Wilderness!* with Albee's single set and four
characters — economic virtues when operating costs and union demands
have soared. Albee, however, like Racine, makes dramatic capital out of
the limitations imposed upon him. Like *Phaedra*, this is an explosion mag-
nified in a confined space.

Superficially, this is a realistic play. Scenically it is totally so. In tone and
language it is something else. As society has cast off many of its traditional
rituals — social, professional, domestic, religious — the theater has shown
a desire to return to ritual forms, or to create new rituals of its own. Pattern
and form, it seems to be suggesting, are essential to the conduct and comprehension of life, however much we delude ourselves into thinking we can
do without them. Thus some modern drama (as we have already seen)
returns to the theater's archetypal beginnings in liturgy, combat, and contest. Albee's ritual, discernible under the superficial realism of the dialogue,
is that of the game.

THE PLAYERS

MARTHA, a large, boisterous woman, 52, looking somewhat younger. Ample, but not fleshy.

GEORGE, her husband, 46. Thin; hair going gray.

HONEY, 26, a petite blond girl, rather plain.

NICK, 30, her husband. Blond, well put-together, good looking.

The Scene: The living room of a house on the campus of a small New England college.

ACT I. FUN AND GAMES

Set in darkness. Crash against front door. MARTHA's *laughter heard. Front door opens, lights are switched on.* MARTHA *enters, followed by* GEORGE.

MARTHA: Je*sus*. . . .

GEORGE: . . . Shhhhhhh. . . .

MARTHA: . . . H. Christ. . . .

GEORGE: For God's sake, Martha, it's two o'clock in the. . . .

MARTHA: Oh, George!

GEORGE: Well, I'm *sorry*, but. . . .

MARTHA: What a cluck! What a cluck you are.

GEORGE: It's late, you know? Late.

MARTHA (*looks about the room. Imitates Bette Davis*): What a dump. Hey, what's that from? "What a dump!"

GEORGE: How would I know what. . . .

MARTHA: Aw, come on! What's it from? *You* know. . . .

GEORGE: . . . Martha. . . .

MARTHA: WHAT'S IT FROM, FOR CHRIST'S SAKE?

GEORGE (*wearily*): What's what from?

MARTHA: I just told you; I just did it. "What a dump!" Hunh? What's that from?

GEORGE: I haven't the faintest idea what. . . .

MARTHA: Dumbbell! It's from some goddamn Bette Davis picture . . . some goddamn Warner Brothers epic. . . .

GEORGE: *I* can't remember all the pictures that. . . .

MARTHA: Nobody's asking you to remember every single goddamn Warner Brothers epic . . . just one! One single little epic! Bette Davis gets peritonitis in the end . . . she's got this big black fright wig she wears all through the picture and she gets peritonitis, and she's married to Joseph Cotten or something. . . .

GEORGE: . . . Some*body*. . . .

MARTHA: . . . some*body* . . . and she wants to go to Chicago all the time, 'cause she's in love with that actor with the scar. . . . But she gets sick, and she sits down in front of her dressing table. . . .

GEORGE: What actor? What scar?

MARTHA: *I* can't remember his name, for God's sake. What's the name of the *picture?* I want to know what the name of the *picture* is. She sits down in front of her dressing table . . . and she's got this peritonitis . . . and she tries to put her lipstick on, but she can't . . . and she gets it all over her face . . . but she decides to go to Chicago anyway, and. . . .

GEORGE: *Chicago!* It's called *Chicago*.

MARTHA: Hunh? What . . . what is?

GEORGE: The picture . . . it's called *Chicago*. . . .

MARTHA: Good grief! Don't you know *anything*? *Chicago* was a 'thirties musical, starring little Miss Alice *Faye*. Don't you know *anything*?

GEORGE: Well, that was probably before my *time*, but. . . .

MARTHA: Can it! Just cut that out! This picture . . . Bette Davis comes home from a hard day at the grocery store. . . .

GEORGE: She works in a grocery store?

MARTHA: She's a housewife; she buys things . . . and she comes home with the groceries, and she walks into the modest living room of the modest cottage modest Joseph Cotten has set her up in. . . .

GEORGE: Are they married?

MARTHA (*impatiently*): Yes. They're married. To each other. Cluck! And she comes in, and she looks around, and she puts her groceries down, and she says, "What a dump!"

GEORGE (*pause*): Oh.

MARTHA (*pause*): She's discontent.

GEORGE (*pause*): Oh.

MARTHA (*pause*): Well, what's the name of the picture?

GEORGE: I really don't know, Martha. . . .

MARTHA: Well, think!

GEORGE: I'm tired, dear . . . it's late . . . and besides. . . .

MARTHA: I don't know what you're so tired about . . . you haven't *done* anything all day; you didn't have any classes, or anything. . . .

GEORGE: Well, I'm tired. . . . If your father didn't set up these goddamn Saturday night orgies all the time. . . .

MARTHA: Well, that's too bad about you, George. . . .

GEORGE (*grumbling*): Well, that's how it is, anyway.

MARTHA: You didn't *do* anything; you never *do* anything; you never *mix*. You just sit around and *talk*.

GEORGE: What do you want me to do? Do you want me to act like you? Do you want me to go around all night *braying* at everybody, the way you do?

MARTHA (*braying*): I DON'T BRAY!

GEORGE (*softly*): All right . . . you don't bray.

MARTHA (*hurt*): I do not *bray*.

GEORGE: All right. I said you didn't bray.

MARTHA (*pouting*): Make me a drink.

GEORGE: What?

MARTHA (*still softly*): I said, make me a drink.

GEORGE (*moving to the portable bar*): Well, I don't suppose a nightcap'd kill either one of us. . . .

MARTHA: A nightcap! Are you kidding? We've got guests.

GEORGE (*disbelieving*): We've got what?

MARTHA: Guests. GUESTS.

GEORGE: GUESTS!

MARTHA: Yes . . . guests . . . people. . . . We've got guests coming over.

GEORGE: When?

MARTHA: NOW!

GEORGE: Good Lord, Martha . . . do you know what time it. . . . Who's coming over?

MARTHA: What's-their-name.

GEORGE: Who?

MARTHA: WHAT'S-THEIR-NAME!

GEORGE: Who what's-their-name?

MARTHA: I don't know what their name is, George. . . . You met them tonight . . . they're new . . . he's in the math department, or something. . . .

GEORGE: Who . . . who are these people?

MARTHA: You met them tonight, George.

GEORGE: I don't remember meeting anyone tonight. . . .

MARTHA: Well you did . . . Will you give me my drink, please. . . . He's in the math department . . . about thirty, blond, and. . . .

GEORGE: . . . and good-looking. . . .

MARTHA: Yes . . . and good-looking. . . .

GEORGE: It figures.

MARTHA: . . . and his wife's a mousey little type, without any hips, or anything.

GEORGE (*vaguely*): Oh.

MARTHA: You remember them now?

GEORGE: Yes, I guess so, Martha. . . . But why in God's name are they coming over here now?

MARTHA (*in a so-there voice*): Because Daddy said we should be nice to them, that's why.

GEORGE (*defeated*): Oh, Lord.

MARTHA: May I have my drink, please? Daddy said we should be nice to them. Thank you.

GEORGE: But why now? It's after two o'clock in the morning, and. . . .

MARTHA: Because Daddy said we should be nice to them!

GEORGE: Yes. But I'm sure your father didn't mean we were supposed to stay up all *night* with these people. I mean, we could have them over some Sunday or something. . . .

MARTHA: Well, never mind. . . . Besides, it *is* Sunday. Very early Sunday.

GEORGE: I mean . . . it's ridiculous. . . .

MARTHA: Well, it's *done!*

GEORGE (*resigned and exasperated*): All right. Well . . . where are they? If we've got guests, where are they?

MARTHA: They'll be here soon.

GEORGE: What did they do . . . go home and get some sleep first, or something?

MARTHA: They'll *be* here!

GEORGE: I wish you'd *tell* me about something sometime. . . . I wish you'd stop *springing* things on me all the time.

MARTHA: I don't *spring* things on you all the time.

GEORGE: Yes, you do . . . you really do . . . you're always *springing* things on me.

MARTHA (*friendly-patronizing*): Oh, George!

GEORGE: Always.

MARTHA: Poor Georgie-Porgie, put-upon pie (*As he sulks.*) Awwwwww . . . what are you doing? Are you sulking? Hunh? Let me see . . . are you sulking? Is that what you're doing?

GEORGE (*very quietly*): Never mind, Martha. . . .

MARTHA: AWWWWWWWWWW!

GEORGE: Just don't bother yourself. . . .

MARTHA: AWWWWWWWWWW! (*No reaction.*) Hey! (*No reaction.*) HEY!

(GEORGE *looks at her, put-upon.*)

Hey. (*She sings.*) Who's afraid of Virginia Woolf,
                          Virginia Woolf,
                          Virginia Woolf. . . .

Ha, ha, ha, HA! (*No reaction.*) What's the matter . . . didn't you think that was funny? Hunh? (*Defiantly.*) I thought it was a scream . . . a real scream. You didn't like it, hunh?

GEORGE: It was all right, Martha. . . .

MARTHA: You laughed your head off when you heard it at the party.

GEORGE: I smiled. I didn't laugh my head off . . . I smiled, you know? . . . it was all right.

MARTHA (*gazing into her drink*): You laughed your goddamn head off.

GEORGE: It was all right. . . .

MARTHA (*ugly*): It was a scream!

GEORGE (*patiently*): It was very funny; yes.

MARTHA (*after a moment's consideration*): You make me puke!

GEORGE: What?

MARTHA: Uh . . . you make me puke!

GEORGE (*thinks about it . . . then . . .*): That wasn't a very nice thing to say, Martha.

MARTHA: That wasn't *what*?

GEORGE: . . . a very nice thing to say.

MARTHA: I like your anger. I think that's what I like about you most . . . your anger. You're such a . . . such a simp! You don't even have the . . . the what? . . .

GEORGE: . . . guts? . . .

MARTHA: PHRASEMAKER! (*Pause . . . then they both laugh.*) Hey, put some more ice in my drink, will you? You never put any ice in my drink. Why is that, hunh?

GEORGE (*takes her drink*): I always put ice in your drink. You eat it, that's all. It's that habit you have . . . chewing your ice cubes . . . like a cocker spaniel. You'll crack your big teeth.

MARTHA: THEY'RE MY BIG TEETH!

GEORGE: Some of them . . . some of them.

MARTHA: I've got more teeth than you've got.

GEORGE: Two more.

MARTHA: Well, two more's a lot more.

GEORGE: I suppose it is. I suppose it's pretty remarkable . . . considering how old you are.

MARTHA: YOU CUT THAT OUT! (*Pause.*) You're not so young yourself.

GEORGE (*with boyish pleasure . . . a chant*): I'm six years younger than you are. . . . I always have been and I always will be.

MARTHA (*glumly*): Well . . . you're going bald.

GEORGE: So are you. (*Pause . . . they both laugh.*) Hello, honey.

MARTHA: Hello. C'mon over here and give your Mommy a big sloppy kiss.

GEORGE: . . . oh, now. . . .

MARTHA: I WANT A BIG SLOPPY KISS!

GEORGE (*preoccupied*): I don't *want* to kiss you, Martha. Where *are* these people? Where are these *people* you invited over?

MARTHA: They stayed on to talk to Daddy. . . . They'll be here. . . . *Why* don't you want to kiss me?

GEORGE (*too matter-of-fact*): Well, dear, if I kissed you I'd get all excited . . . I'd get beside myself, and I'd take you, by force, right here on the living room rug, and then our little guests would walk in, and . . . well, just think what your father would say about *that*.

MARTHA: You pig!

GEORGE (*haughtily*): Oink! Oink!

MARTHA: Ha, ha, ha, HA! Make me another drink . . . lover.

GEORGE (*taking her glass*): My God, you can swill it down, can't you?

MARTHA (*imitating a tiny child*): I'm firsty.

GEORGE: Jesus!

MARTHA (*swinging around*): Look, sweetheart, I can drink you under any goddamn table you want . . . so don't worry about me!

GEORGE: Martha, I gave you the prize years ago. . . . There isn't an abomination award going that you. . . .

MARTHA: I swear . . . if you existed I'd divorce you. . . .

GEORGE: Well, just stay on your feet, that's all. . . . These people are your guests, you know, and. . . .

MARTHA: I can't even see you . . . I haven't been able to see you for years. . . .

GEORGE: . . . if you pass out, or throw up, or something . . .

MARTHA: . . . I mean, you're a blank, a cipher. . . .

GEORGE: . . . and try to keep your clothes on, too. There aren't many more sickening sights than you with a couple of drinks in you and your skirt up over your head, you know. . . .

MARTHA: . . . a zero. . . .

GEORGE: . . . your *heads*, I should say. . . .

(*The front doorbell chimes.*)

MARTHA: Party! Party!

GEORGE (*murderously*): I'm really looking forward to this, Martha. . . .

MARTHA (*same*): Go answer the door.

GEORGE (*not moving*): You answer it.

MARTHA: Get to that door, you. (*He does not move.*) I'll fix you, you. . . .

GEORGE (*fake-spits*): . . . to you. . . .

(*Door chime again.*)

MARTHA (*shouting . . . to the door*): C'MON IN! (*To* GEORGE, *between her teeth.*) I said, get over there!

GEORGE (*moves a little toward the door, smiling slightly*): All right, love . . . whatever love wants. (*Stops.*) Just don't start on the bit, that's all.

MARTHA: The bit? The bit? What kind of language is that? What are you talking about?

GEORGE: The bit. Just don't start in on the bit.

MARTHA: You imitating one of your students, for God's sake? What are you trying to do? WHAT BIT?

GEORGE: Just don't start in on the bit about the kid, that's all.

MARTHA: What do you take me for?

GEORGE: Much too much.

MARTHA (*really angered*): Yeah? Well, I'll start in on the kid if I want to.

GEORGE: Just leave the kid out of this.

MARTHA (*threatening*): He's mine as much as he is yours. I'll talk about him if I want to.

GEORGE: I'd advise against it, Martha.

MARTHA: Well, good for you. (*Knock.*) C'mon in. Get over there and open the door!

GEORGE: You've been advised.

MARTHA: Yeah . . . sure. Get over there!

GEORGE (*moving toward the door*): All right, love . . . whatever love wants. Isn't it nice the way some people have manners, though, even in this day and age? Isn't it nice that some people won't just come breaking into other people's houses even if they *do* hear some sub-human monster yowling at 'em from inside . . . ?

MARTHA: SCREW YOU!

(*Simultaneously with* MARTHA's *last remark,* GEORGE *flings open the front door.* HONEY *and* NICK *are framed in the entrance. There is a brief silence, then. . . .*)

GEORGE (*ostensibly a pleased recognition of* HONEY *and* NICK, *but really satisfaction at having* MARTHA's *explosion overheard*): Ahhhhhhhhh!

MARTHA (*a little too loud . . . to cover*): HI! Hi, there . . . c'mon in!

HONEY AND NICK (*ad lib*): Hello, here we are . . . hi . . . *etc.*

GEORGE (*very matter-of-factly*): You must be our little guests.

MARTHA: Ha, ha, ha, HA! Just ignore old sour-puss over there. C'mon in, kids . . . give your coats and stuff to sour-puss.

NICK (*without expression*): Well, now, perhaps we shouldn't have come. . . .

HONEY: Yes . . . it *is* late, and. . . .

MARTHA: Late! Are you kidding? Throw your stuff down anywhere and c'mon in.

GEORGE (*vaguely . . . walking away*): Anywhere . . . furniture, floor . . . doesn't make any difference around this place.

NICK (*to* HONEY): I told you we shouldn't have come.

MARTHA (*stentorian*): I said c'mon in! Now c'mon!

HONEY (*giggling a little as she and* NICK *advance*): Oh, dear.

GEORGE (*imitating* HONEY's *giggle*): Hee, hee, hee, hee.

MARTHA (*swinging on* GEORGE): Look, muckmouth . . . you cut that out!

GEORGE (*innocence and hurt*): Martha! (*To* HONEY *and* NICK.) Martha's a devil with
  language; she really is.

MARTHA: Hey, *kids* . . . sit down.

HONEY (*as she sits*): Oh, isn't this lovely!

NICK (*perfunctorily*): Yes indeed ·. . . very handsome.

MARTHA: Well, thanks.

NICK (*indicating the abstract painting*): Who . . . who did the . . . ?

MARTHA: That? Oh, that's by. . . .

GEORGE: . . . some Greek with a mustache Martha attacked one night in. . . .

HONEY (*to save the situation*): Oh, ho, ho, ho, HO.

NICK: It's got a . . . a. . . .

GEORGE: A quiet intensity?

NICK: Well, no . . . a. . . .

GEORGE: Oh. (*Pause.*) Well, then, a certain noisy relaxed quality, maybe?

NICK (*knows what* GEORGE *is doing, but stays grimly, coolly polite*): No. What I
  meant was. . . .

GEORGE: How about . . . uh . . . a quietly noisy relaxed intensity.

HONEY: Dear! You're being joshed.

NICK (*cold*): I'm aware of that.

  (*A brief, awkward silence.*)

GEORGE (*truly*): I *am* sorry.

  (NICK *nods condescending forgiveness.*)

GEORGE: What it is, actually, is it's a pictorial representation of the order of
  Martha's mind.

MARTHA: Ha, ha, ha, HA! Make the kids a drink, George. What do you want, kids?
  What do you want to drink, hunh?

NICK: Honey? What would you like?

HONEY: I don't know, dear . . . A little brandy, maybe. "Never mix — never
  worry." (*She giggles.*)

GEORGE: Brandy? Just brandy? Simple; simple. (*Moves to the portable bar.*) What
  about you . . . uh. . . .

NICK: Bourbon on the rocks, if you don't mind.

GEORGE (*as he makes drinks*): Mind? No, I don't mind. I don't think I mind. Martha? Rubbing alcohol for you?

MARTHA: Sure. "Never mix — never worry."

GEORGE: Martha's tastes in liquor have come down . . . simplified over the years
  . . . crystallized. Back when I was courting Martha — well, I don't know if that's
  exactly the right word for it — but back when I was courting Martha. . . .

MARTHA (*cheerfully*): Screw, sweetie!

GEORGE (*returning with* HONEY's *and* NICK's *drinks*): At any rate, back when I was
  courting Martha, she'd order the damnedest things! You wouldn't believe it! We'd
  go into a bar . . . you know, a *bar* . . . a whiskey, beer, and bourbon *bar* . . . and
  what she'd do would be, she'd screw up her face, think real hard, and come up
  with . . . brandy Alexanders, crème de cacao frappés, gimlets, flaming punch
  bowls . . . seven-layer liqueur things.

MARTHA: They were good . . . I liked them.

GEORGE: Real lady-like little drinkies.

MARTHA: Hey, where's my rubbing alcohol?

GEORGE (*returning to the portable bar*): But the years have brought to Martha a sense of essentials . . . the knowledge that cream is for coffee, lime juice for pies . . . and alcohol (*brings* MARTHA *her drink*) pure and simple . . . here you are, angel . . . for the pure and simple. (*Raises his glass.*) For the mind's blind eye, the heart's ease, and the liver's craw. Down the hatch, all.

MARTHA (*to them all*): Cheers, dears. (*They all drink.*) You have a poetic nature, George . . . a Dylan Thomas-y quality that gets me right where I live.

GEORGE: Vulgar girl! With guests here!

MARTHA: Ha, ha, ha, HA! (*To* HONEY *and* NICK.) Hey; hey!

(*Sings, conducts with her drink in her hand.* HONEY *joins in toward the end.*)

> Who's afraid of Virginia Woolf,
> Virginia Woolf,
> Virginia Woolf,
> Who's afraid of Virginia Woolf. . . .

(MARTHA *and* HONEY *laugh;* NICK *smiles.*)

HONEY: Oh, wasn't that funny? That was so funny. . . .

NICK (*snapping to*): Yes . . . yes, it was.

MARTHA: I thought I'd bust a gut; I really did. . . . I really thought I'd bust a gut laughing. George didn't like it. . . . George didn't think it was funny at all.

GEORGE: Lord, Martha, do we have to go through this again?

MARTHA: I'm trying to shame you into a sense of humor, angel, that's all.

GEORGE (*over-patiently, to* HONEY *and* NICK): Martha didn't think I laughed loud enough. Martha thinks that unless . . . as she demurely puts it . . . that unless you "bust a gut" you aren't amused. You know? Unless you carry on like a hyena you aren't having any fun.

HONEY: Well, I certainly had fun . . . it was a *wonderful* party.

NICK (*attempting enthusiasm*): Yes . . . it certainly was.

HONEY (*to* MARTHA): And your father! Oh! He is so marvelous!

NICK (*as above*): Yes . . . yes, he is.

HONEY: Oh, I tell you.

MARTHA (*genuinely proud*): He's quite a guy, isn't he? Quite a guy.

GEORGE (*at* NICK): And you'd better believe it!

HONEY (*admonishing* GEORGE): Ohhhhhhhhh! He's a wonderful man.

GEORGE: I'm not trying to tear him down. He's a God, we all know that.

MARTHA: You lay off my father!

GEORGE: Yes, love. (*To* NICK.) All I mean is . . . when you've had as many of these faculty parties as I have. . . .

NICK (*killing the attempted rapport*): I rather appreciated it. I mean, aside from enjoying it, I appreciated it. You know, when you're new at a place. . . .

(GEORGE *eyes him suspiciously.*)

Meeting everyone, getting introduced around . . . getting to know some of the men. . . . When I was teaching in Kansas. . . .

HONEY: You won't believe it, but we had to make our way all by *ourselves* . . . isn't that right, dear?

NICK: Yes, it is. . . . We. . . .

HONEY: . . . We had to make our own way. . . . I had to go up to wives . . . in the library, or at the supermarket . . . and say, "Hello, I'm new here . . . you must be Mrs. So-and-so, Doctor So-and-so's wife." It really wasn't very nice at all.

MARTHA: Well, *Daddy* knows how to run things.

NICK (*not enough enthusiasm*): He's a remarkable man.

MARTHA: You bet your sweet life.

GEORGE (*to* NICK . . . *a confidence, but not whispered*): Let me tell you a secret, baby. There are easier things in the world, if you happen to be teaching at a university, there are easier things than being married to the daughter of the president of that university. There are easier things in this world.

MARTHA (*loud . . . to no one in particular*): It *should* be an extraordinary opportunity . . . for *some* men it would be the chance of a lifetime!

GEORGE (*to* NICK . . . *a solemn wink*): There are, believe me, easier things in this world.

NICK: Well, I can understand how it might make for some . . . awkwardness, perhaps . . . conceivably, but. . . .

MARTHA: *Some* men would give their right arm for the chance!

GEORGE (*quietly*): Alas, Martha, in reality it works out that the sacrifice is usually of a somewhat more private portion of the anatomy.

MARTHA (*a snarl of dismissal and contempt*): NYYYYAAAAHHHHH!

HONEY (*rising quickly*): I wonder if you could show me where the . . . (*Her voice trails off.*)

GEORGE (*to* MARTHA, *indicating* HONEY): Martha . . .

NICK (*to* HONEY): Are you all right?

HONEY: Of course, dear. I want to . . . put some powder on my nose.

GEORGE (*as* MARTHA *is not getting up*): Martha, won't you show her where we keep the . . . euphemism?

MARTHA: Hm? What? Oh! Sure! (*Rises.*) I'm sorry, c'mon. I want to show you the house.

HONEY: I think I'd like to. . . .

MARTHA: . . . wash up? Sure . . . c'mon with me. (*Takes* HONEY *by the arm. To the men.*) You two do some men talk for a while.

HONEY (*to* NICK): We'll be back, dear.

MARTHA (*to* GEORGE): Honestly, George, you burn me up!

GEORGE (*happily*): All right.

MARTHA: You really do, George.

GEORGE: O.K. Martha . . . O.K. Just . . . trot along.

MARTHA: You really do.

GEORGE: Just don't shoot your mouth off . . . about . . . you-know-what.

MARTHA (*surprisingly vehement*): I'll talk about any goddamn thing I want to, George!

GEORGE: O.K. O.K. Vanish.

MARTHA: Any goddamn thing I want to! (*Practically dragging* HONEY *out with her.*) C'mon. . . .

GEORGE: Vanish. (*The women have gone.*) So? What'll it be?

NICK: Oh, I don't know . . . I'll stick to bourbon, I guess.

GEORGE (*takes* NICK's *glass, goes to portable bar*): That what you were drinking over at Parnassus?

NICK: Over at . . . ?

GEORGE: Parnassus.

NICK: I don't understand. . . .

GEORGE: Skip it. (*Hands him his drink*.) One bourbon.

NICK: Thanks.

GEORGE: It's just a private joke between li'l ol' Martha and me. (*They sit*.) So? (*Pause*.) So . . . you're in the math department, eh?

NICK: No . . . uh, no.

GEORGE: Martha said you were. I think that's what she said. (*Not too friendly*.) What made you decide to be a teacher?

NICK: Oh . . . well, the same things that . . . uh . . . motivated you, I imagine.

GEORGE: What were they?

NICK (*formal*): Pardon?

GEORGE: I said, what were they? What were the things that motivated me?

NICK (*laughing uneasily*): Well . . . I'm sure I don't know.

GEORGE: You just finished saying that the things that motivated you were the same things that motivated me.

NICK (*with a little pique*): I said I *imagined* they were.

GEORGE: Oh. (*Off-hand*.) Did you? (*Pause*.) Well . . . (*Pause*.) You like it here?

NICK (*looking about the room*): Yes . . . it's . . . it's fine.

GEORGE: I mean the University.

NICK: Oh. . . . I thought you meant. . . .

GEORGE: Yes . . . I can see you did. (*Pause*.) I meant the University.

NICK: Well, I . . . I like it . . . fine. (*As* GEORGE *just stares at him*.) Just fine. (*Same*.) You . . . you've been here quite a long time, haven't you?

GEORGE (*absently, as if he had not heard*): What? Oh . . . yes. Ever since I married . . . uh, What's-her-name . . . uh, Martha. Even before that. (*Pause*.) Forever. (*To himself*.) Dashed hopes, and good intentions. Good, better, best, bested. (*Back to* NICK.) How do you like that for a declension, young man? Eh?

NICK: Sir, I'm sorry if we. . . .

GEORGE (*with an edge in his voice*): You didn't answer my question.

NICK: Sir?

GEORGE: Don't you condescend to me! (*Toying with him*.) I asked how you liked that for a declension: Good; better; best; bested. Hm? Well?

NICK (*with some distaste*): I really don't know what to say.

GEORGE (*feigned incredulousness*): You really don't know what to *say*?

NICK (*snapping it out*): All right . . . what do you want me to say? Do you want me to say it's funny, so you can contradict me and say it's sad? or do you want me to say it's sad so you can turn around and say no, it's funny. You can play that damn little game any way you want to, you know!

GEORGE (*feigned awe*): Very good! Very good!

NICK (*even angrier than before*): And when my wife comes back, I think we'll just. . . .

GEORGE (*sincere*): Now, now . . . calm down, my boy. Just . . . calm . . . down. (*Pause*.) All right? (*Pause*.) You want another drink? Here, give me your glass.

NICK: I still have one. I *do* think that when my wife comes downstairs. . . .

GEORGE: Here . . . I'll freshen it. Give me your glass. (*Takes it*.)

NICK: What I mean is . . . you two . . . you and your wife . . . seem to be having *some* sort of a. . . .

GEORGE: Martha and I are having . . . nothing. Martha and I are merely . . . exercising . . . that's all . . . we're merely walking what's left of our wits. Don't pay any attention to it.

NICK (*undecided*): Still. . . .

GEORGE (*an abrupt change of pace*): Well, now . . . let's sit down and talk, hunh?

NICK (*cool again*): It's just that I don't like to . . . become involved . . . (*an afterthought*) uh . . . in other people's affairs.

GEORGE (*comforting a child*): Well, you'll get over that . . . small college and all. Musical beds is the faculty sport around here.

NICK: Sir?

GEORGE: I said, musical beds is the faculty. . . . Never mind. I wish you wouldn't go "Sir" like that . . . not with the question mark at the end of it. You know? Sir? I know it's meant to be a sign of respect for your (*winces*) elders . . . but . . . uh . . . the way you do it. . . . Uh . . . Sir? . . . Madam?

NICK (*with a small, noncommittal smile*): No disrespect intended.

GEORGE: How old *are* you?

NICK: Twenty-eight.

GEORGE: I'm forty something. (*Waits for reaction . . . gets none.*) Aren't you surprised? I mean . . . don't I look older? Doesn't this . . . *gray* quality suggest the fifties? Don't I sort of fade into backgrounds . . . get lost in the cigarette smoke? Hunh?

NICK (*looking around for an ash tray*): I think you look . . . fine.

GEORGE: I've always been lean . . . I haven't put on five pounds since I was your age. I don't have a paunch, either. . . . What I've got . . . I've got this little distension just below the belt . . . but it's hard . . . It's not soft flesh. I use the handball courts. How much do *you* weigh?

NICK: I. . . .

GEORGE: Hundred and fifty-five, sixty . . . something like that? Do you play handball?

NICK: Well, yes . . . no . . . I mean, not very well.

GEORGE: Well, then . . . we shall play some time. Martha is a hundred and eight . . . years *old*. She weighs somewhat more than that. How old is *your* wife?

NICK (*a little bewildered*): She's twenty-six.

GEORGE: Martha is a remarkable woman. I would imagine she weighs around a hundred and ten.

NICK: Your . . . wife . . . weighs . . . ?

GEORGE: No, no, my boy. Yours! *Your* wife. My wife is Martha.

NICK: Yes . . . I know.

GEORGE: If you were married to Martha you would know what it means. (*Pause.*) But then, if I were married to your wife I would know what that means, too . . . wouldn't I?

NICK (*after a pause*): Yes.

GEORGE: Martha says you're in the Math Department, or something.

NICK (*as if for the hundredth time*): No . . . I'm not.

GEORGE: Martha is seldom mistaken . . . maybe you *should* be in the Math Department, or something.

NICK: I'm a biologist. I'm in the Biology Department.

GEORGE (*after a pause*): Oh. (*Then, as if remembering something.*) OH!

NICK: Sir?

GEORGE: You're the one! You're the one's going to make all that trouble . . . making everyone the same, rearranging the chromozones, or whatever it is. Isn't that right?

NICK (*with that small smile*): Not exactly: chromo*somes*.

GEORGE: I'm very mistrustful. Do you believe . . . (*shifting in his chair*) . . . do you believe that people learn nothing from history? Not that there is nothing to learn, mind you, but that people learn nothing? I am in the History Department.

NICK: Well. . . .

GEORGE: I am a Doctor. A.B. . . . M.A. . . . PH.D. . . . ABMAPHID! Abmaphid has been variously described as a wasting disease of the frontal lobes, and as a wonder drug. It is actually both. I'm really very mistrustful. Biology, hunh?

(NICK *does not answer . . . nods . . . looks.*)

I read somewhere that science fiction is really not fiction at all . . . that you people are rearranging my genes, so that everyone will be like everyone else. Now, I won't have that! It would be a . . . shame. I mean . . . look at me! Is it really such a good idea . . . if everyone was forty something and looked fifty-five? You didn't answer my question about history.

NICK: This genetic business you're talking about . . .

GEORGE: Oh, that. (*Dismisses it with a wave of his hand.*) That's very upsetting . . . very . . . disappointing. But history is a great deal more . . . disappointing. I am in the History Department.

NICK: Yes . . . you told me.

GEORGE: I know I told you. . . . I shall probably tell you several more times. Martha tells me often, that I am *in* the History Department . . . as opposed to *being* the History Department . . . in the sense of *running* the History Department. I do not run the History Department.

NICK: Well, I don't run the Biology Department.

GEORGE: You're twenty-one!

NICK: Twenty-eight.

GEORGE: Twenty-eight! Perhaps when you're forty something and look fifty-five, you will run the History Department. . . .

NICK: . . . Biology. . . .

GEORGE: . . . the Biology Department. I *did* run the History Department, for four years, during the war, but that was because everybody was away. Then . . . everybody came back . . . because nobody got killed. That's New England for you. Isn't that amazing? Not one single man in this whole place got his head shot off. That's pretty irrational. (*Broods.*) Your wife *doesn't* have any hips . . . has she . . . does she?

NICK: What?

GEORGE: I don't mean to suggest that I'm hip-happy. . . . I'm not one of those thirty-six, twenty-two, seventy-eight men. Nosiree . . . not me. Everything in proportion. I was implying that your wife is . . . slim-hipped.

NICK: Yes . . . she is.

GEORGE (*looking at the ceiling*): What are they *doing* up there? I assume that's where they are.

NICK (*false heartiness*): You know women.

GEORGE (*gives* NICK *a long stare, of feigned incredulity . . . then his attention moves*): Not one son-of-a-bitch got killed. Of course, nobody bombed Washington. No . . . that's not fair. You have any kids?

NICK: Uh . . . no . . . not yet. (*Pause.*) You?

GEORGE (*a kind of challenge*): That's for me to know and you to find out.

NICK: Indeed?

GEORGE: No kids, hunh?

NICK: Not yet.

GEORGE: People do . . . uh . . . have kids. That's what I meant about history. You people are going to make them in test tubes, aren't you? You biologists. Babies. Then the rest of us . . . them as wants to . . . can screw to their heart's content. What will happen to the tax deduction? Has anyone figured that out yet?

(NICK, *who can think of nothing better to do, laughs mildly*.)

But you *are* going to have kids . . . anyway. In spite of history.

NICK (*hedging*): Yes . . . certainly. We . . . want to wait . . . a little . . . until we're settled.

GEORGE: And this . . . (*with a handsweep taking in not only the room, the house, but the whole countryside*) . . . this is your heart's content — Illyria . . . Penguin Island . . . Gomorrah. . . . You think you're going to be happy here in New Carthage, eh?

NICK (*a little defensively*): I hope we'll stay here.

GEORGE: And every definition has its boundaries, eh? Well, it isn't a bad college, I guess. I mean . . . it'll do. It isn't M.I.T. . . . it isn't U.C.L.A. . . . it isn't the Sorbonne . . . or Moscow U. either, for that matter.

NICK: I don't mean . . . forever.

GEORGE: Well, don't you let that get bandied about. The old man wouldn't like it. Martha's father expects loyalty and devotion out of his . . . staff. I was going to use another word. Martha's father expects his . . . staff . . . to cling to the walls of this place, like the ivy . . . to come here and grow old . . . to fall in the line of service. One man, a professor of Latin and Elocution, actually fell in the cafeteria line, one lunch. He was buried, as many of us have been, and as many more of us will be, under the shrubbery around the chapel. It is said . . . and I have no reason to doubt it . . . that we make excellent fertilizer. But the old man is not going to be buried under the shrubbery . . . the old man is not going to die. Martha's father has the staying power of one of those Micronesian tortoises. There are rumors . . . which you must not breathe in front of Martha, for she foams at the mouth . . . that the old man, her father, is over two hundred years old. There is probably an irony involved in this, but I am not drunk enough to figure out what it is. How many kids you going to have?

NICK: I . . . I don't know. . . . My wife is. . . .

GEORGE: Slim-hipped. (*Rises.*) Have a drink.

NICK: Yes.

GEORGE: MARTHA! (*No answer.*) DAMN IT! (*To* NICK.) You asked me if I knew women. . . . Well, one of the things I do *not* know about them is what they talk about while the men are talking. (*Vaguely.*) I must find out some time.

MARTHA'S VOICE: WHADD'YA WANT?

GEORGE (*to* NICK): Isn't that a wonderful sound? What I mean is . . . what do you think they really *talk* about . . . or don't you care?

NICK: Themselves, I would imagine.

MARTHA'S VOICE: GEORGE?

GEORGE (*to* NICK): Do you find women . . . puzzling?

NICK: Well . . . yes and no.

GEORGE (*with a knowing nod*): Unh-hunh. (*Moves toward the hall, almost bumps into* HONEY, *re-entering*.) Oh! Well, here's one of you, at least.

(HONEY *moves toward* NICK. GEORGE *goes to the hall*.)

HONEY (*to* GEORGE): She'll be right down. (*To* NICK.) You must see this house, dear . . . this is such a wonderful old house.

NICK: Yes, I. . . .

GEORGE: MARTHA!

MARTHA'S VOICE: FOR CHRIST'S SAKE, HANG ON A MINUTE, WILL YOU?

HONEY (*to* GEORGE): She'll be right down . . . she's changing.

GEORGE (*incredulous*): She's *what?* She's changing?

HONEY: Yes.

GEORGE: Her clothes?

HONEY: Her dress.

GEORGE (*suspicious*): Why?

HONEY (*with a nervous little laugh*): Why, I imagine she wants to be . . . comfortable.

GEORGE (*with a threatening look toward the hall*): Oh she does, does she?

HONEY: Well, heavens, I should think. . . .

GEORGE: YOU DON'T KNOW!

NICK (*as* HONEY *starts*): You feel all right?

HONEY (*reassuring, but with the echo of a whine. A long-practiced tone*): Oh, yes, dear . . . perfectly fine.

GEORGE (*fuming . . . to himself*): So she wants to be comfortable, does she? Well, we'll see about that.

HONEY (*to* GEORGE, *brightly*): I didn't know until just a minute ago that you had a son.

GEORGE (*wheeling, as if struck from behind*): WHAT?

HONEY: A son! I hadn't known.

NICK: You to know and me to find out. Well, he must be quite a big. . . .

HONEY: Twenty-one . . . twenty-one tomorrow . . . tomorrow's his birthday.

NICK (*a victorious smile*): Well!

GEORGE (*to* HONEY): She told you about him?

HONEY (*flustered*): Well, *yes*. Well, I mean. . . .

GEORGE (*nailing it down*): She told you about him.

HONEY (*a nervous giggle*): Yes.

GEORGE (*strangely*): You say she's changing?

HONEY: Yes. . . .

GEORGE: And she mentioned . . . ?

HONEY (*cheerful, but a little puzzled*): . . . your son's birthday . . . yes.

GEORGE (*more or less to himself*): O.K., Martha . . . O.K.

NICK: You look pale, Honey. Do you want a . . . ?

HONEY: Yes, dear . . . a little more brandy, maybe. Just a drop.

GEORGE: O.K., Martha.

NICK: May I use the . . . uh . . . bar?

GEORGE: Hm? Oh, yes . . . yes . . . by all means. Drink away . . . you'll need it as the years go on. (*For* MARTHA, *as if she were in the room*.) You goddamn destructive. . . .

HONEY (*to cover*): What time is it, dear?

NICK: Two-thirty.

HONEY: Oh, it's so late . . . we *should* be getting home.

GEORGE (*nastily, but he is so preoccupied he hardly notices his own tone*): For what? You keeping the baby sitter up, or something?

NICK (*almost a warning*): I told you we didn't have children.

GEORGE: Hm? (*Realizing.*) Oh, I'm sorry. I wasn't even listening . . . or thinking . . . (*with a flick of his hand*) . . . whichever one applies.

NICK (*softly, to* HONEY): We'll go in a little while.

GEORGE (*driving*): Oh no, now . . . you mustn't. Martha is changing . . . and Martha is not changing for *me*. Martha hasn't changed for *me* in years. If Martha is changing, it means we'll be here for . . . days. You are being accorded an honor, and you must not forget that Martha is the daughter of our beloved boss. She is his . . . right ball, you might say.

NICK: You might not understand this . . . but I wish you wouldn't talk that way in front of my wife.

HONEY: Oh, now. . . .

GEORGE (*incredulous*): Really? Well, you're quite right. . . . We'll leave that sort of talk to Martha.

MARTHA (*entering*): What sort of talk?

(MARTHA *has changed her clothes, and she looks, now, more comfortable and . . . and this is most important . . . most voluptuous*.)

GEORGE: There you are, my pet.

NICK (*impressed; rising*): Well, now. . . .

GEORGE: Why, Martha . . . your Sunday chapel dress!

HONEY (*slightly disapproving*): Oh, that's most attractive.

MARTHA (*showing off*): You like it? Good! (*To* GEORGE.) What the hell do you mean screaming up the stairs at me like that?

GEORGE: We got lonely, darling . . . we got lonely for the soft purr of your little voice.

MARTHA (*deciding not to rise to it*): Oh. Well, then, you just trot over to the barie-poo. . . .

GEORGE (*taking the tone from her*): . . . and make your little mommy a gweat big dwink.

MARTHA (*giggles*): That's right. (*To* NICK.) Well, did you two have a nice little talk? You men solve the problems of the world, as usual?

NICK: Well, no, we . . .

GEORGE (*quickly*): What we did, actually, if you really want to know, what we did actually is try to figure out what you two were talking about.

(HONEY *giggles*, MARTHA *laughs*.)

MARTHA (*to* HONEY): Aren't they something? Aren't these . . . (*cheerfully disdainful*) . . . *men* the absolute end? (*To* GEORGE.) Why didn't you sneak upstairs and listen in?

GEORGE: Oh, I wouldn't have *listened*, Martha. . . . I would have *peeked*.

(HONEY *giggles*, MARTHA *laughs*.)

NICK (*to* GEORGE, *with false heartiness*): It's a conspiracy.

GEORGE: And now we'll never know. Shucks!

MARTHA (*to* NICK, *as* HONEY *beams*): Hey, you must be quite a boy, getting your Masters when you were . . . what? . . . twelve? You hear that, George?

NICK: Twelve-and-a-half, actually. No, nineteen really. (*To* HONEY.) Honey, you needn't have mentioned that. It. . . .

HONEY: Ohhhh . . . I'm *proud* of you. . . .

GEORGE (*seriously, if sadly*): That's very . . . impressive.

MARTHA (*aggressively*): You're damned right!

GEORGE (*between his teeth*): I said I was impressed, Martha. I'm beside myself with jealousy. What do you want me to do, throw up? (*To* NICK.) That really is very impressive. (*To* HONEY.) You should be right proud.

HONEY (*coy*): Oh, he's a pretty nice fella.

GEORGE (*to* NICK): I wouldn't be surprised if you *did* take over the History Department one of these days.

NICK: The Biology Department.

GEORGE: The *Biology* Department . . . of course. I seem preoccupied with history. Oh! What a remark. (*He strikes a pose, his hand over his heart, his head raised, his voice stentorian*.) "I am preoccupied with history."

MARTHA (*as* HONEY *and* NICK *chuckle*): Ha, ha, ha, HA!

GEORGE (*with some disgust*): I think I'll make *myself* a drink.

MARTHA: George is not preoccupied with *history*. . . . George is preoccupied with the *History Department*. George is preoccupied with the History Department because. . . .

GEORGE: . . . because he is *not* the History Department, but is only *in* the History Department. We know, Martha . . . we went all through it while you were up-stairs . . . getting up. There's no need to go through it again.

MARTHA: That's right, baby . . . keep it clean. (*To the others*.) George is bogged down in the History Department. He's an old bog in the History Department, that's what George is. A bog. . . . A fen. . . . A G.D. swamp. Ha, ha, ha, HA! A SWAMP! Hey, swamp! Hey SWAMPY!

GEORGE (*with a great effort controls himself . . . then, as if she had said nothing more than "George, dear."* . . .): Yes, Martha? Can I get you something?

MARTHA (*amused at his game*): Well . . . uh . . . sure, you can light my cigarette, if you're of a mind to.

GEORGE (*considers, then moves off*): No . . . there are limits. I mean, man can put up with only so much without he descends a rung or two on the old evolutionary ladder . . . (*now a quick aside to* NICK) . . . which is up your line . . . (*then back to* MARTHA) . . . sinks, Martha, and it's a funny ladder . . . you can't reverse yourself . . . start back up once you're descending.

(MARTHA *blows him an arrogant kiss*.)

Now . . . I'll hold your hand when it's dark and you're afraid of the bogey man, and I'll tote your gin bottles out after midnight, so no one'll see . . . but I will not light your cigarette. And that, as they say, is that.

(*Brief silence*.)

MARTHA (*under her breath*): Jesus! (*Then, immediately, to* NICK.) Hey, you played football, hunh?

HONEY (*as* NICK *seems sunk in thought*): Dear. . . .

NICK: Oh! Oh, yes . . . I was a . . . quarterback . . . but I was much more . . . adept . . . at boxing, really.

MARTHA (*with great enthusiasm*): BOXING! You hear that, George?

GEORGE (*resignedly*): Yes, Martha.

MARTHA (*to* NICK, *with peculiar intensity and enthusiasm*): You musta been pretty good at it . . . I mean, you don't look like you got hit in the face at all.

HONEY (*proudly*): He was intercollegiate state middleweight champion.

NICK (*embarrassed*): Honey. . . .

HONEY: Well, you were.

MARTHA: You look like you still got a pretty good body *now*, too . . . is that right? Have you?

GEORGE (*intensely*): Martha . . . decency forbids. . . .

MARTHA (*to* GEORGE . . . *still staring at* NICK, *though*): SHUT UP! (*Now, back to* NICK.) Well, have you? Have you kept your body?

NICK (*unselfconscious . . . almost encouraging her*): It's still pretty good. I work out.

MARTHA (*with a half-smile*): Do you!

NICK: Yeah.

HONEY: Oh, yes . . . he has a very . . . firm body.

MARTHA (*still with that smile . . . a private communication with* NICK): Have you! Oh, I think that's very nice.

NICK (*narcissistic, but not directly for* MARTHA): Well, you never know . . . (*shrugs*) . . . you know . . . once you have it. . . .

MARTHA: . . . you never know when it's going to come in handy.

NICK: I was going to say . . . why give it up until you have to.

MARTHA: I couldn't agree with you more.

(*They both smile, and there is a rapport of some unformed sort established.*)

I couldn't agree with you more.

GEORGE: Martha, your obscenity is more than. . . .

MARTHA: George, here, doesn't cotton much to body talk . . . do you sweetheart? (*No reply.*) George isn't too happy when we get to muscle. You know . . . flat bellies, pectorals. . . .

GEORGE (*to* HONEY): Would you like to take a walk around the garden?

HONEY (*chiding*): Oh, now. . . .

GEORGE (*incredulous*): You're amused? (*Shrugs.*) All right.

MARTHA: Paunchy over there isn't too happy when the conversation moves to muscle. How much do you weigh?

NICK: A hundred and fifty-five, a hundred and. . . .

MARTHA: Still at the old middleweight limit, eh? That's pretty good. (*Swings around.*) Hey George, tell 'em about the boxing match *we* had.

GEORGE (*slamming his drink down, moving toward the hall*): Christ!

MARTHA: George! Tell 'em about it!

GEORGE (*with a sick look on his face*): You tell them, Martha. You're good at it. (*Exits.*)

HONEY: Is he . . . all right?

MARTHA (*laughs*): Him? Oh sure. George and I had this boxing match . . . Oh, Lord, twenty years ago . . . a couple of years after we were married.

NICK: A boxing match? The two of you?

HONEY: Really?

MARTHA: Yup . . . the two of us . . . really.

HONEY (*with a little shivery giggle of anticipation*): I can't imagine it.

MARTHA: Well, like I say, it was twenty years ago, and it wasn't in a ring, or anything like that, you know what I mean. It was wartime, and Daddy was on this physical fitness kick . . . Daddy's always admired physical fitness . . . says a man is only part brain . . . he has a body, too, and it's his responsibility to keep both of them up . . . you know?

NICK: Unh-hunh.

MARTHA: Says the brain can't work unless the body's working, too.

NICK: Well, that's not exactly so. . . .

MARTHA: Well, maybe that *isn't* what he says . . . something like it. *But* . . . it was wartime, and Daddy got the idea all the men should learn how to box . . . self-defense. I suppose the idea was if the Germans landed on the coast, or something, the whole faculty'd go out and punch 'em to death. . . . I don't know.

NICK: It was probably more the principle of the thing.

MARTHA: No kidding. Anyway, so Daddy had a couple of us over one Sunday and we went out in the back, and Daddy put on the gloves himself. Daddy's a strong man. . . . Well, *you* know.

NICK: Yes . . . Yes.

MARTHA: And he asked George to box with him. Aaaaannnnd . . . George didn't *want* to . . . probably something about not wanting to bloody-up his meal ticket. . . .

NICK: Unh-hunh.

MARTHA: . . . Anyway, George said he didn't want to, and Daddy was saying, "Come on, young man . . . what sort of son-in-law *are* you?" . . . and stuff like that.

NICK: Yeah.

MARTHA: So, while this was going on . . . I don't know why I *did* it . . . I got into a pair of gloves myself . . . you know, I didn't lace 'em up, or anything . . . and I snuck up behind George, just kidding, and I yelled "Hey George!" and at the same time I let go sort of a roundhouse right . . . just kidding, you know?

NICK: Unh-hunh.

MARTHA: . . . and George wheeled around real quick, and he caught it right in the jaw . . . POW! (NICK *laughs.*) I hadn't meant it . . . honestly. Anyway . . . POW! Right in the jaw . . . and he was off balance . . . he must have been . . . and he stumbled back a few steps, and then, CRASH, he landed . . . flat . . . in a huckleberry bush!

(NICK *laughs.* HONEY *goes tsk, tsk, tsk, tsk, and shakes her head.*)

It was awful, really. It was funny, but it was awful. (*She thinks, gives a muffled laugh in rueful contemplation of the incident.*) I think it's colored our whole life. Really I do! It's an excuse, anyway.

(GEORGE *enters now, his hands behind his back. No one sees him.*)

It's what he uses for being bogged down, anyway . . . why he hasn't *gone* anywhere.

(GEORGE *advances.* HONEY *sees him.*)

MARTHA: And it was an *accident* . . . a real, goddamn accident!

(GEORGE *takes from behind his back a short-barreled shotgun, and calmly aims it at the back of* MARTHA's *head.* HONEY *screams . . . rises.* NICK *rises, and, simultaneously,* MARTHA *turns her head to face* GEORGE. GEORGE *pulls the trigger.*)

GEORGE: POW!!!

(*Pop! From the barrel of the gun blossoms a large red and yellow Chinese parasol.* HONEY *screams again, this time less, and mostly from relief and confusion.*)

You're dead! Pow! You're dead!
NICK (*laughing*): Good Lord.

(HONEY *is beside herself.* MARTHA *laughs too . . . almost breaks down, her great laugh booming.* GEORGE *joins in the general laughter and confusion. It dies, eventually.*)

HONEY: Oh! My goodness!
MARTHA (*joyously*): Where'd you get that, you bastard?
NICK (*his hand out for the gun*): Let me see that, will you?

(GEORGE *hands him the gun.*)

HONEY: I've never been so frightened in my life! Never!
GEORGE (*a trifle abstracted*): Oh, I've had it awhile. Did you like that?
MARTHA (*giggling*): You bastard.
HONEY (*wanting attention*): I've *never* been so frightened . . . never.
NICK: This is quite a gadget.
GEORGE (*leaning over* MARTHA): You liked that, did you?
MARTHA: Yeah . . . that was pretty good. (*Softer.*) C'mon . . . give me a kiss.
GEORGE (*indicating* NICK *and* HONEY): Later, sweetie.

(But MARTHA *will not be dissuaded. They kiss,* GEORGE *standing, leaning over* MARTHA's *chair. She takes his hand, places it on her stage-side breast. He breaks away.*)

Oh-ho! That's what you're after, is it? What are we going to have . . . blue games for the guests? Hunh? Hunh?
MARTHA (*angry-hurt*): You . . . prick!
GEORGE (*a Pyrrhic victory*): Everything in its place, Martha . . . everything in its own good time.
MARTHA (*an unspoken epithet*): You. . . .
GEORGE (*over to* NICK, *who still has the gun*): Here, let me show you . . . it goes back in, like this. (*Closes the parasol, reinserts it in the gun.*)
NICK: That's damn clever.
GEORGE (*puts the gun down*): Drinks now! Drinks for all! (*Takes* NICK's *glass without question . . . goes to* MARTHA.)
MARTHA (*still angry-hurt*): I'm not finished.
HONEY (*as* GEORGE *puts out his hand for her glass*): Oh, I think I need something.

(*He takes her glass, moves back to the portable bar.*)

NICK: Is that Japanese?

GEORGE: Probably.

HONEY (*to* MARTHA): I was never so frightened in my life. Weren't you frightened? Just for a second?

MARTHA (*smothering her rage at* GEORGE): I don't remember.

HONEY: Ohhhh, now . . . I bet you were.

GEORGE: Did you really think I was going to kill you, Martha?

MARTHA (*dripping contempt*): You? . . . Kill me? . . . That's a laugh.

GEORGE: Well, now, I might . . . some day.

MARTHA: Fat chance.

NICK (*as* GEORGE *hands him his drink*): Where's the john?

GEORGE: Through the hall there . . . and down to your left.

HONEY: Don't you come back with any guns, or anything, now.

NICK (*laughs*): Oh, no.

MARTHA: You don't need any props, do you, baby?

NICK: Unh-unh.

MARTHA (*suggestive*): I'll bet not. No fake Jap gun for you, eh?

NICK (*smiles at* MARTHA. *Then, to* GEORGE, *indicating a side table near the hall*): May I leave my drink here?

GEORGE (*as* NICK *exits without waiting for a reply*): Yeah . . . sure . . . why not? We've got half-filled glasses everywhere in the house, wherever Martha forgets she's left them . . . in the linen closet, on the edge of the bathtub. . . . I even found one in the freezer, once.

MARTHA (*amused in spite of herself*): You did not!

GEORGE: *Yes* I did.

MARTHA (*ibid*): You did *not!*

GEORGE (*giving* HONEY *her brandy*): Yes I *did*. (*To* HONEY.) Brandy doesn't give you a hangover?

HONEY: I never mix. And then, I don't drink very much, either.

GEORGE (*grimaces behind her back*): Oh . . . that's good. Your . . . your husband was telling me all about the . . . chromosomes.

MARTHA (*ugly*): The what?

GEORGE: The chromosomes, Martha . . . the genes, or whatever they are. (*To* HONEY.) You've got quite a . . . terrifying husband.

HONEY (*as if she's being joshed*): Ohhhhhhhhh. . . .

GEORGE: No, really. He's quite terrifying, with his chromosomes, and all.

MARTHA: He's in the Math Department.

GEORGE: No, Martha . . . he's a biologist.

MARTHA (*her voice rising*): He's in the *Math* Department!

HONEY (*timidly*): Uh . . . biology.

MARTHA (*unconvinced*): Are *you* sure?

HONEY (*with a little giggle*): Well, I ought to. (*Then as an afterthought.*) Be.

MARTHA (*grumpy*): I suppose *so*. I don't know who said he was in the Math Department.

GEORGE: You did, Martha.

MARTHA (*by way of irritable explanation*): Well, I can't be expected to remember *everything*. I meet fifteen new teachers and their goddamn wives . . . present company outlawed, of course . . . (HONEY *nods, smiles sillily*) . . . and I'm supposed to remember *everything*. (*Pause.*) So? He's a biologist. Good for him. Biology's even better. It's less . . . abstruse.

GEORGE: Abstract.

MARTHA: ABSTRUSE! In the sense of recondite. (*Sticks her tongue out at* GEORGE.) Don't you tell me words. Biology's even better. It's . . . right at the *meat* of things.

(NICK *re-enters*.)

You're right at the meat of things, baby.

NICK (*taking his drink from the side table*): Oh?

HONEY (*with that giggle*): They thought you were in the Math Department.

NICK: Well, maybe I ought to be.

MARTHA: You stay right where you are . . . you stay right at the . . . *meat* of things.

GEORGE: You're obsessed with that phrase, Martha. . . . It's ugly.

MARTHA (*ignoring* GEORGE . . . *to* NICK): You stay right there. (*Laughs.*) Hell, you can take over the History Department just as easy from there as anywhere else. God knows, *some*body's going to take over the History Department, *some* day, and it ain't going to be Georgie-boy, there . . . that's for sure. Are ya, swampy . . . are ya, hunh?

GEORGE: In my mind, Martha, you are buried in cement, right up to your neck. (MARTHA *giggles*.) No . . . right up to your nose . . . that's much quieter.

MARTHA (*to* NICK): Georgie-boy, here, says you're terrifying. Why are you terrifying?

NICK (*with a small smile*): I didn't know I was.

HONEY (*a little thickly*): It's because of your chromosomes, dear.

NICK: Oh, the chromosome business. . . .

MARTHA (*to* NICK): What's all this about chromosomes?

NICK: Well, chromosomes are. . . .

MARTHA: I know what chromosomes are, sweetie, I love 'em.

NICK: Oh. . . . Well, then.

GEORGE: Martha eats them . . . for breakfast . . . she sprinkles them on her cereal. (*To* MARTHA, *now*.) It's very simple, Martha, this young man is working on a system whereby chromosomes can be altered . . . well not all by himself — he probably has one or two co-conspirators — the genetic makeup of a sperm cell changed, reordered . . . *to* order, actually . . . for hair and eye color, stature, potency . . . I imagine . . . hairiness, features, health . . . and *mind*. Most important . . . Mind. All imbalances will be corrected, sifted out . . . propensity for various diseases will be gone, longevity assured. We will have a race of men . . . test-tube-bred . . . incubator-born . . . superb and sublime.

MARTHA (*impressed*): Hunh!

HONEY: How exciting!

GEORGE: *But!* Everyone will tend to be rather the same. . . . Alike. Everyone . . . and I'm sure I'm not wrong here . . . will tend to look like this young man *here*.

MARTHA: *That's* not a bad idea.

NICK (*impatient*): All right, now. . . .

GEORGE: It will, on the surface of it, be all rather pretty . . . quite jolly. But of course there will be a dank side to it, too. A certain amount of regulation will be necessary . . . uh . . . for the experiment to succeed. A certain number of sperm tubes will have to be cut.

MARTHA: Hunh! . . .

GEORGE: Millions upon millions of them . . . millions of tiny little slicing operations that will leave just the smallest scar, on the underside of the scrotum (MARTHA *laughs*.) but which will assure the sterility of the imperfect . . . the ugly, the stupid . . . the . . . unfit.

NICK (*grimly*): Now look . . . !

GEORGE: . . . with this, we will have, in time, a race of glorious men.

MARTHA: Hunh!

GEORGE: I suspect we will not have much music, much painting, but we will have a civilization of men, smooth, blond, and right at the middleweight limit.

MARTHA: Awww. . . .

GEORGE: . . . a race of scientists and mathematicians, each dedicated to and working for the greater glory of the supercivilization.

MARTHA: Goody.

GEORGE: There will be a certain . . . loss of liberty, I imagine, as a result of this experiment . . . but diversity will no longer be the goal. Cultures and races will eventually vanish . . . the ants will take over the world.

NICK: Are you finished?

GEORGE (*ignoring him*): And I, naturally, am rather opposed to all this. History, which is my field . . . history, of which I am one of the most famous bogs. . . .

MARTHA: Ha, ha, HA!

GEORGE: . . . will lose its glorious variety and unpredictability. I, and with me the . . . the surprise, the multiplexity, the sea-changing rhythm of . . . history, will be eliminated. There will be order and constancy . . . and I am unalterably opposed to it. I will not give up Berlin!

MARTHA: You'll give up Berlin, sweetheart. You going to defend it with your paunch?

HONEY: I don't see what Berlin has to *do* with anything.

GEORGE: There is a saloon in West Berlin where the barstools are five feet high. And the earth . . . the floor . . . is so . . . far . . . below you. I will not give up things like that. No . . . I won't. I will fight you, young man . . . one hand on my scrotum, to be sure . . . but with my free hand I will battle you to the death.

MARTHA (*mocking, laughing*): Bravo!

NICK (*to* GEORGE): That's right. And I am going to be the wave of the future.

MARTHA: You bet you are, baby.

HONEY (*quite drunk — to* NICK): I don't see why you want to do all those things, dear. You never told me.

NICK (*angry*): Oh for God's sake!

HONEY (*shocked*): OH!

GEORGE: The most profound indication of a social malignancy . . . no sense of humor. None of the monoliths could take a joke. Read history. I know something about history.

NICK (*to* GEORGE, *trying to make light of it all*): You . . . you don't know much about science, do you?

GEORGE: I know something about history. I know when I'm being threatened.

MARTHA (*salaciously — to* NICK): So, everyone's going to look like you, eh?

NICK: Oh, sure. I'm going to be a personal screwing machine!

MARTHA: Isn't that nice.

HONEY (*her hands over her ears*): Dear, you mustn't . . . you mustn't . . . you mustn't.

NICK (*impatiently*): I'm sorry, Honey.

HONEY: Such language. It's. . . .

NICK: I'm *sorry*. All right?

HONEY (*pouting*): Well . . . all right. (*Suddenly she giggles insanely, subsides. To* GEORGE.) . . . When is your son? (*Giggles again.*)

GEORGE: What?

NICK (*distastefully*): Something about your son.

GEORGE: SON!

HONEY: When is . . . where is your son . . . coming home? (*Giggles.*)

GEORGE: Ohhhh. (*Too formal.*) Martha? When is our son coming home?

MARTHA: Never mind.

GEORGE: No, no . . . I want to know . . . you brought it out into the open. When is he coming home, Martha?

MARTHA: I said never mind. I'm sorry I brought it up.

GEORGE: Him up . . . not it. You brought *him* up. Well, more or less. When's the little bugger going to appear, hunh? I mean isn't tomorrow meant to be his birthday, or something?

MARTHA: I don't want to talk about it!

GEORGE (*falsely innocent*): But Martha. . . .

MARTHA: I DON'T WANT TO TALK ABOUT IT!

GEORGE: I'll bet you don't. (*To* HONEY *and* NICK.) Martha does not want to talk about it . . . him. Martha is sorry she brought it up . . . him.

HONEY (*idiotically*): When's the little bugger coming home? (*Giggles.*)

GEORGE: Yes, Martha . . . since you had the bad taste to bring the matter up in the first place . . . when *is* the little bugger coming home?

NICK: Honey, do you think you . . . ?

MARTHA: George talks disparagingly about the little bugger because . . . well, because he has problems.

GEORGE: The little bugger has problems? What problems has the little bugger got?

MARTHA: Not the little bugger . . . stop calling him that! You! You've got problems.

GEORGE (*feigned disdain*): I've never heard of anything more ridiculous in my life.

HONEY: Neither have I!

NICK: Honey. . . .

MARTHA: George's biggest problem about the little . . . ha, ha, ha, HA! . . . about our son, about our great big son, is that deep down in the private-most pit of his gut, he's not completely sure it's his own kid.

GEORGE (*deeply serious*): My God, you're a wicked woman.

MARTHA: And I've told you a million times, baby . . . I wouldn't conceive with anyone but you . . . you know that, baby.

GEORGE: A deeply wicked person.

HONEY (*deep in drunken grief*): My, my, my, my. Oh, my.

NICK: I'm not sure that this is a subject for. . . .

GEORGE: Martha's lying. I want you to know that, right now. Martha's lying. (MARTHA *laughs*.) There are very few things in this world that I *am* sure of . . . national boundaries, the level of the ocean, political allegiances, practical morality . . . none of these would I stake my stick on any more . . . but the one thing in this whole sinking world that I am sure of is my partnership, my chromosomological partnership in the . . . creation of our . . . blond-eyed, blue-haired . . . son.

HONEY: Oh, I'm so glad!

MARTHA: That was a very pretty speech, George.

GEORGE: Thank you, Martha.

MARTHA: You rose to the occasion . . . good. Real good.

HONEY: Well . . . real well.

NICK: Honey. . . .

GEORGE: Martha knows . . . she knows better.

MARTHA (*proudly*): I know better. I been to college like everybody else.

GEORGE: Martha been to college. Martha been to a convent when she were a little twig of a thing, too.

MARTHA: And I was an atheist. (*Uncertainly.*) I still am.

GEORGE: Not an atheist, Martha . . . a pagan. (*To* HONEY *and* NICK.) Martha is the only true pagan on the eastern seaboard. (MARTHA *laughs.*)

HONEY: Oh, that's nice. Isn't that nice, dear?

NICK (*humoring her*): Yes . . . wonderful.

GEORGE: And Martha paints blue circles around her things.

NICK: You do?

MARTHA (*defensively, for the joke's sake*): Sometimes. (*Beckoning.*) You wanna see?

GEORGE (*admonishing*): Tut, tut, tut.

MARTHA: Tut, tut yourself . . . you old floozie!

HONEY: He's not a floozie . . . he can't be a floozie . . . you're a floozie. (*Giggles.*)

MARTHA (*shaking a finger at* HONEY): Now you watch yourself!

HONEY (*cheerfully*): All right. I'd like a nipper of brandy, please.

NICK: Honey, I think you've had enough, now. . . .

GEORGE: Nonsense! Everybody's ready, I think. (*Takes glasses, etc.*)

HONEY (*echoing* GEORGE): Nonsense.

NICK (*shrugging*): O.K.

MARTHA (*to* GEORGE): Our son does *not* have blue hair . . . or blue eyes, for that matter. He has green eyes . . . like me.

GEORGE: He has blue eyes, Martha.

MARTHA (*determined*): Green.

GEORGE (*patronizing*): Blue, Martha.

MARTHA (*ugly*): GREEN! (*To* HONEY *and* NICK.) He has the loveliest green eyes . . . they aren't all flaked with brown and gray, you know . . . hazel . . . they're real green . . . deep, pure green eyes . . . like mine.

NICK (*peers*): Your eyes are . . . brown, aren't they?

MARTHA: Green! (*A little too fast.*) Well, in some lights they *look* brown, but they're green. Not green like his . . . more hazel. George has watery blue eyes . . . milky blue.

GEORGE: Make up your mind, Martha.

MARTHA: I was giving you the benefit of the doubt. (*Now back to the others.*) Daddy has green eyes, too.

GEORGE: He does not! Your father has tiny red eyes . . . like a white mouse. In fact, he *is* a white mouse.

MARTHA: You wouldn't dare say a thing like that if he was here! You're a coward!

GEORGE (*to* HONEY *and* NICK): You know . . . that great shock of white hair, and those little beady red eyes . . . a great big white mouse.

MARTHA: George hates Daddy . . . not for anything Daddy's done to him, but for his own. . . .

GEORGE (*nodding . . . finishing it for her*): . . . inadequacies.

MARTHA (*cheerfully*): That's right. You hit it . . . right on the snout. (*Seeing* GEORGE *exiting.*) Where do you think *you're* going?

GEORGE: We need some more booze, angel.

MARTHA: Oh. (*Pause.*) So, go.

GEORGE (*exiting*): Thank you.

MARTHA (*seeing that* GEORGE *has gone*): He's a good bartender . . . a good bar nurse. The S.O.B., he hates my father. You know that?

NICK (*trying to make light of it*): Oh, come on.

MARTHA (*offended*): You think I'm kidding? You think I'm joking? I never joke . . . I don't have a sense of humor. (*Almost pouting.*) I have a fine sense of the ridiculous, but no sense of humor. (*Affirmatively.*) I have no sense of humor!

HONEY (*happily*): I haven't, either.

NICK (*half-heartedly*): Yes, you have, Honey . . . a quiet one.

HONEY (*proudly*): Thank you.

MARTHA: You want to know *why* the S.O.B. hates my father? You want me to tell you? All right. . . . I will now tell you why the S.O.B. hates my father.

HONEY (*swinging to some sort of attention*): Oh, good!

MARTHA (*sternly, to* HONEY): *Some* people feed on the calamities of others.

HONEY (*offended*): They do not!

NICK: Honey. . . .

MARTHA: All right! Shut up! Both of you! (*Pause.*) All right, now. Mommy died early, see, and I sort of grew up with Daddy. (*Pause — thinks.*) . . . I went away to school, and stuff, but I more or less grew up with him. Jesus, I admired that guy! I worshipped him . . . I absolutely worshipped him. I still do. And he was pretty fond of me, too . . . you know? We had a real . . . rapport going . . . a real rapport.

NICK: Yeah, yeah.

MARTHA: And Daddy built this college . . . I mean, he built it up from what it was . . . it's his whole life. He *is* the college.

NICK: Unh-hunh.

MARTHA: The college is him. You know what the endowment was when he took over, and what it is *now*? You look it up some time.

NICK: I know . . . I read about it. . . .

MARTHA: Shut up and listen . . . (*As an afterthought.*) . . . cutie. So after I got done with college and stuff, I came back here and sort of . . . sat around, for a while. I wasn't married, or anything. Wellllll, I'd *been* married . . . sort of . . . for a week, my sophomore year at Miss Muff's Academy for Young Ladies . . . college. A kind of junior Lady Chatterley arrangement, as it turned out . . . the marriage. (NICK *laughs.*) He mowed the lawn at Miss Muff's, sitting up there, all naked, on a big power mower, mowing away. But Daddy and Miss Muff got together and put an end to that . . . real quick . . . annulled . . . which is a laugh . . . because theoretically you can't get an annulment if there's entrance. Ha! Anyway, so I was revirginized, finished at Miss Muff's . . . where they had one less gardener's boy, and a real shame, that was . . . and I came back here and sort of sat around for a while. I was hostess for Daddy and I took care of him . . . and it was . . . nice. It was very nice.

NICK: Yes . . . yes.

MARTHA: What do you mean, yes, yes? How would you know?

(NICK *shrugs helplessly.*)

Lover.

(NICK *smiles a little*.)

And I got the idea, about then, that I'd marry into the college . . . which didn't seem to be quite as stupid as it turned out. I mean, Daddy had a sense of history . . . of continuation. . . . Why don't you come over here and sit by me?

NICK (*indicating* HONEY, *who is barely with it*): I . . . don't think I . . . should. . . . I. . . .

MARTHA: Suit yourself. A sense of continuation . . . history . . . and he'd always had it in the back of his mind to . . . *groom* someone to take over . . . some time, when he quit. A succession . . . you know what I mean?

NICK: Yes, I do.

MARTHA: Which is natural enough. When you've made something, you want to pass it on, to somebody. So, I was sort of on the lookout, for . . . prospects with the new men. An heir-apparent. (*Laughs*.) It wasn't *Daddy's* idea that I had to necessarily marry the guy. I mean, I wasn't the albatross . . . you didn't have to take me to get the prize, or anything like that. It was something *I* had in the back of *my* mind. And a lot of the new men were married . . . naturally.

NICK: Sure.

MARTHA (*with a strange smile*): Like you, baby.

HONEY (*a mindless echo*): Like you, baby.

MARTHA (*ironically*): But then George came along . . . along came George.

GEORGE (*re-entering, with liquor*): And along came George, bearing hooch. What are you doing now, Martha?

MARTHA (*unfazed*): I'm telling a story. Sit down . . . you'll learn something.

GEORGE (*stays standing. Puts the liquor on the portable bar*): All rightie.

HONEY: You've come back!

GEORGE: That's right.

HONEY: Dear! He's come back!

NICK: Yes, I see . . . I see.

MARTHA: Where was I?

HONEY: I'm *so* glad.

NICK: Shhhhh.

HONEY (*imitating him*): Shhhhh.

MARTHA: Oh yeah. And along came George. That's right. Who was young . . . intelligent . . . and . . . bushy-tailed, and . . . sort of cute . . . if you can imagine it. . . .

GEORGE: . . . and younger than you. . . .

MARTHA: . . . and younger than me. . . .

GEORGE: . . . by six years . . .

MARTHA: . . . by six years. . . . It doesn't bother me, George. . . . And along he came, bright-eyed, into the History Department. And you know what I did, dumb cluck that I am? You know what I did? I fell for him.

HONEY (*dreamy*): Oh, that's nice.

GEORGE: Yes, she did. You should have seen it. She'd sit outside of my room, on the lawn, at night, and she'd howl and claw at the turf . . . I couldn't work.

MARTHA (*laughs, really amused*): I actually fell for him . . . it . . . that, there.

GEORGE: Martha's a Romantic at heart.

MARTHA: That I am. So, I actually fell for him. And the match seemed . . . practical, too. You know, Daddy was looking for someone to. . . .

GEORGE: Just a minute, Martha. . . .

MARTHA: . . . take over, some time, when he was ready to. . . .

GEORGE (*stony*): Just a minute, Martha.

MARTHA: . . . retire, and so I thought. . . .

GEORGE: STOP IT, MARTHA!

MARTHA (*irritated*): Whadda you want?

GEORGE (*too patiently*): I'd thought you were telling the story of our courtship, Martha . . . I didn't know you were going to start in on the other business.

MARTHA (*so-thereish*): Well, I am!

GEORGE: I wouldn't, if I were you.

MARTHA: Oh . . . you wouldn't? Well, you're not!

GEORGE: Now, you've already sprung a leak about you-know-what. . . .

MARTHA (*a duck*): What? What?

GEORGE: . . . about the apple of our eye . . . the sprout . . . the little bugger . . . (*Spits it out.*) . . . our son . . . and if you start in on this other business, I warn you, Martha, it's going to make me angry.

MARTHA (*laughing at him*): Oh, it is, is it?

GEORGE: I warn you.

MARTHA (*incredulous*): You *what*?

GEORGE (*very quietly*): I warn you.

NICK: Do you really think we have to go through . . . ?

MARTHA: I stand warned! (*Pause . . . then, to* HONEY *and* NICK.) So, anyway, I married the S.O.B., and I had it all planned out. . . . He was the groom . . . he was going to be groomed. He'd take over some day . . . first, he'd take over the History Department, and then, when Daddy retired, he'd take over the college . . . you know? That's the way it was supposed to be.

(*To* GEORGE, *who is at the portable bar with his back to her.*)

You getting angry, baby? Hunh? (*Now back.*) That's the way it was *supposed* to be. Very simple. And Daddy seemed to think it was a pretty good idea, too. For a while. Until he watched for a couple of years! (*To* GEORGE *again.*) You getting angrier? (*Now back.*) Until he watched for a couple of years and started thinking maybe it wasn't such a good idea after all . . . that maybe Georgie-boy didn't have the *stuff* . . . that he didn't have it in him!

GEORGE (*still with his back to them all*): Stop it, Martha.

MARTHA (*viciously triumphant*): The hell I will! You see, George didn't have much . . . push . . . he wasn't particularly . . . aggressive. In fact he was sort of a . . . (*Spits the word at* GEORGE's *back.*) . . . a FLOP! A great . . . big . . . fat . . . FLOP!

(CRASH! *Immediately after* FLOP! GEORGE *breaks a bottle against the portable bar and stands there, still with his back to them all, holding the remains of the bottle by the neck. There is a silence, with everyone frozen. Then. . . .*)

GEORGE (*almost crying*): I said stop, Martha.

MARTHA (*after considering what course to take*): I hope that was an empty bottle, George. You don't want to waste good liquor . . . not on your salary.

(GEORGE *drops the broken bottle on the floor, not moving.*)

Not on an Associate Professor's salary. (*To* NICK *and* HONEY.) I mean, he'd be . . . no good . . . at trustees' dinners, fund raising. He didn't have any . . . personality, you know what I mean? Which was disappointing to Daddy, as you can imagine. So, here I am, stuck with this flop. . . .

GEORGE (*turning around*): . . . don't go on, Martha. . . .

MARTHA: . . . this BOG in the History Department. . . .

GEORGE: . . . don't, Martha, don't. . . .

MARTHA (*her voice rising to match his*): . . . who's married to the President's daughter, who's expected to *be* somebody, not just some nobody, some bookworm, somebody who's so damn . . . contemplative, he can't make anything out of himself, somebody without the *guts* to make anybody proud of him . . . ALL RIGHT, GEORGE!

GEORGE (*under her, then covering, to drown her*): I said, don't. All right . . . all right: (*sings*)
Who's afraid of Virginia Woolf,
Virginia Woolf,
Virginia Woolf,
Who's afraid of Virginia Woolf,
early in the morning.

GEORGE AND HONEY (*who joins him drunkenly*):

Who's afraid of Virginia Woolf,
Virginia Woolf,
Virginia Woolf . . . (*etc.*)

MARTHA: STOP IT!

(*A brief silence.*)

HONEY (*rising, moving toward the hall*): I'm going to be sick . . . I'm going to be sick . . . I'm going to vomit. (*Exits.*)

NICK (*going after her*): Oh, for God's sake! (*Exits.*)

MARTHA (*going after them, looks back at* GEORGE, *contemptuously*): Jesus! (*Exits.* GEORGE *is alone on stage.*)

CURTAIN

ACT II. WALPURGISNACHT

GEORGE, *by himself;* NICK *re-enters.*

NICK (*after a silence*): I . . . guess . . . she's all right. (*No answer.*) She . . . really shouldn't drink. (*No answer.*) She's . . . frail. (*No answer.*) Uh . . . slim-hipped, as you'd have it. (GEORGE *smiles vaguely.*) I'm really very sorry.

GEORGE (*quietly*): Where's my little yum yum? Where's Martha?

NICK: She's making coffee . . . in the kitchen. She . . . gets sick quite easily.

GEORGE (*preoccupied*): Martha? Oh no, Martha hasn't been sick a day in her life, unless you count the time she spends in the rest home. . . .

NICK (*he, too, quietly*): No, no; *my* wife . . . *my* wife gets sick quite easily. Your wife is Martha.

GEORGE (*with some rue*): Oh, yes . . . I know.

NICK (*a statement of fact*): She doesn't really spend any time in a rest home.

GEORGE: Your wife?

NICK: No. Yours.

GEORGE: Oh! Mine. (*Pause.*) No, no, she doesn't . . . *I* would; I mean if I were . . . her . . . she . . . *I* would. But I'm not . . . and so I don't. (*Pause.*) I'd like to, though. It gets pretty bouncy around here sometimes.

NICK (*coolly*): Yes . . . I'm sure.

GEORGE: Well, you saw an example of it.

NICK: I try not to. . . .

GEORGE: Get involved. Um? Isn't that right?

NICK: Yes . . . that's right.

GEORGE: I'd imagine not.

NICK: I find it . . . embarrassing.

GEORGE (*sarcastic*): Oh, you do, hunh?

NICK: Yes. Really. Quite.

GEORGE (*mimicking him*): Yes. Really. Quite. (*Then aloud, but to himself.*) IT'S DISGUSTING!

NICK: Now look! I didn't have anything. . . .

GEORGE: DISGUSTING! (*Quietly, but with great intensity.*) Do you think I like having that . . . whatever-it-is . . . ridiculing me, tearing me down, in front of . . . (*waves his hand in a gesture of contemptuous dismissal*) YOU? Do you think I *care* for it?

NICK (*cold — unfriendly*): Well, no . . . I don't imagine you care for it at all.

GEORGE: Oh, you don't imagine it, hunh?

NICK (*antagonistic*): No . . . I don't. I don't imagine you do!

GEORGE (*withering*): Your sympathy disarms me . . . your . . . your compassion makes me weep! Large, salty, unscientific tears!

NICK (*with great disdain*): I just don't see why you feel you have to subject *other* people to it.

GEORGE: *I?*

NICK: If you and your . . . wife . . . want to go at each other, like a couple of. . . .

GEORGE: *I!* Why *I* want to!

NICK: . . . animals, I don't see why you don't do it when there aren't any. . . .

GEORGE (*laughing through his anger*): Why, you smug, self-righteous little. . . .

NICK (*a genuine threat*): CAN . . . IT . . . MISTER!

(*Silence.*)

Just . . . watch it!

GEORGE: . . . scientist.

NICK: I've never hit an older man.

GEORGE (*considers it*): Oh. (*Pause.*) You just hit younger men . . . and children . . . women . . . birds. (*Sees that* NICK *is not amused.*) Well, you're quite right, of course. It isn't the prettiest spectacle . . . seeing a couple of middle-age types hacking away at each other, all red in the face and winded, missing half the time.

NICK: Oh, you two don't miss . . . you two are pretty good. Impressive.

GEORGE: And impressive things impress you, don't they? You're . . . easily impressed . . . sort of a . . . pragmatic idealism.

NICK (*a tight smile*): No, it's that sometimes I can admire things that I don't admire. Now, flagellation isn't my idea of good times, but. . . .

GEORGE: . . . but you can admire a good flagellator . . . a real pro.

NICK: Unh-hunh . . . yeah.

GEORGE: Your wife throws up a lot, eh?

NICK: I didn't say that. . . . I said she gets sick quite easily.

GEORGE: Oh. I thought by sick you meant. . . .

NICK: Well, it's true. . . . She . . . she does throw up a lot. Once she starts . . . there's practically no stopping her. . . . I mean, she'll go right on . . . for hours. Not all the time, but . . . regularly.

GEORGE: You can tell time by her, hunh?

NICK: Just about.

GEORGE: Drink?

NICK: Sure. (*With no emotion, except the faintest distaste, as* GEORGE *takes his glass to the bar.*) I married her because she was pregnant.

GEORGE: (*Pause.*) Oh? (*Pause.*) But you said you didn't have any children. . . . When I asked you, you said. . . .

NICK: She wasn't . . . really. It was a hysterical pregnancy. She blew up, and then she went down.

GEORGE: And while she was up, you married her.

NICK: And then she went down.

(*They both laugh, and are a little surprised that they do.*)

GEORGE: Uh . . . Bourbon *is* right.

NICK: Uh . . . yes, Bourbon.

GEORGE (*at the bar, still*): When I was sixteen and going to prep school, during the Punic Wars, a bunch of us used to go into New York on the first day of vacations, before we fanned out to our homes, and in the evening this bunch of us used to go to this gin mill owned by the gangster-father of one of us — for this was during the Great Experiment, or Prohibition, as it is more frequently called, and it was a bad time for the liquor lobby, but a fine time for the crooks and the cops — and we would go to this gin mill, and we would drink with the grown-ups and listen to the jazz. And one time, in the bunch of us, there was this boy who was fifteen, and he had killed his mother with a shotgun some years before — accidentally, completely accidentally, without even an unconscious motivation, I have no doubt, no doubt at all — and this one evening this boy went with us, and we ordered our drinks, and when it came his turn he said, I'll have bergin . . . give me some bergin, please . . . bergin and water. Well, we all laughed . . . he was blond and he had the face of a cherub, and we all laughed, and his cheeks went red and the color rose in his neck, and the assistant crook who had taken our order told people at the next table what the boy had said, and then they laughed, and then more people were told and the laughter grew, and more people and more laughter, and no one was laughing more than us, and none of us more than the boy who had shot his mother. And soon, everyone in the gin mill knew what the laughter was about, and everyone started ordering bergin, and laughing when they ordered it. And soon, of course, the laughter became less general, but it did not subside, entirely, for a very long time, for always at this table or that someone would order bergin and a new area of laughter would rise. We drank free that night, and we were bought champagne by the management, by the gangster-father of one of us. And, of course, we suffered the next day, each of us, alone, on his train, away from New York, each of us with a grown-up's hangover . . . but it was the grandest day of my . . . youth. (*Hands* NICK *a drink on the word.*)

NICK (*very quietly*): Thank you. What . . . what happened to the boy . . . the boy who had shot his mother?

GEORGE: I won't tell you.

NICK: All right.

GEORGE: The following summer, on a country road, with his learner's permit in his pocket and his father on the front seat to his right, he swerved the car, to avoid a porcupine, and drove straight into a large tree.

NICK (*faintly pleading*): No.

GEORGE: He was not killed, of course. And in the hospital, when he was conscious and out of danger, and when they told him that his father *was* dead, he began to laugh, I have been told, and his laughter grew and he would not stop, and it was not until after they jammed a needle in his arm, not until after that, until his consciousness slipped away from him, that his laughter subsided . . . stopped. And when he was recovered from his injuries enough so that he could be moved without damage should he struggle, he was put in an asylum. That was thirty years ago.

NICK: Is he . . . still there?

GEORGE: Oh, yes. And I'm told that for these thirty years he has . . . not . . . uttered . . . one . . . sound.

(A *rather long silence: five seconds, please*.)

MARTHA! (*Pause*.) MARTHA!

NICK: I told you . . . she's making coffee.

GEORGE: For your hysterical wife, who goes up and down.

NICK: Went. Up and down.

GEORGE: Went. No more?

NICK: No more. Nothing.

GEORGE (*after a sympathetic pause*): The saddest thing about men. . . . Well, no, one of the saddest things about men is the way they age . . . some of them. Do you know what it is with insane people? Do you? . . . the quiet ones?

NICK: No.

GEORGE: They don't change . . . they don't grow old.

NICK: They must.

GEORGE: Well, eventually, probably, yes. But they don't . . . in the usual sense. They maintain a . . . a firm-skinned serenity . . . the . . . the underuse of everything leaves them . . . quite whole.

NICK: Are you recommending it?

GEORGE: No. Some things are sad, though. (*Imitates a pep-talker*.) But ya jest gotta buck up an' face 'em, 'at's all. Buck up! (*Pause*.) Martha doesn't have hysterical pregnancies.

NICK: My wife had *one*.

GEORGE: Yes. Martha doesn't have pregnancies at all.

NICK: Well, no . . . I don't imagine so . . . now. Do you have any other kids? Do you have any daughters, or anything?

GEORGE (*as if it's a great joke*): Do we have any *what*?

NICK: Do you have any . . . I mean, do you have only one . . . kid . . . uh . . . your son?

GEORGE (*with a private knowledge*): Oh no . . . just one . . . one boy . . . our son.

NICK: Well . . . (*shrugs*) . . . that's nice.

GEORGE: Oh ho, ho. Yes, well, he's a . . . comfort, a bean bag.

NICK: A what?

GEORGE: A bean bag. Bean bag. You wouldn't understand. (*Over-distinct*.) Bean . . . bag.

NICK: I *heard* you . . . I didn't say I was deaf . . . I said I didn't understand.

GEORGE: You didn't say that at all.

NICK: I meant I was *implying* I didn't understand. (*Under his breath.*) For Christ's sake!

GEORGE: You're getting testy.

NICK (*testy*): I'm sorry.

GEORGE: All I said was, our son . . . the apple of our three eyes, Martha being a Cyclops . . . our son is a bean bag, and you get testy.

NICK: I'm sorry! It's late, I'm tired, I've been drinking since nine o'clock, my wife is vomiting, there's been a lot of screaming going on around here. . . .

GEORGE: And so you're testy. Naturally. Don't . . . worry about it. Anybody who comes here ends up getting . . . testy. It's expected . . . don't be upset.

NICK (*testy*): I'm not upset!

GEORGE: You're testy.

NICK: Yes.

GEORGE: I'd like to set you straight about something . . . while the little ladies are out of the room . . . I'd like to set you straight about what Martha said.

NICK: I don't . . . make judgments, so there's no need, really, unless you. . . .

GEORGE: Well, I want to. I know you don't like to become involved . . . I know you like to . . . preserve your scientific detachment in the face of — for lack of a better word — Life . . . and all . . . but still, I want to tell you.

NICK (*a tight, formal smile*): I'm a . . . guest. You go right ahead.

GEORGE (*mocking appreciation*): Oh . . . well, thanks. Now! That makes me feel all warm and runny inside.

NICK: Well, if you're going to . . .

MARTHA'S VOICE: HEY!

NICK: . . . if you're going to start that kind of stuff again. . . .

GEORGE: Hark! Forest sounds.

NICK: Hm?

GEORGE: Animal noises.

MARTHA (*sticking her head in*): Hey!

NICK: Oh!

GEORGE: Well, here's nursie.

MARTHA (*to* NICK): We're sitting up . . . we're having coffee, and we'll be back in.

NICK (*not rising*): Oh . . . is there anything I should do?

MARTHA: Nayh. You just stay here and listen to George's side of things. Bore yourself to death.

GEORGE: Monstre!

MARTHA: Cochon!

GEORGE: Bête!

MARTHA: Canaille!

GEORGE: Putain!

MARTHA (*with a gesture of contemptuous dismissal*): Yaaaahhhh! You two types amuse yourselves . . . we'll be in. (*As she goes.*) You clean up the mess you made, George?

GEORGE (MARTHA *goes.* GEORGE *speaks to the empty hallway*): No, Martha, I did not clean up the mess I made. I've been trying for years to clean up the mess I made.

NICK: Have you?

GEORGE: Hm?

NICK: *Have* you been trying for years?

GEORGE (*after a long pause . . . looking at him*): Accommodation, malleability, adjustment . . . those do seem to be in the order of things, don't they?

NICK: Don't try to put me in the same class with you!

GEORGE (*Pause.*) Oh. (*Pause.*) No, of course not. Things are simpler with you . . . you marry a woman because she's all blown up . . . while I, in my clumsy, old-fashioned way. . . .

NICK: There was more to it than that!

GEORGE: Sure! I'll bet she has money, too!

NICK (*Looks hurt. Then, determined, after a pause*): Yes.

GEORGE: Yes? (*Joyfully.*) YES! You mean I was right? I hit it?

NICK: Well, you see. . . .

GEORGE: My God, what archery! First try, too. How about that!

NICK: You see. . . .

GEORGE: There were other things.

NICK: Yes.

GEORGE: To compensate.

NICK: Yes.

GEORGE: There always are. (*Sees that* NICK *is reacting badly.*) No, I'm sure there are. I didn't mean to be . . . flip. There are *always* compensating factors . . . as in the case of Martha and myself. . . . Now, on the surface of it. . . .

NICK: We sort of grew up together, you know. . . .

GEORGE: . . . it looks to be a kind of knock-about, drag-out affair, on the *surface* of it. . . .

NICK: We knew each other from, oh God, I don't know, when we were *six*, or something. . . .

GEORGE: . . . but somewhere back there, at the beginning of it, right when I first came to New Carthage, back then. . . .

NICK (*with some irritation*): I'm *sorry*.

GEORGE: Hm? Oh. No, no . . . *I'm* sorry.

NICK: No . . . it's . . . it's all right.

GEORGE: No . . . you go ahead.

NICK: No . . . please.

GEORGE: I insist. . . . You're a guest. You go first.

NICK: Well, it seems a little silly . . . now.

GEORGE: Nonsense! (*Pause.*) But if you were six, she must have been four, or something.

NICK: Maybe I was eight . . . she was six. We . . . we used to play . . . doctor.

GEORGE: That's a good healthy heterosexual beginning.

NICK (*laughing*): Yup.

GEORGE: The scientist even then, eh?

NICK (*laughs*): Yeah. And it was . . . always taken for granted . . . you know . . . by our families, and by us, too, I guess. And . . . so, we did.

GEORGE (*Pause.*) Did what?

NICK: We got married.

GEORGE: When you were eight?

NICK: No. No, of course not. Much later.

GEORGE: I wondered.

NICK: I wouldn't say there was any . . . particular *passion* between us, even at the beginning . . . of our marriage, I mean.

GEORGE: Well, certainly no surprise, no earth-shaking discoveries, after doctor, and all.

NICK (*uncertainly*): No. . . .

GEORGE: Everything's all pretty much the same, anyway . . . in *spite* of what they say about Chinese women.

NICK: What is that?

GEORGE: Let me freshen you up. (*Takes* NICK's *glass*.)

NICK: Oh, thanks. After a while you don't get any drunker, do you?

GEORGE: Well, you *do* . . . but it's different . . . everything slows down . . . you get sodden . . . unless you can up-chuck . . . like your wife . . . then you can sort of start all over again.

NICK: Everybody drinks a lot here in the East. (*Thinks about it.*) Everybody drinks a lot in the Middle West, too.

GEORGE: We drink a great deal in this country, and I suspect we'll be drinking a great deal more, too . . . if we survive. We should be Arabs or Italians . . . the Arabs don't drink, and the Italians don't get drunk much, except on religious holidays. We should live on Crete, or something.

NICK (*sarcastically . . . as if killing a joke*): And that, of course, would make us cretins.

GEORGE (*mild surprise*): So it would. (*Hands* NICK *his drink.*) Tell me about your wife's money.

NICK (*suddenly suspicious*): Why?

GEORGE: Well . . . don't, then.

NICK: What do you want to know about my wife's money for? (*Ugly.*) Hunh?

GEORGE: Well, I thought it would be nice.

NICK: No you didn't.

GEORGE (*still deceptively bland*): All right. . . . I want to know about your wife's money because . . . well, because I'm fascinated by the methodology . . . by the pragmatic accommodation by which you wave-of-the-future boys are going to take over.

NICK: You're starting in again.

GEORGE: Am I? No I'm not. Look . . . Martha has money too. I mean, her father's been robbing this place blind for years, and. . . .

NICK: No, he hasn't. He has not.

GEORGE: He hasn't?

NICK: No.

GEORGE (*shrugs*): Very well. . . . Martha's father has *not* been robbing this place blind for years, and Martha does not have any money. O.K.?

NICK: We were talking about *my* wife's money . . . not yours.

GEORGE: O.K. . . . talk.

NICK: No. (*Pause.*) My father-in-law . . . was a man of the Lord, and he was very rich.

GEORGE: What faith?

NICK: He . . . my father-in-law . . . was called by God when he was six, or something, and he started preaching, and he baptized people, and he saved them, and he travelled around a lot, and he became pretty famous . . . not like some of them, but he became pretty famous . . . and when he died he had a lot of money.

GEORGE: God's money.

NICK: No . . . his own.

GEORGE: What happened to God's money?

NICK: He spent God's money . . . and he saved his own. He built hospitals, and he sent off Mercy ships, and he brought the outhouses indoors, and he brought the people outdoors, into the sun, and he built three churches, or whatever they were, and two of them burned down . . . and he ended up pretty rich.

GEORGE (*after considering it*): Well, I think that's very nice.

NICK: Yes. (*Pause. Giggles a little.*) And so, my wife's got some money.

GEORGE: But not God's money.

NICK: No. Her own.

GEORGE: Well, I think that's very nice.

(NICK *giggles a little.*)

Martha's got money because Martha's father's second wife . . . not Martha's mother, but after Martha's mother died . . . was a very old lady with warts who was very rich.

NICK: She was a witch.

GEORGE: She was a *good* witch, and she married the white mouse . . .

(NICK *begins to giggle.*)

. . . with the tiny red eyes . . . and he must have nibbled her warts, or something like that, because she went up in a puff of smoke almost immediately. POUF!

NICK: POUF!

GEORGE: POUF! And all that was left, aside from some wart medicine, was a big fat will. . . . A peach pie, with some for the township of New Carthage, some for the college, some for Martha's daddy, and just this much for Martha.

NICK (*quite beside himself*): Maybe . . . maybe my father-in-law and the witch with the warts should have gotten together, because he was a mouse, too.

GEORGE (*urging* NICK *on*): He was?

NICK (*breaking down*): Sure . . . he was a church mouse! (*They both laugh a great deal, but it is sad laughter . . . eventually they subside, fall silent.*) Your wife never mentioned a stepmother.

GEORGE (*considers it*): Well . . . maybe it isn't true.

NICK (*narrowing his eyes*): And maybe it is.

GEORGE: Might be . . . might not. Well, I think your story's a lot nicer . . . about your pumped-up little wife, and your father-in-law who was a priest. . . .

NICK: He was not a priest . . . he was a man of God.

GEORGE: Yes.

NICK: And my wife wasn't pumped up . . . she blew up.

GEORGE: Yes, yes.

NICK (*giggling*): Get things straight.

GEORGE: I'm sorry . . . I will. I'm sorry.

NICK: O.K.

GEORGE: You realize, of course, that I've been drawing you out on this stuff, not because I'm interested in your terrible lifehood, but only because you represent a direct and pertinent threat to my lifehood, and I want to get the goods on you.

NICK (*still amused*): Sure . . . sure.

GEORGE: I mean . . . I've warned you . . . you stand warned.

NICK: I stand warned. (*Laughs.*) It's you sneaky types worry me the most, you know. You ineffectual sons of bitches . . . you're the worst.

GEORGE: Yes . . . we are. Sneaky. An elbow in your steely-blue eye . . . a knee in your solid gold groin . . . we're the worst.

NICK: Yup.

GEORGE: Well, I'm glad you don't believe me. . . . I know you've got history on your side, and all. . . .

NICK: Unh-unh. *You've* got history on *your* side. . . . I've got biology on mine. History, biology.

GEORGE: I know the difference.

NICK: You don't act it.

GEORGE: No? I thought we'd decided that you'd take over the History Department first, before you took over the whole works. You know . . . a step at a time.

NICK (*stretching . . . luxuriating . . . playing the game*): Nyaah . . . what I thought I'd do is . . . I'd sort of insinuate myself generally, play around for a while, find all the weak spots, shore 'em up, but with my own name plate on 'em . . . become sort of a fact, and then turn into a . . . a what . . . ?

GEORGE: An inevitability.

NICK: Exactly. . . . An inevitability. You know. . . . Take over a few courses from the older men, start some special groups for myself . . . plow a few pertinent wives. . . .

GEORGE: Now that's it! You can take over all the courses you want to, and get as much of the young elite together in the gymnasium as you like, but until you start plowing pertinent wives, you really aren't working. The way to a man's heart is through his wife's belly, and don't you forget it.

NICK (*playing along*): Yeah. . . . I know.

GEORGE: And the women around here are no better than puntas — you know, South American ladies of the night. You know what they do in South America . . . in Rio? The puntas? Do you know? They hiss . . . like geese. . . . They stand around in the street and they hiss at you . . . like a bunch of geese.

NICK: Gangle.

GEORGE: Hm?

NICK: Gangle . . . gangle of geese . . . not bunch . . . gangle.

GEORGE: Well, if you're going to get all cute about it, all ornithological, it's gaggle . . . not gangle, *gaggle*.

NICK: Gaggle? Not gangle?

GEORGE: Yes, gaggle.

NICK (*crestfallen*): Oh.

GEORGE: Oh. Yes. . . . Well they stand around on the street and they hiss at you, like a bunch of geese. All the faculty wives, downtown in New Carthage, in front of the A&P, hissing away like a bunch of geese. That's the way to power — plow 'em all!

NICK (*still playing along*): I'll bet you're right.

GEORGE: Well, I am.

NICK: And I'll bet your wife's the biggest goose in the gangle, isn't she . . . ? Her father president, and all.

GEORGE: You bet your historical inevitability she is!

NICK: Yessirree. (*Rubs his hands together.*) Well now, I'd just better get her off in a corner and mount her like a goddamn dog, eh?

GEORGE: Why, you'd certainly better.

NICK (*looks at* GEORGE *a minute, his expression a little sick*): You know, I almost think you're serious.

GEORGE (*toasting him*): No, baby . . . *you* almost think you're serious, and it scares the hell out of you.

NICK (*exploding in disbelief*): ME!

GEORGE (*quietly*): Yes . . . you.

NICK: You're kidding!

GEORGE (*like a father*): I wish I were. . . . I'll give you some good advice if you want me to. . . .

NICK: Good advice! From you? Oh boy! (*Starts to laugh.*)

GEORGE: You haven't learned yet. . . . Take it wherever you can get it. . . . Listen to me, now.

NICK: Come off it!

GEORGE: I'm giving you good advice, now.

NICK: Good God . . . !

GEORGE: There's quicksand here, and you'll be dragged down, just as. . . .

NICK: Oh boy . . . !

GEORGE: . . . before you know it . . . sucked down. . . .

(NICK *laughs derisively.*)

You disgust me on principle, and you're a smug son of a bitch personally, but I'm trying to give you a survival kit. DO YOU HEAR ME?

NICK (*still laughing*): I hear you. You come in loud.

GEORGE: ALL RIGHT!

NICK: Hey, Honey.

GEORGE (*silence. Then quietly*): All right . . . O.K. You want to play it by ear, right? Everything's going to work out anyway, because the time-table's history, right?

NICK: Right . . . right. You just tend to your knitting, grandma. . . . I'll be O.K.

GEORGE (*after a silence*): I've tried to . . . tried to reach you . . . to. . . .

NICK (*contemptuously*): . . . make contact?

GEORGE: Yes.

NICK (*still*): . . . communicate?

GEORGE: Yes. Exactly.

NICK: Aw . . . that *is* touching . . . that is . . . downright moving . . . that's what it is. (*With sudden vehemence.*) UP YOURS!

GEORGE (*brief pause*): Hm?

NICK (*threatening*): You heard me!

GEORGE (*at* NICK, *not to him*): You take the trouble to construct a civilization . . . to . . . to build a society, based on the principles of . . . of principle . . . you endeavor to make communicable sense out of natural order, morality out of the unnatural disorder of man's mind . . . you make government and art, and realize that they are, must be, both the same . . . you bring things to the saddest of all points . . . to the point where there *is* something to lose . . . then all at once, through all the music, through all the sensible sounds of men building, attempting, comes the *Dies Irae*. And what is it? What does the trumpet sound? Up yours. I suppose there's justice to it, after all the years. . . . Up yours.

NICK (*brief pause . . . then applauding*): Ha, ha! Bravo! Ha, ha! (*Laughs on.*)

(And MARTHA *re-enters, leading* HONEY, *who is wan but smiling bravely*.)

HONEY (*grandly*): Thank you . . . thank you.

MARTHA: Here we are, a little shaky, but on our feet.

GEORGE: Goodie.

NICK: What? Oh . . . OH! Hi, Honey . . . you better?

HONEY: A little bit, dear. . . . I'd better sit down, though.

NICK: Sure . . . c'mon . . . you sit by me.

HONEY: Thank you, dear.

GEORGE (*beneath his breath*): Touching . . . touching.

MARTHA (*to* GEORGE): Well? Aren't you going to apologize?

GEORGE (*squinting*): For what, Martha?

MARTHA: For making the little lady throw up, what else?

GEORGE: I did not make her throw up.

MARTHA: You most certainly did!

GEORGE: I did not!

HONEY (*papal gesture*): No, now . . . no.

MARTHA (*to* GEORGE): Well, who do you think did . . . Sexy over there? You think he made his *own* little wife sick?

GEORGE (*helpfully*): Well, you make *me* sick.

MARTHA: THAT'S DIFFERENT!

HONEY: No, now. I . . . I throw up . . . I mean, I get sick . . . occasionally, all by myself . . . without any reason.

GEORGE: Is that a fact?

NICK: You're . . . you're delicate, Honey.

HONEY (*proudly*): I've always done it.

GEORGE: Like Big Ben.

NICK (*a warning*): Watch it!

HONEY: And the doctors say there's nothing wrong with me . . . organically. You know?

NICK: Of course there isn't.

HONEY: Why, just before we got married, I developed . . . appendicitis . . . or everybody *thought* it was appendicitis . . . but it turned out to be . . . it was a . . . (*laughs briefly*) . . . false alarm.

(GEORGE *and* NICK *exchange glances*.)

MARTHA (*to* GEORGE): Get me a drink.

(GEORGE *moves to the bar*.)

George makes everybody sick. . . . When our son was just a little boy, he used to. . . .

GEORGE: Don't, Martha. . . .

MARTHA: . . . he used to throw up all the time, because of George. . . .

GEORGE: I said, don't!

MARTHA: It got so bad that whenever George came into the room he'd start right in retching, and. . . .

GEORGE: . . . the real reason (*spits out the words*) our son . . . used to throw up all the time, wife and lover, was nothing more complicated than that he couldn't stand you fiddling at him all the time, breaking into his bedroom with your kimono flying, fiddling at him all the time, with your liquor breath on him, and your hands all over his. . . .

MARTHA: YEAH? And I suppose that's why he ran away from home twice in one month, too. (Now to the guests.) Twice in one month! Six times in one year!

GEORGE (also to the guests): Our son ran away from home all the time because Martha here used to corner him.

MARTHA (braying): I NEVER CORNERED THE SON OF A BITCH IN MY LIFE!

GEORGE (handing MARTHA her drink): He used to run up to me when I'd get home, and he'd say, "Mama's always coming at me." That's what he'd say.

MARTHA: Liar!

GEORGE (shrugging): Well, that's the way it was . . . you were always coming at him. I thought it was very embarrassing.

NICK: If you thought it was so embarrassing, what are you talking about it for?

HONEY (admonishing): Dear . . . !

MARTHA: Yeah! (To NICK.) Thanks, sweetheart.

GEORGE (to them all): I didn't want to talk about him at all . . . I would have been perfectly happy not to discuss the whole subject. . . . I never want to talk about it.

MARTHA: Yes you do.

GEORGE: When we're alone, maybe.

MARTHA: We're alone!

GEORGE: Uh . . . no, Love . . . we've got guests.

MARTHA (with a covetous look at NICK): We sure have.

HONEY: Could I have a little brandy? I think I'd like a little brandy.

NICK: Do you think you should?

HONEY: Oh yes . . . yes, dear.

GEORGE (moving to the bar again): Sure! Fill 'er up!

NICK: Honey, I don't think you. . . .

HONEY (petulance creeping in): It will steady me, dear. I feel a little unsteady.

GEORGE: Hell, you can't walk steady on half a bottle . . . got to do it right.

HONEY: Yes. (To MARTHA.) I love brandy . . . I really do.

MARTHA (somewhat abstracted): Good for you.

NICK (giving up): Well, if you think it's a good idea. . . .

HONEY (really testy): I know what's best for me, dear.

NICK (not even pleasant): Yes . . . I'm sure you do.

HONEY (GEORGE hands her a brandy): Oh, goodie! Thank you (To NICK.) Of course I do, dear.

GEORGE (pensively): I used to drink brandy.

MARTHA (privately): You used to drink bergin, too.

GEORGE (sharp): Shut up, Martha!

MARTHA (her hand over her mouth in a little girl gesture): Oooooops.

NICK (something having clicked, vaguely): Hm?

GEORGE (burying it): Nothing . . . nothing.

MARTHA (she, too): You two men have it out while we were gone? George tell you his side of things? He bring you to tears, hunh?

NICK: Well . . . no. . . .

GEORGE: No, what we did, actually, was . . . we sort of danced around.

MARTHA: Oh, yeah? Cute!

HONEY: Oh, I love dancing.

NICK: He didn't mean that, Honey.

HONEY: Well, I didn't think he did! Two grown men dancing . . . heavens!

MARTHA: You mean he didn't start in on how he would have amounted to something if it hadn't been for Daddy? How his high moral sense wouldn't even let him *try* to better himself? No?

NICK (*qualified*): No. . . .

MARTHA: And he didn't run on about how he tried to publish a goddam book, and Daddy wouldn't let him.

NICK: A book? No.

GEORGE: Please, Martha. . . .

NICK (*egging her on*): A book? What book?

GEORGE (*pleading*): Please. Just a book.

MARTHA (*mock incredulity*): Just a book!

GEORGE: *Please*, Martha!

MARTHA (*almost disappointed*): Well, I guess you didn't get the whole sad story. What's the matter with you, George? You given up?

GEORGE (*calm . . . serious*): No . . . no. It's just I've got to figure out some new way to fight you, Martha. Guerrilla tactics, maybe . . . internal subversion . . . I don't know. Something.

MARTHA: Well, you figure it out, and you let me know when you do.

GEORGE (*cheery*): All right, Love.

HONEY: Why don't we dance? I'd love some dancing.

NICK: Honey. . . .

HONEY: I would! I'd love some dancing.

NICK: Honey. . . .

HONEY: I *want* some! I want some dancing!

GEORGE: All right . . . ! For heaven's sake . . . we'll have some dancing.

HONEY (*all sweetness again. To* MARTHA): Oh, I'm so glad . . . I just love dancing. Don't you?

MARTHA (*with a glance at* NICK): Yeah . . . yeah, that's not a bad idea.

NICK (*genuinely nervous*): Gee.

GEORGE: Gee.

HONEY: I dance like the wind.

MARTHA (*without comment*): Yeah?

GEORGE (*picking a record*): Martha had her daguerreotype in the paper once . . . oh, 'bout twenty-five years ago. . . . Seems she took second prize in one o' them seven-day dancin' contest things . . . biceps all bulging, holding up her partner.

MARTHA: Will you put a record on and shut up?

GEORGE: Certainly, Love. (*To all.*) How are we going to work this? Mixed doubles?

MARTHA: Well, you certainly don't think I'm going to dance with *you*, do you?

GEORGE (*considers it*): Noooooo . . . not with him around . . . that's for sure. And not with twinkle-toes here, either.

HONEY: I'll dance with anyone. . . . I'll dance by myself.

NICK: Honey. . . .

HONEY: I dance like the wind.

GEORGE: All right, kiddies . . . choose up and hit the sack.

(*Music starts. . . . Second movement, Beethoven's 7th Symphony*)

HONEY (*up, dancing by herself*): De, de de *da* da, da-da de, da *da*-da de da . . . wonderful . . . !

NICK: Honey. . . .

MARTHA: All right, George . . . cut that out!

HONEY: Dum, de de da da, da-da de, dum de *da* da da. . . . Wheeeee . . . !

MARTHA: Cut it out, George!

GEORGE (*pretending not to hear*): What, Martha? What?

NICK: Honey. . . .

MARTHA (*as* GEORGE *turns up the volume*): CUT IT OUT, GEORGE!

GEORGE: WHAT?

MARTHA (*gets up, moves quickly, threateningly, to* GEORGE): All right, you son of a bitch. . . .

GEORGE (*record off, at once. Quietly*): What did you say, Love?

MARTHA: You son of a. . . .

HONEY (*in an arrested posture*): You stopped! Why did you stop?

NICK: Honey. . . .

HONEY (*to* NICK, *snapping*): Stop that!

GEORGE: I thought it was fitting, Martha.

MARTHA: Oh you did, hunh?

HONEY: You're always *at* me when I'm having a good time.

NICK (*trying to remain civil*): I'm sorry, Honey.

HONEY: Just . . . leave me alone!

GEORGE: Well, why don't *you* choose, Martha? (*Moves away from the phonograph . . . leaves it to* MARTHA.) Martha's going to run things . . . the little lady's going to lead the band.

HONEY: I like to dance and you don't want me to.

NICK: *I* like you to dance.

HONEY: Just . . . leave me alone. (*She sits . . . takes a drink.*)

GEORGE: Martha's going to put on some rhythm she understands . . . Sacre du Printemps, maybe. (*Moves . . . sits by* HONEY.) Hi, sexy.

HONEY (*a little giggle-scream*): Oooooohhhhh!

GEORGE (*laughs mockingly*): Ha, ha, ha, ha, ha. Choose it, Martha . . . do your stuff!

MARTHA (*concentrating on the machine*): You're damn right!

GEORGE (*to* HONEY): You want to dance with me, angel-tits?

NICK: What did you call my wife?

GEORGE (*derisively*): Oh boy!

HONEY (*petulantly*): No! If I can't do my interpretive dance, I don't want to dance with anyone. I'll just sit here and. . . . (*Shrugs . . . drinks.*)

MARTHA (*record on . . . a jazzy slow pop tune*): O.K. stuff, let's go. (*Grabs* NICK.)

NICK: Hm? Oh . . . hi.

MARTHA: Hi. (*They dance, close together, slowly.*)

HONEY (*pouting*): We'll just sit here and watch.

GEORGE: That's *right!*

MARTHA (*to* NICK): Hey, you *are* strong, aren't you?

NICK: Unh-hunh.

MARTHA: I like that.

NICK: Unh-hunh.

HONEY: They're dancing like they've danced before.

GEORGE: It's a familiar dance . . . they both know it. . . .

MARTHA: Don't be shy.

NICK: I'm . . . not. . . .

GEORGE (*to* HONEY): It's a very old ritual, monkey-nipples . . . old as they come.
HONEY: I . . . I don't know what you mean.

(NICK *and* MARTHA *move apart now, and dance on either side of where* GEORGE *and* HONEY *are sitting; they face each other, and while their feet move but little, their bodies undulate congruently. . . . It is as if they were pressed together.*)

MARTHA: I like the way you move.
NICK: I like the way you move, too.
GEORGE (*to* HONEY): They like the way they move.
HONEY (*not entirely with it*): That's nice.
MARTHA (*to* NICK): I'm surprised George didn't give you his side of things.
GEORGE (*to* HONEY): Aren't they cute?
NICK: Well, he didn't.
MARTHA: That surprises me.

(*Perhaps* MARTHA'*s statements are more or less in time to the music.*)

NICK: Does it?
MARTHA: Yeah . . . he usually does . . . when he gets the chance.
NICK: Well, what do you know.
MARTHA: It's really a very sad story.
GEORGE: You have ugly talents, Martha.
NICK: Is it?
MARTHA: It would make you weep.
GEORGE: Hideous gifts.
NICK: Is that so?
GEORGE: Don't encourage her.
MARTHA: Encourage me.
NICK: Go on.

(*They may undulate toward each other and then move back.*)

GEORGE: I warn you . . . don't encourage her.
MARTHA: He warns you . . . don't encourage me.
NICK: I heard him . . . tell me more.
MARTHA (*consciously making rhymed speech*): Well, Georgie-boy had lots of big am-
    bitions
    In spite of something funny in his past. . . .
GEORGE (*quietly warning*): Martha. . . .
MARTHA: Which Georgie-boy here turned into a novel. . . .
    His first attempt and also his last. . . .
    Hey! I rhymed! I rhymed!
GEORGE: I warn you, Martha.
NICK: Yeah . . . you rhymed. Go on, go on.
MARTHA: But Daddy took a look at Georgie's novel. . . .
GEORGE: You're looking for a punch in the mouth. . . . You know that, Martha.
MARTHA: Do tell! . . . and he was very shocked by what he read.
NICK: He was?
MARTHA: Yes . . . he was. . . . A novel all about a naughty boychild. . . .
GEORGE (*rising*): I will not tolerate this!
NICK (*offhand, to* GEORGE): Oh, can it.

MARTHA: . . . ha, ha!
  naughty boychild
  who . . . uh . . . who killed his mother and his father dead.
GEORGE: STOP IT, MARTHA!
MARTHA: And Daddy said . . . Look here, I will not let you publish such a thing. . . .
GEORGE (*rushes to phonograph . . . rips the record off*): That's it! The dancing's over. That's it. Go on now!
NICK: What do you think you're doing, hunh?
HONEY (*happily*): Violence! Violence!
MARTHA (*loud: a pronouncement*): And Daddy said . . . Look here, kid, you don't think for a second I'm going to let you publish this crap, do you? Not on your life, baby . . . not while you're teaching here. . . . You publish that goddam book and you're out . . . on your ass!
GEORGE: DESIST! DESIST!
MARTHA: Ha, ha, ha, HA!
NICK (*laughing*): De . . . sist!
HONEY: Oh, violence . . . violence!
MARTHA: Why, the idea! A teacher at a respected, conservative institution like this, in a town like New Carthage, publishing a book like that? If you respect your position here, young man, young . . . whippersnapper, you'll just withdraw that manuscript. . . .
GEORGE: I will not be made mock of!
NICK: He will not be made mock of, for Christ's sake. (*Laughs.*)

(HONEY *joins in the laughter, not knowing exactly why.*)

GEORGE: I will not!

(*All three are laughing at him.*)

(*Infuriated.*) THE GAME IS OVER!
MARTHA (*pushing on*): Imagine such a thing! A book about a boy who murders his mother and kills his father, and pretends it's all an accident!
HONEY (*beside herself with glee*): An accident!
NICK (*remembering something related*): Hey . . . wait a minute. . . .
MARTHA (*her own voice now*): And you want to know the clincher? You want to know what big brave Georgie said to Daddy?
GEORGE: NO! NO! NO! NO!
NICK: Wait a minute now. . . .
MARTHA: Georgie said . . . but Daddy . . . I mean . . . ha, ha, ha, ha . . . but *Sir*, it isn't a *novel* at all. . . . (*Other voice.*) Not a novel? (*Mimicking* GEORGE'S *voice.*) No, Sir . . . it isn't a novel at all. . . .
GEORGE (*advancing on her*): You will not say this!
NICK (*sensing the danger*): Hey.
MARTHA: The hell I won't. Keep away from me, you bastard! (*Backs off a little . . . uses* GEORGE'S *voice again.*) No, Sir, this isn't a novel at all . . . this is the truth . . . this really happened. . . . TO ME!
GEORGE (*on her*): I'LL KILL YOU!

(*Grabs her by the throat. They struggle.*)

NICK: HEY! (*Comes between them.*)

HONEY (*wildly*): VIOLENCE! VIOLENCE!

(GEORGE, MARTHA, *and* NICK *struggle . . . yells, etc.*)

MARTHA: IT HAPPENED! TO ME! TO ME!
GEORGE: YOU SATANIC BITCH!
NICK: STOP THAT! STOP THAT!
HONEY: VIOLENCE! VIOLENCE!

(*The other three struggle.* GEORGE's *hands are on* MARTHA's *throat.* NICK *grabs him, tears him from* MARTHA, *throws him on the floor.* GEORGE, *on the floor;* NICK *over him;* MARTHA *to one side, her hand on her throat.*)

NICK: That's enough now!
HONEY (*disappointment in her voice*): Oh . . . oh . . . oh. . . .

(GEORGE *drags himself into a chair. He is hurt, but it is more a profound humiliation than a physical injury.*)

GEORGE (*they watch him . . . a pause. . . .*): All right . . . all right . . . very quiet now . . . we will all be . . . very quiet.
MARTHA (*softly, with a slow shaking of her head*): Murderer. Mur . . . der . . . er.
NICK (*softly to* MARTHA): O.K. now . . . that's enough.

(*A brief silence. They all move around a little, self-consciously, like wrestlers flexing after a fall.*)

GEORGE (*composure seemingly recovered, but there is a great nervous intensity*): Well! That's one game. What shall we do now, hunh?

(MARTHA *and* NICK *laugh nervously.*)

Oh come on . . . let's think of something else. We've played Humiliate the Host . . . we've gone through that one . . . what shall we do now?
NICK: Aw . . . look. . . .
GEORGE: AW LOOK! (*Whines it.*) Awww . . . looooook. (*Alert.*) I mean, come on! We must know other games, college type types like us . . . that can't be the . . . limit of our vocabulary, can it?
NICK: I think maybe. . . .
GEORGE: Let's see now . . . what else can we do? There are other games. How about . . . how about . . . Hump the Hostess? HUNH?? How about that? How about Hump the Hostess? (*To* NICK.) You wanna play that one? You wanna play Hump the Hostess? HUNH? HUNH?
NICK (*a little frightened*): Calm down, now.

(MARTHA *giggles quietly.*)

GEORGE: Or is that for later . . . mount her like a goddamn dog?
HONEY (*wildly toasting everybody*): Hump the Hostess!
NICK (*to* HONEY . . . *sharply*): Just shut up . . . will you?

(HONEY *does, her glass in mid-air.*)

GEORGE: You don't wanna play that now, hunh? You wanna save that game till later? Well, what'll we play now? We gotta play a game.
MARTHA (*quietly*): Portrait of a man drowning.

GEORGE (*affirmatively, but to none of them*): I am not drowning.

HONEY (*to* NICK, *tearfully indignant*): You told me to shut up!

NICK (*impatiently*): I'm sorry.

HONEY (*between her teeth*): No you're not.

NICK (*to* HONEY, *even more impatiently*): I'm sorry.

GEORGE (*claps his hands together, once, loud*): I've got it! I'll tell you what game we'll play. We're done with Humiliate the Host . . . this round, anyway . . . we're done with that . . . and we don't want to play Hump the Hostess, yet . . . not yet . . . So I know what we'll play . . . We'll play a round of Get the Guests. How about that? How about a little game of Get the Guests?

MARTHA (*turning away, a little disgusted*): Jesus, George.

GEORGE: Book dropper! Child mentioner!

HONEY: I don't like these games.

NICK: Yeah. . . . I think maybe we've had enough of games, now. . . .

GEORGE: Oh, no . . . oh, no . . . we haven't. We've had only one game. . . . Now we're going to have another. You can't fly on one game.

NICK: I think maybe. . . .

GEORGE (*with great authority*): SILENCE! (*It is respected.*) Now, how are we going to play Get the Guests?

MARTHA: For God's sake, George. . . .

GEORGE: You be quiet!

(MARTHA *shrugs.*)

I wonder. . . . I wonder. (*Puzzles . . . then. . . .*) O.K.! Well . . . Martha . . . in her indiscreet way . . . well, not really indiscreet, because Martha is a naïve, at heart . . . anyway, Martha told you all about my first novel. True or false? Hunh? I mean, true or false that there ever was such a thing. HA! But, Martha told you about it . . . my first novel, my . . . memory book . . . which I'd sort of preferred she hadn't, but hell, that's blood under the bridge. BUT! what she didn't do . . . what Martha didn't tell you about is she didn't tell us all about my *second* novel.

(MARTHA *looks at him with puzzled curiosity.*)

No, you didn't know about that, did you, Martha? About my second novel, true or false. True or false?

MARTHA (*sincerely*): No.

GEORGE: No. (*He starts quietly but as he goes on, his tone becomes harsher, his voice louder.*) Well, it's an allegory, really — probably — but it can be read as straight, cozy prose . . . and it's all about a nice young couple who come out of the middle west. It's a bucolic you see. AND, this nice young couple comes out of the middle west, and he's blond and about thirty, and he's a scientist, a teacher, a scientist . . . and his mouse is a wifey little type who gargles brandy all the time . . . and . . .

NICK: Just a minute here. . . .

GEORGE: . . . and they got to know each other when they was only teensie little types, and they used to get under the vanity table and poke around, and. . . .

NICK: I said JUST A MINUTE!

GEORGE: This is my game! You played yours . . . you people. This is my game!

HONEY (*dreamy*): I want to hear the story. I love stories.

MARTHA: George, for heaven's sake. . . .

GEORGE: AND! And Mousie's father was a holy man, see, and he ran sort of a traveling clip joint, based on Christ and all those girls, and he took the faithful . . . that's all . . . just took 'em. . . .

HONEY (*puzzling*): This is familiar. . . .

NICK (*voice shaking a little*): No kidding!

GEORGE: . . . and he died eventually, Mousie's pa, and they pried him open, and all sorts of money fell out. . . . Jesus money, Mary money. . . . LOOT!

HONEY (*dreamy, puzzling*): I've heard this story before.

NICK (*with quiet intensity . . . to waken her*): Honey. . . .

GEORGE: But that's in the backwash, in the early part of the book. Anyway, Blondie and his frau out of the plain states came. (*Chuckles.*)

MARTHA: Very funny, George. . . .

GEORGE: . . . thank you . . . and settled in a town just like nouveau Carthage here. . . .

NICK (*threatening*): I don't think you'd better go on, mister. . . .

GEORGE: Do you not!

NICK (*less certainly*): No. I . . . I don't think you'd better.

HONEY: I love familiar stories . . . they're the best.

GEORGE: How right you are. But Blondie was in disguise, really, all got up as a teacher, 'cause his baggage ticket had bigger things writ on it . . . H.I. HI! Historical inevitability.

NICK: There's no need for you to go any further, now. . . .

HONEY (*puzzling to make sense out of what she is hearing*): Let them go on.

GEORGE: We shall. And he had this baggage with him, and part of this baggage was in the form of his mouse. . . .

NICK: We don't have to listen to this!

HONEY: Why not?

GEORGE: Your bride has a point. And one of the things nobody could understand about Blondie was his baggage . . . his mouse, I mean, here he was, pan-Kansas swimming champeen, or something, and he had this mouse, of whom he was solicitous to a point that faileth human understanding . . . given that she was sort of a simp, in the long run. . . .

NICK: This isn't fair of you. . . .

GEORGE: Perhaps not. Like, as I said, his mouse, she tooted brandy immodestly and spent half of her time in the upchuck. . . .

HONEY (*focussing*): I know these people. . . .

GEORGE: Do you! . . . But she was a money baggage amongst other things . . . Godly money ripped from the golden teeth of the unfaithful, a pragmatic extension of the big dream . . . and she was put up with. . . .

HONEY (*some terror*): I don't like this story. . . .

NICK (*surprisingly pleading*): Please . . . please don't.

MARTHA: Maybe you better stop, George. . . .

GEORGE: . . . and she was put up with. . . . STOP? Ha-ha.

NICK: Please . . . please don't.

GEORGE: Beg, baby.

MARTHA: George. . . .

GEORGE: . . . and . . . oh, we get a flashback here, to How They Got Married.

NICK: NO!

GEORGE (*triumphant*): YES!

NICK (*almost whining*): Why?

GEORGE: How They Got Married. Well, how they got married is this. . . . The Mouse got all puffed up one day, and she went over to Blondie's house, and she stuck out her puff, and she said . . . look at me.

HONEY (*white . . . on her feet*): I . . . don't . . . like this.

NICK (*to* GEORGE): Stop it!

GEORGE: Look at me . . . I'm all puffed up. Oh my goodness, said Blondie. . . .

HONEY (*as from a distance*): . . . and so they were married. . . .

GEORGE: . . . and so they were married. . . .

HONEY: . . . and then. . . .

GEORGE: . . . and then. . . .

HONEY (*hysteria*): WHAT? . . . and then, WHAT?

NICK: NO! No!

GEORGE (*as if to a baby*): . . . and then the puff went *away* . . . like magic . . . pouf!

NICK (*almost sick*): Jesus God. . . .

HONEY: . . . the puff went away. . . .

GEORGE (*softly*): . . . pouf.

NICK: Honey . . . I didn't mean to . . . honestly, I didn't mean to. . . .

HONEY: You . . . you told them. . . .

NICK: Honey . . . I didn't mean to. . . .

HONEY (*with outlandish horror*): You . . . told them! You told them! OOOO-HHHH! Oh, no, no, no, no! You couldn't have told them . . . oh, noooo!

NICK: Honey, I didn't mean to. . . .

HONEY (*grabbing at her belly*): Ohhhhh . . . nooooo.

NICK: Honey . . . baby . . . I'm sorry . . . I didn't mean to. . . .

GEORGE (*abruptly and with some disgust*): And that's how you play Get the Guests.

HONEY: I'm going to . . . I'm going to be . . . sick. . . .

GEORGE: Naturally!

NICK: Honey. . . .

HONEY (*hysterical*): Leave me alone . . . I'm going . . . to . . . be . . . sick. (*She runs out of the room.*)

MARTHA (*shaking her head, watching* HONEY's *retreating form*): God Almighty.

GEORGE (*shrugging*): The patterns of history.

NICK (*quietly shaking*): You shouldn't have done that . . . you shouldn't have done that at all.

GEORGE (*calmly*): I hate hypocrisy.

NICK: That was cruel . . . and vicious. . . .

GEORGE: . . . she'll get over it. . . .

NICK: . . . and damaging . . . !

GEORGE: . . . she'll recover. . . .

NICK: DAMAGING!! TO ME!!

GEORGE (*with wonder*): To you!

NICK: TO ME!!

GEORGE: To you!!

NICK: YES!!

GEORGE: Oh beautiful . . . beautiful. By God, you gotta have a swine to show you where the truffles are. (*So calmly.*) Well, you just rearrange your alliances, boy. You just pick up the pieces where you can . . . you just look around and make the best of things . . . you scramble back up on your feet.

MARTHA (*quietly, to* NICK): Go look after your wife.

GEORGE: Yeah . . . go pick up the pieces and plan some new strategy.

NICK (*to* GEORGE, *as he moves toward the hall*): You're going to regret this.

GEORGE: Probably. I regret everything.

NICK: I mean, I'm going to make you regret this.

GEORGE (*softly*): No doubt. Acute embarrassment, eh?

NICK: I'll play the charades like you've got 'em set up. . . . I'll play in your language.
. . . I'll be what you say I am.

GEORGE: You are already . . . you just don't know it.

NICK (*shaking within*): No . . . no. Not really. But I'll *be* it, mister. . . . I'll show
you something come to life you'll wish you hadn't set up.

GEORGE: Go clean up the mess.

NICK (*quietly . . . intensely*): You just wait, mister.

(*He exits. Pause.* GEORGE *smiles at* MARTHA.)

MARTHA: Very good, George.

GEORGE: Thank you, Martha.

MARTHA: Really good.

GEORGE: I'm glad you liked it.

MARTHA: I mean. . . . You did a good job . . . you really fixed it.

GEORGE: Unh-hunh.

MARTHA: It's the most . . . life you've shown in a long time.

GEORGE: You bring out the best in me, baby.

MARTHA: Yeah . . . pigmy hunting!

GEORGE: PIGMY!

MARTHA: You're really a bastard.

GEORGE: I? I?

MARTHA: Yeah . . . you.

GEORGE: Baby, if quarterback there is a pigmy, you've certainly changed your style.
What are you after now . . . giants?

MARTHA: You make me sick.

GEORGE: It's perfectly all right for you. . . . I mean, you can make your own rules
. . . you can go around like a hopped-up Arab, slashing away at everything in
sight, scarring up half the world if you want to. But somebody else try it . . . no
sir!

MARTHA: You miserable. . . .

GEORGE (*mocking*): Why baby, I did it all for you. I thought you'd like it, sweetheart
. . . it's sort of to your taste . . . blood, carnage and all. Why, I thought you'd get
all excited . . . sort of heave and pant and come running at me, your melons
bobbling.

MARTHA: You've really screwed up, George.

GEORGE (*spitting it out*): Oh, for God's sake, Martha!

MARTHA: I mean it . . . you really have.

GEORGE (*barely contained anger now*): You can sit there in that chair of yours, you
can sit there with the gin running out of your mouth, and you can humiliate me,
you can tear me apart . . . ALL NIGHT . . . and that's perfectly all right . . . that's
O.K. . . .

MARTHA: YOU CAN STAND IT!

GEORGE: I CANNOT STAND IT!

MARTHA: YOU CAN STAND IT!! YOU MARRIED ME FOR IT!!

(*A silence.*)

GEORGE (*quietly*): That is a desperately sick lie.

MARTHA: DON'T YOU KNOW IT, EVEN YET?

GEORGE (*shaking his head*): Oh . . . Martha.

MARTHA: My arm has gotten tired whipping you.

GEORGE (*stares at her in disbelief*): You're mad.

MARTHA: For twenty-three years!

GEORGE: You're deluded . . . Martha, you're deluded.

MARTHA: IT'S NOT WHAT I'VE WANTED!

GEORGE: I thought at least you were . . . on to yourself. I didn't know. I . . . didn't know.

MARTHA (*anger taking over*): I'm on to myself.

GEORGE (*as if she were some sort of bug*): No . . . no . . . you're . . . sick.

MARTHA (*rises — screams*): I'LL SHOW YOU WHO'S SICK!

GEORGE: All right, Martha . . . you're going too far.

MARTHA (*screams again*): I'LL SHOW YOU WHO'S SICK. I'LL SHOW YOU.

GEORGE (*he shakes her*): Stop it! (*Pushes her back in her chair.*) Now, stop it!

MARTHA (*calmer*): I'll show you who's sick. (*Calmer.*) Boy, you're really having a field day, hunh? Well, I'm going to finish you . . . before I'm through with you. . . .

GEORGE: . . . you and the quarterback . . . you both gonna finish me . . . ?

MARTHA: . . . before I'm through with you you'll wish you'd died in that automobile, you bastard.

GEORGE (*emphasizing with his forefinger*): And you'll wish you'd never mentioned our son!

MARTHA (*dripping contempt*): You. . . .

GEORGE: Now, I said I warned you.

MARTHA: I'm impressed.

GEORGE: I warned you not to go too far.

MARTHA: I'm just beginning.

GEORGE (*calmly, matter-of-factly*): I'm numbed enough . . . and I don't mean by liquor, though maybe that's been part of the process — a gradual, over-the-years going to sleep of the brain cells — I'm numbed enough, now, to be able to take you when we're alone. I don't listen to you . . . or when I *do* listen to you, I sift everything, I bring everything down to reflex response, so I don't really *hear* you, which is the only way to manage it. But you've taken a new tack, Martha, over the past couple of centuries — or however long it's been I've lived in this house with you — that makes it just too much . . . too much. I don't mind your dirty underthings in public . . . well, I *do* mind, but I've reconciled myself to that . . . but you've moved bag and baggage into your own fantasty world now, and you've started playing variations on your own distortions, and, as a result. . . .

MARTHA: Nuts!

GEORGE: Yes . . . you have.

MARTHA: Nuts!

GEORGE: Well, you can go on like that as long as you want to. And, when you're done. . . .

MARTHA: Have you ever listened to your sentences, George? Have you ever listened

to the way you talk? You're so frigging . . . convoluted . . . that's what you are.
You talk like you were writing one of your stupid papers.

GEORGE: Actually, I'm rather worried about you. About your mind.

MARTHA: Don't you worry about my mind, sweetheart!

GEORGE: I think I'll have you committed.

MARTHA: You WHAT?

GEORGE (*quietly . . . distinctly*): I think I'll have you committed.

MARTHA (*breaks into long laughter*): Oh baby, aren't you something!

GEORGE: I've got to find some way to really get at you.

MARTHA: You've got at me, George . . . you don't have to do anything. Twenty-three years of you has been quite enough.

GEORGE: Will you go quietly, then?

MARTHA: You know what's happened, George? You want to know what's *really happened*? (*Snaps her fingers.*) It's snapped, finally. Not me . . . *it*. The whole arrangement. You can go along . . . forever, and everything's . . . manageable. You make all sorts of excuses to yourself . . . *you* know . . . this is life . . . the hell with it . . . maybe tomorrow he'll be dead . . . maybe tomorrow *you'll* be dead . . . all sorts of excuses. But then, one day, one night, something happens . . . and SNAP! It breaks. And you just don't give a damn any more. I've tried with you, baby . . . really, I've tried.

GEORGE: Come off it, Martha.

MARTHA: I've tried . . . I've really tried.

GEORGE (*with some awe*): You're a monster . . . you *are*.

MARTHA: I'm loud, and I'm vulgar, and I wear the pants in this house because somebody's got to, but I am *not* a monster. I am *not*.

GEORGE: You're a spoiled, self-indulgent, willful, dirty-minded, liquor-ridden. . . .

MARTHA: SNAP! It went snap. Look, I'm not going to try to get through to you any more. . . . I'm not going to try. There was a second back there, maybe, there was a second, just a second, when I could have gotten through to you, when maybe we could have cut through all this crap. But that's past, and now I'm not going to try.

GEORGE: Once a month, Martha! I've gotten used to it . . . once a month and we get misunderstood Martha, the good-hearted girl underneath the barnacles, the little Miss that the touch of kindness'd bring to bloom again. And I've believed it more times than I want to remember, because I don't want to think I'm that much of a sucker. I don't believe you . . . I just don't believe you. There is no moment . . . there is no moment any more when we could . . . come together.

MARTHA (*armed again*): Well, maybe you're right, baby. You can't come together with nothing, and you're nothing! SNAP! It went snap tonight at Daddy's party. (*Dripping contempt, but there is fury and loss under it.*) I sat there at Daddy's party, and I watched you . . . I watched you sitting there, and I watched the younger men around you, the men who were going to go somewhere. And I sat there and I watched you, and *you* weren't *there*! And it snapped! It finally snapped! And I'm going to howl it out, and I'm not going to give a damn what I do, and I'm going to make the damned biggest explosion you ever heard.

GEORGE (*very pointedly*): You try it and I'll beat you at your own game.

MARTHA (*hopefully*): Is that a threat, George? Hunh?

GEORGE: That's a threat, Martha.

MARTHA (*fake-spits at him*): You're going to get it, baby.

GEORGE: Be careful, Martha . . . I'll rip you to pieces.

MARTHA: You aren't man enough . . . you haven't got the guts.

GEORGE: Total war?

MARTHA: Total.

(*Silence. They both seem relieved . . . elated.* NICK *re-enters.*)

NICK (*brushing his hands off*): Well . . . she's . . . resting.

GEORGE (*quietly amused at* NICK's *calm, off-hand manner*): Oh?

MARTHA: Yeah? She all right?

NICK: I think so . . . now. I'm . . . terribly sorry. . . .

MARTHA: Forget about it.

GEORGE: Happens all the time around here.

NICK: She'll be all right.

MARTHA: She lying down? You put her upstairs? On a bed?

NICK (*making himself a drink*): Well, no, actually. Uh . . . may I? She's . . . in the bathroom . . . on the bathroom floor . . . she's lying there.

GEORGE (*considers it*): Well . . . that's not very nice.

NICK: She likes it. She says it's . . . cool.

GEORGE: Still, I don't think. . . .

MARTHA (*overruling him*): If she wants to lie on the bathroom floor, let her. (*To* NICK, *seriously.*) Maybe she'd be more comfortable in the tub?

NICK (*he, too, seriously*): No, she says she likes the floor . . . she took up the mat, and she's lying on the tiles. She . . . she lies on the floor a lot . . . she really does.

MARTHA (*pause*): Oh.

NICK: She . . . she gets lots of headaches and things, and she always lies on the floor. (*To* GEORGE.) Is there . . . ice?

GEORGE: What?

NICK: Ice. Is there ice?

GEORGE (*as if the word were unfamiliar to him*): Ice?

NICK: Ice. Yes.

MARTHA: Ice.

GEORGE (*as if he suddenly understood*): Ice!

MARTHA: Attaboy.

GEORGE (*without moving*): Oh, yes . . . I'll get some.

MARTHA: Well, go. (*Mugging . . . to* NICK.) Besides, we want to be alone.

GEORGE (*moving to take the bucket*): I wouldn't be surprised, Martha . . . I wouldn't be surprised.

MARTHA (*as if insulted*): Oh, you wouldn't, hunh?

GEORGE: Not a bit, Martha.

MARTHA (*violent*): NO?

GEORGE (*he too*): NO! (*Quietly again.*) You'll try anything, Martha. (*Picks up the ice bucket.*)

NICK (*to cover*): Actually, she's very . . . frail, and. . . .

GEORGE: . . . slim-hipped.

NICK (*remembering*): Yes . . . exactly.

GEORGE (*at the hallway . . . not kindly*): That why you don't have any kids? (*He exits.*)

NICK (*to* GEORGE's *retreating form*): Well, I don't know that that's . . . (*trails off*) . . . if that has anything to do with any . . . thing.

MARTHA: Well, if it does, who cares? Hunh?
NICK: Pardon?

(MARTHA *blows him a kiss.*)

NICK (*still concerned with* GEORGE'S *remark*): I . . . what? . . . I'm sorry.
MARTHA: I said . . . (*Blows him another kiss.*)
NICK (*uncomfortable*): Oh . . . yes.
MARTHA: Hey . . . hand me a cigarette . . . lover. (NICK *fishes in his pocket.*) That's
a good boy. (*He gives her one.*) Unh . . . thanks.

(*He lights it for her. As he does, she slips her hand between his legs, somewhere
between the knee and the crotch, bringing her hand around to the outside of his
leg.*)

Ummmmmmmmm.

(*He seems uncertain, but does not move. She smiles, moves her hand a little.*)

Now, for being such a good boy, you can give me a kiss. C'mon.
NICK (*nervously*): Look . . . I don't think we should. . . .
MARTHA: C'mon, baby . . . a friendly kiss.
NICK (*still uncertain*): Well. . . .
MARTHA: . . . you won't get hurt, little boy. . . .
NICK: . . . not so little. . . .
MARTHA: I'll bet you're not. C'mon. . . .
NICK (*weakening*): But what if he should come back in, and . . . or . . . ?
MARTHA (*all the while her hand is moving up and down his leg*): George? Don't
worry about him. Besides, who could object to a friendly little kiss? It's all in the
faculty.

(*They both laugh, quietly . . .* NICK *a little nervously.*)

We're a close-knit family here . . . Daddy always says so. . . . Daddy wants us to
get to know each other . . . that's what he had the party for tonight. So c'mon
. . . let's get to know each other a little bit.
NICK: It isn't that I don't want to . . . believe me. . . .
MARTHA: You're a scientist, aren't you? C'mon . . . make an experiment . . . make
a little experiment. Experiment on old Martha.
NICK (*giving in*): . . . not very old. . . .
MARTHA: That's right, not very old, but lots of good experience . . . lots of it.
NICK: I'll . . . I'll bet.
MARTHA (*as they draw slowly closer*): It'll be a nice change for you, too.
NICK: Yes, it would.
MARTHA: And you could go back to your little wife all refreshed.
NICK (*closer . . . almost whispering*): She wouldn't know the difference.
MARTHA: Well, nobody else's going to know, either.

(*They come together. What might have been a joke rapidly becomes serious,
with* MARTHA *urging it in that direction. There is no frenetic quality, but rather
a slow, continually involving intertwining. Perhaps* MARTHA *is still more or less
in her chair, and* NICK *is sort of beside and on the chair.*

    GEORGE *enters . . . stops . . . watches a moment . . . smiles . . . laughs si-
lently, nods his head, turns, exits, without being noticed.*)

NICK, *who has already had his hand on* MARTHA's *breast, now puts his hand inside her dress*.)

MARTHA (*slowing him down*): Hey . . . hey. Take it easy, boy. Down, baby. Don't rush it, hunh?

NICK (*his eyes still closed*): Oh, c'mon, now. . . .

MARTHA (*pushing him away*): Unh-unh. Later, baby . . . later.

NICK: I told you . . . I'm a biologist.

MARTHA (*soothing him*): I know. I can tell. Later, hunh?

(GEORGE *is heard off-stage, singing "Who's afraid of Virginia Woolf?"* MARTHA *and* NICK *go apart,* NICK *wiping his mouth,* MARTHA *checking her clothes. Safely later,* GEORGE *re-enters with the ice bucket*.)

GEORGE: . . . of Virginia Woolf,
                         Virginia Woolf,
                         Virginia. . . .
    . . . ah! Here we are . . . ice for the lamps of China, Manchuria thrown in. (*To* NICK.) You better watch those yellow bastards, my love . . . they aren't amused. Why don't you come on over to our side, and we'll blow the hell out of 'em. Then we can split up the money between us and be on Easy Street. What d'ya say?

NICK (*not at all sure what is being talked about*): Well . . . sure. Hey! Ice!

GEORGE (*with hideously false enthusiasm*): Right! (*Now to* MARTHA, *purring*.) Hello, Martha . . . my dove. . . . You look . . . radiant.

MARTHA (*off-hand*): Thank you.

GEORGE (*very cheerful*): Well now, let me see. I've got the ice. . . .

MARTHA: . . . gotten. . . .

GEORGE: Got, Martha. Got is perfectly correct . . . it's just a little . . . archaic, like you.

MARTHA (*suspicious*): What are you so cheerful about?

GEORGE (*ignoring the remark*): Let's see now . . . I've got the ice. Can I make someone a drink? Martha, can I make you a drink?

MARTHA (*bravura*): Yeah, why not?

GEORGE (*taking her glass*): Indeed . . . why not? (*Examines the glass*.) Martha! You've been nibbling away at the glass.

MARTHA: I have not!

GEORGE (*to* NICK, *who is at the bar*): I see you're making your own, which is fine . . . fine. I'll just hootch up Martha, here, and then we'll be all set.

MARTHA (*suspicious*): All set for what?

GEORGE (*pause . . . considers*): Why, I don't know. We're having a party, aren't we? (*To* NICK, *who has moved from the bar*.) I passed your wife in the hall. I mean, I passed the john and I looked in on her. Peaceful . . . so peaceful. Sound asleep . . . and she's actually . . . sucking her thumb.

MARTHA: Awwwwww!

GEORGE: Rolled up like a fetus, sucking away.

NICK (*a little uncomfortably*): I suppose she's all right.

GEORGE (*expansively*): Of course she is! (*Hands* MARTHA *her drink*.) There you are.

MARTHA (*still on her guard*): Thanks.

GEORGE: And now one for me. It's my turn.

MARTHA: Never, baby . . . it's never your turn.

GEORGE (*too cheerful*): Oh, now, I wouldn't say that, Martha.

MARTHA: You moving on the principle the worm turns? Well, the worm part's O.K.
. . . cause that fits you fine, but the turning part . . . unh-unh! You're in a
straight line, buddy-boy, and it doesn't lead anywhere . . . (*a vague afterthought*)
. . . except maybe the grave.

GEORGE (*chuckles, takes his drink*): Well, you just hold that thought, Martha . . .
hug it close . . . run your hands over it. Me, I'm going to sit down . . . if you'll
excuse me. . . . I'm going to sit down over there and read a book. (*He moves to a
chair facing away from the center of the room, but not too far from the front door.*)

MARTHA: You're gonna do *what?*

GEORGE (*quietly, distinctly*): I am going to read a book. Read. Read. Read? You've
heard of it? (*Picks up a book.*)

MARTHA (*standing*): Whaddya mean you're gonna read? What's the matter with you?

GEORGE (*too calmly*): There's nothing the matter with me, Martha. . . . I'm going
to read a book. That's all.

MARTHA (*oddly furious*): We've got company!

GEORGE (*over-patiently*): I know, my dear . . . (*looks at his watch*) . . . but . . .
it's after four o'clock, and I always read around this time. Now, you . . . (*dismisses her with a little wave*) . . . go about your business. . . . I'll sit here very
quietly. . . .

MARTHA: You read in the afternoon! You read at four o'clock in the afternoon . . .
you don't read at four o'clock in the morning! Nobody reads at four o'clock in the
morning!

GEORGE (*absorbing himself in his book*): Now, now, now.

MARTHA (*incredulously, to* NICK): He's going to read a book. . . . The son of a bitch
is going to read a book!

NICK (*smiling a little*): So it would seem.

(*Moves to* MARTHA, *puts his arm around her waist.* GEORGE *cannot see this, of
course.*)

MARTHA (*getting an idea*): Well, we can amuse ourselves, can't we?

NICK: I imagine so.

MARTHA: We're going to amuse ourselves, George.

GEORGE (*not looking up*): Unh-hunh. That's nice.

MARTHA: You might not like it.

GEORGE (*never looking up*): No, no, now . . . you go right ahead . . . you entertain
your guests.

MARTHA: I'm going to entertain myself, too.

GEORGE: Good . . . good.

MARTHA: Ha, ha. You're a riot, George.

GEORGE: Unh-hunh.

MARTHA: Well, I'm a riot, too, George.

GEORGE: Yes you are, Martha.

(NICK *takes* MARTHA's *hand, pulls her to him. They stop for a moment, then
kiss, not briefly.*)

MARTHA (*after*): You know what I'm doing, George?

GEORGE: No, Martha . . . what are you doing?

MARTHA: I'm entertaining. I'm entertaining one of the guests. I'm necking with one of the guests.

GEORGE (*seemingly relaxed and preoccupied, never looking*): Oh, that's nice. Which one?

MARTHA (*livid*): Oh, by God you're funny. (*Breaks away from* NICK . . . *moves into* GEORGE's *side-line of vision by herself. Her balance is none too good, and she bumps into or brushes against the door chimes by the door. They chime.*)

GEORGE: Someone at the door, Martha.

MARTHA: Never mind that. I said I was necking with one of the guests.

GEORGE: Good . . . good. You go right on.

MARTHA (*pauses . . . not knowing quite what to do*): Good?

GEORGE: Yes, good . . . good for you.

MARTHA (*her eyes narrowing, her voice becoming hard*): Oh, I see what you're up to, you lousy little. . . .

GEORGE: I'm up to page a hundred and. . . .

MARTHA: Cut it! Just cut it out! (*She hits against the door chimes again; they chime.*) Goddamn bongs.

GEORGE: They're chimes, Martha. Why don't you go back to your necking and stop bothering me? I want to read.

MARTHA: Why, you miserable. . . . I'll show *you*.

GEORGE (*swings around to face her . . . says, with great loathing*): No . . . show him, Martha . . . he hasn't seen it. *Maybe* he hasn't seen it. (*Turns to* NICK.) You haven't seen it yet, have you?

NICK (*turning away, a look of disgust on his face*): I . . . I have no respect for you.

GEORGE: And none for yourself, either. . . . (*Indicating* MARTHA.) I don't know what the younger generation's coming to.

NICK: You don't . . . you don't even. . . .

GEORGE: Care? You're quite right. . . . I couldn't care less. So, you just take this bag of laundry here, throw her over your shoulder, and. . . .

NICK: You're disgusting.

GEORGE (*incredulous*): Because *you're* going to hump Martha, *I'm* disgusting? (*He breaks down in ridiculing laughter.*)

MARTHA (*to* GEORGE): You Mother! (*To* NICK.) Go wait for me, hunh? Go wait for me in the kitchen. (*But* NICK *does not move.* MARTHA *goes to him, puts her arms around him.*) C'mon, baby . . . please. Wait for me . . . in the kitchen . . . be a good baby.

(NICK *takes her kiss, glares at* GEORGE . . . *who has turned his back again . . . and exits.*)

(MARTHA *swings around to* GEORGE.) Now you listen to me. . . .

GEORGE: I'd rather read, Martha, if you don't mind. . . .

MARTHA (*her anger has her close to tears, her frustration to fury*): Well, I do mind. Now, you pay attention to me! You come off this kick you're on, or I swear to God I'll do it. I swear to God I'll follow that guy into the kitchen, and then I'll take him upstairs, and. . . .

GEORGE (*swinging around to her again . . . loud . . . loathing*): SO WHAT, MARTHA?

MARTHA (*considers him for a moment . . . then, nodding her head, backing off slowly*): O.K. . . . O.K. . . . You asked for it . . . and you're going to get it.

GEORGE (*softly, sadly*): Lord, Martha, if you want the boy that much . . . have him

. . . but do it honestly, will you? Don't cover it over with all this . . . all this . . . footwork.

MARTHA (*hopeless*): I'll make you sorry you made me want to marry you. (*At the hallway.*) I'll make you regret the day you ever decided to come to this college. I'll make you sorry you ever let yourself down. (*She exits.*)

(*Silence.* GEORGE *sits still, staring straight ahead. Listening . . . but there is no sound. Outwardly calm, he returns to his book, reads a moment, then looks up . . . considers. . . .*)

GEORGE: "And the west, encumbered by crippling alliances, and burdened with a morality too rigid to accommodate itself to the swing of events, must . . . eventually . . . fall."

(*He laughs, briefly, ruefully . . . rises, with the book in his hand. He stands still . . . then, quickly, he gathers all the fury he has been containing within himself . . . he shakes . . . he looks at the book in his hand and, with a cry that is part growl, part howl, he hurls it at the chimes. They crash against one another, ringing wildly. A brief pause, then* HONEY *enters.*)

HONEY (*the worse for wear, half asleep, still sick, weak, still staggering a little . . . vaguely, in something of a dream world*): Bells. Ringing. I've been hearing bells.

GEORGE: Jesus!

HONEY: I couldn't sleep . . . for the bells. Ding-ding, bong . . . it woke me up. What time is it?

GEORGE (*quietly beside himself*): Don't bother me.

HONEY (*confused and frightened*): I was asleep, and the bells started . . . they BOOMED! Poe-bells . . . they were Poe-bells . . . Bing-bing-bong-BOOM!

GEORGE : BOOM!

HONEY: I was asleep, and I was dreaming of . . . something . . . and I heard the sounds coming, and I didn't know what it was.

GEORGE (*never quite to her*): It was the sound of bodies. . . .

HONEY: And I didn't want to wake up, but the sound kept coming. . . .

GEORGE: . . . go back to sleep. . . .

HONEY: . . . and it FRIGHTENED ME!

GEORGE (*quietly . . . to* MARTHA, *as if she were in the room*): I'm going to get you . . . Martha.

HONEY: And it was so . . . cold. The wind was . . . the wind was so cold! And I was lying somewhere, and the covers kept slipping away from me, and I didn't want them to. . . .

GEORGE: Somehow, Martha.

HONEY: . . . and there was someone there . . . !

GEORGE: There was no one there.

HONEY (*frightened*): And I didn't want someone there . . . I was . . . naked . . . !

GEORGE: You don't know what's going on, do you?

HONEY (*still with her dream*): I DON'T WANT ANY . . . NO . . . !

GEORGE: You don't know what's been going on around here while you been having your snoozette, do you?

HONEY: NO! . . . I DON'T WANT ANY . . . I DON'T WANT THEM . . . GO 'WAY. . . . (*Begins to cry.*) I DON'T WANT . . . ANY . . . CHILDREN. . . . I . . . don't . . . want . . . any . . . children. I'm afraid! I don't want to be hurt. . . . PLEASE!

GEORGE (*nodding his head . . . speaks with compassion*): I should have known.

HONEY (*snapping awake from her reverie*): What! What?

GEORGE: I should have known . . . the whole business . . . the headaches . . . the whining . . . the. . . .

HONEY (*terrified*): What are you talking about?

GEORGE (*ugly again*): Does *he* know that? Does that . . . stud you're married to know about that, hunh?

HONEY: About what? Stay away from me!

GEORGE: Don't worry, baby . . . I wouldn't. . . . Oh, my God, that *would* be a joke, wouldn't it! But don't worry, baby. HEY! How you do it? Hunh? How do you make your secret little murders stud-boy doesn't know about, hunh? Pills? PILLS? You got a secret supply of pills? Or what? Apple jelly? WILL POWER?

HONEY: I feel sick.

GEORGE: You going to throw up again? You going to lie down on the cold tiles, your knees pulled up under your chin, your thumb stuck in your mouth . . . ?

HONEY (*panicked*): Where is he?

GEORGE: Where's who? There's nobody here, baby.

HONEY: I want my husband! I want a drink!

GEORGE: Well, you just crawl over to the bar and make yourself one.

(*From off-stage comes the sound of* MARTHA's *laughter and the crashing of dishes.*)

(*Yelling.*) That's right! Go at it!

HONEY: I want . . . something. . . .

GEORGE: You know what's going on in there, little Miss? Hunh? You hear all that? You know what's going on in there?

HONEY: I don't want to know anything!

GEORGE: There are a couple of people in there. . . .

(MARTHA's *laughter again.*)

. . . they are in there, in the kitchen. . . . Right there, with the onion skins and the coffee grounds . . . sort of . . . sort of a . . . sort of a dry run for the wave of the future.

HONEY (*beside herself*): I . . . don't . . . understand . . . you . . .

GEORGE (*a hideous elation*): It's very simple. . . . When people can't abide things as they are, when they can't abide the present, they do one of two things . . . either they . . . either they turn to a contemplation of the past, as I have done, or they set about to . . . alter the future. And when you want to change something . . . you BANG! BANG! BANG! BANG!

HONEY: Stop it!

GEORGE: And you, you simpering bitch . . . you don't want *children*?

HONEY: You leave me . . . alone. Who . . . WHO RANG?

GEORGE: What?

HONEY: What were the bells? Who rang?

GEORGE: You don't want to know, do you? You don't want to listen to it, hunh?

HONEY (*shivering*): I don't want to listen to you. . . . I want to know who rang.

GEORGE: Your husband is . . . and you want to know who *rang*?

HONEY: Who rang? Someone rang!

GEORGE (*his jaw drops open . . . he is whirling with an idea*): . . . Someone. . . .

HONEY: RANG!

GEORGE: . . . someone . . . rang . . . yes . . . yessss. . . .

HONEY: The . . . bells . . . rang. . . .

GEORGE (*his mind racing ahead*): The bells rang . . . and it was someone. . . .

HONEY: Somebody. . . .

GEORGE (*he is home, now*): . . . somebody rang . . . it was somebody . . . with . . . I'VE GOT IT! I'VE GOT IT, MARTHA . . . ! Somebody with a message . . . and the message was . . . our son . . . OUR SON! (*Almost whispered.*) It was a message . . . the bells rang and it was a message, and it was about . . . our son . . . and the message . . . was . . . and the message was . . . our . . . son . . . is . . . DEAD!

HONEY (*almost sick*): Oh . . . no.

GEORGE (*cementing it in his mind*): Our son is . . . dead. . . . And . . . Martha doesn't know. . . . I haven't told . . . Martha.

HONEY: No . . . no . . . no.

GEORGE (*slowly, deliberately*): Our son is dead, and Martha doesn't know.

HONEY: Oh. God in heaven . . . no.

GEORGE (*to* HONEY . . . *slowly, deliberately, dispassionately*): And you're not going to tell her.

HONEY (*in tears*): Your son is dead.

GEORGE: I'll tell her myself . . . in good time. I'll tell her myself.

HONEY (*so faintly*): I'm going to be sick.

GEORGE (*turning away from her . . . he, too, softly*): Are you? That's nice.

(MARTHA'S *laugh is heard again.*)

Oh, listen to that.

HONEY: I'm going to die.

GEORGE (*quite by himself now*): Good . . . good . . . you go right ahead. (*Very softly, so* MARTHA *could not possibly hear.*) Martha? Martha? I have some . . . terrible news for you. (*There is a strange half-smile on his lips.*) It's about our . . . son. He's dead. Can you hear me, Martha? Our boy is dead. (*He begins to laugh, very softly . . . it is mixed with crying.*)

CURTAIN

ACT III. THE EXORCISM

MARTHA *enters, talking to herself.*

MARTHA: Hey, hey. . . . Where is everybody . . . ? (*It is evident she is not bothered.*) So? Drop me; pluck me like a goddamn . . . whatever-it-is . . . creeping vine, and throw me over your shoulder like an old shoe . . . George? (*Looks about her.*) George? (*Silence.*) George! What are you doing: Hiding, or something? (*Silence.*) GEORGE!! (*Silence.*) Oh, fa Chri. . . . (*Goes to the bar, makes herself a drink and amuses herself with the following performance.*) Deserted! Abandon-ed! Left out in the cold like an old pussycat. HA! Can I get you a drink, Martha? Why, thank you, George; that's very kind of you. No, Martha, no; why I'd do anything for you. Would you, George? Why, I'd do anything for you, too.

Would you, Martha? Why, certainly, George. Martha, I've misjudged you. And I've misjudged you, too, George. WHERE IS EVERYBODY!!! Hump the Hostess! (*Laughs greatly at this, falls into a chair; calms down, looks defeated, says, softly.*) Fat chance. (*Even softer.*) Fat chance. (*Baby-talk now.*) Daddy? Daddy? Martha is abandon-ed. Left to her own vices at . . . (*peers at a clock*) . . . something o'clock in the old A.M. Daddy White-Mouse; do you really have red eyes? Do you? Let me see. Ohhhhh! You do! You do! Daddy, you have red eyes . . . because you cry all the time, don't you, Daddy. Yes; you do. You cry alllll the time. I'LL GIVE ALL YOU BASTARDS FIVE TO COME OUT FROM WHERE YOU'RE HIDING!! (*Pause.*) I cry all the time too, Daddy. I cry alllll the time; but deep inside, so no one can see me. I cry all the time. And Georgie cries all the time, too. We both cry all the time, and then, what we do, we cry, and we take our tears, and we put 'em in the ice box, in the goddamn ice trays (*begins to laugh*) until they're all frozen (*laughs even more*) and then . . . we put them . . . in our . . . drinks. (*More laughter, which is something else, too. After sobering silence.*) Up the drain, down the spout, dead, gone and forgotten. . . . Up the spout, not down the spout; *Up* the spout: THE POKER NIGHT. Up the spout. . . . (*Sadly.*) I've got windshield wipers on my eyes, because I married you . . . baby! . . . Martha, you'll be a song-writer yet. (*Jiggles the ice in her glass.*) CLINK! (*Does it again.*) CLINK! (*Giggles, repeats it several times.*) CLINK! . . . CLINK! . . . CLINK! . . . CLINK!

(NICK *enters while* MARTHA *is clinking; he stands in the hall entrance and watches her; finally he comes in.*)

NICK: My God, you've gone crazy too.

MARTHA: Clink?

NICK: I said, you've gone crazy too.

MARTHA (*considers it*): Probably . . . probably.

NICK: You've all gone crazy: I come downstairs, and what happens. . . .

MARTHA: What happens?

NICK: . . . my wife's gone into the can with a liquor bottle, and she winks at me . . . winks at me! . . .

MARTHA (*sadly*): She's never wunk at you; what a shame. . . .

NICK: She is lying down on the floor again, the tiles, all curled up, and she starts peeling the label off the liquor bottle, the brandy bottle. . . .

MARTHA: . . . we'll never get the deposit back that way. . . .

NICK: . . . and I ask her what she's doing, and she goes: shhhhhh! nobody knows I'm here; and I come back in here, and you're sitting there going Clink! for God's sake. Clink!

MARTHA: CLINK!

NICK: You've all gone crazy.

MARTHA: Yes. Sad but true.

NICK: Where is your husband?

MARTHA: He is vanish-ed. Pouf!

NICK: You're all crazy: nuts.

MARTHA (*affects a brogue*): Awww, 'tis the refuge we take when the unreality of the world weighs too heavy on our tiny heads. (*Normal voice again.*) Relax; sink into it; you're no better than anybody else.

NICK (*wearily*): I think I am.

MARTHA (*her glass to her mouth*): You're certainly a flop in some departments.

NICK (*wincing*): I beg your pardon . . . ?

MARTHA (*unnecessarily loud*): I said, you're certainly a flop in some. . . .

NICK (*he, too, too loud*): I'm sorry you're disappointed.

MARTHA (*braying*): I didn't say I was disappointed! Stupid!

NICK: You should try me some time when we haven't been drinking for ten hours, and maybe. . . .

MARTHA (*still braying*): I wasn't talking about your potential; I was talking about your goddamn performance.

NICK (*softly*): Oh.

MARTHA (*she softer, too*): Your potential's fine. It's dandy. (*Wiggles her eyebrows.*) Absolutely dandy. I haven't seen such a dandy potential in a long time. Oh, but baby, you sure are a flop.

NICK (*snapping it out*): Everybody's a flop to you! Your husband's a flop, *I'm* a flop. . . .

MARTHA (*dismissing him*): You're all flops. I am the Earth Mother, and you're all flops. (*More or less to herself.*) I disgust me. I pass my life in crummy, totally pointless infidelities . . . (*laughs ruefully*) would-be infidelities. Hump the Hostess? That's a laugh. A bunch of boozed-up . . . impotent lunk-heads. Martha makes goo-goo eyes, and the lunk-heads grin, and roll their beautiful, beautiful eyes back, and grin some more, and Martha licks her chops, and the lunk-heads slap over to the bar to pick up a little courage, *and* they pick up a little courage, and they bounce back over to old Martha, who does a little dance for them, which heats them all up . . . mentally . . . and so they slap over to the bar again, and pick up a little more courage, and their wives and sweethearts stick their noses up in the air . . . right through the ceiling, sometimes . . . which sends the lunk-heads back to the soda fountain again where they fuel up some more, while Martha-poo sits there with her dress up over her head . . . suffocating — you don't know how *stuffy* it is with your dress up over your head — suffocating! waiting for the lunk-heads; so, *finally* they get their courage up . . . but that's all, baby! Oh my, there is sometimes some very nice potential, but, oh my! My, my, my. (*Brightly.*) But that's how it is in a civilized society. (*To herself again.*) All the gorgeous lunk-heads. Poor babies. (*To* NICK, *now; earnestly.*) There is only one man in my life who has ever . . . made me happy. Do you know that? One!

NICK: The . . . the what-do-you-call-it? . . . uh . . . the lawn mower, or something?

MARTHA: No; I'd forgotten him. But when I think about him and me it's almost like being a voyeur. Hunh. No; I didn't mean him; I meant George, of course. (*No response from* NICK.) Uh . . . George; my husband.

NICK (*disbelieving*): You're kidding.

MARTHA: Am I?

NICK: You must be. Him?

MARTHA: Him.

NICK (*as if in on a joke*): Sure; sure.

MARTHA: You don't believe it.

NICK (*mocking*): Why, of course I do.

MARTHA: You always deal in appearances?

NICK (*derisively*): Oh, for God's sake. . . .

MARTHA: . . . George who is out somewhere there in the dark. . . . George who is good to me, and whom I revile; who understands me, and whom I push off; who can make me laugh, and I choke it back in my throat; who can hold me, at night, so that it's warm, and whom I will bite so there's blood; who keeps learning the games we play as quickly as I can change the rules; who can make me happy and I do not wish to be happy, and yes I do wish to be happy. George and Martha: sad, sad, sad.

NICK (*echoing, still not believing*): Sad.

MARTHA: . . . whom I will not forgive for having come to rest; for having seen me and having said: yes; this will do; who has made the hideous, the hurting, the insulting mistake of loving me and must be punished for it. George and Martha: sad, sad, sad.

NICK (*puzzled*): Sad.

MARTHA: . . . who tolerates, which is intolerable; who is kind, which is cruel; who understands, which is beyond comprehension. . . .

NICK: George and Martha: sad, sad, sad.

MARTHA: Some day . . . hah! some *night* . . . some stupid, liquor-ridden night . . . I will go too far . . . and I'll either break the man's back . . . or push him off for good . . . which is what I deserve.

NICK: I don't think he's got a vertebra intact.

MARTHA (*laughing at him*): You don't, huh? You don't think so. Oh, little boy, you got yourself hunched over that microphone of yours. . . .

NICK: Microscope. . . .

MARTHA: . . . yes . . . and you don't see anything, do you? You see everything but the goddamn mind; you see all the little specks and crap, but you don't see what goes on, do you?

NICK: I know when a man's had his back broken; I can see that.

MARTHA: Can you!

NICK: You're damn right.

MARTHA: Oh . . . you know so little. And you're going to take over the world, hunh?

NICK: All right, now. . . .

MARTHA: You think a man's got his back broken 'cause he makes like a clown and walks bent, hunh? Is that *really* all you know?

NICK: I said, all *right!*

MARTHA: Ohhhh! The stallion's mad, hunh. The gelding's all upset. Ha, ha, ha, HA!

NICK (*softly; wounded*): You . . . you swing wild, don't you.

MARTHA (*triumphant*): HAH!

NICK: Just . . . anywhere.

MARTHA: HAH! I'm a Gatling gun. Hahahahahahahahaha!

NICK (*in wonder*): Aimless . . . butchery. Pointless.

MARTHA: Aw! You poor little bastard.

NICK: Hit out at everything.

(*The door chimes chime.*)

MARTHA: Go answer the door.

NICK (*amazed*): What did you say?

MARTHA: I said, go answer the door. What are you, deaf?

NICK (*trying to get it straight*): You . . . want me . . . to go answer the door?

MARTHA: That's right, lunk-head; answer the door. There must be something you can do well; or, are you too drunk to do that, too? Can't you get the latch up, either?

NICK: Look, there's no need. . . .

(Door chimes again.)

MARTHA *(shouting)*: Answer it! *(Softer.)* You can be houseboy around here for a while. You can start off being houseboy right now.

NICK: Look, lady, I'm no flunky to you.

MARTHA *(cheerfully)*: Sure you are! You're ambitious, aren't you, boy? You didn't chase me around the kitchen and up the goddamn stairs out of mad, driven passion, did you now? You were thinking a little bit about your career, weren't you? Well, you can just houseboy your way up the ladder for a while.

NICK: There's no limit to you, is there?

(Door chimes again.)

MARTHA *(calmly, surely)*: No, baby; none. Go answer the door. (NICK *hesitates.*) Look, boy; once you stick your nose in it, you're not going to pull out just whenever you feel like it. You're in for a while. Now, git!

NICK: Aimless . . . wanton . . . pointless. . . .

MARTHA: Now, now, now; just do what you're told; show old Martha there's something you *can* do. Hunh? Attaboy.

NICK *(considers, gives in, moves toward the door)*: *(Chimes again.)* I'm coming, for Christ's sake!

MARTHA *(claps her hands)*: Ha HA! Wonderful; marvelous. *(Sings.)* "Just a gigolo, everywhere I go, people always say. . . ."

NICK: STOP THAT!

MARTHA *(giggles)*: Sorry, baby; go on now; open the little door.

NICK *(with great rue)*: Christ.

(He flings open the door, and a hand thrusts into the opening a great bunch of snapdragons; they stay there for a moment. NICK strains his eyes to see who is behind them.)

MARTHA: Oh, how lovely!

GEORGE *(appearing in the doorway, the snapdragons covering his face; speaks in a hideously cracked falsetto)*: Flores; flores para los muertos. Flores.

MARTHA: Ha, ha, ha, HA!

GEORGE *(a step into the room; lowers the flowers; sees NICK; his face becomes gleeful; he opens his arms)*: Sonny! You've come home for your birthday! At last!

NICK *(backing off)*: Stay away from me.

MARTHA: Ha, ha, ha, HA! That's the houseboy, for God's sake.

GEORGE: Really? That's not our own little sonny-Jim? Our own little all-American something-or-other?

MARTHA *(giggling)*: Well, I certainly hope not; he's been acting awful funny, if he is.

GEORGE *(almost manic)*: Ohhhh! I'll bet! Chippie-chippie-chippie, hunh? *(Affecting embarrassment.)* I . . . I brungya dese flowers, Mart'a, 'cause I . . . wull, 'cause you'se . . . awwwwww hell. Gee.

MARTHA: Pansies! Rosemary! Violence! My wedding bouquet!

NICK *(starting to move away)*: Well, if you two kids don't mind, I think I'll just. . . .

MARTHA: Ach! You just stay where you are. Make my hubby a drink.

NICK: I don't think I will.

GEORGE: No, Martha, no; that would be too much; he's your houseboy, baby, not mine.

NICK: I'm nobody's houseboy. . . .

GEORGE AND MARTHA: . . . Now! (*Sing.*) I'm nobody's houseboy now. . . . (*Both laugh.*)

NICK: Vicious. . . .

GEORGE (*finishing it for him*): . . . children. Hunh? That right? Vicious children, with their oh-so-sad games, hopscotching their way through life, etcetera, etcetera. Is that it?

NICK: Something like it.

GEORGE: Screw, baby.

MARTHA: Him can't. Him too fulla booze.

GEORGE: Weally? (*Handing the snapdragons to* NICK.) Here; dump these in some gin. (NICK *takes them, looks at them, drops them on the floor at his feet.*)

MARTHA (*sham dismay*): Awwwwwww.

GEORGE: What a terrible thing to do . . . to Martha's snapdragons.

MARTHA: Is that what they are?

GEORGE: Yup. And here I went out into the moonlight to pick 'em for Martha tonight, and for our sonny-boy tomorrow, for his birfday.

MARTHA (*passing on information*): There is no moon now. I saw it go down from the bedroom.

GEORGE (*feigned glee*): From the bedroom! (*Normal tone.*) Well, there was a moon.

MARTHA (*too patient; laughing a little*): There couldn't have been a moon.

GEORGE: Well, there was. There is.

MARTHA: There is no moon; the moon went down.

GEORGE: There is a moon; the moon is up.

MARTHA (*straining to keep civil*): I'm afraid you're mistaken.

GEORGE (*too cheerful*): No; no.

MARTHA (*between her teeth*): There is no goddamn moon.

GEORGE: My dear Martha . . . I did not pick snapdragons in the stony dark. I did not go stumbling around Daddy's greenhouse in the pitch.

MARTHA: Yes . . . you did. You would.

GEORGE: Martha, I do not pick flowers in the blink. I have never robbed a hothouse without there is a light from heaven.

MARTHA (*with finality*): There is no moon; the moon went down.

GEORGE (*with great logic*): That may very well be, Chastity; the moon may very well have gone down . . . but it came back up.

MARTHA: The moon does *not* come back up; when the moon has gone down it stays down.

GEORGE (*getting a little ugly*): You don't know anything. IF the moon went down, then it came back up.

MARTHA: BULL!

GEORGE: Ignorance! Such . . . ignorance.

MARTHA: Watch who you're calling ignorant!

GEORGE: Once . . . once, when I was sailing past Majorca, drinking on deck with a correspondent who was talking about Roosevelt, the moon went down, thought about it for a little . . . considered it, you know what I mean? . . . and then, POP, came up again. Just like that.

MARTHA: That is not true! That is such a lie!

GEORGE: You must not call everything a lie, Martha. (*To* NICK.) Must she?

NICK: Hell, I don't know when you people are lying, or what.

MARTHA: You're damned right!

GEORGE: You're not supposed to.

MARTHA: Right!

GEORGE: At any rate, I was sailing past Majorca. . . .

MARTHA: You never sailed past Majorca. . . .

GEORGE: Martha. . . .

MARTHA: You were never in the goddamn Mediterranean at all . . . ever. . . .

GEORGE: I certainly was! My Mommy and Daddy took me there as a college graduation present.

MARTHA: Nuts!

NICK: Was this after you killed them?

(GEORGE *and* MARTHA *swing around and look at him; there is a brief, ugly pause.*)

GEORGE (*defiantly*): Maybe.

MARTHA: Yeah; maybe not, too.

NICK: Jesus!

(GEORGE *swoops down, picks up the bunch of snapdragons, shakes them like a feather duster in* NICK's *face, and moves away a little.*)

GEORGE: HAH!

NICK: Damn you.

GEORGE (*to* NICK): Truth and illusion. Who knows the difference, eh, toots? Eh?

MARTHA: You were never in the Mediterranean . . . truth or illusion . . . either way.

GEORGE: If I wasn't in the Mediterranean, how did I get to the Aegean? Hunh?

MARTHA: OVERLAND!

NICK: Yeah!

GEORGE: Don't you side with her, houseboy.

NICK: I am not a houseboy.

GEORGE: Look! I know the game! You don't make it in the sack, you're a houseboy.

NICK: I AM NOT A HOUSEBOY!

GEORGE: No? Well then, you must have made it in the sack. Yes? (*He is breathing a little heavy; behaving a little manic.*) Yes? Someone's lying around here; somebody isn't playing the game straight. Yes? Come on; come on; who's lying? Martha? Come on!

NICK (*after a pause; to* MARTHA, *quietly with intense pleading*): Tell him I'm not a houseboy.

MARTHA (*after a pause, quietly, lowering her head*): No; you're not a houseboy.

GEORGE (*with great, sad relief*): So be it.

MARTHA (*pleading*): Truth and illusion, George; you don't know the difference.

GEORGE: No; but we must carry on as though we did.

MARTHA: Amen.

GEORGE (*flourishing the flowers*): SNAP WENT THE DRAGONS!!

(NICK *and* MARTHA *laugh weakly.*)

Hunh? Here we go round the mulberry bush, hunh?

NICK (*tenderly, to* MARTHA): Thank you.

MARTHA: Skip it.

GEORGE (*loud*): I said, here we go round the mulberry bush!

MARTHA (*impatiently*): Yeah, yeah; we know; snap go the dragons.

GEORGE (*taking a snapdragon, throwing it, spear-like, stemfirst at* MARTHA): SNAP!

MARTHA: Don't, George.

GEORGE (*throws another*): SNAP!

NICK: Don't do that.

GEORGE: Shut up, stud.

NICK: I'm not a stud!

GEORGE (*throws one at* NICK): SNAP! Then you're a houseboy. Which is it? Which are you? Hunh? Make up your mind. Either way. . . . (*Throws another at him.*) SNAP! *you disgust me.*

MARTHA: Does it matter to you, George!?

GEORGE (*throws one at her*): SNAP! No, actually, it doesn't. Either way . . . I've had it.

MARTHA: Stop throwing those goddamn things at me!

GEORGE: Either way. (*Throws another at her.*) SNAP!

NICK (*to* MARTHA): Do you want me to . . . do something to him?

MARTHA: You leave him alone!

GEORGE: If you're a houseboy, baby, you can pick up after me; if you're a stud, you can go protect your plow. Either way. Either way. . . . Everything.

NICK: Oh for God's. . . .

MARTHA (*a little afraid*): Truth or illusion, George. Doesn't it matter to you . . . at all?

GEORGE (*without throwing anything*): SNAP! (*Silence.*) You got your answer, baby?

MARTHA (*sadly*): Got it.

GEORGE: You just gird your blue-veined loins, girl. (*Sees* NICK *moving toward the hall.*) Now; we got one more game to play. And it's called Bringing Up Baby.

NICK (*more-or-less under his breath*): Oh, for Lord's sake. . . .

MARTHA: George. . . .

GEORGE: I don't want any fuss. (*To* NICK.) You don't want any scandal around here, do you, big boy? You don't want to wreck things, do you? Hunh? You want to keep to your timetable, don't you? Then sit! (NICK *sits.*) (*To* MARTHA.) And you, pretty Miss, you like fun and games, don't you? You're a sport from way back, aren't you?

MARTHA (*quietly, giving in*): All right, George; all right.

GEORGE (*seeing them both cowed; purrs*): Goooooooood; gooooood. (*Looks about him.*) But, we're not all here. (*Snaps his fingers a couple of times at* NICK.) You; you . . . uh . . . you; your little wifelet isn't here.

NICK: Look; she's had a rough night, now; she's in the can, and she's. . . .

GEORGE: Well, we can't play without everyone here. Now that's a fact. We gotta have your little wife. (*Hog-calls toward the hall.*) SOOOWWWIIIEEE!! SOOOWWWIIIEEE!!

NICK (*as* MARTHA *giggles nervously*): Cut that!

GEORGE (*swinging around, facing him*): Then get your butt out of that chair and bring the little dip back in here. (*As* NICK *does not move.*) Now be a good puppy. Fetch, good puppy, go fetch.

(NICK *rises, opens his mouth to say something, thinks better of it, exits.*)

One more game.

MARTHA (*after* NICK *goes*): I don't like what's going to happen.

GEORGE (*surprisingly tender*): Do you know what it is?

MARTHA (*pathetic*): No. But I don't like it.

GEORGE: Maybe you will, Martha.

MARTHA: No.

GEORGE: Oh, it's a real fun game, Martha.

MARTHA (*pleading*): No more games.

GEORGE (*quietly triumphant*): One more, Martha. One more game, and then bed-die-bye. Everybody pack up his tools and baggage and stuff and go home. And you and me, well, we gonna climb them well-worn stairs.

MARTHA (*almost in tears*): No, George; no.

GEORGE (*soothing*): Yes, baby.

MARTHA: No, George; please?

GEORGE: It'll all be done with before you know it.

MARTHA: No, George.

GEORGE: No climb stairs with Georgie?

MARTHA (*a sleepy child*): No more games . . . please. It's games I don't want. No more games.

GEORGE: Aw, sure you do, Martha . . . original game-girl and all, 'course you do.

MARTHA: Ugly games . . . ugly. And now this new one?

GEORGE (*stroking her hair*): You'll love it, baby.

MARTHA: No, George.

GEORGE: You'll have a ball.

MARTHA (*tenderly; moves to touch him*): Please, George, no more games; I. . . .

GEORGE (*slapping her moving hand with vehemence*): Don't you touch me! You keep your paws clean for the undergraduates!

MARTHA (*A cry of alarm, but faint.*)

GEORGE (*grabbing her hair, pulling her head back*): Now, you listen to me, Martha; you have had quite an evening . . . quite a night for yourself, and you can't just cut it off whenever you've got enough blood in your mouth. We are going on, and I'm going to have at you, and it's going to make your performance tonight look like an Easter pageant. Now I want you to get yourself a little alert. (*Slaps her lightly with his free hand.*) I want a little life in you, baby. (*Again.*)

MARTHA (*struggling*): Stop it!

GEORGE (*again*): Pull yourself together! (*Again.*) I want you on your feet and slug-ging, sweetheart, because I'm going to knock you around, and I want you up for it. (*Again; he pulls away, releases her; she rises.*)

MARTHA: All right, George. What do you want, George?

GEORGE: An equal battle, baby; that's all.

MARTHA: You'll get it!

GEORGE: I want you mad.

MARTHA: I'M MAD!!

GEORGE: Get madder!

MARTHA: DON'T WORRY ABOUT IT!

GEORGE: Good for you, girl; now, we're going to play this one to the death.

MARTHA: Yours!

GEORGE: You'd be surprised. Now, here come the tots; you be ready for this.

MARTHA (*she paces, actually looks a bit like a fighter*): I'm ready for you.

(NICK *and* HONEY *re-enter;* NICK *supporting* HONEY, *who still retains her brandy bottle and glass.*)

NICK (*unhappily*): Here we are.

HONEY (*cheerfully*): Hip, hop. Hip, hop.

NICK: You a bunny, Honey? (*She laughs greatly, sits.*)

HONEY: I'm a bunny, Honey.

GEORGE (*to* HONEY): Well, now; how's the bunny?

HONEY: Bunny funny! (*She laughs again.*)

NICK (*under his breath*): Jesus.

GEORGE: Bunny funny? Good for bunny!

MARTHA: Come on, George!

GEORGE (*to* MARTHA): Honey funny bunny! (HONEY *screams with laughter.*)

NICK: Jesus God. . . .

GEORGE (*slaps his hands together, once*): All right! Here we go! Last game! All sit. (NICK *sits.*) Sit down, Martha. This is a civilized game.

MARTHA (*cocks her fist, doesn't swing. Sits*): Just get on with it.

HONEY (*to* GEORGE): I've decided I don't remember anything. (*To* NICK.) Hello, Dear.

GEORGE: Hunh? What?

MARTHA: It's almost dawn, for God's sake. . . .

HONEY (*ibid*): I don't remember anything, and you don't remember anything, either. Hello, Dear.

GEORGE: You what?

HONEY (*ibid, an edge creeping into her voice*): You heard me, nothing. Hello, Dear.

GEORGE (*to* HONEY, *referring to* NICK): You do know that's your husband, there, don't you?

HONEY (*with great dignity*): Well, I certainly know *that.*

GEORGE (*close to* HONEY's *ear*): It's just some things you can't remember . . . hunh?

HONEY (*a great laugh to cover; then quietly, intensely to* GEORGE): *Don't* remember; not *can't.* (*At* NICK, *cheerfully.*) Hello, Dear.

GEORGE (*to* NICK): Well, speak to your little wifelet, your little bunny, for God's sake.

NICK (*softly, embarrassed*): Hello, Honey.

GEORGE: Awww, that was nice. I think we've been having a . . . a real good evening . . . all things considered. . . . We've sat around, and got to know each other, and had fun and games . . . curl-up-on-the-floor, for example. . . .

HONEY: . . . the tiles. . . .

GEORGE: . . . the tiles. . . . Snap the Dragon.

HONEY: . . . peel the label. . . .

GEORGE: . . . peel the . . . what?

MARTHA: Label. Peel the label.

HONEY (*apologetically, holding up her brandy bottle*): I peel labels.

GEORGE: We all peel labels, sweetie; and when you get through the skin, all three layers, through the muscle, slosh aside the organs (*an aside to* NICK) them which is still sloshable — (*back to* HONEY) and get down to bone . . . you know what you do then?

HONEY (*terribly interested*): No!

GEORGE: When you get down to bone, you haven't got all the way, yet. There's something inside the bone . . . the marrow . . . and that's what you gotta get at. (*A strange smile at* MARTHA.)

HONEY: Oh! I see.

GEORGE: The marrow. But bones are pretty resilient, especially in the young. Now, take our son. . . .

HONEY (*strangely*): Who?

GEORGE: Our son. . . . Martha's and my little joy!

NICK (*moving toward the bar*): Do you mind if I . . . ?

GEORGE: No, no; you go right ahead.

MARTHA: George. . . .

GEORGE (*too kindly*): Yes, Martha?

MARTHA: Just what are you doing?

GEORGE: Why love, I was talking about our son.

MARTHA: Don't.

GEORGE: Isn't Martha something? Here we are, on the eve of our boy's home-coming, the eve of his twenty-first birfday, the eve of his majority . . . and Martha says don't talk about him.

MARTHA: Just . . . don't.

GEORGE: But I want to, Martha! It's very important we talk about him. Now bunny and the . . . well, whichever he is . . . here don't know much about junior, and I think they should.

MARTHA: Just . . . don't.

GEORGE (*snapping his fingers at* NICK): You. Hey, you! You want to play Bringing Up Baby, don't you!

NICK (*hardly civil*): Were you snapping at me?

GEORGE: That's right. (*Instructing him.*) You want to hear about our bouncey boy.

NICK (*pause; then, shortly*): Yeah; sure.

GEORGE (*to* HONEY): And you, my dear? You want to hear about him, too, don't you?

HONEY (*pretending not to understand*): Whom?

GEORGE: Martha's and my son.

HONEY (*nervously*): Oh, you have a child?

(MARTHA *and* NICK *laugh uncomfortably.*)

GEORGE: Oh, indeed; do we ever! Do you want to talk about him, Martha, or shall I? Hunh?

MARTHA (*a smile that is a sneer*): Don't, George.

GEORGE: All rightie. Well, now; let's see. He's a nice kid, really, in spite of his home life; I mean, most kids'd grow up neurotic, what with Martha here carrying on the way she does: sleeping 'til four in the P.M., climbing all over the poor bastard, trying to break the bathroom door down to wash him in the tub when he's sixteen, dragging strangers into the house at all hours. . . .

MARTHA (*rising*): O.K. YOU!

GEORGE (*mock concern*): Martha!

MARTHA: That's enough!

GEORGE: Well, do you want to take over?

HONEY (*to* NICK): Why would anybody want to wash somebody who's sixteen years old?

NICK (*slamming his drink down*): Oh, for Christ's sake, Honey!

HONEY (*stage whisper*): Well, why?!

GEORGE: Because it's her baby-poo.

MARTHA: ALL RIGHT!! (*By rote; a kind of almost-tearful recitation.*) Our son. You want our son? You'll have it.

GEORGE: You want a drink, Martha?

MARTHA (*pathetically*): Yes.

NICK (*to* MARTHA *kindly*): We don't have to hear about it . . . if you don't want to.

GEORGE: Who says so? You in a position to set the rules around here?

NICK (*pause; tight-lipped*): No.

GEORGE: Good boy; you'll go far. All right, Martha; your recitation, please.

MARTHA (*from far away*): What, George?

GEORGE (*prompting*): "Our son. . . ."

MARTHA: All right. Our son. Our son was born in a September night, a night not unlike tonight, though tomorrow, and twenty . . . one . . . years ago.

GEORGE (*beginning of quiet asides*): You see? I told you.

MARTHA: It was an easy birth. . . .

GEORGE: Oh, Martha; no. You labored . . . how you labored.

MARTHA: It was an easy birth . . . once it had been . . . accepted, relaxed into.

GEORGE: Ah . . . yes. Better.

MARTHA: It was an easy birth, once it had been accepted, and I was young.

GEORGE: And I was younger. . . . (*Laughs quietly to himself.*)

MARTHA: And I was young, and he was a healthy child, a red, bawling child, with slippery firm limbs. . . .

GEORGE: . . . Martha thinks she saw him at delivery. . . .

MARTHA: . . . with slippery, firm limbs, and a full head of black, fine, fine hair which, oh, later, later, became blond as the sun, our son.

GEORGE: He was a healthy child.

MARTHA: And I had wanted a child . . . oh, I had wanted a child.

GEORGE (*prodding her*): A son? A daughter?

MARTHA: A child! (*Quieter.*) A child. And I had my child.

GEORGE: Our child.

MARTHA (*with great sadness*): Our child. And we raised him . . . (*laughs, briefly, bitterly*) yes, we did; we raised him. . . .

GEORGE: With teddy bears and an antique bassinet from Austria . . . and *no nurse.*

MARTHA: . . . with teddy bears and transparent floating goldfish, and a pale blue bed with cane at the headboard when he was older, cane which he wore through . . . finally . . . with his little hands . . . in his . . . sleep. . . .

GEORGE: . . . nightmares. . . .

MARTHA: . . . *sleep.* . . . He was a restless child. . . .

GEORGE: . . . (*Soft chuckle, head-shaking of disbelief.*) . . . Oh Lord . . .

MARTHA: . . . sleep . . . and a croup tent . . . a pale green croup tent, and the shining kettle hissing in the one light of the room that time he was sick . . . those four days . . . and animal crackers, and the bow and arrow he kept under his bed. . . .

GEORGE: . . . the arrows with rubber cups at their tip. . . .

MARTHA: . . . at their tip, which he kept beneath his bed. . . .

GEORGE: Why? Why, Martha?

MARTHA: . . . for fear . . . for fear of. . . .

GEORGE: For fear. Just that: for fear.

MARTHA (*vaguely waving him off; going on*): . . . and . . . and sandwiches on Sunday night, and Saturdays . . . (*pleased recollection*) . . . and Saturdays the banana boat, the whole peeled banana, scooped out on top, with green grapes for the crew, a double line of green grapes, and along the sides, stuck to the boat with toothpicks, orange slices. . . . SHIELDS.

GEORGE: And for the oar?

MARTHA (*uncertainly*): A . . . carrot?

GEORGE: Or a swizzle stick, whatever was easier.

MARTHA: No. A carrot. And his eyes were green . . . green with . . . if you peered so deep into them . . . so deep . . . bronze . . . bronze parentheses around the irises . . . such green eyes!

GEORGE: . . . blue, green, brown. . . .

MARTHA: . . . and he loved the sun! . . . He was tan before and after everyone . . . and in the sun his hair . . . became . . . fleece.

GEORGE (*echoing her*): . . . fleece. . . .

MARTHA: . . . beautiful, beautiful boy.

GEORGE: Absolve, Domine, animas omnium fidelium defunctorum ab omni vinculo delictorum.[1]

MARTHA: . . . and school . . . and summer camp . . . and sledding . . . and swimming. . . .

GEORGE: Et gratia tua illis succurrente, mereantur evadere judicium ultionis.[2]

MARTHA (*laughing, to herself*): . . . and how he broke his arm . . . how funny it was . . . oh, no, it hurt him! . . . but, oh, it was funny . . . in a field, his very first cow, the first he'd ever seen . . . and he went into the field, to the cow, where the cow was grazing, head down, busy . . . and he moo'd at it! (*Laughs, ibid.*) He moo'd at it . . . and the beast, oh, surprised, swung its head up and moo'd at him, all three years of him, and he ran, startled, and he stumbled . . . fell . . . and broke his poor arm. (*Laughs, ibid.*) Poor lamb.

GEORGE: Et lucis aeternae beatitudine perfrui.[3]

MARTHA: George cried! Helpless . . . George . . . cried. I carried the poor lamb. George snuffling beside me, I carried the child, having fashioned a sling . . . and across the great fields.

GEORGE: In Paradisum deducant te Angeli.[4]

MARTHA: And as he grew . . . and as he grew . . . oh! so wise! . . . he walked evenly between us . . . (*she spreads her hands*) . . . a hand out to each of us for what we could offer by way of support, affection, teaching, even love . . . and these hands, still, to hold us off a bit, for mutual protection, to protect us all from George's . . . weakness . . . and my . . . necessary greater strength . . . to protect himself . . . and *us*.

GEORGE: In memoria aeterna erit justus: ab auditione mala non timebit.[5]

MARTHA: So wise; so wise.

NICK (*to* GEORGE): What is this? What are you doing?

GEORGE: Shhhhh.

HONEY: Shhhhh.

NICK (*shrugging*): O.K.

---

[1] (Lat.) Absolve, O Lord, the souls of all the faithful departed from every bond of sin (here, as in all the Latin passages that follow, George is quoting from the "Masses for the Dead" in the Roman Catholic *Missal*)

[2] And by the help of Thy grace, let them be found worthy to escape the sentence of vengeance

[3] And to enjoy the full beatitude of the light eternal

[4] May the Angels lead thee into Paradise

[5] The just shall be in everlasting remembrance: he shall not fear the evil hearing

MARTHA: So beautiful; so wise.

GEORGE (*laughs quietly*): All truth being relative.

MARTHA: It was true! Beautiful; wise; perfect.

GEORGE: There's a real mother talking.

HONEY (*suddenly; almost tearfully*): I want a child.

NICK: Honey. . . .

HONEY (*more forcefully*): I want a child!

GEORGE: On principle?

HONEY (*in tears*): I want a child. I want a baby.

MARTHA (*waiting out the interruption, not really paying it any mind*): Of course, this state, this perfection . . . couldn't last. Not with George . . . not with George around.

GEORGE (*to the others*): There; you see? I knew she'd shift.

HONEY: Be still!

GEORGE (*mock awe*): Sorry . . . mother.

NICK: Can't you be still?

GEORGE (*making a sign at* NICK): Dominus vobiscum.[6]

MARTHA: Not with George around. A drowning man takes down those nearest. George tried, but, oh, God, how I fought him. God, how I fought him.

GEORGE (*a satisfied laugh*): Ahhhhhhh.

MARTHA: Lesser states can't stand those above them. Weakness, imperfection cries out against strength, goodness and innocence. And George tried.

GEORGE: How did I try, Martha? How did I try?

MARTHA: How did you . . . what? . . . No! No . . . he grew . . . our son grew . . . up; he is grown up; he is away at school, college. He is fine, everything is fine.

GEORGE (*mocking*): Oh, come on, Martha!

MARTHA: No. That's all.

GEORGE: Just a minute! You can't cut a story off like that, sweetheart. You started to say something . . . now you say it!

MARTHA: No!

GEORGE: Well, I will.

MARTHA: No!

GEORGE: You see, Martha, here, stops just when the going gets good . . . just when things start getting a little rough. Now, Martha, here, is a misunderstood little girl; she really is. Not only does she have a husband who is a bog . . . a younger-than-she-is bog albeit . . . not only does she have a husband who is a bog, she has as well a tiny problem with spiritous liquors — like she can't get enough. . . .

MARTHA (*without energy*): No more, George.

GEORGE: . . . and on top of all that, poor weighed-down girl, PLUS a father who really doesn't give a damn whether she lives or dies, who couldn't care less *what* happens to his only daughter . . . on top of all that she has a *son*. She has a son who fought her every inch of the way, who didn't want to be turned into a weapon against his father, who didn't want to be used as a goddamn club whenever Martha didn't get things like she wanted them!

MARTHA (*rising to it*): Lies! Lies!!

GEORGE: Lies? All right. A son who would *not* disown his father, who came to him for advice, for information, for love that wasn't mixed with sickness — and you

[6] The Lord be with you

know what I mean, Martha! — who could not tolerate the slashing, braying residue that called itself his MOTHER. MOTHER? HAH!!

MARTHA (*cold*): All right, you. A son who was so ashamed of his father he asked me
once if it — possibly — wasn't true, as he had heard, from some cruel boys,
maybe, that he was not our child; who could not tolerate the shabby failure his
father had become. . . .

GEORGE: Lies!

MARTHA: Lies? Who would not bring his girl friends to the house. . . .

GEORGE: . . . in shame of his mother. . . .

MARTHA: . . . of his father! Who writes letters only to me!

GEORGE: Oh, so you think! To me! At my office!

MARTHA: Liar!

GEORGE: I have a stack of them!

MARTHA: YOU HAVE NO LETTERS!

GEORGE: And you have?

MARTHA: He has no letters. A son . . . a son who spends his summers away . . .
away from his family . . . ON ANY PRETEXT . . . because he can't stand the
shadow of a man flickering around the edges of a house. . . .

GEORGE: . . . who spends his summers away . . . and he does! . . . who spends his
summers away because there isn't room for him in a house full of empty bottles,
lies, strange men, and a harridan who. . . .

MARTHA: Liar!!

GEORGE: Liar?

MARTHA: . . . A son who I have raised as best I can against . . . vicious odds,
against the corruption of weakness and petty revenges. . . .

GEORGE: . . . A son who is, deep in his gut, sorry to have been born. . . .

(*Both together.*)

MARTHA: I have tried, oh God I have tried; the one thing . . . the one thing I've tried to carry pure and un-scathed through the sewer of this marriage; through the sick nights, and the pathetic, stupid days, through the derision and the laugh-ter . . . *God*, the laughter, through one failure after another, one failure compounding another failure, each attempt more sickening, more numbing than the one before; the one thing, the one *person* I have tried to protect, to raise above the mire of this vile, crushing marriage; the one light in all this hopeless . . . *dark*ness . . . our SON.	GEORGE: Libera me, Domine, de morte aeterna, in die illa tremenda: Quando caeli movendi sunt et terra: Dum veneris judicare saeculum per ignem. Tremens factus sum ego, et timeo, dum discussio venerit, atque ventura ira. Quando caeli movendi sunt et terra. Dies illa, dies irae, cal-amitatis et miseriae; dies magna et amara valde. Dum veneris judicare saeculum per ignem. Requiem ae-ternam dona eis, Domine: et lux perpetua luceat eis. Libera me Domine de morte aeterna in die illa tremenda: quando caeli movendi sunt et terra; Dum veneris judicare saeculum per ignem.[7]

(*End together.*)

[7] Deliver me, O Lord, from eternal death on that dreadful day when the heavens and the
earth shall be moved, and Thou shalt come to judge the world by fire. I am seized with fear

HONEY (*her hands to her ears*): STOP IT!! STOP IT!!

GEORGE (*with a hand sign*): Kyrie, eleison. Christe, eleison. Kyrie, eleison.[8]

HONEY: JUST STOP IT!!

GEORGE: Why, baby? Don't you like it?

HONEY (*quite hysterical*): You . . . can't . . . do . . . this!

GEORGE (*triumphant*): Who says!

HONEY: I! Say!

GEORGE: Tell us why, baby.

HONEY: No!

NICK: Is this game over?

HONEY: Yes! Yes, it is.

GEORGE: Ho-ho! Not by a long shot. (*To* MARTHA.) We got a little surprise for you, baby. It's about sunny-Jim.

MARTHA: No more, George.

GEORGE: YES!

NICK: Leave her be!

GEORGE: I'M RUNNING THIS SHOW! (*To* MARTHA.) Sweetheart, I'm afraid I've got some bad news for you . . . for us, of course. Some rather sad news.

(HONEY *begins weeping, head in hands*.)

MARTHA (*afraid, suspicious*): What is this?

GEORGE (*oh, so patiently*): Well, Martha, while you were out of the room, while the . . . two of you were out of the room . . . I mean, I don't know where, hell, you both must have been somewhere. (*Little laugh*.) . . . While you were out of the room, for a while . . . well, Missey and I were sittin' here havin' a little talk, you know: a chaw and a talk . . . and the doorbell rang. . . .

HONEY (*head still in hands*): Chimed.

GEORGE: Chimed . . . and . . . well, it's hard to tell you, Martha. . . .

MARTHA (*a strange throaty voice*): Tell me.

HONEY: Please . . . don't.

MARTHA: Tell me.

GEORGE: . . . and . . . what it was . . . it was good old Western Union, some little boy about seventy.

MARTHA (*involved*): Crazy Billy?

GEORGE: Yes, Martha, that's right . . . crazy Billy . . . and he had a telegram, and it was for us, and I have to tell you about it.

MARTHA (*as if from a distance*): Why didn't they phone it? Why did they bring it; why didn't they telephone it?

GEORGE: Some telegrams you have to deliver, Martha; some telegrams you can't phone.

MARTHA (*rising*): What do you mean?

GEORGE: Martha. . . . I can hardly bring myself to say it. . . .

---

and trembling when I reflect upon the judgment and the wrath to come. When the heavens and the earth shall be moved. That day, a day of wrath, of wasting and of misery, a dreadful and exceeding bitter day. When Thou shalt come to judge the world by fire. Eternal rest grant unto them, O Lord, and let perpetual light shine upon them. Deliver me, O Lord, from eternal death on that dreadful day when the heavens and the earth shall be moved, and Thou shalt come to judge the world by fire

[8] Lord, have mercy. Christ, have mercy. Lord, have mercy

HONEY: Don't.

GEORGE (*to* HONEY): Do you want to do it?

HONEY (*defending herself against an attack of bees*): No no no no no.

GEORGE (*sighing heavily*): All right. Well, Martha . . . I'm afraid our boy isn't coming home for his birthday.

MARTHA: Of course he is.

GEORGE: No, Martha.

MARTHA: Of course he is. I say he is!

GEORGE: He . . . can't.

MARTHA: He is! I say so!

GEORGE: Martha . . . (*long pause*) . . . our son is . . . dead.

(*Silence.*)

He was . . . killed . . . late in the afternoon. . . .

(*Silence.*)

(*a tiny chuckle*) on a country road, with his learner's permit in his pocket, he swerved, to avoid a porcupine, and drove straight into a. . . .

MARTHA (*rigid fury*): YOU . . . CAN'T . . . DO . . . THAT!

GEORGE: . . . large tree.

MARTHA: YOU CANNOT DO THAT!

NICK (*softly*): Oh my God. (HONEY *is weeping louder.*)

GEORGE (*quietly, dispassionately*): I thought you should know.

NICK: Oh my God; no.

MARTHA (*quivering with rage and loss*): NO! NO! YOU CANNOT DO THAT! YOU CAN'T DECIDE THAT FOR YOURSELF! I WILL NOT LET YOU DO THAT!

GEORGE: We'll have to leave around noon, I suppose. . . .

MARTHA: I WILL NOT LET YOU DECIDE THESE THINGS!

GEORGE: . . . because there are matters of identification, naturally, and arrangements to be made. . . .

MARTHA (*leaping at* GEORGE, *but ineffectual*): YOU CAN'T DO THIS!

(NICK *rises, grabs hold of* MARTHA, *pins her arms behind her back.*)

I WON'T LET YOU DO THIS, GET YOUR HANDS OFF ME!

GEORGE (*as* NICK *holds on; right in* MARTHA'S *face*): You don't seem to understand, Martha; I haven't done anything. Now, pull yourself together. Our son is DEAD! Can you get that into your head?

MARTHA: YOU CAN'T DECIDE THESE THINGS.

NICK: Lady, please.

MARTHA: LET ME GO!

GEORGE: Now listen, Martha; listen carefully. We got a telegram; there was a car accident, and he's dead. POUF! Just like that! Now, how do you like it?

MARTHA (*a howl which weakens into a moan*): NOOOOOOOoooooo.

GEORGE (*to* NICK): Let her go. (MARTHA *slumps to the floor in a sitting position.*) She'll be all right now.

MARTHA (*pathetic*): No; no, he is *not* dead; he is not *dead*.

GEORGE: He is dead. Kyrie, eleison. Christe, eleison. Kyrie, eleison.

MARTHA: You can*not*. You may not decide these things.

NICK (*leaning over her; tenderly*): He hasn't decided anything, lady. It's not his doing. He doesn't have the power. . . .

GEORGE: That's right, Martha; I'm not a God. I don't have the power over life and death, do I?

MARTHA: YOU CAN'T KILL HIM! YOU CAN'T HAVE HIM DIE!

HONEY: Lady . . . please. . . .

MARTHA: YOU CAN'T!

GEORGE: There was a telegram, Martha.

MARTHA (*up; facing him*): Show it to me! Show me the telegram!

GEORGE (*long pause; then, with a straight face*): I ate it.

MARTHA (*a pause; then with the greatest disbelief possible, tinged with hysteria*): What did you just say to me?

GEORGE (*barely able to stop exploding with laughter*): I . . . ate . . . it.

(MARTHA *stares at him for a long moment, then spits in his face.*)

GEORGE (*with a smile*): Good for you, Martha.

NICK (*to* GEORGE): Do you think that's the way to treat her at a time like this? Making an ugly goddamn joke like that? Hunh?

GEORGE (*snapping his fingers at* HONEY): Did I eat the telegram or did I not?

HONEY (*terrified*): Yes; yes, you ate it. I watched . . . I watched you . . . you . . . you ate it all down.

GEORGE (*prompting*): . . . like a good boy.

HONEY: . . . like a . . . g-g-g-good . . . boy. Yes.

MARTHA (*to* GEORGE, *coldly*): You're not going to get away with this.

GEORGE (*with disgust*): YOU KNOW THE RULES, MARTHA! FOR CHRIST'S SAKE, YOU KNOW THE RULES!

MARTHA: NO!

NICK (*with the beginnings of a knowledge he cannot face*): What are you two talking about?

GEORGE: I can kill him, Martha, if I want to.

MARTHA: HE IS OUR CHILD!

GEORGE: Oh yes, and you bore him, and it was a good delivery. . . .

MARTHA: HE IS OUR CHILD!

GEORGE: AND I HAVE KILLED HIM!

MARTHA: NO!

GEORGE: YES!

(*Long silence.*)

NICK (*very quietly*): I think I understand this.

GEORGE (*ibid*): Do you?

NICK (*ibid*): Jesus Christ, I think I understand this.

GEORGE (*ibid*): Good for you, buster.

NICK (*violently*): JESUS CHRIST I THINK I UNDERSTAND THIS!

MARTHA (*great sadness and loss*): You have no right . . . you have no right at all. . . .

GEORGE (*tenderly*): I have the right, Martha. We never spoke of it; that's all. I could kill him any time I wanted to.

MARTHA: But why? Why?

GEORGE: You broke our rule, baby. You mentioned him . . . you mentioned him to someone else.

MARTHA (*tearfully*): I did *not*. I never did.

GEORGE: Yes, you did.

MARTHA: Who? WHO?

HONEY (*crying*): To me. You mentioned him to me.

MARTHA (*crying*): I FORGET! Sometimes . . . sometimes when it's night, when it's late, and . . . and everybody else is . . . talking . . . I forget and I . . . want to mention him . . . but I . . . HOLD ON . . . I hold on . . . but I've wanted to . . . so often . . . oh, George, you've *pushed* it . . . there was no need . . . there was no need for *this*. I *men*tioned him . . . all right . . . but you didn't have to push it over the EDGE. You didn't have to . . . kill him.

GEORGE: Requiescat in pace.[9]

HONEY: Amen.

MARTHA: You didn't have to have him die, George.

GEORGE: Requiem aeternam dona eis, Domine.[10]

HONEY: Et lux perpetua luceat eis.[11]

MARTHA: That wasn't . . . needed.

(*A long silence.*)

GEORGE (*softly*): It will be dawn soon. I think the party's over.

NICK (*to* GEORGE; *quietly*): You couldn't have . . . any?

GEORGE: We couldn't.

MARTHA (*a hint of communion in this*): We couldn't.

GEORGE (*to* NICK *and* HONEY): Home to bed, children; it's way past your bedtime.

NICK (*his hand out to* HONEY): Honey?

HONEY (*rising, moving to him*): Yes.

GEORGE: (MARTHA *is sitting on the floor by a chair now.*) You two go now.

NICK: Yes.

HONEY: Yes.

NICK: I'd like to. . . .

GEORGE: Good night.

NICK: (*Pause.*) Good night.

(NICK *and* HONEY *exit;* GEORGE *closes the door after them; looks around the room; sighs, picks up a glass or two, takes it to the bar. This whole last section very softly, very slowly.*)

GEORGE: Do you want anything, Martha?

MARTHA (*still looking away*): No . . . nothing.

GEORGE: All right. (*Pause.*) Time for bed.

MARTHA: Yes.

GEORGE: Are you tired?

MARTHA: Yes.

GEORGE: I am.

MARTHA: Yes.

GEORGE: Sunday tomorrow; all day.

MARTHA: Yes.

---

[9] May he rest in peace
[10] Eternal rest grant unto them, O Lord
[11] And let perpetual light shine upon them

(*A long silence between them.*)

Did you . . . did you . . . have to?
GEORGE (*pause*): Yes.
MARTHA: It was . . . ? You had to?
GEORGE (*pause*): Yes.
MARTHA: I don't know.
GEORGE: It was . . . time.
MARTHA: Was it?
GEORGE: Yes.
MARTHA (*pause*): I'm cold.
GEORGE: It's late.
MARTHA: Yes.
GEORGE (*long silence*): It will be better.
MARTHA (*long silence*): I don't . . . know.
GEORGE: It will be . . . maybe.
MARTHA: I'm . . . not . . . sure.
GEORGE: No.
MARTHA: Just . . . us?
GEORGE: Yes.
MARTHA: I don't suppose, maybe, we could. . . .
GEORGE: No, Martha.
MARTHA: Yes. No.
GEORGE: Are you all right?
MARTHA: Yes. No.
GEORGE (*puts his hand gently on her shoulder; she puts her head back and he sings to her, very softly*):

> Who's afraid of Virginia Woolf,
> Virginia Woolf,
> Virginia Woolf,

MARTHA: I . . . am . . . George. . . .
GEORGE: Who's afraid of Virginia Woolf. . . .
MARTHA: I . . . am . . . George. . . . I . . . am. . . .

(GEORGE *nods, slowly.*)

(*Silence; tableau.*)

CURTAIN

AFTERWORD

Who's Afraid of Virginia Woolf? is a very funny play, but it is also sad, painful, difficult, and of uncertain dramatic integrity. Its spectacle of the family living room as battleground and torture chamber is a match for Strindberg's *The Dance of Death* and O'Neill's *Long Day's Journey into Night,* and in sordid explicitness and brutality of language it leaves its predecessors far behind. But the verbal sharpshooting slows the dramatic movement, and a night of fun and games is an uneasy vehicle for a semiallegory of religious overtones and inconclusive outcome. There is a tension in the play between the raw realism of a domestic hell and the redemptive ritual that perhaps saves both the marriage and western civilization. Large, boisterous, loud, lusty, and ruthless, Martha fills the role of Earth Mother, for whom all men are flops, and George, as a critic has suggested, may be a Christ figure, because a number of his entries and exits are timed to coincide with somebody using "Jesus Christ" as a profanity. But the Earth Mother is a barren bitch and the Christ figure a cuckold and a child-killer. The imagery is charged, but it fails to make a coherent marriage myth. The imaginary child and the exorcism of it represent a reaching out for a meaning transcending naturalistic psychology, but one that the rest of the play can only doubtfully accommodate. "Hi-jinks and high seriousness fail to fuse," wrote Robert Brustein in his review in *The New Republic* after the Broadway opening in October, 1962. That is too curt a verdict on the structural tension in the play, but Brustein has a point. The tension may be calculated, but it threatens to pull the play apart.

We find the tension in individual scenes as well. There is a strain, not between two dramatic modes but between two motifs, in a little scene in Act II, but there is the same quality of mystifying "significance" as in the play as a whole. George is reading a book while his wife is upstairs making love to their guest. He comes to a sentence he reads aloud to himself: "And the west, encumbered by crippling alliances and burdened with a morality too rigid to accommodate itself to the swing of events, must . . . eventually . . . fall." Then in a fury he hurls the book away. No other scene more sharply focuses the George-Martha relationship and the "historical inevitability" motif that is the ideological issue between George and Nick. Nick is a bright and handsome young scientist on the make, an athlete with brains, "the wave of the future," with visions of a Brave New World managed by eugenicist-technocrats. George, graying and paunchy, is a middle-aged history professor and an academic failure, but a champion of traditional humanistic values and a believer in the "glorious unpredictability . . . the surprise, the multiplexity, the sea-changing rhythm of . . . history." The words he reads discount mankind's freedom to control events, the efficacy of moral will, and they prophesy the fall of what George has devoted his professional life to understand. Like Nick, the writer of the sentence is on the side of historical inevitability against George's affirmation of the "endeavor to make communicable sense out of natural order, morality out of the unnatural disorder of man's mind." George's fury, then, is paradoxically both the impotent rage of a man who identifies himself with a losing cause and a scholar's angry impatience with an untenable theory of history. Presumably, it is also an expression of the sexual jealousy he feels for Nick, whom he associates with the mechanistic thought of the passage. (There is a touch of vulgar and ignorant cliché in George's fear of what genetic science is up to these days.)

But how do the words he reads relate to his marriage? It is a "crippling alliance" in the sense that it has psychologically emasculated him, but what is "rigid" about the morality of an adulterous wife and a condoning husband? Do we react to the final game, "Bringing Up Baby," as a saving act of a flexible imagination because we feel that our entire cultural tradition is behind George's therapeutic game-playing? Does the exorcism vindicate George's values over Nick's by changing the predictable course of events in George's and Martha's marriage toward a final break or disaster, and by reestablishing it instead on their joint, humble acceptance of a difficult reality? And is this tentative redemption a parable of some vision Albee has of the spiritual crisis in our culture and its wished-for resolution? Is New Carthage, the academic community, moribund in its emotional and intellectual sterility — like its classical namesake, ripe for destruction? In an interview printed in the *Paris Review* in 1966, Albee said he chose the Christian names of George Washington and his wife for his two main characters because the play "contains an attempt to examine the success or failure of American revolutionary principles." This is elliptical, but Albee's point could be that the principles of self-determination, private property rights, and the right of the individual to "life, liberty, and the pursuit of happiness," for which the American Revolution was fought and which have made self-fulfillment the highest value in our national ethos, are incompatible with the virtues of tolerance, humility, and self-abnegation that make marriage viable. Are George and Martha the prototypal American couple? There is more than one reason why one hesitates to answer "yes."

The critical and popular success of the play raises other questions. Here is a play about two unattractive faculty couples having a three-and-a-half hour drunken orgy of obscene violence, playing a series of coarse games in provocation and retaliation. The object of the games is to hurt and humiliate others. In the last of the games an imaginary child is "killed" in Latin litany. The significance of all this is hidden in an abstruse highbrow joke involving Walt Disney's three little pigs and a British stream-of-consciousness novelist. What is the condition of the culture that hails such a play as "brilliant" and "crucial" and turns it into an international box office hit on stage and screen? What is the "nature" to which the play holds up a "mirror"? What fearful "form and pressure," shaping "the very age and body" of our time, does the mirror reflect?

We have a choice of answers, each reductive. We can say, with the member of the Pulitzer advisory board who vetoed the jury's nomination of the play for the 1962–63 award, that it is "a filthy play" and refuse to be the victims of some sardonic game of Alienate the Audience that Albee is playing for reasons of his own. We can go further and deplore the play's success, saying it proves that we have abandoned standards not just of good taste but of intellectual and dramatic coherence as well, that Hamlet's criteria for meaningful theater sadly no longer apply, and that we have arrived at the age of a theater of pointless cruelty. Or we can take its success as a sign that we have the courage to face ugly reality in our own lives

when we endure the spectacle of the sterile violence of love failed —
though cynics will ask whether we do, indeed, "endure" or are simply vulgarly amused. Many, no doubt, have gone to see *Who's Afraid of Virginia
Woolf?* in order to be shocked or titillated, or to derive some obscure comfort from observing a marriage worse than their own, or to be thought
broad-minded, or to keep up with the intelligentsia. Some have come away
offended or puzzled or pleased; others as from a vision of their own private
purgatory. The play poses questions that are not easily answered and raises
controversies in which one does not lightly choose sides. It is more easily
described than interpreted and evaluated. Whatever else it may mean, the
variety of responses suggests that *Who's Afraid of Virginia Woolf?*, like so
many other serious contemporary plays, resists classification by traditional
genres, and that modern drama is a drama of uncertain values, the true
mirror of a troubled age.

The form of the play is realistic in the sense that we are never required
to accept what we see and hear as happening anywhere else than in the
real world. The four characters engage in some unusual behavior and talk,
but their world is not some grotesque version of a familiar reality, like the
living room in *The American Dream*, one of Albee's early, one-act, absurdist parables. The authentic quality of the professorial home is so evident, in
fact, that the play has been faulted for not being the fair and accurate
picture of the domestic manners and mores of faculty families that the
realism of setting and language seems to imply it is. But the charge is beside the point. Albee is not trying to produce an unretouched picture of
academic married life as current sociological fact, and he is not telling the
story of what typically happens when a college professor and his wife invite
fellow guests from a dinner party over for a nightcap. His lines are marvel-
ously speakable, ranging in style from raw expletive and drunken inanity to
lonely eloquence and tired monosyllables, but the situation in which they
are spoken is so monotonously brutal and limited that their effect is not
primarily felt to be realistic. Rather, they represent speech that has been
tensed and heightened to aggressive gesture — words as weapons. And violent speech is just one of the play's several images of radical dislocations in
social relationships. People play vicious games of mutual insult and injury,
betray intimate confidences, throw and smash things, get drunk and sick,
leave the party they host, and make loveless love. The incessant and feverish hostility in word and deed in *Who's Afraid of Virginia Woolf?* functions
metaphorically like the surrealistic distortions of normal family relationships in *The American Dream*. Both plays express the reality behind the
bland decencies of conventional middle-class family life. Both contain social satire, but both go beyond satire. Compassion comes closer than contempt, than ridicule, than indignation, to define Albee's attitude toward his
characters.

That realism for its own sake was not Albee's goal is suggested by a comment he made in the *Paris Review* interview on the Mike Nichols screen

version of his play (with Elizabeth Taylor and Richard Burton). He liked the film very much, said Albee, though he felt it slighted the "intellectual" in favor of the "emotional level" of the play. But he did not approve of the film's roadhouse scenes. He did not elaborate on his opinion, but we can guess his reasons. In moving his cameras out of the living room set in the interest of movement and visual change and a broader social scene, Nichols weakened the claustrophobic effect of the play's single setting. The suggestion that George and Martha are trapped in their "dump" was lost in the film. In achieving an added dimension of realism, it frustrated a part of Albee's artistic intent.

Nor was that intent the searching anatomy of a sick marriage that Ibsen and Strindberg established as something of a dramatic subgenre in the closing years of the nineteenth century. Like the two Scandinavians, Albee takes for his subject the conflicts within and between the members of a small middle-class family, and, also like his predecessors, he reveals the origin of the conflicts in retrospective dialogue. Albee's foursome, however, are in various stages of drunkenness, and though the dialogue evidence of this could be said to be a realistic feature, it also means that the quality of their speech is different from that of Strindberg's and particularly Ibsen's characters. Most of it is spontaneous and freewheeling verbal infighting rather than coherent talk about topics and issues. It is vituperative rather than discursive. Except for the narratives in the games passages, it gives the impression, as dialogue never does in Ibsen and Srindberg, of drift rather than of directedness. Also, in older realism the past that is shown to be responsible for the present crisis is supposed to be true history, but George's and Martha's past is a mixture of fact and fantasy. The factual status of George's killing his parents remains ambiguous until the end, and when George "kills" his and Martha's child, he destroys an illusion that has been a reality of their life together. Neither of them has ever believed in the actual existence of the child — they are not psychotics — but their sharing a deliberate fantasy has given their marriage content. The parent game, like all their games, has been deadly serious.

Aeschylus's *Oresteia* began the tradition of domestic drama written on the premise that tensions in the intimate family group are the source of individual maladjustment. In modern times the premise has been reinforced by Freudian psychology. The central fact of the family situation in *Who's Afraid of Virginia Woolf?* is the absence of an actual child from the archetypal triad of husband/father, wife/mother, and child; or, more accurately, the central fact is the child's imaginary nature. This is neither Aeschylean nor Freudian nor Ibsenite, and it means that what is revealed about George's and Martha's relationship to their respective parents is less important as an explanation of the conditioning past than as a thematic image adjunctive to the imaginary child motif. Incest and adultery, child-killing and parent-killing, do not shape a plot but are metaphors for disruptions of the archetypal patterns of family life. Since Nick and Honey are also childless, the barrenness motif comes to represent a whole society's emotional climate. The gamesmanship that makes up social life in the play consists of aggressive responses to barrenness as literal and symbolic fact, and the end of the games is the end of illusion. Significantly, George's and Martha's child dies just before reaching maturity.

A final difference, then, between *Who's Afraid of Virginia Woolf?* and Ibsen's and Strindberg's family dramas is that the subject of Albee's play really is not either psychology or social realism. The play is not, like Ibsen's plays, about the subordination of the wife in bourgeois marriage, or neurotic sex, or the tragic consequences of a husband's choice of vocational over romantic and domestic values; nor does it, like Strindberg's plays, show marriage as a struggle between husband and wife for dominance. George's and Martha's strange and ambivalent relationship does not lend itself to close analysis, and to approach the play as if it were a diagnostic study of an unhappy marriage would be to miss just about every important meaning in it. The ritualization of violent emotion in games of truth and illusion is the real subject of Albee's play, and marriage is its vehicle because it institutionalizes human intimacy.

There is no way of refuting the charge that Albee's play is "filthy." The recent trend toward total permissiveness of speech and action on stage may have rendered the charge obsolete, but it has not made it meaningless. We have not abolished the concept of filthy art; we have begun to take such art seriously. The way to justify a play like *Who's Afraid of Virginia Woolf?* is to say that the drinking and the promiscuity, the obscenities and the profanities, are ways in which the characters are striking back at an existence of love denied and betrayed. A ritual is a formal act by which private emotion is made communal, and George and Martha achieve a kind of negative communion by taking turns as aggressor and victim, sadist and masochist, in elaborate games of mutual hurt, one of the rules of which is that a player can change the rules without telling the other. Instead of affection there is anger; instead of trust, cheating tricks. But their psychic violence establishes a bond of mutual understanding, even a kind of tenderness, between them. They stay together, because each needs the other as an assurance of his or her own identity. Their ritual of hatred is a form of coexistence. Martha needs George to hurt and to be hurt by, but she can make him "visible" only by turning him into a victim of her braying bitchiness, and George fondles his failures in her sight and invents past guilt in order to make himself available to attack. Victimization means existence, and for Martha the fact that George is there to listen to her saying "If you existed, I'd divorce you" means that she has a husband. Only when he is not there to hear can she afford to be sentimental about their relationship:

George who is out there somewhere in the dark. . . . George who is good to me, and whom I revile; who understands me, and whom I push off; who can make me laugh, and I choke it back in my throat; who can hold me at night, so that it's warm, and whom I will bite so there's blood; who keeps learning the games we play as quickly as I can change the rules; who can make me happy and I do not wish to be happy, and yes I do wish to be happy. George and Martha: sad, sad, sad.

Her verbal assaults are acts of love, pleas for love. The exact psychic process that accounts for this stalemated ambivalence of feeling is not explained, but it is put to work dramatically. Albee's profoundest insight in the play is that hatred can be a form of love, and that humiliation, betrayal, adultery, and violence can be efforts to reach another person in a genuine offering of self.

The ritualization of this action of psychological paradox is pervasive, though much of the time it is submerged in the texture of raucous colloquialism. It is most evident in three formal devices, the first of which Albee imposes on his play by authorial fiat, while the other two are the work of the characters. The first device is the sequence of act titles. "Fun and Games" is a self-explanatory piece of irony. "Walpurgisnacht" is the word for the witches' sabbath in popular German superstition and the title of a scene in Part I of Goethe's *Faust*, in which Faust and Mephisto indulge in a blasphemous sexual orgy with young and old witches. The action of "The Exorcism" is the laying to rest of the evil spirits aroused in "Walpurgisnacht." The spiritual action is descending in the first two acts; in the third it rises from the depths of the night of Walpurgis to a scene of forgiveness, reconciliation, acceptance, and tentative communion, as Sunday dawn follows the Night of Wrath and the two couples are left to work out their marital salvation.

Within this structure of acts is the sequence of the four games George and Martha play with each other and their two guests. The first two games are revelations that involve, directly or indirectly, the betrayal of secrets between husband and wife. The third game is adulterous love-making, ending in an act of uncompleted intercourse offstage. The fourth begins as a narrative of idyllic parental reminiscence, which gradually grows ugly and ominous and ends in the murder of the imaginary child. Of the three revelations in game one, "Humiliate the Host," the first two (the emblematic boxing match — "it's colored our whole life" — and the story of George's failure as his father-in-law's heir-apparent in the college power structure) are made in Act I. The third (the story of George's novel) is made in Act II. As "Humiliate the Host" is played in both of the first two acts, so "Bringing Up Baby," the fourth and final game, links the last two, for George gets the idea for it at the end of Act II and plays it in Act III. Honey's sickness in the end of Act I and in the middle and end of Act II is a motif that both ties the games together and provides breaks within and between them. The fact that she does not get sick after the fourth game in Act III suggests the restoration of health after George's session of violent therapy. The games are further linked by their alliterative names. Shifting roles in the games weave patterns of psychological action and reaction. In "Humiliate the Host" Martha is aggressor, George victim, and Nick and

Honey are passive spectator-listeners. In "Get the Guests" George is aggressor, Nick and Honey are victims, and Martha is spectator-listener. Martha and Nick play "Hump the Hostess" together, but George's attitude toward the initial stages of their love-making leaves it uncertain who is victim and who aggressor in this game, and Honey, off-stage, is not even aware that it is being played. George directs "Bringing Up Baby" against Martha, but the game involves Nick and Honey by analogy. The games occasion uses and abuses of language, and they dramatize the truth-illusion theme by demonstrating that in the games people play they become the roles they assume or are forced to assume: Social life is play-acting.

The third ritualizing device is the passage in counterpoint in the exorcism scene in Act III, when George intones the Latin phrases of the Roman Catholic Mass for the Dead against Martha's desperate assertion that their son has been the one pure thing "through the sewer of this marriage," the one thing raised above "the mire of this vile, crushing marriage." It is both a moving and a climactic passage. The beauty of Martha's illusion measures the enormity of her betrayal of her and George's secret child to strangers — she loses the child because she has exposed it — and the solemn Latin phrases sanctify George's act of exorcism, giving religious significance to the psychological rehabilitation it seeks to effect. The counterpoint motif is anticipated at the end of Act I, where it is tied to the verbal and musical leitmotiv of the joke about Virginia Woolf.

The exorcism is a form of the "guerilla warfare," the "internal subversion," which represents George's new tactics after "total war" has been declared between him and Martha. By facing her guilt of betrayal, Martha is "subverted" to accept the task George, practicing his profession as teacher, imposes on her — confronting "Virginia Woolf." * At the end of "Get the Guests," Nick had been forced to make a similar admission of guilty betrayal, and in "Bringing Up Baby" Honey is forced to recognize the truth about her hysterical pregnancy before her marriage and her self-induced barrenness afterward and brought to say she wants a child. The last words she and Nick say to one another before their final exit are "Yes. . . . Yes. . . . Yes." There is in this a hint of new life in more than one sense — as if the killing of the invented child in the older marriage may make possible the birth of a real child in the younger marriage.

The final tableau is of George cradling Martha's head as he softly sings

---

* In the *Paris Review* interview, Albee said he found the title of his play scrawled in soap on a mirror in a tavern toilet and decided to use it instead of his original title, "The Exorcism," because he felt it was the sort of allusive joke that intellectuals are likely to make and because it could suggest the meaning, "Who is afraid of living life without illusions?" Presumably, Virginia Woolf, the author of *Mrs. Dalloway*, *To the Lighthouse*, and other novels of journeys through an inner landscape, stands for a courageous and uncompromising realist of the spirit, a scrupulous recorder of the minutest movements of the mind, and, as a suicide in 1941, a rejector of the violence of a world at war. Of Disney's three little pigs, the two younger are foolish illusionists for thinking that their flimsy structures can stand up to the huffing and puffing of the big, bad wolf — they *ought* to be afraid of him — while their older brother, the bricklayer, is the stern and wise realist.

the reassuring words of the title song. Martha is tired and afraid; the night's journey has been long and hard. George understands her fears and perhaps shares them, and the words he sings may be foolish, but the tableau itself is that of calm after storm, of rest after battle, of a new promise after the past has been consigned to death. The litany has silenced both brawls and baby talk; and instead of the illusions that barrenness is life, hatred is love, and games are reality, there is the sad wisdom of resignation to uncertainty. "Truth and illusion, George," says Martha when she is on the brink of recognition at the end of Act III. "You don't know the difference."

GEORGE: No; but we must carry on as though we did.
MARTHA: Amen.

If her "Amen" is spoken in flippant disbelief, it is ironic. At the end, she must learn to live by George's formula, which gives dignity to and makes moral sense of a life lived in defiance of the process of historical inevitability.

Read thus (and this reading is not offered as final or exhaustive), the ending of Who's Afraid of Virginia Woolf? can be taken to signify a stage of new faith in Albee's development, though the content of the faith is not easily defined. But the ending here certainly departs from, if it does not negate, the nihilism of the short, absurdist plays that preceded Who's Afraid of Virginia Woolf? The exorcism of the child is a deliberate spiritual act, and it has consequences. It is an assertion of the moral will against surrendering either to the escapism of a cowardly imagination or to the automated paradise of perfected eugenics. It re-relates life to a supernatural dimension, the very existence of which is denied by the absurdist view of man as a solitary prisoner in a dark void. And as an act of ritual language used redemptively it transcends the breakdown in communication signaled by the incoherence, the nonreferential quality, and the dead stereotypes of absurdist dialogue. It seems to say that the human condition is as real as appearances suggest it is, and that, though painful, difficult, and indefinite, it is not hopeless. Small talk, profanity, verbal injury, and the Mass for the Dead are all part of the same, single world of discourse, within which alone human contact is possible.

Imamu Amiri Baraka

DUTCHMAN

FOREWORD

The black theater movement was slow to evolve in the United States. But even before black theater developed there were distinguished black performers. Ira Aldridge, in the nineteenth century, earned himself the title of the "African Roscius" and an international reputation in tragedy; he died en route to a command performance in Russia. Paul Robeson, in the twentieth century, established his *Othello* as the longest-running Shakespearean production to that date, and became known to a wider public through film. Eugene O'Neill, in *The Emperor Jones*, created a major role for a black actor. These, however, were the exceptions. The popular theater of the nineteenth century, which drew much of its humor from racial stereotypes, created no rewarding black roles, and it was not until the 1920s that the theater began to deal with specifically black situations. Within the last few decades plays by black playwrights, dealing with issues important to blacks, have made a growing impact on the American scene. Predictably, many of these works have been polemics. The conflict of race has provided some of the most bitter problem plays of our time.

CHARACTERS

CLAY, twenty-year-old Negro
LULA, thirty-year-old white woman
RIDERS OF COACH, white and black
YOUNG NEGRO
CONDUCTOR

In the flying underbelly of the city. Steaming hot, and summer on top, outside. Underground. The subway heaped in modern myth.

Opening scene is a man sitting in a subway seat, holding a magazine but looking vacantly just above its wilting pages. Occasionally he looks blankly toward the window on his right. Dim lights and darkness whistling by against the glass. (Or paste the lights, as admitted props, right on the subway windows. Have them move, even dim and flicker. But give the sense of speed. Also stations, whether the train is stopped or the glitter and activity of these stations merely flashes by the windows.)

The man is sitting alone. That is, only his seat is visible, though the rest of the car is outfitted as a complete subway car. But only his seat is shown. There might be, for a time, as the play begins, a loud scream of the actual train. And it can recur throughout the play, or continue on a lower key once the dialogue starts.

The train slows after a time, pulling to a brief stop at one of the stations. The man looks idly up, until he sees a woman's face staring at him through the window; when it realizes that the man has noticed the face, it begins very premeditatedly to smile. The man smiles too, for a moment, without a trace of self-consciousness. Almost an instinctive though undesirable response. Then a kind of awkwardness or embarrassment sets in, and the man makes to look away, is further embarrassed, so he brings back his eyes to where the face was, but by now the train is moving again, and the face would seem to be left behind by the way the man turns his head to look back through the other windows at the slowly fading platform. He smiles then; more comfortably confident, hoping perhaps that his memory of this brief encounter will be pleasant. And then he is idle again.

SCENE I

Train roars. Lights flash outside the windows.

LULA enters from the rear of the car in bright, skimpy summer clothes and sandals. She carries a net bag full of paper books, fruit, and other anonymous articles. She is wearing sunglasses, which she pushes up on her forehead from time to time. LULA is a tall, slender, beautiful woman with long red hair hanging straight down her back, wearing only loud lipstick in somebody's good taste. She is eating an apple, very daintily. Coming down the car toward CLAY.

She stops beside CLAY's seat and hangs languidly from the strap, still manag-

ing to eat the apple. It is apparent that she is going to sit in the seat next to
CLAY, *and that she is only waiting for him to notice her before she sits.*

    CLAY *sits as before, looking just beyond his magazine, now and again pulling
the magazine slowly back and forth in front of his face in a hopeless effort to fan
himself. Then he sees the woman hanging there beside him and he looks up into
her face, smiling quizzically.*

LULA: Hello.
CLAY: Uh, hi're you?
LULA: I'm going to sit down. . . . O.K.?
CLAY: Sure.
LULA (*swings down onto the seat, pushing her legs straight out as if she is very
    weary*): Oooof! Too much weight.
CLAY: Ha, doesn't look like much to me. (*Leaning back against the window, a little
    surprised and maybe stiff.*)
LULA: It's so anyway.

    (*And she moves her toes in the sandals, then pulls her right leg up on the left
knee, better to inspect the bottoms of the sandals and the back of her heel. She
appears for a second not to notice that* CLAY *is sitting next to her or that she has
spoken to him just a second before.* CLAY *looks at the magazine, then out the
black window. As he does this, she turns very quickly toward him.*)

Weren't you staring at me through the window?
CLAY (*wheeling around and very much stiffened*): What?
LULA: Weren't you staring at me through the window? At the last stop?
CLAY: Staring at you? What do you mean?
LULA: Don't you know what staring means?
CLAY: I saw you through the window . . . if that's what it means. I don't know if I
    was staring. Seems to me you were staring through the window at me.
LULA: I was. But only after I'd turned around and saw you staring through that
    window down in the vicinity of my ass and legs.
CLAY: Really?
LULA: Really. I guess you were just taking those idle potshots. Nothing else to do.
    Run your mind over people's flesh.
CLAY: Oh boy. Wow, now I admit I was looking in your direction. But the rest of
    that weight is yours.
LULA: I suppose.
CLAY: Staring through train windows is weird business. Much weirder than staring
    very sedately at abstract asses.
LULA: That's why I came looking through the window . . . so you'd have more than
    that to go on. I even smiled at you.
CLAY: That's right.
LULA: I even got into this train, going some other way than mine. Walked down the
    aisle . . . searching you out.
CLAY: Really? That's pretty funny.
LULA: That's pretty funny. . . . God, you're dull.
CLAY: Well, I'm sorry, lady, but I really wasn't prepared for party talk.
LULA: No, you're not. What are you prepared for? (*Wrapping the apple core in a
    Kleenex and dropping it on the floor.*)

CLAY (*takes her conversation as pure sex talk. He turns to confront her squarely with this idea*): I'm prepared for anything. How about you?

LULA (*laughing loudly and cutting it off abruptly*): What do you think you're doing?

CLAY: What?

LULA: You think I want to pick you up, get you to take me somewhere and screw me, huh?

CLAY: Is that the way I look?

LULA: You look like you been trying to grow a beard. That's exactly what you look like. You look like you live in New Jersey with your parents and are trying to grow a beard. That's what. You look like you've been reading Chinese poetry and drinking lukewarm sugarless tea. (*Laughs, uncrossing and recrossing her legs.*) You look like death eating a soda cracker.

CLAY (*cocking his head from one side to the other, embarrassed and trying to make some comeback, but also intrigued by what the woman is saying . . . even the sharp city coarseness of her voice, which is still a kind of gentle sidewalk throb*): Really? I look like all that?

LULA: Not all of it. (*She feigns a seriousness to cover an actual somber tone.*) I lie a lot. (*Smiling.*) It helps me control the world.

CLAY (*relieved and laughing louder than the humor*): Yeah, I bet.

LULA: But it's true, most of it, right? Jersey? Your bumpy neck?

CLAY: How'd you know all that? Huh? Really, I mean about Jersey . . . and even the beard. I met you before? You know Warren Enright?

LULA: You tried to make it with your sister when you were ten.

(CLAY *leans back hard against the back of the seat, his eyes opening now, still trying to look amused.*)

But I succeeded a few weeks ago. (*She starts to laugh again.*)

CLAY: What're you talking about? Warren tell you that? You're a friend of Georgia's?

LULA: I told you I lie. I don't know your sister. I don't know Warren Enright.

CLAY: You mean you're just picking these things out of the air?

LULA: Is Warren Enright a tall skinny black boy with a phony English accent?

CLAY: I figured you knew him.

LULA: But I don't. I just figured you would know somebody like that. (*Laughs.*)

CLAY: Yeah, yeah.

LULA: You're probably on your way to his house now.

CLAY: That's right.

LULA (*putting her hand on* CLAY's *closest knee, drawing it from the knee up to the thigh's hinge, then removing it, watching his face very closely, and continuing to laugh, perhaps more gently than before*): Dull, dull, dull. I bet you think I'm exciting.

CLAY: You're O.K.

LULA: Am I exciting you now?

CLAY: Right. That's not what's supposed to happen?

LULA: How do I know? (*She returns her hand, without moving it, then takes it away and plunges it in her bag to draw out an apple.*) You want this?

CLAY: Sure.

LULA (*she gets one out of the bag for herself*): Eating apples together is always the first step. Or walking up uninhabited Seventh Avenue in the twenties on weekends. (*Bites and giggles, glancing at* CLAY *and speaking in loose sing-song.*) Can get you involved . . . boy! Get us involved. Um-huh. (*Mock seriousness.*) Would you like to get involved with me, Mister Man?

CLAY (*trying to be as flippant as* LULA, *whacking happily at the apple*): Sure. Why not? A beautiful woman like you. Huh, I'd be a fool not to.

LULA: And I bet you're sure you know what you're talking about. (*Taking him a little roughly by the wrist, so he cannot eat the apple, then shaking the wrist.*) I bet you're sure of almost everything anybody ever asked you about . . . right? (*Shakes his wrist harder.*) Right?

CLAY: Yeah, right. . . . Wow, you're pretty strong, you know? Whatta you, a lady wrestler or something?

LULA: What's wrong with lady wrestlers? And don't answer because you never knew any. Huh. (*Cynically.*) That's for sure. They don't have any lady wrestlers in that part of Jersey. That's for sure.

CLAY: Hey, you still haven't told me how you know so much about me.

LULA: I told you I didn't know anything about *you* . . . you're a well-known type.

CLAY: Really?

LULA: Or at least I know the type very well. And your skinny English friend too.

CLAY: Anonymously?

LULA (*settles back in seat, single-mindedly finishing her apple and humming snatches of rhythm and blues song*): What?

CLAY: Without knowing us specifically?

LULA: Oh boy. (*Looking quickly at* CLAY.) What a face. You know, you could be a handsome man.

CLAY: I can't argue with you.

LULA (*vague, off-center response*): What?

CLAY (*raising his voice, thinking the train noise has drowned part of his sentence*): I can't argue with you.

LULA: My hair is turning gray. A gray hair for each year and type I've come through.

CLAY: Why do you want to sound so old?

LULA: But it's always gentle when it starts. (*Attention drifting.*) Hugged against tenements, day or night.

CLAY: What?

LULA (*refocusing*): Hey, why don't you take me to that party you're going to?

CLAY: You must be a friend of Warren's to know about the party.

LULA: Wouldn't you like to take me to the party? (*Imitates clinging vine.*) Oh, come on, ask me to your party.

CLAY: Of course I'll ask you to come with me to the party. And I'll bet you're a friend of Warren's.

LULA: Why not be a friend of Warren's? Why not? (*Taking his arm.*) Have you asked me yet?

CLAY: How can I ask you when I don't know your name?

LULA: Are you talking to my name?

CLAY: What is it, a secret?

LULA: I'm Lena the Hyena.

CLAY: The famous woman poet?

LULA: Poetess! The same!

CLAY: Well, you know so much about me . . . what's my name?

LULA: Morris the Hyena.

CLAY: The famous woman poet?

LULA: The same. (*Laughing and going into her bag.*) You want another apple?

CLAY: Can't make it, lady.. I only have to keep one doctor away a day.

LULA: I bet your name is . . . something like . . . uh, Gerald or Walter. Huh?

CLAY: God, no.

LULA: Lloyd, Norman? One of those hopeless colored names creeping out of New Jersey. Leonard? Gag. . . .

CLAY: Like Warren?

LULA: Definitely. Just exactly like Warren. Or Everett.

CLAY: Gag. . . .

LULA: Well, for sure, it's not Willie.

CLAY: It's Clay.

LULA: Clay? Really? Clay what?

CLAY: Take your pick. Jackson, Johnson, or Williams.

LULA: Oh, really? Good for you. But it's got to be Williams. You're too pretentious to be a Jackson or Johnson.

CLAY: Thass right.

LULA: But Clay's O.K.

CLAY: So's Lena.

LULA: It's Lula.

CLAY: Oh?

LULA: Lula the Hyena.

CLAY: Very good.

LULA (*starts laughing again*): Now you say to me, "Lula, Lula, why don't you go to this party with me tonight?" It's your turn, and let those be your lines.

CLAY: Lula, why don't you go to this party with me tonight, huh?

LULA: Say my name twice before you ask, and no huh's.

CLAY: Lula, Lula, why don't you go to this party with me tonight?

LULA: I'd like to go, Clay, but how can you ask me to go when you barely know me?

CLAY: That is strange, isn't it?

LULA: What kind of reaction is that? You're supposed to say, "Aw, come on, we'll get to know each other better at the party."

CLAY: That's pretty corny.

LULA: What are you into anyway? (*Looking at him half sullenly but still amused.*) What thing are you playing at, Mister? Mister Clay Williams? (*Grabs his thigh, up near the crotch.*) What are *you* thinking about?

CLAY: Watch it now, you're gonna excite me for real.

LULA (*taking her hand away and throwing her apple core through the window*): I bet. (*She slumps in the seat and is heavily silent.*)

CLAY: I thought you knew everything about me? What happened?

(LULA *looks at him, then looks slowly away, then over where the other aisle would be. Noise of the train. She reaches in her bag and pulls out one of the paper books. She puts it on her leg and thumbs the pages listlessly.* CLAY *cocks his head to see the title of the book. Noise of the train.* LULA *flips pages and her eyes drift. Both remain silent.*)

Are you going to the party with me, Lula?

LULA (*bored and not even looking*): I don't even know you.

CLAY: You said you know my type.

LULA (*strangely irritated*): Don't get smart with me, Buster. I know you like the palm of my hand.

CLAY: The one you eat the apples with?

LULA: Yeh. And the one I open doors late Saturday evening with. That's my door. Up at the top of the stairs. Five flights. Above a lot of Italians and lying Americans. And scrape carrots with. Also . . . (*looks at him*) the same hand I unbutton my dress with, or let my skirt fall down. Same hand. Lover.

CLAY: Are you angry about anything? Did I say something wrong?

LULA: Everything you say is wrong. (*Mock smile.*) That's what makes you so attractive. Ha. In that funnybook jacket with all the buttons. (*More animate, taking hold of his jacket.*) What've you got that jacket and tie on in all this heat for? And why're you wearing a jacket and tie like that? Did your people ever burn witches or start revolutions over the price of tea? Boy, those narrow-shoulder clothes come from a tradition you ought to feel oppressed by. A three-button suit. What right do you have to be wearing a three-button suit and striped tie? Your grandfather was a slave, he didn't go to Harvard.

CLAY: My grandfather was a night watchman.

LULA: And you went to a colored college where everybody thought they were Averell Harriman.

CLAY: All except me.

LULA: And who did you think you were? Who do you think you are now?

CLAY (*laughs as if to make light of the whole trend of the conversation*): Well, in college I thought I was Baudelaire. But I've slowed down since.

LULA: I bet you never once thought you were a black nigger.

(*Mock serious, then she howls with laughter.* CLAY *is stunned but after initial reaction, he quickly tries to appreciate the humor.* LULA *almost shrieks.*)

A black Baudelaire.

CLAY: That's right.

LULA: Boy, are you corny. I take back what I said before. Everything you say is not wrong. It's perfect. You should be on television.

CLAY: You act like you're on television already.

LULA: That's because I'm an actress.

CLAY: I thought so.

LULA: Well, you're wrong. I'm no actress. I told you I always lie. I'm nothing, honey, and don't you ever forget it. (*Lighter.*) Although my mother was a Communist. The only person in my family ever to amount to anything.

CLAY: My mother was a Republican.

LULA: And your father voted for the man rather than the party.

CLAY: Right!

LULA: Yea for him. Yea, yea for him.

CLAY: Yea!

LULA: And yea for America where he is free to vote for the mediocrity of his choice! Yea!

CLAY: Yea!

LULA: And yea for both your parents who even though they differ about so crucial a matter as the body politic still forged a union of love and sacrifice that was destined to flower at the birth of the noble Clay . . . what's your middle name?

CLAY: Clay.

LULA: A union of love and sacrifice that was destined to flower at the birth of the noble Clay Clay Williams. Yea! And most of all yea yea for you, Clay Clay. The Black Baudelaire! Yes! (*And with knifelike cynicism.*) My Christ. My Christ.

CLAY: Thank you, ma'am.

LULA: May the people accept you as a ghost of the future. And love you, that you might not kill them when you can.

CLAY: What?

LULA: You're a murderer, Clay, and you know it. (*Her voice darkening with significance.*) You know goddamn well what I mean.

CLAY: I do?

LULA: So we'll pretend the air is light and full of perfume.

CLAY (*sniffing at her blouse*): It is.

LULA: And we'll pretend the people cannot see you. That is, the citizens. And that you are free of your own history. And I am free of my history. We'll pretend that we are both anonymous beauties smashing along through the city's entrails. (*She yells as loud as she can.*) GROOVE!

BLACK

SCENE II

Scene is the same as before, though now there are other seats visible in the car. And throughout the scene other people get on the subway. There are maybe one or two seated in the car as the scene opens, though neither CLAY nor LULA notices them. CLAY's tie is open. LULA is hugging his arm.

CLAY: The party!

LULA: I know it'll be something good. You can come in with me, looking casual and significant. I'll be strange, haughty, and silent, and walk with long slow strides.

CLAY: Right.

LULA: When you get drunk, pat me once, very lovingly on the flanks, and I'll look at you cryptically, licking my lips.

CLAY: It sounds like something we can do.

LULA: You'll go around talking to young men about your mind, and to old men about your plans. If you meet a very close friend who is also with someone like me, we can stand together, sipping our drinks and exchanging codes of lust. The atmosphere will be slithering in love and half-love and very open moral decision.

CLAY: Great. Great.

LULA: And everyone will pretend they don't know your name, and then . . . (*she pauses heavily*) later, when they have to, they'll claim a friendship that denies your sterling character.

CLAY (*kissing her neck and fingers*): And then what?

LULA: Then? Well, then we'll go down the street, late night, eating apples and winding very deliberately toward my house.

CLAY: Deliberately?

LULA: I mean, we'll look in all the shopwindows, and make fun of the queers. Maybe we'll meet a Jewish Buddhist and flatten his conceits over some very pretentious coffee.

CLAY: In honor of whose God?

LULA: Mine.

CLAY: Who is . . . ?

LULA: Me . . . and you?

CLAY: A corporate Godhead.

LULA: Exactly. Exactly. (*Notices one of the other people entering.*)

CLAY: Go on with the chronicle. Then what happens to us?

LULA (*a mild depression, but she still makes her description triumphant and increasingly direct*): To my house, of course.

CLAY: Of course.

LULA: And up the narrow steps of the tenement.

CLAY: You live in a tenement?

LULA: Wouldn't live anywhere else. Reminds me specifically of my novel form of insanity.

CLAY: Up the tenement stairs.

LULA: And with my apple-eating hand I push open the door and lead you, my tender big-eyed prey, into my . . . God, what can I call it . . . into my hovel.

CLAY: Then what happens?

LULA: After the dancing and games, after the long drinks and long walks, the real fun begins.

CLAY: Ah, the real fun. (*Embarrassed, in spite of himself.*) Which is . . . ?

LULA (*laughs at him*): Real fun in the dark house. Hah! real fun in the dark house, high up above the street and the ignorant cowboys. I lead you in, holding your wet hand gently in my hand . . .

CLAY: Which is not wet?

LULA: Which is dry as ashes.

CLAY: And cold?

LULA: Don't think you'll get out of your responsibility that way. It's not cold at all. You Fascist! Into my dark living room. Where we'll sit and talk endlessly, endlessly.

CLAY: About what?

LULA: About what? About your manhood, what do you think? What do you think we've been talking about all this time?

CLAY: Well, I didn't know it was that. That's for sure. Every other thing in the world but that. (*Notices another person entering, looks quickly, almost involuntarily up and down the car, seeing the other people in the car.*) Hey, I didn't even notice when those people got on.

LULA: Yeah, I know.

CLAY: Man, this subway is slow.

LULA: Yeah, I know.

CLAY: Well, go on. We were talking about my manhood.

LULA: We still are. All the time.

CLAY: We were in your living room.

LULA: My dark living room. Talking endlessly.

CLAY: About my manhood.

LULA: I'll make you a map of it. Just as soon as we get to my house.

CLAY: Well, that's great.

LULA: One of the things we do while we talk. And screw.

CLAY (*trying to make his smile broader and less shaky*): We finally got there.

LULA: And you'll call my rooms black as a grave. You'll say, "This place is like Juliet's tomb."

CLAY (*laughs*): I might.

LULA: I know. You've probably said it before.

CLAY: And is that all? The whole grand tour?

LULA: Not all. You'll say to me very close to my face, many, many times, you'll say, even whisper, that you love me.

CLAY: Maybe I will.

LULA: And you'll be lying.

CLAY: I wouldn't lie about something like that.

LULA: Hah. It's the only kind of thing you will lie about. Especially if you think it'll keep me alive.

CLAY: Keep you alive? I don't understand.

LULA (*bursting out laughing, but too shrilly*): Don't understand? Well, don't look at me. It's the path I take, that's all. Where both feet take me when I set them down. One in front of the other.

CLAY: Morbid. Morbid. You sure you're not an actress? All that self-aggrandizement.

LULA: Well, I told you I wasn't an actress . . . but I also told you I lie all the time. Draw your own conclusions.

CLAY: Morbid. Morbid. You sure you're not an actress? All scribed? There's no more?

LULA: I've told you all I know. Or almost all.

CLAY: There's no funny parts?

LULA: I thought it was all funny.

CLAY: But you mean peculiar, not ha-ha.

LULA: You don't know what I mean.

CLAY: Well, tell me the almost part then. You said almost all. What else? I want the whole story.

LULA (*searching aimlessly through her bag. She begins to talk breathlessly, with a light and silly tone*): All stories are whole stories. All of 'em. Our whole story . . . nothing but change. How could things go on like that forever? Huh? (*Slaps him on the shoulder, begins finding things in her bag, taking them out and throwing them over her shoulder into the aisle.*) Except I do go on as I do. Apples and long walks with deathless intelligent lovers. But you mix it up. Look out the window, all the time. Turning pages. Change change change. Till, shit, I don't know you. Wouldn't, for that matter. You're too serious. I bet you're even too serious to be psychoanalyzed. Like all those Jewish poets from Yonkers, who leave their mothers looking for other mothers, or others' mothers, on whose baggy tits they lay their fumbling heads. Their poems are always funny, and all about sex.

CLAY: They sound great. Like movies.

LULA: But you change. (*Blankly.*) And things work on you till you hate them.

(*More people come into the train. They come closer to the couple, some of them not sitting, but swinging drearily on the straps, staring at the two with uncertain interest.*)

CLAY: Wow. All these people, so suddenly. They must all come from the same place.

LULA: Right. That they do.

CLAY: Oh? You know about them too?

LULA: Oh yeah. About them more than I know about you. Do they frighten you?

CLAY: Frighten me? Why should they frighten me?

LULA: 'Cause you're an escaped nigger.

CLAY: Yeah?

LULA: 'Cause you crawled through the wire and made tracks to my side.

CLAY: Wire?

LULA: Don't they have wire around plantations?

CLAY: You must be Jewish. All you can think about is wire. Plantations didn't have any wire. Plantations were big open whitewashed places like heaven, and everybody on 'em was grooved to be there. Just strummin' and hummin' all day.

LULA: Yes, yes.

CLAY: And that's how the blues was born.

LULA: Yes, yes. And that's how the blues was born. (*Begins to make up a song that becomes quickly hysterical. As she sings she rises from her seat, still throwing things out of her bag into the aisle, beginning a rhythmical shudder and twistlike wiggle, which she continues up and down the aisle, bumping into many of the standing people and tripping over the feet of those sitting. Each time she runs into a person she lets out a very vicious piece of profanity, wiggling and stepping all the time.*) And that's how the blues was born. Yes. Yes. Son of a bitch, get out of the way. Yes. Quack. Yes. Yes. And that's how the blues was born. Ten little niggers sitting on a limb, but none of them ever looked like him. (*Points to* CLAY, *returns toward the seat, with her hands extended for him to rise and dance with her.*) And that's how blues was born. Yes. Come on, Clay. Let's do the nasty. Rub bellies. Rub bellies.

CLAY (*waves his hands to refuse. He is embarrassed, but determined to get a kick out of the proceedings*): Hey, what was in those apples? Mirror, mirror on the wall, who's the fairest one of all? Snow White, baby, and don't you forget it.

LULA (*grabbing for his hands, which he draws away*): come on, Clay. Let's rub bellies on the train. The nasty. The nasty. Do the gritty grind, like your ol' rag-head mammy. Grind till you lose your mind. Shake it, shake it, shake it, shake it! OOOOweeee! Come on, Clay. Let's do the choo-choo train shuffle, the navel scratcher.

CLAY: Hey, you coming on like the lady who smoked up her grass skirt.

LULA (*becoming annoyed that he will not dance, and becoming more animated as if to embarrass him still further*): Come on, Clay . . . let's do the thing. Uhh! Uhh! Clay! Clay! You middle-class black bastard. Forget your social-working mother for a few seconds and let's knock stomachs. Clay, you liver-lipped white man. You would-be Christian. You ain't no nigger, you're just a dirty white man. Get up, Clay. Dance with me, Clay.

CLAY: Lula! Sit down, now. Be cool.

LULA (*mocking him, in wild dance*): Be cool. Be cool. That's all you know . . . shaking that wildroot cream-oil on your knotty head, jackets buttoning up to your chin, so full of white man's words. Christ. God. Get up and scream at these people. Like scream meaningless shit in these hopeless faces. (*She screams at people in train, still dancing.*) Red trains cough Jewish underwear for keeps! Expanding smells of silence. Gravy snot whistling like sea birds. Clay. Clay, you got to break out. Don't sit there dying the way they want you to die. Get up.

CLAY: Oh, sit the fuck down. (*He moves to restrain her.*) Sit down, goddamn it.

LULA (*twisting out of his reach*): Screw yourself, Uncle Tom. Thomas Woolly-Head. (*Begins to dance a kind of jig, mocking* CLAY *with loud forced humor.*) There is Uncle Tom . . . I mean, Uncle Thomas Woolly-Head. With old white matted mane. He hobbles on his wooden cane. Old Tom. Old Tom. Let the white man hump his ol' mama, and he jes' shuffle off in the woods and hide his gentle gray head. Ol' Thomas Woolly-Head.

(*Some of the other riders are laughing now. A drunk gets up and joins* LULA *in her dance, singing, as best he can, her "song."* CLAY *gets up out of his seat and visibly scans the faces of the other riders.*)

CLAY: Lula! Lula!

(*She is dancing and turning, still shouting as loud as she can. The drunk too is shouting, and waving his hands wildly.*)

Lula . . . you dumb bitch. Why don't you stop it? (*He rushes half stumbling from his seat, and grabs one of her flailing arms.*)

LULA: Let me go! You black son of a bitch. (*She struggles against him.*) Let me go! Help!

(CLAY *is dragging her towards her seat, and the drunk seeks to interfere. He grabs* CLAY *around the shoulders and begins wrestling with him.* CLAY *clubs the drunk to the floor without releasing* LULA, *who is still screaming.* CLAY *finally gets her to the seat and throws her into it.*)

CLAY: Now you shut the hell up. (*Grabbing her shoulders.*) Just shut up. You don't know what you're talking about. You don't know anything. So just keep your stupid mouth closed.

LULA: You're afraid of white people. And your father was. Uncle Tom Big Lip!

CLAY (*slaps her as hard as he can, across the mouth.* LULA's *head bangs against the back of the seat. When she raises it again,* CLAY *slaps her again*): Now shut up and let me talk.

(*He turns toward the other riders, some of whom are sitting on the edge of their seats. The drunk is on one knee, rubbing his head, and singing softly the same song. He shuts up too when he sees* CLAY *watching him. The others go back to newspapers or stare out the windows.*)

Shit, you don't have any sense, Lula, nor feelings either. I could murder you now. Such a tiny ugly throat. I could squeeze it flat, and watch you turn blue, on a humble. For dull kicks. And all these weak-faced ofays squatting around here, staring over their papers at me. Murder them too. Even if they expected it. That man there . . . (*Points to well-dressed man.*) I could rip that *Times* right out of his hand, as skinny and middle-classed as I am, I could rip that paper out of his hand and just as easily rip out his throat. It takes no great effort. For what? To kill you soft idiots? You don't understand anything but luxury.

LULA: You fool!

CLAY (*pushing her against the seat*): I'm not telling you again, Tallulah Bankhead! Luxury. In your face and your fingers. You telling me what I ought to do. (*Sudden scream frightening the whole coach.*) Well, don't! Don't you tell me anything! If I'm a middle-class fake white man . . . let me be. And let me be in the way I want. (*Through his teeth.*) I'll rip your lousy breasts off! Let me be who I feel like being. Uncle Tom. Thomas. Whoever. It's none of your business. You don't know anything except what's there for you to see. An act. Lies. Device. Not the pure heart, the pumping black heart. You don't ever know that. And I sit here, in this buttoned-up suit, to keep myself from cutting all your throats. I mean wantonly. You great liberated whore! you fuck some black man, and right away you're an expert on black people. What a lotta shit that is. The only thing you know is that you come if he bangs you hard enough. And that's all. The belly rub? You wanted to do the belly rub? Shit, you don't even know how. You don't know how. That ol' dipty-dip shit you do, rolling your ass like an elephant. That's not my kind of belly rub. Belly rub is not Queens. Belly rub is dark places, with big hats and overcoats held up with one arm. Belly rub hates you. Old bald-headed four-eyed ofays popping their fingers . . . and don't know yet what they're doing. They say, "I love Bessie Smith." And don't even understand that Bessie Smith is saying, "Kiss my ass, kiss my black unruly ass." Before love, suffering, desire, anything you can explain, she's saying, and very plainly, "Kiss my black ass." And if you don't know that, it's you that's doing the kissing.

Charlie Parker? Charlie Parker. All the hip white boys scream for Bird. And Bird saying, "Up your ass, feeble-minded ofay! Up your ass." And they sit there talking about the tortured genius of Charlie Parker. Bird would've played not a note of music if he just walked up to East Sixty-seventh Street and killed the first ten white people he saw. Not a note! And I'm the great would-be poet. Yes. That's right! Poet. Some kind of bastard literature . . . all it needs is a simple knife thrust. Just let me bleed you, you loud whore, and one poem vanished. A whole people of neurotics, struggling to keep from being sane. And the only thing that would cure the neurosis would be your murder. Simple as that. I mean if I murdered you, then other white people would begin to understand me. You understand? No. I guess not. If Bessie Smith had killed some white people she wouldn't have needed that music. She could have talked very straight and plain about the world. No metaphors. No grunts. No wiggles in the dark of her soul. Just straight two and two are four. Money. Power. Luxury. Like that. All of them. Crazy niggers turning their backs on sanity. When all it needs is that simple act. Murder. Just murder! Would make us all sane.

(*Suddenly weary.*) Ahhh. Shit. But who needs it? I'd rather be a fool. Insane. Safe with my words, and no deaths, and clean, hard thoughts, urging me to new conquests. My people's madness. Hah! That's a laugh. My people. They don't need me to claim them. They got legs and arms of their own. Personal insanities. Mirrors. They don't need all those words. They don't need any defense. But listen, though, one more thing. And you tell this to your father, who's probably the kind of man who needs to know at once. So he can plan ahead. Tell him not to preach so much rationalism and cold logic to these niggers. Let them alone. Let them sing curses at you in code and see your filth as simple lack of style. Don't make the mistake, through some irresponsible surge of Christian charity, of talking too much about the advantages of Western rationalism, or the great intellectual legacy of the white man, or maybe they'll begin to listen. And then, maybe one day, you'll find they actually do understand exactly what you are talking about, all these fantasy people. All these blues people. And on that day, as sure as shit, when you really believe you can "accept" them into your fold, as half-white trusties late of the subject peoples. With no more blues, except the very old ones, and not a watermelon in sight, the great missionary heart will have triumphed, and all of those ex-coons will be stand-up Western men, with eyes for clean hard useful lives, sober, pious and sane, and they'll murder you. They'll murder you, and have very rational explanations. Very much like your own. They'll cut your throats, and drag you out to the edge of your cities so the flesh can fall away from your bones, in sanitary isolation.

LULA (*her voice takes on a different, more businesslike quality*): I've heard enough.

CLAY (*reaching for his books*): I bet you have. I guess I better collect my stuff and get off this train. Looks like we won't be acting out that little pageant you outlined before.

LULA: No. We won't. You're right about that, at least. (*She turns to look quickly around the rest of the car.*) All right!

(*The others respond.*)

CLAY (*bending across the girl to retrieve his belongings*): Sorry, baby, I don't think we could make it.

(*As he is bending over her, the girl brings up a small knife and plunges it into* CLAY's *chest. Twice. He slumps across her knees, his mouth working stupidly.*)

LULA: Sorry is right. (*Turning to the others in the car who have already gotten up from their seats.*) Sorry is the rightest thing you've said. Get this man off me! Hurry, now!

(*The others come and drag* CLAY's *body down the aisle.*)

Open the door and throw his body out.

(*They throw him off.*)

And all of you get off at the next stop.

(LULA *busies herself straightening her things. Getting everything in order. She takes out a notebook and makes a quick scribbling note. Drops in in her bag. The train apparently stops and all the others get off, leaving her alone in the coach.*

Very soon a young Negro of about twenty comes into the coach, with a couple of books under his arm. He sits a few seats in back of LULA. *When he is seated she turns and gives him a long slow look. He looks up from his book and drops the book on his lap. Then an old Negro conductor comes into the car, doing a sort of restrained soft shoe, and half mumbling the words of some song. He looks at the young man, briefly, with a quick greeting.*)

CONDUCTOR: Hey, brother!
YOUNG MAN: Hey.

(*The conductor continues down the aisle with his little dance and the mumbled song. LULA turns to stare at him and follows his movements down the aisle. The conductor tips his hat when he reaches her seat, and continues out the car.*)

CURTAIN

AFTERWORD

The setting in *Dutchman* is "the subway heaped in modern myth," and its action is a brief, underground passage to violence, starting all over again as the play ends. In tough, bright, four-letter idiom, the two characters who virtually make up its cast articulate *the* social dialogue in America today. Part polemic, part anecdote, and part allegory, *Dutchman* is the most coherent and the most grimly powerful of Imamu Amiri Baraka's first four plays.

"My ideas," says Baraka, "revolve around the rotting and destruction of America, so I can't really expect anyone who is part of that to accept my ideas." The remark is depressing, for it automatically incriminates anyone who disagrees with his views. Argue, for example, that *Dutchman* is a defeatist play because it denies the viability of black-white dialogue, or that it only perpetuates attitudes of hatred, or that it oversimplifies the causes of racial conflict by assuming that all oppression is white and all whites oppressors, and you have immediately identified yourself with the forces of destruction and corruption. Discussion is deadlocked the moment it begins.

We should be and can be more discriminating than that about the play. Obviously, its "ideas" are a function of the fable about a black man and a white woman and their murderous sexual encounter on a New York subway train. But it is part of the tragedy of our current social situation that this kind of objective approach has become suspect or worse. We are so involved in our racial dilemma that polemics overwhelm the drama. There is a pressure on us to feel that only what the play *says* is important, not what it *is*. Whether this means that *Dutchman* will become dated once our racial tensions are resolved is unimportant today, an issue for some happier America of the future to decide. In the meantime, its social relevance is so appallingly urgent that to deal with it as a literary construct can only seem stupidly frivolous and *irrelevant*. When a house is on fire, the voice and the syntax in which the cry of alarm is raised don't matter. The only responsible way of discussing *Dutchman* is as a black assault on white attitudes toward race. It calls for social action, not for literary criticism. Never mind the art, pay attention to the anger. Time is running out.

But Baraka chose to express his anger in drama rather than in some other form. Presumably he did so because he "saw" his subject dramatically and because he hoped a play would reach a larger audience than an essay in a periodical. Whatever his reasons, he has written a play and not a sociological thesis. That Clay's name suggests pliability, that Lula is a seductive apple-eater who is and is not an actress, that much of their talk is about sex, that the setting is subterranean and moving at high speed, that the old Negro conductor calls the second young man "brother," and that the shape of the play is circular are the kind of things we should attend to if we want to find out what Baraka is saying. A polemical author does not with impunity decide to use representations of people and their conversation as a medium; that commits him. And if we inspect the commitments his dramatic art makes for him, we are not thereby removing his play to some serene area of esthetics, safely protected from the social crisis; we are sharing the playwright's vision of that crisis, and the vision is polemically more forceful — though it may not be easy to say exactly what we have been told — than an abstracted paraphrase of it in a militant essay. An irresponsible and irrelevant approach to *Dutchman* is one that ignores the stageable particulars of Baraka's dramatic imagination and makes a leap for the expected generalizations about black frustration and alienated belligerence. To reduce to stereotypes a play that is about victimization by conceptual and attitudinal stereotypes would be a sad as well as a dangerous paradox.

Clay and Lula meet under circumstances indistinguishable from a casual pickup for quick sex, but the sequel is less sordid and far more serious. The real subject of their edgy, flittering talk is, as Lula soon points out, Clay's manhood. The overt quality of tentative, mutual seduction is profoundly relevant, for anxieties about sex underlie much of the American mythology about race, and the question of Clay's manhood is a racial question. Clay and Lula are believable characters as strangers meeting accidentally, but they are also figures in a mythical enactment of the confrontation of blacks and whites. The significance of talk and action expands as the realism of the beginning yields to the ritual of the ending. Myth is a concretion in narration, epic or dramatic, of patterns of communal thought and feeling. It is the embodiment in imaginative form of abstracts that distinguish a large social unit (class, nation, culture, race) and control its life and ethos in subtle, sometimes subconscious, ways. *Dutchman* dramatizes the myth of black manhood in America. More specifically, and in Baraka's own words, it is about "the difficulty of becoming a man in America."

The archetypal action in this myth is role-playing, the deliberate assumption of identities. But the roles are only partly chosen. Lula stage-manages their play-acting, but her own roles, as well as Clay's, are also imposed by past interracial relationships. The most crucial game Lula wants to play is that of making believe that they are both free from their respective pasts.

And we'll pretend the people cannot see you. That is, the citizens. And that you are free of your own history. And I am free of my history. We'll pretend that we are both anonymous beauties smashing along through the city's entrails. (*She yells as loud as she can.*) GROOVE!

But, as Clay says just before he is killed, the "acting out the little pageant you outlined before" will not come off. Their history *does* hold them and halts the action.

To see exactly why the pageant fails involves a synopsis of Baraka's dialectical dialogue. Lula begins their encounter by casting Clay in the role he has already assumed and then mocking his performance. He is the young, middle-class Negro from the suburbs, socially respectable, intellectually ambitious, so anonymous in his trueness to type that Lula can invent facts about him and be right. She rehearses him, giving him lines to speak and gestures to make, in the role he is to play at the party they are going to. They are to be the emancipated, interracial couple, deliberately acting out the old subversive daydreams, flouting dark taboos: the white woman attracted to black virility, the black man cautiously eager for sex with a white woman.

When Clay seems to accept his assigned part in their pageant, Lula changes her tactics. Her game is not to seduce Clay but to challenge him to racial awareness. The arousal to sex is an arousal to black manhood. The roles she gives him to play are meant to confront him with the unreality of what he is trying to be. She denies him the right to the whiteness he presumes to because she wants him to be a "black nigger." She insults him in order to liberate him. She seeks to provoke him into rejecting a way of life and a set of values that are based on a tradition that is no tradition for him: "Boy, those narrow-shoulder clothes come from a tradition you ought to feel oppressed by. . . . Your grandfather was a slave, he didn't go to Harvard." The "black Baudelaire" is a grotesque. By mimicking middle-class white ways Clay has become the "ghost of the future," for the integrated pseudo-white is dead even before he has become what he is trying to become. Clay ought to be the "murderer" his people's past entitles him to be; he ought to act out the suppressed violence of the outraged. Till he accepts his blackness in proud and free defiance, she can see him only as an "escaped nigger" who has "crawled through the wire and made tracks to my side." In Scene II, she offers him the role that is his by right: that of the uninhibited and joyous sensualist who dares to join her in her aisle dance, defying social convention. When he hesitates, she taunts him again. "You ain't no nigger, you're just a dirty white man. Get up, Clay. Dance with me, Clay. . . . Get up and scream at these people. . . . Clay, you got to break out. Don't sit there dying the way they want you to die. Get up." When he doesn't, she calls him an Uncle Tom — silly, scared, submissive, smiling, harmless. She rejects him for rejecting the visibility she holds out to him.

But Lula has got Negro history wrong. Clay's grandfather happened to be a night watchman, not a slave, and there were no wires around Southern plantations. She is extrapolating from white images of evil tyranny, as if the evil of slavery was Hitler's evil and not hers. Trapped in the white history she wants to atone for, she needs to believe she understands black psychology. By redeeming his own past on terms she prescribes, Clay is to redeem hers.

In his long answering monologue, Clay makes two points. The first is that blacks are already beyond being the "murderers" she wants them to be. What whites treasure in black culture — everything denoted by "the blues" — is only an alternative to warfare, and so is the black aping of white ways. Blacks already know they are "fantasy people." They are veteran actors, and Lula's coaching is naive presumption. "I sit here," Clay tells her, "in this buttoned-up suit, to keep myself from cutting all your throats." Whether blues-singers or pseudo-white suburbanites, blacks are "a whole people of neurotics, struggling to keep from being sane. . . . Murder! Just murder. Would make us all sane." Clay's second point is that if white liberals keep preaching "rationalism and cold logic" to the blacks, urging them to rise in the name of "the great intellectual legacy" of Western culture, they may find that their pupils have learned their lesson too well. For the logic of that legacy, the lesson of history, is that revolution follows oppression and oppression follows revolution in an endless cycle.

So leave us alone, says Clay. In your own interest, let us continue in our phony mimicry of whiteness, if that is what we opt for. Let us remain as neurotic blues people or as sex maniacs or Uncle Toms or noble militants against a past which you well-meaning whites join us in repudiating because of what it has done to us. The alternative is murder, for hatred is the core of blackness in white America. The old soft-shoeing conductor at the end is engaged in the same subterfuge as other blacks who choose roles in struggling against the sanity of violence. That is why he can greet the young Negro as "brother," though the latter is an intellectual and he is just a menial. "You telling me what I ought to do," says Clay to Lula. ". . . Well, don't! Don't you tell me anything! If I'm a middle-class fake white man . . . let me be. And let me be in the way I want."

Clay's and Lula's "little pageant" ends in murder because Clay refuses to submit to the sexual and ideological seduction she tempts him with. To succumb to the temptation would amount to a fall not from innocence, certainly, but from an experience of American life that at least leaves him the dignity of having a choice of roles. At the end of his tirade, Lula has realized that no dialogue is possible across the gap that separates black and white, and she kills him not so much in fear or hatred, perhaps, as in sheer frustration. The terrible logic of the play compels the conclusion that there is no way to mutual understanding, for Lula is not a bigoted racist or a condescending sentimentalist or an officious assimilationist. She is hard-headed, clever, attractive, and liberal. There is tenderness behind her toughness, a yearning for union: "Dance with me, Clay." If *she* fails, who can hope to succeed?

Like other successful allegories, *Dutchman* is open to other interpretations, though hardly to one that does not recognize the absolute impasse of the ending. Like other modern dramatists Baraka is much less interested in accounting for human behavior than in showing it; Clay and Lula are in the play to articulate their feelings, not to reveal their reasons for being pawns in a plot. And so it isn't really very much to the point to ask if Lula is part of a conspiracy involving both whites and blacks (there are blacks among the passengers who help her get rid of Clay's body) to provoke intransigent blacks like Clay to violence in order to justify murdering them. It is more meaningful to ask if Clay's attitude of sly pliancy is meant to represent a passive response to the black struggle for self-fulfillment and if the play is saying that his kind must be eliminated before the struggle can be won. That is, is Clay Baraka's hero, or is he the villain? And is Lula the villainess, trying to shape Clay into what, in her bitchy sexiness, she wants him to be, or is she, like Clay, the victim of the racial impasse? These, it could be argued, are genuine ambiguities in the play, but rather than muddling its meaning they darken the problem it poses. That Baraka offers no solution is another reason why the play should not be taken to be simple propaganda or polemics. It is, instead, a frightening image of social conflict in play form.

It is also, perhaps, a prophecy. In legend, the Flying Dutchman was a skipper who, frustrated by head winds in his efforts to round Cape Horn, swore he would keep trying even if it took him all eternity. He was punished for his blasphemy by being taken at his word. His doom is to sail through storms forever, on a ship manned by a crew of dead men who obey his orders but never speak. Superstitious sailors used to say that seeing the Flying Dutchman was an omen of disaster. The analogy between legend and play does not work out as a set of one-to-one correspondences,* but the subway train, like the legendary ship, keeps journeying on, and the spectacle of violence mutely accepted is an omen of things to come that are already on the point of becoming reality.

---

* But some such correspondences may be suggested. Lula, like the Dutch skipper, is engaged in a futile effort. Today's racial turbulence is the "storm" we are all traveling through toward an uncertain destination. Lula's "crew" are the mute passengers who throw Clay's body off the train on her order. The subway trip with its recurrent violence is "cursed."

Peter Weiss

The Persecution and Assassination of

JEAN-PAUL MARAT

as Performed by the Inmates of the Asylum of Charenton
under the Direction of

THE MARQUIS DE SADE

English Version by Geoffrey Skelton
Verse Adaptation by Adrian Mitchell

FOREWORD

Changing concepts of the drama have revised the actor-audience relationship. An audience watching *Major Barbara* or *Death of a Salesman*,
however strong its emotional or intellectual involvement, is still physically
detached; it observes an action performed at some remove, in a contained
space. With Brecht, the case is clearly different. In *The Caucasian Chalk
Circle* the audience is addressed directly and asked to function, not as a
group of passive spectators, but as a tribunal. Post-Brechtian drama has
moved more strongly in this direction. The barrier of the proscenium arch
has been broken down, physically or metaphorically. New stage forms set
performers among the audience or surround the audience with action. In
such experiments as the "living theater" the audience may be asked to contribute physically to the action. *Marat/Sade* must be read in the context of
this new staging, for the "theater of cruelty" insists that the audience must
not be *permitted* to remain impassive. It must be involved by violent assaults on its senses, and sometimes on its person. It must be exposed to
scenes calculated to provoke cries of horror and disgust. It must become a
contributing factor in the performance. In *Marat/Sade* this closely interlocking relationship causes us to examine our own sanity.

For performers, this change of relationship has created new demands
and responsibilities. They may often be asked to improvise, to react spon-
taneously to an audience response. Even in a play with a closely articulated
text, they may create their roles on an improvisatory basis, using the text

not as a starting-point but as a destination. The director's function has changed correspondingly. No longer does he or she come to the first rehearsal with the whole production mapped out. Rather, the task is now to channel what the actors' and actresses' instincts create. In this kind of free-flow situation, the director suggests and encourages, but does not dictate.

CHARACTERS

MARQUIS DE SADE, Sixty-eight years old, extremely corpulent, grey hair, smooth complexion. He moves heavily, breathes at times with difficulty, as if asthmatic. His clothing is of good quality, but worn. He is wearing white breeches with bows, a wide-sleeved white shirt with ornamental front and lace cuffs and white buckled shoes.

JEAN-PAUL MARAT, In his fiftieth year, suffering from a skin disease. He is draped in a white cloth and has a white bandage round his temples.

SIMONNE EVRARD, Marat's mistress, of indeterminate age. The player of the role is wearing a hospital uniform, with an apron and a headcloth. Her posture is crooked, her movements odd and constrained. When she has nothing to do, she stands wringing a cloth in her hands. She seizes every opportunity to change Marat's bandage.

CHARLOTTE CORDAY, Aged twenty-four.

Her clothing consists of a thin white blouse of Empire cut. The blouse does not conceal the bosom, but she wears a flimsy white cloth over it. Her long auburn hair hangs down on the right side of her neck. She wears pink leather boots with high heels, and when she is "on stage" a ribboned hat is tied to her. She is attended throughout by two Sisters, who support her, comb her hair and arrange her clothes. She moves like a somnambulist.

DUPERRET, Girondist Deputy. The player of the role wears, in addition to his hospital shirt, a short waistcoat and the smooth tight trousers of an "Incroyable." His clothing is also white, with some ornamentation. He is held in the mental home as an erotomaniac, and takes advantage of his role as Corday's lover at every suitable opportunity.

JACQUES ROUX, Former priest, radical

Socialist. He wears a white hospital shirt with an overall shaped like a monk's robe. The sleeves of his shirt are tied together in front of him over his hands, and he can move only in the limits of this straitjacket.

THE FOUR SINGERS: KOKOL, Bass; POL-POCH, Baritone; CUCURUCU, Tenor; ROSSIGNOL, Soprano. Part crowd types, part comedians. They have decked out their hospital uniforms with grotesque bits of costume and wear the cap of the Revolution. Rossignol, with her tricolour sash and sabre, represents the figure of Marianne. They have singing voices and perform in mime.

PATIENTS, As extras, voices, mimes and chorus. According to need they appear either in their white hospital uniforms or in primitive costumes with strong colour contrasts. Any not required in the play devote themselves to physical exercises. Their presence must set the atmosphere behind the acting area. They make habitual movements, turn in circles, hop, mutter to themselves, wail, scream and so on.

HERALD, Wears a harlequin smock over his hospital shirt. His two-pointed cap is hung with bells and spangles. He is draped with numerous instruments with which he can make a noise as necessary.

He holds in his hand a beribboned staff.

FIVE MUSICIANS, Inmates of the mental home, clad in white. They play harmonium, lute, flute, trumpet and drums.

MALE NURSES, In light grey uniforms with long white aprons which give them the appearance of butchers. They carry batons in the pockets of their aprons.

SISTERS, Also dressed in light grey, with long white aprons, starched collars and large white bonnets. They carry rosaries. The Sisters are played by athletic-looking men.

COULMIER, Director of the mental home, in elegant light grey clothing, with coat and top hat. He wears pince-nez and carries a walking stick. He likes to adopt a Napoleonic pose.

COULMIER'S WIFE and DAUGHTER, Form a composite pattern of colour from pale mauve to pearl grey, sprinkled with jewels and glittering silver.

ACT I

The asylum bell rings behind the stage. The curtain rises.

1. ASSEMBLY

The stage shows the bath hall of the asylum. To right and left bathtubs and showers. Against the back wall a many-tiered platform with benches and massage tables. In the middle area of the stage benches are placed for the actors, sisters and male nurses. The walls are covered with white tiles to a height of about ten feet. There are window openings high up in the side walls. There is a metal framework in front of the platform and around the baths at the sides. Curtains are fixed to each side of the framework before the platform and these can be pulled when the patients are to be hidden. Front stage centre there is a circular arena. To the right of it a dais for MARAT's bath, to the left a dais for SADE's chair. Left front a raised tribunal for COULMIER and his FAMILY. On another tribunal right front the musicians stand ready.

SADE *is occupied with last-minute preparations for the entry of the actors.*

The MALE NURSES *are completing a few routine operations of bathing and massage.* PATIENTS *are sitting or lying on the platform at the back.*

SADE *gives a sign. Through a side door at right back the actors enter, led by* COULMIER *and his* FAMILY *and escorted by* SISTERS *and* MALE NURSES.

The PATIENTS *rise to their feet. The ceremonious procession comes forward. The asylum bell is still tolling.*

MARAT, *wrapped in a white sheet and accompanied by* SIMONNE, *is led to the bath.* CORDAY, *sunk into herself, is taken to a bench by two* SISTERS.

DUPERRET, ROUX *and the* FOUR SINGERS *take up their positions as* COULMIER *reaches the stage. The* HERALD *stands in the middle of the stage.* SADE *stands near his raised chair. The tolling of the bell ceases. The procession moves towards the acting area.*

COULMIER *enters the acting area.*

The PATIENTS *in the background stand tensely. One of them adopts an eccentric pose, another comes slowly forward with outstretched arms.*

FANFARE

2. PROLOGUE

COULMIER: As Director of the Clinic of Charenton
  I would like to welcome you to this salon
  To one of our residents a vote
  of thanks is due Monsieur de Sade who wrote
  and has produced this play for your delectation   5
  and for our patients' rehabilitation
  We ask your kindly indulgence for
  a cast never on stage before
  coming to Charenton But each inmate
  I can assure you will try to pull his weight   10
  We're modern enlightened and we don't agree
  with locking up patients We prefer therapy
  through education and especially art
  so that our hospital may play its part
  faithfully following according to our lights   15
  the Declaration of Human Rights
  I agree with our author Monsieur de Sade
  that his play set in our modern bath house won't be marred
  by all these instruments for mental and physical hygiene
  Quite on the contrary they set the scene   20
  For in Monsieur de Sade's play he has tried
  to show how Jean-Paul Marat died
  and how he waited in his bath before
  Charlotte Corday came knocking at his door

3. PREPARATION

HERALD *knocks three times with his staff and gives the* ORCHESTRA *a sign. Ceremonious music begins.* COULMIER *moves to his* FAMILY. SADE *mounts his dais.* MARAT *is placed in his bath.* SIMONNE *puts his bandage straight. The* SISTERS *arrange* CORDAY's *costume. The* GROUP *assumes the pose of a heroic tableau.*

4. PRESENTATION

The music stops. HERALD *knocks three times with his staff.*

HERALD: Already seated in his place
    here is Marat observe his face

(*points his staff at* MARAT)

Fifty years old and not yet dead
he wears a bandage around his head

(*points staff at bandage*)

His flesh burns it is yellow as cheese   5

(*points at his neck*)

because disfigured by a skin disease
And only water cooling every limb

(*points to bath*)

prevents his fever from consuming him

(MARAT *takes his pen and begins to write.*)

To act this most important role we chose
a lucky paranoiac one of those   10
who've made unprecedented strides since we
introduced them to hydrotherapy.
The lady who is acting as his nurse

(*points at* SIMONNE. *She bends with a jerky movement over* MARAT, *loosens his bandage and puts on a new one.*)

whose touch certainly makes him no worse
is Simonne Evrard not Charlotte Corday   15
Marat and Evrard united one day
They shared one vision of the just and true
and furthermore they shared her money too
Here's Charlotte Corday waiting for her entry

(*points to* CORDAY *who smooths her clothes and ties her neckcloth*)

She comes from Caen her family landed gentry   20
Her dress is pretty shoes chic and you'll note
she readjusts the cloth around her throat

(*points at it.* CORDAY *adjusts it.*)

Historians agree so it's not lewd in us
to say that she's phenomenally pulchritudinous

(She draws herself up.)

Unfortunately the girl who plays the role here   25
has sleeping sickness also melancholia
Our hope must be for this afflicted soul

(With closed eyes, she inclines her head far backwards.)

that she does not forget her role

(with emphasis, turning to CORDAY*)*

Ah here comes Monsieur Duperret

(indicates DUPERRET*)*

with silken hose and fresh toupee   30
To the Revolution's murderous insanity
he brings a touch of high urbanity
Though as a well-known Girondist
his name's upon Marat's black list
he's handsome cheerful full of zest   35
and needs more watching than the rest

*(*DUPERRET *approaches* CORDAY, *pawing her furtively. The* HERALD *raps him on the hand with his staff. A* SISTER *pulls back* DUPERRET.)*

Jailed for taking a radical view
of anything you can name the former priest Jacques Roux

(indicates ROUX *who pushes out his elbows and raises his head)*

Ally of Marat's revolution but
unfortunately the censor's cut
most of his rabble-rousing theme   40
Our moral guardians found it too extreme
ROUX: Liberty

(opens his mouth and pushes his elbows out vigorously. COULMIER *raises his forefinger threateningly.)*

HERALD: Ladies and gentlemen our players
are drawn from many social layers   45

(He waves his staff over the audience and the group of actors.)

Our singers for example of these four
each must be classified as bottom drawer
But now they've left the alcoholic mists
of slums and gin cellars our vocalists

(points to the FOUR SINGERS*)*

Cucurucu Polpoch Kokol   50
and on the streets no longer Rossignol

(Each named changes his pose with a studied bow, ROSSIGNOL *curtsies.)*

Now meet this gentleman from high society

(points at SADE *who turns his back on the public in a bored way)*

who under the lurid star of notoriety
came to live with us just five years ago
It's to his genius that we owe this show   55
The former Marquis Monsieur de Sade
whose books were banned his essays barred
while he's been persecuted and reviled
thrown into jail and for some years exiled
The introduction's over now the play   60
of Jean-Paul Marat can get under way
Tonight the date
is the thirteenth of July eighteen-o-eight
And on this night our cast intend
showing how fifteen years ago night without end   65
fell on that man that invalid

(points at MARAT*)*

And you are going to see him bleed

(points at MARAT's *breast)*

and see this woman after careful thought

(points at CORDAY*)*

take up the dagger and cut him short
Homage to Marat   70

(Music starts. CORDAY *is led by the* SISTERS *from the arena to a bench in the background.* SIMONNE *seats herself on the edge of the dais behind* MARAT's *bath.* SADE *goes to his seat and sits down.* ROUX *and* DUPERRET *withdraw to a bench.*

   The FOUR SINGERS *take their position for the homage to* MARAT.*)*

5. HOMAGE TO MARAT

KOKOL AND POLPOCH *(recitative):* Four years after the Revolution
  and the old king's execution
  four years after remember how
  those courtiers took their final bow
CHORUS *(singing in the background):* String up every aristocrat   5
  Out with the priests and let them live on their fat
CUCURUCU AND ROSSIGNOL *(recitative):* Four years after we started fighting
  Marat keeps on with his writing
  Four years after the Bastille fell
  he still recalls the old battle yell   10
CHORUS *(singing in the background):* Down with all of the ruling class
  Throw all the generals out on their arse
ROUX: Long live the Revolution

(The FOUR SINGERS *and other* PATIENTS *form an adoring group around the bath. A wreath of leaves is held up.)*

PATIENT (*in background*): Marat we won't dig our own bloody graves
PATIENT (*in background*): Marat we've got to be clothed and fed   15
PATIENT (*in background*): Marat we're sick of working like slaves
PATIENT (*in background*): Marat we've got to have cheaper bread
KOKOL (*indicating wreath*): We crown you with these leaves Marat because of
    the laurel shortage
  The laurels all went to decorate
  academics generals and heads of state   20
  And their heads are enormous

(*The wreath is placed on* MARAT's *head, he is lifted from the bath and carried
on the shoulders of two patients.*)

CHORUS: Good old Marat
  By your side we'll stand or fall
  You're the only one that we can trust at all   25

(MARAT *is carried around the arena.* SIMONNE *walks beside him looking up to
him anxiously. The* FOUR SINGERS *and the* PATIENTS *in the procession carry
out studied gestures of homage.*)

ROSSIGNOL (*naively, taking the play seriously*): Don't scratch your scabs or
    they'll never get any better
FOUR SINGERS (*song*): Four years he fought and he fought unafraid
  sniffing down traitors by traitors betrayed
  Marat in the courtroom Marat underground
  sometimes the otter and sometimes the hound   30

  Fighting all the gentry and fighting every priest
  businessman the bourgeois the military beast
  Marat always ready to stifle every scheme
  of the sons of the arse-licking dying regime

  We've got new generals our leaders are new   35
  They sit and they argue and all that they do
  is sell their own colleagues and ride on their backs
  and jail them and break them or give them all the axe

  Screaming in language no man understands
  of rights that we grabbed with our own bleeding hands   40
  when we wiped out the bosses and stormed through the wall
  of the prison they told us would outlast us all
CHORUS AND FOUR SINGERS: Marat we're poor and the poor stay poor
  Marat don't make us wait any more
  We want our rights and we don't care how
  We want our revolution NOW   45

(MARAT *is ceremoniously placed back in the bath. The wreath is taken from
his head.*

  SIMONNE *busily changes his bandages and rearranges the cloth about his
shoulders. Music ends.*

  SADE *sits unmoving, looking across the stage with a mocking expression on
his face.*)

HERALD: The Revolution came and went
  and unrest was replaced by discontent

6. STIFLED UNREST

PATIENT: We've got rights the right to starve
PATIENT: We've got jobs waiting for work
PATIENT: We're all brothers lousy and dirty
PATIENT: We're all free and equal to die like dogs
ROSSIGNOL: And now our lovely new leaders come   5
  they give us banknotes which we're told
  are money just as good as gold
  but they're only good for wiping your bum

(COULMIER *jumps up from his seat.*)

ROUX (*in the middle of the stage*): Who controls the markets
  Who locks up the granaries   10
  Who got the loot from the palaces
  Who sits tight on the estates
  that were going to be divided between the poor

(COULMIER *looks around. A* SISTER *pulls* ROUX *back.*)

PATIENTS (*in the background, and beating out the rhythm emphatically*):
  Who keeps us prisoner
  Who locks us in   15
  We're all normal and we want our freedom
CHORUS: Freedom Freedom Freedom

(*The unrest grows.*)

COULMIER (*knocking with his stick on the railing*): Monsieur de Sade

(SADE *takes no notice*)

It appears I must act as the voice of reason
What's going to happen when right at the start of the play   20
the patients are so disturbed
Please keep your production under control
Times have changed times are different
and these days we should take a subtler view
of old grievances   25

(*The* PATIENTS *are pushed back by the* MALE NURSES.
  Some SISTERS *place themselves in front of the* PATIENTS *and sing a tran-
quillizing litany.*)

7. CORDAY IS INTRODUCED

Midstage, CORDAY, *who is sitting slumped down on the bench, is being prepared by the* SISTERS *for her entrance.*

HERALD: Here sits Marat the people's choice
  dreaming and listening to his fever's voice
  You see his hand curled round his pen
  and the screams from the street are all forgotten
  He stares at the map of France eyes marching from town to town

(Points to the map, which MARAT *rolls up)*

while you wait

(Turns round. In the background a whispering begins and spreads.)

CHORUS *(whispers)*: Corday Corday
HERALD: while you wait for this woman to cut him down

(Points with his staff to CORDAY. ORCHESTRA *plays the* CORDAY *theme.)*

HERALD *(waiting for the* SISTERS *to complete their preparations)*: And none of us
  And none of us

*(CORDAY *is led forward by the* SISTERS)*

And none of us can alter the fact do what we will
  that she stands outside his door ready and poised to kill

(he taps the floor three times with his staff.
    CORDAY *is put in position in the arena. This all resembles a ritual act. The*
  music ends. The SISTERS *step back.)*

CORDAY *(sleepily and hesitantly)*: Poor Marat in your bathtub
  your body soaked saturated with poison

(waking up)

Poison spurting from your hiding place
poisoning the people
arousing them to looting and murder
Marat
I have come
I
Charlotte Corday from Caen
where a huge army of liberation is massing
and Marat I come as the first of them Marat

(Pause. A chord on the lute leads in the musical accompaniment.)

Once both of us saw the world must go
and change as we read in great Rousseau
but change meant one thing to you I see
and something quite different to me
The very same words we both have said
to give our ideals wings to spread
  but my way was true
    while for you
the highway led over mountains of dead

Once both of us spoke a single tongue
of brotherly love we sweetly sung
but love meant one thing to you I see   35
and something quite different to me
but now I'm aware that I was blind
and now I can see into your mind
   and so I say no
   and I go   40
to murder you Marat and free all mankind

(*Music ends.* CORDAY *stands with her head bowed. The* SISTERS *lead her back.*)

8. I AM THE REVOLUTION

MARAT (*tyrannically*): Simonne Simonne
  More cold water
  Change my bandage
  O this itching is unbearable

(SIMONNE *stands ready behind him and carries out with maniacal movements
her rehearsed tasks. She changes his bandage, fans him with the shoulder cloth
and tips a jug over the bath.*)

SIMONNE: Jean-Paul don't scratch yourself   5
  you'll tear your skin to shreds
  give up writing Jean-Paul
  it won't do any good
MARAT: My call
  My fourteenth of July call   10
  to the people of France
SIMONNE: Jean-Paul please be more careful
  look how red the water's getting
MARAT: And what's a bath full of blood
  compared to the bloodbaths still to come   15
  Once we thought a few hundred corpses would be enough
  then we saw thousands were still too few
  and today we can't even count all the dead
  Everywhere you look
  everywhere   20

(MARAT *raises himself up in the bath. The* FOUR SINGERS *stretched out on the
floor play cards, taking no notice of* MARAT.)

There they are
Behind he walls
Up on the rooftops
Down in the cellars
Hypocrites   25
They wear the people's cap on their heads
but their underwear's embroidered with crowns
and if so much as a shop gets looted

they squeal
Beggars villains gutter rats
Simonne Simonne
my head's on fire
I can't breathe
There is a rioting mob inside me
Simonne
I am the Revolution

(CORDAY *is led forward by the* SISTERS.)

9. CORDAY'S FIRST VISIT

HERALD *taps three times with his staff on the floor and points at* CORDAY, *who is led on to the arena.*

 DUPERRET *follows* CORDAY *and remains with bent knee at the edge of the arena.* SIMONNE *stands between her and the bath.*

HERALD: Corday's first visit

(ORCHESTRA *plays the* CORDAY *theme.*)

CORDAY: I have come to speak to Citizen Marat
 I have an important message for him
 about the situation in Caen my home
 where his enemies are gathering
SIMONNE: We don't want any visitors
 We want a bit of peace
 If you've got anything to say to Marat
 put it in writing
CORDAY: What I have to say cannot be said in writing
 I want to stand in front of him and look at him

(*amorously*)

I want to see his body tremble and his forehead bubble with sweat
I want to thrust right between his ribs the dagger
which I carry between my breasts

(*obsessively*)

I shall take the dagger in both hands
and push it through his flesh
and then I will hear

(*approaches* MARAT)

what he has got to say to me

(*She stands directly in front of the bath. She raises dagger and is poised to strike.* SIMONNE *stands paralysed.* SADE *rises from his seat.*)

SADE: Not yet Corday
 You have to come to his door three times

(CORDAY *stops short, hides the dagger and withdraws to her bench. The* SIS-
TERS *and* DUPERRET *follow her as she leaves.*)

10. SONG AND MIME OF CORDAY'S ARRIVAL IN PARIS

As an accompaniment to the song, PATIENTS *come forward as mimes. They
walk singly around the arena. With simple disguises they present types in the
streets. One is an "Incroyable," another a "Merveilleuse" or a banner-bearer, a
salesman and cutler, an acrobat or flower seller, and there are also some prostitutes.*

    CORDAY *circles the arena in the opposite direction. She represents the coun-
try girl who has come to town for the first time.*

FOUR SINGERS (*on the edge of the arena, to a musical accompaniment.
  Song*): Charlotte Corday came to our town
  heard the people talking saw the banners wave
  Weariness had almost dragged her down
  weariness had dragged her down

  Charlotte Corday had to be brave   5
  She could never stay at comfortable hotels
  Had to find a man with knives to sell
  had to find a man with knives

  Charlotte Corday passed the pretty stores
  Perfume and cosmetics powders and wigs   10
  unguent for curing syphilis sores
  unguent for curing your sores

  She saw a dagger its handle was white
  walked into the cutlery seller's door
  When she saw the dagger the dagger was bright   15
  Charlotte saw the dagger was bright

  When the man asked her who is it for
  it is common knowledge to each of you
  Charlotte smiled and paid him his forty sous
  Charlotte smiled and paid forty sous   20

(*Mime of the purchase of the knife.* CORDAY *chooses the dagger, takes it and
pays. She conceals the dagger under her neckcloth. The* SALESMAN *looks down
her bosom with an admiring gesture.*)

  Charlotte Corday walked alone
  Paris birds sang sugar calls
  Charlotte walked down lanes of stone
  through the haze from perfume stalls
  Charlotte smelt the dead's gangrene   25
  Heard the singing guillotine

(*The mime procession grows larger and develops into a dance of death. The
music underlines the monotonous rhythm.*

Two PATIENTS, *covered with a cloth, represent a horse. They pull a cart in which stand the condemned receiving last rites from a priest.*

The PATIENTS *accompanying the cart make ecstatic and contorted movements. Some are seized with convulsions and throw themselves down in fits. One hears stifled giggles and groans and the stamping of feet to music.)*

Don't soil your pretty little shoes
The gutter's deep and red
Climb up climb up and ride along with me
the tumbrel driver said   30

But she never said a word
never turned her head

Don't soil your pretty little pants
I only go one way
Climb up climb up and ride along with me   35
There's no gold coach today

But she never said a word
never turned her head
CORDAY (*in front of the arena, turned to the public. Behind her the stamping
        continues*): What kind of town is this
The sun can hardly pierce the haze   40
not a haze made out of rain and fog
but steaming thick and hot
like the mist in a slaughterhouse
Why are they howling
What are they dragging through the streets   45
They carry stakes but what's impaled on those stakes
Why do they hop what are they dancing for
Why are they racked with laughter
Why do the children scream
What are those heaps they fight over   50
those heaps with eyes and mouths
What kind of town is this
hacked buttocks lying in the street
What are all these faces

(*Behind her the dance of death takes place. The* FOUR SINGERS *join the dancers.*

    The cart is turned into a place of execution. Two PATIENTS *represent the guillotine. The execution is prepared in gruesome detail.*

    CORDAY *sits slumped at the foremost edge of the arena.*)

Soon these faces will close around me   55
These eyes and mouths will call me to join them

(*The mime depicts the piercing and bursting of the fat belly of the priest. The condemned man leans across the execution block. His hands are sawn off.*)

11. DEATH'S TRIUMPH

MARAT (*speaking to the audience*): Now it's happening and you can't stop it
    happening
The people used to suffer everything
now they take their revenge
You are watching that revenge
and you don't remember that you drove the people to it   5
Now you protest
but it's too late
to start crying over spilt blood
What is the blood of these aristocrats
compared with the blood the people shed for you   10
Many of them had their throats slit by your gangs
Many of them died more slowly in your workshops

(*The hands of the victim fall off. Howls. The executioners start sawing off his head.*)

So what is this sacrifice
compared with the sacrifices the people made
to keep you fat   15
What are a few looted mansions
compared with their looted lives
You don't care
if the foreign armies with whom you're making secret deals
march in and massacre the people   20
You hope the people will be wiped out so you can flourish
and when they are wiped out not a muscle will twitch in your puffy bourgeois
    faces
which are now all twisted up with anger and disgust

(COULMIER *rises. The head falls off. Triumphant screams. The* PATIENTS *play ball with the head.*)

COULMIER: Monsieur de Sade
we can't allow this   25
you really cannot call this education
It isn't making my patients any better
they're all becoming over-excited
After all we invited the public here
to show them that our patients   30
are not all social lepers

(SADE *does not react. He gazes with a mocking smile across the stage and cues the* HERALD.)

HERALD (*tapping his staff before* COULMIER *has finished speaking*): We only show
    these people massacred
because this indisputably occurred
Please calmly watch these barbarous displays
which could not happen nowadays   35

The men of that time mostly now demised
were primitive we are more civilised

(HERALD *points with his staff at the execution scene. Trumpet call. Procession of nobles forms quickly, lining up for execution.*)

CORDAY (*rising*): Up there on the scaffold
you stand completely still and stare
farther than your executioners can see
That is how I will stand
when it's all over

40

(*She closes her eyes and appears to be sleeping.*)

SADE: Look at them Marat
these men who once owned everything
See how they turn their defeat into victory
Now that their pleasures have been taken away
the guillotine saves them from endless boredom
Gaily they offer their heads as if for coronation
Is not that the pinnacle of perversion

45

(*The victims kneel in front of the execution block.* SADE *gestures to the whole group to retreat. The* PATIENTS *withdraw. The cart is taken away.* CORDAY *is led to her bench. A curtain is drawn to hide the* PATIENTS.)

12. CONVERSATION CONCERNING LIFE AND DEATH

Order is restored at the back. The SISTERS *murmur a short litany.*

MARAT (*speaking to* SADE *across the empty arena*): I read in your books de Sade
in one of your immortal works
that the basis of all of life is death
SADE: Correct Marat
But man has given a false importance to death
Any animal plant or man who dies
adds to Nature's compost heap
becomes the manure without which
nothing could grow nothing could be created
Death is simply part of the process
Every death even the cruellest death
drowns in the total indifference of Nature
Nature herself would watch unmoved
if we destroyed the entire human race

5

10

(*rising*)

I hate Nature
this passionless spectator this unbreakable iceberg-face
that can bear everything
this goads us to greater and greater acts

15

(*breathing heavily*)

Haven't we always beaten down those weaker than ourselves
Haven't we torn at their throats   20
with continuous villainy and lust
Haven't we experimented in our laboratories
before applying the final solution
Let me remind you of the execution of Damiens
after his unsuccessful attempt to assassinate   25
Louis the Fifteenth (now deceased)
Remember how Damiens died
How gentle the guillotine is
compared with his torture
It lasted four hours while the crowd goggled   30
and Casanova at an upper window
felt under the skirts of the ladies watching

(*pointing in the direction of the tribunal where* COULMIER *sits*)

His chest arms thighs and calves were slit open
Molten lead was poured into each slit
boiling oil they poured over him burning tar wax sulphur   35
They burnt off his hands
tied ropes to his arms and legs
harnessed four horses to him and geed them up
They pulled at him for an hour but they'd never done it before
and he wouldn't come apart   40
until they sawed through his shoulders and hips
So he lost the first arm then the second
and he watched what they did to him and then turned to us
and shouted so everyone could understand
And when they tore off the first leg and then the second leg   45
he still lived though his voice was getting weak
and at the end he hung there a bloody torso with a nodding head
just groaning and staring at the crucifix
which the father confessor was holding up to him

(*In the background a half-murmured litany is heard.*)

That   50
was a festival with which
today's festivals can't compete
Even our inquisition gives us no pleasure
nowadays
Although we've only just started   55
there's no passion in our post-revolutionary murders
Now they are all official
We condemn to death without emotion
and there's no singular personal death to be had
only an anonymous cheapened death   60
which we could dole out to entire nations
on a mathematical basis

until the time comes
for all life
to be extinguished
MARAT: Citizen Marquis
you may have fought for us last September
when we dragged out of the gaols
the aristocrats who plotted against us
but you still talk like a grand seigneur
and what you call the indifference of Nature
is your own lack of compassion
SADE: Compassion
Now Marat you are talking like an aristocrat
Compassion is the property of the privileged classes
When the pitier lowers himself
to give to a beggar
he throbs with contempt
To protect his riches he pretends to be moved
and his gift to the beggar amounts to no more than a kick

(*Lute chord.*)

No Marat
no small emotions please
Your feelings were never petty
For you just as for me
only the most extreme actions matter
MARAT: If I am extreme I am not extreme in the same way as you
Against Nature's silence I use action
In the vast indifference I invent a meaning
I don't watch unmoved I intervene
and say that this and this are wrong
and I work to alter them and improve them
The important thing
is to pull yourself up by your own hair
to turn yourself inside out
and see the whole world with fresh eyes

13. MARAT'S LITURGY

The curtain is drawn open. PATIENTS *move forward and arrange themselves in a closed group.*

HERALD: Marat's liturgy
MARAT: Remember how it used to be
The kings were our dear fathers
under whose care we lived in peace
and their deeds were glorified
by official poets
Piously the simpleminded breadwinners
passed on the lesson to their children

CHORUS (*murmuring in the background as* MARAT *continues*): The kings are our
    dear fathers
  under whose care we live in peace   10
  The kings are our dear fathers
  under whose care we live in peace
MARAT: And the children repeated the lesson they believed it
  as anyone believes
  what they hear over and over again   15

(CHORUS *repeats*)

And over and over again the priests said

(*accompanied by chorus of* PATIENTS)

Our love embraces all mankind
of every colour race and creed
Our love is international universal
we are all brothers every one   20

(*continuing alone*)

And the priests looked down into the pit of injustice
and they turned their faces away and said

(*accompanied by chorus of* PATIENTS)

Our kingdom is not as the kingdom of this world
Our life on earth is but a pilgrimage
The soul lives on humility and patience   25

(*continuing alone*)

at the same time screwing from the poor their last centime
They settled down among their treasures
and ate and drank with princes
and to the starving they said

(*accompanied by chorus of* PATIENTS)

Suffer   30
Suffer as he suffered on the cross
for it is the will of God

(A *mime is performed.* PATIENTS *and the* FOUR SINGERS *come forward.
Church dignitaries are depicted:* CUCURUCU *carries a cross made of brooms
tied together and leads* POLPOCH *with a rope around his neck behind him.*
KOKOL *swings a bucket as a censer.* ROSSIGNOL *counts her beads.*)

(*continuing alone*)

And anyone believes what they hear over and over again
so the poor instead of bread made do with a picture
of the bleeding scourged and nailed-up Christ   35
and prayed to that image of their helplessness
And the priests said

(Accompanied by chorus of PATIENTS. *The litanies of the* SISTERS *can also be heard.)*

Raise your hands to heaven bend your knees
and bear your suffering without complaint
Pray for those who torture you 40
for prayer and blessing are the only stairways
which you can climb to Paradise

(speaking alone)

And so they chained down the poor in their ignorance
so that they wouldn't stand up and fight their bosses
who ruled in the name of the lie of divine right 45
CHORUS: Amen
COULMIER *(rising and calling above the Amen)*: Monsieur de Sade
I must interrupt this argument
We agreed to make some cuts in this passage
After all nobody now objects to the church 50
since our emperor is surrounded by high-ranking clergy
and since it's been proved over and over again
that the poor need the spiritual comfort of the priests
There's no question of anyone being oppressed
Quite on the contrary everything's done to relieve suffering 55
with clothing collections medical aid and soup kitchens
and in this very clinic we're dependent on the goodwill
not only of the temporal government
but even more on the goodness and understanding of the church
HERALD *(raising his staff)*: If our performance causes aggravation 60
we hope you'll swallow down your indignation
and please remember that we show
only those things which happened long ago
Remember things were very different then
of course today we're all God-fearing men 65

(makes the sign of the cross)

14. A REGRETTABLE INTERVENTION

A PATIENT, *a clergyman's collar round his neck, detaches himself from the group and hops forward on his knees.*

PATIENT *(stammering incoherently)*: Pray pray
O pray to him
Our Satan which art in hell
thy kingdom come
thy will be done 5
on earth as it is in hell
forgive us our good deeds
and deliver us from holiness
Lead us

Lead us into temptation   10
for ever and ever
    Amen

(COULMIER *has sprung to his feet.*
    MALE NURSES *throw themselves on the* PATIENT, *overpower him, put him
under a shower, then bind him and drag him to the back.*)

HERALD (*swinging his rattle*): The regrettable incident you've just seen
was unavoidable indeed foreseen
by our playwright who managed to compose   15
some extra lines in case the need arose
Please understand this man was once the very
well-thought-of abbot of a monastery
It should remind us all that as they say
God moves like man in a mysterious way   20

(*He swings his rattle.*
    COULMIER *sits down. The* PATIENTS *retreat and stretch out on the benches,
supervised by the* SISTERS *and* MALE NURSES.)

15. CONTINUATION OF THE CONVERSATION
BETWEEN MARAT AND SADE

SADE: Before deciding what is wrong and what is right
first we must find out what we are
I
do not know myself
No sooner have I discovered something   5
than I begin to doubt it
and I have to destroy it again
What we do is just a shadow of what we want to do
and the only truths we can point to
are the ever-changing truths of our own experience   10
I do not know if I am hangman or victim
for I imagine the most horrible tortures
and as I describe them I suffer them myself
There is nothing that I could not do and everything fills me with horror
And I see that other people also   15
suddenly change themselves into strangers
and are driven to unpredictable acts
A little while ago I saw my tailor
a gentle cultured man who liked to talk philosophy
I saw him foam at the mouth   20
and raging and screaming attack with a cudgel
a man from Switzerland
a large man heavily armed
and destroy him utterly
and then I saw him   25
tear open the breast of the defeated man

saw him take out the still beating heart
and swallow it

(A PATIENT, *in pacing across the stage, comes face to face with* COULMIER *and*
addresses part of his speech directly to him.)

PATIENT: A mad animal
Man's a mad animal   30
I'm a thousand years old and in my time
I've helped commit a million murders
The earth is spread
The earth is spread thick
with squashed human guts   35
We few survivors
We few survivors
walk over a quaking bog of corpses
always under our feet
every step we take   40
rotted bones ashes matted hair
under our feet
broken teeth skulls split open
A mad animal
I'm a mad animal   45

(SADE *comes up to him and leads him gently to the back as he continues*)

Prisons don't help
Chains don't help
I escape
through all the walls
through all the shit and the splintered bones   50
You'll see it all one day
I'm not through yet
I have plans
MARAT: (*Searches for his cue.*)
HERALD (*prompting*): O this itching
MARAT: O this itching this itching (*hesitates*)   55
HERALD (*prompting*): This fever
MARAT: This fever beats in my head like a drum
   my skin simmers and scorches
   Simonne
   Simonne dip the cloth in vinegar and water   60
   cool my forehead

(SIMONNE *hastens to him and goes through her motions.*)

SADE: Marat I know
   that you'd give up your fame and all the love of the people
   for a few days of health
   You lie in your bath   65
   as if you were in the pink water of the womb

You swim all huddled up
alone with your ideas about the world
which no longer fit the world outside
And why should you care about the world outside   70
For me the only reality is imagination
the world inside myself
The Revolution
no longer interests me
MARAT: Wrong Sade wrong   75
No restless ideas
can break down the walls
I never believed the pen alone
could destroy institutions
However hard we try to bring in the new   80
it comes into being only
in the midst of clumsy deals
We're all so clogged with dead ideas
passed from generation to generation
that even the best of us   85
don't know the way out
We invented the Revolution
but we don't know how to run it
Look everyone wants to keep something from the past
a souvenir of the old regime   90
     This man decides to keep a painting
     This one keeps his mistress
     This man keeps his horse
     He (*pointing*) keeps his garden
     He (*pointing*) keeps his estate   95
     He keeps his country house
     He keeps his factories
     This man couldn't part with his shipyards
     This one kept his army
     and that one keeps his king   100
And so we stand here
and write into the declaration of the rights of man
the holy right of property
And now we find where that leads
Every man's equally free to fight   105
fraternally and with equal arms of course
Every man his own millionaire
Man against man group against group
in happy mutual robbery

(*The* PATIENTS *stand up slowly, some step forward. The* SINGERS *take up their positions.*)

And ahead of them the great springtime of mankind   110
the budding of trade and the blossoming of industry

and one enormous financial upsurge
We stand here more oppressed than when we begun

(*points across the auditorium*)

and they think that the Revolution's been won

16. The People's Reaction

THE FOUR SINGERS (*with musical accompaniment*): Why do they have the gold
  Why do they have all the power
  Why do they have friends at the top
  Why do they have jobs at the top
  We've got nothing always had nothing   5
  nothing but holes and millions of them
KOKOL: Living in holes
POLPOCH: Dying in holes
CUCURUCU: Holes in our bellies
ROSSIGNOL: and holes in our clothes   10
THE FOUR SINGERS AND CHORUS: Marat we're poor and the poor stay poor
  Marat don't make us wait any more
  We want our rights and we don't care how
  We want our Revolution NOW
HERALD:

(*coming forward quickly, swinging his staff. Music ends. The* FOUR SINGERS
and CHORUS *withdraw.*)

Observe how easily a crowd turns mob   15
through ignorance of its wise ruler's job
Rather than bang an empty drum
of protest citizens be dumb
Work for and trust the powerful few
what's best for them is best for you   20
Ladies and gentlemen we'd like to see
people and government in harmony
a harmony which I should say
we've very nearly reached today

(DUPERRET *and the* SISTERS *busy themselves with* CORDAY, *who cannot be
awakened. They pull her to her feet and hold her up and try to get her
moving.*)

17. First Conversation Between Corday and Duperret

CORDAY *is led forward by the two* SISTERS, *supporting her under the arms.*
DUPERRET *walks behind, supporting* CORDAY's *back with his hands.*

HERALD (*plays a few runs on his Pan-flute*): And now nobility meets grace
  Our author brings them face to face
  The beautiful and brave Charlotte Corday

(turns round in concern, nods in relief and points his staff at CORDAY*)*

The handsome Monsieur Duperret

(With the help of the SISTERS*,* CORDAY *enters the arena.* DUPERRET *walks beside her. The* SISTERS *withdraw.* CORDAY *and* DUPERRET *greet each other with exaggerated ceremony.)*

In Caen where she spent the best years of her youth   5
in a convent devoted to the way of truth
Duperret's name she heard them recommend
as a most sympathetic helpful friend

*(*DUPERRET *uses the scene to make amorous advances to* CORDAY*. The* HERALD *addresses* DUPERRET*.)*

Confine your passion to the lady's mind
Your love's platonic not the other kind   10

(He gives the ORCHESTRA *a sign with his staff.* CORDAY *stands with head held back, eyes closed. The* ORCHESTRA *plays the* CORDAY *theme. The* HERALD *withdraws. He waits a few seconds and watches* CORDAY*.)*

CORDAY *(with her eyes closed)*: Ah dearest Duperret

(she hesitates then starts again as if singing an aria)

Ah dearest Duperret what can we do
How can we stop this dreadful calamity
In the streets everyone is saying
Marat's to be   15

(She hesitates. DUPERRET *gently caresses her hips and back.)*

Marat's to be tribune and dictator
He still pretends that his iron grip
will relax as soon as the worst is over
But we know what Marat really wants
anarchy and confusion   20

*(*CORDAY *stands sunk into herself.)*

DUPERRET *(embracing* CORDAY*, also as if singing an aria, but with great ardour)*: Dearest Charlotte you must return
return to your friends the pious nuns
and live in prayer and contemplation
You cannot fight
the hard-faced enemies surrounding us   25

(One of the SISTERS *approaches* DUPERRET *and pulls back his hand, which he had placed on her bosom.* CORDAY *stands sunk into herself.)*

You talk about Marat but who's this Marat
A street salesman a funfair barker
a layabout from Corsica sorry I mean Sardinia
Marat the name sounds Jewish to me

perhaps derived from the waters of Marah in the Bible 30
But who listens to him
Only the mob down in the streets
Up here Marat can be no danger to us

(DUPERRET *embraces* CORDAY's *hips.*
    The FOUR SINGERS *are filling in time with all sorts of pranks, throwing dice and showing each other card tricks.*)

CORDAY (*suddenly awake and full of power*): Dearest Duperret you're trying to
    test me
but I know what I must do 35

(*Tries to free herself from* DUPERRET's *embrace. The two* SISTERS *standing behind the podium interfere and pull back* DUPERRET's *hands.*)

Duperret go to Caen
Barbaroux and Buzot are waiting for you there
Go now and travel quickly
Do not wait till this evening
for this evening everything will be too late 40
DUPERRET (*passionately, in aria style as before*): Dearest Charlotte my place
    is here

(*throws himself on his knees and hugs her legs*)

How could I leave the city which holds you
Dearest Charlotte
my place is here

(*he forgets himself and becomes wilder in his embracing. The* HERALD *pushes him with his staff and then taps on the floor.*)

HERALD (*prompting*): And why should I run 45
DUPERRET: And why should I run
now when it can't last much longer

(*stroking* CORDAY *vigorously*)

Already the English lie off Dunkirk and Toulon
The Prussians
HERALD (*prompting*): The Spaniards 50
DUPERRET: The Spaniards have occupied Roussillon
    Paris
HERALD (*prompting*): Mayence
DUPERRET: Mayence is surrounded by the Prussians
    Condé and Valenciennes have fallen to the English 55
HERALD (*correcting*): Austrians
DUPERRET: To the Austrians
    The Vendée is up in arms

(*with much ardour and vigorous embraces*)

They can't hold out much longer
these fanatical upstarts 60

with no vision and no culture
They can't hold out much longer
No dear Charlotte here I stay

(*snuggles up to her and puts his head into her lap*)

waiting for the promised day
when with Marat's mob interred   65
France once more speaks the forbidden word
Freedom

(DUPERRET *raises himself, clinging to* CORDAY, *tries to kiss her.* CORDAY *extricates herself, the two* SISTERS *come to her aid, pushing* DUPERRET *away and pulling her back to her bench. The music ends.*)

18. SADE TURNS HIS BACK ON ALL THE NATIONS

SADE (*shouting to* MARAT): You hear that Marat
   Freedom
   They all say they want what's best for France
   My patriotism's bigger than yours
   They're all ready to die for the honour of France   5
   Radical or moderate
   they're all after the taste of blood

   (*rising*)

   The luke-warm liberals and the angry radicals
   all believe in the greatness of France
   Marat   10
   can't you see this patriotism is lunacy
   Long ago I left heroics to the heroes
   and I care no more for this country
   than for any other country
COULMIER (*calling over them with raised forefinger*): Take care   15
PATIENT (*in the background*): Long live Napoleon and the nation

   (*a shrill laugh in the background*)

KOKOL (*at back calling*): Long live all emperors kings bishops and popes

   (*signs of disorder in the background*)

POLPOCH: Long live watery broth and the straitjacket
ROSSIGNOL: Long live Marat
ROUX: Long live the Revolution (*shouting above the disorder*)   20
SADE: It's easy to get mass movements going
   movements that move in vicious circles

   (*Shrill whistles in background.*
     A PATIENT *begins to run in a circle, a second and third join in.* MALE
   NURSES *pursue them and halt them.*)

SADE: I don't believe in idealists

who charge down blind alleys
I don't believe in any of the sacrifices   25
that have been made for any cause
I believe only in myself

MARAT (*turning violently to* SADE): I believe only in that thing which you betray
We've overthrown our wealthy rabble of rulers
disarmed many of them though   30
many escaped
But now those rulers have been replaced by others
who used to carry torches and banners with us
and now long for the good old days
It becomes clear   35
that the Revolution was fought
for merchants and shopkeepers
the bourgeoisie
a new victorious class
and underneath them   40
ourselves
who always lose the lottery

FOUR SINGERS: Those fat monkeys covered in banknotes
have champagne and brandy on tap
They're up to their eyeballs in franc notes   45
We're up to our noses in crap

Those gorilla-mouthed fakers
are longing to see us all rot
The gentry may lose a few acres
but we lose the little we've got   50

Revolution it's more like a ruin
They're all stuffed with glorious food
They think about nothing but screwing
but we are the ones who get screwed

19. First Rabble-Rousing of Jacques Roux

ROUX (*springing on a bench in background, shouting*): Pick up your arms
Fight for your rights
Grab what you need and grab it now
or wait a hundred years
and see what the authorities arrange   5

(PATIENTS *approach* ROUX *from the tribunal*)

Up there they despise you
because you never had the cash
to learn to read and write
You're good enough for the dirty work of the Revolution
but they screw their noses up at you   10
because your sweat stinks

You have to sit way down there
so they won't have to see you
And down there
in ignorance and stink   15
you're allowed to do your bit
towards bringing in the golden age
in which you'll all do the same old dirty work
Up there in the sunlight
their poets sing   20
about the power of life
and the expensive rooms in which they scheme
are hung with exquisite paintings
So stand up
Defend yourselves from their whips   25
Stand up stand in front of them
and let them see how many of you there are

(*The* FOUR SINGERS *sit down in the arena and pass a bottle around.*
     The two SISTERS *grab* ROUX *from behind and pull him down from the dais.*)

COULMIER (*springing up*): Do we have to listen to this sort of thing
     We're citizens of a new enlightened age
     We're all revolutionaries nowadays   30
     but this is plain treachery we can't allow it
HERALD (*sounding a shrill whistle*): The cleric you've been listening to
     is that notorious priest Jacques Roux

(*points with his staff at* ROUX)

who to adopt the new religious fashion
has quit the pulpit and with earthier passion   35
rages from soapboxes A well-trained priest
his rhetoric is slick to say the least
'If you'd make paradise your only chance
is not to build on clouds but solid France'
The mob eats from his hand while Roux   40
knows what he wants but not what he should do
Talk's cheap The price of action is colossal
so Roux decides to be the chief apostle
of Jean-Paul Marat Seems good policy
since Marat's heading straight for Calvary   45
and crucifixion all good Christians know
is the most sympathetic way to go
ROUX (*frees himself and jumps forward*): We demand
     the opening of the granaries to feed the poor
     We demand   50
     the public ownership of workshops and factories

(*The* FOUR SINGERS *listen to the disturbance, but soon lose interest. They
quarrel for the last drop of the bottle.*)

We demand

the conversion of the churches into schools
so that now at last something useful can be taught in them

(COULMIER *wrings his hands and signifies protest*)

We demand that everyone should do all they can   55
to put an end to war
This damned war
which is run for the benefit of profiteers'
and leads only to more wars

(COULMIER *runs across to* SADE *and speaks to him, but* SADE *does not react.*)

We demand   60
that the people who started the war
should pay the cost of it

(*The* FOUR SINGERS *continue their antics.*)

Once and for all
the idea of glorious victories
won by the glorious army   65
must be wiped out
Neither side is glorious
On either side they're just frightened men messing their pants
and they all want the same thing
Not to lie under the earth   70
but to walk upon it
without crutches

COULMIER (*shouting over him*): This is outright defeatism
At this very moment our soldiers are laying down their lives
for the freedom of the world and for our freedom   75

(*turning violently to* SADE)

This scene was cut
SADE (*calling out, without concerning himself with* COULMIER's *protest*):
Bravo Jacques Roux
I like your monk's habit
Nowadays it's best
to preach revolution   80
wearing a robe

(ROUX *is overpowered by the two* NURSES *and dragged off.* DUPERRET *makes violent passes at* CORDAY, *who remains impassive. The* PATIENTS *come forward restlessly.*)

ROUX (*as he is being strapped to a bench*): Marat
Your hour has come
Now Marat show yourself
Come out and lead the people   85
They are waiting for you
It must be now

For the Revolution
which burns up everything
in blinding brightness
will only last as long as a lightning flash

90

20. Monsieur de Sade Is Whipped

ROUX *jumps up, the bench strapped to his back. He is overpowered. The* PA-
TIENTS *are pushed back.* SADE *comes slowly into the arena. He speaks without
bothering about the noise.*

SADE: Marat
Today they need you because you are going to suffer for them
They need you and they honour the urn which holds your ashes
Tomorrow they will come back and smash that urn
and they will ask
Marat who was Marat
Marat
Now I will tell you
what I think of this Revolution
which I helped to make

5

10

(It has become very quiet in the background.)

When I lay in the Bastille
my ideas were already formed
I sweated them out
under the blows of my own whip
out of hatred for myself
and the limitations of my mind
In prison I created in my mind
monstrous representatives of a dying class
who could only exercise their power
in spectacularly staged orgies
I recorded the mechanics of their atrocities
in the minutest detail
and brought out everything wicked and brutal
that lay inside me
In a criminal society
I dug the criminal out of myself
so I could understand him and so understand
the times we live in
My imaginary giants committed
desecrations and tortures
I committed them myself
and like them allowed myself to be bound and beaten
And even now I should like to take
this beauty here

15

20

25

30

(pointing to CORDAY, *who is brought forward)*

who stands there so expectantly   35
and let her beat me
while I talk to you about the Revolution

(*The* SISTERS *place* CORDAY *in the arena.* SADE *hands her a many-stranded*
whip. He tears off his shirt and offers his back to CORDAY. *He stands facing*
the audience. CORDAY *stands behind him. The* PATIENTS *advance slowly from*
the background. The ladies on COULMIER's *dais stand up expectantly.*)

At first I saw in the Revolution a chance
for a tremendous outburst of revenge
an orgy greater than all my dreams   40

(CORDAY *slowly raises the whip and lashes him.* SADE *cowers.*)

But then I saw
when I sat in the courtroom myself

(*Whiplash.* SADE *gasps.*)

not as I had been before the accused
but as a judge
I couldn't bring myself   45
to deliver the prisoners to the hangman

(*Whiplash.*)

I did all I could to release them or let them escape
I saw I wasn't capable of murder

(*Whiplash.* SADE *groans asthmatically.*)

although murder
was the final proof of my existence   50
and now

(*Whiplash. He gasps and groans.*)

the very thought of it
horrifies me
In September when I saw
the official sacking of the Carmelite Convent   55
I had to bend over in the courtyard
and vomit

(CORDAY *stops, herself breathing heavily.*)

as I saw my own prophecies coming true

(*He falls down on his knees.* CORDAY *stands before him.*)

and women running by
holding in their dripping hands
the severed genitals of men   60

(CORDAY *flogs him again. He groans and falls forward.*)

And then in the next few months

(*hindered by his asthma*)

as the tumbrels ran regularly to the scaffolds
and the blade dropped and was winched up and dropped again

(*Whiplash.*)

all the meaning drained out of this revenge   65
It had become mechanical

(*Another blow. He crumples.* CORDAY *stands very erect.*)

It was inhuman it was dull
and curiously technocratic

(*Whiplash.*)

And now Marat

(*Whiplash.* SADE *breathes heavily.*)

now I see where   70
this Revolution is leading

(CORDAY *stands breathlessly, holding the whip over* SADE. *The two* SISTERS
*move forward and pull her back. She does not resist, dragging the whip behind
her.*
     SADE *continues, lying on his knees.*)

To the withering of the individual man
and a slow merging into uniformity
to the death of choice
to self denial   75
to deadly weakness
in a state
which has no contact with individuals
but which is impregnable
So I turn away   80
I am one of those who has to be defeated
and from this defeat I want to seize
all I can get with my own strength
I step out of my place
and watch what happens   85
without joining in
observing
noting down my observations
and all around me
stillness   90

(*pauses, breathing heavily*)

And when I vanish
I want all trace of my existence
to be wiped out

(*He takes his shirt and returns to his chair, slowly dressing.*)

21. Poor Old Marat

MARAT (*bent forward, sunk into himself*): Simonne Simonne

(*staring as if blind*)

Why is it getting so dark
Give me a fresh cloth for my forehead
Put a new towel round my shoulders
I don't know
If I am freezing or burning to death

(SIMONNE *stands ready and bends over him with her jerky movements, puts a hand to his brow, changes the cloths, fans him. The* PATIENTS *cower behind the arena.*)

Simonne
Fetch Bas so I can dictate my call
my call to the people of France

(SIMONNE *shakes her head in horror and puts a hand over her mouth.*)

Simonne
Where are my papers
I saw them only a moment ago
Why is it so dark
SIMONNE (*pushing the papers lying on the board nearer*): They're here can't you
    see Jean-Paul
MARAT: Where's the ink
Where's my pen
SIMONNE (*indicating*): Here's your pen Jean-Paul
and here's the ink
where it always is
That was only a cloud over the sun
or perhaps smoke
They are burning the corpses

(*The* ORCHESTRA *plays. The* FOUR SINGERS *come forward.*)

FOUR SINGERS (*singing to music*): Poor old Marat they hunt you down
The bloodhounds are sniffing all over the town
Just yesterday your printing press
was smashed Now they're asking your home address

Poor old Marat in you we trust
You work till your eyes turn as red as rust
but while you write they're on your track
The boots mount the staircase the door's flung back

(*together with* CHORUS)

Marat we're poor and the poor stay poor
Marat don't make us wait any more
We want our rights and we don't care how
We want our Revolution NOW

(*Music Finale.* SINGERS *withdraw. The* PATIENTS *close the curtain.*)

22. SECOND CONVERSATION BETWEEN CORDAY AND DUPERRET

The SISTERS *and* DUPERRET *busy themselves with* CORDAY. *Together they raise her up. The* SISTERS *arrange her clothes and tie on her hat. The* HERALD *comes forward and knocks his staff on the floor three times.*

HERALD (*plays a few runs on his Pan-flute*): Now that these painful matters have
    been clarified
let's turn and look upon the sunny side
Fever sores blows not one of them destroys
the universal rule of love's sweet joys
Anger and woe don't give a true reflection   5
of life there's also spiritual affection
Recall this couple and their love so pure

(CORDAY *is led to the centre by* SISTERS. DUPERRET *has his arm around her.
    The* HERALD *points his staff.*)

she with her neatly-groomed coiffure

(*points to it*)

and her face intriguingly pale and clear

(*points to it*)

and her eyes ashine with the trace of a tear   10

(*points to them*)

her lips sensual and ripe seeming to silently cry for protection

(*points to them*)

and his embraces proving his affection

(*Points to* DUPERRET, *who lifts* CORDAY's *foot and kisses her shoe, then covers
her leg in kisses.* CORDAY *pushes him back.*)

See how he moves with natural grace

(DUPERRET *loses his balance and, without grace, sits on his behind, but rises
immediately and strikes a comic amorous pose before* CORDAY, *who turns her
face from him in disgust.*)

and how his heart sprints on at passion's pace

(*points to* DUPERRET's *breast*)

Let's gaze at the sweet blending of the strong and fair sex   15
before their heads fall off their necks

(ORCHESTRA *plays* CORDAY *theme. She hesitates, looking for her words.
    The* HERALD *prompts her.*)

HERALD: One day it will come to pass
CORDAY (*in the aria style*): One day it will come to pass
    Man will live in harmony with himself
    and with his fellow-man   20

DUPERRET (*covers her hand and arm with kisses*): One day it will come

(*He strokes her hair, singing in the aria style.*)

a society which will pool its energy
to defend and protect
each person for the possession of each person
and in which each individual   25
although united with all the others

(*putting a hand under* CORDAY's *dress. She defends herself.*)

only obeys himself
and so stays free

(DUPERRET *tries to kiss* CORDAY's *mouth. She avoids him.*)

CORDAY: A society
in which every man is trusted with the right   30
of governing himself himself
DUPERRET (*holding* CORDAY *and embracing her violently*): One day it will come
a constitution in which the natural inequalities of man

(CORDAY *leans back.* DUPERRET *jumps after her, continuing.*)

are subject to a higher order
(*breathless*) so that all   35

(*One of the* SISTERS *gets hold of* CORDAY *and leads her back.* CORDAY *is placed in a heroic pose.*)

however varied their physical and mental powers may be
by agreement legally
get their fair share

(*He utters a sigh of relief, and then he also falls into a suitable pose so that they form a pleasant tableau.*)

23. THESE LIES THEY TELL

MARAT *raises himself up.* CORDAY *is led back by the* SISTERS, DUPERRET *follows her.*

MARAT: These lies they tell about the ideal state
The rich will never give away their property
of their own free will
And if by force of circumstances
they have to give up just a little   5
here and there
they do it only because they know
they'll soon win it back again
The rumour spreads
that the workers can soon expect higher wages   10
Why

(*The head of a* PATIENT *appears from behind the curtain, which is opened from inside.*)

Because this raises production and increases demand
to fill the rich man's gold-chest
Don't imagine
that you can beat them without using force   15

(*The* PATIENTS *rise one by one and advance slowly, listening intently.* COR-
DAY *lies stretched out on the dais,* DUPERRET *leans over her.*)

Don't be deceived
when our Revolution has been finally stamped out
and they tell you
things are better now
Even if there's no poverty to be seen   20
because the poverty's been hidden
even if you ever got more wages
and could afford to buy
more of these new and useless goods
which these new industries foist on you   25
and even if it seems to you
that you never had so much
that is only the slogan of those
who still have much more than you

(*The* PATIENTS *and* FOUR SINGERS *advance slowly.*)

Don't be taken in   30
when they pat you paternally on the shoulder and say
that there's no inequality worth speaking of
and no more reason
for fighting

(COULMIER *looks around, worried.*)

Because if you believe them   35

(*turns towards the audience*)

they will be completely in charge
in their marble homes and granite banks
from which they rob the people of the world
under the pretence of bringing them culture

(COULMIER *leaves the platform and hurries towards* SADE. *He speaks to him.*
SADE *does not react.*)

Watch out   40
for as soon as it pleases them
they'll send you out
to protect their gold
in wars

(SADE *rises and moves to the arena*.)

whose weapons rapidly developed
by servile scientists
will become more and more deadly
until they can with a flick of a finger
tear a million of you to pieces

SADE: Lying there
scratched and swollen
your brow burning

(COULMIER *nods with satisfaction and returns to the platform*.)

in your world your bath
you still believe that justice is possible
you still believe all men are equal
Do you still believe that all occupations
are equally valuable equally satisfying
and that no man wants to be greater than the others
How does the old song go

24. SONG AND MIME OF THE GLORIFICATION OF THE BENEFICIARY

The FOUR SINGERS *perform a mime, in which they illustrate the cash value of
all the things* SADE *names*.

SADE: One always bakes the most delicate cakes
Two is the really superb masseur
Three sets your hair with exceptional flair
Four's brandy goes to the Emperor
Five knows each trick of advanced rhetoric
Six bred a beautiful brand-new rose
Seven can cook every dish in the book
And eight cuts you flawlessly elegant clothes
Do you think those eight would be happy
if each of them could climb so high
and no higher
before banging their heads on equality
if each could be only a small link
in a long and heavy chain
Do you still think it's possible
to unite mankind
when already you see how the few idealists
who did join together in the name of harmony
are now out of tune
and would like to kill each other over trifles

MARAT (*raising himself*): But they aren't trifles
They are matters of principle
and it's usual in a revolution
for the half-hearted and the fellow-travellers
to be dropped

(*Mime ends.* MARAT *stands up in the bath.*)

We can't begin to build till we've burnt the old building down
however dreadful that may seem to those
who lounge in make-believe contentment
wearing their scruples as protective clothing
Listen   30
Can you hear through the walls
how they plot and whisper

(MARAT *gets out of the bath and stumbles around the arena as if about to
faint. Some* NURSES *seize him and put him back into the bath.*)

Do you see how they lurk everywhere
waiting for the chance to strike
THE FOUR SINGERS (*to music accompaniment, singly, speaking in conversational tones while promenading*): What has gone wrong with   35
the men who are ruling
I'd like to know who
they think they are fooling
They told us that torture
was over and gone   40
but everyone knows
the same torture goes on
The king's gone away
The priests emigrating
The nobles are buried   45
so why are we waiting

25. CORDAY'S SECOND VISIT

CORDAY *is prepared by the* SISTERS, *who lead her forward.* DUPERRET *follows
them.* MARAT *sits waiting in his bath.* SIMONNE *changes his cloths.* SADE
stands in front of his chair. CORDAY *is placed on the arena in a pose. She
holds up her hand as if about to knock. The* SISTERS *stand behind her ready to
support her.* DUPERRET *sits down. The* FOUR SINGERS *stop in front of the
musicians.*
     The HERALD *gives* CORDAY *a sign with his staff, she moves her hand as if
knocking, and the* HERALD *knocks three times with his staff on the floor.*
     The ORCHESTRA *plays the* CORDAY *theme.*

HERALD: Now Charlotte Corday stands outside
     Marat's front door the second time she's tried

(*points to* CORDAY. SIMONNE *straightens and goes a few steps towards*
CORDAY.)

CORDAY (*quietly*): I have come
     to deliver this letter

(*draws a letter from her bodice*)

in which I ask again   5
to be received by Marat

(*hesitates*)

I am unhappy
and therefore have a right to his aid

(CORDAY *holds the letter out to* SIMONNE. SIMONNE, *confused, takes a step towards* CORDAY, *returns to the back and begins to change* MARAT's *bandage.*)

CORDAY (*repeating loudly*): I have a right to his aid

(*She stretches out her hand.* SIMONNE *wavers nervously about, then runs to* CORDAY *and snatches the letter from her.*)

MARAT: Who was that at the door Simonne   10

(SIMONNE *hesitates in confusion between* CORDAY *and* MARAT.)

HERALD (*prompting*): A girl from Caen with a letter
a petitioner

(CORDAY *is now standing sunk into herself.* DUPERRET *rises and puts his arm around her waist. The two* SISTERS *come up.* CORDAY *is led off.*)

SIMONNE (*confused and angry*): I won't let anyone in
They only bring us trouble
All these people with their convulsions and complaints   15
As if you had nothing better to do
than be their lawyer and doctor and confessor

(*She tears the letter up and puts the pieces in her apron. She puts a fresh cloth around* MARAT's *shoulders.*)

SADE (*goes into the arena and stops near the bath. Musical accompaniment*):
That's how it is Marat
That's how she sees your Revolution
They have toothache   20
and their teeth should be pulled

(*The* FOUR SINGERS *mime the characters in his speech. They mime very slowly, with economical gestures illustrating suffering.*)

Their soup's burnt
They shout for better soup
A woman finds her husband too short
she wants a taller one   25
A man finds his wife too skinny
he wants a plumper one
A man's shoes pinch
but his neighbour's shoes fit comfortably
A poet runs out of poetry
and desperately gropes for new images   30
For hours an angler casts his line
Why aren't the fish biting
And so they join the Revolution
thinking the Revolution will give them everything   35

a fish
a poem
a new pair of shoes
a new wife
a new husband   40
and the best soup in the world
So they storm all the citadels
and there they are
and everything is just the same
no fish biting   45
verses botched
shoes pinching
a worn and stinking partner in bed
and the soup burnt
and all that heroism   50
which drove us down to the sewers
well we can talk about it to our grandchildren
if we have any grandchildren

(*Music changes to a quartet with tragic flavour.*)

THE FOUR SINGERS (*taking up their positions*): Marat Marat it's all in vain
   You studied the body and probed the brain   55
   In vain you spent your energies
   for how can Marat cure his own disease

   Marat Marat where is our path
   or is it not visible from your bath
   Your enemies are closing in   60
   Without you the people can never win

(MARAT *lays himself wearily across the board.*)

Marat Marat can you explain
how once in the daylight your thought seemed plain
Has your affliction left you dumb
Your thoughts lie in shadows now night has come   65

(*The music changes to a dramatic growling.*
   MARAT *is in a fever.* SIMONNE *feels his brow, fans him, changes his bandage.*)

26. THE FACES OF MARAT

(*The whole stage trembles and roars. The mimes appear with a cart. The cart is drawn by a man and a woman who represent* MARAT'*s parents. The characters in the cart stand for Science, the Army, the Church, the Nouveaux Riches. The* PRIEST *blesses the owner of the sack of gold looted from the aristocrats. The figures are bedecked with medals and with primitive insignia. The costumes are extremely grotesque.*

MARAT (*raising himself up*): They are coming
  Listen to them
  and look carefully at
  these gathering figures
  Listen closely
  Watch
  Yes I hear you
  all the voices I ever heard
  Yes I see you
  all the old faces

(*The loud noise continues.*)

HERALD (*tapping his staff*): Ladies and gentlemen silence I pray
  Let's hear what these people are aching to say

(*pointing to figures*)

  about this man

(*pointing to* MARAT)

  whom they all understood
  before they bury him for good
  First the schoolmaster of that charming place

(*points to* SCHOOLMASTER)

  in which this man

(*points to* MARAT)

  spent his childhood days
SCHOOLMASTER (*sings in falsetto voice*): Even as a child
  this Marat
  made groups of his friends
  rush screaming at each other
  they fought with wooden swords
  but real blood flowed

(*cries are heard in the background*)

  and they took prisoners
  and bound and tortured them
  and nobody knew why
HERALD (*pointing to the figure representing* MARAT'S MOTHER): Now let us hear
  this lady for she can
  give us the inside story of this man
  She smelt him from the very first
  for from her womb young Marat burst
MOTHER (*in a complaining voice*): Wouldn't eat his food
  Lay around for days saying nothing
  Broke a lot of canes on his hide we did

(*she laughs shrilly. Laughter is heard in the background, also the sound of whipping.*)

Locked him up in the cellar of course 35
but nothing helped
There was no getting at him
Oh

(she starts laughing again)

FATHER *(springing forward, in a hurried voice)*: When I bit him he bit back
    his own father 40
    Threw himself down when I wanted to hang him up
    and when I spat at him he lay there stiff as a poker
    cold as ice

(starts to laugh harshly)

MARAT: Yes I see you
    hated father hated mother 45

*(The two figures squat down, still shaking with laughter. They rock to and fro
as if sitting in a boat.)*

What's that boat you're rocking in
I see you
I hear you
Why do you laugh like executioners

(The two figures sit rocking, their laughter dies.)

SIMONNE *(approaching the bath)*: Jean-Paul you're feverish 50
    Stop writing Jean-Paul
    or it'll kill you
    Lie still
    You must take more care of yourself
MARAT: I'm not feverish 55
    Now I see clearly
    those figures were always hallucinations
    Why doesn't Bas come
    Fetch him
    My call to the nation 60
    I must write my call
    Bas
SCHOOLMASTER *(jumping forward)*: When he was five this loudmouth boasted
    I can do anything teacher can do
    and what's more I know more 65
    and at fifteen I've conquered the uni-v-v-v-versities
    and outdone all the p-p-professors
    and at the age of twenty I've mastered
    the entire in-in-in-intellectual cosmos
    That's what he boasted 70
    as true as I stand here

(swings his cane)

MARAT: Simonne
 where are my old manuscripts
 My novel about the young Count Potovsky
 and my book about the chains of slavery
SIMONNE (*defensively*): Leave all that stuff
 It'll only bring you trouble
MARAT (*raising himself up*): I want to see them
 Look for them
 bring them to me
SCHOOLMASTER: Scribblings of a pickpocket
 pilfered thoughts
 frivolities tirades
MILITARY REPRESENTATIVE: One book published under the name of a count
 The other under the name of a prince
 Just look at him
 this charlatan
 greedy for titles and court distinctions
 who turned on those he once flattered
 only because they did not recognize him
A SCIENTIST: What did he do in England this shady Marat
 Wasn't he a dandy in the highest society
 who had to run away
 because he was caught red-handed embezzling and stealing
 Didn't he smuggle himself back into well-known circles
 and get himself appointed physician
 to the Count d' Artois
 or was it only to his horses
 Didn't we see him going about with aristocrats
 He charged thirty-six livres for a consultation
 and on top of that enjoyed the favours of
 certain well-born ladies

(COULMIER'S WIFE *and* DAUGHTER *applaud*.)

A NEWLY RICH: And when at last they let him drop
 back to his kind the simple poor
 and when he spoke and couldn't stop
 each word from branding him a boor
 and when they found he was a quack
 with watered drugs and pills of chalk
 and when they threw him on his back
 he raised his battered head to squawk
  Property is Robbery

(*cries in the background*)

 Down with all Tyrants

(*The cry is taken up in the background.*)

MARAT: Bas fetch Bas

75

80

85

90

95

100

105

110

(VOLTAIRE *emerges from the darkness, suitably masked and with corkscrew curls*.)

CHORUS: Bas

HERALD (*as* VOLTAIRE *advances*): It is a privilege indeed 115
    to introduce Voltaire He wrote Candide

VOLTAIRE (*monotonously*): We have received from a certain Marat
    a slim volume
    entitled Man
    This Marat claims in a somewhat revolutionary essay 120
    that the soul exists in the walls of the brain
    and from that strategic point controls
    the hypodraulic mechanism of the body
    by means of a network of tinkling nerve threads
    At the same time apparently the soul is receiving 125
    messages from the mechanamism of the body
    messages conveyed by pistons plugs and wires
    which the soul transforms into consciousness through separate
    centimentrifuges operating asimultaneously
    In other words 130
    it is the opinion of this gentleman
    that a corn fills the corridors of the brain with pain of the soul
    and that a troubled soul curdles the liver and kidneys
    For this kind of ring-a-ring-a-roses
    we can spare not even our laughter 135

(CUCURUCU *and* ROSSIGNOL *laugh ironically Ha Ha Ha. A figure with a palm branch moves forward.*)

HERALD: We're equally happy to welcome today
    that eminent scientist Lavoisier

(*points to him*)

LAVOISIER (*monotonously*): The Academy has received from a certain Marat
    some theories concerning fire light and electricity
    This Marat seems entirely certain 140
    that he knows a great deal better than the Academy
    For fire he says is not an element
    but a liquid fluidium caused by heat
    which only ignites because of air
    Light he proceeds to say is not light 145
    but a path of vibratorating rays
    left behind by light
    Certainly an extraordinary scientist
    He goes further
    Heat according to him is not of course heat 150
    but simply more vibratoratory rays
    which become heat only
    when they collide with a body and set in motionability

its minuscule molecules
He wants to pronounce   155
the whole of firm and fixed creation invalid
And instead he wants to introduce
a universe of unbridled activation
in which electrified magnetic forces
whizz about and rub against each other   160
No wonder that the author sits there in his bath
attempting to determine the validity of the proposition
The more you scratch the more you itch

(KOKOL *and* POLPOCH *laugh ironically Ha Ha Ha.* FATHER *and* MOTHER *join in the laughter. The figures mime the attitude of judges about to give a verdict.*)

VOLTAIRE: So this frustrated Newton's eyes
PRIEST: turned to the streets He thought it best   165
SCHOOLMASTER: to join the revolutionaries
NEWLY RICH: and beat his dilettante breast
PRIEST: crying out The oppressed must rise
LAVOISIER: He meant of course I am oppressed

(*Rocking to and fro and laughing, the* FATHER *and* MOTHER *pull back the cart with the figures.* ROUX *hurries to the front, a belated advocate.*)

ROUX: Woe to the man who is different   170
who tries to break down all the barriers
Woe to the man
who tries to stretch the imagination of man
He shall be mocked he shall be scourged
by the blinkered guardians of morality   175
You wanted enlightenment and warmth
and so you studied light and heat

(*unrest in background*)

You wondered how forces can be controlled
so you studied electricity
You wanted to know what man is for   180
so you asked yourself What is this soul
this dump for hollow ideals and mangled morals
You decided that the soul is in the brain

(*The* PATIENTS *form into a group and advance.*)

and that it can learn to think
For to you the soul is a practical thing   185
a tool for ruling and mastering life
And you came one day to the Revolution
because you saw the most important vision
That our circumstances must be changed fundamentally
and without these changes   190
everything we try to do must fail

(COULMIER *jumps up. The* SISTERS *and* MALE NURSES *run towards* ROUX *and pull him into the background.* SADE *stands erect in front of his chair and smiles.* CORDAY *lies sleeping on her bench.* DUPERRET *sits by her on the floor.*)

CHORUS (*to music while the* SISTERS *sing a litany*): Marat we're poor and the
    poor stay poor
Marat don't make us wait any more
We want our rights and we don't care how
We want our Revolution NOW   195

(*Music ends.*)

HERALD (*swinging his rattle*): The end comes soon Before we watch the crime
    let's interpose a drinking thinking time
while you recall that what our cast presents
is simply this a series of events
but that our end which might seem prearranged   200
could be delayed or even changed
We will since it's a play not actual history
postpone it with an interval We guarantee
that after your refreshments and debating
you'll find Marat still in his bathtub waiting   205

(*points to* MARAT)

CURTAIN

ACT II

The handbell is rung behind the curtain. Curtain goes up.

27. THE NATIONAL ASSEMBLY

The setting is the same, but with the following changes: DUPERRET *sits on the steps leading to* SADE's *raised chair, between the two* PATIENTS *representing prostitutes. On the left are seated the* PATIENTS *who represent the Girondists in the National Assembly.* SADE *stands underneath* COULMIER's *platform. The bath has been removed from* MARAT's *dais. On it are the* FOUR SINGERS *and the* PATIENTS *who represent the Jacobites.* PATIENTS *sit on benches alongside the arena. There are more* PATIENTS *in the background listening. The entire group composes a tableau. The bath, in which* MARAT *stands, is wheeled in through the door at the back right.*
    CHORUS *in sections:*
    A drawn-out cat-call.
    A long monotonous whistle.
    A muffled trampling of feet.
    MARAT *is pushed in his bath to the centre of the arena. He stands straight and looks towards the* HERALD.

HERALD: Marat is still in his bathtub confined
  but politicians crowd into his mind
  He speaks to them his last polemic fight
  to say who should be tribune. It is almost night

(He gives the ORCHESTRA *a sign with his staff. A flourish. The people in the tableau spring to life, stamp their feet, whistle and shout.)*

KOKOL: Down with Marat
CUCURUCU: Don't let him speak   5
ROSSIGNOL: Listen to him he's got the right to speak
POLPOCH: Long live Marat
KOKOL: Long live Robespierre
CUCURUCU: Long live Danton   10
MARAT *(addressing the audience. During his entire speech he never turns to those present on the stage. It is obvious that his speech is imaginary):* Fellow citizens
  members of the National Assembly
  our country is in danger
  From every corner of Europe armies invade us
  led by profiteers   15
  who want to strangle us
  and already quarrel over the spoils
  And what are we doing

(apathetic noises)

Our minister of war
  whose integrity you never doubted   20
  has sold the corn meant for our armies
  for his own profit to foreign powers
  and now it feeds the troops
  who are invading us

(Cries and whistles.)

KOKOL: Lies
CUCURUCU: Throw him out   25
MARAT: The chief of our army Dumouriez
ROSSIGNOL: Bravo
POLPOCH: Long live Dumouriez
MARAT: against whom I've warned you continually   30
  and whom you recently hailed as a hero
  has gone over to the enemy
KOKOL: Shame
ROSSIGNOL: Bravo
CUCURUCU: Liar   35

(shuffling of feet)

MARAT: Most of the generals
  who wear our uniform
  are sympathetic with the emigrés

and when the emigrés return
    our generals will be out to welcome them   40
KOKOL: Execute them
CUCURUCU: Down with Marat
ROSSIGNOL: Bravo
POLPOCH: Long live Marat
MARAT: Our trusted minister of finance   45
    the celebrated Monsieur Cambon
    is issuing fake banknotes thus increasing inflation
    and diverting a fortune into his own pocket

(*whistles and stamping*)

ROSSIGNOL: Long live free enterprise
MARAT: And I am told   50
    that Perregeaux our most intelligent banker
    is in league with the English
    and in his armoured vaults
    is organising a centre of espionage against us
COULMIER (*jumping up to protest*): That's enough   55
    We're living in eighteen hundred and eight
    and the names which were dragged through the gutter then
    have been deservedly rehabilitated
    by the command of the Emperor
ROSSIGNOL: Go on   60
KOKOL: Shut up Marat
CUCURUCU: Shut his mouth
POLPOCH: Long live Marat
MARAT (*interrupting*): The people can't pay the inflated price of bread
    Our soldiers march in rags   65
    The counter-revolution has started a new civil war
    and what are we doing
    The farms we confiscated from the churches have so far produced nothing
    to feed the dispossessed
    and years have passed since I proposed these farms   70
    should be divided into allotments
    and given farm implements and seed
    And why have we seen no communal workshops
    which were to be started in the old monasteries and country houses
    Those who have jobs   75
    must sweat for agents stockbrokers and speculators

(*wild cries*)

Fellow citizens
    did we fight for the freedom of those
    who now exploit us again
KOKOL: Sit down   80
ROSSIGNOL: Hear hear
CUCURUCU: Sit down
POLPOCH: Hear hear

MARAT: Our country is in danger
    We talk about France
    but who is France for   85
    We talk about freedom
    but who's this freedom for
    Members of the National Assembly
    you will never shake off the past   90
    you'll never understand
    the great upheaval in which you find yourselves

    (*whistles and cries of Boo*)

    Why aren't there thousands of public seats
    in this assembly
    so anyone who wants   95
    can hear what's being discussed
DUPERRET: What is he trying to do
    He's trying to rouse the people again
    Look who sits on the public benches
    Knitting-women concierges and washer-women   100
    with no one to employ them any more
    And who has he got on his side
    Pickpockets layabouts parasites
    who loiter in the boulevards

    (*indignation among the onlookers*)

    and hang around the cafés   105
CUCURUCU: Wish we could
DUPERRET: Released prisoners
    escaped lunatics

    (*tumult and whistling*)

    Does he want to rule our country
    with these
MARAT: You are liars   110
    You hate the people

    (*cries of indignation*)

ROSSIGNOL: Well done Marat
POLPOCH: That's true
MARAT: You'll never stop talking of the people   115
    as a rough and formless mass
    Why
    Because you live apart from them
    You let yourselves be dragged into the Revolution
    knowing nothing about its principles   120
    Has not our respected Danton himself announced
    that instead of banning riches
    we should try

to make poverty respectable
And Robespierre   125
who turns white when the word force is used
doesn't he sit at high-class tables
making cultural conversation
by candlelight

(*tongue clicking*)

KOKOL: Shame   130
CUCURUCU: Down with Robespierre
POLPOCH: Long live Marat
ROSSIGNOL: Down with Danton
MARAT: And you still long to ape them
    those powdered chimpanzees   135
    Necker Lafayette Talleyrand
COULMIER (*interrupting*): That's enough
    If you use any more of these passages
    we agreed to cut
    I will stop your play   140
MARAT (*breaking in*): and all the rest of them
    What we need now is a true deputy of the people
    one who's incorruptible
    one we can trust
    Things are breaking down things are chaotic 145
    that is good
    that's the first step
    Now we must take the next step
    and choose a man
    who will rule for you   150
ROSSIGNOL: Marat for dictator
POLPOCH: Marat in his bathtub
KOKOL: Send him down the sewers
CUCURUCU: Dictator of the rats
MARAT: Dictator The word must be abolished   155
    I hate anything to do with masters and slaves
    I am talking about a leader
    who in this hour of crisis

(*His words are drowned in the mighty tumult.*)

DUPERRET: He's trying to incite them
    to new murders   160
MARAT: We do not murder
    we kill in self-defence
    We are fighting
    for our lives
DUPERRET: Oh if only we could have constructive thought   165
    instead of agitation
    If only beauty and concord could once more replace
    hysteria and fanaticism

(*The* FOUR SINGERS *throw themselves on* DUPERRET *and stop his mouth.*)

ROUX (*jumping up in the background*): Look what's happening
    Join together   170
    'Cast down your enemies
    disarm them
    For if they win
    they will spare
    not one of you   175
    and all that you have won so far
    will be lost

(*Enthusiastic calls, whistles and trampling.*)

CALLS (*in spoken chorus, simultaneously*): Marat Marat Marat Marat
    Boo
    A laurel wreath for Marat   180
    Down with Marat
    A victory parade for Marat
    Down with him
    Long live the streets
    Long live the lamp-posts   185
    Long live the bakers' shops
    Long live freedom

(*Disorder and screams. The* PATIENTS *tumble forward.* MARAT's *bath is pushed on to the platform right.*)

KOKOL AND POLPOCH (*dancing*): Hit at the rich until they crash
    Throw down their god and divide their cash
CUCURUCU AND ROSSIGNOL (*dancing*): We wouldn't mind a tasty meal   190
    of paté de foie and filleted eel
CHORUS: Marat Marat Marat Marat Marat

(SADE *raises his hands. They all freeze. Roll of drums and beginning of music.*)

28. POOR MARAT IN YOUR BATHTUB SEAT

MARAT *sinks back into his bath. Exhausted, he leans forward on the board.*
    The spectators' benches are pushed back, the SISTERS *and* NURSES *force back the* PATIENTS. *In front of the arena the* FOUR SINGERS *dance a slow Carmagnole.*

FOUR SINGERS (*accompanied, singing and dancing*): Poor Marat in your bathtub
    seat
    your life on this planet is near complete
    Closer and closer to you death creeps
    though there on her bench Charlotte Corday sleeps

    Poor Marat if she slept too late   5
    while dreaming of fairy-tale heads of state

maybe your sickness would disappear
Charlotte Corday would not find you here

Poor Marat stay wide awake
and be on your guard for the people's sake   10
Stare through the failing evening light
for this is the evening before the night

(*Drums. In the background order has been restored after a fashion. The* PA-
TIENTS *should be standing upright, their hands crossed above their heads.*
SISTERS *are standing before them, folding their hands and praying. The murmur of prayers can be heard. The* FOUR SINGERS *dance on a while and then
stretch themselves out on the arena before* MARAT's *bath.*)

MARAT (*with fear in his voice*): What is that knocking Simonne

   (*tyrannic again*)

Simonne
more cold water   15

   (SIMONNE *sits huddled up at the edge of the platform and doesn't react.*)

Simonne
Where is Bas
SADE: Give up Marat
   You said yourself
   nothing can be achieved by scribbling   20
   Long ago I abandoned my masterpiece
   a roll of paper thirty yards long
   which I filled completely with minute handwriting
   in my dungeon years ago
   It vanished when the Bastille fell   25
   it vanished as everything written
   everything thought and planned
   will disappear

   (MARAT *lies with his face on the board and covers his ears with his hands.*)

SADE (*continues*): Marat
   Look at me   30
   Marat can you call this living
   in your bath
   in your mortification

   (*By order of the* SISTERS *the* PATIENTS *change their position and stretch up
   their hands.*)

MARAT (*raising himself up*): I had time for nothing but work
   Day and night were not enough for me   35
   When I investigated a wrong it grew branches
   and every branch grew twigs
   Wherever I turned
   I found corruption

(A PATIENT *falls over in the ranks*. A NURSE *carries him off*.)

When I wrote
I always wrote with action in mind   40
kept sight of the fact
that writing was just a preparation
When I wrote
I always wrote in a fever   45
hearing the roar of action
When I was preparing
my books on the chains of slavery
I sat for three months
twenty-one hours a day   50
collecting material dreaming of material
paper piling high parchment crackling
until I sank into the swamps of overwork
That manuscript was suppressed
They were always ready   55
to pick up my statements
to slander them maim them
After each pamphlet was published
I had to go into hiding
They came with cannons   60
A thousand men of the National Guard
surrounded my house
And even today
I still wait for the knocking at the door
wait   65
for the bayonet to point at my breast
Simonne
Simonne
Fetch Bas
so that I can dictate my call   70
my fourteenth of July call
SADE: Why all these calls to the nation
It's too late Marat
forget your call
it contains only lies   75
What do you still want from the Revolution
Where is it going
Look at these lost revolutionaries

(*Pointing to the* FOUR SINGERS *who lie stretched out on the floor, scratching
themselves, yawning and trying to get the last drop out of the empty bottle.*)

What will you order them to do
Where will you lead them   80

(*In the background the* PATIENTS, *on the* SISTERS' *command, must stand on
one leg.*)

Once you attacked the authorities who turned
the law into instruments of oppression
Do you want someone to rule you
to control the words you write
and tell you   85
what work you must do
and repeat to you the new laws
over and over
until you can recite them in your sleep

(*The* PATIENTS *in the background walk in a circle while the* SISTERS *pray. The* FOUR SINGERS *begin to hum unconcernedly, lying at first on the floor with legs waving in the air. Then* ROSSIGNOL *and* CUCURUCU *get up and dance to the hummed melody.*)

MARAT (*falling across the board again*): Why is everything so confused now
Everything I wrote or spoke   90
was considered and true
each argument was sound
And now
doubt   95
Why does everything sound false
THE FOUR SINGERS (*singing and dancing*): Poor old Marat you lie prostrate
while others are gambling with France's fate
Your words have turned into a flood
which covers all France with her people's blood   100

(*Music ends. The* FOUR SINGERS *dance back to the centre of the stage. The* PATIENTS *are led to their platform. The* SISTERS *try to wake* CORDAY. *Loud knocking three times.*)

29. Preparations for the Third Visit

HERALD: Corday
wake up

(*Pause. The name* CORDAY *is whispered in the background. The whispering swells up and spreads over the whole stage. The* SISTERS *shake* CORDAY, DU- PERRET *calls her name.* SIMONNE *stands awkwardly by the bath and gazes across at* CORDAY.)

CHORUS: Corday
Corday
Corday   5
HERALD (*signals to the* ORCHESTRA *with his staff*): Corday you have an appoint-
ment to keep
and there is no more time for sleep
Charlotte Corday awake and stand
Take the dagger in your hand

(*Pause. The* SISTERS *raise* CORDAY *to her feet.* CORDAY *stands with lowered head and wobbly legs. The* SISTERS *support her and lead her slowly forward. Her legs drag along the floor.* DUPERRET *walks behind her with his hands around her hips.*)

HERALD: Come on Charlotte do your deed   10
    soon you'll get all the sleep you need

(CORDAY *is pushed into the arena. The two* SISTERS *stand at her side holding her firmly.* DUPERRET, *standing behind her, supports her back. Music ends.*)

CORDAY (*her eyes still closed, speaking, softly, nervously*): Now I know what it is
    like
  when the head is cut off the body
  Oh this moment
  hands tied behind the back   15
  feet bound together
  neck bared
  hair cut off
  knees on the boards
  the head already laid   20
  in the metal slot
  looking down into the dripping basket
  The sound of the blade rising
  and from its slanting edge
  the blood still drops   25
  and then the downward slide
  to split us in two

  (*pause*)

  They say
  that the head
  held high in the executioner's hand
  still lives   30
  that the eyes still see
  that the tongue still writhes
  and down below the arms and legs still shudder
DUPERRET (*accompanied by lute. He is still holding his hand on her hip*):
    Charlotte awaken from your nightmare   35
  Wake up Charlotte and look at the trees
  look at the rose-coloured evening sky
  in which your lovely bosom heaves

(*Pause. He lifts his hand and strokes her on the bosom. He notices the dagger under the cloth.*)

  Forget your worries abandon each care
  and breathe in the warmth of the summertime air   40
  What are you hiding

A dagger
throw it away

(*the music ends*)

CORDAY (*pushes his hand away*): We should all carry weapons nowadays
    in self-defence   45
DUPERRET (*beseechingly*): No one will attack you Charlotte
    Charlotte throw the dagger away
    go away
    go back to Caen
CORDAY (*drawing herself up and pushing the* SISTERS' *hands away*): In my room
    in Caen   50
    on the table under the open window
    lies open The Book of Judith
    Dressed in her legendary beauty
    she entered the tent of the enemy
    and with a single blow   55
    slew him
DUPERRET: Charlotte
    what are you planning
CORDAY (*forlorn again*): Look at this city
    Its prisons are crowded   60
    with our friends
    I was among them just now
    in my sleep
    They all stand huddled together there
    and hear through the windows   65
    the guards talking about executions
    Now they talk of people as gardeners talk of leaves for burning
    Their names are crossed off the top of a list
    and as the list grows shorter
    more names are added at the bottom   70
    I stood with them
    and we waited
    for our own names to be called
DUPERRET: Charlotte
    let us leave together   75
    this very evening
CORDAY (*as if she has not heard him*): What kind of town is this
    What sort of streets are these
    Who invented this
    who profits by it   80
    I saw peddlers
    at every corner
    they're selling little guillotines
    with tiny sharp blades
    and dolls filled with red liquid   85
    which spurts from the neck
    when the sentence is carried out

What kind of children are these
who can play
with this toy so efficiently
and who is judging
who is judging

(PATIENTS move to a group at centre. CORDAY raises her hand to knock.)

30. CORDAY'S THIRD AND LAST VISIT

The HERALD *knocks three times on the floor with his staff while* CORDAY *carries out the knocking movement with her hand.* MARAT *starts up and looks in* CORDAY's *direction.* SIMONNE *places herself protectively in front of the bath.*

DUPERRET: What do you want at this door
    Do you know who lives here
CORDAY: The man
    for whose sake I have come here
DUPERRET: What do you want from him
    Turn back Charlotte

(goes on his knees before her)

CORDAY: I have a task
    which I must carry out
    Go

(Pushes him with her foot.)

leave me alone

(DUPERRET embraces her legs. She kicks out at him several times. DUPERRET *moves back on his knees.)*

HERALD: Now for the third time you observe
    the girl whose job it is to serve

(points to CORDAY)

as Charlotte Corday stands once more
waiting outside Marat's door
Duperret you see before her languish

(points to DUPERRET)

prostrated by their parting's anguish

(raising a forefinger)

For what has happened cannot be undone
although that might be wished by everyone

(pointing to CORDAY)

We tried restraining her with peaceful sleep
and with the claims of a passion still more deep
Simonne as well as best she could she tried

(*pointing to* SIMONNE)

but this girl here

(*points to* CORDAY)

would not be turned aside
That man is now forgotten and we can

(*points to* DUPERRET, *who moves backwards on his knees from the dais*)

do nothing more Corday is focussed on this man   25

(*points to* MARAT)

MARAT: No

(*raising himself high*)

I am right
and I will say it once more
Simonne
where is Bas   30
It is urgent
my call

(SIMONNE *moves aside, stops still and stares bewitched at* CORDAY.)

SADE (*approaches the bath*): Marat
what are all your pamphlets and speeches
compared with her   35
she stands there and will come to you
to kiss you and embrace you
Marat
an untouched virgin stands before you and offers herself to you
See how she smiles   40

(CORDAY *stands erect and smiling, throwing her hair aside. She has her hand
on the neckcloth in the place where the dagger is hidden.*)

how her teeth shine
how she shakes her auburn hair aside
Marat
forget the rest
there's nothing else   45
beyond the body
Look
she stands there
her breast naked under the thin cloth
and perhaps she carries a knife   50
to intensify the love-play

(CORDAY *moves a step closer to the bath, swaying lightly.* SIMONNE *stands
frozen, mechanically wringing the cloth in her hands.*)

MARAT: Simonne Simonne
who was knocking at the door

SADE: A maiden
  from the rural desert of a convent
  Imagine   55
  those pure girls lying on hard floors
  in rough shifts
  and the heated air from the fields
  forcing its way to them through the barred windows   60
  Imagine
  them lying there
  with moist thighs and breasts
  dreaming of those
  who control life in the outside world   65

(*The* FOUR SINGERS *come forward and begin a copulation mime.*
    ROSSIGNOL *mounts the strongest of her companions and performs acrobatics
with them.*)

SADE (*to musical accompaniment*): And then she was tired of her isolation
  and stirred up by the new age
  and gathered up in the great tide
  and wanted to be part of the Revolution
  And what's the point of a revolution
  without general copulation   70
CHORUS: And what's the point of a revolution
  without general
  copulation copulation copulation

(*continues as a round. Mime ends.*)

SADE: Marat   75
  as I sat there in the Bastille
  for thirteen long years
  I learned
  that this is a world of bodies
  each body pulsing with a terrible power   80
  each body alone and racked with its own unrest
  In that loneliness
  marooned in a stone sea
  I heard lips whispering continually
  and felt all the time
  in the palms of my hands and in my skin   85
  touching and stroking
  Shut behind thirteen bolted doors
  my feet fettered
  I dreamed only
  of the orifices of the body   90
  put there
  so one may hook and twine oneself in them

(A PATIENT *comes forward on tip-toe and stops behind the arena, listening
tensely. Other* PATIENTS *follow.*)

Continually I dreamed of this confrontation
and it was a dream of the most savage jealous   95
and cruellest imagining
Marat
these cells of the inner self
are worse than the deepest stone dungeon
and as long as they are locked   100
all your Revolution remains
only a prison mutiny
to be put down
by corrupted fellow-prisoners
CHORUS (*repeating with musical accompaniment*): And what's the point of a
    revolution   105
without general copulation

(*Music ends.*)

CORDAY (*to* SIMONNE. *Lute accompaniment*): Have you given my letter to
    Marat
Let me in it is vital
I must tell him what's happening in Caen
where they are gathering to destroy him   110
MARAT: Who's at the door
SIMONNE: The girl from Caen
MARAT: Let her come in

(SIMONNE *stands aside, shaking her head vigorously. She squats down at the
edge of the dais behind the bath and hides her head in her hands.* CORDAY
*moves towards the bath, swaying and smiling. Her hand still rests on her
neckcloth.* SADE *leaves the arena and goes to his dais, where he remains,
standing, watching tensely.*)

CORDAY (*softly*): Marat
I will tell you the names of my heroes   115
but I am not betraying them
for I am speaking to a dead man
MARAT (*raising himself up*): Speak more clearly
I can't understand you
Come closer   120
CORDAY (*coming closer to the bath with a fixed smile, her body slowly swaying.
    She pushes a hand under her neckcloth*): I name you names
Marat
the names of those
who have gathered at Caen

(*falling into a sing-song*)

I name Barbaroux   125
and Buzot
and Pétion
and Louvet

(As she speaks the names her face is distorted increasingly by an expression of hate and lust.)

and Brissot
and Vergniaud
and Guadet
and Gensonné   130
MARAT: Who are you
Come closer

(MARAT raises himself up high. The cloth falls from his shoulders. CORDAY moves closer to him, swaying. Her left hand is stretched out as if to caress. In the right hand she holds the dagger under the neckcloth.)

CORDAY *(humming words which sound like caresses)*: I am coming Marat   135
You cannot see me Marat
because you are dead
MARAT *(crying out, raising himself up high, half-naked)*: Bas
Take this down
Saturday the thirteenth of July seventeen hundred and ninety three   140
A call to the people of France

(CORDAY stands immediately before MARAT. She moves her left hand close to his skin over his chest, his shoulders, his neck. MARAT sits arched over the back of the bath, a pen still in his hand. CORDAY pulls the dagger from her neck-cloth. She holds it with both hands and raises her arms high to strike.
The HERALD blows shrilly on his whistle.
All players remain unmoving in their positions.
CORDAY sinks back into herself. MARAT sits quietly, leaning forward.)

31. INTERRUPTUS

HERALD: Now it's a part of Sade's dramatic plan
to interrupt the climax so this man
Marat can hear and gasp with his last breath
at how the world will go after his death
With a musical history we'll bring him up to date   5
From seventeen-ninety-three to eighteen-eight

(Music starts with very quick military march. The FOUR SINGERS sing and perform grotesquely in time to the music. The HERALD displays banners showing the date of the events as they are described.)

FOUR SINGERS: Now your enemies fall
We're beheading them all (1793)
Duperret
and Corday
executed in the same old way   10
Robespierre has to get on (1794)
he gets rid of Danton
That was spring
comes July   15

and old Robespierre has to die
Three rebellions a year (1795)
but we're still of good cheer
Malcontents
all have been
taught their lesson by the guillotine
There's a shortage of wheat (1796)
We're too happy to eat
Austria
cracks and then
she surrenders to our men

Fifteen glorious years
Fifteen glorious years
Years of peace
years of war
each year greater
than the year before
Marat
we're marching on

What brave soldiers we've got (1797)
Now the traitors are shot
Generals
boldly take
power in Paris
for the people's sake
Egypt's beaten down flat (1798)
Bonaparte did that
Cheer him as
they retreat
even though we lose our fleet
Bonaparte comes back (1799)
gives our rulers the sack
He's the man (1800)
brave the true
Bonaparte would die for you
Europe's free of her chains (1801)
Only England remains
but we want (1802)
wars to cease
so there's fourteen months of peace

(PATIENTS *join in, marching on the spot.*)

Fifteen glorious years
Fifteen glorious years
Years of peace
years of war
each year greater
than the year before

Marat
we're marching on

England must be insane (1803)
wants to fight us again   65
so we march
off to war
Bonaparte is our emperor (1804)
Nelson bothers our fleet
but he's shot off his feet   70
We're on top
yes we are
and we spit on Trafalgar
Now the Prussians retreat (1806)
Russia faces defeat (1807)   75
All the world
bends its knee
to Napoleon
and his family
Fight on land and on sea (1808)   80
All men want to be free
If they don't
never mind
we'll abolish all mankind

Fifteen glorious years   85
Fifteen glorious years
Years of peace
years of war
each year greater
than the one before   90
Marat
we're marching on
behind Napoleon

32. THE MURDER

The entire cast have resumed their positions exactly as before the song.

CORDAY *clasps the knife with both hands above her head. Very slowly she lowers it towards* MARAT. SADE *follows her movements precisely, bending from the waist. She kills* MARAT. PATIENTS *let out one single scream.* CORDAY *crumples on the stage.* SADE *stands contemplating the scene.* MARAT *hangs as in David's classical picture, with his right hand over the edge of the bath. In his right hand he still holds his pen, in his left his papers.*

33. EPILOGUE

The ORCHESTRA *starts to play soft ceremonious music.*

The SISTERS *come forward and take charge of* CORDAY. MARAT *steps out of his bath.* COULMIER *comes forward.*

COULMIER: Enlightened ladies pious gentlemen
  let's close the history book and then
  return to eighteen-eight the present day
  of which though not unclouded we may say
  it promises that mankind soon will cease   5
  to fear the storms of war the squalls of peace

(*The music turns more and more into a monotonous march. The* PATIENTS *in
the background mark time. Their unrest increases.*)

  For today we live in far different times
  We have no oppressors no violent crimes
  and although we're at war anyone can see
  it can only end in victory   10
FOUR SINGERS: And if most have a little and few have a lot
  you can see how much nearer our goal we have got
  We can say what we like without favour or fear
  and what we can't say we can breathe in your ear
ROUX (*through the singing*): When will you learn to see   15
  When will you learn to take sides
  When will you show them
FOUR SINGERS: And though we're locked up we're no longer enslaved
  and the honour of France is eternally saved
  The useless debate the political brawl   20
  are over there's one man to speak for us all
  For he helps us in sickness and destitution
  he's the leader who ended the Revolution
  and everyone knows why we're cheering for
  Napoleon our mighty Emperor   25

(*During the song* COULMIER *and his* FAMILY *have congratulated* SADE *and
chatted with him.* SADE *presents various members of the cast. At this point
the music grows louder. The column of* PATIENTS *begins to march forward.*
SISTERS *and* NURSES *try to restrain it. Several times the column advances four
paces and takes three paces back. The music and marching rhythm grow in
power.* COULMIER *moves anxiously to the side gesticulating.*)

ALL: Led by him our soldiers go
  over deserts and through the snow
  A victory here and a victory there
  Invincible glorious always victorious
  for the good of all people everywhere   30

(*The column advances still further, stamping some paces forward and some
back. The* HERALD *begins to throw buckets etc. around.* NURSES *try to restrain
him.* COULMIER's FAMILY *flee, screaming and shouting.*)

ALL (*in confused but rhythmic shouts in time to the marching*): Charenton
  Charenton
  Napoleon Napoleon
  Nation Nation

Revolution Revolution
Copulation Copulation

35

(*The shouting grows. The column reaches the front. The struggle between* NURSES *and* HERALD *develops and catches the attention of the others. Suddenly the whole stage is fighting.* SADE *watches with a faint smile, almost indulgent. The actors have moved to the side. Music, shouting and tramping increase to a tempest. A strong wind blows in through the upper side windows. The huge curtains billow far into the room. The* NURSES *go among the* PATIENTS *wielding their batons.* ROUX *springs forward and places himself before the marchers, his back to them, still with fettered arms.*)

ROUX: When will you learn to see
When will you learn to take sides

(*He tries to force them back, but is drawn in and vanishes from sight in the still advancing ranks.*

The PATIENTS *are fully at the mercy of their mad marchlike dance. Many of them hop and spin in ecstasy.* COULMIER *incites the* NURSES *to extreme violence.* PATIENTS *are struck down. The* HERALD *is now in front of the* ORCHESTRA, *leaping about in time to the music.* SADE *stands upright on his chair, laughing triumphantly.*

In desperation COULMIER *gives the signal to close the curtain.*)

CURTAIN

AFTERWORD

At a performance of *Marat/Sade* we watch inmates of the insane asylum at Charenton in 1808 perform Sade's play about the assassination of Marat in Paris in 1793. After the killing, the patient-victim "steps out of his bath," his role done. But Sade's play for his fellow inmates arouses them to riot, and Weiss's play ends in violent confusion. What we have seen is a refraction of the French Revolution through a lunatic theatrical that gets out of hand.

Just about everything that is difficult and meaningful in *Marat/Sade* follows from its refractive structure. Its free verse recitations and songs are never involuted or abstract. It is not a study in intricate character psychology or personal relationships. And if the confrontations of ideologies in Marat's and Sade's conversations do not make a complete and coherent debate on the meaning of revolution, neither are they obscure. The play assaults our senses and teases our minds because Sade's ritual reenactment of the past in psychodrama is constantly being subverted by its performers. Irrational acts intrude upon rehearsed histrionics, autocratic systems upon enacted and real revolution, the reality of 1808 upon the imaginary 1793, and our reflections on the intrusions upon our observation of the action.

Saying that Weiss's play has a play-within-a-play structure does not really describe it adequately — certainly not if the term is taken to imply a stable relationship between two levels of action. Rather than one action enclosing another (the way the mousetrap scene in *Hamlet* is framed by the story of Hamlet's revenge, or the way the legend of Grusha in *The Caucasian Chalk Circle* is contained by the kolkhoz action), there is in *Marat/Sade* incessant interflow of an inner action about revolution and an outer action about lunatics. The reversible equation of revolution and lunacy is the core concept of the play, the historical hero as mad actor its master metaphor, and disorder — in the state (revolution) and in the self (lunacy) — both its subject and its unifying theatrical image. Quite properly, the total stage action reaches us as a cacophony of voices set in a kaleidoscope of pantomimes. The disorder on the stage eludes a firm cognitive grasp. As a play about a disintegrating theatrical performance it could be said to self-destruct, and its proven power over audiences becomes a mordant paradox that reflects on our vision of history as progress and on our sense of a coherent dramatic tradition.

Not much that is important can be said about such a play in the traditional vocabulary of drama criticism. Categories of critical analysis like plot structure, dialogue texture, and character motivation become all but irrelevant. Part narrative, part discourse, and part ritual incantation, *Marat/Sade* is above all a play of intense visuality that works by the rationale of theatrical montage. By missing the spectacle, a reader of *Marat/Sade* loses more of the meaning of the play than with most plays. But in the theater the viewer may lose much of the verbal meaning under the powerful spell of the spectacle. Even in an ideally complete experience of the play, its structure is a labyrinth from which there is no carrying away clear meanings in safe and easy exit. The play reorders no hierarchy of values, assumes no absolutes, and will not let us rest in any single point of view. One wonders what Molière and Ibsen would have thought of it.

It tells no coherent story about credible characters who reveal themselves in the imaginary present tense in which conventional dramatic action occurs. The Charenton bathhouse is an illusionistic set, but the illusion is made precarious by the obvious relevance for the 1960s of Roux's tirades ("We demand that everyone should do all they can / to put an end to war / This damned war / which is run for the benefit of profiteers / and leads only to more wars") and of Coulmier's (and the Herald's) repeated assurances that the Napoleonic, unlike the Revolutionary, era is enlightened, humane, and liberal. Listening to the voice of the 1808 establishment we hear that of our own, benevolently complacent. And in the staging of Sade's play, there is hardly any attempt at illusionism at all. As a piece of equipment that naturally belongs in the bathhouse, Marat's bathtub is an equivocal prop: Corday's first arrival in Paris is staged next to it. The play creates no suspense, for Coulmier's Prologue — if not our memory of the historical facts — tells us that Corday will kill Marat before the play is over. What intervenes between the Prologue and the assassination

is not a causally connected sequence of events leading up to and accounting for the assassination, but a succession of choric songs and commentaries, tiradic outbursts, philosophical discussions, and insane pantomime
delaying its accomplishment.

The result is that Weiss's play is, among other things, about the difficulties of staging Sade's play. Some of the interruptions are impromptu inter-
ferences by the onstage audience of asylum inmates and by Coulmier inter-
fering with the interferers and admonishing Sade to keep his production
under control. But others are in Sade's script, so that Sade and Weiss become collaborators in the use of play-writing tactics that continually digress
from the straight progress of the nominally central title action. Time shifts
not just between 1793 and 1808; there are also the flashback appearances of
Marat's parents and other figures from his past, some historical (Voltaire,
Lavoisier) and some fictitious (the Schoolmaster). No scene in the play is
unaffected by the form of a theater using itself *as* itself rather than as a
piece of offstage space peopled not by actors but by the real-life characters
they impersonate. Corday almost disrupts the measured progress of Sade's
ritualized version of the murder of Marat by trying to commit the murder
prematurely. The Herald, dressed in motley like a medieval court jester or
the harlequin figure from the *commedia dell'arte* of the late Renaissance,
introduces a scene between Corday and Duperret by promising us relief
from the "painful matters" that have just preceded: the persecution of
Marat in a scene replete with imagery of deadly fever, loathsome disease,
darkened sun, and burning corpses. What we are to see next will recall for
us the couple's "love so pure," "the sweet blending of the strong and fair
sex." But what we actually get is a grotesque tableau, mock-heroic and
mock-romantic, of an erotomaniac frantically fondling a somnambulist.

The scene illustrates Weiss's main design: the interpenetration of the
play about the lunatics at Charenton and the play about the assassination
in Paris as mutually ironic commentaries. The modern actor playing Marat
impersonates not the revolutionary leader but a paranoiac impersonating
Marat. His paranoia is ironically vindicated when he is "killed." Corday is
not Corday but a semiconscious melancholiac who has to be prompted in
her part. Sade acts himself but interacts with his fellow patients who are
playing the roles of the historical figures his play is about. The Charenton
action is a screen between us and the events of the French Revolution, but
the idea of the Revolution fills the minds of the Charenton inmates. Their
chaotic violence is a parody of the Revolution, but the parody moves by
the same emotional dynamic as the Revolution's quest for a perfected social order. The ironic vision of the Revolution as something happening in a
madman's brain is balanced by the disturbing vision of a revolt for liberty
being suppressed by the post-Revolution establishment — lunacy, as Susan
Sontag has observed, being here a metaphor for passion. When the patients usurp the stage in an ending Sade may or may not have planned,
they represent the oppressed people of France, having traded king for emperor, still dispossessed, still not free, and still wanting "Revolution NOW."

But their violence is now no longer a programmed dramatization of events that occurred fifteen years earlier, censored and licensed by the director of Charenton for patient "rehabilitation" and audience "delectation." It is a spontaneous actuality in 1808, a revolt against Coulmier's own regime, forcing his family to flee the stage in screaming terror. And the spectacle implicates us, for we are in the seats presumably occupied by the 1808 audience threatened by the bathhouse riot: the fashionable ladies and gentlemen who have come out from Paris to attend one of the notorious Marquis de Sade's theatrical productions "in the 'hiding-place for the moral rejects of civilized society.' "* Coulmier addresses his welcoming Prologue to them, but he is looking at us. Politics and insanity; metaphysics and mad antics; the streets of Paris in 1793 and the bathhouse at Charenton in 1808; the real Marat and Marat the paranoiac; Sade the detached playwright and Sade letting himself be whipped by Corday; Roux, the socialist priest, half in and half out of Sade's play; and the modern audience watching a spectacle that is a threat and an accusation — these are among the shifting constituents in the play's large complex of unresolved tensions.

In an attempt to impose some kind of stable shape on this flux, we may try to distinguish among circles of action, defining each by a separate conflict. Working from the center and out, we find Corday versus Marat, Marat versus Sade, Sade versus Coulmier, patients as performers versus patients as patients, inmates versus audience. But the paradigm collapses when we test it against what actually goes on. Our circles expand and contract and open up, letting characters pass freely from one to another. If we decide we need a separate circle for the Herald and the Four Singers as choric figures, where does it fit in? Their choric functions are not the same. The Herald stage-manages Sade's play about events in Paris in 1793, speaks in ironic echo of Coulmier's self-congratulatory "modern" voice, and is in both capacities presumably Sade's manipulated puppet. The Four Singers, a ribald and unsavory quartet from the Paris gutters, are both spokesmen for and victims of the Revolution, and it is never clear whether or not they perform under Sade's control and whether they realize that they are only members of the asylum cast reenacting Marat's death or think they are witnessing the actual assassination of the real Marat. The characters of the inmost circle arrange themselves in a symmetrical pattern of two complementary couples. The victim Marat, the would-be dictator confined to his bathtub, physically passive but impatient to act, is cared for by the spastic Simonne, urging him to rest. The assassin Corday, nearly passive in her somnolence, is caressed and urged to abstain from action by the hyperactive Duperret. Duperret, the lover, fails to keep Corday from murdering Marat, just as Simonne, Marat's mistress, fails to protect her lover. The assassination itself is both a double martyrdom and — by gesture and verbal image — Corday's act of love. All this is a tidy visualization of historical ironies. But when he debates Sade, Marat moves out of this

---

* From Weiss's "Note on the Historical Background to the Play."

circle, or, alternatively, Sade enters it, as he does also when he ironically assumes Marat's role as Corday's victim in the whipping scene. Our concept of the play as a system of concentric circles of action is useful only up to a point, because the multi-leveled structure is too fluid and flexible to be held in a fixed pattern. It cannot, for example, sort out the ambiguities that make up the crucial idea of "audience" in the play.

Weiss himself has said that the "encounter" between Marat and Sade is "the subject" of his play. His remark makes it all the more tempting to turn from the perplexities of the theatricalist form to the drama of ideas he implies is the reason for the play's being. The encounter is between Marat's passionate commitment to collective action for social reform and Sade's skeptical withdrawal into anarchic individualism. The issue is the utility or futility of revolution. With just as much right as Marat, Sade can claim to "be" the Revolution, since in his prison fantasies he has already acted out its cruelest horrors. His imagination, "the world inside myself," is his "only reality." Alone in its "stillness," he finds in murder "the final proof of my existence."

> In a criminal society
> I dug the criminal out of myself
> so I could understand him and so understand
> the times we live in

Man is a criminal in solitary confinement, for "the cells of the inner self / are worse than the deepest stone dungeons," and consequently (he tells Marat):

> all your Revolution remains
> only a prison mutiny
> to be put down
> by corrupted fellow-prisoners

Because the root of social evil is not in any political and economic system but in humanity itself, revolution is futile and self-perpetuating violence. The "basis for all life is death," but with the guillotine the Revolution has made dying wholesale and mechanical, passionless and therefore meaningless. In contrast, the ghastly ceremony of the four-hour execution of Damiens, King Louis XV's would-be assassin, was a recognition of the significance of individual suffering. The Revolution leads "To the withering of the individual man / . . . to the death of choice." Sade thinks of himself as "one of those who has to be defeated," for in his chosen stance as alienated observer, passive in his conviction of the unredeemable depravity of the human species, he denies everything the Revolution assumes. For him, as for one of his fellow inmate-prisoners, "man is a mad animal," incapable of progress.

Sade's nihilistic solipsism puts him beyond both indignation and despair. Against it, Marat, the romantic activist, asserts human-made absolutes of value. "What you call the indifference of Nature," he tells Sade, "is your own lack of compassion"; and to Sade's contemptuous "Compassion is the property of the privileged classes," Marat replies:

> Against Nature's silence I use action
> In the vast indifference I invent a meaning
> I don't watch unmoved I intervene
> and say that this and this are wrong
> and I work to alter them and improve them

When Sade says that the leaders of the Revolution "would like to kill each other over trifles," Marat retorts, "But they aren't trifles / They are matters of principle." The Revolution must go on, for the bourgeoisie has set itself up as tyrannical exploiters in the place of the executed king and nobles: "We do not murder / we kill in self-defense / We are fighting for our lives." On the fourth anniversary of the fall of the Bastille, the prison symbol of the old regime where Sade himself was confined for years, Marat is writing still another "call to the people of France" for more bloodshed in the name of freedom and justice. Evil must be eliminated, and it *can* be eliminated, for evil is not in people themselves but in what Marat's follower Roux calls "circumstances," in systems and institutions that can be changed. Marat's philosophy is essentially Rousseau's. People, his position implies, are capable of acting for the good of all, of submerging personal interest in the interest of the community. The ideological clash between Sade and Marat has less to do with politics as the means and ends of social change than with irreconcilable differences between two views of human nature.

Marat/Sade ends with Roux's call to the audience for social commitment: "When will you learn to see / When will you learn to take sides." For those for whom the heart of the play is the Marat-Sade debates, Roux's question poses itself as a categorical imperative. But which of the two does Weiss want us to side with: Marat, the social activist who kills from an idealistic belief in a better future; or Sade, the isolated absurdist who inflicts violence only upon himself? Marat, the pre-Marxist; or Sade, the pre-Freudian (in the critic Samuel A. Weiss's illuminating if not exhaustive contrast)? To the extent that we sense the insistent topicality of their encounter, we take sides according to our own convictions about social values and human nature, and if the play leaves us neutral or undecided, we feel guilty — the way anyone does who remains uncommitted these days. But if we return the encounter to its place within the turning prism of the lunatic performance, we may begin to doubt the possibility of determining its rights and wrongs, truths and errors. We may come to say with Sade:

> I
> do not know myself
> No sooner have I discovered something
> than I begin to doubt it
> . . . I do not know if I am hangman or victim

or with Marat:

> Why is everything so confused now
> Everything I wrote or spoke
> was considered and true
> each argument was sound
> And now
> I doubt
> Why does everything sound false

It is difficult not to feel that Sade is the more agile and cogent debater, but then we reflect that he is also the presumed author of Marat's lines and may naturally have reserved the best lines for himself. Are the debates, then, only internal dialogues between two sides in Sade's divided mind, the tortured reaching for unreachable truth by a man who has come to doubt his own doubts? How committed is he to his sardonic disengagement? What do we make of the fact that Sade himself is an inmate of Charenton, a certified madman, whose name has become a byword for unspeakable sexual perversions? How seriously are we supposed to take a controversy between two lunatics? Do not the line divisions, which arbitrarily (except, significantly, in the songs) break up units of meaning, serve to subtly remind us that much of the time the characters do not really know what they are saying? Since writing *Marat/Sade*, Weiss has publicly sided with Marat's belief in the value of social revolution. But regardless of his personal political beliefs, his play is not reducible to thesis drama. There is in it no character whom we can safely accept as the authoritative voice of the playwright. A consideration of the ideologies confronting one another in the Marat-Sade debates may take us to the heart of the labyrinth, but it does not show us the way out. The play is a dramatic inquiry, left unresolved at the end.

This skeptical open-endedness has become something of a signature of contemporary drama on philosophical themes. But of the three names, Luigi Pirandello, Bertolt Brecht, and Antonin Artaud, that first come to mind when we seek to relate *Marat/Sade* to the traditions of modern drama, only the earliest of them, Pirandello, is a confirmed skeptic. Weiss's Pirandellian heritage is evident in his use of the stage as a vehicle for radical relativism: In *Marat/Sade* as in Pirandello, art and life, role and reality, illusion and truth, sanity and insanity, then and now, coalesce in endless and slippery configurations of paradox. As in Pirandello's *Six Characters in Search of an Author*, the primary situation in *Marat/Sade* is a moment from the past frozen in the timeless present of dramatic art. From Brecht, Weiss has taken *Verfremdung* devices, such as choric narrative and a multitude of brief, disjunctive scenes, that keep us from mistaking the theatrical spectacle for realistic mimesis and from losing ourselves in empathy when we should be provoked to thought about human nature and social justice.

But Artaud, the French poet-director and theorist of "the drama of cruelty," is the name that figures most frequently in critical discussions of the influences on *Marat/Sade*. Susan Sontag, for example, sees Weiss's play as representing an unlikely but brilliant marriage of Brecht's "theater of intelligence" and Artaud's "theater of magic, of gesture, of 'cruelty,' of feeling." Artaud's influence on Weiss is real enough. A play about Sade with a play *by* Sade inside it has, not surprisingly, its moments of cruelty, even in the literal sense. And in its escape from the tyranny of the dramatic text, Weiss's play comes close to realizing the "total theater" envisioned by Artaud in *The Theater and Its Double* (1938) — a theater speaking to "total man," "staging events not men," a myth-embodying theater of all the senses, inducing a "delirium" of the spirit, a "mirage," a "virtual reality," prefiguring the primary reality, ecstatic and terrible, that Artaud calls his theater's "double." Artaud wanted to restore the kind of theater that Friedrich Nietzsche postulated as the origin of western drama in *The Birth of Tragedy* (1871, 1886), though Artaud derived his theater from oriental models rather than from Nietzsche's synthesis of Apollonian artifice and the passional wisdom of Dionysus.

But Artaud's influence of *Marat/Sade* is more a matter of form than of substance, and much of the influence comes filtered through absurdist drama: its restless kinetic energy and its chaotic irrationality. (*Marat/Sade* obviously has nothing in common with the small, claustrophobic, quiescent worlds of Beckett and Pinter.) And in addition to Artaud, not just Pirandello and Brecht but also other, older dramatists and dramas have contributed to Weiss's distinctive use of the theater: the Greek tragic dithyramb and chorus, the medieval passion play with its stylized staging, Shakespeare's panoramic dramaturgy, the improvisations in the Italian *commedia dell'arte*. The justly celebrated Peter Brook production of Weiss's play was faithful to its Artaudian spirit in making it an occasion for a theater that nearly overwhelms sight and hearing. But the cool and complex intellectualism that never quite lets go its control of the violent spectacles in *Marat/Sade* has no counterpart in Artaud's theater of sensuousness and passion. Not the least vital of the many tensions in Weiss's play is that between its ironic vision of western history and its spectacular physicality.

Marat/Sade is a play that seeks to comprehend the diversity of the modern experience in a single artistic form. To that end, it draws upon a variety of old and new dramatic styles and conventions. Its ideological pluralism is both a function of and analogous to the heterogeneity of its sources in earlier traditions of the theater. Its unity strains, but it holds, and without the strain it would have been not just a smaller but a much less relevant play in a world that has become a confused battleground for cultural heritages. That it withholds a final "meaning" seems almost tragically right: It puts before us a mirror image that is grotesque, violent, and perplexing. It has already become a central item in the modern repertory.

Appendix

BIOGRAPHICAL NOTES

EDWARD FRANKLIN ALBEE (1928–   ), one of the first successful practitioners of absurd drama in this country, is the adopted child of a New York family, whose wealth comes from a chain of theaters. He does not know his real parents. By his own account, he was a "problem child," who went through the dismissals from schools (he left Trinity College without a degree) and the sequence of odd jobs (one as a Western Union messenger boy) that in the mind of the public have become obligatory early experience for a successful American writer. In 1958 what Albee calls a "creative explosion" led to the writing of *The Zoo Story* in three weeks. It was first produced in Germany in 1959. A later, off-Broadway production received favorable reviews. *The American Dream*, an assault on a whole spectrum of middle-class values, was begun in 1959 but laid aside, completed in 1960, and produced on Broadway early in 1961. In the meantime Albee had written two other short plays, *The Sandbox* (with the same family that appears in *The American Dream*) and the antiracist *Death of Bessie Smith*. His first full-length Broadway play, *Who's Afraid of Virginia Woolf?* (1962), raised a storm of controversy and acclaim in both America and Europe. In 1963 two members of the Pulitzer Prize drama jury resigned in protest against the refusal of the advisory board to make public the jury's nomination and the board's veto of the play for the 1962 award. Hostility to the play centered on its alleged "obscenity." *The Ballad of the Sad Café*, a dramatization of Carson McCullers's novella, was written before *Virginia Woolf* but first produced in 1963. Albee's most recent plays have not added to his already high reputation. They include *Tiny Alice* (1964), a religious allegory-fantasy variously judged and interpreted; two adaptations, *Malcolm* (1966) and *Everything in the Garden* (1967); *A Delicate Balance* (1966), generally favorably received and awarded the Pulitzer Prize; the two one-acters *Box* and *Quotations from Chairman Mao Tse-tung* (both 1968); *All Over* (1971); and *Seascape* (1975). The question of his future career is, as one critic has said, "no more than the question of the use to which he will put his abilities."

Suggested Reading

Albee, Edward F. "Which Theatre Is the Absurd One?" *The New York Times Magazine*, Feb. 25, 1962.

Amacher, Richard E. *Edward Albee*. New York: Twayne, 1969.

Baxandall, Lee. "The Theatre of Edward Albee." *Tulane Drama Review* 9 (1965):19–40.

Bigsby, C. W. E. *Confrontation and Commitment*. Columbia, Mo.: University of Missouri Press, 1968.

Bigsby, C. W. E., ed. *Edward Albee: A Collection of Critical Essays*. Englewood Cliffs, N.J.: Prentice-Hall (Spectrum), 1975.

Cohn, Ruby. *Edward Albee*. Minneapolis, Minn.: University of Minnesota Press, 1969.

Flanagan, William. "Edward Albee: An Interview." *Paris Review* 10 (1966):93–121.

Hayman, Ronald. *Edward Albee*. New York: Ungar, 1973.

Paolucci, Anne. *From Tension to Tonic: The Plays of Edward Albee*. Carbondale, Ill.: Southern Illinois University Press, 1972.

Porter, Thomas E. "Fun and Games in Suburbia: *Who's Afraid of Virginia Woolf?*" In *Myth and Modern American Drama*. Detroit: Wayne State University Press, 1969.

Rutenberg, Michael E. *Edward Albee: Playwright in Protest*. New York: DBS Publications, 1969.

Recording of Who's Afraid of Virginia Woolf?

Uta Hagen, Arthur Hill. Columbia Records (4 records, DOL287, mono, and DOS687, stereo).

Film Version of Who's Afraid of Virginia Woolf?

American (Warner Brothers), 1966. With Richard Burton, Elizabeth Taylor, directed by Mike Nichols (129 min., 16mm, sound, black-and-white). Warner Brothers, Non-Theatrical Div., 4000 Warner Blvd., Burbank, CA 91505. (Rental.)

IMAMU AMIRI BARAKA (LEROI JONES) (1934–   ) was born in Newark, N.J., the son of a postal superintendent and a social worker. Feeling "displaced" at Rutgers, he transferred to Howard University after his freshman year. After post-graduate work at Columbia and the New School for Social Research, he served for a time in the Air Force. Baraka thinks of himself primarily as a poet and has published three volumes of verse. In addition to poems and plays, he has also written a history of jazz, *Blues People*; *System of Dante's Hell*, a semiautobiographical, expressionistic novel; *Home*, a collection of essays tracing his movement toward black militancy; *Raise Race Rays Raze: Essays Since 1965* (1971), a virulently antiwhite collection; and he has edited a documentary on *Congress of African Peoples*, Atlanta (1970). The first four of his five plays were written in 1964. Only *Dutchman* has received wide critical acclaim. It won the off-Broadway Obie Award and was performed at the Festival of Two Worlds at Spoleto, Italy. *The Baptism* is an incoherent satirical allegory about ritual murder in a white church. In *The Toilet*, set in a dingy institutional latrine, a love relationship between a black and a white boy ends in violence. In *The Slave*, a poet-leader of the blacks, who are fighting a war against the whites, enters the home of his former white wife to get his children back. *Madheart (A Morality Play)* (1966) is a violent allegory (of autobiographical implications) on racial conflict. The setting in *Slave Ship* (1969), a brutal reenactment of the past, is indicated by the title. *Jello* (1970), a play about Jack Benny and his black "servant" Rochester, was refused publication in *Black Fire*, a collection of essays, poems, short stories, and plays, co-edited by Baraka, but it has since appeared. Critical comments on Baraka's work have raised the question of whether the artistic control that marks his best works is being subverted by his racial rage. In the last few years he has published no new plays.

Suggested Reading

Benston, Kimberly W. *Baraka: The Renegade and the Mask*. New Haven: Yale University Press, 1967.

Bigsby, C. W. E. *Confrontation and Commitment*. Columbia, Mo.: University of Missouri Press, 1968.

Costello, Donald P. "LeRoi Jones: Black Man as Victim." *Commonweal* 88 (1968):436–440.

Dennison, George. "The Demagogy of LeRoi Jones." *Commentary* 39 (1965):67–70.

Hutson, Theodore R. *From LeRoi Jones to Amiri Baraka*. Durham, N.C.: Duke University Press, 1973.

Negro Digest, "Islam and Black Art: An Interview with LeRoi Jones," by Mervin X and Faruk. (January 1969), pp. 4–10.

Weales, Gerald C. "The Negro Revolution," in *The Jumping-off Place: American Drama in the 1960's*. New York: Macmillan, 1969.

Film Version of Dutchman

British, 1967. Directed by Anthony Harvey (55 min., 16mm, sound, black-and-white). Walter Reade 16, 241 E. 34th St., New York, NY 10016. (Rental.) Budget Films, 4590 Santa Monica Blvd., Los Angeles, CA 90029. (Rental.)

SAMUEL BECKETT (1906–   ) was born near Dublin, Ireland, and educated in that city. While teaching English in Paris in the late 1920s, he became part of James Joyce's circle and was for a time Joyce's secretary. He got his M.A. degree from Trinity College in Dublin in 1931, in the same year that he published a critical study of the French novelist Marcel Proust. In the mid-1930s he traveled around Europe and began writing short fiction. During World War II he worked in the French Resistance. Since the war he has lived mostly in France, and most of his plays and novels were originally written in French. The first production of *Waiting for Godot* in 1953 quickly established it as the prototype of "absurd drama" — showing life as drained of meaning, an endless round of dull routines and sudden violence, with the human being caught in a metaphysical void. Between 1947 and 1949, the years when he wrote *Godot*, he also wrote (in French) three avant-garde novels, full of linguistic equilibristics à la Joyce. *Endgame* (1957), *All That Fall* (1957), *Krapp's Last Tape* (1958), and *Happy Days* (1961) are his most important plays after *Waiting for Godot* (published in French in 1952). In recent years, Beckett's plays have become shorter and sparser and less and less dependent on language. Beckett was awarded the Nobel Prize in 1969. There is general agreement that his work has been the most original and influential of any single writer's in the postwar period.

Suggested Reading

Coe, Richard N. *Samuel Beckett*, rev. ed. New York: Grove Press, 1970. (First publ. by Oliver and Boyd, London, 1964; rev. ed., 1968)

Cohn, Ruby. *Back to Beckett*. Princeton, N.J.: Princeton University Press, 1973.

———, ed. *Samuel Beckett: A Collection of Criticism*. New York: McGraw-Hill, 1975.

———. *Samuel Beckett: The Comic Gamut*. New Brunswick, N.J.: Rutgers University Press, 1962.

Esslin, Martin. *The Theatre of the Absurd*, rev. ed. Garden City, N.Y.: Doubleday (Anchor), 1969.

———, ed. *Samuel Beckett: A Collection of Critical Essays*. Englewood Cliffs, N.J.: Prentice-Hall (Spectrum), 1965.

Fletcher, John B., and John Spurling. *Beckett: A Study of His Plays*. New York: Hill and Wang, 1972.

Grossvogel, David I. *The Blasphemers*. Ithaca, N.Y.: Cornell University Press, 1965. (Originally publ. as *Four Playwrights and a Postscript*, 1962.)

Guicharnaud, Jacques (with June Beckelman). *Modern French Theatre from Giraudoux to Beckett*. New Haven: Yale University Press, 1961.

Kenner, Hugh. *A Reader's Guide to Samuel Beckett*. New York: Farrar, Straus and Giroux, 1973.

———. *Samuel Beckett: A Critical Study*, new ed. Berkeley and Los Angeles: University of California Press, 1968.

Webb, Eugene. *The Plays of Samuel Beckett*. Seattle, Wash.: University of Washington Press, 1972.

Film Version of Act Without Words

1970. Animated (10 min., 16 mm, sound, color). Pyramid Film Productions, P.O. Box 1048, 317 Georgina Ave., Santa Monica, CA 90406.

BERTOLT BRECHT (1898–1956) was born in the South German town of Augsburg in Bavaria. He studied medicine, served in World War I, began writing expressionistic plays, and in the 1920s was part of a group of avant-garde and leftist poets, playwrights, actors, and artists in Berlin. After becoming a Marxist about 1925, he began writing didactic plays of doctrinaire political content. Artistically, the most successful of these (and the least didactic) is *The Three-Penny Opera* (1928), an adaptation to modern conditions of John Gay's eighteenth-century *Beggar's Opera*, with music by Kurt Weill. In 1928 he married the actress Helene Weigel, who, after World War II, was to create the title role in *Mother Courage*. Brecht and his family fled Germany the day after the Reichstag fire that initiated the Nazi reign of terror in 1933. He spent the first six years of exile from Hitler's Germany in Denmark. In 1939, when a Nazi invasion of Denmark began to seem likely, he moved to Sweden, and later to Finland. In 1941, when Finland, as Germany's ally, went to war against Russia, the Brechts fled to California, where they remained until 1947. For a while Brecht worked in Hollywood. But the postwar United States did not provide a hospitable climate for a European Marxist, and in 1947 Brecht moved to Zürich where he wrote and produced plays for the National Swiss Theater. In 1949 he moved to East Berlin, ostensibly, at least, supporting the Communist regime. Here he worked with his own ensemble in a theater at Schiffbauerdamm until his death.

In the years of his exile just before and during World War II Brecht wrote his four greatest plays — *Galileo* (1938–39), *Mother Courage* (1941), *The Good Woman of Setzuan* (1943), and *The Caucasian Chalk Circle* (1944–45) — swift, fluid, theatrically inventive, and largely non-illusionistic parables on the dilemmas confronting the embattled human spirit in a world of war, tyranny, corruption, stupidity, and greed. Brecht has been a profound influence on modern theater not only as playwright and director but also as theorist of a new kind of non-Aristotelian drama, in which acting is demonstration rather than impersonation, the mode of the drama episodic narrative rather than unilinear enactment, the proper audience attitude rational observation rather than entranced involvement, and the purpose of the performance the arousal of the audience to social action rather than the release of its empathies in catharsis. But it is possible to argue that his actual practice in his best plays does not conform to his theory. At its greatest, Brecht's art is too spaciously humanistic to be confined by political or esthetic dogma.

Suggested Reading

Brecht, Bertolt. "On the Experimental Theatre." *Tulane Drama Review* 6 (1961):3–17.
————. *Seven Plays by Bertolt Brecht*. Edited and with an introduction by Eric Bentley. New York: Grove Press, 1961.
Demetz, Peter, ed. *Brecht: A Collection of Critical Essays*. Englewood Cliffs, N.J.: Prentice-Hall (Spectrum), 1962.
Esslin, Martin. *Brecht, the Man and His Works*, new rev. ed. Garden City, N.Y.: Doubleday (Anchor), 1971.
Ewen, Frederic. *Bertolt Brecht: His Life, His Art, and His Times*. New York: Citadel Press, 1967.
Fuegi, John. *The Essential Brecht*. Los Angeles: Hennessey & Ingalls, 1972.
Gray, Ronald. *Bertolt Brecht*. New York: Grove Press, 1961.
Hill, Claude. *Bertolt Brecht*. New York: Twayne, 1975.
Spalter, Max. *Brecht's Tradition*. Baltimore: Johns Hopkins Press, 1967.
Weideli, Walter. *The Art of Bertolt Brecht*. New York: New York University Press, 1963.
Willett, John, ed. and tr. *Brecht on Theatre*. New York: Hill and Wang (Dramabook), 1964.
————. *The Theatre of Bertolt Brecht*, 3rd ed. rev. London: Methuen, 1967.

ANTON PAVLOVICH CHEKHOV (1860–1904) was born in Taganrog on the Sea of Azov in southern Russia, the grandson of a serf and the son of a grocer. A harsh boyhood was followed by medical studies in Moscow. He received his degree in 1884, but he never practiced medicine very regularly and in his last years not at all. In order to pay for his studies and support his family, he began to write and sell small, comical narrative sketches. In 1886, a successful collection of short stories, somewhat in the manner of de Maupassant, brought him acceptance in leading literary circles. His early one-act plays, most of them comedies, were quite successful, his first full-length play, *Ivanov* (1887), somewhat less so, and his next serious dramas failed. In 1890, tired with literary life, he traveled to the penal colony on the island of Sakhalin in the Sea of Okhotsk, off the east coast of Siberia. He returned home by way of Singapore and Ceylon. In 1898, *The Seagull*, which had been a humiliating fiasco in St. Petersburg two years earlier, was a brilliant success in the newly opened Moscow Art Theater, under the direction of Konstantin Stanislavsky. *The Seagull* established not only Chekhov's reputation as a major playwright but also the success of the Stanislavsky "method" of realistic, inner-motivated acting, and secured the finances of the new theater. Stanislavsky and Chekhov, however, did not always agree on the interpretation of Chekhov's plays. In 1901 Chekhov married one of the leading actresses in the Moscow Art Theater, but his bad health — he had contracted tuberculosis in his early twenties — forced them to live apart for long periods: While she acted in Moscow, he spent the cold months of the year in Yalta on the Crimea. He wrote three additional plays for the Moscow Art Theater: *Uncle Vanya* (1899, a revision of *The Wood Demon*, which he had written ten years earlier), *The Three Sisters* (1901), and, his greatest success, *The Cherry Orchard* (1904). He died at a sanatorium in southern Germany.

Chekhov's major plays continue both to succeed in the theater and to elude final criticism. The social conditions they reflect are no longer actual, if they ever were. In disjointed dialogue and understated plots they chronicle small and stagnant lives and have no apparent theses. Rather than photographs and stenograms of reality or social problem plays, they are images that reduce to ironic order the unchanneled flow of banality that makes up most of human life.

Suggested Reading

Gillès, Daniel. *Chekhov: Observer Without Illusion*. Translated from the French by Charles Lain Markmann. New York: Funk and Wagnalls, 1968.
Jackson, Robert L. *Chekhov: A Collection of Critical Essays*. Englewood Cliffs, N.J.: Prentice-Hall (Spectrum), 1967.
Magarshack, David. *Chekhov the Dramatist*. New York: Hill and Wang (Dramabook), 1960.
Melchinger, Siegfried. *Anton Chekhov*. Translated from the German by Edith Tarcov. New York: Ungar, 1972.
Simmons, Ernest J. *Chekhov*. Boston: Little, Brown, 1962.
Toumanova, Princess Nina Andronikova. *Anton Chekhov: The Voice of Twilight Russia*. New York: Columbia University Press, 1960.
Valency, Maurice J. *The Breaking String: The Plays of Anton Chekhov*. New York: Oxford University Press, 1966.

Recording of The Cherry Orchard

Jessica Tandy, Hume Cronyn. Caedmon Records (3 records, TRS314, stereo).

Film Version of The Cherry Orchard

American, 1967. (43 min., 16mm, sound, color or black-and-white.) Encyclopaedia Britannica Educational Corp., 425 Michigan Ave., Chicago, IL 60611. (Sale, and available on a non-exclusive basis from many rental agencies throughout the U.S. Check local commercial film libraries, public library film collections, and college audio-visual centers.)

SIR GEORGE ETHEREGE (?1635–?1691). Very little that is certain is known about Etherege's life. He was probably born at Maidenhead, Berkshire, the son of a Bermuda planter. There is some evidence that he attended Cambridge, lived abroad for a while, and studied law at the Inns of Court. After the success of his plays, he led for some time the life of a fashionable rake, often in the company of the witty and dissolute Earl of Rochester. About 1680 he was knighted and married a wealthy widow. In his later years, he held diplomatic posts in the Hague and in Ratisbon, Germany. His amusing letters to friends in England describe his boredom with life in both places. His improprieties in Ratisbon forced him to leave. He died in Paris, according to one story from injuries suffered when he fell down a flight of stairs.

Etherege wrote only three plays, *The Comical Revenge, or, Love in a Tub* (1664), *She Would if She Could* (1668), and *The Man of Mode* (1676). Of these, the last is by far the best integrated and most sophisticated, but all three rely heavily on sexual intrigue and witty repartee. *The Comical Revenge* is one of the earliest examples of Restoration comedy of sexual manners, a forerunner of the elegant comedies of manners by Congreve and Sheridan.

Suggested Reading

Carnochan, W. B., ed. *The Man of Mode*. Lincoln, Neb.: University of Nebraska Press, 1966.
Fujimura, Thomas H. *The Restoration Comedy of Wit*. New York: Barnes & Noble, 1952.

Holland, Norman. *The First Modern Comedies*. Cambridge, Mass.: Harvard University Press, 1959.

Powell, Jocelyn. "George Etherege and the Form of a Comedy." In *Restoration Theatre*, edited by John Russell and Bernard Harris. New York: St. Martin's Press, 1965.

Rosenfeld, Sybil. *The Letterbook of Sir George Etherege*. London: Oxford University Press, 1928.

Underwood, Dale. *Etherege and the Seventeenth-Century Comedy of Manners*. New Haven, Conn.: Yale University Press, 1957.

EVERYMAN. Nothing is known about the author of *Everyman*, and scholars disagree on whether it is derived from or is the source for *Elckerlijk*, a Flemish morality play printed in 1495. A certain Peter Dorland of Diest has been suggested as the author of the latter.

Suggested Reading

Bevington, David M. *From Mankind to Marlowe: Growth of Structure in the Popular Drama of Tudor England*. Cambridge, Mass.: Harvard University Press, 1962.

Cawley, A. C., ed. *Everyman and Medieval Miracle Plays*. New York: Dutton, 1959.

Chambers, E. K. *English Literature at the Close of the Middle Ages*. New York: Oxford University Press, 1945.

Cormican, L. A. "Morality Tradition and the Interludes." In *The Age of Chaucer*, edited by Boris Ford. London: Penguin Books, 1954.

Craig, Hardin. *English Religious Drama of the Middle Ages*. Oxford, Eng.: Clarendon Press, 1955.

Ryan, Lawrence V. "Doctrine and Dramatic Structure in *Everyman*." *Speculum* 22 (1957):722–735.

Wickham, Glynne. *The Medieval Theatre*. New York: St. Martin's Press, 1974.

Williams, Arnold. *The Drama of Medieval England*. East Lansing, Mich.: Michigan State University Press, 1961.

Recording of Everyman

Burgess Meredith. Caedmon Records (1 record, TC1031, mono).

Film Version of Everyman

1971. (55 min., 16mm, sound, color.) Lewison (Paul), 8899 Beverly Blvd., Suite 101, Los Angeles, CA 90048.

SIR WILLIAM SCHWENK GILBERT (1836–1911) was at first intended for a legal career, but his inclinations led him in other directions. By the time he was called to the English bar, in 1863, he was already contributing comic verse to a leading journal. This led to successful work for the stage, and his meeting with Sir Arthur Sullivan in 1870 inaugurated one of the most distinguished and productive partnerships in the history of the musical theater. The music of their first collaboration, *Thespis*, has been lost, but their subsequent works have remained popular favorites to the present day. *Trial by Jury* was followed by a succession of works produced by Richard D'Oyly Carte: *The Sorcerer*, *H.M.S. Pinafore*, *The Pirates of Penzance*, and *Patience*. D'Oyly Carte held the partnership together, in spite of temperamental differences that made a breach always imminent, and in 1881 built the Savoy Theater as their permanent London home. There followed *Iolanthe*; *Princess Ida*; *The Mikado*, perhaps their most popular work; *Ruddigore*; *The Yeoman of the Guard*, their closest approach to grand opera; and *The Gondoliers*. In 1889 Gilbert and Sullivan broke up over a contractual dispute. Though they reunited in 1893 for *Utopia Limited* and in 1896 for *The Grand Duke*, these works have never been considered the equal of their earlier successes.

Some aspects of Gilbert's humor — his punning, his sexual coyness, his overuse of certain recurrent comic types — are inevitably dated. Many of his topical references are now unintelligible to the layman. The larger aspects of his work, however — his infectious fantasy and his merciless satire of individual and institutional pomposity — still have a broad appeal, and the quality of Sullivan's music has elevated several of these operettas to a place in some of the world's leading opera houses.

Suggested Reading

Bailey, Leslie. *The Gilbert and Sullivan Book*. London: Cassell, 1952.
Gilbert, Sir William Schwenk, and Sir Arthur Seymour Sullivan. *The Complete Plays of Gilbert and Sullivan*. New York: The Modern Library, 1936.
———. *The Savoy Operas*. Introduction by David Cecil with notes by Derek Hudson. New York: Oxford University Press, 1962–63.
Pearson, Hesketh. *Gilbert: His Life and Strife*. New York: Harper, 1957.

Recording of Trial by Jury

D'Oyly Carte Opera Company. London Records (1 record, Lon1167, stereo).

HENRIK IBSEN (1828–1906) was born in Skien, a small town in southern Norway. His father, a merchant of some social standing in the town, lost his money when the boy was eight, and the family thereafter lived in reduced circumstances. At sixteen Ibsen was apprenticed to a druggist in another small town. Two years later a servant-girl in the household gave birth to his illegitimate child. There is good reason to believe that these early experiences of financial hardship and social disgrace conditioned the shrewd sense of business, the reticence, and the excessive outer propriety that characterized Ibsen in later life, and both financial ruin and bastardy are recurrent motifs in his plays. He wrote his first play in 1848, under the influence of the liberalism of the February revolution in France of that year. Having soon abandoned a plan to study medicine, he was a free-lance journalist for a few years and flirted briefly with political radicalism. In the 1850s and early 1860s he held positions as salaried playwright and director at theaters in Bergen and Christiania (Oslo). Norway's failure to help Denmark in her war against Prussia in 1864 disillusioned him deeply (though he did not himself volunteer for service), and he and his wife and son left Norway for twenty-seven years of self-imposed exile in Italy and Germany. By the time he returned in 1891 he was a world figure. He died in Christiania after several years' illness.

Ibsen's iconoclasm, compact dramaturgy, and use of realistic symbols have earned him his reputation as "the father of modern drama." His canon, however, includes other kinds of plays than those on which, until fairly recently, his reputation was almost exclusively based. Most of his early plays were works of national romanticism, dealing with sagas and peasants. His first popular success was the philosophical dramatic poem *Brand* (1866), which was followed by the complementary, antithetical *Peer Gynt* (1867). Together, these two verse dramas provide a clue to much that has been found obscure in the realistic plays that followed. Ibsen himself considered *Emperor and Galilean* (1873), a ten-act "world-historical drama" about the conflict between paganism and Christianity in the soul of the fourth-century Roman emperor Julian the Apostate, his most important work — a judgment no one else has shared. In the late 1870s and 1880s he wrote the social problem plays in prose by which he first attained international fame. The most important of these are *A Doll's House* (1879), *Ghosts* (1881), *An Enemy of the People* (1882), *The Wild Duck* (1884), *Rosmersholm* (1886), and *Hedda Gabler* (1890). Actually, the last three of these subordinate social problematics to individual psychology, and they mark, in some ways, a transition to Ibsen's final phase, in which he continued to anatomize the marriage relationship in heavily symbolic plays of little external action and of some autobiographical import. The most important of his last four plays are *The Master Builder* (1892) and *When We Dead Awaken* (1899).

Suggested Reading

Bradbrook, Muriel. *Ibsen the Norwegian*. London: Chatto & Windus, 1948.
Downs, Brian W. *Ibsen: the Intellectual Background*. Cambridge, Eng.: Cambridge University Press, 1946.
———. *A Study of Six Plays by Ibsen*. Cambridge, Eng.: Cambridge University Press, 1950.
Egan, Michael, ed. *Ibsen: The Critical Heritage*. London: Routledge and Kegan Paul, 1972.
Fjelde, Rolf, ed. *Ibsen: A Collection of Critical Essays*. Englewood Cliffs, N.J.: Prentice-Hall (Spectrum), 1965.

Hurt, James. *Catiline's Dream: An Essay on Ibsen's Plays*. Urbana, Ill.: University of Illinois Press, 1972.

Knight, George Wilson. *Henrik Ibsen*. New York: Grove Press, 1963.

Koht, Halvdan. *Life of Ibsen*. Translated and edited by Einar Haugen and A. E. Santaniello. New York: B. Blom, 1971.

Lucas, Frank L. *The Drama of Ibsen and Strindberg*. London: Cassell, 1962.

McFarlane, James W., ed. *Henrik Ibsen: A Critical Anthology*. Harmondsworth, Eng.: Penguin, 1970.

————, tr. and ed. *Ibsen* [the collected works in English]. London, New York: Oxford University Press, 1960.

————. *Ibsen and the Temper of Norwegian Literature*. London: Oxford University Press, 1960.

Meyer, Michael L. *Ibsen: A Biography*. New York: Doubleday, 1971.

Northam, John. *Ibsen: A Critical Study*. Cambridge, Eng.: Cambridge University Press, 1973.

————. *Ibsen's Dramatic Method*. London: Faber and Faber, 1953.

Sprinchorn, Evert, ed. *Ibsen: Letters and Speeches*. New York: Hill and Wang (Dramabook), 1964.

Tennant, P. F. D. *Ibsen's Dramatic Technique*. Cambridge, Eng.: Bowes & Bowes, 1948.

Weigand, Hermann. *The Modern Ibsen*. New York: Dutton, 1960 (first publ. 1925).

Recording of A Doll's House

Claire Bloom. Caedmon Records (3 records, TRS343, stereo).

Film Versions of A Doll's House

American, 1967. (61 min., 16mm, sound, color or black-and-white.) Encyclopaedia Britannica Educational Corp., 425 Michigan Ave., Chicago, IL 60611. (Sale, and available on a non-exclusive basis from many rental agencies throughout the U.S. Check local commercial film libraries, public library film collections, and college audio-visual centers.)

American (Columbia), 1972. With Jane Fonda, directed by Joseph Losey (108 min., 16mm, sound, color). (Available on a nonexclusive basis from many rental agencies throughout the U.S. Check local commercial film libraries, public library film collections, and college audio-visual centers.)

British, 1973. With Claire Bloom, Sir Ralph Richardson (95 min., 16 mm, sound, color). Films Incorporated, 4420 Oakton St.; Skokie, IL 60076. (Rental.)

ARTHUR MILLER (1915–   ) was born in New York City. His father lost his money during the Depression. After graduating from the University of Michigan in 1938, Miller held a variety of jobs, including writing plays for radio, before joining the Federal Theater project in New York. In 1944 he wrote the script for the movie *The Story of G.I. Joe. Focus*, a novel about anti-Semitism, was a bestseller in 1945. An early play failed on Broadway in 1944, but in 1947 *All My Sons* won the Drama Critics' Award, and *Death of a Salesman* (1949) won the Pulitzer Prize, and became one of the most enduring hits of the post–World War II era. In the early 1950s Miller appeared before the House Committee on Un-American Activities but refused to aid it in its witch hunt for left-wing writers. Both his adaptation of Ibsen's *An Enemy of the People* (1950) and *The Crucible* (1953), a play about the Salem witch trials, bear witness to his involvement with liberal politics during the years of McCarthyism. His later plays include *A View From the Bridge* (1955, revised 1957), *After the Fall* (1964), *The Price* (1968), and *The Creation of the World and Other Business* (1972), a dramatic fantasy on motifs in Genesis in the Bible, and quite unlike Miller's earlier plays of social realism. The conflict between private and public morals has remained a frequent motif in Miller's plays. Between 1956 and 1961 he was married to the movie actress Marilyn Monroe. In 1961 he wrote the script for *The Misfits*, in which she starred with Clark Gable.

Suggested Reading

Corrigan, Robert W. "The Achievement of Arthur Miller." *Comparative Drama* 2 (1968):141–60.

———, ed. *Arthur Miller: A Collection of Critical Essays*. Englewood Cliffs, N.J.: Prentice-Hall (Spectrum), 1969.

Huftel, Sheila. *Arthur Miller: The Burning Glass*. New York: Citadel Press, 1965.

Miller, Arthur. "Introduction." *Collected Plays*. New York: Viking, 1957.

Moss, Leonard. *Arthur Miller*. New York: Twayne, 1967.

Nelson, Benjamin. *Arthur Miller: Portrait of a Playwright*. New York: McKay, 1970.

Popkin, Henry. "Arthur Miller: The Strange Encounter." *Sewanee Review* 68 (Winter, 1960):34–60.

Vidal, Gore, et al. *"Death of a Salesman:* A Symposium." *Tulane Drama Review* 2 (May, 1958):63–69.

Recording of Death of a Salesman

Lee J. Cobb, Mildred Dunnock, Dustin Hoffman. Caedmon Records (3 records, TRS310, stereo).

Film Versions of Death of a Salesman

American (Columbia), 1951. With Frederic March, Mildred Dunnock. (115 min., 16mm, sound, black-and-white.) (Available on a nonexclusive basis from many rental agencies throughout the U.S. Check local commercial film libraries, public library film collections, and college audio-visual centers.)

American (Columbia), 1966. (111 min., 16mm, sound, black-and-white.) Columbia Broadcasting System, 383 Madison Ave., New York, NY 10017. (Rental.)

JEAN BAPTISTE POQUELIN (MOLIÈRE) (1622–1673) was the son of a well-to-do upholsterer attached to the royal court. Both upholstering and law studies proved abortive careers, and in 1643 young Poquelin co-founded a theatrical company and took the name Molière (its significance is unknown) as a stage name. Unsuccessful in Paris, the company toured the provinces between 1645 and 1658. These were Molière's years of apprenticeship. In 1659 he experienced his first success as a playwright with the brief satire *The Affected Ladies*. In 1661 the company, enjoying royal patronage, established itself in its own theater, the Palais-Royal, in Paris. Until his death, Molière continued to write plays for his company, mainly comedies, and to act, mainly in comic parts. Many of his plays enraged the pious and the learned, and Louis XIV's favor proved fickle. As a result, the fortunes of the company remained insecure, despite Molière's popularity with the enlightened part of his audience. His marriage to a much younger woman appears to have been unhappy, and his children died in infancy. Grim irony attended his death: he suffered a hemorrhage while performing the title role of his own comedy *The Hypochondriac* and died a few hours afterwards.

Like Shakespeare's, the best of Molière's plays belong to world literature. Their farcical plots are vehicles for intimate studies of self-duped eccentrics whose single-minded psychological biases (or "humors") reduce them to stiff human grotesques, unable and unwilling to accommodate themselves to the norms of joyous and healthy social relationships. In Molière's comedies, as in the tragedies of his contemporary Racine, character is destiny. Besides *Tartuffe*, the best known among them are *School for Wives* (1662), *The Misanthrope* (1666), *The Miser* (1668), *The Gentleman Burgher* (1670), and *The Learned Ladies* (1672).

Suggested Reading

Fernandez, Ramon. *Molière: The Man Seen Through His Plays*. Translated by Wilson Follet. New York: Hill and Wang (Dramabook), 1958.

Gossman, Lionel. *Men and Masks: A Study of Molière*. Baltimore: Johns Hopkins Press, 1963.

Guicharnaud, Jacques, ed. *Molière: A Collection of Critical Essays*. Englewood Cliffs, N.J.: Prentice-Hall (Spectrum), 1964.

Hubert, Judd D. *Molière and the Comedy of Intellect*. Berkeley: University of California Press, 1962.

Lewis, D. Wyndham. *Molière, the Comic Mask*. London: Eyre and Spottiswoode, 1959.

Moore, Will. *Molière, a New Criticism*. Oxford: Clarendon Press, 1962.

Turnell, Martin. *The Classical Moment: Studies in* Corneille, Molière, *and* Racine. Norfolk, Conn.: New Directions, 1948.

Recording of Tartuffe

Willima Hutt, Douglas Rain. Stratford Shakespeare Festival Foundation of Canada. Caedmon Records (3 records, TRS332, stereo).

Film Version of Tartuffe

German, 1927. With Emil Jannings, directed by F. W. Murnau (70 min., 8 or 16mm, silent, black-and-white). (Sale, and available on a nonexclusive basis from many rental agencies throughout the U.S. Check local commercial film libraries, public library film collections, and college audio-visual centers.)

EUGENE O'NEILL (1888–1953), America's most important playwright, was born in a hotel room overlooking Times Square in New York City, the son of an actor who gained both popularity and wealth from a lifetime career as the title character in a melodramatization of *The Count of Monte Cristo.* Home life was disharmonious and unsettled as the family followed the itinerary of his father's acting company. At the end of his freshman year at Princeton, O'Neill was expelled for a prank. For the next five years he drifted — as a gold prospector in Honduras, a sailor on voyages to Europe and South America, a waterfront bum in New York, a bit actor, and a cub reporter. In 1912 he contracted tuberculosis and spent several months in a sanatorium where he read widely in modern drama. Strindberg, particularly, was a revelation. O'Neill began to write one-act plays, enrolled in Professor George Pierce Baker's famous dramatic workshop at Harvard, and in 1916 saw *Bound East for Cardiff* produced by a group of semiprofessionals at Provincetown, Massachusetts. Like most of his early plays, it was based on his sea-going experience. In 1920, his first full-length, professionally produced play, *Beyond the Horizon,* won the Pulitzer Prize. Extremely prolific, he turned out a rapid succession of plays both realistic — *Anna Christie* (1921, second Pulitzer Prize) and *Desire Under the Elms* (1924) — and expressionistic — *The Emperor Jones* (1920) and *The Hairy Ape* (1922). His plays from the late 1920s were increasingly experimental — *The Great God Brown* (1926), *Marco Millions, Lazarus Laughed* (both 1927). In 1927 he left the "little theater" groups that had produced his early plays and began his long association with the Theater Guild. In 1928 the Guild staged *Strange Interlude,* a long psychological study of a woman in her various life roles; the play made use of time-stopping, introspective asides and brought him his third Pulitzer Prize. The trilogy *Mourning Becomes Electra,* a heavily Freudian adaptation of Aeschylus's *Oresteia* set in Civil War America, appeared in 1931. *Ah, Wilderness!* (1933) is a pleasantly nostalgic piece about adolescent rebellion in small-town New England in the early years of the century. In 1936 he received the Nobel Prize of Literature, the first American author to do so. Following the failure of *Days Without End* (1934), O'Neill and his third wife retired to California. He was silent for twelve years until *The Iceman Cometh* (1946), a wholly naturalistic play making Dr. Relling's point (in Ibsen's *The Wild Duck*) about the necessity for a life of illusions, reinstated him as the leading American playwright. O'Neill's last years were darkened by family tragedies and by ill health. He suffered from a degenerative disorder of the brain that impaired his motor ability and made writing increasingly difficult, but which left his mind clear. Some time near the end of his life, he destroyed most of the manuscripts for an enormous tragic cycle dealing with an Irish immigrant family. Its collective title was to be "A Tale of Possessors, Self-dispossessed." Since his death, the two plays of the cycle that survived (*A Touch of the Poet, More Stately Mansions,* the latter left unfinished) have been produced, without adding much stature to his reputation. *Long Day's Journey Into Night* (published and produced posthumously in 1956), perhaps the best of all his plays, was not a part of the cycle. It is a brooding study of the conflicts in a small family, based on the troubled relationships among the young O'Neill (the time is 1912), his parents, and his older brother. It was the fourth of O'Neill's plays to win the Pulitzer Prize.

There is little verbal artistry in O'Neill's plays, and many critics find his most ambitious plays pretentious and overlong. But there is almost no disagreement about his superb sense of theater or about the total commitment he brings, in a variety of dramatic forms, to his quest for meaning in our existence in a mysterious universe that fails to answer to our desires. Few modern playwrights have pursued the tragic vision more persistently than O'Neill. *Ah, Wilderness!* is his only comedy, but it, too, draws on O'Neill's own early experience. Only in this play is his reminiscing mellow rather than anguished.

Suggested Reading

Bogard, Travis. *Contour in Time: The Plays of Eugene O'Neill*. New York: Oxford University Press, 1972.

Cargill, Oscar, N. Bryllion Fagin, and William J. Fisher, eds. *O'Neill and His Plays: Four Decades of Criticism*. New York: New York University Press, 1961.

Carpenter, Frederic L. *Eugene O'Neill*. New York: Twayne, 1964.

Engel, Edwin A. *The Haunted Heroes of Eugene O'Neill*. Cambridge, Mass.: Harvard University Press, 1953.

Falk, Doris V. *Eugene O'Neill and the Tragic Tension*. New Brunswick, N.J.: Rutgers University Press, 1958.

Gassner, John, ed. *O'Neill: A Collection of Critical Essays*. Englewood Cliffs, N.J.: Prentice-Hall (Spectrum), 1964.

Gelb, Arthur and Barbara. *O'Neill*. Enlarged ed. with "Epilogue." New York: Harper and Row, 1973.

Leech, Clifford. *Eugene O'Neill*. New York: Grove Press, 1963.

Recording of Ah, Wildnerness!

Circle in the Square Theatre. Caedmon Records (3 records, TRS340, stereo).

Film Version of Ah, Wilderness!

American (Metro-Goldwyn-Mayer), 1935. With Wallace Beery, Lionel Barrymore. (101 min., 16mm, sound, black-and-white.) Films, Incorporated, 4420 Oakton St., Skokie, IL 60076. (Rental.)

HAROLD PINTER (1930–   ) was born in a working class area of East End London, where his father was a tailor. The family is of Jewish-Portuguese origin. In the late 1940s he spent a couple of unhappy terms at the Royal Academy of Dramatic Art and stood trial twice as a conscientious objector to military service. Between 1949 and 1957 he acted in touring companies, including a long stint in Ireland. In 1956 he married the actress Vivien Merchant. They have since separated. His first play, *The Room*, was written at a friend's request in 1957 and produced in Bristol that same year. *The Dumb Waiter* was also written in 1957 but not produced till 1960. Before he turned to drama, he had been writing poems and short fiction. His next play, *The Birthday Party*, lasted only six performances in London in 1958. *The Caretaker* (1960) was his first critically and commercially successful play. Pinter himself wrote the script for the fine film version in 1963. Of his many other plays (most of them long one-acters), *A Slight Ache* (1959), *A Night Out* (1960), *Homecoming* (1965), and *No Man's Land* (1975) are the most notable. Pinter has also written radio and television scripts and has done some directing and occasionally acted in his own plays.

The adjective "Pinteresque" has become something of a cliché in drama criticism, in recognition of the distinct dramatic mode Pinter has created within the general movement of the absurd theater. There is more variety in Pinter's work than the cliché suggests, but his best plays do have certain characteristics in common: actions and situations that resist rational explanation; the motifs of dispossesion, uncertain identity, and someone's private space being invaded by an alien intruder; a pervasive mood of unease or terror; dialogues that are repetitive, spasmodic, semipetulant, funny, unpredictable, contradictory, and authentic in diction and cadence. Depending on how one feels, Pinter's plays seem either endlessly interpretable or resistant to any interpretation at all. They certainly are ideologically and generically elusive. Perhaps the least misleading label for them — as for so many contemporary plays — is "tragicomedies." A comment by the American critic Walter Kerr fairly sums up current critical consensus on Pinter. He is, says Kerr, "the only man working in the theater today who writes existential plays existentially."

Suggested Reading

Burkman, Katherine H. *The Dramatic World of Harold Pinter*. Columbus, Ohio: Ohio State University Press, 1971.

Dukore, Bernard F. *Where Laughter Stops: Pinter's Tragicomedy*. Columbia, Mo.: University of Missouri Press, 1976.

Esslin, Martin. *The Peopled Wound: The Work of Harold Pinter*. Garden City, N.Y.: Double-day (Anchor), 1970.

Ganz, Arthur, ed. *Pinter: A Collection of Critical Essays*. Englewood Cliffs, N.J.: Prentice-Hall (Spectrum), 1972.

Hayman, Ronald. *Harold Pinter*. New York: Ungar, 1973.

Hinchliffe, Arnold P. *Harold Pinter*. New York: Twayne, 1967.

Kennedy, Andrew K. "*Pinter*." In *Six Dramatists in Search of a Language*. Cambridge, Eng.: Cambridge University Press, 1975.

Quigley, Austin E. *The Pinter Problem*. Princeton, N.J.: Princeton University Press, 1975.

Taylor, John R. *Harold Pinter*. London: Longmans, 1969.

LUIGI PIRANDELLO (1867–1936) was the son of a rich owner of sulphur mines in the town of Agrigento on the south coast of Sicily. After studies at the University of Rome he went on to take his doctorate at the University of Bonn, Germany, on a philological study of his home dialect. His early literary production — composed for pleasure, not to make a living — included poems and prose fiction, mostly short stories. By family arrangement he married the daughter of his father's partner. Both families lost their money when the mines were flooded in 1904, and Pirandello was forced to make a living as an instructor at a women's teacher's college in Rome. Soon after, his wife's mind gave way. Too poor to put her in a private institution and too conscientious to put her in a public one, Pirandello endured life with a lunatic till her death in 1918. By then he had attained fame as a playwright and could give up teaching. By the early twenties he was an international celebrity. In 1925 he founded his own art theater, which successfully toured some of the world's great stages. Pirandello's brooding, restless, cerebral inquiries into the nature of reality seem quite alien to the muscular aggressiveness of Mussolini's Italy, but Pirandello himself was not hostile to Fascism. "I am a Fascist because I am an Italian," he said once in an interview in New York. His acceptance of the Nobel Prize in Literature in 1934 was officially approved by Mussolini.

It does not seem unreasonable to assume a connection between his domestic tragedy and the philosophical relativism of his plays. To the unhappy, the belief that all experience is illusory is not a remote solace. The titles of several of his best known plays suggest his paradoxical skepticism: *It Is So! (If You Think So)* (1917), *Each In His Own Way* (1924), and *As You Desire Me* and *Tonight We Improvise* (both 1930). Another famous and characteristic play is *Henry IV* (1922), along with *Six Characters* generally considered his best work.

Suggested Reading

Bishop, Thomas. *Pirandello and the French Theater*. New York: New York University Press, 1960.

Büdel, Oscar. *Pirandello*. London: Bowes & Bowes, 1969.

Cambon, Glauco, ed. *Pirandello: A Collection of Critical Essays*. Englewood Cliffs, N.J.: Prentice-Hall (Spectrum), 1967.

MacClintock, Lander. *The Age of Pirandello*. Bloomington, Ind.: Indiana University Press, 1951.

Matthaei, Renate. *Luigi Pirandello*. Translated by Simon and Erika Young. New York: Ungar, 1973.

Nelson, Robert J. *Play within a Play*. New Haven, Conn.: Yale University Press, 1958.

Starkie, Walter. *Luigi Pirandello: 1867–1936*, 3rd ed., rev. Berkeley, Cal.: University of California Press, 1965.

Vittorini, Domenico. *The Drama of Luigi Pirandello*. Philadelphia: University of Pennsylvania Press, 1935.

JEAN RACINE (1639–1699) was the son of a civil servant in a small town near Paris. Both his parents died while he was still a child. His grandparents had him educated in a school, just south of Paris, run by a Roman Catholic reformist sect known as the Jansenists (after its Dutch founder, Cornelius Jansen). The Jansenists strictly followed St. Augustine's teachings about the irremediable corruption of human nature and the impossibility, therefore, of saving the soul by faith or by good works without the grace of God. The austerity of their life and their insistence that religion is more than the logic of scholasticism make the Jansenists representative of something like a "Puritan" movement within Catholicism. Their ethical seriousness and their awareness of man's spiritual dilemmas left deep marks on Racine's plays. They did not, however, succeed in recruiting him for the priesthood. As a student in Paris, Racine made friends with writers and soon began to write himself. Molière's troupe produced Racine's first play in 1664, but the next year Racine broke with both Molière and his Jansenist mentors at the academy of Port-Royal. Over the next thirteen years he wrote eight tragedies and one comedy. Seven of the tragedies take their subjects from classical history or myth. In 1672 he was elected a member of the French Academy. His plays were successful, but hostile literary factions intrigued against him, and in 1677, after writing *Phaedra*, he retired from the theater, reconciled himself with the Jansenists, married, and became one of King Louis XIV's two historiographers. In 1689, Mme. de Maintenon, the king's pious mistress, induced him to write two tragedies based on stories from the Bible, for performance by the students at a girls' school of which she was a patron. These two plays, *Esther* and *Athalie*, make use of a chorus. Illness and the loss of the king's favor because of disagreement over religion darkened Racine's last years. Among the most representative and indispensable works of French neo-classicism are the greatest of Racine's tragedies: *Andromache* (1667), *Britannicus* (1669), *Berenice* (1670), *Phaedra* (1677), and *Athalie* (1691).

Suggested Reading

Barthes, Roland. *On Racine*. Translated by Richard Howard. New York: Hill and Wang (Dramabook), 1964.
Bowra, Sir Maurice. *The Simplicity of Racine*. Oxford, Eng.: Clarendon Press, 1956.
Knight, R. C., ed. *Racine: Modern Judgements*. London: Macmillan, 1969.
Lapp, J. C. *Aspects of Racinian Tragedy*. Toronto: University of Toronto Press, 1956.
Mander, Gertrud. *Molière*. Translated by Diane Stone Peters. New York: Ungar, 1973.
Mourgues, Odette de. *Racine, or The Triumph of Relevance*. Cambridge, Eng.: Cambridge University Press, 1967.
Turnell, Martin. *The Classical Moment: Studies in Corneille, Molière, and Racine*. Norfolk, Conn.: New Directions, 1948.
Weinberg, B. *The Art of Jean Racine*. Chicago: University of Chicago Press, 1963.

Recording of Phaedra

Marian Seldes. Excerpts in French and English. Folkway Records (1 record, FL9909, mono).

Film Version of Phaedra

Greek, 1962. Directed by Jules Dassin, with Melina Mercouri, Anthony Perkins. (115 min., 16mm, sound, black-and-white.) United Artists, 729 Seventh Ave., New York, NY 10019. (Rental.) This is not Racine's text, but an interesting modern version of the legend.

WILLIAM SHAKESPEARE (1564–1616). Enough is known about Shakespeare, both as citizen and as man of the theater, to refute all speculation that he was not the author of the plays ascribed to him. His life is better documented than that of most of his literary contemporaries. The evidence consists of church and court records and of references, both friendly and unfriendly, to his professional life. The late seventeenth and early eighteenth centuries knew a number of colorful legends about his early life, but these have not been verified by modern scholarship.

He was the son of a substantial tradesman in Stratford-on-Avon. Presumably he received a good grammar-school education (including training in Latin) till he was about sixteen. At eighteen he married Anne Hathaway, who was eight years older than he and with whom he had three children. In the early 1590s he turned up in London as a rising young poet and actor-playwright, a member of the company of the Chamberlain's Men, later (1603) known as the King's Men. When the company built the Globe Theater in 1599, Shakespeare was listed as the second of nine shareholders. In or shortly before 1612 he retired to Stratford, apparently a prosperous man. Friends and colleagues (including Ben Jonson) speak affectionately of him as a witty and cheerful companion.

The First Folio edition of Shakespeare's plays in 1623 established the conventional division of the canon into comedies, histories, and tragedies. (The First Folio includes thirty-six plays, but modern scholars count thirty-seven plays as wholly or almost wholly his.) It is a convenient division, particularly because it is traditional, but it takes no note of Shakespeare's development as a dramatist or of the generic variety within some single plays, and it obscures the range of plays within the same category. *Romeo and Juliet*, from about 1595, is a different kind of tragedy from *King Lear* and *Coriolanus*, from about 1606 and 1608, respectively. A history play like *Richard II* could qualify as tragedy and major parts of *Henry IV, Part 1* as comedy. And "comedy" is not a very accurate collective term for plays as different as *The Comedy of Errors*, *A Midsummer Night's Dream*, *The Merry Wives of Windsor*, *The Merchant of Venice*, *Twelfth Night*, *Measure for Measure*, and *The Tempest*.

The exact chronology of Shakespeare's plays remains uncertain, but there is general agreement that most of the histories were written early, that *Hamlet* is the earliest of the major tragedies and only a little later than such "high" romantic comedies as *As You Like It* and *Twelfth Night*, that the period of "dark" or "problem" comedies of moral ambiguity, like *Troilus and Cressida* and *Measure for Measure*, partly coincides with the period of the mature tragedies, and that the allegorical romances on the themes of forgiveness and reconciliation (often treated by modern critics as a fourth category of plays, in addition to the Folio divisions), like *The Winter's Tale* and *The Tempest*, reflect a post-tragic view of life and are among Shakespeare's last plays.

Suggested Reading

Bentley, Gerald E. *Shakespeare: A Biographical Handbook*. New Haven, Conn.: Yale University Press, 1961.

Bradley, A. C. *Shakespearean Tragedy*. New York: Meridian Books, 1955 (first publ. 1904).

Campbell, Oscar J., and Edward G. Quinn, *The Reader's Encyclopedia of Shakespeare*. New York: Crowell, 1966.

Charney, Maurice. *Style in "Hamlet."* Princeton, N.J.: Princeton University Press, 1969.

Chute, Marchette. *Shakespeare of London*. New York: Dutton, 1949.

Dean, Leonard F., ed. *Shakespeare: Modern Essays in Criticism*. New York: Oxford University Press, 1957.

Fergusson, Francis. "*Hamlet, Prince of Denmark:* The Analogy of Action." In *The Idea of a Theater*. Princeton, N.J.: Princeton University Press, 1949.

Granville-Barker, H. *Prefaces to Shakespeare*. Princeton, N.J.: Princeton University Press, 1946.

────── and G. B. Harrison. *A Companion to Shakespeare Studies*. Garden City, N.Y.: Doubleday (Anchor), 1960.

Harbage, Alfred, ed. *Shakespeare: The Tragedies: A Collection of Critical Essays*. Englewood Cliffs, N.J.: Prentice-Hall (Spectrum), 1964.

Holland, Norman N. *The Shakespearean Imaginaton*. Bloomington, Ind.: Indiana University Press, 1964.

Jones, Ernest. *Hamlet and Oedipus*. New York: Norton, 1949.

Knight, G. Wilson. *The Wheel of Fire*. London: Methuen, 1949.

Knights, L. C. *An Approach to Hamlet*. Stanford, Cal.: Stanford University Press, 1961.

Levenson, J. C. *Discussions of Hamlet*. Boston: D. C. Heath, 1960.

Mack, Maynard. "The World of *Hamlet.*" *Yale Review* 41 (1952):502–523.

Nagler, A. M. *Shakespeare's Stage*. New Haven, Conn.: Yale University Press, 1964.

Prosser, Eleanor. *Hamlet and Revenge*. Stanford, Cal.: Stanford University Press, 1967.

Sacks, Claire, and Edgar Whan, eds. *Hamlet: Enter Critic*. New York: Appleton-Century-Crofts, 1960.

Schoenbaum, Samuel. *William Shakespeare: A Documentary Life*. New York: Oxford University Press, 1975.

Webster, Margaret. *Shakespeare Without Tears*, rev. ed. Cleveland, Ohio: World Publishing Company, 1955.

Wilson, J. Dover. *What Happens in Hamlet?* New York: Cambridge University Press, 1951.

Recordings of Hamlet

Complete play:
Richard Burton, Eileen Herlie, Alfred Drake, Hume Cronyn. Columbia Records (4 records DOL302, mono, and DOS702, stereo).
Marlowe Society. Argo Records (5 records, RG256–60, mono).
Paul Scofield. Caedmon Records (4 records, SRS232, stereo).
Famous scenes:
Burton, Herlie, Drake, Cronyn. Columbia Records (OL8020, mono, and OS2620, stereo).

Film Versions of Hamlet

British (J. Arthur Rank), 1948. Directed by Sir Laurence Olivier (152 min., 16mm, sound, black-and-white). (Available on a nonexclusive basis from many rental agencies throughout the U.S. Check local commercial film libraries, public library film collections, and college audio-visual centers.)
American (Encyclopaedia Britannica Educational Corp.), 1959. (120 min., 16mm, sound, color, 4 parts.) Encyclopaedia Britannica Educational Corp., 425 Michigan Ave., Chicago, IL 60611. (Sale or rental.)
German, 1964. With Maximilian Schell, directed by Edward Dmytryk and Franz Peter Wirth (127 min., 16mm, sound, black-and-white, dubbed dialogue). (Available on a nonexclusive basis from many rental agencies throughout the U.S. Check local commercial film libraries, public library film collections, and college audio-visual centers.)
Russian, 1966. Directed by Grigori Kozintsev (148 min., 16mm, sound, black-and-white, subtitles). United Artists, 16729 Seventh Ave., New York, NY 10019. (Rental.)

(GEORGE) BERNARD SHAW (1856–1950) was born in Dublin of impoverished English parents. His formal education ended when he was fifteen. In 1876 he arrived in London, and over the next nine years he wrote five unsuccessful novels, joined the Fabian Society, a group of socialist intellectuals, and became a radical journalist. Between 1885 and 1898 he wrote art, music, and drama criticism for leading periodicals. *The Quintessence of Ibsenism* (1891) is enthusiastic propaganda for Ibsen's drama as liberal dialectics, but it says perhaps more about Shaw himself than about Ibsen. The long series of his plays began in 1892 with *Widowers' Houses* and ended in 1948. Once he was established as a playwright, his life was lacking in external events; his biography becomes the biography of a mind and is recorded in his voluminous writings. He married in 1898. In 1905 he settled in Ayot St. Lawrence in Hertfordshire, where he spent most of his time until his death. He received the Nobel Prize for Literature in 1925. He was a vegetarian and teetotaller and against vivisection and vaccination. He willed the bulk of his estate to a project for English spelling reform.

In a certain sense, the social criticism that informs Shaw's earliest plays remained his deepest concern. His views, however, never became the orthodoxy of any one ideological camp, and many of his plays and his nondramatic pronouncements on politics have provoked liberals and reactionaries alike. His prefaces to his plays, in impeccably lucid, incisive prose, are often as good clues to his thought as the plays themselves. The plays are dramas of dialectics rather than of plot and character, though the best of them have repeatedly proved their ability to hold popular audiences with their dramatic and theatrical craftsmanship. Their distinctive strength is the way in which they wittily and caustically expose all sorts of shams and nonsense in modern thought and feeling. The best of them are more serious than their flamboyant heterodoxy suggests. Of these, the following are the most representative: *Arms and the Man, Candida* (both 1894), *Cæsar and Cleopatra* (1898), *Man and Superman* (1903), *Major Barbara* (1905), *The Doctor's Dilemma* (1906), *Pygmalion* (1912), *Heartbreak House* (1916), *Back to Methuselah* (1921), and *Saint Joan* (1923).

Suggested Reading

Bentley, Eric. *Bernard Shaw*, 2nd ed. London: Methuen, 1967.
Berst, Charles. *Bernard Shaw and the Art of Drama*. Urbana, Ill.: University of Illinois Press, 1973.

Chesterton, G. K. *George Bernard Shaw*. New York: Hill and Wang (Dramabook), 1956 (first publ. 1909).

Crompton, Louis. *Shaw the Dramatist*. Lincoln, Neb.: University of Nebraska Press, 1969.

Dukore, Bernard F. *Bernard Shaw, Playwright: Aspects of Shavian Drama*. Columbia, Mo.: University of Missouri Press, 1973.

Evans, T. F., ed. *Shaw: The Critical Heritage*. London, Boston: Routledge & Kegan Paul, 1976.

Henderson, Archibald. *George Bernard Shaw: Man of the Century*. New York: Appleton-Century-Crofts, 1956.

Kaufmann, R. J., ed. *G. B. Shaw: A Collection of Critical Essays*. Englewood Cliffs, N.J.: Prentice-Hall (Spectrum), 1965.

Kronenberger, Louis, ed. *George Bernard Shaw: A Critical Survey*. Cleveland, Ohio: World Publishing Company, 1953.

Meisel, Martin. *Shaw and the 19th-Century Theater*. Princeton, N.J.: Princeton University Press, 1963.

Ohmann, Richard M. *Shaw, the Style and the Man*. Middletown, Conn.: Wesleyan University Press, 1962.

Shaw, Bernard. *Shaw on Theater*. Edited by E. J. West. New York: Hill and Wang (Dramabook), 1958.

Valency, Maurice. *The Cart and the Trumpet: The Plays of George Bernard Shaw*. New York: Oxford University Press, 1973.

Whitman, Robert F. *Shaw and the Play of Ideas*. Ithaca, N.Y.: Cornell University Press, 1977.

Wilson, Colin. *Bernard Shaw: A Reassessment*. New York: Atheneum, 1969.

Zimbardo, Rose, ed. *Twentieth Century Interpretations of Major Barbara*. Englewood Cliffs, N.J.: Prentice-Hall (Spectrum), 1970.

Recording of Major Barbara

Maggie Smith, Robert Morley. Caedmon Records (4 records, TRS319, stereo).

Film Version of Major Barbara

British, 1941. With Wendy Hiller, Rex Harrison (115 min., 16mm, sound, black-and-white). Janus Films, 745 Fifth Ave., New York, NY 10022. (Rental.)

SOPHOCLES (?496–406 B.C.) was born in Colonus, then a suburb of Athens. His home town is the setting for *Oedipus at Colonus*, the last of the nearly 120 plays he is said to have written. Only seven are extant today, and only three of these can be dated with any certainty: *Antigone*, 442 B.C.; *Philoctetes*, 409; and *Oedipus at Colonus*, close to 406. Of the others, *Ajax* is thought to be an early play, *Oedipus the King* is usually dated 430–425, *Electra* is probably later than *Oedipus the King*, and for *Trachiniae* there is no agreement on date. In the annual competition among playwrights writing for the Dionysiac festival, Sophocles won the prize eighteen times. His trilogies, unlike Aeschylus's, consisted of plays unrelated in subject matter. He was the first tragic writer to put three characters (in addition to the chorus) on stage at the same time.

Chronologically, Sophocles is the second of the three great Athenian tragedians — some thirty years younger than Aeschylus, some fifteen years older than Euripides. His manhood roughly coincides with the flowering of Athenian civilization between the defeat of the Persians in 480 B.C. and the surrender to Sparta at the end of the Peloponnesian War in 404. He was active in political and military affairs. His fame as a playwright may have earned him his public employments. Sophocles himself reports that his friend Pericles said that he was a better poet than a general. By all accounts, Sophocles was handsome, charming, popular, and well-to-do. Aristophanes, the writer of comedies and Sophocles' younger contemporary, summed up the tenor of his life in calling him "contented among the living, contented among the dead" — a curious but provocative judgment in view of the fact that it concerns one of the greatest of tragic poets.

Suggested Reading

Adams, Sinclair M. *Sophocles the Playwright*. Toronto: University of Toronto Press, 1957.

Bieber, Margarete. *The History of the Greek and Roman Theater*, 2nd rev. ed. Princeton, N.J.: Princeton University Press, 1960.

Bowra, C. M. *Sophoclean Tragedy*. Oxford, Eng.: Clarendon Press, 1944.

Butcher, S. H. *Aristotle's Theory of Poetry and Fine Arts*. New York: Dover Publications, 1951.

Fergusson, Francis. "*Oedipus Rex*: The Tragic Rhythm of Action." In *The Idea of a Theater*. Princeton, N.J.: Princeton University Press, 1949.

Kirkwood, Gordon M. *A Study of Sophoclean Drama*. Ithaca, N.Y.: Cornell University Press, 1958.

Kitto, H. D. F. *Greek Tragedy: A Literary Study*. Garden City, N.Y.: Doubleday (Anchor), 1954.

Knox, Bernard M. W. *The Heroic Temper*. Berkeley, Cal.: University of California Press, 1964.

Stone, John Alexander. *Sophocles and Racine: A Comparative Study in Dramatic Technique*. Geneva, Switzerland: Droz, 1964.

Waldock, A. J. A. *Sophocles the Dramatist*. Cambridge, Eng.: Cambridge University Press, 1951.

Whitman, Cedric H. *Sophocles: A Study in Heroic Humanism*. Cambridge, Mass.: Harvard University Press, 1951.

Woodard, Thomas, ed. *Sophocles: A Collection of Critical Essays*. Englewood Cliffs, N.J.: Prentice-Hall (Spectrum), 1966.

Recordings of Oedipus the King

Amherst College Students. Folkway Records (1 record, FL9862, mono).

Douglas Campbell, Stratford Players. Caedmon Records (2 records, TC2012, mono).

Film Versions of Oedipus the King

Canadian, 1957. Directed by Sir Tyrone Guthrie (88 min., 16mm, sound color). Contemporary/McGraw-Hill Films, 1221 Ave. of the Americas, New York, NY 10020. (Rental or sale.)

American (Encyclopaedia Britannica Educational Corp.), 1959. (90 min., 16mm, sound, color, 3 parts.) Encyclopaedia Britannica Educational Corp., 425 Michigan Ave., Chicago, IL 60611. (Sale, and available on a nonexclusive basis from many rental agencies throughout the U.S. Check local commercial film libraries, public library film collections, and college audio-visual centers.)

British, 1968. With Christopher Plummer, Orson Welles (97 min., 16mm, sound, color). (Available on a nonexclusive basis from many rental agencies throughout the U.S. Check local commercial film libraries, public library film collections, and college audio-visual centers.)

(JOHAN) AUGUST STRINDBERG (1849–1912) was born in Stockholm, the son of a stolid, middle-class, businessman father and a working-class mother. The couple had children together before their marriage, but the future playwright was born in wedlock. Strindberg tried halfheartedly for an advanced university degree at Uppsala and then for a career in acting. The eight years of his young manhood when he worked as a librarian, became a scholar of some note, and wrote his earliest plays and tales were probably the happiest period in his restless, haunted life. In 1877 he married for the first time. Two years later he made a name for himself with *The Red Room*, a novel of satiric realism. The same year he left Sweden to pursue a writing career abroad. In 1884 he returned home to stand trial on a charge of blasphemy, brought on by *Married*, a collection of short stories. He was acquitted, but the affair strained his hypersensitive nerves. There followed a period of frenetic literary activity, partly in Sweden, partly on the Continent. His thinly disguised autobiographies from the 1880s (*Son of Bondwoman*, *A Fool's Apology*) and the naturalistic plays *The Father* (1887), *Miss Julie* (1888), and *Creditors* (1888) reflect the tortured ambivalence of his attitude toward women, which contributed to the dissolution of his marriage in 1891. Through most of the 1890s Strindberg suffered from a persecution complex, sometimes attended by hallucinations, though authorities disagree as to whether his condition was ever such as to justify calling him a lunatic. Between voluntary stays at mental hospitals he studied and wrote on botany and chemistry — but also on alchemy and demonology. His second marriage failed in 1894. *Inferno* (1897), a somewhat fictionalized autobiography, records the critical years of his psychopathy. From 1902 until his death Strindberg lived in Stockholm, indubitably sane though hardly serene. His third marriage ended in divorce in 1904, but his amazing literary creativity never again left him: plays, novels, tales, short stories, historical writings, and essays on philology, anthropology, politics, and other topics poured from his pen. Among the plays are *To Damascus*, I–III (1898, 1904), an early and moderate experiment in expressionism; *Easter* (1901), a modern parable of Christian expiation; *The Dance of Death*, I–II (1901), an only overtly realistic play of marital horrors; *A Dream Play* (1901), a radically expressionistic descant on the theme that recurs like a refrain throughout: "Human kind is to be pitied"; a long series of Shakespearean chronicle plays with subjects from the lives of Swedish kings from the sixteenth to the eighteenth centuries; and, finally, a group of esoteric, sometimes fantastic "chamber plays" that were performed at the Intimate Theater, Strindberg's own stage in Stockholm, under the management of a younger friend. Of these, in addition to *The Ghost Sonata* (1907), *The Storm* and *The Pelican* (both also 1907) are the most important.

Suggested Reading

Brandell, Gunnar. *Strindberg in Inferno*. Translated by Barry Jacobs. Cambridge, Mass.: Harvard University Press, 1974.

Brustein, Robert. "August Strindberg." In *The Theatre of Revolt*. Boston: Little, Brown, 1962.

Dahlström, C. E. W. L. *Strindberg's Dramatic Expressionism*. Ann Arbor, Mich.: University of Michigan Press, 1930.

Johnson, Walter G. *August Strindberg*. Boston: Twayne, 1976.

Klaf, Franklin S. *Strindberg: The Origin of Psychology in Modern Drama*. New York: Citadel Press, 1963.

Lamm, Martin. *August Strindberg*. Translated and edited by Harry G. Carlson. New York: B. Blom, 1971.

Madsen, Borge Gedso. *Strindberg's Naturalistic Theatre*. Seattle, Wash.: University of Washington Press, 1962.

Mortensen, Brita M. E., and Downs, Brian W. *Strindberg: An Introduction to His Life and Work*. Cambridge, Eng.: Cambridge University Press, 1949.

Ollén, Gunnar. *August Strindberg*. Translated from German by Peter Tirner. New York: Ungar, 1972.

Reinert, Otto, ed. *Strindberg: A Collection of Critical Essays*. Englewood Cliffs, N.J.: Prentice-Hall (Spectrum), 1971.

Smedmark, Carl R., ed. *Essays on Strindberg*. Stockholm: J. Beckman for The Strindberg Society, 1966.

Sprigge, Elizabeth. *The Strange Life of August Strindberg*. London: Hamish Hamilton, 1949.

Steene, Birgitta. *The Greatest Fire: A Study of August Strindberg*. Carbondale, Ill.: Southern Illinois University Press, 1973.

JOHN MILLINGTON SYNGE (1871–1909) was of Protestant Anglo-Irish landowner stock. His father, a barrister, died when Synge was only a year old. In his teens, he turned away from his mother's joyless, puritanical religion. He received the B.A. degree from Trinity College in Dublin in 1892, went to Germany to prepare himself for a career in music, became instead a student of languages (including Gaelic) at the Sorbonne in Paris, and began to write poetry. Late in 1896 he met Yeats in Paris, and his career took a new turn. Yeats, already recognized as one of the leaders of the Irish literary revival, urged Synge to go to the Aran Islands and there to discover and express his native Irish heritage. Between 1898 and 1902 Synge spent several months on the Arans, off the west coast. Life among the peasants and fishermen on the islands sparked his genius, though of his six plays only *Riders to the Sea* (1904) has an island setting. His first play was *The Shadow of the Glen* (1903). Neither of the two plays is a romantic-patriotic dramatization of old Celtic legend, according to the formula favored by the young Yeats. When the Irish National Theatre Society moved into the Abbey Street theater in 1904, Synge — with Yeats and Lady Gregory — became one of its directors. His plays had begun to gain him a European reputation even before the riots at the Abbey during the first run of *The Playboy of the Western World* (1907), a lusty tragicomedy with a realistic peasant setting. Synge's health had always been frail. In 1906 he became engaged to Molly Allgood, one of the Abbey actresses, but he died of Hodgkin's disease before they could marry. At the time of his death he was finishing *Deirdre of the Sorrows*, a lyrical tragedy based on Irish mythology.

Of the playwrights of the early years of this century, perhaps none did more than Synge to give new vitality to dramatic realism with new subject matter and a new kind of lyricism in prose dialogue.

Suggested Reading

Bushrui, S. B., ed. *Sunshine and the Moon's Delight: A Centenary Tribute to John Millington Synge*. Gerrard Cross, Buckinghamshire: Colin Smythe, Ltd., and Beirut, Lebanon: the American University of Beirut, 1972.

Ellis-Fermor, Una. *The Irish Dramatic Movement*. London: Methuen, 1954.

Gerstenberger, Donna. *John Millington Synge*. New York: Twayne, 1965.

Greene, David H., and Edward M. Stephens. *J. M. Synge, 1871–1909*. New York: Macmillan, 1959.

Grene, Nicholas. *Synge: A Critical Study of the Plays*. Totowa, N.J.: Rowman and Littlefield, 1975.

Johnston, Denis. *John Millington Synge*. New York: Columbia University Press, 1965.

Price, Alan. *Synge and Anglo-Irish Drama*. London: Methuen, 1961.

Saddlemyer, Ann, ed. *J. M. Synge, Collected Works*, vols. 3 and 4 (Plays). London: Oxford University Press, 1968.

Skelton, Robin. *J. M. Synge and His World*. New York: Viking, 1971.

Yeats, W. B. "The Death of Synge." In *Dramatis Personae*. London: Macmillan, 1936.

———. "The Irish Dramatic Movement." In *Explorations*. London: Macmillan, 1962.

Recording of Riders to the Sea

Radio Eireann Players of Dublin. Spoken Arts Records (1 record, SPA743, mono).

PETER WEISS (1916–   ) was born in Nowawes near Berlin but has resided in Sweden since fleeing the Nazis just before World War II. He continues to write in German. He began his artistic career as a surrealist painter strongly influenced by Max Ernst and Salvador Dali. Surrealism was the mode of his early film-making as well, but later he turned to documentaries as a means of exploring the theme of personal alienation. Both styles, and their literary corollaries in Franz Kafka and Henry Miller, have continued to influence Weiss, first as novelist and later as playwright.

Though his early work as artist and film producer had attracted attention, Weiss had difficulty finding publishers for his novels, but the award of a literary prize for *Point of Escape* (1963) established his reputation in Germany. His first play, *Night with Guests* (1962), has not yet been produced. His second, *Marat / Sade*, opened in April, 1964, at the Schiller Theater in West Berlin to an enthusiastic reception. The following year the Royal Shakespeare Company, under the direction of Peter Brook, staged the play in London; and in December, 1965, the same production opened in New York, ran for 145 performances, and won the Drama Critics Circle Award for 1965–66. The production has been filmed and has played successfully in art movie houses.

Like *Marat / Sade*, Weiss's later plays also deal with social issues through a combination of visual happenings and documentary technique. *The Investigation* (1966) consists of excerpts from the transcripts of the 1964–65 trial of those responsible for the mass extermination at Auschwitz during the last war. *The Song of the Lusitanian Bogey* (1967) uses verse, discordant melody, and ballet to depict the struggle in Angola between native "primitivism" and Portuguese "civilization." Weiss's two most recent plays are *Discourse on Vietnam* (1968), the complete title of which runs to 46 words, and which presents a Marxist interpretation of 2,000 years of Vietnamese history and ends with the escalation of the war on the orders of an American president; and *Trotsky in Exile* (1970), an anti-Stalinist view of the historical events.

Suggested Reading

Cohn, Ruby. "*Marat / Sade:* An Education in Theatre." *Educational Theatre Journal* 19 (1967):478–485.
Hilton, Ian. *Peter Weiss: A Search for Affinities*. London: Wolff, 1970.
Moeller, Hans Bernard. "German Theatre 1964: Weiss' Reasoning in a Madhouse." *Symposium* 20 (1966):163–173.
Roloff, Michael. "An Interview with Peter Weiss." *Partisan Review* 22 (1965):220–232.
Sontag, Susan. "Marat / Sade / Artaud." *Partisan Review* 22 (1965):210–219.
Weiss, Samuel A. "Peter Weiss's *Marat / Sade*." *Drama Survey* 5 (1966–67):123–130.

Recording of Marat / Sade

Ian Richardson, Patrick McGee, Glenda Jackson, and the Royal Shakespeare Company of Great Britain. Caedmon Records (3 records, TRS312, stereo).

Film Version of Marat / Sade

British, 1967. With the Royal Shakespeare Company of Great Britain, directed by Peter Brook (115 min., 16mm, sound, color). United Artists, 16729 Seventh Ave., New York, NY 10019. (Rental.)

OSCAR FINGAL O'FLAHERTIE WILLS WILDE (1854–1900) was born in Dublin to diversely talented parents. His father was Ireland's leading eye and ear surgeon, and a respected writer; his mother was a poet of the Free Ireland movement and an authority on Celtic folklore. Wilde's university education took him from Trinity College, Dublin, to Oxford, where he distinguished himself as a classical scholar and wit and won the coveted Newdigate Prize for poetry. By the early 1880s he was established in London's smart social life as the most colorful advocate of the aesthetic movement. His poems attracted less attention than his picturesque dress and his loudly proclaimed opinions that life should follow the rules of art. Gilbert and Sullivan's *Patience*, which satirized the movement, probably did not intend to ridicule Wilde personally, but the public unhesitatingly identified him with Bunthorne, the "fleshly poet" of the operetta. Wilde's lecture tour of the United States in 1882 thus served as advance publicity for the American production of *Patience*. He married in 1884; his second son, Vyvyan, was later to write movingly about his father. For the next few years Wilde worked as editor and reviewer, also publishing a number of short stories. His only novel, *The Picture of Dorian Gray*, was hailed as brilliant but morally subversive.

In his last and most productive decade Wilde turned to the stage, writing the series of works based on upper-class London society for which he is chiefly famous: *Lady Windermere's Fan*, *A Woman of No Importance*, *An Ideal Husband* and *The Importance of Being Earnest*. A disturbing exception was the perversely brilliant *Salome*, written originally in French and banned on moral grounds; it has continued to excite, and defeat, actors and directors ever since.

The events of Wilde's private life conspired to shatter his brilliantly successful career. His homosexual tendencies, long known to his immediate circle, were brought into the open by his involvement with Lord Alfred Douglas ("Bosie"), son of the bitter and eccentric Marquess of Queensberry. Accused by the father of sodomy, Wilde instituted proceedings for libel, which plunged him into the two most scandalous trials of the decade. Repudiated by the society that had once cultivated him — Lord Alfred Douglas was not charged — Wilde was sentenced to two years' hard labor. *The Ballad of Reading Gaol* and *De Profundis*, products of this period, record his humiliation and despair. Released as a bankrupt in 1897 he went to France, where he died a few years later ignored by all except a few close friends. At the end of his life he was received into the Roman Catholic Church; his grave in the Père Lachaise Cemetery in Paris has become a center of literary pilgrimage.

Suggested Reading

Beckson, Karl E., ed. *Oscar Wilde: The Critical Heritage*. New York: Barnes & Noble, 1970.
Ellmann, Richard. *Oscar Wilde: A Collection of Critical Essays*. Englewood Cliffs, N.J.: Prentice-Hall (Spectrum), 1969.
Hyde, Harford Montgomery. *Oscar Wilde: A Biography*. New York: Farrar, Strauss and Giroux, 1975.
Wilde, Oscar. *Complete Works of Oscar Wilde*. Edited by J. B. Foreman, introduction by Vyvyan Holland. London: Collins, 1966.

Recordings of The Importance of Being Earnest

Dame Gladys Cooper, Joan Greenwood. Caedmon Records (2 records, TRS329, stereo).
Sir John Gielgud, Dame Edith Evans. Angel Recordings (2 records, ANG3504, mono).

Film Version of The Importance of Being Earnest

British, 1952. Directed by Anthony Asquith, with Joan Greenwood, Sir Michael Redgrave (95 min., 16mm, sound, color). Janus Films, 745 Fifth Ave., New York, NY 10022. (Rental.)

WILLIAM BUTLER YEATS (1865–1939) was the son of a distinguished Dublin portrait painter. His childhood was divided between London and his mother's home in Sligo County in western Ireland, a country that was to influence motif and imagery in his poetry. In 1880 the family moved back to Dublin. Yeats had little formal schooling. His early verse (like *The Wanderings of Oisin*, 1888) was in the contemporary manner of the Pre-Raphaelites and their successors — sensuously romantic, but a little soft and vague. In 1899, with Lady Augusta Gregory and Edward Martyn, both playwrights, Yeats founded the Irish Literary Theater (reorganized as the Irish National Theater Society in 1902) and was its leader for many years. He dreamed of making it the center for plays about Irish mythology and national sentiment, but though his own plays were produced there and though the Abbey Theater became one of modern Europe's great stages, he never realized his dream. He did, however, have a decisive influence on the playwriting careers of John Millington Synge and Sean O'Casey, two other leading figures in the Irish literary renaissance. From about 1916 (thanks, in part, to Ezra Pound), Yeats's own plays were influenced by the symbolic and stylized Japanese Nō theater. Yeats called his plays in this manner "Plays for Dancers." In 1925 he published *A Vision*, a comprehensive, semiphilosophical system of psycho-astrology. His poems in the late 1920s and '30s gained in depth of thought and in taut, sparse strength of imagery — but also in difficulty, because of his growing reliance on a private stock of symbols and metaphors derived from his study of mysticism and the occult. In 1923 he received the Nobel Prize for literature. For some years after 1922 Yeats was a senator in the newly independent Irish republic, though many aspects of politics in a modern democracy were distasteful to his aristocratic and tradition-oriented allegiances. The great love of his youth was the beautiful Irish actress and patriot Maud Gonne, who played the title role in his most nationalistic play, *Cathleen ni Houlihan* (1902). Yeats married an Englishwoman in 1917. He died in the south of France, but he now lies buried in Sligo, according to his wish in his last poem, "Under Ben Bulben."

The years have proved many of Yeats's plays more stageworthy than his contemporaries thought they were. Still, it is as a lyric poet and not as a playwright that he is ranked among the greats of modern English literature. His early and still most popular plays are based on themes from Irish myth and folklore: *The Countess Cathleen* (1892), *The Land of Heart's Desire* (1894), *Cathleen ni Houlihan* (1902), *The Hour Glass* (1902), and *On Baile's Strand* (1904), the first of several plays about a legendary Irish king. *At the Hawk's Well* (1914), *Purgatory* (1939), and *The Death of Cuchulain* (1939) are early and late examples of Yeats's terse, emblematic, and enigmatic manner in drama. Among his other plays are successful adaptations of Sophocles' two plays about Oedipus (1928, 1934).

Suggested Reading

Clark, David R. *W. B. Yeats and the Theatre of Desolate Reality*. Dublin: Dolmen Press, 1965.
Ellis-Fermor, Una. *The Irish Dramatic Movement*. London: Methuen, 1954.

Ellmann, Richard. *Yeats, the Man and the Masks*. New York: Dutton, 1948.

Hone, Joseph. *W. B. Yeats, 1865–1939*, 2nd ed. London: Macmillan, 1962.

Moore, John R. *Masks of Love and Death: Yeats as Dramatist*. Ithaca, N.Y.: Cornell University Press, 1971.

————. "An Old Man's Tragedy — Yeats's *Purgatory*." *Modern Drama* 5 (1963):440–450.

Nathan, Leonard E. *The Tragic Drama of William Butler Yeats: Figures in a Dance*. New York and London: Columbia University Press, 1965.

Schmitt, Natalie C. "Curing Oneself of the Work of Time: W. B. Yeats's *Purgatory*." *Comparative Drama* 7 (1974):310–333.

Unterecker, John, ed. *Yeats: A Collection of Critical Essays*. Englewood Cliffs, N.J.: Prentice-Hall (Spectrum), 1963.

Ure, Peter. *Yeats the Playwright*. New York: Barnes & Noble, 1963.

Vendler, Helen Hennessy. *Yeats's "Vision" and the Later Plays*. Cambridge, Mass.: Harvard University Press, 1963.

Wilson, F. A. C. *W. B. Yeats and Tradition*. New York: Macmillan, 1958.

Recording of Purgatory

In *Five One Act Plays*. Caedmon Records (3 records, TRS315, stereo).

SUGGESTED GENERAL REFERENCES

Theory

Abel, Lionel. *Metatheatre*. New York: Hill and Wang (Dramabook), 1963.

Artaud, Antonin. *The Theater and Its Double*. Translated by Mary Caroline Richards. New York: Grove Press, 1958.

Barnet, Sylvan, Morton Berman, and William Burto, eds. *Aspects of the Drama: A Handbook*. Boston: Little, Brown, 1962.

Bentley, Eric, ed. *The Theory of the Modern Stage*. Harmondsworth, Eng.: Penguin, 1968.

————. *The Life of the Drama*. New York: Atheneum, 1964.

Brook, Peter. *The Empty Space*. London and New York: Atheneum, 1968.

Brooks, Cleanth, and Robert B. Heilman. *Understanding Drama: Twelve Plays*. New York: Henry Holt, 1948.

Butcher, S. H. *Aristotle's Theory of Poetry and Fine Art*. New York: Dover Publications, 1951.

Calderwood, James L., and Harold E. Toliver, eds. *Perspectives on Drama*. New York: Oxford University Press, 1968.

Clark, Barrett H., ed. *European Theories of Drama, with a Supplement on the American Drama*. New York: Crown Publishers, 1947.

Cole, Toby, ed. *Playwrights on Playwriting: The Meaning and Making of Modern Drama from Ibsen to Ionesco*. New York: Hill and Wang (Dramabook), 1960.

Corrigan, Robert W., ed. *Comedy: Meaning and Form*. San Francisco: Chandler, 1965.

————, ed. *Tragedy: Vision and Form*. San Francisco: Chandler, 1965.

Corrigan, Robert W., and James L. Rosenberg, eds. *The Context and Craft of Drama*. San Francisco: Chandler, 1964.

Dawson, S. W. *Drama and the Dramatic*. London: Methuen, 1970.

Dukore, Bernard F. *Dramatic Theory and Criticism: Greeks to Grotowski*. New York: Holt, Rinehart and Winston, 1974.

Eliot, T. S. *Poetry and Drama*. Cambridge, Mass.: Harvard University Press, 1951.

Ellis-Fermor, Una. *The Frontiers of Drama*, 2nd ed. London: Methuen, 1964.

Ellmann, Richard, and Charles Feidelson, Jr., eds. *The Modern Tradition: Backgrounds of Modern Literature*. New York: Oxford University Press, 1965.

Esslin, Martin. *An Anatomy of Drama*. New York: Hill and Wang, 1977.

Fergusson, Francis. *The Human Image in Dramatic Literature*. Garden City, N.Y.: Doubleday (Anchor), 1957.

————. *The Idea of a Theater*. Garden City, N.Y.: Doubleday (Anchor), 1949.

Frye, Northrop. *Anatomy of Criticism*. Princeton, N.J.: Princeton University Press, 1957.

Guthke, Carl Siegfried. *Modern Tragicomedy*. New York: Random House, 1966.

Heilman, Robert B. *Tragedy and Melodrama: Versions of Experience*. Seattle, Wash.: University of Washington Press, 1968.

Kerr, Walter. *Tragedy and Comedy*. New York: Simon and Schuster, 1967.

Lauter, Paul, ed. *Theories of Comedy*. Garden City, N.Y.: Doubleday (Anchor), 1964.

Leech, Clifford. *Tragedy*. London: Methuen, 1969.

Lucas, F. L. *Tragedy*. New York: Collier Books, 1962.

Nicoll, Allardyce. *The Theatre and Dramatic Theory*. New York: Barnes & Noble, 1962.

Nietzsche, Friedrich. *The Birth of Tragedy* and *The Genealogy of Morals*. Translated by Francis Golffing. Garden City, N.Y.: Doubleday (Anchor), 1956.

Olson, Elder. *Tragedy and the Theory of Drama*. Detroit, Mich.: Wayne State University Press, 1966.

Peacock, Ronald. *The Art of Drama*. London: Routledge & Kegan Paul, 1957.

Sewall, Richard B. *The Vision of Tragedy*. New Haven, Conn.: Yale University Press, 1959.

Sewall, Richard B., and Lawrence Michel, eds. *Tragedy: Modern Essays in Criticism*. Englewood Cliffs, N.J.: Prentice-Hall (Spectrum), 1963.

Styan, J. L. *The Dark Comedy*. Cambridge, Eng.: Cambridge University Press, 1962.

———. *The Elements of Drama*. Cambridge, Eng.: Cambridge University Press, 1960.

Van Laan, Thomas F. *The Idiom of Drama*. Ithaca, N.Y., and London: Cornell University Press, 1970.

Williams, Raymond. *Drama in Performance*. Harmondsworth, Eng.: Penguin, 1972.

———. *Modern Tragedy*. Stanford, Cal.: Stanford University Press, 1966.

History and Criticism

Arnott, Peter. *The Ancient Greek and Roman Theatre*. New York: Peter Smith, 1971.

Bentley, Eric. *In Search of Theater*. New York: Alfred A. Knopf, 1953.

———. *The Playwright as Thinker*. New York: Meridian Books, 1957.

Bogard, Travis, and William I. Oliver, eds. *Modern Drama: Essays in Criticism*. New York: Oxford University Press, 1965.

Brustein, Robert. *The Theatre of Revolt*. Boston: Atlantic-Little, Brown, 1962.

Cohn, Ruby. *Currents in Contemporary Drama*. Bloomington, Ind.: University of Indiana Press, 1969.

Corrigan, Robert W., ed. *Theatre in the Twentieth Century*. New York: Grove Press, 1963.

Esslin, Martin. *The Theatre of the Absurd*, revised, updated ed. Garden City, N.Y.: Doubleday (Anchor), 1969.

Freedman, Morris, ed. *Essays in the Modern Drama*. Boston: D. C. Heath, 1964.

———. *The Moral Impulse: Modern Drama from Ibsen to the Present*. Carbondale, Ill.: Southern Illinois University Press, 1967.

Gassner, John. *Form and Idea in Modern Theatre*. New York: Dryden Press, 1956.

———. *Masters of the Drama*, 3rd rev. ed. New York: Dover Publications, 1954.

———. *The Theatre in Our Times*. New York: Crown Publishers, 1954.

Grossvogel, David I. *The Blasphemers* (original title: *Four Playwrights and a Postscript: Brecht, Ionesco, Beckett, Genet*). Ithaca, N.Y.: Cornell University Press, 1962.

Knight, G. Wilson. *The Golden Labyrinth*. New York: Norton, 1962.

Krutch, Joseph Wood. *"Modernism" in Modern Drama*. Ithaca, N.Y.: Cornell University Press, 1953.

Lucas, Frank L. *The Drama of Chekhov, Synge, Yeats, and Pirandello*. London: Cassell, 1963.

Lumley, Frederick. *New Trends in 20th Century Drama*, 4th new ed. New York: Oxford University Press, 1972.

Nicoll, Allardyce. *World Drama from Aeschylus to Anouilh*. London: G. G. Harrap, 1949.

Steiner, George. *The Death of Tragedy*. New York: Alfred A. Knopf, 1961.

Valency, Maurice. *The Flower and the Castle: An Introduction to Modern Drama*. New York: Macmillan, 1963.

Wellwarth, George E. *The Theater of Protest and Paradox*. New York: New York University Press, 1964.

Williams, Raymond. *Drama from Ibsen to Brecht*. London: Chatto & Windus, 1969.

Theater Arts

Brockett, Oscar G. *History of the Theatre*, 3rd ed. Boston: Allyn and Bacon, 1977.

———. *The Essential Theatre*. New York: Holt, Rinehart and Winston, 1976.

Cole, Toby, and Helen Krich Chinoy, eds. *Actors on Acting*. New York: Crown Publishers, 1949.

Gorelik, Mordecai. *New Theatres for Old*. New York: S. French, 1940.

Hunningher, Benjamin. *The Origin of the Theater*. New York: Hill and Wang (Dramabook), 1961.

Macgowan, Kenneth, and William Melnitz. *The Living Stage: A History of the World Theater*. Englewood Cliffs, N.J.: Prentice-Hall, 1955. (A shorter version is *The Golden Ages of the Theater*, 1959.)

Nagler, Alois M. *A Source Book in Theatrical History*. New York: Dover, 1959.

Nicoll, Allardyce. *The Development of the Theatre*, 5th rev. ed. New York: Harcourt, Brace & World, 1966.

Stanislavsky, Constantin. *An Actor Prepares*. Translated by Elizabeth Reynolds Hapgood. New York: Theatre Arts Books, 1936.

Reference

Bowman, Walter P., and Robert Hamilton Ball. *Theatre Language: A Dictionary of Terms in English of the Drama and Stage from Medieval to Modern Times*. New York: Theatre Arts Books, 1936.

Gassner, John, and Edward Quinn. *The Reader's Encyclopedia of World Drama*. New York: Crowell, 1969.

Hartnoll, Phyllis, ed. *The Oxford Companion to the Theatre*, 3rd ed. London: Oxford University Press, 1967.

Hathorn, Richmond. *Crowell's Handbook of Classical Drama*. New York: Crowell, 1967.

Matlaw, Myron. *Modern World Drama: An Encyclopedia*. New York: E. P. Dutton & Co., 1972.

Some Useful Collections of Plays

Bentley, Eric, ed. *The Play: A Critical Anthology*. Englewood Cliffs, N.J.: Prentice-Hall, 1951.

———, ed. *The Modern Theatre*, I–VI. Garden City, N.Y.: Doubleday (Anchor), 1955–1960.

Block, Haskell, and Robert Shedd, eds. *Masters of Modern Drama*. New York: Random House, 1961.

Clayes, Stanley, David Spencer, E. Bradlee Watson, and Benfield Pressey, eds. *Contemporary Drama Series* [five collections]. New York: Charles Scribner's Sons, 1941–1962.

Corrigan, Robert W., ed. *The Modern Theatre*. New York: Macmillan, 1964.

Downer, Alan S., ed. *The Art of the Play*. New York: Henry Holt, 1955.

Gassner, John, ed. *Treasury of the Theatre*, I–II, 3rd ed. New York: Simon and Schuster, 1967.

Grene, David, and Richmond Lattimore, eds. *The Complete Greek Tragedies*, I–IV. Chicago: University of Chicago Press, 1959.

Alvin Kernan, ed. *Character and Conflict: An Introduction to Drama*, 2nd ed. New York: Harcourt, Brace & World, 1969.

———, ed. *Classics of the Modern Theater*. New York: Harcourt, Brace & World, 1965.

Films and Records

See *Feature Films on 8 and 16. A Directory of Feature Films Available for Rental, Lease, and Sale in the U.S.*, 2nd ed. Compiled and edited by James L. Limbacher. New Haven, Conn.: Reader's Press, 1968. See also *Index to 16mm Educational Films*, 5th ed. University Park, Los Angeles, Cal.: National Information Center for Educational Media (NICEM), University of Southern California, 1975. (Vol. I: Subject Heading Outline, Index to Subject Headings, Subject Guide, Producer / Distributor Code Section. Vol. II: Alphabetical Guide to 16mm Film, A–L. Vol. III: the same, M–Z.)

For a catalogue of recordings of some of the plays (complete or excerpted) included in this volume, see *Index to Educational Audio Tapes*, 4th ed. University Park, Los Angeles, Cal.: National Information Center for Educational Media (NICEM), University of Southern California, 1977.

TO THE STUDENT

As educational publishers we realize it is our responsibility to try to improve the textbooks we publish. In order to make *Twenty-Three Plays* a better book next time, we need to know what you, our ultimate consumer, think of what we've already done. Please help us by filling out this questionnaire and returning it to Little, Brown and Company, College English Developmental Group, 34 Beacon St., Boston, Mass. 02106.

School_____ City and State_____

Instructor's name _____ Course title_____

Other texts assigned_____

Please give us your reaction to the selections:

	Keep	Drop	Didn't read	Read in high school
OEDIPUS THE KING	—	—	—	—
EVERYMAN	—	—	—	—
HAMLET	—	—	—	—
TARTUFFE	—	—	—	—
PHAEDRA	—	—	—	—
THE MAN OF MODE	—	—	—	—
TRIAL BY JURY	—	—	—	—
A DOLL'S HOUSE	—	—	—	—
THE IMPORTANCE OF BEING EARNEST	—	—	—	—
THE CHERRY ORCHARD	—	—	—	—
MAJOR BARBARA	—	—	—	—
THE GHOST SONATA	—	—	—	—
RIDERS TO THE SEA	—	—	—	—
PURGATORY	—	—	—	—
SIX CHARACTERS IN SEARCH OF AN AUTHOR	—	—	—	—
AH, WILDERNESS!	—	—	—	—
THE CAUCASIAN CHALK CIRCLE	—	—	—	—
DEATH OF A SALESMAN	—	—	—	—

ACT WITHOUT WORDS I   ___ ___ ___ ___

THE DUMB WAITER   ___ ___ ___ ___

WHO'S AFRAID OF VIRGINIA WOOLF?   ___ ___ ___ ___

DUTCHMAN   ___ ___ ___ ___

MARAT / SADE   ___ ___ ___ ___

General comments: _____

_____

1. Are there any plays or playwrights not included that you would like to see included next

time?_____ _____

2. Did you read the Introduction?_____ Was it helpful?_____

_____

3. Did you read the Forewords for each play? _____

How might they be improved?_____

4. Did you read the Afterwords for each play?_____

How might they be improved?_____

5. Was the essay "The Realistic Theater and Its Aftermath" useful?_____

6. Did you use the Index of Dramatic Terms?_____

7. Did you find the Biographical Notes and the Suggested References helpful? _____

_____

8. Please add any comments or suggestions on how we might improve this book:_____

_____

_____

Your name_____ Date_____

Mailing address_____

May we quote you, either in promotion for this book or in future publishing

ventures?   yes_____   no_____

Thank you.